DATABASE MANAGEMENT SYSTEMS

DATABASE MANAGEMENT SYSTEMS

Third Edition

Raghu Ramakrishnan
University of Wisconsin
Madison, Wisconsin, USA

■

Johannes Gehrke
Cornell University
Ithaca, New York, USA

McGraw Hill Education (India) Private Limited
NEW DELHI

McGraw Hill Education Offices
New Delhi New York St Louis San Francisco Auckland Bogotá Caracas
Kuala Lumpur Lisbon London Madrid Mexico City Milan Montreal
San Juan Santiago Singapore Sydney Tokyo Toronto

McGraw Hill Education (India) Private Limited

DATABASE MANAGEMENT SYSTEMS, THIRD EDITION

McGraw Hill Education (India) Edition 2014

Fifth reprint 2015
RQQACRAVDXRLA

Reprinted in India by arrangement with The McGraw-Hill Companies, Inc., New York

Sales territories: India, Pakistan, Nepal, Bangladesh, Sri Lanka and Bhutan

Library of Congress Cataloging-in-Publication Data

Ramakrishnan, Raghu.
Database management systems / Raghu Ramakrishnan, Johannes Gehrke. —3rd ed.

p. cm.
Includes index.
ISBN 0-07-246563-8—ISBN 0-07-115110-9 (ISE)
1. Database management. I. Gehrke, Johannes. II. Title.
QA76.9.D3 R237 2003
005.74—dc21
2002075205

ISBN-13: 978-93-392-1311-4
ISBN-10: 93-392-1311-4

Published by McGraw Hill Education (India) Private Limited, P-24, Green Park Extension New Delhi 110 016, and printed at Magic International Private Limited, Greater Noida 201 306

Visit us at: www.mheducation.co.in

To Apu, Ketan, and Vivek with love

To Keiko and Elisa

CONTENTS

PREFACE

The advantage of doing one's praising for oneself is that one can lay it on so thick and exactly in the right places.

—Samuel Butler

Database management systems are now an indispensable tool for managing information, and a course on the principles and practice of database systems is now an integral part of computer science curricula. This book covers the fundamentals of modern database management systems, in particular relational database systems.

We have attempted to present the material in a clear, simple style. A quantitative approach is used throughout with many detailed examples. An extensive set of exercises (for which solutions are available online to instructors) accompanies each chapter and reinforces students' ability to apply the concepts to real problems.

The book can be used with the accompanying software and programming assignments in two distinct kinds of introductory courses:

1. **Applications Emphasis:** A course that covers the principles of database systems, and emphasizes how they are used in developing data-intensive applications. Two new chapters on application development (one on database-backed applications, and one on Java and Internet application architectures) have been added to the third edition, and the entire book has been extensively revised and reorganized to support such a course. A running case-study and extensive online materials (e.g., code for SQL queries and Java applications, online databases and solutions) make it easy to teach a hands-on application-centric course.

2. **Systems Emphasis:** A course that has a strong systems emphasis and assumes that students have good programming skills in C and C++. In this case the accompanying Minibase software can be used as the basis for projects in which students are asked to implement various parts of a relational DBMS. Several central modules in the project software (e.g., heap files, buffer manager, B+ trees, hash indexes, various join methods)

are described in sufficient detail in the text to enable students to implement them, given the (C++) class interfaces.

Many instructors will no doubt teach a course that falls between these two extremes. The restructuring in the third edition offers a very modular organization that facilitates such hybrid courses. The also book contains enough material to support advanced courses in a two-course sequence.

Organization of the Third Edition

The book is organized into six main parts plus a collection of advanced topics, as shown in Figure 0.1. The Foundations chapters introduce database systems, the

(1) Foundations	Both
(2) Application Development	Applications emphasis
(3) Storage and Indexing	Systems emphasis
(4) Query Evaluation	Systems emphasis
(5) Transaction Management	Systems emphasis
(6) Database Design and Tuning	Applications emphasis
(7) Additional Topics	Both

Figure 0.1 Organization of Parts in the Third Edition

ER model and the relational model. They explain how databases are created and used, and cover the basics of database design and querying, including an in-depth treatment of SQL queries. While an instructor can omit some of this material at their discretion (e.g., relational calculus, some sections on the ER model or SQL queries), this material is relevant to every student of database systems, and we recommend that it be covered in as much detail as possible.

Each of the remaining five main parts has either an application or a systems emphasis. Each of the three Systems parts has an overview chapter, designed to provide a self-contained treatment, e.g., Chapter 8 is an overview of storage and indexing. The overview chapters can be used to provide stand-alone coverage of the topic, or as the first chapter in a more detailed treatment. Thus, in an application-oriented course, Chapter 8 might be the only material covered on file organizations and indexing, whereas in a systems-oriented course it would be supplemented by a selection from Chapters 9 through 11. The Database Design and Tuning part contains a discussion of performance tuning and designing for secure access. These application topics are best covered after giving students a good grasp of database system architecture, and are therefore placed later in the chapter sequence.

Suggested Course Outlines

The book can be used in two kinds of introductory database courses, one with an applications emphasis and one with a systems emphasis.

The *introductory applications-oriented course* could cover the Foundations chapters, then the Application Development chapters, followed by the overview systems chapters, and conclude with the Database Design and Tuning material. Chapter dependencies have been kept to a minimum, enabling instructors to easily fine tune what material to include. The Foundations material, Part I, should be covered first, and within Parts III, IV, and V, the overview chapters should be covered first. The only remaining dependencies between chapters in Parts I to VI are shown as arrows in Figure 0.2. The chapters in Part I should be covered in sequence. However, the coverage of algebra and calculus can be skipped in order to get to SQL queries sooner (although we believe this material is important and recommend that it should be covered before SQL).

The *introductory systems-oriented course* would cover the Foundations chapters and a selection of Applications and Systems chapters. An important point for systems-oriented courses is that the timing of programming projects (e.g., using Minibase) makes it desirable to cover some systems topics early. Chapter dependencies have been carefully limited to allow the Systems chapters to be covered as soon as Chapters 1 and 3 have been covered. The remaining Foundations chapters and Applications chapters can be covered subsequently.

The book also has ample material to support a multi-course sequence. Obviously, choosing an applications or systems emphasis in the introductory course results in dropping certain material from the course; the material in the book supports a comprehensive two-course sequence that covers both applications and systems aspects. The Additional Topics range over a broad set of issues, and can be used as the core material for an advanced course, supplemented with further readings.

Supplementary Material

This book comes with extensive online supplements:

- **Online Chapter:** To make space for new material such as application development, information retrieval, and XML, we've moved the coverage of QBE to an online chapter. Students can freely download the chapter from the book's web site, and solutions to exercises from this chapter are included in solutions manual.

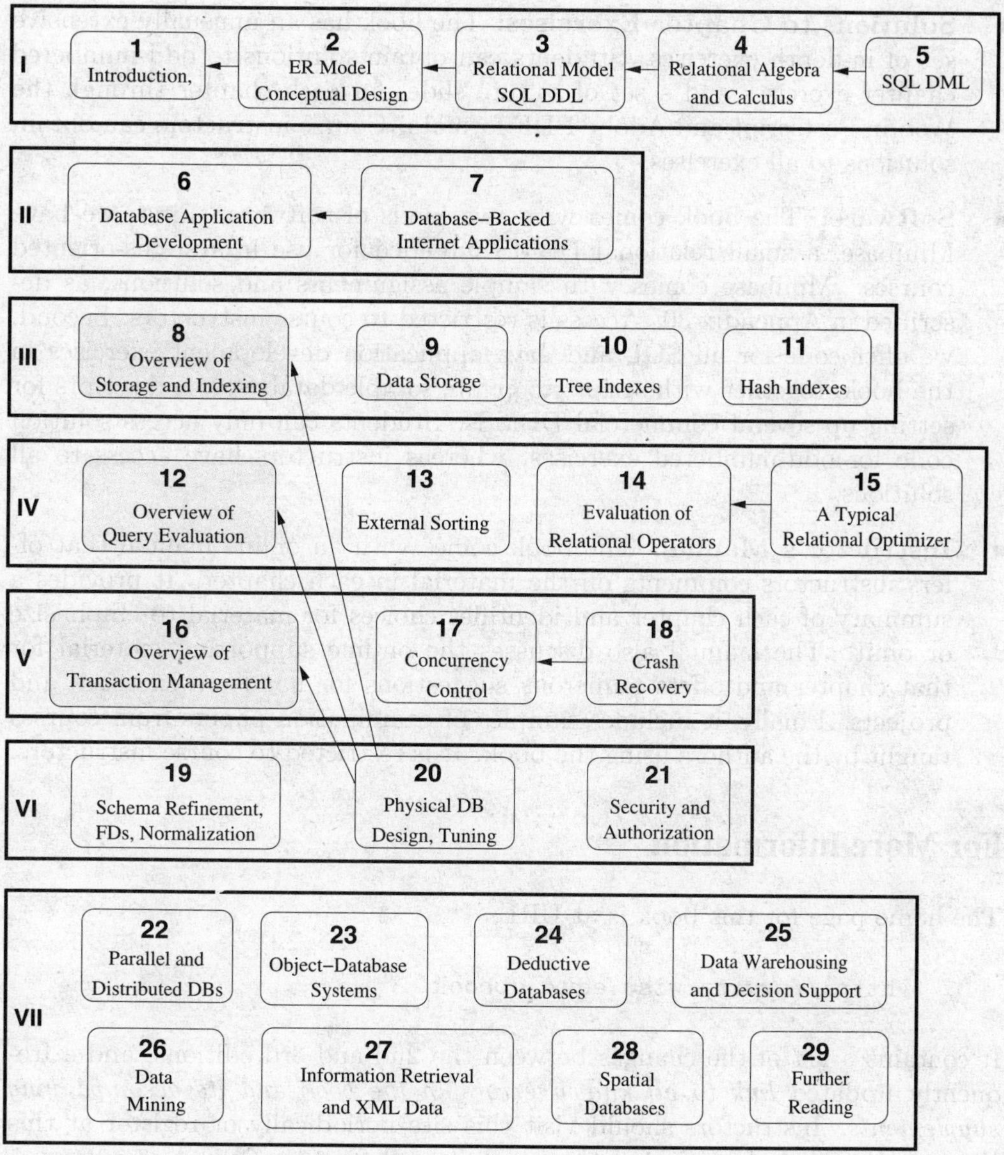

Figure 0.2 Chapter Organization and Dependencies

- **Lecture Slides:** Lecture slides are freely available for all chapters in Postscript, and PDF formats. Course instructors can also obtain these slides in Microsoft Powerpoint format, and can adapt them to their teaching needs. Instructors also have access to all figures used in the book (in xfig format), and can use them to modify the slides.

- **Solutions to Chapter Exercises:** The book has an unusually extensive set of in-depth exercises. Students can obtain solutions to odd-numbered chapter exercises and a set of lecture slides for each chapter through the Web in Postscript and Adobe PDF formats. Course instructors can obtain solutions to all exercises.

- **Software:** The book comes with two kinds of software. First, we have Minibase, a small relational DBMS intended for use in systems-oriented courses. Minibase comes with sample assignments and solutions, as described in Appendix 30. Access is restricted to course instructors. Second, we offer code for all SQL and Java application development exercises in the book, together with scripts to create sample databases, and scripts for setting up several commercial DBMSs. Students can only access solution code for odd-numbered exercises, whereas instructors have access to all solutions.

- **Instructor's Manual:** The book comes with an online manual that offers instructors comments on the material in each chapter. It provides a summary of each chapter and identifies choices for material to emphasize or omit. The manual also discusses the on-line supporting material for that chapter and offers numerous suggestions for hands-on exercises and projects. Finally, it includes samples of examination papers from courses taught by the authors using the book. It is restricted to course instructors.

For More Information

The home page for this book is at URL:

`http://www.cs.wisc.edu/~dbbook`

It contains a list of the changes between the 2nd and 3rd editions, and a frequently updated *link to all known errors in the book and its accompanying supplements.* Instructors should visit this site periodically or register at this site to be notified of important changes by email.

Acknowledgments

This book grew out of lecture notes for CS564, the introductory (senior/graduate level) database course at UW-Madison. David DeWitt developed this course and the Minirel project, in which students wrote several well-chosen parts of a relational DBMS. My thinking about this material was shaped by teaching CS564, and Minirel was the inspiration for Minibase, which is more comprehensive (e.g., it has a query optimizer and includes visualization software) but tries to retain the spirit of Minirel. Mike Carey and I jointly designed much of Minibase. My lecture notes (and in turn this book) were influenced by Mike's lecture notes and by Yannis Ioannidis's lecture slides.

Joe Hellerstein used the beta edition of the book at Berkeley and provided invaluable feedback, assistance on slides, and hilarious quotes. Writing the chapter on object-database systems with Joe was a lot of fun.

C. Mohan provided invaluable assistance, patiently answering a number of questions about implementation techniques used in various commercial systems, in particular indexing, concurrency control, and recovery algorithms. Moshe Zloof answered numerous questions about QBE semantics and commercial systems based on QBE. Ron Fagin, Krishna Kulkarni, Len Shapiro, Jim Melton, Dennis Shasha, and Dirk Van Gucht reviewed the book and provided detailed feedback, greatly improving the content and presentation. Michael Goldweber at Beloit College, Matthew Haines at Wyoming, Michael Kifer at SUNY StonyBrook, Jeff Naughton at Wisconsin, Praveen Seshadri at Cornell, and Stan Zdonik at Brown also used the beta edition in their database courses and offered feedback and bug reports. In particular, Michael Kifer pointed out an error in the (old) algorithm for computing a minimal cover and suggested covering some SQL features in Chapter 2 to improve modularity. Gio Wiederhold's bibliography, converted to Latex format by S. Sudarshan, and Michael Ley's online bibliography on databases and logic programming were a great help while compiling the chapter bibliographies. Shaun Flisakowski and Uri Shaft helped me frequently in my never-ending battles with Latex.

I owe a special thanks to the many, many students who have contributed to the Minibase software. Emmanuel Ackaouy, Jim Pruyne, Lee Schumacher, and Michael Lee worked with me when I developed the first version of Minibase (much of which was subsequently discarded, but which influenced the next version). Emmanuel Ackaouy and Bryan So were my TAs when I taught CS564 using this version and went well beyond the limits of a TAship in their efforts to refine the project. Paul Aoki struggled with a version of Minibase and offered lots of useful comments as a TA at Berkeley. An entire class of CS764 students (our graduate database course) developed much of the current version of Minibase in a large class project that was led and coordinated by Mike Carey and me. Amit Shukla and Michael Lee were my TAs when I first taught CS564 using this version of Minibase and developed the software further.

Several students worked with me on independent projects, over a long period of time, to develop Minibase components. These include visualization packages for the buffer manager and B+ trees (Huseyin Bektas, Harry Stavropoulos, and Weiqing Huang); a query optimizer and visualizer (Stephen Harris, Michael Lee, and Donko Donjerkovic); an ER diagram tool based on the Opossum schema editor (Eben Haber); and a GUI-based tool for normalization (Andrew Prock and Andy Therber). In addition, Bill Kimmel worked to integrate and fix a large body of code (storage manager, buffer manager, files and access methods, relational operators, and the query plan executor) produced by the CS764 class project. Ranjani Ramamurty considerably extended Bill's work on cleaning up and integrating the various modules. Luke Blanshard, Uri Shaft, and Shaun Flisakowski worked on putting together the release version of the code and developed test suites and exercises based on the Minibase software. Krishna Kunchithapadam tested the optimizer and developed part of the Minibase GUI.

Clearly, the Minibase software would not exist without the contributions of a great many talented people. With this software available freely in the public domain, I hope that more instructors will be able to teach a systems-oriented database course with a blend of implementation and experimentation to complement the lecture material.

I'd like to thank the many students who helped in developing and checking the solutions to the exercises and provided useful feedback on draft versions of the book. In alphabetical order: X. Bao, S. Biao, M. Chakrabarti, C. Chan, W. Chen, N. Cheung, D. Colwell, C. Fritz, V. Ganti, J. Gehrke, G. Glass, V. Gopalakrishnan, M. Higgins, T. Jasmin, M. Krishnaprasad, Y. Lin, C. Liu, M. Lusignan, H. Modi, S. Narayanan, D. Randolph, A. Ranganathan, J. Reminga, A. Therber, M. Thomas, Q. Wang, R. Wang, Z. Wang, and J. Yuan. Arcady Grenader, James Harrington, and Martin Reames at Wisconsin and Nina Tang at Berkeley provided especially detailed feedback.

Charlie Fischer, Avi Silberschatz, and Jeff Ullman gave me invaluable advice on working with a publisher. My editors at McGraw-Hill, Betsy Jones and Eric Munson, obtained extensive reviews and guided this book in its early stages. Emily Gray and Brad Kosirog were there whenever problems cropped up. At Wisconsin, Ginny Werner really helped me to stay on top of things.

Finally, this book was a thief of time, and in many ways it was harder on my family than on me. My sons expressed themselves forthrightly. From my (then) five-year-old, Ketan: "Dad, stop working on that silly book. You don't have any time for *me*." Two-year-old Vivek: "You working *boook*? No no no come play basketball me!" All the seasons of their discontent were visited upon my wife, and Apu nonetheless cheerfully kept the family going in its usual chaotic, happy way all the many evenings and weekends I was wrapped up in this book. (Not to mention the days when I was wrapped up in being a faculty member!) As in all things, I can trace my parents' hand in much of this; my father, with his love of learning, and my mother, with her love of us, shaped me. My brother Kartik's contributions to this book consisted chiefly of phone calls in which he kept me from working, but if I don't acknowledge him, he's liable to be annoyed. I'd like to thank my family for being there and giving meaning to everything I do. (There! I knew I'd find a legitimate reason to thank Kartik.)

Acknowledgments for the Second Edition

Emily Gray and Betsy Jones at McGraw-Hill obtained extensive reviews and provided guidance and support as we prepared the second edition. Jonathan Goldstein helped with the bibliography for spatial databases. The following reviewers provided valuable feedback on content and organization: Liming Cai at Ohio University, Costas Tsatsoulis at University of Kansas, Kwok-Bun Yue at University of Houston, Clear Lake, William Grosky at Wayne State University, Sang H. Son at University of Virginia, James M. Slack at Minnesota State University, Mankato, Herman Balsters at University of Twente, Netherlands, Karen C. Davis at University of Cincinnati, Joachim Hammer at University of Florida, Fred Petry at Tulane University, Gregory Speegle at Baylor University, Salih Yurttas at Texas A&M University, and David Chao at San Francisco State University.

A number of people reported bugs in the first edition. In particular, we wish to thank the following: Joseph Albert at Portland State University, Han-yin Chen at University of Wisconsin, Lois Delcambre at Oregon Graduate Institute, Maggie Eich at Southern Methodist University, Raj Gopalan at Curtin University of Technology, Davood Rafiei at University of Toronto, Michael Schrefl at University of South Australia, Alex Thomasian at University of Connecticut, and Scott Vandenberg at Siena College.

A special thanks to the many people who answered a detailed survey about how commercial systems support various features: At IBM, Mike Carey, Bruce Lindsay, C. Mohan, and James Teng; at Informix, M. Muralikrishna and Michael Ubell; at Microsoft, David Campbell, Goetz Graefe, and Peter Spiro; at Oracle, Hakan Jacobsson, Jonathan D. Klein, Muralidhar Krishnaprasad, and M. Ziauddin; and at Sybase, Marc Chanliau, Lucien Dimino, Sangeeta Doraiswamy, Hanuma Kodavalla, Roger MacNicol, and Tirumanjanam Rengarajan.

After reading about himself in the acknowledgment to the first edition, Ketan (now 8) had a simple question: "How come you didn't dedicate the book to us? Why mom?" Ketan, I took care of this inexplicable oversight. Vivek (now 5) was more concerned about the extent of his fame: "Daddy, is my name in *evvy* copy of your book? Do they have it in *evvy* compooter science department in the world?" Vivek, I hope so. Finally, this revision would not have made it without Apu's and Keiko's support.

Acknowledgments for the Third Edition

We thank Raghav Kaushik for his contribution to the discussion of XML, and Alex Thomasian for his contribution to the coverage of concurrency control. A special thanks to Jim Melton for giving us a pre-publication copy of his book on object-oriented extensions in the SQL:1999 standard, and catching several bugs in a draft of this edition. Marti Hearst at Berkeley generously permitted us to adapt some of her slides on Information Retrieval, and Alon Levy and Dan Suciu were kind enough to let us adapt some of their lectures on XML. Mike Carey offered input on Web services.

Emily Lupash at McGraw-Hill has been a source of constant support and encouragement. She coordinated extensive reviews from Ming Wang at Embry-Riddle Aeronautical University, Cheng Hsu at RPI, Paul Bergstein at Univ. of Massachusetts, Archana Sathaye at SJSU, Bharat Bhargava at Purdue, John Fendrich at Bradley, Ahmet Ugur at Central Michigan, Richard Osborne at Univ. of Colorado, Akira Kawaguchi at CCNY, Mark Last at Ben Gurion, Vassilis Tsotras at Univ. of California, and Ronald Eaglin at Univ. of Central Florida. It is a pleasure to acknowledge the thoughtful input we received from the reviewers, which greatly improved the design and content of this edition. Gloria Schiesl and Jade Moran dealt cheerfully and efficiently with last-minute snafus, and, with Sherry Kane, made a very tight schedule possible. Michelle Whitaker iterated many times on the cover and end-sheet design.

On a personal note for Raghu, Ketan, following the canny example of the camel that shared a tent, observed that "it is only fair" that Raghu dedicate this edition solely to him and Vivek, since "mommy already had it dedicated only to her." Despite this blatant attempt to hog the limelight, enthusiastically supported by Vivek and viewed with the indulgent affection of a doting father, this book is also dedicated to Apu, for being there through it all.

For Johannes, this revision would not have made it without Keiko's support and inspiration and the motivation from looking at Elisa's peacefully sleeping face.

PART I

FOUNDATIONS

1

OVERVIEW OF DATABASE SYSTEMS

- What is a DBMS, in particular, a relational DBMS?
- Why should we consider a DBMS to manage data?
- How is application data represented in a DBMS?
- How is data in a DBMS retrieved and manipulated?
- How does a DBMS support concurrent access and protect data during system failures?
- What are the main components of a DBMS?
- Who is involved with databases in real life?
- **Key concepts:** database management, data independence, database design, data model; relational databases and queries; schemas, levels of abstraction; transactions, concurrency and locking, recovery and logging; DBMS architecture; database administrator, application programmer, end user

Has everyone noticed that all the letters of the word *database* are typed with the left hand? Now the layout of the QWERTY typewriter keyboard was designed, among other things, to facilitate the even use of both hands. It follows, therefore, that writing about databases is not only unnatural, but a lot harder than it appears.

—Anonymous

The amount of information available to us is literally exploding, and the value of data as an organizational asset is widely recognized. To get the most out of their large and complex datasets, users require tools that simplify the tasks of

The area of database management systems is a microcosm of computer science in general. The issues addressed and the techniques used span a wide spectrum, including languages, object-orientation and other programming paradigms, compilation, operating systems, concurrent programming, data structures, algorithms, theory, parallel and distributed systems, user interfaces, expert systems and artificial intelligence, statistical techniques, and dynamic programming. We cannot go into all these aspects of database management in one book, but we hope to give the reader a sense of the excitement in this rich and vibrant discipline.

managing the data and extracting useful information in a timely fashion. Otherwise, data can become a liability, with the cost of acquiring it and managing it far exceeding the value derived from it.

A **database** is a collection of data, typically describing the activities of one or more related organizations. For example, a university database might contain information about the following:

- *Entities* such as students, faculty, courses, and classrooms.
- *Relationships* between entities, such as students' enrollment in courses, faculty teaching courses, and the use of rooms for courses.

A **database management system**, or **DBMS**, is software designed to assist in maintaining and utilizing large collections of data. The need for such systems, as well as their use, is growing rapidly. The alternative to using a DBMS is to store the data in files and write application-specific code to manage it. The use of a DBMS has several important advantages, as we will see in Section 1.4.

1.1 MANAGING DATA

The goal of this book is to present an in-depth introduction to database management systems, with an emphasis on how to *design* a database and *use* a DBMS effectively. Not surprisingly, many decisions about how to use a DBMS for a given application depend on what capabilities the DBMS supports efficiently. Therefore, to use a DBMS well, it is necessary to also understand how a DBMS *works*.

Many kinds of database management systems are in use, but this book concentrates on **relational database systems (RDBMSs)**, which are by far the dominant type of DBMS today. The following questions are addressed in the core chapters of this book:

1. **Database Design and Application Development:** How can a user describe a real-world enterprise (e.g., a university) in terms of the data stored in a DBMS? What factors must be considered in deciding how to organize the stored data? How can we develop applications that rely upon a DBMS? (Chapters 2, 3, 6, 7, 19, 20, and 21.)
2. **Data Analysis:** How can a user answer questions about the enterprise by posing queries over the data in the DBMS? (Chapters 4 and 5.)[1]
3. **Concurrency and Robustness:** How does a DBMS allow many users to access data concurrently, and how does it protect the data in the event of system failures? (Chapters 16, 17, and 18.)
4. **Efficiency and Scalability:** How does a DBMS store large datasets and answer questions against this data efficiently? (Chapters 8, 9, 10, 11, 12, 13, 14, and 15.)

Later chapters cover important and rapidly evolving topics, such as parallel and distributed database management, data warehousing and complex queries for decision support, data mining, databases and information retrieval, XML repositories, object databases, spatial data management, and rule-oriented DBMS extensions.

In the rest of this chapter, we introduce these issues. In Section 1.2, we begin with a brief history of the field and a discussion of the role of database management in modern information systems. We then identify the benefits of storing data in a DBMS instead of a file system in Section 1.3, and discuss the advantages of using a DBMS to manage data in Section 1.4. In Section 1.5, we consider how information about an enterprise should be organized and stored in a DBMS. A user probably thinks about this information in high-level terms that correspond to the entities in the organization and their relationships, whereas the DBMS ultimately stores data in the form of (many, many) bits. The gap between how users think of their data and how the data is ultimately stored is bridged through several *levels of abstraction* supported by the DBMS. Intuitively, a user can begin by describing the data in fairly high-level terms, then refine this description by considering additional storage and representation details as needed.

In Section 1.6, we consider how users can retrieve data stored in a DBMS and the need for techniques to efficiently compute answers to questions involving such data. In Section 1.7, we provide an overview of how a DBMS supports concurrent access to data by several users and how it protects the data in the event of system failures.

[1] An online chapter on Query-by-Example (QBE) is also available.

We then briefly describe the internal structure of a DBMS in Section 1.8, and mention various groups of people associated with the development and use of a DBMS in Section 1.9.

1.2 A HISTORICAL PERSPECTIVE

From the earliest days of computers, storing and manipulating data have been a major application focus. The first general-purpose DBMS, designed by Charles Bachman at General Electric in the early 1960s, was called the Integrated Data Store. It formed the basis for the *network data model*, which was standardized by the Conference on Data Systems Languages (CODASYL) and strongly influenced database systems through the 1960s. Bachman was the first recipient of ACM's Turing Award (the computer science equivalent of a Nobel Prize) for work in the database area; he received the award in 1973.

In the late 1960s, IBM developed the Information Management System (IMS) DBMS, used even today in many major installations. IMS formed the basis for an alternative data representation framework called the *hierarchical data model*. The SABRE system for making airline reservations was jointly developed by American Airlines and IBM around the same time, and it allowed several people to access the same data through a computer network. Interestingly, today the same SABRE system is used to power popular Web-based travel services such as Travelocity.

In 1970, Edgar Codd, at IBM's San Jose Research Laboratory, proposed a new data representation framework called the *relational data model*. This proved to be a watershed in the development of database systems: It sparked the rapid development of several DBMSs based on the relational model, along with a rich body of theoretical results that placed the field on a firm foundation. Codd won the 1981 Turing Award for his seminal work. Database systems matured as an academic discipline, and the popularity of relational DBMSs changed the commercial landscape. Their benefits were widely recognized, and the use of DBMSs for managing corporate data became standard practice.

In the 1980s, the relational model consolidated its position as the dominant DBMS paradigm, and database systems continued to gain widespread use. The SQL query language for relational databases, developed as part of IBM's System R project, is now the standard query language. SQL was standardized in the late 1980s, and the current standard, SQL:1999, was adopted by the American National Standards Institute (ANSI) and International Organization for Standardization (ISO). Arguably, the most widely used form of concurrent programming is the concurrent execution of database programs (called *transactions*). Users write programs as if they are to be run by themselves, and the responsibility for running them concurrently is given to the DBMS. James Gray won the 1999 Turing award for his contributions to database transaction management.

In the late 1980s and the 1990s, advances were made in many areas of database systems. Considerable research was carried out into more powerful query languages and richer data models, with emphasis placed on supporting complex analysis of data from all parts of an enterprise. Several vendors (e.g., IBM's DB2, Oracle 8, Informix[2] UDS) extended their systems with the ability to store new data types such as images and text, and to ask more complex queries. Specialized systems have been developed by numerous vendors for creating *data warehouses*, consolidating data from several databases, and for carrying out specialized analysis.

An interesting phenomenon is the emergence of several **enterprise resource planning (ERP)** and **management resource planning (MRP)** packages, which add a substantial layer of application-oriented features on top of a DBMS. Widely used packages include systems from Baan, Oracle, PeopleSoft, SAP, and Siebel. These packages identify a set of common tasks (e.g., inventory management, human resources planning, financial analysis) encountered by a large number of organizations and provide a general application layer to carry out these tasks. The data is stored in a relational DBMS and the application layer can be customized to different companies, leading to lower overall costs for the companies, compared to the cost of building the application layer from scratch.

Most significant, perhaps, DBMSs have entered the Internet Age. While the first generation of websites stored their data exclusively in operating systems files, the use of a DBMS to store data accessed through a Web browser is becoming widespread. Queries are generated through Web-accessible forms and answers are formatted using a markup language such as HTML to be easily displayed in a browser. All the database vendors are adding features to their DBMS aimed at making it more suitable for deployment over the Internet.

Database management continues to gain importance as more and more data is brought online and made ever more accessible through computer networking. Today the field is being driven by exciting visions such as multimedia databases, interactive video, streaming data, digital libraries, a host of scientific projects such as the human genome mapping effort and NASA's Earth Observation System project, and the desire of companies to consolidate their decision-making processes and *mine* their data repositories for useful information about their businesses. Commercially, database management systems represent one of the

[2]Informix was recently acquired by IBM.

largest and most vigorous market segments. Thus the study of database systems could prove to be richly rewarding in more ways than one!

1.3 FILE SYSTEMS VERSUS A DBMS

To understand the need for a DBMS, let us consider a motivating scenario: A company has a large collection (say, 500 GB[3]) of data on employees, departments, products, sales, and so on. This data is accessed concurrently by several employees. Questions about the data must be answered quickly, changes made to the data by different users must be applied consistently, and access to certain parts of the data (e.g., salaries) must be restricted.

We can try to manage the data by storing it in operating system files. This approach has many drawbacks, including the following:

- We probably do not have 500 GB of main memory to hold all the data. We must therefore store data in a storage device such as a disk or tape and bring relevant parts into main memory for processing as needed.
- Even if we have 500 GB of main memory, on computer systems with 32-bit addressing, we cannot refer directly to more than about 4 GB of data. We have to program some method of identifying all data items.
- We have to write special programs to answer each question a user may want to ask about the data. These programs are likely to be complex because of the large volume of data to be searched.
- We must protect the data from inconsistent changes made by different users accessing the data concurrently. If applications must address the details of such concurrent access, this adds greatly to their complexity.
- We must ensure that data is restored to a consistent state if the system crashes while changes are being made.
- Operating systems provide only a password mechanism for security. This is not sufficiently flexible to enforce security policies in which different users have permission to access different subsets of the data.

A DBMS is a piece of software designed to make the preceding tasks easier. By storing data in a DBMS rather than as a collection of operating system files, we can use the DBMS's features to manage the data in a robust and efficient manner. As the volume of data and the number of users grow—hundreds of gigabytes of data and thousands of users are common in current corporate databases—DBMS support becomes indispensable.

[3]A kilobyte (KB) is 1024 bytes, a megabyte (MB) is 1024 KBs, a gigabyte (GB) is 1024 MBs, a terabyte (TB) is 1024 GBs, and a petabyte (PB) is 1024 terabytes.

1.4 ADVANTAGES OF A DBMS

Using a DBMS to manage data has many advantages:

- **Data Independence:** Application programs should not, ideally, be exposed to details of data representation and storage. The DBMS provides an abstract view of the data that hides such details.

- **Efficient Data Access:** A DBMS utilizes a variety of sophisticated techniques to store and retrieve data efficiently. This feature is especially important if the data is stored on external storage devices.

- **Data Integrity and Security:** If data is always accessed through the DBMS, the DBMS can enforce integrity constraints. For example, before inserting salary information for an employee, the DBMS can check that the department budget is not exceeded. Also, it can enforce *access controls* that govern what data is visible to different classes of users.

- **Data Administration:** When several users share the data, centralizing the administration of data can offer significant improvements. Experienced professionals who understand the nature of the data being managed, and how different groups of users use it, can be responsible for organizing the data representation to minimize redundancy and for fine-tuning the storage of the data to make retrieval efficient.

- **Concurrent Access and Crash Recovery:** A DBMS schedules concurrent accesses to the data in such a manner that users can think of the data as being accessed by only one user at a time. Further, the DBMS protects users from the effects of system failures.

- **Reduced Application Development Time:** Clearly, the DBMS supports important functions that are common to many applications accessing data in the DBMS. This, in conjunction with the high-level interface to the data, facilitates quick application development. DBMS applications are also likely to be more robust than similar stand-alone applications because many important tasks are handled by the DBMS (and do not have to be debugged and tested in the application).

Given all these advantages, is there ever a reason *not* to use a DBMS? Sometimes, yes. A DBMS is a complex piece of software, optimized for certain kinds of workloads (e.g., answering complex queries or handling many concurrent requests), and its performance may not be adequate for certain specialized applications. Examples include applications with tight real-time constraints or just a few well-defined critical operations for which efficient custom code must be written. Another reason for not using a DBMS is that an application may need to manipulate the data in ways not supported by the query language. In such a situation, the abstract view of the data presented by the DBMS does not match the application's needs and actually gets in the way. As an example, relational databases do not support flexible analysis of text data (although vendors are now extending their products in this direction).

If specialized performance or data manipulation requirements are central to an application, the application may choose not to use a DBMS, especially if the added benefits of a DBMS (e.g., flexible querying, security, concurrent access, and crash recovery) are not required. In most situations calling for large-scale data management, however, DBMSs have become an indispensable tool.

1.5 DESCRIBING AND STORING DATA IN A DBMS

The user of a DBMS is ultimately concerned with some real-world enterprise, and the data to be stored describes various aspects of this enterprise. For example, there are students, faculty, and courses in a university, and the data in a university database describes these entities and their relationships.

A **data model** is a collection of high-level data description constructs that hide many low-level storage details. A DBMS allows a user to define the data to be stored in terms of a data model. Most database management systems today are based on the **relational data model**, which we focus on in this book.

While the data model of the DBMS hides many details, it is nonetheless closer to how the DBMS stores data than to how a user thinks about the underlying enterprise. A **semantic data model** is a more abstract, high-level data model that makes it easier for a user to come up with a good initial description of the data in an enterprise. These models contain a wide variety of constructs that help describe a real application scenario. A DBMS is not intended to support all these constructs directly; it is typically built around a data model with just a few basic constructs, such as the relational model. A database design in terms of a semantic model serves as a useful starting point and is subsequently translated into a database design in terms of the data model the DBMS actually supports.

A widely used semantic data model called the entity-relationship (ER) model allows us to pictorially denote entities and the relationships among them. We cover the ER model in Chapter 2.

An Example of Poor Design: The relational schema for Students illustrates a poor design choice; you should *never* create a field such as *age*, whose value is constantly changing. A better choice would be *DOB* (for *date of birth*); age can be computed from this. We continue to use *age* in our examples, however, because it makes them easier to read.

1.5.1 The Relational Model

In this section we provide a brief introduction to the relational model. The central data description construct in this model is a **relation**, which can be thought of as a set of **records**.

A description of data in terms of a data model is called a **schema**. In the relational model, the schema for a relation specifies its name, the name of each **field** (or **attribute** or **column**), and the type of each field. As an example, student information in a university database may be stored in a relation with the following schema:

Students(*sid:* `string`, *name:* `string`, *login:* `string`,
age: `integer`, *gpa:* `real`)

The preceding schema says that each record in the Students relation has five fields, with field names and types as indicated. An example instance of the Students relation appears in Figure 1.1.

sid	*name*	*login*	*age*	*gpa*
53666	Jones	jones@cs	18	3.4
53688	Smith	smith@ee	18	3.2
53650	Smith	smith@math	19	3.8
53831	Madayan	madayan@music	11	1.8
53832	Guldu	guldu@music	12	2.0

Figure 1.1 An Instance of the Students Relation

Each row in the Students relation is a record that describes a student. The description is not complete—for example, the student's height is not included—but is presumably adequate for the intended applications in the university database. Every row follows the schema of the Students relation. The schema can therefore be regarded as a template for describing a student.

We can make the description of a collection of students more precise by specifying **integrity constraints**, which are conditions that the records in a relation must satisfy. For example, we could specify that every student has a unique *sid* value. Observe that we cannot capture this information by simply adding another field to the Students schema. Thus, the ability to specify uniqueness of the values in a field increases the accuracy with which we can describe our data. The expressiveness of the constructs available for specifying integrity constraints is an important aspect of a data model.

Other Data Models

In addition to the relational data model (which is used in numerous systems, including IBM's DB2, Informix, Oracle, Sybase, Microsoft's Access, FoxBase, Paradox, Tandem, and Teradata), other important data models include the hierarchical model (e.g., used in IBM's IMS DBMS), the network model (e.g., used in IDS and IDMS), the object-oriented model (e.g., used in Objectstore and Versant), and the object-relational model (e.g., used in DBMS products from IBM, Informix, ObjectStore, Oracle, Versant, and others). While many databases use the hierarchical and network models and systems based on the object-oriented and object-relational models are gaining acceptance in the marketplace, the dominant model today is the relational model.

In this book, we focus on the relational model because of its wide use and importance. Indeed, the object-relational model, which is gaining in popularity, is an effort to combine the best features of the relational and object-oriented models, and a good grasp of the relational model is necessary to understand object-relational concepts. (We discuss the object-oriented and object-relational models in Chapter 23.)

1.5.2 Levels of Abstraction in a DBMS

The data in a DBMS is described at three levels of abstraction, as illustrated in Figure 1.2. The database description consists of a schema at each of these three levels of abstraction: the *conceptual*, *physical*, and *external*.

A **data definition language** (DDL) is used to define the external and conceptual schemas. We discuss the DDL facilities of the most widely used database language, SQL, in Chapter 3. All DBMS vendors also support SQL commands to describe aspects of the physical schema, but these commands are not part of the SQL language standard. Information about the conceptual, external, and physical schemas is stored in the **system catalogs** (Section 12.1). We discuss the three levels of abstraction in the rest of this section.

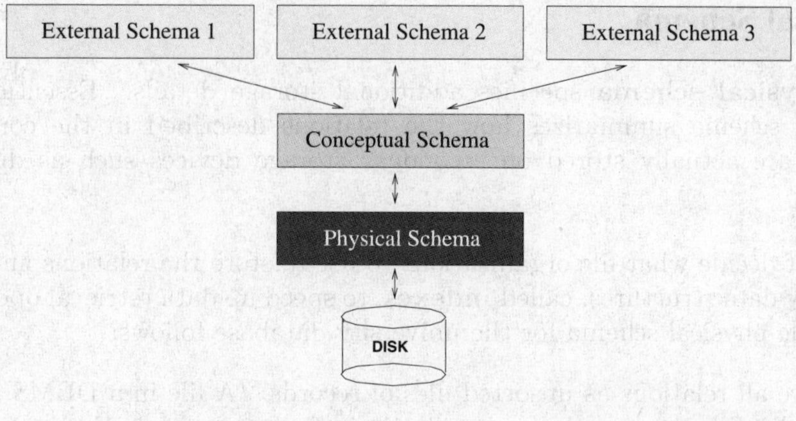

Figure 1.2 Levels of Abstraction in a DBMS

Conceptual Schema

The **conceptual schema** (sometimes called the **logical schema**) describes the stored data in terms of the data model of the DBMS. In a relational DBMS, the conceptual schema describes all relations that are stored in the database. In our sample university database, these relations contain information about *entities*, such as students and faculty, and about *relationships*, such as students' enrollment in courses. All student entities can be described using records in a Students relation, as we saw earlier. In fact, each collection of entities and each collection of relationships can be described as a relation, leading to the following conceptual schema:

Students(*sid:* `string`, *name:* `string`, *login:* `string`,
age: `integer`, *gpa:* `real`)
Faculty(*fid:* `string`, *fname:* `string`, *sal:* `real`)
Courses(*cid:* `string`, *cname:* `string`, *credits:* `integer`)
Rooms(*rno:* `integer`, *address:* `string`, *capacity:* `integer`)
Enrolled(*sid:* `string`, *cid:* `string`, *grade:* `string`)
Teaches(*fid:* `string`, *cid:* `string`)
Meets_In(*cid:* `string`, *rno:* `integer`, *time:* `string`)

The choice of relations, and the choice of fields for each relation, is not always obvious, and the process of arriving at a good conceptual schema is called **conceptual database design**. We discuss conceptual database design in Chapters 2 and 19.

Physical Schema

The **physical schema** specifies additional storage details. Essentially, the physical schema summarizes how the relations described in the conceptual schema are actually stored on secondary storage devices such as disks and tapes.

We must decide what file organizations to use to store the relations and create auxiliary data structures, called **indexes**, to speed up data retrieval operations. A sample physical schema for the university database follows:

- Store all relations as unsorted files of records. (A file in a DBMS is either a collection of records or a collection of pages, rather than a string of characters as in an operating system.)
- Create indexes on the first column of the Students, Faculty, and Courses relations, the *sal* column of Faculty, and the *capacity* column of Rooms.

Decisions about the physical schema are based on an understanding of how the data is typically accessed. The process of arriving at a good physical schema is called **physical database design**. We discuss physical database design in Chapter 20.

External Schema

External schemas, which usually are also in terms of the data model of the DBMS, allow data access to be customized (and authorized) at the level of individual users or groups of users. Any given database has exactly one conceptual schema and one physical schema because it has just one set of stored relations, but it may have several external schemas, each tailored to a particular group of users. Each external schema consists of a collection of one or more **views** and relations from the conceptual schema. A view is conceptually a relation, but the records in a view are not stored in the DBMS. Rather, they are computed using a definition for the view, in terms of relations stored in the DBMS. We discuss views in more detail in Chapters 3 and 25.

The external schema design is guided by end user requirements. For example, we might want to allow students to find out the names of faculty members teaching courses as well as course enrollments. This can be done by defining the following view:

Courseinfo(*cid:* `string`, *fname:* `string`, *enrollment:* `integer`)

A user can treat a view just like a relation and ask questions about the records in the view. Even though the records in the view are not stored explicitly, they are computed as needed. We did not include Courseinfo in the conceptual schema because we can compute Courseinfo from the relations in the conceptual schema, and to store it in addition would be redundant. Such redundancy, in addition to the wasted space, could lead to inconsistencies. For example, a tuple may be inserted into the Enrolled relation, indicating that a particular student has enrolled in some course, without incrementing the value in the *enrollment* field of the corresponding record of Courseinfo (if the latter also is part of the conceptual schema and its tuples are stored in the DBMS).

1.5.3 Data Independence

A very important advantage of using a DBMS is that it offers **data independence**. That is, application programs are insulated from changes in the way the data is structured and stored. Data independence is achieved through use of the three levels of data abstraction; in particular, the conceptual schema and the external schema provide distinct benefits in this area.

Relations in the external schema (view relations) are in principle generated on demand from the relations corresponding to the conceptual schema.[4] If the underlying data is reorganized, that is, the conceptual schema is changed, the definition of a view relation can be modified so that the same relation is computed as before. For example, suppose that the Faculty relation in our university database is replaced by the following two relations:

Faculty_public(*fid:* `string`, *fname:* `string`, *office:* `integer`)
Faculty_private(*fid:* `string`, *sal:* `real`)

Intuitively, some confidential information about faculty has been placed in a separate relation and information about offices has been added. The Courseinfo view relation can be redefined in terms of Faculty_public and Faculty_private, which together contain all the information in Faculty, so that a user who queries Courseinfo will get the same answers as before.

Thus, users can be shielded from changes in the logical structure of the data, or changes in the choice of relations to be stored. This property is called **logical data independence**.

In turn, the conceptual schema insulates users from changes in physical storage details. This property is referred to as **physical data independence**. The conceptual schema hides details such as how the data is actually laid out on disk, the file structure, and the choice of indexes. As long as the conceptual

[4] In practice, they could be precomputed and stored to speed up queries on view relations, but the computed view relations must be updated whenever the underlying relations are updated.

schema remains the same, we can change these storage details without altering applications. (Of course, performance might be affected by such changes.)

1.6 QUERIES IN A DBMS

The ease with which information can be obtained from a database often determines its value to a user. In contrast to older database systems, relational database systems allow a rich class of questions to be posed easily; this feature has contributed greatly to their popularity. Consider the sample university database in Section 1.5.2. Here are some questions a user might ask:

1. What is the name of the student with student ID 123456?
2. What is the average salary of professors who teach course CS564?
3. How many students are enrolled in CS564?
4. What fraction of students in CS564 received a grade better than B?
5. Is any student with a GPA less than 3.0 enrolled in CS564?

Such questions involving the data stored in a DBMS are called **queries**. A DBMS provides a specialized language, called the **query language**, in which queries can be posed. A very attractive feature of the relational model is that it supports powerful query languages. **Relational calculus** is a formal query language based on mathematical logic, and queries in this language have an intuitive, precise meaning. **Relational algebra** is another formal query language, based on a collection of **operators** for manipulating relations, which is equivalent in power to the calculus.

A DBMS takes great care to evaluate queries as efficiently as possible. We discuss query optimization and evaluation in Chapters 12, 14, and 15. Of course, the efficiency of query evaluation is determined to a large extent by how the data is stored physically. Indexes can be used to speed up many queries—in fact, a good choice of indexes for the underlying relations can speed up each query in the preceding list. We discuss data storage and indexing in Chapters 8, 9, 10, and 11.

A DBMS enables users to create, modify, and query data through a **data manipulation language** (DML). Thus, the query language is only one part of the DML, which also provides constructs to insert, delete, and modify data. We will discuss the DML features of SQL in Chapter 5. The DML and DDL are collectively referred to as the **data sublanguage** when embedded within a **host language** (e.g., C or COBOL).

1.7 TRANSACTION MANAGEMENT

Consider a database that holds information about airline reservations. At any given instant, it is possible (and likely) that several travel agents are looking up information about available seats on various flights and making new seat reservations. When several users access (and possibly modify) a database concurrently, the DBMS must order their requests carefully to avoid conflicts. For example, when one travel agent looks up Flight 100 on some given day and finds an empty seat, another travel agent may simultaneously be making a reservation for that seat, thereby making the information seen by the first agent obsolete.

Another example of concurrent use is a bank's database. While one user's application program is computing the total deposits, another application may transfer money from an account that the first application has just 'seen' to an account that has not yet been seen, thereby causing the total to appear larger than it should be. Clearly, such anomalies should not be allowed to occur. However, disallowing concurrent access can degrade performance.

Further, the DBMS must protect users from the effects of system failures by ensuring that all data (and the status of active applications) is restored to a consistent state when the system is restarted after a crash. For example, if a travel agent asks for a reservation to be made, and the DBMS responds saying that the reservation has been made, the reservation should not be lost if the system crashes. On the other hand, if the DBMS has not yet responded to the request, but is making the necessary changes to the data when the crash occurs, the partial changes should be undone when the system comes back up.

A **transaction** is *any one execution* of a user program in a DBMS. (Executing the same program several times will generate several transactions.) This is the basic unit of change as seen by the DBMS: Partial transactions are not allowed, and the effect of a group of transactions is equivalent to some serial execution of all transactions. We briefly outline how these properties are guaranteed, deferring a detailed discussion to later chapters.

1.7.1 Concurrent Execution of Transactions

An important task of a DBMS is to schedule concurrent accesses to data so that each user can safely ignore the fact that others are accessing the data concurrently. The importance of this task cannot be underestimated because a database is typically shared by a large number of users, who submit their requests to the DBMS independently and simply cannot be expected to deal with arbitrary changes being made concurrently by other users. A DBMS allows users to think of their programs as if they were executing in isolation, one after the other in some order chosen by the DBMS. For example, if a program that deposits cash into an account is submitted to the DBMS at the same time as another program that debits money from the same account, either of these programs could be run first by the DBMS, but their steps will not be interleaved in such a way that they interfere with each other.

A **locking protocol** is a set of rules to be followed by each transaction (and enforced by the DBMS) to ensure that, even though actions of several transactions might be interleaved, the net effect is identical to executing all transactions in some serial order. A **lock** is a mechanism used to control access to database objects. Two kinds of **locks** are commonly supported by a DBMS: **shared locks** on an object can be held by two different transactions at the same time, but an **exclusive lock** on an object ensures that no other transactions hold *any* lock on this object.

Suppose that the following locking protocol is followed: *Every transaction begins by obtaining a shared lock on each data object that it needs to read and an exclusive lock on each data object that it needs to modify, then releases all its locks after completing all actions.* Consider two transactions $T1$ and $T2$ such that $T1$ wants to modify a data object and $T2$ wants to read the same object. Intuitively, if $T1$'s request for an exclusive lock on the object is granted first, $T2$ cannot proceed until $T1$ releases this lock, because $T2$'s request for a shared lock will not be granted by the DBMS until then. Thus, all of $T1$'s actions will be completed before any of $T2$'s actions are initiated. We consider locking in more detail in Chapters 16 and 17.

1.7.2 Incomplete Transactions and System Crashes

Transactions can be interrupted before running to completion for a variety of reasons, e.g., a system crash. A DBMS must ensure that the changes made by such incomplete transactions are removed from the database. For example, if the DBMS is in the middle of transferring money from account A to account B and has debited the first account but not yet credited the second when the crash occurs, the money debited from account A must be restored when the system comes back up after the crash.

To do so, the DBMS maintains a **log** of all writes to the database. A crucial property of the log is that each write action must be recorded in the log (on disk) *before* the corresponding change is reflected in the database itself—otherwise, if the system crashes just after making the change in the database but before the change is recorded in the log, the DBMS would be unable to detect and undo this change. This property is called **Write-Ahead Log**, or **WAL**. To ensure this property, the DBMS must be able to selectively force a page in memory to disk.

The log is also used to ensure that the changes made by a successfully completed transaction are not lost due to a system crash, as explained in Chapter 18. Bringing the database to a consistent state after a system crash can be a slow process, since the DBMS must ensure that the effects of all transactions that completed prior to the crash are restored, and that the effects of incomplete transactions are undone. The time required to recover from a crash can be reduced by periodically forcing some information to disk; this periodic operation is called a **checkpoint**.

1.7.3 Points to Note

In summary, there are three points to remember with respect to DBMS support for concurrency control and recovery:

1. Every object that is read or written by a transaction is first locked in shared or exclusive mode, respectively. Placing a lock on an object restricts its availability to other transactions and thereby affects performance.

2. For efficient log maintenance, the DBMS must be able to selectively force a collection of pages in main memory to disk. Operating system support for this operation is not always satisfactory.

3. Periodic checkpointing can reduce the time needed to recover from a crash. Of course, this must be balanced against the fact that checkpointing too often slows down normal execution.

1.8 STRUCTURE OF A DBMS

Figure 1.3 shows the structure (with some simplification) of a typical DBMS based on the relational data model.

The DBMS accepts SQL commands generated from a variety of user interfaces, produces query evaluation plans, executes these plans against the database, and returns the answers. (This is a simplification: SQL commands can be embedded in host-language application programs, e.g., Java or COBOL programs. We ignore these issues to concentrate on the core DBMS functionality.)

When a user issues a query, the parsed query is presented to a **query optimizer**, which uses information about how the data is stored to produce an efficient execution plan for evaluating the query. An **execution plan** is a

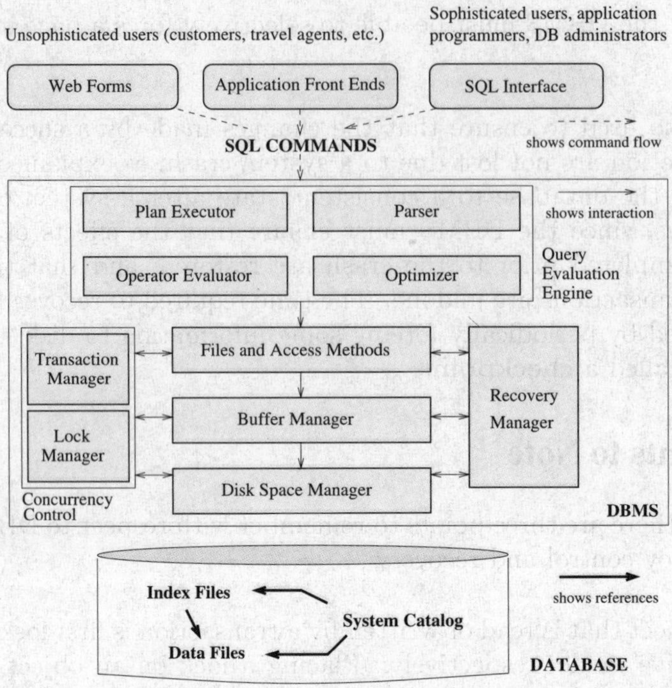

Figure 1.3 Architecture of a DBMS

blueprint for evaluating a query, usually represented as a tree of relational operators (with annotations that contain additional detailed information about which access methods to use, etc.). We discuss query optimization in Chapters 12 and 15. Relational operators serve as the building blocks for evaluating queries posed against the data. The implementation of these operators is discussed in Chapters 12 and 14.

The code that implements relational operators sits on top of the file and access methods layer. This layer supports the concept of a **file**, which, in a DBMS, is a collection of pages or a collection of records. **Heap files**, or files of unordered pages, as well as indexes are supported. In addition to keeping track of the pages in a file, this layer organizes the information within a page. File and page level storage issues are considered in Chapter 9. File organizations and indexes are considered in Chapter 8.

The files and access methods layer code sits on top of the **buffer manager**, which brings pages in from disk to main memory as needed in response to read requests. Buffer management is discussed in Chapter 9.

The lowest layer of the DBMS software deals with management of space on disk, where the data is stored. Higher layers allocate, deallocate, read, and write pages through (routines provided by) this layer, called the **disk space manager**. This layer is discussed in Chapter 9.

The DBMS supports concurrency and crash recovery by carefully scheduling user requests and maintaining a log of all changes to the database. DBMS components associated with concurrency control and recovery include the **transaction manager**, which ensures that transactions request and release locks according to a suitable locking protocol and schedules the execution transactions; the **lock manager**, which keeps track of requests for locks and grants locks on database objects when they become available; and the **recovery manager**, which is responsible for maintaining a log and restoring the system to a consistent state after a crash. The disk space manager, buffer manager, and file and access method layers must interact with these components. We discuss concurrency control and recovery in detail in Chapter 16.

1.9 PEOPLE WHO WORK WITH DATABASES

Quite a variety of people are associated with the creation and use of databases. Obviously, there are **database implementors**, who build DBMS software, and **end users** who wish to store and use data in a DBMS. Database implementors work for vendors such as IBM or Oracle. End users come from a diverse and increasing number of fields. As data grows in complexity and volume, and is increasingly recognized as a major asset, the importance of maintaining it professionally in a DBMS is being widely accepted. Many end users simply use applications written by database application programmers (see below) and so require little technical knowledge about DBMS software. Of course, sophisticated users who make more extensive use of a DBMS, such as writing their own queries, require a deeper understanding of its features.

In addition to end users and implementors, two other classes of people are associated with a DBMS: *application programmers* and *database administrators.*

Database application programmers develop packages that facilitate data access for end users, who are usually not computer professionals, using the host or data languages and software tools that DBMS vendors provide. (Such tools include report writers, spreadsheets, statistical packages, and the like.) Application programs should ideally access data through the external schema. It is possible to write applications that access data at a lower level, but such applications would compromise data independence.

A personal database is typically maintained by the individual who owns it and uses it. However, corporate or enterprise-wide databases are typically important enough and complex enough that the task of designing and maintaining the database is entrusted to a professional, called the **database administrator (DBA)**. The DBA is responsible for many critical tasks:

- **Design of the Conceptual and Physical Schemas:** The DBA is responsible for interacting with the users of the system to understand what data is to be stored in the DBMS and how it is likely to be used. Based on this knowledge, the DBA must design the conceptual schema (decide what relations to store) and the physical schema (decide how to store them). The DBA may also design widely used portions of the external schema, although users probably augment this schema by creating additional views.

- **Security and Authorization:** The DBA is responsible for ensuring that unauthorized data access is not permitted. In general, not everyone should be able to access all the data. In a relational DBMS, users can be granted permission to access only certain views and relations. For example, although you might allow students to find out course enrollments and who teaches a given course, you would not want students to see faculty salaries or each other's grade information. The DBA can enforce this policy by giving students permission to read only the Courseinfo view.

- **Data Availability and Recovery from Failures:** The DBA must take steps to ensure that if the system fails, users can continue to access as much of the uncorrupted data as possible. The DBA must also work to restore the data to a consistent state. The DBMS provides software support for these functions, but the DBA is responsible for implementing procedures to back up the data periodically and maintain logs of system activity (to facilitate recovery from a crash).

- **Database Tuning:** Users' needs are likely to evolve with time. The DBA is responsible for modifying the database, in particular the conceptual and physical schemas, to ensure adequate performance as requirements change.

1.10 REVIEW QUESTIONS

Answers to the review questions can be found in the listed sections.

- What are the main benefits of using a DBMS to manage data in applications involving extensive data access? **(Sections 1.1, 1.4)**

- When would you store data in a DBMS instead of in operating system files and vice-versa? **(Section 1.3)**

- What is a data model? What is the relational data model? What is data independence and how does a DBMS support it? **(Section 1.5)**
- Explain the advantages of using a query language instead of custom programs to process data. **(Section 1.6)**
- What is a transaction? What guarantees does a DBMS offer with respect to transactions? **(Section 1.7)**
- What are locks in a DBMS, and why are they used? What is write-ahead logging, and why is it used? What is checkpointing and why is it used? **(Section 1.7)**
- Identify the main components in a DBMS and briefly explain what they do. **(Section 1.8)**
- Explain the different roles of database administrators, application programmers, and end users of a database. Who needs to know the most about database systems? **(Section 1.9)**

EXERCISES

Exercise 1.1 Why would you choose a database system instead of simply storing data in operating system files? When would it make sense *not* to use a database system?

Exercise 1.2 What is logical data independence and why is it important?

Exercise 1.3 Explain the difference between logical and physical data independence.

Exercise 1.4 Explain the difference between external, internal, and conceptual schemas. How are these different schema layers related to the concepts of logical and physical data independence?

Exercise 1.5 What are the responsibilities of a DBA? If we assume that the DBA is never interested in running his or her own queries, does the DBA still need to understand query optimization? Why?

Exercise 1.6 Scrooge McNugget wants to store information (names, addresses, descriptions of embarrassing moments, etc.) about the many ducks on his payroll. Not surprisingly, the volume of data compels him to buy a database system. To save money, he wants to buy one with the fewest possible features, and he plans to run it as a stand-alone application on his PC clone. Of course, Scrooge does not plan to share his list with anyone. Indicate which of the following DBMS features Scrooge should pay for; in each case, also indicate why Scrooge should (or should not) pay for that feature in the system he buys.

1. A security facility.
2. Concurrency control.
3. Crash recovery.
4. A view mechanism.

5. A query language.

Exercise 1.7 Which of the following plays an important role in *representing* information about the real world in a database? Explain briefly.

1. The data definition language.
2. The data manipulation language.
3. The buffer manager.
4. The data model.

Exercise 1.8 Describe the structure of a DBMS. If your operating system is upgraded to support some new functions on OS files (e.g., the ability to force some sequence of bytes to disk), which layer(s) of the DBMS would you have to rewrite to take advantage of these new functions?

Exercise 1.9 Answer the following questions:

1. What is a transaction?
2. Why does a DBMS interleave the actions of different transactions instead of executing transactions one after the other?
3. What must a user guarantee with respect to a transaction and database consistency? What should a DBMS guarantee with respect to concurrent execution of several transactions and database consistency?
4. Explain the strict two-phase locking protocol.
5. What is the WAL property, and why is it important?

PROJECT-BASED EXERCISES

Exercise 1.10 Use a Web browser to look at the HTML documentation for Minibase. Try to get a feel for the overall architecture.

BIBLIOGRAPHIC NOTES

The evolution of database management systems is traced in [289]. The use of data models for describing real-world data is discussed in [423], and [425] contains a taxonomy of data models. The three levels of abstraction were introduced in [186, 712]. The network data model is described in [186], and [775] discusses several commercial systems based on this model. [721] contains a good annotated collection of systems-oriented papers on database management.

Other texts covering database management systems include [204, 245, 305, 339, 475, 574, 689, 747, 762]. [204] provides a detailed discussion of the relational model from a conceptual standpoint and is notable for its extensive annotated bibliography. [574] presents a performance-oriented perspective, with references to several commercial systems. [245] and [689] offer broad coverage of database system concepts, including a discussion of the hierarchical and network data models. [339] emphasizes the connection between database query languages and logic programming. [762] emphasizes data models. Of these texts, [747] provides the most detailed discussion of theoretical issues. Texts devoted to theoretical aspects include [3, 45, 501]. Handbook [744] includes a section on databases that contains introductory survey articles on a number of topics.

2

INTRODUCTION TO DATABASE DESIGN

- What are the steps in designing a database?
- Why is the ER model used to create an initial design?
- What are the main concepts in the ER model?
- What are guidelines for using the ER model effectively?
- How does database design fit within the overall design framework for complex software within large enterprises?
- What is UML and how is it related to the ER model?

Key concepts: database design, conceptual, logical, and physical design; entity-relationship (ER) model, entity set, relationship set, attribute, instance, key; integrity constraints, one-to-many and many-to-many relationships, participation constraints; weak entities, class hierarchies, aggregation; UML, class diagrams, database diagrams, component diagrams.

> The great successful men of the world have used their imaginations. They think ahead and create their mental picture, and then go to work materializing that picture in all its details, filling in here, adding a little there, altering this bit and that bit, but steadily building, steadily building.
>
> —Robert Collier

The *entity-relationship (ER) data model* allows us to describe the data involved in a real-world enterprise in terms of objects and their relationships and is widely used to develop an initial database design. It provides useful concepts that allow us to move from an informal description of what users want from their database to a more detailed, precise description that can be implemented in a DBMS. In this chapter, we introduce the ER model and discuss how its features allow us to model a wide range of data faithfully.

We begin with an overview of database design in Section 2.1 in order to motivate our discussion of the ER model. Within the larger context of the overall design process, the ER model is used in a phase called *conceptual database design.* We then introduce the ER model in Sections 2.2, 2.3, and 2.4. In Section 2.5, we discuss database design issues involving the ER model. We briefly discuss conceptual database design for large enterprises in Section 2.6. In Section 2.7, we present an overview of UML, a design and modeling approach that is more general in its scope than the ER model.

In Section 2.8, we introduce a case study that is used as a running example throughout the book. The case study is an end-to-end database design for an Internet shop. We illustrate the first two steps in database design (requirements analysis and conceptual design) in Section 2.8. In later chapters, we extend this case study to cover the remaining steps in the design process.

We note that many variations of ER diagrams are in use and no widely accepted standards prevail. The presentation in this chapter is representative of the family of ER models and includes a selection of the most popular features.

2.1 DATABASE DESIGN AND ER DIAGRAMS

We begin our discussion of database design by observing that this is typically just one part, although a central part in data-intensive applications, of a larger software system design. Our primary focus is the design of the database, however, and we will not discuss other aspects of software design in any detail. We revisit this point in Section 2.7.

The database design process can be divided into six steps. The ER model is most relevant to the first three steps.

1. **Requirements Analysis:** The very first step in designing a database application is to understand what data is to be stored in the database, what applications must be built on top of it, and what operations are most frequent and subject to performance requirements. In other words, we must find out what the users want from the database. This is usually an informal process that involves discussions with user groups, a study of the current operating environment and how it is expected to change, analysis of any available documentation on existing applications that are expected to be replaced or complemented by the database, and so on.

> **Database Design Tools:** Design tools are available from RDBMS vendors as well as third-party vendors. For example, see the following link for details on design and analysis tools from Sybase:
> `http://www.sybase.com/products/application_tools`
> The following provides details on Oracle's tools:
> `http://www.oracle.com/tools`

Several methodologies have been proposed for organizing and presenting the information gathered in this step, and some automated tools have been developed to support this process.

2. **Conceptual Database Design:** The information gathered in the requirements analysis step is used to develop a high-level description of the data to be stored in the database, along with the constraints known to hold over this data. This step is often carried out using the ER model and is discussed in the rest of this chapter. The ER model is one of several high-level, or **semantic**, data models used in database design. The goal is to create a simple description of the data that closely matches how users and developers think of the data (and the people and processes to be represented in the data). This facilitates discussion among all the people involved in the design process, even those who have no technical background. At the same time, the initial design must be sufficiently precise to enable a straightforward translation into a data model supported by a commercial database system (which, in practice, means the relational model).

3. **Logical Database Design:** We must choose a DBMS to implement our database design, and convert the conceptual database design into a database schema in the data model of the chosen DBMS. We will consider only relational DBMSs, and therefore, the task in the logical design step is to convert an ER schema into a relational database schema. We discuss this step in detail in Chapter 3; the result is a conceptual schema, sometimes called the **logical schema**, in the relational data model.

2.1.1 Beyond ER Design

The ER diagram is just an approximate description of the data, constructed through a subjective evaluation of the information collected during requirements analysis. A more careful analysis can often refine the logical schema obtained at the end of Step 3. Once we have a good logical schema, we must consider performance criteria and design the physical schema. Finally, we must address security issues and ensure that users are able to access the data they need, but not data that we wish to hide from them. The remaining three steps of database design are briefly described next:

4. **Schema Refinement:** The fourth step in database design is to analyze the collection of relations in our relational database schema to identify potential problems, and to refine it. In contrast to the requirements analysis and conceptual design steps, which are essentially subjective, schema refinement can be guided by some elegant and powerful theory. We discuss the theory of *normalizing* relations—restructuring them to ensure some desirable properties—in Chapter 19.

5. **Physical Database Design:** In this step, we consider typical expected workloads that our database must support and further refine the database design to ensure that it meets desired performance criteria. This step may simply involve building indexes on some tables and clustering some tables, or it may involve a substantial redesign of parts of the database schema obtained from the earlier design steps. We discuss physical design and database tuning in Chapter 20.

6. **Application and Security Design:** Any software project that involves a DBMS must consider aspects of the application that go beyond the database itself. Design methodologies like UML (Section 2.7) try to address the complete software design and development cycle. Briefly, we must identify the entities (e.g., users, user groups, departments) and processes involved in the application. We must describe the role of each entity in every process that is reflected in some application task, as part of a complete workflow for that task. For each role, we must identify the parts of the database that must be accessible and the parts of the database that must *not* be accessible, and we must take steps to ensure that these access rules are enforced. A DBMS provides several mechanisms to assist in this step, and we discuss this in Chapter 21.

In the implementation phase, we must code each task in an application language (e.g., Java), using the DBMS to access data. We discuss application development in Chapters 6 and 7.

In general, our division of the design process into steps should be seen as a classification of the *kinds* of steps involved in design. Realistically, although we might begin with the six step process outlined here, a complete database design will probably require a subsequent **tuning** phase in which all six kinds of design steps are interleaved and repeated until the design is satisfactory.

2.2 ENTITIES, ATTRIBUTES, AND ENTITY SETS

An **entity** is an object in the real world that is distinguishable from other objects. Examples include the following: the Green Dragonzord toy, the toy department, the manager of the toy department, the home address of the manager of the toy department. It is often useful to identify a collection of similar entities. Such a collection is called an **entity set**. Note that entity sets need not be disjoint; the collection of toy department employees and the collection of appliance department employees may both contain employee John Doe (who happens to work in both departments). We could also define an entity set called Employees that contains both the toy and appliance department employee sets.

An entity is described using a set of **attributes**. All entities in a given entity set have the same attributes; this is what we mean by *similar*. (This statement is an oversimplification, as we will see when we discuss inheritance hierarchies in Section 2.4.4, but it suffices for now and highlights the main idea.) Our choice of attributes reflects the level of detail at which we wish to represent information about entities. For example, the Employees entity set could use name, social security number (ssn), and parking lot (lot) as attributes. In this case we will store the name, social security number, and lot number for each employee. However, we will not store, say, an employee's address (or gender or age).

For each attribute associated with an entity set, we must identify a **domain** of possible values. For example, the domain associated with the attribute *name* of Employees might be the set of 20-character strings.[1] As another example, if the company rates employees on a scale of 1 to 10 and stores ratings in a field called *rating*, the associated domain consists of integers 1 through 10. Further, for each entity set, we choose a *key*. A **key** is a minimal set of attributes whose values uniquely identify an entity in the set. There could be more than one **candidate** key; if so, we designate one of them as the **primary** key. For now we assume that each entity set contains at least one set of attributes that uniquely identifies an entity in the entity set; that is, the set of attributes contains a key. We revisit this point in Section 2.4.3.

The Employees entity set with attributes *ssn, name,* and *lot* is shown in Figure 2.1. An entity set is represented by a rectangle, and an attribute is represented by an oval. Each attribute in the primary key is underlined. The domain information could be listed along with the attribute name, but we omit this to keep the figures compact. The key is *ssn.*

2.3 RELATIONSHIPS AND RELATIONSHIP SETS

A **relationship** is an association among two or more entities. For example, we may have the relationship that Attishoo works in the pharmacy department.

[1]To avoid confusion, we assume that attribute names do not repeat across entity sets. This is not a real limitation because we can always use the entity set name to resolve ambiguities if the same attribute name is used in more than one entity set.

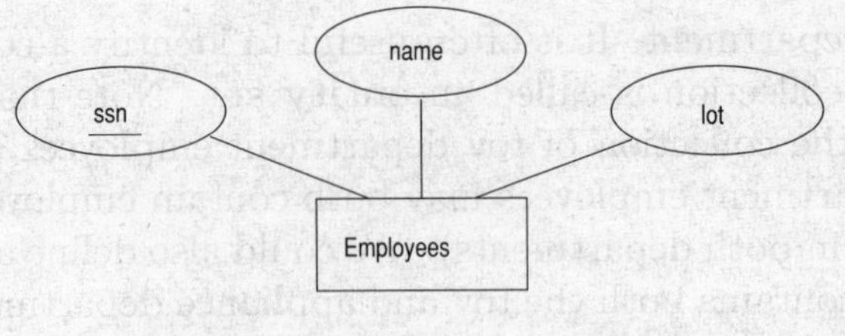

Figure 2.1 The Employees Entity Set

As with entities, we may wish to collect a set of similar relationships into a **relationship set**. A relationship set can be thought of as a set of n-tuples:

$$\{(e_1, \ldots, e_n) \mid e_1 \in E_1, \ldots, e_n \in E_n\}$$

Each n-tuple denotes a relationship involving n entities e_1 through e_n, where entity e_i is in entity set E_i. In Figure 2.2 we show the relationship set Works In, in which each relationship indicates a department in which an employee works. Note that several relationship sets might involve the same entity sets. For example, we could also have a Manages relationship set involving Employees and Departments.

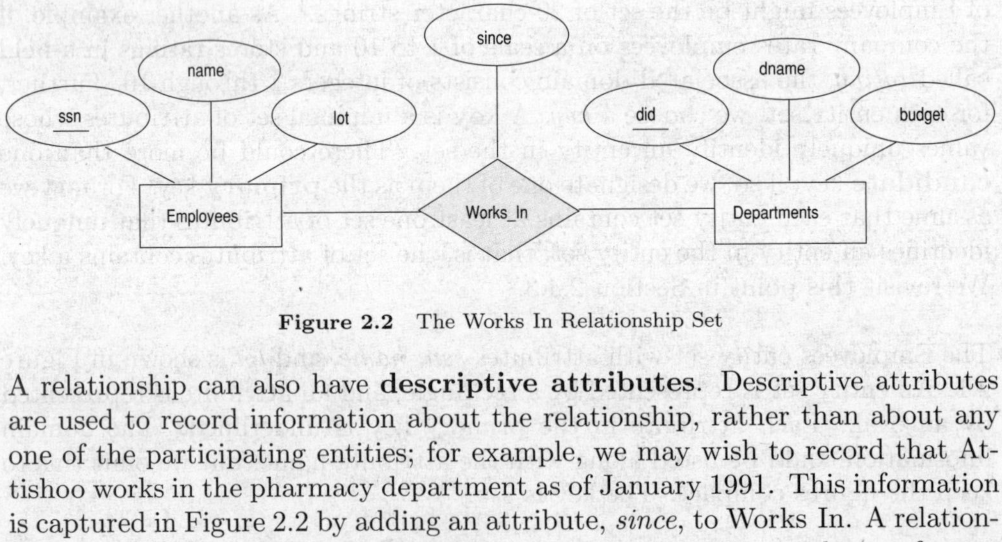

Figure 2.2 The Works In Relationship Set

A relationship can also have **descriptive attributes**. Descriptive attributes are used to record information about the relationship, rather than about any one of the participating entities; for example, we may wish to record that Attishoo works in the pharmacy department as of January 1991. This information is captured in Figure 2.2 by adding an attribute, *since*, to Works In. A relationship must be uniquely identified by the participating entities, without reference to the descriptive attributes. In the Works In relationship set, for example, each Works In relationship must be uniquely identified by the combination of employee *ssn* and department *did*. Thus, for a given employee-department pair, we cannot have more than one associated *since* value.

An **instance** of a relationship set is a set of relationships. Intuitively, an instance can be thought of as a 'snapshot' of the relationship set at some instant in time. An instance of the Works In relationship set is shown in Figure 2.3. Each Employees entity is denoted by its *ssn*, and each Departments entity is denoted by its *did*, for simplicity. The *since* value is shown beside each relationship. (The 'many-to-many' and 'total participation' comments in the figure are discussed later, when we discuss integrity constraints.)

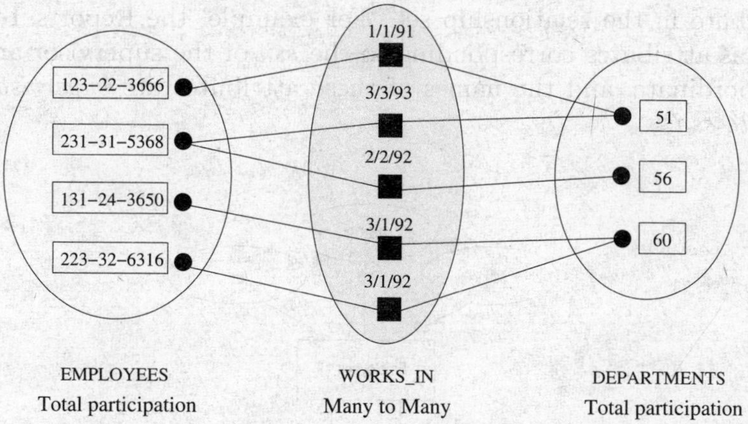

Figure 2.3 An Instance of the Works In Relationship Set

As another example of an ER diagram, suppose that each department has offices in several locations and we want to record the locations at which each employee works. This relationship is **ternary** because we must record an association between an employee, a department, and a location. The ER diagram for this variant of Works In, which we call Works In2, is shown in Figure 2.4.

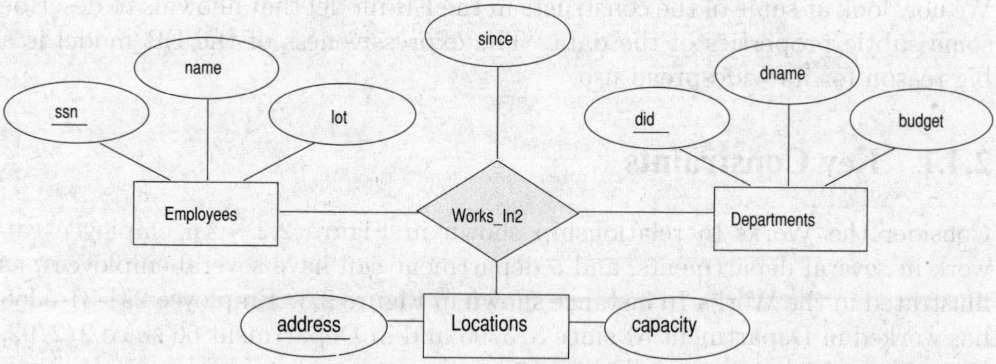

Figure 2.4 A Ternary Relationship Set

The entity sets that participate in a relationship set need not be distinct; sometimes a relationship might involve two entities in the same entity set. For example, consider the Reports To relationship set shown in Figure 2.5. Since employees report to other employees, every relationship in Reports To is of the form (emp_1, emp_2), where both emp_1 and emp_2 are entities in Employees. However, they play different **roles**: emp_1 reports to the managing employee emp_2, which is reflected in the **role indicators** *supervisor* and *subordinate* in Figure 2.5. If an entity set plays more than one role, the role indicator concatenated with an attribute name from the entity set gives us a unique name for each attribute in the relationship set. For example, the Reports To relationship set has attributes corresponding to the *ssn* of the supervisor and the *ssn* of the subordinate, and the names of these attributes are *supervisor ssn* and *subordinate ssn*.

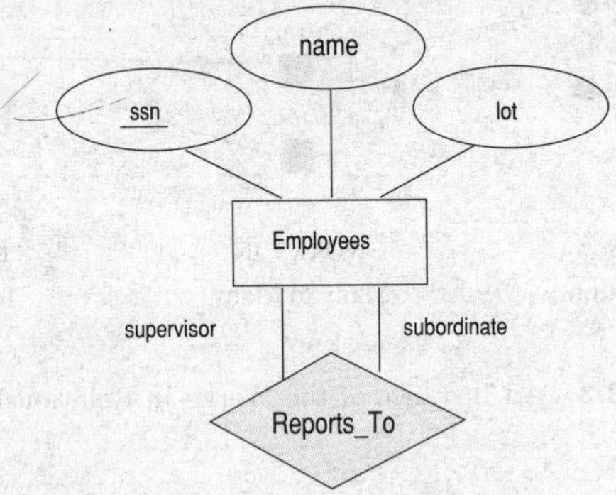

Figure 2.5 The Reports To Relationship Set

2.4 ADDITIONAL FEATURES OF THE ER MODEL

We now look at some of the constructs in the ER model that allow us to describe some subtle properties of the data. The expressiveness of the ER model is a big reason for its widespread use.

2.4.1 Key Constraints

Consider the Works In relationship shown in Figure 2.2. An employee can work in several departments, and a department can have several employees, as illustrated in the Works In instance shown in Figure 2.3. Employee 231-31-5368 has worked in Department 51 since 3/3/93 and in Department 56 since 2/2/92. Department 51 has two employees.

Now consider another relationship set called Manages between the Employees and Departments entity sets such that each department has at most one manager, although a single employee is allowed to manage more than one department. The restriction that each department has at most one manager is an example of a **key constraint**, and it implies that each Departments entity appears in at most one Manages relationship in any allowable instance of Manages. This restriction is indicated in the ER diagram of Figure 2.6 by using an arrow from Departments to Manages. Intuitively, the arrow states that given a Departments entity, we can uniquely determine the Manages relationship in which it appears.

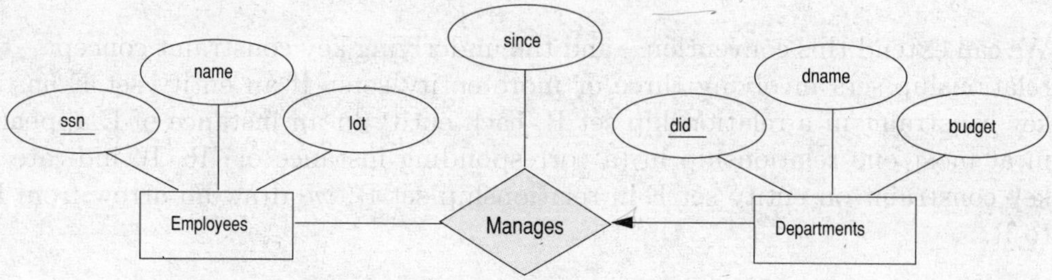

Figure 2.6 Key Constraint on Manages

An instance of the Manages relationship set is shown in Figure 2.7. While this is also a potential instance for the Works In relationship set, the instance of Works In shown in Figure 2.3 violates the key constraint on Manages.

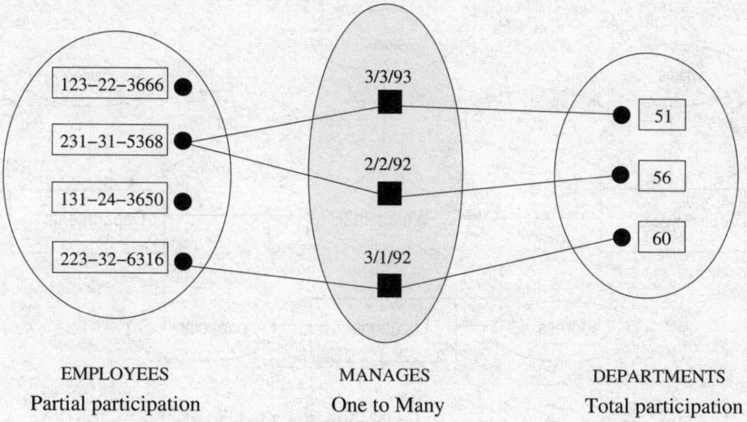

Figure 2.7 An Instance of the Manages Relationship Set

A relationship set like Manages is sometimes said to be **one-to-many**, to indicate that *one* employee can be associated with *many* departments (in the capacity of a manager), whereas each department can be associated with at most one employee as its manager. In contrast, the Works In relationship set, in which an employee is allowed to work in several departments and a department is allowed to have several employees, is said to be **many-to-many**.

If we add the restriction that each employee can manage at most one department to the Manages relationship set, which would be indicated by adding an arrow from Employees to Manages in Figure 2.6, we have a **one-to-one** relationship set.

Key Constraints for Ternary Relationships

We can extend this convention—and the underlying key constraint concept—to relationship sets involving three or more entity sets: If an entity set E has a key constraint in a relationship set R, each entity in an instance of E appears in at most one relationship in (a corresponding instance of) R. To indicate a key constraint on entity set E in relationship set R, we draw an arrow from E to R.

In Figure 2.8, we show a ternary relationship with key constraints. Each employee works in at most one department and at a single location. An instance of the Works In3 relationship set is shown in Figure 2.9. Note that each department can be associated with several employees and locations and each location can be associated with several departments and employees; however, each employee is associated with a single department and location.

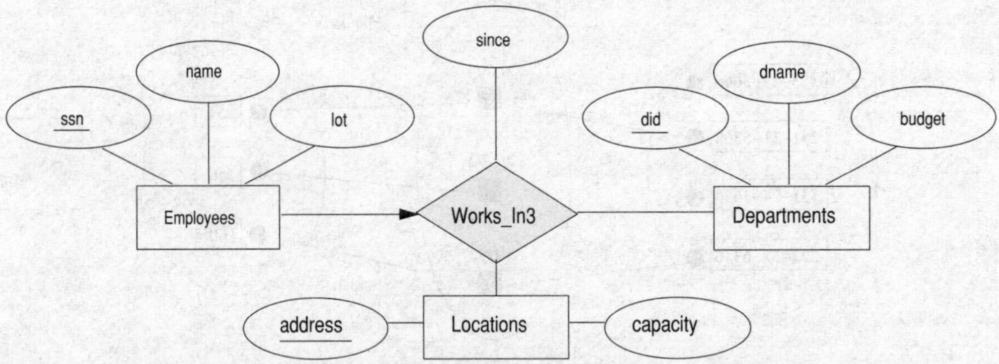

Figure 2.8 A Ternary Relationship Set with Key Constraints

2.4.2 Participation Constraints

The key constraint on Manages tells us that a department has at most one manager. A natural question to ask is whether every department has a manager. Let us say that every department is required to have a manager. This requirement is an example of a **participation constraint**; the participation of the entity set Departments in the relationship set Manages is said to be **total**. A participation that is not total is said to be **partial**. As an example, the

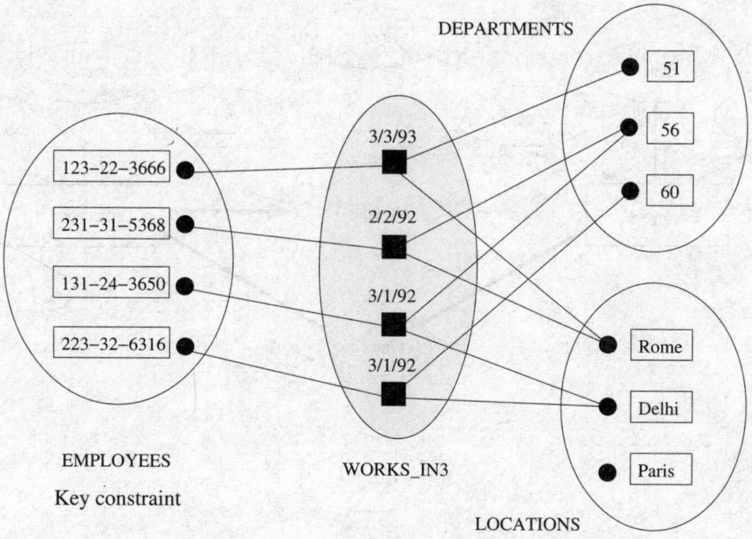

Figure 2.9 An Instance of Works In3

participation of the entity set Employees in Manages is partial, since not every employee gets to manage a department.

Revisiting the Works In relationship set, it is natural to expect that each employee works in at least one department and that each department has at least one employee. This means that the participation of both Employees and Departments in Works In is total. The ER diagram in Figure 2.10 shows both the Manages and Works In relationship sets and all the given constraints. If the participation of an entity set in a relationship set is total, the two are connected by a thick line; independently, the presence of an arrow indicates a key constraint. The instances of Works In and Manages shown in Figures 2.3 and 2.7 satisfy all the constraints in Figure 2.10.

2.4.3 Weak Entities

Thus far, we have assumed that the attributes associated with an entity set include a key. This assumption does not always hold. For example, suppose that employees can purchase insurance policies to cover their dependents. We wish to record information about policies, including who is covered by each policy, but this information is really our only interest in the dependents of an employee. If an employee quits, any policy owned by the employee is terminated and we want to delete all the relevant policy and dependent information from the database.

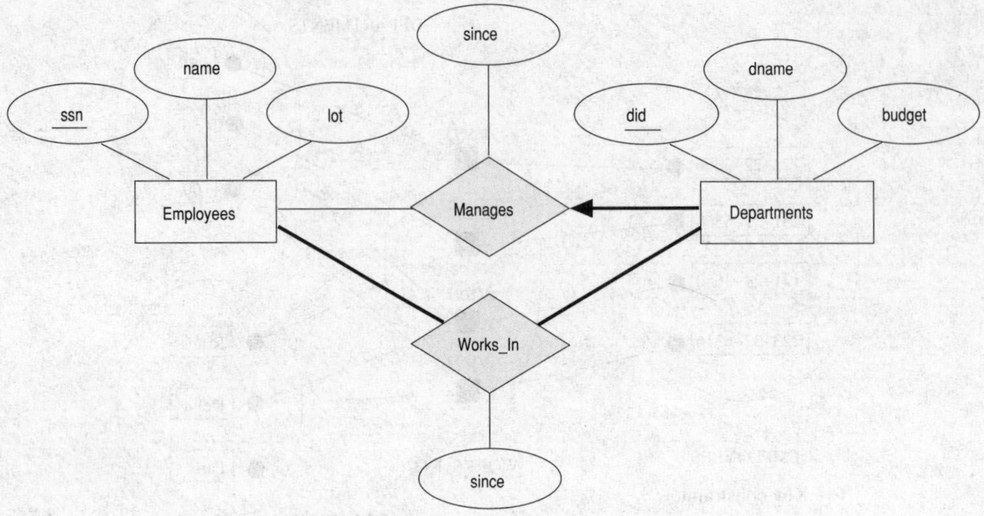

Figure 2.10 Manages and Works_In

We might choose to identify a dependent by name alone in this situation, since it is reasonable to expect that the dependents of a given employee have different names. Thus the attributes of the Dependents entity set might be *pname* and *age*. The attribute *pname* does *not* identify a dependent uniquely. Recall that the key for Employees is *ssn*; thus we might have two employees called Smethurst and each might have a son called Joe.

Dependents is an example of a **weak entity set**. A weak entity can be identified uniquely only by considering some of its attributes in conjunction with the primary key of another entity, which is called the **identifying owner**.

The following restrictions must hold:

- The owner entity set and the weak entity set must participate in a one-to-many relationship set (one owner entity is associated with one or more weak entities, but each weak entity has a single owner). This relationship set is called the **identifying relationship set** of the weak entity set.

- The weak entity set must have total participation in the identifying relationship set.

For example, a Dependents entity can be identified uniquely only if we take the key of the *owning* Employees entity and the *pname* of the Dependents entity. The set of attributes of a weak entity set that uniquely identify a weak entity for a given owner entity is called a *partial key* of the weak entity set. In our example, *pname* is a partial key for Dependents.

The Dependents weak entity set and its relationship to Employees is shown in Figure 2.11. The total participation of Dependents in Policy is indicated by linking them with a dark line. The arrow from Dependents to Policy indicates that each Dependents entity appears in at most one (indeed, exactly one, because of the participation constraint) Policy relationship. To underscore the fact that Dependents is a weak entity and Policy is its identifying relationship, we draw both with dark lines. To indicate that *pname* is a partial key for Dependents, we underline it using a broken line. This means that there may well be two dependents with the same *pname* value.

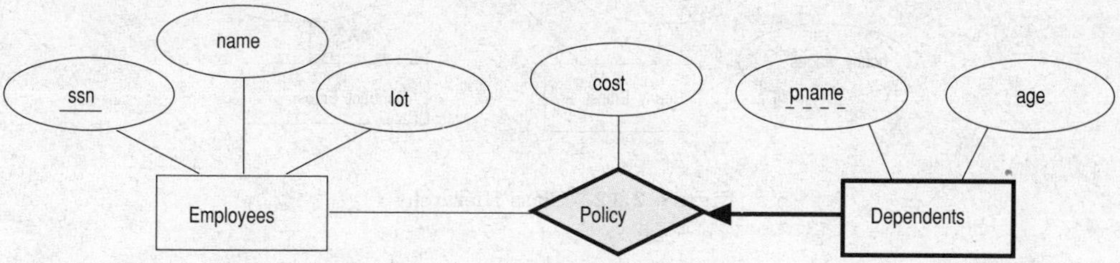

Figure 2.11 A Weak Entity Set

2.4.4 Class Hierarchies

Sometimes it is natural to classify the entities in an entity set into subclasses. For example, we might want to talk about an Hourly_Emps entity set and a Contract_Emps entity set to distinguish the basis on which they are paid. We might have attributes *hours_worked* and *hourly_wage* defined for Hourly_Emps and an attribute *contractid* defined for Contract_Emps.

We want the semantics that every entity in one of these sets is also an Employees entity and, as such, must have all the attributes of Employees defined. Therefore, the attributes defined for an Hourly_Emps entity are the attributes for Employees plus Hourly_Emps. We say that the attributes for the entity set Employees are **inherited** by the entity set Hourly_Emps and that Hourly_Emps **ISA** (read *is a*) Employees. In addition—and in contrast to class hierarchies in programming languages such as C++—there is a constraint on queries over instances of these entity sets: A query that asks for all Employees entities must consider all Hourly_Emps and Contract_Emps entities as well. Figure 2.12 illustrates the class hierarchy.

The entity set Employees may also be classified using a different criterion. For example, we might identify a subset of employees as Senior_Emps. We can modify Figure 2.12 to reflect this change by adding a second ISA node as a child of Employees and making Senior_Emps a child of this node. Each of these entity sets might be classified further, creating a multilevel ISA hierarchy.

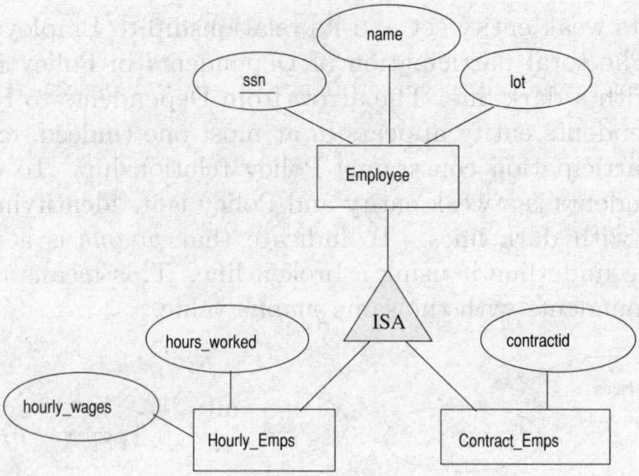

Figure 2.12 Class Hierarchy

A class hierarchy can be viewed in one of two ways:

- Employees is **specialized** into subclasses. Specialization is the process of identifying subsets of an entity set (the **superclass**) that share some distinguishing characteristic. Typically, the superclass is defined first, the subclasses are defined next, and subclass-specific attributes and relationship sets are then added.

- Hourly_Emps and Contract_Emps are **generalized** by Employees. As another example, two entity sets Motorboats and Cars may be generalized into an entity set Motor_Vehicles. Generalization consists of identifying some common characteristics of a collection of entity sets and creating a new entity set that contains entities possessing these common characteristics. Typically, the subclasses are defined first, the superclass is defined next, and any relationship sets that involve the superclass are then defined.

We can specify two kinds of constraints with respect to ISA hierarchies, namely, *overlap* and *covering* constraints. **Overlap constraints** determine whether two subclasses are allowed to contain the same entity. For example, can Attishoo be both an Hourly_Emps entity and a Contract_Emps entity? Intuitively, no. Can he be both a Contract_Emps entity and a Senior_Emps entity? Intuitively, yes. We denote this by writing 'Contract_Emps `OVERLAPS` Senior_Emps.' In the absence of such a statement, we assume by default that entity sets are constrained to have no overlap.

Covering constraints determine whether the entities in the subclasses collectively include all entities in the superclass. For example, does every Employees entity have to belong to one of its subclasses? Intuitively, no. Does every Motor_Vehicles entity have to be either a Motorboats entity or a Cars entity? Intuitively, yes; a characteristic property of generalization hierarchies is that every instance of a superclass is an instance of a subclass. We denote this by writing 'Motorboats `AND` Cars `COVER` Motor_Vehicles.' In the absence of such a statement, we assume by default that there is no covering constraint; we can have motor vehicles that are not motorboats or cars.

There are two basic reasons for identifying subclasses (by specialization or generalization):

1. We might want to add descriptive attributes that make sense only for the entities in a subclass. For example, *hourly_wages* does not make sense for a Contract_Emps entity, whose pay is determined by an individual contract.

2. We might want to identify the set of entities that participate in some relationship. For example, we might wish to define the Manages relationship so that the participating entity sets are Senior_Emps and Departments, to ensure that only senior employees can be managers. As another example, Motorboats and Cars may have different descriptive attributes (say, tonnage and number of doors), but as Motor_Vehicles entities, they must be licensed. The licensing information can be captured by a Licensed_To relationship between Motor_Vehicles and an entity set called Owners.

2.4.5 Aggregation

As defined thus far, a relationship set is an association between entity sets. Sometimes, we have to model a relationship between a collection of entities and *relationships.* Suppose that we have an entity set called Projects and that each Projects entity is sponsored by one or more departments. The Sponsors relationship set captures this information. A department that sponsors a project might assign employees to monitor the sponsorship. Intuitively, Monitors should be a relationship set that associates a Sponsors relationship (rather than a Projects or Departments entity) with an Employees entity. However, we have defined relationships to associate two or more *entities.*

To define a relationship set such as Monitors, we introduce a new feature of the ER model, called *aggregation.* **Aggregation** allows us to indicate that a relationship set (identified through a dashed box) participates in another relationship set. This is illustrated in Figure 2.13, with a dashed box around Sponsors (and its participating entity sets) used to denote aggregation. This effectively allows us to treat Sponsors as an entity set for purposes of defining the Monitors relationship set.

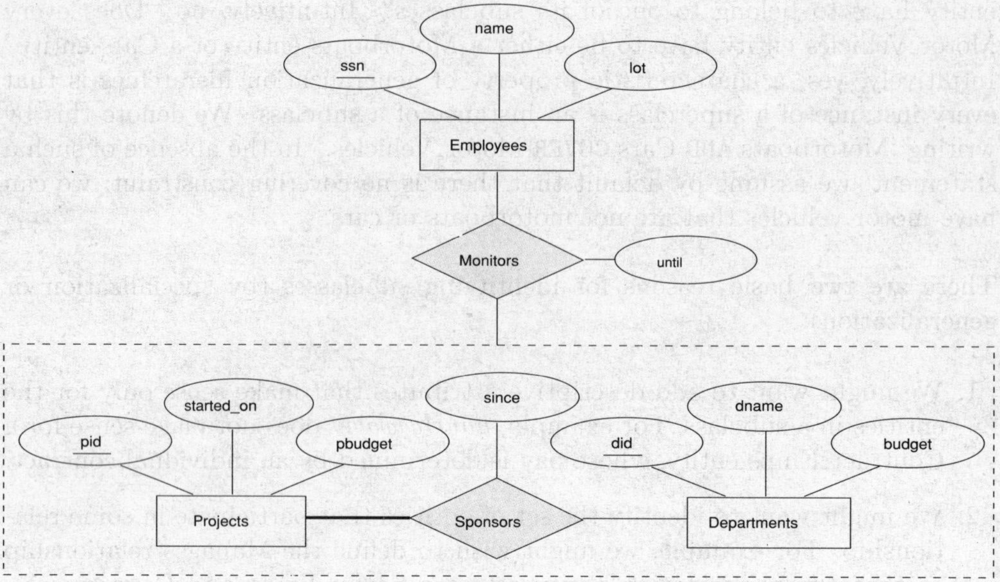

Figure 2.13 Aggregation

When should we use aggregation? Intuitively, we use it when we need to express a relationship among relationships. But can we not express relationships involving other relationships without using aggregation? In our example, why not make Sponsors a ternary relationship? The answer is that there are really two distinct relationships, Sponsors and Monitors, each possibly with attributes of its own. For instance, the Monitors relationship has an attribute *until* that records the date until when the employee is appointed as the sponsorship monitor. Compare this attribute with the attribute *since* of Sponsors, which is the date when the sponsorship took effect. The use of aggregation versus a ternary relationship may also be guided by certain integrity constraints, as explained in Section 2.5.4.

2.5 CONCEPTUAL DESIGN WITH THE ER MODEL

Developing an ER diagram presents several choices, including the following:

- Should a concept be modeled as an entity or an attribute?
- Should a concept be modeled as an entity or a relationship?
- What are the relationship sets and their participating entity sets? Should we use binary or ternary relationships?
- Should we use aggregation?

We now discuss the issues involved in making these choices.

2.5.1 Entity versus Attribute

While identifying the attributes of an entity set, it is sometimes not clear whether a property should be modeled as an attribute or as an entity set (and related to the first entity set using a relationship set). For example, consider adding address information to the Employees entity set. One option is to use an attribute *address*. This option is appropriate if we need to record only one address per employee, and it suffices to think of an address as a string. An alternative is to create an entity set called Addresses and to record associations between employees and addresses using a relationship (say, Has_Address). This more complex alternative is necessary in two situations:

- We have to record more than one address for an employee.
- We want to capture the structure of an address in our ER diagram. For example, we might break down an address into city, state, country, and Zip code, in addition to a string for street information. By representing an address as an entity with these attributes, we can support queries such as "Find all employees with an address in Madison, WI."

For another example of when to model a concept as an entity set rather than an attribute, consider the relationship set (called Works_In4) shown in Figure 2.14.

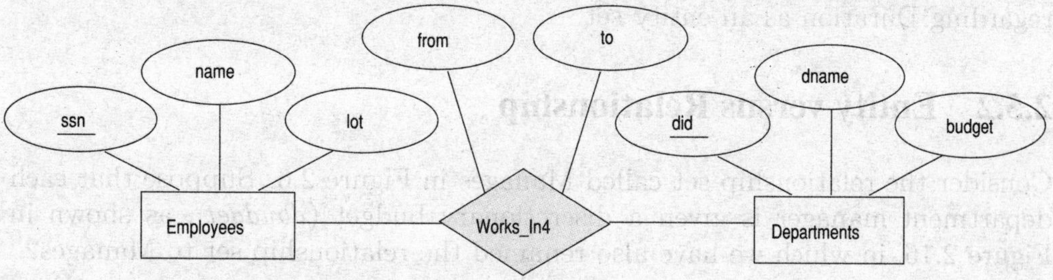

Figure 2.14 The Works_In4 Relationship Set

It differs from the Works_In relationship set of Figure 2.2 only in that it has attributes *from* and *to*, instead of *since*. Intuitively, it records the interval during which an employee works for a department. Now suppose that it is possible for an employee to work in a given department over more than one period.

This possibility is ruled out by the ER diagram's semantics, because a relationship is uniquely identified by the participating entities (recall from Section

2.3). The problem is that we want to record several values for the descriptive attributes for each instance of the Works In2 relationship. (This situation is analogous to wanting to record several addresses for each employee.) We can address this problem by introducing an entity set called, say, Duration, with attributes *from* and *to*, as shown in Figure 2.15.

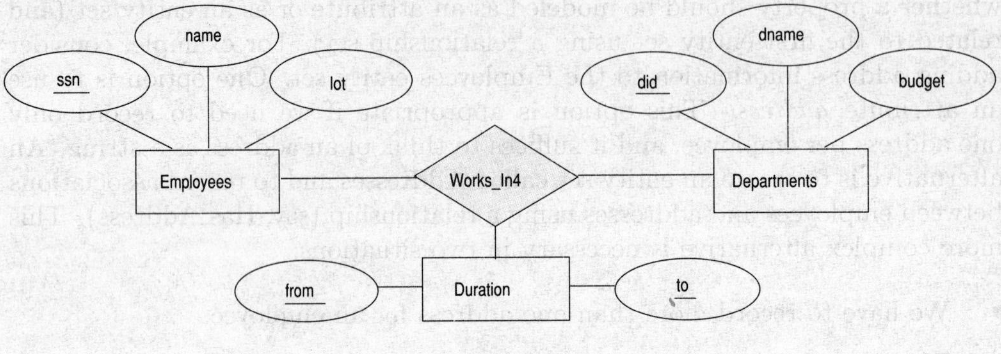

Figure 2.15 The Works In4 Relationship Set

In some versions of the ER model, attributes are allowed to take on sets as values. Given this feature, we could make Duration an attribute of Works In, rather than an entity set; associated with each Works In relationship, we would have a set of intervals. This approach is perhaps more intuitive than modeling Duration as an entity set. Nonetheless, when such set-valued attributes are translated into the relational model, which does not support set-valued attributes, the resulting relational schema is very similar to what we get by regarding Duration as an entity set.

2.5.2 Entity versus Relationship

Consider the relationship set called Manages in Figure 2.6. Suppose that each department manager is given a discretionary budget (*dbudget*), as shown in Figure 2.16, in which we have also renamed the relationship set to Manages2.

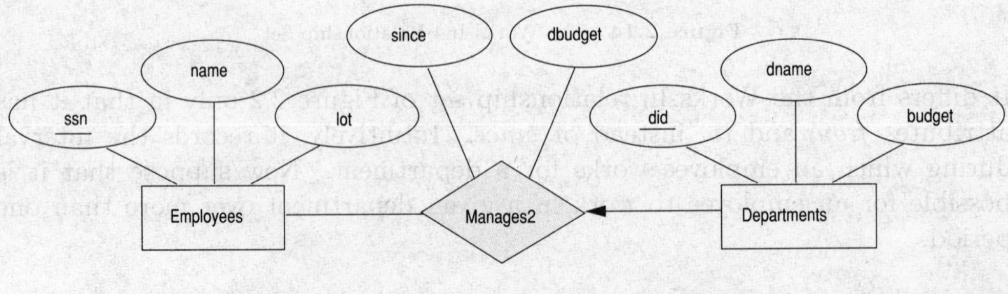

Figure 2.16 Entity versus Relationship

Given a department, we know the manager, as well as the manager's starting date and budget for that department. This approach is natural if we assume that a manager receives a separate discretionary budget for each department that he or she manages.

But what if the discretionary budget is a sum that covers *all* departments managed by that employee? In this case, each Manages2 relationship that involves a given employee will have the same value in the *dbudget* field, leading to redundant storage of the same information. Another problem with this design is that it is misleading; it suggests that the budget is associated with the relationship, when it is actually associated with the manager.

We can address these problems by introducing a new entity set called Managers (which can be placed below Employees in an ISA hierarchy, to show that every manager is also an employee). The attributes *since* and *dbudget* now describe a manager entity, as intended. As a variation, while every manager has a budget, each manager may have a different starting date (as manager) for each department. In this case *dbudget* is an attribute of Managers, but *since* is an attribute of the relationship set between managers and departments.

The imprecise nature of ER modeling can thus make it difficult to recognize underlying entities, and we might associate attributes with relationships rather than the appropriate entities. In general, such mistakes lead to redundant storage of the same information and can cause many problems. We discuss redundancy and its attendant problems in Chapter 19, and present a technique called *normalization* to eliminate redundancies from tables.

2.5.3 Binary versus Ternary Relationships

Consider the ER diagram shown in Figure 2.17. It models a situation in which an employee can own several policies, each policy can be owned by several employees, and each dependent can be covered by several policies.

Suppose that we have the following additional requirements:

- A policy cannot be owned jointly by two or more employees.
- Every policy must be owned by some employee.
- Dependents is a weak entity set, and each dependent entity is uniquely identified by taking *pname* in conjunction with the *policyid* of a policy entity (which, intuitively, covers the given dependent).

The first requirement suggests that we impose a key constraint on Policies with respect to Covers, but this constraint has the unintended side effect that a

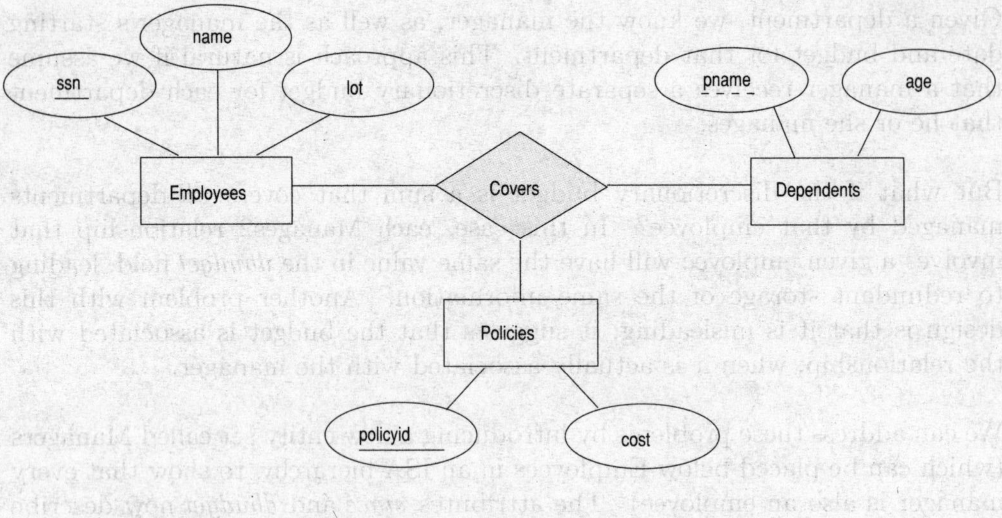

Figure 2.17 Policies as an Entity Set

policy can cover only one dependent. The second requirement suggests that we impose a total participation constraint on Policies. This solution is acceptable if each policy covers at least one dependent. The third requirement forces us to introduce an identifying relationship that is binary (in our version of ER diagrams, although there are versions in which this is not the case).

Even ignoring the third requirement, the best way to model this situation is to use two binary relationships, as shown in Figure 2.18.

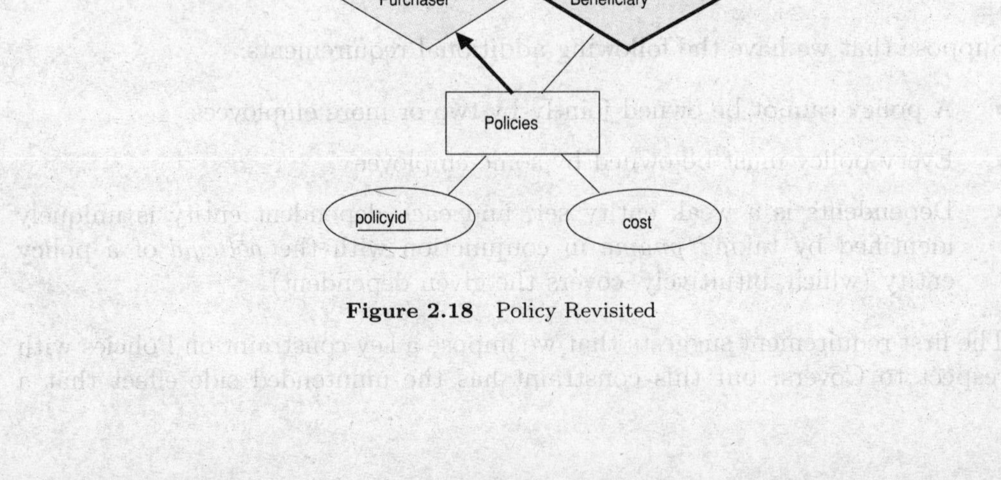

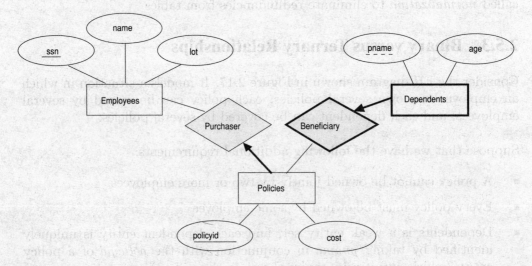

Figure 2.18 Policy Revisited

This example really has two relationships involving Policies, and our attempt to use a single ternary relationship (Figure 2.17) is inappropriate. There are situations, however, where a relationship inherently associates more than two entities. We have seen such an example in Figures 2.4 and 2.15.

As a typical example of a ternary relationship, consider entity sets Parts, Suppliers, and Departments, and a relationship set Contracts (with descriptive attribute *qty*) that involves all of them. A contract specifies that a supplier will supply (some quantity of) a part to a department. This relationship cannot be adequately captured by a collection of binary relationships (without the use of aggregation). With binary relationships, we can denote that a supplier 'can supply' certain parts, that a department 'needs' some parts, or that a department 'deals with' a certain supplier. No combination of these relationships expresses the meaning of a contract adequately, for at least two reasons:

- The facts that supplier S can supply part P, that department D needs part P, and that D will buy from S do not necessarily imply that department D indeed buys part P from supplier S!
- We cannot represent the *qty* attribute of a contract cleanly.

2.5.4 Aggregation versus Ternary Relationships

As we noted in Section 2.4.5, the choice between using aggregation or a ternary relationship is mainly determined by the existence of a relationship that relates a *relationship set* to an entity set (or second relationship set). The choice may also be guided by certain integrity constraints that we want to express. For example, consider the ER diagram shown in Figure 2.13. According to this diagram, a project can be sponsored by any number of departments, a department can sponsor one or more projects, and each sponsorship is monitored by one or more employees. If we don't need to record the *until* attribute of Monitors, then we might reasonably use a ternary relationship, say, Sponsors2, as shown in Figure 2.19.

Consider the constraint that each sponsorship (of a project by a department) be monitored by at most one employee. We cannot express this constraint in terms of the Sponsors2 relationship set. On the other hand, we can easily express the constraint by drawing an arrow from the aggregated relationship Sponsors to the relationship Monitors in Figure 2.13. Thus, the presence of such a constraint serves as another reason for using aggregation rather than a ternary relationship set.

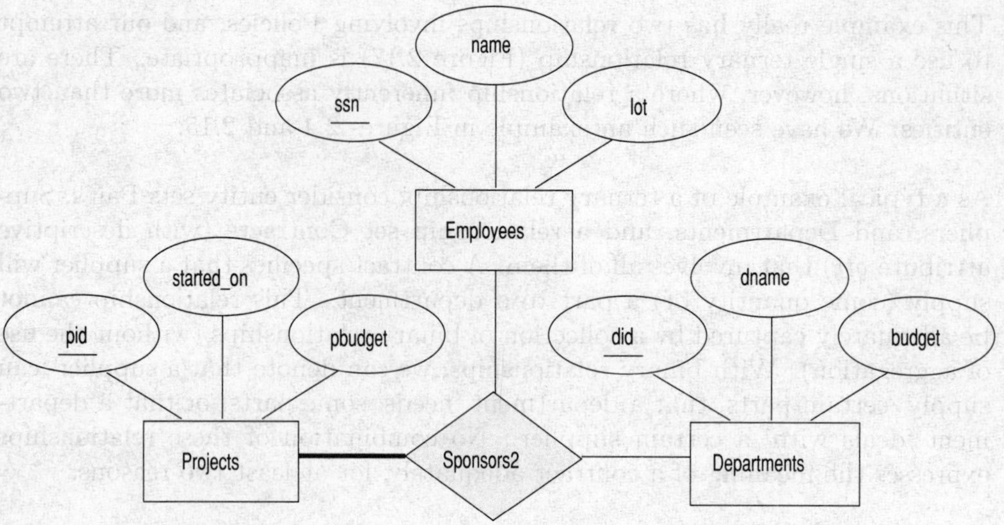

Figure 2.19 Using a Ternary Relationship instead of Aggregation

2.6 CONCEPTUAL DESIGN FOR LARGE ENTERPRISES

We have thus far concentrated on the constructs available in the ER model for describing various application concepts and relationships. The process of conceptual design consists of more than just describing small fragments of the application in terms of ER diagrams. For a large enterprise, the design may require the efforts of more than one designer and span data and application code used by a number of user groups. Using a high-level, semantic data model, such as ER diagrams, for conceptual design in such an environment offers the additional advantage that the high-level design can be diagrammatically represented and easily understood by the many people who must provide input to the design process.

An important aspect of the design process is the methodology used to structure the development of the overall design and ensure that the design takes into account all user requirements and is consistent. The usual approach is that the requirements of various user groups are considered, any conflicting requirements are somehow resolved, and a single set of global requirements is generated at the end of the requirements analysis phase. Generating a single set of global requirements is a difficult task, but it allows the conceptual design phase to proceed with the development of a logical schema that spans all the data and applications throughout the enterprise.

An alternative approach is to develop separate conceptual schemas for different user groups and then *integrate* these conceptual schemas. To integrate multiple conceptual schemas, we must establish correspondences between entities, relationships, and attributes, and we must resolve numerous kinds of conflicts (e.g., naming conflicts, domain mismatches, differences in measurement units). This task is difficult in its own right. In some situations, schema integration cannot be avoided; for example, when one organization merges with another, existing databases may have to be integrated. Schema integration is also increasing in importance as users demand access to *heterogeneous* data sources, often maintained by different organizations.

2.7 THE UNIFIED MODELING LANGUAGE

There are many approaches to end-to-end software system design, covering all the steps from identifying the business requirements to the final specifications for a complete application, including workflow, user interfaces, and many aspects of software systems that go well beyond databases and the data stored in them. In this section, we briefly discuss an approach that is becoming popular, called the **unified modeling language (UML) approach**.

UML, like the ER model, has the attractive feature that its constructs can be drawn as diagrams. It encompasses a broader spectrum of the software design process than the ER model:

- **Business Modeling:** In this phase, the goal is to describe the business processes involved in the software application being developed.
- **System Modeling:** The understanding of business processes is used to identify the requirements for the software application. One part of the requirements is the database requirements.
- **Conceptual Database Modeling:** This step corresponds to the creation of the ER design for the database. For this purpose, UML provides many constructs that parallel the ER constructs.
- **Physical Database Modeling:** UML also provides pictorial representations for physical database design choices, such as the creation of table spaces and indexes. (We discuss physical database design in later chapters, but not the corresponding UML constructs.)
- **Hardware System Modeling:** UML diagrams can be used to describe the hardware configuration used for the application.

There are many kinds of diagrams in UML. **Use case** diagrams describe the actions performed by the system in response to user requests, and the people involved in these actions. These diagrams specify the external functionality that the system is expected to support.

Activity diagrams show the flow of actions in a business process. **Statechart** diagrams describe dynamic interactions between system objects. These diagrams, used in business and system modeling, describe how the external functionality is to be implemented, consistent with the business rules and processes of the enterprise.

Class diagrams are similar to ER diagrams, although they are more general in that they are intended to model *application* entities (intuitively, important program components) and their logical relationships in addition to data entities and their relationships.

Both entity sets and relationship sets can be represented as classes in UML, together with key constraints, weak entities, and class hierarchies. The term *relationship* is used slightly differently in UML, and UML's relationships are binary. This sometimes leads to confusion over whether relationship sets in an ER diagram involving three or more entity sets can be directly represented in UML. The confusion disappears once we understand that all relationship sets (in the ER sense) are represented as classes in UML; the binary UML 'relationships' are essentially just the links shown in ER diagrams between entity sets and relationship sets.

Relationship sets with key constraints are usually omitted from UML diagrams, and the relationship is indicated by directly linking the entity sets involved. For example, consider Figure 2.6. A UML representation of this ER diagram would have a class for Employees, a class for Departments, and the relationship Manages is shown by linking these two classes. The link can be labeled with a name and cardinality information to show that a department can have only one manager.

As we will see in Chapter 3, ER diagrams are translated into the relational model by mapping each entity set into a table and each relationship set into a table. Further, as we will see in Section 3.5.3, the table corresponding to a one-to-many relationship set is typically omitted by including some additional information about the relationship in the table for one of the entity sets involved. Thus, UML class diagrams correspond closely to the tables created by mapping an ER diagram.

Indeed, every class in a UML class diagram is mapped into a table in the corresponding UML database diagram. UML's **database diagrams** show how classes are represented in the database and contain additional details about the structure of the database such as integrity constraints and indexes. Links (UML's 'relationships') between UML classes lead to various integrity constraints between the corresponding tables. Many details specific to the relational model (e.g., *views*, *foreign keys*, *null-allowed fields*) and that reflect physical design choices (e.g., indexed fields) can be modeled in UML database diagrams.

UML's **component** diagrams describe storage aspects of the database, such as *tablespaces* and *database partitions*), as well as interfaces to applications that access the database. Finally, **deployment** diagrams show the hardware aspects of the system.

Our objective in this book is to concentrate on the data stored in a database and the related design issues. To this end, we deliberately take a simplified view of the other steps involved in software design and development. Beyond the specific discussion of UML, the material in this section is intended to place the design issues that we cover within the context of the larger software design process. We hope that this will assist readers interested in a more comprehensive discussion of software design to complement our discussion by referring to other material on their preferred approach to overall system design.

2.8 CASE STUDY: THE INTERNET SHOP

We now introduce an illustrative, 'cradle-to-grave' design case study that we use as a running example throughout this book. DBDudes Inc., a well-known database consulting firm, has been called in to help Barns and Nobble (B&N) with its database design and implementation. B&N is a large bookstore specializing in books on horse racing, and it has decided to go online. DBDudes first verifies that B&N is willing and able to pay its steep fees and then schedules a lunch meeting—billed to B&N, naturally—to do requirements analysis.

2.8.1 Requirements Analysis

The owner of B&N, unlike many people who need a database, has thought extensively about what he wants and offers a concise summary:

"I would like my customers to be able to browse my catalog of books and place orders over the Internet. Currently, I take orders over the phone. I have mostly corporate customers who call me and give me the ISBN number of a book and a quantity; they often pay by credit card. I then prepare a shipment that contains the books they ordered. If I don't have enough copies in stock, I order additional copies and delay the shipment until the new copies arrive; I want to ship a customer's entire order together. My catalog includes all the books I sell. For each book, the catalog contains its ISBN number, title, author, purchase price, sales price, and the year the book was published. Most of my customers are regulars, and I have records with their names and addresses.

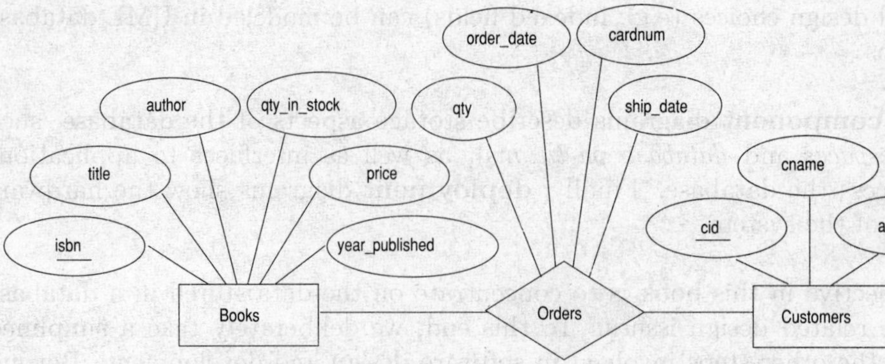

Figure 2.20 ER Diagram of the Initial Design

New customers have to call me first and establish an account before they can use my website.

On my new website, customers should first identify themselves by their unique customer identification number. Then they should be able to browse my catalog and to place orders online."

DBDudes's consultants are a little surprised by how quickly the requirements phase is completed—it usually takes weeks of discussions (and many lunches and dinners) to get this done—but return to their offices to analyze this information.

2.8.2 Conceptual Design

In the conceptual design step, DBDudes develops a high level description of the data in terms of the ER model. The initial design is shown in Figure 2.20. Books and customers are modeled as entities and related through orders that customers place. Orders is a relationship set connecting the Books and Customers entity sets. For each order, the following attributes are stored: quantity, order date, and ship date. As soon as an order is shipped, the ship date is set; until then the ship date is set to *null*, indicating that this order has not been shipped yet.

DBDudes has an internal design review at this point, and several questions are raised. To protect their identities, we will refer to the design team leader as Dude 1 and the design reviewer as Dude 2.

Dude 2: What if a customer places two orders for the same book in one day?
Dude 1: The first order is handled by creating a new Orders relationship and

the second order is handled by updating the value of the quantity attribute in this relationship.
Dude 2: What if a customer places two orders for different books in one day?
Dude 1: No problem. Each instance of the Orders relationship set relates the customer to a different book.
Dude 2: Ah, but what if a customer places two orders for the same book on different days?
Dude 1: We can use the attribute order date of the orders relationship to distinguish the two orders.
Dude 2: Oh no you can't. The attributes of Customers and Books must jointly contain a key for Orders. So this design does not allow a customer to place orders for the same book on different days.
Dude 1: Yikes, you're right. Oh well, B&N probably won't care; we'll see.

DBDudes decides to proceed with the next phase, logical database design; we rejoin them in Section 3.8.

2.9 REVIEW QUESTIONS

Answers to the review questions can be found in the listed sections.

- Name the main steps in database design. What is the goal of each step? In which step is the ER model mainly used? **(Section 2.1)**
- Define these terms: *entity*, *entity set*, *attribute*, *key*. **(Section 2.2)**
- Define these terms: *relationship*, *relationship set*, *descriptive attributes*. **(Section 2.3)**
- Define the following kinds of constraints, and give an example of each: *key constraint*, *participation constraint*. What is a *weak entity*? What are *class hierarchies*? What is *aggregation*? Give an example scenario motivating the use of each of these ER model design constructs. **(Section 2.4)**
- What guidelines would you use for each of these choices when doing ER design: Whether to use an attribute or an entity set, an entity or a relationship set, a binary or ternary relationship, or aggregation. **(Section 2.5)**
- Why is designing a database for a large enterprise especially hard? **(Section 2.6)**
- What is UML? How does database design fit into the overall design of a data-intensive software system? How is UML related to ER diagrams? **(Section 2.7)**

EXERCISES

Exercise 2.1 Explain the following terms briefly: *attribute, domain, entity, relationship, entity set, relationship set, one-to-many relationship, many-to-many relationship, participation constraint, overlap constraint, covering constraint, weak entity set, aggregation*, and *role indicator*.

Exercise 2.2 A university database contains information about professors (identified by social security number, or SSN) and courses (identified by courseid). Professors teach courses; each of the following situations concerns the Teaches relationship set. For each situation, draw an ER diagram that describes it (assuming no further constraints hold).

1. Professors can teach the same course in several semesters, and each offering must be recorded.
2. Professors can teach the same course in several semesters, and only the most recent such offering needs to be recorded. (Assume this condition applies in all subsequent questions.)
3. Every professor must teach some course.
4. Every professor teaches exactly one course (no more, no less).
5. Every professor teaches exactly one course (no more, no less), and every course must be taught by some professor.
6. Now suppose that certain courses can be taught by a team of professors jointly, but it is possible that no one professor in a team can teach the course. Model this situation, introducing additional entity sets and relationship sets if necessary.

Exercise 2.3 Consider the following information about a university database:

- Professors have an SSN, a name, an age, a rank, and a research specialty.
- Projects have a project number, a sponsor name (e.g., NSF), a starting date, an ending date, and a budget.
- Graduate students have an SSN, a name, an age, and a degree program (e.g., M.S. or Ph.D.).
- Each project is managed by one professor (known as the project's principal investigator).
- Each project is worked on by one or more professors (known as the project's co-investigators).
- Professors can manage and/or work on multiple projects.
- Each project is worked on by one or more graduate students (known as the project's research assistants).
- When graduate students work on a project, a professor must supervise their work on the project. Graduate students can work on multiple projects, in which case they will have a (potentially different) supervisor for each one.
- Departments have a department number, a department name, and a main office.
- Departments have a professor (known as the chairman) who runs the department.
- Professors work in one or more departments, and for each department that they work in, a time percentage is associated with their job.
- Graduate students have one major department in which they are working on their degree.

- Each graduate student has another, more senior graduate student (known as a student advisor) who advises him or her on what courses to take.

Design and draw an ER diagram that captures the information about the university. Use only the basic ER model here; that is, entities, relationships, and attributes. Be sure to indicate any key and participation constraints.

Exercise 2.4 A company database needs to store information about employees (identified by *ssn*, with *salary* and *phone* as attributes), departments (identified by *dno*, with *dname* and *budget* as attributes), and children of employees (with *name* and *age* as attributes). Employees *work* in departments; each department is *managed by* an employee; a child must be identified uniquely by *name* when the parent (who is an employee; assume that only one parent works for the company) is known. We are not interested in information about a child once the parent leaves the company.

Draw an ER diagram that captures this information.

Exercise 2.5 Notown Records has decided to store information about musicians who perform on its albums (as well as other company data) in a database. The company has wisely chosen to hire you as a database designer (at your usual consulting fee of $2500/day).

- Each musician that records at Notown has an SSN, a name, an address, and a phone number. Poorly paid musicians often share the same address, and no address has more than one phone.
- Each instrument used in songs recorded at Notown has a name (e.g., guitar, synthesizer, flute) and a musical key (e.g., C, B-flat, E-flat).
- Each album recorded on the Notown label has a title, a copyright date, a format (e.g., CD or MC), and an album identifier.
- Each song recorded at Notown has a title and an author.
- Each musician may play several instruments, and a given instrument may be played by several musicians.
- Each album has a number of songs on it, but no song may appear on more than one album.
- Each song is performed by one or more musicians, and a musician may perform a number of songs.
- Each album has exactly one musician who acts as its producer. A musician may produce several albums, of course.

Design a conceptual schema for Notown and draw an ER diagram for your schema. The preceding information describes the situation that the Notown database must model. Be sure to indicate all key and cardinality constraints and any assumptions you make. Identify any constraints you are unable to capture in the ER diagram and briefly explain why you could not express them.

Exercise 2.6 Computer Sciences Department frequent fliers have been complaining to Dane County Airport officials about the poor organization at the airport. As a result, the officials decided that all information related to the airport should be organized using a DBMS, and you have been hired to design the database. Your first task is to organize the information about all the airplanes stationed and maintained at the airport. The relevant information is as follows:

- Every airplane has a registration number, and each airplane is of a specific model.
- The airport accommodates a number of airplane models, and each model is identified by a model number (e.g., DC-10) and has a capacity and a weight.
- A number of technicians work at the airport. You need to store the name, SSN, address, phone number, and salary of each technician.
- Each technician is an expert on one or more plane model(s), and his or her expertise may overlap with that of other technicians. This information about technicians must also be recorded.
- Traffic controllers must have an annual medical examination. For each traffic controller, you must store the date of the most recent exam.
- All airport employees (including technicians) belong to a union. You must store the union membership number of each employee. You can assume that each employee is uniquely identified by a social security number.
- The airport has a number of tests that are used periodically to ensure that airplanes are still airworthy. Each test has a Federal Aviation Administration (FAA) test number, a name, and a maximum possible score.
- The FAA requires the airport to keep track of each time a given airplane is tested by a given technician using a given test. For each testing event, the information needed is the date, the number of hours the technician spent doing the test, and the score the airplane received on the test.

1. Draw an ER diagram for the airport database. Be sure to indicate the various attributes of each entity and relationship set; also specify the key and participation constraints for each relationship set. Specify any necessary overlap and covering constraints as well (in English).
2. The FAA passes a regulation that tests on a plane must be conducted by a technician who is an expert on that model. How would you express this constraint in the ER diagram? If you cannot express it, explain briefly.

Exercise 2.7 The Prescriptions-R-X chain of pharmacies has offered to give you a free lifetime supply of medicine if you design its database. Given the rising cost of health care, you agree. Here's the information that you gather:

- Patients are identified by an SSN, and their names, addresses, and ages must be recorded.
- Doctors are identified by an SSN. For each doctor, the name, specialty, and years of experience must be recorded.
- Each pharmaceutical company is identified by name and has a phone number.
- For each drug, the trade name and formula must be recorded. Each drug is sold by a given pharmaceutical company, and the trade name identifies a drug uniquely from among the products of that company. If a pharmaceutical company is deleted, you need not keep track of its products any longer.
- Each pharmacy has a name, address, and phone number.
- Every patient has a primary physician. Every doctor has at least one patient.
- Each pharmacy sells several drugs and has a price for each. A drug could be sold at several pharmacies, and the price could vary from one pharmacy to another.

- Doctors prescribe drugs for patients. A doctor could prescribe one or more drugs for several patients, and a patient could obtain prescriptions from several doctors. Each prescription has a date and a quantity associated with it. You can assume that, if a doctor prescribes the same drug for the same patient more than once, only the last such prescription needs to be stored.
- Pharmaceutical companies have long-term contracts with pharmacies. A pharmaceutical company can contract with several pharmacies, and a pharmacy can contract with several pharmaceutical companies. For each contract, you have to store a start date, an end date, and the text of the contract.
- Pharmacies appoint a supervisor for each contract. There must always be a supervisor for each contract, but the contract supervisor can change over the lifetime of the contract.

1. Draw an ER diagram that captures the preceding information. Identify any constraints not captured by the ER diagram.
2. How would your design change if each drug must be sold at a fixed price by all pharmacies?
3. How would your design change if the design requirements change as follows: If a doctor prescribes the same drug for the same patient more than once, several such prescriptions may have to be stored.

Exercise 2.8 Although you always wanted to be an artist, you ended up being an expert on databases because you love to cook data and you somehow confused *database* with *data baste.* Your old love is still there, however, so you set up a database company, ArtBase, that builds a product for art galleries. The core of this product is a database with a schema that captures all the information that galleries need to maintain. Galleries keep information about artists, their names (which are unique), birthplaces, age, and style of art. For each piece of artwork, the artist, the year it was made, its unique title, its type of art (e.g., painting, lithograph, sculpture, photograph), and its price must be stored. Pieces of artwork are also classified into groups of various kinds, for example, portraits, still lifes, works by Picasso, or works of the 19th century; a given piece may belong to more than one group. Each group is identified by a name (like those just given) that describes the group. Finally, galleries keep information about customers. For each customer, galleries keep that person's unique name, address, total amount of dollars spent in the gallery (very important!), and the artists and groups of art that the customer tends to like.

Draw the ER diagram for the database.

Exercise 2.9 Answer the following questions.

- Explain the following terms briefly: *UML, use case diagrams, statechart diagrams, class diagrams, database diagrams, component diagrams*, and *deployment diagrams.*
- Explain the relationship between ER diagrams and UML.

BIBLIOGRAPHIC NOTES

Several books provide a good treatment of conceptual design; these include [63] (which also contains a survey of commercial database design tools) and [730].

The ER model was proposed by Chen [172], and extensions have been proposed in a number of subsequent papers. Generalization and aggregation were introduced in [693]. [390, 589] contain good surveys of semantic data models. Dynamic and temporal aspects of semantic data models are discussed in [749].

[731] discusses a design methodology based on developing an ER diagram and then translating it to the relational model. Markowitz considers referential integrity in the context of ER to relational mapping and discusses the support provided in some commercial systems (as of that date) in [513, 514].

The entity-relationship conference proceedings contain numerous papers on conceptual design, with an emphasis on the ER model; for example, [698].

The OMG home page (`www.omg.org`) contains the specification for UML and related modeling standards. Numerous good books discuss UML; for example [105, 278, 640] and there is a yearly conference dedicated to the advancement of UML, the International Conference on the Unified Modeling Language.

View integration is discussed in several papers, including [97, 139, 184, 244, 535, 551, 550, 685, 697, 748]. [64] is a survey of several integration approaches.

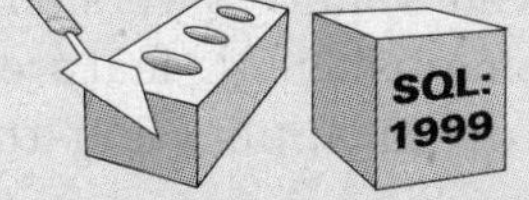

3

THE RELATIONAL MODEL

- How is data represented in the relational model?
- What integrity constraints can be expressed?
- How can data be created and modified?
- How can data be manipulated and queried?
- How can we create, modify, and query tables using SQL?
- How do we obtain a relational database design from an ER diagram?
- What are views and why are they used?
- **Key concepts:** relation, schema, instance, tuple, field, domain, degree, cardinality; SQL DDL, `CREATE TABLE`, `INSERT`, `DELETE`, `UPDATE`; integrity constraints, domain constraints, key constraints, `PRIMARY KEY`, `UNIQUE`, foreign key constraints, `FOREIGN KEY`; referential integrity maintenance, deferred and immediate constraints; relational queries; logical database design, translating ER diagrams to relations, expressing ER constraints using SQL; views, views and logical independence, security; creating views in SQL, updating views, querying views, dropping views

TABLE: An arrangement of words, numbers, or signs, or combinations of them, as in parallel columns, to exhibit a set of facts or relations in a definite, compact, and comprehensive form; a synopsis or scheme.

—Webster's *Dictionary of the English Language*

Codd proposed the relational data model in 1970. At that time, most database systems were based on one of two older data models (the hierarchical model

SQL. Originally developed as the query language of the pioneering System-R relational DBMS at IBM, structured query language (SQL) has become the most widely used language for creating, manipulating, and querying relational DBMSs. Since many vendors offer SQL products, there is a need for a standard that defines 'official SQL.' The existence of a standard allows users to measure a given vendor's version of SQL for completeness. It also allows users to distinguish SQL features specific to one product from those that are standard; an application that relies on nonstandard features is less portable.

The first SQL standard was developed in 1986 by the American National Standards Institute (ANSI) and was called SQL-86. There was a minor revision in 1989 called SQL-89 and a major revision in 1992 called SQL-92. The International Standards Organization (ISO) collaborated with ANSI to develop SQL-92. Most commercial DBMSs currently support (the core subset of) SQL-92 and are working to support the recently adopted SQL:1999 version of the standard, a major extension of SQL-92. Our coverage of SQL is based on SQL:1999, but is applicable to SQL-92 as well; features unique to SQL:1999 are explicitly noted.

and the network model); the relational model revolutionized the database field and largely supplanted these earlier models. Prototype relational database management systems were developed in pioneering research projects at IBM and UC-Berkeley by the mid-1970s, and several vendors were offering relational database products shortly thereafter. Today, the relational model is by far the dominant data model and the foundation for the leading DBMS products, including IBM's DB2 family, Informix, Oracle, Sybase, Microsoft's Access and SQLServer, FoxBase, and Paradox. Relational database systems are ubiquitous in the marketplace and represent a multibillion dollar industry.

The relational model is very simple and elegant: a database is a collection of one or more *relations*, where each relation is a table with rows and columns. This simple tabular representation enables even novice users to understand the contents of a database, and it permits the use of simple, high-level languages to query the data. The major advantages of the relational model over the older data models are its simple data representation and the ease with which even complex queries can be expressed.

While we concentrate on the underlying concepts, we also introduce the **Data Definition Language (DDL)** features of SQL, the standard language for creating, manipulating, and querying data in a relational DBMS. This allows us to ground the discussion firmly in terms of real database systems.

We discuss the concept of a relation in Section 3.1 and show how to create relations using the SQL language. An important component of a data model is the set of constructs it provides for specifying conditions that must be satisfied by the data. Such conditions, called *integrity constraints* (ICs), enable the DBMS to reject operations that might corrupt the data. We present integrity constraints in the relational model in Section 3.2, along with a discussion of SQL support for ICs. We discuss how a DBMS enforces integrity constraints in Section 3.3.

In Section 3.4, we turn to the mechanism for accessing and retrieving data from the database, *query languages*, and introduce the querying features of SQL, which we examine in greater detail in a later chapter.

We then discuss converting an ER diagram into a relational database schema in Section 3.5. We introduce *views*, or tables defined using queries, in Section 3.6. Views can be used to define the external schema for a database and thus provide the support for logical data independence in the relational model. In Section 3.7, we describe SQL commands to destroy and alter tables and views.

Finally, in Section 3.8 we extend our design case study, the Internet shop introduced in Section 2.8, by showing how the ER diagram for its conceptual schema can be mapped to the relational model, and how the use of views can help in this design.

3.1 INTRODUCTION TO THE RELATIONAL MODEL

The main construct for representing data in the relational model is a **relation**. A relation consists of a **relation schema** and a **relation instance**. The relation instance is a table, and the relation schema describes the column heads for the table. We first describe the relation schema and then the relation instance. The schema specifies the relation's name, the name of each **field** (or **column**, or **attribute**), and the **domain** of each field. A domain is referred to in a relation schema by the **domain name** and has a set of associated **values**.

We use the example of student information in a university database from Chapter 1 to illustrate the parts of a relation schema:

Students(*sid:* `string`, *name:* `string`, *login:* `string`,
age: `integer`, *gpa:* `real`)

This says, for instance, that the field named *sid* has a domain named `string`. The set of values associated with domain `string` is the set of all character strings.

We now turn to the instances of a relation. An **instance** of a relation is a set of **tuples**, also called **records**, in which each tuple has the same number of fields as the relation schema. A relation instance can be thought of as a *table* in which each tuple is a *row*, and all rows have the same number of fields. (The term *relation instance* is often abbreviated to just *relation*, when there is no confusion with other aspects of a relation such as its schema.)

An instance of the Students relation appears in Figure 3.1. The instance $S1$

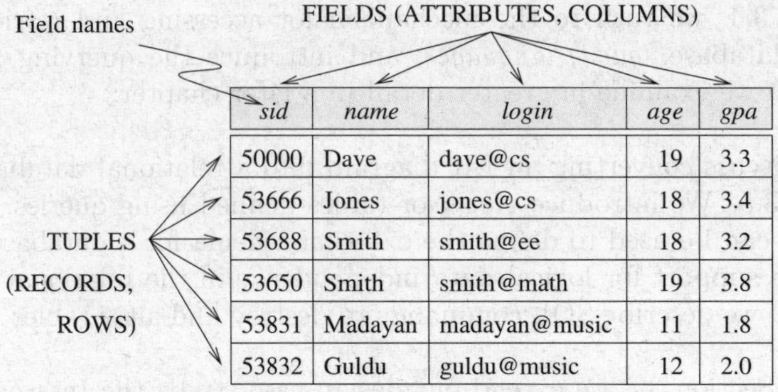

sid	*name*	*login*	*age*	*gpa*
50000	Dave	dave@cs	19	3.3
53666	Jones	jones@cs	18	3.4
53688	Smith	smith@ee	18	3.2
53650	Smith	smith@math	19	3.8
53831	Madayan	madayan@music	11	1.8
53832	Guldu	guldu@music	12	2.0

Figure 3.1 An Instance $S1$ of the Students Relation

contains six tuples and has, as we expect from the schema, five fields. Note that no two rows are identical. This is a requirement of the relational model—each relation is defined to be a *set* of unique tuples or rows.

In practice, commercial systems allow tables to have duplicate rows, but we assume that a relation is indeed a set of tuples unless otherwise noted. The order in which the rows are listed is not important. Figure 3.2 shows the same relation instance. If the fields are named, as in our schema definitions and

sid	*name*	*login*	*age*	*gpa*
53831	Madayan	madayan@music	11	1.8
53832	Guldu	guldu@music	12	2.0
53688	Smith	smith@ee	18	3.2
53650	Smith	smith@math	19	3.8
53666	Jones	jones@cs	18	3.4
50000	Dave	dave@cs	19	3.3

Figure 3.2 An Alternative Representation of Instance $S1$ of Students

figures depicting relation instances, the order of fields does not matter either. However, an alternative convention is to list fields in a specific order and refer to a field by its position. Thus, *sid* is field 1 of Students, *login* is field 3, and so on. If this convention is used, the order of fields is significant. Most database systems use a combination of these conventions. For example, in SQL, the named fields convention is used in statements that retrieve tuples and the ordered fields convention is commonly used when inserting tuples.

A relation schema specifies the domain of each field or column in the relation instance. These **domain constraints** in the schema specify an important condition that we want each instance of the relation to satisfy: The values that appear in a column must be drawn from the domain associated with that column. Thus, the domain of a field is essentially the *type* of that field, in programming language terms, and restricts the values that can appear in the field.

More formally, let R(f_1:`D1`, ..., f_n:`Dn`) be a relation schema, and for each f_i, $1 \leq i \leq n$, let Dom_i be the set of values associated with the domain named `Di`. An instance of R that satisfies the domain constraints in the schema is a set of tuples with n fields:

$$\{ \langle f_1 : d_1, \ \ldots \ , f_n : d_n \rangle \ \mid \ d_1 \in Dom_1, \ \ldots \ , d_n \in Dom_n \ \}$$

The angular brackets $\langle \ldots \rangle$ identify the fields of a tuple. Using this notation, the first Students tuple shown in Figure 3.1 is written as ⟨*sid:* 50000, *name:* Dave, *login:* dave@cs, *age:* 19, *gpa:* 3.3⟩. The curly brackets $\{\ldots\}$ denote a set (of tuples, in this definition). The vertical bar | should be read 'such that,' the symbol $\in$ should be read 'in,' and the expression to the right of the vertical bar is a condition that must be satisfied by the field values of each tuple in the set. Therefore, an instance of R is defined as a set of tuples. The fields of each tuple must correspond to the fields in the relation schema.

Domain constraints are so fundamental in the relational model that we henceforth consider only relation instances that satisfy them; therefore, *relation instance* means *relation instance that satisfies the domain constraints in the relation schema.*

The **degree**, also called **arity**, of a relation is the number of fields. The **cardinality** of a relation instance is the number of tuples in it. In Figure 3.1, the degree of the relation (the number of columns) is five, and the cardinality of this instance is six.

A **relational database** is a collection of relations with distinct relation names. The **relational database schema** is the collection of schemas for the relations in the database. For example, in Chapter 1, we discussed a university database with relations called Students, Faculty, Courses, Rooms, Enrolled, Teaches, and Meets In. An **instance** of a relational database is a collection of relation instances, one per relation schema in the database schema; of course, each relation instance must satisfy the domain constraints in its schema.

3.1.1 Creating and Modifying Relations Using SQL

The SQL language standard uses the word *table* to denote *relation*, and we often follow this convention when discussing SQL. The subset of SQL that supports the creation, deletion, and modification of tables is called the Data Definition Language (DDL). Further, while there is a command that lets users define new domains, analogous to type definition commands in a programming language, we postpone a discussion of domain definition until Section 5.7. For now, we only consider domains that are built-in types, such as `integer`.

The `CREATE TABLE` statement is used to define a new table.[1] To create the Students relation, we can use the following statement:

```
CREATE TABLE Students ( sid    CHAR(20),
                        name   CHAR(30),
                        login  CHAR(20),
                        age    INTEGER,
                        gpa    REAL )
```

Tuples are inserted using the `INSERT` command. We can insert a single tuple into the Students table as follows:

```
INSERT
INTO   Students  (sid, name, login, age, gpa)
VALUES (53688, 'Smith', 'smith@ee', 18, 3.2)
```

We can optionally omit the list of column names in the `INTO` clause and list the values in the appropriate order, but it is good style to be explicit about column names.

We can delete tuples using the `DELETE` command. We can delete all Students tuples with *name* equal to Smith using the command:

```
DELETE
FROM   Students S
WHERE  S.name = 'Smith'
```

[1] SQL also provides statements to destroy tables and to change the columns associated with a table; we discuss these in Section 3.7.

We can modify the column values in an existing row using the `UPDATE` command. For example, we can increment the age and decrement the gpa of the student with *sid* 53688:

```
UPDATE Students S
SET    S.age = S.age + 1, S.gpa = S.gpa − 1
WHERE  S.sid = 53688
```

These examples illustrate some important points. The `WHERE` clause is applied first and determines which rows are to be modified. The `SET` clause then determines how these rows are to be modified. If the column being modified is also used to determine the new value, the value used in the expression on the right side of equals (=) is the *old* value, that is, before the modification. To illustrate these points further, consider the following variation of the previous query:

```
UPDATE Students S
SET    S.gpa = S.gpa − 0.1
WHERE  S.gpa >= 3.3
```

If this query is applied on the instance $S1$ of Students shown in Figure 3.1, we obtain the instance shown in Figure 3.3.

sid	*name*	*login*	*age*	*gpa*
50000	Dave	dave@cs	19	3.2
53666	Jones	jones@cs	18	3.3
53688	Smith	smith@ee	18	3.2
53650	Smith	smith@math	19	3.7
53831	Madayan	madayan@music	11	1.8
53832	Guldu	guldu@music	12	2.0

Figure 3.3 Students Instance $S1$ after Update

3.2 INTEGRITY CONSTRAINTS OVER RELATIONS

A database is only as good as the information stored in it, and a DBMS must therefore help prevent the entry of incorrect information. An **integrity constraint (IC)** is a condition specified on a database schema and restricts the data that can be stored in an instance of the database. If a database instance satisfies all the integrity constraints specified on the database schema, it is a **legal** instance. A DBMS **enforces** integrity constraints, in that it permits only legal instances to be stored in the database.

Integrity constraints are specified and enforced at different times:

1. When the DBA or end user defines a database schema, he or she specifies the ICs that must hold on any instance of this database.

2. When a database application is run, the DBMS checks for violations and disallows changes to the data that violate the specified ICs. (In some situations, rather than disallow the change, the DBMS might make some compensating changes to the data to ensure that the database instance satisfies all ICs. In any case, changes to the database are not allowed to create an instance that violates any IC.) It is important to specify exactly when integrity constraints are checked relative to the statement that causes the change in the data and the transaction that it is part of. We discuss this aspect in Chapter 16, after presenting the transaction concept, which we introduced in Chapter 1, in more detail.

Many kinds of integrity constraints can be specified in the relational model. We have already seen one example of an integrity constraint in the *domain constraints* associated with a relation schema (Section 3.1). In general, other kinds of constraints can be specified as well; for example, no two students have the same *sid* value. In this section we discuss the integrity constraints, other than domain constraints, that a DBA or user can specify in the relational model.

3.2.1 Key Constraints

Consider the Students relation and the constraint that no two students have the same student id. This IC is an example of a key constraint. A **key constraint** is a statement that a certain *minimal* subset of the fields of a relation is a unique identifier for a tuple. A set of fields that uniquely identifies a tuple according to a key constraint is called a **candidate key** for the relation; we often abbreviate this to just *key*. In the case of the Students relation, the (set of fields containing just the) *sid* field is a candidate key.

Let us take a closer look at the above definition of a (candidate) key. There are two parts to the definition:[2]

1. Two distinct tuples in a legal instance (an instance that satisfies all ICs, including the key constraint) cannot have identical values in all the fields of a key.

2. No subset of the set of fields in a key is a unique identifier for a tuple.

[2]The term *key* is rather overworked. In the context of access methods, we speak of *search keys*, which are quite different.

The first part of the definition means that, in *any* legal instance, the values in the key fields uniquely identify a tuple in the instance. When specifying a key constraint, the DBA or user must be sure that this constraint will not prevent them from storing a 'correct' set of tuples. (A similar comment applies to the specification of other kinds of ICs as well.) The notion of 'correctness' here depends on the nature of the data being stored. For example, several students may have the same name, although each student has a unique student id. If the *name* field is declared to be a key, the DBMS will not allow the Students relation to contain two tuples describing different students with the same name!

The second part of the definition means, for example, that the set of fields {*sid, name*} is not a key for Students, because this set properly contains the key {*sid*}. The set {*sid, name*} is an example of a **superkey**, which is a set of fields that contains a key.

Look again at the instance of the Students relation in Figure 3.1. Observe that two different rows always have different *sid* values; *sid* is a key and uniquely identifies a tuple. However, this does not hold for nonkey fields. For example, the relation contains two rows with *Smith* in the *name* field.

Note that every relation is guaranteed to have a key. Since a relation is a set of tuples, the set of *all* fields is always a superkey. If other constraints hold, some subset of the fields may form a key, but if not, the set of all fields is a key.

A relation may have several candidate keys. For example, the *login* and *age* fields of the Students relation may, taken together, also identify students uniquely. That is, {*login, age*} is also a key. It may seem that *login* is a key, since no two rows in the example instance have the same *login* value. However, the key must identify tuples uniquely in all possible legal instances of the relation. By stating that {*login, age*} is a key, the user is declaring that two students may have the same login or age, but not both.

Out of all the available candidate keys, a database designer can identify a **primary** key. Intuitively, a tuple can be referred to from elsewhere in the database by storing the values of its primary key fields. For example, we can refer to a Students tuple by storing its *sid* value. As a consequence of referring to student tuples in this manner, tuples are frequently accessed by specifying their *sid* value. In principle, we can use any key, not just the primary key, to refer to a tuple. However, using the primary key is preferable because it is what the DBMS expects—this is the significance of designating a particular candidate key as a primary key—and optimizes for. For example, the DBMS may create an index with the primary key fields as the search key, to make the retrieval of a tuple given its primary key value efficient. The idea of referring to a tuple is developed further in the next section.

Specifying Key Constraints in SQL

In SQL, we can declare that a subset of the columns of a table constitute a key by using the `UNIQUE` constraint. At most one of these candidate keys can be declared to be a *primary key*, using the `PRIMARY KEY` constraint. (SQL does not require that such constraints be declared for a table.)

Let us revisit our example table definition and specify key information:

```
CREATE TABLE Students ( sid    CHAR(20),
                        name   CHAR(30),
                        login  CHAR(20),
                        age    INTEGER,
                        gpa    REAL,
                        UNIQUE (name, age),
                        CONSTRAINT StudentsKey PRIMARY KEY (sid) )
```

This definition says that *sid* is the primary key and the combination of *name* and *age* is also a key. The definition of the primary key also illustrates how we can name a constraint by preceding it with `CONSTRAINT` *constraint-name*. If the constraint is violated, the constraint name is returned and can be used to identify the error.

3.2.2 Foreign Key Constraints

Sometimes the information stored in a relation is linked to the information stored in another relation. If one of the relations is modified, the other must be checked, and perhaps modified, to keep the data consistent. An IC involving both relations must be specified if a DBMS is to make such checks. The most common IC involving two relations is a *foreign key* constraint.

Suppose that, in addition to Students, we have a second relation:

Enrolled(*studid:* `string`, *cid:* `string`, *grade:* `string`)

To ensure that only bona fide students can enroll in courses, any value that appears in the *studid* field of an instance of the Enrolled relation should also appear in the *sid* field of some tuple in the Students relation. The *studid* field of Enrolled is called a **foreign key** and **refers** to Students. The foreign key in the referencing relation (Enrolled, in our example) must match the primary key of the referenced relation (Students); that is, it must have the same number of columns and compatible data types, although the column names can be different.

This constraint is illustrated in Figure 3.4. As the figure shows, there may well be some Students tuples that are not referenced from Enrolled (e.g., the student with *sid=50000*). However, every *studid* value that appears in the instance of the Enrolled table appears in the primary key column of a row in the Students table.

Foreign key: studid

cid	grade	studid
Carnatic101	C	53831
Reggae203	B	53832
Topology112	A	53650
History105	B	53666

Enrolled (Referencing relation)

Primary key: sid

sid	*name*	*login*	*age*	*gpa*
50000	Dave	dave@cs	19	3.3
53666	Jones	jones@cs	18	3.4
53688	Smith	smith@ee	18	3.2
53650	Smith	smith@math	19	3.8
53831	Madayan	madayan@music	11	1.8
53832	Guldu	guldu@music	12	2.0

Students (Referenced relation)

Figure 3.4 Referential Integrity

If we try to insert the tuple ⟨*55555, Art104, A*⟩ into $E1$, the IC is violated because there is no tuple in $S1$ with *sid* 55555; the database system should reject such an insertion. Similarly, if we delete the tuple ⟨*53666, Jones, jones@cs, 18, 3.4*⟩ from $S1$, we violate the foreign key constraint because the tuple ⟨*53666, History105, B*⟩ in $E1$ contains *studid* value 53666, the *sid* of the deleted Students tuple. The DBMS should disallow the deletion or, perhaps, also delete the Enrolled tuple that refers to the deleted Students tuple. We discuss foreign key constraints and their impact on updates in Section 3.3.

Finally, we note that a foreign key could refer to the same relation. For example, we could extend the Students relation with a column called *partner* and declare this column to be a foreign key referring to Students. Intuitively, every student could then have a partner, and the *partner* field contains the partner's *sid*. The observant reader will no doubt ask, "What if a student does not (yet) have a partner?" This situation is handled in SQL by using a special value called **null**. The use of *null* in a field of a tuple means that value in that field is either unknown or not applicable (e.g., we do not know the partner yet or there is no partner). The appearance of *null* in a foreign key field does not violate the foreign key constraint. However, *null* values are not allowed to appear in a primary key field (because the primary key fields are used to identify a tuple uniquely). We discuss *null* values further in Chapter 5.

Specifying Foreign Key Constraints in SQL

Let us define Enrolled(*studid:* `string`, *cid:* `string`, *grade:* `string`):

```
CREATE TABLE Enrolled ( studid CHAR(20),
                        cid    CHAR(20),
                        grade  CHAR(10),
                        PRIMARY KEY (studid, cid),
                        FOREIGN KEY (studid) REFERENCES Students )
```

The foreign key constraint states that every *studid* value in Enrolled must also appear in Students, that is, *studid* in Enrolled is a foreign key referencing Students. Specifically, every *studid* value in Enrolled must appear as the value in the primary key field, *sid*, of Students. Incidentally, the primary key constraint for Enrolled states that a student has exactly one grade for each course he or she is enrolled in. If we want to record more than one grade per student per course, we should change the primary key constraint.

3.2.3 General Constraints

Domain, primary key, and foreign key constraints are considered to be a fundamental part of the relational data model and are given special attention in most commercial systems. Sometimes, however, it is necessary to specify more general constraints.

For example, we may require that student ages be within a certain range of values; given such an IC specification, the DBMS rejects inserts and updates that violate the constraint. This is very useful in preventing data entry errors. If we specify that all students must be at least 16 years old, the instance of Students shown in Figure 3.1 is illegal because two students are underage. If we disallow the insertion of these two tuples, we have a legal instance, as shown in Figure 3.5.

sid	*name*	*login*	*age*	*gpa*
53666	Jones	jones@cs	18	3.4
53688	Smith	smith@ee	18	3.2
53650	Smith	smith@math	19	3.8

Figure 3.5 An Instance *S*2 of the Students Relation

The IC that students must be older than 16 can be thought of as an extended domain constraint, since we are essentially defining the set of permissible *age* values more stringently than is possible by simply using a standard domain such as `integer`. In general, however, constraints that go well beyond domain, key, or foreign key constraints can be specified. For example, we could require that every student whose age is greater than 18 must have a gpa greater than 3.

Current relational database systems support such general constraints in the form of *table constraints* and *assertions.* Table constraints are associated with a single table and checked whenever that table is modified. In contrast, assertions involve several tables and are checked whenever any of these tables is modified. Both table constraints and assertions can use the full power of SQL queries to specify the desired restriction. We discuss SQL support for *table constraints* and *assertions* in Section 5.7 because a full appreciation of their power requires a good grasp of SQL's query capabilities.

3.3 ENFORCING INTEGRITY CONSTRAINTS

As we observed earlier, ICs are specified when a relation is created and enforced when a relation is modified. The impact of domain, `PRIMARY KEY`, and `UNIQUE` constraints is straightforward: If an insert, delete, or update command causes a violation, it is rejected. Every potential IC violation is generally checked at the end of each SQL statement execution, although it can be *deferred* until the end of the transaction executing the statement, as we will see in Section 3.3.1.

Consider the instance *S*1 of Students shown in Figure 3.1. The following insertion violates the primary key constraint because there is already a tuple with the *sid* 53688, and it will be rejected by the DBMS:

```
INSERT
INTO   Students  (sid, name, login, age, gpa)
VALUES (53688, 'Mike', 'mike@ee', 17, 3.4)
```

The following insertion violates the constraint that the primary key cannot contain *null*:

```
INSERT
INTO   Students  (sid, name, login, age, gpa)
VALUES (null, 'Mike', 'mike@ee', 17, 3.4)
```

Of course, a similar problem arises whenever we try to insert a tuple with a value in a field that is not in the domain associated with that field, that is, whenever we violate a domain constraint. Deletion does not cause a violation of domain, primary key or unique constraints. However, an update can cause violations, similar to an insertion:

```
UPDATE Students S
SET    S.sid = 50000
WHERE  S.sid = 53688
```

This update violates the primary key constraint because there is already a tuple with *sid* 50000.

The impact of foreign key constraints is more complex because SQL sometimes tries to rectify a foreign key constraint violation instead of simply rejecting the change. We discuss the **referential integrity enforcement steps** taken by the DBMS in terms of our Enrolled and Students tables, with the foreign key constraint that Enrolled.*sid* is a reference to (the primary key of) Students.

In addition to the instance *S*1 of Students, consider the instance of Enrolled shown in Figure 3.4. Deletions of Enrolled tuples do not violate referential integrity, but insertions of Enrolled tuples could. The following insertion is illegal because there is no Students tuple with *sid* 51111:

```
INSERT
INTO   Enrolled (cid, grade, studid)
VALUES ('Hindi101', 'B', 51111)
```

On the other hand, insertions of Students tuples do not violate referential integrity, and deletions of Students tuples could cause violations. Further, updates on either Enrolled or Students that change the *studid* (respectively, *sid*) value could potentially violate referential integrity.

SQL provides several alternative ways to handle foreign key violations. We must consider three basic questions:

1. *What should we do if an Enrolled row is inserted, with a* studid *column value that does not appear in any row of the Students table?*

   In this case, the `INSERT` command is simply rejected.

2. *What should we do if a Students row is deleted?*

   The options are:

   - Delete all Enrolled rows that refer to the deleted Students row.
   - Disallow the deletion of the Students row if an Enrolled row refers to it.
   - Set the *studid* column to the *sid* of some (existing) 'default' student, for every Enrolled row that refers to the deleted Students row.

- For every Enrolled row that refers to it, set the *studid* column to *null*. In our example, this option conflicts with the fact that *studid* is part of the primary key of Enrolled and therefore cannot be set to *null*. Therefore, we are limited to the first three options in our example, although this fourth option (setting the foreign key to *null*) is available in general.

3. *What should we do if the primary key value of a Students row is updated?*

The options here are similar to the previous case.

SQL allows us to choose any of the four options on `DELETE` and `UPDATE`. For example, we can specify that when a Students row is *deleted*, all Enrolled rows that refer to it are to be deleted as well, but that when the *sid* column of a Students row is *modified*, this update is to be rejected if an Enrolled row refers to the modified Students row:

```
CREATE TABLE Enrolled ( studid CHAR(20),
                        cid    CHAR(20),
                        grade  CHAR(10),
                        PRIMARY KEY (studid, cid),
                        FOREIGN KEY (studid) REFERENCES Students
                                   ON DELETE CASCADE
                                   ON UPDATE NO ACTION )
```

The options are specified as part of the foreign key declaration. The default option is `NO ACTION`, which means that the action (`DELETE` or `UPDATE`) is to be rejected. Thus, the `ON UPDATE` clause in our example could be omitted, with the same effect. The `CASCADE` keyword says that, if a Students row is deleted, all Enrolled rows that refer to it are to be deleted as well. If the `UPDATE` clause specified `CASCADE`, and the *sid* column of a Students row is updated, this update is also carried out in each Enrolled row that refers to the updated Students row.

If a Students row is deleted, we can switch the enrollment to a 'default' student by using `ON DELETE SET DEFAULT`. The default student is specified as part of the definition of the *sid* field in Enrolled; for example, *sid* `CHAR(20) DEFAULT` *'53666'*. Although the specification of a default value is appropriate in some situations (e.g., a default parts supplier if a particular supplier goes out of business), it is really not appropriate to switch enrollments to a default student. The correct solution in this example is to also delete all enrollment tuples for the deleted student (that is, `CASCADE`) or to reject the update.

SQL also allows the use of *null* as the default value by specifying `ON DELETE SET NULL`.

3.3.1 Transactions and Constraints

As we saw in Chapter 1, a program that runs against a database is called a transaction, and it can contain several statements (queries, inserts, updates, etc.) that access the database. If (the execution of) a statement in a transaction violates an integrity constraint, should the DBMS detect this right away or should all constraints be checked together just before the transaction completes?

By default, a constraint is checked at the end of every SQL statement that could lead to a violation, and if there is a violation, the statement is rejected. Sometimes this approach is too inflexible. Consider the following variants of the Students and Courses relations; every student is required to have an honors course, and every course is required to have a grader, who is some student.

```
CREATE TABLE Students ( sid     CHAR(20),
                        name    CHAR(30),
                        login   CHAR(20),
                        age     INTEGER,
                        honors  CHAR(10) NOT NULL,
                        gpa     REAL )
                        PRIMARY KEY (sid),
                        FOREIGN KEY (honors) REFERENCES Courses (cid))

CREATE TABLE Courses (  cid     CHAR(10),
                        cname   CHAR(10),
                        credits INTEGER,
                        grader  CHAR(20) NOT NULL,
                        PRIMARY KEY (cid)
                        FOREIGN KEY (grader) REFERENCES Students (sid))
```

Whenever a Students tuple is inserted, a check is made to see if the honors course is in the Courses relation, and whenever a Courses tuple is inserted, a check is made to see that the grader is in the Students relation. How are we to insert the very first course or student tuple? One cannot be inserted without the other. The only way to accomplish this insertion is to **defer** the constraint checking that would normally be carried out at the end of an INSERT statement.

SQL allows a constraint to be in DEFERRED or IMMEDIATE mode.

```
SET CONSTRAINT ConstraintFoo DEFERRED
```

A constraint in deferred mode is checked at commit time. In our example, the foreign key constraints on Boats and Sailors can both be declared to be in deferred mode. We can then insert a boat with a nonexistent sailor as the captain (temporarily making the database inconsistent), insert the sailor (restoring consistency), then commit and check that both constraints are satisfied.

3.4 QUERYING RELATIONAL DATA

A **relational database query** (query, for short) is a question about the data, and the answer consists of a new relation containing the result. For example, we might want to find all students younger than 18 or all students enrolled in Reggae203. A **query language** is a specialized language for writing queries.

SQL is the most popular commercial query language for a relational DBMS. We now present some SQL examples that illustrate how easily relations can be queried. Consider the instance of the Students relation shown in Figure 3.1. We can retrieve rows corresponding to students who are younger than 18 with the following SQL query:

```
SELECT *
FROM   Students S
WHERE  S.age < 18
```

The symbol '*' means that we retain all fields of selected tuples in the result. Think of S as a variable that takes on the value of each tuple in Students, one tuple after the other. The condition *S.age* < *18* in the `WHERE` clause specifies that we want to select only tuples in which the *age* field has a value less than 18. This query evaluates to the relation shown in Figure 3.6.

sid	*name*	*login*	*age*	*gpa*
53831	Madayan	madayan@music	11	1.8
53832	Guldu	guldu@music	12	2.0

Figure 3.6 Students with *age* < 18 on Instance *S*1

This example illustrates that the domain of a field restricts the operations that are permitted on field values, in addition to restricting the values that can appear in the field. The condition *S.age* < *18* involves an arithmetic comparison of an *age* value with an integer and is permissible because the domain of *age* is the set of integers. On the other hand, a condition such as *S.age* = *S.sid* does not make sense because it compares an integer value with a string value, and this comparison is defined to fail in SQL; a query containing this condition produces no answer tuples.

In addition to selecting a subset of tuples, a query can extract a subset of the fields of each selected tuple. We can compute the names and logins of students who are younger than 18 with the following query:

```
SELECT S.name, S.login
FROM   Students S
WHERE  S.age < 18
```

Figure 3.7 shows the answer to this query; it is obtained by applying the selection to the instance $S1$ of Students (to get the relation shown in Figure 3.6), followed by removing unwanted fields. Note that the order in which we perform these operations does matter—if we remove unwanted fields first, we cannot check the condition *S.age* < *18*, which involves one of those fields.

name	*login*
Madayan	madayan@music
Guldu	guldu@music

Figure 3.7 Names and Logins of Students under 18

We can also combine information in the Students and Enrolled relations. If we want to obtain the names of all students who obtained an A and the id of the course in which they got an A, we could write the following query:

```
SELECT S.name, E.cid
FROM   Students S, Enrolled E
WHERE  S.sid = E.studid AND E.grade = 'A'
```

This query can be understood as follows: "If there is a Students tuple S and an Enrolled tuple E such that S.sid = E.studid (so that S describes the student who is enrolled in E) and E.grade = 'A', then print the student's name and the course id." When evaluated on the instances of Students and Enrolled in Figure 3.4, this query returns a single tuple, ⟨*Smith, Topology112*⟩.

We cover relational queries and SQL in more detail in subsequent chapters.

3.5 LOGICAL DATABASE DESIGN: ER TO RELATIONAL

The ER model is convenient for representing an initial, high-level database design. Given an ER diagram describing a database, a standard approach is taken to generating a relational database schema that closely approximates the ER design. (The translation is approximate to the extent that we cannot capture all the constraints implicit in the ER design using SQL, unless we use certain SQL constraints that are costly to check.) We now describe how to translate an ER diagram into a collection of tables with associated constraints, that is, a relational database schema.

3.5.1 Entity Sets to Tables

An entity set is mapped to a relation in a straightforward way: Each attribute of the entity set becomes an attribute of the table. Note that we know both the domain of each attribute and the (primary) key of an entity set.

Consider the Employees entity set with attributes *ssn*, *name*, and *lot* shown in Figure 3.8. A possible instance of the Employees entity set, containing three

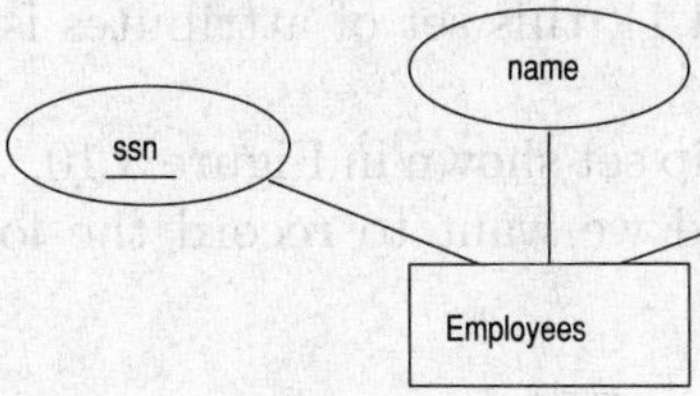

Figure 3.8 The Employees Entity Set

Employees entities, is shown in Figure 3.9 in a tabular format.

ssn	*name*	*lot*
123-22-3666	Attishoo	48
231-31-5368	Smiley	22
131-24-3650	Smethurst	35

Figure 3.9 An Instance of the Employees Entity Set

The following SQL statement captures the preceding information, including the domain constraints and key information:

```
CREATE TABLE Employees ( ssn    CHAR(11),
                         name   CHAR(30),
                         lot    INTEGER,
                         PRIMARY KEY (ssn) )
```

3.5.2 Relationship Sets (without Constraints) to Tables

A relationship set, like an entity set, is mapped to a relation in the relational model. We begin by considering relationship sets without key and participation constraints, and we discuss how to handle such constraints in subsequent sections. To represent a relationship, we must be able to identify each participating entity and give values to the descriptive attributes of the relationship. Thus, the attributes of the relation include:

- The primary key attributes of each participating entity set, as foreign key fields.
- The descriptive attributes of the relationship set.

The set of nondescriptive attributes is a superkey for the relation. If there are no key constraints (see Section 2.4.1), this set of attributes is a candidate key.

Consider the Works_In2 relationship set shown in Figure 3.10. Each department has offices in several locations and we want to record the locations at which each employee works.

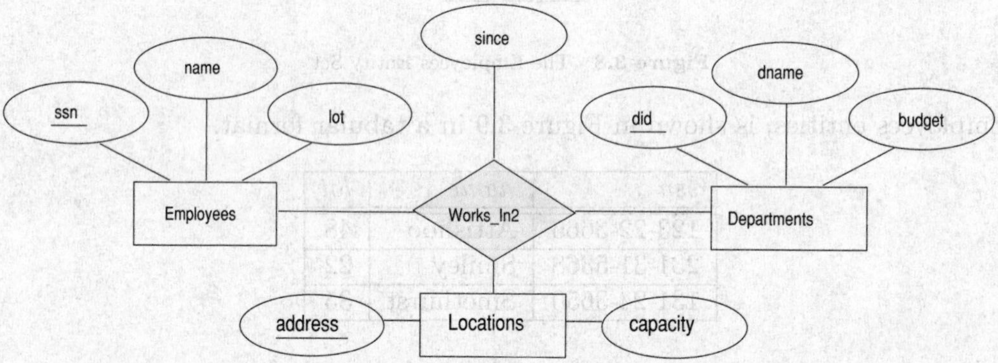

Figure 3.10 A Ternary Relationship Set

All the available information about the Works_In2 table is captured by the following SQL definition:

```
CREATE TABLE Works_In2 ( ssn      CHAR(11),
                         did      INTEGER,
                         address  CHAR(20),
                         since    DATE,
                         PRIMARY KEY (ssn, did, address),
                         FOREIGN KEY (ssn) REFERENCES Employees,
```

```
                    FOREIGN KEY (address) REFERENCES Locations,
                    FOREIGN KEY (did) REFERENCES Departments )
```

Note that the *address*, *did*, and *ssn* fields cannot take on *null* values. Because these fields are part of the primary key for Works_In2, a NOT NULL constraint is implicit for each of these fields. This constraint ensures that these fields uniquely identify a department, an employee, and a location in each tuple of Works_In. We can also specify that a particular action is desired when a referenced Employees, Departments, or Locations tuple is deleted, as explained in the discussion of integrity constraints in Section 3.2. In this chapter, we assume that the default action is appropriate except for situations in which the semantics of the ER diagram require some other action.

Finally, consider the Reports_To relationship set shown in Figure 3.11. The

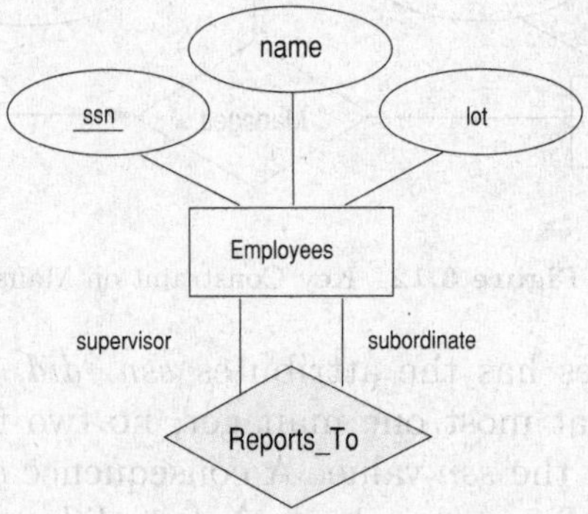

Figure 3.11 The Reports_To Relationship Set

role indicators *supervisor* and *subordinate* are used to create meaningful field names in the CREATE statement for the Reports_To table:

```
CREATE TABLE Reports_To (
        supervisor_ssn   CHAR(11),
        subordinate_ssn  CHAR(11),
        PRIMARY KEY (supervisor_ssn, subordinate_ssn),
        FOREIGN KEY (supervisor_ssn) REFERENCES Employees(ssn),
        FOREIGN KEY (subordinate_ssn) REFERENCES Employees(ssn) )
```

Observe that we need to explicitly name the referenced field of Employees because the field name differs from the name(s) of the referring field(s).

3.5.3 Translating Relationship Sets with Key Constraints

If a relationship set involves n entity sets and some m of them are linked via arrows in the ER diagram, the key for any one of these m entity sets constitutes a key for the relation to which the relationship set is mapped. Hence we have m candidate keys, and one of these should be designated as the primary key. The translation discussed in Section 2.3 from relationship sets to a relation can be used in the presence of key constraints, taking into account this point about keys.

Consider the relationship set Manages shown in Figure 3.12. The table cor-

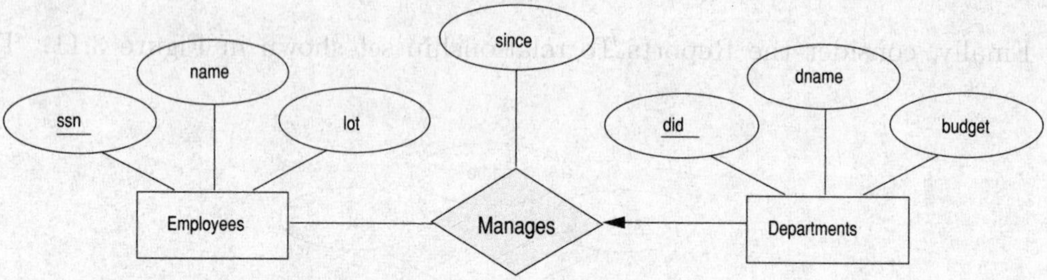

Figure 3.12 Key Constraint on Manages

responding to Manages has the attributes *ssn, did, since.* However, because each department has at most one manager, no two tuples can have the same *did* value but differ on the *ssn* value. A consequence of this observation is that *did* is itself a key for Manages; indeed, the set *did, ssn* is not a key (because it is not minimal). The Manages relation can be defined using the following SQL statement:

```
CREATE TABLE Manages ( ssn    CHAR(11),
                       did    INTEGER,
                       since  DATE,
                       PRIMARY KEY (did),
                       FOREIGN KEY (ssn) REFERENCES Employees,
                       FOREIGN KEY (did) REFERENCES Departments )
```

A second approach to translating a relationship set with key constraints is often superior because it avoids creating a distinct table for the relationship set. The idea is to include the information about the relationship set in the table corresponding to the entity set with the key, taking advantage of the key constraint. In the Manages example, because a department has at most one manager, we can add the key fields of the Employees tuple denoting the manager and the *since* attribute to the Departments tuple.

This approach eliminates the need for a separate Manages relation, and queries asking for a department's manager can be answered without combining information from two relations. The only drawback to this approach is that space could be wasted if several departments have no managers. In this case the added fields would have to be filled with *null* values. The first translation (using a separate table for Manages) avoids this inefficiency, but some important queries require us to combine information from two relations, which can be a slow operation.

The following SQL statement, defining a Dept_Mgr relation that captures the information in both Departments and Manages, illustrates the second approach to translating relationship sets with key constraints:

```
CREATE TABLE Dept_Mgr ( did      INTEGER,
                        dname    CHAR(20),
                        budget   REAL,
                        ssn      CHAR(11),
                        since    DATE,
                        PRIMARY KEY (did),
                        FOREIGN KEY (ssn) REFERENCES Employees )
```

Note that *ssn* can take on *null* values.

This idea can be extended to deal with relationship sets involving more than two entity sets. In general, if a relationship set involves n entity sets and some m of them are linked via arrows in the ER diagram, the relation corresponding to any one of the m sets can be augmented to capture the relationship.

We discuss the relative merits of the two translation approaches further after considering how to translate relationship sets with participation constraints into tables.

3.5.4 Translating Relationship Sets with Participation Constraints

Consider the ER diagram in Figure 3.13, which shows two relationship sets, Manages and Works_In.

Every department is required to have a manager, due to the participation constraint, and at most one manager, due to the key constraint. The following SQL statement reflects the second translation approach discussed in Section 3.5.3, and uses the key constraint:

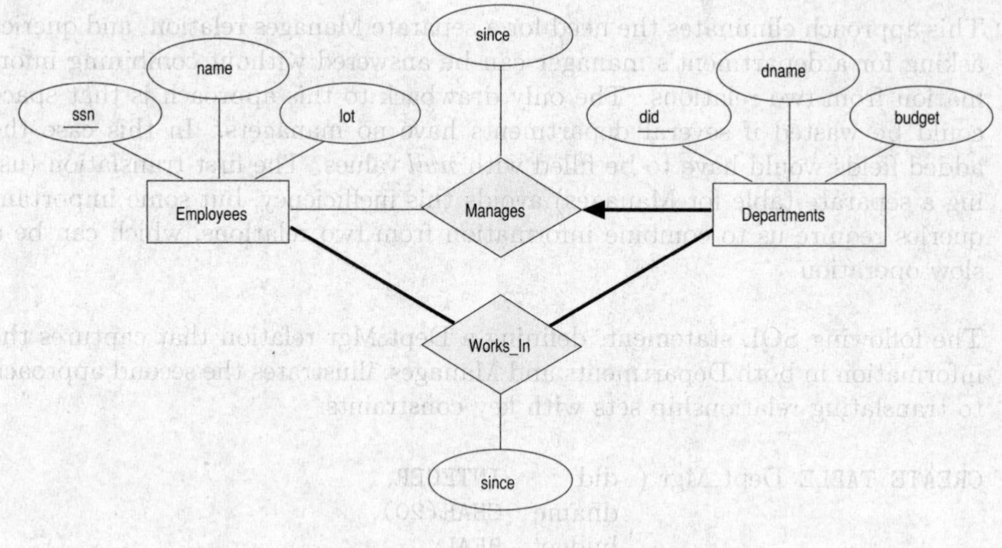

Figure 3.13 Manages and Works_In

```
CREATE TABLE Dept_Mgr ( did     INTEGER,
                        dname   CHAR(20),
                        budget  REAL,
                        ssn     CHAR(11) NOT NULL,
                        since   DATE,
                        PRIMARY KEY (did),
                        FOREIGN KEY (ssn) REFERENCES Employees
                                ON DELETE NO ACTION )
```

It also captures the participation constraint that every department must have a manager: Because *ssn* cannot take on *null* values, each tuple of Dept_Mgr identifies a tuple in Employees (who is the manager). The `NO ACTION` specification, which is the default and need not be explicitly specified, ensures that an Employees tuple cannot be deleted while it is pointed to by a Dept_Mgr tuple. If we wish to delete such an Employees tuple, we must first change the Dept_Mgr tuple to have a new employee as manager. (We could have specified `CASCADE` instead of `NO ACTION`, but deleting all information about a department just because its manager has been fired seems a bit extreme!)

The constraint that every department must have a manager cannot be captured using the first translation approach discussed in Section 3.5.3. (Look at the definition of Manages and think about what effect it would have if we added `NOT NULL` constraints to the *ssn* and *did* fields. *Hint:* The constraint would prevent the firing of a manager, but does not ensure that a manager is initially appointed for each department!) This situation is a strong argument in favor of using the second approach for one-to-many relationships such as Manages, especially when the entity set with the key constraint also has a total participation constraint.

Unfortunately, there are many participation constraints that we cannot capture using SQL, short of using *table constraints* or *assertions*. Table constraints and assertions can be specified using the full power of the SQL query language (as discussed in Section 5.7) and are very expressive but also very expensive to check and enforce. For example, we cannot enforce the participation constraints on the Works_In relation without using these general constraints. To see why, consider the Works_In relation obtained by translating the ER diagram into relations. It contains fields *ssn* and *did*, which are foreign keys referring to Employees and Departments. To ensure total participation of Departments in Works_In, we have to guarantee that every *did* value in Departments appears in a tuple of Works_In. We could try to guarantee this condition by declaring that *did* in Departments is a foreign key referring to Works_In, but this is not a valid foreign key constraint because *did* is not a candidate key for Works_In.

To ensure total participation of Departments in Works_In using SQL, we need an assertion. We have to guarantee that every *did* value in Departments appears in a tuple of Works_In; further, this tuple of Works_In must also have non-*null* values in the fields that are foreign keys referencing other entity sets involved in the relationship (in this example, the *ssn* field). We can ensure the second part of this constraint by imposing the stronger requirement that *ssn* in Works_In cannot contain *null* values. (Ensuring that the participation of Employees in Works_In is total is symmetric.)

Another constraint that requires assertions to express in SQL is the requirement that each Employees entity (in the context of the Manages relationship set) must manage at least one department.

In fact, the Manages relationship set exemplifies most of the participation constraints that we can capture using key and foreign key constraints. Manages is a binary relationship set in which exactly one of the entity sets (Departments) has a key constraint, and the total participation constraint is expressed on that entity set.

We can also capture participation constraints using key and foreign key constraints in one other special situation: a relationship set in which all participating entity sets have key constraints and total participation. The best translation approach in this case is to map all the entities as well as the relationship into a single table; the details are straightforward.

3.5.5 Translating Weak Entity Sets

A weak entity set always participates in a one-to-many binary relationship and has a key constraint and total participation. The second translation approach discussed in Section 3.5.3 is ideal in this case, but we must take into account that the weak entity has only a partial key. Also, when an owner entity is deleted, we want all owned weak entities to be deleted.

Consider the Dependents weak entity set shown in Figure 3.14, with partial key *pname*. A Dependents entity can be identified uniquely only if we take the key of the *owning* Employees entity and the *pname* of the Dependents entity, and the Dependents entity must be deleted if the owning Employees entity is deleted.

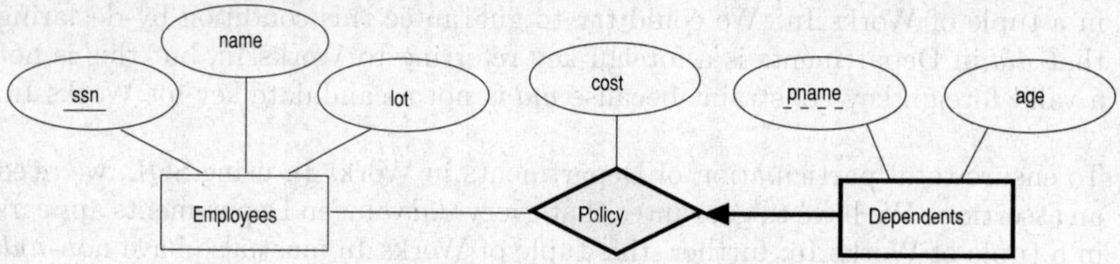

Figure 3.14 The Dependents Weak Entity Set

We can capture the desired semantics with the following definition of the Dep_Policy relation:

```
CREATE TABLE Dep_Policy ( pname  CHAR(20),
                          age    INTEGER,
                          cost   REAL,
                          ssn    CHAR(11),
                          PRIMARY KEY (pname, ssn),
                          FOREIGN KEY (ssn) REFERENCES Employees
                                 ON DELETE CASCADE )
```

Observe that the primary key is ⟨*pname, ssn*⟩, since Dependents is a weak entity. This constraint is a change with respect to the translation discussed in Section 3.5.3. We have to ensure that every Dependents entity is associated with an Employees entity (the owner), as per the total participation constraint on Dependents. That is, *ssn* cannot be *null*. This is ensured because *ssn* is part of the primary key. The CASCADE option ensures that information about an employee's policy and dependents is deleted if the corresponding Employees tuple is deleted.

3.5.6 Translating Class Hierarchies

We present the two basic approaches to handling ISA hierarchies by applying them to the ER diagram shown in Figure 3.15:

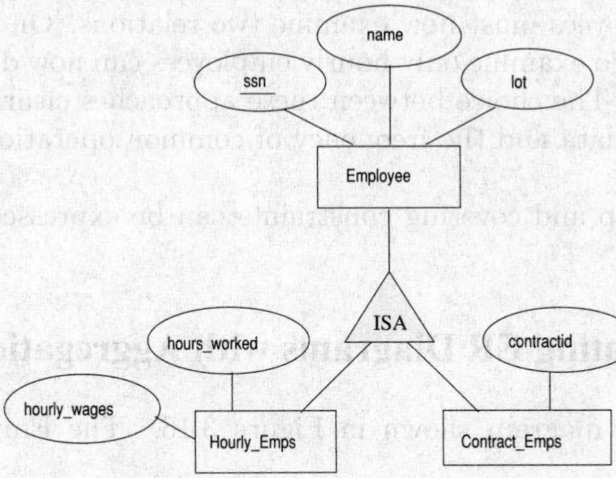

Figure 3.15 Class Hierarchy

1. We can map each of the entity sets Employees, Hourly_Emps, and Contract_Emps to a distinct relation. The Employees relation is created as in Section 2.2. We discuss Hourly_Emps here; Contract_Emps is handled similarly. The relation for Hourly_Emps includes the *hourly_wages* and *hours_worked* attributes of Hourly_Emps. It also contains the key attributes of the superclass (*ssn*, in this example), which serve as the primary key for Hourly_Emps, as well as a foreign key referencing the superclass (Employees). For each Hourly_Emps entity, the value of the *name* and *lot* attributes are stored in the corresponding row of the superclass (Employees). Note that if the superclass tuple is deleted, the delete must be cascaded to Hourly_Emps.

2. Alternatively, we can create just two relations, corresponding to Hourly_Emps and Contract_Emps. The relation for Hourly_Emps includes all the attributes of Hourly_Emps as well as all the attributes of Employees (i.e., *ssn, name, lot, hourly_wages, hours_worked*).

The first approach is general and always applicable. Queries in which we want to examine all employees and do not care about the attributes specific to the subclasses are handled easily using the Employees relation. However, queries in which we want to examine, say, hourly employees, may require us to combine Hourly_Emps (or Contract_Emps, as the case may be) with Employees to retrieve *name* and *lot*.

The second approach is not applicable if we have employees who are neither hourly employees nor contract employees, since there is no way to store such employees. Also, if an employee is both an Hourly_Emps and a Contract_Emps entity, then the *name* and *lot* values are stored twice. This duplication can lead to some of the anomalies that we discuss in Chapter 19. A query that needs to examine all employees must now examine two relations. On the other hand, a query that needs to examine only hourly employees can now do so by examining just one relation. The choice between these approaches clearly depends on the semantics of the data and the frequency of common operations.

In general, overlap and covering constraints can be expressed in SQL only by using assertions.

3.5.7 Translating ER Diagrams with Aggregation

Consider the ER diagram shown in Figure 3.16. The Employees, Projects,

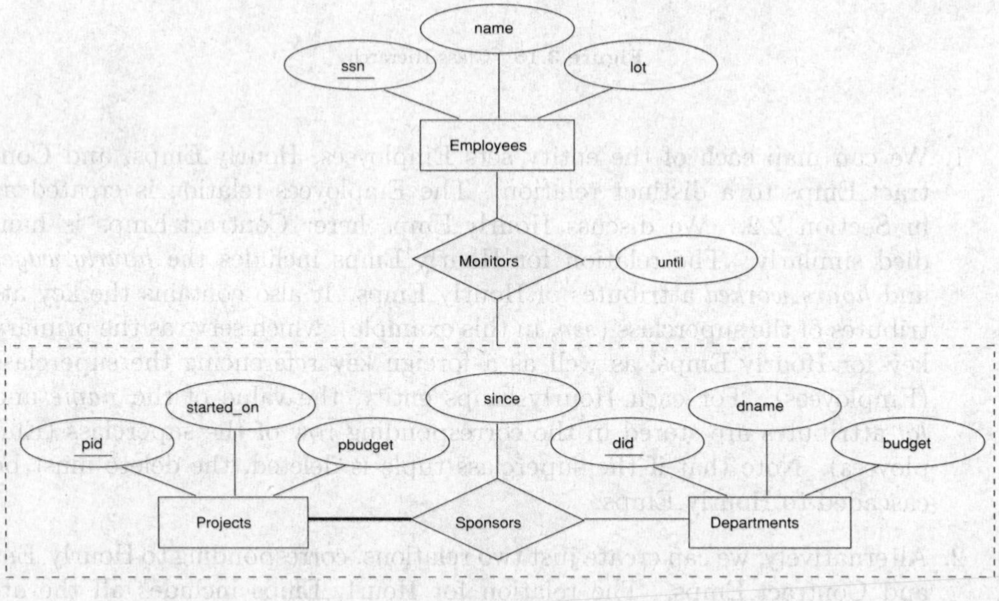

Figure 3.16 Aggregation

and Departments entity sets and the Sponsors relationship set are mapped as described in previous sections. For the Monitors relationship set, we create a relation with the following attributes: the key attributes of Employees (*ssn*), the key attributes of Sponsors (*did, pid*), and the descriptive attributes of Monitors (*until*). This translation is essentially the standard mapping for a relationship set, as described in Section 3.5.2.

There is a special case in which this translation can be refined by dropping the Sponsors relation. Consider the Sponsors relation. It has attributes *pid, did,* and *since*; and in general we need it (in addition to Monitors) for two reasons:

1. We have to record the descriptive attributes (in our example, *since*) of the Sponsors relationship.
2. Not every sponsorship has a monitor, and thus some ⟨*pid, did*⟩ pairs in the Sponsors relation may not appear in the Monitors relation.

However, if Sponsors has no descriptive attributes and has total participation in Monitors, every possible instance of the Sponsors relation can be obtained from the ⟨*pid, did*⟩ columns of Monitors; Sponsors can be dropped.

3.5.8 ER to Relational: Additional Examples

Consider the ER diagram shown in Figure 3.17. We can use the key constraints

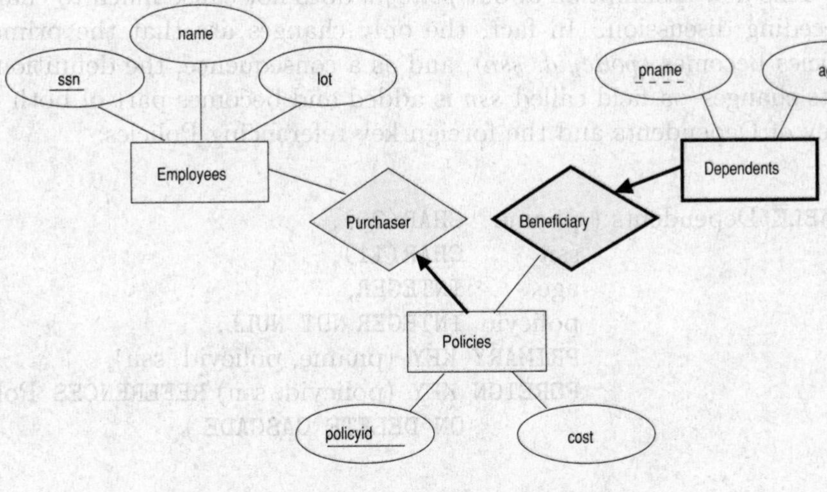

Figure 3.17 Policy Revisited

to combine Purchaser information with Policies and Beneficiary information with Dependents, and translate it into the relational model as follows:

```
CREATE TABLE Policies ( policyid INTEGER,
                        cost     REAL,
                        ssn      CHAR(11) NOT NULL,
                        PRIMARY KEY (policyid),
                        FOREIGN KEY (ssn) REFERENCES Employees
                                 ON DELETE CASCADE )
```

```
CREATE TABLE Dependents ( pname    CHAR(20),
                          age      INTEGER,
                          policyid INTEGER,
                          PRIMARY KEY (pname, policyid),
                          FOREIGN KEY (policyid) REFERENCES Policies
                                   ON DELETE CASCADE )
```

Notice how the deletion of an employee leads to the deletion of all policies owned by the employee and all dependents who are beneficiaries of those policies. Further, each dependent is required to have a covering policy—because *policyid* is part of the primary key of Dependents, there is an implicit NOT NULL constraint. This model accurately reflects the participation constraints in the ER diagram and the intended actions when an employee entity is deleted.

In general, there could be a chain of identifying relationships for weak entity sets. For example, we assumed that *policyid* uniquely identifies a policy. Suppose that *policyid* distinguishes only the policies owned by a given employee; that is, *policyid* is only a partial key and Policies should be modeled as a weak entity set. This new assumption about *policyid* does not cause much to change in the preceding discussion. In fact, the only changes are that the primary key of Policies becomes ⟨*policyid, ssn*⟩, and as a consequence, the definition of Dependents changes—a field called *ssn* is added and becomes part of both the primary key of Dependents and the foreign key referencing Policies:

```
CREATE TABLE Dependents ( pname    CHAR(20),
                          ssn      CHAR(11),
                          age      INTEGER,
                          policyid INTEGER NOT NULL,
                          PRIMARY KEY (pname, policyid, ssn),
                          FOREIGN KEY (policyid, ssn) REFERENCES Policies
                                   ON DELETE CASCADE )
```

3.6 INTRODUCTION TO VIEWS

A **view** is a table whose rows are not explicitly stored in the database but are computed as needed from a **view definition**. Consider the Students and Enrolled relations. Suppose we are often interested in finding the names and student identifiers of students who got a grade of B in some course, together with the course identifier. We can define a view for this purpose. Using SQL notation:

```
CREATE VIEW B-Students (name, sid, course)
       AS SELECT S.sname, S.sid, E.cid
```

```
FROM   Students S, Enrolled E
WHERE  S.sid = E.studid AND E.grade = 'B'
```

The view B-Students has three fields called *name*, *sid*, and *course* with the same domains as the fields *sname* and *sid* in *Students* and *cid* in Enrolled. (If the optional arguments *name*, *sid*, and *course* are omitted from the `CREATE VIEW` statement, the column names *sname*, *sid*, and *cid* are inherited.)

This view can be used just like a **base table**, or explicitly stored table, in defining new queries or views. Given the instances of Enrolled and Students shown in Figure 3.4, B-Students contains the tuples shown in Figure 3.18. Conceptually, whenever B-Students is used in a query, the view definition is first evaluated to obtain the corresponding instance of B-Students, then the rest of the query is evaluated treating B-Students like any other relation referred to in the query. (We discuss how queries on views are evaluated in practice in Chapter 25.)

name	*sid*	*course*
Jones	53666	History105
Guldu	53832	Reggae203

Figure 3.18 An Instance of the B-Students View

3.6.1 Views, Data Independence, Security

Consider the levels of abstraction we discussed in Section 1.5.2. The *physical* schema for a relational database describes how the relations in the conceptual schema are stored, in terms of the file organizations and indexes used. The *conceptual* schema is the collection of schemas of the relations stored in the database. While some relations in the conceptual schema can also be exposed to applications, that is, be part of the *external* schema of the database, additional relations in the *external* schema can be defined using the view mechanism. The view mechanism thus provides the support for *logical data independence* in the relational model. That is, it can be used to define relations in the external schema that mask changes in the conceptual schema of the database from applications. For example, if the schema of a stored relation is changed, we can define a view with the old schema and applications that expect to see the old schema can now use this view.

Views are also valuable in the context of *security*: We can define views that give a group of users access to just the information they are allowed to see. For example, we can define a view that allows students to see the other students' name and age but not their gpa, and allows all students to access this view but not the underlying Students table (see Chapter 21).

3.6.2 Updates on Views

The motivation behind the view mechanism is to tailor how users see the data. Users should not have to worry about the view versus base table distinction. This goal is indeed achieved in the case of queries on views; a view can be used just like any other relation in defining a query. However, it is natural to want to specify updates on views as well. Here, unfortunately, the distinction between a view and a base table must be kept in mind.

The SQL-92 standard allows updates to be specified only on views that are defined on a single base table using just selection and projection, with no use of aggregate operations.[3] Such views are called **updatable views**. This definition is oversimplified, but it captures the spirit of the restrictions. An update on such a restricted view can always be implemented by updating the underlying base table in an unambiguous way. Consider the following view:

```
CREATE VIEW GoodStudents (sid, gpa)
     AS SELECT S.sid, S.gpa
        FROM   Students S
        WHERE  S.gpa > 3.0
```

We can implement a command to modify the gpa of a GoodStudents row by modifying the corresponding row in Students. We can delete a GoodStudents row by deleting the corresponding row from Students. (In general, if the view did not include a key for the underlying table, several rows in the table could 'correspond' to a single row in the view. This would be the case, for example, if we used *S.sname* instead of *S.sid* in the definition of GoodStudents. A command that affects a row in the view then affects all corresponding rows in the underlying table.)

We can insert a GoodStudents row by inserting a row into Students, using *null* values in columns of Students that do not appear in GoodStudents (e.g., *sname*, *login*). Note that primary key columns are not allowed to contain *null* values. Therefore, if we attempt to insert rows through a view that does not contain the primary key of the underlying table, the insertions will be rejected. For example, if GoodStudents contained *sname* but not *sid*, we could not insert rows into Students through insertions to GoodStudents.

[3] There is also the restriction that the DISTINCT operator cannot be used in updatable view definitions. By default, SQL does not eliminate duplicate copies of rows from the result of a query; the DISTINCT operator requires duplicate elimination. We discuss this point further in Chapter 5.

Updatable Views in SQL:1999 The new SQL standard has expanded the class of view definitions that are updatable, taking primary key constraints into account. In contrast to SQL-92, a view definition that contains more than one table in the `FROM` clause may be updatable under the new definition. Intuitively, we can update a field of a view if it is obtained from exactly one of the underlying tables, and the primary key of that table is included in the fields of the view.

SQL:1999 distinguishes between views whose rows can be modified (*updatable views*) and views into which new rows can be inserted (**insertable-into views**): Views defined using the SQL constructs `UNION`, `INTERSECT`, and `EXCEPT` (which we discuss in Chapter 5) cannot be inserted into, even if they are updatable. Intuitively, updatability ensures that an updated tuple in the view can be traced to exactly one tuple in one of the tables used to define the view. The updatability property, however, may still not enable us to decide into which table to insert a new tuple.

An important observation is that an `INSERT` or `UPDATE` may change the underlying base table so that the resulting (i.e., inserted or modified) row is not in the view! For example, if we try to insert a row ⟨*51234, 2.8*⟩ into the view, this row can be (padded with *null* values in the other fields of Students and then) added to the underlying Students table, but it will not appear in the GoodStudents view because it does not satisfy the view condition $gpa > 3.0$. The SQL default action is to allow this insertion, but we can disallow it by adding the clause `WITH CHECK OPTION` to the definition of the view. In this case, only rows that will actually appear in the view are permissible insertions.

We caution the reader, that when a view is defined in terms of another view, the interaction between these view definitions with respect to updates and the `CHECK OPTION` clause can be complex; we not go into the details.

Need to Restrict View Updates

While the SQL rules on updatable views are more stringent than necessary, there are some fundamental problems with updates specified on views and good reason to limit the class of views that can be updated. Consider the Students relation and a new relation called Clubs:

Clubs(*cname:* `string`, *jyear:* `date`, *mname:* `string`)

cname	*jyear*	*mname*
Sailing	1996	Dave
Hiking	1997	Smith
Rowing	1998	Smith

Figure 3.19 An Instance *C* of Clubs

sid	*name*	*login*	*age*	*gpa*
50000	Dave	dave@cs	19	3.3
53666	Jones	jones@cs	18	3.4
53688	Smith	smith@ee	18	3.2
53650	Smith	smith@math	19	3.8

Figure 3.20 An Instance *S*3 of Students

name	*login*	*club*	*since*
Dave	dave@cs	Sailing	1996
Smith	smith@ee	Hiking	1997
Smith	smith@ee	Rowing	1998
Smith	smith@math	Hiking	1997
Smith	smith@math	Rowing	1998

Figure 3.21 Instance of ActiveStudents

A tuple in Clubs denotes that the student called *mname* has been a member of the club *cname* since the date *jyear*.[4] Suppose that we are often interested in finding the names and logins of students with a gpa greater than 3 who belong to at least one club, along with the club name and the date they joined the club. We can define a view for this purpose:

```
CREATE VIEW ActiveStudents (name, login, club, since)
       AS SELECT S.sname, S.login, C.cname, C.jyear
          FROM   Students S, Clubs C
          WHERE  S.sname = C.mname AND S.gpa > 3
```

Consider the instances of Students and Clubs shown in Figures 3.19 and 3.20. When evaluated using the instances *C* and *S*3, ActiveStudents contains the rows shown in Figure 3.21.

Now suppose that we want to delete the row ⟨*Smith, smith@ee, Hiking, 1997*⟩ from ActiveStudents. How are we to do this? ActiveStudents rows are not stored explicitly but computed as needed from the Students and Clubs tables using the view definition. So we must change either Students or Clubs (or both) in such a way that evaluating the view definition on the modified instance does not produce the row ⟨*Smith, smith@ee, Hiking, 1997.*⟩ This task can be accomplished in one of two ways: by either deleting the row ⟨*53688, Smith, smith@ee, 18, 3.2*⟩ from Students or deleting the row ⟨*Hiking, 1997, Smith*⟩

[4]We remark that Clubs has a poorly designed schema (chosen for the sake of our discussion of view updates), since it identifies students by name, which is not a candidate key for Students.

from Clubs. But neither solution is satisfactory. Removing the Students row has the effect of also deleting the row ⟨*Smith, smith@ee, Rowing, 1998*⟩ from the view ActiveStudents. Removing the Clubs row has the effect of also deleting the row ⟨*Smith, smith@math, Hiking, 1997*⟩ from the view ActiveStudents. Neither side effect is desirable. In fact, the only reasonable solution is to *disallow* such updates on views.

Views involving more than one base table can, in principle, be safely updated. The B-Students view we introduced at the beginning of this section is an example of such a view. Consider the instance of B-Students shown in Figure 3.18 (with, of course, the corresponding instances of Students and Enrolled as in Figure 3.4). To insert a tuple, say ⟨*Dave, 50000, Reggae203*⟩ B-Students, we can simply insert a tuple ⟨*Reggae203, B, 50000*⟩ into Enrolled since there is already a tuple for *sid* 50000 in Students. To insert ⟨*John, 55000, Reggae203*⟩, on the other hand, we have to insert ⟨*Reggae203, B, 55000*⟩ into Enrolled and also insert ⟨*55000, John,* null, null, null⟩ into Students. Observe how *null* values are used in fields of the inserted tuple whose value is not available. Fortunately, the view schema contains the primary key fields of both underlying base tables; otherwise, we would not be able to support insertions into this view. To delete a tuple from the view B-Students, we can simply delete the corresponding tuple from Enrolled.

Although this example illustrates that the SQL rules on updatable views are unnecessarily restrictive, it also brings out the complexity of handling view updates in the general case. For practical reasons, the SQL standard has chosen to allow only updates on a very restricted class of views.

3.7 DESTROYING/ALTERING TABLES AND VIEWS

If we decide that we no longer need a base table and want to destroy it (i.e., delete all the rows *and* remove the table definition information), we can use the `DROP TABLE` command. For example, `DROP TABLE` Students `RESTRICT` destroys the Students table unless some view or integrity constraint refers to Students; if so, the command fails. If the keyword `RESTRICT` is replaced by `CASCADE`, Students is dropped and any referencing views or integrity constraints are (recursively) dropped as well; one of these two keywords must always be specified. A view can be dropped using the `DROP VIEW` command, which is just like `DROP TABLE`.

`ALTER TABLE` modifies the structure of an existing table. To add a column called *maiden-name* to Students, for example, we would use the following command:

```
ALTER TABLE Students
      ADD COLUMN maiden-name CHAR(10)
```

The definition of Students is modified to add this column, and all existing rows are padded with *null* values in this column. ALTER TABLE can also be used to delete columns and add or drop integrity constraints on a table; we do not discuss these aspects of the command beyond remarking that dropping columns is treated very similarly to dropping tables or views.

3.8 CASE STUDY: THE INTERNET STORE

The next design step in our running example, continued from Section 2.8, is logical database design. Using the standard approach discussed in Chapter 3, DBDudes maps the ER diagram shown in Figure 2.20 to the relational model, generating the following tables:

```
CREATE TABLE Books ( isbn             CHAR(10),
                     title            CHAR(80),
                     author           CHAR(80),
                     qty_in_stock     INTEGER,
                     price            REAL,
                     year_published   INTEGER,
                     PRIMARY KEY (isbn))

CREATE TABLE Orders ( isbn        CHAR(10),
                      cid         INTEGER,
                      cardnum     CHAR(16),
                      qty         INTEGER,
                      order_date  DATE,
                      ship_date   DATE,
                      PRIMARY KEY (isbn,cid),
                      FOREIGN KEY (isbn) REFERENCES Books,
                      FOREIGN KEY (cid) REFERENCES Customers )

CREATE TABLE Customers ( cid      INTEGER,
                         cname    CHAR(80),
                         address  CHAR(200),
                         PRIMARY KEY (cid)
```

The design team leader, who is still brooding over the fact that the review exposed a flaw in the design, now has an inspiration. The Orders table contains the field *order_date* and the key for the table contains only the fields *isbn* and *cid*. Because of this, a customer cannot order the same book on different days, a restriction that was not intended. Why not add the *order date* attribute to the key for the Orders table? This would eliminate the unwanted restriction:

```
CREATE TABLE Orders (   isbn          CHAR(10),
                        ...
                        PRIMARY KEY (isbn,cid,ship date),
                        ...)
```

The reviewer, Dude 2, is not entirely happy with this solution, which he calls a 'hack'. He points out that no natural ER diagram reflects this design and stresses the importance of the ER diagram as a design document. Dude 1 argues that, while Dude 2 has a point, it is important to present B&N with a preliminary design and get feedback; everyone agrees with this, and they go back to B&N.

The owner of B&N now brings up some additional requirements he did not mention during the initial discussions: "Customers should be able to purchase several different books in a single order. For example, if a customer wants to purchase three copies of 'The English Teacher' and two copies of 'The Character of Physical Law,' the customer should be able to place a single order for both books."

The design team leader, Dude 1, asks how this affects the shippping policy. Does B&N still want to ship all books in an order together? The owner of B&N explains their shipping policy: "As soon as we have have enough copies of an ordered book we ship it, even if an order contains several books. So it could happen that the three copies of 'The English Teacher' are shipped today because we have five copies in stock, but that 'The Character of Physical Law' is shipped tomorrow, because we currently have only one copy in stock and another copy arrives tomorrow. In addition, my customers could place more than one order per day, and they want to be able to identify the orders they placed."

The DBDudes team thinks this over and identifies two new requirements: First, it must be possible to order several different books in a single order and second, a customer must be able to distinguish between several orders placed the same day. To accomodate these requirements, they introduce a new attribute into the Orders table called *ordernum*, which uniquely identifies an order and therefore the customer placing the order. However, since several books could be purchased in a single order, *ordernum* and *isbn* are both needed to determine *qty* and *ship date* in the Orders table.

Orders are assigned order numbers sequentially and orders that are placed later have higher order numbers. If several orders are placed by the same customer on a single day, these orders have different order numbers and can thus be distinguished. The SQL DDL statement to create the modified Orders table follows:

```
CREATE TABLE Orders ( ordernum     INTEGER,
                      isbn         CHAR(10),
                      cid          INTEGER,
                      cardnum      CHAR(16),
                      qty          INTEGER,
                      order_date   DATE,
                      ship_date    DATE,
                      PRIMARY KEY (ordernum, isbn),
                      FOREIGN KEY (isbn) REFERENCES Books
                      FOREIGN KEY (cid) REFERENCES Customers )
```

The owner of B&N is quite happy with this design for Orders, but has realized something else. (DBDudes is not surprised; customers almost always come up with several new requirements as the design progresses.) While he wants all his employees to be able to look at the details of an order, so that they can respond to customer enquiries, he wants customers' credit card information to be secure. To address this concern, DBDudes creates the following view:

```
CREATE VIEW OrderInfo (isbn, cid, qty, order_date, ship_date)
    AS SELECT O.cid, O.qty, O.order_date, O.ship_date
       FROM   Orders O
```

The plan is to allow employees to see this table, but not Orders; the latter is restricted to B&N's Accounting division. We'll see how this is accomplished in Section 21.7.

3.9 REVIEW QUESTIONS

Answers to the review questions can be found in the listed sections.

- What is a relation? Differentiate between a relation schema and a relation instance. Define the terms *arity* and *degree* of a relation. What are domain constraints? **(Section 3.1)**
- What SQL construct enables the definition of a relation? What constructs allow modification of relation instances? **(Section 3.1.1)**
- What are *integrity constraints*? Define the terms *primary key constraint* and *foreign key constraint.* How are these constraints expressed in SQL? What other kinds of constraints can we express in SQL? **(Section 3.2)**

- What does the DBMS do when constraints are violated? What is *referential integrity*? What options does SQL give application programmers for dealing with violations of referential integrity? **(Section 3.3)**
- When are integrity constraints enforced by a DBMS? How can an application programmer control the time that constraint violations are checked during transaction execution? **(Section 3.3.1)**
- What is a *relational database query*? **(Section 3.4)**
- How can we translate an ER diagram into SQL statements to create tables? How are entity sets mapped into relations? How are relationship sets mapped? How are constraints in the ER model, weak entity sets, class hierarchies, and aggregation handled? **(Section 3.5)**
- What is a *view*? How do views support logical data independence? How are views used for security? How are queries on views evaluated? Why does SQL restrict the class of views that can be updated? **(Section 3.6)**
- What are the SQL constructs to modify the structure of tables and destroy tables and views? Discuss what happens when we destroy a view. **(Section 3.7)**

EXERCISES

Exercise 3.1 Define the following terms: *relation schema, relational database schema, domain, relation instance, relation cardinality,* and *relation degree.*

Exercise 3.2 How many distinct tuples are in a relation instance with cardinality 22?

Exercise 3.3 Does the relational model, as seen by an SQL query writer, provide physical and logical data independence? Explain.

Exercise 3.4 What is the difference between a candidate key and the primary key for a given relation? What is a superkey?

Exercise 3.5 Consider the instance of the Students relation shown in Figure 3.1.

1. Give an example of an attribute (or set of attributes) that you can deduce is *not* a candidate key, based on this instance being legal.
2. Is there any example of an attribute (or set of attributes) that you can deduce *is* a candidate key, based on this instance being legal?

Exercise 3.6 What is a foreign key constraint? Why are such constraints important? What is referential integrity?

Exercise 3.7 Consider the relations Students, Faculty, Courses, Rooms, Enrolled, Teaches, and Meets_In defined in Section 1.5.2.

1. List all the foreign key constraints among these relations.
2. Give an example of a (plausible) constraint involving one or more of these relations that is not a primary key or foreign key constraint.

Exercise 3.8 Answer each of the following questions briefly. The questions are based on the following relational schema:

> Emp(*eid:* `integer`, *ename:* `string`, *age:* `integer`, *salary:* `real`)
> Works(*eid:* `integer`, *did:* `integer`, *pct_time:* `integer`)
> Dept(*did:* `integer`, *dname:* `string`, *budget:* `real`, *managerid:* `integer`)

1. Give an example of a foreign key constraint that involves the Dept relation. What are the options for enforcing this constraint when a user attempts to delete a Dept tuple?
2. Write the SQL statements required to create the preceding relations, including appropriate versions of all primary and foreign key integrity constraints.
3. Define the Dept relation in SQL so that every department is guaranteed to have a manager.
4. Write an SQL statement to add John Doe as an employee with $eid = 101$, $age = 32$ and $salary = 15,000$.
5. Write an SQL statement to give every employee a 10 percent raise.
6. Write an SQL statement to delete the Toy department. Given the referential integrity constraints you chose for this schema, explain what happens when this statement is executed.

Exercise 3.9 Consider the SQL query whose answer is shown in Figure 3.6.

1. Modify this query so that only the *login* column is included in the answer.
2. If the clause `WHERE` *S.gpa >= 2* is added to the original query, what is the set of tuples in the answer?

Exercise 3.10 Explain why the addition of `NOT NULL` constraints to the SQL definition of the Manages relation (in Section 3.5.3) would not enforce the constraint that each department must have a manager. What, if anything, is achieved by requiring that the *ssn* field of Manages be non-*null*?

Exercise 3.11 Suppose that we have a ternary relationship R between entity sets A, B, and C such that A has a key constraint and total participation and B has a key constraint; these are the only constraints. A has attributes $a1$ and $a2$, with $a1$ being the key; B and C are similar. R has no descriptive attributes. Write SQL statements that create tables corresponding to this information so as to capture as many of the constraints as possible. If you cannot capture some constraint, explain why.

Exercise 3.12 Consider the scenario from Exercise 2.2, where you designed an ER diagram for a university database. Write SQL statements to create the corresponding relations and capture as many of the constraints as possible. If you cannot capture some constraints, explain why.

Exercise 3.13 Consider the university database from Exercise 2.3 and the ER diagram you designed. Write SQL statements to create the corresponding relations and capture as many of the constraints as possible. If you cannot capture some constraints, explain why.

Exercise 3.14 Consider the scenario from Exercise 2.4, where you designed an ER diagram for a company database. Write SQL statements to create the corresponding relations and capture as many of the constraints as possible. If you cannot capture some constraints, explain why.

Exercise 3.15 Consider the Notown database from Exercise 2.5. You have decided to recommend that Notown use a relational database system to store company data. Show the SQL statements for creating relations corresponding to the entity sets and relationship sets in your design. Identify any constraints in the ER diagram that you are unable to capture in the SQL statements and briefly explain why you could not express them.

Exercise 3.16 Translate your ER diagram from Exercise 2.6 into a relational schema, and show the SQL statements needed to create the relations, using only key and null constraints. If your translation cannot capture any constraints in the ER diagram, explain why.

In Exercise 2.6, you also modified the ER diagram to include the constraint that tests on a plane must be conducted by a technician who is an expert on that model. Can you modify the SQL statements defining the relations obtained by mapping the ER diagram to check this constraint?

Exercise 3.17 Consider the ER diagram that you designed for the Prescriptions-R-X chain of pharmacies in Exercise 2.7. Define relations corresponding to the entity sets and relationship sets in your design using SQL.

Exercise 3.18 Write SQL statements to create the corresponding relations to the ER diagram you designed for Exercise 2.8. If your translation cannot capture any constraints in the ER diagram, explain why.

Exercise 3.19 Briefly answer the following questions based on this schema:

Emp(*eid:* `integer`, *ename:* `string`, *age:* `integer`, *salary:* `real`)
Works(*eid:* `integer`, *did:* `integer`, *pct_time:* `integer`)
Dept(*did:* `integer`, *budget:* `real`, *managerid:* `integer`)

1. Suppose you have a view SeniorEmp defined as follows:

```
CREATE VIEW SeniorEmp (sname, sage, salary)
       AS SELECT E.ename, E.age, E.salary
          FROM   Emp E
          WHERE  E.age > 50
```

   Explain what the system will do to process the following query:

```
SELECT S.sname
FROM   SeniorEmp S
WHERE  S.salary > 100,000
```

2. Give an example of a view on Emp that could be automatically updated by updating Emp.
3. Give an example of a view on Emp that would be impossible to update (automatically) and explain why your example presents the update problem that it does.

Exercise 3.20 Consider the following schema:

Suppliers(*sid:* `integer`, *sname:* `string`, *address:* `string`)
Parts(*pid:* `integer`, *pname:* `string`, *color:* `string`)
Catalog(*sid:* `integer`, *pid:* `integer`, *cost:* `real`)

The Catalog relation lists the prices charged for parts by Suppliers. Answer the following questions:

- Give an example of an updatable view involving one relation.
- Give an example of an updatable view involving two relations.
- Give an example of an insertable-into view that is updatable.
- Give an example of an insertable-into view that is not updatable.

PROJECT-BASED EXERCISES

Exercise 3.21 Create the relations Students, Faculty, Courses, Rooms, Enrolled, Teaches, and Meets_In in Minibase.

Exercise 3.22 Insert the tuples shown in Figures 3.1 and 3.4 into the relations Students and Enrolled. Create reasonable instances of the other relations.

Exercise 3.23 What integrity constraints are enforced by Minibase?

Exercise 3.24 Run the SQL queries presented in this chapter.

BIBLIOGRAPHIC NOTES

The relational model was proposed in a seminal paper by Codd [187]. Childs [176] and Kuhns [454] foreshadowed some of these developments. Gallaire and Minker's book [296] contains several papers on the use of logic in the context of relational databases. A system based on a variation of the relational model in which the entire database is regarded abstractly as a single relation, called the *universal relation*, is described in [746]. Extensions of the relational model to incorporate *null* values, which indicate an unknown or missing field value, are discussed by several authors; for example, [329, 396, 622, 754, 790].

Pioneering projects include System R [40, 150] at IBM San Jose Research Laboratory (now IBM Almaden Research Center), Ingres [717] at the University of California at Berkeley, PRTV [737] at the IBM UK Scientific Center in Peterlee, and QBE [801] at IBM T. J. Watson Research Center.

A rich theory underpins the field of relational databases. Texts devoted to theoretical aspects include those by Atzeni and DeAntonellis [45]; Maier [501]; and Abiteboul, Hull, and Vianu [3]. [415] is an excellent survey article.

Integrity constraints in relational databases have been discussed at length. [190] addresses semantic extensions to the relational model, and integrity, in particular referential integrity. [360] discusses semantic integrity constraints. [203] contains papers that address various aspects of integrity constraints, including in particular a detailed discussion of referential integrity. A vast literature deals with enforcing integrity constraints. [51] compares the cost of enforcing integrity constraints via compile-time, run-time, and post-execution checks. [145] presents an SQL-based language for specifying integrity constraints and identifies conditions under which integrity rules specified in this language can be violated. [713] discusses the technique of integrity constraint checking by query modification. [180] discusses real-time integrity constraints. Other papers on checking integrity constraints in databases include [82, 122, 138, 517]. [681] considers the approach of verifying the correctness of programs that access the database instead of run-time checks. Note that this list of references is far from complete; in fact, it does not include any of the many papers on checking recursively specified integrity constraints. Some early papers in this widely studied area can be found in [296] and [295].

For references on SQL, see the bibliographic notes for Chapter 5. This book does not discuss specific products based on the relational model, but many fine books discuss each of the major commercial systems; for example, Chamberlin's book on DB2 [149], Date and McGoveran's book on Sybase [206], and Koch and Loney's book on Oracle [443].

Several papers consider the problem of translating updates specified on views into updates on the underlying table [59, 208, 422, 468, 778]. [292] is a good survey on this topic. See the bibliographic notes for Chapter 25 for references to work querying views and maintaining materialized views.

[731] discusses a design methodology based on developing an ER diagram and then translating to the relational model. Markowitz considers referential integrity in the context of ER to relational mapping and discusses the support provided in some commercial systems (as of that date) in [513, 514].

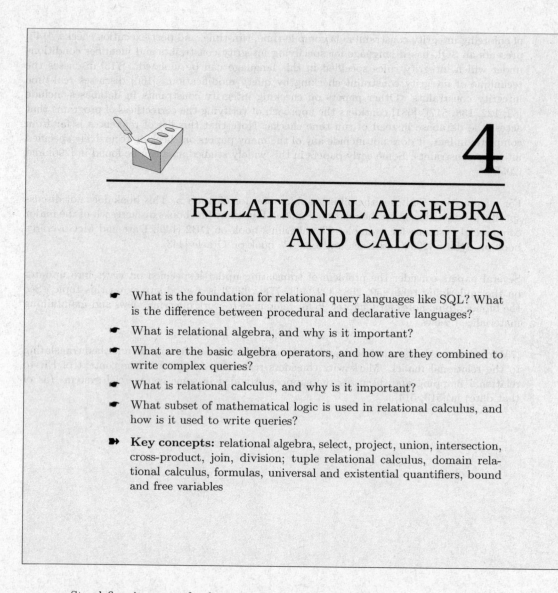

4 RELATIONAL ALGEBRA AND CALCULUS

- What is the foundation for relational query languages like SQL? What is the difference between procedural and declarative languages?
- What is relational algebra, and why is it important?
- What are the basic algebra operators, and how are they combined to write complex queries?
- What is relational calculus, and why is it important?
- What subset of mathematical logic is used in relational calculus, and how is it used to write queries?
- **Key concepts:** relational algebra, select, project, union, intersection, cross-product, join, division; tuple relational calculus, domain relational calculus, formulas, universal and existential quantifiers, bound and free variables

Stand firm in your refusal to remain conscious during algebra. In real life, I assure you, there is no such thing as algebra.

—Fran Lebowitz, *Social Studies*

This chapter presents two formal query languages associated with the relational model. **Query languages** are specialized languages for asking questions, or **queries**, that involve the data in a database. After covering some preliminaries in Section 4.1, we discuss *relational algebra* in Section 4.2. Queries in relational algebra are composed using a collection of operators, and each query describes a step-by-step procedure for computing the desired answer; that is, queries are specified in an *operational* manner. In Section 4.3, we discuss *relational calculus*, in which a query describes the desired answer without specifying how the answer is to be computed; this nonprocedural style of querying is called *declarative*. We usually refer to relational algebra and relational calculus as algebra and calculus, respectively. We compare the expressive power of algebra and calculus in Section 4.4. These formal query languages have greatly influenced commercial query languages such as SQL, which we discuss in later chapters.

4.1 PRELIMINARIES

We begin by clarifying some important points about relational queries. The inputs and outputs of a query are relations. A query is evaluated using *instances* of each input relation and it produces an instance of the output relation. In Section 3.4, we used field names to refer to fields because this notation makes queries more readable. An alternative is to always list the fields of a given relation in the same order and refer to fields by position rather than by field name.

In defining relational algebra and calculus, the alternative of referring to fields by position is more convenient than referring to fields by name: Queries often involve the computation of intermediate results, which are themselves relation instances; and if we use field names to refer to fields, the definition of query language constructs must specify the names of fields for all intermediate relation instances. This can be tedious and is really a secondary issue, because we can refer to fields by position anyway. On the other hand, field names make queries more readable.

Due to these considerations, we use the positional notation to formally define relational algebra and calculus. We also introduce simple conventions that allow intermediate relations to 'inherit' field names, for convenience.

We present a number of sample queries using the following schema:

Sailors(*sid:* `integer`, *sname:* `string`, *rating:* `integer`, *age:* `real`)
Boats(*bid:* `integer`, *bname:* `string`, *color:* `string`)
Reserves(*sid:* `integer`, *bid:* `integer`, *day:* `date`)

The key fields are underlined, and the domain of each field is listed after the field name. Thus, *sid* is the key for Sailors, *bid* is the key for Boats, and all three fields together form the key for Reserves. Fields in an instance of one of these relations are referred to by name, or positionally, using the order in which they were just listed.

In several examples illustrating the relational algebra operators, we use the instances $S1$ and $S2$ (of Sailors) and $R1$ (of Reserves) shown in Figures 4.1, 4.2, and 4.3, respectively.

sid	*sname*	*rating*	*age*
22	Dustin	7	45.0
31	Lubber	8	55.5
58	Rusty	10	35.0

Figure 4.1 Instance $S1$ of Sailors

sid	*sname*	*rating*	*age*
28	yuppy	9	35.0
31	Lubber	8	55.5
44	guppy	5	35.0
58	Rusty	10	35.0

Figure 4.2 Instance $S2$ of Sailors

sid	*bid*	*day*
22	101	10/10/96
58	103	11/12/96

Figure 4.3 Instance $R1$ of Reserves

4.2 RELATIONAL ALGEBRA

Relational algebra is one of the two formal query languages associated with the relational model. Queries in algebra are composed using a collection of operators. A fundamental property is that every operator in the algebra accepts (one or two) relation instances as arguments and returns a relation instance as the result. This property makes it easy to *compose* operators to form a complex query—a **relational algebra expression** is recursively defined to be a relation, a unary algebra operator applied to a single expression, or a binary algebra operator applied to two expressions. We describe the basic operators of the algebra (selection, projection, union, cross-product, and difference), as well as some additional operators that can be defined in terms of the basic operators but arise frequently enough to warrant special attention, in the following sections.

Each relational query describes a step-by-step procedure for computing the desired answer, based on the order in which operators are applied in the query. The procedural nature of the algebra allows us to think of an algebra expression as a recipe, or a plan, for evaluating a query, and relational systems in fact use algebra expressions to represent query evaluation plans.

4.2.1 Selection and Projection

Relational algebra includes operators to *select* rows from a relation (σ) and to *project* columns (π). These operations allow us to manipulate data in a single relation. Consider the instance of the Sailors relation shown in Figure 4.2, denoted as *S2*. We can retrieve rows corresponding to expert sailors by using the σ operator. The expression

$$\sigma_{rating>8}(S2)$$

evaluates to the relation shown in Figure 4.4. The subscript *rating>8* specifies the selection criterion to be applied while retrieving tuples.

sid	*sname*	*rating*	*age*
28	yuppy	9	35.0
58	Rusty	10	35.0

Figure 4.4 $\sigma_{rating>8}(S2)$

sname	*rating*
yuppy	9
Lubber	8
guppy	5
Rusty	10

Figure 4.5 $\pi_{sname,rating}(S2)$

The selection operator σ specifies the tuples to retain through a *selection condition.* In general, the selection condition is a Boolean combination (i.e., an expression using the logical connectives $\wedge$ and $\vee$) of *terms* that have the form *attribute* op *constant* or *attribute1* op *attribute2*, where op is one of the comparison operators $<, <=, =, \neq, >=$, or $>$. The reference to an attribute can be by position (of the form *.i* or *i*) or by name (of the form *.name* or *name*). The schema of the result of a selection is the schema of the input relation instance.

The projection operator π allows us to extract columns from a relation; for example, we can find out all sailor names and ratings by using π. The expression

$$\pi_{sname,rating}(S2)$$

evaluates to the relation shown in Figure 4.5. The subscript *sname,rating* specifies the fields to be retained; the other fields are 'projected out.' The schema of the result of a projection is determined by the fields that are projected in the obvious way.

Suppose that we wanted to find out only the ages of sailors. The expression

$$\pi_{age}(S2)$$

evaluates to the relation shown in Figure 4.6. The important point to note is that, although three sailors are aged 35, a single tuple with *age=35.0* appears in the result of the projection. This follows from the definition of a relation as a *set* of tuples. In practice, real systems often omit the expensive step of eliminating *duplicate tuples*, leading to relations that are multisets. However, our discussion of relational algebra and calculus assumes that duplicate elimination is always done so that relations are always sets of tuples.

Since the result of a relational algebra expression is always a relation, we can substitute an expression wherever a relation is expected. For example, we can compute the names and ratings of highly rated sailors by combining two of the preceding queries. The expression

$$\pi_{sname,rating}(\sigma_{rating>8}(S2))$$

produces the result shown in Figure 4.7. It is obtained by applying the selection to $S2$ (to get the relation shown in Figure 4.4) and then applying the projection.

age
35.0
55.5

Figure 4.6 $\pi_{age}(S2)$

sname	*rating*
yuppy	9
Rusty	10

Figure 4.7 $\pi_{sname,rating}(\sigma_{rating>8}(S2))$

4.2.2 Set Operations

The following standard operations on sets are also available in relational algebra: *union* ($\cup$), *intersection* ($\cap$), *set-difference* ($-$), and *cross-product* ($\times$).

- **Union:** $R \cup S$ returns a relation instance containing all tuples that occur in *either* relation instance R or relation instance S (or both). R and S must be *union-compatible*, and the schema of the result is defined to be identical to the schema of R.

  Two relation instances are said to be **union-compatible** if the following conditions hold:
  - they have the same number of the fields, and
  - corresponding fields, taken in order from left to right, have the same *domains*.

  Note that field names are not used in defining union-compatibility. For convenience, we will assume that the fields of $R \cup S$ inherit names from R, if the fields of R have names. (This assumption is implicit in defining the schema of $R \cup S$ to be identical to the schema of R, as stated earlier.)

- **Intersection:** $R \cap S$ returns a relation instance containing all tuples that occur in *both* R and S. The relations R and S must be union-compatible, and the schema of the result is defined to be identical to the schema of R.

- **Set-difference:** $R - S$ returns a relation instance containing all tuples that occur in R but not in S. The relations R and S must be union-compatible, and the schema of the result is defined to be identical to the schema of R.

- **Cross-product:** $R \times S$ returns a relation instance whose schema contains all the fields of R (in the same order as they appear in R) followed by all the fields of S (in the same order as they appear in S). The result of $R \times S$ contains one tuple $\langle r, s \rangle$ (the concatenation of tuples r and s) for each pair of tuples $r \in R$, $s \in S$. The cross-product opertion is sometimes called **Cartesian product**.

  We use the convention that the fields of $R \times S$ inherit names from the corresponding fields of R and S. It is possible for both R and S to contain one or more fields having the same name; this situation creates a *naming conflict*. The corresponding fields in $R \times S$ are unnamed and are referred to solely by position.

In the preceding definitions, note that each operator can be applied to relation instances that are computed using a relational algebra (sub)expression.

We now illustrate these definitions through several examples. The union of $S1$ and $S2$ is shown in Figure 4.8. Fields are listed in order; field names are also inherited from $S1$. $S2$ has the same field names, of course, since it is also an instance of Sailors. In general, fields of $S2$ may have different names; recall that we require only domains to match. Note that the result is a *set* of tuples. Tuples that appear in both $S1$ and $S2$ appear only once in $S1 \cup S2$. Also, $S1 \cup R1$ is not a valid operation because the two relations are not union-compatible. The intersection of $S1$ and $S2$ is shown in Figure 4.9, and the set-difference $S1 - S2$ is shown in Figure 4.10.

sid	*sname*	*rating*	*age*
22	Dustin	7	45.0
31	Lubber	8	55.5
58	Rusty	10	35.0
28	yuppy	9	35.0
44	guppy	5	35.0

Figure 4.8 $S1 \cup S2$

The result of the cross-product $S1 \times R1$ is shown in Figure 4.11. Because $R1$ and $S1$ both have a field named *sid*, by our convention on field names, the corresponding two fields in $S1 \times R1$ are unnamed, and referred to solely by the position in which they appear in Figure 4.11. The fields in $S1 \times R1$ have the same domains as the corresponding fields in $R1$ and $S1$. In Figure 4.11, *sid* is

sid	*sname*	*rating*	*age*
31	Lubber	8	55.5
58	Rusty	10	35.0

Figure 4.9 $S1 \cap S2$

sid	*sname*	*rating*	*age*
22	Dustin	7	45.0

Figure 4.10 $S1 - S2$

listed in parentheses to emphasize that it is not an inherited field name; only the corresponding domain is inherited.

(*sid*)	*sname*	*rating*	*age*	(*sid*)	*bid*	*day*
22	Dustin	7	45.0	22	101	10/10/96
22	Dustin	7	45.0	58	103	11/12/96
31	Lubber	8	55.5	22	101	10/10/96
31	Lubber	8	55.5	58	103	11/12/96
58	Rusty	10	35.0	22	101	10/10/96
58	Rusty	10	35.0	58	103	11/12/96

Figure 4.11 $S1 \times R1$

4.2.3 Renaming

We have been careful to adopt field name conventions that ensure that the result of a relational algebra expression inherits field names from its argument (input) relation instances in a natural way whenever possible. However, name conflicts can arise in some cases; for example, in $S1 \times R1$. It is therefore convenient to be able to give names explicitly to the fields of a relation instance that is defined by a relational algebra expression. In fact, it is often convenient to give the instance itself a name so that we can break a large algebra expression into smaller pieces by giving names to the results of subexpressions.

We introduce a **renaming** operator ρ for this purpose. The expression $\rho(R(\overline{F}), E)$ takes an arbitrary relational algebra expression E and returns an instance of a (new) relation called R. R contains the same tuples as the result of E and has the same schema as E, but some fields are renamed. The field names in relation R are the same as in E, except for fields renamed in the *renaming list* $\overline{F}$, which is a list of terms having the form *oldname* $\rightarrow$ *newname* or *position* $\rightarrow$ *newname*. For ρ to be well-defined, references to fields (in the form of *oldnames* or *positions* in the renaming list) may be unambiguous and no two fields in the result may have the same name. Sometimes we want to only rename fields or (re)name the relation; we therefore treat both R and $\overline{F}$ as optional in the use of ρ. (Of course, it is meaningless to omit both.)

For example, the expression $\rho(C(1 \rightarrow sid1, 5 \rightarrow sid2),\ S1 \times R1)$ returns a relation that contains the tuples shown in Figure 4.11 and has the following schema: C(*sid1:* `integer`, *sname:* `string`, *rating:* `integer`, *age:* `real`, *sid2:* `integer`, *bid:* `integer`, *day:* `dates`).

It is customary to include some additional operators in the algebra, but all of them can be defined in terms of the operators we have defined thus far. (In fact, the renaming operator is needed only for syntactic convenience, and even the $\cap$ operator is redundant; $R \cap S$ can be defined as $R - (R - S)$.) We consider these additional operators and their definition in terms of the basic operators in the next two subsections.

4.2.4 Joins

The *join* operation is one of the most useful operations in relational algebra and the most commonly used way to combine information from two or more relations. Although a join can be defined as a cross-product followed by selections and projections, joins arise much more frequently in practice than plain cross-products. Further, the result of a cross-product is typically much larger than the result of a join, and it is very important to recognize joins and implement them without materializing the underlying cross-product (by applying the selections and projections 'on-the-fly'). For these reasons, joins have received a lot of attention, and there are several variants of the join operation.[1]

Condition Joins

The most general version of the join operation accepts a *join condition* c and a pair of relation instances as arguments and returns a relation instance. The *join condition* is identical to a *selection condition* in form. The operation is defined as follows:

$$R \bowtie_c S = \sigma_c(R \times S)$$

Thus $\bowtie$ is defined to be a cross-product followed by a selection. Note that the condition c can (and typically *does*) refer to attributes of both R and S. The reference to an attribute of a relation, say, R, can be by position (of the form $R.i$) or by name (of the form $R.name$).

As an example, the result of $S1 \bowtie_{S1.sid<R1.sid} R1$ is shown in Figure 4.12. Because *sid* appears in both $S1$ and $R1$, the corresponding fields in the result of the cross-product $S1 \times R1$ (and therefore in the result of $S1 \bowtie_{S1.sid<R1.sid} R1$)

[1]Several variants of joins are not discussed in this chapter. An important class of joins, called *outer joins*, is discussed in Chapter 5.

are unnamed. Domains are inherited from the corresponding fields of $S1$ and $R1$.

(*sid*)	*sname*	*rating*	*age*	(*sid*)	*bid*	*day*
22	Dustin	7	45.0	58	103	11/12/96
31	Lubber	8	55.5	58	103	11/12/96

Figure 4.12 $S1 \bowtie_{S1.sid<R1.sid} R1$

Equijoin

A common special case of the join operation $R \bowtie S$ is when the *join condition* consists solely of equalities (connected by $\wedge$) of the form $R.name1 = S.name2$, that is, equalities between two fields in R and S. In this case, obviously, there is some redundancy in retaining both attributes in the result. For join conditions that contain only such equalities, the join operation is refined by doing an additional projection in which $S.name2$ is dropped. The join operation with this refinement is called **equijoin**.

The schema of the result of an equijoin contains the fields of R (with the same names and domains as in R) followed by the fields of S that do not appear in the join conditions. If this set of fields in the result relation includes two fields that inherit the same name from R and S, they are unnamed in the result relation.

We illustrate $S1 \bowtie_{R.sid=S.sid} R1$ in Figure 4.13. Note that only one field called *sid* appears in the result.

sid	*sname*	*rating*	*age*	*bid*	*day*
22	Dustin	7	45.0	101	10/10/96
58	Rusty	10	35.0	103	11/12/96

Figure 4.13 $S1 \bowtie_{R.sid=S.sid} R1$

Natural Join

A further special case of the join operation $R \bowtie S$ is an equijoin in which equalities are specified on *all* fields having the same name in R and S. In this case, we can simply omit the join condition; the default is that the join condition is a collection of equalities on all common fields. We call this special case a *natural join*, and it has the nice property that the result is guaranteed not to have two fields with the same name.

The equijoin expression $S1 \bowtie_{R.sid=S.sid} R1$ is actually a natural join and can simply be denoted as $S1 \bowtie R1$, since the only common field is *sid*. If the two relations have no attributes in common, $S1 \bowtie R1$ is simply the cross-product.

4.2.5 Division

The division operator is useful for expressing certain kinds of queries for example, "Find the names of sailors who have reserved all boats." Understanding how to use the basic operators of the algebra to define division is a useful exercise. However, the division operator does not have the same importance as the other operators—it is not needed as often, and database systems do not try to exploit the semantics of division by implementing it as a distinct operator (as, for example, is done with the join operator).

We discuss division through an example. Consider two relation instances A and B in which A has (exactly) two fields x and y and B has just one field y, with the same domain as in A. We define the *division* operation A/B as the set of all x values (in the form of unary tuples) such that for *every* y value in (a tuple of) B, there is a tuple $\langle x,y \rangle$ in A.

Another way to understand division is as follows. For each x value in (the first column of) A, consider the set of y values that appear in (the second field of) tuples of A with that x value. If this set contains (all y values in) B, the x value is in the result of A/B.

An analogy with integer division may also help to understand division. For integers A and B, A/B is the largest integer Q such that $Q * B \leq A$. For relation instances A and B, A/B is the largest relation instance Q such that $Q \times B \subseteq A$.

Division is illustrated in Figure 4.14. It helps to think of A as a relation listing the parts supplied by suppliers and of the B relations as listing parts. A/Bi computes suppliers who supply *all* parts listed in relation instance Bi.

Expressing A/B in terms of the basic algebra operators is an interesting exercise, and the reader should try to do this before reading further. The basic idea is to compute all x values in A that are not *disqualified*. An x value is *disqualified* if by attaching a y value from B, we obtain a tuple $\langle x,y \rangle$ that is not in A. We can compute disqualified tuples using the algebra expression

$$\pi_x((\pi_x(A) \times B) - A)$$

Thus, we can define A/B as

$$\pi_x(A) - \pi_x((\pi_x(A) \times B) - A)$$

A

sno	*pno*
s1	p1
s1	p2
s1	p3
s1	p4
s2	p1
s2	p2
s3	p2
s4	p2
s4	p4

B1

pno
p2

B2

pno
p2
p4

B3

pno
p1
p2
p4

A/B1

sno
s1
s2
s3
s4

A/B2

sno
s1
s4

A/B3

sno
s1

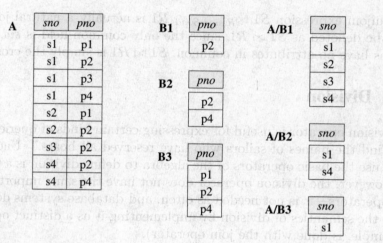

Figure 4.14 Examples Illustrating Division

To understand the division operation in full generality, we have to consider the case when both x and y are replaced by a set of attributes. The generalization is straightforward and left as an exercise for the reader. We discuss two additional examples illustrating division (Queries Q9 and Q10) later in this section.

4.2.6 More Examples of Algebra Queries

We now present several examples to illustrate how to write queries in relational algebra. We use the Sailors, Reserves, and Boats schema for all our examples in this section. We use parentheses as needed to make our algebra expressions unambiguous. Note that all the example queries in this chapter are given a unique query number. The query numbers are kept unique across both this chapter and the SQL query chapter (Chapter 5). This numbering makes it easy to identify a query when it is revisited in the context of relational calculus and SQL and to compare different ways of writing the same query. (All references to a query can be found in the subject index.)

In the rest of this chapter (and in Chapter 5), we illustrate queries using the instances $S3$ of Sailors, $R2$ of Reserves, and $B1$ of Boats, shown in Figures 4.15, 4.16, and 4.17, respectively.

(Q1) Find the names of sailors who have reserved boat 103.

This query can be written as follows:

$$\pi_{sname}((\sigma_{bid=103}Reserves) \bowtie Sailors)$$

sid	*sname*	*rating*	*age*
22	Dustin	7	45.0
29	Brutus	1	33.0
31	Lubber	8	55.5
32	Andy	8	25.5
58	Rusty	10	35.0
64	Horatio	7	35.0
71	Zorba	10	16.0
74	Horatio	9	35.0
85	Art	3	25.5
95	Bob	3	63.5

Figure 4.15 An Instance $S3$ of Sailors

sid	*bid*	*day*
22	101	10/10/98
22	102	10/10/98
22	103	10/8/98
22	104	10/7/98
31	102	11/10/98
31	103	11/6/98
31	104	11/12/98
64	101	9/5/98
64	102	9/8/98
74	103	9/8/98

Figure 4.16 An Instance $R2$ of Reserves

We first compute the set of tuples in Reserves with $bid = 103$ and then take the natural join of this set with Sailors. This expression can be evaluated on instances of Reserves and Sailors. Evaluated on the instances $R2$ and $S3$, it yields a relation that contains just one field, called *sname*, and three tuples $\langle Dustin \rangle$, $\langle Horatio \rangle$, and $\langle Lubber \rangle$. (Observe that two sailors are called Horatio and only one of them has reserved a red boat.)

bid	*bname*	*color*
101	Interlake	blue
102	Interlake	red
103	Clipper	green
104	Marine	red

Figure 4.17 An Instance $B1$ of Boats

We can break this query into smaller pieces using the renaming operator ρ:

$$\rho(Temp1, \sigma_{bid=103} Reserves)$$
$$\rho(Temp2, Temp1 \bowtie Sailors)$$
$$\pi_{sname}(Temp2)$$

Notice that because we are only using ρ to give names to intermediate relations, the renaming list is optional and is omitted. $Temp1$ denotes an intermediate relation that identifies reservations of boat 103. $Temp2$ is another intermediate relation, and it denotes sailors who have made a reservation in the set $Temp1$. The instances of these relations when evaluating this query on the instances $R2$ and $S3$ are illustrated in Figures 4.18 and 4.19. Finally, we extract the *sname* column from $Temp2$.

sid	*bid*	*day*
22	103	10/8/98
31	103	11/6/98
74	103	9/8/98

Figure 4.18 Instance of *Temp1*

sid	*sname*	*rating*	*age*	*bid*	*day*
22	Dustin	7	45.0	103	10/8/98
31	Lubber	8	55.5	103	11/6/98
74	Horatio	9	35.0	103	9/8/98

Figure 4.19 Instance of *Temp2*

The version of the query using ρ is essentially the same as the original query; the use of ρ is just syntactic sugar. However, there are indeed several distinct ways to write a query in relational algebra. Here is another way to write this query:

$$\pi_{sname}(\sigma_{bid=103}(Reserves \bowtie Sailors))$$

In this version we first compute the natural join of Reserves and Sailors and then apply the selection and the projection.

This example offers a glimpse of the role played by algebra in a relational DBMS. Queries are expressed by users in a language such as SQL. The DBMS translates an SQL query into (an extended form of) relational algebra and then looks for other algebra expressions that produce the same answers but are cheaper to evaluate. If the user's query is first translated into the expression

$$\pi_{sname}(\sigma_{bid=103}(Reserves \bowtie Sailors))$$

a good query optimizer will find the equivalent expression

$$\pi_{sname}((\sigma_{bid=103}Reserves) \bowtie Sailors)$$

Further, the optimizer will recognize that the second expression is likely to be less expensive to compute because the sizes of intermediate relations are smaller, thanks to the early use of selection.

(Q2) Find the names of sailors who have reserved a red boat.

$$\pi_{sname}((\sigma_{color='red'}Boats) \bowtie Reserves \bowtie Sailors)$$

This query involves a series of two joins. First, we choose (tuples describing) red boats. Then, we join this set with Reserves (natural join, with equality specified on the *bid* column) to identify reservations of red boats. Next, we join the resulting intermediate relation with Sailors (natural join, with equality specified on the *sid* column) to retrieve the names of sailors who have made reservations for red boats. Finally, we project the sailors' names. The answer, when evaluated on the instances $B1$, $R2$, and $S3$, contains the names Dustin, Horatio, and Lubber.

An equivalent expression is:

$$\pi_{sname}(\pi_{sid}((\pi_{bid}\sigma_{color='red'}Boats) \bowtie Reserves) \bowtie Sailors)$$

The reader is invited to rewrite both of these queries by using ρ to make the intermediate relations explicit and compare the schemas of the intermediate relations. The second expression generates intermediate relations with fewer fields (and is therefore likely to result in intermediate relation instances with fewer tuples as well). A relational query optimizer would try to arrive at the second expression if it is given the first.

(Q3) Find the colors of boats reserved by Lubber.

$$\pi_{color}((\sigma_{sname='Lubber'}Sailors) \bowtie Reserves \bowtie Boats)$$

This query is very similar to the query we used to compute sailors who reserved red boats. On instances $B1$, $R2$, and $S3$, the query returns the colors green and red.

(Q4) Find the names of sailors who have reserved at least one boat.

$$\pi_{sname}(Sailors \bowtie Reserves)$$

The join of Sailors and Reserves creates an intermediate relation in which tuples consist of a Sailors tuple 'attached to' a Reserves tuple. A Sailors tuple appears in (some tuple of) this intermediate relation only if at least one Reserves tuple has the same *sid* value, that is, the sailor has made some reservation. The answer, when evaluated on the instances $B1$, $R2$ and $S3$, contains the three tuples $\langle Dustin \rangle$, $\langle Horatio \rangle$, and $\langle Lubber \rangle$. Even though two sailors called Horatio have reserved a boat, the answer contains only one copy of the tuple $\langle Horatio \rangle$, because the answer is a *relation*, that is, a *set* of tuples, with no duplicates.

At this point it is worth remarking on how frequently the natural join operation is used in our examples. This frequency is more than just a coincidence based on the set of queries we have chosen to discuss; the natural join is a very natural, widely used operation. In particular, natural join is frequently used when joining two tables on a foreign key field. In Query Q4, for example, the join equates the *sid* fields of Sailors and Reserves, and the *sid* field of Reserves is a foreign key that refers to the *sid* field of Sailors.

(Q5) Find the names of sailors who have reserved a red or a green boat.

$$\rho(Tempboats, (\sigma_{color='red'}Boats) \cup (\sigma_{color='green'}Boats))$$
$$\pi_{sname}(Tempboats \bowtie Reserves \bowtie Sailors)$$

We identify the set of all boats that are either red or green (Tempboats, which contains boats with the *bids* 102, 103, and 104 on instances $B1$, $R2$, and $S3$). Then we join with Reserves to identify *sids* of sailors who have reserved one of these boats; this gives us *sids* 22, 31, 64, and 74 over our example instances. Finally, we join (an intermediate relation containing this set of *sids*) with Sailors to find the names of Sailors with these *sids*. This gives us the names Dustin, Horatio, and Lubber on the instances $B1$, $R2$, and $S3$. Another equivalent definition is the following:

$$\rho(Tempboats, (\sigma_{color='red' \vee color='green'} Boats))$$
$$\pi_{sname}(Tempboats \bowtie Reserves \bowtie Sailors)$$

Let us now consider a very similar query.

(Q6) Find the names of sailors who have reserved a red and a green boat. It is tempting to try to do this by simply replacing $\cup$ by $\cap$ in the definition of Tempboats:

$$\rho(Tempboats2, (\sigma_{color='red'} Boats) \cap (\sigma_{color='green'} Boats))$$
$$\pi_{sname}(Tempboats2 \bowtie Reserves \bowtie Sailors)$$

However, this solution is incorrect—it instead tries to compute sailors who have reserved a boat that is both red and green. (Since *bid* is a key for Boats, a boat can be only one color; this query will always return an empty answer set.) The correct approach is to find sailors who have reserved a red boat, then sailors who have reserved a green boat, and then take the intersection of these two sets:

$$\rho(Tempred, \pi_{sid}((\sigma_{color='red'} Boats) \bowtie Reserves))$$
$$\rho(Tempgreen, \pi_{sid}((\sigma_{color='green'} Boats) \bowtie Reserves))$$
$$\pi_{sname}((Tempred \cap Tempgreen) \bowtie Sailors)$$

The two temporary relations compute the *sids* of sailors, and their intersection identifies sailors who have reserved both red and green boats. On instances $B1$, $R2$, and $S3$, the *sids* of sailors who have reserved a red boat are 22, 31, and 64. The *sids* of sailors who have reserved a green boat are 22, 31, and 74. Thus, sailors 22 and 31 have reserved both a red boat and a green boat; their names are Dustin and Lubber.

This formulation of Query Q6 can easily be adapted to find sailors who have reserved red *or* green boats (Query Q5); just replace $\cap$ by $\cup$:

$$\rho(Tempred, \pi_{sid}((\sigma_{color='red'} Boats) \bowtie Reserves))$$
$$\rho(Tempgreen, \pi_{sid}((\sigma_{color='green'} Boats) \bowtie Reserves))$$
$$\pi_{sname}((Tempred \cup Tempgreen) \bowtie Sailors)$$

In the formulations of Queries Q5 and Q6, the fact that *sid* (the field over which we compute union or intersection) is a key for Sailors is very important. Consider the following attempt to answer Query Q6:

$$\rho(Tempred, \pi_{sname}((\sigma_{color='red'} Boats) \bowtie Reserves \bowtie Sailors))$$
$$\rho(Tempgreen, \pi_{sname}((\sigma_{color='green'} Boats) \bowtie Reserves \bowtie Sailors))$$
$$Tempred \cap Tempgreen$$

This attempt is incorrect for a rather subtle reason. Two distinct sailors with the same name, such as Horatio in our example instances, may have reserved red and green boats, respectively. In this case, the name Horatio (incorrectly) is included in the answer even though no one individual called Horatio has reserved a red boat and a green boat. The cause of this error is that *sname* is used to identify sailors (while doing the intersection) in this version of the query, but *sname* is not a key.

(Q7) Find the names of sailors who have reserved at least two boats.

$$\rho(Reservations, \pi_{sid,sname,bid}(Sailors \bowtie Reserves))$$
$$\rho(Reservationpairs(1 \rightarrow sid1, 2 \rightarrow sname1, 3 \rightarrow bid1, 4 \rightarrow sid2,$$
$$5 \rightarrow sname2, 6 \rightarrow bid2), Reservations \times Reservations)$$
$$\pi_{sname1}\sigma_{(sid1=sid2)\wedge(bid1\neq bid2)} Reservationpairs$$

First, we compute tuples of the form $\langle sid, sname, bid \rangle$, where sailor *sid* has made a reservation for boat *bid*; this set of tuples is the temporary relation Reservations. Next we find all pairs of Reservations tuples where the same sailor has made both reservations and the boats involved are distinct. Here is the central idea: To show that a sailor has reserved two boats, we must find two Reservations tuples involving the same sailor but distinct boats. Over instances $B1$, $R2$, and $S3$, each of the sailors with *sids* 22, 31, and 64 have reserved at least two boats. Finally, we project the names of such sailors to obtain the answer, containing the names Dustin, Horatio, and Lubber.

Notice that we included *sid* in Reservations because it is the key field identifying sailors, and we need it to check that two Reservations tuples involve the same sailor. As noted in the previous example, we cannot use *sname* for this purpose.

(Q8) Find the sids of sailors with age over 20 who have not reserved a red boat.

$$\pi_{sid}(\sigma_{age>20} Sailors) -$$
$$\pi_{sid}((\sigma_{color='red'} Boats) \bowtie Reserves \bowtie Sailors)$$

This query illustrates the use of the set-difference operator. Again, we use the fact that *sid* is the key for Sailors. We first identify sailors aged over 20 (over instances $B1$, $R2$, and $S3$, *sids* 22, 29, 31, 32, 58, 64, 74, 85, and 95) and then discard those who have reserved a red boat (*sids* 22, 31, and 64), to obtain the answer (*sids* 29, 32, 58, 74, 85, and 95). If we want to compute the names of such sailors, we must first compute their *sids* (as shown earlier) and then join with Sailors and project the *sname* values.

(Q9) Find the names of sailors who have reserved all boats.

The use of the word *all* (or *every*) is a good indication that the division operation might be applicable:

$$\rho(Tempsids, (\pi_{sid,bid}Reserves)/(\pi_{bid}Boats))$$
$$\pi_{sname}(Tempsids \bowtie Sailors)$$

The intermediate relation Tempsids is defined using division and computes the set of *sids* of sailors who have reserved every boat (over instances $B1$, $R2$, and $S3$, this is just *sid* 22). Note how we define the two relations that the division operator (/) is applied to—the first relation has the schema *(sid,bid)* and the second has the schema *(bid)*. Division then returns all *sids* such that there is a tuple $\langle sid, bid \rangle$ in the first relation for each *bid* in the second. Joining Tempsids with Sailors is necessary to associate names with the selected *sids*; for sailor 22, the name is Dustin.

(Q10) Find the names of sailors who have reserved all boats called Interlake.

$$\rho(Tempsids, (\pi_{sid,bid}Reserves)/(\pi_{bid}(\sigma_{bname='Interlake'}Boats)))$$
$$\pi_{sname}(Tempsids \bowtie Sailors)$$

The only difference with respect to the previous query is that now we apply a selection to Boats, to ensure that we compute *bids* only of boats named *Interlake* in defining the second argument to the division operator. Over instances $B1$, $R2$, and $S3$, Tempsids evaluates to *sids* 22 and 64, and the answer contains their names, Dustin and Horatio.

4.3 RELATIONAL CALCULUS

Relational calculus is an alternative to relational algebra. In contrast to the algebra, which is procedural, the calculus is nonprocedural, or *declarative*, in that it allows us to describe the set of answers without being explicit about how they should be computed. Relational calculus has had a big influence on the design of commercial query languages such as SQL and, especially, Query-by-Example (QBE).

The variant of the calculus we present in detail is called the **tuple relational calculus (TRC)**. Variables in TRC take on tuples as values. In another variant, called the **domain relational calculus (DRC)**, the variables range over field values. TRC has had more of an influence on SQL, while DRC has strongly influenced QBE. We discuss DRC in Section 4.3.2.[2]

4.3.1 Tuple Relational Calculus

A **tuple variable** is a variable that takes on tuples of a particular relation schema as values. That is, every value assigned to a given tuple variable has the same number and type of fields. A tuple relational calculus query has the form $\{\ T \mid p(T)\ \}$, where T is a tuple variable and $p(T)$ denotes a *formula* that describes T; we will shortly define formulas and queries rigorously. The result of this query is the set of all tuples t for which the formula $p(T)$ evaluates to `true` with $T = t$. The language for writing formulas $p(T)$ is thus at the heart of TRC and essentially a simple subset of *first-order logic*. As a simple example, consider the following query.

(Q11) Find all sailors with a rating above 7.

$$\{S \mid S \in Sailors \wedge S.rating > 7\}$$

When this query is evaluated on an instance of the Sailors relation, the tuple variable S is instantiated successively with each tuple, and the test $S.rating > 7$ is applied. The answer contains those instances of S that pass this test. On instance $S3$ of Sailors, the answer contains Sailors tuples with *sid* 31, 32, 58, 71, and 74.

Syntax of TRC Queries

We now define these concepts formally, beginning with the notion of a formula. Let *Rel* be a relation name, R and S be tuple variables, a be an attribute of R, and b be an attribute of S. Let `op` denote an operator in the set $\{<, >, =, \leq, \geq, \neq\}$. An **atomic formula** is one of the following:

- $R \in Rel$
- $R.a$ `op` $S.b$
- $R.a$ `op` *constant*, or *constant* `op` $R.a$

A **formula** is recursively defined to be one of the following, where p and q are themselves formulas and $p(R)$ denotes a formula in which the variable R appears:

[2]The material on DRC is referred to in the (online) chapter on QBE; with the exception of this chapter, the material on DRC and TRC can be omitted without loss of continuity.

- any atomic formula
- $\neg p$, $p \wedge q$, $p \vee q$, or $p \Rightarrow q$
- $\exists R(p(R))$, where R is a tuple variable
- $\forall R(p(R))$, where R is a tuple variable

In the last two clauses, the **quantifiers** $\exists$ and $\forall$ are said to **bind** the variable R. A variable is said to be **free** in a formula or *subformula* (a formula contained in a larger formula) if the (sub)formula does not contain an occurrence of a quantifier that binds it.[3]

We observe that every variable in a TRC formula appears in a subformula that is atomic, and every relation schema specifies a domain for each field; this observation ensures that each variable in a TRC formula has a well-defined domain from which values for the variable are drawn. That is, each variable has a well-defined *type*, in the programming language sense. Informally, an atomic formula $R \in Rel$ gives R the type of tuples in Rel, and comparisons such as $R.a$ `op` $S.b$ and $R.a$ `op` *constant* induce type restrictions on the field $R.a$. If a variable R does not appear in an atomic formula of the form $R \in Rel$ (i.e., it appears only in atomic formulas that are comparisons), we follow the convention that the type of R is a tuple whose fields include all (and only) fields of R that appear in the formula.

We do not define types of variables formally, but the type of a variable should be clear in most cases, and the important point to note is that comparisons of values having different types should always fail. (In discussions of relational calculus, the simplifying assumption is often made that there is a single domain of constants and this is the domain associated with each field of each relation.)

A **TRC query** is defined to be expression of the form $\{T \mid p(T)\}$, where T is the only free variable in the formula p.

Semantics of TRC Queries

What does a TRC query mean? More precisely, what is the set of answer tuples for a given TRC query? The **answer** to a TRC query $\{T \mid p(T)\}$, as noted earlier, is the set of all tuples t for which the formula $p(T)$ evaluates to `true` with variable T assigned the tuple value t. To complete this definition, we must state which assignments of tuple values to the free variables in a formula make the formula evaluate to `true`.

[3]We make the assumption that each variable in a formula is either free or bound by exactly one occurrence of a quantifier, to avoid worrying about details such as nested occurrences of quantifiers that bind some, but not all, occurrences of variables.

A query is evaluated on a given instance of the database. Let each free variable in a formula F be bound to a tuple value. For the given assignment of tuples to variables, with respect to the given database instance, F evaluates to (or simply 'is') `true` if one of the following holds:

- F is an atomic formula $R \in Rel$, and R is assigned a tuple in the instance of relation Rel.
- F is a comparison $R.a$ `op` $S.b$, $R.a$ `op` *constant*, or *constant* `op` $R.a$, and the tuples assigned to R and S have field values $R.a$ and $S.b$ that make the comparison `true`.
- F is of the form $\neg p$ and p is not `true`, or of the form $p \wedge q$, and both p and q are `true`, or of the form $p \vee q$ and one of them is `true`, or of the form $p \Rightarrow q$ and q is `true` whenever[4] p is `true`.
- F is of the form $\exists R(p(R))$, and there is some assignment of tuples to the free variables in $p(R)$, including the variable R,[5] that makes the formula $p(R)$ `true`.
- F is of the form $\forall R(p(R))$, and there is some assignment of tuples to the free variables in $p(R)$ that makes the formula $p(R)$ `true` no matter what tuple is assigned to R.

Examples of TRC Queries

We now illustrate the calculus through several examples, using the instances $B1$ of Boats, $R2$ of Reserves, and $S3$ of Sailors shown in Figures 4.15, 4.16, and 4.17. We use parentheses as needed to make our formulas unambiguous. Often, a formula $p(R)$ includes a condition $R \in Rel$, and the meaning of the phrases *some tuple R* and *for all tuples R* is intuitive. We use the notation $\exists R \in Rel(p(R))$ for $\exists R(R \in Rel \wedge p(R))$. Similarly, we use the notation $\forall R \in Rel(p(R))$ for $\forall R(R \in Rel \Rightarrow p(R))$.

(Q12) Find the names and ages of sailors with a rating above 7.

$$\{P \mid \exists S \in Sailors(S.rating > 7 \wedge P.name = S.sname \wedge P.age = S.age)\}$$

This query illustrates a useful convention: P is considered to be a tuple variable with exactly two fields, which are called *name* and *age*, because these are the only fields of P mentioned and P does not range over any of the relations in the query; that is, there is no subformula of the form $P \in Relname$. The result of this query is a relation with two fields, *name* and *age*. The atomic

[4] *Whenever* should be read more precisely as 'for all assignments of tuples to the free variables.'

[5] Note that some of the free variables in $p(R)$ (e.g., the variable R itself) may be bound in F.

formulas *P.name* = *S.sname* and *P.age* = *S.age* give values to the fields of an answer tuple P. On instances $B1$, $R2$, and $S3$, the answer is the set of tuples $\langle Lubber, 55.5\rangle$, $\langle Andy, 25.5\rangle$, $\langle Rusty, 35.0\rangle$, $\langle Zorba, 16.0\rangle$, and $\langle Horatio, 35.0\rangle$.

(Q13) Find the sailor name, boat id, and reservation date for each reservation.

$$\{P \mid \exists R \in Reserves\ \ \exists S \in Sailors$$
$$(R.sid = S.sid \wedge P.bid = R.bid \wedge P.day = R.day \wedge P.sname = S.sname)\}$$

For each Reserves tuple, we look for a tuple in Sailors with the same *sid.* Given a pair of such tuples, we construct an answer tuple P with fields *sname, bid,* and *day* by copying the corresponding fields from these two tuples. This query illustrates how we can combine values from different relations in each answer tuple. The answer to this query on instances $B1$, $R2$, and $S3$ is shown in Figure 4.20.

sname	*bid*	*day*
Dustin	101	10/10/98
Dustin	102	10/10/98
Dustin	103	10/8/98
Dustin	104	10/7/98
Lubber	102	11/10/98
Lubber	103	11/6/98
Lubber	104	11/12/98
Horatio	101	9/5/98
Horatio	102	9/8/98
Horatio	103	9/8/98

Figure 4.20 Answer to Query Q13

(Q1) Find the names of sailors who have reserved boat 103.

$$\{P \mid \exists S \in Sailors\ \ \exists R \in Reserves(R.sid = S.sid \wedge R.bid = 103$$
$$\wedge P.sname = S.sname)\}$$

This query can be read as follows: "Retrieve all sailor tuples for which there exists a tuple in Reserves having the same value in the *sid* field and with *bid* = 103." That is, for each sailor tuple, we look for a tuple in Reserves that shows that this sailor has reserved boat 103. The answer tuple P contains just one field, *sname.*

(Q2) Find the names of sailors who have reserved a red boat.

$$\{P \mid \exists S \in Sailors\ \ \exists R \in Reserves(R.sid = S.sid \wedge P.sname = S.sname$$

$$\wedge \exists B \in Boats(B.bid = R.bid \wedge B.color ='red'))\}$$

This query can be read as follows: "Retrieve all sailor tuples S for which there exist tuples R in Reserves and B in Boats such that $S.sid = R.sid$, $R.bid = B.bid$, and $B.color ='red'$." Another way to write this query, which corresponds more closely to this reading, is as follows:

$$\{P \mid \exists S \in Sailors \;\; \exists R \in Reserves \;\; \exists B \in Boats$$
$$(R.sid = S.sid \wedge B.bid = R.bid \wedge B.color ='red' \wedge P.sname = S.sname)\}$$

(Q7) Find the names of sailors who have reserved at least two boats.

$$\{P \mid \exists S \in Sailors \;\; \exists R1 \in Reserves \;\; \exists R2 \in Reserves$$
$$(S.sid = R1.sid \wedge R1.sid = R2.sid \wedge R1.bid \neq R2.bid$$
$$\wedge P.sname = S.sname)\}$$

Contrast this query with the algebra version and see how much simpler the calculus version is. In part, this difference is due to the cumbersome renaming of fields in the algebra version, but the calculus version really is simpler.

(Q9) Find the names of sailors who have reserved all boats.

$$\{P \mid \exists S \in Sailors \;\; \forall B \in Boats$$
$$(\exists R \in Reserves(S.sid = R.sid \wedge R.bid = B.bid \wedge P.sname = S.sname))\}$$

This query was expressed using the division operator in relational algebra. Note how easily it is expressed in the calculus. The calculus query directly reflects how we might express the query in English: "Find sailors S such that for all boats B there is a Reserves tuple showing that sailor S has reserved boat B."

(Q14) Find sailors who have reserved all red boats.

$$\{S \mid S \in Sailors \wedge \forall B \in Boats$$
$$(B.color ='red' \Rightarrow (\exists R \in Reserves(S.sid = R.sid \wedge R.bid = B.bid)))\}$$

This query can be read as follows: For each candidate (sailor), if a boat is red, the sailor must have reserved it. That is, for a candidate sailor, a boat being red must imply that the sailor has reserved it. Observe that since we can return an entire sailor tuple as the answer instead of just the sailor's name, we avoided introducing a new free variable (e.g., the variable P in the previous example) to hold the answer values. On instances $B1$, $R2$, and $S3$, the answer contains the Sailors tuples with *sid*s 22 and 31.

We can write this query without using implication, by observing that an expression of the form $p \Rightarrow q$ is logically equivalent to $\neg p \vee q$:

$$\{S \mid S \in Sailors \wedge \forall B \in Boats$$

$$(B.color \neq 'red' \vee (\exists R \in Reserves(S.sid = R.sid \wedge R.bid = B.bid)))\}$$

This query should be read as follows: "Find sailors S such that, for all boats B, either the boat is not red or a Reserves tuple shows that sailor S has reserved boat B."

4.3.2 Domain Relational Calculus

A **domain variable** is a variable that ranges over the values in the domain of some attribute (e.g., the variable can be assigned an integer if it appears in an attribute whose domain is the set of integers). A DRC query has the form $\{\langle x_1, x_2, \ldots, x_n \rangle \mid p(\langle x_1, x_2, \ldots, x_n \rangle)\}$, where each x_i is either a *domain variable* or a constant and $p(\langle x_1, x_2, \ldots, x_n \rangle)$ denotes a **DRC formula** whose only free variables are the variables among the x_i, $1 \leq i \leq n$. The result of this query is the set of all tuples $\langle x_1, x_2, \ldots, x_n \rangle$ for which the formula evaluates to `true`.

A DRC formula is defined in a manner very similar to the definition of a TRC formula. The main difference is that the variables are now domain variables. Let op denote an operator in the set $\{<, >, =, \leq, \geq, \neq\}$ and let X and Y be domain variables. An **atomic formula** in DRC is one of the following:

- $\langle x_1, x_2, \ldots, x_n \rangle \in Rel$, where Rel is a relation with n attributes; each x_i, $1 \leq i \leq n$ is either a variable or a constant
- X op Y
- X op *constant*, or *constant* op X

A **formula** is recursively defined to be one of the following, where p and q are themselves formulas and $p(X)$ denotes a formula in which the variable X appears:

- any atomic formula
- $\neg p$, $p \wedge q$, $p \vee q$, or $p \Rightarrow q$
- $\exists X(p(X))$, where X is a domain variable
- $\forall X(p(X))$, where X is a domain variable

The reader is invited to compare this definition with the definition of TRC formulas and see how closely these two definitions correspond. We will not define the semantics of DRC formulas formally; this is left as an exercise for the reader.

Examples of DRC Queries

We now illustrate DRC through several examples. The reader is invited to compare these with the TRC versions.

(Q11) Find all sailors with a rating above 7.

$$\{\langle I, N, T, A\rangle \mid \langle I, N, T, A\rangle \in Sailors \wedge T > 7\}$$

This differs from the TRC version in giving each attribute a (variable) name. The condition $\langle I, N, T, A\rangle \in Sailors$ ensures that the domain variables I, N, T, and A are restricted to be fields of the *same* tuple. In comparison with the TRC query, we can say $T > 7$ instead of $S.rating > 7$, but we must specify the tuple $\langle I, N, T, A\rangle$ in the result, rather than just S.

(Q1) Find the names of sailors who have reserved boat 103.

$$\{\langle N\rangle \mid \exists I, T, A(\langle I, N, T, A\rangle \in Sailors$$
$$\wedge \exists Ir, Br, D(\langle Ir, Br, D\rangle \in Reserves \wedge Ir = I \wedge Br = 103))\}$$

Note that only the *sname* field is retained in the answer and that only N is a free variable. We use the notation $\exists Ir, Br, D(\ldots)$ as a shorthand for $\exists Ir(\exists Br(\exists D(\ldots)))$. Very often, all the quantified variables appear in a single relation, as in this example. An even more compact notation in this case is $\exists\langle Ir, Br, D\rangle \in Reserves$. With this notation, which we use henceforth, the query would be as follows:

$$\{\langle N\rangle \mid \exists I, T, A(\langle I, N, T, A\rangle \in Sailors$$
$$\wedge \exists\langle Ir, Br, D\rangle \in Reserves(Ir = I \wedge Br = 103))\}$$

The comparison with the corresponding TRC formula should now be straightforward. This query can also be written as follows; note the repetition of variable I and the use of the constant 103:

$$\{\langle N\rangle \mid \exists I, T, A(\langle I, N, T, A\rangle \in Sailors$$
$$\wedge \exists D(\langle I, 103, D\rangle \in Reserves))\}$$

(Q2) Find the names of sailors who have reserved a red boat.

$$\{\langle N\rangle \mid \exists I, T, A(\langle I, N, T, A\rangle \in Sailors$$
$$\wedge \exists\langle I, Br, D\rangle \in Reserves \wedge \exists\langle Br, BN, 'red'\rangle \in Boats)\}$$

(Q7) Find the names of sailors who have reserved at least two boats.

$$\{\langle N\rangle \mid \exists I, T, A(\langle I, N, T, A\rangle \in Sailors \wedge$$
$$\exists Br1, Br2, D1, D2(\langle I, Br1, D1\rangle \in Reserves$$
$$\wedge \langle I, Br2, D2\rangle \in Reserves \wedge Br1 \neq Br2))\}$$

Note how the repeated use of variable I ensures that the same sailor has reserved both the boats in question.

(Q9) Find the names of sailors who have reserved all boats.

$$\{\langle N\rangle \mid \exists I,T,A(\langle I,N,T,A\rangle \in Sailors \wedge$$
$$\forall B,BN,C(\neg(\langle B,BN,C\rangle \in Boats) \vee$$
$$(\exists\langle Ir,Br,D\rangle \in Reserves(I = Ir \wedge Br = B)))))\}$$

This query can be read as follows: "Find all values of N such that some tuple $\langle I,N,T,A\rangle$ in Sailors satisfies the following condition: For every $\langle B,BN,C\rangle$, either this is not a tuple in Boats or there is some tuple $\langle Ir,Br,D\rangle$ in Reserves that proves that Sailor I has reserved boat B." The $\forall$ quantifier allows the domain variables B, BN, and C to range over all values in their respective attribute domains, and the pattern '$\neg(\langle B,BN,C\rangle \in Boats)\vee$' is necessary to restrict attention to those values that appear in tuples of Boats. This pattern is common in DRC formulas, and the notation $\forall\langle B,BN,C\rangle \in Boats$ can be used as a shortcut instead. This is similar to the notation introduced earlier for $\exists$. With this notation, the query would be written as follows:

$$\{\langle N\rangle \mid \exists I,T,A(\langle I,N,T,A\rangle \in Sailors \wedge \forall\langle B,BN,C\rangle \in Boats$$
$$(\exists\langle Ir,Br,D\rangle \in Reserves(I = Ir \wedge Br = B)))\}$$

(Q14) Find sailors who have reserved all red boats.

$$\{\langle I,N,T,A\rangle \mid \langle I,N,T,A\rangle \in Sailors \wedge \forall\langle B,BN,C\rangle \in Boats$$
$$(C = 'red' \Rightarrow \exists\langle Ir,Br,D\rangle \in Reserves(I = Ir \wedge Br = B))\}$$

Here, we find all sailors such that, for every red boat, there is a tuple in Reserves that shows the sailor has reserved it.

4.4 EXPRESSIVE POWER OF ALGEBRA AND CALCULUS

We presented two formal query languages for the relational model. Are they equivalent in power? Can every query that can be expressed in relational algebra also be expressed in relational calculus? The answer is yes, it can. Can every query that can be expressed in relational calculus also be expressed in relational algebra? Before we answer this question, we consider a major problem with the calculus as we presented it.

Consider the query $\{S \mid \neg(S \in Sailors)\}$. This query is syntactically correct. However, it asks for all tuples S such that S is not in (the given instance of)

Sailors. The set of such S tuples is obviously infinite, in the context of infinite domains such as the set of all integers. This simple example illustrates an *unsafe* query. It is desirable to restrict relational calculus to disallow unsafe queries.

We now sketch how calculus queries are restricted to be safe. Consider a set I of relation instances, with one instance per relation that appears in the query Q. Let $Dom(Q, I)$ be the set of all constants that appear in these relation instances I or in the formulation of the query Q itself. Since we allow only finite instances I, $Dom(Q, I)$ is also finite.

For a calculus formula Q to be considered safe, at a minimum we want to ensure that, for any given I, the set of answers for Q contains only values in $Dom(Q, I)$. While this restriction is obviously required, it is not enough. Not only do we want the set of answers to be composed of constants in $Dom(Q, I)$, we wish to *compute* the set of answers by examining only tuples that contain constants in $Dom(Q, I)$! This wish leads to a subtle point associated with the use of quantifiers $\forall$ and $\exists$: Given a TRC formula of the form $\exists R(p(R))$, we want to find all values for variable R that make this formula `true` by checking only tuples that contain constants in $Dom(Q, I)$. Similarly, given a TRC formula of the form $\forall R(p(R))$, we want to find any values for variable R that make this formula `false` by checking only tuples that contain constants in $Dom(Q, I)$.

We therefore define a *safe* TRC formula Q to be a formula such that:

1. For any given I, the set of answers for Q contains only values that are in $Dom(Q, I)$.
2. For each subexpression of the form $\exists R(p(R))$ in Q, if a tuple r (assigned to variable R) makes the formula `true`, then r contains only constants in $Dom(Q, I)$.
3. For each subexpression of the form $\forall R(p(R))$ in Q, if a tuple r (assigned to variable R) contains a constant that is not in $Dom(Q, I)$, then r must make the formula `true`.

Note that this definition is not *constructive*, that is, it does not tell us how to check if a query is safe.

The query $Q = \{S \mid \neg(S \in Sailors)\}$ is unsafe by this definition. $Dom(Q, I)$ is the set of all values that appear in (an instance I of) Sailors. Consider the instance $S1$ shown in Figure 4.1. The answer to this query obviously includes values that do not appear in $Dom(Q, S1)$.

Returning to the question of expressiveness, we can show that every query that can be expressed using a *safe* relational calculus query can also be expressed as a relational algebra query. The expressive power of relational algebra is often used as a metric of how powerful a relational database query language is. If a query language can express all the queries that we can express in relational algebra, it is said to be **relationally complete**. A practical query language is expected to be relationally complete; in addition, commercial query languages typically support features that allow us to express some queries that cannot be expressed in relational algebra.

4.5 REVIEW QUESTIONS

Answers to the review questions can be found in the listed sections.

- What is the input to a relational query? What is the result of evaluating a query? **(Section 4.1)**
- Database systems use some variant of relational algebra to represent query evaluation plans. Explain why algebra is suitable for this purpose. **(Section 4.2)**
- Describe the selection operator. What can you say about the cardinality of the input and output tables for this operator? (That is, if the input has k tuples, what can you say about the output?) Describe the projection operator. What can you say about the cardinality of the input and output tables for this operator? **(Section 4.2.1)**
- Describe the set operations of relational algebra, including union ($\cup$), intersection ($\cap$), set-difference ($-$), and cross-product ($\times$). For each, what can you say about the cardinality of their input and output tables? **(Section 4.2.2)**
- Explain how the renaming operator is used. Is it required? That is, if this operator is not allowed, is there any query that can no longer be expressed in algebra? **(Section 4.2.3)**
- Define all the variations of the join operation. Why is the join operation given special attention? Cannot we express every join operation in terms of cross-product, selection, and projection? **(Section 4.2.4)**
- Define the division operation in terms of the basic relational algebra operations. Describe a typical query that calls for division. Unlike join, the division operator is not given special treatment in database systems. Explain why. **(Section 4.2.5)**

- Relational calculus is said to be a *declarative* language, in contrast to algebra, which is a *procedural* language. Explain the distinction. **(Section 4.3)**
- How does a relational calculus query 'describe' result tuples? Discuss the subset of first-order predicate logic used in tuple relational calculus, with particular attention to universal and existential quantifiers, bound and free variables, and restrictions on the query formula. **(Section 4.3.1)**.
- What is the difference between tuple relational calculus and domain relational calculus? **(Section 4.3.2)**.
- What is an *unsafe* calculus query? Why is it important to avoid such queries? **(Section 4.4)**
- Relational algebra and relational calculus are said to be equivalent in expressive power. Explain what this means, and how it is related to the notion of *relational completeness.* **(Section 4.4)**

EXERCISES

Exercise 4.1 Explain the statement that relational algebra operators can be *composed.* Why is the ability to compose operators important?

Exercise 4.2 Given two relations $R1$ and $R2$, where $R1$ contains N1 tuples, $R2$ contains N2 tuples, and N2 > N1 > 0, give the minimum and maximum possible sizes (in tuples) for the resulting relation produced by each of the following relational algebra expressions. In each case, state any assumptions about the schemas for $R1$ and $R2$ needed to make the expression meaningful:

(1) $R1 \cup R2$, (2) $R1 \cap R2$, (3) $R1 - R2$, (4) $R1 \times R2$, (5) $\sigma_{a=5}(R1)$, (6) $\pi_a(R1)$, and (7) $R1/R2$

Exercise 4.3 Consider the following schema:

Suppliers(*sid:* `integer`, *sname:* `string`, *address:* `string`)
Parts(*pid:* `integer`, *pname:* `string`, *color:* `string`)
Catalog(*sid:* `integer`, *pid:* `integer`, *cost:* `real`)

The key fields are underlined, and the domain of each field is listed after the field name. Therefore *sid* is the key for Suppliers, *pid* is the key for Parts, and *sid* and *pid* together form the key for Catalog. The Catalog relation lists the prices charged for parts by Suppliers. Write the following queries in relational algebra, tuple relational calculus, and domain relational calculus:

1. Find the *names* of suppliers who supply some red part.
2. Find the *sids* of suppliers who supply some red or green part.
3. Find the *sids* of suppliers who supply some red part or are at 221 Packer Ave.
4. Find the *sids* of suppliers who supply some red part and some green part.

5. Find the *sids* of suppliers who supply every part.
6. Find the *sids* of suppliers who supply every red part.
7. Find the *sids* of suppliers who supply every red or green part.
8. Find the *sids* of suppliers who supply every red part or supply every green part.
9. Find pairs of *sids* such that the supplier with the first *sid* charges more for some part than the supplier with the second *sid*.
10. Find the *pids* of parts supplied by at least two different suppliers.
11. Find the *pids* of the most expensive parts supplied by suppliers named Yosemite Sham.
12. Find the *pids* of parts supplied by every supplier at less than \$200. (If any supplier either does not supply the part or charges more than \$200 for it, the part is not selected.)

Exercise 4.4 Consider the Supplier-Parts-Catalog schema from the previous question. State what the following queries compute:

1. $\pi_{sname}(\pi_{sid}(\sigma_{color='red'} Parts) \bowtie (\sigma_{cost<100} Catalog) \bowtie Suppliers)$
2. $\pi_{sname}(\pi_{sid}((\sigma_{color='red'} Parts) \bowtie (\sigma_{cost<100} Catalog) \bowtie Suppliers))$
3. $(\pi_{sname}((\sigma_{color='red'} Parts) \bowtie (\sigma_{cost<100} Catalog) \bowtie Suppliers)) \cap$

   $(\pi_{sname}((\sigma_{color='green'} Parts) \bowtie (\sigma_{cost<100} Catalog) \bowtie Suppliers))$
4. $(\pi_{sid}((\sigma_{color='red'} Parts) \bowtie (\sigma_{cost<100} Catalog) \bowtie Suppliers)) \cap$

   $(\pi_{sid}((\sigma_{color='green'} Parts) \bowtie (\sigma_{cost<100} Catalog) \bowtie Suppliers))$
5. $\pi_{sname}((\pi_{sid,sname}((\sigma_{color='red'} Parts) \bowtie (\sigma_{cost<100} Catalog) \bowtie Suppliers)) \cap$

   $(\pi_{sid,sname}((\sigma_{color='green'} Parts) \bowtie (\sigma_{cost<100} Catalog) \bowtie Suppliers)))$

Exercise 4.5 Consider the following relations containing airline flight information:

Flights(*flno:* `integer`, *from:* `string`, *to:* `string`,
distance: `integer`, *departs:* `time`, *arrives:* `time`)
Aircraft(*aid:* `integer`, *aname:* `string`, *cruisingrange:* `integer`)
Certified(*eid:* `integer`, *aid:* `integer`)
Employees(*eid:* `integer`, *ename:* `string`, *salary:* `integer`)

Note that the Employees relation describes pilots and other kinds of employees as well; every pilot is certified for some aircraft (otherwise, he or she would not qualify as a pilot), and only pilots are certified to fly.

Write the following queries in relational algebra, tuple relational calculus, and domain relational calculus. Note that some of these queries may not be expressible in relational algebra (and, therefore, also not expressible in tuple and domain relational calculus)! For such queries, informally explain why they cannot be expressed. (See the exercises at the end of Chapter 5 for additional queries over the airline schema.)

1. Find the *eids* of pilots certified for some Boeing aircraft.
2. Find the *names* of pilots certified for some Boeing aircraft.
3. Find the *aids* of all aircraft that can be used on non-stop flights from Bonn to Madras.

4. Identify the flights that can be piloted by every pilot whose salary is more than $100,000.
5. Find the names of pilots who can operate planes with a range greater than 3,000 miles but are not certified on any Boeing aircraft.
6. Find the *eids* of employees who make the highest salary.
7. Find the *eids* of employees who make the second highest salary.
8. Find the *eids* of employees who are certified for the largest number of aircraft.
9. Find the *eids* of employees who are certified for exactly three aircraft.
10. Find the total amount paid to employees as salaries.
11. Is there a sequence of flights from Madison to Timbuktu? Each flight in the sequence is required to depart from the city that is the destination of the previous flight; the first flight must leave Madison, the last flight must reach Timbuktu, and there is no restriction on the number of intermediate flights. Your query must determine whether a sequence of flights from Madison to Timbuktu exists for *any* input Flights relation instance.

Exercise 4.6 What is *relational completeness*? If a query language is relationally complete, can you write any desired query in that language?

Exercise 4.7 What is an *unsafe* query? Give an example and explain why it is important to disallow such queries.

BIBLIOGRAPHIC NOTES

Relational algebra was proposed by Codd in [187], and he showed the equivalence of relational algebra and TRC in [189]. Earlier, Kuhns [454] considered the use of logic to pose queries. LaCroix and Pirotte discussed DRC in [459]. Klug generalized the algebra and calculus to include aggregate operations in [439]. Extensions of the algebra and calculus to deal with aggregate functions are also discussed in [578]. Merrett proposed an extended relational algebra with quantifiers such as *the number of* that go beyond just universal and existential quantification [530]. Such generalized quantifiers are discussed at length in [52].

5

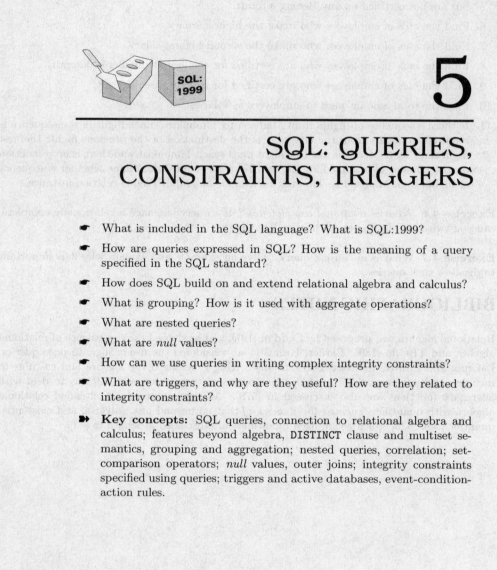

SQL: QUERIES, CONSTRAINTS, TRIGGERS

- What is included in the SQL language? What is SQL:1999?
- How are queries expressed in SQL? How is the meaning of a query specified in the SQL standard?
- How does SQL build on and extend relational algebra and calculus?
- What is grouping? How is it used with aggregate operations?
- What are nested queries?
- What are *null* values?
- How can we use queries in writing complex integrity constraints?
- What are triggers, and why are they useful? How are they related to integrity constraints?
- **Key concepts:** SQL queries, connection to relational algebra and calculus; features beyond algebra, `DISTINCT` clause and multiset semantics, grouping and aggregation; nested queries, correlation; set-comparison operators; *null* values, outer joins; integrity constraints specified using queries; triggers and active databases, event-condition-action rules.

What men or gods are these? What maidens loth?
What mad pursuit? What struggle to escape?
What pipes and timbrels? What wild ecstasy?

—John Keats, *Ode on a Grecian Urn*

Structured Query Language (SQL) is the most widely used commercial relational database language. It was originally developed at IBM in the SEQUEL-

> **SQL Standards Conformance:** SQL:1999 has a collection of features called Core SQL that a vendor must implement to claim conformance with the SQL:1999 standard. It is estimated that all the major vendors can comply with Core SQL with little effort. Many of the remaining features are organized into **packages**.
>
> For example, packages address each of the following (with relevant chapters in parentheses): *enhanced date and time*, *enhanced integrity management and active databases* (this chapter), *external language interfaces* (Chapter 6), *OLAP* (Chapter 25), and *object features* (Chapter 23). The SQL/MM standard complements SQL:1999 by defining additional packages that support *data mining* (Chapter 26), *spatial data* (Chapter 28) and *text documents* (Chapter 27). Support for XML data and queries is forthcoming.

XRM and System-R projects (1974–1977). Almost immediately, other vendors introduced DBMS products based on SQL, and it is now a de facto standard. SQL continues to evolve in response to changing needs in the database area. The current ANSI/ISO standard for SQL is called SQL:1999. While not all DBMS products support the full SQL:1999 standard yet, vendors are working toward this goal and most products already support the core features. The SQL:1999 standard is very close to the previous standard, SQL-92, with respect to the features discussed in this chapter. Our presentation is consistent with both SQL-92 and SQL:1999, and we explicitly note any aspects that differ in the two versions of the standard.

5.1 OVERVIEW

The SQL language has several aspects to it.

- **The Data Manipulation Language (DML):** This subset of SQL allows users to pose queries and to insert, delete, and modify rows. Queries are the main focus of this chapter. We covered DML commands to insert, delete, and modify rows in Chapter 3.
- **The Data Definition Language (DDL):** This subset of SQL supports the creation, deletion, and modification of definitions for tables and views. *Integrity constraints* can be defined on tables, either when the table is created or later. We cocvered the DDL features of SQL in Chapter 3. Although the standard does not discuss indexes, commercial implementations also provide commands for creating and deleting indexes.
- **Triggers and Advanced Integrity Constraints:** The new SQL:1999 standard includes support for *triggers*, which are actions executed by the

DBMS whenever changes to the database meet conditions specified in the trigger. We cover triggers in this chapter. SQL allows the use of queries to specify complex integrity constraint specifications. We also discuss such constraints in this chapter.

- **Embedded and Dynamic SQL:** Embedded SQL features allow SQL code to be called from a host language such as C or COBOL. Dynamic SQL features allow a query to be constructed (and executed) at run-time. We cover these features in Chapter 6.

- **Client-Server Execution and Remote Database Access:** These commands control how a *client* application program can connect to an SQL database *server*, or access data from a database over a network. We cover these commands in Chapter 7.

- **Transaction Management:** Various commands allow a user to explicitly control aspects of how a transaction is to be executed. We cover these commands in Chapter 21.

- **Security:** SQL provides mechanisms to control users' access to data objects such as tables and views. We cover these in Chapter 21.

- **Advanced features:** The SQL:1999 standard includes object-oriented features (Chapter 23), recursive queries (Chapter 24), decision support queries (Chapter 25), and also addresses emerging areas such as data mining (Chapter 26), spatial data (Chapter 28), and text and XML data management (Chapter 27).

5.1.1 Chapter Organization

The rest of this chapter is organized as follows. We present basic SQL queries in Section 5.2 and introduce SQL's set operators in Section 5.3. We discuss nested queries, in which a relation referred to in the query is itself defined within the query, in Section 5.4. We cover aggregate operators, which allow us to write SQL queries that are not expressible in relational algebra, in Section 5.5. We discuss *null* values, which are special values used to indicate unknown or nonexistent field values, in Section 5.6. We discuss complex integrity constraints that can be specified using the SQL DDL in Section 5.7, extending the SQL DDL discussion from Chapter 3; the new constraint specifications allow us to fully utilize the query language capabilities of SQL.

Finally, we discuss the concept of an *active database* in Sections 5.8 and 5.9. An **active database** has a collection of **triggers**, which are specified by the DBA. A trigger describes actions to be taken when certain situations arise. The DBMS monitors the database, detects these situations, and invokes the trigger.

The SQL:1999 standard requires support for triggers, and several relational DBMS products already support some form of triggers.

About the Examples

We will present a number of sample queries using the following table definitions:

Sailors(*sid:* `integer`, *sname:* `string`, *rating:* `integer`, *age:* `real`)
Boats(*bid:* `integer`, *bname:* `string`, *color:* `string`)
Reserves(*sid:* `integer`, *bid:* `integer`, *day:* `date`)

We give each query a unique number, continuing with the numbering scheme used in Chapter 4. The first new query in this chapter has number Q15. Queries Q1 through Q14 were introduced in Chapter 4.[1] We illustrate queries using the instances $S3$ of Sailors, $R2$ of Reserves, and $B1$ of Boats introduced in Chapter 4, which we reproduce in Figures 5.1, 5.2, and 5.3, respectively.

All the example tables and queries that appear in this chapter are available online on the book's webpage at

`http://www.cs.wisc.edu/~dbbook`

The online material includes instructions on how to set up Oracle, IBM DB2, Microsoft SQL Server, and MySQL, and scripts for creating the example tables and queries.

5.2 THE FORM OF A BASIC SQL QUERY

This section presents the syntax of a simple SQL query and explains its meaning through a *conceptual evaluation strategy.* A conceptual evaluation strategy is a way to evaluate the query that is intended to be easy to understand rather than efficient. A DBMS would typically execute a query in a different and more efficient way.

The basic form of an SQL query is as follows:

```
SELECT [ DISTINCT ] select-list
FROM   from-list
WHERE  qualification
```

[1]All references to a query can be found in the subject index for the book.

sid	*sname*	*rating*	*age*
22	Dustin	7	45.0
29	Brutus	1	33.0
31	Lubber	8	55.5
32	Andy	8	25.5
58	Rusty	10	35.0
64	Horatio	7	35.0
71	Zorba	10	16.0
74	Horatio	9	35.0
85	Art	3	25.5
95	Bob	3	63.5

Figure 5.1 An Instance *S*3 of Sailors

sid	*bid*	*day*
22	101	10/10/98
22	102	10/10/98
22	103	10/8/98
22	104	10/7/98
31	102	11/10/98
31	103	11/6/98
31	104	11/12/98
64	101	9/5/98
64	102	9/8/98
74	103	9/8/98

Figure 5.2 An Instance *R*2 of Reserves

bid	*bname*	*color*
101	Interlake	blue
102	Interlake	red
103	Clipper	green
104	Marine	red

Figure 5.3 An Instance *B*1 of Boats

Every query must have a SELECT clause, which specifies columns to be retained in the result, and a FROM clause, which specifies a cross-product of tables. The optional WHERE clause specifies selection conditions on the tables mentioned in the FROM clause.

Such a query intuitively corresponds to a relational algebra expression involving selections, projections, and cross-products. The close relationship between SQL and relational algebra is the basis for query optimization in a relational DBMS, as we will see in Chapters 12 and 15. Indeed, execution plans for SQL queries are represented using a variation of relational algebra expressions (Section 15.1).

Let us consider a simple example.

(Q15) Find the names and ages of all sailors.

```
SELECT DISTINCT S.sname, S.age
FROM    Sailors S
```

The answer is a *set* of rows, each of which is a pair ⟨*sname, age*⟩. If two or more sailors have the same name and age, the answer still contains just one pair with that name and age. This query is equivalent to applying the projection operator of relational algebra.

If we omit the keyword DISTINCT, we would get a copy of the row $\langle s,a \rangle$ for each sailor with name s and age a; the answer would be a *multiset* of rows. A **multiset** is similar to a set in that it is an unordered collection of elements, but there could be several copies of each element, and the number of copies is significant—two multisets could have the same elements and yet be different because the number of copies is different for some elements. For example, {a, b, b} and {b, a, b} denote the same multiset, and differ from the multiset {a, a, b}.

The answer to this query with and without the keyword DISTINCT on instance $S3$ of Sailors is shown in Figures 5.4 and 5.5. The only difference is that the tuple for Horatio appears twice if DISTINCT is omitted; this is because there are two sailors called Horatio and age 35.

sname	*age*
Dustin	45.0
Brutus	33.0
Lubber	55.5
Andy	25.5
Rusty	35.0
Horatio	35.0
Zorba	16.0
Art	25.5
Bob	63.5

Figure 5.4 Answer to Q15

sname	*age*
Dustin	45.0
Brutus	33.0
Lubber	55.5
Andy	25.5
Rusty	35.0
Horatio	35.0
Zorba	16.0
Horatio	35.0
Art	25.5
Bob	63.5

Figure 5.5 Answer to Q15 without DISTINCT

Our next query is equivalent to an application of the selection operator of relational algebra.

(Q11) Find all sailors with a rating above 7.

```
SELECT S.sid, S.sname, S.rating, S.age
FROM   Sailors AS S
WHERE  S.rating > 7
```

This query uses the optional keyword AS to introduce a range variable. Incidentally, when we want to retrieve all columns, as in this query, SQL provides a convenient shorthand: We can simply write `SELECT *`. This notation is useful for interactive querying, but it is poor style for queries that are intended to be reused and maintained because the schema of the result is not clear from the query itself; we have to refer to the schema of the underlying Sailors table.

As these two examples illustrate, the `SELECT` clause is actually used to do *projection*, whereas *selections* in the relational algebra sense are expressed using the `WHERE` clause! This mismatch between the naming of the selection and projection operators in relational algebra and the syntax of SQL is an unfortunate historical accident.

We now consider the syntax of a basic SQL query in more detail.

- The **from-list** in the `FROM` clause is a list of table names. A table name can be followed by a **range variable**; a range variable is particularly useful when the same table name appears more than once in the from-list.

- The **select-list** is a list of (expressions involving) column names of tables named in the from-list. Column names can be prefixed by a range variable.

- The **qualification** in the `WHERE` clause is a boolean combination (i.e., an expression using the logical connectives `AND`, `OR`, and `NOT`) of conditions of the form *expression* `op` *expression*, where `op` is one of the comparison operators $\{<, <=, =, <>, >=, >\}$.[2] An *expression* is a *column* name, a *constant*, or an (arithmetic or string) expression.

- The `DISTINCT` keyword is optional. It indicates that the table computed as an answer to this query should not contain *duplicates*, that is, two copies of the same row. The default is that duplicates are not eliminated.

Although the preceding rules describe (informally) the syntax of a basic SQL query, they do not tell us the *meaning* of a query. The answer to a query is itself a relation—which is a *multiset* of rows in SQL!—whose contents can be understood by considering the following conceptual evaluation strategy:

1. Compute the cross-product of the tables in the **from-list**.

2. Delete rows in the cross-product that fail the **qualification** conditions.

3. Delete all columns that do not appear in the **select-list**.

4. If `DISTINCT` is specified, eliminate duplicate rows.

[2] Expressions with `NOT` can always be replaced by equivalent expressions without `NOT` given the set of comparison operators just listed.

This straightforward conceptual evaluation strategy makes explicit the rows that must be present in the answer to the query. However, it is likely to be quite inefficient. We will consider how a DBMS actually evaluates queries in later chapters; for now, our purpose is simply to explain the meaning of a query. We illustrate the conceptual evaluation strategy using the following query:

(Q1) Find the names of sailors who have reserved boat number 103.

It can be expressed in SQL as follows.

```
SELECT S.sname
FROM   Sailors S, Reserves R
WHERE  S.sid = R.sid AND R.bid=103
```

Let us compute the answer to this query on the instances *R*3 of Reserves and *S*4 of Sailors shown in Figures 5.6 and 5.7, since the computation on our usual example instances (*R*2 and *S*3) would be unnecessarily tedious.

sid	*bid*	*day*
22	101	10/10/96
58	103	11/12/96

Figure 5.6 Instance *R*3 of Reserves

sid	*sname*	*rating*	*age*
22	dustin	7	45.0
31	lubber	8	55.5
58	rusty	10	35.0

Figure 5.7 Instance *S*4 of Sailors

The first step is to construct the cross-product $S4 \times R3$, which is shown in Figure 5.8.

sid	*sname*	*rating*	*age*	*sid*	*bid*	*day*
22	dustin	7	45.0	22	101	10/10/96
22	dustin	7	45.0	58	103	11/12/96
31	lubber	8	55.5	22	101	10/10/96
31	lubber	8	55.5	58	103	11/12/96
58	rusty	10	35.0	22	101	10/10/96
58	rusty	10	35.0	58	103	11/12/96

Figure 5.8 $S4 \times R3$

The second step is to apply the qualification *S.sid* = *R.sid* AND *R.bid=103*. (Note that the first part of this qualification requires a join operation.) This step eliminates all but the last row from the instance shown in Figure 5.8. The third step is to eliminate unwanted columns; only *sname* appears in the SELECT clause. This step leaves us with the result shown in Figure 5.9, which is a table with a single column and, as it happens, just one row.

sname
rusty

Figure 5.9 Answer to Query Q1 on R3 and S4

5.2.1 Examples of Basic SQL Queries

We now present several example queries, many of which were expressed earlier in relational algebra and calculus (Chapter 4). Our first example illustrates that the use of range variables is optional, unless they are needed to resolve an ambiguity. Query Q1, which we discussed in the previous section, can also be expressed as follows:

```
SELECT sname
FROM   Sailors S, Reserves R
WHERE  S.sid = R.sid AND bid=103
```

Only the occurrences of *sid* have to be qualified, since this column appears in both the Sailors and Reserves tables. An equivalent way to write this query is:

```
SELECT sname
FROM   Sailors, Reserves
WHERE  Sailors.sid = Reserves.sid AND bid=103
```

This query shows that table names can be used implicitly as row variables. Range variables need to be introduced explicitly only when the FROM clause contains more than one occurrence of a relation.[3] However, we recommend the explicit use of range variables and full qualification of all occurrences of columns with a range variable to improve the readability of your queries. We will follow this convention in all our examples.

(Q16) Find the sids of sailors who have reserved a red boat.

```
SELECT  R.sid
FROM    Boats B, Reserves R
WHERE   B.bid = R.bid AND B.color = 'red'
```

This query contains a join of two tables, followed by a selection on the color of boats. We can think of B and R as rows in the corresponding tables that

[3]The table name cannot be used as an implicit range variable once a range variable is introduced for the relation.

'prove' that a sailor with sid R.sid reserved a red boat B.bid. On our example instances $R2$ and $S3$ (Figures 5.1 and 5.2), the answer consists of the *sids* 22, 31, and 64. If we want the names of sailors in the result, we must also consider the Sailors relation, since Reserves does not contain this information, as the next example illustrates.

(Q2) Find the names of sailors who have reserved a red boat.

```
SELECT   S.sname
FROM     Sailors S, Reserves R, Boats B
WHERE    S.sid = R.sid AND R.bid = B.bid AND B.color = 'red'
```

This query contains a join of three tables followed by a selection on the color of boats. The join with Sailors allows us to find the name of the sailor who, according to Reserves tuple R, has reserved a red boat described by tuple B.

(Q3) Find the colors of boats reserved by Lubber.

```
SELECT B.color
FROM   Sailors S, Reserves R, Boats B
WHERE  S.sid = R.sid AND R.bid = B.bid AND S.sname = 'Lubber'
```

This query is very similar to the previous one. Note that in general there may be more than one sailor called Lubber (since *sname* is not a key for Sailors); this query is still correct in that it will return the colors of boats reserved by *some* Lubber, if there are several sailors called Lubber.

(Q4) Find the names of sailors who have reserved at least one boat.

```
SELECT S.sname
FROM   Sailors S, Reserves R
WHERE  S.sid = R.sid
```

The join of Sailors and Reserves ensures that for each selected *sname*, the sailor has made some reservation. (If a sailor has not made a reservation, the second step in the conceptual evaluation strategy would eliminate all rows in the cross-product that involve this sailor.)

5.2.2 Expressions and Strings in the SELECT Command

SQL supports a more general version of the **select-list** than just a list of columns. Each item in a **select-list** can be of the form *expression* AS *column name*, where *expression* is any arithmetic or string expression over column names (possibly prefixed by range variables) and constants, and *column name* is a new name for this column in the output of the query. It can also contain *aggregates* such as *sum* and *count*, which we will discuss in Section 5.5. The SQL standard also includes expressions over date and time values, which we will not discuss. Although not part of the SQL standard, many implementations also support the use of built-in functions such as *sqrt*, *sin*, and *mod*.

(Q17) Compute increments for the ratings of persons who have sailed two different boats on the same day.

```
SELECT S.sname, S.rating+1 AS rating
FROM   Sailors S, Reserves R1, Reserves R2
WHERE  S.sid = R1.sid AND S.sid = R2.sid
       AND R1.day = R2.day AND R1.bid <> R2.bid
```

Also, each item in a *qualification* can be as general as *expression1* = *expression2*.

```
SELECT S1.sname AS name1, S2.sname AS name2
FROM   Sailors S1, Sailors S2
WHERE  2*S1.rating = S2.rating-1
```

For string comparisons, we can use the comparison operators (=, <, >, etc.) with the ordering of strings determined alphabetically as usual. If we need to sort strings by an order other than alphabetical (e.g., sort strings denoting month names in the calendar order January, February, March, etc.), SQL supports a general concept of a **collation**, or sort order, for a character set. A collation allows the user to specify which characters are 'less than' which others and provides great flexibility in string manipulation.

In addition, SQL provides support for pattern matching through the `LIKE` operator, along with the use of the wild-card symbols % (which stands for zero or more arbitrary characters) and   (which stands for exactly one, arbitrary, character). Thus, ' AB%' denotes a pattern matching every string that contains at least three characters, with the second and third characters being A and B respectively. Note that unlike the other comparison operators, blanks can be significant for the `LIKE` operator (depending on the collation for the underlying character set). Thus, *'Jeff'* = *'Jeff '* is true while *'Jeff'* `LIKE` *'Jeff '* is false. An example of the use of `LIKE` in a query is given below.

(Q18) Find the ages of sailors whose name begins and ends with B and has at least three characters.

```
SELECT S.age
```

Regular Expressions in SQL: Reflecting the increased importance of text data, SQL:1999 includes a more powerful version of the LIKE operator called SIMILAR. This operator allows a rich set of regular expressions to be used as patterns while searching text. The regular expressions are similar to those supported by the Unix operating system for string searches, although the syntax is a little different.

Relational Algebra and SQL: The set operations of SQL are available in relational algebra. The main difference, of course, is that they are *multiset* operations in SQL, since tables are multisets of tuples.

```
FROM    Sailors S
WHERE   S.sname LIKE 'B_%B'
```

The only such sailor is Bob, and his age is 63.5.

5.3 UNION, INTERSECT, AND EXCEPT

SQL provides three set-manipulation constructs that extend the basic query form presented earlier. Since the answer to a query is a multiset of rows, it is natural to consider the use of operations such as union, intersection, and difference. SQL supports these operations under the names UNION, INTERSECT, and EXCEPT.[4] SQL also provides other set operations: IN (to check if an element is in a given set), op ANY, op ALL (to compare a value with the elements in a given set, using comparison operator op), and EXISTS (to check if a set is empty). IN and EXISTS can be prefixed by NOT, with the obvious modification to their meaning. We cover UNION, INTERSECT, and EXCEPT in this section, and the other operations in Section 5.4.

Consider the following query:

(Q5) Find the names of sailors who have reserved a red or a green boat.

```
SELECT  S.sname
FROM    Sailors S, Reserves R, Boats B
WHERE   S.sid = R.sid AND R.bid = B.bid
        AND (B.color = 'red' OR B.color = 'green')
```

[4]Note that although the SQL standard includes these operations, many systems currently support only UNION. Also, many systems recognize the keyword MINUS for EXCEPT.

This query is easily expressed using the OR connective in the WHERE clause. However, the following query, which is identical except for the use of 'and' rather than 'or' in the English version, turns out to be much more difficult:

(Q6) Find the names of sailors who have reserved both a red and a green boat.

If we were to just replace the use of OR in the previous query by AND, in analogy to the English statements of the two queries, we would retrieve the names of sailors who have reserved a boat that is both red and green. The integrity constraint that *bid* is a key for Boats tells us that the same boat cannot have two colors, and so the variant of the previous query with AND in place of OR will always return an empty answer set. A correct statement of Query Q6 using AND is the following:

```
SELECT S.sname
FROM   Sailors S, Reserves R1, Boats B1, Reserves R2, Boats B2
WHERE  S.sid = R1.sid AND R1.bid = B1.bid
       AND S.sid = R2.sid AND R2.bid = B2.bid
       AND B1.color='red' AND B2.color = 'green'
```

We can think of R1 and B1 as rows that prove that sailor S.sid has reserved a red boat. R2 and B2 similarly prove that the same sailor has reserved a green boat. S.sname is not included in the result unless five such rows S, R1, B1, R2, and B2 are found.

The previous query is difficult to understand (and also quite inefficient to execute, as it turns out). In particular, the similarity to the previous OR query (Query Q5) is completely lost. A better solution for these two queries is to use UNION and INTERSECT.

The OR query (Query Q5) can be rewritten as follows:

```
SELECT S.sname
FROM   Sailors S, Reserves R, Boats B
WHERE  S.sid = R.sid AND R.bid = B.bid AND B.color = 'red'
UNION
SELECT S2.sname
FROM   Sailors S2, Boats B2, Reserves R2
WHERE  S2.sid = R2.sid AND R2.bid = B2.bid AND B2.color = 'green'
```

This query says that we want the union of the set of sailors who have reserved red boats and the set of sailors who have reserved green boats. In complete symmetry, the AND query (Query Q6) can be rewritten as follows:

```
SELECT S.sname
```

```
FROM    Sailors S, Reserves R, Boats B
WHERE   S.sid = R.sid AND R.bid = B.bid AND B.color = 'red'
INTERSECT
SELECT  S2.sname
FROM    Sailors S2, Boats B2, Reserves R2
WHERE   S2.sid = R2.sid AND R2.bid = B2.bid AND B2.color = 'green'
```

This query actually contains a subtle bug—if there are two sailors such as Horatio in our example instances *B*1, *R*2, and *S*3, one of whom has reserved a red boat and the other has reserved a green boat, the name Horatio is returned even though no one individual called Horatio has reserved both a red and a green boat. Thus, the query actually computes sailor names such that some sailor with this name has reserved a red boat and some sailor with the same name (perhaps a different sailor) has reserved a green boat.

As we observed in Chapter 4, the problem arises because we are using *sname* to identify sailors, and *sname* is not a key for Sailors! If we select *sid* instead of *sname* in the previous query, we would compute the set of *sid*s of sailors who have reserved both red and green boats. (To compute the names of such sailors requires a nested query; we will return to this example in Section 5.4.4.)

Our next query illustrates the set-difference operation in SQL.

(Q19) Find the sids *of all sailors who have reserved red boats but not green boats.*

```
SELECT  S.sid
FROM    Sailors S, Reserves R, Boats B
WHERE   S.sid = R.sid AND R.bid = B.bid AND B.color = 'red'
EXCEPT
SELECT  S2.sid
FROM    Sailors S2, Reserves R2, Boats B2
WHERE   S2.sid = R2.sid AND R2.bid = B2.bid AND B2.color = 'green'
```

Sailors 22, 64, and 31 have reserved red boats. Sailors 22, 74, and 31 have reserved green boats. Hence, the answer contains just the *sid* 64.

Indeed, since the Reserves relation contains sid information, there is no need to look at the Sailors relation, and we can use the following simpler query:

```
SELECT  R.sid
FROM    Boats B, Reserves R
WHERE   R.bid = B.bid AND B.color = 'red'
EXCEPT
```

```
SELECT R2.sid
FROM   Boats B2, Reserves R2
WHERE  R2.bid = B2.bid AND B2.color = 'green'
```

Observe that this query relies on referential integrity; that is, there are no reservations for nonexisting sailors. Note that UNION, INTERSECT, and EXCEPT can be used on *any* two tables that are union-compatible, that is, have the same number of columns and the columns, taken in order, have the same types. For example, we can write the following query:

(Q20) Find all sids of sailors who have a rating of 10 or reserved boat 104.

```
SELECT S.sid
FROM   Sailors S
WHERE  S.rating = 10
UNION
SELECT R.sid
FROM   Reserves R
WHERE  R.bid = 104
```

The first part of the union returns the *sids* 58 and 71. The second part returns 22 and 31. The answer is, therefore, the set of *sids* 22, 31, 58, and 71. A final point to note about UNION, INTERSECT, and EXCEPT follows. In contrast to the default that duplicates are not eliminated unless DISTINCT is specified in the basic query form, the default for UNION queries is that duplicates *are* eliminated! To retain duplicates, UNION ALL must be used; if so, the number of copies of a row in the result is always $m + n$, where m and n are the numbers of times that the row appears in the two parts of the union. Similarly, INTERSECT ALL retains duplicates—the number of copies of a row in the result is $min(m, n)$—and EXCEPT ALL also retains duplicates—the number of copies of a row in the result is $m - n$, where m corresponds to the first relation.

5.4 NESTED QUERIES

One of the most powerful features of SQL is nested queries. A **nested query** is a query that has another query embedded within it; the embedded query is called a **subquery**. The embedded query can of course be a nested query itself; thus queries that have very deeply nested structures are possible. When writing a query, we sometimes need to express a condition that refers to a table that must itself be computed. The query used to compute this subsidiary table is a subquery and appears as part of the main query. A subquery typically appears within the WHERE clause of a query. Subqueries can sometimes appear in the FROM clause or the HAVING clause (which we present in Section 5.5).

> **Relational Algebra and SQL:** Nesting of queries is a feature that is not available in relational algebra, but nested queries can be translated into algebra, as we will see in Chapter 15. Nesting in SQL is inspired more by relational calculus than algebra. In conjunction with some of SQL's other features, such as (multi)set operators and aggregation, nesting is a very expressive construct.

This section discusses only subqueries that appear in the WHERE clause. The treatment of subqueries appearing elsewhere is quite similar. Some examples of subqueries that appear in the FROM clause are discussed later in Section 5.5.1.

5.4.1 Introduction to Nested Queries

As an example, let us rewrite the following query, which we discussed earlier, using a nested subquery:

(Q1) Find the names of sailors who have reserved boat 103.

```
SELECT S.sname
FROM   Sailors S
WHERE  S.sid IN ( SELECT R.sid
                  FROM   Reserves R
                  WHERE  R.bid = 103 )
```

The nested subquery computes the (multi)set of *sids* for sailors who have reserved boat 103 (the set contains 22, 31, and 74 on instances $R2$ and $S3$), and the top-level query retrieves the names of sailors whose *sid* is in this set. The IN operator allows us to test whether a value is in a given set of elements; an SQL query is used to generate the set to be tested. Note that it is very easy to modify this query to find all sailors who have *not* reserved boat 103—we can just replace IN by NOT IN!

The best way to understand a nested query is to think of it in terms of a conceptual evaluation strategy. In our example, the strategy consists of examining rows in Sailors and, for each such row, evaluating the subquery over Reserves. In general, the conceptual evaluation strategy that we presented for defining the semantics of a query can be extended to cover nested queries as follows: Construct the cross-product of the tables in the FROM clause of the top-level query as before. For each row in the cross-product, while testing the qualification in the WHERE clause, (re)compute the subquery.[5] Of course, the subquery might itself contain another nested subquery, in which case we apply the same idea one more time, leading to an evaluation strategy with several levels of nested loops.

As an example of a multiply nested query, let us rewrite the following query.

(Q2) Find the names of sailors who have reserved a red boat.

```
SELECT S.sname
FROM   Sailors S
WHERE  S.sid IN ( SELECT R.sid
                  FROM   Reserves R
                  WHERE  R.bid IN ( SELECT B.bid
                                    FROM   Boats B
                                    WHERE  B.color = 'red' )
```

The innermost subquery finds the set of *bids* of red boats (102 and 104 on instance $B1$). The subquery one level above finds the set of *sids* of sailors who have reserved one of these boats. On instances $B1$, $R2$, and $S3$, this set of *sids* contains 22, 31, and 64. The top-level query finds the names of sailors whose *sid* is in this set of *sids*; we get Dustin, Lubber, and Horatio.

To find the names of sailors who have not reserved a red boat, we replace the outermost occurrence of IN by NOT IN, as illustrated in the next query.

(Q21) Find the names of sailors who have not *reserved a red boat.*

```
SELECT S.sname
FROM   Sailors S
WHERE  S.sid NOT IN ( SELECT R.sid
                      FROM   Reserves R
                      WHERE  R.bid IN ( SELECT B.bid
                                        FROM   Boats B
                                        WHERE  B.color = 'red' )
```

This query computes the names of sailors whose *sid* is *not* in the set 22, 31, and 64.

In contrast to Query Q21, we can modify the previous query (the nested version of Q2) by replacing the inner occurrence (rather than the outer occurence) of

[5]Since the inner subquery in our example does not depend on the 'current' row from the outer query in any way, you might wonder why we have to recompute the subquery for each outer row. For an answer, see Section 5.4.2.

IN with NOT IN. This modified query would compute the names of sailors who have reserved a boat that is not red, that is, if they have a reservation, it is not for a red boat. Let us consider how. In the inner query, we check that *R.bid* is *not* either 102 or 104 (the *bids* of red boats). The outer query then finds the *sids* in Reserves tuples where the *bid* is not 102 or 104. On instances *B*1, *R*2, and *S*3, the outer query computes the set of *sids* 22, 31, 64, and 74. Finally, we find the names of sailors whose *sid* is in this set.

We can also modify the nested query Q2 by replacing both occurrences of IN with NOT IN. This variant finds the names of sailors who have not reserved a boat that is not red, that is, who have reserved only red boats (if they've reserved any boats at all). Proceeding as in the previous paragraph, on instances *B*1, *R*2, and *S*3, the outer query computes the set of *sids* (in Sailors) other than 22, 31, 64, and 74. This is the set 29, 32, 58, 71, 85, and 95. We then find the names of sailors whose *sid* is in this set.

5.4.2 Correlated Nested Queries

In the nested queries seen thus far, the inner subquery has been completely independent of the outer query. In general, the inner subquery could depend on the row currently being examined in the outer query (in terms of our conceptual evaluation strategy). Let us rewrite the following query once more.

(Q1) Find the names of sailors who have reserved boat number 103.

```
SELECT S.sname
FROM   Sailors S
WHERE  EXISTS ( SELECT *
                FROM   Reserves R
                WHERE  R.bid = 103
                       AND R.sid = S.sid )
```

The EXISTS operator is another set comparison operator, such as IN. It allows us to test whether a set is nonempty, an implicit comparison with the empty set. Thus, for each Sailor row *S*, we test whether the set of Reserves rows *R* such that *R.bid = 103* AND *S.sid = R.sid* is nonempty. If so, sailor *S* has reserved boat 103, and we retrieve the name. The subquery clearly depends on the current row *S* and must be re-evaluated for each row in Sailors. The occurrence of *S* in the subquery (in the form of the literal *S.sid*) is called a *correlation*, and such queries are called *correlated queries*.

This query also illustrates the use of the special symbol * in situations where all we want to do is to check that a qualifying row exists, and do not really want to retrieve any columns from the row. This is one of the two uses of * in the SELECT clause that is good programming style; the other is as an argument of the COUNT aggregate operation, which we describe shortly.

As a further example, by using NOT EXISTS instead of EXISTS, we can compute the names of sailors who have not reserved a red boat. Closely related to EXISTS is the UNIQUE predicate. When we apply UNIQUE to a subquery, the resulting condition returns true if no row appears twice in the answer to the subquery, that is, there are no duplicates; in particular, it returns true if the answer is empty. (And there is also a NOT UNIQUE version.)

5.4.3 Set-Comparison Operators

We have already seen the set-comparison operators EXISTS, IN, and UNIQUE, along with their negated versions. SQL also supports op ANY and op ALL, where op is one of the arithmetic comparison operators {<, <=, =, <>, >=, >}. (SOME is also available, but it is just a synonym for ANY.)

(Q22) Find sailors whose rating is better than some sailor called Horatio.

```
SELECT S.sid
FROM   Sailors S
WHERE  S.rating > ANY ( SELECT S2.rating
                        FROM   Sailors S2
                        WHERE  S2.sname = 'Horatio' )
```

If there are several sailors called Horatio, this query finds all sailors whose rating is better than that of *some* sailor called Horatio. On instance $S3$, this computes the *sids* 31, 32, 58, 71, and 74. What if there were *no* sailor called Horatio? In this case the comparison *S.rating* > ANY ... is defined to return false, and the query returns an empty answer set. To understand comparisons involving ANY, it is useful to think of the comparison being carried out repeatedly. In this example, *S.rating* is successively compared with each rating value that is an answer to the nested query. Intuitively, the subquery must return a row that makes the comparison true, in order for *S.rating* > ANY ... to return true.

(Q23) Find sailors whose rating is better than every sailor called Horatio.

We can obtain all such queries with a simple modification to Query Q22: Just replace ANY with ALL in the WHERE clause of the outer query. On instance $S3$, we would get the *sids* 58 and 71. If there were no sailor called Horatio, the comparison *S.rating* > ALL ... is defined to return true! The query would then return the names of all sailors. Again, it is useful to think of the comparison being carried out repeatedly. Intuitively, the comparison must be true for every returned row for *S.rating* > ALL ... to return true.

As another illustration of ALL, consider the following query.

(Q24) Find the sailors with the highest rating.

```
SELECT S.sid
FROM   Sailors S
WHERE  S.rating >= ALL ( SELECT S2.rating
                         FROM   Sailors S2 )
```

The subquery computes the set of all rating values in Sailors. The outer WHERE condition is satisfied only when *S.rating* is greater than or equal to each of these rating values, that is, when it is the largest rating value. In the instance *S*3, the condition is satisfied only for *rating* 10, and the answer includes the *sid*s of sailors with this rating, i.e., 58 and 71.

Note that IN and NOT IN are equivalent to = ANY and <> ALL, respectively.

5.4.4 More Examples of Nested Queries

Let us revisit a query that we considered earlier using the INTERSECT operator.

(Q6) Find the names of sailors who have reserved both a red and a green boat.

```
SELECT S.sname
FROM   Sailors S, Reserves R, Boats B
WHERE  S.sid = R.sid AND R.bid = B.bid AND B.color = 'red'
       AND S.sid IN ( SELECT S2.sid
                      FROM   Sailors S2, Boats B2, Reserves R2
                      WHERE  S2.sid = R2.sid AND R2.bid = B2.bid
                             AND B2.color = 'green' )
```

This query can be understood as follows: "Find all sailors who have reserved a red boat and, further, have *sid*s that are included in the set of *sid*s of sailors who have reserved a green boat." This formulation of the query illustrates how queries involving INTERSECT can be rewritten using IN, which is useful to know if your system does not support INTERSECT. Queries using EXCEPT can be similarly rewritten by using NOT IN. To find the *sid*s of sailors who have reserved red boats but not green boats, we can simply replace the keyword IN in the previous query by NOT IN.

As it turns out, writing this query (Q6) using INTERSECT is more complicated because we have to use *sid*s to identify sailors (while intersecting) and have to return sailor names:

```
SELECT S.sname
FROM   Sailors S
WHERE  S.sid IN (( SELECT R.sid
                   FROM   Boats B, Reserves R
                   WHERE  R.bid = B.bid AND B.color = 'red' )
                   INTERSECT
                   (SELECT R2.sid
                   FROM   Boats B2, Reserves R2
                   WHERE  R2.bid = B2.bid AND B2.color = 'green' ))
```

Our next example illustrates how the *division* operation in relational algebra can be expressed in SQL.

(Q9) Find the names of sailors who have reserved all boats.

```
SELECT S.sname
FROM   Sailors S
WHERE  NOT EXISTS (( SELECT B.bid
                     FROM   Boats B )
                     EXCEPT
                     (SELECT R.bid
                     FROM   Reserves R
                     WHERE  R.sid = S.sid ))
```

Note that this query is correlated—for each sailor S, we check to see that the set of boats reserved by S includes every boat. An alternative way to do this query without using EXCEPT follows:

```
SELECT S.sname
FROM   Sailors S
WHERE  NOT EXISTS ( SELECT B.bid
                    FROM   Boats B
                    WHERE  NOT EXISTS ( SELECT R.bid
                                        FROM   Reserves R
                                        WHERE  R.bid = B.bid
                                               AND R.sid = S.sid ))
```

Intuitively, for each sailor we check that there is no boat that has not been reserved by this sailor.

> **SQL:1999 Aggregate Functions:** The collection of aggregate functions is greatly expanded in the new standard, including several statistical functions such as standard deviation, covariance, and percentiles. However, the new aggregate functions are in the SQL/OLAP package and may not be supported by all vendors.

5.5 AGGREGATE OPERATORS

In addition to simply retrieving data, we often want to perform some computation or summarization. As we noted earlier in this chapter, SQL allows the use of arithmetic expressions. We now consider a powerful class of constructs for computing *aggregate values* such as `MIN` and `SUM`. These features represent a significant extension of relational algebra. SQL supports five aggregate operations, which can be applied on any column, say A, of a relation:

1. `COUNT` ([`DISTINCT`] A): The number of (unique) values in the A column.
2. `SUM` ([`DISTINCT`] A): The sum of all (unique) values in the A column.
3. `AVG` ([`DISTINCT`] A): The average of all (unique) values in the A column.
4. `MAX` (A): The maximum value in the A column.
5. `MIN` (A): The minimum value in the A column.

Note that it does not make sense to specify `DISTINCT` in conjunction with `MIN` or `MAX` (although SQL does not preclude this).

(Q25) Find the average age of all sailors.

```
SELECT AVG (S.age)
FROM   Sailors S
```

On instance *S*3, the average age is 37.4. Of course, the `WHERE` clause can be used to restrict the sailors considered in computing the average age.

(Q26) Find the average age of sailors with a rating of 10.

```
SELECT AVG (S.age)
FROM   Sailors S
WHERE  S.rating = 10
```

There are two such sailors, and their average age is 25.5. `MIN` (or `MAX`) can be used instead of `AVG` in the above queries to find the age of the youngest (oldest) sailor. However, finding both the name and the age of the oldest sailor is more tricky, as the next query illustrates.

(Q27) Find the name and age of the oldest sailor.

Consider the following attempt to answer this query:

```
SELECT S.sname, MAX (S.age)
FROM   Sailors S
```

The intent is for this query to return not only the maximum age but also the name of the sailors having that age. However, this query is illegal in SQL—if the SELECT clause uses an aggregate operation, then it must use *only* aggregate operations unless the query contains a GROUP BY clause! (The intuition behind this restriction should become clear when we discuss the GROUP BY clause in Section 5.5.1.) Therefore, we cannot use MAX (S.age) as well as S.sname in the SELECT clause. We have to use a nested query to compute the desired answer to Q27:

```
SELECT S.sname, S.age
FROM   Sailors S
WHERE  S.age = ( SELECT MAX (S2.age)
                 FROM Sailors S2 )
```

Observe that we have used the result of an aggregate operation in the subquery as an argument to a comparison operation. Strictly speaking, we are comparing an age value with the result of the subquery, which is a relation. However, because of the use of the aggregate operation, the subquery is guaranteed to return a single tuple with a single field, and SQL converts such a relation to a field value for the sake of the comparison. The following equivalent query for Q27 is legal in the SQL standard but, unfortunately, is not supported in many systems:

```
SELECT S.sname, S.age
FROM   Sailors S
WHERE  ( SELECT MAX (S2.age)
         FROM Sailors S2 ) = S.age
```

We can count the number of sailors using COUNT. This example illustrates the use of * as an argument to COUNT, which is useful when we want to count all rows.

(Q28) Count the number of sailors.

```
SELECT COUNT (*)
```

```
FROM    Sailors S
```

We can think of * as shorthand for all the columns (in the cross-product of the **from-list** in the FROM clause). Contrast this query with the following query, which computes the number of distinct sailor names. (Remember that *sname* is not a key!)

(Q29) Count the number of different sailor names.

```
SELECT COUNT ( DISTINCT S.sname )
FROM    Sailors S
```

On instance *S*3, the answer to Q28 is 10, whereas the answer to Q29 is 9 (because two sailors have the same name, Horatio). If DISTINCT is omitted, the answer to Q29 is 10, because the name Horatio is counted twice. If COUNT does not include DISTINCT, then COUNT(*) gives the same answer as COUNT(x), where x is any set of attributes. In our example, without DISTINCT Q29 is equivalent to Q28. However, the use of COUNT (*) is better querying style, since it is immediately clear that all records contribute to the total count.

Aggregate operations offer an alternative to the ANY and ALL constructs. For example, consider the following query:

(Q30) Find the names of sailors who are older than the oldest sailor with a rating of 10.

```
SELECT S.sname
FROM   Sailors S
WHERE  S.age > ( SELECT MAX ( S2.age )
                 FROM   Sailors S2
                 WHERE  S2.rating = 10 )
```

On instance *S*3, the oldest sailor with rating 10 is sailor 58, whose age is 35. The names of older sailors are Bob, Dustin, Horatio, and Lubber. Using ALL, this query could alternatively be written as follows:

```
SELECT S.sname
FROM   Sailors S
WHERE  S.age > ALL ( SELECT S2.age
                     FROM   Sailors S2
                     WHERE  S2.rating = 10 )
```

However, the ALL query is more error prone—one could easily (and incorrectly!) use ANY instead of ALL, and retrieve sailors who are older than *some* sailor with

> **Relational Algebra and SQL:** Aggregation is a fundamental operation that cannot be expressed in relational algebra. Similarly, SQL's grouping construct cannot be expressed in algebra.

a rating of 10. The use of ANY intuitively corresponds to the use of MIN, instead of MAX, in the previous query.

5.5.1 The GROUP BY and HAVING Clauses

Thus far, we have applied aggregate operations to all (qualifying) rows in a relation. Often we want to apply aggregate operations to each of a number of **groups** of rows in a relation, where the number of groups depends on the relation instance (i.e., is not known in advance). For example, consider the following query.

(Q31) Find the age of the youngest sailor for each rating level.

If we know that ratings are integers in the range 1 to 10, we could write 10 queries of the form:

```
SELECT MIN (S.age)
FROM   Sailors S
WHERE  S.rating = i
```

where $i = 1, 2, \ldots, 10$. Writing 10 such queries is tedious. More important, we may not know what rating levels exist in advance.

To write such queries, we need a major extension to the basic SQL query form, namely, the GROUP BY clause. In fact, the extension also includes an optional HAVING clause that can be used to specify qualifications over groups (for example, we may be interested only in rating levels > 6. The general form of an SQL query with these extensions is:

```
SELECT    [ DISTINCT ] select-list
FROM      from-list
WHERE     qualification
GROUP BY  grouping-list
HAVING    group-qualification
```

Using the GROUP BY clause, we can write Q31 as follows:

```
SELECT    S.rating, MIN (S.age)
```

```
FROM      Sailors S
GROUP BY  S.rating
```

Let us consider some important points concerning the new clauses:

- The **select-list** in the SELECT clause consists of (1) a list of column names and (2) a list of terms having the form **aggop** (*column-name*) AS *new-name*. We already saw AS used to rename output columns. Columns that are the result of aggregate operators do not already have a column name, and therefore giving the column a name with AS is especially useful.

  Every column that appears in (1) must also appear in **grouping-list**. The reason is that each row in the result of the query corresponds to one *group*, which is a collection of rows that agree on the values of columns in grouping-list. In general, if a column appears in list (1), but not in **grouping-list**, there can be multiple rows within a group that have different values in this column, and it is not clear what value should be assigned to this column in an answer row.

  We can sometimes use primary key information to verify that a column has a unique value in all rows within each group. For example, if the **grouping-list** contains the primary key of a table in the **from-list**, every column of that table has a unique value within each group. In SQL:1999, such columns are also allowed to appear in part (1) of the **select-list**.

- The expressions appearing in the **group-qualification** in the HAVING clause must have a *single* value per group. The intuition is that the HAVING clause determines whether an answer row is to be generated for a given group. To satisfy this requirement in SQL-92, a column appearing in the **group-qualification** must appear as the argument to an aggregation operator, or it must also appear in **grouping-list**. In SQL:1999, two new set functions have been introduced that allow us to check whether *every* or *any* row in a group satisfies a condition; this allows us to use conditions similar to those in a WHERE clause.

- If GROUP BY is omitted, the entire table is regarded as a single group.

We explain the semantics of such a query through an example.

(Q32) Find the age of the youngest sailor who is eligible to vote (i.e., is at least 18 years old) for each rating level with at least two such sailors.

```
SELECT    S.rating, MIN (S.age) AS minage
FROM      Sailors S
WHERE     S.age >= 18
GROUP BY  S.rating
HAVING    COUNT (*) > 1
```

We will evaluate this query on instance $S3$ of Sailors, reproduced in Figure 5.10 for convenience. The instance of Sailors on which this query is to be evaluated is shown in Figure 5.10. Extending the conceptual evaluation strategy presented in Section 5.2, we proceed as follows. The first step is to construct the cross-product of tables in the **from-list**. Because the only relation in the from-list in Query Q32 is Sailors, the result is just the instance shown in Figure 5.10.

sid	*sname*	*rating*	*age*
22	Dustin	7	45.0
29	Brutus	1	33.0
31	Lubber	8	55.5
32	Andy	8	25.5
58	Rusty	10	35.0
64	Horatio	7	35.0
71	Zorba	10	16.0
74	Horatio	9	35.0
85	Art	3	25.5
95	Bob	3	63.5
96	Frodo	3	25.5

Figure 5.10 Instance $S3$ of Sailors

The second step is to apply the qualification in the `WHERE` clause, $S.age >= 18$. This step eliminates the row $\langle 71, zorba, 10, 16 \rangle$. The third step is to eliminate unwanted columns. Only columns mentioned in the `SELECT` clause, the `GROUP BY` clause, or the `HAVING` clause are necessary, which means we can eliminate *sid* and *sname* in our example. The result is shown in Figure 5.11. Observe that there are two identical rows with *rating* 3 and *age* 25.5—SQL does not eliminate duplicates except when required to do so by use of the `DISTINCT` keyword! The number of copies of a row in the intermediate table of Figure 5.11 is determined by the number of rows in the original table that had these values in the projected columns.

The fourth step is to sort the table according to the `GROUP BY` clause to identify the groups. The result of this step is shown in Figure 5.12.

The fifth step is to apply the group-qualification in the `HAVING` clause, that is, the condition `COUNT (*)` > 1. This step eliminates the groups with *rating* equal to 1, 9, and 10. Observe that the order in which the `WHERE` and `GROUP BY` clauses are considered is significant: If the `WHERE` clause were not considered first, the group with *rating=10* would have met the group-qualification in the `HAVING` clause. The sixth step is to generate one answer row for each remaining group. The answer row corresponding to a group consists of a subset

rating	*age*
7	45.0
1	33.0
8	55.5
8	25.5
10	35.0
7	35.0
9	35.0
3	25.5
3	63.5
3	25.5

Figure 5.11 After Evaluation Step 3

rating	*age*
1	33.0
3	25.5
3	25.5
3	63.5
7	45.0
7	35.0
8	55.5
8	25.5
9	35.0
10	35.0

Figure 5.12 After Evaluation Step 4

of the grouping columns, plus one or more columns generated by applying an aggregation operator. In our example, each answer row has a *rating* column and a *minage* column, which is computed by applying `MIN` to the values in the *age* column of the corresponding group. The result of this step is shown in Figure 5.13.

rating	*minage*
3	25.5
7	35.0
8	25.5

Figure 5.13 Final Result in Sample Evaluation

If the query contains `DISTINCT` in the `SELECT` clause, duplicates are eliminated in an additional, and final, step.

SQL:1999 has introduced two new set functions, `EVERY` and `ANY`. To illustrate these functions, we can replace the `HAVING` clause in our example by

```
HAVING   COUNT (*) > 1 AND EVERY ( S.age <= 60 )
```

The fifth step of the conceptual evaluation is the one affected by the change in the `HAVING` clause. Consider the result of the fourth step, shown in Figure 5.12. The `EVERY` keyword requires that every row in a group must satisfy the attached condition to meet the group-qualification. The group for *rating* 3 does meet this criterion and is dropped; the result is shown in Figure 5.14.

SQL:1999 Extensions: Two new set functions, EVERY and ANY, have been added. When they are used in the HAVING clause, the basic intuition that the clause specifies a condition to be satisfied by each group, taken as a whole, remains unchanged. However, the condition can now involve tests on individual tuples in the group, whereas it previously relied exclusively on aggregate functions over the group of tuples.

It is worth contrasting the preceding query with the following query, in which the condition on *age* is in the WHERE clause instead of the HAVING clause:

```
SELECT   S.rating, MIN (S.age) AS minage
FROM     Sailors S
WHERE    S.age >= 18 AND S.age <= 60
GROUP BY S.rating
HAVING   COUNT (*) > 1
```

Now, the result after the third step of conceptual evaluation no longer contains the row with *age* 63.5. Nonetheless, the group for *rating* 3 satisfies the condition COUNT (*) > 1, since it still has two rows, and meets the group-qualification applied in the fifth step. The final result for this query is shown in Figure 5.15.

rating	*minage*
7	45.0
8	55.5

Figure 5.14 Final Result of EVERY Query

rating	*minage*
3	25.5
7	45.0
8	55.5

Figure 5.15 Result of Alternative Query

5.5.2 More Examples of Aggregate Queries

(Q33) For each red boat, find the number of reservations for this boat.

```
SELECT   B.bid, COUNT (*) AS reservationcount
FROM     Boats B, Reserves R
WHERE    R.bid = B.bid AND B.color = 'red'
GROUP BY B.bid
```

On instances *B*1 and *R*2, the answer to this query contains the two tuples ⟨102, 3⟩ and ⟨104, 2⟩.

Observe that this version of the preceding query is illegal:

```
SELECT   B.bid, COUNT (*) AS reservationcount
FROM     Boats B, Reserves R
WHERE    R.bid = B.bid
GROUP BY B.bid
HAVING   B.color = 'red'
```

Even though the group-qualification *B.color = 'red'* is single-valued per group, since the grouping attribute *bid* is a key for Boats (and therefore determines *color*), SQL disallows this query.[6] Only columns that appear in the GROUP BY clause can appear in the HAVING clause, unless they appear as arguments to an aggregate operator in the HAVING clause.

(Q34) Find the average age of sailors for each rating level that has at least two sailors.

```
SELECT   S.rating, AVG (S.age) AS avgage
FROM     Sailors S
GROUP BY S.rating
HAVING   COUNT (*) > 1
```

After identifying groups based on *rating*, we retain only groups with at least two sailors. The answer to this query on instance *S*3 is shown in Figure 5.16.

rating	*avgage*
3	44.5
7	40.0
8	40.5
10	25.5

Figure 5.16 Q34 Answer

rating	*avgage*
3	45.5
7	40.0
8	40.5
10	35.0

Figure 5.17 Q35 Answer

rating	*avgage*
3	45.5
7	40.0
8	40.5

Figure 5.18 Q36 Answer

The following alternative formulation of Query Q34 illustrates that the HAVING clause can have a nested subquery, just like the WHERE clause. Note that we can use *S.rating* inside the nested subquery in the HAVING clause because it has a single value for the current group of sailors:

```
SELECT   S.rating, AVG ( S.age ) AS avgage
FROM     Sailors S
GROUP BY S.rating
HAVING   1 < ( SELECT COUNT (*)
               FROM   Sailors S2
               WHERE  S.rating = S2.rating )
```

[6]This query can be easily rewritten to be legal in SQL:1999 using EVERY in the HAVING clause.

(Q35) Find the average age of sailors who are of voting age (i.e., at least 18 years old) for each rating level that has at least two sailors.

```
SELECT    S.rating, AVG ( S.age ) AS avgage
FROM      Sailors S
WHERE     S. age >= 18
GROUP BY  S.rating
HAVING    1 < ( SELECT COUNT (*)
                FROM   Sailors S2
                WHERE  S.rating = S2.rating )
```

In this variant of Query Q34, we first remove tuples with *age* <= 18 and group the remaining tuples by *rating*. For each group, the subquery in the HAVING clause computes the number of tuples in Sailors (without applying the selection *age* <= 18) with the same *rating* value as the current group. If a group has less than two sailors, it is discarded. For each remaining group, we output the average age. The answer to this query on instance $S3$ is shown in Figure 5.17. Note that the answer is very similar to the answer for Q34, with the only difference being that for the group with rating 10, we now ignore the sailor with age 16 while computing the average.

(Q36) Find the average age of sailors who are of voting age (i.e., at least 18 years old) for each rating level that has at least two such *sailors.*

```
SELECT    S.rating, AVG ( S.age ) AS avgage
FROM      Sailors S
WHERE     S. age > 18
GROUP BY  S.rating
HAVING    1 < ( SELECT COUNT (*)
                FROM   Sailors S2
                WHERE  S.rating = S2.rating AND S2.age >= 18 )
```

This formulation of the query reflects its similarity to Q35. The answer to Q36 on instance $S3$ is shown in Figure 5.18. It differs from the answer to Q35 in that there is no tuple for rating 10, since there is only one tuple with rating 10 and *age* $\geq$ 18.

Query Q36 is actually very similar to Q32, as the following simpler formulation shows:

```
SELECT    S.rating, AVG ( S.age ) AS avgage
FROM      Sailors S
WHERE     S. age > 18
GROUP BY  S.rating
```

```
HAVING   COUNT (*) > 1
```

This formulation of Q36 takes advantage of the fact that the WHERE clause is applied before grouping is done; thus, only sailors with *age* > 18 are left when grouping is done. It is instructive to consider yet another way of writing this query:

```
SELECT Temp.rating, Temp.avgage
FROM   ( SELECT    S.rating, AVG ( S.age ) AS avgage,
                   COUNT (*) AS ratingcount
         FROM      Sailors S
         WHERE     S. age > 18
         GROUP BY  S.rating ) AS Temp
WHERE Temp.ratingcount > 1
```

This alternative brings out several interesting points. First, the FROM clause can also contain a nested subquery according to the SQL standard.[7] Second, the HAVING clause is not needed at all. Any query with a HAVING clause can be rewritten without one, but many queries are simpler to express with the HAVING clause. Finally, when a subquery appears in the FROM clause, using the AS keyword to give it a name is necessary (since otherwise we could not express, for instance, the condition *Temp.ratingcount > 1*).

(Q37) Find those ratings for which the average age of sailors is the minimum over all ratings.

We use this query to illustrate that aggregate operations cannot be nested. One might consider writing it as follows:

```
SELECT   S.rating
FROM     Sailors S
WHERE    AVG (S.age) = ( SELECT    MIN (AVG (S2.age))
                         FROM      Sailors S2
                         GROUP BY  S2.rating )
```

A little thought shows that this query will not work even if the expression MIN (AVG (S2.age)), which is illegal, were allowed. In the nested query, Sailors is partitioned into groups by rating, and the average age is computed for each rating value. For each group, applying MIN to this average age value for the group will return the same value! A correct version of this query follows. It essentially computes a temporary table containing the average age for each rating value and then finds the rating(s) for which this average age is the minimum.

[7] Not all commercial database systems currently support nested queries in the FROM clause.

The Relational Model and SQL: Null values are not part of the basic relational model. Like SQL's treatment of tables as multisets of tuples, this is a departure from the basic model.

```
SELECT Temp.rating, Temp.avgage
FROM   ( SELECT   S.rating, AVG (S.age) AS avgage,
         FROM     Sailors S
         GROUP BY S.rating) AS Temp
WHERE  Temp.avgage = ( SELECT MIN (Temp.avgage) FROM Temp )
```

The answer to this query on instance $S3$ is $\langle 10, 25.5 \rangle$.

As an exercise, consider whether the following query computes the same answer.

```
SELECT   Temp.rating, MIN ( Temp.avgage )
FROM     ( SELECT   S.rating, AVG (S.age) AS avgage,
           FROM     Sailors S
           GROUP BY S.rating ) AS Temp
GROUP BY Temp.rating
```

5.6 NULL VALUES

Thus far, we have assumed that column values in a row are always known. In practice column values can be unknown. For example, when a sailor, say Dan, joins a yacht club, he may not yet have a rating assigned. Since the definition for the Sailors table has a *rating* column, what row should we insert for Dan? What is needed here is a special value that denotes *unknown*. Suppose the Sailor table definition was modified to include a *maiden-name* column. However, only married women who take their husband's last name have a maiden name. For women who do not take their husband's name and for men, the *maiden-name* column is *inapplicable*. Again, what value do we include in this column for the row representing Dan?

SQL provides a special column value called *null* to use in such situations. We use *null* when the column value is either *unknown* or *inapplicable*. Using our Sailor table definition, we might enter the row $\langle 98, Dan, null, 39 \rangle$ to represent Dan. The presence of *null* values complicates many issues, and we consider the impact of *null* values on SQL in this section.

5.6.1 Comparisons Using Null Values

Consider a comparison such as *rating = 8*. If this is applied to the row for Dan, is this condition true or false? Since Dan's rating is unknown, it is reasonable to say that this comparison should evaluate to the value `unknown`. In fact, this is the case for the comparisons *rating* > 8 and *rating* < 8 as well. Perhaps less obviously, if we compare two *null* values using <, >, =, and so on, the result is always `unknown`. For example, if we have *null* in two distinct rows of the sailor relation, any comparison returns `unknown`.

SQL also provides a special comparison operator `IS NULL` to test whether a column value is *null*; for example, we can say *rating* `IS NULL`, which would evaluate to `true` on the row representing Dan. We can also say *rating* `IS NOT NULL`, which would evaluate to `false` on the row for Dan.

5.6.2 Logical Connectives AND, OR, and NOT

Now, what about boolean expressions such as *rating* = 8 `OR` *age* < 40 and *rating* = 8 `AND` *age* < 40? Considering the row for Dan again, because *age* < 40, the first expression evaluates to true regardless of the value of *rating*, but what about the second? We can only say `unknown`.

But this example raises an important point—once we have *null* values, we must define the logical operators `AND`, `OR`, and `NOT` using a *three-valued* logic in which expressions evaluate to `true`, `false`, or `unknown`. We extend the usual interpretations of `AND`, `OR`, and `NOT` to cover the case when one of the arguments is `unknown` as follows. The expression `NOT unknown` is defined to be `unknown`. `OR` of two arguments evaluates to `true` if either argument evaluates to `true`, and to `unknown` if one argument evaluates to `false` and the other evaluates to `unknown`. (If both arguments are `false`, of course, `OR` evaluates to `false`.) `AND` of two arguments evaluates to `false` if either argument evaluates to `false`, and to `unknown` if one argument evaluates to `unknown` and the other evaluates to `true` or `unknown`. (If both arguments are `true`, `AND` evaluates to `true`.)

5.6.3 Impact on SQL Constructs

Boolean expressions arise in many contexts in SQL, and the impact of *null* values must be recognized. For example, the qualification in the `WHERE` clause eliminates rows (in the cross-product of tables named in the `FROM` clause) for which the qualification does not evaluate to `true`. Therefore, in the presence of *null* values, any row that evaluates to `false` or `unknown` is eliminated. Eliminating rows that evaluate to `unknown` has a subtle but significant impact on queries, especially nested queries involving `EXISTS` or `UNIQUE`.

Another issue in the presence of *null* values is the definition of when two rows in a relation instance are regarded as *duplicates*. The SQL definition is that two rows are duplicates if corresponding columns are either equal, or both contain *null*. Contrast this definition with the fact that if we compare two *null* values using =, the result is `unknown`! In the context of duplicates, this comparison is implicitly treated as `true`, which is an anomaly.

As expected, the arithmetic operations +, −, ∗, and / all return *null* if one of their arguments is *null*. However, nulls can cause some unexpected behavior with aggregate operations. `COUNT(*)` handles *null* values just like other values; that is, they get counted. All the other aggregate operations (`COUNT`, `SUM`, `AVG`, `MIN`, `MAX`, and variations using `DISTINCT`) simply discard *null* values—thus `SUM` cannot be understood as just the addition of all values in the (multi)set of values that it is applied to; a preliminary step of discarding all *null* values must also be accounted for. As a special case, if one of these operators—other than `COUNT`—is applied to *only* null values, the result is again *null*.

5.6.4 Outer Joins

Some interesting variants of the join operation that rely on *null* values, called **outer joins**, are supported in SQL. Consider the join of two tables, say Sailors $\bowtie_c$ Reserves. Tuples of Sailors that do not match some row in Reserves according to the join condition c do not appear in the result. In an outer join, on the other hand, Sailor rows without a matching Reserves row appear exactly once in the result, with the result columns inherited from Reserves assigned *null* values.

In fact, there are several variants of the outer join idea. In a **left outer join**, Sailor rows without a matching Reserves row appear in the result, but not vice versa. In a **right outer join**, Reserves rows without a matching Sailors row appear in the result, but not vice versa. In a **full outer join**, both Sailors and Reserves rows without a match appear in the result. (Of course, rows with a match always appear in the result, for all these variants, just like the usual joins, sometimes called *inner* joins, presented in Chapter 4.)

SQL allows the desired type of join to be specified in the `FROM` clause. For example, the following query lists ⟨*sid, bid*⟩ pairs corresponding to sailors and boats they have reserved:

```
SELECT S.sid, R.bid
FROM   Sailors S NATURAL LEFT OUTER JOIN Reserves R
```

The `NATURAL` keyword specifies that the join condition is equality on all common attributes (in this example, *sid*), and the `WHERE` clause is not required (unless we want to specify additional, non-join conditions). On the instances of Sailors and Reserves shown in Figure 5.6, this query computes the result shown in Figure 5.19.

sid	*bid*
22	101
31	*null*
58	103

Figure 5.19 Left Outer Join of *Sailor1* and *Reserves1*

5.6.5 Disallowing Null Values

We can disallow *null* values by specifying `NOT NULL` as part of the field definition; for example, *sname* `CHAR(20) NOT NULL`. In addition, the fields in a primary key are not allowed to take on *null* values. Thus, there is an implicit `NOT NULL` constraint for every field listed in a `PRIMARY KEY` constraint.

Our coverage of *null* values is far from complete. The interested reader should consult one of the many books devoted to SQL for a more detailed treatment of the topic.

5.7 COMPLEX INTEGRITY CONSTRAINTS IN SQL

In this section we discuss the specification of complex integrity constraints that utilize the full power of SQL queries. The features discussed in this section complement the integrity constraint features of SQL presented in Chapter 3.

5.7.1 Constraints over a Single Table

We can specify complex constraints over a single table using **table constraints**, which have the form `CHECK` *conditional-expression.* For example, to ensure that *rating* must be an integer in the range 1 to 10, we could use:

```
CREATE TABLE Sailors ( sid    INTEGER,
                       sname  CHAR(10),
                       rating INTEGER,
                       age    REAL,
                       PRIMARY KEY (sid),
                       CHECK ( rating >= 1 AND rating <= 10 ))
```

To enforce the constraint that Interlake boats cannot be reserved, we could use:

```
CREATE TABLE Reserves ( sid     INTEGER,
                        bid     INTEGER,
                        day     DATE,
                        FOREIGN KEY (sid) REFERENCES Sailors
                        FOREIGN KEY (bid) REFERENCES Boats
                        CONSTRAINT noInterlakeRes
                        CHECK ( 'Interlake' <>
                                  ( SELECT B.bname
                                    FROM   Boats B
                                    WHERE  B.bid = Reserves.bid )))
```

When a row is inserted into Reserves or an existing row is modified, the *conditional expression* in the CHECK constraint is evaluated. If it evaluates to false, the command is rejected.

5.7.2 Domain Constraints and Distinct Types

A user can define a new domain using the CREATE DOMAIN statement, which uses CHECK constraints.

```
CREATE DOMAIN ratingval INTEGER DEFAULT 1
                    CHECK ( VALUE >= 1 AND VALUE <= 10 )
```

INTEGER is the underlying, or *source*, type for the domain ratingval, and every ratingval value must be of this type. Values in ratingval are further restricted by using a CHECK constraint; in defining this constraint, we use the keyword VALUE to refer to a value in the domain. By using this facility, we can constrain the values that belong to a domain using the full power of SQL queries. Once a domain is defined, the name of the domain can be used to restrict column values in a table; we can use the following line in a schema declaration, for example:

```
rating  ratingval
```

The optional DEFAULT keyword is used to associate a default value with a domain. If the domain ratingval is used for a column in some relation and no value is entered for this column in an inserted tuple, the default value 1 associated with ratingval is used.

SQL's support for the concept of a domain is limited in an important respect. For example, we can define two domains called SailorId and BoatId, each

> **SQL:1999 Distinct Types:** Many systems, e.g., Informix UDS and IBM DB2, already support this feature. With its introduction, we expect that the support for domains will be *deprecated*, and eventually eliminated, in future versions of the SQL standard. It is really just one part of a broad set of object-oriented features in SQL:1999, which we discuss in Chapter 23.

using `INTEGER` as the underlying type. The intent is to force a comparison of a `SailorId` value with a `BoatId` value to always fail (since they are drawn from different domains); however, since they both have the same base type, `INTEGER`, the comparison will succeed in SQL. This problem is addressed through the introduction of **distinct types** in SQL:1999:

```
CREATE TYPE ratingtype AS INTEGER
```

This statement defines a new *distinct* type called **ratingtype**, with **INTEGER** as its source type. Values of type **ratingtype** can be compared with each other, but they cannot be compared with values of other types. In particular, **ratingtype** values are treated as being distinct from values of the source type, `INTEGER`—we cannot compare them to integers or combine them with integers (e.g., add an integer to a **ratingtype** value). If we want to define operations on the new type, for example, an *average* function, we must do so explicitly; none of the existing operations on the source type carry over. We discuss how such functions can be defined in Section 23.4.1.

5.7.3 Assertions: ICs over Several Tables

Table constraints are associated with a single table, although the conditional expression in the `CHECK` clause can refer to other tables. Table constraints are required to hold *only* if the associated table is nonempty. Thus, when a constraint involves two or more tables, the table constraint mechanism is sometimes cumbersome and not quite what is desired. To cover such situations, SQL supports the creation of **assertions**, which are constraints not associated with any one table.

As an example, suppose that we wish to enforce the constraint that the number of boats plus the number of sailors should be less than 100. (This condition might be required, say, to qualify as a 'small' sailing club.) We could try the following table constraint:

```
CREATE TABLE Sailors ( sid    INTEGER,
                       sname  CHAR(10),
```

```
rating  INTEGER,
age     REAL,
PRIMARY KEY (sid),
CHECK ( rating >= 1 AND rating <= 10)
CHECK ( ( SELECT COUNT (S.sid) FROM Sailors S )
      + ( SELECT COUNT (B.bid) FROM Boats B )
      < 100 ))
```

This solution suffers from two drawbacks. It is associated with Sailors, although it involves Boats in a completely symmetric way. More important, if the Sailors table is empty, this constraint is defined (as per the semantics of table constraints) to always hold, even if we have more than 100 rows in Boats! We could extend this constraint specification to check that Sailors is nonempty, but this approach becomes cumbersome. The best solution is to create an assertion, as follows:

```
CREATE ASSERTION smallClub
CHECK (( SELECT COUNT (S.sid) FROM Sailors S )
      + ( SELECT COUNT (B.bid) FROM Boats B)
      < 100 )
```

5.8 TRIGGERS AND ACTIVE DATABASES

A **trigger** is a procedure that is automatically invoked by the DBMS in response to specified changes to the database, and is typically specified by the DBA. A database that has a set of associated triggers is called an **active database**. A trigger description contains three parts:

- **Event**: A change to the database that **activates** the trigger.
- **Condition**: A query or test that is run when the trigger is activated.
- **Action**: A procedure that is executed when the trigger is activated and its condition is true.

A trigger can be thought of as a 'daemon' that monitors a database, and is executed when the database is modified in a way that matches the *event* specification. An insert, delete, or update statement could activate a trigger, regardless of which user or application invoked the activating statement; users may not even be aware that a trigger was executed as a side effect of their program.

A *condition* in a trigger can be a true/false statement (e.g., all employee salaries are less than $100,000) or a query. A query is interpreted as *true* if the answer set is nonempty and *false* if the query has no answers. If the condition part evaluates to true, the action associated with the trigger is executed.

A trigger *action* can examine the answers to the query in the condition part of the trigger, refer to old and new values of tuples modified by the statement activating the trigger, execute new queries, and make changes to the database. In fact, an action can even execute a series of data-definition commands (e.g., create new tables, change authorizations) and transaction-oriented commands (e.g., commit) or call host-language procedures.

An important issue is when the action part of a trigger executes in relation to the statement that activated the trigger. For example, a statement that inserts records into the Students table may activate a trigger that is used to maintain statistics on how many students younger than 18 are inserted at a time by a typical insert statement. Depending on exactly what the trigger does, we may want its action to execute *before* changes are made to the Students table or *afterwards*: A trigger that initializes a variable used to count the number of qualifying insertions should be executed before, and a trigger that executes once per qualifying inserted record and increments the variable should be executed after each record is inserted (because we may want to examine the values in the new record to determine the action).

5.8.1 Examples of Triggers in SQL

The examples shown in Figure 5.20, written using Oracle Server syntax for defining triggers, illustrate the basic concepts behind triggers. (The SQL:1999 syntax for these triggers is similar; we will see an example using SQL:1999 syntax shortly.) The trigger called *init count* initializes a counter variable before every execution of an `INSERT` statement that adds tuples to the Students relation. The trigger called *incr count* increments the counter for each inserted tuple that satisfies the condition $age < 18$.

One of the example triggers in Figure 5.20 executes before the activating statement, and the other example executes after it. A trigger can also be scheduled to execute *instead of* the activating statement; or in *deferred* fashion, at the end of the transaction containing the activating statement; or in *asynchronous* fashion, as part of a separate transaction.

The example in Figure 5.20 illustrates another point about trigger execution: A user must be able to specify whether a trigger is to be executed once per modified record or once per activating statement. If the action depends on individual changed records, for example, we have to examine the *age* field of the inserted Students record to decide whether to increment the count, the trigger-

```
CREATE TRIGGER init count BEFORE INSERT ON Students      /* Event */
    DECLARE
        count INTEGER;
    BEGIN                                                /* Action */
        count := 0;
    END

CREATE TRIGGER incr count AFTER INSERT ON Students       /* Event */
    WHEN (new.age < 18)   /* Condition; 'new' is just-inserted tuple */
    FOR EACH ROW
    BEGIN        /* Action; a procedure in Oracle's PL/SQL syntax */
        count := count + 1;
    END
```

Figure 5.20 Examples Illustrating Triggers

ing event should be defined to occur for each modified record; the `FOR EACH ROW` clause is used to do this. Such a trigger is called a **row-level trigger**. On the other hand, the *init count* trigger is executed just once per `INSERT` statement, regardless of the number of records inserted, because we have omitted the `FOR EACH ROW` phrase. Such a trigger is called a **statement-level trigger**.

In Figure 5.20, the keyword `new` refers to the newly inserted tuple. If an existing tuple were modified, the keywords `old` and `new` could be used to refer to the values before and after the modification. SQL:1999 also allows the action part of a trigger to refer to the *set* of changed records, rather than just one changed record at a time. For example, it would be useful to be able to refer to the set of inserted Students records in a trigger that executes once after the `INSERT` statement; we could count the number of inserted records with $age < 18$ through an SQL query over this set. Such a trigger is shown in Figure 5.21 and is an alternative to the triggers shown in Figure 5.20.

The definition in Figure 5.21 uses the syntax of SQL:1999, in order to illustrate the similarities and differences with respect to the syntax used in a typical current DBMS. The keyword clause `NEW TABLE` enables us to give a table name (InsertedTuples) to the set of newly inserted tuples. The `FOR EACH STATEMENT` clause specifies a statement-level trigger and can be omitted because it is the default. This definition does not have a `WHEN` clause; if such a clause is included, it follows the `FOR EACH STATEMENT` clause, just before the action specification.

The trigger is evaluated once for each SQL statement that inserts tuples into Students, and inserts a single tuple into a table that contains statistics on modifications to database tables. The first two fields of the tuple contain constants (identifying the modified table, Students, and the kind of modifying statement, an INSERT), and the third field is the number of inserted Students tuples with *age* < 18. (The trigger in Figure 5.20 only computes the count; an additional trigger is required to insert the appropriate tuple into the statistics table.)

```
CREATE TRIGGER set count AFTER INSERT ON Students          /* Event */
REFERENCING NEW TABLE AS InsertedTuples
FOR EACH STATEMENT
    INSERT                                                 /* Action */
        INTO StatisticsTable(ModifiedTable, ModificationType, Count)
        SELECT 'Students', 'Insert', COUNT *
        FROM InsertedTuples I
        WHERE I.age < 18
```

Figure 5.21 Set-Oriented Trigger

5.9 DESIGNING ACTIVE DATABASES

Triggers offer a powerful mechanism for dealing with changes to a database, but they must be used with caution. The effect of a collection of triggers can be very complex, and maintaining an active database can become very difficult. Often, a judicious use of integrity constraints can replace the use of triggers.

5.9.1 Why Triggers Can Be Hard to Understand

In an active database system, when the DBMS is about to execute a statement that modifies the database, it checks whether some trigger is activated by the statement. If so, the DBMS processes the trigger by evaluating its condition part, and then (if the condition evaluates to true) executing its action part.

If a statement activates more than one trigger, the DBMS typically processes all of them, in some arbitrary order. An important point is that the execution of the action part of a trigger could in turn activate another trigger. In particular, the execution of the action part of a trigger could again activate the same trigger; such triggers are called **recursive triggers**. The potential for such *chain* activations and the unpredictable order in which a DBMS processes activated triggers can make it difficult to understand the effect of a collection of triggers.

5.9.2 Constraints versus Triggers

A common use of triggers is to maintain database consistency, and in such cases, we should always consider whether using an integrity constraint (e.g., a foreign key constraint) achieves the same goals. The meaning of a constraint is not defined operationally, unlike the effect of a trigger. This property makes a constraint easier to understand, and also gives the DBMS more opportunities to optimize execution. A constraint also prevents the data from being made inconsistent by *any* kind of statement, whereas a trigger is activated by a specific kind of statement (`INSERT`, `DELETE`, or `UPDATE`). Again, this restriction makes a constraint easier to understand.

On the other hand, triggers allow us to maintain database integrity in more flexible ways, as the following examples illustrate.

> Suppose that we have a table called Orders with fields *itemid*, *quantity*, *customerid*, and *unitprice*. When a customer places an order, the first three field values are filled in by the user (in this example, a sales clerk). The fourth field's value can be obtained from a table called Items, but it is important to include it in the Orders table to have a complete record of the order, in case the price of the item is subsequently changed. We can define a trigger to look up this value and include it in the fourth field of a newly inserted record. In addition to reducing the number of fields that the clerk has to type in, this trigger eliminates the possibility of an entry error leading to an inconsistent price in the Orders table.

> Continuing with this example, we may want to perform some additional actions when an order is received. For example, if the purchase is being charged to a credit line issued by the company, we may want to check whether the total cost of the purchase is within the current credit limit. We can use a trigger to do the check; indeed, we can even use a `CHECK` constraint. Using a trigger, however, allows us to implement more sophisticated policies for dealing with purchases that exceed a credit limit. For instance, we may allow purchases that exceed the limit by no more than 10% if the customer has dealt with the company for at least a year, and add the customer to a table of candidates for credit limit increases.

5.9.3 Other Uses of Triggers

Many potential uses of triggers go beyond integrity maintenance. Triggers can alert users to unusual events (as reflected in updates to the database). For example, we may want to check whether a customer placing an order has made enough purchases in the past month to qualify for an additional discount; if so, the sales clerk must be informed so that he (or she) can tell the customer and possibly generate additional sales! We can relay this information by using a trigger that checks recent purchases and prints a message if the customer qualifies for the discount.

Triggers can generate a log of events to support auditing and security checks. For example, each time a customer places an order, we can create a record with the customer's ID and current credit limit and insert this record in a customer history table. Subsequent analysis of this table might suggest candidates for an increased credit limit (e.g., customers who have never failed to pay a bill on time and who have come within 10% of their credit limit at least three times in the last month).

As the examples in Section 5.8 illustrate, we can use triggers to gather statistics on table accesses and modifications. Some database systems even use triggers internally as the basis for managing replicas of relations (Section 22.11.1). Our list of potential uses of triggers is not exhaustive; for example, triggers have also been considered for workflow management and enforcing business rules.

5.10 REVIEW QUESTIONS

Answers to the review questions can be found in the listed sections.

- What are the parts of a basic SQL query? Are the input and result tables of an SQL query sets or multisets? How can you obtain a set of tuples as the result of a query? **(Section 5.2)**
- What are range variables in SQL? How can you give names to output columns in a query that are defined by arithmetic or string expressions? What support does SQL offer for string pattern matching? **(Section 5.2)**
- What operations does SQL provide over (multi)sets of tuples, and how would you use these in writing queries? **(Section 5.3)**
- What are nested queries? What is *correlation* in nested queries? How would you use the operators `IN`, `EXISTS`, `UNIQUE`, `ANY`, and `ALL` in writing nested queries? Why are they useful? Illustrate your answer by showing how to write the *division* operator in SQL. **(Section 5.4)**
- What aggregate operators does SQL support? **(Section 5.5)**
- What is *grouping*? Is there a counterpart in relational algebra? Explain this feature, and discuss the interaction of the `HAVING` and `WHERE` clauses. Mention any restrictions that must be satisfied by the fields that appear in the `GROUP BY` clause. **(Section 5.5.1)**

- What are *null* values? Are they supported in the relational model, as described in Chapter 3? How do they affect the meaning of queries? Can primary key fields of a table contain *null* values? **(Section 5.6)**
- What types of SQL constraints can be specified using the query language? Can you express primary key constraints using one of these new kinds of constraints? If so, why does SQL provide for a separate primary key constraint syntax? **(Section 5.7)**
- What is a *trigger*, and what are its three parts? What are the differences between row-level and statement-level triggers? **(Section 5.8)**
- Why can triggers be hard to understand? Explain the differences between triggers and integrity constraints, and describe when you would use triggers over integrity constrains and vice versa. What are triggers used for? **(Section 5.9)**

EXERCISES

Online material is available for all exercises in this chapter on the book's webpage at

`http://www.cs.wisc.edu/~dbbook`

This includes scripts to create tables for each exercise for use with Oracle, IBM DB2, Microsoft SQL Server, and MySQL.

Exercise 5.1 Consider the following relations:

Student(*snum:* `integer`, *sname:* `string`, *major:* `string`, *level:* `string`, *age:* `integer`)
Class(*name:* `string`, *meets_at:* `time`, *room:* `string`, *fid:* `integer`)
Enrolled(*snum:* `integer`, *cname:* `string`)
Faculty(*fid:* `integer`, *fname:* `string`, *deptid:* `integer`)

The meaning of these relations is straightforward; for example, Enrolled has one record per student-class pair such that the student is enrolled in the class.

Write the following queries in SQL. No duplicates should be printed in any of the answers.

1. Find the names of all Juniors (level = JR) who are enrolled in a class taught by I. Teach.
2. Find the age of the oldest student who is either a History major or enrolled in a course taught by I. Teach.
3. Find the names of all classes that either meet in room R128 or have five or more students enrolled.
4. Find the names of all students who are enrolled in two classes that meet at the same time.

5. Find the names of faculty members who teach in every room in which some class is taught.
6. Find the names of faculty members for whom the combined enrollment of the courses that they teach is less than five.
7. Print the level and the average age of students for that level, for each level.
8. Print the level and the average age of students for that level, for all levels except JR.
9. For each faculty member that has taught classes only in room R128, print the faculty member's name and the total number of classes she or he has taught.
10. Find the names of students enrolled in the maximum number of classes.
11. Find the names of students not enrolled in any class.
12. For each age value that appears in Students, find the level value that appears most often. For example, if there are more FR level students aged 18 than SR, JR, or SO students aged 18, you should print the pair (18, FR).

Exercise 5.2 Consider the following schema:

> Suppliers(*sid:* `integer`, *sname:* `string`, *address:* `string`)
> Parts(*pid:* `integer`, *pname:* `string`, *color:* `string`)
> Catalog(*sid:* `integer`, *pid:* `integer`, *cost:* `real`)

The Catalog relation lists the prices charged for parts by Suppliers. Write the following queries in SQL:

1. Find the *pname*s of parts for which there is some supplier.
2. Find the *sname*s of suppliers who supply every part.
3. Find the *sname*s of suppliers who supply every red part.
4. Find the *pname*s of parts supplied by Acme Widget Suppliers and no one else.
5. Find the *sid*s of suppliers who charge more for some part than the average cost of that part (averaged over all the suppliers who supply that part).
6. For each part, find the *sname* of the supplier who charges the most for that part.
7. Find the *sid*s of suppliers who supply only red parts.
8. Find the *sid*s of suppliers who supply a red part and a green part.
9. Find the *sid*s of suppliers who supply a red part or a green part.
10. For every supplier that only supplies green parts, print the name of the supplier and the total number of parts that she supplies.
11. For every supplier that supplies a green part and a red part, print the name and price of the most expensive part that she supplies.

Exercise 5.3 The following relations keep track of airline flight information:

> Flights(*flno:* `integer`, *from:* `string`, *to:* `string`, *distance:* `integer`,
> *departs:* `time`, *arrives:* `time`, *price:* `integer`)
> Aircraft(*aid:* `integer`, *aname:* `string`, *cruisingrange:* `integer`)
> Certified(*eid:* `integer`, *aid:* `integer`)
> Employees(*eid:* `integer`, *ename:* `string`, *salary:* `integer`)

Note that the Employees relation describes pilots and other kinds of employees as well; every pilot is certified for some aircraft, and only pilots are certified to fly. Write each of the following queries in SQL. (*Additional queries using the same schema are listed in the exercises for Chapter 4.*)

1. Find the names of aircraft such that all pilots certified to operate them earn more than $80,000.
2. For each pilot who is certified for more than three aircraft, find the *eid* and the maximum *cruisingrange* of the aircraft for which she or he is certified.
3. Find the names of pilots whose *salary* is less than the price of the cheapest route from Los Angeles to Honolulu.
4. For all aircraft with *cruisingrange* over 1000 miles, find the name of the aircraft and the average salary of all pilots certified for this aircraft.
5. Find the names of pilots certified for some Boeing aircraft.
6. Find the *aid*s of all aircraft that can be used on routes from Los Angeles to Chicago.
7. Identify the routes that can be piloted by every pilot who makes more than $100,000.
8. Print the *ename*s of pilots who can operate planes with *cruisingrange* greater than 3000 miles but are not certified on any Boeing aircraft.
9. A customer wants to travel from Madison to New York with no more than two changes of flight. List the choice of departure times from Madison if the customer wants to arrive in New York by 6 p.m.
10. Compute the difference between the average salary of a pilot and the average salary of all employees (including pilots).
11. Print the name and salary of every nonpilot whose salary is more than the average salary for pilots.
12. Print the names of employees who are certified only on aircrafts with cruising range longer than 1000 miles.
13. Print the names of employees who are certified only on aircrafts with cruising range longer than 1000 miles, but on at least two such aircrafts.
14. Print the names of employees who are certified only on aircrafts with cruising range longer than 1000 miles and who are certified on some Boeing aircraft.

Exercise 5.4 Consider the following relational schema. An employee can work in more than one department; the *pct_time* field of the Works relation shows the percentage of time that a given employee works in a given department.

Emp(<u>*eid:* `integer`</u>, *ename:* `string`, *age:* `integer`, *salary:* `real`)
Works(<u>*eid:* `integer`, *did:* `integer`</u>, *pct_time:* `integer`)
Dept(<u>*did:* `integer`</u>, *budget:* `real`, *managerid:* `integer`)

Write the following queries in SQL:

1. Print the names and ages of each employee who works in both the Hardware department and the Software department.
2. For each department with more than 20 full-time-equivalent employees (i.e., where the part-time and full-time employees add up to at least that many full-time employees), print the *did* together with the number of employees that work in that department.

sid	*sname*	*rating*	*age*
18	jones	3	30.0
41	jonah	6	56.0
22	ahab	7	44.0
63	moby	*null*	15.0

Figure 5.22 An Instance of Sailors

3. Print the name of each employee whose salary exceeds the budget of all of the departments that he or she works in.
4. Find the *managerids* of managers who manage only departments with budgets greater than $1 million.
5. Find the *enames* of managers who manage the departments with the largest budgets.
6. If a manager manages more than one department, he or she *controls* the sum of all the budgets for those departments. Find the *managerids* of managers who control more than $5 million.
7. Find the *managerids* of managers who control the largest amounts.
8. Find the *enames* of managers who manage only departments with budgets larger than $1 million, but at least one department with budget less than $5 million.

Exercise 5.5 Consider the instance of the Sailors relation shown in Figure 5.22.

1. Write SQL queries to compute the average rating, using AVG; the sum of the ratings, using SUM; and the number of ratings, using COUNT.
2. If you divide the sum just computed by the count, would the result be the same as the average? How would your answer change if these steps were carried out with respect to the *age* field instead of *rating*?
3. Consider the following query: *Find the names of sailors with a higher rating than all sailors with age* < 21. The following two SQL queries attempt to obtain the answer to this question. Do they both compute the result? If not, explain why. Under what conditions would they compute the same result?

```
SELECT S.sname
FROM   Sailors S
WHERE  NOT EXISTS ( SELECT *
                    FROM   Sailors S2
                    WHERE  S2.age < 21
                           AND S.rating <= S2.rating )
SELECT *
FROM   Sailors S
WHERE  S.rating > ANY ( SELECT S2.rating
                        FROM   Sailors S2
                        WHERE  S2.age < 21 )
```

4. Consider the instance of Sailors shown in Figure 5.22. Let us define instance S1 of Sailors to consist of the first two tuples, instance S2 to be the last two tuples, and S to be the given instance.

(a) Show the left outer join of S with itself, with the join condition being *sid=sid*.

(b) Show the right outer join of S with itself, with the join condition being *sid=sid*.

(c) Show the full outer join of S with itself, with the join condition being *sid=sid*.

(d) Show the left outer join of S1 with S2, with the join condition being *sid=sid*.

(e) Show the right outer join of S1 with S2, with the join condition being *sid=sid*.

(f) Show the full outer join of S1 with S2, with the join condition being *sid=sid*.

Exercise 5.6 Answer the following questions:

1. Explain the term *impedance mismatch* in the context of embedding SQL commands in a host language such as C.
2. How can the value of a host language variable be passed to an embedded SQL command?
3. Explain the `WHENEVER` command's use in error and exception handling.
4. Explain the need for cursors.
5. Give an example of a situation that calls for the use of embedded SQL; that is, interactive use of SQL commands is not enough, and some host language capabilities are needed.
6. Write a C program with embedded SQL commands to address your example in the previous answer.
7. Write a C program with embedded SQL commands to find the standard deviation of sailors' ages.
8. Extend the previous program to find all sailors whose age is within one standard deviation of the average age of all sailors.
9. Explain how you would write a C program to compute the transitive closure of a graph, represented as an SQL relation Edges(*from, to*), using embedded SQL commands. (You need not write the program, just explain the main points to be dealt with.)
10. Explain the following terms with respect to cursors: *updatability, sensitivity,* and *scrollability.*
11. Define a cursor on the Sailors relation that is updatable, scrollable, and returns answers sorted by *age*. Which fields of Sailors can such a cursor *not* update? Why?
12. Give an example of a situation that calls for dynamic SQL; that is, even embedded SQL is not sufficient.

Exercise 5.7 Consider the following relational schema and briefly answer the questions that follow:

Emp(*eid:* `integer`, *ename:* `string`, *age:* `integer`, *salary:* `real`)
Works(*eid:* `integer`, *did:* `integer`, *pct_time:* `integer`)
Dept(*did:* `integer`, *budget:* `real`, *managerid:* `integer`)

1. Define a table constraint on Emp that will ensure that every employee makes at least $10,000.
2. Define a table constraint on Dept that will ensure that all managers have *age* > 30.
3. Define an assertion on Dept that will ensure that all managers have *age* > 30. Compare this assertion with the equivalent table constraint. Explain which is better.

4. Write SQL statements to delete all information about employees whose salaries exceed that of the manager of one or more departments that they work in. Be sure to ensure that all the relevant integrity constraints are satisfied after your updates.

Exercise 5.8 Consider the following relations:

> Student(*snum:* `integer`, *sname:* `string`, *major:* `string`,
> *level:* `string`, *age:* `integer`)
> Class(*name:* `string`, *meets_at:* `time`, *room:* `string`, *fid:* `integer`)
> Enrolled(*snum:* `integer`, *cname:* `string`)
> Faculty(*fid:* `integer`, *fname:* `string`, *deptid:* `integer`)

The meaning of these relations is straightforward; for example, Enrolled has one record per student-class pair such that the student is enrolled in the class.

1. Write the SQL statements required to create these relations, including appropriate versions of all primary and foreign key integrity constraints.
2. Express each of the following integrity constraints in SQL unless it is implied by the primary and foreign key constraint; if so, explain how it is implied. If the constraint cannot be expressed in SQL, say so. For each constraint, state what operations (inserts, deletes, and updates on specific relations) must be monitored to enforce the constraint.
   (a) Every class has a minimum enrollment of 5 students and a maximum enrollment of 30 students.
   (b) At least one class meets in each room.
   (c) Every faculty member must teach at least two courses.
   (d) Only faculty in the department with *deptid=33* teach more than three courses.
   (e) Every student must be enrolled in the course called Math101.
   (f) The room in which the earliest scheduled class (i.e., the class with the smallest *meets_at* value) meets should not be the same as the room in which the latest scheduled class meets.
   (g) Two classes cannot meet in the same room at the same time.
   (h) The department with the most faculty members must have fewer than twice the number of faculty members in the department with the fewest faculty members.
   (i) No department can have more than 10 faculty members.
   (j) A student cannot add more than two courses at a time (i.e., in a single update).
   (k) The number of CS majors must be more than the number of Math majors.
   (l) The number of distinct courses in which CS majors are enrolled is greater than the number of distinct courses in which Math majors are enrolled.
   (m) The total enrollment in courses taught by faculty in the department with *deptid=33* is greater than the number of Math majors.
   (n) There must be at least one CS major if there are any students whatsoever.
   (o) Faculty members from different departments cannot teach in the same room.

Exercise 5.9 Discuss the strengths and weaknesses of the trigger mechanism. Contrast triggers with other integrity constraints supported by SQL.

Exercise 5.10 Consider the following relational schema. An employee can work in more than one department; the *pct_time* field of the Works relation shows the percentage of time that a given employee works in a given department.

Emp(*eid:* `integer`, *ename:* `string`, *age:* `integer`, *salary:* `real`)
Works(*eid:* `integer`, *did:* `integer`, *pct_time:* `integer`)
Dept(*did:* `integer`, *budget:* `real`, *managerid:* `integer`)

Write SQL-92 integrity constraints (domain, key, foreign key, or `CHECK` constraints; or assertions) or SQL:1999 triggers to ensure each of the following requirements, considered independently.

1. Employees must make a minimum salary of $1000.
2. Every manager must be also be an employee.
3. The total percentage of all appointments for an employee must be under 100%.
4. A manager must always have a higher salary than any employee that he or she manages.
5. Whenever an employee is given a raise, the manager's salary must be increased to be at least as much.
6. Whenever an employee is given a raise, the manager's salary must be increased to be at least as much. Further, whenever an employee is given a raise, the department's budget must be increased to be greater than the sum of salaries of all employees in the department.

PROJECT-BASED EXERCISE

Exercise 5.11 Identify the subset of SQL queries that are supported in Minibase.

BIBLIOGRAPHIC NOTES

The original version of SQL was developed as the query language for IBM's System R project, and its early development can be traced in [107, 151]. SQL has since become the most widely used relational query language, and its development is now subject to an international standardization process.

A very readable and comprehensive treatment of SQL-92 is presented by Melton and Simon in [524], and the central features of SQL:1999 are covered in [525]. We refer readers to these two books for an authoritative treatment of SQL. A short survey of the SQL:1999 standard is presented in [237]. Date offers an insightful critique of SQL in [202]. Although some of the problems have been addressed in SQL-92 and later revisions, others remain. A formal semantics for a large subset of SQL queries is presented in [560]. SQL:1999 is the current International Organization for Standardization (ISO) and American National Standards Institute (ANSI) standard. Melton is the editor of the ANSI and ISO SQL:1999 standard, document ANSI/ISO/IEC 9075-:1999. The corresponding ISO document is ISO/IEC 9075-:1999. A successor, planned for 2003, builds on SQL:1999 SQL:2003 is close to ratification (as of June 2002). Drafts of the SQL:2003 deliberations are available at the following URL:

`ftp://sqlstandards.org/SC32/`

[774] contains a collection of papers that cover the active database field. [794] includes a good in-depth introduction to active rules, covering semantics, applications and design issues. [251] discusses SQL extensions for specifying integrity constraint checks through triggers. [123] also discusses a procedural mechanism, called an *alerter*, for monitoring a database. [185] is a recent paper that suggests how triggers might be incorporated into SQL extensions. Influential active database prototypes include Ariel [366], HiPAC [516], ODE [18], Postgres [722], RDL [690], and Sentinel [36]. [147] compares various architectures for active database systems.

[32] considers conditions under which a collection of active rules has the same behavior, independent of evaluation order. Semantics of active databases is also studied in [285] and [792]. Designing and managing complex rule systems is discussed in [60, 225]. [142] discusses rule management using Chimera, a data model and language for active database systems.

PART II

APPLICATION DEVELOPMENT

6

DATABASE APPLICATION DEVELOPMENT

- How do application programs connect to a DBMS?
- How can applications manipulate data retrieved from a DBMS?
- How can applications modify data in a DBMS?
- What are cursors?
- What is JDBC and how is it used?
- What is SQLJ and how is it used?
- What are stored procedures?
- **Key concepts:** Embedded SQL, Dynamic SQL, cursors; JDBC, connections, drivers, ResultSets, java.sql, SQLJ; stored procedures, SQL/PSM

He profits most who serves best.

—Motto for Rotary International

In Chapter 5, we looked at a wide range of SQL query constructs, treating SQL as an independent language in its own right. A relational DBMS supports an *interactive SQL* interface, and users can directly enter SQL commands. This simple approach is fine as long as the task at hand can be accomplished entirely with SQL commands. In practice, we often encounter situations in which we need the greater flexibility of a general-purpose programming language in addition to the data manipulation facilities provided by SQL. For example, we may want to integrate a database application with a nice graphical user interface, or we may want to integrate with other existing applications.

Applications that rely on the DBMS to manage data run as separate processes that connect to the DBMS to interact with it. Once a connection is established, SQL commands can be used to insert, delete, and modify data. SQL queries can be used to retrieve desired data, but we need to bridge an important difference in how a database system sees data and how an application program in a language like Java or C sees data: The result of a database query is a set (or multiset) or records, but Java has no set or multiset data type. This mismatch is resolved through additional SQL constructs that allow applications to obtain a handle on a collection and iterate over the records one at a time.

We introduce Embedded SQL, Dynamic SQL, and cursors in Section 6.1. Embedded SQL allows us to access data using static SQL queries in application code (Section 6.1.1); with Dynamic SQL, we can create the queries at run-time (Section 6.1.3). Cursors bridge the gap between set-valued query answers and programming languages that do not support set-values (Section 6.1.2).

The emergence of Java as a popular application development language, especially for Internet applications, has made accessing a DBMS from Java code a particularly important topic. Section 6.2 covers JDBC, a programming interface that allows us to execute SQL queries from a Java program and use the results in the Java program. JDBC provides greater portability than Embedded SQL or Dynamic SQL, and offers the ability to connect to several DBMSs without recompiling the code. Section 6.4 covers SQLJ, which does the same for static SQL queries, but is easier to program in than Java with JDBC.

Often, it is useful to execute application code at the database server, rather than just retrieve data and execute application logic in a separate process. Section 6.5 covers stored procedures, which enable application logic to be stored and executed at the database server. We conclude the chapter by discussing our B&N case study in Section 6.6.

While writing database applications, we must also keep in mind that typically many application programs run concurrently. The transaction concept, introduced in Chapter 1, is used to encapsulate the effects of an application on the database. An application can select certain transaction properties through SQL commands to control the degree to which it is exposed to the changes of other concurrently running applications. We touch on the transaction concept at many points in this chapter, and, in particular, cover transaction-related aspects of JDBC. A full discussion of transaction properties and SQL's support for transactions is deferred until Chapter 16.

Examples that appear in this chapter are available online at

```
http://www.cs.wisc.edu/~dbbook
```

6.1 ACCESSING DATABASES FROM APPLICATIONS

In this section, we cover how SQL commands can be executed from within a program in a **host language** such as C or Java. The use of SQL commands within a host language program is called **Embedded SQL**. Details of Embedded SQL also depend on the host language. Although similar capabilities are supported for a variety of host languages, the syntax sometimes varies.

We first cover the basics of Embedded SQL with static SQL queries in Section 6.1.1. We then introduce cursors in Section 6.1.2. We discuss Dynamic SQL, which allows us to construct SQL queries at runtime (and execute them) in Section 6.1.3.

6.1.1 Embedded SQL

Conceptually, embedding SQL commands in a host language program is straightforward. SQL statements (i.e., not declarations) can be used wherever a statement in the host language is allowed (with a few restrictions). SQL statements must be clearly marked so that a preprocessor can deal with them before invoking the compiler for the host language. Also, any host language variables used to pass arguments into an SQL command must be declared in SQL. In particular, some special host language variables *must* be declared in SQL (so that, for example, any error conditions arising during SQL execution can be communicated back to the main application program in the host language).

There are, however, two complications to bear in mind. First, the data types recognized by SQL may not be recognized by the host language and vice versa. This mismatch is typically addressed by casting data values appropriately before passing them to or from SQL commands. (SQL, like other programming languages, provides an operator to cast values of one type into values of another type.) The second complication has to do with SQL being **set-oriented**, and is addressed using cursors (see Section 6.1.2. Commands operate on and produce tables, which are sets

In our discussion of Embedded SQL, we assume that the host language is C for concreteness, because minor differences exist in how SQL statements are embedded in different host languages.

Declaring Variables and Exceptions

SQL statements can refer to variables defined in the host program. Such host-language variables must be prefixed by a colon (:) in SQL statements and be declared between the commands `EXEC SQL BEGIN DECLARE SECTION` and `EXEC`

SQL END DECLARE SECTION. The declarations are similar to how they would look in a C program and, as usual in C, are separated by semicolons. For example, we can declare variables *c_sname*, *c_sid*, *c_rating*, and *c_age* (with the initial *c* used as a naming convention to emphasize that these are host language variables) as follows:

```
EXEC SQL BEGIN DECLARE SECTION
char c_sname[20];
long c_sid;
short c_rating;
float c_age;
EXEC SQL END DECLARE SECTION
```

The first question that arises is which SQL types correspond to the various C types, since we have just declared a collection of C variables whose values are intended to be read (and possibly set) in an SQL run-time environment when an SQL statement that refers to them is executed. The SQL-92 standard defines such a correspondence between the host language types and SQL types for a number of host languages. In our example, *c_sname* has the type CHARACTER(20) when referred to in an SQL statement, *c_sid* has the type INTEGER, *c_rating* has the type SMALLINT, and *c_age* has the type REAL.

We also need some way for SQL to report what went wrong if an error condition arises when executing an SQL statement. The SQL-92 standard recognizes two special variables for reporting errors, SQLCODE and SQLSTATE. SQLCODE is the older of the two and is defined to return some negative value when an error condition arises, without specifying further just what error a particular negative integer denotes. SQLSTATE, introduced in the SQL-92 standard for the first time, associates predefined values with several common error conditions, thereby introducing some uniformity to how errors are reported. One of these two variables *must* be declared. The appropriate C type for SQLCODE is long and the appropriate C type for SQLSTATE is char[6], that is, a character string five characters long. (Recall the null-terminator in C strings.) In this chapter, we assume that SQLSTATE is declared.

Embedding SQL Statements

All SQL statements embedded within a host program must be clearly marked, with the details dependent on the host language; in C, SQL statements must be prefixed by EXEC SQL. An SQL statement can essentially appear in any place in the host language program where a host language statement can appear.

As a simple example, the following Embedded SQL statement inserts a row, whose column values are based on the values of the host language variables contained in it, into the Sailors relation:

```
EXEC SQL
INSERT INTO Sailors VALUES (:c_sname, :c_sid, :c_rating, :c_age);
```

Observe that a semicolon terminates the command, as per the convention for terminating statements in C.

The SQLSTATE variable should be checked for errors and exceptions after each Embedded SQL statement. SQL provides the WHENEVER command to simplify this tedious task:

```
EXEC SQL WHENEVER [ SQLERROR | NOT FOUND ] [ CONTINUE | GOTO stmt ]
```

The intent is that the value of SQLSTATE should be checked after each Embedded SQL statement is executed. If SQLERROR is specified and the value of SQLSTATE indicates an exception, control is transferred to *stmt*, which is presumably responsible for error and exception handling. Control is also transferred to *stmt* if NOT FOUND is specified and the value of SQLSTATE is 02000, which denotes NO DATA.

6.1.2 Cursors

A major problem in embedding SQL statements in a host language like C is that an *impedance mismatch* occurs because SQL operates on *sets* of records, whereas languages like C do not cleanly support a set-of-records abstraction. The solution is to essentially provide a mechanism that allows us to retrieve rows one at a time from a relation.

This mechanism is called a **cursor**. We can declare a cursor on any relation or on any SQL query (because every query returns a set of rows). Once a cursor is declared, we can **open** it (which positions the cursor just before the first row); **fetch** the next row; **move** the cursor (to the next row, to the row after the next n, to the first row, or to the previous row, etc., by specifying additional parameters for the FETCH command); or **close** the cursor. Thus, a cursor essentially allows us to retrieve the rows in a table by positioning the cursor at a particular row and reading its contents.

Basic Cursor Definition and Usage

Cursors enable us to examine, in the host language program, a collection of rows computed by an Embedded SQL statement:

- We usually need to open a cursor if the embedded statement is a SELECT (i.e., a query). However, we can avoid opening a cursor if the answer contains a single row, as we see shortly.
- INSERT, DELETE, and UPDATE statements typically require no cursor, although some variants of DELETE and UPDATE use a cursor.

As an example, we can find the name and age of a sailor, specified by assigning a value to the host variable *c_sid*, declared earlier, as follows:

```
EXEC SQL SELECT S.sname, S.age
         INTO   :c_sname, :c_age
         FROM   Sailors S
         WHERE  S.sid = :c_sid;
```

The INTO clause allows us to assign the columns of the single answer row to the host variables *c_sname* and *c_age*. Therefore, we do not need a cursor to embed this query in a host language program. But what about the following query, which computes the names and ages of all sailors with a rating greater than the current value of the host variable *c_minrating*?

```
SELECT S.sname, S.age
FROM   Sailors S
WHERE  S.rating > :c_minrating
```

This query returns a collection of rows, not just one row. When executed interactively, the answers are printed on the screen. If we embed this query in a C program by prefixing the command with EXEC SQL, how can the answers be bound to host language variables? The INTO clause is inadequate because we must deal with several rows. The solution is to use a cursor:

```
DECLARE sinfo CURSOR FOR
SELECT S.sname, S.age
FROM   Sailors S
WHERE  S.rating > :c_minrating;
```

This code can be included in a C program, and once it is executed, the cursor *sinfo* is defined. Subsequently, we can open the cursor:

```
OPEN sinfo;
```

The value of *c_minrating* in the SQL query associated with the cursor is the value of this variable when we open the cursor. (The cursor declaration is processed at compile-time, and the OPEN command is executed at run-time.)

A cursor can be thought of as 'pointing' to a row in the collection of answers to the query associated with it. When a cursor is opened, it is positioned just before the first row. We can use the FETCH command to read the first row of cursor *sinfo* into host language variables:

```
FETCH sinfo INTO :c_sname, :c_age;
```

When the FETCH statement is executed, the cursor is positioned to point at the next row (which is the first row in the table when FETCH is executed for the first time after opening the cursor) and the column values in the row are copied into the corresponding host variables. By repeatedly executing this FETCH statement (say, in a while-loop in the C program), we can read all the rows computed by the query, one row at a time. Additional parameters to the FETCH command allow us to position a cursor in very flexible ways, but we do not discuss them.

How do we know when we have looked at all the rows associated with the cursor? By looking at the special variables SQLCODE or SQLSTATE, of course. SQLSTATE, for example, is set to the value 02000, which denotes NO DATA, to indicate that there are no more rows if the FETCH statement positions the cursor after the last row.

When we are done with a cursor, we can close it:

```
CLOSE sinfo;
```

It can be opened again if needed, and the value of : *c minrating* in the SQL query associated with the cursor would be the value of the host variable *c minrating* at that time.

Properties of Cursors

The general form of a cursor declaration is:

```
DECLARE cursorname [INSENSITIVE] [SCROLL] CURSOR
        [ WITH HOLD ]
        FOR some query
        [ ORDER BY order-item-list ]
        [ FOR READ ONLY | FOR UPDATE ]
```

A cursor can be declared to be a **read-only cursor** (FOR READ ONLY) or, if it is a cursor on a base relation or an updatable view, to be an **updatable cursor** (FOR UPDATE). If it is updatable, simple variants of the UPDATE and

DELETE commands allow us to update or delete the row on which the cursor is positioned. For example, if *sinfo* is an updatable cursor and open, we can execute the following statement:

```
UPDATE  Sailors S
SET     S.rating = S.rating - 1
WHERE   CURRENT of sinfo;
```

This Embedded SQL statement modifies the *rating* value of the row currently pointed to by cursor *sinfo*; similarly, we can delete this row by executing the next statement:

```
DELETE  Sailors S
WHERE   CURRENT of sinfo;
```

A cursor is updatable by default unless it is a scrollable or insensitive cursor (see below), in which case it is read-only by default.

If the keyword SCROLL is specified, the cursor is **scrollable**, which means that variants of the FETCH command can be used to position the cursor in very flexible ways; otherwise, only the basic FETCH command, which retrieves the next row, is allowed.

If the keyword INSENSITIVE is specified, the cursor behaves as if it is ranging over a private copy of the collection of answer rows. Otherwise, and by default, other actions of some transaction could modify these rows, creating unpredictable behavior. For example, while we are fetching rows using the *sinfo* cursor, we might modify *rating* values in Sailor rows by concurrently executing the command:

```
UPDATE  Sailors S
SET     S.rating = S.rating - 1
```

Consider a Sailor row such that (1) it has not yet been fetched, and (2) its original *rating* value would have met the condition in the WHERE clause of the query associated with *sinfo*, but the new *rating* value does not. Do we fetch such a Sailor row? If INSENSITIVE is specified, the behavior is as if all answers were computed and stored when *sinfo* was opened; thus, the update command has no effect on the rows fetched by *sinfo* if it is executed after *sinfo* is opened. If INSENSITIVE is not specified, the behavior is implementation dependent in this situation.

A **holdable** cursor is specified using the WITH HOLD clause, and is not closed when the transaction is committed. The motivation for this comes from long transactions in which we access (and possibly change) a large number of rows of a table. If the transaction is aborted for any reason, the system potentially has to redo a lot of work when the transaction is restarted. Even if the transaction is not aborted, its locks are held for a long time and reduce the concurrency of the system. The alternative is to break the transaction into several smaller transactions, but remembering our position in the table between transactions (and other similar details) is complicated and error-prone. Allowing the application program to commit the transaction it initiated, while retaining its handle on the active table (i.e., the cursor) solves this problem: The application can commit its transaction and start a new transaction and thereby save the changes it has made thus far.

Finally, in what order do `FETCH` commands retrieve rows? In general this order is unspecified, but the optional `ORDER BY` clause can be used to specify a sort order. Note that columns mentioned in the `ORDER BY` clause cannot be updated through the cursor!

The **order-item-list** is a list of **order-items**; an order-item is a column name, optionally followed by one of the keywords `ASC` or `DESC`. Every column mentioned in the `ORDER BY` clause must also appear in the **select-list** of the query associated with the cursor; otherwise it is not clear what columns we should sort on. The keywords `ASC` or `DESC` that follow a column control whether the result should be sorted—with respect to that column—in ascending or descending order; the default is `ASC`. This clause is applied as the last step in evaluating the query.

Consider the query discussed in Section 5.5.1, and the answer shown in Figure 5.13. Suppose that a cursor is opened on this query, with the clause:

```
ORDER BY minage ASC, rating DESC
```

The answer is sorted first in ascending order by *minage*, and if several rows have the same *minage* value, these rows are sorted further in descending order by *rating*. The cursor would fetch the rows in the order shown in Figure 6.1.

rating	*minage*
8	25.5
3	25.5
7	35.0

Figure 6.1 Order in which Tuples Are Fetched

6.1.3 Dynamic SQL

Consider an application such as a spreadsheet or a graphical front-end that needs to access data from a DBMS. Such an application must accept commands from a user and, based on what the user needs, generate appropriate SQL statements to retrieve the necessary data. In such situations, we may not be able to predict in advance just what SQL statements need to be executed, even though there is (presumably) some algorithm by which the application can construct the necessary SQL statements once a user's command is issued.

SQL provides some facilities to deal with such situations; these are referred to as **Dynamic SQL**. We illustrate the two main commands, PREPARE and EXECUTE, through a simple example:

```
char c sqlstring[] = {"DELETE FROM Sailors WHERE rating>5"};
EXEC SQL PREPARE readytogo FROM :c sqlstring;
EXEC SQL EXECUTE readytogo;
```

The first statement declares the C variable *c sqlstring* and initializes its value to the string representation of an SQL command. The second statement results in this string being parsed and compiled as an SQL command, with the resulting executable bound to the SQL variable *readytogo*. (Since *readytogo* is an SQL variable, just like a cursor name, it is not prefixed by a colon.) The third statement executes the command.

Many situations require the use of Dynamic SQL. However, note that the preparation of a Dynamic SQL command occurs at run-time and is run-time overhead. Interactive and Embedded SQL commands can be prepared once at compile-time and then re-executed as often as desired. Consequently you should limit the use of Dynamic SQL to situations in which it is essential.

There are many more things to know about Dynamic SQL—how we can pass parameters from the host language program to the SQL statement being prepared, for example—but we do not discuss it further.

6.2 AN INTRODUCTION TO JDBC

Embedded SQL enables the integration of SQL with a general-purpose programming language. As described in Section 6.1.1, a DBMS-specific preprocessor transforms the Embedded SQL statements into function calls in the host language. The details of this translation vary across DBMSs, and therefore even though the source code can be compiled to work with different DBMSs, the final executable works only with one specific DBMS.

ODBC and **JDBC**, short for Open DataBase Connectivity and Java DataBase Connectivity, also enable the integration of SQL with a general-purpose programming language. Both ODBC and JDBC expose database capabilities in a standardized way to the application programmer through an **application programming interface (API)**. In contrast to Embedded SQL, ODBC and JDBC allow a single executable to access different DBMSs *without recompilation.* Thus, while Embedded SQL is DBMS-independent only at the source code level, applications using ODBC or JDBC are DBMS-independent at the source code level and at the level of the executable. In addition, using ODBC or JDBC, an application can access not just one DBMS but several different ones simultaneously.

ODBC and JDBC achieve portability at the level of the executable by introducing an extra level of indirection. All direct interaction with a specific DBMS happens through a DBMS-specific **driver**. A driver is a software program that translates the ODBC or JDBC calls into DBMS-specific calls. Drivers are loaded dynamically on demand since the DBMSs the application is going to access are known only at run-time. Available drivers are registered with a **driver manager**.

One interesting point to note is that a driver does not necessarily need to interact with a DBMS that understands SQL. It is sufficient that the driver translates the SQL commands from the application into equivalent commands that the DBMS understands. Therefore, in the remainder of this section, we refer to a data storage subsystem with which a driver interacts as a **data source**.

An application that interacts with a data source through ODBC or JDBC selects a data source, dynamically loads the corresponding driver, and establishes a connection with the data source. There is no limit on the number of open connections, and an application can have several open connections to different data sources. Each connection has transaction semantics; that is, changes from one connection are visible to other connections only after the connection has committed its changes. While a connection is open, transactions are executed by submitting SQL statements, retrieving results, processing errors, and finally committing or rolling back. The application disconnects from the data source to terminate the interaction.

In the remainder of this chapter, we concentrate on JDBC.

JDBC Drivers: The most up-to-date source of JDBC drivers is the Sun JDBC Driver page at
`http://industry.java.sun.com/products/jdbc/drivers`
JDBC drivers are available for all major database sytems.

6.2.1 Architecture

The architecture of JDBC has four main components: the *application*, the *driver manager*, several data source specific *drivers*, and the corresponding *data sources*.

The *application* initiates and terminates the connection with a data source. It sets transaction boundaries, submits SQL statements, and retrieves the results—all through a well-defined interface as specified by the JDBC API. The primary goal of the *driver manager* is to load JDBC drivers and pass JDBC function calls from the application to the correct driver. The driver manager also handles JDBC initialization and information calls from the applications and can log all function calls. In addition, the driver manager performs some rudimentary error checking. The *driver* establishes the connection with the data source. In addition to submitting requests and returning request results, the driver translates data, error formats, and error codes from a form that is specific to the data source into the JDBC standard. The *data source* processes commands from the driver and returns the results.

Depending on the relative location of the data source and the application, several architectural scenarios are possible. Drivers in JDBC are classified into four types depending on the architectural relationship between the application and the data source:

- **Type I—Bridges:** This type of driver translates JDBC function calls into function calls of another API that is not native to the DBMS. An example is a JDBC-ODBC bridge; an application can use JDBC calls to access an ODBC compliant data source. The application loads only one driver, the bridge. Bridges have the advantage that it is easy to piggyback the application onto an existing installation, and no new drivers have to be installed. But using bridges has several drawbacks. The increased number of layers between data source and application affects performance. In addition, the user is limited to the functionality that the ODBC driver supports.

- **Type II—Direct Translation to the Native API via Non-Java Driver:** This type of driver translates JDBC function calls directly into method invocations of the API of one specific data source. The driver is usually written using a combination of C++ and Java; it is dynamically linked and specific to the data source. This architecture performs significantly better than a JDBC-ODBC bridge. One disadvantage is that the database driver that implements the API needs to be installed on each computer that runs the application.

- **Type III—Network Bridges:** The driver talks over a network to a middleware server that translates the JDBC requests into DBMS-specific method invocations. In this case, the driver on the client site (i.e., the network bridge) is not DBMS-specific. The JDBC driver loaded by the application can be quite small, as the only functionality it needs to implement is sending of SQL statements to the middleware server. The middleware server can then use a Type II JDBC driver to connect to the data source.

- **Type IV—Direct Translation to the Native API via Java Driver:** Instead of calling the DBMS API directly, the driver communicates with the DBMS through Java sockets. In this case, the driver on the client side is written in Java, but it is DBMS-specific. It translates JDBC calls into the native API of the database system. This solution does not require an intermediate layer, and since the implementation is all Java, its performance is usually quite good.

6.3 JDBC CLASSES AND INTERFACES

JDBC is a collection of Java classes and interfaces that enables database access from programs written in the Java language. It contains methods for connecting to a remote data source, executing SQL statements, examining sets of results from SQL statements, transaction management, and exception handling. The classes and interfaces are part of the `java.sql` package. Thus, all code fragments in the remainder of this section should include the statement `import java.sql.*` at the beginning of the code; we omit this statement in the remainder of this section. JDBC 2.0 also includes the `javax.sql` package, the **JDBC Optional Package**. The package `javax.sql` adds, among other things, the capability of connection pooling and the `RowSet` interface. We discuss connection pooling in Section 6.3.2, and the `ResultSet` interface in Section 6.3.4.

We now illustrate the individual steps that are required to submit a database query to a data source and to retrieve the results.

6.3.1 JDBC Driver Management

In JDBC, data source drivers are managed by the `Drivermanager` class, which maintains a list of all currently loaded drivers. The `Drivermanager` class has methods `registerDriver`, `deregisterDriver`, and `getDrivers` to enable dynamic addition and deletion of drivers.

The first step in connecting to a data source is to load the corresponding JDBC driver. This is accomplished by using the Java mechanism for dynamically loading classes. The static method `forName` in the `Class` class returns the Java class as specified in the argument string and executes its `static` constructor. The static constructor of the dynamically loaded class loads an instance of the `Driver` class, and this `Driver` object registers itself with the `DriverManager` class.

The following Java example code explicitly loads a JDBC driver:

```
Class.forName(``oracle/jdbc.driver.OracleDriver'');
```

There are two other ways of registering a driver. We can include the driver with `-Djdbc.drivers=oracle/jdbc.driver` at the command line when we start the Java application. Alternatively, we can explicitly instantiate a driver, but this method is used only rarely, as the name of the driver has to be specified in the application code, and thus the application becomes sensitive to changes at the driver level.

After registering the driver, we connect to the data source.

6.3.2 Connections

A session with a data source is started through creation of a `Connection` object. A connection identifies a logical session with a data source; multiple connections within the same Java program can refer to different data sources or the same data source. Connections are specified through a **JDBC URL**, a URL that uses the jdbc protocol. Such a URL has the form

```
jdbc:<subprotocol>:<otherParameters>
```

The code example shown in Figure 6.2 establishes a connection to an Oracle database assuming that the strings `userId` and `password` are set to valid values.

In JDBC, connections can have different properties. For example, a connection can specify the granularity of transactions. If `autocommit` is set for a connection, then each SQL statement is considered to be its own transaction. If `autocommit` is off, then a series of statements that compose a transaction can be committed using the `commit()` method of the `Connection` class, or aborted using the `rollback()` method. The `Connection` class has methods to set the

```
String url = "jdbc:oracle:www.bookstore.com:3083"
Connection connection;
try {
    Connection connection =
        DriverManager.getConnection(url,userId,password);
}
catch(SQLException excpt) {
    System.out.println(excpt.getMessage());
    return;
}
```

Figure 6.2 Establishing a Connection with JDBC

> **JDBC Connections:** Remember to close connections to data sources and return shared connections to the connection pool. Database systems have a limited number of resources available for connections, and orphan connections can often only be detected through time-outs—and while the database system is waiting for the connection to time-out, the resources used by the orphan connection are wasted.

autocommit mode (`Connection.setAutoCommit`) and to retrieve the current autocommit mode (`getAutoCommit`). The following methods are part of the `Connection` interface and permit setting and getting other properties:

- `public int getTransactionIsolation() throws SQLException` and `public void setTransactionIsolation(int l) throws SQLException`. These two functions get and set the current level of isolation for transactions handled in the current connection. All five SQL levels of isolation (see Section 16.6 for a full discussion) are possible, and argument l can be set as follows:
  - `TRANSACTION_NONE`
  - `TRANSACTION_READ_UNCOMMITTED`
  - `TRANSACTION_READ_COMMITTED`
  - `TRANSACTION_REPEATABLE_READ`
  - `TRANSACTION_SERIALIZABLE`
- `public boolean getReadOnly() throws SQLException` and `public void setReadOnly(boolean readOnly) throws SQLException`. These two functions allow the user to specify whether the transactions executed through this connection are read only.

- `public boolean isClosed() throws SQLException`.
  Checks whether the current connection has already been closed.

- `setAutoCommit` and `get AutoCommit`.
  We already discussed these two functions.

Establishing a connection to a data source is a costly operation since it involves several steps, such as establishing a network connection to the data source, authentication, and allocation of resources such as memory. In case an application establishes many different connections from different parties (such as a Web server), connections are often **pooled** to avoid this overhead. A **connection pool** is a set of established connections to a data source. Whenever a new connection is needed, one of the connections from the pool is used, instead of creating a new connection to the data source.

Connection pooling can be handled either by specialized code in the application, or the optional `javax.sql` package, which provides functionality for connection pooling and allows us to set different parameters, such as the capacity of the pool, and shrinkage and growth rates. Most application servers (see Section 7.7.2) implement the `javax.sql` package or a proprietary variant.

6.3.3 Executing SQL Statements

We now discuss how to create and execute SQL statements using JDBC. In the JDBC code examples in this section, we assume that we have a `Connection` object named `con`. JDBC supports three different ways of executing statements: `Statement`, `PreparedStatement`, and `CallableStatement`. The `Statement` class is the base class for the other two statment classes. It allows us to query the data source with any static or dynamically generated SQL query. We cover the `PreparedStatement` class here and the `CallableStatement` class in Section 6.5, when we discuss stored procedures.

The `PreparedStatement` class dynamically generates precompiled SQL statements that can be used several times; these SQL statements can have parameters, but their structure is fixed when the `PreparedStatement` object (representing the SQL statement) is created.

Consider the sample code using a `PreparedStatment` object shown in Figure 6.3. The SQL query specifies the query string, but uses '?' for the values of the parameters, which are set later using methods `setString`, `setFloat`, and `setInt`. The '?' placeholders can be used anywhere in SQL statements where they can be replaced with a value. Examples of places where they can appear include the `WHERE` clause (e.g., '`WHERE author=?`'), or in SQL `UPDATE` and `INSERT` statements, as in Figure 6.3. The method `setString` is one way

```
// initial quantity is always zero
String sql = "INSERT INTO Books VALUES(?, ?, ?, ?, 0, ?)";
PreparedStatement pstmt = con.prepareStatement(sql);

// now instantiate the parameters with values
// assume that isbn, title, etc. are Java variables that
// contain the values to be inserted
pstmt.clearParameters();
pstmt.setString(1, isbn);
pstmt.setString(2, title);
pstmt.setString(3, author);
pstmt.setFloat(5, price);
pstmt.setInt(6, year);

int numRows = pstmt.executeUpdate();
```

Figure 6.3 SQL Update Using a `PreparedStatement` Object

to set a parameter value; analogous methods are available for `int`, `float`, and `date`. It is good style to always use `clearParameters()` before setting parameter values in order to remove any old data.

There are different ways of submitting the query string to the data source. In the example, we used the `executeUpdate` command, which is used if we know that the SQL statement does not return any records (SQL `UPDATE`, `INSERT`, `ALTER`, and `DELETE` statements). The `executeUpdate` method returns an integer indicating the number of rows the SQL statement modified; it returns 0 for successful execution without modifying any rows.

The `executeQuery` method is used if the SQL statement returns data, such as in a regular `SELECT` query. JDBC has its own cursor mechanism in the form of a `ResultSet` object, which we discuss next. The `execute` method is more general than `executeQuery` and `executeUpdate`; the references at the end of the chapter provide pointers with more details.

6.3.4 ResultSets

As discussed in the previous section, the statement `executeQuery` returns a `ResultSet` object, which is similar to a cursor. `ResultSet` cursors in JDBC 2.0 are very powerful; they allow forward and reverse scrolling and in-place editing and insertions.

In its most basic form, the ResultSet object allows us to read one row of the output of the query at a time. Initially, the ResultSet is positioned before the first row, and we have to retrieve the first row with an explicit call to the next() method. The next method returns false if there are no more rows in the query answer, and true otherwise. The code fragment shown in Figure 6.4 illustrates the basic usage of a ResultSet object.

```
ResultSet rs=stmt.executeQuery(sqlQuery);
// rs is now a cursor
// first call to rs.next() moves to the first record
// rs.next() moves to the next row
String sqlQuery;
ResultSet rs = stmt.executeQuery(sqlQuery)
while (rs.next()) {
    // process the data
}
```

Figure 6.4 Using a ResultSet Object

While next() allows us to retrieve the logically next row in the query answer, we can move about in the query answer in other ways too:

- previous() moves back one row.
- absolute(int num) moves to the row with the specified number.
- relative(int num) moves forward or backward (if num is negative) relative to the current position. relative(-1) has the same effect as previous.
- first() moves to the first row, and last() moves to the last row.

Matching Java and SQL Data Types

In considering the interaction of an application with a data source, the issues we encountered in the context of Embedded SQL (e.g., passing information between the application and the data source through shared variables) arise again. To deal with such issues, JDBC provides special data types and specifies their relationship to corresponding SQL data types. Figure 6.5 shows the **accessor methods** in a ResultSet object for the most common SQL datatypes. With these accessor methods, we can retrieve values from the current row of the query result referenced by the ResultSet object. There are two forms for each accessor method: One method retrieves values by column index, starting at one, and the other retrieves values by column name. The following example shows how to access fields of the current ResultSet row using accesssor methods.

SQL Type	Java class	ResultSet get method
BIT	Boolean	getBoolean()
CHAR	String	getString()
VARCHAR	String	getString()
DOUBLE	Double	getDouble()
FLOAT	Double	getDouble()
INTEGER	Integer	getInt()
REAL	Double	getFloat()
DATE	java.sql.Date	getDate()
TIME	java.sql.Time	getTime()
TIMESTAMP	java.sql.TimeStamp	getTimestamp()

Figure 6.5 Reading SQL Datatypes from a ResultSet Object

```
ResultSet rs=stmt.executeQuery(sqlQuery);
String sqlQuery;
ResultSet rs = stmt.executeQuery(sqlQuery)
while (rs.next()) {
    isbn = rs.getString(1);
    title = rs.getString("TITLE");
    // process isbn and title
}
```

6.3.5 Exceptions and Warnings

Similar to the `SQLSTATE` variable, most of the methods in `java.sql` can throw an exception of the type `SQLException` if an error occurs. The information includes `SQLState`, a string that describes the error (e.g., whether the statement contained an SQL syntax error). In addition to the standard `getMessage()` method inherited from `Throwable`, `SQLException` has two additional methods that provide further information, and a method to get (or chain) additional exceptions:

- `public String getSQLState()` returns an SQLState identifier based on the SQL:1999 specification, as discussed in Section 6.1.1.
- `public int getErrorCode()` retrieves a vendor-specific error code.
- `public SQLException getNextException()` gets the next exception in a chain of exceptions associated with the current SQLException object.

An SQLWarning is a subclass of SQLException. Warnings are not as severe as errors and the program can usually proceed without special handling of warnings. Warnings are not thrown like other exceptions, and they are not caught as part of the `try–catch` block around a `java.sql` statement. We need to specifically test whether warnings exist. `Connection`, `Statement`, and `ResultSet` objects all have a `getWarnings()` method with which we can retrieve SQL warnings if they exist. Duplicate retrieval of warnings can be avoided through `clearWarnings()`. `Statement` objects clear warnings automatically on execution of the next statement; `ResultSet` objects clear warnings every time a new tuple is accessed.

Typical code for obtaining SQLWarnings looks similar to the code shown in Figure 6.6.

```
try {
    stmt = con.createStatement();
    warning = con.getWarnings();
    while( warning != null) {
        // handleSQLWarnings                    //code to process warning
        warning = warning.getNextWarning();     //get next warning
    }
    con.clearWarnings();

    stmt.executeUpdate( queryString );
    warning = stmt.getWarnings();
    while( warning != null) {
        // handleSQLWarnings                    //code to process warning
        warning = warning.getNextWarning();     //get next warning
    }
} // end try
catch ( SQLException SQLe) {
    // code to handle exception
} // end catch
```

Figure 6.6 Processing JDBC Warnings and Exceptions

6.3.6 Examining Database Metadata

We can use the `DatabaseMetaData` object to obtain information about the database system itself, as well as information from the database catalog. For example, the following code fragment shows how to obtain the name and driver version of the JDBC driver:

```
DatabaseMetaData md = con.getMetaData();

System.out.println("Driver Information:");
```

```
System.out.println("Name:" + md.getDriverName()
            + "; version:" + md.getDriverVersion());
```

The `DatabaseMetaData` object has many more methods (in JDBC 2.0, exactly 134); we list some methods here:

- `public ResultSet getCatalogs() throws SQLException`. This function returns a ResultSet that can be used to iterate over all the catalog relations. The functions `getIndexInfo()` and `getTables()` work analogously.
- `public int getMaxConnections() throws SQLException`. This function returns the maximum number of connections possible.

We will conclude our discussion of JDBC with an example code fragment that examines all database metadata shown in Figure 6.7.

```
DatabaseMetaData dmd = con.getMetaData();
ResultSet tablesRS = dmd.getTables(null,null,null,null);
string tableName;

while(tablesRS.next()) {
    tableName = tablesRS.getString("TABLE_NAME");

        // print out the attributes of this table
        System.out.println("The attributes of table "
                    + tableName + " are:");
        ResultSet columnsRS = dmd.getColums(null,null,tableName, null);
        while (columnsRS.next()) {
            System.out.print(colummsRS.getString("COLUMN_NAME")
                        + " ");
        }

        // print out the primary keys of this table
        System.out.println("The keys of table " + tableName + " are:");
        ResultSet keysRS = dmd.getPrimaryKeys(null,null,tableName);
        while (keysRS.next()) {
            System.out.print(keysRS.getString("COLUMN_NAME") + " ");
        }
}
```

Figure 6.7 Obtaining Information about a Data Source

6.4 SQLJ

SQLJ (short for 'SQL-Java') was developed by the SQLJ Group, a group of database vendors and Sun. SQLJ was developed to complement the dynamic way of creating queries in JDBC with a static model. It is therefore very close to Embedded SQL. Unlike JDBC, having semi-static SQL queries allows the compiler to perform SQL syntax checks, strong type checks of the compatibility of the host variables with the respective SQL attributes, and consistency of the query with the database schema—tables, attributes, views, and stored procedures—all at compilation time. For example, in both SQLJ and Embedded SQL, variables in the host language always are bound statically to the same arguments, whereas in JDBC, we need separate statements to bind each variable to an argument and to retrieve the result. For example, the following SQLJ statement binds host language variables title, price, and author to the return values of the cursor `books`.

```
#sql books = {
    SELECT title, price INTO :title, :price
    FROM Books WHERE author = :author
};
```

In JDBC, we can dynamically decide which host language variables will hold the query result. In the following example, we read the title of the book into variable ftitle if the book was written by Feynman, and into variable otitle otherwise:

```
// assume we have a ResultSet cursor rs
author = rs.getString(3);

if (author=="Feynman") {
    ftitle = rs.getString(2);
}
else {
    otitle = rs.getString(2);
}
```

When writing SQLJ applications, we just write regular Java code and embed SQL statements according to a set of rules. SQLJ applications are pre-processed through an SQLJ translation program that replaces the embedded SQLJ code with calls to an SQLJ Java library. The modified program code can then be compiled by any Java compiler. Usually the SQLJ Java library makes calls to a JDBC driver, which handles the connection to the database system.

An important philosophical difference exists between Embedded SQL and SQLJ and JDBC. Since vendors provide their own proprietary versions of SQL, it is advisable to write SQL queries according to the SQL-92 or SQL:1999 standard. However, when using Embedded SQL, it is tempting to use vendor-specific SQL constructs that offer functionality beyond the SQL-92 or SQL:1999 standards. SQLJ and JDBC force adherence to the standards, and the resulting code is much more portable across different database systems.

In the remainder of this section, we give a short introduction to SQLJ.

6.4.1 Writing SQLJ Code

We will introduce SQLJ by means of examples. Let us start with an SQLJ code fragment that selects records from the Books table that match a given author.

```
String title; Float price; String author;
#sql iterator Books (String title, Float price);
Books books;

// the application sets the author
// execute the query and open the cursor
#sql books = {
    SELECT title, price INTO :title, :price
    FROM Books WHERE author = :author
};

// retrieve results
while (books.next()) {
    System.out.println(books.title() + ", " + books.price());
}
books.close();
```

The corresponding JDBC code fragment looks as follows (assuming we also declared `price`, `name`, and `author`:

```
PreparedStatement stmt = connection.prepareStatement(
"SELECT title, price FROM Books WHERE author = ?");

// set the parameter in the query and execute it
stmt.setString(1, author);
ResultSet rs = stmt.executeQuery();

// retrieve the results
while (rs.next()) {
```

```
System.out.println(rs.getString(1) + ", " + rs.getFloat(2));
}
```

Comparing the JDBC and SQLJ code, we see that the SQLJ code is much easier to read than the JDBC code. Thus, SQLJ reduces software development and maintenance costs.

Let us consider the individual components of the SQLJ code in more detail. All SQLJ statements have the special prefix `#sql`. In SQLJ, we retrieve the results of SQL queries with **iterator** objects, which are basically cursors. An iterator is an instance of an iterator class. Usage of an iterator in SQLJ goes through five steps:

- **Declare the Iterator Class:** In the preceding code, this happened through the statement
  `#sql iterator Books (String title, Float price);`
  This statement creates a new Java class that we can use to instantiate objects.

- **Instantiate an Iterator Object from the New Iterator Class:** We instantiated our iterator in the statement `Books books;`.

- **Initialize the Iterator Using a SQL Statement:** In our example, this happens through the statement `#sql books = ....`

- **Iteratively, Read the Rows From the Iterator Object:** This step is very similar to reading rows through a `ResultSet` object in JDBC.

- **Close the Iterator Object.**

There are two types of iterator classes: named iterators and positional iterators. For **named iterators**, we specify both the variable type and the name of each column of the iterator. This allows us to retrieve individual columns by name as in our previous example where we could retrieve the title column from the Books table using the expression `books.title()`. For **positional iterators**, we need to specify only the variable type for each column of the iterator. To access the individual columns of the iterator, we use a `FETCH ... INTO` construct, similar to Embedded SQL. Both iterator types have the same performance; which iterator to use depends on the programmer's taste.

Let us revisit our example. We can make the iterator a positional iterator through the following statement:

```
#sql iterator Books (String, Float);
```

We then retrieve the individual rows from the iterator as follows:

```
while (true) {
    #sql { FETCH :books INTO :title, :price, };
    if (books.endFetch()) {
        break;
    }

    // process the book
}
```

6.5 STORED PROCEDURES

It is often important to execute some parts of the application logic directly in the process space of the database system. Running application logic directly at the database has the advantage that the amount of data that is transferred between the database server and the client issuing the SQL statement can be minimized, while at the same time utilizing the full power of the database server.

When SQL statements are issued from a remote application, the records in the result of the query need to be transferred from the database system back to the application. If we use a cursor to remotely access the results of an SQL statement, the DBMS has resources such as locks and memory tied up while the application is processing the records retrieved through the cursor. In contrast, a **stored procedure** is a program that is executed through a single SQL statement that can be locally executed and completed within the process space of the database server. The results can be packaged into one big result and returned to the application, or the application logic can be performed directly at the server, without having to transmit the results to the client at all.

Stored procedures are also beneficial for software engineering reasons. Once a stored procedure is registered with the database server, different users can re-use the stored procedure, eliminating duplication of efforts in writing SQL queries or application logic, and making code maintenance easy. In addition, application programmers do not need to know the the database schema if we encapsulate all database access into stored procedures.

Although they are called stored *procedures*, they do not have to be procedures in a programming language sense; they can be functions.

6.5.1 Creating a Simple Stored Procedure

Let us look at the example stored procedure written in SQL shown in Figure 6.8. We see that stored procedures must have a name; this stored procedure has the name 'ShowNumberOfOrders.' Otherwise, it just contains an SQL statement that is precompiled and stored at the server.

```
CREATE PROCEDURE ShowNumberOfOrders
SELECT C.cid, C.cname, COUNT(*)
       FROM      Customers C, Orders O
       WHERE     C.cid = O.cid
       GROUP BY  C.cid, C.cname
```

Figure 6.8 A Stored Procedure in SQL

Stored procedures can also have parameters. These parameters have to be valid SQL types, and have one of three different **modes**: IN, OUT, or INOUT. IN parameters are arguments to the stored procedure. OUT parameters are returned from the stored procedure; it assigns values to all OUT parameters that the user can process. INOUT parameters combine the properties of IN and OUT parameters: They contain values to be passed to the stored procedures, and the stored procedure can set their values as return values. Stored procedures enforce strict type conformance: If a parameter is of type INTEGER, it cannot be called with an argument of type VARCHAR.

Let us look at an example of a stored procedure with arguments. The stored procedure shown in Figure 6.9 has two arguments: book_isbn and addedQty. It updates the available number of copies of a book with the quantity from a new shipment.

```
CREATE PROCEDURE AddInventory (
                 IN book_isbn CHAR(10),
                 IN addedQty INTEGER)
UPDATE Books
       SET    qty_in_stock = qty_in_stock + addedQty
       WHERE  book_isbn = isbn
```

Figure 6.9 A Stored Procedure with Arguments

Stored procedures do not have to be written in SQL; they can be written in any host language. As an example, the stored procedure shown in Figure 6.10 is a Java function that is dynamically executed by the database server whenever it is called by the client:

6.5.2 Calling Stored Procedures

Stored procedures can be called in interactive SQL with the CALL statement:

```
CREATE PROCEDURE RankCustomers(IN number INTEGER)
LANGUAGE Java
EXTERNAL NAME 'file:///c:/storedProcedures/rank.jar'
```

Figure 6.10 A Stored Procedure in Java

```
CALL storedProcedureName(argument1, argument2, ..., argumentN);
```

In Embedded SQL, the arguments to a stored procedure are usually variables in the host language. For example, the stored procedure `AddInventory` would be called as follows:

```
EXEC SQL BEGIN DECLARE SECTION
char isbn[10];
long qty;
EXEC SQL END DECLARE SECTION

// set isbn and qty to some values
EXEC SQL CALL AddInventory(:isbn,:qty);
```

Calling Stored Procedures from JDBC

We can call stored procedures from JDBC using the `CallableStatment` class. `CallableStatement` is a subclass of `PreparedStatement` and provides the same functionality. A stored procedure could contain multiple SQL statements or a series of SQL statements—thus, the result could be many different `ResultSet` objects. We illustrate the case when the stored procedure result is a single `ResultSet`.

```
CallableStatement cstmt=
            con.prepareCall("{call ShowNumberOfOrders}");
ResultSet rs = cstmt.executeQuery()
while (rs.next())
    ...
```

Calling Stored Procedures from SQLJ

The stored procedure 'ShowNumberOfOrders' is called as follows using SQLJ:

```
// create the cursor class
#sql Iterator CustomerInfo(int cid, String cname, int count);

// create the cursor
```

```
CustomerInfo customerinfo;

// call the stored procedure
#sql customerinfo = {CALL ShowNumberOfOrders};
while (customerinfo.next()) {
    System.out.println(customerinfo.cid() + "," +
                       customerinfo.count());
}
```

6.5.3 SQL/PSM

All major database systems provide ways for users to write stored procedures in a simple, general purpose language closely aligned with SQL. In this section, we briefly discuss the SQL/PSM standard, which is representative of most vendor-specific languages. In PSM, we define **modules**, which are collections of stored procedures, temporary relations, and other declarations.

In SQL/PSM, we declare a stored procedure as follows:

```
CREATE PROCEDURE name (parameter1,..., parameterN)
    local variable declarations
    procedure code;
```

We can declare a function similarly as follows:

```
CREATE FUNCTION name (parameter1,..., parameterN)
            RETURNS sqlDataType
    local variable declarations
    function code;
```

Each parameter is a triple consisting of the mode (IN, OUT, or INOUT as discussed in the previous section), the parameter name, and the SQL datatype of the parameter. We can seen very simple SQL/PSM procedures in Section 6.5.1. In this case, the local variable declarations were empty, and the procedure code consisted of an SQL query.

We start out with an example of a SQL/PSM function that illustrates the main SQL/PSM constructs. The function takes as input a customer identified by her *cid* and a year. The function returns the rating of the customer, which is defined as follows: Customers who have bought more than ten books during the year are rated 'two'; customer who have purchased between 5 and 10 books are rated 'one', otherwise the customer is rated 'zero'. The following SQL/PSM code computes the rating for a given customer and year.

```
CREATE PROCEDURE RateCustomer
```

```
                (IN custId INTEGER, IN year INTEGER)
                RETURNS INTEGER
DECLARE rating INTEGER;
DECLARE numOrders INTEGER;
SET numOrders =
      (SELECT COUNT(*) FROM Orders O WHERE O.cid = custId);
IF (numOrders>10) THEN rating=2;
ELSEIF (numOrders>5) THEN rating=1;
ELSE rating=0;
END IF;
RETURN rating;
```

Let us use this example to give a short overview of some SQL/PSM constructs:

- We can declare local variables using the DECLARE statement. In our example, we declare two local variables: 'rating', and 'numOrders'.
- PSM/SQL functions return values via the RETURN statement. In our example, we return the value of the local variable 'rating'.
- We can assign values to variables with the SET statement. In our example, we assigned the return value of a query to the variable 'numOrders'.
- SQL/PSM has branches and loops. Branches have the following form:

  ```
  IF (condition) THEN statements;
  ELSEIF statements;
  ...
  ELSEIF statements;
  ELSE statements; END IF
  ```

  Loops are of the form

  ```
  LOOP
        statements;
  END LOOP
  ```

- Queries can be used as part of expressions in branches; queries that return a single value can be assigned to variables as in our example above.
- We can use the same cursor statements as in Embedded SQL (OPEN, FETCH, CLOSE), but we do not need the EXEC SQL constructs, and variables do not have to be prefixed by a colon ':'.

We only gave a very short overview of SQL/PSM; the references at the end of the chapter provide more information.

6.6 CASE STUDY: THE INTERNET BOOK SHOP

DBDudes finished logical database design, as discussed in Section 3.8, and now consider the queries that they have to support. They expect that the application logic will be implemented in Java, and so they consider JDBC and SQLJ as possible candidates for interfacing the database system with application code.

Recall that DBDudes settled on the following schema:

> Books(*isbn:* CHAR(10), *title:* CHAR(8), *author:* CHAR(80),
> *qty_in_stock:* INTEGER, *price:* REAL, *year_published:* INTEGER)
> Customers(*cid:* INTEGER, *cname:* CHAR(80), *address:* CHAR(200))
> Orders(*ordernum:* INTEGER, *isbn:* CHAR(10), *cid:* INTEGER,
> *cardnum:* CHAR(16), *qty:* INTEGER, *order_date:* DATE, *ship_date:* DATE)

Now, DBDudes considers the types of queries and updates that will arise. They first create a list of tasks that will be performed in the application. Tasks performed by customers include the following.

- Customers search books by author name, title, or ISBN.
- Customers register with the website. Registered customers might want to change their contact information. DBDudes realize that they have to augment the Customers table with additional information to capture login and password information for each customer; we do not discuss this aspect any further.
- Customers check out a final shopping basket to complete a sale.
- Customers add and delete books from a 'shopping basket' at the website.
- Customers check the status of existing orders and look at old orders.

Administrative tasks performed by employees of B&N are listed next.

- Employees look up customer contact information.
- Employees add new books to the inventory.
- Employees fulfill orders, and need to update the shipping date of individual books.
- Employees analyze the data to find profitable customers and customers likely to respond to special marketing campaigns.

Next, DBDudes consider the types of queries that will arise out of these tasks. To support searching for books by name, author, title, or ISBN, DBDudes decide to write a stored procedure as follows:

```
CREATE PROCEDURE SearchByISBN (IN book isbn CHAR(10))
    SELECT B.title, B.author, B.qty in stock, B.price, B.year published
    FROM   Books B
    WHERE  B.isbn = book isbn
```

Placing an order involves inserting one or more records into the Orders table. Since DBDudes has not yet chosen the Java-based technology to program the application logic, they assume for now that the individual books in the order are stored at the application layer in a Java array. To finalize the order, they write the following JDBC code shown in Figure 6.11, which inserts the elements from the array into the Orders table. Note that this code fragment assumes several Java variables have been set beforehand.

```
String sql = "INSERT INTO Orders VALUES(?, ?, ?, ?, ?, ?)";
PreparedStatement pstmt = con.prepareStatement(sql);
con.setAutoCommit(false);

try {
    // orderList is a vector of Order objects
    // ordernum is the current order number
    // cid is the ID of the customer, cardnum is the credit card number
    for (int i=0; i¡orderList.length(); i++)
        // now instantiate the parameters with values
        Order currentOrder = orderList[i];
        pstmt.clearParameters();
        pstmt.setInt(1, ordernum);
        pstmt.setString(2, Order.getIsbn());
        pstmt.setInt(3, cid);
        pstmt.setString(4, creditCardNum);
        pstmt.setInt(5, Order.getQty());
        pstmt.setDate(6, null);

        pstmt.executeUpdate();
    }
    con.commit();
catch (SQLException e){
    con.rollback();
    System.out.println(e.getMessage());
}
```

Figure 6.11 Inserting a Completed Order into the Database

DBDudes writes other JDBC code and stored procedures for all of the remaining tasks. They use code similar to some of the fragments that we have seen in this chapter.

- Establishing a connection to a database, as shown in Figure 6.2.
- Adding new books to the inventory, as shown in Figure 6.3.
- Processing results from SQL queries as shown in Figure 6.4.
- For each customer, showing how many orders he or she has placed. We showed a sample stored procedure for this query in Figure 6.8.
- Increasing the available number of copies of a book by adding inventory, as shown in Figure 6.9.
- Ranking customers according to their purchases, as shown in Figure 6.10.

DBDudes takes care to make the application robust by processing exceptions and warnings, as shown in Figure 6.6.

DBDudes also decide to write a trigger, which is shown in Figure 6.12. Whenever a new order is entered into the Orders table, it is inserted with ship_date set to NULL. The trigger processes each row in the order and calls the stored procedure 'UpdateShipDate'. This stored procedure (whose code is not shown here) updates the (anticipated) ship_date of the new order to 'tomorrow', in case qty_in_stock of the corresponding book in the Books table is greater than zero. Otherwise, the stored procedure sets the ship_date to two weeks.

```
CREATE TRIGGER update_ShipDate
        AFTER INSERT ON Orders                    /* Event */
    FOR EACH ROW
    BEGIN CALL UpdateShipDate(new); END           /* Action */
```

Figure 6.12 Trigger to Update the Shipping Date of New Orders

6.7 REVIEW QUESTIONS

Answers to the review questions can be found in the listed sections.

- Why is it not straightforward to integrate SQL queries with a host programming language? **(Section 6.1.1)**
- How do we declare variables in Embedded SQL? **(Section 6.1.1)**

- How do we use SQL statements within a host language? How do we check for errors in statement execution? **(Section 6.1.1)**
- Explain the impedance mismatch between host languages and SQL, and describe how cursors address this. **(Section 6.1.2)**
- What properties can cursors have? **(Section 6.1.2)**
- What is Dynamic SQL and how is it different from Embedded SQL? **(Section 6.1.3)**
- What is JDBC and what are its advantages? **(Section 6.2)**
- What are the components of the JDBC architecture? Describe four different architectural alternatives for JDBC drivers. **(Section 6.2.1)**
- How do we load JDBC drivers in Java code? **(Section 6.3.1)**
- How do we manage connections to data sources? What properties can connections have? **(Section 6.3.2)**
- What alternatives does JDBC provide for executing SQL DML and DDL statements? **(Section 6.3.3)**
- How do we handle exceptions and warnings in JDBC? **(Section 6.3.5)**
- What functionality provides the `DatabaseMetaData` class? **(Section 6.3.6)**
- What is SQLJ and how is it different from JDBC? **(Section 6.4)**
- Why are stored procedures important? How do we declare stored procedures and how are they called from application code? **(Section 6.5)**

EXERCISES

Exercise 6.1 Briefly answer the following questions.

1. Explain the following terms: Cursor, Embedded SQL, JDBC, SQLJ, stored procedure.
2. What are the differences between JDBC and SQLJ? Why do they both exist?
3. Explain the term *stored procedure*, and give examples why stored procedures are useful.

Exercise 6.2 Explain how the following steps are performed in JDBC:

1. Connect to a data source.
2. Start, commit, and abort transactions.
3. Call a stored procedure.

How are these steps performed in SQLJ?

Exercise 6.3 Compare exception handling and handling of warnings in embedded SQL, dynamic SQL, JDBC, and SQLJ.

Exercise 6.4 Answer the following questions.

1. Why do we need a precompiler to translate embedded SQL and SQLJ? Why do we not need a precompiler for JDBC?
2. SQLJ and embedded SQL use variables in the host language to pass parameters to SQL queries, whereas JDBC uses placeholders marked with a '?'. Explain the difference, and why the different mechanisms are needed.

Exercise 6.5 A dynamic web site generates HTML pages from information stored in a database. Whenever a page is requested, is it dynamically assembled from static data and data in a database, resulting in a database access. Connecting to the database is usually a time-consuming process, since resources need to be allocated, and the user needs to be authenticated. Therefore, **connection pooling**—setting up a pool of persistent database connections and then reusing them for different requests can significantly improve the performance of database-backed websites. Since servlets can keep information beyond single requests, we can create a connection pool, and allocate resources from it to new requests.

Write a connection pool class that provides the following methods:

- Create the pool with a specified number of open connections to the database system.
- Obtain an open connection from the pool.
- Release a connection to the pool.
- Destroy the pool and close all connections.

PROJECT-BASED EXERCISES

In the following exercises, you will create database-backed applications. In this chapter, you will create the parts of the application that access the database. In the next chapter, you will extend this code to other aspects of the application. Detailed information about these exercises and material for more exercises can be found online at

`http://www.cs.wisc.edu/~dbbook`

Exercise 6.6 Recall the Notown Records database that you worked with in Exercise 2.5 and Exercise 3.15. You have now been tasked with designing a website for Notown. It should provide the following functionality:

- Users can search for records by name of the musician, title of the album, and name of the song.
- Users can register with the site, and registered users can log on to the site. Once logged on, users should not have to log on again unless they are inactive for a long time.
- Users who have logged on to the site can add items to a shopping basket.
- Users with items in their shopping basket can check out and make a purchase.

Notown wants to use JDBC to access the database. Write JDBC code that performs the necessary data access and manipulation. You will integrate this code with application logic and presentation in the next chapter.

If Notown had chosen SQLJ instead of JDBC, how would your code change?

Exercise 6.7 Recall the database schema for Prescriptions-R-X that you created in Exercise 2.7. The Prescriptions-R-X chain of pharmacies has now engaged you to design their new website. The website has two different classes of users: doctors and patients. Doctors should be able to enter new prescriptions for their patients and modify existing prescriptions. Patients should be able to declare themselves as patients of a doctor; they should be able to check the status of their prescriptions online; and they should be able to purchase the prescriptions online so that the drugs can be shipped to their home address.

Follow the analogous steps from Exercise 6.6 to write JDBC code that performs the necessary data access and manipulation. You will integrate this code with application logic and presentation in the next chapter.

Exercise 6.8 Recall the university database schema that you worked with in Exercise 5.1. The university has decided to move enrollment to an online system. The website has two different classes of users: faculty and students. Faculty should be able to create new courses and delete existing courses, and students should be able to enroll in existing courses.

Follow the analogous steps from Exercise 6.6 to write JDBC code that performs the necessary data access and manipulation. You will integrate this code with application logic and presentation in the next chapter.

Exercise 6.9 Recall the airline reservation schema that you worked on in Exercise 5.3. Design an online airline reservation system. The reservation system will have two types of users: airline employees, and airline passengers. Airline employees can schedule new flights and cancel existing flights. Airline passengers can book existing flights from a given destination.

Follow the analogous steps from Exercise 6.6 to write JDBC code that performs the necessary data access and manipulation. You will integrate this code with application logic and presentation in the next chapter.

BIBLIOGRAPHIC NOTES

Information on ODBC can be found on Microsoft's web page (`www.microsoft.com/data/odbc`), and information on JDBC can be found on the Java web page (`java.sun.com/products/jdbc`). There exist many books on ODBC, for example, Sanders' ODBC Developer's Guide [652] and the Microsoft ODBC SDK [533]. Books on JDBC include works by Hamilton et al. [359], Reese [621], and White et al. [773].

7 INTERNET APPLICATIONS

- ☛ How do we name resources on the Internet?
- ☛ How do Web browsers and webservers communicate?
- ☛ How do we present documents on the Internet? How do we differentiate between formatting and content?
- ☛ What is a three-tier application architecture? How do we write three-tiered applications?
- ☛ Why do we have application servers?
- ➽ **Key concepts:** Uniform Resource Identifiers (URI), Uniform Resource Locators (URL); Hypertext Transfer Protocol (HTTP), stateless protocol; Java; HTML; XML, XML DTD; three-tier architecture, client-server architecture; HTML forms; JavaScript; cascading style sheets, XSL; application server; Common Gateway Interface (CGI); servlet; JavaServer Page (JSP); cookie

Wow! They've got the Internet on computers now!

—Homer Simpson, *The Simpsons*

7.1 INTRODUCTION

The proliferation of computer networks, including the Internet and corporate 'intranets,' has enabled users to access a large number of data sources. This increased access to databases is likely to have a great practical impact; data and services can now be offered directly to customers in ways impossible until recently. Examples of such **electronic commerce** applications include purchasing books through a Web retailer such as Amazon.com, engaging in online auctions at a site such as eBay, and exchanging bids and specifications for products between companies. The emergence of standards such as XML for describing the content of documents is likely to further accelerate electronic commerce and other online applications.

While the first generation of Internet sites were collections of HTML files, most major sites today store a large part (if not all) of their data in database systems. They rely on DBMSs to provide fast, reliable responses to user requests received over the Internet. This is especially true of sites for electronic commerce and other business applications.

In this chapter, we present an overview of concepts that are central to Internet application development. We start out with a basic overview of how the Internet works in Section 7.2. We introduce HTML and XML, two data formats that are used to present data on the Internet, in Sections 7.3 and 7.4. In Section 7.5, we introduce three-tier architectures, a way of structuring Internet applications into different layers that encapsulate different functionality. In Sections 7.6 and 7.7, we describe the presentation layer and the middle layer in detail; the DBMS is the third layer. We conclude the chapter by discussing our B&N case study in Section 7.8.

Examples that appear in this chapter are available online at

```
http://www.cs.wisc.edu/~dbbook
```

7.2 INTERNET CONCEPTS

The Internet has emerged as a universal connector between globally distributed software systems. To understand how it works, we begin by discussing two basic issues: how sites on the Internet are identified, and how programs at one site communicate with other sites.

We first introduce Uniform Resource Identifiers, a naming schema for locating resources on the Internet in Section 7.2.1. We then talk about the most popular protocol for accessing resources over the Web, the hypertext transfer protocol (HTTP) in Section 7.2.2.

7.2.1 Uniform Resource Identifiers

Uniform Resource Identifiers (URIs), are strings that uniquely identify resources on the Internet. A **resource** is any kind of information that can

Distributed Applications and Service-Oriented Architectures: The advent of XML, due to its loosely-coupled nature, has made information exchange between different applications feasible to an extent previously unseen. By using XML for information exchange, applications can be written in different programming languages, run on different operating systems, and yet they can still share information with each other. There are also standards for externally describing the intended content of an XML file or message, most notably the recently adopted W3C XML Schemas standard.

A promising concept that has arisen out of the XML revolution is the notion of a **Web service**. A Web service is an application that provides a well-defined service, packaged as a set of remotely callable procedures accessible through the Internet. Web services have the potential to enable powerful new applications by *composing* existing Web services—all communicating seamlessly thanks to the use of standardized XML-based information exchange. Several technologies have been developed or are currently under development that facilitate design and implementation of distributed applications. **SOAP** is a W3C standard for XML-based invocation of remote services (think XML RPC) that allows distributed applications to communicate either synchronously or asynchronously via structured, typed XML messages. SOAP calls can ride on a variety of underlying transport layers, including HTTP (part of what is making SOAP so successful) and various reliable messaging layers. Related to the SOAP standard are W3C's **Web Services Description Language (WSDL)** for describing Web service interfaces, and **Universal Description, Discovery, and Integration (UDDI)**, a WSDL-based Web services registry standard (think yellow pages for Web services).

SOAP-based Web services are the foundation for Microsoft's recently released **.NET** framework, their application development infrastructure and associated run-time system for developing distributed applications, as well as for the Web services offerings of major software vendors such as IBM, BEA, and others. Many large software application vendors (major companies like PeopleSoft and SAP) have announced plans to provide Web service interfaces to their products and the data that they manage, and many are hoping that XML and Web services will finally provide the answer to the long-standing problem of enterprise application integration. Web services are also being looked to as a natural foundation for the next generation of business process management (or workflow) systems.

be identified by a URI, and examples include webpages, images, downloadable files, services that can be remotely invoked, mailboxes, and so on. The most common kind of resource is a static file (such as a HTML document), but a resource may also be a dynamically-generated HTML file, a movie, the output of a program, etc.

A URI has three parts:

- The (name of the) protocol used to access the resource.
- The host computer where the resource is located.
- The path name of the resource itself on the host computer.

Consider an example URI, such as `http://www.bookstore.com/index.html`. This URI can be interpreted as follows. Use the HTTP protocol (explained in the next section) to retrieve the document `index.html` located at the computer `www.bookstore.com`. This example URI is an instance of a **Universal Resource Locator (URL)**, a subset of the more general URI naming scheme; the distinction is not important for our purposes. As another example, the following HTML fragment shows a URI that is an email address:

```
<a href="mailto:webmaster@bookstore.com">Email the webmaster.</A>
```

7.2.2 The Hypertext Transfer Protocol (HTTP)

A **communication protocol** is a set of standards that defines the structure of messages between two communicating parties so that they can understand each other's messages. The **Hypertext Transfer Protocol** (HTTP) is the most common communication protocol used over the Internet. It is a client-server protocol in which a client (usually a Web browser) sends a request to an HTTP server, which sends a response back to the client. When a user requests a webpage (e.g., clicks on a hyperlink), the browser sends **HTTP request messages** for the objects in the page to the server. The server receives the requests and responds with **HTTP response messages**, which include the objects. It is important to recognize that HTTP is used to transmit all kinds of resources, not just files, but most resources on the Internet today are either static files or files output from server-side scripts.

A variant of the HTTP protocol called the **Secure Sockets Layer (SSL)** protocol uses encryption to exchange information securely between client and server. We postpone a discussion of SSL to Section 21.5.2 and present the basic HTTP protocol in this chapter.

As an example, consider what happens if a user clicks on the following link: `http://www.bookstore.com/index.html`. We first explain the structure of an HTTP request message and then the structure of an HTTP response message.

HTTP Requests

The client (Web browser) establishes a connection with the webserver that hosts the resource and sends a HTTP request message. The following example shows a sample HTTP request message:

```
GET index.html HTTP/1.1
User-agent: Mozilla/4.0
Accept: text/html, image/gif, image/jpeg
```

The general structure of an HTTP request consists of several lines of ASCII text, with an empty line at the end. The first line, the **request line**, has three fields: the **HTTP method field**, the **URI field**, and the **HTTP version field**. The **method** field can take on values **GET** and **POST**; in the example the message requests the object `index.html`. (We discuss the differences between HTTP `GET` and HTTP `POST` in detail in Section 7.11.) The version field indicates which version of HTTP is used by the client and can be used for future extensions of the protocol. The **user agent** indicates the type of the client (e.g., versions of Netscape or Internet Explorer); we do not discuss this option further. The third line, starting with `Accept`, indicates what types of files the client is willing to accept. For example, if the page `index.html` contains a movie file with the extension `.mpg`, the server will not send this file to the client, as the client is not ready to accept it.

HTTP Responses

The server responds with an **HTTP response** message. It retrieves the page `index.html`, uses it to assemble the HTTP response message, and sends the message to the client. A sample HTTP response looks like this:

```
HTTP/1.1 200 OK
Date: Mon, 04 Mar 2002 12:00:00 GMT
Content-Length: 1024
Content-Type: text/html
Last-Modified: Mon, 22 Jun 1998 09:23:24 GMT
<HTML>
<HEAD>
</HEAD>
<BODY>
```

```
<H1>Barns and Nobble Internet Bookstore</H1>
Our inventory:
<H3>Science</H3>
<B>The Character of Physical Law</B>
...
```

The HTTP response message has three parts: a status line, several header lines, and the body of the message (which contains the actual object that the client requested). The **status line** has three fields (analogous to the request line of the HTTP request message): the HTTP version (`HTTP/1.1`), a status code (`200`), and an associated server message (`OK`). Common status codes and associated messages are:

- `200 OK`: The request succeeded and the object is contained in the body of the response message";
- `400 Bad Request`: A generic error code indicating that the request could not be fulfilled by the server.
- `404 Not Found`: The requested object does not exist on the server.
- `505 HTTP Version Not Supported`: The HTTP protocol version that the client uses is not supported by the server. (Recall that the HTTP protocol version sent in the client's request.)

Our example has three **header lines**: The date header line indicates the time and date when the HTTP response was created (not that this is not the object creation time). The `Last-Modified` header line indicates when the object was created. The `Content-Length` header line indicates the number of bytes in the object being sent after the last header line. The `Content-Type` header line indicates that the object in the entity body is HTML text.

The client (the Web browser) receives the response message, extracts the HTML file, parses it, and displays it. In doing so, it might find additional URIs in the file, and it then uses the HTTP protocol to retrieve each of these resources, establishing a new connection each time.

One important issue is that the HTTP protocol is a **stateless protocol**. Every message—from the client to the HTTP server and vice-versa—is self-contained, and the connection established with a request is maintained only until the response message is sent. The protocol provides no mechanism to automatically 'remember' previous interactions between client and server.

The stateless nature of the HTTP protocol has a major impact on how Internet applications are written. Consider a user who interacts with our example bookstore application. Assume that the bookstore permits users to log into the site and then carry out several actions, such as ordering books or changing their address, without logging in again (until the login expires or the user logs out). How do we keep track of whether a user is logged in or not? Since HTTP is stateless, we cannot switch to a different state (say the 'logged in' state) at the protocol level. Instead, for every request that the user (more precisely, his or her Web browser) sends to the server, we must encode any *state* information required by the application, such as the user's login status. Alternatively, the server-side application code must maintain this state information and look it up on a per-request basis. This issue is explored further in Section 7.7.5.

Note that the statelessness of HTTP is a tradeoff between ease of implementation of the HTTP protocol and ease of application development. The designers of HTTP chose to keep the protocol itself simple, and deferred any functionality beyond the request of objects to application layers above the HTTP protocol.

7.3 HTML DOCUMENTS

In this section and the next, we focus on introducing HTML and XML. In Section 7.6, we consider how applications can use HTML and XML to create forms that capture user input, communicate with an HTTP server, and convert the results produced by the data management layer into one of these formats.

HTML is a simple language used to describe a document. It is also called a **markup language** because HTML works by augmenting regular text with 'marks' that hold special meaning for a Web browser. Commands in the language, called **tags**, consist (usually) of a **start tag** and an **end tag** of the form `<TAG>` and `</TAG>`, respectively. For example, consider the HTML fragment shown in Figure 7.1. It describes a webpage that shows a list of books. The document is enclosed by the tags `<HTML>` and `</HTML>`, marking it as an HTML document. The remainder of the document—enclosed in `<BODY>` ... `</BODY>`—contains information about three books. Data about each book is represented as an unordered list (`UL`) whose entries are marked with the `LI` tag. HTML defines the set of valid tags as well as the meaning of the tags. For example, HTML specifies that the tag `<TITLE>` is a valid tag that denotes the title of the document. As another example, the tag `<UL>` always denotes an unordered list.

Audio, video, and even programs (written in Java, a highly portable language) can be included in HTML documents. When a user retrieves such a document using a suitable browser, images in the document are displayed, audio and video clips are played, and embedded programs are executed at the user's machine; the result is a rich multimedia presentation. The ease with which HTML docu-

```
<HTML>
<HEAD>
</HEAD>
<BODY>
<H1>Barns and Nobble Internet Bookstore</H1>
Our inventory:
<H3>Science</H3>
    <B>The Character of Physical Law</B>
    <UL>
        <LI>Author: Richard Feynman</LI>
        <LI>Published 1980</LI>
        <LI>Hardcover</LI>
    </UL>
<H3>Fiction</H3>
    <B>Waiting for the Mahatma</B>
    <UL>
        <LI>Author: R.K. Narayan</LI>
        <LI>Published 1981</LI>
    </UL>
    <B>The English Teacher</B>
    <UL>
        <LI>Author: R.K. Narayan</LI>
        <LI>Published 1980</LI>
        <LI>Paperback</LI>
    </UL>
</BODY>
</HTML>
```

Figure 7.1 Book Listing in HTML

ments can be created—there are now visual editors that automatically generate HTML—and accessed using Internet browsers has fueled the explosive growth of the Web.

7.4 XML DOCUMENTS

In this section, we introduce XML as a document format, and consider how applications can utilize XML. Managing XML documents in a DBMS poses several new challenges; we discuss this aspect of XML in Chapter 27.

While HTML can be used to mark up documents for display purposes, it is not adequate to describe the structure of the content for more general applications. For example, we can send the HTML document shown in Figure 7.1 to another application that displays it, but the second application cannot distinguish the first names of authors from their last names. (The application can try to recover such information by looking at the text inside the tags, but this defeats the purpose of using tags to describe document structure.) Therefore, HTML is unsuitable for the exchange of complex documents containing product specifications or bids, for example.

Extensible Markup Language (XML) is a markup language developed to remedy the shortcomings of HTML. In contrast to a fixed set of tags whose meaning is specified by the language (as in HTML), XML allows users to define new collections of tags that can be used to structure any type of data or document the user wishes to transmit. XML is an important bridge between the document-oriented view of data implicit in HTML and the schema-oriented view of data that is central to a DBMS. It has the potential to make database systems more tightly integrated into Web applications than ever before.

XML emerged from the confluence of two technologies, SGML and HTML. The **Standard Generalized Markup Language (SGML)** is a metalanguage that allows the definition of data and document interchange languages such as HTML. The SGML standard was published in 1988, and many organizations that manage a large number of complex documents have adopted it. Due to its generality, SGML is complex and requires sophisticated programs to harness its full potential. XML was developed to have much of the power of SGML while remaining relatively simple. Nonetheless, XML, like SGML, allows the definition of new document markup languages.

Although XML does not prevent a user from designing tags that encode the display of the data in a Web browser, there is a style language for XML called **Extensible Style Language (XSL)**. XSL is a standard way of describing how an XML document that adheres to a certain vocabulary of tags should be displayed.

7.4.1 Introduction to XML

We use the small XML document shown in Figure 7.2 as an example.

- **Elements:** Elements, also called **tags**, are the primary building blocks of an XML document. The start of the content of an element `ELM` is marked with `<ELM>`, which is called the **start tag**, and the end of the content end is marked with `</ELM>`, called the **end tag**. In our example document,

> **The Design Goals of XML:** XML was developed starting in 1996 by a working group under guidance of the World Wide Web Consortium (W3C) XML Special Interest Group. The design goals for XML included the following:
>
> 1. XML should be compatible with SGML.
> 2. It should be easy to write programs that process XML documents.
> 3. The design of XML should be formal and concise.

the element `BOOKLIST` encloses all information in the sample document. The element BOOK demarcates all data associated with a single book. XML elements are case sensitive: the element BOOK is different from Book. Elements must be properly nested. Start tags that appear inside the content of other tags must have a corresponding end tag. For example, consider the following XML fragment:

```
<BOOK>
    <AUTHOR>
        <FIRSTNAME>Richard</FIRSTNAME>
        <LASTNAME>Feynman</LASTNAME>
    </AUTHOR>
</BOOK>
```

The element `AUTHOR` is completely nested inside the element `BOOK`, and both the elements `LASTNAME` and `FIRSTNAME` are nested inside the element `AUTHOR`.

- **Attributes:** An element can have descriptive attributes that provide additional information about the element. The values of attributes are set inside the start tag of an element. For example, let `ELM` denote an element with the attribute `att`. We can set the value of `att` to `value` through the following expression: `<ELM att="value">`. All attribute values must be enclosed in quotes. In Figure 7.2, the element `BOOK` has two attributes. The attribute `GENRE` indicates the genre of the book (science or fiction) and the attribute `FORMAT` indicates whether the book is a hardcover or a paperback.

- **Entity References:** Entities are shortcuts for portions of common text or the content of external files, and we call the usage of an entity in the XML document an **entity reference**. Wherever an entity reference appears in the document, it is textually replaced by its content. Entity references start with a '`&`' and end with a '`;`'. Five predefined entities in XML are placeholders for characters with special meaning in XML. For example, the

```
<?xml version="1.0" encoding="UTF-8" standalone="yes"?>
<BOOKLIST>
<BOOK GENRE=”Science” FORMAT=”Hardcover”>
    <AUTHOR>
        <FIRSTNAME>Richard</FIRSTNAME>
        <LASTNAME>Feynman</LASTNAME>
    </AUTHOR>
    <TITLE>The Character of Physical Law</TITLE>
    <PUBLISHED>1980</PUBLISHED>
</BOOK>
<BOOK> GENRE=”Fiction”>
    <AUTHOR>
        <FIRSTNAME>R.K.</FIRSTNAME>
        <LASTNAME>Narayan</LASTNAME>
    </AUTHOR>
    <TITLE>Waiting for the Mahatma</TITLE>
    <PUBLISHED>1981</PUBLISHED>
</BOOK>
<BOOK GENRE=”Fiction”>
    <AUTHOR>
        <FIRSTNAME>R.K.</FIRSTNAME>
        <LASTNAME>Narayan</LASTNAME>
    </AUTHOR>
    <TITLE>The English Teacher</TITLE>
    <PUBLISHED>1980</PUBLISHED>
</BOOK>
</BOOKLIST>
```

Figure 7.2 Book Information in XML

$<$ character that marks the beginning of an XML command is reserved and has to be represented by the entity `lt`. The other four reserved characters are $\&$, $>$, ”, and ’; they are represented by the entities `amp`, `gt`, `quot`, and `apos`. For example, the text ‘1 $<$ 5’ has to be encoded in an XML document as follows: `'1<5'`. We can also use entities to insert arbitrary Unicode characters into the text. **Unicode** is a standard for character representations, similar to ASCII. For example, we can display the Japanese Hiragana character *a* using the entity reference `&#x3042`.

- **Comments:** We can insert comments anywhere in an XML document. Comments start with `<!-` and end with `->`. Comments can contain arbitrary text except the string `--`.

- **Document Type Declarations (DTDs):** In XML, we can define our own markup language. A DTD is a set of rules that allows us to specify our own set of elements, attributes, and entities. Thus, a DTD is basically a grammar that indicates what tags are allowed, in what order they can appear, and how they can be nested. We discuss DTDs in detail in the next section.

We call an XML document **well-formed** if it has no associated DTD but follows these structural guidelines:

- The document starts with an XML declaration. An example of an XML declaration is the first line of the XML document shown in Figure 7.2.
- A **root element** contains all the other elements. In our example, the root element is the element `BOOKLIST`.
- All elements must be properly nested. This requirement states that start and end tags of an element must appear within the same enclosing element.

7.4.2 XML DTDs

A DTD is a set of rules that allows us to specify our own set of elements, attributes, and entities. A DTD specifies which elements we can use and constraints on these elements, for example, how elements can be nested and where elements can appear in the document. We call a document **valid** if a DTD is associated with it and the document is structured according to the rules set by the DTD. In the remainder of this section, we use the example DTD shown in Figure 7.3 to illustrate how to construct DTDs.

```
<!DOCTYPE BOOKLIST [
<!ELEMENT BOOKLIST (BOOK)*>
    <!ELEMENT BOOK (AUTHOR,TITLE,PUBLISHED?)>
        <!ELEMENT AUTHOR (FIRSTNAME,LASTNAME)>
            <!ELEMENT FIRSTNAME (#PCDATA)>
            <!ELEMENT LASTNAME (#PCDATA)>
        <!ELEMENT TITLE (#PCDATA)>
        <!ELEMENT PUBLISHED (#PCDATA)>
    <!ATTLIST BOOK GENRE (Science|Fiction) #REQUIRED>
    <!ATTLIST BOOK FORMAT (Paperback|Hardcover) "Paperback">
]>
```

Figure 7.3 Bookstore XML DTD

A DTD is enclosed in `<!DOCTYPE name [DTDdeclaration]>`, where `name` is the name of the outermost enclosing tag, and DTDdeclaration is the text of the rules of the DTD. The DTD starts with the outermost element—the *root element*—which is `BOOKLIST` in our example. Consider the next rule:

<!ELEMENT BOOKLIST (BOOK)*>

This rule tells us that the element `BOOKLIST` consists of zero or more `BOOK` elements. The `*` after `BOOK` indicates how many `BOOK` elements can appear inside the `BOOKLIST` element. A `*` denotes zero or more occurrences, a `+` denotes one or more occurrences, and a `?` denotes zero or one occurrence. For example, if we want to ensure that a `BOOKLIST` has at least one book, we could change the rule as follows:

<!ELEMENT BOOKLIST (BOOK)+>

Let us look at the next rule:

<!ELEMENT BOOK (AUTHOR,TITLE,PUBLISHED?)>

This rule states that a `BOOK` element contains a `AUTHOR` element, a `TITLE` element, and an optional `PUBLISHED` element. Note the use of the `?` to indicate that the information is optional by having zero or one occurrence of the element. Let us move ahead to the following rule:

<!ELEMENT LASTNAME (#PCDATA)>

Until now we considered only elements that contained other elements. This rule states that `LASTNAME` is an element that does not contain other elements, but contains actual text. Elements that only contain other elements are said to have **element content**, whereas elements that also contain `#PCDATA` are said to have **mixed content**. In general, an element type declaration has the following structure:

<!ELEMENT (contentType)>

Five possible content types are:

- Other elements.
- The special symbol `#PCDATA`, which indicates (parsed) character data.
- The special symbol `EMPTY`, which indicates that the element has no content. Elements that have no content are not required to have an end tag.
- The special symbol `ANY`, which indicates that any content is permitted. This content should be avoided whenever possible since it disables all checking of the document structure inside the element.

- A **regular expression** constructed from the preceding four choices. A regular expression is one of the following:
  - exp1, exp2, exp3: A list of regular expressions.
  - exp*: An optional expression (zero or more occurrences).
  - exp?: An optional expression (zero or one occurrences).
  - exp+: A mandatory expression (one or more occurrences).
  - exp1 | exp2: exp1 or exp2.

Attributes of elements are declared outside the element. For example, consider the following attribute declaration from Figure 7.3:

<!ATTLIST BOOK GENRE (Science|Fiction) #REQUIRED>>

This XML DTD fragment specifies the attribute GENRE, which is an attribute of the element BOOK. The attribute can take two values: Science or Fiction. Each BOOK element must be described in its start tag by a GENRE attribute since the attribute is required as indicated by #REQUIRED. Let us look at the general structure of a DTD attribute declaration:

<!ATTLIST elementName (attName attType default)+>

The keyword ATTLIST indicates the beginning of an attribute declaration. The string elementName is the name of the element with which the following attribute definition is associated. What follows is the declaration of one or more attributes. Each attribute has a name, as indicated by attName, and a type, as indicated by attType. XML defines several possible types for an attribute. We discuss only **string types** and **enumerated types** here. An attribute of type string can take any string as a value. We can declare such an attribute by setting its type field to CDATA. For example, we can declare a third attribute of type string of the element BOOK as follows:

<!ATTLIST BOOK edition CDATA "1">

If an attribute has an enumerated type, we list all its possible values in the attribute declaration. In our example, the attribute GENRE is an enumerated attribute type; its possible attribute values are 'Science' and 'Fiction'.

The last part of an attribute declaration is called its **default specification**. The DTD in Figure 7.3 shows two different default specifications: #REQUIRED and the string 'Paperback'. The default specification #REQUIRED indicates that the attribute is required and whenever its associated element appears somewhere in the XML document a value for the attribute must be specified. The default specification indicated by the string 'Paperback' indicates that the attribute is not required; whenever its associated element appears without setting

```
<?xml version="1.0" encoding="UTF-8" standalone="no"?>
<!DOCTYPE BOOKLIST SYSTEM "books.dtd">
<BOOKLIST>
    <BOOK GENRE="Science" FORMAT="Hardcover">
        <AUTHOR>
        ...
```

Figure 7.4 Book Information in XML

> **XML Schema:** The DTD mechanism has several limitations, in spite of its widespread use. For example, elements and attributes cannot be assigned types in a flexible way, and elements are always ordered, even if the application does not require this. XML Schema is a new W3C proposal that provides a more powerful way to describe document structure than DTDs; it is a superset of DTDs, allowing legacy data to be handled easily. An interesting aspect is that it supports uniqueness and foreign key constraints.

a value for the attribute, the attribute automatically takes the value 'Paperback'. For example, we can make the attribute value 'Science' the default value for the GENRE attribute as follows:

```
<!ATTLIST BOOK GENRE (Science|Fiction) "Science">
```

In our bookstore example, the XML document with a reference to the DTD is shown in Figure 7.4.

7.4.3 Domain-Specific DTDs

Recently, DTDs have been developed for several specialized domains—including a wide range of commercial, engineering, financial, industrial, and scientific domains—and a lot of the excitement about XML has its origins in the belief that more and more standardized DTDs will be developed. Standardized DTDs would enable seamless data exchange among heterogeneous sources, a problem solved today either by implementing specialized protocols such as **Electronic Data Interchange (EDI)** or by implementing ad hoc solutions.

Even in an environment where all XML data is valid, it is not possible to straightforwardly integrate several XML documents by matching elements in their DTDs, because even when two elements have identical names in two different DTDs, the meaning of the elements could be completely different. If both documents use a single, standard DTD, we avoid this problem. The development of standardized DTDs is more a social process than a research problem, since the major players in a given domain or industry segment have to collaborate.

For example, the **mathematical markup language (MathML)** has been developed for encoding mathematical material on the Web. There are two types of MathML elements. The 28 **presentation elements** describe the layout structure of a document; examples are the `mrow` element, which indicates a horizontal row of characters, and the `msup` element, which indicates a base and a subscript. The 75 **content elements** describe mathematical concepts. An example is the `plus` element, which denotes the addition operator. (A third type of element, the `math` element, is used to pass parameters to the MathML processor.) MathML allows us to encode mathematical objects in both notations since the requirements of the user of the objects might be different. Content elements encode the precise mathematical meaning of an object without ambiguity, and the description can be used by applications such as computer algebra systems. On the other hand, good notation can suggest the logical structure to a human and emphasize key aspects of an object; presentation elements allow us to describe mathematical objects at this level.

For example, consider the following simple equation:

$$x^2 - 4x - 32 = 0$$

Using presentation elements, the equation is represented as follows:

```
<mrow>
    <mrow> <msup><mi>x</mi><mn>2</mn></msup>
        <mo>-</mo>
        <mrow><mn>4</mn>
            <mo>&invisibletimes;</mo>
            <mi>x</mi>
        </mrow>
        <mo>-</mo><mn>32</mn>
    </mrow><mo>=</mo><mn>0</mn>
</mrow>
```

Using content elements, the equation is described as follows:

```
<reln><eq/>
    <apply>
        <minus/>
        <apply> <power/> <ci>x</ci> <cn>2</cn> </apply>
        <apply> <times/> <cn>4</cn> <ci>x</ci> </apply>
        <cn>32</cn>
```

```
    </apply> <cn>0</cn>
  </reln>
```

Note the additional power that we gain from using MathML instead of encoding the formula in HTML. The common way of displaying mathematical objects inside an HTML object is to include images that display the objects, for example, as in the following code fragment:

```
<IMG SRC="images/equation.gif" ALT=" x**2 - 4x - 32 = 10 " >
```

The equation is encoded inside an `IMG` tag with an alternative display format specified in the `ALT` tag. Using this encoding of a mathematical object leads to the following presentation problems. First, the image is usually sized to match a certain font size, and on systems with other font sizes the image is either too small or too large. Second, on systems with a different background color, the picture does not blend into the background and the resolution of the image is usually inferior when printing the document. Apart from problems with changing presentations, we cannot easily search for a formula or formula fragments on a page, since there is no specific markup tag.

7.5 THE THREE-TIER APPLICATION ARCHITECTURE

In this section, we discuss the overall architecture of data-intensive Internet applications. Data-intensive Internet applications can be understood in terms of three different functional components: *data management, application logic,* and *presentation.* The component that handles data mangement usually utilizes a DBMS for data storage, but application logic and presentation involve much more than just the DBMS itself.

We start with a short overview of the history of database-backed application architectures, and introduce single-tier and client-server architectures in Section 7.5.1. We explain the three-tier architecture in detail in Section 7.5.2, and show its advantages in Section 7.5.3.

7.5.1 Single-Tier and Client-Server Architectures

In this section, we provide some perspective on the three-tier architecture by discussing single-tier and client-server architectures, the predecessors of the three-tier architecture. Initially, data-intensive applications were combined into a single tier, including the DBMS, application logic, and user interface, as illustrated in Figure 7.5. The application typically ran on a mainframe, and users accessed it through *dumb terminals* that could perform only data input and display. This approach has the benefit of being easily maintained by a central administrator.

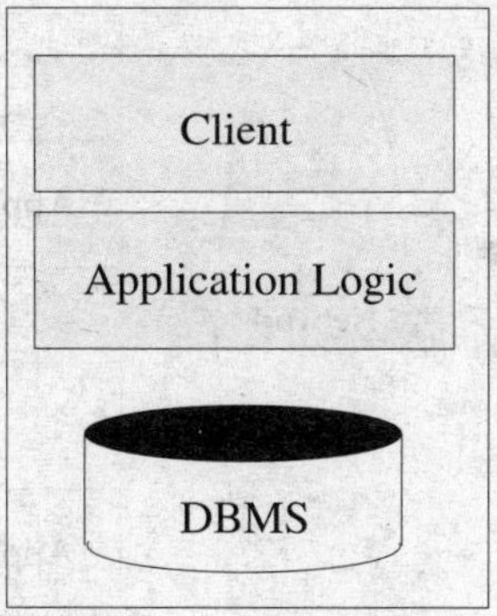

Figure 7.5 A Single-Tier Architecture

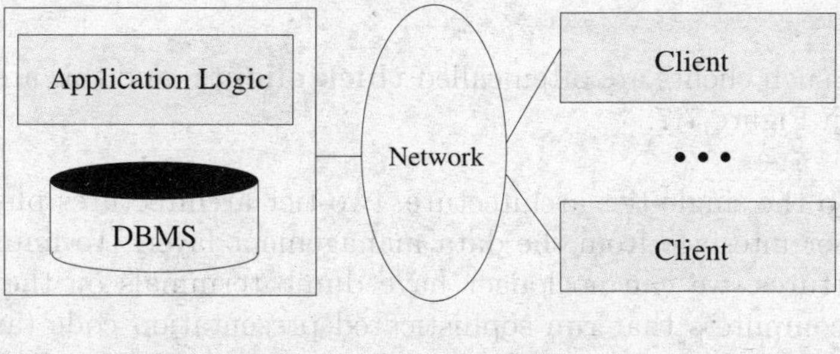

Figure 7.6 A Two-Server Architecture: Thin Clients

Single-tier architectures have an important drawback: Users expect graphical interfaces that require much more computational power than simple dumb terminals. Centralized computation of the graphical displays of such interfaces requires much more computational power than a single server has available, and thus single-tier architectures do not scale to thousands of users. The commoditization of the PC and the availability of cheap client computers led to the development of the two-tier architecture.

Two-tier architectures, often also referred to as **client-server architectures,** consist of a **client computer** and a **server computer**, which interact through a well-defined protocol. What part of the functionality the client implements, and what part is left to the server, can vary. In the traditional **client-server architecture**, the client implements just the graphical user interface, and the server implements both the business logic and the data management; such clients are often called **thin clients**, and this architecture is illustrated in Figure 7.6.

Other divisions are possible, such as more powerful clients that implement both user interface and business logic, or clients that implement user interface and part of the business logic, with the remaining part being implemented at the

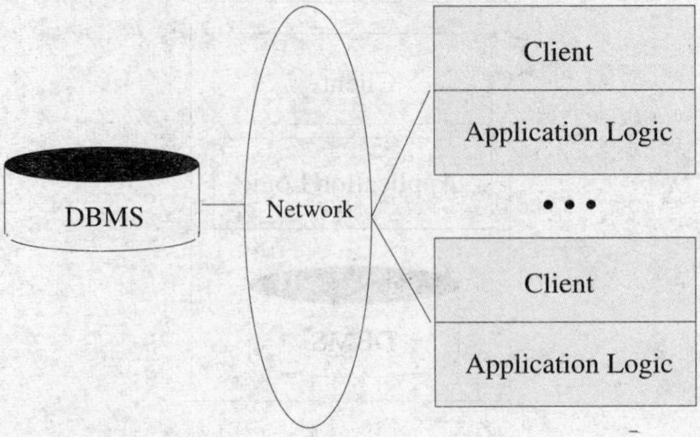

Figure 7.7 A Two-Tier Architecture: Thick Clients

server level; such clients are often called **thick clients**, and this architecture is illustrated in Figure 7.7.

Compared to the single-tier architecture, two-tier architectures physically separate the user interface from the data management layer. To implement two-tier architectures, we can no longer have dumb terminals on the client side; we require computers that run sophisticated presentation code (and possibly, application logic).

Over the last ten years, a large number of client-server development tools such Microsoft Visual Basic and Sybase Powerbuilder have been developed. These tools permit rapid development of client-server software, contributing to the success of the client-server model, especially the thin-client version.

The thick-client model has several disadvantages when compared to the thin-client model. First, there is no central place to update and maintain the business logic, since the application code runs at many client sites. Second, a large amount of trust is required between the server and the clients. As an example, the DBMS of a bank has to trust the (application executing at an) ATM machine to leave the database in a consistent state. (One way to address this problem is through *stored procedures*, trusted application code that is registered with the DBMS and can be called from SQL statements. We discuss stored procedures in detail in Section 6.5.)

A third disadvantage of the thick-client architecture is that it does not scale with the number of clients; it typically cannot handle more than a few hundred clients. The application logic at the client issues SQL queries to the server and the server returns the query result to the client, where further processing takes place. Large query results might be transferred between client and server.

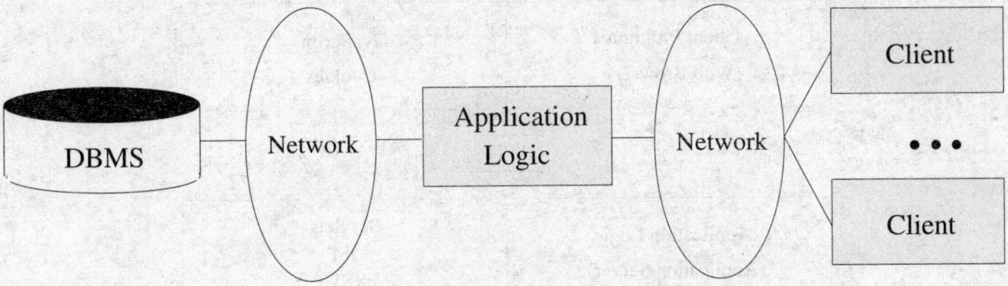

Figure 7.8 A Standard Three-Tier Architecture

(Stored procedures can mitigate this bottleneck.) Fourth, thick-client systems do not scale as the application accesses more and more database systems. Assume there are x different database systems that are accessed by y clients, then there are $x \cdot y$ different connections open at any time, clearly not a scalable solution.

These disadvantages of thick-client systems and the widespread adoption of standard, very thin clients—notably, Web browsers—have led to the widespread use thin-client architectures.

7.5.2 Three-Tier Architectures

The thin-client two-tier architecture essentially separates presentation issues from the rest of the application. The three-tier architecture goes one step further, and also separates application logic from data management:

- **Presentation Tier:** Users require a natural interface to make requests, provide input, and to see results. The widespread use of the Internet has made Web-based interfaces increasingly popular.
- **Middle Tier:** The application logic executes here. An enterprise-class application reflects complex business processes, and is coded in a general purpose language such as C++ or Java.
- **Data Management Tier:** Data-intensive Web applications involve DBMSs, which are the subject of this book.

Figure 7.8 shows a basic three-tier architecture. Different technologies have been developed to enable distribution of the three tiers of an application across multiple hardware platforms and different physical sites. Figure 7.9 shows the technologies relevant to each tier.

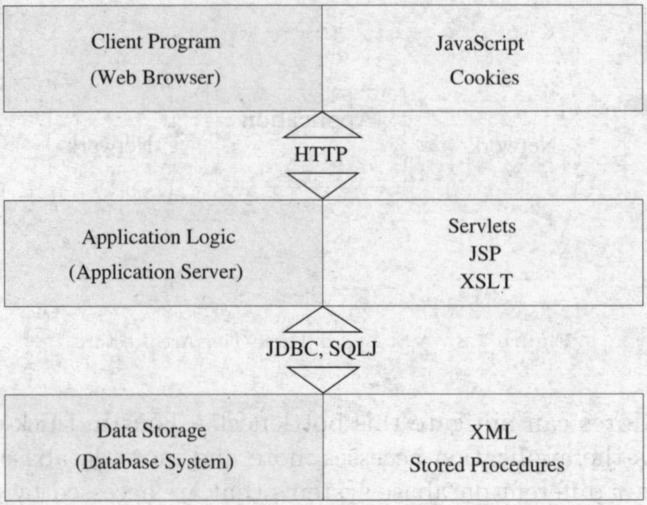

Figure 7.9 Technologies for the Three Tiers

Overview of the Presentation Tier

At the presentation layer, we need to provide forms through which the user can issue requests, and display responses that the middle tier generates. The hypertext markup language (HTML) discussed in Section 7.3 is the basic data presentation language.

It is important that this layer of code be easy to adapt to different display devices and formats; for example, regular desktops versus handheld devices versus cell phones. This adaptivity can be achieved either at the middle tier through generation of different pages for different types of client, or directly at the client through **style sheets** that specify how the data should be presented. In the latter case, the middle tier is responsible for producing the appropriate data in response to user requests, whereas the presentation layer decides *how* to display that information.

We cover presentation tier technologies, including style sheets, in Section 7.6.

Overview of the Middle Tier

The middle layer runs code that implements the business logic of the application: It controls what data needs to be input before an action can be executed, determines the control flow between multi-action steps, controls access to the database layer, and often assembles dynamically generated HTML pages from database query results.

The middle tier code is responsible for supporting all the different roles involved in the application. For example, in an Internet shopping site implementation, we would like customers to be able to browse the catalog and make purchases, administrators to be able to inspect current inventory, and possibly data analysts to ask summary queries about purchase histories. Each of these roles can require support for several complex actions.

For example, consider the a customer who wants to buy an item (after browsing or searching the site to find it). Before a sale can happen, the customer has to go through a series of steps: She has to add items to her shopping basket, she has to provide her shipping address and credit card number (unless she has an account at the site), and she has to finally confirm the sale with tax and shipping costs added. Controlling the flow among these steps and remembering already executed steps is done at the middle tier of the application. The data carried along during this series of steps might involve database accesses, but usually it is not yet permanent (for example, a shopping basket is not stored in the database until the sale is confirmed).

We cover the middle tier in detail in Section 7.7.

7.5.3 Advantages of the Three-Tier Architecture

The three-tier architecture has the following advantages:

- **Heterogeneous Systems:** Applications can utilize the strengths of different platforms and different software components at the different tiers. It is easy to modify or replace the code at any tier without affecting the other tiers.
- **Thin Clients:** Clients only need enough computation power for the presentation layer. Typically, clients are Web browsers.
- **Integrated Data Access:** In many applications, the data must be accessed from several sources. This can be handled transparently at the middle tier, where we can centrally manage connections to all database systems involved.
- **Scalability to Many Clients:** Each client is lightweight and all access to the system is through the middle tier. The middle tier can share database connections across clients, and if the middle tier becomes the bottle-neck, we can deploy several servers executing the middle tier code; clients can connect to any one of these servers, if the logic is designed appropriately. This is illustrated in Figure 7.10, which also shows how the middle tier accesses multiple data sources. Of course, we rely upon the DBMS for each

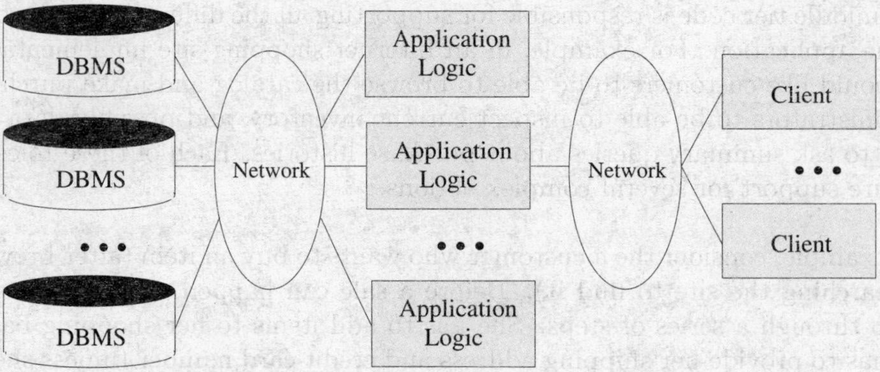

Figure 7.10 Middle-Tier Replication and Access to Multiple Data Sources

data source to be scalable (and this might involve additional parallelization or replication, as discussed in Chapter 22).

- **Software Development Benefits:** By dividing the application cleanly into parts that address presentation, data access, and business logic, we gain many advantages. The business logic is centralized, and is therefore easy to maintain, debug, and change. Interaction between tiers occurs through well-defined, standardized APIs. Therefore, each application tier can be built out of reusable components that can be individually developed, debugged, and tested.

7.6 THE PRESENTATION LAYER

In this section, we describe technologies for the client side of the three-tier architecture. We discuss HTML forms as a special means of passing arguments from the client to the middle tier (i.e., from the presentation tier to the middle tier) in Section 7.6.1. In Section 7.6.2, we introduce JavaScript, a Java-based scripting language that can be used for light-weight computation in the client tier (e.g., for simple animations). We conclude our discussion of client-side technologies by presenting style sheets in Section 7.6.3. Style sheets are languages that allow us to present the same webpage with different formatting for clients with different presentation capabilities; for example, Web browsers versus cell phones, or even a Netscape browser versus Microsoft's Internet Explorer.

7.6.1 HTML Forms

HTML forms are a common way of communicating data from the client tier to the middle tier. The general format of a form is the following:

```
<FORM ACTION="page.jsp" METHOD="GET" NAME="LoginForm">
```

```
...
</FORM>
```

A single HTML document can contain more than one form. Inside an HTML form, we can have any HTML tags except another `FORM` element.

The `FORM` tag has three important attributes:

- `ACTION`: Specifies the URI of the page to which the form contents are submitted; if the `ACTION` attribute is absent, then the URI of the current page is used. In the sample above, the form input would be submited to the page named `page.jsp`, which should provide logic for processing the input from the form. (We will explain methods for reading form data at the middle tier in Section 7.7.)
- `METHOD`: The HTTP/1.0 method used to submit the user input from the filled-out form to the webserver. There are two choices, `GET` and `POST`; we postpone their discussion to the next section.
- `NAME`: This attribute gives the form a name. Although not necessary, naming forms is good style. In Section 7.6.2, we discuss how to write client-side programs in JavaScript that refer to forms by name and perform checks on form fields.

Inside HTML forms, the `INPUT`, `SELECT`, and `TEXTAREA` tags are used to specify user input elements; a form can have many elements of each type. The simplest user input element is an `INPUT` field, a standalone tag with no terminating tag. An example of an `INPUT` tag is the following:

```
<INPUT TYPE="text" NAME="title">
```

The `INPUT` tag has several attributes. The three most important ones are `TYPE`, `NAME`, and `VALUE`. The `TYPE` attribute determines the type of the input field. If the `TYPE` attribute has value `text`, then the field is a text input field. If the `TYPE` attribute has value `password`, then the input field is a text field where the entered characters are displayed as stars on the screen. If the `TYPE` attribute has value `reset`, it is a simple button that resets all input fields within the form to their default values. If the `TYPE` attribute has value `submit`, then it is a button that sends the values of the different input fields in the form to the server. Note that `reset` and `submit` input fields affect the entire form.

The `NAME` attribute of the `INPUT` tag specifies the symbolic name for this field and is used to identify the value of this input field when it is sent to the server. `NAME` has to be set for `INPUT` tags of all types except `submit` and `reset`. In the preceding example, we specified `title` as the `NAME` of the input field.

The `VALUE` attribute of an input tag can be used for text or password fields to specify the default contents of the field. For submit or reset buttons, `VALUE` determines the label of the button.

The form in Figure 7.11 shows two text fields, one regular text input field and one password field. It also contains two buttons, a reset button labeled 'Reset Values' and a submit button labeled 'Log on.' Note that the two input fields are named, whereas the reset and submit button have no `NAME` attributes.

```
<FORM ACTION="page.jsp" METHOD="GET" NAME="LoginForm">
    <INPUT TYPE="text" NAME="username" VALUE="Joe"><P>
    <INPUT TYPE="password" NAME="password"><P>
    <INPUT TYPE="reset" VALUE="Reset Values"><P>
    <INPUT TYPE="submit" VALUE="Log on">
</FORM>
```

Figure 7.11 HTML Form with Two Text Fields and Two Buttons

HTML forms have other ways of specifying user input, such as the aforementioned `TEXTAREA` and `SELECT` tags; we do not discuss them.

Passing Arguments to Server-Side Scripts

As mentioned at the beginning of Section 7.6.1, there are two different ways to submit HTML Form data to the webserver. If the method `GET` is used, then the contents of the form are assembled into a query URI (as discussed next) and sent to the server. If the method `POST` is used, then the contents of the form are encoded as in the `GET` method, but the contents are sent in a separate data block instead of appending them directly to the URI. Thus, in the `GET` method the form contents are directly visible to the user as the constructed URI, whereas in the `POST` method, the form contents are sent inside the HTTP request message body and are not visible to the user.

Using the `GET` method gives users the opportunity to bookmark the page with the constructed URI and thus directly jump to it in subsequent sessions; this is not possible with the `POST` method. The choice of `GET` versus `POST` should be determined by the application and its requirements.

Let us look at the encoding of the URI when the `GET` method is used. The encoded URI has the following form:

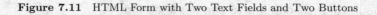

action?name1=value1&name2=value2&name3=value3

The `action` is the URI specified in the `ACTION` attribute to the `FORM` tag, or the current document URI if no `ACTION` attribute was specified. The 'name=value' pairs are the user inputs from the `INPUT` fields in the form. For form `INPUT` fields where the user did not input anything, the name is stil present with an empty value (`name=`). As a concrete example, consider the password submission form at the end of the previous section. Assume that the user inputs 'John Doe' as username, and 'secret' as password. Then the request URI is:

page.jsp?username=John+Doe&password=secret

The user input from forms can contain general ASCII characters, such as the space character, but URIs have to be single, consecutive strings with no spaces. Therefore, special characters such as spaces, '=', and other unprintable characters are encoded in a special way. To create a URI that has form fields encoded, we perform the following three steps:

1. Convert all special characters in the names and values to '%xyz,' where 'xyz' is the ASCII value of the character in hexadecimal. Special characters include =, &, %, +, and other unprintable characters. Note that we could encode *all* characters by their ASCII value.

2. Convert all space characters to the '+' character.

3. Glue corresponding names and values from an individual HTML `INPUT` tag together with '=' and then paste name-value pairs from different HTML `INPUT` tags together using '&' to create a request URI of the form: action?name1=value1&name2=value2&name3=value3

Note that in order to process the input elements from the HTML form at the middle tier, we need the `ACTION` attribute of the `FORM` tag to point to a page, script, or program that will process the values of the form fields the user entered. We discuss ways of receiving values from form fields in Sections 7.7.1 and 7.7.3.

7.6.2 JavaScript

JavaScript is a scripting language at the client tier with which we can add programs to webpages that run directly at the client (i.e., at the machine running the Web browser). JavaScript is often used for the following types of computation at the client:

- **Browser Detection:** JavaScript can be used to detect the browser type and load a browser-specific page.

- **Form Validation:** JavaScript is used to perform simple consistency checks on form fields. For example, a JavaScript program might check whether a form input that asks for an email address contains the character '@,' or if all required fields have been input by the user.

- **Browser Control:** This includes opening pages in customized windows; examples include the annoying pop-up advertisements that you see at many websites, which are programmed using JavaScript.

JavaScript is usually embedded into an HTML document with a special tag, the `SCRIPT` tag. The `SCRIPT` tag has the attribute `LANGUAGE`, which indicates the language in which the script is written. For JavaScript, we set the language attribute to `JavaScript`. Another attribute of the `SCRIPT` tag is the `SRC` attribute, which specifies an external file with JavaScript code that is automatically embedded into the HTML document. Usually JavaScript source code files use a '.js' extension. The following fragment shows a JavaScript file included in an HTML document:

```
<SCRIPT LANGUAGE="JavaScript" SRC="validateForm.js"> </SCRIPT>
```

The `SCRIPT` tag can be placed inside HTML comments so that the JavaScript code is not displayed verbatim in Web browsers that do not recognize the `SCRIPT` tag. Here is another JavaScipt code example that creates a pop-up box with a welcoming message. We enclose the JavaScipt code inside HTML comments for the reasons just mentioned.

```
<SCRIPT LANGUAGE="JavaScript">
<!--
    alert("Welcome to our bookstore");
//-->
</SCRIPT>
```

JavaScript provides two different commenting styles: single-line comments that start with the '//' character, and multi-line comments starting with '/*' and ending with '*/' characters.[1]

JavaScript has variables that can be numbers, boolean values (true or false), strings, and some other data types that we do not discuss. Global variables have to be declared in advance of their usage with the keyword `var`, and they can be used anywhere inside the HTML documents. Variables local to a JavaScript function (explained next) need not be declared. Variables do not have a fixed type, but implicitly have the type of the data to which they have been assigned.

[1]Actually, '<!--' also marks the start of a single-line comment, which is why we did not have to mark the HTML starting comment '<!--' in the preceding example using JavaScript comment notation. In contrast, the HTML closing comment "-->" has to be commented out in JavaScript as it is interpreted otherwise.

JavaScript has the usual assignment operators (=, + =, etc.), the usual arithmetic operators (+, −, ∗, /, %), the usual comparison operators (==, ! =, >=, etc.), and the usual boolean operators (&& for logical `AND`, || for logical `OR`, and ! for negation). Strings can be concatenated using the '+' character. The type of an object determines the behavior of operators; for example 1+1 is 2, since we are adding numbers, whereas "1"+"1" is "11," since we are concatenating strings. JavaScript contains the usual types of statements, such as assignments, conditional statements (`if (condition) {statements;} else {statements; }`), and loops (`for`-loop, `do-while`, and `while`-loop).

JavaScript allows us to create functions using the `function` keyword: `function f(arg1, arg2) {statements;}`. We can call functions from JavaScript code, and functions can return values using the keyword `return`.

We conclude this introduction to JavaScript with a larger example of a JavaScript function that tests whether the login and password fields of a HTML form are not empty. Figure 7.12 shows the JavaScript function and the HTML form. The JavaScript code is a function called `testLoginEmpty()` that tests whether either of the two input fields in the form named `LoginForm` is empty. In the function `testLoginEmpty`, we first use variable `loginForm` to refer to the form `LoginForm` using the implicitly defined variable `document`, which refers to the current HTML page. (JavaScript has a library of objects that are implicitly defined.) We then check whether either of the strings `loginForm.userif.value` or `loginForm.password.value` is empty.

The function `testLoginEmpty` is checked within a form event handler. An **event handler** is a function that is called if an event happens on an object in a webpage. The event handler we use is `onSubmit`, which is called if the submit button is pressed (or if the user presses return in a text field in the form). If the event handler returns `true`, then the form contents are submitted to the server, otherwise the form contents are not submitted to the server.

JavaScript has functionality that goes beyond the basics that we explained in this section; the interested reader is referred to the bibliographic notes at the end of this chapter.

7.6.3 Style Sheets

Different clients have different displays, and we need correspondingly different ways of displaying the same information. For example, in the simplest case, we might need to use different font sizes or colors that provide high-contrast on a black-and-white screen. As a more sophisticated example, we might need to re-arrange objects on the page to accommodate small screens in personal

```
<SCRIPT LANGUAGE="JavaScript">
<!--
function testLoginEmpty()
{
    loginForm = document.LoginForm
    if ((loginForm.userid.value == "") ||
            (loginForm.password.value == "")) {
        alert('Please enter values for userid and password.');
        return false;
    }
    else
        return true;
}
//-->
</SCRIPT>
<H1 ALIGN = "CENTER">Barns and Nobble Internet Bookstore</H1>
<H3 ALIGN = "CENTER">Please enter your userid and password:</H3>
<FORM NAME = "LoginForm" METHOD="POST"
        ACTION="TableOfContents.jsp"
        onSubmit="return testLoginEmpty()">
    Userid: <INPUT TYPE="TEXT" NAME="userid"><P>
    Password: <INPUT TYPE="PASSWORD" NAME="password"><P>
    <INPUT TYPE="SUBMIT" VALUE="Login" NAME="SUBMIT">
    <INPUT TYPE="RESET" VALUE="Clear Input" NAME="RESET">
</FORM>
```

Figure 7.12 Form Validation with JavaScript

digital assistants (PDAs). As another example, we might highlight different information to focus on some important part of the page. A **style sheet** is a method to adapt the same document contents to different presentation formats. A style sheet contains instructions that tell a Web browser (or whatever the client uses to display the webpage) how to translate the data of a document into a presentation that is suitable for the client's display.

Style sheets separate the **transformative** aspect of the page from the **rendering** aspects of the page. During transformation, the objects in the XML document are rearranged to form a different structure, to omit parts of the XML document, or to merge two different XML documents into a single document. During rendering, we take the existing hierarchical structure of the XML document and format the document according to the user's display device.

```
BODY {BACKGROUND-COLOR: yellow}
H1 {FONT-SIZE: 36pt}
H3 {COLOR: blue}
P {MARGIN-LEFT: 50px; COLOR: red}
```

Figure 7.13 An Example Style sheet

The use of style sheets has many advantages. First, we can reuse the same document many times and display it differently depending on the context. Second, we can tailor the display to the reader's preference such as font size, color style, and even level of detail. Third, we can deal with different output formats, such as different output devices (laptops versus cell phones), different display sizes (letter versus legal paper), and different display media (paper versus digital display). Fourth, we can standardize the display format within a corporation and thus apply style sheet conventions to documents at any time. Further, changes and improvements to these display conventions can be managed at a central place.

There are two style sheet languages: XSL and CSS. CSS was created for HTML with the goal of separating the display characteristics of different formatting tags from the tags themselves. XSL is an extension of CSS to arbitrary XML documents; besides allowing us to define ways of formatting objects, XSL contains a transformation language that enables us to rearrange objects. The target files for CSS are HTML files, whereas the target files for XSL are XML files.

Cascading Style Sheets

A **Cascading Style Sheet (CSS)** defines how to display HTML elements. (In Section 7.13, we introduce a more general style sheet language designed for XML documents.) Styles are normally stored in style sheets, which are files that contain style definitions. Many different HTML documents, such as all documents in a website, can refer to the same CSS. Thus, we can change the format of a website by changing a single file. This is a very convenient way of changing the layout of many webpages at the same time, and a first step toward the separation of content from presentation.

An example style sheet is shown in Figure 7.13. It is included into an HTML file with the following line:

```
<LINK REL="style sheet" TYPE="text/css" HREF="books.css" />
```

Each line in a CSS sheet consists of three parts; a selector, a property, and a value. They are syntactically arranged in the following way:

`selector` {property: value}

The `selector` is the element or tag whose format we are defining. The `property` indicates the tag's attribute whose value we want to set in the style sheet, and the `property` is the actual value of the attribute. As an example, consider the first line of the example style sheet shown in Figure 7.13:

`BODY {BACKGROUND-COLOR: yellow}`

This line has the same effect as changing the HTML code to the following:

`<BODY BACKGROUND-COLOR="yellow">.`

The value should always be quoted, as it could consist of several words. More than one property for the same selector can be separated by semicolons as shown in the last line of the example in Figure 7.13:

`P {MARGIN-LEFT: 50px; COLOR: red}`

Cascading style sheets have an extensive syntax; the bibliographic notes at the end of the chapter point to books and online resources on CSSs.

XSL

XSL is a language for expressing style sheets. An XSL style sheet is, like CSS, a file that describes how to display an XML document of a given type. XSL shares the functionality of CSS and is compatible with it (although it uses a different syntax).

The capabilities of XSL vastly exceed the functionality of CSS. XSL contains the **XSL Transformation** language, or XSLT, a language that allows us to transform the input XML document into a XML document with another structure. For example, with XSLT we can change the order of elements that we are displaying (e.g., by sorting them), process elements more than once, suppress elements in one place and present them in another, and add generated text to the presentation.

XSL also contains the **XML Path Language (XPath)**, a language that allows us to refer to parts of an XML document. We discuss XPath in Section

27. XSL also contains XSL Formatting Object, a way of formatting the output of an XSL transformation.

7.7 THE MIDDLE TIER

In this section, we discuss technologies for the middle tier. The first generation of middle-tier applications were stand-alone programs written in a general-purpose programming language such as C, C++, and Perl. Programmers quickly realized that interaction with a stand-alone application was quite costly; the overheads include starting the application every time it is invoked and switching processes between the webserver and the application. Therefore, such interactions do not scale to large numbers of concurrent users. This led to the development of the **application server**, which provides the run-time environment for several technologies that can be used to program middle-tier application components. Most of today's large-scale websites use an application server to run application code at the middle tier.

Our coverage of technologies for the middle tier mirrors this evolution. We start in Section 7.7.1 with the Common Gateway Interface, a protocol that is used to transmit arguments from HTML forms to application programs running at the middle tier. We introduce application servers in Section 7.7.2. We then describe technologies for writing application logic at the middle tier: Java servlets (Section 7.7.3) and Java Server Pages (Section 7.7.4). Another important functionality is the maintenance of state in the middle tier component of the application as the client component goes through a series of steps to complete a transaction (for example, the purchase of a market basket of items or the reservation of a flight). In Section 7.7.5, we discuss Cookies, one approach to maintaining state.

7.7.1 CGI: The Common Gateway Interface

The Common Gateway Interface connects HTML forms with application programs. It is a protocol that defines how arguments from forms are passed to programs at the server side. We do not go into the details of the actual CGI protocol since libraries enable application programs to get arguments from the HTML form; we shortly see an example in a CGI program. Programs that communicate with the webserver via CGI are often called **CGI scripts**, since many such application programs were written in a scripting language such as Perl.

As an example of a program that interfaces with an HTML form via CGI, consider the sample page shown in Figure 7.14. This webpage contains a form where a user can fill in the name of an author. If the user presses the 'Send

```
<HTML><HEAD><TITLE>The Database Bookstore</TITLE></HEAD>
<BODY>
<FORM ACTION="find_books.cgi" METHOD=POST>
    Type an author name:
    <INPUT TYPE="text" NAME="authorName"
           SIZE=30 MAXLENGTH=50>
    <INPUT TYPE="submit" value="Send it">
    <INPUT TYPE="reset" VALUE="Clear form">
</FORM>
</BODY></HTML>
```

Figure 7.14 A Sample Web Page Where Form Input Is Sent to a CGI Script

it' button, the Perl script 'findBooks.cgi' shown in Figure 7.14 is executed as a separate process. The CGI protocol defines how the communication between the form and the script is performed. Figure 7.15 illustrates the processes created when using the CGI protocol.

Figure 7.16 shows the example CGI script, written in Perl. We omit error-checking code for simplicity. Perl is an interpreted language that is often used for CGI scripting and many Perl libraries, called **modules**, provide high-level interfaces to the CGI protocol. We use one such library, called the **DBI library**, in our example. The CGI module is a convenient collection of functions for creating CGI scripts. In part 1 of the sample script, we extract the argument of the HTML form that is passed along from the client as follows:

```
$authorName = $dataIn->param('authorName');
```

Note that the parameter name `authorName` was used in the form in Figure 7.14 to name the first input field. Conveniently, the CGI protocol abstracts the actual implementation of how the webpage is returned to the Web browser; the webpage consists simply of the output of our program, and we start assembling the output HTML page in part 2. Everything the script writes in `print`-statements is part of the dynamically constructed webpage returned to the browser. We finish in part 3 by appending the closing format tags to the resulting page.

7.7.2 Application Servers

Application logic can be enforced through server-side programs that are invoked using the CGI protocol. However, since each page request results in the creation of a new process, this solution does not scale well to a large number of simultaneous requests. This performance problem led to the development of

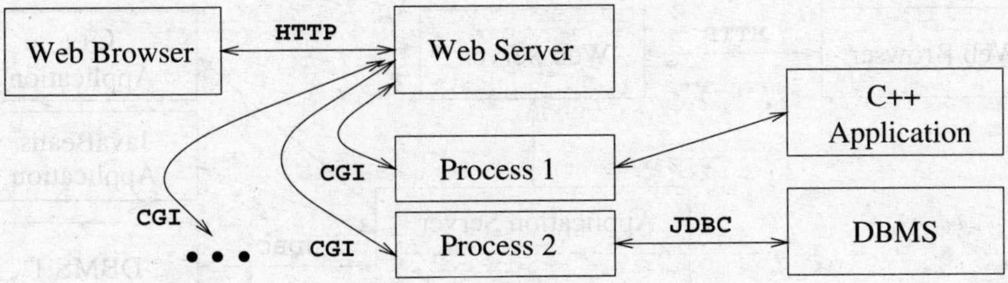

Figure 7.15 Process Structure with CGI Scripts

```
#!/usr/bin/perl
use CGI;

### part 1
$dataIn = new CGI;
$dataIn-¿header();
$authorName = $dataIn-¿param(‘authorName’);

### part 2
print("<HTML><TITLE>Argument passing test</TITLE>");
print("The user passed the following argument:");
print("authorName: ", $authorName);

### part 3
print ("</HTML>");
exit;
```

Figure 7.16 A Simple Perl Script

specialized programs called **application servers**. An application server maintains a pool of threads or processes and uses these to execute requests. Thus, it avoids the startup cost of creating a new process for each request.

Application servers have evolved into flexible middle-tier packages that provide many functions in addition to eliminating the process-creation overhead. They facilitate concurrent access to several heterogeneous data sources (e.g., by providing JDBC drivers), and provide **session management** services. Often, business processes involve several steps. Users expect the system to maintain continuity during such a multistep session. Several session identifiers such as **cookies**, URI extensions, and hidden fields in HTML forms can be used to identify a session. Application servers provide functionality to detect when a session starts and ends and keep track of the sessions of individual users. They

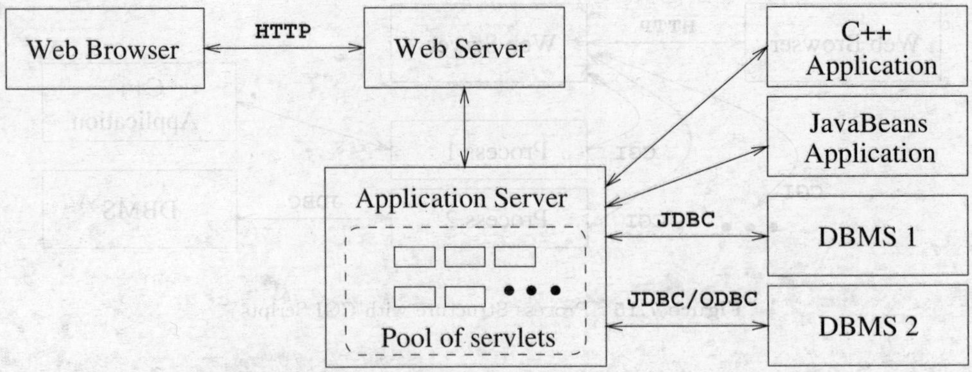

Figure 7.17 Process Structure in the Application Server Architecture

also help to ensure secure database access by supporting a general user-id mechanism. (For more on security, see Chapter 21.)

A possible architecture for a website with an application server is shown in Figure 7.17. The client (a Web browser) interacts with the webserver through the HTTP protocol. The webserver delivers static HTML or XML pages directly to the client. To assemble dynamic pages, the webserver sends a request to the application server. The application server contacts one or more data sources to retrieve necessary data or sends update requests to the data sources. After the interaction with the data sources is completed, the application server assembles the webpage and reports the result to the webserver, which retrieves the page and delivers it to the client.

The execution of business logic at the webserver's site, **server-side processing**, has become a standard model for implementing more complicated business processes on the Internet. There are many different technologies for server-side processing and we only mention a few in this section; the interested reader is referred to the bibliographic notes at the end of the chapter.

7.7.3 Servlets

Java servlets are pieces of Java code that run on the middle tier, in either webservers or application servers. There are special conventions on how to read the input from the user request and how to write output generated by the servlet. Servlets are truly platform-independent, and so they have become very popular with Web developers.

Since servlets are Java programs, they are very versatile. For example, servlets can build webpages, access databases, and maintain state. Servlets have access

```
import java.io.*;
import javax.servlet.*;
import javax.servlet.http.*;

public class ServletTemplate extends HttpServlet {
    public void doGet(HttpServletRequest request,
            HttpServletResponse response)
            throws ServletException, IOException {
        PrintWriter out = response.getWriter();
        // Use 'out' to send content to browser
        out.println("Hello World");
    }
}
```

Figure 7.18 Servlet Template

to all Java APIs, including JDBC. All servlets must implement the `Servlet` interface. In most cases, servlets extend the specific `HttpServlet` class for servers that communicate with clients via HTTP. The `HttpServlet` class provides methods such as `doGet` and `doPost` to receive arguments from HTML forms, and it sends its output back to the client via HTTP. Servlets that communicate through other protocols (such as ftp) need to extend the class `GenericServlet`.

Servlets are compiled Java classes executed and maintained by a **servlet container**. The servlet container manages the lifespan of individual servlets by creating and destroying them. Although servlets can respond to any type of request, they are commonly used to extend the applications hosted by webservers. For such applications, there is a useful library of HTTP-specific servlet classes.

Servlets usually handle requests from HTML forms and maintain state between the client and the server. We discuss how to maintain state in Section 7.7.5. A template of a generic servlet structure is shown in Figure 7.18. This simple servlet just outputs the two words "Hello World," but it shows the general structure of a full-fledged servlet. The `request` object is used to read HTML form data. The `response object` is used to specify the HTTP response status code and headers of the HTTP response. The object `out` is used to compose the content that is returned to the client.

Recall that HTTP sends back the status line, a header, a blank line, and then the context. Right now our servlet just returns plain text. We can extend our servlet by setting the content type to HTML, generating HTML as follows:

```
PrintWriter out = response.getWriter();
String docType =
    "<!DOCTYPE HTML PUBLIC "-//W3C//DTD HTML 4.0 " +
    "Transitional//EN"> \n";
out.println(docType +
    "<HTML>\n" +
    "<HEAD><TITLE>Hello WWW</TITLE></HEAD>\n" +
    "<BODY>\n" +
    "<H1>Hello WWW</H1>\n" +
    "</BODY></HTML>");
```

What happens during the life of a servlet? Several methods are called at different stages in the development of a servlet. When a requested page is a servlet, the webserver forwards the request to the servlet container, which creates an instance of the servlet if necessary. At servlet creation time, the servlet container calls the `init()` method, and before deallocating the servlet, the servlet container calls the servlet's `destroy()` method.

When a servlet container calls a servlet because of a requested page, it starts with the `service()` method, whose default behavior is to call one of the following methods based on the HTTP transfer method: `service()` calls `doGet()` for a HTTP GET request, and it calls `doPost()` for a HTTP POST request. This automatic dispatching allows the servlet to perform different tasks on the request data depending on the HTTP transfer method. Usually, we do not override the `service()` method, unless we want to program a servlet that handles both HTTP POST and HTTP GET requests identically.

We conclude our discussion of servlets with an example, shown in Figure 7.19, that illustrates how to pass arguments from an HTML form to a servlet.

7.7.4 JavaServer Pages

In the previous section, we saw how to use Java programs in the middle tier to encode application logic and dynamically generate webpages. If we needed to generate HTML output, we wrote it to the `out` object. Thus, we can think about servlets as Java code embodying application logic, with embedded HTML for output.

JavaServer pages (JSPs) interchange the roles of output and application logic. JavaServer pages are written in HTML with servlet-like code embedded in special HTML tags. Thus, in comparison to servlets, JavaServer pages are better suited to quickly building interfaces that have some logic inside, whereas servlets are better suited for complex application logic.

```
import java.io.*;
import javax.servlet.*;
import javax.servlet.http.*;
import java.util.*;

public class ReadUserName extends HttpServlet {
    public void doGet(HttpServletRequest request,
            HttpServletResponse response)
        throws ServletException, IOException {

        response.setContentType("text/html");
        PrintWriter out = response.getWriter();

        out.println("<BODY>\n" +
            "<H1 ALIGN=CENTER> Username: </H1>\n" +
            "<UL>\n" +
            " <LI>title: "
            + request.getParameter("userid") + "\n" +
            + request.getParameter("password") + "\n" +
            "</UL>\n" +
            "</BODY></HTML>");
    }

    public void doPost(HttpServletRequest request,
            HttpServletResponse response)
        throws ServletException, IOException {
        doGet(request, response);
    }
}
```

Figure 7.19 Extracting the User Name and Password From a Form

While there is a big difference for the programmer, the middle tier handles JavaServer pages in a very simple way: They are usually compiled into a servlet, which is then handled by a servlet container analogous to other servlets.

The code fragment in Figure 7.20 shows a simple JSP example. In the middle of the HTML code, we access information that was passed from a form.

```
<!DOCTYPE HTML PUBLIC "-//W3C//DTD HTML 4.0
        Transitional//EN">
<HTML>
<HEAD><TITLE>Welcome to Barnes and Nobble</TITLE></HEAD>
<BODY>
    <H1>Welcome back!</H1>
    <% String name="NewUser";
        if (request.getParameter("username") != null) {
            name=request.getParameter("username");
        }
    %>
    You are logged on as user <%=name%>
    <P>
    Regular HTML for all the rest of the on-line store's webpage.
</BODY>
</HTML>
```

Figure 7.20 Reading Form Parameters in JSP

7.7.5 Maintaining State

As discussed in previous sections, there is a need to maintain a user's **state** across different pages. As an example, consider a user who wants to make a purchase at the Barnes and Nobble website. The user must first add items into her shopping basket, which persists while she navigates through the site. Thus, we use the notion of state mainly to remember information as the user navigates through the site.

The HTTP protocol is stateless. We call an interaction with a webserver **stateless** if no information is retained from one request to the next request. We call an interaction with a webserver **stateful**, or we say that **state is maintained**, if some memory is stored between requests to the server, and different actions are taken depending on the contents stored.

In our example of Barnes and Nobble, we need to maintain the shopping basket of a user. Since state is not encapsulated in the HTTP protocol, it has to be maintained either at the server or at the client. Since the HTTP protocol is stateless by design, let us review the advantages and disadvantages of this design decision. First, a stateless protocol is easy to program and use, and it is great for applications that require just retrieval of static information. In addition, no extra memory is used to maintain state, and thus the protocol itself is very efficient. On the other hand, without some additional mechanism at the presentation tier and the middle tier, we have no record of previous requests, and we cannot program shopping baskets or user logins.

Since we cannot maintain state in the HTTP protocol, where should we mtaintain state? There are basically two choices. We can maintain state in the middle tier, by storing information in the local main memory of the application logic, or even in a database system. Alternatively, we can maintain state on the client side by storing data in the form of a *cookie*. We discuss these two ways of maintaining state in the next two sections.

Maintaining State at the Middle Tier

At the middle tier, we have several choices as to *where* we maintain state. First, we could store the state at the bottom tier, in the database server. The state survives crashes of the system, but a database access is required to query or update the state, a potential performance bottleneck. An alternative is to store state in main memory at the middle tier. The drawbacks are that this information is volatile and that it might take up a lot of main memory. We can also store state in local files at the middle tier, as a compromise between the first two approaches.

A rule of thumb is to use state maintenance at the middle tier or database tier only for data that needs to persist over many different user sessions. Examples of such data are past customer orders, click-stream data recording a user's movement through the website, or other permanent choices that a user makes, such as decisions about personalized site layout, types of messages the user is willing to receive, and so on. As these examples illustrate, state information is often centered around users who interact with the website.

Maintaining State at the Presentation Tier: Cookies

Another possibility is to store state at the presentation tier and pass it to the middle tier with every HTTP request. We essentially work around around the statelessness of the HTTP protocol by sending additional information with every request. Such information is called a cookie.

A **cookie** is a collection of ⟨*name*, *value*⟩–pairs that can be manipulated at the presentation and middle tiers. Cookies are easy to use in Java servlets and JavaServer Pages and provide a simple way to make non-essential data persistent at the client. They survive several client sessions because they persist in the browser cache even after the browser is closed.

One disadvantage of cookies is that they are often perceived as as being invasive, and many users disable cookies in their Web browser; browsers allow users to prevent cookies from being saved on their machines. Another disadvantage is that the data in a cookie is currently limited to 4KB, but for most applications this is not a bad limit.

We can use cookies to store information such as the user's shopping basket, login information, and other non-permanent choices made in the current session.

Next, we discuss how cookies can be manipulated from servlets at the middle tier.

The Servlet Cookie API

A cookie is stored in a small text file at the client and contains ⟨*name*, *value*⟩–pairs, where both name and value are strings. We create a new cookie through the Java `Cookie` class in the middle tier application code:

```
Cookie cookie = new Cookie("username","guest");
cookie.setDomain("www.bookstore.com");
cookie.setSecure(false);            // no SSL required
cookie.setMaxAge(60*60*24*7*31);    // one month lifetime
response.addCookie(cookie);
```

Let us look at each part of this code. First, we create a new Cookie object with the specified ⟨*name*, *value*⟩–pair. Then we set attributes of the cookie; we list some of the most common attributes below:

- `setDomain` and `getDomain`: The domain specifies the website that will receive the cookie. The default value for this attribute is the domain that created the cookie.
- `setSecure` and `getSecure`: If this flag is `true`, then the cookie is sent only if we are using a secure version of the HTTP protocol, such as SSL.
- `setMaxAge` and `getMaxAge`: The `MaxAge` attribute determines the lifetime of the cookie in seconds. If the value of `MaxAge` is less than or equal to zero, the cookie is deleted when the browser is closed.

- `setName` and `getName`: We did not use these functions in our code fragment; they allow us to name the cookie.
- `setValue` and `getValue`: These functions allow us to set and read the value of the cookie.

The cookie is added to the `request` object within the Java servlet to be sent to the client. Once a cookie is received from a site (`www.bookstore.com` in this example), the client's Web browser appends it to all HTTP requests it sends to this site, until the cookie expires.

We can access the contents of a cookie in the middle-tier code through the `request` object `getCookies()` method, which returns an array of Cookie objects. The following code fragment reads the array and looks for the cookie with name 'username.'

```
Cookie[] cookies = request.getCookies();
String theUser;
for(int i=0; i < cookies.length; i++) {
    Cookie cookie = cookies[i];
    if (cookie.getName().equals("username"))
        theUser = cookie.getValue();
}
```

A simple test can be used to check whether the user has turned off cookies: Send a cookie to the user, and then check whether the `request` object that is returned still contains the cookie. Note that a cookie should never contain an unencrypted password or other private, unencrypted data, as the user can easily inspect, modify, and erase any cookie at any time, including in the middle of a session. The application logic needs to have sufficient consistency checks to ensure that the data in the cookie is valid.

7.8 CASE STUDY: THE INTERNET BOOK SHOP

DBDudes now moves on to the implementation of the application layer and considers alternatives for connecting the DBMS to the World Wide Web.

DBDudes begins by considering session management. For example, users who log in to the site, browse the catalog, and select books to buy do not want to re-enter their customer identification numbers. Session management has to extend to the whole process of selecting books, adding them to a shopping cart, possibly removing books from the cart, and checking out and paying for the books.

DBDudes then considers whether webpages for books should be static or dynamic. If there is a static webpage for each book, then we need an extra database field in the Books relation that points to the location of the file. Even though this enables special page designs for different books, it is a very labor-intensive solution. DBDudes convinces B&N to dynamically assemble the webpage for a book from a standard template instantiated with information about the book in the Books relation. Thus, DBDudes do not use static HTML pages, such as the one shown in Figure 7.1, to display the inventory.

DBDudes considers the use of XML as a data exchange format between the database server and the middle tier, or the middle tier and the client tier. Representation of the data in XML at the middle tier as shown in Figures 7.2 and 7.3 would allow easier integration of other data sources in the future, but B&N decides that they do not anticipate a need for such integration, and so DBDudes decide not to use XML data exchange at this time.

DBDudes designs the application logic as follows. They think that there will be four different webpages:

- `index.jsp`: The home page of Barns and Nobble. This is the main entry point for the shop. This page has search text fields and buttons that allow the user to search by author name, ISBN, or title of the book. There is also a link to the page that shows the shopping cart, `cart.jsp`.
- `login.jsp`: Allows registered users to log in. Here DBDudes use an HTML form similar to the one displayed in Figure 7.11. At the middle tier, they use a code fragment similar to the piece shown in Figure 7.19 and JavaServerPages as shown in Figure 7.20.
- `search.jsp`: Lists all books in the database that match the search condition specified by the user. The user can add listed items to the shopping basket; each book has a button next to it that adds it. (If the item is already in the shopping basket, it increments the quantity by one.) There is also a counter that shows the total number of items currently in the shopping basket. (DBDudes makes a note that that a quantity of five for a single item in the shopping basket should indicate a total purchase quantity of five as well.) The `search.jsp` page also contains a button that directs the user to `cart.jsp`.
- `cart.jsp`: Lists all the books currently in the shopping basket. The listing should include all items in the shopping basket with the product name, price, a text box for the quantity (which the user can use to change quantities of items), and a button to remove the item from the shopping basket. This page has three other buttons: one button to continue shopping (which returns the user to page `index.jsp`), a second button to update the shop-

ping basket with the altered quantities from the text boxes, and a third button to place the order, which directs the user to the page `confirm.jsp`.

- `confirm.jsp`: Lists the complete order so far and allows the user to enter his or her contact information or customer ID. There are two buttons on this page: one button to cancel the order and a second button to submit the final order. The cancel button empties the shopping basket and returns the user to the home page. The submit button updates the database with the new order, empties the shopping basket, and returns the user to the home page.

DBDudes also considers the use of JavaScript at the presentation tier to check user input before it is sent to the middle tier. For example, in the page `login.jsp`, DBDudes is likely to write JavaScript code similar to that shown in Figure 7.12.

This leaves DBDudes with one final decision: how to connect applications to the DBMS. They consider the two main alternatives presented in Section 7.7: CGI scripts versus using an application server infrastructure. If they use CGI scripts, they would have to encode session management logic—not an easy task. If they use an application server, they can make use of all the functionality that the application server provides. Therefore, they recommend that B&N implement server-side processing using an application server.

B&N accepts the decision to use an application server, but decides that no code should be specific to any particular application server, since B&N does not want to lock itself into one vendor. DBDudes agrees proceeds to build the following pieces:

- DBDudes designs top level pages that allow customers to navigate the website as well as various search forms and result presentations.
- Assuming that DBDudes selects a Java-based application server, they have to write Java servlets to process form-generated requests. Potentially, they could reuse existing (possibly commercially available) JavaBeans. They can use JDBC as a database interface; examples of JDBC code can be found in Section 6.2. Instead of programming servlets, they could resort to Java Server Pages and annotate pages with special JSP markup tags.
- DBDudes select an application server that uses proprietary markup tags, but due to their arrangement with B&N, they are not allowed to use such tags in their code.

For completeness, we remark that if DBDudes and B&N had agreed to use CGI scripts, DBDudes would have had the following tasks:

- Create the top level HTML pages that allow users to navigate the site and various forms that allow users to search the catalog by ISBN, author name, or title. An example page containing a search form is shown in Figure 7.1. In addition to the input forms, DBDudes must develop appropriate presentations for the results.
- Develop the logic to track a customer session. Relevant information must be stored either at the server side or in the customer's browser using cookies.
- Write the scripts that process user requests. For example, a customer can use a form called 'Search books by title' to type in a title and search for books with that title. The CGI interface communicates with a script that processes the request. An example of such a script written in Perl using the DBI library for data access is shown in Figure 7.16.

Our discussion thus far covers only the customer interface, the part of the website that is exposed to B&N's customers. DBDudes also needs to add applications that allow the employees and the shop owner to query and access the database and to generate summary reports of business activities.

Complete files for the case study can be found on the webpage for this book.

7.9 REVIEW QUESTIONS

Answers to the review questions can be found in the listed sections.

- What are URIs and URLs? **(Section 7.2.1)**
- How does the HTTP protocol work? What is a stateless protocol? **(Section 7.2.2)**
- Explain the main concepts of HTML. Why is it used only for data presentation and not data exchange? **(Section 7.3)**
- What are some shortcomings of HTML, and how does XML address them? **(Section 7.4)**
- What are the main components of an XML document? **(Section 7.4.1)**
- Why do we have XML DTDs? What is a well-formed XML document? What is a valid XML document? Give an example of an XML document that is valid but not well-formed, and vice versa. **(Section 7.4.2)**
- What is the role of domain-specific DTDs? **(Section 7.4.3)**
- What is a three-tier architecture? What advantages does it offer over single-tier and two-tier architectures? Give a short overview of the functionality at each of the three tiers. **(Section 7.5)**

- Explain how three-tier architectures address each of the following issues of database-backed Internet applications: heterogeneity, thin clients, data integration, scalability, software development. **(Section 7.5.3)**
- Write an HTML form. Describe all the components of an HTML form. **(Section 7.6.1)**
- What is the difference between the HTML `GET` and `POST` methods? How does URI encoding of an HTML form work? **(Section 7.11)**
- What is JavaScript used for? Write a JavaScipt function that checks whether an HTML form element contains a syntactically valid email address. **(Section 7.6.2)**
- What problem do style sheets address? What are the advantages of using style sheets? **(Section 7.6.3)**
- What are Cascading Style Sheets? Explain the components of Cascading Style Sheets. What is XSL and how it is different from CSS? **(Sections 7.6.3 and 7.13)**
- What is CGI and what problem does it address? **(Section 7.7.1)**
- What are application servers and how are they different from webservers? **(Section 7.7.2)**
- What are servlets? How do servlets handle data from HTML forms? Explain what happens during the lifetime of a servlet. **(Section 7.7.3)**
- What is the difference between servlets and JSP? When should we use servlets and when should we use JSP? **(Section 7.7.4)**
- Why do we need to maintain state at the middle tier? What are cookies? How does a browser handle cookies? How can we access the data in cookies from servlets? **(Section 7.7.5)**

EXERCISES

Exercise 7.1 Briefly answer the following questions:

1. Explain the following terms and describe what they are used for: HTML, URL, XML, Java, JSP, XSL, XSLT, servlet, cookie, HTTP, CSS, DTD.
2. What is CGI? Why was CGI introduced? What are the disadvantages of an architecture using CGI scripts?
3. What is the difference between a webserver and an application server? What funcionality do typical application servers provide?
4. When is an XML document well-formed? When is an XML document valid?

Exercise 7.2 Briefly answer the following questions about the HTTP protocol:

1. What is a communication protocol?
2. What is the structure of an HTTP request message? What is the structure of an HTTP response message? Why do HTTP messages carry a version field?
3. What is a stateless protocol? Why was HTTP designed to be stateless?
4. Show the HTTP request message generated when you request the home page of this book (`http://www.cs.wisc.edu/~dbbook`). Show the HTTP response message that the server generates for that page.

Exercise 7.3 In this exercise, you are asked to write the functionality of a generic shopping basket; you will use this in several subsequent project exercises. Write a set of JSP pages that displays a shopping basket of items and allows users to add, remove, and change the quantity of items. To do this, use a cookie storage scheme that stores the following information:

- The UserId of the user who owns the shopping basket.
- The number of products stored in the shopping basket.
- A product id and a quantity for each product.

When manipulating cookies, remember to set the `Expires` property such that the cookie can persist for a session or indefinitely. Experiment with cookies using JSP and make sure you know how to retrieve, set values, and delete the cookie.

You need to create five JSP pages to make your prototype complete:

- **Index Page** (`index.jsp`): This is the main entry point. It has a link that directs the user to the Products page so they can start shopping.
- **Products Page** (`products.jsp`): Shows a listing of all products in the database with their descriptions and prices. This is the main page where the user fills out the shopping basket. Each listed product should have a button next to it, which adds it to the shopping basket. (If the item is already in the shopping basket, it increments the quantity by one.) There should also be a counter to show the total number of items currently in the shopping basket. Note that if a user has a quantity of five of a single item in the shopping basket, the counter should indicate a total quantity of five. The page also contains a button that directs the user to the Cart page.
- **Cart Page** (`cart.jsp`): Shows a listing of all items in the shopping basket cookie. The listing for each item should include the product name, price, a text box for the quantity (the user can change the quantity of items here), and a button to remove the item from the shopping basket. This page has three other buttons: one button to continue shopping (which returns the user to the Products page), a second button to update the cookie with the altered quantities from the text boxes, and a third button to place or confirm the order, which directs the user to the Confirm page.
- **Confirm Page** (`confirm.jsp`): Lists the final order. There are two buttons on this page. One button cancels the order and the other submits the completed order. The cancel button just deletes the cookie and returns the user to the Index page. The submit button updates the database with the new order, deletes the cookie, and returns the user to the Index page.

Exercise 7.4 In the previous exercise, replace the page `products.jsp` with the following *search page* `search.jsp`. This page allows users to search products by name or description. There should be both a text box for the search text and radio buttons to allow the user to choose between search-by-name and search-by-description (as well as a submit button to retrieve the results). The page that handles search results should be modeled after `products.jsp` (as described in the previous exercise) and be called `products.jsp`. It should retrieve all records where the search text is a substring of the name or description (as chosen by the user). To integrate this with the previous exercise, simply replace all the links to `products.jsp` with `search.jsp`.

Exercise 7.5 Write a simple authentication mechanism (without using encrypted transfer of passwords, for simplicity). We say a user is authenticated if she has provided a valid username-password combination to the system; otherwise, we say the user is not authenticated. Assume for simplicity that you have a database schema that stores only a customer id and a password:

Passwords(<u>cid: `integer`</u>, username: `string`, password: `string`)

1. How and where are you going to track when a user is 'logged on' to the system?
2. Design a page that allows a registered user to log on to the system.
3. Design a page header that checks whether the user visiting this page is logged in.

Exercise 7.6 (Due to Jeff Derstadt) TechnoBooks.com is in the process of reorganizing its website. A major issue is how to efficiently handle a large number of search results. In a human interaction study, it found that modem users typically like to view 20 search results at a time, and it would like to program this logic into the system. Queries that return batches of sorted results are called *top N queries*. (See Section 25.5 for a discussion of database support for top N queries.) For example, results 1-20 are returned, then results 21-40, then 41-60, and so on. Different techniques are used for performing top N queries and TechnoBooks.com would like you to implement two of them.

Infrastructure: Create a database with a table called Books and populate it with some books, using the format that follows. This gives you 111 books in your database with a title of AAA, BBB, CCC, DDD, or EEE, but the keys are not sequential for books with the same title.

Books(<u>*bookid:* `INTEGER`</u>, *title:* `CHAR(80)`, *author:* `CHAR(80)`, *price:* `REAL`)

```
For i = 1 to 111 {
        Insert the tuple (i, "AAA", "AAA Author", 5.99)
        i = i + 1
        Insert the tuple (i, "BBB", "BBB Author", 5.99)
        i = i + 1
        Insert the tuple (i, "CCC", "CCC Author", 5.99)
        i = i + 1
        Insert the tuple (i, "DDD", "DDD Author", 5.99)
        i = i + 1
        Insert the tuple (i, "EEE", "EEE Author", 5.99)
}
```

Placeholder Technique: The simplest approach to top N queries is to store a placeholder for the first and last result tuples, and then perform the same query. When the new query results are returned, you can iterate to the placeholders and return the previous or next 20 results.

Tuples Shown	Lower Placeholder	Previous Set	Upper Placeholder	Next Set
1-20	1	None	20	21-40
21-40	21	1-20	40	41-60
41-60	41	21-40	60	61-80

Write a webpage in JSP that displays the contents of the Books table, sorted by the Title and BookId, and showing the results 20 at a time. There should be a link (where appropriate) to get the previous 20 results or the next 20 results. To do this, you can encode the placeholders in the Previous or Next Links as follows. Assume that you are displaying records 21–40. Then the previous link is `display.jsp?lower=21` and the next link is `display.jsp?upper=40`.

You should not display a previous link when there are no previous results; nor should you show a Next link if there are no more results. When your page is called again to get another batch of results, you can perform the same query to get all the records, iterate through the result set until you are at the proper starting point, then display 20 more results.

What are the advantages and disadvantages of this technique?

Query Constraints Technique: A second technique for performing top N queries is to push boundary constraints into the query (in the `WHERE` clause) so that the query returns only results that have not yet been displayed. Although this changes the query, fewer results are returned and it saves the cost of iterating up to the boundary. For example, consider the following table, sorted by (title, primary key).

Batch	Result Number	Title	Primary Key
1	1	AAA	105
1	2	BBB	13
1	3	CCC	48
1	4	DDD	52
1	5	DDD	101
2	6	DDD	121
2	7	EEE	19
2	8	EEE	68
2	9	FFF	2
2	10	FFF	33
3	11	FFF	58
3	12	FFF	59
3	13	GGG	93
3	14	HHH	132
3	15	HHH	135

In batch 1, rows 1 through 5 are displayed, in batch 2 rows 6 through 10 are displayed, and so on. Using the placeholder technique, all 15 results would be returned for each batch. Using the constraint technique, batch 1 displays results 1-5 but returns results 1-15, batch 2 will display results 6-10 but returns only results 6-15, and batch 3 will display results 11-15 but return only results 11-15.

The constraint can be pushed into the query because of the sorting of this table. Consider the following query for batch 2 (displaying results 6-10):

```
EXEC SQL SELECT B.Title
FROM     Books B
WHERE    (B.Title = 'DDD' AND B.BookId > 101) OR (B.Title > 'DDD')
ORDER BY B.Title, B.BookId
```

This query first selects all books with the title 'DDD,' but with a primary key that is greater than that of record 5 (record 5 has a primary key of 101). This returns record 6. Also, any book that has a title after 'DDD' alphabetically is returned. You can then display the first five results.

The following information needs to be retained to have Previous and Next buttons that return more results:

- **Previous:** The title of the *first* record in the previous set, and the primary key of the *first* record in the previous set.
- **Next:** The title of the *first* record in the next set; the primary key of the *first* record in the next set.

These four pieces of information can be encoded into the Previous and Next buttons as in the previous part. Using your database table from the first part, write a JavaServer Page that displays the book information 20 records at a time. The page should include *Previous* and *Next* buttons to show the previous or next record set if there is one. Use the constraint query to get the Previous and Next record sets.

PROJECT-BASED EXERCISES

In this chapter, you continue the exercises from the previous chapter and create the parts of the application that reside at the middle tier and at the presentation tier. More information about these exercises and material for more exercises can be found online at

`http://www.cs.wisc.edu/~dbbook`

Exercise 7.7 Recall the Notown Records website that you worked on in Exercise 6.6. Next, you are asked to develop the actual pages for the Notown Records website. Design the part of the website that involves the presentation tier and the middle tier, and integrate the code that you wrote in Exercise 6.6 to access the database.

1. Describe in detail the set of webpages that users can access. Keep the following issues in mind:
   - All users start at a common page.
   - For each action, what input does the user provide? How will the user provide it—by clicking on a link or through an HTML form?
   - What sequence of steps does a user go through to purchase a record? Describe the high-level application flow by showing how each user action is handled.

2. Write the webpages in HTML without dynamic content.
3. Write a page that allows users to log on to the site. Use cookies to store the information permanently at the user's browser.
4. Augment the log-on page with JavaScript code that checks that the username consists only of the characters from a to z.
5. Augment the pages that allow users to store items in a shopping basket with a condition that checks whether the user has logged on to the site. If the user has not yet logged on, there should be no way to add items to the shopping cart. Implement this functionality using JSP by checking cookie information from the user.
6. Create the remaining pages to finish the website.

Exercise 7.8 Recall the online pharmacy project that you worked on in Exercise 6.7 in Chapter 6. Follow the analogous steps from Exercise 7.7 to design the application logic and presentation layer and finish the website.

Exercise 7.9 Recall the university database project that you worked on in Exercise 6.8 in Chapter 6. Follow the analogous steps from Exercise 7.7 to design the application logic and presentation layer and finish the website.

Exercise 7.10 Recall the airline reservation project that you worked on in Exercise 6.9 in Chapter 6. Follow the analogous steps from Exercise 7.7 to design the application logic and presentation layer and finish the website.

BIBLIOGRAPHIC NOTES

The latest version of the standards mentioned in this chapter can be found at the website of the World Wide Web Consortium (`www.w3.org`). It contains links to information about HTML, cascading style sheets, XML, XSL, and much more. The book by Hall is a general introduction to Web programming technologies [357]; a good starting point on the Web is `www.Webdeveloper.com`. There are many introductory books on CGI programming, for example [210, 198]. The JavaSoft (`java.sun.com`) home page is a good starting point for Servlets, JSP, and all other Java-related technologies. The book by Hunter [394] is a good introduction to Java Servlets. Microsoft supports Active Server Pages (ASP), a comparable technology to JSP. More information about ASP can be found on the Microsoft Developer's Network home page (`msdn.microsoft.com`).

There are excellent websites devoted to the advancement of XML, for example `www.xml.com` and `www.ibm.com/xml`, that also contain a plethora of links with information about the other standards. There are good introductory books on many different aspects of XML, for example [195, 158, 597, 474, 381, 320]. Information about UNICODE can be found on its home page `http://www.unicode.org`.

Information about JavaServer Pages and servlets can be found on the JavaSoft home page at `java.sun.com` at `java.sun.com/products/jsp` and at `java.sun.com/products/servlet`.

PART III

STORAGE AND INDEXING

8

OVERVIEW OF STORAGE AND INDEXING

- How does a DBMS store and access persistent data?
- Why is I/O cost so important for database operations?
- How does a DBMS organize files of data records on disk to minimize I/O costs?
- What is an index, and why is it used?
- What is the relationship between a file of data records and any indexes on this file of records?
- What are important properties of indexes?
- How does a hash-based index work, and when is it most effective?
- How does a tree-based index work, and when is it most effective?
- How can we use indexes to optimize performance for a given workload?
- **Key concepts:** external storage, buffer manager, page I/O; file organization, heap files, sorted files; indexes, data entries, search keys, clustered index, clustered file, primary index; index organization, hash-based and tree-based indexes; cost comparison, file organizations and common operations; performance tuning, workload, composite search keys, use of clustering,

If you don't find it in the index, look very carefully through the entire catalog.

—Sears, Roebuck, and Co., Consumers' Guide, 1897

The basic abstraction of data in a DBMS is a collection of records, or a *file*, and each file consists of one or more pages. The *files and access methods* software layer organizes data carefully to support fast access to desired subsets of records. Understanding how records are organized is essential to using a database system effectively, and it is the main topic of this chapter.

A **file organization** is a method of arranging the records in a file when the file is stored on disk. Each file organization makes certain operations efficient but other operations expensive.

Consider a file of employee records, each containing *age, name*, and *sal* fields, which we use as a running example in this chapter. If we want to retrieve employee records in order of increasing age, sorting the file by age is a good file organization, but the sort order is expensive to maintain if the file is frequently modified. Further, we are often interested in supporting more than one operation on a given collection of records. In our example, we may also want to retrieve all employees who make more than $5000. We have to scan the entire file to find such employee records.

A technique called *indexing* can help when we have to access a collection of records in multiple ways, in addition to efficiently supporting various kinds of selection. Section 8.2 introduces indexing, an important aspect of file organization in a DBMS. We present an overview of index data structures in Section 8.3; a more detailed discussion is included in Chapters 10 and 11.

We illustrate the importance of choosing an appropriate file organization in Section 8.4 through a simplified analysis of several alternative file organizations. The cost model used in this analysis, presented in Section 8.4.1, is used in later chapters as well. In Section 8.5, we highlight some important choices to be made in creating indexes. Choosing a good collection of indexes to build is arguably the single most powerful tool a database administrator has for improving performance.

8.1 DATA ON EXTERNAL STORAGE

A DBMS stores vast quantities of data, and the data must persist across program executions. Therefore, data is stored on external storage devices such as disks and tapes, and fetched into main memory as needed for processing. The unit of information read from or written to disk is a *page*. The size of a page is a DBMS parameter, and typical values are 4KB or 8KB.

The cost of page I/O (*input* from disk to main memory and *output* from memory to disk) dominates the cost of typical database operations, and database systems are carefully optimized to minimize this cost. While the details of how files of records are physically stored on disk and how main memory is utilized are covered in Chapter 9, the following points are important to keep in mind:

- Disks are the most important external storage devices. They allow us to retrieve any page at a (more or less) fixed cost per page. However, if we read several pages in the order that they are stored physically, the cost can be much less than the cost of reading the same pages in a random order.
- Tapes are sequential access devices and force us to read data one page after the other. They are mostly used to archive data that is not needed on a regular basis.
- Each record in a file has a unique identifier called a **record id**, or **rid** for short. An rid has the property that we can identify the disk address of the page containing the record by using the rid.

Data is read into memory for processing, and written to disk for persistent storage, by a layer of software called the *buffer manager*. When the *files and access methods* layer (which we often refer to as just the file layer) needs to process a page, it asks the buffer manager to fetch the page, specifying the page's rid. The buffer manager fetches the page from disk if it is not already in memory.

Space on disk is managed by the *disk space manager*, according to the DBMS software architecture described in Section 1.8. When the files and access methods layer needs additional space to hold new records in a file, it asks the disk space manager to allocate an additional disk page for the file; it also informs the disk space manager when it no longer needs one of its disk pages. The disk space manager keeps track of the pages in use by the file layer; if a page is freed by the file layer, the space manager tracks this, and reuses the space if the file layer requests a new page later on.

In the rest of this chapter, we focus on the files and access methods layer.

8.2 FILE ORGANIZATIONS AND INDEXING

The **file of records** is an important abstraction in a DBMS, and is implemented by the files and access methods layer of the code. A file can be created, destroyed, and have records inserted into and deleted from it. It also supports scans; a **scan** operation allows us to step through all the records in the file one at a time. A relation is typically stored as a file of records.

The file layer stores the records in a file in a collection of disk pages. It keeps track of pages allocated to each file, and as records are inserted into and deleted from the file, it also tracks available space within pages allocated to the file.

The simplest file structure is an unordered file, or **heap file**. Records in a heap file are stored in random order across the pages of the file. A heap file organization supports retrieval of all records, or retrieval of a particular record specified by its rid; the file manager must keep track of the pages allocated for the file. (We defer the details of how a heap file is implemented to Chapter 9.)

An **index** is a data structure that organizes data records on disk to optimize certain kinds of retrieval operations. An index allows us to efficiently retrieve all records that satisfy search conditions on the **search key** fields of the index. We can also create additional indexes on a given collection of data records, each with a different search key, to speed up search operations that are not efficiently supported by the file organization used to store the data records.

Consider our example of employee records. We can store the records in a file organized as an index on employee age; this is an alternative to sorting the file by age. Additionally, we can create an auxiliary index file based on salary, to speed up queries involving salary. The first file contains employee records, and the second contains records that allow us to locate employee records satisfying a query on salary.

We use the term **data entry** to refer to the records stored in an index file. A data entry with search key value k, denoted as $k*$, contains enough information to locate (one or more) data records with search key value k. We can efficiently search an index to find the desired data entries, and then use these to obtain data records (if these are distinct from data entries).

There are three main alternatives for what to store as a data entry in an index:

1. A data entry $k*$ is an actual data record (with search key value k).
2. A data entry is a $\langle k,\ rid \rangle$ pair, where *rid* is the record id of a data record with search key value k.
3. A data entry is a $\langle k,\ rid\text{-}list \rangle$ pair, where *rid-list* is a list of record ids of data records with search key value k.

Of course, if the index is used to store actual data records, Alternative (1), each entry $k*$ is a data record with search key value k. We can think of such an index as a special file organization. Such an **indexed file organization** can be used instead of, for example, a sorted file or an unordered file of records.

Alternatives (2) and (3), which contain data entries that point to data records, are independent of the file organization that is used for the indexed file (i.e., the file that contains the data records). Alternative (3) offers better space utilization than Alternative (2), but data entries are variable in length, depending on the number of data records with a given search key value.

If we want to build more than one index on a collection of data records—for example, we want to build indexes on both the *age* and the *sal* fields for a collection of employee records—at most one of the indexes should use Alternative (1) because we should avoid storing data records multiple times.

8.2.1 Clustered Indexes

When a file is organized so that the ordering of data records is the same as or close to the ordering of data entries in some index, we say that the index is **clustered**; otherwise, it clustered is an **unclustered** index. An index that uses Alternative (1) is clustered, by definition. An index that uses Alternative (2) or (3) can be a clustered index only if the data records are sorted on the search key field. Otherwise, the order of the data records is random, defined purely by their physical order, and there is no reasonable way to arrange the data entries in the index in the same order.

In practice, files are rarely kept sorted since this is too expensive to maintain when the data is updated. So, in practice, a clustered index is an index that uses Alternative (1), and indexes that use Alternatives (2) or (3) are unclustered. We sometimes refer to an index using Alternative (1) as a **clustered file**, because the data entries are actual data records, and the index is therefore a file of data records. (As observed earlier, searches and scans on an index return only its data entries, even if it contains additional information to organize the data entries.)

The cost of using an index to answer a range search query can vary tremendously based on whether the index is clustered. If the index is clustered, i.e., we are using the search key of a clustered file, the rids in qualifying data entries point to a contiguous collection of records, and we need to retrieve only a few data pages. If the index is unclustered, each qualifying data entry could contain a rid that points to a distinct data page, leading to as many data page I/Os as the number of data entries that match the range selection, as illustrated in Figure 8.1. This point is discussed further in Chapter 13.

8.2.2 Primary and Secondary Indexes

An index on a set of fields that includes the *primary key* (see Chapter 3) is called a **primary index**; other indexes are called **secondary** indexes. (The terms *primary index* and *secondary index* are sometimes used with a different

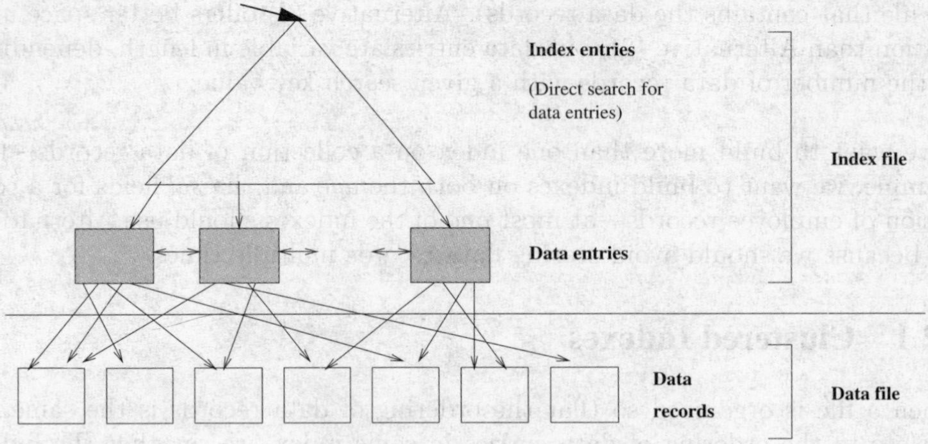

Figure 8.1 Unclustered Index Using Alternative (2)

meaning: An index that uses Alternative (1) is called a *primary index*, and one that uses Alternatives (2) or (3) is called a *secondary index*. We will be consistent with the definitions presented earlier, but the reader should be aware of this lack of standard terminology in the literature.)

Two data entries are said to be **duplicates** if they have the same value for the search key field associated with the index. A primary index is guaranteed not to contain duplicates, but an index on other (collections of) fields can contain duplicates. In general, a secondary index contains duplicates. If we know that no duplicates exist, that is, we know that the search key contains some candidate key, we call the index a **unique** index.

An important issue is how data entries in an index are organized to support efficient retrieval of data entries. We discuss this next.

8.3 INDEX DATA STRUCTURES

One way to organize data entries is to hash data entries on the search key. Another way to organize data entries is to build a tree-like data structure that directs a search for data entries. We introduce these two basic approaches in this section. We study tree-based indexing in more detail in Chapter 10 and hash-based indexing in Chapter 11.

We note that the choice of hash or tree indexing techniques can be combined with any of the three alternatives for data entries.

8.3.1 Hash-Based Indexing

We can organize records using a technique called *hashing* to quickly find records that have a given search key value. For example, if the file of employee records is hashed on the *name* field, we can retrieve all records about Joe.

In this approach, the records in a file are grouped in **buckets**, where a bucket consists of a **primary page** and, possibly, additional pages linked in a chain. The bucket to which a record belongs can be determined by applying a special function, called a **hash function**, to the search key. Given a bucket number, a hash-based index structure allows us to retrieve the primary page for the bucket in one or two disk I/Os.

On inserts, the record is inserted into the appropriate bucket, with 'overflow' pages allocated as necessary. To search for a record with a given search key value, we apply the hash function to identify the bucket to which such records belong and look at all pages in that bucket. If we do not have the search key value for the record, for example, the index is based on *sal* and we want records with a given age value, we have to scan all pages in the file.

In this chapter, we assume that applying the hash function to (the search key of) a record allows us to identify and retrieve the page containing the record with one I/O. In practice, hash-based index structures that adjust gracefully to inserts and deletes and allow us to retrieve the page containing a record in one to two I/Os (see Chapter 11) are known.

Hash indexing is illustrated in Figure 8.2, where the data is stored in a file that is hashed on *age*; the data entries in this first index file are the actual data records. Applying the hash function to the age field identifies the page that the record belongs to. The hash function h for this example is quite simple; it converts the search key value to its binary representation and uses the two least significant bits as the bucket identifier.

Figure 8.2 also shows an index with search key *sal* that contains ⟨*sal, rid*⟩ pairs as data entries. The *rid* (short for *record id*) component of a data entry in this second index is a pointer to a record with search key value *sal* (and is shown in the figure as an arrow pointing to the data record).

Using the terminology introduced in Section 8.2, Figure 8.2 illustrates Alternatives (1) and (2) for data entries. The file of employee records is hashed on *age*, and Alternative (1) is used for for data entries. The second index, on *sal*, also uses hashing to locate data entries, which are now ⟨*sal, rid of employee record*⟩ pairs; that is, Alternative (2) is used for data entries.

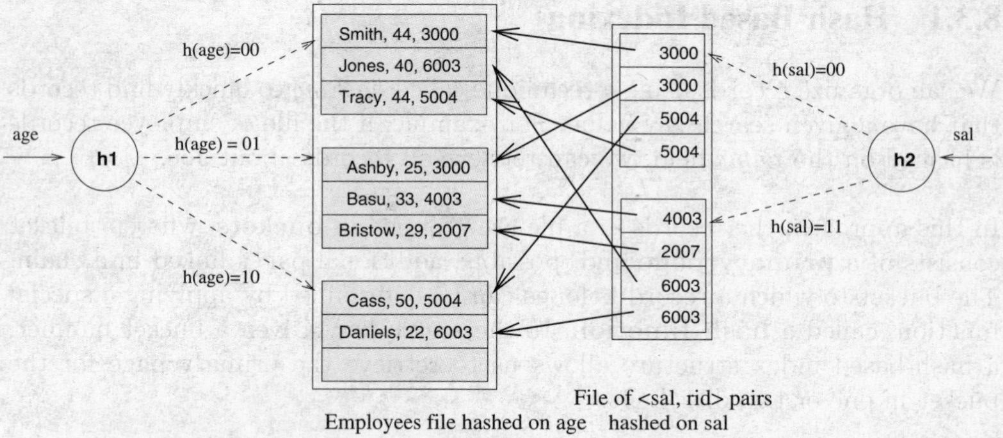

Figure 8.2 Index-Organized File Hashed on *age*, with Auxiliary Index on *sal*

Note that the search key for an index can be any sequence of one or more fields, and it need not uniquely identify records. For example, in the salary index, two data entries have the same search key value 6003. (There is an unfortunate overloading of the term *key* in the database literature. A *primary key* or *candidate key*—fields that uniquely identify a record; see Chapter 3—is unrelated to the concept of a search key.)

8.3.2 Tree-Based Indexing

An alternative to hash-based indexing is to organize records using a tree-like data structure. The data entries are arranged in sorted order by search key value, and a hierarchical search data structure is maintained that directs searches to the correct page of data entries.

Figure 8.3 shows the employee records from Figure 8.2, this time organized in a tree-structured index with search key *age*. Each node in this figure (e.g., nodes labeled A, B, L1, L2) is a physical page, and retrieving a node involves a disk I/O.

The lowest level of the tree, called the **leaf level**, contains the data entries; in our example, these are employee records. To illustrate the ideas better, we have drawn Figure 8.3 as if there were additional employee records, some with age less than 22 and some with age greater than 50 (the lowest and highest age values that appear in Figure 8.2). Additional records with age less than 22 would appear in leaf pages to the left page L1, and records with age greater than 50 would appear in leaf pages to the right of page L3.

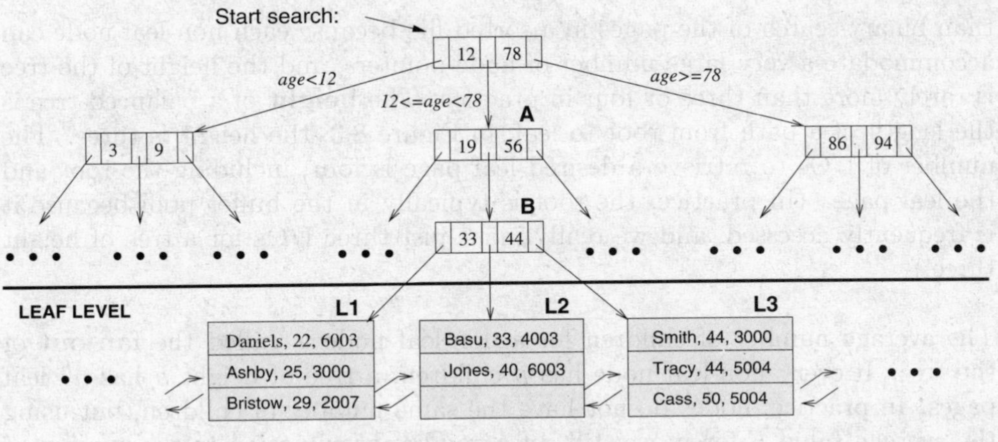

Figure 8.3 Tree-Structured Index

This structure allows us to efficiently locate all data entries with search key values in a desired range. All searches begin at the topmost node, called the **root**, and the contents of pages in non-leaf levels direct searches to the correct leaf page. Non-leaf pages contain node pointers separated by search key values. The node pointer to the left of a key value k points to a subtree that contains only data entries less than k. The node pointer to the right of a key value k points to a subtree that contains only data entries greater than or equal to k.

In our example, suppose we want to find all data entries with $24 < age < 50$. Each edge from the root node to a child node in Figure 8.2 has a label that explains what the corresponding subtree contains. (Although the labels for the remaining edges in the figure are not shown, they should be easy to deduce.) In our example search, we look for data entries with search key value > 24, and get directed to the middle child, node A. Again, examining the contents of this node, we are directed to node B. Examining the contents of node B, we are directed to leaf node L1, which contains data entries we are looking for.

Observe that leaf nodes L2 and L3 also contain data entries that satisfy our search criterion. To facilitate retrieval of such qualifying entries during search, all leaf pages are maintained in a doubly-linked list. Thus, we can fetch page L2 using the 'next' pointer on page L1, and then fetch page L3 using the 'next' pointer on L2.

Thus, the number of disk I/Os incurred during a search is equal to the length of a path from the root to a leaf, plus the number of leaf pages with qualifying data entries. The **B+ tree** is an index structure that ensures that all paths from the root to a leaf in a given tree are of the same length, that is, the structure is always balanced in height. Finding the correct leaf page is faster than binary search of the pages in a sorted file because each non-leaf node can accommodate a very large number of node-pointers, and the height of the tree is rarely more than three or four in practice. The **height** of a balanced tree is the length of a path from root to leaf; in Figure 8.3, the height is three. The number of I/Os to retrieve a desired leaf page is four, including the root and the leaf page. (In practice, the root is typically in the buffer pool because it is frequently accessed, and we really incur just three I/Os for a tree of height three.)

The average number of children for a non-leaf node is called the **fan-out** of the tree. If every non-leaf node has n children, a tree of height h has n^h leaf pages. In practice, nodes do not have the same number of children, but using the average value F for n, we still get a good approximation to the number of leaf pages, F^h. In practice, F is at least 100, which means a tree of height four contains 100 million leaf pages. Thus, we can search a file with 100 million leaf pages and find the page we want using four I/Os; in contrast, binary search of the same file would take $log_2 100,000,000$ (over 25) I/Os.

8.4 COMPARISON OF FILE ORGANIZATIONS

We now compare the costs of some simple operations for several basic file organizations on a collection of employee records. We assume that the files and indexes are organized according to the composite search key $\langle age,sal \rangle$, and that all selection operations are specified on these fields. The organizations that we consider are the following:

- File of randomly ordered employee records, or heap file.
- File of employee records sorted on $\langle age, sal \rangle$.
- Clustered B+ tree file with search key $\langle age, sal \rangle$.
- Heap file with an unclustered B+ tree index on $\langle age, sal \rangle$.
- Heap file with an unclustered hash index on $\langle age, sal \rangle$.

Our goal is to emphasize the importance of the choice of an appropriate file organization, and the above list includes the main alternatives to consider in practice. Obviously, we can keep the records unsorted or sort them. We can also choose to build an index on the data file. Note that even if the data file is sorted, an index whose search key differs from the sort order behaves like an index on a heap file!

The operations we consider are these:

- **Scan:** Fetch all records in the file. The pages in the file must be fetched from disk into the buffer pool. There is also a CPU overhead per record for locating the record on the page (in the pool).

- **Search with Equality Selection:** Fetch all records that satisfy an equality selection; for example, "Find the employee record for the employee with *age* 23 and *sal* 50." Pages that contain qualifying records must be fetched from disk, and qualifying records must be located within retrieved pages.

- **Search with Range Selection:** Fetch all records that satisfy a range selection; for example, "Find all employee records with *age* greater than 35."

- **Insert a Record:** Insert a given record into the file. We must identify the page in the file into which the new record must be inserted, fetch that page from disk, modify it to include the new record, and then write back the modified page. Depending on the file organization, we may have to fetch, modify, and write back other pages as well.

- **Delete a Record:** Delete a record that is specified using its rid. We must identify the page that contains the record, fetch it from disk, modify it, and write it back. Depending on the file organization, we may have to fetch, modify, and write back other pages as well.

8.4.1 Cost Model

In our comparison of file organizations, and in later chapters, we use a simple cost model that allows us to estimate the cost (in terms of execution time) of different database operations. We use B to denote the number of data pages when records are packed onto pages with no wasted space, and R to denote the number of records per page. The average time to read or write a disk page is D, and the average time to process a record (e.g., to compare a field value to a selection constant) is C. In the hashed file organization, we use a function, called a *hash function*, to map a record into a range of numbers; the time required to apply the hash function to a record is H. For tree indexes, we will use F to denote the fan-out, which typically is at least 100 as mentioned in Section 8.3.2.

Typical values today are $D = 15$ milliseconds, C and $H = 100$ nanoseconds; we therefore expect the cost of I/O to dominate. I/O is often (even typically) the dominant component of the cost of database operations, and so considering I/O costs gives us a good first approximation to the true costs. Further, CPU speeds are steadily rising, whereas disk speeds are not increasing at a similar pace. (On the other hand, as main memory sizes increase, a much larger fraction of the needed pages are likely to fit in memory, leading to fewer I/O requests!) We have chosen to concentrate on the I/O component of the cost model, and we assume the simple constant C for in-memory per-record processing cost. Bear the following observations in mind:

- Real systems must consider other aspects of cost, such as CPU costs (and network transmission costs in a distributed database).

- Even with our decision to focus on I/O costs, an accurate model would be too complex for our purposes of conveying the essential ideas in a simple way. We therefore use a simplistic model in which we just count the number of pages read from or written to disk as a measure of I/O. We ignore the important issue of **blocked access** in our analysis—typically, disk systems allow us to read a block of contiguous pages in a single I/O request. The cost is equal to the time required to *seek* the first page in the block and transfer all pages in the block. Such blocked access can be much cheaper than issuing one I/O request per page in the block, especially if these requests do not follow consecutively, because we would have an additional seek cost for each page in the block.

We discuss the implications of the cost model whenever our simplifying assumptions are likely to affect our conclusions in an important way.

8.4.2 Heap Files

Scan: The cost is $B(D+RC)$ because we must retrieve each of B pages taking time D per page, and for each page, process R records taking time C per record.

Search with Equality Selection: Suppose that we know in advance that exactly one record matches the desired equality selection, that is, the selection is specified on a candidate key. On average, we must scan half the file, assuming that the record exists and the distribution of values in the search field is uniform. For each retrieved data page, we must check all records on the page to see if it is the desired record. The cost is $0.5B(D + RC)$. If no record satisfies the selection, however, we must scan the entire file to verify this.

If the selection is not on a candidate key field (e.g., "Find employees aged 18"), we always have to scan the entire file because records with $age = 18$ could be dispersed all over the file, and we have no idea how many such records exist.

Search with Range Selection: The entire file must be scanned because qualifying records could appear anywhere in the file, and we do not know how many qualifying records exist. The cost is $B(D + RC)$.

Insert: We assume that records are always inserted at the end of the file. We must fetch the last page in the file, add the record, and write the page back. The cost is $2D + C$.

Delete: We must find the record, remove the record from the page, and write the modified page back. We assume that no attempt is made to compact the file to reclaim the free space created by deletions, for simplicity.[1] The cost is the cost of searching plus $C + D$.

We assume that the record to be deleted is specified using the record id. Since the page id can easily be obtained from the record id, we can directly read in the page. The cost of searching is therefore D.

If the record to be deleted is specified using an equality or range condition on some fields, the cost of searching is given in our discussion of equality and range selections. The cost of deletion is also affected by the number of qualifying records, since all pages containing such records must be modified.

8.4.3 Sorted Files

Scan: The cost is $B(D + RC)$ because all pages must be examined. Note that this case is no better or worse than the case of unordered files. However, the order in which records are retrieved corresponds to the sort order, that is, all records in *age* order, and for a given age, by *sal* order.

Search with Equality Selection: We assume that the equality selection matches the sort order $\langle age, sal \rangle$. In other words, we assume that a selection condition is specified on at least the first field in the composite key (e.g., $age = 30$). If not (e.g., selection $sal = 50$ or $department =$ "*Toy*"), the sort order does not help us and the cost is identical to that for a heap file.

We can locate the first page containing the desired record or records, should any qualifying records exist, with a binary search in $log_2 B$ steps. (This analysis assumes that the pages in the sorted file are stored sequentially, and we can retrieve the ith page on the file directly in one disk I/O.) Each step requires a disk I/O and two comparisons. Once the page is known, the first qualifying record can again be located by a binary search of the page at a cost of $Clog_2 R$. The cost is $Dlog_2 B + Clog_2 R$, which is a significant improvement over searching heap files.

[1] In practice, a directory or other data structure is used to keep track of free space, and records are inserted into the first available free slot, as discussed in Chapter 9. This increases the cost of insertion and deletion a little, but not enough to affect our comparison.

If several records qualify (e.g., "Find all employees aged 18"), they are guaranteed to be adjacent to each other due to the sorting on *age*, and so the cost of retrieving all such records is the cost of locating the first such record ($Dlog_2B + Clog_2R$) plus the cost of reading all the qualifying records in sequential order. Typically, all qualifying records fit on a single page. If no records qualify, this is established by the search for the first qualifying record, which finds the page that would have contained a qualifying record, had one existed, and searches that page.

Search with Range Selection: Again assuming that the range selection matches the composite key, the first record that satisfies the selection is located as for search with equality. Subsequently, data pages are sequentially retrieved until a record is found that does not satisfy the range selection; this is similar to an equality search with many qualifying records.

The cost is the cost of search plus the cost of retrieving the set of records that satisfy the search. The cost of the search includes the cost of fetching the first page containing qualifying, or matching, records. For small range selections, all qualifying records appear on this page. For larger range selections, we have to fetch additional pages containing matching records.

Insert: To insert a record while preserving the sort order, we must first find the correct position in the file, add the record, and then fetch and rewrite all subsequent pages (because all the old records are shifted by one slot, assuming that the file has no empty slots). On average, we can assume that the inserted record belongs in the middle of the file. Therefore, we must read the latter half of the file and then write it back after adding the new record. The cost is that of searching to find the position of the new record plus $2 \cdot (0.5B(D + RC))$, that is, search cost plus $B(D + RC)$.

Delete: We must search for the record, remove the record from the page, and write the modified page back. We must also read and write all subsequent pages because all records that follow the deleted record must be moved up to compact the free space.[2] The cost is the same as for an insert, that is, search cost plus $B(D + RC)$. Given the rid of the record to delete, we can fetch the page containing the record directly.

If records to be deleted are specified by an equality or range condition, the cost of deletion depends on the number of qualifying records. If the condition is specified on the sort field, qualifying records are guaranteed to be contiguous, and the first qualifying record can be located using binary search.

[2]Unlike a heap file, there is no inexpensive way to manage free space, so we account for the cost of compacting a file when a record is deleted.

8.4.4 Clustered Files

In a clustered file, extensive empirical study has shown that pages are usually at about 67 percent occupancy. Thus, the number of physical data pages is about $1.5B$, and we use this observation in the following analysis.

Scan: The cost of a scan is $1.5B(D + RC)$ because all data pages must be examined; this is similar to sorted files, with the obvious adjustment for the increased number of data pages. Note that our cost metric does not capture potential differences in cost due to sequential I/O. We would expect sorted files to be superior in this regard, although a clustered file using ISAM (rather than B+ trees) would be close.

Search with Equality Selection: We assume that the equality selection matches the search key $\langle age, sal \rangle$. We can locate the first page containing the desired record or records, should any qualifying records exist, in $log_F 1.5B$ steps, that is, by fetching all pages from the root to the appropriate leaf. In practice, the root page is likely to be in the buffer pool and we save an I/O, but we ignore this in our simplified analysis. Each step requires a disk I/O and two comparisons. Once the page is known, the first qualifying record can again be located by a binary search of the page at a cost of $Clog_2 R$. The cost is $Dlog_F 1.5B + Clog_2 R$, which is a significant improvement over searching even sorted files.

If several records qualify (e.g., "Find all employees aged 18"), they are guaranteed to be adjacent to each other due to the sorting on *age*, and so the cost of retrieving all such records is the cost of locating the first such record ($Dlog_F 1.5B + Clog_2 R$) plus the cost of reading all the qualifying records in sequential order.

Search with Range Selection: Again assuming that the range selection matches the composite key, the first record that satisfies the selection is located as it is for search with equality. Subsequently, data pages are sequentially retrieved (using the next and previous links at the leaf level) until a record is found that does not satisfy the range selection; this is similar to an equality search with many qualifying records.

Insert: To insert a record, we must first find the correct leaf page in the index, reading every page from root to leaf. Then, we must add the new record. Most of the time, the leaf page has sufficient space for the new record, and all we need to do is to write out the modified leaf page. Occasionally, the leaf is full and we need to retrieve and modify other pages, but this is sufficiently rare that we can ignore it in this simplified analysis. The cost is therefore the cost of search plus one write, $Dlog_F 1.5B + Clog_2 R + D$.

Delete: We must search for the record, remove the record from the page, and write the modified page back. The discussion and cost analysis for insert applies here as well.

8.4.5 Heap File with Unclustered Tree Index

The number of leaf pages in an index depends on the size of a data entry. We assume that each data entry in the index is a tenth the size of an employee data record, which is typical. The number of leaf pages in the index is $0.1(1.5B) = 0.15B$, if we take into account the 67 percent occupancy of index pages. Similarly, the number of data entries on a page $10(0.67R) = 6.7R$, taking into account the relative size and occupancy.

Scan: Consider Figure 8.1, which illustrates an unclustered index. To do a full scan of the file of employee records, we can scan the leaf level of the index and for each data entry, fetch the corresponding data record from the underlying file, obtaining data records in the sort order $\langle age, sal \rangle$.

We can read all data entries at a cost of $0.15B(D + 6.7RC)$ I/Os. Now comes the expensive part: We have to fetch the employee record for each data entry in the index. The cost of fetching the employee records is one I/O per record, since the index is unclustered and each data entry on a leaf page of the index could point to a different page in the employee file. The cost of this step is $BR(D + C)$, which is prohibitively high. If we want the employee records in sorted order, we would be better off ignoring the index and scanning the employee file directly, and then sorting it. A simple rule of thumb is that a file can be sorted by a two-pass algorithm in which each pass requires reading and writing the entire file. Thus, the I/O cost of sorting a file with B pages is $4B$, which is much less than the cost of using an unclustered index.

Search with Equality Selection: We assume that the equality selection matches the sort order $\langle age, sal \rangle$. We can locate the first page containing the desired data entry or entries, should any qualifying entries exist, in $log_F 0.15B$ steps, that is, by fetching all pages from the root to the appropriate leaf. Each step requires a disk I/O and two comparisons. Once the page is known, the first qualifying data entry can again be located by a binary search of the page at a cost of $Clog_2 6.7R$. The first qualifying data record can be fetched from the employee file with another I/O. The cost is $Dlog_F 0.15B + Clog_2 6.7R + D$, which is a significant improvement over searching sorted files.

If several records qualify (e.g., "Find all employees aged 18"), they are *not* guaranteed to be adjacent to each other. The cost of retrieving all such records is the cost of locating the first qualifying data entry ($Dlog_F 0.15B + Clog_2 6.7R$) plus one I/O per qualifying record. The cost of using an unclustered index is therefore very dependent on the number of qualifying records.

Search with Range Selection: Again assuming that the range selection matches the composite key, the first record that satisfies the selection is located as it is for search with equality. Subsequently, data entries are sequentially retrieved (using the next and previous links at the leaf level of the index) until a data entry is found that does not satisfy the range selection. For each qualifying data entry, we incur one I/O to fetch the corresponding employee records. The cost can quickly become prohibitive as the number of records that satisfy the range selection increases. As a rule of thumb, if 10 percent of data records satisfy the selection condition, we are better off retrieving all employee records, sorting them, and then retaining those that satisfy the selection.

Insert: We must first insert the record in the employee heap file, at a cost of $2D + C$. In addition, we must insert the corresponding data entry in the index. Finding the right leaf page costs $Dlog_F 0.15B + Clog_2 6.7R$, and writing it out after adding the new data entry costs another D.

Delete: We need to locate the data record in the employee file and the data entry in the index, and this search step costs $Dlog_F 0.15B + Clog_2 6.7R + D$. Now, we need to write out the modified pages in the index and the data file, at a cost of $2D$.

8.4.6 Heap File With Unclustered Hash Index

As for unclustered tree indexes, we assume that each data entry is one tenth the size of a data record. We consider only static hashing in our analysis, and for simplicity we assume that there are no overflow chains.[3]

In a static hashed file, pages are kept at about 80 percent occupancy (to leave space for future insertions and minimize overflows as the file expands). This is achieved by adding a new page to a bucket when each existing page is 80 percent full, when records are initially loaded into a hashed file structure. The number of pages required to store data entries is therefore 1.25 times the number of pages when the entries are densely packed, that is, $1.25(0.10B) = 0.125B$. The number of data entries that fit on a page is $10(0.80R) = 8R$, taking into account the relative size and occupancy.

[3]The dynamic variants of hashing are less susceptible to the problem of overflow chains, and have a slightly higher average cost per search, but are otherwise similar to the static version.

Scan: As for an unclustered tree index, all data entries can be retrieved inexpensively, at a cost of $0.125B(D + 8RC)$ I/Os. However, for each entry, we incur the additional cost of one I/O to fetch the corresponding data record; the cost of this step is $BR(D + C)$. This is prohibitively expensive, and further, results are unordered. So no one ever scans a hash index.

Search with Equality Selection: This operation is supported very efficiently for matching selections, that is, equality conditions are specified for each field in the composite search key $\langle age, sal \rangle$. The cost of identifying the page that contains qualifying data entries is H. Assuming that this bucket consists of just one page (i.e., no overflow pages), retrieving it costs D. If we assume that we find the data entry after scanning half the records on the page, the cost of scanning the page is $0.5(8R)C = 4RC$. Finally, we have to fetch the data record from the employee file, which is another D. The total cost is therefore $H + 2D + 4RC$, which is even lower than the cost for a tree index.

If several records qualify, they are *not* guaranteed to be adjacent to each other. The cost of retrieving all such records is the cost of locating the first qualifying data entry ($H+D+4RC$) plus one I/O per qualifying record. The cost of using an unclustered index therefore depends heavily on the number of qualifying records.

Search with Range Selection: The hash structure offers no help, and the entire heap file of employee records must be scanned at a cost of $B(D + RC)$.

Insert: We must first insert the record in the employee heap file, at a cost of $2D + C$. In addition, the appropriate page in the index must be located, modified to insert a new data entry, and then written back. The additional cost is $H + 2D + C$.

Delete: We need to locate the data record in the employee file and the data entry in the index; this search step costs $H + 2D + 4RC$. Now, we need to write out the modified pages in the index and the data file, at a cost of $2D$.

8.4.7 Comparison of I/O Costs

Figure 8.4 compares I/O costs for the various file organizations that we discussed. A heap file has good storage efficiency and supports fast scanning and insertion of records. However, it is slow for searches and deletions.

A sorted file also offers good storage efficiency, but insertion and deletion of records is slow. Searches are faster than in heap files. It is worth noting that, in a real DBMS, a file is almost never kept fully sorted.

File Type	*Scan*	*Equality Search*	*Range Search*	*Insert*	*Delete*
Heap	BD	$0.5BD$	BD	$2D$	$Search + D$
Sorted	BD	$Dlog_2B$	$Dlog_2B + \#$ *matching pages*	$Search + BD$	$Search + BD$
Clustered	$1.5BD$	$Dlog_F1.5B$	$Dlog_F1.5B + \#$ *matching pages*	$Search + D$	$Search + D$
Unclustered tree index	$BD(R + 0.15)$	$D(1 + log_F0.15B)$	$D(log_F0.15B + \#$ *matching records*$)$	$D(3 + log_F0.15B)$	$Search + 2D$
Unclustered hash index	$BD(R + 0.125)$	$2D$	BD	$4D$	$Search + 2D$

Figure 8.4 A Comparison of I/O Costs

A clustered file offers all the advantages of a sorted file *and* supports inserts and deletes efficiently. (There is a space overhead for these benefits, relative to a sorted file, but the trade-off is well worth it.) Searches are even faster than in sorted files, although a sorted file can be faster when a large number of records are retrieved sequentially, because of blocked I/O efficiencies.

Unclustered tree and hash indexes offer fast searches, insertion, and deletion, but scans and range searches with many matches are slow. Hash indexes are a little faster on equality searches, but they do not support range searches.

In summary, Figure 8.4 demonstrates that no one file organization is uniformly superior in all situations.

8.5 INDEXES AND PERFORMANCE TUNING

In this section, we present an overview of choices that arise when using indexes to improve performance in a database system. The choice of indexes has a tremendous impact on system performance, and must be made in the context of the expected **workload**, or typical mix of queries and update operations.

A full discussion of indexes and performance requires an understanding of database query evaluation and concurrency control. We therefore return to this topic in Chapter 20, where we build on the discussion in this section. In particular, we discuss examples involving multiple tables in Chapter 20 because they require an understanding of join algorithms and query evaluation plans.

8.5.1 Impact of the Workload

The first thing to consider is the expected workload and the common operations. Different file organizations and indexes, as we have seen, support different operations well.

In general, an index supports efficient retrieval of data entries that satisfy a given selection condition. Recall from the previous section that there are two important kinds of selections: equality selection and range selection. Hash-based indexing techniques are optimized only for equality selections and fare poorly on range selections, where they are typically worse than scanning the entire file of records. Tree-based indexing techniques support both kinds of selection conditions efficiently, explaining their widespread use.

Both tree and hash indexes can support inserts, deletes, and updates quite efficiently. Tree-based indexes, in particular, offer a superior alternative to maintaining fully sorted files of records. In contrast to simply maintaining the data entries in a sorted file, our discussion of (B+ tree) tree-structured indexes in Section 8.3.2 highlights two important advantages over sorted files:

1. We can handle inserts and deletes of data entries efficiently.
2. Finding the correct leaf page when searching for a record by search key value is much faster than binary search of the pages in a sorted file.

The one relative disadvantage is that the pages in a sorted file can be allocated in physical order on disk, making it much faster to retrieve several pages in sequential order. Of course, inserts and deletes on a sorted file are extremely expensive. A variant of B+ trees, called Indexed Sequential Access Method (ISAM), offers the benefit of sequential allocation of leaf pages, plus the benefit of fast searches. Inserts and deletes are not handled as well as in B+ trees, but are much better than in a sorted file. We will study tree-structured indexing in detail in Chapter 10.

8.5.2 Clustered Index Organization

As we saw in Section 8.2.1, a clustered index is really a file organization for the underlying data records. Data records can be large, and we should avoid replicating them; so there can be at most one clustered index on a given collection of records. On the other hand, we can build several unclustered indexes on a data file. Suppose that employee records are sorted by *age*, or stored in a clustered file with search key *age*. If, in addition, we have an index on the *sal* field, the latter must be an unclustered index. We can also build an unclustered index on, say, *department*, if there is such a field.

Clustered indexes, while less expensive to maintain than a fully sorted file, are nonetheless expensive to maintain. When a new record has to be inserted into a full leaf page, a new leaf page must be allocated and some existing records have to be moved to the new page. If records are identified by a combination of page id and slot, as is typically the case in current database systems, all places in the database that point to a moved record (typically, entries in other indexes for the same collection of records) must also be updated to point to the new location. Locating all such places and making these additional updates can involve several disk I/Os. Clustering must be used sparingly and only when justified by frequent queries that benefit from clustering. In particular, there is no good reason to build a clustered file using hashing, since range queries cannot be answered using hash-indexes.

In dealing with the limitation that at most one index can be clustered, it is often useful to consider whether the information in an index's search key is sufficient to answer the query. If so, modern database systems are intelligent enough to avoid fetching the actual data records. For example, if we have an index on *age*, and we want to compute the average age of employees, the DBMS can do this by simply examining the data entries in the index. This is an example of an **index-only evaluation**. In an index-only evaluation of a query we need not access the data records in the files that contain the relations in the query; we can evaluate the query completely through indexes on the files. An important benefit of index-only evaluation is that it works equally efficiently with only unclustered indexes, as only the data entries of the index are used in the queries. Thus, unclustered indexes can be used to speed up certain queries if we recognize that the DBMS will exploit index-only evaluation.

Design Examples Illustrating Clustered Indexes

To illustrate the use of a clustered index on a range query, consider the following example:

```
SELECT   E.dno
FROM     Employees E
WHERE    E.age > 40
```

If we have a B+ tree index on *age*, we can use it to retrieve only tuples that satisfy the selection *E.age*> 40. Whether such an index is worthwhile depends first of all on the selectivity of the condition. What fraction of the employees are older than 40? If virtually everyone is older than 40, we gain little by using an index on *age*; a sequential scan of the relation would do almost as well. However, suppose that only 10 percent of the employees are older than 40. Now, is an index useful? The answer depends on whether the index is clustered. If the index is unclustered, we could have one page I/O per qualifying employee, and this could be more expensive than a sequential scan, even if only 10 percent of the employees qualify! On the other hand, a clustered B+ tree index on *age* requires only 10 percent of the I/Os for a sequential scan (ignoring the few I/Os needed to traverse from the root to the first retrieved leaf page and the I/Os for the relevant index leaf pages).

As another example, consider the following refinement of the previous query:

```
SELECT    E.dno, COUNT(*)
FROM      Employees E
WHERE     E.age > 10
GROUP BY  E.dno
```

If a B+ tree index is available on *age*, we could retrieve tuples using it, sort the retrieved tuples on *dno*, and so answer the query. However, this may not be a good plan if virtually all employees are more than 10 years old. This plan is especially bad if the index is not clustered.

Let us consider whether an index on *dno* might suit our purposes better. We could use the index to retrieve all tuples, grouped by *dno*, and for each *dno* count the number of tuples with *age* > 10. (This strategy can be used with both hash and B+ tree indexes; we only require the tuples to be *grouped*, not necessarily *sorted*, by *dno*.) Again, the efficiency depends crucially on whether the index is clustered. If it is, this plan is likely to be the best if the condition on *age* is not very selective. (Even if we have a clustered index on *age*, if the condition on *age* is not selective, the cost of sorting qualifying tuples on *dno* is likely to be high.) If the index is not clustered, we could perform one page I/O per tuple in Employees, and this plan would be terrible. Indeed, if the index is not clustered, the optimizer will choose the straightforward plan based on sorting on *dno*. Therefore, this query suggests that we build a clustered index on *dno* if the condition on *age* is not very selective. If the condition is very selective, we should consider building an index (not necessarily clustered) on *age* instead.

Clustering is also important for an index on a search key that does not include a candidate key, that is, an index in which several data entries can have the same key value. To illustrate this point, we present the following query:

```
SELECT E.dno
FROM   Employees E
WHERE  E.hobby='Stamps'
```

If many people collect stamps, retrieving tuples through an unclustered index on *hobby* can be very inefficient. It may be cheaper to simply scan the relation to retrieve all tuples and to apply the selection on-the-fly to the retrieved tuples. Therefore, if such a query is important, we should consider making the index on *hobby* a clustered index. On the other hand, if we assume that *eid* is a key for Employees, and replace the condition *E.hobby='Stamps'* by *E.eid=552*, we know that at most one Employees tuple will satisfy this selection condition. In this case, there is no advantage to making the index clustered.

The next query shows how aggregate operations can influence the choice of indexes:

```
SELECT   E.dno, COUNT(*)
FROM     Employees E
GROUP BY E.dno
```

A straightforward plan for this query is to sort Employees on *dno* to compute the count of employees for each *dno*. However, if an index—hash or B+ tree—on *dno* is available, we can answer this query by scanning only the index. For each *dno* value, we simply count the number of data entries in the index with this value for the search key. Note that it does not matter whether the index is clustered because we never retrieve tuples of Employees.

8.5.3 Composite Search Keys

The search key for an index can contain several fields; such keys are called **composite search keys** or **concatenated keys**. As an example, consider a collection of employee records, with fields *name, age*, and *sal*, stored in sorted order by *name*. Figure 8.5 illustrates the difference between a composite index with key $\langle age, sal \rangle$, a composite index with key $\langle sal, age \rangle$, an index with key *age*, and an index with key *sal*. All indexes shown in the figure use Alternative (2) for data entries.

If the search key is composite, an **equality query** is one in which *each* field in the search key is bound to a constant. For example, we can ask to retrieve all data entries with $age = 20$ and $sal = 10$. The hashed file organization supports only equality queries, since a hash function identifies the bucket containing desired records only if a value is specified for each field in the search key.

With respect to a composite key index, in a **range query** not all fields in the search key are bound to constants. For example, we can ask to retrieve all data entries with $age = 20$; this query implies that any value is acceptable for the *sal* field. As another example of a range query, we can ask to retrieve all data entries with $age < 30$ and $sal > 40$.

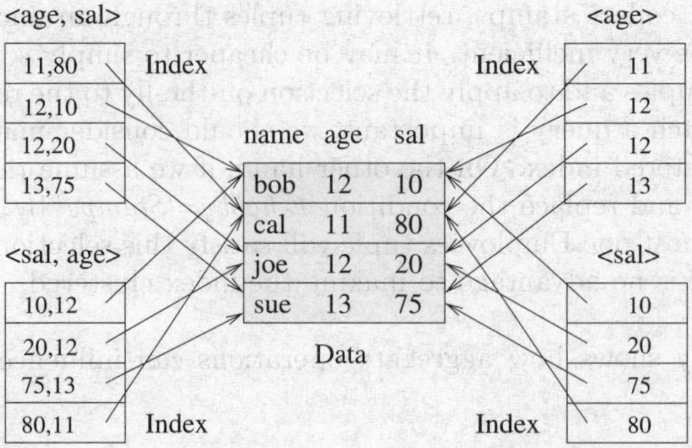

Figure 8.5 Composite Key Indexes

Note that the index cannot help on the query *sal* > 40, because, intuitively, the index organizes records by *age* first and then *sal*. If *age* is left unspecified, qualifying records could be spread across the entire index. We say that an index **matches** a selection condition if the index can be used to retrieve just the tuples that satisfy the condition. For selections of the form *condition* $\wedge \ldots \wedge$ *condition*, we can define when an index matches the selection as follows:[4] For a hash index, a selection matches the index if it includes an equality condition ('field = constant') on every field in the composite search key for the index. For a tree index, a selection matches the index if it includes an equality or range condition on a *prefix* of the composite search key. (As examples, $\langle age \rangle$ and $\langle age, sal, department \rangle$ are prefixes of key $\langle age, sal, department \rangle$, but $\langle age, department \rangle$ and $\langle sal, department \rangle$ are not.)

Trade-offs in Choosing Composite Keys

A composite key index can support a broader range of queries because it matches more selection conditions. Further, since data entries in a composite index contain more information about the data record (i.e., more fields than a single-attribute index), the opportunities for index-only evaluation strategies are increased. (Recall from Section 8.5.2 that an index-only evaluation does not need to access data records, but finds all required field values in the data entries of indexes.)

On the negative side, a composite index must be updated in response to any operation (insert, delete, or update) that modifies *any* field in the search key. A composite index is also likely to be larger than a single-attribute search key

[4]For a more general discussion, see Section 14.2.)

index because the size of entries is larger. For a composite B+ tree index, this also means a potential increase in the number of levels, although key compression can be used to alleviate this problem (see Section 10.8.1).

Design Examples of Composite Keys

Consider the following query, which returns all employees with $20 < age < 30$ and $3000 < sal < 5000$:

```
SELECT E.eid
FROM   Employees E
WHERE  E.age BETWEEN 20 AND 30
       AND E.sal BETWEEN 3000 AND 5000
```

A composite index on $\langle age, sal\rangle$ could help if the conditions in the WHERE clause are fairly selective. Obviously, a hash index will not help; a B+ tree (or ISAM) index is required. It is also clear that a clustered index is likely to be superior to an unclustered index. For this query, in which the conditions on *age* and *sal* are equally selective, a composite, clustered B+ tree index on $\langle age, sal\rangle$ is as effective as a composite, clustered B+ tree index on $\langle sal, age\rangle$. However, the order of search key attributes can sometimes make a big difference, as the next query illustrates:

```
SELECT E.eid
FROM   Employees E
WHERE  E.age = 25
       AND E.sal BETWEEN 3000 AND 5000
```

In this query a composite, clustered B+ tree index on $\langle age, sal\rangle$ will give good performance because records are sorted by *age* first and then (if two records have the same *age* value) by *sal*. Thus, all records with $age = 25$ are clustered together. On the other hand, a composite, clustered B+ tree index on $\langle sal, age\rangle$ will not perform as well. In this case, records are sorted by *sal* first, and therefore two records with the same *age* value (in particular, with $age = 25$) may be quite far apart. In effect, this index allows us to use the range selection on *sal*, but not the equality selection on *age*, to retrieve tuples. (Good performance on both variants of the query can be achieved using a single *spatial* index. We discuss spatial indexes in Chapter 28.)

Composite indexes are also useful in dealing with many aggregate queries. Consider:

```
SELECT AVG (E.sal)
```

```
FROM    Employees E
WHERE   E.age = 25
        AND E.sal BETWEEN 3000 AND 5000
```

A composite B+ tree index on $\langle age, sal \rangle$ allows us to answer the query with an index-only scan. A composite B+ tree index on $\langle sal, age \rangle$ also allows us to answer the query with an index-only scan, although more index entries are retrieved in this case than with an index on $\langle age, sal \rangle$.

Here is a variation of an earlier example:

```
SELECT    E.dno, COUNT(*)
FROM      Employees E
WHERE     E.sal=10,000
GROUP BY  E.dno
```

An index on *dno* alone does not allow us to evaluate this query with an index-only scan, because we need to look at the *sal* field of each tuple to verify that $sal = 10,000$. However, we can use an index-only plan if we have a composite B+ tree index on $\langle sal, dno \rangle$ or $\langle dno, sal \rangle$. In an index with key $\langle sal, dno \rangle$, all data entries with $sal = 10,000$ are arranged contiguously (whether or not the index is clustered). Further, these entries are sorted by *dno*, making it easy to obtain a count for each *dno* group. Note that we need to retrieve only data entries with $sal = 10,000$.

It is worth observing that this strategy does not work if the WHERE clause is modified to use $sal > 10,000$. Although it suffices to retrieve only index data entries—that is, an index-only strategy still applies—these entries must now be sorted by *dno* to identify the groups (because, for example, two entries with the same *dno* but different *sal* values may not be contiguous). An index with key $\langle dno, sal \rangle$ is better for this query: Data entries with a given *dno* value are stored together, and each such group of entries is itself sorted by *sal*. For each *dno* group, we can eliminate the entries with *sal* not greater than 10,000 and count the rest. (Using this index is less efficient than an index-only scan with key $\langle sal, dno \rangle$ for the query with $sal = 10,000$, because we must read all data entries. Thus, the choice between these indexes is influenced by which query is more common.)

As another example, suppose we want to find the minimum *sal* for each *dno*:

```
SELECT    E.dno, MIN(E.sal)
FROM      Employees E
GROUP BY  E.dno
```

An index on *dno* alone does not allow us to evaluate this query with an index-only scan. However, we can use an index-only plan if we have a composite B+ tree index on $\langle dno, sal \rangle$. Note that all data entries in the index with a given *dno* value are stored together (whether or not the index is clustered). Further, this group of entries is itself sorted by *sal*. An index on $\langle sal, dno \rangle$ enables us to avoid retrieving data records, but the index data entries must be sorted on *dno*.

8.5.4 Index Specification in SQL:1999

A natural question to ask at this point is how we can create indexes using SQL. The SQL:1999 standard does *not* include any statement for creating or dropping index structures. In fact, the standard does not even require SQL implementations to support indexes! In practice, of course, every commercial relational DBMS supports one or more kinds of indexes. The following command to create a B+ tree index—we discuss B+ tree indexes in Chapter 10—is illustrative:

```
CREATE INDEX IndAgeRating ON Students
       WITH  STRUCTURE = BTREE,
             KEY = (age, gpa)
```

This specifies that a B+ tree index is to be created on the Students table using the concatenation of the *age* and *gpa* columns as the key. Thus, key values are pairs of the form $\langle age, gpa \rangle$, and there is a distinct entry for each such pair. Once created, the index is automatically maintained by the DBMS adding or removing data entries in response to inserts or deletes of records on the Students relation.

8.6 REVIEW QUESTIONS

Answers to the review questions can be found in the listed sections.

- Where does a DBMS store persistent data? How does it bring data into main memory for processing? What DBMS component reads and writes data from main memory, and what is the unit of I/O? **(Section 8.1)**

- What is a *file organization*? What is an *index*? What is the relationship between files and indexes? Can we have several indexes on a single file of records? Can an index itself store data records (i.e., act as a file)? **(Section 8.2)**

- What is the *search key* for an index? What is a *data entry* in an index? **(Section 8.2)**

- What is a *clustered* index? What is a *primary index*? How many clustered indexes can you build on a file? How many unclustered indexes can you build? **(Section 8.2.1)**
- How is data organized in a hash-based index? When would you use a hash-based index? **(Section 8.3.1)**
- How is data organized in a tree-based index? When would you use a tree-based index? **(Section 8.3.2)**
- Consider the following operations: *scans, equality and range selections, inserts, and deletes*, and the following file organizations: *heap files, sorted files, clustered files, heap files with an unclustered tree index on the search key*, and *heap files with an unclustered hash index.* Which file organization is best suited for each operation? **(Section 8.4)**
- What are the main contributors to the cost of database operations? Discuss a simple cost model that reflects this. **(Section 8.4.1)**
- How does the expected workload influence physical database design decisions such as what indexes to build? Why is the choice of indexes a central aspect of physical database design? **(Section 8.5)**
- What issues are considered in using clustered indexes? What is an *index-only* evaluation method? What is its primary advantage? **(Section 8.5.2)**
- What is a *composite search key*? What are the pros and cons of composite search keys? **(Section 8.5.3)**
- What SQL commands support index creation? **(Section 8.5.4)**

EXERCISES

Exercise 8.1 Answer the following questions about data on external storage in a DBMS:

1. Why does a DBMS store data on external storage?
2. Why are I/O costs important in a DBMS?
3. What is a record id? Given a record's id, how many I/Os are needed to fetch it into main memory?
4. What is the role of the buffer manager in a DBMS? What is the role of the disk space manager? How do these layers interact with the file and access methods layer?

Exercise 8.2 Answer the following questions about files and indexes:

1. What operations are supported by the file of records abstraction?
2. What is an index on a file of records? What is a search key for an index? Why do we need indexes?

sid	*name*	*login*	*age*	*gpa*
53831	Madayan	madayan@music	11	1.8
53832	Guldu	guldu@music	12	2.0
53666	Jones	jones@cs	18	3.4
53688	Smith	smith@ee	19	3.2
53650	Smith	smith@math	19	3.8

Figure 8.6 An Instance of the Students Relation, Sorted by *age*

3. What alternatives are available for the data entries in an index?
4. What is the difference between a primary index and a secondary index? What is a duplicate data entry in an index? Can a primary index contain duplicates?
5. What is the difference between a clustered index and an unclustered index? If an index contains data records as 'data entries,' can it be unclustered?
6. How many clustered indexes can you create on a file? Would you always create at least one clustered index for a file?
7. Consider Alternatives (1), (2) and (3) for 'data entries' in an index, as discussed in Section 8.2 . Are all of them suitable for secondary indexes? Explain.

Exercise 8.3 Consider a relation stored as a randomly ordered file for which the only index is an unclustered index on a field called *sal*. If you want to retrieve all records with $sal > 20$, is using the index always the best alternative? Explain.

Exercise 8.4 Consider the instance of the Students relation shown in Figure 8.6, sorted by *age*: For the purposes of this question, assume that these tuples are stored in a sorted file in the order shown; the first tuple is on page 1 the second tuple is also on page 1; and so on. Each page can store up to three data records; so the fourth tuple is on page 2.

Explain what the data entries in each of the following indexes contain. If the order of entries is significant, say so and explain why. If such an index cannot be constructed, say so and explain why.

1. An unclustered index on *age* using Alternative (1).
2. An unclustered index on *age* using Alternative (2).
3. An unclustered index on *age* using Alternative (3).
4. A clustered index on *age* using Alternative (1).
5. A clustered index on *age* using Alternative (2).
6. A clustered index on *age* using Alternative (3).
7. An unclustered index on *gpa* using Alternative (1).
8. An unclustered index on *gpa* using Alternative (2).
9. An unclustered index on *gpa* using Alternative (3).
10. A clustered index on *gpa* using Alternative (1).
11. A clustered index on *gpa* using Alternative (2).
12. A clustered index on *gpa* using Alternative (3).

File Type	*Scan*	*Equality Search*	*Range Search*	*Insert*	*Delete*
Heap file					
Sorted file					
Clustered file					
Unclustered tree index					
Unclustered hash index					

Figure 8.7 I/O Cost Comparison

Exercise 8.5 Explain the difference between Hash indexes and B+-tree indexes. In particular, discuss how equality and range searches work, using an example.

Exercise 8.6 Fill in the I/O costs in Figure 8.7.

Exercise 8.7 If you were about to create an index on a relation, what considerations would guide your choice? Discuss:

1. The choice of primary index.
2. Clustered versus unclustered indexes.
3. Hash versus tree indexes.
4. The use of a sorted file rather than a tree-based index.
5. Choice of search key for the index. What is a composite search key, and what considerations are made in choosing composite search keys? What are index-only plans, and what is the influence of potential index-only evaluation plans on the choice of search key for an index?

Exercise 8.8 Consider a delete specified using an equality condition. For each of the five file organizations, what is the cost if no record qualifies? What is the cost if the condition is not on a key?

Exercise 8.9 What main conclusions can you draw from the discussion of the five basic file organizations discussed in Section 8.4? Which of the five organizations would you choose for a file where the most frequent operations are as follows?

1. Search for records based on a range of field values.
2. Perform inserts and scans, where the order of records does not matter.
3. Search for a record based on a particular field value.

Exercise 8.10 Consider the following relation:

Emp(*eid:* `integer`, *sal:* `integer`, *age:* `real`, *did:* `integer`)

There is a clustered index on *eid* and an unclustered index on *age*.

1. How would you use the indexes to enforce the constraint that *eid* is a key?
2. Give an example of an update that is *definitely speeded up* because of the available indexes. (English description is sufficient.)

3. Give an example of an update that is *definitely slowed down* because of the indexes. (English description is sufficient.)
4. Can you give an example of an update that is neither speeded up nor slowed down by the indexes?

Exercise 8.11 Consider the following relations:

Emp(*eid:* `integer`, *ename:* `varchar`, *sal:* `integer`, *age:* `integer`, *did:* `integer`)
Dept(*did:* `integer`, *budget:* `integer`, *floor:* `integer`, *mgr_eid:* `integer`)

Salaries range from \$10,000 to \$100,000, ages vary from 20 to 80, each department has about five employees on average, there are 10 floors, and budgets vary from \$10,000 to \$1 million. You can assume uniform distributions of values.

For each of the following queries, which of the listed index choices would you choose to speed up the query? If your database system does not consider index-only plans (i.e., data records are always retrieved even if enough information is available in the index entry), how would your answer change? Explain briefly.

1. Query: *Print ename, age, and sal for all employees.*
   (a) Clustered hash index on $\langle ename, age, sal\rangle$ fields of Emp.
   (b) Unclustered hash index on $\langle ename, age, sal\rangle$ fields of Emp.
   (c) Clustered B+ tree index on $\langle ename, age, sal\rangle$ fields of Emp.
   (d) Unclustered hash index on $\langle eid, did\rangle$ fields of Emp.
   (e) No index.
2. Query: *Find the dids of departments that are on the 10th floor and have a budget of less than \$15,000.*
   (a) Clustered hash index on the $floor$ field of Dept.
   (b) Unclustered hash index on the $floor$ field of Dept.
   (c) Clustered B+ tree index on $\langle floor, budget\rangle$ fields of Dept.
   (d) Clustered B+ tree index on the *budget* field of Dept.
   (e) No index.

PROJECT-BASED EXERCISES

Exercise 8.12 Answer the following questions:

1. What indexing techniques are supported in Minibase?
2. What alternatives for data entries are supported?
3. Are clustered indexes supported?

BIBLIOGRAPHIC NOTES

Several books discuss file organization in detail [29, 312, 442, 531, 648, 695, 775].

Bibliographic notes for hash-indexes and B+-trees are included in Chapters 10 and 11.

9

STORING DATA: DISKS AND FILES

- What are the different kinds of memory in a computer system?
- What are the physical characteristics of disks and tapes, and how do they affect the design of database systems?
- What are RAID storage systems, and what are their advantages?
- How does a DBMS keep track of space on disks? How does a DBMS access and modify data on disks? What is the significance of *pages* as a unit of storage and transfer?
- How does a DBMS create and maintain files of records? How are records arranged on pages, and how are pages organized within a file?
- **Key concepts:** memory hierarchy, persistent storage, random versus sequential devices; physical disk architecture, disk characteristics, seek time, rotational delay, transfer time; RAID, striping, mirroring, RAID levels; disk space manager; buffer manager, buffer pool, replacement policy, prefetching, forcing; file implementation, page organization, record organization

A memory is what is left when something happens and does not completely unhappen.

—Edward DeBono

This chapter initiates a study of the internals of an RDBMS. In terms of the DBMS architecture presented in Section 1.8, it covers the disk space manager, the buffer manager, and implementation-oriented aspects of the *files and access methods* layer.

Section 9.1 introduces disks and tapes. Section 9.2 describes RAID disk systems. Section 9.3 discusses how a DBMS manages disk space, and Section 9.4 explains how a DBMS fetches data from disk into main memory. Section 9.5 discusses how a collection of pages is organized into a file and how auxiliary data structures can be built to speed up retrieval of records from a file. Section 9.6 covers different ways to arrange a collection of records on a page, and Section 9.7 covers alternative formats for storing individual records.

9.1 THE MEMORY HIERARCHY

Memory in a computer system is arranged in a hierarchy, as shown in Figure 9.1. At the top, we have **primary storage**, which consists of cache and main memory and provides very fast access to data. Then comes **secondary storage**, which consists of slower devices, such as magnetic disks. **Tertiary storage** is the slowest class of storage devices; for example, optical disks and tapes. Currently, the cost of a given amount of main memory is about 100 times

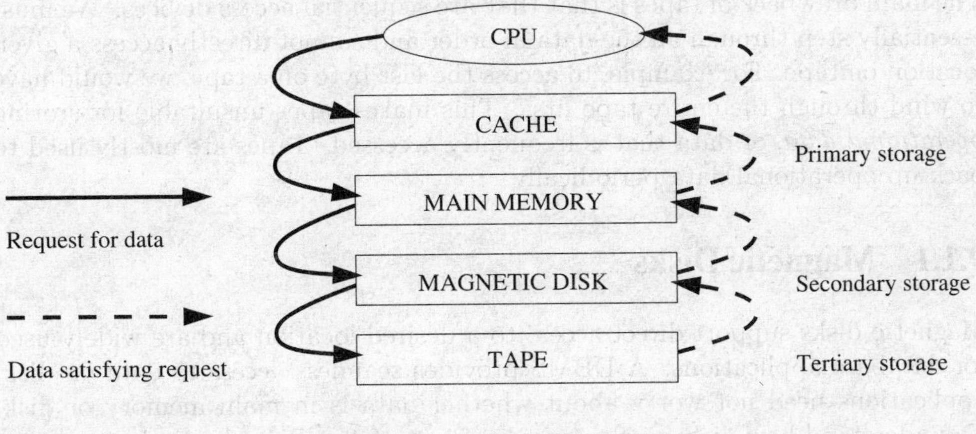

Figure 9.1 The Memory Hierarchy

the cost of the same amount of disk space, and tapes are even less expensive than disks. Slower storage devices such as tapes and disks play an important role in database systems because the amount of data is typically very large. Since buying enough main memory to store all data is prohibitively expensive, we must store data on tapes and disks and build database systems that can retrieve data from lower levels of the memory hierarchy into main memory as needed for processing.

There are reasons other than cost for storing data on secondary and tertiary storage. On systems with 32-bit addressing, only 2^{32} bytes can be directly referenced in main memory; the number of data objects may exceed this number! Further, data must be maintained across program executions. This requires storage devices that retain information when the computer is restarted (after a shutdown or a crash); we call such storage **nonvolatile**. Primary storage is usually volatile (although it is possible to make it nonvolatile by adding a battery backup feature), whereas secondary and tertiary storage are nonvolatile.

Tapes are relatively inexpensive and can store very large amounts of data. They are a good choice for *archival* storage, that is, when we need to maintain data for a long period but do not expect to access it very often. A Quantum DLT 4000 drive is a typical tape device; it stores 20 GB of data and can store about twice as much by compressing the data. It records data on 128 *tape tracks*, which can be thought of as a linear sequence of adjacent bytes, and supports a sustained transfer rate of 1.5 MB/sec with uncompressed data (typically 3.0 MB/sec with compressed data). A single DLT 4000 tape drive can be used to access up to seven tapes in a stacked configuration, for a maximum compressed data capacity of about 280 GB.

The main drawback of tapes is that they are sequential access devices. We must essentially step through all the data in order and cannot directly access a given location on tape. For example, to access the last byte on a tape, we would have to wind through the entire tape first. This makes tapes unsuitable for storing *operational data*, or data that is frequently accessed. Tapes are mostly used to back up operational data periodically.

9.1.1 Magnetic Disks

Magnetic disks support direct access to a desired location and are widely used for database applications. A DBMS provides seamless access to data on disk; applications need not worry about whether data is in main memory or disk. To understand how disks work, consider Figure 9.2, which shows the structure of a disk in simplified form.

Data is stored on disk in units called **disk blocks**. A disk block is a contiguous sequence of bytes and is the unit in which data is written to a disk and read from a disk. Blocks are arranged in concentric rings called **tracks**, on one or more **platters**. Tracks can be recorded on one or both surfaces of a platter; we refer to platters as single-sided or double-sided, accordingly. The set of all tracks with the same diameter is called a **cylinder**, because the space occupied by these tracks is shaped like a cylinder; a cylinder contains one track per platter surface. Each track is divided into arcs, called **sectors**, whose size is a

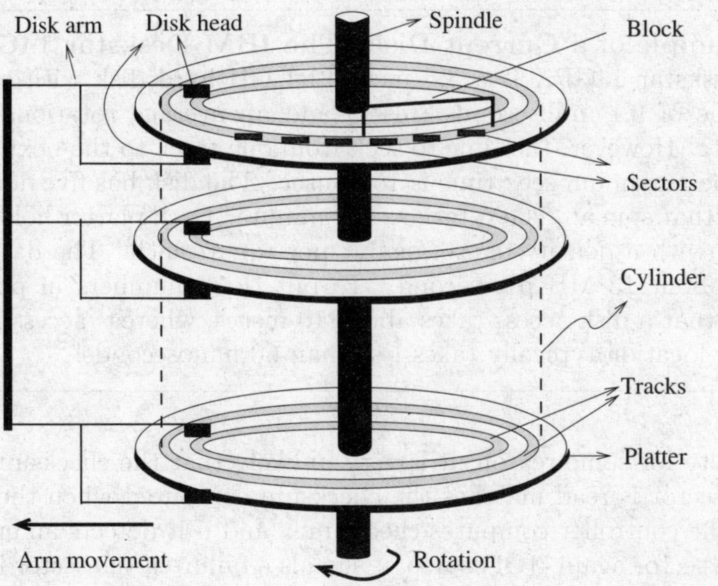

Figure 9.2 Structure of a Disk

characteristic of the disk and cannot be changed. The size of a disk block can be set when the disk is initialized as a multiple of the sector size.

An array of **disk heads**, one per recorded surface, is moved as a unit; when one head is positioned over a block, the other heads are in identical positions with respect to their platters. To read or write a block, a disk head must be positioned on top of the block.

Current systems typically allow at most one disk head to read or write at any one time. All the disk heads cannot read or write in parallel—this technique would increase data transfer rates by a factor equal to the number of disk heads and considerably speed up sequential scans. The reason they cannot is that it is very difficult to ensure that all the heads are perfectly aligned on the corresponding tracks. Current approaches are both expensive and more prone to faults than disks with a single active head. In practice, very few commercial products support this capability and then only in a limited way; for example, two disk heads may be able to operate in parallel.

A **disk controller** interfaces a disk drive to the computer. It implements commands to read or write a sector by moving the arm assembly and transferring data to and from the disk surfaces. A **checksum** is computed for when data is written to a sector and stored with the sector. The checksum is computed again when the data on the sector is read back. If the sector is corrupted or the

An Example of a Current Disk: The IBM Deskstar 14GPX. The IBM Deskstar 14GPX is a 3.5 inch, 14.4 GB hard disk with an average seek time of 9.1 milliseconds (msec) and an average rotational delay of 4.17 msec. However, the time to seek from one track to the next is just 2.2 msec, the maximum seek time is 15.5 msec. The disk has five double-sided platters that spin at 7200 rotations per minute. Each platter holds 3.35 GB of data, with a density of 2.6 gigabit per square inch. The data transfer rate is about 13 MB per second. To put these numbers in perspective, observe that a disk access takes about 10 msecs, whereas accessing a main memory location typically takes less than 60 nanoseconds!

read is faulty for some reason, it is very unlikely that the checksum computed when the sector is read matches the checksum computed when the sector was written. The controller computes checksums, and if it detects an error, it tries to read the sector again. (Of course, it signals a failure if the sector is corrupted and read fails repeatedly.)

While direct access to any desired location in main memory takes approximately the same time, determining the time to access a location on disk is more complicated. The time to access a disk block has several components. **Seek time** is the time taken to move the disk heads to the track on which a desired block is located. As the size of a platter decreases, seek times also decrease, since we have to move a disk head a shorter distance. Typical platter diameters are 3.5 inches and 5.25 inches. **Rotational delay** is the waiting time for the desired block to rotate under the disk head; it is the time required for half a rotation on average and is usually less than seek time. **Transfer time** is the time to actually read or write the data in the block once the head is positioned, that is, the time for the disk to rotate over the block.

9.1.2 Performance Implications of Disk Structure

1. Data must be in memory for the DBMS to operate on it.
2. The unit for data transfer between disk and main memory is a block; if a single item on a block is needed, the entire block is transferred. Reading or writing a disk block is called an **I/O** (for input/output) operation.
3. The time to read or write a block varies, depending on the location of the data:

$$\textit{access time} = \textit{seek time} + \textit{rotational delay} + \textit{transfer time}$$

These observations imply that the time taken for database operations is affected significantly by how data is stored on disks. The time for moving blocks to or from disk usually dominates the time taken for database operations. To minimize this time, it is necessary to locate data records strategically on disk because of the geometry and mechanics of disks. In essence, if two records are frequently used together, we should place them close together. The 'closest' that two records can be on a disk is to be on the same block. In decreasing order of closeness, they could be on the same track, the same cylinder, or an adjacent cylinder.

Two records on the same block are obviously as close together as possible, because they are read or written as part of the same block. As the platter spins, other blocks on the track being read or written rotate under the active head. In current disk designs, all the data on a track can be read or written in one revolution. After a track is read or written, another disk head becomes active, and another track in the same cylinder is read or written. This process continues until all tracks in the current cylinder are read or written, and then the arm assembly moves (in or out) to an adjacent cylinder. Thus, we have a natural notion of 'closeness' for blocks, which we can extend to a notion of *next* and *previous* blocks.

Exploiting this notion of next by arranging records so they are read or written sequentially is very important in reducing the time spent in disk I/Os. Sequential access minimizes seek time and rotational delay and is much faster than random access. (This observation is reinforced and elaborated in Exercises 9.5 and 9.6, and the reader is urged to work through them.)

9.2 REDUNDANT ARRAYS OF INDEPENDENT DISKS

Disks are potential bottlenecks for system performance and storage system reliability. Even though disk performance has been improving continuously, microprocessor performance has advanced much more rapidly. The performance of microprocessors has improved at about 50 percent or more per year, but disk access times have improved at a rate of about 10 percent per year and disk transfer rates at a rate of about 20 percent per year. In addition, since disks contain mechanical elements, they have much higher failure rates than electronic parts of a computer system. If a disk fails, all the data stored on it is lost.

A **disk array** is an arrangement of several disks, organized to increase performance and improve reliability of the resulting storage system. Performance is increased through data striping. Data striping distributes data over several disks to give the impression of having a single large, very fast disk. Reliability is improved through **redundancy**. Instead of having a single copy of the data, redundant information is maintained. The redundant information is carefully organized so that, in case of a disk failure, it can be used to reconstruct the contents of the failed disk. Disk arrays that implement a combination of data striping and redundancy are called **redundant arrays of independent disks**, or in short, **RAID**.[1] Several RAID organizations, referred to as **RAID levels**, have been proposed. Each RAID level represents a different trade-off between reliability and performance.

In the remainder of this section, we first discuss data striping and redundancy and then introduce the RAID levels that have become industry standards.

9.2.1 Data Striping

A disk array gives the user the abstraction of having a single, very large disk. If the user issues an I/O request, we first identify the set of physical disk blocks that store the data requested. These disk blocks may reside on a single disk in the array or may be distributed over several disks in the array. Then the set of blocks is retrieved from the disk(s) involved. Thus, how we distribute the data over the disks in the array influences how many disks are involved when an I/O request is processed.

In **data striping**, the data is segmented into equal-size partitions distributed over multiple disks. The size of the partition is called the **striping unit**. The partitions are usually distributed using a round-robin algorithm: If the disk array consists of D disks, then partition i is written onto disk `i mod D`.

As an example, consider a striping unit of one bit. Since any D successive data bits are spread over all D data disks in the array, all I/O requests involve all disks in the array. Since the smallest unit of transfer from a disk is a block, each I/O request involves transfer of at least D blocks. Since we can read the D blocks from the D disks in parallel, the transfer rate of each request is D times the transfer rate of a single disk; each request uses the aggregated bandwidth of all disks in the array. But the disk access time of the array is basically the access time of a single disk, since all disk heads have to move for all requests. Therefore, for a disk array with a striping unit of a single bit, the number of requests per time unit that the array can process and the average response time for each individual request are similar to that of a single disk.

As another example, consider a striping unit of a disk block. In this case, I/O requests of the size of a disk block are processed by one disk in the array. If many I/O requests of the size of a disk block are made, and the requested

[1]Historically, the I in RAID stood for inexpensive, as a large number of small disks was much more economical than a single very large disk. Today, such very large disks are not even manufactured—a sign of the impact of RAID.

Redundancy Schemes: Alternatives to the parity scheme include schemes based on **Hamming codes** and **Reed-Solomon codes**. In addition to recovery from single disk failures, Hamming codes can identify which disk failed. Reed-Solomon codes can recover from up to two simultaneous disk failures. A detailed discussion of these schemes is beyond the scope of our discussion here; the bibliography provides pointers for the interested reader.

blocks reside on different disks, we can process all requests in parallel and thus reduce the average response time of an I/O request. Since we distributed the striping partitions round-robin, large requests of the size of many contiguous blocks involve all disks. We can process the request by all disks in parallel and thus increase the transfer rate to the aggregated bandwidth of all D disks.

9.2.2 Redundancy

While having more disks increases storage system performance, it also lowers overall storage system reliability. Assume that the **mean-time-to-failure (MTTF)**, of a single disk is $50,000$ hours (about 5.7 years). Then, the MTTF of an array of 100 disks is only $50,000/100 = 500$ hours or about 21 days, assuming that failures occur independently and the failure probability of a disk does not change over time. (Actually, disks have a higher failure probability early and late in their lifetimes. Early failures are often due to undetected manufacturing defects; late failures occur since the disk wears out. Failures do not occur independently either: consider a fire in the building, an earthquake, or purchase of a set of disks that come from a 'bad' manufacturing batch.)

Reliability of a disk array can be increased by storing redundant information. If a disk fails, the redundant information is used to reconstruct the data on the failed disk. Redundancy can immensely increase the MTTF of a disk array. When incorporating redundancy into a disk array design, we have to make two choices. First, we have to decide where to store the redundant information. We can either store the redundant information on a small number of **check disks** or distribute the redundant information uniformly over all disks.

The second choice we have to make is how to compute the redundant information. Most disk arrays store parity information: In the **parity scheme**, an extra check disk contains information that can be used to recover from failure of any one disk in the array. Assume that we have a disk array with D disks and consider the first bit on each data disk. Suppose that i of the D data bits are 1. The first bit on the check disk is set to 1 if i is odd; otherwise, it is set to

0. This bit on the check disk is called the **parity** of the data bits. The check disk contains parity information for each set of corresponding D data bits.

To recover the value of the first bit of a failed disk we first count the number of bits that are 1 on the $D-1$ nonfailed disks; let this number be j. If j is odd and the parity bit is 1, or if j is even and the parity bit is 0, then the value of the bit on the failed disk must have been 0. Otherwise, the value of the bit on the failed disk must have been 1. Thus, with parity we can recover from failure of any one disk. Reconstruction of the lost information involves reading all data disks and the check disk.

For example, with an additional 10 disks with redundant information, the MTTF of our example storage system with 100 data disks can be increased to more than 250 years! What is more important, a large MTTF implies a small failure probability during the actual usage time of the storage system, which is usually much smaller than the reported lifetime or the MTTF. (Who actually uses 10-year-old disks?)

In a RAID system, the disk array is partitioned into **reliability groups**, where a reliability group consists of a set of *data disks* and a set of *check disks*. A common *redundancy scheme* (see box) is applied to each group. The number of check disks depends on the RAID level chosen. In the remainder of this section, we assume for ease of explanation that there is only one reliability group. The reader should keep in mind that actual RAID implementations consist of several reliability groups, and the number of groups plays a role in the overall reliability of the resulting storage system.

9.2.3 Levels of Redundancy

Throughout the discussion of the different RAID levels, we consider sample data that would just fit on four disks. That is, with no RAID technology our storage system would consist of exactly four data disks. Depending on the RAID level chosen, the number of additional disks varies from zero to four.

Level 0: Nonredundant

A RAID Level 0 system uses data striping to increase the maximum bandwidth available. No redundant information is maintained. While being the solution with the lowest cost, reliability is a problem, since the MTTF decreases linearly with the number of disk drives in the array. RAID Level 0 has the best write performance of all RAID levels, because absence of redundant information implies that no redundant information needs to be updated! Interestingly, RAID Level 0 does not have the best read performance of all RAID levels, since systems with redundancy have a choice of scheduling disk accesses, as explained in the next section.

In our example, the RAID Level 0 solution consists of only four data disks. Independent of the number of data disks, the effective space utilization for a RAID Level 0 system is always 100 percent.

Level 1: Mirrored

A RAID Level 1 system is the most expensive solution. Instead of having one copy of the data, two identical copies of the data on two different disks are maintained. This type of redundancy is often called **mirroring**. Every write of a disk block involves a write on both disks. These writes may not be performed simultaneously, since a global system failure (e.g., due to a power outage) could occur while writing the blocks and then leave both copies in an inconsistent state. Therefore, we always write a block on one disk first and then write the other copy on the mirror disk. Since two copies of each block exist on different disks, we can distribute reads between the two disks and allow *parallel reads* of different disk blocks that conceptually reside on the same disk. A read of a block can be scheduled to the disk that has the smaller expected access time. RAID Level 1 does not stripe the data over different disks, so the transfer rate for a single request is comparable to the transfer rate of a single disk.

In our example, we need four data and four check disks with mirrored data for a RAID Level 1 implementation. The effective space utilization is 50 percent, independent of the number of data disks.

Level 0+1: Striping and Mirroring

RAID Level 0+1—sometimes also referred to as *RAID Level 10*—combines striping and mirroring. As in RAID Level 1, read requests of the size of a disk block can be scheduled both to a disk and its mirror image. In addition, read requests of the size of several contiguous blocks benefit from the aggregated bandwidth of all disks. The cost for writes is analogous to RAID Level 1.

As in RAID Level 1, our example with four data disks requires four check disks and the effective space utilization is always 50 percent.

Level 2: Error-Correcting Codes

In RAID Level 2, the striping unit is a single bit. The redundancy scheme used is Hamming code. In our example with four data disks, only three check disks are needed. In general, the number of check disks grows logarithmically with the number of data disks.

Striping at the bit level has the implication that in a disk array with D data disks, the smallest unit of transfer for a read is a set of D blocks. Therefore, Level 2 is good for workloads with many large requests, since for each request, the aggregated bandwidth of all data disks is used. But RAID Level 2 is bad for small requests of the size of an individual block for the same reason. (See the example in Section 9.2.1.) A write of a block involves reading D blocks into main memory, modifying $D + C$ blocks, and writing $D + C$ blocks to disk, where C is the number of check disks. This sequence of steps is called a *read-modify-write* cycle.

For a RAID Level 2 implementation with four data disks, three check disks are needed. In our example, the effective space utilization is about 57 percent. The effective space utilization increases with the number of data disks. For example, in a setup with 10 data disks, four check disks are needed and the effective space utilization is 71 percent. In a setup with 25 data disks, five check disks are required and the effective space utilization grows to 83 percent.

Level 3: Bit-Interleaved Parity

While the redundancy schema used in RAID Level 2 improves in terms of cost over RAID Level 1, it keeps more redundant information than is necessary. Hamming code, as used in RAID Level 2, has the advantage of being able to identify which disk has failed. But disk controllers can easily detect which disk has failed. Therefore, the check disks do not need to contain information to identify the failed disk. Information to recover the lost data is sufficient. Instead of using several disks to store Hamming code, RAID Level 3 has a single check disk with parity information. Thus, the reliability overhead for RAID Level 3 is a single disk, the lowest overhead possible.

The performance characteristics of RAID Levels 2 and 3 are very similar. RAID Level 3 can also process only one I/O at a time, the minimum transfer unit is D blocks, and a write requires a read-modify-write cycle.

Level 4: Block-Interleaved Parity

RAID Level 4 has a striping unit of a disk block, instead of a single bit as in RAID Level 3. Block-level striping has the advantage that read requests of the size of a disk block can be served entirely by the disk where the requested block resides. Large read requests of several disk blocks can still utilize the aggregated bandwidth of the D disks.

The write of a single block still requires a read-modify-write cycle, but only one data disk and the check disk are involved. The parity on the check disk can be updated without reading all D disk blocks, because the new parity can be obtained by noticing the differences between the old data block and the new data block and then applying the difference to the parity block on the check disk:

$$\texttt{NewParity} = (\texttt{OldData}\ \text{XOR}\ \texttt{NewData})\ \text{XOR}\ \texttt{OldParity}$$

The read-modify-write cycle involves reading of the old data block and the old parity block, modifying the two blocks, and writing them back to disk, resulting in four disk accesses per write. Since the check disk is involved in each write, it can easily become the bottleneck.

RAID Level 3 and 4 configurations with four data disks require just a single check disk. In our example, the effective space utilization is 80 percent. The effective space utilization increases with the number of data disks, since always only one check disk is necessary.

Level 5: Block-Interleaved Distributed Parity

RAID Level 5 improves on Level 4 by distributing the parity blocks uniformly over all disks, instead of storing them on a single check disk. This distribution has two advantages. First, several write requests could be processed in parallel, since the bottleneck of a unique check disk has been eliminated. Second, read requests have a higher level of parallelism. Since the data is distributed over all disks, read requests involve all disks, whereas in systems with a dedicated check disk the check disk never participates in reads.

A RAID Level 5 system has the best performance of all RAID levels with redundancy for small and large read and large write requests. Small writes still require a read-modify-write cycle and are thus less efficient than in RAID Level 1.

In our example, the corresponding RAID Level 5 system has five disks overall and thus the effective space utilization is the same as in RAID Levels 3 and 4.

Level 6: P+Q Redundancy

The motivation for RAID Level 6 is the observation that recovery from failure of a single disk is not sufficient in very large disk arrays. First, in large disk arrays, a second disk might fail before replacement of an already failed disk could take place. In addition, the probability of a disk failure during recovery of a failed disk is not negligible.

A RAID Level 6 system uses Reed-Solomon codes to be able to recover from up to two simultaneous disk failures. RAID Level 6 requires (conceptually) two check disks, but it also uniformly distributes redundant information at the block level as in RAID Level 5. Thus, the performance characteristics for small and large read requests and for large write requests are analogous to RAID Level 5. For small writes, the read-modify-write procedure involves six instead of four disks as compared to RAID Level 5, since two blocks with redundant information need to be updated.

For a RAID Level 6 system with storage capacity equal to four data disks, six disks are required. In our example, the effective space utilization is 66 percent.

9.2.4 Choice of RAID Levels

If data loss is not an issue, RAID Level 0 improves overall system performance at the lowest cost. RAID Level 0+1 is superior to RAID Level 1. The main application areas for RAID Level 0+1 systems are small storage subsystems where the cost of mirroring is moderate. Sometimes, RAID Level 0+1 is used for applications that have a high percentage of writes in their workload, since RAID Level 0+1 provides the best write performance. RAID Levels 2 and 4 are always inferior to RAID Levels 3 and 5, respectively. RAID Level 3 is appropriate for workloads consisting mainly of large transfer requests of several contiguous blocks. The performance of a RAID Level 3 system is bad for workloads with many small requests of a single disk block. RAID Level 5 is a good general-purpose solution. It provides high performance for large as well as small requests. RAID Level 6 is appropriate if a higher level of reliability is required.

9.3 DISK SPACE MANAGEMENT

The lowest level of software in the DBMS architecture discussed in Section 1.8, called the **disk space manager**, manages space on disk. Abstractly, the disk space manager supports the concept of a **page** as a unit of data and provides commands to allocate or deallocate a page and read or write a page. The size of a page is chosen to be the size of a disk block and pages are stored as disk blocks so that reading or writing a page can be done in one disk I/O.

It is often useful to allocate a sequence of pages as a *contiguous* sequence of blocks to hold data frequently accessed in sequential order. This capability is essential for exploiting the advantages of sequentially accessing disk blocks, which we discussed earlier in this chapter. Such a capability, if desired, must be provided by the disk space manager to higher-level layers of the DBMS.

The disk space manager hides details of the underlying hardware (and possibly the operating system) and allows higher levels of the software to think of the data as a collection of pages.

9.3.1 Keeping Track of Free Blocks

A database grows and shrinks as records are inserted and deleted over time. The disk space manager keeps track of which disk blocks are in use, in addition to keeping track of which pages are on which disk blocks. Although it is likely that blocks are initially allocated sequentially on disk, subsequent allocations and deallocations could in general create 'holes.'

One way to keep track of block usage is to maintain a list of free blocks. As blocks are deallocated (by the higher-level software that requests and uses these blocks), we can add them to the free list for future use. A pointer to the first block on the free block list is stored in a known location on disk.

A second way is to maintain a bitmap with one bit for each disk block, which indicates whether a block is in use or not. A bitmap also allows very fast identification and allocation of contiguous areas on disk. This is difficult to accomplish with a linked list approach.

9.3.2 Using OS File Systems to Manage Disk Space

Operating systems also manage space on disk. Typically, an operating system supports the abstraction of a *file as a sequence of bytes*. The OS manages space on the disk and translates requests, such as "Read byte i of file f," into corresponding low-level instructions: "Read block m of track t of cylinder c of disk d." A database disk space manager could be built using OS files. For example, the entire database could reside in one or more OS files for which a number of blocks are allocated (by the OS) and initialized. The disk space manager is then responsible for managing the space in these OS files.

Many database systems do not rely on the OS file system and instead do their own disk management, either from scratch or by extending OS facilities. The reasons are practical as well as technical. One practical reason is that a DBMS vendor who wishes to support several OS platforms cannot assume features specific to any OS, for portability, and would therefore try to make the DBMS code as self-contained as possible. A technical reason is that on a 32-bit system, the largest file size is 4 GB, whereas a DBMS may want to access a single file larger than that. A related problem is that typical OS files cannot span disk devices, which is often desirable or even necessary in a DBMS. Additional technical reasons why a DBMS does not rely on the OS file system are outlined in Section 9.4.2.

9.4 BUFFER MANAGER

To understand the role of the buffer manager, consider a simple example. Suppose that the database contains 1 million pages, but only 1000 pages of main memory are available for holding data. Consider a query that requires a scan of the entire file. Because all the data cannot be brought into main memory at one time, the DBMS must bring pages into main memory as they are needed and, in the process, decide what existing page in main memory to replace to make space for the new page. The policy used to decide which page to replace is called the **replacement policy**.

In terms of the DBMS architecture presented in Section 1.8, the **buffer manager** is the software layer responsible for bringing pages from disk to main memory as needed. The buffer manager manages the available main memory by partitioning it into a collection of pages, which we collectively refer to as the **buffer pool**. The main memory pages in the buffer pool are called **frames**; it is convenient to think of them as slots that can hold a page (which usually resides on disk or other secondary storage media).

Higher levels of the DBMS code can be written without worrying about whether data pages are in memory or not; they ask the buffer manager for the page, and it is brought into a frame in the buffer pool if it is not already there. Of course, the higher-level code that requests a page must also release the page when it is no longer needed, by informing the buffer manager, so that the frame containing the page can be reused. The higher-level code must also inform the buffer manager if it modifies the requested page; the buffer manager then makes sure that the change is propagated to the copy of the page on disk. Buffer management is illustrated in Figure 9.3.

In addition to the buffer pool itself, the buffer manager maintains some bookkeeping information and two variables for each frame in the pool: *pin count* and *dirty*. The number of times that the page currently in a given frame has been requested but not released—the number of current users of the page—is recorded in the *pin count* variable for that frame. The Boolean variable *dirty* indicates whether the page has been modified since it was brought into the buffer pool from disk.

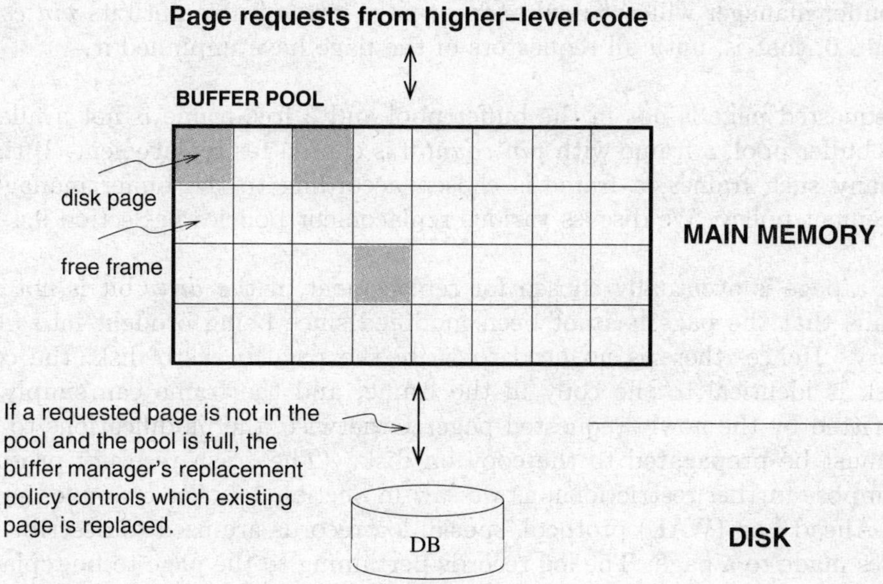

Figure 9.3 The Buffer Pool

Initially, the *pin count* for every frame is set to 0, and the *dirty* bits are turned off. When a page is requested the buffer manager does the following:

1. Checks the buffer pool to see if some frame contains the requested page and, if so, increments the *pin count* of that frame. If the page is not in the pool, the buffer manager brings it in as follows:
   (a) Chooses a frame for replacement, using the replacement policy, and increments its *pin count.*
   (b) If the *dirty* bit for the replacement frame is on, writes the page it contains to disk (that is, the disk copy of the page is overwritten with the contents of the frame).
   (c) Reads the requested page into the replacement frame.
2. Returns the (main memory) address of the frame containing the requested page to the requestor.

Incrementing *pin count* is often called **pinning** the requested page in its frame. When the code that calls the buffer manager and requests the page subsequently calls the buffer manager and releases the page, the *pin count* of the frame containing the requested page is decremented. This is called **unpinning** the page. If the requestor has modified the page, it also informs the buffer manager of this at the time that it unpins the page, and the *dirty* bit for the frame is set.

The buffer manager will not read another page into a frame until its *pin count* becomes 0, that is, until all requestors of the page have unpinned it.

If a requested page is not in the buffer pool and a free frame is not available in the buffer pool, a frame with *pin count* 0 is chosen for replacement. If there are many such frames, a frame is chosen according to the buffer manager's replacement policy. We discuss various replacement policies in Section 9.4.1.

When a page is eventually chosen for replacement, if the *dirty* bit is not set, it means that the page has not been modified since being brought into main memory. Hence, there is no need to write the page back to disk; the copy on disk is identical to the copy in the frame, and the frame can simply be overwritten by the newly requested page. Otherwise, the modifications to the page must be propagated to the copy on disk. (The crash recovery protocol may impose further restrictions, as we saw in Section 1.7. For example, in the Write-Ahead Log (WAL) protocol, special log records are used to describe the changes made to a page. The log records pertaining to the page to be replaced may well be in the buffer; if so, the protocol requires that they be written to disk *before* the page is written to disk.)

If no page in the buffer pool has *pin count* 0 and a page that is not in the pool is requested, the buffer manager must wait until some page is released before responding to the page request. In practice, the transaction requesting the page may simply be aborted in this situation! So pages should be released—by the code that calls the buffer manager to request the page—as soon as possible.

A good question to ask at this point is, "What if a page is requested by several different transactions?" That is, what if the page is requested by programs executing independently on behalf of different users? Such programs could make conflicting changes to the page. The locking protocol (enforced by higher-level DBMS code, in particular the transaction manager) ensures that each transaction obtains a shared or exclusive lock before requesting a page to read or modify. Two different transactions cannot hold an exclusive lock on the same page at the same time; this is how conflicting changes are prevented. The buffer manager simply assumes that the appropriate lock has been obtained before a page is requested.

9.4.1 Buffer Replacement Policies

The policy used to choose an unpinned page for replacement can affect the time taken for database operations considerably. Of the many alternative policies, each is suitable in different situations.

The best-known replacement policy is **least recently used** (LRU). This can be implemented in the buffer manager using a queue of pointers to frames with *pin count* 0. A frame is added to the end of the queue when it becomes a candidate for replacement (that is, when the *pin count* goes to 0). The page chosen for replacement is the one in the frame at the head of the queue.

A variant of LRU, called **clock** replacement, has similar behavior but less overhead. The idea is to choose a page for replacement using a *current* variable that takes on values 1 through N, where N is the number of buffer frames, in circular order. We can think of the frames being arranged in a circle, like a clock's face, and *current* as a clock hand moving across the face. To approximate LRU behavior, each frame also has an associated *referenced* bit, which is turned on when the page *pin count* goes to 0.

The *current* frame is considered for replacement. If the frame is not chosen for replacement, *current* is incremented and the next frame is considered; this process is repeated until some frame is chosen. If the *current* frame has *pin count* greater than 0, then it is not a candidate for replacement and *current* is incremented. If the *current* frame has the *referenced* bit turned on, the clock algorithm turns the *referenced* bit off and increments *current*—this way, a recently referenced page is less likely to be replaced. If the *current* frame has *pin count* 0 and its *referenced* bit is off, then the page in it is chosen for replacement. If all frames are pinned in some sweep of the clock hand (that is, the value of *current* is incremented until it repeats), this means that no page in the buffer pool is a replacement candidate.

The LRU and clock policies are not always the best replacement strategies for a database system, particularly if many user requests require sequential scans of the data. Consider the following illustrative situation. Suppose the buffer pool has 10 frames, and the file to be scanned has 10 or fewer pages. Assuming, for simplicity, that there are no competing requests for pages, only the first scan of the file does any I/O. Page requests in subsequent scans always find the desired page in the buffer pool. On the other hand, suppose that the file to be scanned has 11 pages (which is one more than the number of available pages in the buffer pool). Using LRU, every scan of the file will result in reading every page of the file! In this situation, called **sequential flooding**, LRU is the *worst* possible replacement strategy.

Other replacement policies include **first in first out** (FIFO) and **most recently used** (MRU), which also entail overhead similar to LRU, and **random**, among others. The details of these policies should be evident from their names and the preceding discussion of LRU and clock.

Buffer Management in Practice: IBM DB2 and Sybase ASE allow buffers to be partitioned into named pools. Each database, table, or index can be bound to one of these pools. Each pool can be configured to use either LRU or clock replacement in ASE; DB2 uses a variant of clock replacement, with the initial clock value based on the nature of the page (e.g., index non-leaves get a higher starting clock value, which delays their replacement). Interestingly, a buffer pool client in DB2 can explicitly indicate that it *hates* a page, making the page the next choice for replacement. As a special case, DB2 applies MRU for the pages fetched in some utility operations (e.g., RUNSTATS), and DB2 V6 also supports FIFO. Informix and Oracle 7 both maintain a single global buffer pool using LRU; Microsoft SQL Server has a single pool using clock replacement. In Oracle 8, tables can be bound to one of two pools; one has high priority, and the system attempts to keep pages in this pool in memory.
Beyond setting a maximum number of pins for a given transaction, there are typically no features for controlling buffer pool usage on a per-transaction basis. Microsoft SQL Server, however, supports a reservation of buffer pages by queries that require large amounts of memory (e.g., queries involving sorting or hashing).

9.4.2 Buffer Management in DBMS versus OS

Obvious similarities exist between virtual memory in operating systems and buffer management in database management systems. In both cases, the goal is to provide access to more data than will fit in main memory, and the basic idea is to bring in pages from disk to main memory as needed, replacing pages no longer needed in main memory. Why can't we build a DBMS using the virtual memory capability of an OS? A DBMS can often predict the order in which pages will be accessed, or **page reference patterns**, much more accurately than is typical in an OS environment, and it is desirable to utilize this property. Further, a DBMS needs more control over when a page is written to disk than an OS typically provides.

A DBMS can often predict reference patterns because most page references are generated by higher-level operations (such as sequential scans or particular implementations of various relational algebra operators) with a known pattern of page accesses. This ability to predict reference patterns allows for a better choice of pages to replace and makes the idea of specialized buffer replacement policies more attractive in the DBMS environment.

Even more important, being able to predict reference patterns enables the use of a simple and very effective strategy called **prefetching of pages**. The

> **Prefetching:** IBM DB2 supports both sequential and list prefetch (prefetching a list of pages). In general, the prefetch size is 32 4KB pages, but this can be set by the user. For some sequential type database utilities (e.g., COPY, RUNSTATS), DB2 prefetches up to 64 4KB pages. For a smaller buffer pool (i.e., less than 1000 buffers), the prefetch quantity is adjusted downward to 16 or 8 pages. The prefetch size can be configured by the user; for certain environments, it may be best to prefetch 1000 pages at a time! Sybase ASE supports asynchronous prefetching of up to 256 pages, and uses this capability to reduce latency during indexed access to a table in a range scan. Oracle 8 uses prefetching for sequential scan, retrieving large objects, and certain index scans. Microsoft SQL Server supports prefetching for sequential scan and for scans along the leaf level of a B+ tree index, and the prefetch size can be adjusted as a scan progresses. SQL Server also uses asynchronous prefetching extensively. Informix supports prefetching with a user-defined prefetch size.

buffer manager can anticipate the next several page requests and fetch the corresponding pages into memory *before* the pages are requested. This strategy has two benefits. First, the pages are available in the buffer pool when they are requested. Second, reading in a contiguous block of pages is much faster than reading the same pages at different times in response to distinct requests. (Review the discussion of disk geometry to appreciate why this is so.) If the pages to be prefetched are not contiguous, recognizing that several pages need to be fetched can nonetheless lead to faster I/O because an order of retrieval can be chosen for these pages that minimizes seek times and rotational delays.

Incidentally, note that the I/O can typically be done concurrently with CPU computation. Once the prefetch request is issued to the disk, the disk is responsible for reading the requested pages into memory pages and the CPU can continue to do other work.

A DBMS also requires the ability to explicitly *force* a page to disk, that is, to ensure that the copy of the page on disk is updated with the copy in memory. As a related point, a DBMS must be able to ensure that certain pages in the buffer pool are written to disk *before* certain other pages to implement the WAL protocol for crash recovery, as we saw in Section 1.7. Virtual memory implementations in operating systems cannot be relied on to provide such control over when pages are written to disk; the OS command to write a page to disk may be implemented by essentially recording the write request and deferring the actual modification of the disk copy. If the system crashes in the interim, the effects can be catastrophic for a DBMS. (Crash recovery is discussed further in Chapter 18.)

Indexes as Files: In Chapter 8, we presented indexes as a way of organizing data records for efficient search. From an implementation standpoint, indexes are just another kind of file, containing records that direct traffic on requests for data records. For example, a tree index is a collection of records organized into one page per node in the tree. It is convenient to actually think of a tree index as *two* files, because it contains two kinds of records: (1) a file of *index entries*, which are records with fields for the index's search key, and fields pointing to a child node, and (2) a file of *data entries*, whose structure depends on the choice of data entry alternative.

9.5 FILES OF RECORDS

We now turn our attention from the way pages are stored on disk and brought into main memory to the way pages are used to store records and organized into logical collections or *files.* Higher levels of the DBMS code treat a page as effectively being a collection of records, ignoring the representation and storage details. In fact, the concept of a collection of records is not limited to the contents of a single page; a file can span several pages. In this section, we consider how a collection of pages can be organized as a file. We discuss how the space on a page can be organized to store a collection of records in Sections 9.6 and 9.7.

9.5.1 Implementing Heap Files

The data in the pages of a heap file is not ordered in any way, and the only guarantee is that one can retrieve all records in the file by repeated requests for the next record. Every record in the file has a unique rid, and every page in a file is of the same size.

Supported operations on a heap file include *create* and *destroy* files, *insert* a record, *delete* a record with a given rid, *get* a record with a given rid, and *scan* all records in the file. To get or delete a record with a given rid, note that we must be able to find the id of the page containing the record, given the id of the record.

We must keep track of the pages in each heap file to support scans, and we must keep track of pages that contain free space to implement insertion efficiently. We discuss two alternative ways to maintain this information. In each of these alternatives, pages must hold two pointers (which are page ids) for file-level bookkeeping in addition to the data.

Linked List of Pages

One possibility is to maintain a heap file as a doubly linked list of pages. The DBMS can remember where the first page is located by maintaining a table containing pairs of ⟨*heap_file_name*, *page_1_addr*⟩ in a known location on disk. We call the first page of the file the *header page*.

An important task is to maintain information about empty slots created by deleting a record from the heap file. This task has two distinct parts: how to keep track of free space within a page and how to keep track of pages that have some free space. We consider the first part in Section 9.6. The second part can be addressed by maintaining a doubly linked list of pages with free space and a doubly linked list of full pages; together, these lists contain *all* pages in the heap file. This organization is illustrated in Figure 9.4; note that each pointer is really a page id.

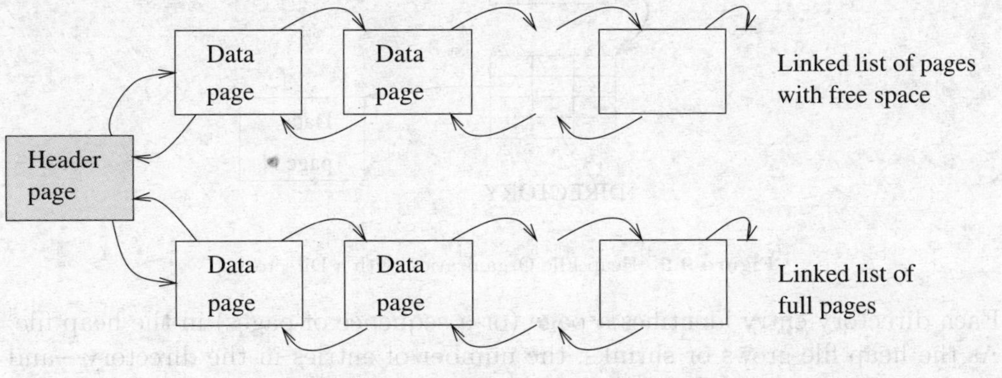

Figure 9.4 Heap File Organization with a Linked List

If a new page is required, it is obtained by making a request to the disk space manager and then added to the list of pages in the file (probably as a page with free space, because it is unlikely that the new record will take up all the space on the page). If a page is to be deleted from the heap file, it is removed from the list and the disk space manager is told to deallocate it. (Note that the scheme can easily be generalized to allocate or deallocate a sequence of several pages and maintain a doubly linked list of these page sequences.)

One disadvantage of this scheme is that virtually all pages in a file will be on the free list if records are of variable length, because it is likely that every page has at least a few free bytes. To insert a typical record, we must retrieve and examine several pages on the free list before we find one with enough free space. The directory-based heap file organization that we discuss next addresses this problem.

Directory of Pages

An alternative to a linked list of pages is to maintain a **directory of pages**. The DBMS must remember where the first directory page of each heap file is located. The directory is itself a collection of pages and is shown as a linked list in Figure 9.5. (Other organizations are possible for the directory itself, of course.)

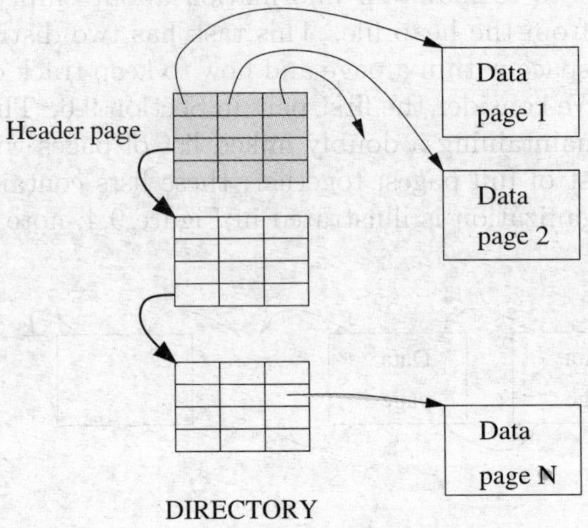

Figure 9.5 Heap File Organization with a Directory

Each directory entry identifies a page (or a sequence of pages) in the heap file. As the heap file grows or shrinks, the number of entries in the directory—and possibly the number of pages in the directory itself—grows or shrinks correspondingly. Note that since each directory entry is quite small in comparison to a typical page, the size of the directory is likely to be very small in comparison to the size of the heap file.

Free space can be managed by maintaining a bit per entry, indicating whether the corresponding page has any free space, or a count per entry, indicating the amount of free space on the page. If the file contains variable-length records, we can examine the free space count for an entry to determine if the record fits on the page pointed to by the entry. Since several entries fit on a directory page, we can efficiently search for a data page with enough space to hold a record to be inserted.

9.6 PAGE FORMATS

The page abstraction is appropriate when dealing with I/O issues, but higher levels of the DBMS see data as a collection of records. In this section, we

> **Rids in Commercial Systems:** IBM DB2, Informix, Microsoft SQL Server, Oracle 8, and Sybase ASE all implement record ids as a page id and slot number. Sybase ASE uses the following page organization, which is typical: Pages contain a header followed by the rows and a slot array. The header contains the page identity, its allocation state, page free space state, and a timestamp. The slot array is simply a mapping of slot number to page offset.
> Oracle 8 and SQL Server use logical record ids rather than page id and slot number in one special case: If a table has a clustered index, then records in the table are identified using the key value for the clustered index. This has the advantage that secondary indexes need not be reorganized if records are moved across pages.

consider how a collection of records can be arranged on a page. We can think of a page as a collection of **slots**, each of which contains a record. A record is identified by using the pair $\langle$*page id*, *slot number*$\rangle$; this is the record id (rid). (We remark that an alternative way to identify records is to assign each record a unique integer as its rid and maintain a table that lists the page and slot of the corresponding record for each rid. Due to the overhead of maintaining this table, the approach of using $\langle$*page id*, *slot number*$\rangle$ as an rid is more common.)

We now consider some alternative approaches to managing slots on a page. The main considerations are how these approaches support operations such as searching, inserting, or deleting records on a page.

9.6.1 Fixed-Length Records

If all records on the page are guaranteed to be of the same length, record slots are uniform and can be arranged consecutively within a page. At any instant, some slots are occupied by records and others are unoccupied. When a record is inserted into the page, we must locate an empty slot and place the record there. The main issues are how we keep track of empty slots and how we locate all records on a page. The alternatives hinge on how we handle the deletion of a record.

The first alternative is to store records in the first N slots (where N is the number of records on the page); whenever a record is deleted, we move the last record on the page into the vacated slot. This format allows us to locate the ith record on a page by a simple offset calculation, and all empty slots appear together at the end of the page. However, this approach does not work if there are external references to the record that is moved (because the rid contains the slot number, which is now changed).

The second alternative is to handle deletions by using an array of bits, one per slot, to keep track of free slot information. Locating records on the page requires scanning the bit array to find slots whose bit is on; when a record is deleted, its bit is turned off. The two alternatives for storing fixed-length records are illustrated in Figure 9.6. Note that in addition to the information about records on the page, a page usually contains additional file-level information (e.g., the id of the next page in the file). The figure does not show this additional information.

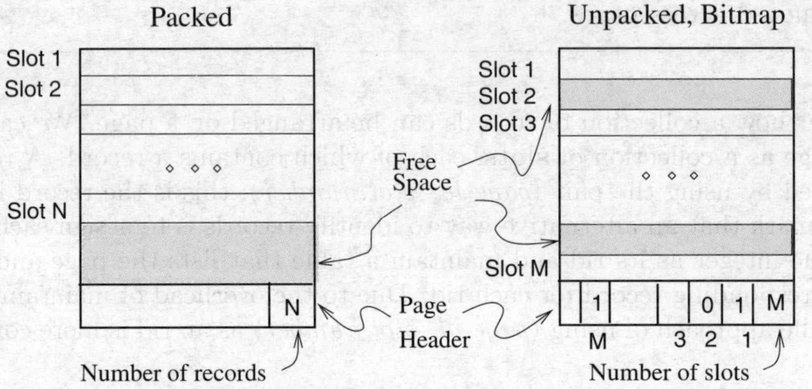

Figure 9.6 Alternative Page Organizations for Fixed-Length Records

The *slotted page* organization described for variable-length records in Section 9.6.2 can also be used for fixed-length records. It becomes attractive if we need to move records around on a page for reasons other than keeping track of space freed by deletions. A typical example is that we want to keep the records on a page sorted (according to the value in some field).

9.6.2 Variable-Length Records

If records are of variable length, then we cannot divide the page into a fixed collection of slots. The problem is that, when a new record is to be inserted, we have to find an empty slot of just the right length—if we use a slot that is too big, we waste space, and obviously we cannot use a slot that is smaller than the record length. Therefore, when a record is inserted, we must allocate just the right amount of space for it, and when a record is deleted, we must move records to fill the hole created by the deletion, to ensure that all the free space on the page is contiguous. Therefore, the ability to move records on a page becomes very important.

The most flexible organization for variable-length records is to maintain a **directory of slots** for each page, with a ⟨*record offset, record length*⟩ pair per slot. The first component (*record offset*) is a 'pointer' to the record, as shown in Figure 9.7; it is the offset in bytes from the start of the data area on the page to the start of the record. Deletion is readily accomplished by setting the record offset to -1. Records can be moved around on the page because the rid, which is the page number and slot number (that is, position in the directory), does not change when the record is moved; only the record offset stored in the slot changes.

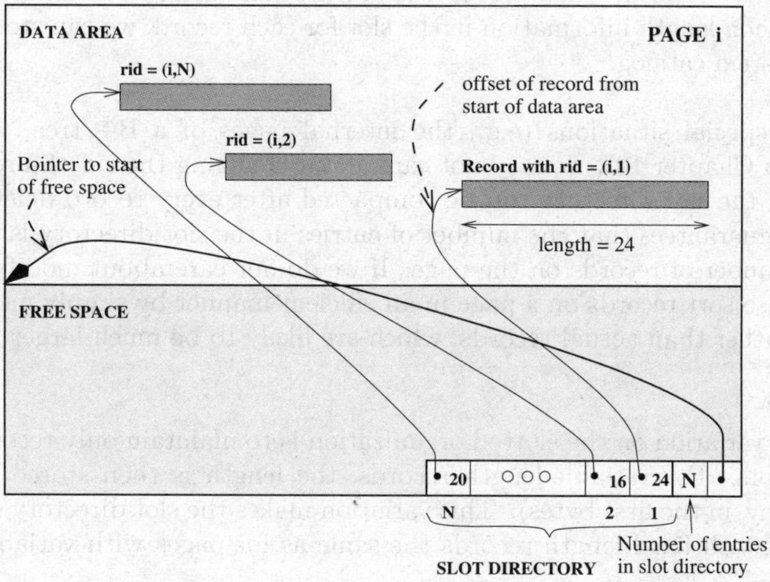

Figure 9.7 Page Organization for Variable-Length Records

The space available for new records must be managed carefully because the page is not preformatted into slots. One way to manage free space is to maintain a pointer (that is, offset from the start of the data area on the page) that indicates the start of the free space area. When a new record is too large to fit into the remaining free space, we have to move records on the page to reclaim the space freed by records deleted earlier. The idea is to ensure that, after reorganization, all records appear in contiguous order, followed by the available free space.

A subtle point to be noted is that the slot for a deleted record cannot always be removed from the slot directory, because slot numbers are used to identify records—by deleting a slot, we change (decrement) the slot number of subsequent slots in the slot directory, and thereby change the rid of records pointed to by subsequent slots. The only way to remove slots from the slot directory is to remove the last slot if the record that it points to is deleted. However, when a record is inserted, the slot directory should be scanned for an element that currently does not point to any record, and this slot should be used for the new record. A new slot is added to the slot directory only if all existing slots point to records. If inserts are much more common than deletes (as is typically the case), the number of entries in the slot directory is likely to be very close to the actual number of records on the page.

This organization is also useful for fixed-length records if we need to move them around frequently; for example, when we want to maintain them in some sorted order. Indeed, when all records are the same length, instead of storing this common length information in the slot for each record, we can store it once in the system catalog.

In some special situations (e.g., the internal pages of a B+ tree, which we discuss in Chapter 10), we may not care about changing the rid of a record. In this case, the slot directory can be compacted after every record deletion; this strategy guarantees that the number of entries in the slot directory is the same as the number of records on the page. If we do not care about modifying rids, we can also sort records on a page in an efficient manner by simply moving slot entries rather than actual records, which are likely to be much larger than slot entries.

A simple variation on the slotted organization is to maintain only record offsets in the slots. For variable-length records, the length is then stored with the record (say, in the first bytes). This variation makes the slot directory structure for pages with fixed-length records the same as for pages with variable-length records.

9.7 RECORD FORMATS

In this section, we discuss how to organize fields within a record. While choosing a way to organize the fields of a record, we must take into account whether the fields of the record are of fixed or variable length and consider the cost of various operations on the record, including retrieval and modification of fields.

Before discussing record formats, we note that in addition to storing individual records, information common to all records of a given record type (such as the number of fields and field types) is stored in the **system catalog**, which can be thought of as a description of the contents of a database, maintained by the DBMS (Section 12.1). This avoids repeated storage of the same information with each record of a given type.

Record Formats in Commercial Aystems: In IBM DB2, fixed-length fields are at fixed offsets from the beginning of the record. Variable-length fields have offset and length in the fixed offset part of the record, and the fields themselves follow the fixed-length part of the record. Informix, Microsoft SQL Server, and Sybase ASE use the same organization with minor variations. In Oracle 8, records are structured as if all fields are potentially of variable length; a record is a sequence of length–data pairs, with a special length value used to denote a *null* value.

9.7.1 Fixed-Length Records

In a fixed-length record, each field has a fixed length (that is, the value in this field is of the same length in all records), and the number of fields is also fixed. The fields of such a record can be stored consecutively, and, given the address of the record, the address of a particular field can be calculated using information about the lengths of preceding fields, which is available in the system catalog. This record organization is illustrated in Figure 9.8.

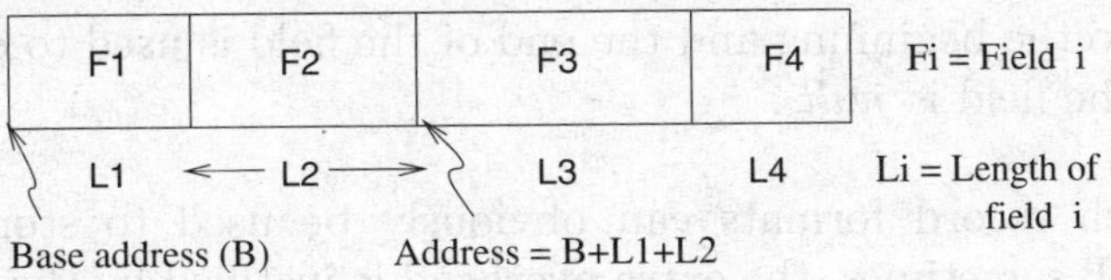

Figure 9.8 Organization of Records with Fixed-Length Fields

9.7.2 Variable-Length Records

In the relational model, every record in a relation contains the same number of fields. If the number of fields is fixed, a record is of variable length only because some of its fields are of variable length.

One possible organization is to store fields consecutively, separated by delimiters (which are special characters that do not appear in the data itself). This organization requires a scan of the record to locate a desired field.

An alternative is to reserve some space at the beginning of a record for use as an array of integer offsets—the *i*th integer in this array is the starting address of the *i*th field value relative to the start of the record. Note that we also store an offset to the end of the record; this offset is needed to recognize where the last field ends. Both alternatives are illustrated in Figure 9.9.

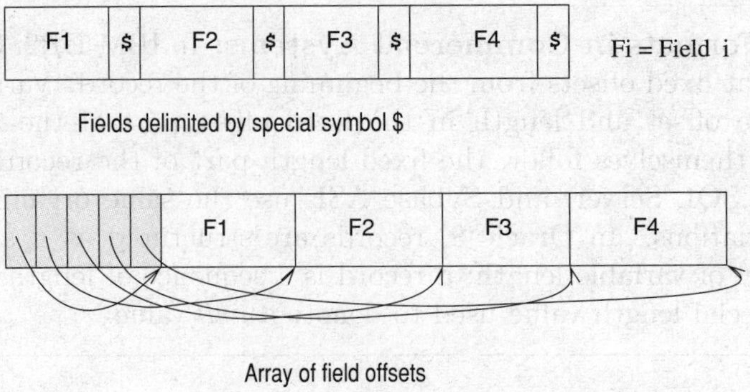

Figure 9.9 Alternative Record Organizations for Variable-Length Fields

The second approach is typically superior. For the overhead of the offset array, we get direct access to any field. We also get a clean way to deal with **null** values. A *null* value is a special value used to denote that the value for a field is unavailable or inapplicable. If a field contains a *null* value, the pointer to the end of the field is set to be the same as the pointer to the beginning of the field. That is, no space is used for representing the *null* value, and a comparison of the pointers to the beginning and the end of the field is used to determine that the value in the field is *null*.

Variable-length record formats can obviously be used to store fixed-length records as well; sometimes, the extra overhead is justified by the added flexibility, because issues such as supporting *null* values and adding fields to a record type arise with fixed-length records as well.

Having variable-length fields in a record can raise some subtle issues, especially when a record is modified.

- Modifying a field may cause it to grow, which requires us to shift all subsequent fields to make space for the modification in all three record formats just presented.
- A modified record may no longer fit into the space remaining on its page. If so, it may have to be moved to another page. If rids, which are used to 'point' to a record, include the page number (see Section 9.6), moving a record to another page causes a problem. We may have to leave a 'forwarding address' on this page identifying the new location of the record. And to ensure that space is always available for this forwarding address, we would have to allocate some minimum space for each record, regardless of its length.

> **Large Records in Real Systems:** In Sybase ASE, a record can be at most 1962 bytes. This limit is set by the 2KB log page size, since records are not allowed to be larger than a page. The exceptions to this rule are BLOBs and CLOBs, which consist of a set of bidirectionally linked pages. IBM DB2 and Microsoft SQL Server also do not allow records to span pages, although large objects are allowed to span pages and are handled separately from other data types. In DB2, record size is limited only by the page size; in SQL Server, a record can be at most 8KB, excluding LOBs. Informix and Oracle 8 allow records to span pages. Informix allows records to be at most 32KB, while Oracle has no maximum record size; large records are organized as a singly directed list.

- A record may grow so large that it no longer fits on *any* one page. We have to deal with this condition by breaking a record into smaller records. The smaller records could be chained together—part of each smaller record is a pointer to the next record in the chain—to enable retrieval of the entire original record.

9.8 REVIEW QUESTIONS

Answers to the review questions can be found in the listed sections.

- Explain the term *memory hierarchy.* What are the differences between primary, secondary, and tertiary storage? Give examples of each. Which of these is *volatile*, and which are *persistent*? Why is persistent storage more important for a DBMS than, say, a program that generates prime numbers? **(Section 9.1)**
- Why are disks used so widely in a DBMS? What are their advantages over main memory and tapes? What are their relative disadvantages? **(Section 9.1.1)**
- What is a *disk block* or *page*? How are blocks arranged in a disk? How does this affect the time to access a block? Discuss *seek time*, *rotational delay*, and *transfer time.* **(Section 9.1.1)**
- Explain how careful placement of pages on the disk to exploit the geometry of a disk can minimize the seek time and rotational delay when pages are read sequentially. **(Section 9.1.2)**
- Explain what a RAID system is and how it improves performance and reliability. Discuss *striping* and its impact on performance and *redundancy* and its impact on reliability. What are the trade-offs between reliability

and performance in the different RAID organizations called *RAID levels*? **(Section 9.2)**

- What is the role of the DBMS *disk space manager*? Why do database systems not rely on the operating system instead? **(Section 9.3)**
- Why does every page request in a DBMS go through the buffer manager? What is the *buffer pool*? What is the difference between a *frame* in a buffer pool, a *page* in a file, and a *block* on a disk? **(Section 9.4)**
- What information does the buffer manager maintain for each page in the buffer pool? What information is maintained for each frame? What is the significance of *pin_count* and the *dirty* flag for a page? Under what conditions can a page in the pool be *replaced*? Under what conditions must a replaced page be written back to disk? **(Section 9.4)**
- Why does the buffer manager have to replace pages in the buffer pool? How is a page chosen for replacement? What is *sequential flooding*, and what replacement policy causes it? **(Section 9.4.1)**
- A DBMS buffer manager can often predict the access pattern for disk pages. How does it utilize this ability to minimize I/O costs? Discuss *prefetching*. What is *forcing*, and why is it required to support the write-ahead log protocol in a DBMS? In light of these points, explain why database systems reimplement many services provided by operating systems. **(Section 9.4.2)**
- Why is the abstraction of a *file of records* important? How is the software in a DBMS layered to take advantage of this? **(Section 9.5)**
- What is a *heap file*? How are pages organized in a heap file? Discuss list versus directory organizations. **(Section 9.5.1)**
- Describe how records are arranged on a page. What is a *slot*, and how are slots used to identify records? How do slots enable us to move records on a page without altering the record's identifier? What are the differences in page organizations for fixed-length and variable-length records? **(Section 9.6)**
- What are the differences in how fields are arranged within fixed-length and variable-length records? For variable-length records, explain how the array of offsets organization provides direct access to a specific field and supports *null* values. **(Section 9.7)**

EXERCISES

Exercise 9.1 What is the most important difference between a disk and a tape?

Exercise 9.2 Explain the terms *seek time, rotational delay,* and *transfer time.*

Exercise 9.3 Both disks and main memory support direct access to any desired location (page). On average, main memory accesses are faster, of course. What is the other important difference (from the perspective of the time required to access a desired page)?

Exercise 9.4 If you have a large file that is frequently scanned sequentially, explain how you would store the pages in the file on a disk.

Exercise 9.5 Consider a disk with a sector size of 512 bytes, 2000 tracks per surface, 50 sectors per track, five double-sided platters, and average seek time of 10 msec.

1. What is the capacity of a track in bytes? What is the capacity of each surface? What is the capacity of the disk?
2. How many cylinders does the disk have?
3. Give examples of valid block sizes. Is 256 bytes a valid block size? 2048? 51,200?
4. If the disk platters rotate at 5400 rpm (revolutions per minute), what is the maximum rotational delay?
5. If one track of data can be transferred per revolution, what is the transfer rate?

Exercise 9.6 Consider again the disk specifications from Exercise 9.5 and suppose that a block size of 1024 bytes is chosen. Suppose that a file containing 100,000 records of 100 bytes each is to be stored on such a disk and that no record is allowed to span two blocks.

1. How many records fit onto a block?
2. How many blocks are required to store the entire file? If the file is arranged sequentially on disk, how many surfaces are needed?
3. How many records of 100 bytes each can be stored using this disk?
4. If pages are stored sequentially on disk, with page 1 on block 1 of track 1, what page is stored on block 1 of track 1 on the next disk surface? How would your answer change if the disk were capable of reading and writing from all heads in parallel?
5. What time is required to read a file containing 100,000 records of 100 bytes each sequentially? Again, how would your answer change if the disk were capable of reading/writing from all heads in parallel (and the data was arranged optimally)?
6. What is the time required to read a file containing 100,000 records of 100 bytes each in a random order? To read a record, the block containing the record has to be fetched from disk. Assume that each block request incurs the average seek time and rotational delay.

Exercise 9.7 Explain what the buffer manager must do to process a read request for a page. What happens if the requested page is in the pool but not pinned?

Exercise 9.8 When does a buffer manager write a page to disk?

Exercise 9.9 What does it mean to say that a page is *pinned* in the buffer pool? Who is responsible for pinning pages? Who is responsible for unpinning pages?

Exercise 9.10 When a page in the buffer pool is modified, how does the DBMS ensure that this change is propagated to disk? (Explain the role of the buffer manager as well as the modifier of the page.)

Exercise 9.11 What happens if a page is requested when all pages in the buffer pool are dirty?

Exercise 9.12 What is *sequential flooding* of the buffer pool?

Exercise 9.13 Name an important capability of a DBMS buffer manager that is not supported by a typical operating system's buffer manager.

Exercise 9.14 Explain the term *prefetching*. Why is it important?

Exercise 9.15 Modern disks often have their own main memory caches, typically about 1 MB, and use this to prefetch pages. The rationale for this technique is the empirical observation that, if a disk page is requested by some (not necessarily database!) application, 80% of the time the next page is requested as well. So the disk gambles by reading ahead.

1. Give a nontechnical reason that a DBMS may not want to rely on prefetching controlled by the disk.
2. Explain the impact on the disk's cache of several queries running concurrently, each scanning a different file.
3. Is this problem addressed by the DBMS buffer manager prefetching pages? Explain.
4. Modern disks support *segmented caches*, with about four to six segments, each of which is used to cache pages from a different file. Does this technique help, with respect to the preceding problem? Given this technique, does it matter whether the DBMS buffer manager also does prefetching?

Exercise 9.16 Describe two possible record formats. What are the trade-offs between them?

Exercise 9.17 Describe two possible page formats. What are the trade-offs between them?

Exercise 9.18 Consider the page format for variable-length records that uses a slot directory.

1. One approach to managing the slot directory is to use a maximum size (i.e., a maximum number of slots) and allocate the directory array when the page is created. Discuss the pros and cons of this approach with respect to the approach discussed in the text.
2. Suggest a modification to this page format that would allow us to sort records (according to the value in some field) without moving records and without changing the record ids.

Exercise 9.19 Consider the two internal organizations for heap files (using lists of pages and a directory of pages) discussed in the text.

1. Describe them briefly and explain the trade-offs. Which organization would you choose if records are variable in length?
2. Can you suggest a single page format to implement both internal file organizations?

Exercise 9.20 Consider a list-based organization of the pages in a heap file in which two lists are maintained: a list of *all* pages in the file and a list of all pages with free space. In contrast, the list-based organization discussed in the text maintains a list of full pages and a list of pages with free space.

1. What are the trade-offs, if any? Is one of them clearly superior?
2. For each of these organizations, describe a suitable page format.

Exercise 9.21 Modern disk drives store more sectors on the outer tracks than the inner tracks. Since the rotation speed is constant, the sequential data transfer rate is also higher on the outer tracks. The seek time and rotational delay are unchanged. Given this information, explain good strategies for placing files with the following kinds of access patterns:

1. Frequent, random accesses to a small file (e.g., catalog relations).
2. Sequential scans of a large file (e.g., selection from a relation with no index).
3. Random accesses to a large file via an index (e.g., selection from a relation via the index).
4. Sequential scans of a small file.

Exercise 9.22 Why do frames in the buffer pool have a pin count instead of a pin flag?

PROJECT-BASED EXERCISES

Exercise 9.23 Study the public interfaces for the disk space manager, the buffer manager, and the heap file layer in Minibase.

1. Are heap files with variable-length records supported?
2. What page format is used in Minibase heap files?
3. What happens if you insert a record whose length is greater than the page size?
4. How is free space handled in Minibase?

BIBLIOGRAPHIC NOTES

Salzberg [648] and Wiederhold [776] discuss secondary storage devices and file organizations in detail.

RAID was originally proposed by Patterson, Gibson, and Katz [587]. The article by Chen et al. provides an excellent survey of RAID [171] . Books about RAID include Gibson's dissertation [317] and the publications from the RAID Advisory Board [605].

The design and implementation of storage managers is discussed in [65, 133, 219, 477, 718]. With the exception of [219], these systems emphasize *extensibility*, and the papers contain much of interest from that standpoint as well. Other papers that cover storage management issues in the context of significant implemented prototype systems are [480] and [588]. The Dali storage manager, which is optimized for main memory databases, is described in [406]. Three techniques for implementing long fields are compared in [96]. The impact of processor cache misses on DBMS performance has received attention lately, as complex queries have become increasingly CPU-intensive. [33] studies this issue, and shows that performance can be significantly improved by using a new arrangement of records within a page, in which records on a page are stored in a column-oriented format (all field values for the first attribute followed by values for the second attribute, etc.).

Stonebraker discusses operating systems issues in the context of databases in [715]. Several buffer management policies for database systems are compared in [181]. Buffer management is also studied in [119, 169, 261, 235].

10

TREE-STRUCTURED INDEXING

- What is the intuition behind tree-structured indexes? Why are they good for range selections?
- How does an ISAM index handle search, insert, and delete?
- How does a B+ tree index handle search, insert, and delete?
- What is the impact of duplicate key values on index implementation?
- What is key compression, and why is it important?
- What is bulk-loading, and why is it important?
- What happens to record identifiers when dynamic indexes are updated? How does this affect clustered indexes?

➽ **Key concepts:** ISAM, static indexes, overflow pages, locking issues; B+ trees, dynamic indexes, balance, sequence sets, node format; B+ tree insert operation, node splits, delete operation, merge versus redistribution, minimum occupancy; duplicates, overflow pages, including rids in search keys; key compression; bulk-loading; effects of splits on rids in clustered indexes.

One that would have the fruit must climb the tree.

Thomas Fuller

We now consider two index data structures, called ISAM and B+ trees, based on tree organizations. These structures provide efficient support for range searches, including sorted file scans as a special case. Unlike sorted files, these index structures support efficient insertion and deletion. They also provide support for equality selections, although they are not as efficient in this case as hash-based indexes, which are discussed in Chapter 11.

An ISAM[1] tree is a static index structure that is effective when the file is not frequently updated, but it is unsuitable for files that grow and shrink a lot. We discuss ISAM in Section 10.2. The B+ tree is a dynamic structure that adjusts to changes in the file gracefully. It is the most widely used index structure because it adjusts well to changes and supports both equality and range queries. We introduce B+ trees in Section 10.3. We cover B+ trees in detail in the remaining sections. Section 10.3.1 describes the format of a tree node. Section 10.4 considers how to search for records by using a B+ tree index. Section 10.5 presents the algorithm for inserting records into a B+ tree, and Section 10.6 presents the deletion algorithm. Section 10.7 discusses how duplicates are handled. We conclude with a discussion of some practical issues concerning B+ trees in Section 10.8.

Notation: In the ISAM and B+ tree structures, leaf pages contain *data entries*, according to the terminology introduced in Chapter 8. For convenience, we denote a data entry with search key value k as $k*$. Non-leaf pages contain *index entries* of the form $\langle$*search key value, page id*$\rangle$ and are used to direct the search for a desired data entry (which is stored in some leaf). We often simply use *entry* where the context makes the nature of the entry (index or data) clear.

10.1 INTUITION FOR TREE INDEXES

Consider a file of Students records sorted by *gpa*. To answer a range selection such as "Find all students with a gpa higher than 3.0," we must identify the first such student by doing a binary search of the file and then scan the file from that point on. If the file is large, the initial binary search can be quite expensive, since cost is proportional to the number of pages fetched; can we improve upon this method?

One idea is to create a second file with one record per page in the original (data) file, of the form $\langle$*first key on page, pointer to page*$\rangle$, again sorted by the key attribute (which is *gpa* in our example). The format of a page in the second *index* file is illustrated in Figure 10.1.

We refer to pairs of the form $\langle$*key, pointer*$\rangle$ as *index entries* or just *entries* when the context is clear. Note that each index page contains one pointer more than

[1]ISAM stands for Indexed Sequential Access Method.

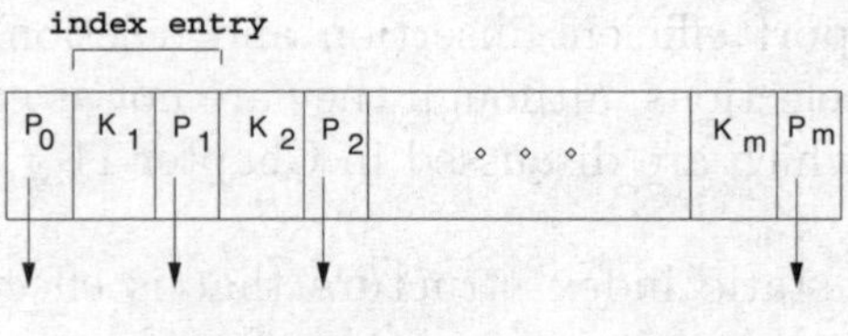

Figure 10.1 Format of an Index Page

the number of keys—each key serves as a *separator* for the contents of the pages pointed to by the pointers to its left and right.

The simple index file data structure is illustrated in Figure 10.2.

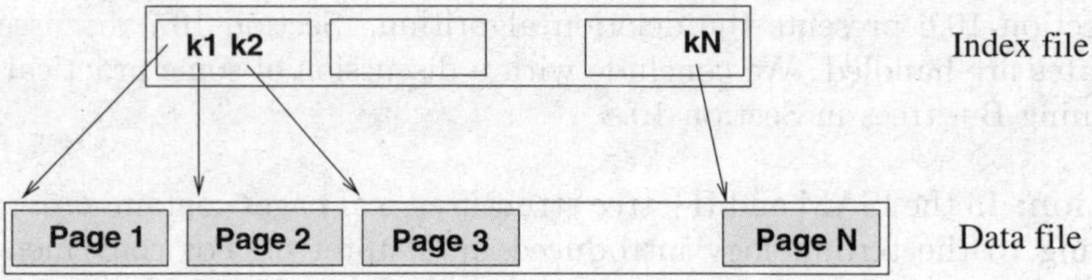

Figure 10.2 One-Level Index Structure

We can do a binary search of the index file to identify the page containing the first key (*gpa*) value that satisfies the range selection (in our example, the first student with *gpa* over 3.0) and follow the pointer to the page containing the first data record with that key value. We can then scan the data file sequentially from that point on to retrieve other qualifying records. This example uses the index to find the first data page containing a Students record with *gpa* greater than 3.0, and the data file is scanned from that point on to retrieve other such Students records.

Because the size of an entry in the index file (key value and page id) is likely to be much smaller than the size of a page, and only one such entry exists per page of the data file, the index file is likely to be much smaller than the data file; therefore, a binary search of the index file is much faster than a binary search of the data file. However, a binary search of the index file could still be fairly expensive, and the index file is typically still large enough to make inserts and deletes expensive.

The potential large size of the index file motivates the tree indexing idea: Why not apply the previous step of building an auxiliary structure on the collection of *index* records and so on recursively until the smallest auxiliary structure fits on one page? This repeated construction of a one-level index leads to a tree structure with several levels of non-leaf pages.

As we observed in Section 8.3.2, the power of the approach comes from the fact that locating a record (given a search key value) involves a traversal from the root to a leaf, with one I/O (at most; some pages, e.g., the root, are likely to be in the buffer pool) per level. Given the typical fan-out value (over 100), trees rarely have more than 3–4 levels.

The next issue to consider is how the tree structure can handle inserts and deletes of data entries. Two distinct approaches have been used, leading to the ISAM and B+ tree data structures, which we discuss in subsequent sections.

10.2 INDEXED SEQUENTIAL ACCESS METHOD (ISAM)

The ISAM data structure is illustrated in Figure 10.3. The data entries of the ISAM index are in the leaf pages of the tree and additional *overflow* pages chained to some leaf page. Database systems carefully organize the layout of pages so that page boundaries correspond closely to the physical characteristics of the underlying storage device. The ISAM structure is completely static (except for the overflow pages, of which it is hoped, there will be few) and facilitates such low-level optimizations.

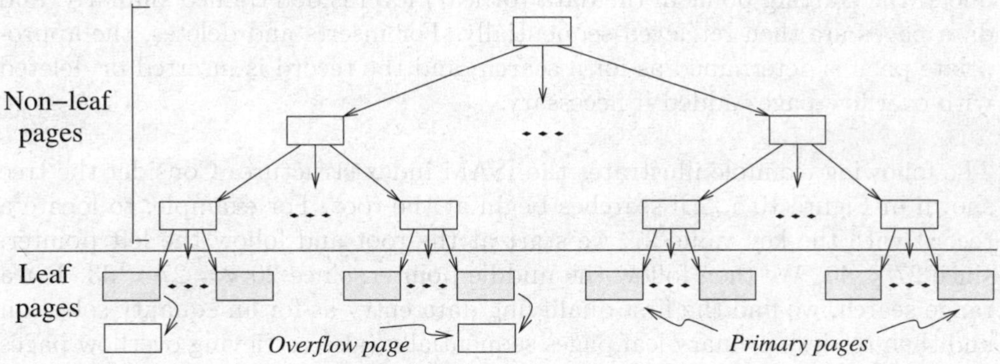

Figure 10.3 ISAM Index Structure

Each tree node is a disk page, and all the data resides in the leaf pages. This corresponds to an index that uses Alternative (1) for data entries, in terms of the alternatives described in Chapter 8; we can create an index with Alternative (2) by storing the data records in a separate file and storing ⟨*key, rid*⟩ pairs in the leaf pages of the ISAM index. When the file is created, all leaf pages are allocated sequentially and sorted on the search key value. (If Alternative (2) or (3) is used, the data records are created and sorted before allocating the leaf pages of the ISAM index.) The non-leaf level pages are then allocated. If there are several inserts to the file subsequently, so that more entries are inserted into a leaf than will fit onto a single page, additional pages are needed because the index structure is static. These additional pages are allocated from an overflow area. The allocation of pages is illustrated in Figure 10.4.

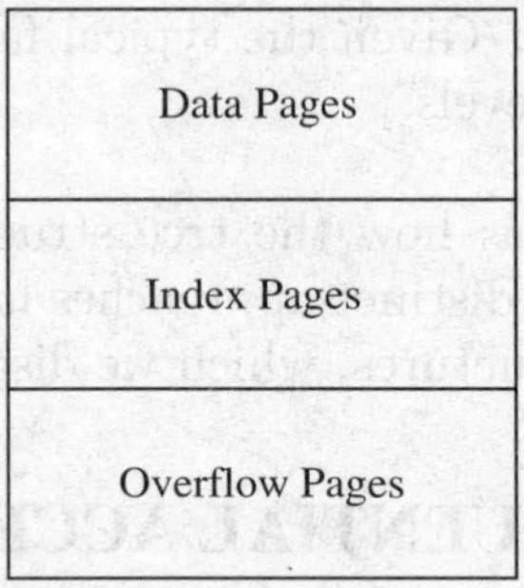

Figure 10.4 Page Allocation in ISAM

The basic operations of insertion, deletion, and search are all quite straightforward. For an equality selection search, we start at the root node and determine which subtree to search by comparing the value in the search field of the given record with the key values in the node. (The search algorithm is identical to that for a B+ tree; we present this algorithm in more detail later.) For a range query, the starting point in the data (or leaf) level is determined similarly, and data pages are then retrieved sequentially. For inserts and deletes, the appropriate page is determined as for a search, and the record is inserted or deleted with overflow pages added if necessary.

The following example illustrates the ISAM index structure. Consider the tree shown in Figure 10.5. All searches begin at the root. For example, to locate a record with the key value 27, we start at the root and follow the left pointer, since $27 < 40$. We then follow the middle pointer, since $20 <= 27 < 33$. For a range search, we find the first qualifying data entry as for an equality selection and then retrieve primary leaf pages sequentially (also retrieving overflow pages as needed by following pointers from the primary pages). The primary leaf pages are assumed to be allocated sequentially—this assumption is reasonable because the number of such pages is known when the tree is created and does not change subsequently under inserts and deletes—and so no 'next leaf page' pointers are needed.

We assume that each leaf page can contain two entries. If we now insert a record with key value 23, the entry 23* belongs in the second data page, which already contains 20* and 27* and has no more space. We deal with this situation by adding an *overflow* page and putting 23* in the overflow page. Chains of overflow pages can easily develop. For instance, inserting 48*, 41*, and 42* leads to an overflow chain of two pages. The tree of Figure 10.5 with all these insertions is shown in Figure 10.6.

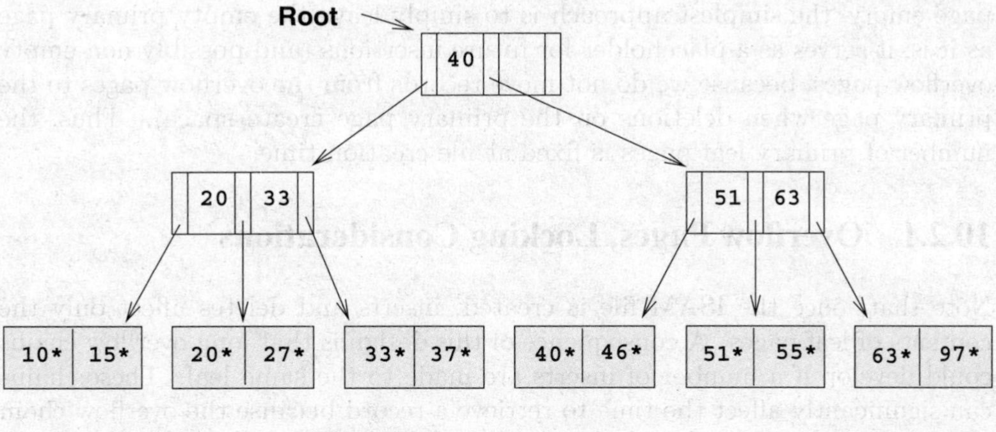

Figure 10.5 Sample ISAM Tree

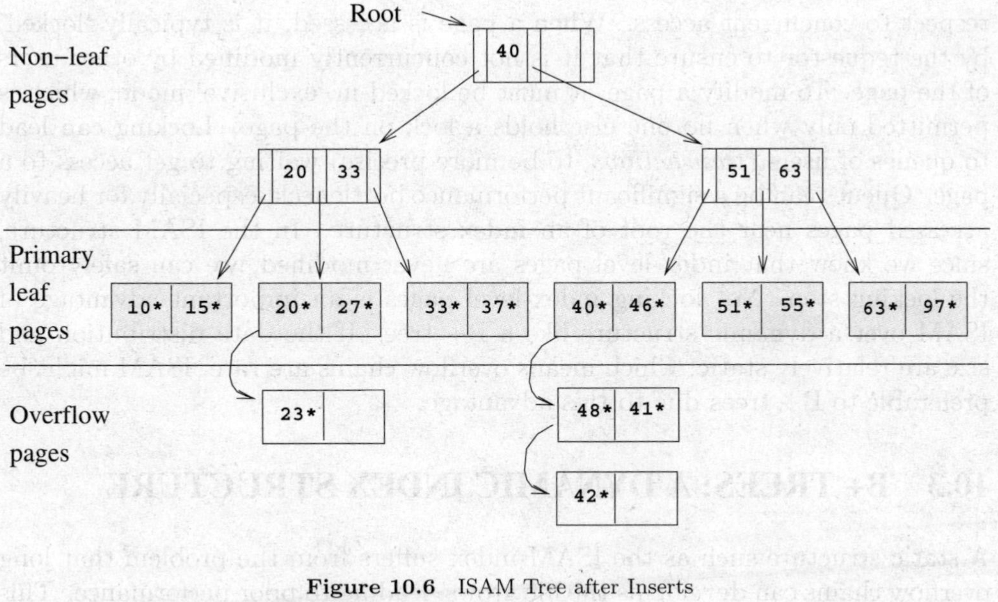

Figure 10.6 ISAM Tree after Inserts

The deletion of an entry $k*$ is handled by simply removing the entry. If this entry is on an overflow page and the overflow page becomes empty, the page can be removed. If the entry is on a primary page and deletion makes the primary page empty, the simplest approach is to simply leave the empty primary page as it is; it serves as a placeholder for future insertions (and possibly non-empty overflow pages, because we do not move records from the overflow pages to the primary page when deletions on the primary page create space). Thus, the number of primary leaf pages is fixed at file creation time.

10.2.1 Overflow Pages, Locking Considerations

Note that, once the ISAM file is created, inserts and deletes affect only the contents of leaf pages. A consequence of this design is that long overflow chains could develop if a number of inserts are made to the same leaf. These chains can significantly affect the time to retrieve a record because the overflow chain has to be searched as well when the search gets to this leaf. (Although data in the overflow chain can be kept sorted, it usually is not, to make inserts fast.) To alleviate this problem, the tree is initially created so that about 20 percent of each page is free. However, once the free space is filled in with inserted records, unless space is freed again through deletes, overflow chains can be eliminated only by a complete reorganization of the file.

The fact that only leaf pages are modified also has an important advantage with respect to concurrent access. When a page is accessed, it is typically 'locked' by the requestor to ensure that it is not concurrently modified by other users of the page. To modify a page, it must be locked in 'exclusive' mode, which is permitted only when no one else holds a lock on the page. Locking can lead to queues of users (*transactions*, to be more precise) waiting to get access to a page. Queues can be a significant performance bottleneck, especially for heavily accessed pages near the root of an index structure. In the ISAM structure, since we know that index-level pages are never modified, we can safely omit the locking step. Not locking index-level pages is an important advantage of ISAM over a dynamic structure like a B+ tree. If the data distribution and size are relatively static, which means overflow chains are rare, ISAM might be preferable to B+ trees due to this advantage.

10.3 B+ TREES: A DYNAMIC INDEX STRUCTURE

A static structure such as the ISAM index suffers from the problem that long overflow chains can develop as the file grows, leading to poor performance. This problem motivated the development of more flexible, dynamic structures that adjust gracefully to inserts and deletes. The **B+ tree** search structure, which is widely used, is a balanced tree in which the internal nodes direct the search and the leaf nodes contain the data entries. Since the tree structure grows and shrinks dynamically, it is not feasible to allocate the leaf pages sequentially as in ISAM, where the set of primary leaf pages was static. To retrieve all leaf pages efficiently, we have to link them using page pointers. By organizing them into a doubly linked list, we can easily traverse the sequence of leaf pages (sometimes called the **sequence set**) in either direction. This structure is illustrated in Figure 10.7.[2]

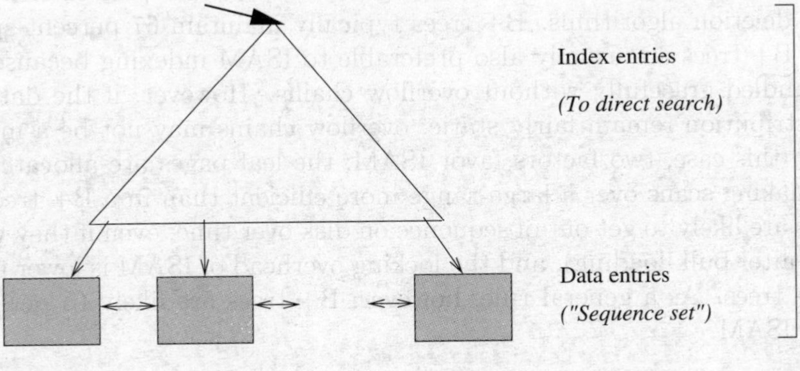

Figure 10.7 Structure of a B+ Tree

The following are some of the main characteristics of a B+ tree:

- Operations (insert, delete) on the tree keep it balanced.
- A minimum occupancy of 50 percent is guaranteed for each node except the root if the deletion algorithm discussed in Section 10.6 is implemented. However, deletion is often implemented by simply locating the data entry and removing it, without adjusting the tree as needed to guarantee the 50 percent occupancy, because files typically grow rather than shrink.
- Searching for a record requires just a traversal from the root to the appropriate leaf. We refer to the length of a path from the root to a leaf—any leaf, because the tree is balanced—as the **height** of the tree. For example, a tree with only a leaf level and a single index level, such as the tree shown in Figure 10.9, has height 1, and a tree that has only the root node has height 0. Because of high fan-out, the height of a B+ tree is rarely more than 3 or 4.

We will study B+ trees in which every node contains m entries, where $d \leq m \leq 2d$. The value d is a parameter of the B+ tree, called the **order** of the

[2] If the tree is created by *bulk-loading* (see Section 10.8.2) an existing data set, the sequence set can be made physically sequential, but this physical ordering is gradually destroyed as new data is added and deleted over time.

tree, and is a measure of the capacity of a tree node. The root node is the only exception to this requirement on the number of entries; for the root, it is simply required that $1 \leq m \leq 2d$.

If a file of records is updated frequently and sorted access is important, maintaining a B+ tree index with data records stored as data entries is almost always superior to maintaining a sorted file. For the space overhead of storing the index entries, we obtain all the advantages of a sorted file plus efficient insertion and deletion algorithms. B+ trees typically maintain 67 percent space occupancy. B+ trees are usually also preferable to ISAM indexing because inserts are handled gracefully without overflow chains. However, if the dataset size and distribution remain fairly static, overflow chains may not be a major problem. In this case, two factors favor ISAM: the leaf pages are allocated in sequence (making scans over a large range more efficient than in a B+ tree, in which pages are likely to get out of sequence on disk over time, even if they were in sequence after bulk-loading), and the locking overhead of ISAM is lower than that for B+ trees. As a general rule, however, B+ trees are likely to perform better than ISAM.

10.3.1 Format of a Node

The format of a node is the same as for ISAM and is shown in Figure 10.1. Non-leaf nodes with m *index entries* contain $m+1$ pointers to children. Pointer P_i points to a subtree in which all key values K are such that $K_i \leq K < K_{i+1}$. As special cases, P_0 points to a tree in which all key values are less than K_1, and P_m points to a tree in which all key values are greater than or equal to K_m. For leaf nodes, entries are denoted as $k*$, as usual. Just as in ISAM, leaf nodes (and *only* leaf nodes!) contain *data entries.* In the common case that Alternative (2) or (3) is used, leaf entries are $\langle K, I(K) \rangle$ pairs, just like non-leaf entries. Regardless of the alternative chosen for leaf entries, the leaf pages are chained together in a doubly linked list. Thus, the leaves form a sequence, which can be used to answer range queries efficiently.

The reader should carefully consider how such a node organization can be achieved using the record formats presented in Section 9.7; after all, each key–pointer pair can be thought of as a record. If the field being indexed is of fixed length, these index entries will be of fixed length; otherwise, we have variable-length records. In either case the B+ tree can itself be viewed as a file of records. If the leaf pages do not contain the actual data records, then the B+ tree is indeed a file of records that is distinct from the file that contains the data. If the leaf pages contain data records, then a file contains the B+ tree as well as the data.

10.4 SEARCH

The algorithm for search finds the leaf node in which a given data entry belongs. A pseudocode sketch of the algorithm is given in Figure 10.8. We use the notation **ptr* to denote the value pointed to by a pointer variable *ptr* and & *(value)* to denote the address of *value*. Note that finding i in *tree_search* requires us to search within the node, which can be done with either a linear search or a binary search (e.g., depending on the number of entries in the node).

In discussing the search, insertion, and deletion algorithms for B+ trees, we assume that there are no *duplicates*. That is, no two data entries are allowed to have the same key value. Of course, duplicates arise whenever the search key does not contain a candidate key and must be dealt with in practice. We consider how duplicates can be handled in Section 10.7.

```
func find (search key value K) returns nodepointer
// Given a search key value, finds its leaf node
return tree_search(root, K);                    // searches from root
endfunc

func tree_search (nodepointer, search key value K) returns nodepointer
// Searches tree for entry
if *nodepointer is a leaf, return nodepointer;
else,
    if K < K_1 then return tree_search(P_0, K);
    else,
        if K ≥ K_m then return tree_search(P_m, K);    // m = # entries
        else,
            find i such that K_i ≤ K < K_{i+1};
            return tree_search(P_i, K)
endfunc
```

Figure 10.8 Algorithm for Search

Consider the sample B+ tree shown in Figure 10.9. This B+ tree is of order d=2. That is, each node contains between 2 and 4 entries. Each non-leaf entry is a ⟨*key value, nodepointer*⟩ pair; at the leaf level, the entries are data records that we denote by $k*$. To search for entry 5*, we follow the left-most child pointer, since $5 < 13$. To search for the entries 14* or 15*, we follow the second pointer, since $13 \leq 14 < 17$, and $13 \leq 15 < 17$. (We do not find 15* on the appropriate leaf and can conclude that it is not present in the tree.) To find 24*, we follow the fourth child pointer, since $24 \leq 24 < 30$.

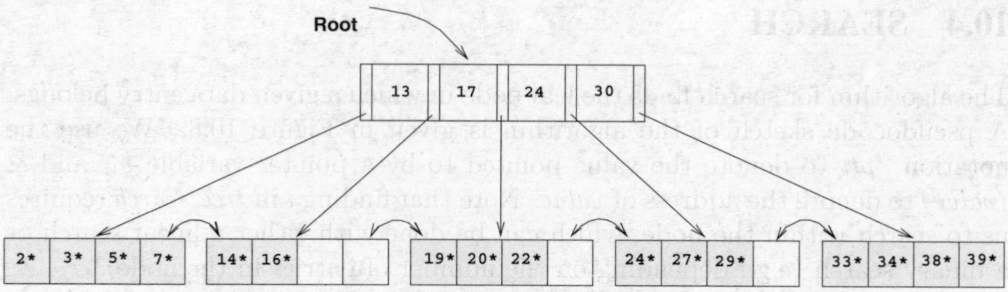

Figure 10.9 Example of a B+ Tree, Order d=2

10.5 INSERT

The algorithm for insertion takes an entry, finds the leaf node where it belongs, and inserts it there. Pseudocode for the B+ tree insertion algorithm is given in Figure 10.10. The basic idea behind the algorithm is that we recursively insert the entry by calling the insert algorithm on the appropriate child node. Usually, this procedure results in going down to the leaf node where the entry belongs, placing the entry there, and returning all the way back to the root node. Occasionally a node is full and it must be split. When the node is split, an entry pointing to the node created by the split must be inserted into its parent; this entry is pointed to by the pointer variable *newchildentry*. If the (old) root is split, a new root node is created and the height of the tree increases by 1.

To illustrate insertion, let us continue with the sample tree shown in Figure 10.9. If we insert entry 8*, it belongs in the left-most leaf, which is already full. This insertion causes a split of the leaf page; the split pages are shown in Figure 10.11. The tree must now be adjusted to take the new leaf page into account, so we insert an entry consisting of the pair ⟨*5, pointer to new page*⟩ into the parent node. Note how the key 5, which discriminates between the split leaf page and its newly created sibling, is 'copied up.' We cannot just 'push up' 5, because every data entry must appear in a leaf page.

Since the parent node is also full, another split occurs. In general we have to split a non-leaf node when it is full, containing $2d$ keys and $2d+1$ pointers, and we have to add another index entry to account for a child split. We now have $2d+1$ keys and $2d+2$ pointers, yielding two minimally full non-leaf nodes, each containing d keys and $d+1$ pointers, and an extra key, which we choose to be the 'middle' key. This key and a pointer to the second non-leaf node constitute an index entry that must be inserted into the parent of the split non-leaf node. The middle key is thus 'pushed up' the tree, in contrast to the case for a split of a leaf page.

```
proc insert (nodepointer, entry, newchildentry)
// Inserts entry into subtree with root '*nodepointer'; degree is d;
//'newchildentry' null initially, and null on return unless child is split

if *nodepointer is a non-leaf node, say N,
    find i such that K_i ≤ entry's key value < K_{i+1};     // choose subtree
    insert(P_i, entry, newchildentry);               // recursively, insert entry
    if newchildentry is null, return;       // usual case; didn't split child
    else,                  // we split child, must insert *newchildentry in N
        if N has space,                                         // usual case
            put *newchildentry on it, set newchildentry to null, return;
        else,            // note difference wrt splitting of leaf page!
            split N:          // 2d + 1 key values and 2d + 2 nodepointers
            first d key values and d + 1 nodepointers stay,
            last d keys and d + 1 pointers move to new node, N2;
            // *newchildentry set to guide searches between N and N2
            newchildentry = & (⟨smallest key value on N2,
                                   pointer to N2⟩);
            if N is the root,                  // root node was just split
                create new node with ⟨pointer to N, *newchildentry⟩;
                make the tree's root-node pointer point to the new node;
            return;

if *nodepointer is a leaf node, say L,
    if L has space,                                             // usual case
    put entry on it, set newchildentry to null, and return;
    else,                              // once in a while, the leaf is full
        split L: first d entries stay, rest move to brand new node L2;
        newchildentry = & (⟨smallest key value on L2, pointer to L2⟩);
        set sibling pointers in L and L2;
        return;
endproc
```

Figure 10.10 Algorithm for Insertion into B+ Tree of Order d

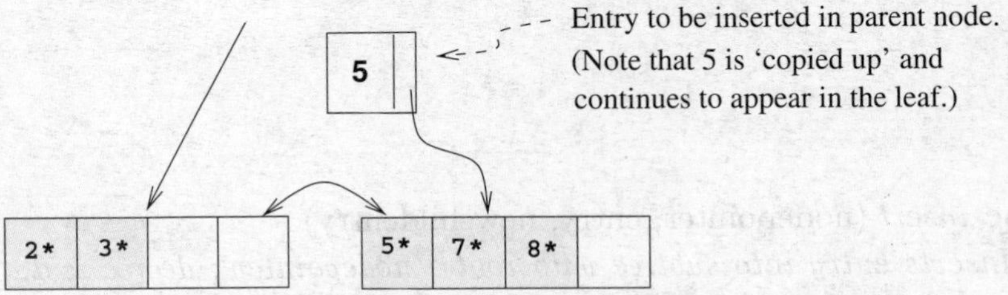
Entry to be inserted in parent node.
(Note that 5 is 'copied up' and
continues to appear in the leaf.)
5
2*
3*
5*
7*
8*

Figure 10.11 Split Leaf Pages during Insert of Entry 8*

The split pages in our example are shown in Figure 10.12. The index entry pointing to the new non-leaf node is the pair ⟨*17, pointer to new index-level page*⟩; note that the key value 17 is 'pushed up' the tree, in contrast to the splitting key value 5 in the leaf split, which was 'copied up.'

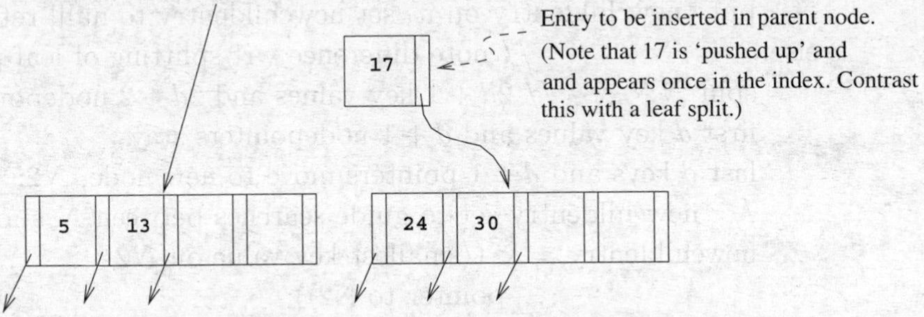
Entry to be inserted in parent node.
(Note that 17 is 'pushed up' and
and appears once in the index. Contrast
this with a leaf split.)
17
5
13
24
30

Figure 10.12 Split Index Pages during Insert of Entry 8*

The difference in handling leaf-level and index-level splits arises from the B+ tree requirement that all data entries $k*$ must reside in the leaves. This requirement prevents us from 'pushing up' 5 and leads to the slight redundancy of having some key values appearing in the leaf level as well as in some index level. However, range queries can be efficiently answered by just retrieving the sequence of leaf pages; the redundancy is a small price to pay for efficiency. In dealing with the index levels, we have more flexibility, and we 'push up' 17 to avoid having two copies of 17 in the index levels.

Now, since the split node was the old root, we need to create a new root node to hold the entry that distinguishes the two split index pages. The tree after completing the insertion of the entry 8* is shown in Figure 10.13.

One variation of the insert algorithm tries to redistribute entries of a node N with a sibling before splitting the node; this improves average occupancy. The **sibling** of a node N, in this context, is a node that is immediately to the left or right of N *and has the same parent as N.*

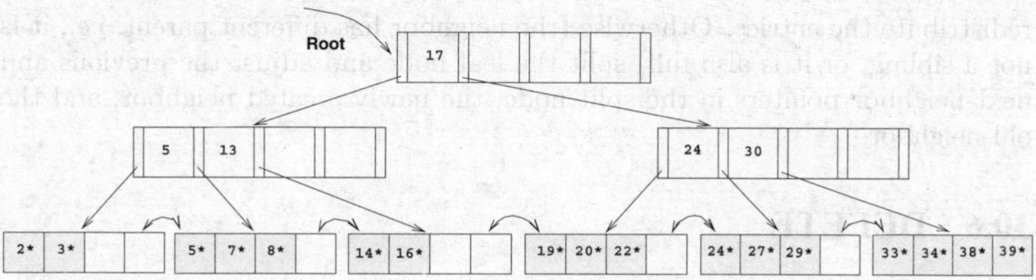

Figure 10.13 B+ Tree after Inserting Entry 8*

To illustrate redistribution, reconsider insertion of entry 8* into the tree shown in Figure 10.9. The entry belongs in the left-most leaf, which is full. However, the (only) sibling of this leaf node contains only two entries and can thus accommodate more entries. We can therefore handle the insertion of 8* with a redistribution. Note how the entry in the parent node that points to the second leaf has a new key value; we 'copy up' the new low key value on the second leaf. This process is illustrated in Figure 10.14.

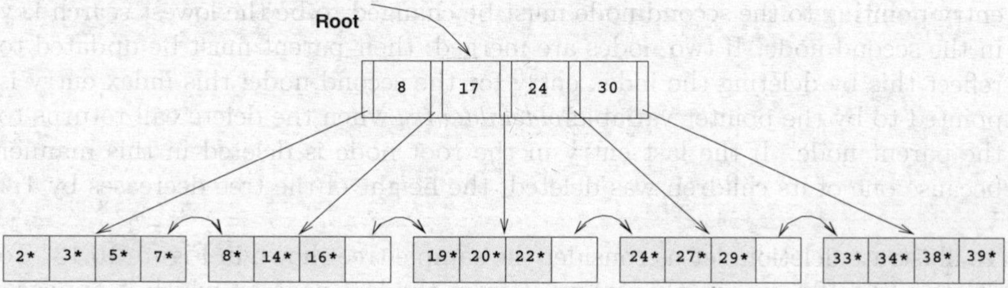

Figure 10.14 B+ Tree after Inserting Entry 8* Using Redistribution

To determine whether redistribution is possible, we have to retrieve the sibling. If the sibling happens to be full, we have to split the node anyway. On average, checking whether redistribution is possible increases I/O for index node splits, especially if we check both siblings. (Checking whether redistribution is possible may reduce I/O if the redistribution succeeds whereas a split propagates up the tree, but this case is very infrequent.) If the file is growing, average occupancy will probably not be affected much even if we do not redistribute. Taking these considerations into account, *not* redistributing entries at non-leaf levels usually pays off.

If a split occurs at the leaf level, however, we have to retrieve a neighbor to adjust the previous and next-neighbor pointers with respect to the newly created leaf node. Therefore, a limited form of redistribution makes sense: If a leaf node is full, fetch a neighbor node; if it has space and has the same parent, redistribute the entries. Otherwise (the neighbor has different parent, i.e., it is not a sibling, or it is also full) split the leaf node and adjust the previous and next-neighbor pointers in the split node, the newly created neighbor, and the old neighbor.

10.6 DELETE

The algorithm for deletion takes an entry, finds the leaf node where it belongs, and deletes it. Pseudocode for the B+ tree deletion algorithm is given in Figure 10.15. The basic idea behind the algorithm is that we recursively delete the entry by calling the delete algorithm on the appropriate child node. We usually go down to the leaf node where the entry belongs, remove the entry from there, and return all the way back to the root node. Occasionally a node is at minimum occupancy before the deletion, and the deletion causes it to go below the occupancy threshold. When this happens, we must either redistribute entries from an adjacent sibling or merge the node with a sibling to maintain minimum occupancy. If entries are redistributed between two nodes, their parent node must be updated to reflect this; the key value in the index entry pointing to the second node must be changed to be the lowest search key in the second node. If two nodes are merged, their parent must be updated to reflect this by deleting the index entry for the second node; this index entry is pointed to by the pointer variable *oldchildentry* when the delete call returns to the parent node. If the last entry in the root node is deleted in this manner because one of its children was deleted, the height of the tree decreases by 1.

To illustrate deletion, let us consider the sample tree shown in Figure 10.13. To delete entry 19*, we simply remove it from the leaf page on which it appears, and we are done because the leaf still contains two entries. If we subsequently delete 20*, however, the leaf contains only one entry after the deletion. The (only) sibling of the leaf node that contained 20* has three entries, and we can therefore deal with the situation by redistribution; we move entry 24* to the leaf page that contained 20* and copy up the new splitting key (27, which is the new low key value of the leaf from which we borrowed 24*) into the parent. This process is illustrated in Figure 10.16.

Suppose that we now delete entry 24*. The affected leaf contains only one entry (22*) after the deletion, and the (only) sibling contains just two entries (27* and 29*). Therefore, we cannot redistribute entries. However, these two leaf nodes together contain only three entries and can be merged. While merging, we can 'toss' the entry (⟨*27, pointer to second leaf page*⟩) in the parent, which pointed to the second leaf page, because the second leaf page is empty after the merge and can be discarded. The right subtree of Figure 10.16 after this step in the deletion of entry 24* is shown in Figure 10.17.

```
proc delete (parentpointer, nodepointer, entry, oldchildentry)
// Deletes entry from subtree with root '*nodepointer'; degree is d;
// 'oldchildentry' null initially, and null upon return unless child deleted
if *nodepointer is a non-leaf node, say N,
    find i such that K_i ≤ entry's key value < K_{i+1};      // choose subtree
    delete(nodepointer, P_i, entry, oldchildentry);          // recursive delete
    if oldchildentry is null, return;          // usual case: child not deleted
    else,                       // we discarded child node (see discussion)
        remove *oldchildentry from N,          // next, check for underflow
        if N has entries to spare,                              // usual case
            set oldchildentry to null, return; // delete doesn't go further
        else,                // note difference wrt merging of leaf pages!
            get a sibling S of N:     // parentpointer arg used to find S
            if S has extra entries,
                redistribute evenly between N and S through parent;
                set oldchildentry to null, return;
            else, merge N and S                       // call node on rhs M
                oldchildentry = & (current entry in parent for M);
                pull splitting key from parent down into node on left;
                move all entries from M to node on left;
                discard empty node M, return;

if *nodepointer is a leaf node, say L,
    if L has entries to spare,                                  // usual case
        remove entry, set oldchildentry to null, and return;
    else,               // once in a while, the leaf becomes underfull
        get a sibling S of L;              // parentpointer used to find S
        if S has extra entries,
            redistribute evenly between L and S;
            find entry in parent for node on right;             // call it M
            replace key value in parent entry by new low-key value in M;
            set oldchildentry to null, return;
        else, merge L and S                           // call node on rhs M
            oldchildentry = & (current entry in parent for M);
            move all entries from M to node on left;
            discard empty node M, adjust sibling pointers, return;
endproc
```

Figure 10.15 Algorithm for Deletion from B+ Tree of Order *d*

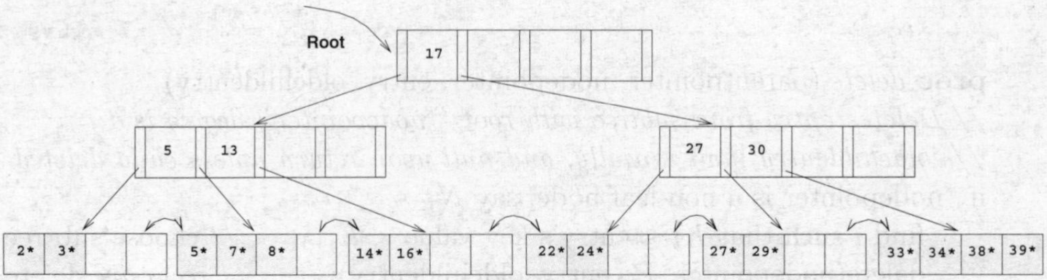

Figure 10.16 B+ Tree after Deleting Entries 19* and 20*

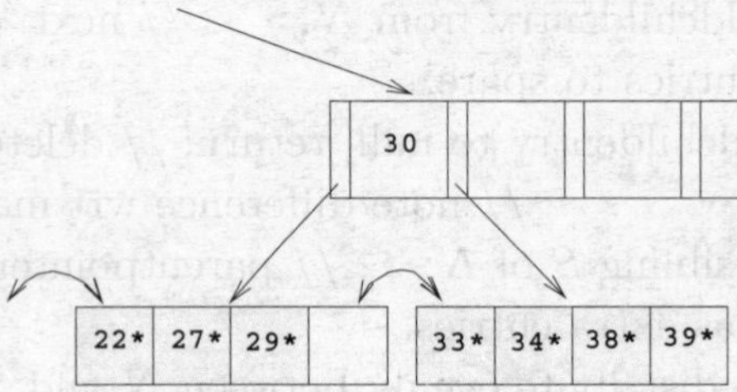

Figure 10.17 Partial B+ Tree during Deletion of Entry 24*

Deleting the entry ⟨*27, pointer to second leaf page*⟩ has created a non-leaf-level page with just one entry, which is below the minimum of $d = 2$. To fix this problem, we must either redistribute or merge. In either case, we must fetch a sibling. The only sibling of this node contains just two entries (with key values 5 and 13), and so redistribution is not possible; we must therefore merge.

The situation when we have to merge two non-leaf nodes is exactly the opposite of the situation when we have to split a non-leaf node. We have to split a non-leaf node when it contains $2d$ keys and $2d + 1$ pointers, and we have to add another key–pointer pair. Since we resort to merging two non-leaf nodes only when we cannot redistribute entries between them, the two nodes must be minimally full; that is, each must contain d keys and $d + 1$ pointers prior to the deletion. After merging the two nodes and removing the key–pointer pair to be deleted, we have $2d - 1$ keys and $2d + 1$ pointers: Intuitively, the left-most pointer on the second merged node lacks a key value. To see what key value must be combined with this pointer to create a complete index entry, consider the parent of the two nodes being merged. The index entry pointing to one of the merged nodes must be deleted from the parent because the node is about to be discarded. The key value in this index entry is precisely the key value we need to complete the new merged node: The entries in the first node being merged, followed by the splitting key value that is 'pulled down' from the parent, followed by the entries in the second non-leaf node gives us a total of $2d$ keys and $2d + 1$ pointers, which is a full non-leaf node. Note how the splitting key value in the parent is pulled down, in contrast to the case of merging two leaf nodes.

Consider the merging of two non-leaf nodes in our example. Together, the non-leaf node and the sibling to be merged contain only three entries, and they have a total of five pointers to leaf nodes. To merge the two nodes, we also need to pull down the index entry in their parent that currently discriminates between these nodes. This index entry has key value 17, and so we create a new entry ⟨*17, left-most child pointer in sibling*⟩. Now we have a total of four entries and five child pointers, which can fit on one page in a tree of order $d = 2$. Note that pulling down the splitting key 17 means that it will no longer appear in the parent node following the merge. After we merge the affected non-leaf node and its sibling by putting all the entries on one page and discarding the empty sibling page, the new node is the only child of the old root, which can therefore be discarded. The tree after completing all these steps in the deletion of entry 24* is shown in Figure 10.18.

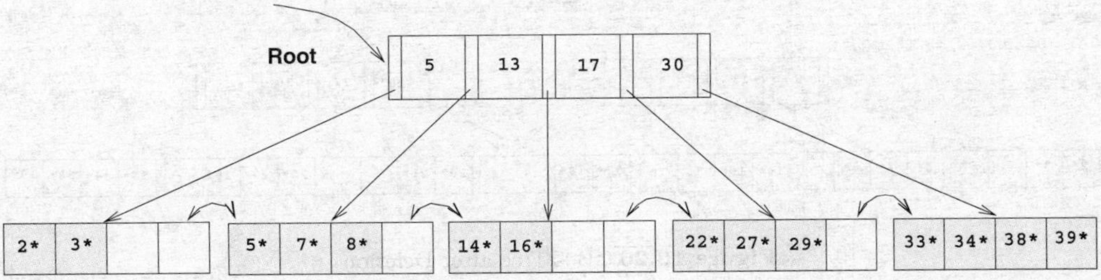

Figure 10.18 B+ Tree after Deleting Entry 24*

The previous examples illustrated redistribution of entries across leaves and merging of both leaf-level and non-leaf-level pages. The remaining case is that of redistribution of entries between non-leaf-level pages. To understand this case, consider the intermediate right subtree shown in Figure 10.17. We would arrive at the same intermediate right subtree if we try to delete 24* from a tree similar to the one shown in Figure 10.16 but with the left subtree and root key value as shown in Figure 10.19. The tree in Figure 10.19 illustrates an intermediate stage during the deletion of 24*. (Try to construct the initial tree.)

In contrast to the case when we deleted 24* from the tree of Figure 10.16, the non-leaf level node containing key value 30 now has a sibling that can spare entries (the entries with key values 17 and 20). We move these entries[3] over from the sibling. Note that, in doing so, we essentially push them through the

[3]It is sufficient to move over just the entry with key value 20, but we are moving over two entries to illustrate what happens when several entries are redistributed.

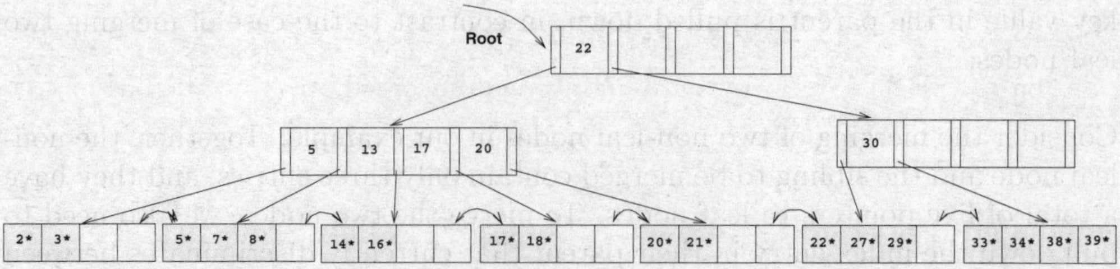

Figure 10.19 A B+ Tree during a Deletion

splitting entry in their parent node (the root), which takes care of the fact that 17 becomes the new low key value on the right and therefore must replace the old splitting key in the root (the key value 22). The tree with all these changes is shown in Figure 10.20.

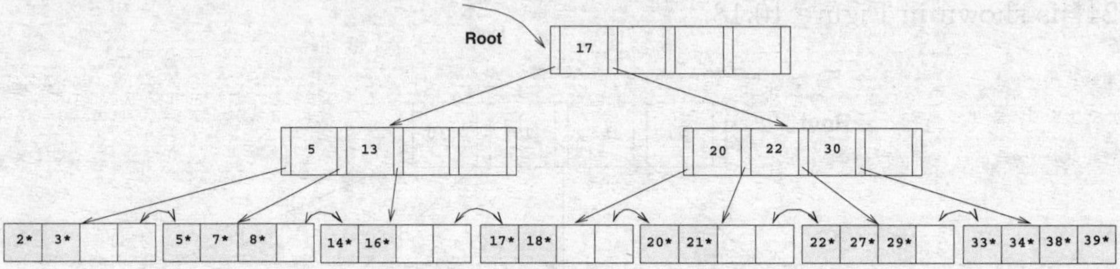

Figure 10.20 B+ Tree after Deletion

In concluding our discussion of deletion, we note that we retrieve only one sibling of a node. If this node has spare entries, we use redistribution; otherwise, we merge. If the node has a second sibling, it may be worth retrieving that sibling as well to check for the possibility of redistribution. Chances are high that redistribution is possible, and unlike merging, redistribution is guaranteed to propagate no further than the parent node. Also, the pages have more space on them, which reduces the likelihood of a split on subsequent insertions. (Remember, files typically grow, not shrink!) However, the number of times that this case arises (the node becomes less than half-full and the first sibling cannot spare an entry) is not very high, so it is not essential to implement this refinement of the basic algorithm that we presented.

10.7 DUPLICATES

The search, insertion, and deletion algorithms that we presented ignore the issue of **duplicate keys**, that is, several data entries with the same key value. We now discuss how duplicates can be handled.

> **Duplicate Handling in Commercial Systems:** In a clustered index in Sybase ASE, the data rows are maintained in sorted order on the page and in the collection of data pages. The data pages are bidirectionally linked in sort order. Rows with duplicate keys are inserted into (or deleted from) the ordered set of rows. This may result in overflow pages of rows with duplicate keys being inserted into the page chain or empty overflow pages removed from the page chain. Insertion or deletion of a duplicate key does not affect the higher index levels unless a split or merge of a non-overflow page occurs. In IBM DB2, Oracle 8, and Microsoft SQL Server, duplicates are handled by adding a row id if necessary to eliminate duplicate key values.

The basic search algorithm assumes that all entries with a given key value reside on a single leaf page. One way to satisfy this assumption is to use *overflow pages* to deal with duplicates. (In ISAM, of course, we have overflow pages in any case, and duplicates are easily handled.)

Typically, however, we use an alternative approach for duplicates. We handle them just like any other entries and several leaf pages may contain entries with a given key value. To retrieve all data entries with a given key value, we must search for the *left-most* data entry with the given key value and then possibly retrieve more than one leaf page (using the leaf sequence pointers). Modifying the search algorithm to find the left-most data entry in an index with duplicates is an interesting exercise (in fact, it is Exercise 10.11).

One problem with this approach is that, when a record is deleted, if we use Alternative (2) for data entries, finding the corresponding data entry to delete in the B+ tree index could be inefficient because we may have to check several duplicate entries ⟨*key*, *rid*⟩ with the same *key* value. This problem can be addressed by considering the *rid* value in the data entry to be *part of the search key*, for purposes of positioning the data entry in the tree. This solution effectively turns the index into a *unique* index (i.e., no duplicates). Remember that a search key can be any sequence of fields—in this variant, the rid of the data record is essentially treated as another field while constructing the search key.

Alternative (3) for data entries leads to a natural solution for duplicates, but if we have a large number of duplicates, a single data entry could span multiple pages. And of course, when a data record is deleted, finding the rid to delete from the corresponding data entry can be inefficient. The solution to this problem is similar to the one discussed previously for Alternative (2): We can maintain the list of rids within each data entry in sorted order (say, by page number and then slot number if a rid consists of a page id and a slot id).

10.8 B+ TREES IN PRACTICE

In this section we discuss several important pragmatic issues.

10.8.1 Key Compression

The height of a B+ tree depends on the *number of data entries* and the *size of index entries.* The size of index entries determines the number of index entries that will fit on a page and, therefore, the *fan-out* of the tree. Since the height of the tree is proportional to $log_{fan-out}$*(# of data entries)*, and the number of disk I/Os to retrieve a data entry is equal to the height (unless some pages are found in the buffer pool), it is clearly important to maximize the fan-out to minimize the height.

An index entry contains a search key value and a page pointer. Hence the size depends primarily on the size of the search key value. If search key values are very long (for instance, the name Devarakonda Venkataramana Sathyanarayana Seshasayee Yellamanchali Murthy, or Donaudampfschifffahrtskapitänsanwärtersmütze), not many index entries will fit on a page: Fan-out is low, and the height of the tree is large.

On the other hand, search key values in index entries are used only to direct traffic to the appropriate leaf. When we want to locate data entries with a given search key value, we compare this search key value with the search key values of index entries (on a path from the root to the desired leaf). During the comparison at an index-level node, we want to identify two index entries with search key values k_1 and k_2 such that the desired search key value k falls between k_1 and k_2. To accomplish this, we need not store search key values in their entirety in index entries.

For example, suppose we have two adjacent index entries in a node, with search key values 'David Smith' and 'Devarakonda ...' To discriminate between these two values, it is sufficient to store the abbreviated forms 'Da' and 'De.' More generally, the meaning of the entry 'David Smith' in the B+ tree is that every value in the subtree pointed to by the pointer to the left of 'David Smith' is less than 'David Smith,' and every value in the subtree pointed to by the pointer to the right of 'David Smith' is (greater than or equal to 'David Smith' and) less than 'Devarakonda ...'

B+ Trees in Real Systems: IBM DB2, Informix, Microsoft SQL Server, Oracle 8, and Sybase ASE all support clustered and unclustered B+ tree indexes, with some differences in how they handle deletions and duplicate key values. In Sybase ASE, depending on the concurrency control scheme being used for the index, the deleted row is removed (with merging if the page occupancy goes below threshold) or simply marked as deleted; a garbage collection scheme is used to recover space in the latter case. In Oracle 8, deletions are handled by marking the row as deleted. To reclaim the space occupied by deleted records, we can rebuild the index online (i.e., while users continue to use the index) or coalesce underfull pages (which does not reduce tree height). Coalesce is in-place, rebuild creates a copy. Informix handles deletions by simply marking records as deleted. DB2 and SQL Server remove deleted records and merge pages when occupancy goes below threshold.

Oracle 8 also allows records from multiple relations to be co-clustered on the same page. The co-clustering can be based on a B+ tree search key or static hashing and up to 32 relations can be stored together.

To ensure such semantics for an entry is preserved, while compressing the entry with key 'David Smith,' we must examine the largest key value in the subtree to the left of 'David Smith' and the smallest key value in the subtree to the right of 'David Smith,' not just the index entries ('Daniel Lee' and 'Devarakonda ...') that are its neighbors. This point is illustrated in Figure 10.21; the value 'Davey Jones' is greater than 'Dav,' and thus, 'David Smith' can be abbreviated only to 'Davi,' not to 'Dav.'

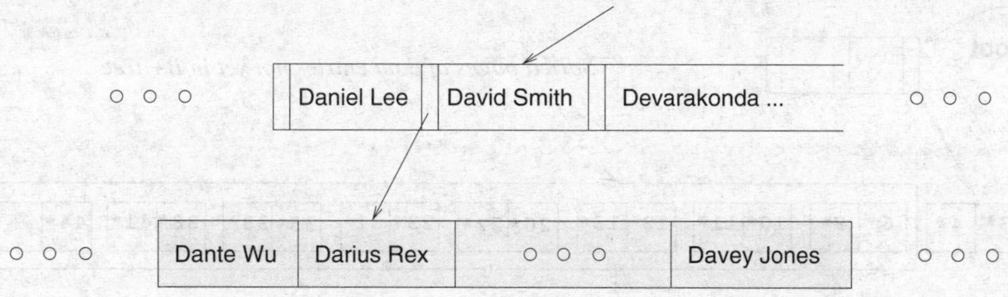

Figure 10.21 Example Illustrating Prefix Key Compression

This technique. called **prefix key compression** or simply **key compression**, is supported in many commercial implementations of B+ trees. It can substantially increase the fan-out of a tree. We do not discuss the details of the insertion and deletion algorithms in the presence of key compression.

10.8.2 Bulk-Loading a B+ Tree

Entries are added to a B+ tree in two ways. First, we may have an existing collection of data records with a B+ tree index on it; whenever a record is added to the collection, a corresponding entry must be added to the B+ tree as well. (Of course, a similar comment applies to deletions.) Second, we may have a collection of data records for which we want to create a B+ tree index on some key field(s). In this situation, we can start with an empty tree and insert an entry for each data record, one at a time, using the standard insertion algorithm. However, this approach is likely to be quite expensive because each entry requires us to start from the root and go down to the appropriate leaf page. Even though the index-level pages are likely to stay in the buffer pool between successive requests, the overhead is still considerable.

For this reason many systems provide a *bulk-loading* utility for creating a B+ tree index on an existing collection of data records. The first step is to sort the data entries $k*$ to be inserted into the (to be created) B+ tree according to the search key k. (If the entries are key–pointer pairs, sorting them does not mean sorting the data records that are pointed to, of course.) We use a running example to illustrate the bulk-loading algorithm. We assume that each data page can hold only two entries, and that each index page can hold two entries and an additional pointer (i.e., the B+ tree is assumed to be of order $d = 1$).

After the data entries have been sorted, we allocate an empty page to serve as the root and insert a pointer to the first page of (sorted) entries into it. We illustrate this process in Figure 10.22, using a sample set of nine sorted pages of data entries.

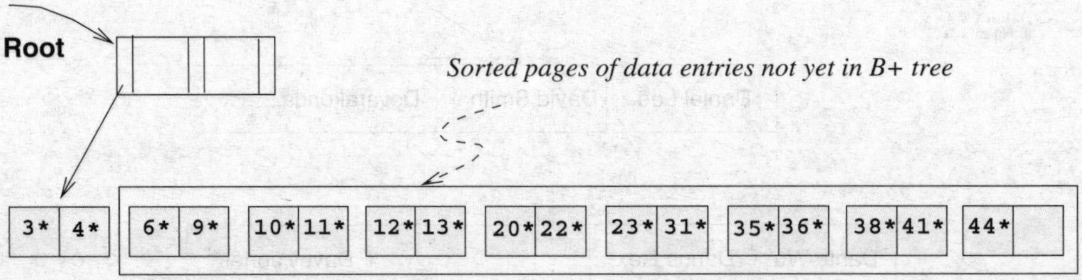

Figure 10.22 Initial Step in B+ Tree Bulk-Loading

We then add one entry to the root page for each page of the sorted data entries. The new entry consists of ⟨*low key value on page, pointer to page*⟩. We proceed until the root page is full; see Figure 10.23.

To insert the entry for the next page of data entries, we must split the root and create a new root page. We show this step in Figure 10.24.

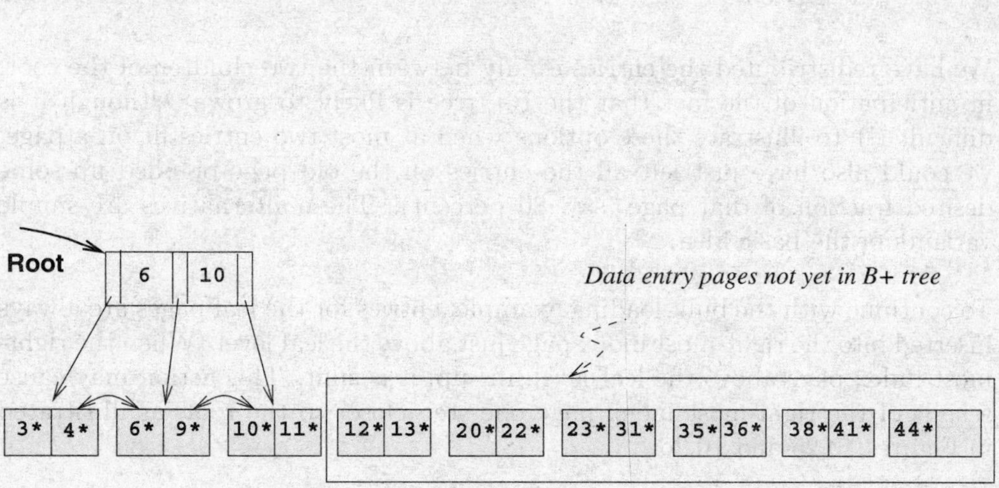

Figure 10.23 Root Page Fills up in B+ Tree Bulk-Loading

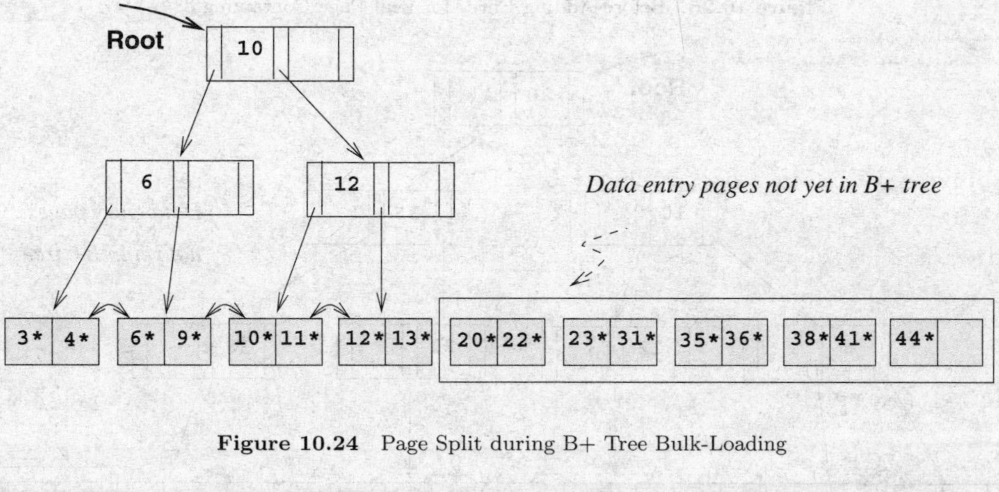

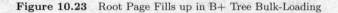

Figure 10.24 Page Split during B+ Tree Bulk-Loading

We have redistributed the entries evenly between the two children of the root, in anticipation of the fact that the B+ tree is likely to grow. Although it is difficult (!) to illustrate these options when at most two entries fit on a page, we could also have just left all the entries on the old page or filled up some desired fraction of that page (say, 80 percent). These alternatives are simple variants of the basic idea.

To continue with the bulk-loading example, entries for the leaf pages are always inserted into the right-most index page just above the leaf level. When the right-most index page above the leaf level fills up, it is split. This action may cause a split of the right-most index page one step closer to the root, as illustrated in Figures 10.25 and 10.26.

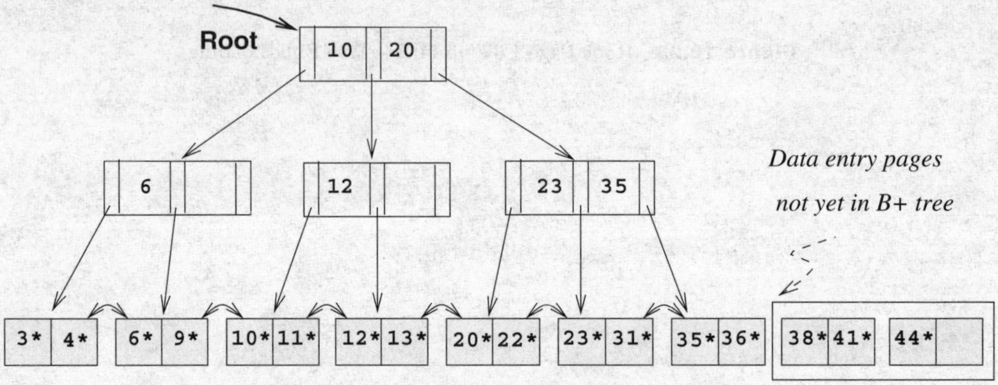

Figure 10.25 Before Adding Entry for Leaf Page Containing 38*

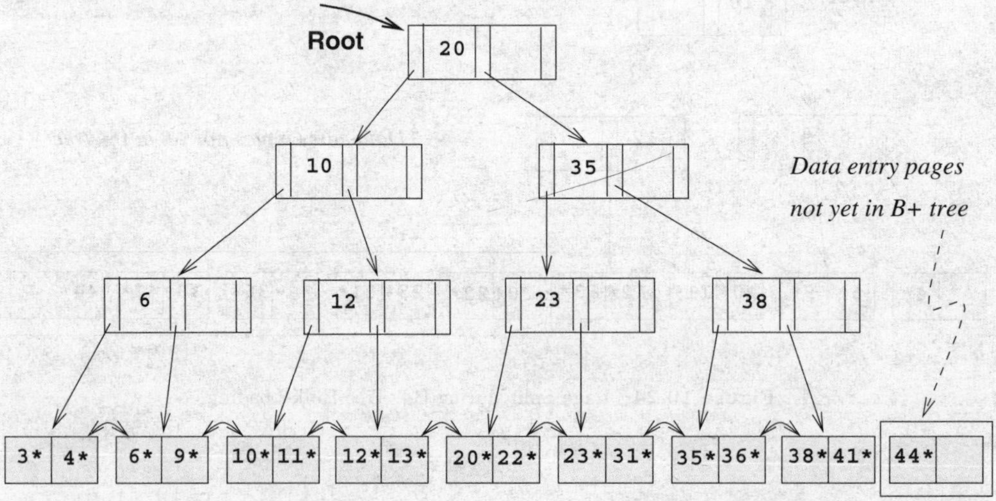

Figure 10.26 After Adding Entry for Leaf Page Containing 38*

Note that splits occur only on the right-most path from the root to the leaf level. We leave the completion of the bulk-loading example as a simple exercise.

Let us consider the cost of creating an index on an existing collection of records. This operation consists of three steps: (1) creating the data entries to insert in the index, (2) sorting the data entries, and (3) building the index from the sorted entries. The first step involves scanning the records and writing out the corresponding data entries; the cost is $(R + E)$ I/Os, where R is the number of pages containing records and E is the number of pages containing data entries. Sorting is discussed in Chapter 13; you will see that the index entries can be generated in sorted order at a cost of about $3E$ I/Os. These entries can then be inserted into the index as they are generated, using the bulk-loading algorithm discussed in this section. The cost of the third step, that is, inserting the entries into the index, is then just the cost of writing out all index pages.

10.8.3 The Order Concept

We presented B+ trees using the parameter d to denote minimum occupancy. It is worth noting that the concept of *order* (i.e., the parameter d), while useful for teaching B+ tree concepts, must usually be relaxed in practice and replaced by a physical space criterion; for example, that nodes must be kept at least half-full.

One reason for this is that leaf nodes and non-leaf nodes can usually hold different numbers of entries. Recall that B+ tree nodes are disk pages and non-leaf nodes contain only search keys and node pointers, while leaf nodes can contain the actual data records. Obviously, the size of a data record is likely to be quite a bit larger than the size of a search entry, so many more search entries than records fit on a disk page.

A second reason for relaxing the order concept is that the search key may contain a character string field (e.g., the *name* field of Students) whose size varies from record to record; such a search key leads to variable-size data entries and index entries, and the number of entries that will fit on a disk page becomes variable.

Finally, even if the index is built on a fixed-size field, several records may still have the same search key value (e.g., several Students records may have the same *gpa* or *name* value). This situation can also lead to variable-size leaf entries (if we use Alternative (3) for data entries). Because of all these complications, the concept of order is typically replaced by a simple physical criterion (e.g., merge if possible when more than half of the space in the node is unused).

10.8.4 The Effect of Inserts and Deletes on Rids

If the leaf pages contain data records—that is, the B+ tree is a clustered index—then operations such as splits, merges, and redistributions can change rids. Recall that a typical representation for a rid is some combination of (physical) page number and slot number. This scheme allows us to move records within a page if an appropriate page format is chosen but not across pages, as is the case with operations such as splits. So unless rids are chosen to be independent of page numbers, an operation such as split or merge in a clustered B+ tree may require compensating updates to other indexes on the same data.

A similar comment holds for any dynamic clustered index, regardless of whether it is tree-based or hash-based. Of course, the problem does not arise with nonclustered indexes, because only index entries are moved around.

10.9 REVIEW QUESTIONS

Answers to the review questions can be found in the listed sections.

- Why are tree-structured indexes good for searches, especially range selections? **(Section 10.1)**
- Describe how search, insert, and delete operations work in ISAM indexes. Discuss the need for overflow pages, and their potential impact on performance. What kinds of update workloads are ISAM indexes most vulnerable to, and what kinds of workloads do they handle well? **(Section 10.2)**
- Only leaf pages are affected in updates in ISAM indexes. Discuss the implications for locking and concurrent access. Compare ISAM and B+ trees in this regard. **(Section 10.2.1)**
- What are the main differences between ISAM and B+ tree indexes? **(Section 10.3)**
- What is the *order* of a B+ tree? Describe the format of nodes in a B+ tree. Why are nodes at the leaf level linked? **(Section 10.3)**
- How many nodes must be examined for equality search in a B+ tree? How many for a range selection? Compare this with ISAM. **(Section 10.4)**
- Describe the B+ tree insertion algorithm, and explain how it eliminates overflow pages. Under what conditions can an insert increase the height of the tree? **(Section 10.5)**
- During deletion, a node might go below the minimum occupancy threshold. How is this handled? Under what conditions could a deletion decrease the height of the tree? **(Section 10.6)**

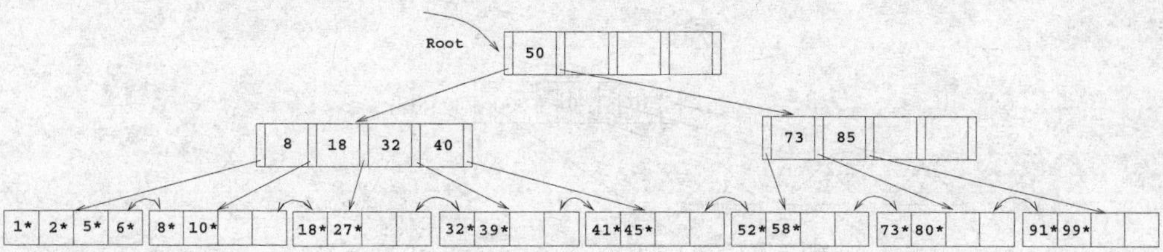

Figure 10.27 Tree for Exercise 10.1

- Why do duplicate search keys require modifications to the implementation of the basic B+ tree operations? **(Section 10.7)**
- What is *key compression*, and why is it important? **(Section 10.8.1)**
- How can a new B+ tree index be efficiently constructed for a set of records? Describe the *bulk-loading* algorithm. **(Section 10.8.2)**
- Discuss the impact of splits in clustered B+ tree indexes. **(Section 10.8.4)**

EXERCISES

Exercise 10.1 Consider the B+ tree index of order $d = 2$ shown in Figure 10.27.

1. Show the tree that would result from inserting a data entry with key 9 into this tree.
2. Show the B+ tree that would result from inserting a data entry with key 3 into the original tree. How many page reads and page writes does the insertion require?
3. Show the B+ tree that would result from deleting the data entry with key 8 from the original tree, assuming that the left sibling is checked for possible redistribution.
4. Show the B+ tree that would result from deleting the data entry with key 8 from the original tree, assuming that the right sibling is checked for possible redistribution.
5. Show the B+ tree that would result from starting with the original tree, inserting a data entry with key 46 and then deleting the data entry with key 52.
6. Show the B+ tree that would result from deleting the data entry with key 91 from the original tree.
7. Show the B+ tree that would result from starting with the original tree, inserting a data entry with key 59, and then deleting the data entry with key 91.
8. Show the B+ tree that would result from successively deleting the data entries with keys 32, 39, 41, 45, and 73 from the original tree.

Exercise 10.2 Consider the B+ tree index shown in Figure 10.28, which uses Alternative (1) for data entries. Each intermediate node can hold up to five pointers and four key values. Each leaf can hold up to four records, and leaf nodes are doubly linked as usual, although these links are not shown in the figure. Answer the following questions.

1. Name all the tree nodes that must be fetched to answer the following query: "Get all records with search key greater than 38."

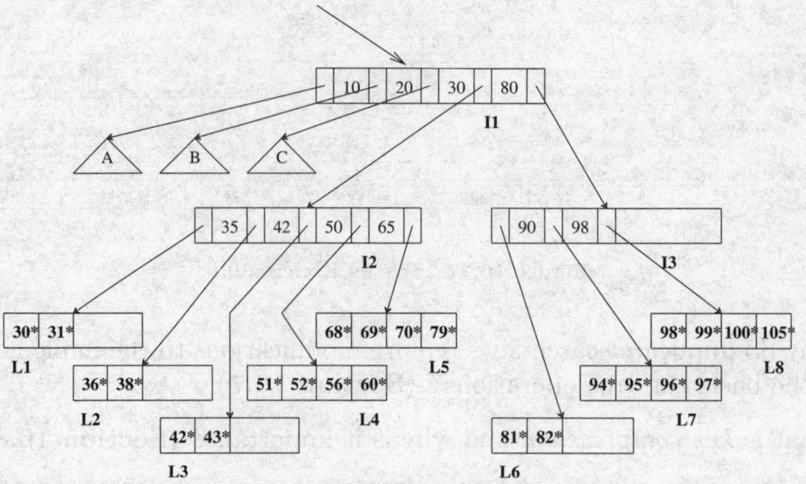

Figure 10.28 Tree for Exercise 10.2

2. Insert a record with search key 109 into the tree.
3. Delete the record with search key 81 from the (original) tree.
4. Name a search key value such that inserting it into the (original) tree would cause an increase in the height of the tree.
5. Note that subtrees A, B, and C are not fully specified. Nonetheless, what can you infer about the contents and the shape of these trees?
6. How would your answers to the preceding questions change if this were an ISAM index?
7. Suppose that this is an ISAM index. What is the minimum number of insertions needed to create a chain of three overflow pages?

Exercise 10.3 Answer the following questions:

1. What is the minimum space utilization for a B+ tree index?
2. What is the minimum space utilization for an ISAM index?
3. If your database system supported both a static and a dynamic tree index (say, ISAM and B+ trees), would you ever consider using the *static* index in preference to the *dynamic* index?

Exercise 10.4 Suppose that a page can contain at most four data values and that all data values are integers. Using only B+ trees of order 2, give examples of each of the following:

1. A B+ tree whose height changes from 2 to 3 when the value 25 is inserted. Show your structure before and after the insertion.
2. A B+ tree in which the deletion of the value 25 leads to a redistribution. Show your structure before and after the deletion.
3. A B+ tree in which the deletion of the value 25 causes a merge of two nodes but without altering the height of the tree.
4. An ISAM structure with four buckets, none of which has an overflow page. Further, every bucket has space for exactly one more entry. Show your structure before and after inserting two additional values, chosen so that an overflow page is created.

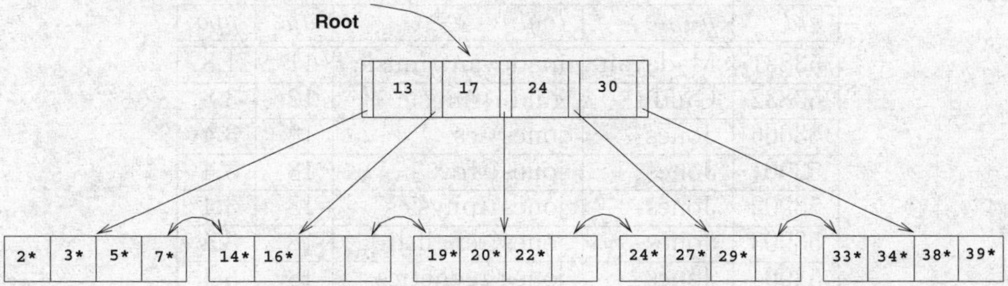

Figure 10.29 Tree for Exercise 10.5

Exercise 10.5 Consider the B+ tree shown in Figure 10.29.

1. Identify a list of five data entries such that:
   (a) Inserting the entries in the order shown and then deleting them in the opposite order (e.g., insert *a*, insert *b*, delete *b*, delete *a*) results in the original tree.
   (b) Inserting the entries in the order shown and then deleting them in the opposite order (e.g., insert *a*, insert *b*, delete *b*, delete *a*) results in a different tree.
2. What is the minimum number of insertions of data entries with distinct keys that will cause the height of the (original) tree to change from its current value (of 1) to 3?
3. Would the minimum number of insertions that will cause the original tree to increase to height 3 change if you were allowed to insert duplicates (multiple data entries with the same key), assuming that overflow pages are not used for handling duplicates?

Exercise 10.6 Answer Exercise 10.5 assuming that the tree is an ISAM tree! (Some of the examples asked for may not exist—if so, explain briefly.)

Exercise 10.7 Suppose that you have a sorted file and want to construct a dense primary B+ tree index on this file.

1. One way to accomplish this task is to scan the file, record by record, inserting each one using the B+ tree insertion procedure. What performance and storage utilization problems are there with this approach?
2. Explain how the bulk-loading algorithm described in the text improves upon this scheme.

Exercise 10.8 Assume that you have just built a dense B+ tree index using Alternative (2) on a heap file containing 20,000 records. The key field for this B+ tree index is a 40-byte string, and it is a candidate key. Pointers (i.e., record ids and page ids) are (at most) 10-byte values. The size of one disk page is 1000 bytes. The index was built in a bottom-up fashion using the bulk-loading algorithm, and the nodes at each level were filled up as much as possible.

1. How many levels does the resulting tree have?
2. For each level of the tree, how many nodes are at that level?
3. How many levels would the resulting tree have if key compression is used and it reduces the average size of each key in an entry to 10 bytes?

sid	*name*	*login*	*age*	*gpa*
53831	Madayan	madayan@music	11	1.8
53832	Guldu	guldu@music	12	3.8
53666	Jones	jones@cs	18	3.4
53901	Jones	jones@toy	18	3.4
53902	Jones	jones@physics	18	3.4
53903	Jones	jones@english	18	3.4
53904	Jones	jones@genetics	18	3.4
53905	Jones	jones@astro	18	3.4
53906	Jones	jones@chem	18	3.4
53902	Jones	jones@sanitation	18	3.8
53688	Smith	smith@ee	19	3.2
53650	Smith	smith@math	19	3.8
54001	Smith	smith@ee	19	3.5
54005	Smith	smith@cs	19	3.8
54009	Smith	smith@astro	19	2.2

Figure 10.30 An Instance of the Students Relation

4. How many levels would the resulting tree have without key compression but with all pages 70 percent full?

Exercise 10.9 The algorithms for insertion and deletion into a B+ tree are presented as recursive algorithms. In the code for *insert*, for instance, a call is made at the parent of a node N to insert into (the subtree rooted at) node N, and when this call returns, the current node is the parent of N. Thus, we do not maintain any 'parent pointers' in nodes of B+ tree. Such pointers are not part of the B+ tree structure for a good reason, as this exercise demonstrates. An alternative approach that uses parent pointers—again, remember that such pointers are *not* part of the standard B+ tree structure!—in each node appears to be simpler:

> Search to the appropriate leaf using the search algorithm; then insert the entry and split if necessary, with splits propagated to parents if necessary (using the parent pointers to find the parents).

Consider this (unsatisfactory) alternative approach:

1. Suppose that an internal node N is split into nodes N and $N2$. What can you say about the parent pointers in the children of the original node N?
2. Suggest two ways of dealing with the inconsistent parent pointers in the children of node N.
3. For each of these suggestions, identify a potential (major) disadvantage.
4. What conclusions can you draw from this exercise?

Exercise 10.10 Consider the instance of the Students relation shown in Figure 10.30. Show a B+ tree of order 2 in each of these cases, assuming that duplicates are handled using overflow pages. Clearly indicate what the data entries are (i.e., do not use the $k*$ convention).

1. A B+ tree index on *age* using Alternative (1) for data entries.
2. A dense B+ tree index on *gpa* using Alternative (2) for data entries. For this question, assume that these tuples are stored in a sorted file in the order shown in the figure: The first tuple is in page 1, slot 1; the second tuple is in page 1, slot 2; and so on. Each page can store up to three data records. You can use ⟨*page-id, slot*⟩ to identify a tuple.

Exercise 10.11 Suppose that duplicates are handled using the approach without overflow pages discussed in Section 10.7. Describe an algorithm to search for the left-most occurrence of a data entry with search key value K.

Exercise 10.12 Answer Exercise 10.10 assuming that duplicates are handled without using overflow pages, using the alternative approach suggested in Section 9.7.

PROJECT-BASED EXERCISES

Exercise 10.13 Compare the public interfaces for heap files, B+ tree indexes, and linear hashed indexes. What are the similarities and differences? Explain why these similarities and differences exist.

Exercise 10.14 This exercise involves using Minibase to explore the earlier (non-project) exercises further.

1. Create the trees shown in earlier exercises and visualize them using the B+ tree visualizer in Minibase.
2. Verify your answers to exercises that require insertion and deletion of data entries by doing the insertions and deletions in Minibase and looking at the resulting trees using the visualizer.

Exercise 10.15 (*Note to instructors: Additional details must be provided if this exercise is assigned; see Appendix 30.*) Implement B+ trees on top of the lower-level code in Minibase.

BIBLIOGRAPHIC NOTES

The original version of the B+ tree was presented by Bayer and McCreight [69]. The B+ tree is described in [442] and [194]. B tree indexes for skewed data distributions are studied in [260]. The VSAM indexing structure is described in [764]. Various tree structures for supporting range queries are surveyed in [79]. An early paper on multiattribute search keys is [498].

References for concurrent access to B+ trees are in the bibliography for Chapter 17.

11

HASH-BASED INDEXING

- What is the intuition behind hash-structured indexes? Why are they especially good for equality searches but useless for range selections?
- What is Extendible Hashing? How does it handle search, insert, and delete?
- What is Linear Hashing? How does it handle search, insert, and delete?
- What are the similarities and differences between Extendible and Linear Hashing?
- **Key concepts:** hash function, bucket, primary and overflow pages, static versus dynamic hash indexes; Extendible Hashing, directory of buckets, splitting a bucket, global and local depth, directory doubling, collisions and overflow pages; Linear Hashing, rounds of splitting, family of hash functions, overflow pages, choice of bucket to split and time to split; relationship between Extendible Hashing's directory and Linear Hashing's family of hash functions, need for overflow pages in both schemes in practice, use of a directory for Linear Hashing.

Not chaos-like, together crushed and bruised,
But, as the world harmoniously confused:
Where order in variety we see.

—Alexander Pope, *Windsor Forest*

In this chapter we consider file organizations that are excellent for equality selections. The basic idea is to use a *hashing function*, which maps values in a search field into a range of *bucket numbers* to find the page on which a desired data entry belongs. We use a simple scheme called *Static Hashing* to introduce the idea. This scheme, like ISAM, suffers from the problem of long overflow chains, which can affect performance. Two solutions to the problem are presented. The *Extendible Hashing* scheme uses a directory to support inserts and deletes efficiently with no overflow pages. The *Linear Hashing* scheme uses a clever policy for creating new buckets and supports inserts and deletes efficiently without the use of a directory. Although overflow pages are used, the length of overflow chains is rarely more than two.

Hash-based indexing techniques cannot support range searches, unfortunately. Tree-based indexing techniques, discussed in Chapter 10, can support range searches efficiently and are almost as good as hash-based indexing for equality selections. Thus, many commercial systems choose to support only tree-based indexes. Nonetheless, hashing techniques prove to be very useful in implementing relational operations such as joins, as we will see in Chapter 14. In particular, the Index Nested Loops join method generates many equality selection queries, and the difference in cost between a hash-based index and a tree-based index can become significant in this context.

The rest of this chapter is organized as follows. Section 11.1 presents Static Hashing. Like ISAM, its drawback is that performance degrades as the data grows and shrinks. We discuss a dynamic hashing technique, called *Extendible Hashing*, in Section 11.2 and another dynamic technique, called *Linear Hashing*, in Section 11.3. We compare Extendible and Linear Hashing in Section 11.4.

11.1 STATIC HASHING

The Static Hashing scheme is illustrated in Figure 11.1. The pages containing the data can be viewed as a collection of **buckets**, with one **primary** page and possibly additional **overflow** pages per bucket. A file consists of buckets 0 through $N-1$, with one primary page per bucket initially. Buckets contain *data entries*, which can be any of the three alternatives discussed in Chapter 8.

To search for a data entry, we apply a **hash function** h to identify the bucket to which it belongs and then search this bucket. To speed the search of a bucket, we can maintain data entries in sorted order by search key value; in this chapter, we do not sort entries, and the order of entries within a bucket has no significance. To insert a data entry, we use the hash function to identify the correct bucket and then put the data entry there. If there is no space for this data entry, we allocate a new *overflow* page, put the data entry on this page, and add the page to the **overflow chain** of the bucket. To delete a data

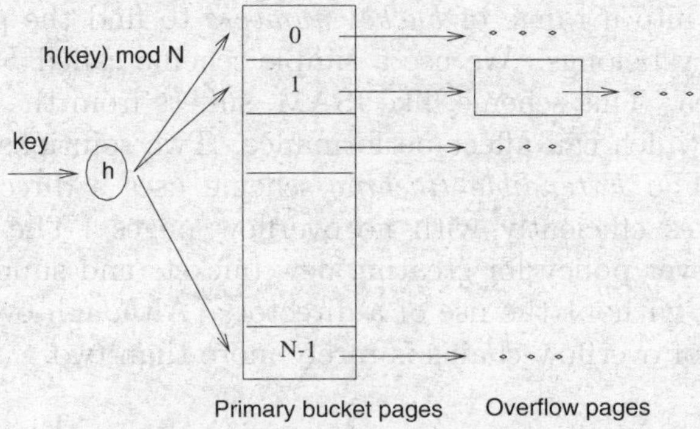

Figure 11.1 Static Hashing

entry, we use the hashing function to identify the correct bucket, locate the data entry by searching the bucket, and then remove it. If this data entry is the last in an overflow page, the overflow page is removed from the overflow chain of the bucket and added to a list of *free pages*.

The hash function is an important component of the hashing approach. It must distribute values in the domain of the search field uniformly over the collection of buckets. If we have N buckets, numbered 0 through $N-1$, a hash function h of the form $h(value) = (a * value + b)$ works well in practice. (The bucket identified is $h(value)\ mod\ N$.) The constants a and b can be chosen to 'tune' the hash function.

Since the number of buckets in a Static Hashing file is known when the file is created, the primary pages can be stored on successive disk pages. Hence, a search ideally requires just one disk I/O, and insert and delete operations require two I/Os (read and write the page), although the cost could be higher in the presence of overflow pages. As the file grows, long overflow chains can develop. Since searching a bucket requires us to search (in general) all pages in its overflow chain, it is easy to see how performance can deteriorate. By initially keeping pages 80 percent full, we can avoid overflow pages if the file does not grow too much, but in general the only way to get rid of overflow chains is to create a new file with more buckets.

The main problem with Static Hashing is that the number of buckets is fixed. If a file shrinks greatly, a lot of space is wasted; more important, if a file grows a lot, long overflow chains develop, resulting in poor performance. Therefore, Static Hashing can be compared to the ISAM structure (Section 10.2), which can also develop long overflow chains in case of insertions to the same leaf. Static Hashing also has the same advantages as ISAM with respect to concurrent access (see Section 10.2.1).

One simple alternative to Static Hashing is to periodically 'rehash' the file to restore the ideal situation (no overflow chains, about 80 percent occupancy). However, rehashing takes time and the index cannot be used while rehashing is in progress. Another alternative is to use **dynamic hashing** techniques such as Extendible and Linear Hashing, which deal with inserts and deletes gracefully. We consider these techniques in the rest of this chapter.

11.1.1 Notation and Conventions

In the rest of this chapter, we use the following conventions. As in the previous chapter, record with search key k, we denote the index data entry by $k*$. For hash-based indexes, the first step in searching for, inserting, or deleting a data entry with search key k is to apply a hash function h to k; we denote this operation by $h(k)$, and the value $h(k)$ identifies the bucket for the data entry $k*$. Note that two different search keys can have the same hash value.

11.2 EXTENDIBLE HASHING

To understand Extendible Hashing, let us begin by considering a Static Hashing file. If we have to insert a new data entry into a full bucket, we need to add an overflow page. If we do not want to add overflow pages, one solution is to reorganize the file at this point by doubling the number of buckets and redistributing the entries across the new set of buckets. This solution suffers from one major defect—the entire file has to be read, and twice as many pages have to be written to achieve the reorganization. This problem, however, can be overcome by a simple idea: Use a **directory** of pointers to buckets, and double the size of the number of buckets by doubling just the directory and splitting *only* the bucket that overflowed.

To understand the idea, consider the sample file shown in Figure 11.2. The directory consists of an array of size 4, with each element being a pointer to a bucket. (The *global depth* and *local depth* fields are discussed shortly, ignore them for now.) To locate a data entry, we apply a hash function to the search field and take the last 2 bits of its binary representation to get a number between 0 and 3. The pointer in this array position gives us the desired bucket; we assume that each bucket can hold four data entries. Therefore, to locate a data entry with hash value 5 (binary 101), we look at directory element 01 and follow the pointer to the data page (bucket B in the figure).

To insert a data entry, we search to find the appropriate bucket. For example, to insert a data entry with hash value 13 (denoted as 13*), we examine directory element 01 and go to the page containing data entries 1*, 5*, and 21*. Since

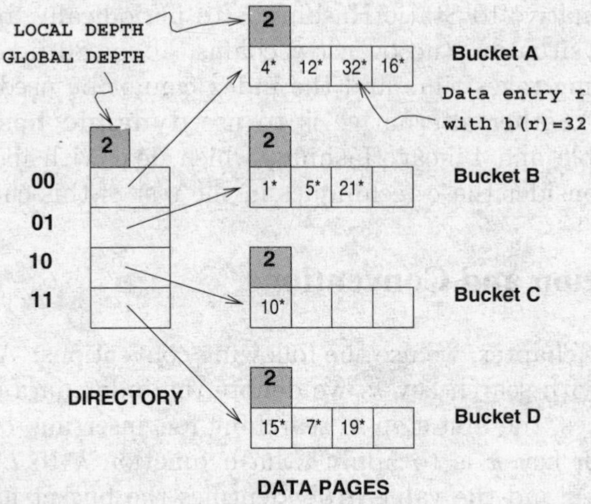

Figure 11.2 Example of an Extendible Hashed File

the page has space for an additional data entry, we are done after we insert the entry (Figure 11.3).

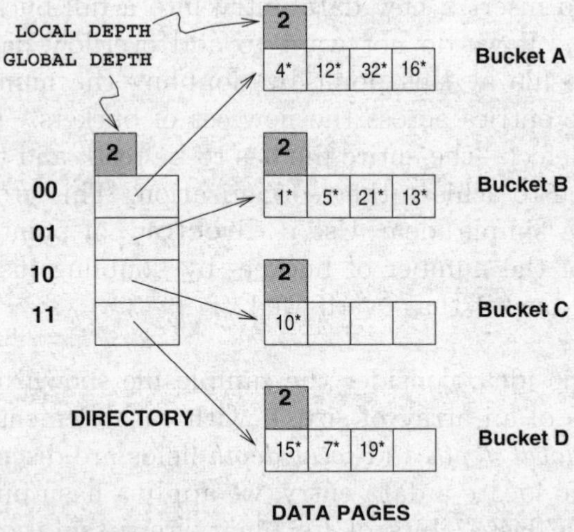

Figure 11.3 After Inserting Entry r with $h(r) = 13$

Next, let us consider insertion of a data entry into a full bucket. The essence of the Extendible Hashing idea lies in how we deal with this case. Consider the insertion of data entry 20* (binary 10100). Looking at directory element 00, we are led to bucket A, which is already full. We must first **split** the bucket by allocating a new bucket[1] and redistributing the contents (including the new entry to be inserted) across the old bucket and its 'split image.' To redistribute entries across the old bucket and its split image, we consider the last *three* bits of $h(r)$; the last two bits are 00, indicating a data entry that belongs to one of these two buckets, and the third bit discriminates between these buckets. The redistribution of entries is illustrated in Figure 11.4.

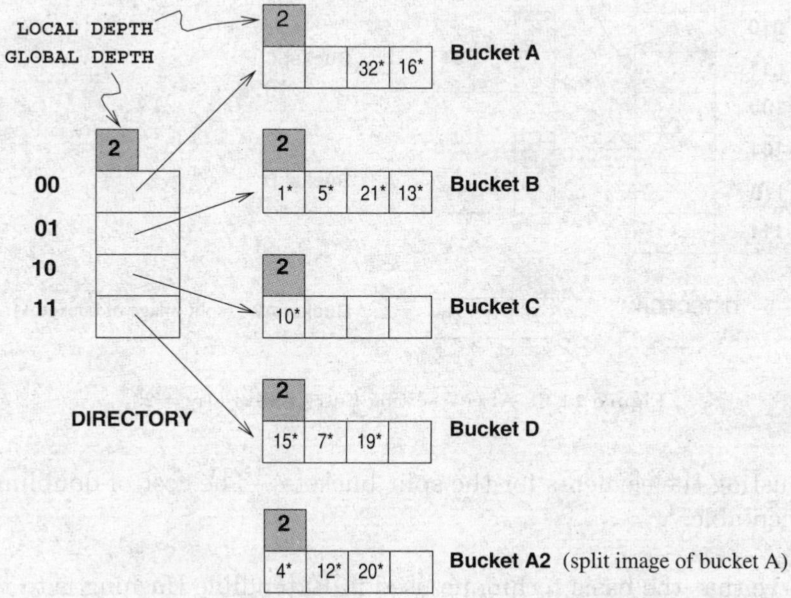

Figure 11.4 While Inserting Entry r with $h(r)$=20

Note a problem that we must now resolve—we need three bits to discriminate between two of our data pages (A and A2), but the directory has only enough slots to store all two-bit patterns. The solution is to *double the directory*. Elements that differ only in the third bit from the end are said to 'correspond': *Corresponding elements* of the directory point to the same bucket with the exception of the elements corresponding to the split bucket. In our example, bucket 0 was split; so, new directory element 000 points to one of the split versions and new element 100 points to the other. The sample file after completing all steps in the insertion of 20* is shown in Figure 11.5.

Therefore, doubling the file requires allocating a new bucket page, writing both this page and the old bucket page that is being split, and doubling the directory array. The directory is likely to be much smaller than the file itself because each element is just a page-id, and can be doubled by simply copying it over

[1] Since there are no overflow pages in Extendible Hashing, a bucket can be thought of as a single page.

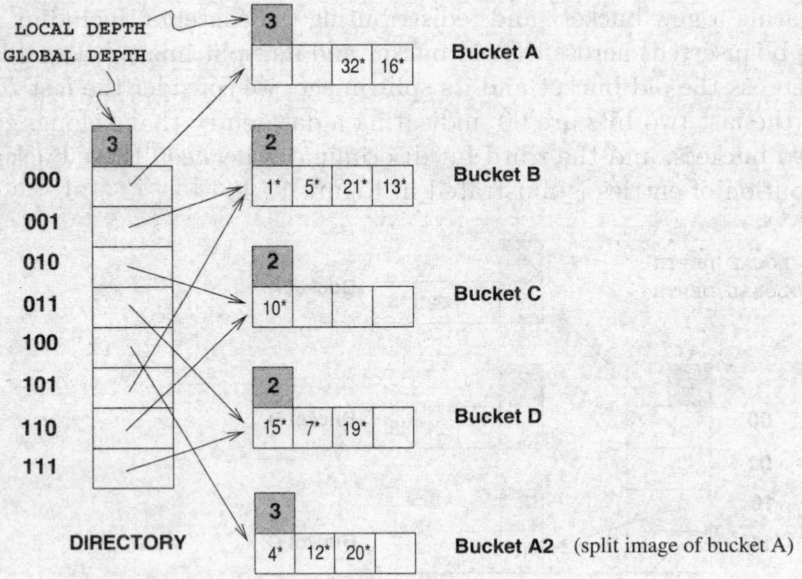

Figure 11.5 After Inserting Entry r with $h(r) = 20$

(and adjusting the elements for the split buckets). The cost of doubling is now quite acceptable.

We observe that the basic technique used in Extendible Hashing is to treat the result of applying a hash function h as a binary number and interpret the last d bits, where d depends on the size of the directory, as an offset into the directory. In our example, d is originally 2 because we only have four buckets; after the split, d becomes 3 because we now have eight buckets. A corollary is that, when distributing entries across a bucket and its split image, we should do so on the basis of the dth bit. (Note how entries are redistributed in our example; see Figure 11.5.) The number d, called the **global depth** of the hashed file, is kept as part of the header of the file. It is used every time we need to locate a data entry.

An important point that arises is whether splitting a bucket necessitates a directory doubling. Consider our example, as shown in Figure 11.5. If we now insert 9*, it belongs in bucket B; this bucket is already full. We can deal with this situation by splitting the bucket and using directory elements 001 and 101 to point to the bucket and its split image, as shown in Figure 11.6.

Hence, a bucket split does not necessarily require a directory doubling. However, if either bucket A or A2 grows full and an insert then forces a bucket split, we are forced to double the directory again.

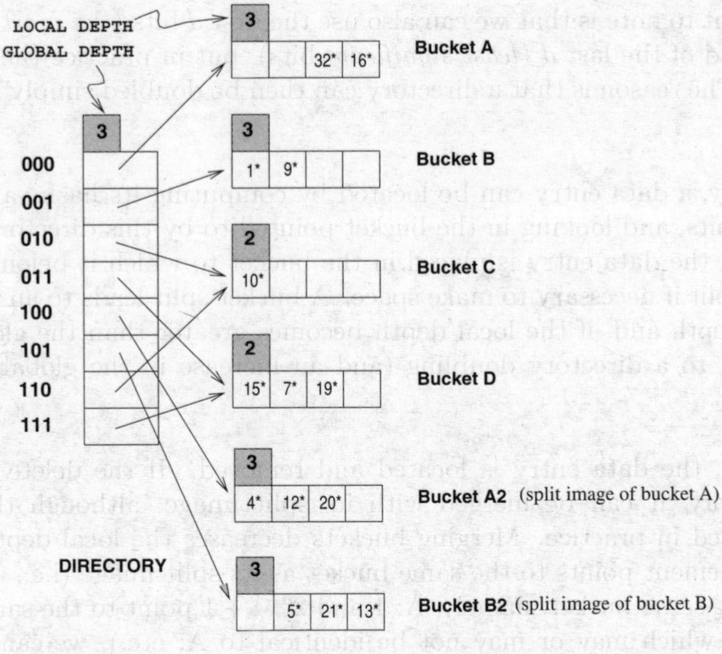

Figure 11.6 After Inserting Entry r with $h(r) = 9$

To differentiate between these cases and determine whether a directory doubling is needed, we maintain a **local depth** for each bucket. If a bucket whose local depth is equal to the global depth is split, the directory must be doubled. Going back to the example, when we inserted 9* into the index shown in Figure 11.5, it belonged to bucket B with local depth 2, whereas the global depth was 3. Even though the bucket was split, the directory did not have to be doubled. Buckets A and A2, on the other hand, have local depth equal to the global depth, and, if they grow full and are split, the directory must then be doubled.

Initially, all local depths are equal to the global depth (which is the number of bits needed to express the total number of buckets). We increment the global depth by 1 each time the directory doubles, of course. Also, whenever a bucket is split (whether or not the split leads to a directory doubling), we increment by 1 the local depth of the split bucket and assign this same (incremented) local depth to its (newly created) split image. Intuitively, if a bucket has local depth l, the hash values of data entries in it agree on the last l bits; further, no data entry in any other bucket of the file has a hash value with the same last l bits. A total of 2^{d-l} directory elements point to a bucket with local depth l; if $d = l$, exactly one directory element points to the bucket and splitting such a bucket requires directory doubling.

A final point to note is that we can also use the first d bits (the *most significant* bits) instead of the last d (*least significant* bits), but in practice the *last d* bits are used. The reason is that a directory can then be doubled simply by copying it.

In summary, a data entry can be located by computing its hash value, taking the last d bits, and looking in the bucket pointed to by this directory element. For inserts, the data entry is placed in the bucket to which it belongs and the bucket is split if necessary to make space. A bucket split leads to an increase in the local depth and, if the local depth becomes greater than the global depth as a result, to a directory doubling (and an increase in the global depth) as well.

For deletes, the data entry is located and removed. If the delete leaves the bucket empty, it can be merged with its split image, although this step is often omitted in practice. Merging buckets decreases the local depth. If each directory element points to the same bucket as its split image (i.e., 0 and 2^{d-1} point to the same bucket, namely, A; 1 and $2^{d-1}+1$ point to the same bucket, namely, B, which may or may not be identical to A; etc.), we can halve the directory and reduce the global depth, although this step is not necessary for correctness.

The insertion examples can be worked out backwards as examples of deletion. (Start with the structure shown after an insertion and delete the inserted element. In each case the original structure should be the result.)

If the directory fits in memory, an equality selection can be answered in a single disk access, as for Static Hashing (in the absence of overflow pages), but otherwise, two disk I/Os are needed. As a typical example, a 100MB file with 100 bytes per data entry and a page size of 4KB contains 1 million data entries and only about 25,000 elements in the directory. (Each page/bucket contains roughly 40 data entries, and we have one directory element per bucket.) Thus, although equality selections can be twice as slow as for Static Hashing files, chances are high that the directory will fit in memory and performance is the same as for Static Hashing files.

On the other hand, the directory grows in spurts and can become large for *skewed data distributions* (where our assumption that data pages contain roughly equal numbers of data entries is not valid). In the context of hashed files, in a **skewed data distribution** the distribution of *hash values of search field values* (rather than the distribution of search field values themselves) is skewed (very 'bursty' or nonuniform). Even if the distribution of search values is skewed, the choice of a good hashing function typically yields a fairly uniform distribution of hash values; skew is therefore not a problem in practice.

Further, **collisions**, or data entries with the same hash value, cause a problem and must be handled specially: When more data entries than will fit on a page have the same hash value, we need overflow pages.

11.3 LINEAR HASHING

Linear Hashing is a dynamic hashing technique, like Extendible Hashing, adjusting gracefully to inserts and deletes. In contrast to Extendible Hashing, it does not require a directory, deals naturally with collisions, and offers a lot of flexibility with respect to the timing of bucket splits (allowing us to trade off slightly greater overflow chains for higher average space utilization). If the data distribution is very skewed, however, overflow chains could cause Linear Hashing performance to be worse than that of Extendible Hashing.

The scheme utilizes a *family* of hash functions h_0, h_1, h_2, ..., with the property that each function's range is twice that of its predecessor. That is, if h_i maps a data entry into one of M buckets, h_{i+1} maps a data entry into one of $2M$ buckets. Such a family is typically obtained by choosing a hash function h and an initial number N of buckets,[2] and defining $h_i(value) = h(value)\ mod\ (2^i N)$. If N is chosen to be a power of 2, then we apply h and look at the last d_i bits; d_0 is the number of bits needed to represent N, and $d_i = d_0 + i$. Typically we choose h to be a function that maps a data entry to some integer. Suppose that we set the initial number N of buckets to be 32. In this case d_0 is 5, and h_0 is therefore $h\ mod\ 32$, that is, a number in the range 0 to 31. The value of d_1 is $d_0 + 1 = 6$, and h_1 is $h\ mod\ (2 * 32)$, that is, a number in the range 0 to 63. Then h_2 yields a number in the range 0 to 127, and so on.

The idea is best understood in terms of **rounds** of splitting. During round number *Level*, only hash functions h_{Level} and $h_{Level+1}$ are in use. The buckets in the file at the beginning of the round are split, one by one from the first to the last bucket, thereby doubling the number of buckets. At any given point within a round, therefore, we have buckets that have been split, buckets that are yet to be split, and buckets created by splits in this round, as illustrated in Figure 11.7.

Consider how we search for a data entry with a given search key value. We apply hash function h_{Level}, and if this leads us to one of the unsplit buckets, we simply look there. If it leads us to one of the split buckets, the entry may be there or it may have been moved to the new bucket created earlier in this round by splitting this bucket; to determine which of the two buckets contains the entry, we apply $h_{Level+1}$.

[2]Note that 0 to $N-1$ is *not* the range of h!

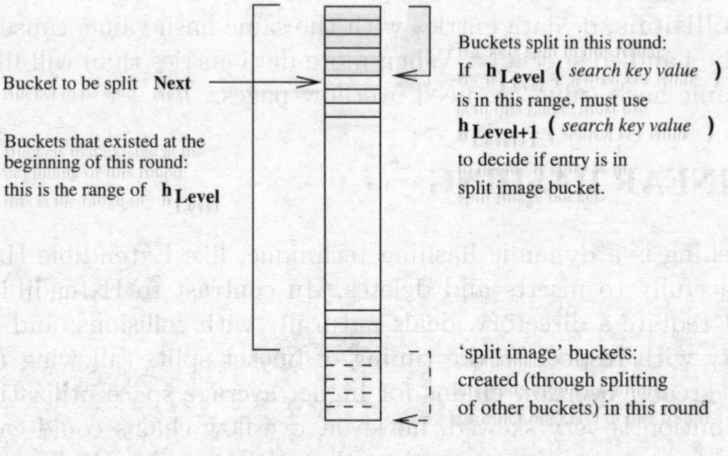

Figure 11.7 Buckets during a Round in Linear Hashing

Unlike Extendible Hashing, when an insert triggers a split, the bucket into which the data entry is inserted is not necessarily the bucket that is split. An overflow page is added to store the newly inserted data entry (which triggered the split), as in Static Hashing. However, since the bucket to split is chosen in round-robin fashion, eventually all buckets are split, thereby redistributing the data entries in overflow chains before the chains get to be more than one or two pages long.

We now describe Linear Hashing in more detail. A counter *Level* is used to indicate the current round number and is initialized to 0. The bucket to split is denoted by *Next* and is initially bucket 0 (the first bucket). We denote the number of buckets in the file at the beginning of round *Level* by N_{Level}. We can easily verify that $N_{Level} = N * 2^{Level}$. Let the number of buckets at the beginning of round 0, denoted by N_0, be N. We show a small linear hashed file in Figure 11.8. Each bucket can hold four data entries, and the file initially contains four buckets, as shown in the figure.

We have considerable flexibility in how to trigger a split, thanks to the use of overflow pages. We can split whenever a new overflow page is added, or we can impose additional conditions based on conditions such as space utilization. For our examples, a split is 'triggered' when inserting a new data entry causes the creation of an overflow page.

Whenever a split is triggered the *Next* bucket is split, and hash function $h_{Level+1}$ redistributes entries between this bucket (say bucket number b) and its split image; the split image is therefore bucket number $b + N_{Level}$. After splitting a bucket, the value of *Next* is incremented by 1. In the example file, insertion of

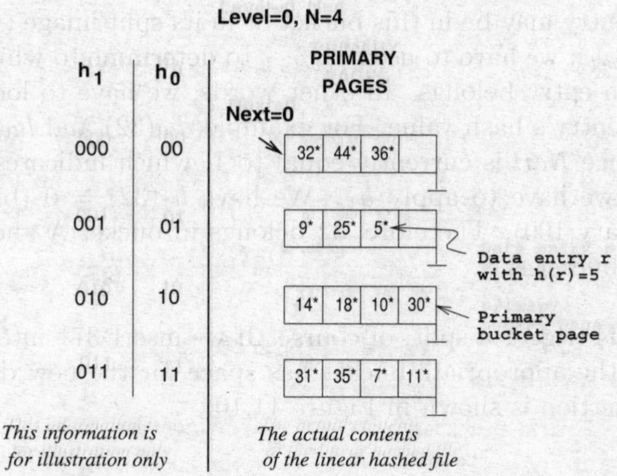

Figure 11.8 Example of a Linear Hashed File

data entry 43* triggers a split. The file after completing the insertion is shown in Figure 11.9.

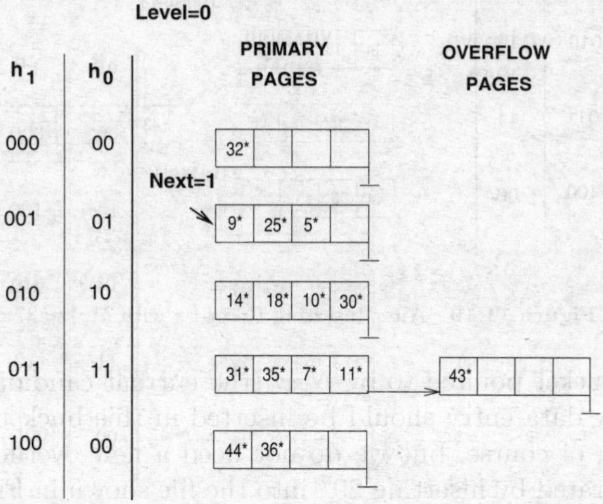

Figure 11.9 After Inserting Record r with $h(r) = 43$

At any time in the middle of a round *Level*, all buckets above bucket *Next* have been split, and the file contains buckets that are their split images, as illustrated in Figure 11.7. Buckets *Next* through N_{Level} have not yet been split. If we use h_{Level} on a data entry and obtain a number b in the range *Next* through N_{Level}, the data entry belongs to bucket b. For example, $h_0(18)$ is 2 (binary 10); since this value is between the current values of *Next* (= 1) and N_1 (= 4), this bucket has not been split. However, if we obtain a number b in the range 0 through

Next, the data entry may be in this bucket or in its split image (which is bucket number $b + N_{Level}$); we have to use $h_{Level+1}$ to determine to which of these two buckets the data entry belongs. In other words, we have to look at one more bit of the data entry's hash value. For example, $h_0(32)$ and $h_0(44)$ are both 0 (binary 00). Since *Next* is currently equal to 1, which indicates a bucket that has been split, we have to apply h_1. We have $h_1(32) = 0$ (binary 000) and $h_1(44) = 4$ (binary 100). Therefore, 32 belongs in bucket A and 44 belongs in its split image, bucket A2.

Not all insertions trigger a split, of course. If we insert 37* into the file shown in Figure 11.9, the appropriate bucket has space for the new data entry. The file after the insertion is shown in Figure 11.10.

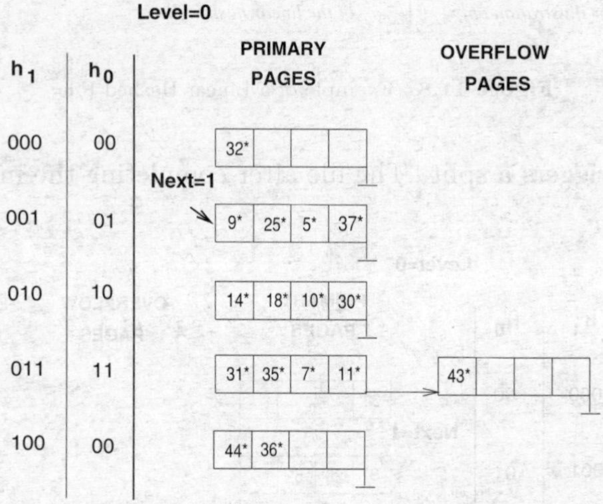

Figure 11.10 After Inserting Record r with $h(r) = 37$

Sometimes the bucket pointed to by *Next* (the current candidate for splitting) is full, and a new data entry should be inserted in this bucket. In this case, a split is triggered, of course, but we do not need a new overflow bucket. This situation is illustrated by inserting 29* into the file shown in Figure 11.10. The result is shown in Figure 11.11.

When *Next* is equal to $N_{Level} - 1$ and a split is triggered, we split the last of the buckets present in the file at the beginning of round *Level*. The number of buckets after the split is twice the number at the beginning of the round, and we start a new round with *Level* incremented by 1 and *Next* reset to 0. Incrementing *Level* amounts to doubling the effective range into which keys are hashed. Consider the example file in Figure 11.12, which was obtained from the file of Figure 11.11 by inserting 22*, 66*, and 34*. (The reader is encouraged to try to work out the details of these insertions.) Inserting 50* causes a split that

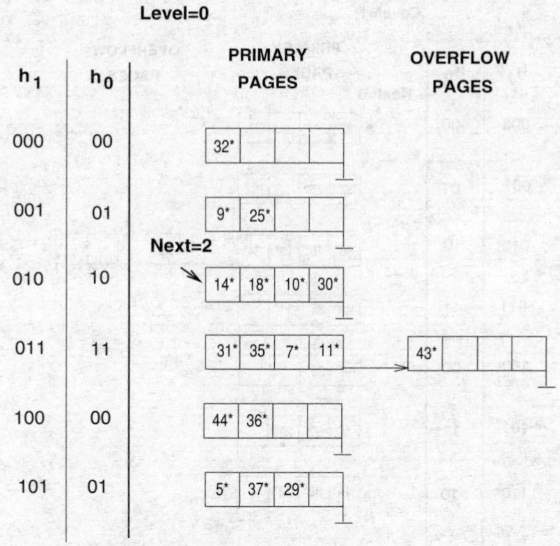

Figure 11.11 After Inserting Record r with $h(r) = 29$

leads to incrementing *Level*, as discussed previously; the file after this insertion is shown in Figure 11.13.

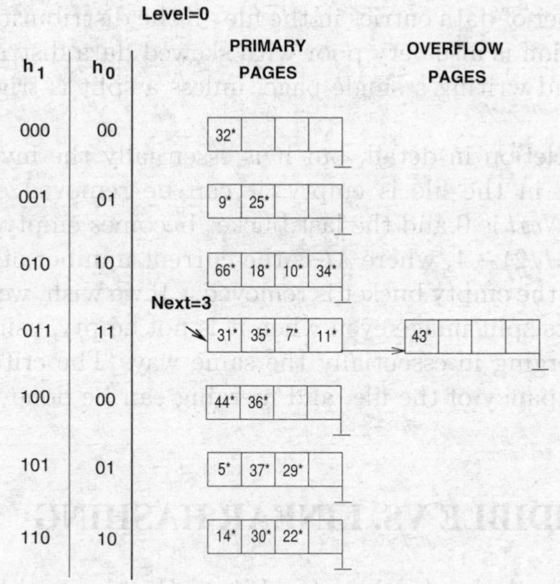

Figure 11.12 After Inserting Records with $h(r) = 22, 66, and 34$

In summary, an equality selection costs just one disk I/O unless the bucket has overflow pages; in practice, the cost on average is about 1.2 disk accesses for

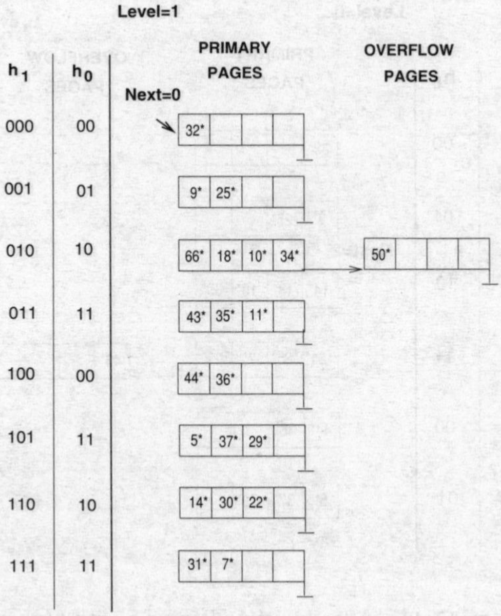

Figure 11.13 After Inserting Record r with $h(r) = 50$

reasonably uniform data distributions. (The cost can be considerably worse—linear in the number of data entries in the file—if the distribution is very skewed. The space utilization is also very poor with skewed data distributions.) Inserts require reading and writing a single page, unless a split is triggered.

We not discuss deletion in detail, but it is essentially the inverse of insertion. If the last bucket in the file is empty, it can be removed and *Next* can be decremented. (If *Next* is 0 and the last bucket becomes empty, *Next* is made to point to bucket $(M/2) - 1$, where M is the current number of buckets, *Level* is decremented, and the empty bucket is removed.) If we wish, we can combine the last bucket with its split image even when it is not empty, using some criterion to trigger this merging in essentially the same way. The criterion is typically based on the occupancy of the file, and merging can be done to improve space utilization.

11.4 EXTENDIBLE VS. LINEAR HASHING

To understand the relationship between Linear Hashing and Extendible Hashing, imagine that we also have a directory in Linear Hashing with elements 0 to $N - 1$. The first split is at bucket 0, and so we add directory element N. In principle, we may imagine that the entire directory has been doubled at this point; however, because element 1 is the same as element $N + 1$, element 2 is the same as element $N + 2$, and so on, we can avoid the actual copying for the rest of the directory. The second split occurs at bucket 1; now directory element $N + 1$ becomes significant and is added. At the end of the round, all the original N buckets are split, and the directory is doubled in size (because all elements point to distinct buckets).

We observe that the choice of hashing functions is actually very similar to what goes on in Extendible Hashing—in effect, moving from h_i to h_{i+1} in Linear Hashing corresponds to doubling the directory in Extendible Hashing. Both operations double the effective range into which key values are hashed; but whereas the directory is doubled in a single step of Extendible Hashing, moving from h_i to h_{i+1}, along with a corresponding doubling in the number of buckets, occurs gradually over the course of a round in Linear Hashing. The new idea behind Linear Hashing is that a directory can be avoided by a clever choice of the bucket to split. On the other hand, by always splitting the appropriate bucket, Extendible Hashing may lead to a reduced number of splits and higher bucket occupancy.

The directory analogy is useful for understanding the ideas behind Extendible and Linear Hashing. However, the directory structure can be avoided for Linear Hashing (but not for Extendible Hashing) by allocating primary bucket pages consecutively, which would allow us to locate the page for bucket i by a simple offset calculation. For uniform distributions, this implementation of Linear Hashing has a lower average cost for equality selections (because the directory level is eliminated). For skewed distributions, this implementation could result in any empty or nearly empty buckets, each of which is allocated at least one page, leading to poor performance relative to Extendible Hashing, which is likely to have higher bucket occupancy.

A different implementation of Linear Hashing, in which a directory is actually maintained, offers the flexibility of not allocating one page per bucket; *null* directory elements can be used as in Extendible Hashing. However, this implementation introduces the overhead of a directory level and could prove costly for large, uniformly distributed files. (Also, although this implementation alleviates the potential problem of low bucket occupancy by not allocating pages for empty buckets, it is not a complete solution because we can still have many pages with very few entries.)

11.5 REVIEW QUESTIONS

Answers to the review questions can be found in the listed sections.

- How does a hash-based index handle an equality query? Discuss the use of the hash function in identifying a bucket to search. Given a bucket number, explain how the record is located on disk.
- Explain how insert and delete operations are handled in a static hash index. Discuss how overflow pages are used, and their impact on performance. How many disk I/Os does an equality search require, in the absence of overflow chains? What kinds of workload does a static hash index handle well, and when it is especially poor? **(Section 11.1)**
- How does Extendible Hashing use a directory of buckets? How does Extendible Hashing handle an equality query? How does it handle insert and delete operations? Discuss the *global depth* of the index and *local depth* of a bucket in your answer. Under what conditions can the directory can get large? **(Section 11.2)**
- What are *collisions*? Why do we need overflow pages to handle them? **(Section 11.2)**
- How does *Linear Hashing* avoid a directory? Discuss the round-robin splitting of buckets. Explain how the split bucket is chosen, and what triggers a split. Explain the role of the family of hash functions, and the role of the *Level* and *Next* counters. When does a round of splitting end? **(Section 11.3)**
- Discuss the relationship between Extendible and Linear Hashing. What are their relative merits? Consider space utilization for skewed distributions, the use of overflow pages to handle collisions in Extendible Hashing, and the use of a directory in Linear Hashing. **(Section 11.4)**

EXERCISES

Exercise 11.1 Consider the Extendible Hashing index shown in Figure 11.14. Answer the following questions about this index:

1. What can you say about the last entry that was inserted into the index?
2. What can you say about the last entry that was inserted into the index if you know that there have been no deletions from this index so far?
3. Suppose you are told that there have been no deletions from this index so far. What can you say about the last entry whose insertion into the index caused a split?
4. Show the index after inserting an entry with hash value 68.
5. Show the original index after inserting entries with hash values 17 and 69.
6. Show the original index after deleting the entry with hash value 21. (Assume that the full deletion algorithm is used.)
7. Show the original index after deleting the entry with hash value 10. Is a merge triggered by this deletion? If not, explain why. (Assume that the full deletion algorithm is used.)

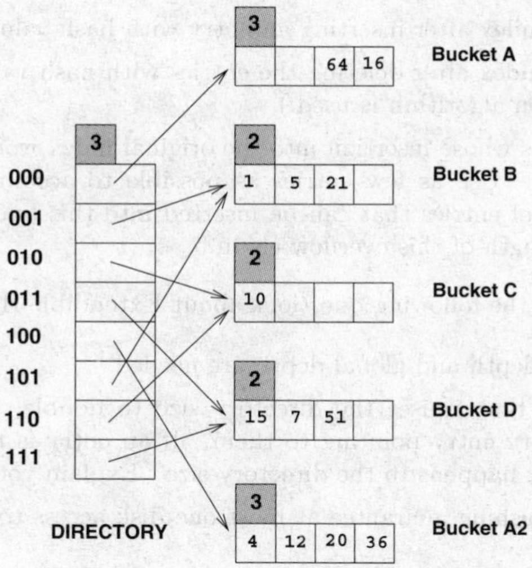

Figure 11.14 Figure for Exercise 11.1

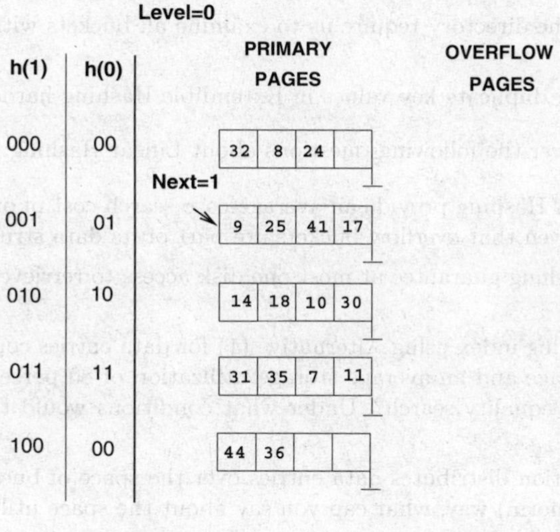

Figure 11.15 Figure for Exercise 11.2

Exercise 11.2 Consider the Linear Hashing index shown in Figure 11.15. Assume that we split whenever an overflow page is created. Answer the following questions about this index:

1. What can you say about the last entry that was inserted into the index?
2. What can you say about the last entry that was inserted into the index if you know that there have been no deletions from this index so far?
3. Suppose you know that there have been no deletions from this index so far. What can you say about the last entry whose insertion into the index caused a split?
4. Show the index after inserting an entry with hash value 4.

5. Show the original index after inserting an entry with hash value 15.
6. Show the original index after deleting the entries with hash values 36 and 44. (Assume that the full deletion algorithm is used.)
7. Find a list of entries whose insertion into the original index would lead to a bucket with two overflow pages. Use as few entries as possible to accomplish this. What is the maximum number of entries that can be inserted into this bucket before a split occurs that reduces the length of this overflow chain?

Exercise 11.3 Answer the following questions about Extendible Hashing:

1. Explain why local depth and global depth are needed.
2. After an insertion that causes the directory size to double, how many buckets have exactly one directory entry pointing to them? If an entry is then deleted from one of these buckets, what happens to the directory size? Explain your answers briefly.
3. Does Extendible Hashing guarantee at most one disk access to retrieve a record with a given key value?
4. If the hash function distributes data entries over the space of bucket numbers in a very skewed (non-uniform) way, what can you say about the size of the directory? What can you say about the space utilization in data pages (i.e., non-directory pages)?
5. Does doubling the directory require us to examine all buckets with local depth equal to global depth?
6. Why is handling duplicate key values in Extendible Hashing harder than in ISAM?

Exercise 11.4 Answer the following questions about Linear Hashing:

1. How does Linear Hashing provide an average-case search cost of only slightly more than one disk I/O, given that overflow buckets are part of its data structure?
2. Does Linear Hashing guarantee at most one disk access to retrieve a record with a given key value?
3. If a Linear Hashing index using Alternative (1) for data entries contains N records, with P records per page and an average storage utilization of 80 percent, what is the worst-case cost for an equality search? Under what conditions would this cost be the actual search cost?
4. If the hash function distributes data entries over the space of bucket numbers in a very skewed (non-uniform) way, what can you say about the space utilization in data pages?

Exercise 11.5 Give an example of when you would use each element (A or B) for each of the following 'A versus B' pairs:

1. A hashed index using Alternative (1) versus heap file organization.
2. Extendible Hashing versus Linear Hashing.
3. Static Hashing versus Linear Hashing.
4. Static Hashing versus ISAM.
5. Linear Hashing versus B+ trees.

Exercise 11.6 Give examples of the following:

1. A Linear Hashing index and an Extendible Hashing index with the same data entries, such that the Linear Hashing index has more pages.

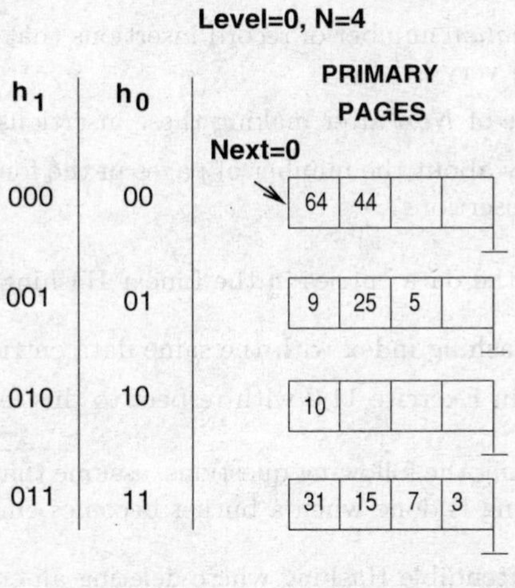

Figure 11.16 Figure for Exercise 11.9

2. A Linear Hashing index and an Extendible Hashing index with the same data entries, such that the Extendible Hashing index has more pages.

Exercise 11.7 Consider a relation R(a, b, c, d) containing 1 million records, where each page of the relation holds 10 records. R is organized as a heap file with unclustered indexes, and the records in R are randomly ordered. Assume that attribute a is a candidate key for R, with values lying in the range 0 to 999,999. For each of the following queries, name the approach that would most likely require the fewest I/Os for processing the query. The approaches to consider follow:

- Scanning through the whole heap file for R.
- Using a B+ tree index on attribute R.a.
- Using a hash index on attribute R.a.

The queries are:

1. Find all R tuples.
2. Find all R tuples such that $a < 50$.
3. Find all R tuples such that $a = 50$.
4. Find all R tuples such that $a > 50$ and $a < 100$.

Exercise 11.8 How would your answers to Exercise 11.7 change if a is not a candidate key for R? How would they change if we assume that records in R are sorted on a?

Exercise 11.9 Consider the snapshot of the Linear Hashing index shown in Figure 11.16. Assume that a bucket split occurs whenever an overflow page is created.

1. What is the *maximum* number of data entries that can be inserted (given the best possible distribution of keys) before you have to split a bucket? Explain very briefly.
2. Show the file after inserting a *single* record whose insertion causes a bucket split.

3. (a) What is the *minimum* number of record insertions that will cause a split of all four buckets? Explain very briefly.
   (b) What is the value of *Next* after making these insertions?
   (c) What can you say about the number of pages in the fourth bucket shown after this series of record insertions?

Exercise 11.10 Consider the data entries in the Linear Hashing index for Exercise 11.9.

1. Show an Extendible Hashing index with the same data entries.
2. Answer the questions in Exercise 11.9 with respect to this index.

Exercise 11.11 In answering the following questions, assume that the full deletion algorithm is used. Assume that merging is done when a bucket becomes empty.

1. Give an example of Extendible Hashing where deleting an entry reduces global depth.
2. Give an example of Linear Hashing in which deleting an entry decrements *Next* but leaves *Level* unchanged. Show the file before and after the deletion.
3. Give an example of Linear Hashing in which deleting an entry decrements *Level*. Show the file before and after the deletion.
4. Give an example of Extendible Hashing and a list of entries e_1, e_2, e_3 such that inserting the entries in order leads to three splits and deleting them in the reverse order yields the original index. If such an example does not exist, explain.
5. Give an example of a Linear Hashing index and a list of entries e_1, e_2, e_3 such that inserting the entries in order leads to three splits and deleting them in the reverse order yields the original index. If such an example does not exist, explain.

PROJECT-BASED EXERCISES

Exercise 11.12 (*Note to instructors: Additional details must be provided if this question is assigned. See Appendix 30.*) Implement Linear Hashing or Extendible Hashing in Minibase.

BIBLIOGRAPHIC NOTES

Hashing is discussed in detail in [442]. Extendible Hashing is proposed in [256]. Litwin proposed Linear Hashing in [483]. A generalization of Linear Hashing for distributed environments is described in [487]. There has been extensive research into hash-based indexing techniques. Larson describes two variations of Linear Hashing in [469] and [470]. Ramakrishna presents an analysis of hashing techniques in [607]. Hash functions that do not produce bucket overflows are studied in [608]. Order-preserving hashing techniques are discussed in [484] and [308]. Partitioned-hashing, in which each field is hashed to obtain some bits of the bucket address, extends hashing for the case of queries in which equality conditions are specified only for some of the key fields. This approach was proposed by Rivest [628] and is discussed in [747]; a further development is described in [616].

PART IV

QUERY EVALUATION

12

OVERVIEW OF QUERY EVALUATION

- What descriptive information does a DBMS store in its catalog?
- What alternatives are considered for retrieving rows from a table?
- Why does a DBMS implement several algorithms for each algebra operation? What factors affect the relative performance of different algorithms?
- What are query evaluation plans and how are they represented?
- Why is it important to find a good evaluation plan for a query? How is this done in a relational DBMS?
- **Key concepts:** catalog, system statistics; fundamental techniques, indexing, iteration, and partitioning; access paths, matching indexes and selection conditions; selection operator, indexes versus scans, impact of clustering; projection operator, duplicate elimination; join operator, index nested-loops join, sort-merge join; query evaluation plan; materialization vs. pipelinining; iterator interface; query optimization, algebra equivalences, plan enumeration; cost estimation

This very remarkable man, commends a most practical plan:
You can do what you want, if you don't think you can't,
So don't think you can't if you can.

—Charles Inge

In this chapter, we present an overview of how queries are evaluated in a relational DBMS. We begin with a discussion of how a DBMS describes the data that it manages, including tables and indexes, in Section 12.1. This descriptive data, or **metadata**, stored in special tables called the **system catalogs**, is used to find the best way to evaluate a query.

SQL queries are translated into an extended form of relational algebra, and query evaluation plans are represented as trees of relational operators, along with labels that identify the algorithm to use at each node. Thus, relational operators serve as building blocks for evaluating queries, and the implementation of these operators is carefully optimized for good performance. We introduce operator evaluation in Section 12.2 and describe evaluation algorithms for various operators in Section 12.3.

In general, queries are composed of several operators, and the algorithms for individual operators can be combined in many ways to evaluate a query. The process of finding a good evaluation plan is called *query optimization.* We introduce query optimization in Section 12.4. The basic task in query optimization, which is to consider several alternative evaluation plans for a query, is motivated through examples in Section 12.5. In Section 12.6, we describe the space of plans considered by a typical relational optimizer.

The ideas are presented in sufficient detail to allow readers to understand how current database systems evaluate typical queries. This chapter provides the necessary background in query evaluation for the discussion of physical database design and tuning in Chapter 20. Relational operator implementation and query optimization are discussed further in Chapters 13, 14, and 15; this in-depth coverage describes how current systems are implemented.

We consider a number of example queries using the following schema:

Sailors(*sid:* `integer`, *sname:* `string`, *rating:* `integer`, *age:* `real`)
Reserves(*sid:* `integer`, *bid:* `integer`, *day:* `dates`, *rname:* `string`)

We assume that each tuple of Reserves is 40 bytes long, that a page can hold 100 Reserves tuples, and that we have 1000 pages of such tuples. Similarly, we assume that each tuple of Sailors is 50 bytes long, that a page can hold 80 Sailors tuples, and that we have 500 pages of such tuples.

12.1 THE SYSTEM CATALOG

We can store a table using one of several alternative file structures, and we can create one or more indexes—each stored as a file—on every table. Conversely, in a relational DBMS, every file contains either the tuples in a table or the entries in an index. The collection of files corresponding to users' tables and indexes represents the *data* in the database.

A relational DBMS maintains information about every table and index that it contains. The descriptive information is itself stored in a collection of special tables called the **catalog tables**. An example of a catalog table is shown in Figure 12.1. The catalog tables are also called the **data dictionary**, the **system catalog**, or simply the *catalog*.

12.1.1 Information in the Catalog

Let us consider what is stored in the system catalog. At a minimum, we have system-wide information, such as the size of the buffer pool and the page size, and the following information about individual tables, indexes, and views:

- For each table:
  - Its *table name*, the *file name* (or some identifier), and the *file structure* (e.g., heap file) of the file in which it is stored.
  - The *attribute name* and *type* of each of its attributes.
  - The *index name* of each index on the table.
  - The *integrity constraints* (e.g., primary key and foreign key constraints) on the table.
- For each index:
  - The *index name* and the *structure* (e.g., B+ tree) of the index.
  - The *search key* attributes.
- For each view:
  - Its *view name* and *definition*.

In addition, statistics about tables and indexes are stored in the system catalogs and updated periodically (*not* every time the underlying tables are modified). The following information is commonly stored:

- **Cardinality:** The number of tuples *NTuples(R)* for each table *R*.
- **Size:** The number of pages *NPages(R)* for each table *R*.
- **Index Cardinality:** The number of distinct key values *NKeys(I)* for each index *I*.
- **Index Size:** The number of pages *INPages(I)* for each index *I*. (For a B+ tree index *I*, we take *INPages* to be the number of leaf pages.)

- **Index Height:** The number of nonleaf levels *IHeight(I)* for each tree index *I*.

- **Index Range:** The minimum present key value *ILow(I)* and the maximum present key value *IHigh(I)* for each index *I*.

We assume that the database architecture presented in Chapter 1 is used. Further, we assume that each file of records is implemented as a separate file of pages. Other file organizations are possible, of course. For example, a page file can contain pages that store records from more than one record file. If such a file organization is used, additional statistics must be maintained, such as the fraction of pages in a file that contain records from a given collection of records.

The catalogs also contain information about *users*, such as accounting information and *authorization* information (e.g., Joe User can modify the Reserves table but only read the Sailors table).

How Catalogs are Stored

An elegant aspect of a relational DBMS is that the system catalog is itself a collection of tables. For example, we might store information about the attributes of tables in a catalog table called Attribute_Cat:

Attribute_Cat(*attr_name:* `string`, *rel_name:* `string`,
type: `string`, *position:* `integer`)

Suppose that the database contains the two tables that we introduced at the begining of this chapter:

Sailors(<u>*sid:* `integer`</u>, *sname:* `string`, *rating:* `integer`, *age:* `real`)
Reserves(<u>*sid:* `integer`, *bid:* `integer`, *day:* `dates`</u>, *rname:* `string`)

Figure 12.1 shows the tuples in the Attribute_Cat table that describe the attributes of these two tables. Note that in addition to the tuples describing Sailors and Reserves, other tuples (the first four listed) describe the four attributes of the Attribute_Cat table itself! These other tuples illustrate an important Point: the catalog tables describe all the tables in the database, *including* the catalog tables themselves. When information about a table is needed, it is obtained from the system catalog. Of course, at the implementation level, whenever the DBMS needs to find the schema of a *catalog* table, the code that retrieves this information must be handled specially. (Otherwise, the code has to retrieve this information from the catalog tables without, presumably, knowing the schema of the catalog tables.)

attr_name	*rel_name*	*type*	*position*
attr_name	Attribute_Cat	string	1
rel_name	Attribute_Cat	string	2
type	Attribute_Cat	string	3
position	Attribute_Cat	integer	4
sid	Sailors	integer	1
sname	Sailors	string	2
rating	Sailors	integer	3
age	Sailors	real	4
sid	Reserves	integer	1
bid	Reserves	integer	2
day	Reserves	dates	3
rname	Reserves	string	4

Figure 12.1 An Instance of the Attribute_Cat Relation

The fact that the system catalog is also a collection of tables is very useful. For example, catalog tables can be queried just like any other table, using the query language of the DBMS! Further, all the techniques available for implementing and managing tables apply directly to catalog tables. The choice of catalog tables and their schemas is not unique and is made by the implementor of the DBMS. Real systems vary in their catalog schema design, but the catalog is always implemented as a collection of tables, and it essentially describes all the data stored in the database.[1]

12.2 INTRODUCTION TO OPERATOR EVALUATION

Several alternative algorithms are available for implementing each relational operator, and for most operators no algorithm is universally superior. Several factors influence which algorithm performs best, including the sizes of the tables involved, existing indexes and sort orders, the size of the available buffer pool, and the buffer replacement policy.

In this section, we describe some common techniques used in developing evaluation algorithms for relational operators, and introduce the concept of *access paths*, which are the different ways in which rows of a table can be retrieved.

[1] Some systems may store additional information in a non-relational form. For example, a system with a sophisticated query optimizer may maintain histograms or other statistical information about the distribution of values in certain attributes of a table. We can think of such information, when it is maintained, as a supplement to the catalog tables.

12.2.1 Three Common Techniques

The algorithms for various relational operators actually have a lot in common. A few simple techniques are used to develop algorithms for each operator:

- **Indexing:** If a selection or join condition is specified, use an index to examine just the tuples that satisfy the condition.
- **Iteration:** Examine all tuples in an input table, one after the other. If we need only a few fields from each tuple and there is an index whose key contains all these fields, instead of examining data tuples, we can scan all index data entries. (Scanning all data entries sequentially makes no use of the index's hash- or tree-based search structure; in a tree index, for example, we would simply examine all leaf pages in sequence.)
- **Partitioning:** By partitioning tuples on a sort key, we can often decompose an operation into a less expensive collection of operations on partitions. *Sorting* and *hashing* are two commonly used partitioning techniques.

We discuss the role of indexing in Section 12.2.2. The iteration and partitioning techniques are seen in Section 12.3.

12.2.2 Access Paths

An **access path** is a way of retrieving tuples from a table and consists of either (1) a file scan or (2) an index plus a *matching* selection condition. Every relational operator accepts one or more tables as input, and the access methods used to retrieve tuples contribute significantly to the cost of the operator.

Consider a simple selection that is a conjunction of conditions of the form *attr* **op** *value*, where **op** is one of the comparison operators $<$, $\leq$, $=$, $\neq$, $\geq$, or $>$. Such selections are said to be in **conjunctive normal form (CNF)**, and each condition is called a **conjunct**.[2] Intuitively, an index **matches** a selection condition if the index can be used to retrieve just the tuples that satisfy the condition.

- A hash index **matches** a CNF selection if there is a term of the form *attribute=value* in the selection for each attribute in the index's search key.
- A tree index **matches** a CNF selection if there is a term of the form *attribute* **op** *value* for each attribute in a *prefix* of the index's search key. ($\langle a \rangle$ and $\langle a, b \rangle$ are prefixes of key $\langle a, b, c \rangle$, but $\langle a, c \rangle$ and $\langle b, c \rangle$ are not.)

[2] We consider more complex selection conditions in Section 14.2.

Note that **op** can be any comparison; it is not restricted to be equality as it is for matching selections on a hash index.

An index can match some subset of the conjuncts in a selection condition (in CNF), even though it does not match the entire condition. We refer to the conjuncts that the index matches as the **primary conjuncts** in the selection.

The following examples illustrate access paths.

- If we have a hash index H on the search key $\langle rname, bid, sid \rangle$, we can use the index to retrieve just the Sailors tuples that satisfy the condition *rname='Joe'* $\wedge$ *bid=5* $\wedge$ *sid=3*. The index matches the entire condition *rname='Joe'* $\wedge$ *bid=5* $\wedge$ *sid= 3*. On the other hand, if the selection condition is *rname='Joe'* $\wedge$ *bid=5*, or some condition on *date*, this index does not match. That is, it cannot be used to retrieve just the tuples that satisfy these conditions.

  In contrast, if the index were a B+ tree, it would match both *rname='Joe'* $\wedge$ *bid=5* $\wedge$ *sid=3* and *rname='Joe'* $\wedge$ *bid=5*. However, it would not match *bid=5* $\wedge$ *sid=3* (since tuples are sorted primarily by *rname*).

- If we have an index (hash or tree) on the search key $\langle bid, sid \rangle$ and the selection condition *rname='Joe'* $\wedge$ *bid=5* $\wedge$ *sid=3*, we can use the index to retrieve tuples that satisfy *bid=5* $\wedge$ *sid=3*; these are the primary conjuncts. The fraction of tuples that satisfy these conjuncts (and whether the index is clustered) determines the number of pages that are retrieved. The additional condition on *rname* must then be applied to each retrieved tuple and will eliminate some of the retrieved tuples from the result.

- If we have an index on the search key $\langle bid, sid \rangle$ and we also have a B+ tree index on *day*, the selection condition *day* < *8/9/2002* $\wedge$ *bid=5* $\wedge$ *sid=3* offers us a choice. Both indexes match (part of) the selection condition, and we can use either to retrieve Reserves tuples. Whichever index we use, the conjuncts in the selection condition that are not matched by the index (e.g., *bid=5* $\wedge$ *sid=3* if we use the B+ tree index on *day*) must be checked for each retrieved tuple.

Selectivity of Access Paths

The **selectivity** of an access path is the number of pages retrieved (index pages plus data pages) if we use this access path to retrieve all desired tuples. If a table contains an index that matches a given selection, there are at least two access paths: the index and a scan of the data file. Sometimes, of course, we can scan the index itself (rather than scanning the data file or using the index to probe the file), giving us a third access path.

The **most selective** access path is the one that retrieves the fewest pages; using the most selective access path minimizes the cost of data retrieval. The selectivity of an access path depends on the primary conjuncts in the selection condition (with respect to the index involved). Each conjunct acts as a filter on the table. The fraction of tuples in the table that satisfy a given conjunct is called the **reduction factor**. When there are several primary conjuncts, the fraction of tuples that satisfy all of them can be approximated by the product of their reduction factors; this effectively treats them as independent filters, and while they may not actually be independent, the approximation is widely used in practice.

Supose we have a hash index H on Sailors with search key $\langle rname, bid, sid \rangle$, and we are given the selection condition *rname='Joe'* $\wedge$ *bid=5* $\wedge$ *sid=3*. We can use the index to retrieve tuples that satisfy all three conjuncts. The catalog contains the number of distinct key values, $NKeys(H)$, in the hash index, as well as the number of pages, $NPages$, in the Sailors table. The fraction of pages satisfying the primary conjuncts is $Npages(Sailors) \cdot \frac{1}{NKeys(H)}$.

If the index has search key $\langle bid, sid \rangle$, the primary conjuncts are *bid=5* $\wedge$ *sid=3*. If we know the number of distinct values in the *bid* column, we can estimate the reduction factor for the first conjunct. This information is available in the catalog if there is an index with *bid* as the search key; if not, optimizers typically use a default value such as 1/10. Multiplying the reduction factors for *bid=5* and *sid=3* gives us (under the simplifying independence assumption) the fraction of tuples retrieved; if the index is clustered, this is also the fraction of pages retrieved. If the index is not clustered, each retrieved tuple could be on a different page. (Review Section 8.4 at this time.)

We estimate the reduction factor for a range condition such as *day* > *8/9/2002* by assuming that values in the column are uniformly distributed. If there is a B+ tree T with key *day*, the reduction factor is $\frac{High(T) - value}{High(T) - Low(T)}$.

12.3 ALGORITHMS FOR RELATIONAL OPERATIONS

We now briefly discuss evaluation algorithms for the main relational operators. While the important ideas are introduced here, a more in-depth treatment is deferred to Chapter 14. As in Chapter 8, we consider only I/O costs and measure I/O costs in terms of the number of page I/Os. In this chapter, we use detailed examples to illustrate how to compute the cost of an algorithm. Although we do not present rigorous cost formulas in this chapter, the reader should be able to apply the underlying ideas to do cost calculations on other similar examples.

12.3.1 Selection

The selection operation is a simple retrieval of tuples from a table, and its implementation is essentially covered in our discussion of access paths. To summarize, given a selection of the form $\sigma_{R.attr}$ **op** $_{value}(R)$, if there is no index on $R.attr$, we have to scan R.

If one or more indexes on R match the selection, we can use the index to retrieve matching tuples, and apply any remaining selection conditions to further restrict the result set. As an example, consider a selection of the form *rname* < *'C%'* on the Reserves table. Assuming that names are uniformly distributed with respect to the initial letter, for simplicity, we estimate that roughly 10% of Reserves tuples are in the result. This is a total of 10,000 tuples, or 100 pages. If we have a clustered B+ tree index on the *rname* field of Reserves, we can retrieve the qualifying tuples with 100 I/Os (plus a few I/Os to traverse from the root to the appropriate leaf page to start the scan). However, if the index is unclustered, we could have up to 10,000 I/Os in the worst case, since each tuple could cause us to read a page.

As a rule of thumb, it is probably cheaper to simply scan the entire table (instead of using an unclustered index) if over 5% of the tuples are to be retrieved.

See Section 14.1 for more details on implementation of selections.

12.3.2 Projection

The projection operation requires us to drop certain fields of the input, which is easy to do. The expensive aspect of the operation is to ensure that no duplicates appear in the result. For example, if we only want the *sid* and *bid* fields from Reserves, we could have duplicates if a sailor has reserved a given boat on several days.

If duplicates need not be eliminated (e.g., the `DISTINCT` keyword is not included in the `SELECT` clause), projection consists of simply retrieving a subset of fields from each tuple of the input table. This can be accomplished by simple iteration on either the table or an index whose key contains all necessary fields. (Note that we do not care whether the index is clustered, since the values we want are in the data entries of the index itself!)

If we have to eliminate duplicates, we typically have to use partitioning. Suppose we want to obtain ⟨*sid, bid*⟩ by projecting from Reserves. We can partition by (1) scanning Reserves to obtain ⟨*sid, bid*⟩ pairs and (2) sorting these pairs using $\langle sid, bid\rangle$ as the sort key. We can then scan the sorted pairs and easily discard duplicates, which are now adjacent.

Sorting large disk-resident datasets is a very important operation in database systems, and is discussed in Chapter 13. Sorting a table typically requires two or three passes, each of which reads and writes the entire table.

The projection operation can be optimized by combining the initial scan of Reserves with the scan in the first pass of sorting. Similarly, the scanning of sorted pairs can be combined with the last pass of sorting. With such an optimized implemention, projection with duplicate elimination requires (1) a first pass in which the entire table is scanned, and only pairs $\langle sid, bid\rangle$ are written out, and (2) a final pass in which all pairs are scanned, but only one copy of each pair is written out. In addition, there might be an intermediate pass in which all pairs are read from and written to disk.

The availability of appropriate indexes can lead to less expensive plans than sorting for duplicate elimination. If we have an index whose search key contains all the fields retained by the projection, we can sort the data entries in the index, rather than the data records themselves. If all the retained attributes appear in a prefix of the search key for a clustered index, we can do even better; we can simply retrieve data entries using the index, and duplicates are easily detected since they are adjacent. These plans are further examples of *index-only* evaluation strategies, which we discussed in Section 8.5.2.

See Section 14.3 for more details on implementation of projections.

12.3.3 Join

Joins are expensive operations and very common. Therefore, they have been widely studied, and systems typically support several algorithms to carry out joins.

Consider the join of Reserves and Sailors, with the join condition $Reserves.sid = Sailors.sid$. Suppose that one of the tables, say Sailors, has an index on the *sid* column. We can scan Reserves and, for each tuple, use the index to *probe* Sailors for matching tuples. This approach is called **index nested loops join**.

Suppose that we have a hash-based index using Alternative (2) on the *sid* attribute of Sailors and that it takes about 1.2 I/Os on average[3] to retrieve the appropriate page of the index. Since *sid* is a key for Sailors, we have at

[3]This is a typical cost for hash-based indexes.

most one matching tuple. Indeed, *sid* in Reserves is a foreign key referring to Sailors, and therefore we have *exactly* one matching Sailors tuple for each Reserves tuple. Let us consider the cost of scanning Reserves and using the index to retrieve the matching Sailors tuple for each Reserves tuple. The cost of scanning Reserves is 1000. There are $100 * 1000$ tuples in Reserves. For each of these tuples, retrieving the index page containing the rid of the matching Sailors tuple costs 1.2 I/Os (on average); in addition, we have to retrieve the Sailors page containing the qualifying tuple. Therefore, we have $100,000 * (1 + 1.2)$ I/Os to retrieve matching Sailors tuples. The total cost is 221,000 I/Os.[4]

If we do not have an index that matches the join condition on either table, we cannot use index nested loops. In this case, we can sort both tables on the join column, and then scan them to find matches. This is called **sort-merge join**.. Assuming that we can sort Reserves in two passes, and Sailors in two passes as well, let us consider the cost of sort-merge join. Consider the join of the tables Reserves and Sailors. Because we read and write Reserves in each pass, the sorting cost is $2 * 2 * 1000 = 4000$ I/Os. Similarly, we can sort Sailors at a cost of $2 * 2 * 500 = 2000$ I/Os. In addition, the second phase of the sort-merge join algorithm requires an additional scan of both tables. Thus the total cost is $4000 + 2000 + 1000 + 500 = 7500$ I/Os.

Observe that the cost of sort-merge join, which does not require a pre-existing index, is lower than the cost of index nested loops join. In addition, the result of the sort-merge join is sorted on the join column(s). Other join algorithms that do not rely on an existing index and are often cheaper than index nested loops join are also known (*block nested loops* and *hash* joins; see Chapter 14). Given this, why consider index nested loops at all?

Index nested loops has the nice property that it is **incremental**. The cost of our example join is incremental in the number of Reserves tuples that we process. Therefore, if some additional selection in the query allows us to consider only a small subset of Reserves tuples, we can avoid computing the join of Reserves and Sailors in its entirety. For instance, suppose that we only want the result of the join for boat 101, and there are very few such reservations. For each such Reserves tuple, we probe Sailors, and we are done. If we use sort-merge join, on the other hand, we have to scan the entire Sailors table at least once, and the cost of this step alone is likely to be much higher than the entire cost of index nested loops join.

Observe that the choice of index nested loops join is based on considering the query as a whole, including the extra selection on Reserves, rather than just

[4] As an exercise, the reader should write formulas for the cost estimates in this example in terms of the properties—e.g., NPages—of the tables and indexes involved.

the join operation by itself. This leads us to our next topic, query optimization, which is the process of finding a good plan for an entire query.

See Section 14.4 for more details.

12.3.4 Other Operations

A SQL query contains group-by and aggregation in addition to the basic relational operations. Different query blocks can be combined with union, set-difference, and set-intersection.

The expensive aspect of set operations such as union and intersection is duplicate elimination, just like for projection. The approach used to implement projection is easily adapted for these operations as well. See Section 14.5 for more details.

Group-by is typically implemented through sorting. Sometimes, the input table has a tree index with a search key that matches the grouping attributes. In this case, we can retrieve tuples using the index in the appropriate order without an explicit sorting step. Aggregate operations are carried out using temporary counters in main memory as tuples are retrieved. See Section 14.6 for more details.

12.4 INTRODUCTION TO QUERY OPTIMIZATION

Query optimization is one of the most important tasks of a relational DBMS. One of the strengths of relational query languages is the wide variety of ways in which a user can express and thus the system can evaluate a query. Although this flexibility makes it easy to write queries, good performance relies greatly on the quality of the query optimizer—a given query can be evaluated in many ways, and the difference in cost between the best and worst plans may be several orders of magnitude. Realistically, we cannot expect to always find the best plan, but we expect to consistently find a plan that is quite good.

A more detailed view of the query optimization and execution layer in the DBMS architecture from Section 1.8 is shown in Figure 12.2. Queries are parsed and then presented to a **query optimizer**, which is responsible for identifying an efficient execution plan. The optimizer generates alternative plans and chooses the plan with the least estimated cost.

The space of plans considered by a typical relational query optimizer can be understood by recognizing that *a query is essentially treated as a* $\sigma - \pi - \bowtie$ *algebra expression*, with the remaining operations (if any, in a given query)

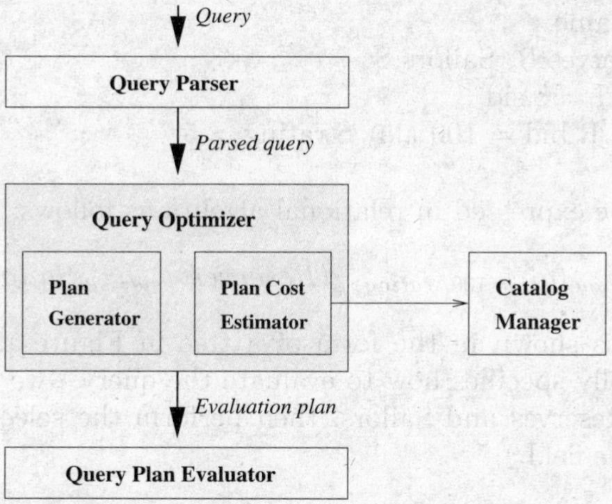

Figure 12.2 Query Parsing, Optimization, and Execution

> **Commercial Optimizers:** Current relational DBMS optimizers are very complex pieces of software with many closely guarded details, and they typically represent 40 to 50 man-years of development effort!

carried out on the result of the $\sigma - \pi - \bowtie$ expression. Optimizing such a relational algebra expression involves two basic steps:

- Enumerating alternative plans for evaluating the expression. Typically, an optimizer considers a subset of all possible plans because the number of possible plans is very large.
- Estimating the cost of each enumerated plan and choosing the plan with the lowest estimated cost.

In this section we lay the foundation for our discussion of query optimization by introducing evaluation plans.

12.4.1 Query Evaluation Plans

A **query evaluation plan** (or simply **plan**) consists of an extended relational algebra tree, with additional annotations at each node indicating the access methods to use for each table and the implementation method to use for each relational operator.

Consider the following SQL query:

```
SELECT S.sname
FROM   Reserves R, Sailors S
WHERE  R.sid = S.sid
       AND R.bid = 100 AND S.rating > 5
```

This query can be expressed in relational algebra as follows:

$$\pi_{sname}(\sigma_{bid=100 \wedge rating>5}(Reserves \bowtie_{sid=sid} Sailors))$$

This expression is shown in the form of a tree in Figure 12.3. The algebra expression partially specifies how to evaluate the query—we first compute the natural join of Reserves and Sailors, then perform the selections, and finally project the *sname* field.

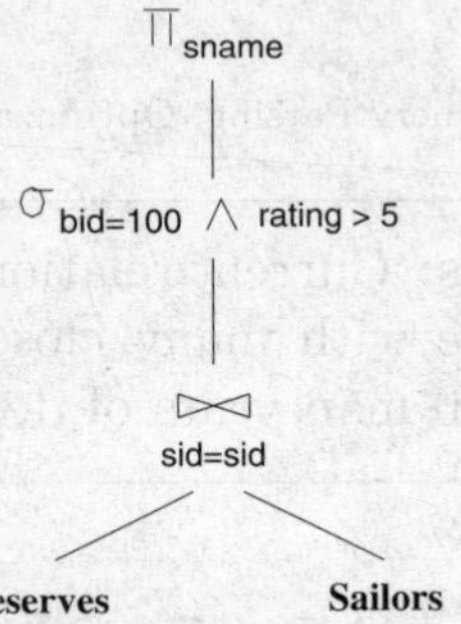

Figure 12.3 Query Expressed as a Relational Algebra Tree

To obtain a fully specified evaluation plan, we must decide on an implementation for each of the algebra operations involved. For example, we can use a page-oriented simple nested loops join with Reserves as the outer table and apply selections and projections to each tuple in the result of the join as it is produced; the result of the join before the selections and projections is never stored in its entirety. This query evaluation plan is shown in Figure 12.4.

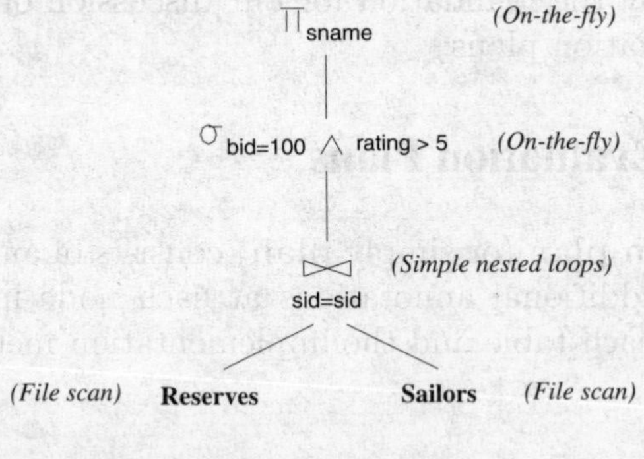

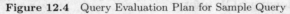

Figure 12.4 Query Evaluation Plan for Sample Query

In drawing the query evaluation plan, we have used the convention that the *outer table* is the *left child* of the join operator. We adopt this convention henceforth.

12.4.2 Multi-operator Queries: Pipelined Evaluation

When a query is composed of several operators, the result of one operator is sometimes **pipelined** to another operator without creating a temporary table to hold the intermediate result. The plan in Figure 12.4 pipelines the output of the join of Sailors and Reserves into the selections and projections that follow. Pipelining the output of an operator into the next operator saves the cost of writing out the intermediate result and reading it back in, and the cost savings can be significant. If the output of an operator is saved in a temporary table for processing by the next operator, we say that the tuples are **materialized**. Pipelined evaluation has lower overhead costs than materialization and is chosen whenever the algorithm for the operator evaluation permits it.

There are many opportunities for pipelining in typical query plans, even simple plans that involve only selections. Consider a selection query in which only part of the selection condition matches an index. We can think of such a query as containing *two* instances of the selection operator: The first contains the primary, or matching, part of the original selection condition, and the second contains the rest of the selection condition. We can evaluate such a query by applying the primary selection and writing the result to a temporary table and then applying the second selection to the temporary table. In contrast, a pipelined evaluation consists of applying the second selection to each tuple in the result of the primary selection as it is produced and adding tuples that qualify to the final result. When the input table to a unary operator (e.g., selection or projection) is pipelined into it, we sometimes say that the operator is applied **on-the-fly**.

As a second and more general example, consider a join of the form $(A \bowtie B) \bowtie C$, shown in Figure 12.5 as a tree of join operations.

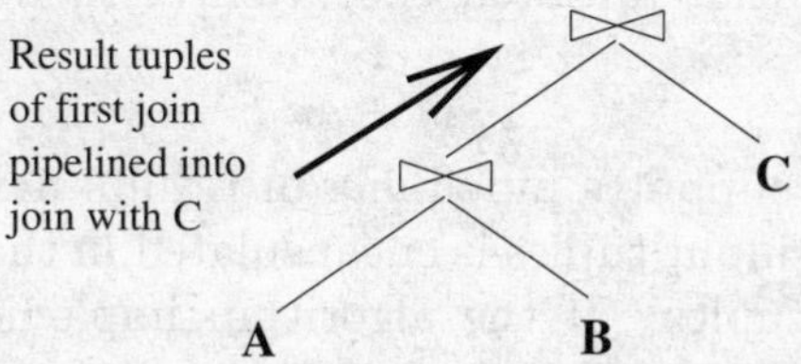

Figure 12.5 A Query Tree Illustrating Pipelining

Both joins can be evaluated in pipelined fashion using some version of a nested loops join. Conceptually, the evaluation is initiated from the root, and the node joining A and B produces tuples as and when they are requested by its parent node. When the root node gets a page of tuples from its left child (the outer table), all the matching inner tuples are retrieved (using either an index or a scan) and joined with matching outer tuples; the current page of outer tuples is then discarded. A request is then made to the left child for the next page of tuples, and the process is repeated. Pipelined evaluation is thus a *control strategy* governing the rate at which different joins in the plan proceed. It has the great virtue of not writing the result of intermediate joins to a temporary file because the results are produced, consumed, and discarded one page at a time.

12.4.3 The Iterator Interface

A query evaluation plan is a tree of relational operators and is executed by calling the operators in some (possibly interleaved) order. Each operator has one or more inputs and an output, which are also nodes in the plan, and tuples must be passed between operators according to the plan's tree structure.

To simplify the code responsible for coordinating the execution of a plan, the relational operators that form the nodes of a plan tree (which is to be evaluated using pipelining) typically support a uniform **iterator** interface, hiding the internal implementation details of each operator. The iterator interface for an operator includes the functions **open**, **get next**, and **close**. The *open* function initializes the state of the iterator by allocating buffers for its inputs and output, and is also used to pass in arguments such as selection conditions that modify the behavior of the operator. The code for the *get next* function calls the *get next* function on each input node and calls operator-specific code to process the input tuples. The output tuples generated by the processing are placed in the output buffer of the operator, and the state of the iterator is updated to keep track of how much input has been consumed. When all output tuples have been produced through repeated calls to *get next*, the *close* function is called (by the code that initiated execution of this operator) to deallocate state information.

The iterator interface supports pipelining of results naturally; the decision to pipeline or materialize input tuples is encapsulated in the operator-specific code that processes input tuples. If the algorithm implemented for the operator allows input tuples to be processed completely when they are received, input tuples are not materialized and the evaluation is pipelined. If the algorithm examines the same input tuples several times, they are materialized. This decision, like other details of the operator's implementation, is hidden by the iterator interface for the operator.

The iterator interface is also used to encapsulate access methods such as B+ trees and hash-based indexes. Externally, access methods can be viewed simply as operators that produce a stream of output tuples. In this case, the *open* function can be used to pass the selection conditions that match the access path.

12.5 ALTERNATIVE PLANS: A MOTIVATING EXAMPLE

Consider the example query from Section 12.4. Let us consider the cost of evaluating the plan shown in Figure 12.4. We ignore the cost of writing out the final result since this is common to all algorithms, and does not affect their relative costs. The cost of the join is $1000 + 1000 * 500 = 501,000$ page I/Os. The selections and the projection are done on-the-fly and do not incur additional I/Os. The total cost of this plan is therefore 501,000 page I/Os. This plan is admittedly naive; however, it is possible to be even more naive by treating the join as a cross-product followed by a selection.

We now consider several alternative plans for evaluating this query. Each alternative improves on the original plan in a different way and introduces some optimization ideas that are examined in more detail in the rest of this chapter.

12.5.1 Pushing Selections

A join is a relatively expensive operation, and a good heuristic is to reduce the sizes of the tables to be joined as much as possible. One approach is to apply selections early; if a selection operator appears after a join operator, it is worth examining whether the selection can be 'pushed' ahead of the join. As an example, the selection *bid=100* involves only the attributes of Reserves and can be applied to Reserves *before* the join. Similarly, the selection *rating*> 5 involves only attributes of Sailors and can be applied to Sailors before the join. Let us suppose that the selections are performed using a simple file scan, that the result of each selection is written to a temporary table on disk, and that the temporary tables are then joined using a sort-merge join. The resulting query evaluation plan is shown in Figure 12.6.

Let us assume that five buffer pages are available and estimate the cost of this query evaluation plan. (It is likely that more buffer pages are available in practice. We chose a small number simply for illustration in this example.) The cost of applying *bid=100* to Reserves is the cost of scanning Reserves (1000 pages) plus the cost of writing the result to a temporary table, say T1.

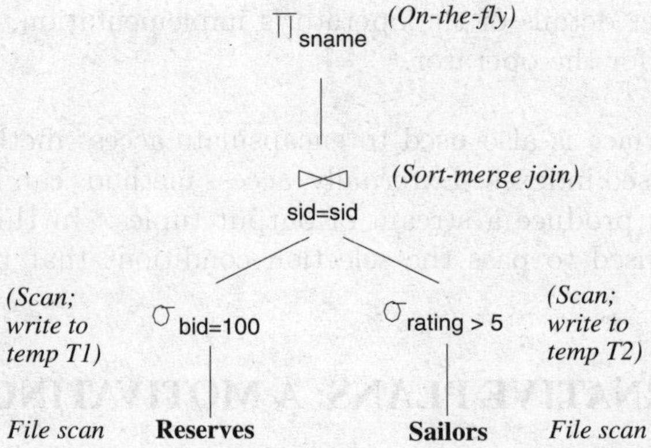

Figure 12.6 A Second Query Evaluation Plan

(Note that the cost of writing the temporary table cannot be ignored—we can ignore only the cost of writing out the *final* result of the query, which is the only component of the cost that is the same for all plans.) To estimate the size of T1, we require additional information. For example, if we assume that the maximum number of reservations of a given boat is one, just one tuple appears in the result. Alternatively, if we know that there are 100 boats, we can assume that reservations are spread out uniformly across all boats and estimate the number of pages in T1 to be 10. For concreteness, assume that the number of pages in T1 is indeed 10.

The cost of applying *rating* > 5 to Sailors is the cost of scanning Sailors (500 pages) plus the cost of writing out the result to a temporary table, say, T2. If we assume that ratings are uniformly distributed over the range 1 to 10, we can approximately estimate the size of T2 as 250 pages.

To do a sort-merge join of T1 and T2, let us assume that a straightforward implementation is used in which the two tables are first completely sorted and then merged. Since five buffer pages are available, we can sort T1 (which has 10 pages) in two passes. Two runs of five pages each are produced in the first pass and these are merged in the second pass. In each pass, we read and write 10 pages; thus, the cost of sorting T1 is $2 * 2 * 10 = 40$ page I/Os. We need four passes to sort T2, which has 250 pages. The cost is $2 * 4 * 250 = 2000$ page I/Os. To merge the sorted versions of T1 and T2, we need to scan these tables, and the cost of this step is $10 + 250 = 260$. The final projection is done on-the-fly, and by convention we ignore the cost of writing the final result.

The total cost of the plan shown in Figure 12.6 is the sum of the cost of the selection ($1000+10+500+250 = 1760$) and the cost of the join ($40+2000+260 = 2300$), that is, 4060 page I/Os.

Sort-merge join is one of several join methods. We may be able to reduce the cost of this plan by choosing a different join method. As an alternative, suppose that we used block nested loops join instead of sort-merge join. Using T1 as the outer table, for every three-page block of T1, we scan all of T2; thus, we scan T2 four times. The cost of the join is therefore the cost of scanning T1 (10) plus the cost of scanning T2 ($4 * 250 = 1000$). The cost of the plan is now $1760 + 1010 = 2770$ page I/Os.

A further refinement is to push the projection, just like we pushed the selections past the join. Observe that only the *sid* attribute of T1 and the *sid* and *sname* attributes of T2 are really required. As we scan Reserves and Sailors to do the selections, we could also eliminate unwanted columns. This on-the-fly projection reduces the sizes of the temporary tables T1 and T2. The reduction in the size of T1 is substantial because only an integer field is retained. In fact, T1 now fits within three buffer pages, and we can perform a block nested loops join with a single scan of T2. The cost of the join step drops to under 250 page I/Os, and the total cost of the plan drops to about 2000 I/Os.

12.5.2 Using Indexes

If indexes are available on the Reserves and Sailors tables, even better query evaluation plans may be available. For example, suppose that we have a clustered static hash index on the *bid* field of Reserves and another hash index on the *sid* field of Sailors. We can then use the query evaluation plan shown in Figure 12.7.

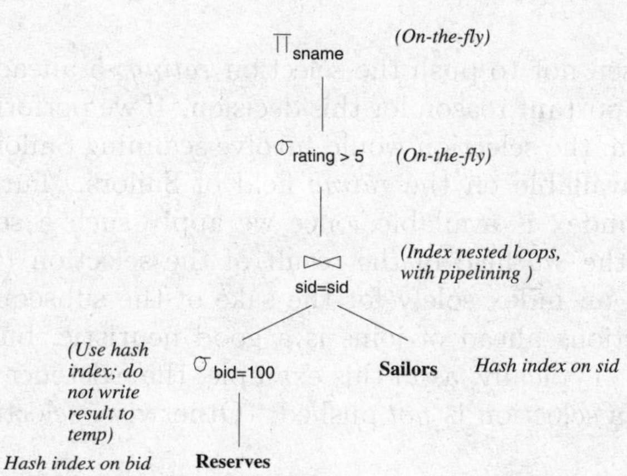

Figure 12.7 A Query Evaluation Plan Using Indexes

The selection *bid*=100 is performed on Reserves by using the hash index on *bid* to retrieve only matching tuples. As before, if we know that 100 boats are available and assume that reservations are spread out uniformly across all boats, we can estimate the number of selected tuples to be $100,000/100 = 1000$. Since the index on *bid* is clustered, these 1000 tuples appear consecutively within the same bucket; therefore, the cost is 10 page I/Os.

For each selected tuple, we retrieve matching Sailors tuples using the hash index on the *sid* field; selected Reserves tuples are not materialized and the join is pipelined. For each tuple in the result of the join, we perform the selection *rating*>5 and the projection of *sname* on-the-fly. There are several important points to note here:

1. Since the result of the selection on Reserves is not materialized; the optimization of projecting out fields that are not needed subsequently is unnecessary (and is not used in the plan shown in Figure 12.7).

2. The join field *sid* is a key for Sailors. Therefore, at most one Sailors tuple matches a given Reserves tuple. The cost of retrieving this matching tuple depends on whether the directory of the hash index on the *sid* column of Sailors fits in memory and on the presence of overflow pages (if any). However, the cost does *not* depend on whether this index is clustered because there is at most one matching Sailors tuple and requests for Sailors tuples are made in random order by *sid* (because Reserves tuples are retrieved by *bid* and are therefore considered in random order by *sid*). For a hash index, 1.2 page I/Os (on average) is a good estimate of the cost for retrieving a data entry. Assuming that the *sid* hash index on Sailors uses Alternative (1) for data entries, 1.2 I/Os is the cost to retrieve a matching Sailors tuple (and if one of the other two alternatives is used, the cost would be 2.2 I/Os).

3. We have chosen not to push the selection *rating*>5 ahead of the join, and there is an important reason for this decision. If we performed the selection before the join, the selection would involve scanning Sailors, assuming that no index is available on the *rating* field of Sailors. Further, whether or not such an index is available, once we apply such a selection, we have no index on the *sid* field of the result of the selection (unless we choose to build such an index solely for the sake of the subsequent join). Thus, pushing selections ahead of joins is a good heuristic, but not always the best strategy. Typically, as in this example, the existence of useful indexes is the reason a selection is *not* pushed. (Otherwise, selections are pushed.)

Let us estimate the cost of the plan shown in Figure 12.7. The selection of Reserves tuples costs 10 I/Os, as we saw earlier. There are 1000 such tuples, and for each, the cost of finding the matching Sailors tuple is 1.2 I/Os, on average. The cost of this step (the join) is therefore 1200 I/Os. All remaining selections and projections are performed on-the-fly. The total cost of the plan is 1210 I/Os.

As noted earlier, this plan does not utilize clustering of the Sailors index. The plan can be further refined if the index on the *sid* field of Sailors is clustered. Suppose we materialize the result of performing the selection *bid*=100 on Reserves and sort this temporary table. This table contains 10 pages. Selecting the tuples costs 10 page I/Os (as before), writing out the result to a temporary table costs another 10 I/Os, and with five buffer pages, sorting this temporary costs $2 * 2 * 10 = 40$ I/Os. (The cost of this step is reduced if we push the projection on *sid*. The *sid* column of materialized Reserves tuples requires only three pages and can be sorted in memory with five buffer pages.) The selected Reserves tuples can now be retrieved in order by *sid*.

If a sailor has reserved the same boat many times, all corresponding Reserves tuples are now retrieved consecutively; the matching Sailors tuple will be found in the buffer pool on all but the first request for it. This improved plan also demonstrates that pipelining is not always the best strategy.

The combination of pushing selections and using indexes illustrated by this plan is very powerful. If the selected tuples from the outer table join with a single inner tuple, the join operation may become trivial, and the performance gains with respect to the naive plan in Figure 12.6 are even more dramatic. The following variant of our example query illustrates this situation:

```
SELECT S.sname
FROM   Reserves R, Sailors S
WHERE  R.sid = S.sid
       AND R.bid = 100 AND S.rating > 5
       AND R.day = '8/9/2002'
```

A slight variant of the plan shown in Figure 12.7, designed to answer this query, is shown in Figure 12.8. The selection *day='8/9/2002'* is applied on-the-fly to the result of the selection *bid=100* on the Reserves table.

Suppose that *bid* and *day* form a key for Reserves. (Note that this assumption differs from the schema presented earlier in this chapter.) Let us estimate the cost of the plan shown in Figure 12.8. The selection *bid=100* costs 10 page I/Os, as before, and the additional selection *day='8/9/2002'* is applied on-the-fly, eliminating all but (at most) one Reserves tuple. There is at most one matching Sailors tuple, and this is retrieved in 1.2 I/Os (an average value). The selection on *rating* and the projection on *sname* are then applied on-the-fly at no additional cost. The total cost of the plan in Figure 12.8 is thus about 11 I/Os. In contrast, if we modify the naive plan in Figure 12.6 to perform the additional selection on *day* together with the selection *bid=100*, the cost remains at 501,000 I/Os.

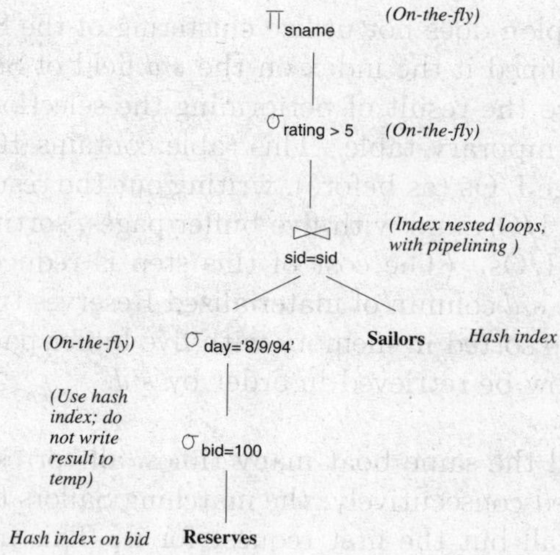

Figure 12.8 A Query Evaluation Plan for the Second Example

12.6 WHAT A TYPICAL OPTIMIZER DOES

A relational query optimizer uses relational algebra equivalences to identify many equivalent expressions for a given query. For each such equivalent version of the query, all available implementation techniques are considered for the relational operators involved, thereby generating several alternative query evaluation plans. The optimizer estimates the cost of each such plan and chooses the one with the lowest estimated cost.

12.6.1 Alternative Plans Considered

Two relational algebra expressions over the same set of input tables are said to be **equivalent** if they produce the same result on all instances of the input tables. Relational algebra equivalences play a central role in identifying alternative plans.

Consider a basic SQL query consisting of a `SELECT` clause, a `FROM` clause, and a `WHERE` clause. This is easily represented as an algebra expression; the fields mentioned in the `SELECT` are projected from the cross-product of tables in the `FROM` clause, after applying the selections in the `WHERE` clause. The use of equivalences enable us to convert this initial representation into equivalent expressions. In particular:

- Selections and cross-products can be combined into joins.
- Joins can be extensively reordered.

- Selections and projections, which reduce the size of the input, can be "pushed" ahead of joins.

The query discussed in Section 12.5 illustrates these points; pushing the selection in that query ahead of the join yielded a dramatically better evaluation plan. We discuss relational algebra equivalences in detail in Section 15.3.

Left-Deep Plans

Consider a query of the form $A \bowtie B \bowtie C \bowtie D$; that is, the natural join of four tables. Three relational algebra operator trees that are equivalent to this query (based on algebra equivalences) are shown in Figure 12.9. By convention, the left child of a join node is the outer table and the right child is the inner table. By adding details such as the join method for each join node, it is straightforward to obtain several query evaluation plans from these trees.

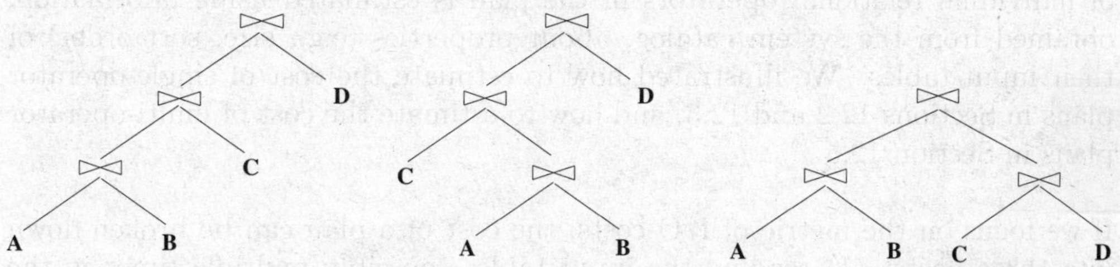

Figure 12.9 Three Join Trees

The first two trees in Figure 12.9 are examples of **linear** trees. In a linear tree, at least one child of a join node is a base table. The first tree is an example of a **left-deep** tree—the *right* child of each join node is a base table. The third tree is an example of a non-linear or **bushy** tree.

Optimizers typically use a dynamic-programming approach (see Section 15.4.2) to efficiently search the class of all **left-deep** plans. The second and third kinds of trees are therefore never considered. Intuitively, the first tree represents a plan in which we join A and B first, then join the result with C, then join the result with D. There are 23[5] other left-deep plans that differ only in the order that tables are joined. If any of these plans has selection and projection conditions other than the joins themselves, these conditions are applied as early as possible (consitent with algebra equivalences) given the choice of a join order for the tables.

Of course, this decision rules out many alternative plans that may cost less than the best plan using a left-deep tree; we have to live with the fact that

[5] The reader should think through the number 23 in this example.

the optimizer will never find such plans. There are two main reasons for this decision to concentrate on **left-deep plans**, or plans based on left-deep trees:

1. As the number of joins increases, the number of alternative plans increases rapidly and it becomes necessary to prune the space of alternative plans.
2. Left-deep trees allow us to generate all **fully pipelined** plans; that is, plans in which all joins are evaluated using pipelining. (Inner tables must always be materialized because we must examine the entire inner table for each tuple of the outer table. So, a plan in which an inner table is the result of a join forces us to materialize the result of that join.)

12.6.2 Estimating the Cost of a Plan

The cost of a plan is the sum of costs for the operators it contains. The cost of individual relational operators in the plan is estimated using information, obtained from the system catalog, about properties (e.g., size, sort order) of their input tables. We illustrated how to estimate the cost of single-operator plans in Sections 12.2 and 12.3, and how to estimate the cost of multi-operator plans in Section 12.5.

If we focus on the metric of I/O costs, the cost of a plan can be broken down into three parts: (1) reading the input tables (possibly multiple times in the case of some join and sorting algorithms), (2) writing intermediate tables, and (possibly) (3) sorting the final result (if the query specifies duplicate elimination or an output order). The third part is common to all plans (unless one of the plans happens to produce output in the required order), and, in the common case that a fully-pipelined plan is chosen, no intermediate tables are written.

Thus, the cost for a fully-pipelined plan is dominated by part (1). This cost depends greatly on the access paths used to read input tables; of course, access paths that are used repeatedly to retrieve matching tuples in a join algorithm are especially important.

For plans that are not fully pipelined, the cost of materializing temporary tables can be significant. The cost of materializing an intermediate result depends on its size, and the size also influences the cost of the operator for which the temporary is an input table. The number of tuples in the result of a selection is estimated by multiplying the input size by the reduction factor for the selection conditions. The number of tuples in the result of a projection is the same as the input, assuming that duplicates are not eliminated; of course, each result tuple is smaller since it contains fewer fields.

The result size for a join can be estimated by multiplying the maximum result size, which is the product of the input table sizes, by the reduction factor of the join condition. The reduction factor for join condition *column1* = *column2* can be approximated by the formula $\frac{1}{\texttt{MAX}\ (NKeys(I1), NKeys(I2))}$ if there are indexes $I1$ and $I2$ on *column1* and *column2*, respectively. This formula assumes that each key value in the smaller index, say $I1$, has a matching value in the other index. Given a value for *column1*, we assume that each of the $NKeys(I2)$ values for *column2* is equally likely. Thus, the number of tuples that have the same value in *column2* as a given value in *column1* is $\frac{1}{NKeys(I2)}$.

12.7 REVIEW QUESTIONS

Answers to the review questions can be found in the listed sections.

- What is *metadata*? What metadata is stored in the *system catalog*? Describe the information stored per relation, and per index. **(Section 12.1)**
- The catalog is itself stored as a collection of relations. Explain why. **(Section 12.1)**
- What three techniques are commonly used in algorithms to evaluate relational operators? **(Section 12.2)**
- What is an access path? When does an index *match* a search condition? **(Section 12.2.2)**
- What are the main approaches to evaluating selections? Discuss the use of indexes, in particular. **(Section 12.3.1)**
- What are the main approaches to evaluating projections? What makes projections potentially expensive? **(Section 12.3.2)**
- What are the main approaches to evaluating joins? Why are joins expensive? **(Section 12.3.3)**
- What is the goal of query optimization? Is it to find the best plan? **(Section 12.4)**
- How does a DBMS represent a relational query evaluation plan? **(Section 12.4.1)**
- What is *pipelined evaluation*? What is its benefit? **(Section 12.4.2)**
- Describe the iterator interface for operators and access methods. What is its purpose? **(Section 12.4.3)**

- Discuss why the difference in cost between alternative plans for a query can be very large. Give specific examples to illustrate the impact of pushing selections, the choice of join methods, and the availability of appropriate indexes. **(Section 12.5)**
- What is the role of relational algebra equivalences in query optimization? **(Section 12.6)**
- What is the space of plans considered by a typical relational query optimizer? Justify the choice of this space of plans. **(Section 12.6.1)**
- How is the cost of a plan estimated? What is the role of the system catalog? What is the *selectivity* of an access path, and how does it influence the cost of a plan? Why is it important to be able to estimate the size of the result of a plan? **(Section 12.6.2)**

EXERCISES

Exercise 12.1 Briefly answer the following questions:

1. Describe three techniques commonly used when developing algorithms for relational operators. Explain how these techniques can be used to design algorithms for the selection, projection, and join operators.
2. What is an access path? When does an index *match* an access path? What is a *primary conjunct*, and why is it important?
3. What information is stored in the system catalogs?
4. What are the benefits of making the system catalogs be relations?
5. What is the goal of query optimization? Why is optimization important?
6. Describe *pipelining* and its advantages.
7. Give an example query and plan in which pipelining *cannot* be used.
8. Describe the *iterator* interface and explain its advantages.
9. What role do statistics gathered from the database play in query optimization?
10. What were the important design decisions made in the System R optimizer?
11. Why do query optimizers consider only left-deep join trees? Give an example of a query and a plan that would not be considered because of this restriction.

Exercise 12.2 Consider a relation R(*a,b,c,d,e*) containing 5,000,000 records, where each data page of the relation holds 10 records. R is organized as a sorted file with secondary indexes. Assume that *R.a* is a candidate key for R, with values lying in the range 0 to 4,999,999, and that R is stored in *R.a* order. For each of the following relational algebra queries, state which of the following three approaches is most likely to be the cheapest:

- Access the sorted file for R directly.
- Use a (clustered) B+ tree index on attribute *R.a*.
- Use a linear hashed index on attribute *R.a*.

1. $\sigma_{a<50,000}(R)$
2. $\sigma_{a=50,000}(R)$
3. $\sigma_{a>50,000 \wedge a<50,010}(R)$
4. $\sigma_{a \neq 50,000}(R)$

Exercise 12.3 For each of the following SQL queries, for each relation involved, list the attributes that must be examined to compute the answer. All queries refer to the following relations:

Emp(*eid:* `integer`, *did:* `integer`, *sal:* `integer`, *hobby:* `char(20)`)
Dept(*did:* `integer`, *dname:* `char(20)`, *floor:* `integer`, *budget:* `real`)

1. `SELECT * FROM` Emp
2. `SELECT * FROM` Emp, Dept
3. `SELECT * FROM` Emp E, Dept D `WHERE` E.did = D.did
4. `SELECT` E.eid, D.dname `FROM` Emp E, Dept D `WHERE` E.did = D.did

Exercise 12.4 Consider the following schema with the Sailors relation:

Sailors(*sid:* `integer`, *sname:* `string`, *rating:* `integer`, *age:* `real`)

For each of the following indexes, list whether the index matches the given selection conditions. If there is a match, list the primary conjuncts.

1. A B+-tree index on the search key ⟨ Sailors.sid ⟩.
   (a) $\sigma_{Sailors.sid<50,000}(Sailors)$
   (b) $\sigma_{Sailors.sid=50,000}(Sailors)$
2. A hash index on the search key ⟨ Sailors.sid ⟩.
   (a) $\sigma_{Sailors.sid<50,000}(Sailors)$
   (b) $\sigma_{Sailors.sid=50,000}(Sailors)$
3. A B+-tree index on the search key ⟨ Sailors.sid, Sailors.age ⟩.
   (a) $\sigma_{Sailors.sid<50,000 \wedge Sailors.age=21}(Sailors)$
   (b) $\sigma_{Sailors.sid=50,000 \wedge Sailors.age>21}(Sailors)$
   (c) $\sigma_{Sailors.sid=50,000}(Sailors)$
   (d) $\sigma_{Sailors.age=21}(Sailors)$
4. A hash-tree index on the search key ⟨ Sailors.sid, Sailors.age ⟩.
   (a) $\sigma_{Sailors.sid=50,000 \wedge Sailors.age=21}(Sailors)$
   (b) $\sigma_{Sailors.sid=50,000 \wedge Sailors.age>21}(Sailors)$
   (c) $\sigma_{Sailors.sid=50,000}(Sailors)$
   (d) $\sigma_{Sailors.age=21}(Sailors)$

Exercise 12.5 Consider again the schema with the Sailors relation:

Sailors(*sid:* **integer**, *sname:* **string**, *rating:* **integer**, *age:* **real**)

Assume that each tuple of Sailors is 50 bytes long, that a page can hold 80 Sailors tuples, and that we have 500 pages of such tuples. For each of the following selection conditions, estimate the number of pages retrieved, given the catalog information in the question.

1. Assume that we have a B+-tree index T on the search key $\langle$ Sailors.sid $\rangle$, and assume that $IHeight(T) = 4$, $INPages(T) = 50$, $Low(T) = 1$, and $High(T) = 100{,}000$.

   (a) $\sigma_{Sailors.sid<50,000}(Sailors)$

   (b) $\sigma_{Sailors.sid=50,000}(Sailors)$

2. Assume that we have a hash index T on the search key $\langle$ Sailors.sid $\rangle$, and assume that $IHeight(T) = 2$, $INPages(T) = 50$, $Low(T) = 1$, and $High(T) = 100{,}000$.

   (a) $\sigma_{Sailors.sid<50,000}(Sailors)$

   (b) $\sigma_{Sailors.sid=50,000}(Sailors)$

Exercise 12.6 Consider the two join methods described in Section 12.3.3. Assume that we join two relations R and S, and that the systems catalog contains appropriate statistics about R and S. Write formulas for the cost estimates of the index nested loops join and sort-merge join using the appropriate variables from the systems catalog in Section 12.1. For index nested loops join, consider both a B+ tree index and a hash index. (For the hash index, you can assume that you can retrieve the index page containing the rid of the matching tuple with 1.2 I/Os on average.)

Note: Additional exercises on the material covered in this chapter can be found in the exercises for Chapters 14 and 15.

BIBLIOGRAPHIC NOTES

See the bibliograpic notes for Chapters 14 and 15.

13

EXTERNAL SORTING

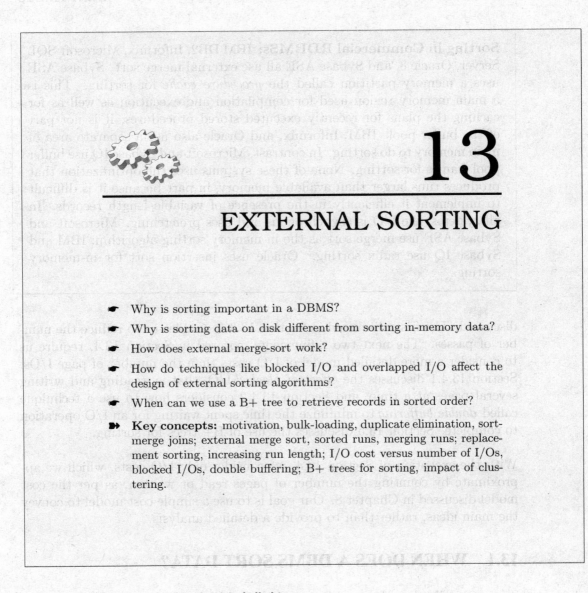

- Why is sorting important in a DBMS?
- Why is sorting data on disk different from sorting in-memory data?
- How does external merge-sort work?
- How do techniques like blocked I/O and overlapped I/O affect the design of external sorting algorithms?
- When can we use a B+ tree to retrieve records in sorted order?
- **Key concepts:** motivation, bulk-loading, duplicate elimination, sort-merge joins; external merge sort, sorted runs, merging runs; replacement sorting, increasing run length; I/O cost versus number of I/Os, blocked I/Os, double buffering; B+ trees for sorting, impact of clustering.

Good order is the foundation of all things.

—Edmund Burke

In this chapter, we consider a widely used and relatively expensive operation, sorting records according to a search key. We begin by considering the many uses of sorting in a database system in Section 13.1. We introduce the idea of external sorting by considering a very simple algorithm in Section 13.2; using repeated passes over the data, even very large datasets can be sorted with a small amount of memory. This algorithm is generalized to develop a realistic external sorting algorithm in Section 13.3. Three important refinements are

Sorting in Commercial RDBMSs: IBM DB2, Informix, Microsoft SQL Server, Oracle 8, and Sybase ASE all use external merge sort. Sybase ASE uses a memory partition called the *procedure cache* for sorting. This is a main memory region used for compilation and execution as well as for caching the plans for recently executed stored procedures; it is not part of the buffer pool. IBM, Informix, and Oracle also use a separate area of main memory to do sorting. In contrast, Microsoft and Sybase IQ use buffer pool frames for sorting. None of these systems uses the optimization that produces runs larger than available memory, in part because it is difficult to implement it efficiently in the presence of variable length records. In all systems, the I/O is asynchronous and uses prefetching. Microsoft and Sybase ASE use merge sort as the in-memory sorting algorithm; IBM and Sybase IQ use radix sorting. Oracle uses insertion sort for in-memory sorting.

discussed. The first, discussed in Section 13.3.1, enables us to reduce the number of passes. The next two refinements, covered in Section 13.4, require us to consider a more detailed model of I/O costs than the number of page I/Os. Section 13.4.1 discusses the effect of *blocked* I/O, that is, reading and writing several pages at a time; and Section 13.4.2 considers how to use a technique called *double buffering* to minimize the time spent waiting for an I/O operation to complete. Section 13.5 discusses the use of B+ trees for sorting.

With the exception of Section 13.4, we consider only I/O costs, which we approximate by counting the number of pages read or written, as per the cost model discussed in Chapter 8. Our goal is to use a simple cost model to convey the main ideas, rather than to provide a detailed analysis.

13.1 WHEN DOES A DBMS SORT DATA?

Sorting a collection of records on some (search) key is a very useful operation. The key can be a single attribute or an ordered list of attributes, of course. Sorting is required in a variety of situations, including the following important ones:

- Users may want answers in some order; for example, by increasing age (Section 5.2).
- Sorting records is the first step in *bulk loading* a tree index (Section 10.8.2).
- Sorting is useful for eliminating *duplicate* copies in a collection of records (Section 14.3).

- A widely used algorithm for performing a very important relational algebra operation, called *join*, requires a sorting step (Section 14.4.2).

Although main memory sizes are growing rapidly the ubiquity of database systems has lead to increasingly larger datasets as well. When the data to be sorted is too large to fit into available main memory, we need an *external sorting* algorithm. Such algorithms seek to minimize the cost of disk accesses.

13.2 A SIMPLE TWO-WAY MERGE SORT

We begin by presenting a simple algorithm to illustrate the idea behind external sorting. This algorithm utilizes only three pages of main memory, and it is presented only for pedagogical purposes. In practice, many more pages of memory are available, and we want our sorting algorithm to use the additional memory effectively; such an algorithm is presented in Section 13.3. When sorting a file, several sorted subfiles are typically generated in intermediate steps. In this chapter, we refer to each sorted subfile as a **run**.

Even if the entire file does not fit into the available main memory, we can sort it by breaking it into smaller subfiles, sorting these subfiles, and then merging them using a minimal amount of main memory at any given time. In the first pass, the pages in the file are read in one at a time. After a page is read in, the records on it are sorted and the sorted page (a sorted run one page long) is written out. Quicksort or any other in-memory sorting technique can be used to sort the records on a page. In subsequent passes, pairs of runs from the output of the previous pass are read in and *merged* to produce runs that are twice as long. This algorithm is shown in Figure 13.1.

If the number of pages in the input file is 2^k, for some k, then:

Pass 0 produces 2^k sorted runs of one page each,
Pass 1 produces 2^{k-1} sorted runs of two pages each,
Pass 2 produces 2^{k-2} sorted runs of four pages each,
and so on, until
Pass k produces one sorted run of 2^k pages.

In each pass, we read every page in the file, process it, and write it out. Therefore we have two disk I/Os per page, per pass. The number of passes is $\lceil log_2 N \rceil + 1$, where N is the number of pages in the file. The overall cost is $2N(\lceil log_2 N \rceil + 1)$ I/Os.

The algorithm is illustrated on an example input file containing seven pages in Figure 13.2. The sort takes four passes, and in each pass, we read and

proc *2-way_extsort* (file)
// *Given a file on disk, sorts it using three buffer pages*
// Produce runs that are one page long: Pass 0
Read each page into memory, sort it, write it out.
// Merge pairs of runs to produce longer runs until only
// one run (containing all records of input file) is left
While the number of runs at end of previous pass is > 1:
    // Pass i = 1, 2, ...
    While there are runs to be merged from previous pass:
        Choose next two runs (from previous pass).
        Read each run into an input buffer; page at a time.
        Merge the runs and write to the output buffer;
        force output buffer to disk one page at a time.

endproc

Figure 13.1 Two-Way Merge Sort

write seven pages, for a total of 56 I/Os. This result agrees with the preceding analysis because $2 \cdot 7(\lceil log_2 7 \rceil + 1) = 56$. The dark pages in the figure illustrate what would happen on a file of eight pages; the number of passes remains at four ($\lceil log_2 8 \rceil + 1 = 4$), but we read and write an additional page in each pass for a total of 64 I/Os. (Try to work out what would happen on a file with, say, five pages.)

This algorithm requires just three buffer pages in main memory, as Figure 13.3 illustrates. This observation raises an important point: Even if we have more buffer space available, this simple algorithm does not utilize it effectively. The external merge sort algorithm that we discuss next addresses this problem.

13.3 EXTERNAL MERGE SORT

Suppose that B buffer pages are available in memory and that we need to sort a large file with N pages. How can we improve on the two-way merge sort presented in the previous section? The intuition behind the generalized algorithm that we now present is to retain the basic structure of making multiple passes while trying to minimize the number of passes. There are two important modifications to the two-way merge sort algorithm:

1. In Pass 0, read in B pages at a time and sort internally to produce $\lceil N/B \rceil$ runs of B pages each (except for the last run, which may contain fewer

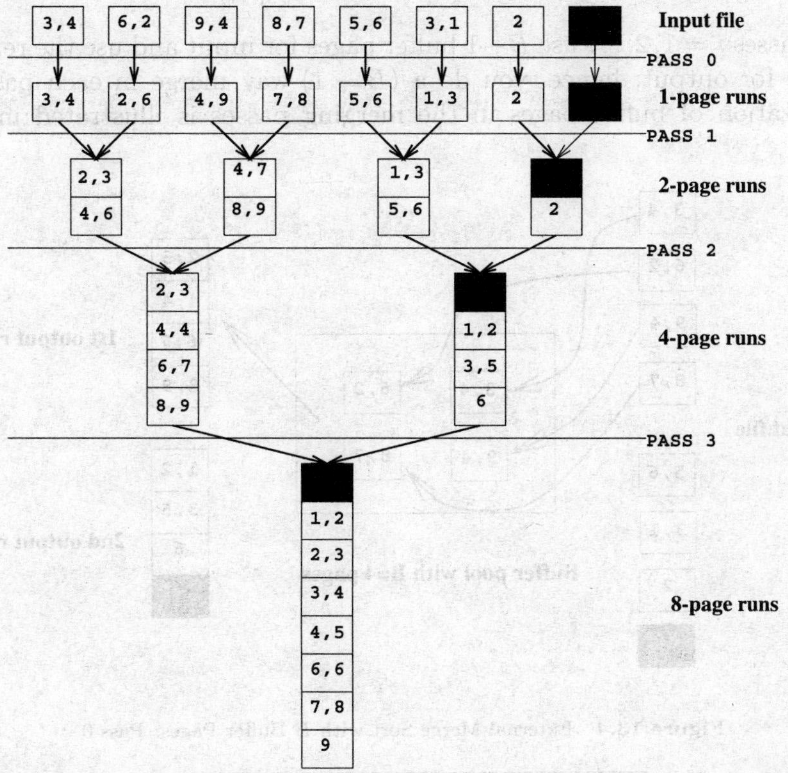

Figure 13.2 Two-Way Merge Sort of a Seven-Page File

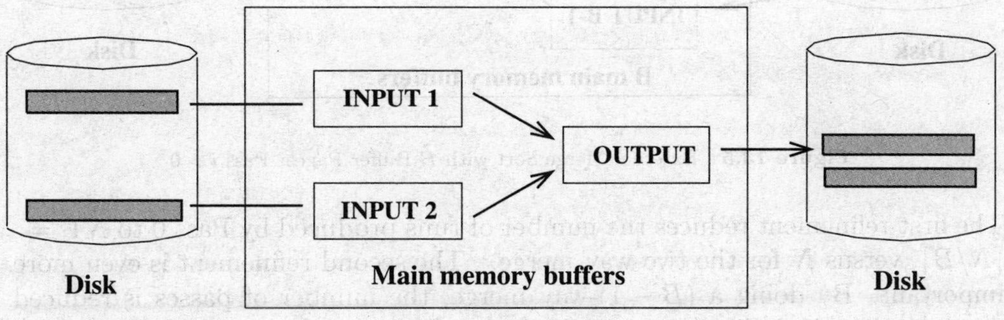

Figure 13.3 Two-Way Merge Sort with Three Buffer Pages

pages). This modification is illustrated in Figure 13.4, using the input file from Figure 13.2 and a buffer pool with four pages.

2. In passes $i = 1, 2, \ldots$ use $B-1$ buffer pages for input and use the remaining page for output; hence, you do a $(B-1)$-way merge in each pass. The utilization of buffer pages in the merging passes is illustrated in Figure 13.5.

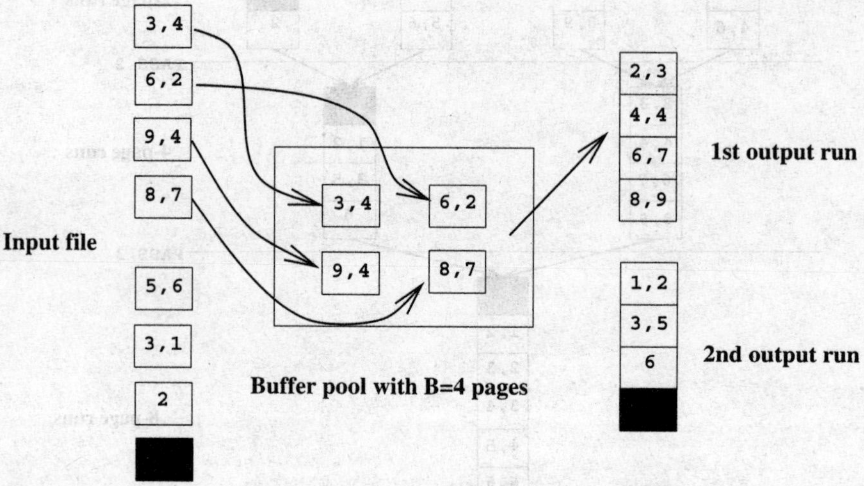

Figure 13.4 External Merge Sort with B Buffer Pages: Pass 0

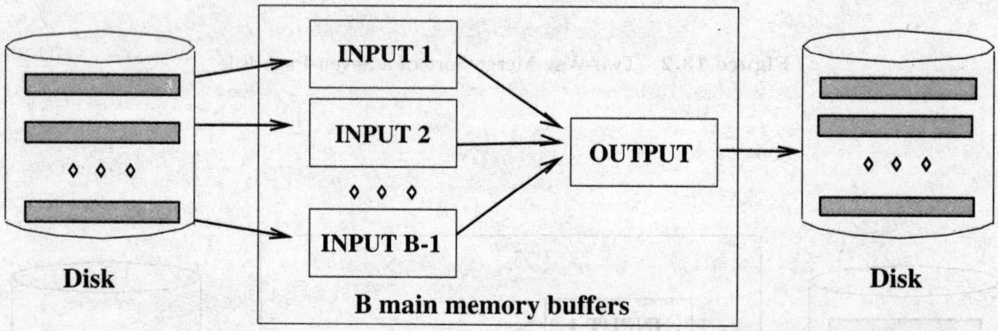

Figure 13.5 External Merge Sort with B Buffer Pages: Pass $i > 0$

The first refinement reduces the number of runs produced by Pass 0 to $N1 = \lceil N/B \rceil$, versus N for the two-way merge.[1] The second refinement is even more important. By doing a $(B-1)$-way merge, the number of passes is reduced dramatically—including the initial pass, it becomes $\lceil log_{B-1}N1 \rceil + 1$ versus $\lceil log_2 N \rceil + 1$ for the two-way merge algorithm presented earlier. Because B is

[1]Note that the technique used for sorting data in buffer pages is orthogonal to external sorting. You could use, say, Quicksort for sorting data in buffer pages.

typically quite large, the savings can be substantial. The external merge sort algorithm is shown is Figure 13.6.

proc *extsort* (file)
// *Given a file on disk, sorts it using three buffer pages*
// Produce runs that are B pages long: Pass 0
Read B pages into memory, sort them, write out a run.
// Merge $B - 1$ runs at a time to produce longer runs until only
// one run (containing all records of input file) is left
While the number of runs at end of previous pass is > 1:
  // Pass $i = 1, 2, \ldots$
  While there are runs to be merged from previous pass:
    Choose next $B - 1$ runs (from previous pass).
    Read each run into an input buffer; page at a time.
    Merge the runs and write to the output buffer;
    force output buffer to disk one page at a time.
endproc

Figure 13.6 External Merge Sort

As an example, suppose that we have five buffer pages available and want to sort a file with 108 pages.

Pass 0 produces $\lceil 108/5 \rceil = 22$ sorted runs of five pages each, except for the last run, which is only three pages long.
Pass 1 does a four-way merge to produce $\lceil 22/4 \rceil$ = six sorted runs of 20 pages each, except for the last run, which is only eight pages long.
Pass 2 produces $\lceil 6/4 \rceil$ = two sorted runs; one with 80 pages and one with 28 pages.
Pass 3 merges the two runs produced in Pass 2 to produce the sorted file.

In each pass we read and write 108 pages; thus the total cost is $2*108*4 = 864$ I/Os. Applying our formula, we have $N1 = \lceil 108/5 \rceil = 22$ and cost $= 2 * N * (\lceil log_{B-1} N1 \rceil + 1) = 2 * 108 * (\lceil log_4 22 \rceil + 1) = 864$, as expected.

To emphasize the potential gains in using all available buffers, in Figure 13.7, we show the number of passes, computed using our formula, for several values of N and B. To obtain the cost, the number of passes should be multiplied by $2N$. In practice, one would expect to have more than 257 buffers, but this table illustrates the importance of a high fan-in during merging.

N	$B = 3$	$B = 5$	$B = 9$	$B = 17$	$B = 129$	$B = 257$
100	7	4	3	2	1	1
1000	10	5	4	3	2	2
10,000	13	7	5	4	2	2
100,000	17	9	6	5	3	3
1,000,000	20	10	7	5	3	3
10,000,000	23	12	8	6	4	3
100,000,000	26	14	9	7	4	4
1,000,000,000	30	15	10	8	5	4

Figure 13.7 Number of Passes of External Merge Sort

Of course, the CPU cost of a multiway merge can be greater than that for a two-way merge, but in general the I/O costs tend to dominate. In doing a $(B - 1)$-way merge, we have to repeatedly pick the 'lowest' record in the $B - 1$ runs being merged and write it to the output buffer. This operation can be implemented simply by examining the first (remaining) element in each of the $B - 1$ input buffers. In practice, for large values of B, more sophisticated techniques can be used, although we do not discuss them here. Further, as we will see shortly, there are other ways to utilize buffer pages to reduce I/O costs; these techniques involve allocating additional pages to each input (and output) run, thereby making the number of runs merged in each pass considerably smaller than the number of buffer pages B.

13.3.1 Minimizing the Number of Runs

In Pass 0 we read in B pages at a time and sort them internally to produce $\lceil N/B \rceil$ runs of B pages each (except for the last run, which may contain fewer pages). With a more aggressive implementation, called **replacement sort**, we can write out runs of approximately $2 \cdot B$ internally sorted pages on average. This improvement is achieved as follows. We begin by reading in pages of the file of tuples to be sorted, say R, until the buffer is full, reserving (say) one page for use as an input buffer and one page for use as an output buffer. We refer to the $B - 2$ pages of R tuples that are not in the input or output buffer as the *current set*. Suppose that the file is to be sorted in ascending order on some search key k. Tuples are appended to the output in ascending order by k value.

The idea is to repeatedly pick the tuple in the current set with the smallest k value that is still greater than the largest k value in the output buffer and append it to the output buffer. For the output buffer to remain sorted, the chosen tuple must satisfy the condition that its k value be greater than or equal to the largest k value currently in the output buffer; of all tuples in the current set that satisfy this condition, we pick the one with the smallest k value and append it to the output buffer. Moving this tuple to the output buffer creates some space in the current set, which we use to add the next input tuple to the current set. (We assume for simplicity that all tuples are the same size.) This process is illustrated in Figure 13.8. The tuple in the current set that is going to be appended to the output next is highlighted, as is the most recently appended output tuple.

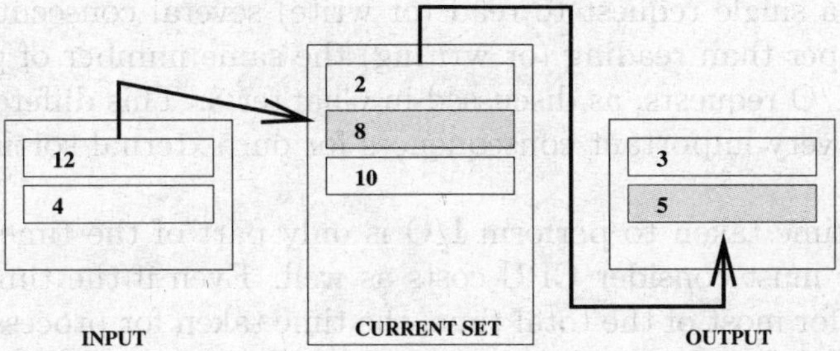

Figure 13.8 Generating Longer Runs

When all tuples in the input buffer have been consumed in this manner, the next page of the file is read in. Of course, the output buffer is written out when it is full, thereby extending the current run (which is gradually built up on disk).

The important question is this: When do we have to terminate the current run and start a new run? As long as some tuple t in the current set has a bigger k value than the most recently appended output tuple, we can append t to the output buffer and the current run can be extended.[2] In Figure 13.8, although a tuple ($k = 2$) in the current set has a smaller k value than the largest output tuple ($k = 5$), the current run can be extended because the current set also has a tuple ($k = 8$) that is larger than the largest output tuple.

When every tuple in the current set is smaller than the largest tuple in the output buffer, the output buffer is written out and becomes the last page in the current run. We then start a new run and continue the cycle of writing tuples from the input buffer to the current set to the output buffer. It is known that this algorithm produces runs that are about $2 \cdot B$ pages long, on average.

This refinement has not been implemented in commercial database systems because managing the main memory available for sorting becomes difficult with

[2]If B is large, the CPU cost of finding such a tuple t can be significant unless appropriate in-memory data structures are used to organize the tuples in the buffer pool. We will not discuss this issue further.

replacement sort, especially in the presence of variable length records. Recent work on this issue, however, shows promise and it could lead to the use of replacement sort in commercial systems.

13.4 MINIMIZING I/O COST VERSUS NUMBER OF I/OS

We have thus far used the number of page I/Os as a cost metric. This metric is only an approximation of true I/O costs because it ignores the effect of *blocked* I/O—issuing a single request to read (or write) several consecutive pages can be much cheaper than reading (or writing) the same number of pages through independent I/O requests, as discussed in Chapter 8. This difference turns out to have some very important consequences for our external sorting algorithm.

Further, the time taken to perform I/O is only part of the time taken by the algorithm; we must consider CPU costs as well. Even if the time taken to do I/O accounts for most of the total time, the time taken for processing records is nontrivial and definitely worth reducing. In particular, we can use a technique called *double buffering* to keep the CPU busy while an I/O operation is in progress.

In this section, we consider how the external sorting algorithm can be refined using blocked I/O and double buffering. The motivation for these optimizations requires us to look beyond the number of I/Os as a cost metric. These optimizations can also be applied to other I/O intensive operations such as joins, which we study in Chapter 14.

13.4.1 Blocked I/O

If the number of page I/Os is taken to be the cost metric, the goal is clearly to minimize the number of passes in the sorting algorithm because each page in the file is read and written in each pass. It therefore makes sense to maximize the fan-in during merging by allocating just one buffer pool page per run (which is to be merged) and one buffer page for the output of the merge. Thus, we can merge $B-1$ runs, where B is the number of pages in the buffer pool. If we take into account the effect of blocked access, which reduces the average cost to read or write *a single page*, we are led to consider whether it might be better to read and write in units of more than one page.

Suppose we decide to read and write in units, which we call **buffer blocks**, of b pages. We must now set aside one buffer block per input run and one buffer block for the output of the merge, which means that we can merge at most $\lfloor \frac{B-b}{b} \rfloor$ runs in each pass. For example, if we have 10 buffer pages, we can either merge nine runs at a time with one-page input and output buffer blocks, or we can merge four runs at a time with two-page input and output buffer blocks. If we choose larger buffer blocks, however, the number of passes increases, while we continue to read and write every page in the file in each pass! In the example, each merging pass reduces the number of runs by a factor of 4, rather than a factor of 9. Therefore, the number of page I/Os increases. This is the price we pay for decreasing the per-page I/O cost and is a trade-off we must take into account when designing an external sorting algorithm.

In practice, however, current main memory sizes are large enough that all but the largest files can be sorted in just two passes, even using blocked I/O. Suppose we have B buffer pages and choose to use a blocking factor of b pages. That is, we read and write b pages at a time, and all our input and output buffer blocks are b pages long. The first pass produces about $N2 = \lceil N/2B \rceil$ sorted runs, each of length $2B$ pages, if we use the optimization described in Section 13.3.1, and about $N1 = \lceil N/B \rceil$ sorted runs, each of length B pages, otherwise. For the purposes of this section, we assume that the optimization is used.

In subsequent passes we can merge $F = \lfloor B/b \rfloor - 1$ runs at a time. The number of passes is therefore $1 + \lceil log_F N2 \rceil$, and in each pass we read and write all pages in the file. Figure 13.9 shows the number of passes needed to sort files of various sizes N, given B buffer pages, using a blocking factor b of 32 pages. It is quite reasonable to expect 5000 pages to be available for sorting purposes; with 4KB pages, 5000 pages is only 20MB. (With 50,000 buffer pages, we can do 1561-way merges; with 10,000 buffer pages, we can do 311-way merges; with 5000 buffer pages, we can do 155-way merges; and with 1000 buffer pages, we can do 30-way merges.)

N	$B=1000$	$B=5000$	$B=10,000$	$B=50,000$
100	1	1	1	1
1000	1	1	1	1
10,000	2	2	1	1
100,000	3	2	2	2
1,000,000	3	2	2	2
10,000,000	4	3	3	2
100,000,000	5	3	3	2
1,000,000,000	5	4	3	3

Figure 13.9 Number of Passes of External Merge Sort with Block Size $b = 32$

To compute the I/O cost, we need to calculate the number of 32-page blocks read or written and multiply this number by the cost of doing a 32-page block I/O. To find the number of block I/Os, we can find the total number of page

I/Os (number of passes multiplied by the number of pages in the file) and divide by the block size, 32. The cost of a 32-page block I/O is the seek time and rotational delay for the first page, plus transfer time for all 32 pages, as discussed in Chapter 8. The reader is invited to calculate the total I/O cost of sorting files of the sizes mentioned in Figure 13.9 with 5000 buffer pages for different block sizes (say, $b = 1$, 32, and 64) to get a feel for the benefits of using blocked I/O.

13.4.2 Double Buffering

Consider what happens in the external sorting algorithm when all the tuples in an input block have been consumed: An I/O request is issued for the next block of tuples in the corresponding input run, and the execution is forced to suspend until the I/O is complete. That is, for the duration of the time taken for reading in one block, the CPU remains idle (assuming that no other jobs are running). The overall time taken by an algorithm can be increased considerably because the CPU is repeatedly forced to wait for an I/O operation to complete. This effect becomes more and more important as CPU speeds increase relative to I/O speeds, which is a long-standing trend in relative speeds. It is therefore desirable to keep the CPU busy while an I/O request is being carried out; that is, to overlap CPU and I/O processing. Current hardware supports such overlapped computation, and it is therefore desirable to design algorithms to take advantage of this capability.

In the context of external sorting, we can achieve this overlap by allocating extra pages to each input buffer. Suppose a block size of $b = 32$ is chosen. The idea is to allocate an additional 32-page block to every input (and the output) buffer. Now, when all the tuples in a 32-page block have been consumed, the CPU can process the next 32 pages of the run by switching to the second, 'double,' block for this run. Meanwhile, an I/O request is issued to fill the empty block. Thus, assuming that the time to consume a block is greater than the time to read in a block, the CPU is never idle! On the other hand, the number of pages allocated to a buffer is doubled (for a given block size, which means the total I/O cost stays the same). This technique, called **double buffering**, can considerably reduce the total time taken to sort a file. The use of buffer pages is illustrated in Figure 13.10.

Note that although double buffering can considerably reduce the response time for a given query, it may not have a significant impact on throughput, because the CPU can be kept busy by working on other queries while waiting for one query's I/O operation to complete.

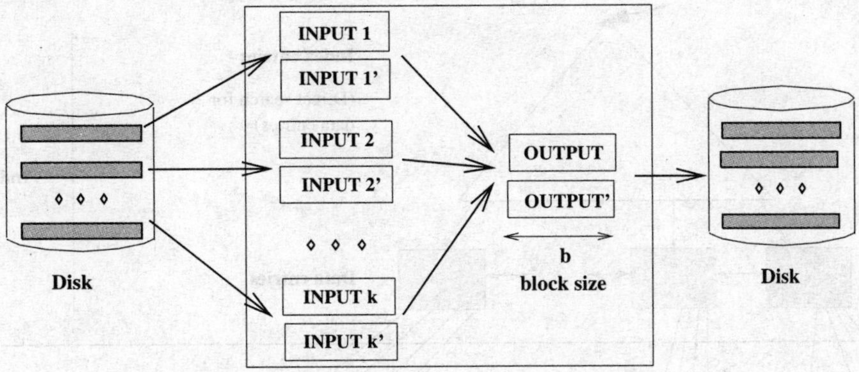

Figure 13.10 Double Buffering

13.5 USING B+ TREES FOR SORTING

Suppose that we have a B+ tree index on the (search) key to be used for sorting a file of records. Instead of using an external sorting algorithm, we could use the B+ tree index to retrieve the records in search key order by traversing the sequence set (i.e., the sequence of leaf pages). Whether this is a good strategy depends on the nature of the index.

13.5.1 Clustered Index

If the B+ tree index is clustered, then the traversal of the sequence set is very efficient. The search key order corresponds to the order in which the data records are stored, and for each page of data records we retrieve, we can read all the records on it in sequence. This correspondence between search key ordering and data record ordering is illustrated in Figure 13.11, with the assumption that data entries are ⟨*key, rid*⟩ pairs (i.e., Alternative (2) is used for data entries).

The cost of using the clustered B+ tree index to retrieve the data records in search key order is the cost to traverse the tree from root to the left-most leaf (which is usually less than four I/Os) plus the cost of retrieving the pages in the sequence set, plus the cost of retrieving the (say, N) pages containing the data records. Note that no data page is retrieved twice, thanks to the ordering of data entries being the same as the ordering of data records. The number of pages in the sequence set is likely to be much smaller than the number of data pages because data entries are likely to be smaller than typical data records. Thus, the strategy of using a clustered B+ tree index to retrieve the records in sorted order is a good one and should be used whenever such an index is available.

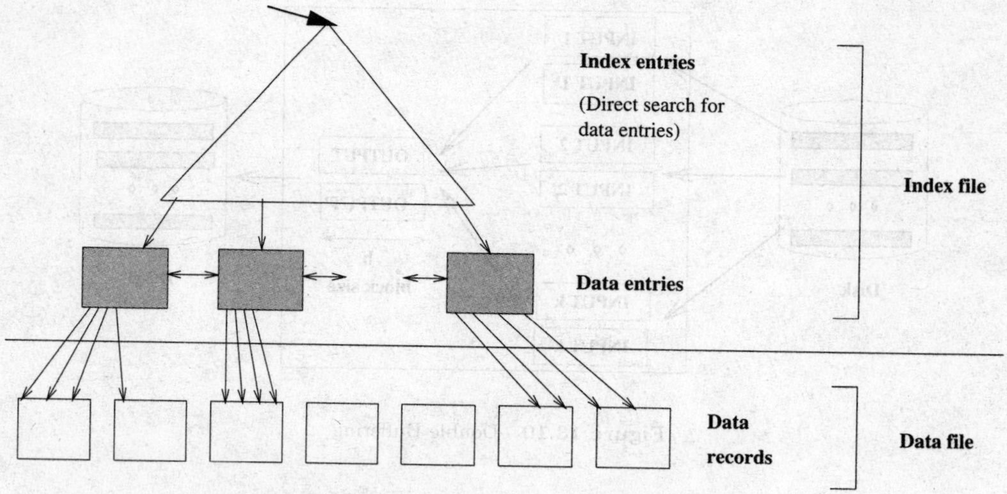

Figure 13.11 Clustered B+ Tree for Sorting

What if Alternative (1) is used for data entries? Then, the leaf pages would contain the actual data records, and retrieving the pages in the sequence set (a total of N pages) would be the only cost. (Note that the space utilization is about 67% in a B+ tree; the number of leaf pages is greater than the number of pages needed to hold the data records in a sorted file, where, in principle, 100% space utilization can be achieved.) In this case, the choice of the B+ tree for sorting is excellent!

13.5.2 Unclustered Index

What if the B+ tree index on the key to be used for sorting is unclustered? This is illustrated in Figure 13.12, with the assumption that data entries are $\langle key, rid \rangle$.

In this case each rid in a leaf page could point to a different data page. Should this happen, the cost (in disk I/Os) of retrieving all data records could equal the number of data records. That is, the worst-case cost is equal to the number of data records, because fetching each record could require a disk I/O. This cost is in addition to the cost of retrieving leaf pages of the B+ tree to get the data entries (which point to the data records).

If p is the average number of records per data page and there are N data pages, the number of data records is $p \cdot N$. If we take f to be the ratio of the size of a data entry to the size of a data record, we can approximate the number of leaf pages in the tree by $f \cdot N$. The total cost of retrieving records in sorted order

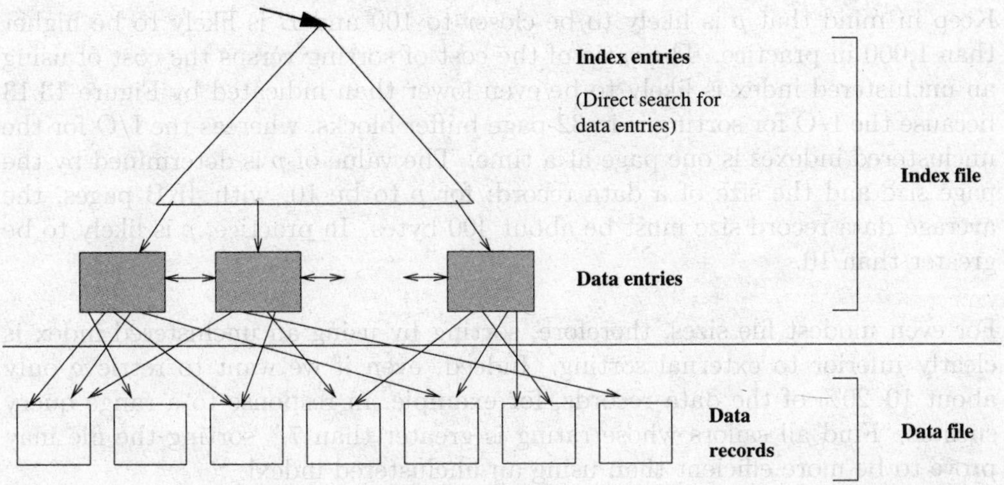

Figure 13.12 Unclustered B+ Tree for Sorting

using an unclustered B+ tree is therefore $(f + p) \cdot N$. Since f is usually 0.1 or smaller and p is typically much larger than 10, $p \cdot N$ is a good approximation.

In practice, the cost may be somewhat less because some rids in a leaf page lead to the same data page, and further, some pages are found in the buffer pool, thereby avoiding an I/O. Nonetheless, the usefulness of an unclustered B+ tree index for sorted retrieval highly depends on the extent to which the order of data entries corresponds and—this is just a matter of chance—to the physical ordering of data records.

We illustrate the cost of sorting a file of records using external sorting and unclustered B+ tree indexes in Figure 13.13. The costs shown for the unclustered index are worst-case numbers, based on the approximate formula $p \cdot N$. For comparison, note that the cost for a clustered index is approximately equal to N, the number of pages of data records.

N	Sorting	$p = 1$	$p = 10$	$p = 100$
100	200	100	1000	10,000
1000	2000	1000	10,000	100,000
10,000	40,000	10,000	100,000	1,000,000
100,000	600,000	100,000	1,000,000	10,000,000
1,000,000	8,000,000	1,000,000	10,000,000	100,000,000
10,000,000	80,000,000	10,000,000	100,000,000	1,000,000,000

Figure 13.13 Cost of External Sorting ($B = 1000, b = 32$) versus Unclustered Index

Keep in mind that p is likely to be closer to 100 and B is likely to be higher than 1,000 in practice. The ratio of the cost of sorting versus the cost of using an unclustered index is likely to be even lower than indicated by Figure 13.13 because the I/O for sorting is in 32-page buffer blocks, whereas the I/O for the unclustered indexes is one page at a time. The value of p is determined by the page size and the size of a data record; for p to be 10, with 4KB pages, the average data record size must be about 400 bytes. In practice, p is likely to be greater than 10.

For even modest file sizes, therefore, sorting by using an unclustered index is clearly inferior to external sorting. Indeed, even if we want to retrieve only about 10–20% of the data records, for example, in response to a range query such as "Find all sailors whose rating is greater than 7," sorting the file may prove to be more efficient than using an unclustered index!

13.6 REVIEW QUESTIONS

Answers to the review questions can be found in the listed sections.

- What database operations utilize sorting? **(Section 13.1)**
- Describe how the *two-way merge sort* algorithm can sort a file of arbitrary length using only three main-memory pages at any time. Explain what a *run* is and how runs are created and merged. Discuss the cost of the algorithm in terms of the number of *passes* and the I/O cost per pass. **(Section 13.2)**
- How does the general *external merge sort* algorithm improve upon the two-way merge sort? Discuss the length of initial runs, and how memory is utilized in subsequent merging passes. Discuss the cost of the algorithm in terms of the number of passes and the I/O cost per pass. **(Section 13.3)**
- Discuss the use of *replacement sort* to increase the average length of initial runs and thereby reduce the number of runs to be merged. How does this affect the cost of external sorting? **(Section 13.3.1)**
- What is *blocked I/O*? Why is it cheaper to read a sequence of pages using blocked I/O than to read them through several independent requests? How does the use of blocking affect the external sorting algorithm, and how does it change the cost formula? **(Section 13.4.1)**
- What is *double buffering*? What is the motivation for using it? **(Section 13.4.2)**
- If we want to sort a file and there is a B+ tree with the same search key, we have the option of retrieving records in order through the index. Compare

the cost of this approach to retrieving the records in random order and then sorting them. Consider both clustered and unclustered B+ trees. What conclusions can you draw from your comparison? **(Section 13.5)**

EXERCISES

Exercise 13.1 Suppose you have a file with 10,000 pages and you have three buffer pages. Answer the following questions for each of these scenarios, assuming that our most general external sorting algorithm is used:

(a) A file with 10,000 pages and three available buffer pages.

(b) A file with 20,000 pages and five available buffer pages.

(c) A file with 2,000,000 pages and 17 available buffer pages.

1. How many runs will you produce in the first pass?
2. How many passes will it take to sort the file completely?
3. What is the total I/O cost of sorting the file?
4. How many buffer pages do you need to sort the file completely in just two passes?

Exercise 13.2 Answer Exercise 13.1 assuming that a two-way external sort is used.

Exercise 13.3 Suppose that you just finished inserting several records into a heap file and now want to sort those records. Assume that the DBMS uses external sort and makes efficient use of the available buffer space when it sorts a file. Here is some potentially useful information about the newly loaded file and the DBMS software available to operate on it:

> The number of records in the file is 4500. The sort key for the file is 4 bytes long. You can assume that rids are 8 bytes long and page ids are 4 bytes long. Each record is a total of 48 bytes long. The page size is 512 bytes. Each page has 12 bytes of control information on it. Four buffer pages are available.

1. How many sorted subfiles will there be after the initial pass of the sort, and how long will each subfile be?
2. How many passes (including the initial pass just considered) are required to sort this file?
3. What is the total I/O cost for sorting this file?
4. What is the largest file, in terms of the number of records, you can sort with just four buffer pages in two passes? How would your answer change if you had 257 buffer pages?
5. Suppose that you have a B+ tree index with the search key being the same as the desired sort key. Find the cost of using the index to retrieve the records in sorted order for each of the following cases:
   - The index uses Alternative (1) for data entries.
   - The index uses Alternative (2) and is unclustered. (You can compute the worst-case cost in this case.)

- How would the costs of using the index change if the file is the largest that you can sort in two passes of external sort with 257 buffer pages? Give your answer for both clustered and unclustered indexes.

Exercise 13.4 Consider a disk with an average seek time of 10ms, average rotational delay of 5ms, and a transfer time of 1ms for a 4K page. Assume that the cost of reading/writing a page is the sum of these values (i.e., 16ms) unless a *sequence* of pages is read/written. In this case, the cost is the average seek time plus the average rotational delay (to find the first page in the sequence) plus 1ms per page (to transfer data). You are given 320 buffer pages and asked to sort a file with 10,000,000 pages.

1. Why is it a bad idea to use the 320 pages to support virtual memory, that is, to 'new' 10,000,000 · 4K bytes of memory, and to use an in-memory sorting algorithm such as Quicksort?
2. Assume that you begin by creating sorted runs of 320 pages each in the first pass. Evaluate the cost of the following approaches for the subsequent merging passes:
   (a) Do 319-way merges.
   (b) Create 256 'input' buffers of 1 page each, create an 'output' buffer of 64 pages, and do 256-way merges.
   (c) Create 16 'input' buffers of 16 pages each, create an 'output' buffer of 64 pages, and do 16-way merges.
   (d) Create eight 'input' buffers of 32 pages each, create an 'output' buffer of 64 pages, and do eight-way merges.
   (e) Create four 'input' buffers of 64 pages each, create an 'output' buffer of 64 pages, and do four-way merges.

Exercise 13.5 Consider the refinement to the external sort algorithm that produces runs of length $2B$ on average, where B is the number of buffer pages. This refinement was described in Section 11.2.1 under the assumption that all records are the same size. Explain why this assumption is required and extend the idea to cover the case of variable-length records.

PROJECT-BASED EXERCISES

Exercise 13.6 (*Note to instructors: Additional details must be provided if this exercise is assigned; see Appendix 30.*) Implement external sorting in Minibase.

BIBLIOGRAPHIC NOTES

Knuth's text [442] is the classic reference for sorting algorithms. Memory management for replacement sort is discussed in [471]. A number of papers discuss parallel external sorting algorithms, including [66, 71, 223, 494, 566, 647].

14 EVALUATING RELATIONAL OPERATORS

- What are the alternative algorithms for selection? Which alternatives are best under different conditions? How are complex selection conditions handled?
- How can we eliminate duplicates in projection? How do sorting and hashing approaches compare?
- What are the alternative join evaluation algorithms? Which alternatives are best under different conditions?
- How are the set operations (union, intersection, set-difference, cross-product) implemented?
- How are aggregate operations and grouping handled?
- How does the size of the buffer pool and the buffer replacement policy affect algorithms for evaluating relational operators?
- **Key concepts:** selections, CNF; projections, sorting versus hashing; joins, block nested loops, index nested loops, sort-merge, hash; union, set-difference, duplicate elimination; aggregate operations, running information, partitioning into groups, using indexes; buffer management, concurrent execution, repeated access patterns

Now, *here*, you see, it takes all the running you can do, to keep in the same place. If you want to get somewhere else, you must run at least twice as fast as that!

—Lewis Carroll, *Through the Looking Glass*

In this chapter, we consider the implementation of individual relational operators in sufficient detail to understand how DBMSs are implemented. The discussion builds on the foundation laid in Chapter 12. We present implementation alternatives for the selection operator in Sections 14.1 and 14.2. It is instructive to see the variety of alternatives and the wide variation in performance of these alternatives, for even such a simple operator. In Section 14.3, we consider the other unary operator in relational algebra, projection.

We then discuss the implementation of binary operators, beginning with joins in Section 14.4. Joins are among the most expensive operators in a relational database system, and their implementation has a big impact on performance. After discussing the join operator, we consider implementation of the binary operators cross-product, intersection, union, and set-difference in Section 14.5. We discuss the implementation of grouping and aggregate operators, which are extensions of relational algebra, in Section 14.6. We conclude with a discussion of how buffer management affects operator evaluation costs in Section 14.7.

The discussion of each operator is largely independent of the discussion of other operators. Several alternative implementation techniques are presented for each operator; the reader who wishes to cover this material in less depth can skip some of these alternatives without loss of continuity.

Preliminaries: Examples and Cost Calculations

We present a number of example queries using the same schema as in Chapter 12:

Sailors(*sid:* `integer`, *sname:* `string`, *rating:* `integer`, *age:* `real`)
Reserves(*sid:* `integer`, *bid:* `integer`, *day:* `dates`, *rname:* `string`)

This schema is a variant of the one that we used in Chapter 5; we added a string field *rname* to Reserves. Intuitively, this field is the name of the person who made the reservation (and may be different from the name of the sailor *sid* for whom the reservation was made; a reservation may be made by a person who is not a sailor on behalf of a sailor). The addition of this field gives us more flexibility in choosing illustrative examples. We assume that each tuple of Reserves is 40 bytes long, that a page can hold 100 Reserves tuples, and that we have 1000 pages of such tuples. Similarly, we assume that each tuple of Sailors is 50 bytes long, that a page can hold 80 Sailors tuples, and that we have 500 pages of such tuples.

Two points must be kept in mind to understand our discussion of costs:

- As discussed in Chapter 8, we consider only I/O costs and measure I/O cost in terms of the number of page I/Os. We also use big-O notation to express the complexity of an algorithm in terms of an input parameter and assume that the reader is familiar with this notation. For example, the cost of a file scan is $O(M)$, where M is the size of the file.
- We discuss several alternate algorithms for each operation. Since each alternative incurs the same cost in writing out the result, should this be necessary, we uniformly ignore this cost in comparing alternatives.

14.1 THE SELECTION OPERATION

In this section, we describe various algorithms to evaluate the selection operator. To motivate the discussion, consider the selection query shown in Figure 14.1, which has the selection condition *rname='Joe'*.

```
SELECT *
FROM   Reserves R
WHERE  R.rname='Joe'
```

Figure 14.1 Simple Selection Query

We can evaluate this query by scanning the entire relation, checking the condition on each tuple, and adding the tuple to the result if the condition is satisfied. The cost of this approach is 1000 I/Os, since Reserves contains 1000 pages. If only a few tuples have *rname='Joe'*, this approach is expensive because it does not utilize the selection to reduce the number of tuples retrieved in any way. How can we improve on this approach? The key is to utilize information in the selection condition and use an index if a suitable index is available. For example, a B+ tree index on *rname* could be used to answer this query considerably faster, but an index on *bid* would not be useful.

In the rest of this section, we consider various situations with respect to the file organization used for the relation and the availability of indexes and discuss appropriate algorithms for the selection operation. We discuss only simple selection operations of the form $\sigma_{R.attr\ \mathbf{op}\ value}(R)$ until Section 14.2, where we consider general selections. In terms of the general techniques listed in Section 12.2, the algorithms for selection use either iteration or indexing.

14.1.1 No Index, Unsorted Data

Given a selection of the form $\sigma_{R.attr\ \mathbf{op}\ value}(R)$, if there is no index on *R.attr* and R is not sorted on *R.attr*, we have to scan the entire relation. Therefore, the most selective access path is a file scan. For each tuple, we must test the condition *R.attr* **op** *value* and add the tuple to the result if the condition is satisfied.

14.1.2 No Index, Sorted Data

Given a selection of the form $\sigma_{R.attr\ \mathbf{op}\ value}(R)$, if there is no index on *R.attr*, but *R* is physically sorted on *R.attr*, we can utilize the sort order by doing a binary search to locate the first tuple that satisfies the selection condition. Further, we can then retrieve all tuples that satisfy the selection condition by starting at this location and scanning *R* until the selection condition is no longer satisfied. The access method in this case is a sorted-file scan with selection condition $\sigma_{R.attr\ \mathbf{op}\ value}(R)$.

For example, suppose that the selection condition is $R.attr1 > 5$, and that *R* is sorted on *attr*1 in ascending order. After a binary search to locate the position in *R* corresponding to 5, we simply scan all remaining records.

The cost of the binary search is $O(log_2 M)$. In addition, we have the cost of the scan to retrieve qualifying tuples. The cost of the scan depends on the number of such tuples and can vary from zero to *M*. In our selection from Reserves (Figure 14.1), the cost of the binary search is $log_2 1000 \approx 10$ I/Os.

In practice, it is unlikely that a relation will be kept sorted if the DBMS supports Alternative (1) for index data entries; that is, allows data records to be stored as index data entries. If the ordering of data records is important, a better way to maintain it is through a B+ tree index that uses Alternative (1).

14.1.3 B+ Tree Index

If a clustered B+ tree index is available on *R.attr*, the best strategy for selection conditions $\sigma_{R.attr\ \mathbf{op}\ value}(R)$ in which **op** is not equality is to use the index. This strategy is also a good access path for equality selections, although a hash index on *R.attr* would be a little better. If the B+ tree index is not clustered, the cost of using the index depends on the number of tuples that satisfy the selection, as discussed later.

We can use the index as follows: We search the tree to find the first index entry that points to a qualifying tuple of *R*. Then we scan the leaf pages of the index to retrieve all entries in which the key value satisfies the selection condition. For each of these entries, we retrieve the corresponding tuple of *R*. (For concreteness in this discussion, we assume that data entries use Alternatives (2) or (3); if Alternative (1) is used, the data entry contains the actual tuple and there is no additional cost—beyond the cost of retrieving data entries—for retrieving tuples.)

The cost of identifying the starting leaf page for the scan is typically two or three I/Os. The cost of scanning the leaf level page for qualifying data entries depends on the number of such entries. The cost of retrieving qualifying tuples from R depends on two factors:

- The number of qualifying tuples.
- Whether the index is clustered. (Clustered and unclustered B+ tree indexes are illustrated in Figures 13.11 and 13.12. The figures should give the reader a feel for the impact of clustering, regardless of the type of index involved.)

If the index is clustered, the cost of retrieving qualifying tuples is probably just one page I/O (since it is likely that all such tuples are contained in a single page). If the index is not clustered, each index entry could point to a qualifying tuple on a different page, and the cost of retrieving qualifying tuples in a straightforward way could be one page I/O per qualifying tuple (unless we get lucky with buffering). We can significantly reduce the number of I/Os to retrieve qualifying tuples from R by first sorting the rids (in the index's data entries) by their *page-id* component. This sort ensures that, when we bring in a page of R, all qualifying tuples on this page are retrieved one after the other. The cost of retrieving qualifying tuples is now the number of pages of R that contain qualifying tuples.

Consider a selection of the form *rname* < *'C%'* on the Reserves relation. Assuming that names are uniformly distributed with respect to the initial letter, for simplicity, we estimate that roughly 10% of Reserves tuples are in the result. This is a total of 10,000 tuples, or 100 pages. If we have a clustered B+ tree index on the *rname* field of Reserves, we can retrieve the qualifying tuples with 100 I/Os (plus a few I/Os to traverse from the root to the appropriate leaf page to start the scan). However, if the index is unclustered, we could have up to 10,000 I/Os in the worst case, since each tuple could cause us to read a page. If we sort the rids of Reserves tuples by the page number and then retrieve pages of Reserves, we avoid retrieving the same page multiple times; nonetheless, the tuples to be retrieved are likely to be scattered across many more than 100 pages. Therefore, the use of an unclustered index for a range selection could be expensive; it might be cheaper to simply scan the entire relation (which is 1000 pages in our example).

14.1.4 Hash Index, Equality Selection

If a hash index is available on *R.attr* and **op** is equality, the best way to implement the selection $\sigma_{R.attr\ \mathbf{op}\ value}(R)$ is obviously to use the index to retrieve qualifying tuples.

The cost includes a few (typically one or two) I/Os to retrieve the appropriate bucket page in the index, plus the cost of retrieving qualifying tuples from *R*. The cost of retrieving qualifying tuples from *R* depends on the number of such tuples and on whether the index is clustered. Since **op** is equality, there is exactly one qualifying tuple if *R.attr* is a (candidate) key for the relation. Otherwise, we could have several tuples with the same value in this attribute.

Consider the selection in Figure 14.1. Suppose that there is an unclustered hash index on the *rname* attribute, that we have 10 buffer pages, and that 100 reservations were made by people named Joe. The cost of retrieving the index page containing the rids of such reservations is one or two I/Os. The cost of retrieving the 100 Reserves tuples can vary between 1 and 100, depending on how these records are distributed across pages of Reserves and the order in which we retrieve these records. If these 100 records are contained in, say, some five pages of Reserves, we have just five additional I/Os if we sort the rids by their page component. Otherwise, it is possible that we bring in one of these five pages, then look at some of the other pages, and find that the first page has been paged out when we need it again. (Remember that several users and DBMS operations share the buffer pool.) This situation could cause us to retrieve the same page several times.

14.2 GENERAL SELECTION CONDITIONS

In our discussion of the selection operation thus far, we have considered selection conditions of the form $\sigma_{R.attr\ \mathbf{op}\ value}(R)$. In general, a selection condition is a Boolean combination (i.e., an expression using the logical connectives $\wedge$ and $\vee$) of **terms** that have the form *attribute* **op** *constant* or *attribute1* **op** *attribute2*. For example, if the `WHERE` clause in the query shown in Figure 14.1 contained the condition *R.rname='Joe'* `AND` *R.bid=r*, the equivalent algebra expression would be $\sigma_{R.rname='Joe' \wedge R.bid=r}(R)$.

In Section 14.2.1, we provide a more rigorous definition of CNF, which we introduced in Section 12.2.2. We consider algorithms for applying selection conditions without disjunction in Section 14.2.2 and then discuss conditions with disjunction in Section 14.2.3.

14.2.1 CNF and Index Matching

To process a selection operation with a general selection condition, we first express the condition in **conjunctive normal form (CNF)**, that is, as a collection of *conjuncts* that are connected through the use of the $\wedge$ operator. Each **conjunct** consists of one or more *terms* (of the form described previously) connected by $\vee$.[1] Conjuncts that contain $\vee$ are said to be **disjunctive** or to **contain disjunction**.

As an example, suppose that we have a selection on Reserves with the condition *(day < 8/9/02 $\wedge$ rname = 'Joe') $\vee$ bid=5 $\vee$ sid=3*. We can rewrite this in conjunctive normal form as *(day < 8/9/02 $\vee$ bid=5 $\vee$ sid=3) $\wedge$ (rname = 'Joe' $\vee$ bid=5 $\vee$ sid=3)*.

We discussed when an index matches a CNF selection in Section 12.2.2 and introduced selectivity of access paths. The reader is urged to review that material now.

14.2.2 Evaluating Selections without Disjunction

When the selection does not contain disjunction, that is, it is a conjunction of terms, we have two evaluation options to consider:

- We can retrieve tuples using a file scan or a single index that matches some conjuncts (and which we estimate to be the most selective access path) and apply all nonprimary conjuncts in the selection to each retrieved tuple. This approach is very similar to how we use indexes for simple selection conditions, and we do not discuss it further. (We emphasize that the number of tuples retrieved depends on the selectivity of the primary conjuncts in the selection, and the remaining conjuncts only reduce the cardinality of the result of the selection.)
- We can try to utilize several indexes. We examine this approach in the rest of this section.

If several indexes containing data entries with rids (i.e., Alternatives (2) or (3)) match conjuncts in the selection, we can use these indexes to compute sets of rids of candidate tuples. We can then intersect these sets of rids, typically by first sorting them, then retrieving those records whose rids are in the intersection. If additional conjuncts are present in the selection, we can apply these conjuncts to discard some of the candidate tuples from the result.

---

[1] Every selection condition can be expressed in CNF. We refer the reader to any standard text on mathematical logic for the details.

Intersecting rid Sets: Oracle 8 uses several techniques to do rid set intersection for selections with `AND`. One is to `AND` bitmaps. Another is to do a hash join of indexes. For example, given $sal < 5 \wedge price > 30$ and indexes on *sal* and *price*, we can join the indexes on the rid column, considering only entries that satisfy the given selection conditions. Microsoft SQL Server implements rid set intersection through index joins. IBM DB2 implements intersection of rid sets using Bloom filters (which are discussed in Section 22.10.2). Sybase ASE does not do rid set intersection for `AND` selections; Sybase ASIQ does it using bitmap operations. Informix also does rid set intersection.

As an example, given the condition *day < 8/9/02* ∧ *bid=5* ∧ *sid=3,* we can retrieve the rids of records that meet the condition *day < 8/9/02* by using a B+ tree index on *day*, retrieve the rids of records that meet the condition *sid=3* by using a hash index on *sid*, and intersect these two sets of rids. (If we sort these sets by the page id component to do the intersection, a side benefit is that the rids in the intersection are obtained in sorted order by the pages that contain the corresponding tuples, which ensures that we do not fetch the same page twice while retrieving tuples using their rids.) We can now retrieve the necessary pages of Reserves to retrieve tuples and check *bid=5* to obtain tuples that meet the condition *day < 8/9/02* ∧ *bid=5* ∧ *sid=3*.

14.2.3 Selections with Disjunction

Now let us consider that one of the conjuncts in the selection condition is a *disjunction of terms.* If even one of these terms requires a file scan because suitable indexes or sort orders are unavailable, testing this conjunct by itself (i.e., without taking advantage of other conjuncts) requires a file scan. For example, suppose that the only available indexes are a hash index on *rname* and a hash index on *sid*, and that the selection condition contains just the (disjunctive) conjunct *(day < 8/9/02* ∨ *rname='Joe')*. We can retrieve tuples satisfying the condition *rname='Joe'* by using the index on *rname*. However, *day < 8/9/02* requires a file scan. So we might as well do a file scan and check the condition *rname='Joe'* for each retrieved tuple. Therefore, the most selective access path in this example is a file scan.

On the other hand, if the selection condition is *(day < 8/9/02* ∨ *rname='Joe')* ∧ *sid=3*, the index on *sid* matches the conjunct *sid=3*. We can use this index to find qualifying tuples and apply *day < 8/9/02* ∨ *rname='Joe'* to just these tuples. The best access path in this example is the index on *sid* with the primary conjunct *sid=3*.

Disjunctions: Microsoft SQL Server considers the use of unions and bitmaps for dealing with disjunctive conditions. Oracle 8 considers four ways to handle disjunctive conditions: (1) Convert the query into a union of queries without `OR`. (2) If the conditions involve the same attribute, such as $sal < 5 \vee sal > 30$, use a nested query with an `IN` list and an index on the attribute to retrieve tuples matching a value in the list. (3) Use bitmap operations, e.g., evaluate $sal < 5 \vee sal > 30$ by generating bitmaps for the values 5 and 30 and `OR` the bitmaps to find the tuples that satisfy one of the conditions. (We discuss bitmaps in Chapter 25.) (4) Simply apply the disjunctive condition as a filter on the set of retrieved tuples. Sybase ASE considers the use of unions for dealing with disjunctive queries and Sybase ASIQ uses bitmap operations.

Finally, if every term in a disjunction has a matching index, we can retrieve candidate tuples using the indexes and then take the union. For example, if the selection condition is the conjunct *(day < 8/9/02 ∨ rname='Joe')* and we have B+ tree indexes on *day* and *rname*, we can retrieve all tuples such that *day < 8/9/02* using the index on *day*, retrieve all tuples such that *rname='Joe'* using the index on *rname*, and then take the union of the retrieved tuples. If all the matching indexes use Alternative (2) or (3) for data entries, a better approach is to take the union of rids and sort them before retrieving the qualifying data records. Thus, in the example, we can find rids of tuples such that *day < 8/9/02* using the index on *day*, find rids of tuples such that *rname='Joe'* using the index on *rname*, take the union of these sets of rids and sort them by page number, and then retrieve the actual tuples from Reserves. This strategy can be thought of as a (complex) access path that matches the selection condition *(day < 8/9/02 ∨ rname='Joe')*.

Most current systems do not handle selection conditions with disjunction efficiently and concentrate on optimizing selections without disjunction.

14.3 THE PROJECTION OPERATION

Consider the query shown in Figure 14.2. The optimizer translates this query into the relational algebra expression $\pi_{sid,bid} Reserves$. In general the projection operator is of the form $\pi_{attr1,attr2,\ldots,attrm}(R)$. To implement projection, we have

```
SELECT DISTINCT R.sid, R.bid
FROM   Reserves R
```

Figure 14.2 Simple Projection Query

to do the following:

1. Remove unwanted attributes (i.e., those not specified in the projection).

2. Eliminate any duplicate tuples produced.

The second step is the difficult one. There are two basic algorithms, one based on sorting and one based on hashing. In terms of the general techniques listed in Section 12.2, both algorithms are instances of partitioning. While the technique of using an index to identify a subset of useful tuples is not applicable for projection, the sorting or hashing algorithms can be applied to data entries in an index, instead of to data records, under certain conditions described in Section 14.3.4.

14.3.1 Projection Based on Sorting

The algorithm based on sorting has the following steps (at least conceptually):

1. Scan R and produce a set of tuples that contain only the desired attributes.

2. Sort this set of tuples using the combination of all its attributes as the key for sorting.

3. Scan the sorted result, comparing adjacent tuples, and discard duplicates.

If we use temporary relations at each step, the first step costs M I/Os to scan R, where M is the number of pages of R, and T I/Os to write the temporary relation, where T is the number of pages of the temporary; T is O(M). (The exact value of T depends on the number of fields retained and the sizes of these fields.) The second step costs O($TlogT$) (which is also O($MlogM$), of course). The final step costs T. The total cost is O($MlogM$). The first and third steps are straightforward and relatively inexpensive. (As noted in the chapter on sorting, the cost of sorting grows linearly with dataset size in practice, given typical dataset sizes and main memory sizes.)

Consider the projection on Reserves shown in Figure 14.2. We can scan Reserves at a cost of 1000 I/Os. If we assume that each tuple in the temporary relation created in the first step is 10 bytes long, the cost of writing this temporary relation is 250 I/Os. Suppose we have 20 buffer pages. We can sort the temporary relation in two passes at a cost of $2 \cdot 2 \cdot 250 = 1000$ I/Os. The scan required in the third step costs an additional 250 I/Os. The total cost is 2500 I/Os.

This approach can be improved on by modifying the sorting algorithm to do projection with duplicate elimination. Recall the structure of the external sorting algorithm presented in Chapter 13. The very first pass (Pass 0) involves a scan of the records that are to be sorted to produce the initial set of (internally) sorted runs. Subsequently, one or more passes merge runs. Two important modifications to the sorting algorithm adapt it for projection:

- We can project out unwanted attributes during the first pass (Pass 0) of sorting. If B buffer pages are available, we can read in B pages of R and write out $(T/M) \cdot B$ *internally sorted* pages of the temporary relation. In fact, with a more aggressive implementation, we can write out approximately $2 \cdot B$ internally sorted pages of the temporary relation on average. (The idea is similar to the refinement of external sorting discussed in Section 13.3.1.)
- We can eliminate duplicates during the merging passes. In fact, this modification reduces the cost of the merging passes since fewer tuples are written out in each pass. (Most of the duplicates are eliminated in the very first merging pass.)

Let us consider our example again. In the first pass we scan Reserves, at a cost of 1000 I/Os and write out 250 pages. With 20 buffer pages, the 250 pages are written out as seven internally sorted runs, each (except the last) about 40 pages long. In the second pass we read the runs, at a cost of 250 I/Os, and merge them. The total cost is 1,500 I/Os, which is much lower than the cost of the first approach used to implement projection.

14.3.2 Projection Based on Hashing

If we have a fairly large number (say, B) of buffer pages relative to the number of pages of R, a hash-based approach is worth considering. There are two phases: partitioning and duplicate elimination.

In the *partitioning* phase, we have one *input* buffer page and $B-1$ *output* buffer pages. The relation R is read into the input buffer page, one page at a time. The input page is processed as follows: For each tuple, we project out the unwanted attributes and then apply a hash function h to the combination of all remaining attributes. The function h is chosen so that tuples are distributed uniformly to one of $B-1$ partitions; there is one output page per partition. After the projection the tuple is written to the output buffer page that it is hashed to by h.

At the end of the partitioning phase, we have $B-1$ partitions, each of which contains a collection of tuples that share a common hash value (computed by applying h to all fields), and have only the desired fields. The partitioning phase is illustrated in Figure 14.3.

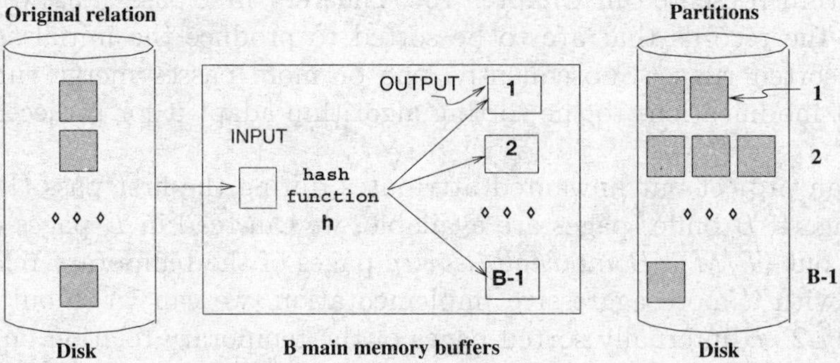

Figure 14.3 Partitioning Phase of Hash-Based Projection

Two tuples that belong to different partitions are guaranteed not to be duplicates because they have different hash values. Thus, if two tuples are duplicates, they are in the same partition. In the *duplicate elimination* phase, we read in the $B - 1$ partitions one at a time to eliminate duplicates. The basic idea is to build an in-memory hash table as we process tuples in order to detect duplicates.

For each partition produced in the first phase:

1. Read in the partition one page at a time. Hash each tuple by applying hash function $h2$ ($\neq h$) to the combination of all fields and then insert it into an in-memory hash table. If a new tuple hashes to the same value as some existing tuple, compare the two to check whether the new tuple is a duplicate. Discard duplicates as they are detected.
2. After the entire partition has been read in, write the tuples in the hash table (which is free of duplicates) to the result file. Then clear the in-memory hash table to prepare for the next partition.

Note that $h2$ is intended to distribute the tuples in a partition across many buckets to minimize *collisions* (two tuples having the same $h2$ values). Since all tuples in a given partition have the same h value, $h2$ cannot be the same as h!

This hash-based projection strategy will not work well if the size of the hash table for a partition (produced in the partitioning phase) is greater than the number of available buffer pages B. One way to handle this *partition overflow* problem is to recursively apply the hash-based projection technique to eliminate the duplicates in each partition that overflows. That is, we divide an overflowing partition into subpartitions, then read each subpartition into memory to eliminate duplicates.

If we assume that h distributes the tuples with perfect uniformity and that the number of pages of tuples *after* the projection (but before duplicate elimination) is T, each partition contains $\frac{T}{B-1}$ pages. (Note that the number of partitions is $B - 1$ because one of the buffer pages is used to read in the relation during the partitioning phase.) The size of a partition is therefore $\frac{T}{B-1}$, and the size of a hash table for a partition is $\frac{T}{B-1} \cdot f$; where f is a *fudge factor* used to capture the (small) increase in size between the partition and a hash table for the partition. The number of buffer pages B must be greater than the partition size $\frac{T}{B-1} \cdot f$ to avoid partition overflow. This observation implies that we require approximately $B > \sqrt{f \cdot T}$ buffer pages.

Now let us consider the cost of hash-based projection. In the partitioning phase, we read R, at a cost of M I/Os. We also write out the projected tuples, a total of T pages, where T is some fraction of M, depending on the fields that are projected out. The cost of this phase is therefore $M + T$ I/Os; the cost of hashing is a CPU cost, and we do not take it into account. In the duplicate elimination phase, we have to read in every partition. The total number of pages in all partitions is T. We also write out the in-memory hash table for each partition after duplicate elimination; this hash table is part of the result of the projection, and we ignore the cost of writing out result tuples, as usual. Thus, the total cost of both phases is $M + 2T$. In our projection on Reserves (Figure 14.2), this cost is $1000 + 2 \cdot 250 = 1500$ I/Os.

14.3.3 Sorting Versus Hashing for Projections

The sorting-based approach is superior to hashing if we have many duplicates or if the distribution of (hash) values is very nonuniform. In this case, some partitions could be much larger than average, and a hash table for such a partition would not fit in memory during the duplicate elimination phase. Also, a useful side effect of using the sorting-based approach is that the result is sorted. Further, since external sorting is required for a variety of reasons, most database systems have a sorting utility, which can be used to implement projection relatively easily. For these reasons, sorting is the standard approach for projection. And perhaps due to a simplistic use of the sorting utility, unwanted attribute removal and duplicate elimination are separate steps in many systems (i.e., the basic sorting algorithm is often used without the refinements we outlined).

We observe that, if we have $B > \sqrt{T}$ buffer pages, where T is the size of the projected relation before duplicate elimination, both approaches have the

Projection in Commercial Systems: Informix uses hashing. IBM DB2, Oracle 8, and Sybase ASE use sorting. Microsoft SQL Server and Sybase ASIQ implement both hash-based and sort-based algorithms.

same I/O cost. Sorting takes two passes. In the first pass, we read M pages of the original relation and write out T pages. In the second pass, we read the T pages and output the result of the projection. Using hashing, in the partitioning phase, we read M pages and write T pages' worth of partitions. In the second phase, we read T pages and output the result of the projection. Thus, considerations such as CPU costs, desirability of sorted order in the result, and skew in the distribution of values drive the choice of projection method.

14.3.4 Use of Indexes for Projections

Neither the hashing nor the sorting approach utilizes any existing indexes. An existing index is useful if the key includes all the attributes we wish to retain in the projection. In this case, we can simply retrieve the key values from the index—without ever accessing the actual relation—and apply our projection techniques to this (much smaller) set of pages. This technique, called an *index-only scan*, and was discussed in Sections 8.5.2 and 12.3.2. If we have an ordered (i.e., a tree) index whose search key includes the wanted attributes as a *prefix*, we can do even better: Just retrieve the data entries in order, discarding unwanted fields, and compare adjacent entries to check for duplicates. The index-only scan technique is discussed further in Section 15.4.1.

14.4 THE JOIN OPERATION

Consider the following query:

```
SELECT *
FROM   Reserves R, Sailors S
WHERE  R.sid = S.sid
```

This query can be expressed in relational algebra using the join operation: $R \bowtie S$. The *join* operation, one of the most useful operations in relational algebra, is the primary means of combining information from two or more relations.

Joins in Commercial Systems: Sybase ASE supports index nested loop and sort-merge join. Sybase ASIQ supports page-oriented nested loop, index nested loop, simple hash, and sort-merge join, in addition to join indexes (which we discuss in Chapter 25). Oracle 8 supports page-oriented nested loops join, sort-merge join, and a variant of hybrid hash join. IBM DB2 supports block nested loop, sort-merge, and hybrid hash join. Microsoft SQL Server supports block nested loops, index nested loops, sort-merge, hash join, and a technique called *hash teams*. Informix supports block nested loops, index nested loops, and hybrid hash join.

Although a join can be defined as a cross-product followed by selections and projections, joins arise much more frequently in practice than plain cross-products. Further, the result of a cross-product is typically much larger than the result of a join, so it is very important to recognize joins and implement them without materializing the underlying cross-product. Joins have therefore received a lot of attention.

We now consider several alternative techniques for implementing joins. We begin by discussing two algorithms (simple nested loops and block nested loops) that essentially enumerate all tuples in the cross-product and discard tuples that do not meet the join conditions. These algorithms are instances of the simple iteration technique mentioned in Section 12.2.

The remaining join algorithms avoid enumerating the cross-product. They are instances of the indexing and partitioning techniques mentioned in Section 12.2. Intuitively, if the join condition consists of equalities, tuples in the two relations can be thought of as belonging to *partitions*, such that only tuples in the same partition can join with each other; the tuples in a partition contain the same values in the join columns. Index nested loops join scans one of the relations and, for each tuple in it, uses an index on the (join columns of the) second relation to locate tuples in the same partition. Thus, only a subset of the second relation is compared with a given tuple of the first relation, and the entire cross-product is not enumerated. The last two algorithms (sort-merge join and hash join) also take advantage of join conditions to partition tuples in the relations to be joined and compare only tuples in the same partition while computing the join, but they do not rely on a pre-existing index. Instead, they either sort or hash the relations to be joined to achieve the partitioning.

We discuss the join of two relations R and S, with the join condition $R_i = S_j$, using positional notation. (If we have more complex join conditions, the basic idea behind each algorithm remains essentially the same. We discuss the details in Section 14.4.4.) We assume M pages in R with p_R tuples per page and N

pages in S with p_S tuples per page. We use R and S in our presentation of the algorithms, and the Reserves and Sailors relations for specific examples.

14.4.1 Nested Loops Join

The simplest join algorithm is a tuple-at-a-time nested loops evaluation. We scan the *outer* relation R, and for each tuple $r \in R$, we scan the entire *inner* relation S. The cost of scanning R is M I/Os. We scan S a total of $p_R \cdot M$ times, and each scan costs N I/Os. Thus, the total cost is $M + p_R \cdot M \cdot N$.

```
foreach tuple r ∈ R do
    foreach tuple s ∈ S do
        if r_i==s_j then add ⟨r, s⟩ to result
```

Figure 14.4 Simple Nested Loops Join

Suppose we choose R to be Reserves and S to be Sailors. The value of M is then 1,000, p_R is 100, and N is 500. The cost of simple nested loops join is $1000 + 100 \cdot 1000 \cdot 500$ page I/Os (plus the cost of writing out the result; we remind the reader again that we uniformly ignore this component of the cost). The cost is staggering: $1000 + (5 \cdot 10^7)$ I/Os. Note that each I/O costs about 10ms on current hardware, which means that this join will take about 140 hours!

A simple refinement is to do this join *page-at-a-time*: For each page of R, we can retrieve each page of S and write out tuples $\langle r, s \rangle$ for all qualifying tuples $r \in$ *R-page* and $s \in$ *S-page*. This way, the cost is M to scan R, as before. However, S is scanned only M times, and so the total cost is $M + M \cdot N$. Thus, the page-at-a-time refinement gives us an improvement of a factor of p_R. In the example join of the Reserves and Sailors relations, the cost is reduced to $1000 + 1000 \cdot 500 = 501,000$ I/Os and would take about 1.4 hours. This dramatic improvement underscores the importance of page-oriented operations for minimizing disk I/O.

From these cost formulas a straightforward observation is that we should choose the outer relation R to be the smaller of the two relations ($R \bowtie B = B \bowtie R$, as long as we keep track of field names). This choice does not change the costs significantly, however. If we choose the smaller relation, Sailors, as the outer relation, the cost of the page-at-a-time algorithm is $500 + 500 \cdot 1000 = 500,500$ I/Os, which is only marginally better than the cost of page-oriented simple nested loops join with Reserves as the outer relation.

Block Nested Loops Join

The simple nested loops join algorithm does not effectively utilize buffer pages. Suppose we have enough memory to hold the smaller relation, say, R, with at least two extra buffer pages left over. We can read in the smaller relation and use one of the extra buffer pages to scan the larger relation S. For each tuple $s \in S$, we check R and output a tuple $\langle r, s \rangle$ for qualifying tuples s (i.e., $r_i = s_j$). The second extra buffer page is used as an output buffer. Each relation is scanned just once, for a total I/O cost of $M + N$, which is optimal.

If enough memory is available, an important refinement is to build an in-memory *hash table* for the smaller relation R. The I/O cost is still $M + N$, but the CPU cost is typically much lower with the hash table refinement.

What if we have too little memory to hold the entire smaller relation? We can generalize the preceding idea by breaking the relation R into *blocks* that can fit into the available buffer pages and scanning all of S for each block of R. R is the *outer* relation, since it is scanned only once, and S is the *inner* relation, since it is scanned multiple times. If we have B buffer pages, we can read in $B - 2$ pages of the outer relation R and scan the inner relation S using one of the two remaining pages. We can write out tuples $\langle r, s \rangle$, where $r \in$ *R-block*, $s \in$ *S-page*, and $r_i = s_j$, using the last buffer page for output.

An efficient way to find **matching pairs** of tuples (i.e., tuples satisfying the join condition $r_i = s_j$) is to build a main-memory hash table for the block of R. Because a hash table for a set of tuples takes a little more space than just the tuples themselves, building a hash table involves a trade-off: The effective block size of R, in terms of the number of tuples per block, is reduced. Building a hash table is well worth the effort. The block nested loops algorithm is described in Figure 14.5. Buffer usage in this algorithm is illustrated in Figure 14.6.

```
foreach block of B − 2 pages of R do
    foreach page of S do {
        for all matching in-memory tuples r ∈ R-block and s ∈ S-page,
        add ⟨r, s⟩ to result
    }
```

Figure 14.5 Block Nested Loops Join

The cost of this strategy is M I/Os for reading in R (which is scanned only once). S is scanned a total of $\lceil \frac{M}{B-2} \rceil$ times—ignoring the extra space required per page due to the in-memory hash table—and each scan costs N I/Os. The total cost is thus $M + N \cdot \lceil \frac{M}{B-2} \rceil$.

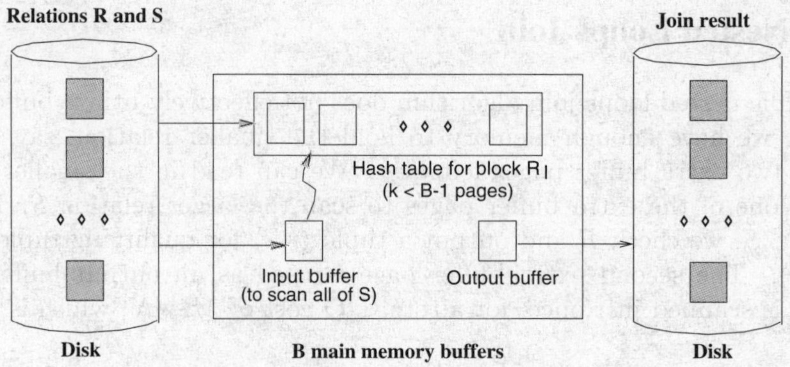

Figure 14.6 Buffer Usage in Block Nested Loops Join

Consider the join of the Reserves and Sailors relations. Let us choose Reserves to be the outer relation R and assume we have enough buffers to hold an in-memory hash table for 100 pages of Reserves (with at least two additional buffers, of course). We have to scan Reserves, at a cost of 1000 I/Os. For each 100-page block of Reserves, we have to scan Sailors. Therefore, we perform 10 scans of Sailors, each costing 500 I/Os. The total cost is $1000 + 10 \cdot 500 = 6000$ I/Os. If we had only enough buffers to hold 90 pages of Reserves, we would have to scan Sailors $\lceil 1000/90 \rceil = 12$ times, and the total cost would be $1000 + 12 \cdot 500 = 7000$ I/Os.

Suppose we choose Sailors to be the outer relation R instead. Scanning Sailors costs 500 I/Os. We would scan Reserves $\lceil 500/100 \rceil = 5$ times. The total cost is $500 + 5 \cdot 1,000 = 5500$ I/Os. If instead we have only enough buffers for 90 pages of Sailors, we would scan Reserves a total of $\lceil 500/90 \rceil = 6$ times. The total cost in this case is $500 + 6 \cdot 1000 = 6500$ I/Os. We note that the block nested loops join algorithm takes a little over a minute on our running example, assuming 10ms per I/O as before.

Impact of Blocked Access

If we consider the effect of blocked access to several pages, there is a fundamental change in the way we allocate buffers for block nested loops. Rather than using just one buffer page for the inner relation, the best approach is to split the buffer pool evenly between the two relations. This allocation results in more passes over the inner relation, leading to more page fetches. However, the time spent on *seeking* for pages is dramatically reduced.

The technique of double buffering (discussed in Chapter 13 in the context of sorting) can also be used, but we do not discuss it further.

Index Nested Loops Join

If there is an index on one of the relations on the join attribute(s), we can take advantage of the index by making the indexed relation be the inner relation. Suppose we have a suitable index on S; Figure 14.7 describes the index nested loops join algorithm.

```
foreach tuple r ∈ R do
    foreach tuple s ∈ S where r_i == s_j
        add ⟨r, s⟩ to result
```

Figure 14.7 Index Nested Loops Join

For each tuple $r \in R$, we use the index to retrieve matching tuples of S. Intuitively, we compare r only with tuples of S that are in the same *partition*, in that they have the same value in the join column. Unlike the other nested loops join algorithms, therefore, the index nested loops join algorithm does not enumerate the cross-product of R and S. The cost of scanning R is M, as before. The cost of retrieving matching S tuples depends on the kind of index and the number of matching tuples; for each R tuple, the cost is as follows:

1. If the index on S is a B+ tree index, the cost to find the appropriate leaf is typically 2–4 I/Os. If the index is a hash index, the cost to find the appropriate bucket is 1–2 I/Os.

2. Once we find the appropriate leaf or bucket, the cost of retrieving matching S tuples depends on whether the index is clustered. If it is, the cost per outer tuple $r \in R$ is typically just one more I/O. If it is not clustered, the cost could be one I/O per matching S-tuple (since each of these could be on a different page in the worst case).

As an example, suppose that we have a hash-based index using Alternative (2) on the *sid* attribute of Sailors and that it takes about 1.2 I/Os on average[2] to retrieve the appropriate page of the index. Since *sid* is a key for Sailors, we have at most one matching tuple. Indeed, *sid* in Reserves is a foreign key referring to Sailors, and therefore we have *exactly* one matching Sailors tuple for each Reserves tuple. Let us consider the cost of scanning Reserves and using the index to retrieve the matching Sailors tuple for each Reserves tuple. The cost of scanning Reserves is 1000. There are $100 \cdot 1000$ tuples in Reserves. For each of these tuples, retrieving the index page containing the rid of the matching Sailors tuple costs 1.2 I/Os (on average); in addition, we have to retrieve the Sailors page containing the qualifying tuple. Therefore, we have

[2]This is a typical cost for hash-based indexes.

100,000 $\cdot(1 + 1.2)$ I/Os to retrieve matching Sailors tuples. The total cost is 221,000 I/Os.

As another example, suppose that we have a hash-based index using Alternative (2) on the *sid* attribute of Reserves. Now we can scan Sailors (500 I/Os), and for each tuple, use the index to retrieve matching Reserves tuples. We have a total of $80 \cdot 500$ Sailors tuples, and each tuple could match with either zero or more Reserves tuples; a sailor may have no reservations or several. For each Sailors tuple, we can retrieve the index page containing the rids of matching Reserves tuples (assuming that we have at most one such index page, which is a reasonable guess) in 1.2 I/Os on average. The total cost thus far is $500 + 40,000 \cdot 1.2 = 48,500$ I/Os.

In addition, we have the cost of retrieving matching Reserves tuples. Since we have 100,000 reservations for 40,000 Sailors, assuming a uniform distribution we can estimate that each Sailors tuple matches with 2.5 Reserves tuples on average. If the index on Reserves is clustered, and these matching tuples are typically on the same page of Reserves for a given sailor, the cost of retrieving them is just one I/O per Sailor tuple, which adds up to 40,000 extra I/Os. If the index is not clustered, each matching Reserves tuple may well be on a different page, leading to a total of $2.5 \cdot 40,000$ I/Os for retrieving qualifying tuples. Therefore, the total cost can vary from 48,500+40,000=88,500 to 48,500+100,000=148,500 I/Os. Assuming 10ms per I/O, this would take about 15 to 25 minutes.

So, even with an unclustered index, if the number of matching inner tuples for each outer tuple is small (on average), the cost of the index nested loops join algorithm is likely to be much less than the cost of a simple nested loops join.

14.4.2 Sort-Merge Join

The basic idea behind the **sort-merge join** algorithm is to *sort* both relations on the join attribute and then look for qualifying tuples $r \in R$ and $s \in S$ by essentially *merging* the two relations. The sorting step groups all tuples with the same value in the join column and thus makes it easy to identify partitions, or groups of tuples with the same value, in the join column. We exploit this partitioning by comparing the R tuples in a partition with only the S tuples in the same partition (rather than with all S tuples), thereby avoiding enumeration of the cross-product of R and S. (This partition-based approach works only for equality join conditions.)

The external sorting algorithm discussed in Chapter 13 can be used to do the sorting, and of course, if a relation is already sorted on the join attribute, we need not sort it again. We now consider the merging step in detail: We scan the relations R and S, looking for qualifying tuples (i.e., tuples Tr in R and Ts in S such that $Tr_i = Ts_j$). The two scans start at the first tuple in each relation. We advance the scan of R as long as the current R tuple is less than the current S tuple (with respect to the values in the join attribute). Similarly, we advance the scan of S as long as the current S tuple is less than the current R tuple. We alternate between such advances until we find an R tuple Tr and a S tuple Ts with $Tr_i = Ts_j$.

When we find tuples Tr and Ts such that $Tr_i = Ts_j$, we need to output the joined tuple. In fact, we could have several R tuples and several S tuples with the same value in the join attributes as the current tuples Tr and Ts. We refer to these tuples as the *current R partition* and the *current S partition*. For each tuple r in the current R partition, we scan all tuples s in the current S partition and output the joined tuple $\langle r, s \rangle$. We then resume scanning R and S, beginning with the first tuples that follow the partitions of tuples that we just processed.

The sort-merge join algorithm is shown in Figure 14.8. We assign only tuple values to the variables Tr, Ts, and Gs and use the special value eof to denote that there are no more tuples in the relation being scanned. Subscripts identify fields, for example, Tr_i denotes the ith field of tuple Tr. If Tr has the value eof, any comparison involving Tr_i is defined to evaluate to `false`.

We illustrate sort-merge join on the Sailors and Reserves instances shown in Figures 14.9 and 14.10, with the join condition being equality on the *sid* attributes.

These two relations are already sorted on *sid*, and the merging phase of the sort-merge join algorithm begins with the scans positioned at the first tuple of each relation instance. We advance the scan of Sailors, since its *sid* value, now 22, is less than the *sid* value of Reserves, which is now 28. The second Sailors tuple has *sid* = 28, which is equal to the *sid* value of the current Reserves tuple. Therefore, we now output a result tuple for each pair of tuples, one from Sailors and one from Reserves, in the current partition (i.e., with *sid* = 28). Since we have just one Sailors tuple with *sid* = 28 and two such Reserves tuples, we write two result tuples. After this step, we position the scan of Sailors at the first tuple after the partition with *sid* = 28, which has *sid* = 31. Similarly, we position the scan of Reserves at the first tuple with *sid* = 31. Since these two tuples have the same *sid* values, we have found the next matching partition, and we must write out the result tuples generated from this partition (there are three such tuples). After this, the Sailors scan is positioned at the tuple with *sid* = 36, and the Reserves scan is positioned at the tuple with *sid* = 58. The rest of the merge phase proceeds similarly.

```
proc smjoin(R, S, 'R_i = S'_j')

if R not sorted on attribute i, sort it;
if S not sorted on attribute j, sort it;

Tr = first tuple in R;                              // ranges over R
Ts = first tuple in S;                              // ranges over S
Gs = first tuple in S;                   // start of current S-partition

while Tr ≠ eof and Gs ≠ eof do {

    while Tr_i < Gs_j do
        Tr = next tuple in R after Tr;               // continue scan of R

    while Tr_i > Gs_j do
        Gs = next tuple in S after Gs                // continue scan of S

    Ts = Gs;                                 // Needed in case Tr_i ≠ Gs_j
    while Tr_i == Gs_j do {                  // process current R partition
        Ts = Gs;                                // reset S partition scan
        while Ts_j == Tr_i do {                 // process current R tuple
            add ⟨Tr, Ts⟩ to result;               // output joined tuples
            Ts = next tuple in S after Ts;} // advance S partition scan
        Tr = next tuple in R after Tr;               // advance scan of R
    }                                      // done with current R partition

    Gs = Ts;                         // initialize search for next S partition

}
```

Figure 14.8 Sort-Merge Join

sid	*sname*	*rating*	*age*
22	dustin	7	45.0
28	yuppy	9	35.0
31	lubber	8	55.5
36	lubber	6	36.0
44	guppy	5	35.0
58	rusty	10	35.0

Figure 14.9 An Instance of Sailors

sid	*bid*	*day*	*rname*
28	103	12/04/96	guppy
28	103	11/03/96	yuppy
31	101	10/10/96	dustin
31	102	10/12/96	lubber
31	101	10/11/96	lubber
58	103	11/12/96	dustin

Figure 14.10 An Instance of Reserves

In general, we have to scan a partition of tuples in the second relation as often as the number of tuples in the corresponding partition in the first relation. The first relation in the example, Sailors, has just one tuple in each partition. (This is not happenstance but a consequence of the fact that *sid* is a key—this example is a key–foreign key join.) In contrast, suppose that the join condition is changed to be *sname=rname*. Now, both relations contain more than one tuple in the partition with *sname=rname='lubber'*. The tuples with *rname='lubber'* in Reserves have to be scanned for each Sailors tuple with *sname='lubber'*.

Cost of Sort-Merge Join

The cost of sorting R is $O(MlogM)$ and the cost of sorting S is $O(NlogN)$. The cost of the merging phase is $M + N$ if no S partition is scanned multiple times (or the necessary pages are found in the buffer after the first pass). This approach is especially attractive if at least one relation is already sorted on the join attribute or has a clustered index on the join attribute.

Consider the join of the relations Reserves and Sailors. Assuming that we have 100 buffer pages (roughly the same number that we assumed were available in our discussion of block nested loops join), we can sort Reserves in just two passes. The first pass produces 10 internally sorted runs of 100 pages each. The second pass merges these 10 runs to produce the sorted relation. Because we read and write Reserves in each pass, the sorting cost is $2 \cdot 2 \cdot 1000 = 4000$ I/Os. Similarly, we can sort Sailors in two passes, at a cost of $2 \cdot 2 \cdot 500 = 2000$ I/Os. In addition, the second phase of the sort-merge join algorithm requires an additional scan of both relations. Thus the total cost is $4000 + 2000 + 1000 + 500 = 7500$ I/Os, which is similar to the cost of the block nested loops algorithm.

Suppose that we have only 35 buffer pages. We can still sort both Reserves and Sailors in two passes, and the cost of the sort-merge join algorithm remains at 7500 I/Os. However, the cost of the block nested loops join algorithm is more than 15,000 I/Os. On the other hand, if we have 300 buffer pages, the cost of the sort-merge join remains at 7500 I/Os, whereas the cost of the block nested loops join drops to 2500 I/Os. (We leave it to the reader to verify these numbers.)

We note that multiple scans of a partition of the second relation are potentially expensive. In our example, if the number of Reserves tuples in a repeatedly scanned partition is small (say, just a few pages), the likelihood of finding the entire partition in the buffer pool on repeated scans is very high, and the I/O cost remains essentially the same as for a single scan. However, if many pages of Reserves tuples are in a given partition, the first page of such a partition may no longer be in the buffer pool when we request it a second time (after first scanning all pages in the partition; remember that each page is unpinned as the scan moves past it). In this case, the I/O cost could be as high as the number of pages in the Reserves partition times the number of tuples in the corresponding Sailors partition!

In the worst-case scenario, the merging phase could require us to read the complete second relation for each *tuple* in the first relation, and the number of I/Os is $O(M \cdot N)$ I/Os! (This scenario occurs when all tuples in both relations contain the same value in the join attribute; it is extremely unlikely.)

In practice, the I/O cost of the merge phase is typically just a single scan of each relation. A single scan can be guaranteed if at least one of the relations involved has no duplicates in the join attribute; this is the case, fortunately, for key–foreign key joins, which are very common.

A Refinement

We assumed that the two relations are sorted first and then merged in a distinct pass. It is possible to improve the sort-merge join algorithm by combining the merging phase of sorting with the merging phase of the join. First, we produce sorted runs of size B for both R and S. If $B > \sqrt{L}$, where L is the size of the larger relation, the number of runs per relation is less than $\sqrt{L}$. Suppose that the number of buffers available for the merging phase is at least $2\sqrt{L}$; that is, more than the total number of runs for R and S. We allocate one buffer page for each run of R *and* one for each run of S. We then merge the runs of R (to generate the sorted version of R), merge the runs of S, and merge the resulting R and S streams as they are generated; we apply the join condition as we merge the R and S streams and discard tuples in the cross-product that do not meet the join condition.

Unfortunately, this idea increases the number of buffers required to $2\sqrt{L}$. However, by using the technique discussed in Section 13.3.1 we can produce sorted runs of size approximately $2 \cdot B$ for both R and S. Consequently, we have fewer than $\sqrt{L}/2$ runs of each relation, given the assumption that $B > \sqrt{L}$. Thus, the total number of runs is less than $\sqrt{L}$, that is, less than B, and we can combine the merging phases with no need for additional buffers.

This approach allows us to perform a sort-merge join at the cost of reading and writing R and S in the first pass and reading R and S in the second pass. The total cost is thus $3 \cdot (M + N)$. In our example, the cost goes down from 7500 to 4500 I/Os.

Blocked Access and Double-Buffering

The blocked I/O and double-buffering optimizations, discussed in Chapter 13 in the context of sorting, can be used to speed up the merging pass as well as the sorting of the relations to be joined; we do not discuss these refinements.

14.4.3 Hash Join

The **hash join** algorithm, like the sort-merge join algorithm, identifies partitions in R and S in a **partitioning phase** and, in a subsequent **probing phase**, compares tuples in an R partition only with tuples in the corresponding S partition for testing equality join conditions. Unlike sort-merge join, hash join uses hashing to identify partitions rather than sorting. The partitioning (also called **building**) phase of hash join is similar to the partitioning in hash-based projection and is illustrated in Figure 14.3. The probing (sometimes called **matching**) phase is illustrated in Figure 14.11.

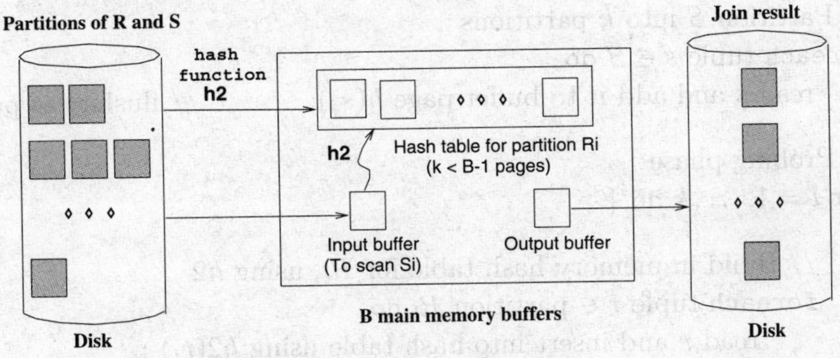

Figure 14.11 Probing Phase of Hash Join

The idea is to hash *both* relations on the join attribute, using the *same* hash function h. If we hash each relation (ideally uniformly) into k partitions, we are assured that R tuples in partition i can join only with S tuples in the same partition i. This observation can be used to good effect: We can read in a (complete) partition of the smaller relation R and scan just the corresponding partition of S for matches. We never need to consider these R and S tuples again. Thus, once R and S are partitioned, we can perform the join by reading in R and S just once, provided enough memory is available to hold all the tuples in any given partition of R.

In practice we build an in-memory hash table for the R partition, using a hash function $h2$ that is different from h (since $h2$ is intended to distribute tuples in a partition based on h), to reduce CPU costs. We need enough memory to hold this hash table, which is a little larger than the R partition itself.

The hash join algorithm is presented in Figure 14.12. (There are several variants on this idea; this version is called *Grace hash join* in the literature.) Consider the cost of the hash join algorithm. In the partitioning phase, we have to scan both R and S once and write them out once. The cost of this phase is therefore $2(M + N)$. In the second phase, we scan each partition once, assuming no partition overflows, at a cost of $M + N$ I/Os. The total cost is therefore $3(M+N)$, given our assumption that each partition fits into memory in the second phase. On our example join of Reserves and Sailors, the total cost is $3 \cdot (500 + 1000) = 4500$ I/Os, and assuming 10ms per I/O, hash join takes under a minute. Compare this with simple nested loops join, which took about 140 *hours*—this difference underscores the importance of using a good join algorithm.

```
// Partition R into k partitions
foreach tuple r ∈ R do
    read r and add it to buffer page h(r_i);        // flushed as page fills

// Partition S into k partitions
foreach tuple s ∈ S do
    read s and add it to buffer page h(s_j);        // flushed as page fills

// Probing phase
for l = 1, ..., k do {

    // Build in-memory hash table for R_l, using h2
    foreach tuple r ∈ partition R_l do
        read r and insert into hash table using h2(r_i) ;

    // Scan S_l and probe for matching R_l tuples
    foreach tuple s ∈ partition S_l do {
        read s and probe table using h2(s_j);
        for matching R tuples r, output ⟨r, s⟩ };

    clear hash table to prepare for next partition;
    }
```

Figure 14.12 Hash Join

Memory Requirements and Overflow Handling

To increase the chances of a given partition fitting into available memory in the probing phase, we must minimize the size of a partition by maximizing the number of partitions. In the partitioning phase, to partition R (similarly,

S) into k partitions, we need at least k output buffers and one input buffer. Therefore, given B buffer pages, the maximum number of partitions is $k = B - 1$. Assuming that partitions are equal in size, this means that the size of each R partition is $\frac{M}{B-1}$ (as usual, M is the number of pages of R). The number of pages in the (in-memory) hash table built during the probing phase for a partition is thus $\frac{f \cdot M}{B-1}$, where f is a *fudge factor* used to capture the (small) increase in size between the partition and a hash table for the partition.

During the probing phase, in addition to the hash table for the R partition, we require a buffer page for scanning the S partition and an output buffer. Therefore, we require $B > \frac{f \cdot M}{B-1} + 2$. *We need approximately* $B > \sqrt{f \cdot M}$ *for the hash join algorithm to perform well.*

Since the partitions of R are likely to be close in size but not identical, the largest partition is somewhat larger than $\frac{M}{B-1}$, and the number of buffer pages required is a little more than $B > \sqrt{f \cdot M}$. There is also the risk that, if the hash function h does not partition R uniformly, the hash table for one or more R partitions may not fit in memory during the probing phase. This situation can significantly degrade performance.

As we observed in the context of hash-based projection, one way to handle this *partition overflow* problem is to recursively apply the hash join technique to the join of the overflowing R partition with the corresponding S partition. That is, we first divide the R and S partitions into subpartitions. Then, we join the subpartitions pairwise. All subpartitions of R probably fit into memory; if not, we apply the hash join technique recursively.

Utilizing Extra Memory: Hybrid Hash Join

The minimum amount of memory required for hash join is $B > \sqrt{f \cdot M}$. If more memory is available, a variant of hash join called **hybrid hash join** offers better performance. Suppose that $B > f \cdot (M/k)$, for some integer k. This means that, if we divide R into k partitions of size M/k, an in-memory hash table can be built for each partition. To partition R (similarly, S) into k partitions, we need k output buffers and one input buffer; that is, $k + 1$ pages. This leaves us with $B - (k + 1)$ extra pages during the partitioning phase.

Suppose that $B - (k + 1) > f \cdot (M/k)$. That is, we have enough extra memory during the partitioning phase to hold an in-memory hash table for a partition of R. The idea behind hybrid hash join is to build an in-memory hash table for the first partition of R during the partitioning phase, which means that we do not write this partition to disk. Similarly, while partitioning S, rather than write out the tuples in the first partition of S, we can directly probe the in-memory table for the first R partition and write out the results. At the end of the partitioning phase, we have completed the join of the first partitions of R and S, in addition to partitioning the two relations; in the probing phase, we join the remaining partitions as in hash join.

The savings realized through hybrid hash join is that we avoid writing the first partitions of R and S to disk during the partitioning phase and reading them in again during the probing phase. Consider our example, with 500 pages in the smaller relation R and 1000 pages in S.[3] If we have $B = 300$ pages, we can easily build an in-memory hash table for the first R partition while partitioning R into two partitions. During the partitioning phase of R, we scan R and write out one partition; the cost is $500 + 250$ if we assume that the partitions are of equal size. We then scan S and write out one partition; the cost is $1000 + 500$. In the probing phase, we scan the second partition of R and of S; the cost is $250 + 500$. The total cost is $750 + 1500 + 750 = 3000$. In contrast, the cost of hash join is 4500.

If we have enough memory to hold an in-memory hash table for all of R, the savings are even greater. For example, if $B > f \cdot N + 2$, that is, $k = 1$, we can build an in-memory hash table for all of R. This means that we read R only once, to build this hash table, and read S once, to probe the R hash table. The cost is $500 + 1000 = 1500$.

Hash Join Versus Block Nested Loops Join

While presenting the block nested loops join algorithm, we briefly discussed the idea of building an in-memory hash table for the inner relation. We now compare this (more CPU-efficient) version of block nested loops join with hybrid hash join.

If a hash table for the entire smaller relation fits in memory, the two algorithms are identical. If both relations are large relative to the available buffer size, we require several passes over one of the relations in block nested loops join; hash join is a more effective application of hashing techniques in this case. The I/O saved in this case by using the hash join algorithm in comparison to a block nested loops join is illustrated in Figure 14.13. In the latter, we read in all of S for each block of R; the I/O cost corresponds to the whole rectangle. In the hash join algorithm, for each block of R, we read only the corresponding block of S; the I/O cost corresponds to the shaded areas in the figure. This difference in I/O due to scans of S is highlighted in the figure.

[3] It is unfortunate, that in our running example, the smaller relation, which we denoted by the variable R in our discussion of hash join, is in fact the Sailors relation, which is more naturally denoted by S!

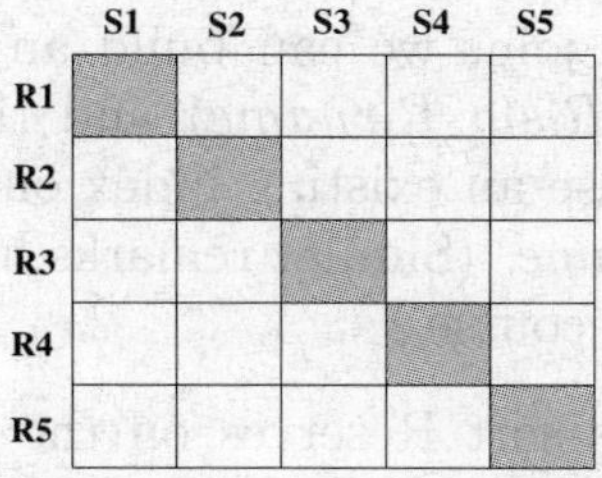

Figure 14.13 Hash Join Vs. Block Nested Loops for Large Relations

We note that this picture is rather simplistic. It does not capture the costs of scanning R in the block nested loops join and the partitioning phase in the hash join, and it focuses on the cost of the probing phase.

Hash Join Versus Sort-Merge Join

Let us compare hash join with sort-merge join. If we have $B > \sqrt{M}$ buffer pages, where M is the number of pages in the *smaller* relation and we assume uniform partitioning, the cost of hash join is $3(M + N)$ I/Os. If we have $B > \sqrt{N}$ buffer pages, where N is the number of pages in the *larger* relation, the cost of sort-merge join is also $3(M + N)$, as discussed in Section 14.4.2. A choice between these techniques is therefore governed by other factors, notably:

- If the partitions in hash join are not uniformly sized, hash join could cost more. Sort-merge join is less sensitive to such data skew.
- If the available number of buffers falls between $\sqrt{M}$ and $\sqrt{N}$, hash join costs less than sort-merge join, since we need only enough memory to hold partitions of the smaller relation, whereas in sort-merge join the memory requirements depend on the size of the larger relation. The larger the difference in size between the two relations, the more important this factor becomes.
- Additional considerations include the fact that the result is sorted in sort-merge join.

14.4.4 General Join Conditions

We have discussed several join algorithms for the case of a simple equality join condition. Other important cases include a join condition that involves equalities over several attributes and inequality conditions. To illustrate the case of several equalities, we consider the join of Reserves R and Sailors S with the join condition $R.sid{=}S.sid \land R.rname{=}S.sname$:

- For index nested loops join, we can build an index on Reserves on the combination of fields $\langle R.sid, R.rname\rangle$ and treat Reserves as the inner relation. We can also use an existing index on this combination of fields, or on *R.sid*, or on *R.rname*. (Similar remarks hold for the choice of Sailors as the inner relation, of course.)
- For sort-merge join, we sort Reserves on the combination of fields $\langle sid, rname\rangle$ and Sailors on the combination of fields $\langle sid, sname\rangle$. Similarly, for hash join, we partition on these combinations of fields.
- The other join algorithms we discussed are essentially unaffected.

If we have an inequality comparison, for example, a join of Reserves R and Sailors S with the join condition $R.rname < S.sname$:

- We require a B+ tree index for index nested loops join.
- Hash join and sort-merge join are not applicable.
- The other join algorithms we discussed are essentially unaffected.

Of course, regardless of the algorithm, the number of qualifying tuples in an inequality join is likely to be much higher than in an equality join.

We conclude our presentation of joins with the observation that no one join algorithm is uniformly superior to the others. The choice of a good algorithm depends on the sizes of the relations being joined, available access methods, and the size of the buffer pool. This choice can have a considerable impact on performance because the difference between a good and a bad algorithm for a given join can be enormous.

14.5 THE SET OPERATIONS

We now briefly consider the implementation of the set operations $R \cap S$, $R \times S$, $R \cup S$, and $R - S$. From an implementation standpoint, intersection and cross-product can be seen as special cases of join (with equality on all fields as the join condition for intersection, and with no join condition for cross-product). Therefore, we will not discuss them further.

The main point to address in the implementation of union is the elimination of duplicates. Set-difference can also be implemented using a variation of the techniques for duplicate elimination. (Union and difference queries on a single relation can be thought of as a selection query with a complex selection condition. The techniques discussed in Section 14.2 are applicable for such queries.)

There are two implementation algorithms for union and set-difference, again based on sorting and hashing. Both algorithms are instances of the partitioning technique mentioned in Section 12.2.

14.5.1 Sorting for Union and Difference

To implement $R \cup S$:

1. Sort R using the combination of all fields; similarly, sort S.
2. Scan the sorted R and S in parallel and merge them, eliminating duplicates.

As a refinement, we can produce sorted runs of R and S and merge these runs in parallel. (This refinement is similar to the one discussed in detail for projection.) The implementation of $R - S$ is similar. During the merging pass, we write only tuples of R to the result, after checking that they do not appear in S.

14.5.2 Hashing for Union and Difference

To implement $R \cup S$:

1. Partition R and S using a hash function h.
2. Process each partition l as follows:
   - Build an in-memory hash table (using hash function $h2 \neq h$) for S_l.
   - Scan R_l. For each tuple, probe the hash table for S_l. If the tuple is in the hash table, discard it; otherwise, add it to the table.
   - Write out the hash table and then clear it to prepare for the next partition.

To implement $R - S$, we proceed similarly. The difference is in the processing of a partition. After building an in-memory hash table for S_l, we scan R_l. For each R_l tuple, we probe the hash table; if the tuple is not in the table, we write it to the result.

14.6 AGGREGATE OPERATIONS

The SQL query shown in Figure 14.14 involves an *aggregate operation*, `AVG`. The other aggregate operations supported in SQL-92 are `MIN`, `MAX`, `SUM`, and `COUNT`.

```
SELECT AVG(S.age)
FROM   Sailors S
```

Figure 14.14 Simple Aggregation Query

The basic algorithm for aggregate operators consists of scanning the entire Sailors relation and maintaining some **running information** about the scanned tuples; the details are straightforward. The running information for each aggregate operation is shown in Figure 14.15. The cost of this operation is the cost of scanning all Sailors tuples.

Aggregate Operation	*Running Information*
SUM	*Total* of the values retrieved
AVG	⟨*Total, Count*⟩ of the values retrieved
COUNT	*Count* of values retrieved
MIN	Smallest value retrieved
MAX	Largest value retrieved

Figure 14.15 Running Information for Aggregate Operations

Aggregate operators can also be used in combination with a GROUP BY clause. If we add GROUP BY *rating* to the query in Figure 14.14, we would have to compute the average age of sailors for each *rating* group. For queries with grouping, there are two good evaluation algorithms that do not rely on an existing index: One algorithm is based on sorting and the other is based on hashing. Both algorithms are instances of the partitioning technique mentioned in Section 12.2.

The *sorting* approach is simple—we sort the relation on the grouping attribute (*rating*) and then scan it again to compute the result of the aggregate operation for each group. The second step is similar to the way we implement aggregate operations without grouping, with the only additional point being that we have to watch for group boundaries. (It is possible to refine the approach by doing aggregation as part of the sorting step; we leave this as an exercise for the reader.) The I/O cost of this approach is just the cost of the sorting algorithm.

In the *hashing* approach we build a hash table (in main memory, if possible) on the grouping attribute. The entries have the form ⟨*grouping-value, running-info*⟩. The running information depends on the aggregate operation, as per the discussion of aggregate operations without grouping. As we scan the relation, for each tuple, we probe the hash table to find the entry for the group to which the tuple belongs and update the running information. When the hash table is complete, the entry for a grouping value can be used to compute the answer tuple for the corresponding group in the obvious way. If the hash table fits in memory, which is likely because each entry is quite small and there is only one entry per grouping value, the cost of the hashing approach is $O(M)$, where M is the size of the relation.

If the relation is so large that the hash table does not fit in memory, we can partition the relation using a hash function h on *grouping-value*. Since all tuples with a given grouping value are in the same partition, we can then process each partition independently by building an in-memory hash table for the tuples in it.

14.6.1 Implementing Aggregation by Using an Index

The technique of using an index to select a subset of useful tuples is not applicable for aggregation. However, under certain conditions, we can evaluate aggregate operations efficiently by using the data entries in an index instead of the data records:

- If the search key for the index includes all the attributes needed for the aggregation query, we can apply the techniques described earlier in this section to the set of data entries in the index, rather than to the collection of data records and thereby avoid fetching data records.
- If the `GROUP BY` clause attribute list forms a prefix of the index search key and the index is a tree index, we can retrieve data entries (and data records, if necessary) in the order required for the grouping operation and thereby avoid a sorting step.

A given index may support one or both of these techniques; both are examples of *index-only* plans. We discuss the use of indexes for queries with grouping and aggregation in the context of queries that also include selections and projections in Section 15.4.1.

14.7 THE IMPACT OF BUFFERING

In implementations of relational operators, effective use of the buffer pool is very important, and we explicitly considered the size of the buffer pool in determining algorithm parameters for several of the algorithms discussed. There are three main points to note:

1. If several operations execute concurrently, they share the buffer pool. This effectively reduces the number of buffer pages available for each operation.
2. If tuples are accessed using an index, especially an unclustered index, the likelihood of finding a page in the buffer pool if it is requested multiple

times depends (in a rather unpredictable way, unfortunately) on the size of the buffer pool and the replacement policy. Further, if tuples are accessed using an unclustered index, each tuple retrieved is likely to require us to bring in a new page; therefore, the buffer pool fills up quickly, leading to a high level of paging activity.

3. If an operation has a *pattern* of repeated page accesses, we can increase the likelihood of finding a page in memory by a good choice of replacement policy or by *reserving* a sufficient number of buffers for the operation (if the buffer manager provides this capability). Several examples of such patterns of repeated access follow:

   - Consider a simple nested loops join. For each tuple of the outer relation, we repeatedly scan all pages in the inner relation. If we have enough buffer pages to hold the entire inner relation, the replacement policy is irrelevant. Otherwise, the replacement policy becomes critical. With LRU, we will *never* find a page when it is requested, because it is paged out. This is the *sequential flooding* problem discussed in Section 9.4.1. With MRU, we obtain the best buffer utilization—the first $B-2$ pages of the inner relation always remain in the buffer pool. (B is the number of buffer pages; we use one page for scanning the outer relation[4] and always replace the last page used for scanning the inner relation.)
   - In a block nested loops join, for each block of the outer relation, we scan the entire inner relation. However, since only one unpinned page is available for the scan of the inner relation, the replacement policy makes no difference.
   - In an index nested loops join, for each tuple of the outer relation, we use the index to find matching inner tuples. If several tuples of the outer relation have the same value in the join attribute, there is a repeated pattern of access on the inner relation; we can maximize the repetition by sorting the outer relation on the join attributes.

14.8 REVIEW QUESTIONS

Answers to the review questions can be found in the listed sections.

- Consider a simple selection query of the form $\sigma_{R.attr}$ **op** $_{value}(R)$. What are the alternative access paths in each of these cases: (i) there is no index and the file is not sorted, (ii) there is no index but the file is sorted. **(Section 14.1)**

[4]Think about the sequence of pins and unpins used to achieve this.

- If a B+ tree index matches the selection condition, how does clustering affect the cost? Discuss this in terms of the selectivity of the condition. **(Section 14.1)**
- Describe *conjunctive normal form* for general selections. Define the terms *conjunct* and *disjunct*. Under what conditions does a general selection condition match an index? **(Section 14.2)**
- Describe the various implementation options for general selections. **(Section 14.2)**
- Discuss the use of sorting versus hashing to eliminate duplicates during projection. **(Section 14.3)**
- When can an index be used to implement projections, without retrieving actual data records? When does the index additionally allow us to eliminate duplicates without sorting or hashing? **(Section 14.3)**
- Consider the join of relations R and S. Describe *simple nested loops join* and *block nested loops join*. What are the similarities and differences? How does the latter reduce I/O costs? Discuss how you would utilize buffers in block nested loops. **(Section 14.4.1)**
- Describe *index nested loops join*. How does it differ from block nested loops join? **(Section 14.4.1)**
- Describe sort-merge join of R and S. What join conditions are supported? What optimizations are possible beyond sorting both R and S on the join attributes and then doing a merge of the two? In particular, discuss how steps in sorting can be combined with the merge pass. **(Section 14.4.2)**
- What is the idea behind *hash join*? What is the additional optimization in *hybrid hash join*? **(Section 14.4.3)**
- Discuss how the choice of join algorithm depends on the number of buffer pages available, the sizes of R and S, and the indexes available. Be specific in your discussion and refer to cost formulas for the I/O cost of each algorithm. **(Sections 14.12–Section 14.13)**
- How are general join conditions handled? **(Section 14.4.4)**
- Why are the set operations $R \cap S$ and $R \times S$ special cases of joins? What is the similarity between the set operations $R \cup S$ and $R - S$? **(Section 14.5)**
- Discuss the use of sorting versus hashing in implementing $R \cup S$ and $R - S$. Compare this with the implementation of projection. **(Section 14.5)**
- Discuss the use of *running information* in implementing aggregate operations. Discuss the use of sorting versus hashing for dealing with grouping. **(Section 14.6)**

- Under what conditions can we use an index to implement aggregate operations without retrieving data records? Under what conditions do indexes allow us to avoid sorting or hashing? **(Section 14.6)**
- Using the cost formulas for the various relational operator evaluation algorithms, discuss which operators are most sensitive to the number of available buffer pool pages. How is this number influenced by the number of operators being evaluated concurrently? **(Section 14.7)**
- Explain how the choice of a good buffer pool replacement policy can influence overall performance. Identify the patterns of access in typical relational operator evaluation and how they influence the choice of replacement policy. **(Section 14.7)**

EXERCISES

Exercise 14.1 Briefly answer the following questions:

1. Consider the three basic techniques, *iteration*, *indexing*, and *partitioning*, and the relational algebra operators *selection*, *projection*, and *join*. For each technique-operator pair, describe an algorithm based on the technique for evaluating the operator.
2. Define the term *most selective access path for a query*.
3. Describe *conjunctive normal form*, and explain why it is important in the context of relational query evaluation.
4. When does a general selection condition *match* an index? What is a *primary term* in a selection condition with respect to a given index?
5. How does hybrid hash join improve on the basic hash join algorithm?
6. Discuss the pros and cons of hash join, sort-merge join, and block nested loops join.
7. If the join condition is not equality, can you use sort-merge join? Can you use hash join? Can you use index nested loops join? Can you use block nested loops join?
8. Describe how to evaluate a grouping query with aggregation operator `MAX` using a sorting-based approach.
9. Suppose that you are building a DBMS and want to add a new aggregate operator called `SECOND LARGEST`, which is a variation of the `MAX` operator. Describe how you would implement it.
10. Give an example of how buffer replacement policies can affect the performance of a join algorithm.

Exercise 14.2 Consider a relation R(a,b,c,d,e) containing 5,000,000 records, where each data page of the relation holds 10 records. R is organized as a sorted file with secondary indexes. Assume that *R.a* is a candidate key for R, with values lying in the range 0 to 4,999,999, and that R is stored in *R.a* order. For each of the following relational algebra queries, state which of the following approaches (or combination thereof) is most likely to be the cheapest:

- Access the sorted file for R directly.

- Use a clustered B+ tree index on attribute $R.a$.
- Use a linear hashed index on attribute $R.a$.
- Use a clustered B+ tree index on attributes $(R.a, R.b)$.
- Use a linear hashed index on attributes $(R.a, R.b)$.
- Use an unclustered B+ tree index on attribute $R.b$.

1. $\sigma_{a<50,000 \wedge b<50,000}(R)$
2. $\sigma_{a=50,000 \wedge b<50,000}(R)$
3. $\sigma_{a>50,000 \wedge b=50,000}(R)$
4. $\sigma_{a=50,000 \wedge a=50,010}(R)$
5. $\sigma_{a \neq 50,000 \wedge b=50,000}(R)$
6. $\sigma_{a<50,000 \vee b=50,000}(R)$

Exercise 14.3 Consider processing the following SQL projection query:

SELECT DISTINCT E.title, E.ename FROM Executives E

You are given the following information:

Executives has attributes *ename*, *title*, *dname*, and *address*; all are string fields of the same length.
The *ename* attribute is a candidate key.
The relation contains 10,000 pages.
There are 10 buffer pages.

Consider the optimized version of the sorting-based projection algorithm: The initial sorting pass reads the input relation and creates sorted runs of tuples containing only attributes *ename* and *title*. Subsequent merging passes eliminate duplicates while merging the initial runs to obtain a single sorted result (as opposed to doing a separate pass to eliminate duplicates from a sorted result containing duplicates).

1. How many sorted runs are produced in the first pass? What is the average length of these runs? (Assume that memory is utilized well and any available optimization to increase run size is used.) What is the I/O cost of this sorting pass?
2. How many additional merge passes are required to compute the final result of the projection query? What is the I/O cost of these additional passes?
3. (a) Suppose that a clustered B+ tree index on *title* is available. Is this index likely to offer a cheaper alternative to sorting? Would your answer change if the index were unclustered? Would your answer change if the index were a hash index?

   (b) Suppose that a clustered B+ tree index on *ename* is available. Is this index likely to offer a cheaper alternative to sorting? Would your answer change if the index were unclustered? Would your answer change if the index were a hash index?

   (c) Suppose that a clustered B+ tree index on ⟨*ename*, *title*⟩ is available. Is this index likely to offer a cheaper alternative to sorting? Would your answer change if the index were unclustered? Would your answer change if the index were a hash index?
4. Suppose that the query is as follows:

   SELECT E.title, E.ename FROM Executives E

That is, you are not required to do duplicate elimination. How would your answers to the previous questions change?

Exercise 14.4 Consider the join $R \bowtie_{R.a=S.b} S$, given the following information about the relations to be joined. The cost metric is the number of page I/Os unless otherwise noted, and the cost of writing out the result should be uniformly ignored.

Relation R contains 10,000 tuples and has 10 tuples per page.
Relation S contains 2000 tuples and also has 10 tuples per page.
Attribute *b* of relation S is the primary key for S.
Both relations are stored as simple heap files.
Neither relation has any indexes built on it.
52 buffer pages are available.

1. What is the cost of joining R and S using a page-oriented simple nested loops join? What is the minimum number of buffer pages required for this cost to remain unchanged?
2. What is the cost of joining R and S using a block nested loops join? What is the minimum number of buffer pages required for this cost to remain unchanged?
3. What is the cost of joining R and S using a sort-merge join? What is the minimum number of buffer pages required for this cost to remain unchanged?
4. What is the cost of joining R and S using a hash join? What is the minimum number of buffer pages required for this cost to remain unchanged?
5. What would be the lowest possible I/O cost for joining R and S using *any* join algorithm, and how much buffer space would be needed to achieve this cost? Explain briefly.
6. How many tuples does the join of R and S produce, at most, and how many pages are required to store the result of the join back on disk?
7. Would your answers to any of the previous questions in this exercise change if you were told that *R.a* is a foreign key that refers to *S.b*?

Exercise 14.5 Consider the join of R and S described in Exercise 14.1.

1. With 52 buffer pages, if unclustered B+ indexes existed on *R.a* and *S.b*, would either provide a cheaper alternative for performing the join (using an index nested loops join) than a block nested loops join? Explain.
   (a) Would your answer change if only five buffer pages were available?
   (b) Would your answer change if S contained only 10 tuples instead of 2000 tuples?
2. With 52 buffer pages, if *clustered* B+ indexes existed on *R.a* and *S.b*, would either provide a cheaper alternative for performing the join (using the *index nested loops* algorithm) than a block nested loops join? Explain.
   (a) Would your answer change if only five buffer pages were available?
   (b) Would your answer change if S contained only 10 tuples instead of 2000 tuples?
3. If only 15 buffers were available, what would be the cost of a sort-merge join? What would be the cost of a hash join?
4. If the size of S were increased to also be 10,000 tuples, but only 15 buffer pages were available, what would be the cost of a sort-merge join? What would be the cost of a hash join?

5. If the size of S were increased to also be 10,000 tuples, and 52 buffer pages were available, what would be the cost of sort-merge join? What would be the cost of hash join?

Exercise 14.6 Answer each of the questions—if some question is inapplicable, explain why—in Exercise 14.1 again but using the following information about R and S:

Relation R contains 200,000 tuples and has 20 tuples per page.
Relation S contains 4,000,000 tuples and also has 20 tuples per page.
Attribute *a* of relation R is the primary key for R.
Each tuple of R joins with exactly 20 tuples of S.
1,002 buffer pages are available.

Exercise 14.7 We described variations of the join operation called *outer joins* in Section 5.6.4 . One approach to implementing an outer join operation is to first evaluate the corresponding (inner) join and then add additional tuples padded with *null* values to the result in accordance with the semantics of the given outer join operator. However, this requires us to compare the result of the inner join with the input relations to determine the additional tuples to be added. The cost of this comparison can be avoided by modifying the join algorithm to add these extra tuples to the result while input tuples are processed during the join. Consider the following join algorithms: *block nested loops join, index nested loops join, sort-merge join,* and *hash join.* Describe how you would modify each of these algorithms to compute the following operations on the Sailors and Reserves tables discussed in this chapter:

1. Sailors `NATURAL LEFT OUTER JOIN` Reserves
2. Sailors `NATURAL RIGHT OUTER JOIN` Reserves
3. Sailors `NATURAL FULL OUTER JOIN` Reserves

PROJECT-BASED EXERCISES

Exercise 14.8 (*Note to instructors: Additional details must be provided if this exercise is assigned; see Appendix 30.*) Implement the various join algorithms described in this chapter in Minibase. (As additional exercises, you may want to implement selected algorithms for the other operators as well.)

BIBLIOGRAPHIC NOTES

The implementation techniques used for relational operators in System R are discussed in [101]. The implementation techniques used in PRTV, which utilized relational algebra transformations and a form of multiple-query optimization, are discussed in [358]. The techniques used for aggregate operations in Ingres are described in [246]. [324] is an excellent survey of algorithms for implementing relational operators and is recommended for further reading.

Hash-based techniques are investigated (and compared with sort-based techniques) in [110], [222], [325], and [677]. Duplicate elimination is discussed in [99]. [277] discusses secondary storage access patterns arising in join implementations. Parallel algorithms for implementing relational operations are discussed in [99, 168, 220, 224, 233, 293, 534].

15

A TYPICAL RELATIONAL QUERY OPTIMIZER

- How are SQL queries translated into relational algebra? As a consequence, what class of relation algebra queries does a query optimizer concentrate on?
- What information is stored in the system catalog of a DBMS and how is it used in query optimization?
- How does an optimizer estimate the cost of a query evaluation plan?
- How does an optimizer generate alternative plans for a query? What is the space of plans considered? What is the role of relational algebra equivalences in generating plans?
- How are nested SQL queries optimized?
- **Key concepts:** SQL to algebra, query block; system catalog, data dictionary, metadata, system statistics, relational representation of catalogs; cost estimation, size estimation, reduction factors; histograms, equiwidth, equidepth, compressed; algebra equivalences, pushing selections, join ordering; plan space, single-relation plans, multi-relation left-deep plans; enumerating plans, dynamic programming approach, alternative approaches

Life is what happens while you're busy making other plans.

—John Lennon

In this chapter, we present a typical relational query optimizer in detail. We begin by discussing how SQL queries are converted into units called *blocks* and how blocks are translated into (extended) relational algebra expressions (Section 15.1). The central task of an optimizer is to find a good plan for evaluating such expressions. Optimizing a relational algebra expression involves two basic steps:

- Enumerating alternative plans for evaluating the expression. Typically, an optimizer considers a subset of all possible plans because the number of possible plans is very large.
- Estimating the cost of each enumerated plan and choosing the plan with the lowest estimated cost.

We discuss how to use system statistics to estimate the properties of the result of a relational operation, in particular result sizes, in Section 15.2. After discussing how to estimate the cost of a given plan, we describe the space of plans considered by a typical relational query optimizer in Sections 15.3 and 15.4. We discuss how nested SQL queries are handled in Section 15.5. We briefly discuss some of the influential choices made in the System R query optimizer in Section 15.6. We conclude with a short discussion of other approaches to query optimization in Section 15.7.

We consider a number of example queries using the following schema:

Sailors(*sid:* `integer`, *sname:* `string`, *rating:* `integer`, *age:* `real`)
Boats(*bid:* `integer`, *bname:* `string`, *color:* `string`)
Reserves(*sid:* `integer`, *bid:* `integer`, *day:* `dates`, *rname:* `string`)

As in Chapter 14, we assume that each tuple of Reserves is 40 bytes long, that a page can hold 100 Reserves tuples, and that we have 1000 pages of such tuples. Similarly, we assume that each tuple of Sailors is 50 bytes long, that a page can hold 80 Sailors tuples, and that we have 500 pages of such tuples.

15.1 TRANSLATING SQL QUERIES INTO ALGEBRA

SQL queries are optimized by decomposing them into a collection of smaller units, called *blocks.* A typical relational query optimizer concentrates on optimizing a single block at a time. In this section, we describe how a query is decomposed into blocks and how the optimization of a single block can be understood in terms of plans composed of relational algebra operators.

15.1.1 Decomposition of a Query into Blocks

When a user submits an SQL query, the query is parsed into a collection of query blocks and then passed on to the query optimizer. A **query block**

```
SELECT    S.sid, MIN (R.day)
FROM      Sailors S, Reserves R, Boats B
WHERE     S.sid = R.sid AND R.bid = B.bid AND B.color = 'red' AND
          S.rating = ( SELECT MAX (S2.rating)
                       FROM   Sailors S2 )
GROUP BY  S.sid
HAVING    COUNT (*) > 1
```

Figure 15.1 Sailors Reserving Red Boats

(or simply **block**) is an SQL query with no nesting and exactly one SELECT clause and one FROM clause and at most one WHERE clause, GROUP BY clause, and HAVING clause. The WHERE clause is assumed to be in conjunctive normal form, as per the discussion in Section 14.2. We use the following query as a running example:

For each sailor with the highest rating (over all sailors) and at least two reservations for red boats, find the sailor id and the earliest date on which the sailor has a reservation for a red boat.

The SQL version of this query is shown in Figure 15.1. This query has two query blocks. The **nested block** is:

```
SELECT MAX (S2.rating)
FROM   Sailors S2
```

The nested block computes the highest sailor rating. The **outer block** is shown in Figure 15.2. Every SQL query can be decomposed into a collection of query blocks without nesting.

```
SELECT    S.sid, MIN (R.day)
FROM      Sailors S, Reserves R, Boats B
WHERE     S.sid = R.sid AND R.bid = B.bid AND B.color = 'red' AND
          S.rating = Reference to nested block
GROUP BY  S.sid
HAVING    COUNT (*) > 1
```

Figure 15.2 Outer Block of Red Boats Query

The optimizer examines the system catalogs to retrieve information about the types and lengths of fields, statistics about the referenced relations, and the access paths (indexes) available for them. The optimizer then considers each query block and chooses a query evaluation plan for that block. We focus mostly on optimizing a single query block and defer a discussion of nested queries to Section 15.5.

15.1.2 A Query Block as a Relational Algebra Expression

The first step in optimizing a query block is to express it as a relational algebra expression. For uniformity, let us assume that `GROUP BY` and `HAVING` are also operators in the extended algebra used for plans and that aggregate operations are allowed to appear in the argument list of the projection operator. The meaning of the operators should be clear from our discussion of SQL. The SQL query of Figure 15.2 can be expressed in the extended algebra as:

$$\begin{aligned}
&\pi_{S.sid,MIN(R.day)}(\\
&HAVING_{COUNT(*)>2}(\\
&GROUP\ BY_{S.sid}(\\
&\sigma_{S.sid=R.sid \wedge R.bid=B.bid \wedge B.color='red' \wedge S.rating=value\ from\ nested\ block}(\\
&Sailors \times Reserves \times Boats))))
\end{aligned}$$

For brevity, we used S, R, and B (rather than Sailors, Reserves, and Boats) to prefix attributes. Intuitively, the selection is applied to the cross-product of the three relations. Then the qualifying tuples are grouped by $S.sid$, and the `HAVING` clause condition is used to discard some groups. For each remaining group, a result tuple containing the attributes (and count) mentioned in the projection list is generated. This algebra expression is a faithful summary of the semantics of an SQL query, which we discussed in Chapter 5.

Every SQL query block can be expressed as an extended algebra expression having this form. The `SELECT` clause corresponds to the projection operator, the `WHERE` clause corresponds to the selection operator, the `FROM` clause corresponds to the cross-product of relations, and the remaining clauses are mapped to corresponding operators in a straightforward manner.

The alternative plans examined by a typical relational query optimizer can be understood by recognizing that *a query is essentially treated as a* $\sigma\pi\times$ *algebra expression*, with the remaining operations (if any, in a given query) carried out on the result of the $\sigma\pi\times$ expression. The $\sigma\pi\times$ expression for the query in Figure 15.2 is:

$$\begin{aligned}
&\pi_{S.sid,R.day}(\\
&\sigma_{S.sid=R.sid \wedge R.bid=B.bid \wedge B.color='red' \wedge S.rating=value\ from\ nested\ block}(\\
&Sailors \times Reserves \times Boats))
\end{aligned}$$

To make sure that the `GROUP BY` and `HAVING` operations in the query can be carried out, the attributes mentioned in these clauses are added to the projection list. Further, since aggregate operations in the `SELECT` clause, such as the `MIN`*(R.day)* operation in our example, are computed after first computing the $\sigma\pi\times$ part of the query, aggregate expressions in the projection list are replaced by the names of the attributes to which they refer. Thus, the optimization of the $\sigma\pi\times$ part of the query essentially ignores these aggregate operations.

The optimizer finds the best plan for the $\sigma\pi\times$ expression obtained in this manner from a query. This plan is evaluated and the resulting tuples are then sorted (alternatively, hashed) to implement the GROUP BY clause. The HAVING clause is applied to eliminate some groups, and aggregate expressions in the SELECT clause are computed for each remaining group. This procedure is summarized in the following extended algebra expression:

$$\pi_{S.sid,MIN(R.day)}($$
$$HAVING_{COUNT(*)>2}($$
$$GROUP\ BY_{S.sid}($$
$$\pi_{S.sid,R.day}($$
$$\sigma_{S.sid=R.sid \wedge R.bid=B.bid \wedge B.color='red' \wedge S.rating=value\ from\ nested\ block}($$
$$Sailors \times Reserves \times Boats)))))$$

Some optimizations are possible if the FROM clause contains just one relation and the relation has some indexes that can be used to carry out the grouping operation. We discuss this situation further in Section 15.4.1.

To a first approximation therefore, the alternative plans examined by a typical optimizer can be understood in terms of the plans considered for $\sigma\pi\times$ queries. An optimizer enumerates plans by applying several equivalences between relational algebra expressions, which we present in Section 15.3. We discuss the space of plans enumerated by an optimizer in Section 15.4.

15.2 ESTIMATING THE COST OF A PLAN

For each enumerated plan, we have to estimate its cost. There are two parts to estimating the cost of an evaluation plan for a query block:

1. For each node in the tree, we must *estimate the cost* of performing the corresponding operation. Costs are affected significantly by whether pipelining is used or temporary relations are created to pass the output of an operator to its parent.

2. For each node in the tree, we must *estimate the size of the result* and whether it is sorted. This result is the input for the operation that corresponds to the parent of the current node, and the size and sort order in turn affect the estimation of size, cost, and sort order for the parent.

We discussed the cost of implementation techniques for relational operators in Chapter 14. As we saw there, estimating costs requires knowledge of various parameters of the input relations, such as the number of pages and available indexes. Such statistics are maintained in the DBMS's system catalogs. In this section, we describe the statistics maintained by a typical DBMS and discuss how result sizes are estimated. As in Chapter 14, we use the number of page I/Os as the metric of cost and ignore issues such as blocked access, for the sake of simplicity.

The estimates used by a DBMS for result sizes and costs are at best approximations to actual sizes and costs. It is unrealistic to expect an optimizer to find the very best plan; it is more important to avoid the worst plans and find a good plan.

15.2.1 Estimating Result Sizes

We now discuss how a typical optimizer estimates the size of the result computed by an operator on given inputs. Size estimation plays an important role in cost estimation as well because the output of one operator can be the input to another operator, and the cost of an operator depends on the size of its inputs.

Consider a query block of the form:

> `SELECT` *attribute list*
> `FROM` *relation list*
> `WHERE` $term_1 \wedge term_2 \wedge \ldots \wedge term_n$

The maximum number of tuples in the result of this query (without duplicate elimination) is the product of the cardinalities of the relations in the `FROM` clause. Every term in the `WHERE` clause, however, eliminates some of these potential result tuples. We can model the effect of the `WHERE` clause on the result size by associating a **reduction factor** with each term, which is the ratio of the (expected) result size to the input size considering only the selection represented by the term. The actual size of the result can be estimated as the maximum size times the product of the reduction factors for the terms in the `WHERE` clause. Of course, this estimate reflects the—unrealistic but simplifying—assumption that the conditions tested by each term are statistically independent.

We now consider how reduction factors can be computed for different kinds of terms in the `WHERE` clause by using the statistics available in the catalogs:

- *column = value*: For a term of this form, the reduction factor can be approximated by $\frac{1}{NKeys(I)}$ if there is an index I on *column* for the relation in question. This formula assumes uniform distribution of tuples among the index key values; this uniform distribution assumption is frequently made in arriving at cost estimates in a typical relational query optimizer. If there is no index on *column*, the System R optimizer arbitrarily assumes that the reduction factor is $\frac{1}{10}$. Of course, it is possible to maintain statistics such as the number of distinct values present for any attribute whether or not there is an index on that attribute. If such statistics are maintained, we can do better than the arbitrary choice of $\frac{1}{10}$.

- *column1 = column2*: In this case the reduction factor can be approximated by $\frac{1}{\texttt{MAX}\ (NKeys(I1), NKeys(I2))}$ if there are indexes $I1$ and $I2$ on *column1* and *column2*, respectively. This formula assumes that each key value in the smaller index, say, $I1$, has a matching value in the other index. Given a value for *column1*, we assume that each of the $NKeys(I2)$ values for *column2* is equally likely. Therefore, the number of tuples that have the same value in *column2* as a given value in *column1* is $\frac{1}{NKeys(I2)}$. If only one of the two columns has an index I, we take the reduction factor to be $\frac{1}{NKeys(I)}$; if neither column has an index, we approximate it by the ubiquitous $\frac{1}{10}$. These formulas are used whether or not the two columns appear in the same relation.

- *column > value*: The reduction factor is approximated by $\frac{High(I)\ -\ value}{High(I)\ -\ Low(I)}$ if there is an index I on *column*. If the column is not of an arithmetic type or there is no index, a fraction less than half is arbitrarily chosen. Similar formulas for the reduction factor can be derived for other range selections.

- *column* IN *(list of values)*: The reduction factor is taken to be the reduction factor for *column = value* multiplied by the number of items in the list. However, it is allowed to be at most half, reflecting the heuristic belief that each selection eliminates at least half the candidate tuples.

These estimates for reduction factors are at best approximations that rely on assumptions such as uniform distribution of values and independent distribution of values in different columns. In recent years more sophisticated techniques based on storing more detailed statistics (e.g., histograms of the values in a column, which we consider later in this section) have been proposed and are finding their way into commercial systems.

Reduction factors can also be approximated for terms of the form *column* IN *subquery* (ratio of the estimated size of the subquery result to the number of distinct values in *column* in the outer relation); NOT *condition* (1−reduction factor for *condition*); *value1*<*column*<*value2*; the disjunction of two conditions; and so on, but we will not discuss such reduction factors.

To summarize, regardless of the plan chosen, we can estimate the size of the final result by taking the product of the sizes of the relations in the FROM clause

Estimating Query Characteristics: IBM DB2, Informix, Microsoft SQL Server, Oracle 8, and Sybase ASE all use histograms to estimate query characteristics such as result size and cost. As an example, Sybase ASE uses one-dimensional, equidepth histograms with some special attention paid to high frequency values, so that their count is estimated accurately. ASE also keeps the average count of duplicates for each prefix of an index to estimate correlations between histograms for composite keys (although it does not maintain such histograms). ASE also maintains estimates of the degree of clustering in tables and indexes. IBM DB2, Informix, and Oracle also use one-dimensional equidepth histograms; Oracle automatically switches to maintaining a count of duplicates for each value when there are few values in a column. Microsoft SQL Server uses one-dimensional equiarea histograms with some optimizations (adjacent buckets with similar distributions are sometimes combined to compress the histogram). In SQL Server, the creation and maintenance of histograms is done automatically with no need for user input.

Although sampling techniques have been studied for estimating result sizes and costs, in current systems, sampling is used only by system utilities to estimate statistics or build histograms but not directly by the optimizer to estimate query characteristics. Sometimes, sampling is used to do load balancing in parallel implementations.

and the reduction factors for the terms in the `WHERE` clause. We can similarly estimate the size of the result of each operator in a plan tree by using reduction factors, since the subtree rooted at that operator's node is itself a query block.

Note that the number of tuples in the result is not affected by projections if duplicate elimination is not performed. However, projections reduce the number of pages in the result because tuples in the result of a projection are smaller than the original tuples; the ratio of tuple sizes can be used as a **reduction factor for projection** to estimate the result size in pages, given the size of the input relation.

Improved Statistics: Histograms

Consider a relation with N tuples and a selection of the form *column* $>$ *value* on a column with an index I. The reduction factor r is approximated by $\frac{High(I) - value}{High(I) - Low(I)}$, and the size of the result is estimated as rN. This estimate relies on the assumption that the distribution of values is uniform.

Estimates can be improved considerably by maintaining more detailed statistics than just the low and high values in the index I. Intuitively, we want to approximate the distribution of key values I as accurately as possible. Consider the two distributions of values shown in Figure 15.3. The first is a nonuniform distribution D of values (say, for an attribute called *age*). The *frequency* of a value is the number of tuples with that *age* value; a distribution is represented by showing the frequency for each possible *age* value. In our example, the lowest *age* value is 0, the highest is 14, and all recorded *age* values are integers in the range 0 to 14. The second distribution approximates D by assuming that each *age* value in the range 0 to 14 appears equally often in the underlying collection of tuples. This approximation can be stored compactly because we need to record only the low and high values for the *age* range (0 and 14 respectively) and the total count of all frequencies (which is 45 in our example).

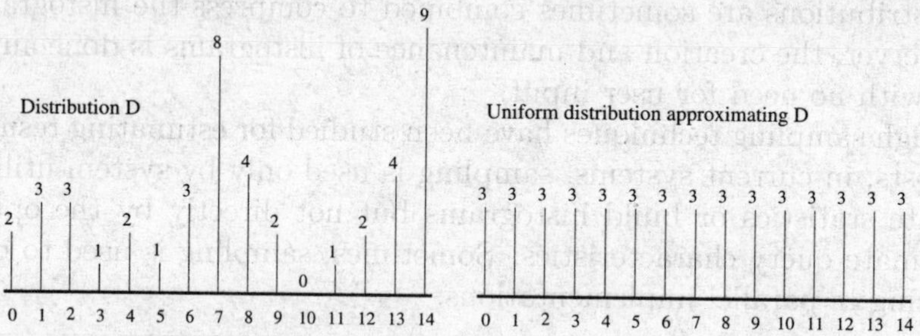

Figure 15.3 Uniform vs. Nonuniform Distributions

Consider the selection *age* > 13. From the distribution D in Figure 15.3, we see that the result has 9 tuples. Using the uniform distribution approximation, on the other hand, we estimate the result size as $\frac{1}{15} \cdot 45 = 3$ tuples. Clearly, the estimate is quite inaccurate.

A **histogram** is a data structure maintained by a DBMS to approximate a data distribution. In Figure 15.4, we show how the data distribution from Figure 15.3 can be approximated by dividing the range of *age* values into subranges called **buckets**, and for each bucket, counting the number of tuples with *age* values within that bucket. Figure 15.4 shows two different kinds of histograms, called *equiwidth* and *equidepth*, respectively.

Consider the selection query *age* > 13 again and the first (equiwidth) histogram. We can estimate the size of the result to be 5 because the selected range includes a third of the range for Bucket 5. Since Bucket 5 represents a total of 15 tuples, the selected range corresponds to $\frac{1}{3} \cdot 15 = 5$ tuples. As this example shows, we assume that the distribution *within* a histogram bucket is uniform. Therefore, when we simply maintain the high and low values for index

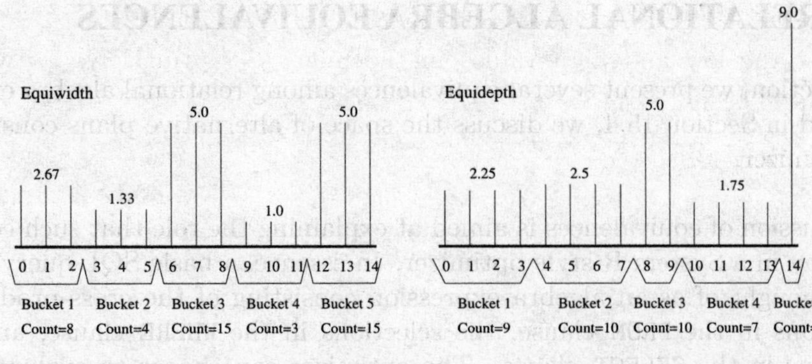

Figure 15.4 Histograms Approximating Distribution D

I, we effectively use a 'histogram' with a single bucket. Using histograms with a small number of buckets instead leads to much more accurate estimates, at the cost of a few hundred bytes per histogram. (Like all statistics in a DBMS, histograms are updated periodically rather than whenever the data is changed.)

One important question is how to divide the value range into buckets. In an **equiwidth** histogram, we divide the range into subranges of equal size (in terms of the *age* value range). We could also choose subranges such that the number of tuples within each subrange (i.e., bucket) is equal. Such a histogram, called an **equidepth** histogram, is also illustrated in Figure 15.4. Consider the selection $age > 13$ again. Using the equidepth histogram, we are led to Bucket 5, which contains only the *age* value 15, and thus we arrive at the exact answer, 9. While the relevant bucket (or buckets) generally contains more than one tuple, equidepth histograms provide better estimates than equiwidth histograms. Intuitively, buckets with very frequently occurring values contain fewer values, and thus the uniform distribution assumption is applied to a smaller range of values, leading to better approximations. Conversely, buckets with mostly infrequent values are approximated less accurately in an equidepth histogram, but for good estimation, the frequent values are important.

Proceeding further with the intuition about the importance of frequent values, another alternative is to maintain separate counts for a small number of very frequent values, say the *age* values 7 and 14 in our example, and maintain an equidepth (or other) histogram to cover the remaining values. Such a histogram is called a **compressed** histogram. Most commercial DBMSs currently use equidepth histograms, and some use compressed histograms.

15.3 RELATIONAL ALGEBRA EQUIVALENCES

In this section, we present several equivalences among relational algebra expressions; and in Section 15.4, we discuss the space of alternative plans considered by a optimizer.

Our discussion of equivalences is aimed at explaining the role that such equivalences play in a System R style optimizer. In essence, a basic SQL query block can be thought of as an algebra expression consisting of the cross-product of all relations in the `FROM` clause, the selections in the `WHERE` clause, and the projections in the `SELECT` clause. The optimizer can choose to evaluate any equivalent expression and still obtain the same result. Algebra equivalences allow us to convert cross-products to joins, choose different join orders, and push selections and projections ahead of joins. For simplicity, we assume that naming conflicts never arise and we need not consider the renaming operator ρ.

15.3.1 Selections

Two important equivalences involve the selection operation. The first one involves **cascading of selections**:

$$\sigma_{c1 \wedge c2 \wedge \ldots c_n}(R) \equiv \sigma_{c1}(\sigma_{c2}(\ldots(\sigma_{c_n}(R))\ldots))$$

Going from the right side to the left, this equivalence allows us to combine several selections into one selection. Intuitively, we can test whether a tuple meets each of the conditions $c_1 \ldots c_n$ at the same time. In the other direction, this equivalence allows us to take a selection condition involving several conjuncts and replace it with several smaller selection operations. Replacing a selection with several smaller selections turns out to be very useful in combination with other equivalences, especially commutation of selections with joins or cross-products, which we discuss shortly. Intuitively, such a replacement is useful in cases where only part of a complex selection condition can be pushed.

The second equivalence states that selections are **commutative**:

$$\sigma_{c1}(\sigma_{c2}(R)) \equiv \sigma_{c2}(\sigma_{c1}(R))$$

In other words, we can test the conditions c_1 and c_2 in either order.

15.3.2 Projections

The rule for **cascading projections** says that successively eliminating columns from a relation is equivalent to simply eliminating all but the columns retained by the final projection:

$$\pi_{a_1}(R) \equiv \pi_{a_1}(\pi_{a_2}(\ldots(\pi_{a_n}(R))\ldots))$$

Each a_i is a set of attributes of relation R, and $a_i \subseteq a_{i+1}$ for $i = 1 \ldots n - 1$. This equivalence is useful in conjunction with other equivalences such as commutation of projections with joins.

15.3.3 Cross-Products and Joins

Two important equivalences involving cross-products and joins. We present them in terms of natural joins for simplicity, but they hold for general joins as well.

First, assuming that fields are identified by name rather than position, these operations are **commutative**:

$$R \times S \equiv S \times R$$

$$R \bowtie S \equiv S \bowtie R$$

This property is very important. It allows us to choose which relation is to be the inner and which the outer in a join of two relations.

The second equivalence states that joins and cross-products are **associative**:

$$R \times (S \times T) \equiv (R \times S) \times T$$

$$R \bowtie (S \bowtie T) \equiv (R \bowtie S) \bowtie T$$

Thus we can either join R and S first and then join T to the result, or join S and T first and then join R to the result. The intuition behind associativity of cross-products is that, regardless of the order in which the three relations are considered, the final result contains the same columns. Join associativity is based on the same intuition, with the additional observation that the selections specifying the join conditions can be cascaded. Thus the same rows appear in the final result, regardless of the order in which the relations are joined.

Together with commutativity, associativity essentially says that we can choose to join any pair of these relations, then join the result with the third relation, and always obtain the same final result. For example, let us verify that

$$R \bowtie (S \bowtie T) \equiv (T \bowtie R) \bowtie S$$

From commutativity, we have:

$$R \bowtie (S \bowtie T) \equiv R \bowtie (T \bowtie S)$$

From associativity, we have:

$$R \bowtie (T \bowtie S) \equiv (R \bowtie T) \bowtie S$$

Using commutativity again, we have:

$$(R \bowtie T) \bowtie S \equiv (T \bowtie R) \bowtie S$$

In other words, when joining several relations, we are free to join the relations in any order we choose. This order-independence is fundamental to how a query optimizer generates alternative query evaluation plans.

15.3.4 Selects, Projects, and Joins

Some important equivalences involve two or more operators.

We can **commute** a selection with a projection if the selection operation involves only attributes retained by the projection:

$$\pi_a(\sigma_c(R)) \equiv \sigma_c(\pi_a(R))$$

Every attribute mentioned in the selection condition c must be included in the set of attributes a.

We can **combine** a selection with a cross-product to form a join, as per the definition of join:

$$R \bowtie_c S \equiv \sigma_c(R \times S)$$

We can **commute** a selection with a cross-product or a join if the selection condition involves only attributes of one of the arguments to the cross-product or join:

$$\sigma_c(R \times S) \equiv \sigma_c(R) \times S$$
$$\sigma_c(R \bowtie S) \equiv \sigma_c(R) \bowtie S$$

The attributes mentioned in c must appear only in R and not in S. Similar equivalences hold if c involves only attributes of S and not R, of course.

In general, a selection σ_c on $R \times S$ can be replaced by a cascade of selections σ_{c_1}, σ_{c_2}, and σ_{c_3} such that c_1 involves attributes of both R and S, c_2 involves only attributes of R, and c_3 involves only attributes of S:

$$\sigma_c(R \times S) \equiv \sigma_{c_1 \wedge c_2 \wedge c_3}(R \times S)$$

Using the cascading rule for selections, this expression is equivalent to

$$\sigma_{c_1}(\sigma_{c_2}(\sigma_{c_3}(R \times S)))$$

Using the rule for commuting selections and cross-products, this expression is equivalent to

$$\sigma_{c1}(\sigma_{c2}(R) \times \sigma_{c3}(S))$$

Thus we can push part of the selection condition c ahead of the cross-product. This observation also holds for selections in combination with joins, of course.

We can **commute** a projection with a cross-product:

$$\pi_a(R \times S) \equiv \pi_{a1}(R) \times \pi_{a2}(S)$$

where a_1 is the subset of attributes in a that appear in R, and a_2 is the subset of attributes in a that appear in S. We can also **commute** a projection with a join if the join condition involves only attributes retained by the projection:

$$\pi_a(R \bowtie_c S) \equiv \pi_{a1}(R) \bowtie_c \pi_{a2}(S)$$

where a_1 is the subset of attributes in a that appear in R, and a_2 is the subset of attributes in a that appear in S. Further, every attribute mentioned in the join condition c must appear in a.

Intuitively, we need to retain only those attributes of R and S that are either mentioned in the join condition c or included in the set of attributes a retained by the projection. Clearly, if a includes all attributes mentioned in c, the previous commutation rules hold. If a does *not* include all attributes mentioned in c, we can generalize the commutation rules by first projecting out attributes that are not mentioned in c or a, performing the join, and then projecting out all attributes that are not in a:

$$\pi_a(R \bowtie_c S) \equiv \pi_a(\pi_{a1}(R) \bowtie_c \pi_{a2}(S))$$

Now, a_1 is the subset of attributes of R that appear in either a or c, and a_2 is the subset of attributes of S that appear in either a or c.

We can in fact derive the more general commutation rule by using the rule for cascading projections and the simple commutation rule, and we leave this as an exercise for the reader.

15.3.5 Other Equivalences

Additional equivalences hold when we consider operations such as set-difference, union, and intersection. Union and intersection are associative and commutative. Selections and projections can be commuted with each of the set operations (set-difference, union, and intersection). We do not discuss these equivalences further.

```
SELECT     S.rating, COUNT (*)
FROM       Sailors S
WHERE      S.rating > 5 AND S.age = 20
GROUP BY   S.rating
HAVING     COUNT DISTINCT (S.sname) > 2
```

Figure 15.5 A Single-Relation Query

15.4 ENUMERATION OF ALTERNATIVE PLANS

We now come to an issue that is at the heart of an optimizer, namely, the space of alternative plans considered for a given query. Given a query, an optimizer essentially enumerates a certain set of plans and chooses the plan with the least estimated cost; the discussion in Section 12.1.1 indicated how the cost of a plan is estimated. The algebraic equivalences discussed in Section 15.3 form the basis for generating alternative plans, in conjunction with the choice of implementation technique for the relational operators (e.g., joins) present in the query. However, not all algebraically equivalent plans are considered, because doing so would make the cost of optimization prohibitively expensive for all but the simplest queries. This section describes the subset of plans considered by a typical optimizer.

There are two important cases to consider: queries in which the FROM clause contains a single relation and queries in which the FROM clause contains two or more relations.

15.4.1 Single-Relation Queries

If the query contains a single relation in the FROM clause, only selection, projection, grouping, and aggregate operations are involved; there are no joins. If we have just one selection or projection or aggregate operation applied to a relation, the alternative implementation techniques and cost estimates discussed in Chapter 14 cover all the plans that must be considered. We now consider how to optimize queries that involve a combination of several such operations, using the following query as an example:

For each rating greater than 5, print the rating and the number of 20-year-old sailors with that rating, provided that there are at least two such sailors with different names.

The SQL version of this query is shown in Figure 15.5. Using the extended algebra notation introduced in Section 15.1.2, we can write this query as:

$$\pi_{S.rating,COUNT(*)}($$

$$HAVING_{COUNTDISTINCT(S.sname)>2}($$
$$GROUP\ BY_{S.rating}($$
$$\pi_{S.rating,S.sname}($$
$$\sigma_{S.rating>5 \wedge S.age=20}($$
$$Sailors)))))$$

Notice that *S.sname* is added to the projection list, even though it is not in the `SELECT` clause, because it is required to test the `HAVING` clause condition.

We are now ready to discuss the plans that an optimizer would consider. The main decision to be made is which access path to use in retrieving Sailors tuples. If we considered only the selections, we would simply choose the most selective access path, based on which available indexes *match* the conditions in the `WHERE` clause (as per the definition in Section 14.2.1). Given the additional operators in this query, we must also take into account the cost of subsequent sorting steps and consider whether these operations can be performed without sorting by exploiting some index. We first discuss the plans generated when there are no suitable indexes and then examine plans that utilize some index.

Plans without Indexes

The basic approach in the absence of a suitable index is to scan the Sailors relation and apply the selection and projection (without duplicate elimination) operations to each retrieved tuple, as indicated by the following algebra expression:

$$\pi_{S.rating,S.sname}($$
$$\sigma_{S.rating>5 \wedge S.age=20}($$
$$Sailors))$$

The resulting tuples are then sorted according to the `GROUP BY` clause (in the example query, on *rating*), and one answer tuple is generated for each group that meets the condition in the `HAVING` clause. The computation of the aggregate functions in the `SELECT` and `HAVING` clauses is done for each group, using one of the techniques described in Section 14.6.

The cost of this approach consists of the costs of each of these steps:

1. Performing a file scan to retrieve tuples and apply the selections and projections.
2. Writing out tuples after the selections and projections.
3. Sorting these tuples to implement the `GROUP BY` clause.

Note that the HAVING clause does not cause additional I/O. The aggregate computations can be done on-the-fly (with respect to I/O) as we generate the tuples in each group at the end of the sorting step for the GROUP BY clause.

In the example query the cost includes the cost of a file scan on Sailors plus the cost of writing out ⟨*S.rating, S.sname*⟩ pairs plus the cost of sorting as per the GROUP BY clause. The cost of the file scan is *NPages(Sailors)*, which is 500 I/Os, and the cost of writing out ⟨*S.rating, S.sname*⟩ pairs is *NPages(Sailors)* times the ratio of the size of such a pair to the size of a Sailors tuple times the reduction factors of the two selection conditions. In our example, the result tuple size ratio is about 0.8, the *rating* selection has a reduction factor of 0.5, and we use the default factor of 0.1 for the *age* selection. Therefore, the cost of this step is 20 I/Os. The cost of sorting this intermediate relation (which we call *Temp*) can be estimated as *3*NPages(Temp)*, which is 60 I/Os, if we assume that enough pages are available in the buffer pool to sort it in two passes. (Relational optimizers often assume that a relation can be sorted in two passes, to simplify the estimation of sorting costs. If this assumption is not met at run-time, the actual cost of sorting may be higher than the estimate.) The total cost of the example query is therefore $500 + 20 + 60 = 580$ I/Os.

Plans Utilizing an Index

Indexes can be utilized in several ways and can lead to plans that are significantly faster than any plan that does not utilize indexes:

1. **Single-Index Access Path:** If several indexes match the selection conditions in the WHERE clause, each matching index offers an alternative access path. An optimizer can choose the access path that it estimates will result in retrieving the fewest pages, apply any projections and nonprimary selection terms (i.e., parts of the selection condition that do not match the index), and proceed to compute the grouping and aggregation operations (by sorting on the GROUP BY attributes).

2. **Multiple-Index Access Path:** If several indexes using Alternatives (2) or (3) for data entries match the selection condition, each such index can be used to retrieve a set of rids. We can *intersect* these sets of rids, then sort the result by page id (assuming that the rid representation includes the page id) and retrieve tuples that satisfy the primary selection terms of all the matching indexes. Any projections and nonprimary selection terms can then be applied, followed by grouping and aggregation operations.

3. **Sorted Index Access Path:** If the list of grouping attributes is a prefix of a tree index, the index can be used to retrieve tuples in the order required by the GROUP BY clause. All selection conditions can be applied on each

retrieved tuple, unwanted fields can be removed, and aggregate operations computed for each group. This strategy works well for clustered indexes.

4. **Index-Only Access Path:** If all the attributes mentioned in the query (in the `SELECT`, `WHERE`, `GROUP BY`, or `HAVING` clauses) are included in the search key for some *dense* index on the relation in the `FROM` clause, an **index-only scan** can be used to compute answers. Because the data entries in the index contain all the attributes of a tuple needed for this query and there is one index entry per tuple, we never need to retrieve actual tuples from the relation. Using just the data entries from the index, we can carry out the following steps as needed in a given query: Apply selection conditions, remove unwanted attributes, sort the result to achieve grouping, and compute aggregate functions within each group. This *index-only* approach works even if the index does not match the selections in the `WHERE` clause. If the index matches the selection, we need examine only a subset of the index entries; otherwise, we must scan all index entries. In either case, we can avoid retrieving actual data records; therefore, the cost of this strategy does not depend on whether the index is clustered. In addition, if the index is a tree index and the list of attributes in the `GROUP BY` clause forms a prefix of the index key, we can retrieve data entries in the order needed for the `GROUP BY` clause and thereby avoid sorting!

We now illustrate each of these four cases, using the query shown in Figure 15.5 as a running example. We assume that the following indexes, all using Alternative (2) for data entries, are available: a B+ tree index on *rating*, a hash index on *age*, and a B+ tree index on $\langle$*rating, sname, age*$\rangle$. For brevity, we do not present detailed cost calculations, but the reader should be able to calculate the cost of each plan. The steps in these plans are scans (a file scan, a scan retrieving tuples by using an index, or a scan of only index entries), sorting, and writing temporary relations; and we have already discussed how to estimate the costs of these operations.

As an example of the first case, we could choose to retrieve Sailors tuples such that $S.age$=20 using the hash index on *age*. The cost of this step is the cost of retrieving the index entries plus the cost of retrieving the corresponding Sailors tuples, which depends on whether the index is clustered. We can then apply the condition $S.rating > 5$ to each retrieved tuple; project out fields not mentioned in the `SELECT`, `GROUP BY`, and `HAVING` clauses; and write the result to a temporary relation. In the example, only the *rating* and *sname* fields need to be retained. The temporary relation is then sorted on the *rating* field to identify the groups, and some groups are eliminated by applying the `HAVING` condition.

> **Utilizing Indexes:** All of the main RDBMSs recognize the importance of index-only plans and look for such plans whenever possible. In IBM DB2, when creating an index a user can specify a set of 'include' columns that are to be kept in the index but are *not* part of the index key. This allows a richer set of index-only queries to be handled, because columns frequently accessed are included in the index even if they are not part of the key. In Microsoft SQL Server, an interesting class of index-only plans is considered: Consider a query that selects attributes *sal* and *age* from a table, given an index on *sal* and another index on *age*. SQL Server uses the indexes by joining the entries on the rid of data records to identify $\langle sal, age \rangle$ pairs that appear in the table.

As an example of the second case, we can retrieve rids of tuples satisfying *rating*>5 using the index on *rating*, retrieve rids of tuples satisfying *age*=20 using the index on *age*, sort the retrieved rids by page number, and then retrieve the corresponding Sailors tuples. We can retain just the *rating* and *name* fields and write the result to a temporary relation, which we can sort on *rating* to implement the `GROUP BY` clause. (A good optimizer might pipeline the projected tuples to the sort operator without creating a temporary relation.) The `HAVING` clause is handled as before.

As an example of the third case, we can retrieve Sailors tuples in which *S.rating* > 5, ordered by *rating*, using the B+ tree index on *rating*. We can compute the aggregate functions in the `HAVING` and `SELECT` clauses on-the-fly because tuples are retrieved in *rating* order.

As an example of the fourth case, we can retrieve *data entries* from the $\langle$*rating, sname, age*$\rangle$ index in which *rating* > 5. These entries are sorted by *rating* (and then by *sname* and *age*, although this additional ordering is not relevant for this query). We can choose entries with *age=20* and compute the aggregate functions in the `HAVING` and `SELECT` clauses on-the-fly because the data entries are retrieved in *rating* order. In this case, in contrast to the previous case, we do not retrieve any Sailors tuples. This property of not retrieving data records makes the index-only strategy especially valuable with unclustered indexes.

15.4.2 Multiple-Relation Queries

Query blocks that contain two or more relations in the `FROM` clause require joins (or cross-products). Finding a good plan for such queries is very important because these queries can be quite expensive. Regardless of the plan chosen, the size of the final result can be estimated by taking the product of the sizes of the relations in the FROM clause and the reduction factors for the terms in the WHERE clause. But, depending on the order in which relations are joined, intermediate relations of widely varying sizes can be created, leading to plans with very different costs.

Enumeration of Left-Deep Plans

As we saw in Chapter 12, current relational systems, following the lead of the System R optimizer, only consider left-deep plans. We now discuss how this class of plans is efficiently searched using dynamic programming.

Consider a query block of the form:

```
SELECT  attribute list
FROM    relation list
WHERE   term1 ∧ term2 ∧ ... ∧ termn
```

A System R style query optimizer enumerates all left-deep plans, with selections and projections considered (but not necessarily applied!) as early as possible. The enumeration of plans can be understood as a multiple-pass algorithm in which we proceed as follows:

Pass 1: We enumerate all single-relation plans (over some relation in the FROM clause). Intuitively, each single-relation plan is a partial left-deep plan for evaluating the query in which the given relation is the first (in the linear join order for the left-deep plan of which it is a part). When considering plans involving a relation A, we identify those selection terms in the WHERE clause that mention only attributes of A. These are the selections that can be performed when first accessing A, before any joins that involve A. We also identify those attributes of A not mentioned in the SELECT clause or in terms in the WHERE clause involving attributes of other relations. These attributes can be projected out when first accessing A, before any joins that involve A. We choose the best access method for A to carry out these selections and projections, as per the discussion in Section 15.4.1.

For each relation, if we find plans that produce tuples in different orders, we retain the cheapest plan for each such ordering of tuples. An ordering of tuples could prove useful at a subsequent step, say, for a sort-merge join or implementing a GROUP BY or ORDER BY clause. Hence, for a single relation, we may retain a file scan (as the cheapest overall plan for fetching all tuples) and a B+ tree index (as the cheapest plan for fetching all tuples in the search key order).

Pass 2: We generate all two-relation plans by considering each single-relation plan retained after Pass 1 as the outer relation and (successively) every other relation as the inner relation. Suppose that A is the outer relation and B the inner relation for a particular two-relation plan. We examine the list of selections in the WHERE clause and identify:

1. Selections that involve only attributes of B and can be applied before the join.
2. Selections that define the join (i.e., are conditions involving attributes of both A and B and no other relation).
3. Selections that involve attributes of other relations and can be applied only after the join.

The first two groups of selections can be considered while choosing an access path for the inner relation B. We also identify the attributes of B that do not appear in the SELECT clause or in any selection conditions in the second or third group and can therefore be projected out before the join.

Note that our identification of attributes that can be projected out before the join and selections that can be applied before the join is based on the relational algebra equivalences discussed earlier. In particular, we rely on the equivalences that allow us to push selections and projections ahead of joins. As we will see, whether we actually perform these selections and projections ahead of a given join depends on cost considerations. The only selections that are really applied *before* the join are those that match the chosen access paths for A and B. The remaining selections and projections are done on-the-fly as part of the join.

An important point to note is that tuples generated by the outer plan are assumed to be *pipelined* into the join. That is, we avoid having the outer plan write its result to a file that is subsequently read by the join (to obtain outer tuples). For some join methods, the join operator might require materializing the outer tuples. For example, a hash join would partition the incoming tuples, and a sort-merge join would sort them if they are not already in the appropriate sort order. Nested loops joins, however, can use outer tuples as they are generated and avoid materializing them. Similarly, sort-merge joins can use outer tuples as they are generated if they are generated in the sorted order required for the join. We include the cost of materializing the outer relation, should this be necessary, in the cost of the join. The adjustments to the join costs discussed in Chapter 14 to reflect the use of pipelining or materialization of the outer are straightforward.

For each single-relation plan for A retained after Pass 1, for each join method that we consider, we must determine the best access method to use for B. The access method chosen for B retrieves, in general, a subset of the tuples in B, possibly with some fields eliminated, as discussed later. Consider relation B.

We have a collection of selections (some of which are the join conditions) and projections on a single relation, and the choice of the best access method is made as per the discussion in Section 15.4.1. The only additional consideration is that the join method might require tuples to be retrieved in some order. For example, in a sort-merge join, we want the inner tuples in sorted order on the join column(s). If a given access method does not retrieve inner tuples in this order, we must add the cost of an additional sorting step to the cost of the access method.

Pass 3: We generate all three-relation plans. We proceed as in Pass 2, except that we now consider plans retained after Pass 2 as outer relations, instead of plans retained after Pass 1.

Additional Passes: This process is repeated with additional passes until we produce plans that contain all the relations in the query. We now have the cheapest overall plan for the query as well as the cheapest plan for producing the answers in some interesting order.

If a multiple-relation query contains a `GROUP BY` clause and aggregate functions such as `MIN`, `MAX`, and `SUM` in the `SELECT` clause, these are dealt with at the very end. If the query block includes a `GROUP BY` clause, a set of tuples is computed based on the rest of the query, as described above, and this set is sorted as per the `GROUP BY` clause. Of course, if there is a plan according to which the set of tuples is produced in the desired order, the cost of this plan is compared with the cost of the cheapest plan (assuming that the two are different) plus the sorting cost. Given the sorted set of tuples, partitions are identified and any aggregate functions in the `SELECT` clause are applied on a per-partition basis, as per the discussion in Chapter 14.

Examples of Multiple-Relation Query Optimization

Consider the query tree shown in Figure 12.3. Figure 15.6 shows the same query, taking into account how selections and projections are considered early.

In looking at this figure, it is worth emphasizing that the selections shown on the leaves are not necessarily done in a distinct step that precedes the join—rather, as we have seen, they are considered as potential matching predicates when considering the available access paths on the relations.

Suppose that we have the following indexes, all unclustered and using Alternative (2) for data entries: a B+ tree index on the *rating* field of Sailors, a hash index on the *sid* field of Sailors, and a B+ tree index on the *bid* field of

Optimization in Commercial Systems: IBM DB2, Informix, Microsoft SQL Server, Oracle 8, and Sybase ASE all search for left-deep trees using dynamic programming, as described here, with several variations. For example, Oracle always considers interchanging the two relations in a hash join, which could lead to right-deep trees or hybrids. DB2 generates some bushy trees as well. Systems often use a variety of strategies for generating plans, going beyond the systematic bottom-up enumeration that we described, in conjunction with a dynamic programming strategy for costing plans and remembering interesting plans (to avoid repeated analysis of the same plan). Systems also vary in the degree of control they give users. Sybase ASE and Oracle 8 allow users to force the choice of join orders and indexes—Sybase ASE even allows users to explicitly edit the execution plan—whereas IBM DB2 does not allow users to direct the optimizer other than by setting an 'optimization level,' which influences how many alternative plans the optimizer considers.

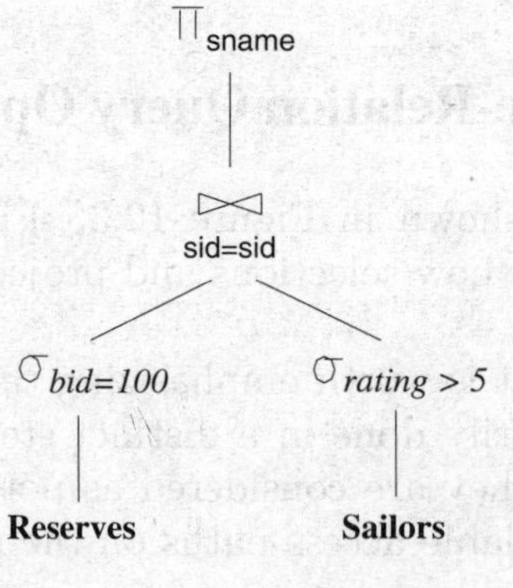

Figure 15.6 A Query Tree

Reserves. In addition, we assume that we can do a sequential scan of both Reserves and Sailors. Let us consider how the optimizer proceeds.

In Pass 1, we consider three access methods for Sailors (B+ tree, hash index, and sequential scan), taking into account the selection $\sigma_{rating>5}$. This selection matches the B+ tree on *rating* and therefore reduces the cost for retrieving tuples that satisfy this selection. The cost of retrieving tuples using the hash index and the sequential scan is likely to be much higher than the cost of using the B+ tree. So the plan retained for Sailors is access via the B+ tree index, and it retrieves tuples in sorted order by *rating*. Similarly, we consider two access methods for Reserves taking into account the selection $\sigma_{bid=100}$. This selection matches the B+ tree index on Reserves, and the cost of retrieving matching tuples via this index is likely to be much lower than the cost of retrieving tuples using a sequential scan; access through the B+ tree index is therefore the only plan retained for Reserves after Pass 1.

In Pass 2, we consider taking the (relation computed by the) plan for Reserves and joining it (as the outer) with Sailors. In doing so, we recognize that now, we need only Sailors tuples that satisfy $\sigma_{rating>5}$ and $\sigma_{sid=value}$, where *value* is some value from an outer tuple. The selection $\sigma_{sid=value}$ matches the hash index on the *sid* field of Sailors, and the selection $\sigma_{rating>5}$ matches the B+ tree index on the *rating* field. Since the equality selection has a much lower reduction factor, the hash index is likely to be the cheaper access method. In addition to the preceding consideration of alternative access methods, we consider alternative join methods. All available join methods are considered. For example, consider a sort-merge join. The inputs must be sorted by *sid*; since neither input is sorted by *sid* or has an access method that can return tuples in this order, the cost of the sort-merge join in this case must include the cost of storing the two inputs in temporary relations and sorting them. A sort-merge join provides results in sorted order by *sid*, but this is not a useful ordering in this example because the projection π_{sname} is applied (on-the-fly) to the result of the join, thereby eliminating the *sid* field from the answer. Therefore, the plan using sort-merge join is retained after Pass 2 only if it is the least expensive plan involving Reserves and Sailors.

Similarly, we also consider taking the plan for Sailors retained after Pass 1 and joining it (as the outer relation) with Reserves. Now we recognize that we need only Reserves tuples that satisfy $\sigma_{bid=100}$ and $\sigma_{sid=value}$, where *value* is some value from an outer tuple. Again, we consider all available join methods.

We finally retain the cheapest plan overall.

As another example, illustrating the case when more than two relations are joined, consider the following query:

```
SELECT    S.sid, COUNT(*) AS numres
FROM      Boats B, Reserves R, Sailors S
WHERE     R.sid = S.sid AND B.bid=R.bid AND B.color = 'red'
GROUP BY  S.sid
```

This query finds the number of red boats reserved by each sailor. This query is shown in the form of a tree in Figure 15.7.

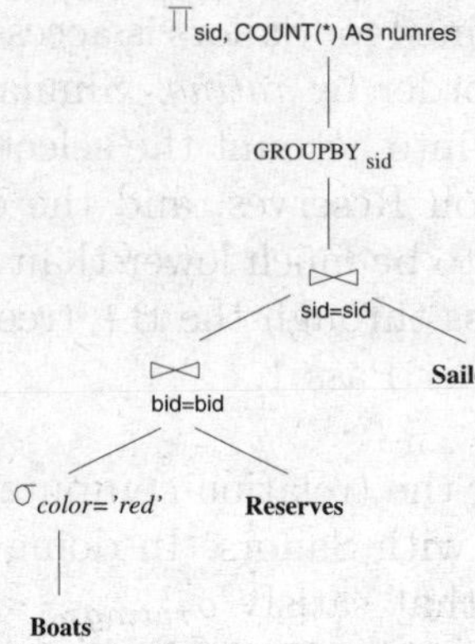

Figure 15.7 A Query Tree

Suppose that the following indexes are available: for Reserves, a B+ tree on the *sid* field and a clustered B+ tree on the *bid* field; for Sailors, a B+ tree index on the *sid* field and a hash index on the *sid* field; and for Boats, a B+ tree index on the *color* field and a hash index on the *color* field. (The list of available indexes is contrived to create a relatively simple, illustrative example.) Let us consider how this query is optimized. The initial focus is on the SELECT, FROM, and WHERE clauses.

In Pass 1, the best plan is found for accessing each relation, regarded as the first relation in an execution plan. For Reserves and Sailors, the best plan is obviously a file scan because no selections match an available index. The best plan for Boats is to use the hash index on *color*, which matches the selection *B.color = 'red'*. The B+ tree on *color* also matches this selection and is retained even though the hash index is cheaper, because it returns tuples in sorted order by *color*.

In Pass 2, for each of the plans generated in Pass 1, taken as the outer relation, we consider joining another relation as the inner one. Hence, we consider each of the following joins: file scan of Reserves (outer) with Boats (inner), file scan of Reserves (outer) with Sailors (inner), file scan of Sailors (outer) with Boats (inner), file scan of Sailors (outer) with Reserves (inner), Boats accessed via B+ tree index on *color* (outer) with Sailors (inner), Boats accessed via hash index on *color* (outer) with Sailors (inner), Boats accessed via B+ tree index on *color* (outer) with Reserves (inner), and Boats accessed via hash index on *color* (outer) with Reserves (inner).

For each such pair, we consider every join method, and for each join method, we consider every available access path for the inner relation. For each pair of relations, we retain the cheapest of the plans considered for every sorted order in which the tuples are generated. For example, with Boats accessed via the hash index on *color* as the outer relation, an index nested loops join accessing Reserves via the B+ tree index on *bid* is likely to be a good plan; observe that there is no hash index on this field of Reserves. Another plan for joining Reserves and Boats is to access Boats using the hash index on *color*, access Reserves using the B+ tree on *bid*, and use a sort-merge join; this plan, in contrast to the previous one, generates tuples in sorted order by *bid*. It is retained even if the previous plan is cheaper, unless an even cheaper plan produces the tuples in sorted order by *bid*. However, the previous plan, which produces tuples in no particular order, would not be retained if this plan is cheaper.

A good heuristic is to avoid considering cross-products if possible. If we apply this heuristic, we would not consider the following 'joins' in Pass 2 of this example: file scan of Sailors (outer) with Boats (inner), Boats accessed via B+ tree index on *color* (outer) with Sailors (inner), and Boats accessed via hash index on *color* (outer) with Sailors (inner).

In Pass 3, for each plan retained in Pass 2, taken as the outer relation, we consider how to join the remaining relation as the inner one. An example of a plan generated at this step is the following: Access Boats via the hash index on *color*, access Reserves via the B+ tree index on *bid*, and join them using a sort-merge join, then take the result of this join as the outer and join with Sailors using a sort-merge join, accessing Sailors via the B+ tree index on the *sid* field. Note that, since the result of the first join is produced in sorted order by *bid*, whereas the second join requires its inputs to be sorted by *sid*, the result of the first join must be sorted by *sid* before being used in the second join. The tuples in the result of the second join are generated in sorted order by *sid*.

The `GROUP BY` clause is considered after all joins, and it requires sorting on the *sid* field. For each plan retained in Pass 3, if the result is not sorted on *sid*, we add the cost of sorting on the *sid* field. The sample plan generated in Pass 3 produces tuples in *sid* order; therefore, it may be the cheapest plan for the query even if a cheaper plan joins all three relations but does not produce tuples in *sid* order.

15.5 NESTED SUBQUERIES

The unit of optimization in a typical system is a *query block*, and nested queries are dealt with using some form of nested loops evaluation. Consider the following nested query in SQL: *Find the names of sailors with the highest rating:*

```
SELECT S.sname
FROM   Sailors S
WHERE  S.rating = ( SELECT MAX (S2.rating)
                    FROM   Sailors S2 )
```

In this simple query, the nested subquery can be evaluated just once, yielding a single value. This value is incorporated into the top-level query as if it had been part of the original statement of the query. For example, if the highest rated sailor has a rating of 8, the `WHERE` clause is effectively modified to `WHERE` *S.rating = 8*.

However, the subquery sometimes returns a relation, or more precisely, a table in the SQL sense (i.e., possibly with duplicate rows). Consider the following query: *Find the names of sailors who have reserved boat number 103:*

```
SELECT S.sname
FROM   Sailors S
WHERE  S.sid IN ( SELECT R.sid
                  FROM   Reserves R
                  WHERE  R.bid = 103 )
```

Again, the nested subquery can be evaluated just once, yielding a collection of *sids*. For each tuple of Sailors, we must now check whether the *sid* value is in the computed collection of *sids*; this check entails a join of Sailors and the computed collection of *sids*, and in principle we have the full range of join methods to choose from. For example, if there is an index on the *sid* field of Sailors, an index nested loops join with the computed collection of *sids* as the outer relation and Sailors as the inner one might be the most efficient join method. However, in many systems, the query optimizer is not smart enough to find this strategy—a common approach is to always do a nested loops join in which the inner relation is the collection of *sids* computed from the subquery (and this collection may not be indexed).

The motivation for this approach is that it is a simple variant of the technique used to deal with *correlated queries* such as the following version of the previous query:

```
SELECT S.sname
```

```
FROM    Sailors S
WHERE   EXISTS ( SELECT *
                 FROM   Reserves R
                 WHERE  R.bid = 103
                 AND S.sid = R.sid )
```

This query is *correlated*—the tuple variable *S* from the top-level query appears in the nested subquery. Therefore, we cannot evaluate the subquery just once. In this case the typical evaluation strategy is to evaluate the nested subquery for each tuple of Sailors.

An important point to note about nested queries is that a typical optimizer is likely to do a poor job, because of the limited approach to nested query optimization. This is highlighted next:

- In a nested query with correlation, the join method is effectively index nested loops, with the inner relation typically a subquery (and therefore potentially expensive to compute). This approach creates two distinct problems. First, the nested subquery is evaluated once per outer tuple; if the same value appears in the correlation field (*S.sid* in our example) of several outer tuples, the same subquery is evaluated many times. The second problem is that the approach to nested subqueries is not *set-oriented.* In effect, a join is seen as a scan of the outer relation with a selection on the inner subquery for each outer tuple. This precludes consideration of alternative join methods, such as a sort-merge join or a hash join, that could lead to superior plans.

- Even if index nested loops is the appropriate join method, nested query evaluation may be inefficient. For example, if there is an index on the *sid* field of Reserves, a good strategy might be to do an index nested loops join with Sailors as the outer relation and Reserves as the inner relation and apply the selection on *bid* on-the-fly. However, this option is not considered when optimizing the version of the query that uses `IN`, because the nested subquery is fully evaluated as a first step; that is, Reserves tuples that meet the *bid* selection are retrieved first.

- Opportunities for finding a good evaluation plan may also be missed because of the implicit ordering imposed by the nesting. For example, if there is an index on the *sid* field of Sailors, an index nested loops join with Reserves as the outer relation and Sailors as the inner one might be the most efficient plan for our example correlated query. However, this join ordering is never considered by an optimizer.

A nested query often has an equivalent query without nesting, and a correlated query often has an equivalent query without correlation. We already saw cor-

> **Nested Queries:** IBM DB2, Informix, Microsoft SQL Server, Oracle 8, and Sybase ASE all use some version of correlated evaluation to handle nested queries, which are an important part of the TPC-D benchmark; IBM and Informix support a version in which the results of subqueries are stored in a 'memo' table and the same subquery is not executed multiple times. All these RDBMSs consider decorrelation and "flattening" of nested queries as an option. Microsoft SQL Server, Oracle 8 and IBM DB2 also use rewriting techniques, e.g., Magic Sets (see Chapter 24) or variants, in conjunction with decorrelation.

related and uncorrelated versions of the example nested query. There is also an equivalent query without nesting:

```
SELECT S.sname
FROM   Sailors S, Reserves R
WHERE  S.sid = R.sid AND R.bid=103
```

A typical SQL optimizer is likely to find a much better evaluation strategy if it is given the unnested or 'decorrelated' version of the example query than if it were given either of the nested versions of the query. Many current optimizers cannot recognize the equivalence of these queries and transform one of the nested versions to the nonnested form. This is, unfortunately, up to the educated user. From an efficiency standpoint, users are advised to consider such alternative formulations of a query.

We conclude our discussion of nested queries by observing that there could be several levels of nesting. In general, the approach we sketched is extended by evaluating such queries from the innermost to the outermost levels, in order, in the absence of correlation. A correlated subquery must be evaluated for each candidate tuple of the higher-level (sub)query that refers to it. The basic idea is therefore similar to the case of one-level nested queries; we omit the details.

15.6 THE SYSTEM R OPTIMIZER

Current relational query optimizers have been greatly influenced by choices made in the design of IBM's System R query optimizer. Important design choices in the System R optimizer include:

1. The use of *statistics* about the database instance to estimate the cost of a query evaluation plan.

2. A decision to consider only plans with binary joins in which the inner relation is a base relation (i.e., not a temporary relation). This heuristic

reduces the (potentially very large) number of alternative plans that must be considered.

3. A decision to focus optimization on the class of SQL queries without nesting and treat nested queries in a relatively ad hoc way.

4. A decision not to perform duplicate elimination for projections (except as a final step in the query evaluation when required by a `DISTINCT` clause).

5. A model of cost that accounted for CPU costs as well as I/O costs.

Our discussion of optimization reflects these design choices, except for the last point in the preceding list, which we ignore to retain our simple cost model based on the number of page I/Os.

15.7 OTHER APPROACHES TO QUERY OPTIMIZATION

We have described query optimization based on an exhaustive search of a large space of plans for a given query. The space of all possible plans grows rapidly with the size of the query expression, in particular with respect to the number of joins, because join-order optimization is a central issue. Therefore, heuristics are used to limit the space of plans considered by an optimizer. A widely used heuristic is that only left-deep plans are considered, which works well for most queries. However, once the number of joins becomes greater than about 15, the cost of optimization using this exhaustive approach becomes prohibitively high, even if we consider only left-deep plans.

Such complex queries are becoming important in decision-support environments, and other approaches to query optimization have been proposed. These include **rule-based optimizers**, which use a set of rules to guide the generation of candidate plans, and **randomized plan generation**, which uses probabilistic algorithms such as *simulated annealing* to explore a large space of plans quickly, with a reasonable likelihood of finding a good plan.

Current research in this area also involves techniques for estimating the size of intermediate relations more accurately; **parametric query optimization**, which seeks to find good plans for a given query for each of several different conditions that might be encountered at run-time; and **multiple-query optimization**, in which the optimizer takes concurrent execution of several queries into account.

15.8 REVIEW QUESTIONS

Answers to the review questions can be found in the listed sections.

- What is an *SQL query block*? Why is it important in the context of query optimization? **(Section 15.1)**
- Describe how a query block is translated into extended relational algebra. Describe and motivate the extensions to relational algebra. Why are $\sigma\pi\times$ expressions the focus of an optimizer? **(Section 15.1)**
- What are the two parts to estimating the cost of a query plan? **(Section 15.2)**
- How is the result size estimated for a $\sigma\pi\times$ expression? Describe the use of *reduction factors*, and explain how they are calculated for different kinds of selections? **(Section 15.2.1)**
- What are *histograms*? How do they help in cost estimation? Explain the differences between the different kinds of histograms, with particular attention to the role of frequent data values. **(Section 15.2.1)**
- When are two relational algebra expressions considered *equivalent*? How is equivalence used in query optimization? What algebra equivalences that justify the common optimizations of pushing selections ahead of joins and re-ordering join expressions? **(Section 15.3)**
- Describe *left-deep* plans and explain why optimizers typically consider only such plans. **(Section 15.4)**
- What plans are considered for (sub)queries with a single relation? Of these, which plans are retained in the dynamic programming approach to enumerating left-deep plans? Discuss access methods and output order in your answer. In particular, explain *index-only plans* and why they are attractive. **(Section 15.4)**
- Explain how query plans are generated for queries with multiple relations. Discuss the space and time complexity of the dynamic programming approach, and how the plan generation process incorporates heuristics like pushing selections and join ordering. How are index-only plans for multiple-relation queries identified? How are pipelining opportunities identified? **(Section 15.4)**
- How are nested subqueries optimized and evaluated? Discuss correlated queries and the additional optimization challenges they present. Why are plans produced for nested queries typically of poor quality? What is the lesson for application programmers? **(Section 15.5)**
- Discuss some of the influential design choices made in the System R optimizer. **(Section 15.6)**
- Briefly survey optimization techniques that go beyond the dynamic programming framework discussed in this chapter. **(Section 15.7)**

EXERCISES

Exercise 15.1 Briefly answer the following questions:

1. In the context of query optimization, what is an *SQL query block*?
2. Define the term *reduction factor*.
3. Describe a situation in which projection should precede selection in processing a project-select query, and describe a situation where the opposite processing order is better. (Assume that duplicate elimination for projection is done via sorting.)
4. If there are unclustered (secondary) B+ tree indexes on both *R.a* and *S.b*, the join $R \bowtie_{a=b} S$ could be processed by doing a sort-merge type of join—without doing any sorting—by using these indexes.
   (a) Would this be a good idea if R and S each has only one tuple per page or would it be better to ignore the indexes and sort R and S? Explain.
   (b) What if R and S each have many tuples per page? Again, explain.
5. Explain the role of *interesting orders* in the System R optimizer.

Exercise 15.2 Consider a relation with this schema:

Employees(<u>*eid:* `integer`</u>, *ename:* `string`, *sal:* `integer`, *title:* `string`, *age:* `integer`)

Suppose that the following indexes, all using Alternative (2) for data entries, exist: a hash index on *eid*, a B+ tree index on *sal*, a hash index on *age*, and a clustered B+ tree index on ⟨*age, sal*⟩. Each Employees record is 100 bytes long, and you can assume that each index data entry is 20 bytes long. The Employees relation contains 10,000 pages.

1. Consider each of the following selection conditions and, assuming that the reduction factor (RF) for each term that matches an index is 0.1, compute the cost of the most selective access path for retrieving all Employees tuples that satisfy the condition:
   (a) $sal > 100$
   (b) $age = 25$
   (c) $age > 20$
   (d) $eid = 1,000$
   (e) $sal > 200 \wedge age > 30$
   (f) $sal > 200 \wedge age = 20$
   (g) $sal > 200 \wedge title = 'CFO'$
   (h) $sal > 200 \wedge age > 30 \wedge title = 'CFO'$
2. Suppose that, for each of the preceding selection conditions, you want to retrieve the average salary of qualifying tuples. For each selection condition, describe the least expensive evaluation method and state its cost.
3. Suppose that, for each of the preceding selection conditions, you want to compute the average salary for each *age* group. For each selection condition, describe the least expensive evaluation method and state its cost.
4. Suppose that, for each of the preceding selection conditions, you want to compute the average age for each *sal* level (i.e., group by *sal*). For each selection condition, describe the least expensive evaluation method and state its cost.

5. For each of the following selection conditions, describe the best evaluation method:
   (a) $sal > 200 \vee age = 20$
   (b) $sal > 200 \vee title = 'CFO'$
   (c) $title = 'CFO' \wedge ename = 'Joe'$

Exercise 15.3 For each of the following SQL queries, for each relation involved, list the attributes that must be examined to compute the answer. All queries refer to the following relations:

Emp(*eid:* `integer`, *did:* `integer`, *sal:* `integer`, *hobby:* `char(20)`)
Dept(*did:* `integer`, *dname:* `char(20)`, *floor:* `integer`, *budget:* `real`)

1. `SELECT COUNT(*) FROM` Emp E, Dept D `WHERE` E.did = D.did
2. `SELECT MAX(`E.sal) `FROM` Emp E, Dept D `WHERE` E.did = D.did
3. `SELECT MAX(`E.sal) `FROM` Emp E, Dept D `WHERE` E.did = D.did `AND` D.floor = 5
4. `SELECT` E.did, `COUNT(*) FROM` Emp E, Dept D `WHERE` E.did = D.did `GROUP BY` D.did
5. `SELECT` D.floor, `AVG(`D.budget) `FROM` Dept D `GROUP BY` D.floor `HAVING COUNT(*)` > 2
6. `SELECT` D.floor, `AVG(`D.budget) `FROM` Dept D `GROUP BY` D.floor `ORDER BY` D.floor

Exercise 15.4 You are given the following information:

Executives has attributes *ename*, *title*, *dname*, and *address*; all are string fields of the same length.
The *ename* attribute is a candidate key.
The relation contains 10,000 pages.
There are 10 buffer pages.

1. Consider the following query:

   `SELECT` E.title, E.ename `FROM` Executives E `WHERE` E.title='CFO'

   Assume that only 10% of Executives tuples meet the selection condition.

   (a) Suppose that a clustered B+ tree index on *title* is (the only index) available. What is the cost of the best plan? (In this and subsequent questions, be sure to describe the plan you have in mind.)
   (b) Suppose that an unclustered B+ tree index on *title* is (the only index) available. What is the cost of the best plan?
   (c) Suppose that a clustered B+ tree index on *ename* is (the only index) available. What is the cost of the best plan?
   (d) Suppose that a clustered B+ tree index on *address* is (the only index) available. What is the cost of the best plan?
   (e) Suppose that a clustered B+ tree index on ⟨*ename, title*⟩ is (the only index) available. What is the cost of the best plan?

2. Suppose that the query is as follows:

   `SELECT` E.ename `FROM` Executives E `WHERE` E.title='CFO' `AND` E.dname='Toy'

Assume that only 10% of Executives tuples meet the condition $E.title = 'CFO'$, only 10% meet $E.dname = 'Toy'$, and that only 5% meet both conditions.

(a) Suppose that a clustered B+ tree index on *title* is (the only index) available. What is the cost of the best plan?

(b) Suppose that a clustered B+ tree index on *dname* is (the only index) available. What is the cost of the best plan?

(c) Suppose that a clustered B+ tree index on $\langle title, dname \rangle$ is (the only index) available. What is the cost of the best plan?

(d) Suppose that a clustered B+ tree index on $\langle title, ename \rangle$ is (the only index) available. What is the cost of the best plan?

(e) Suppose that a clustered B+ tree index on $\langle dname, title, ename \rangle$ is (the only index) available. What is the cost of the best plan?

(f) Suppose that a clustered B+ tree index on $\langle ename, title, dname \rangle$ is (the only index) available. What is the cost of the best plan?

3. Suppose that the query is as follows:

```
SELECT E.title, COUNT(*) FROM Executives E GROUP BY E.title
```

(a) Suppose that a clustered B+ tree index on *title* is (the only index) available. What is the cost of the best plan?

(b) Suppose that an unclustered B+ tree index on *title* is (the only index) available. What is the cost of the best plan?

(c) Suppose that a clustered B+ tree index on *ename* is (the only index) available. What is the cost of the best plan?

(d) Suppose that a clustered B+ tree index on $\langle ename, title \rangle$ is (the only index) available. What is the cost of the best plan?

(e) Suppose that a clustered B+ tree index on $\langle title, ename \rangle$ is (the only index) available. What is the cost of the best plan?

4. Suppose that the query is as follows:

```
SELECT E.title, COUNT(*) FROM Executives E
WHERE E.dname > 'W%' GROUP BY E.title
```

Assume that only 10% of Executives tuples meet the selection condition.

(a) Suppose that a clustered B+ tree index on *title* is (the only index) available. What is the cost of the best plan? If an additional index (on any search key you want) is available, would it help produce a better plan?

(b) Suppose that an unclustered B+ tree index on *title* is (the only index) available. What is the cost of the best plan?

(c) Suppose that a clustered B+ tree index on *dname* is (the only index) available. What is the cost of the best plan? If an additional index (on any search key you want) is available, would it help to produce a better plan?

(d) Suppose that a clustered B+ tree index on $\langle dname, title \rangle$ is (the only index) available. What is the cost of the best plan?

(e) Suppose that a clustered B+ tree index on $\langle title, dname \rangle$ is (the only index) available. What is the cost of the best plan?

Exercise 15.5 Consider the query $\pi_{A,B,C,D}(R \bowtie_{A=C} S)$. Suppose that the projection routine is based on sorting and is smart enough to eliminate all but the desired attributes during the initial pass of the sort and also to toss out duplicate tuples on-the-fly while sorting, thus eliminating two potential extra passes. Finally, assume that you know the following:

R is 10 pages long, and R tuples are 300 bytes long.
S is 100 pages long, and S tuples are 500 bytes long.
C is a key for S, and A is a key for R.
The page size is 1024 bytes.
Each S tuple joins with exactly one R tuple.
The combined size of attributes A, B, C, and D is 450 bytes.
A and B are in R and have a combined size of 200 bytes; C and D are in S.

1. What is the cost of writing out the final result? (As usual, you should ignore this cost in answering subsequent questions.)
2. Suppose that three buffer pages are available, and the only join method that is implemented is simple (page-oriented) nested loops.
   (a) Compute the cost of doing the projection followed by the join.
   (b) Compute the cost of doing the join followed by the projection.
   (c) Compute the cost of doing the join first and then the projection on-the-fly.
   (d) Would your answers change if 11 buffer pages were available?

Exercise 15.6 Briefly answer the following questions:

1. Explain the role of relational algebra equivalences in the System R optimizer.
2. Consider a relational algebra expression of the form $\sigma_c(\pi_l(R \times S))$. Suppose that the equivalent expression with selections and projections pushed as much as possible, taking into account only relational algebra equivalences, is in one of the following forms. In each case give an illustrative example of the selection conditions and the projection lists (c, l, $c1$, $l1$, etc.).
   (a) *Equivalent maximally pushed form:* $\pi_{l1}(\sigma_{c1}(R) \times S)$.
   (b) *Equivalent maximally pushed form:* $\pi_{l1}(\sigma_{c1}(R) \times \sigma_{c2}(S))$.
   (c) *Equivalent maximally pushed form:* $\sigma_c(\pi_{l1}(\pi_{l2}(R) \times S))$.
   (d) *Equivalent maximally pushed form:* $\sigma_{c1}(\pi_{l1}(\sigma_{c2}(\pi_{l2}(R)) \times S))$.
   (e) *Equivalent maximally pushed form:* $\sigma_{c1}(\pi_{l1}(\pi_{l2}(\sigma_{c2}(R)) \times S))$.
   (f) *Equivalent maximally pushed form:* $\pi_l(\sigma_{c1}(\pi_{l1}(\pi_{l2}(\sigma_{c2}(R)) \times S)))$.

Exercise 15.7 Consider the following relational schema and SQL query. The schema captures information about employees, departments, and company finances (organized on a per department basis).

Emp(*eid:* `integer`, *did:* `integer`, *sal:* `integer`, *hobby:* `char(20)`)
Dept(*did:* `integer`, *dname:* `char(20)`, *floor:* `integer`, *phone:* `char(10)`)
Finance(*did:* `integer`, *budget:* `real`, *sales:* `real`, *expenses:* `real`)

Consider the following query:

```
SELECT D.dname, F.budget
FROM   Emp E, Dept D, Finance F
WHERE  E.did=D.did AND D.did=F.did AND D.floor=1
       AND E.sal ≥ 59000 AND E.hobby = 'yodeling'
```

1. Identify a relational algebra tree (or a relational algebra expression if you prefer) that reflects the order of operations a decent query optimizer would choose.
2. List the join orders (i.e., orders in which pairs of relations can be joined to compute the query result) that a relational query optimizer will consider. (Assume that the optimizer follows the heuristic of never considering plans that require the computation of cross-products.) Briefly explain how you arrived at your list.
3. Suppose that the following additional information is available: Unclustered B+ tree indexes exist on *Emp.did*, *Emp.sal*, *Dept.floor*, *Dept.did*, and *Finance.did*. The system's statistics indicate that employee salaries range from 10,000 to 60,000, employees enjoy 200 different hobbies, and the company owns two floors in the building. There are a total of 50,000 employees and 5,000 departments (each with corresponding financial information) in the database. The DBMS used by the company has just one join method available, index nested loops.
   (a) For each of the query's base relations (Emp, Dept, and Finance) estimate the number of tuples that would be initially selected from that relation if all of the non-join predicates on that relation were applied to it before any join processing begins.
   (b) Given your answer to the preceding question, which of the join orders considered by the optimizer has the lowest estimated cost?

Exercise 15.8 Consider the following relational schema and SQL query:

Suppliers(*sid:* `integer`, *sname:* `char(20)`, *city:* `char(20)`)
Supply(*sid:* `integer`, *pid:* `integer`)
Parts(*pid:* `integer`, *pname:* `char(20)`, *price:* `real`)

```
SELECT S.sname, P.pname
FROM   Suppliers S, Parts P, Supply Y
WHERE  S.sid = Y.sid AND Y.pid = P.pid AND
       S.city = 'Madison' AND P.price ≤ 1,000
```

1. What information about these relations does the query optimizer need to select a good query execution plan for the given query?
2. How many different join orders, assuming that cross-products are disallowed, does a System R style query optimizer consider when deciding how to process the given query? List each of these join orders.
3. What indexes might be of help in processing this query? Explain briefly.
4. How does adding `DISTINCT` to the `SELECT` clause affect the plans produced?
5. How does adding `ORDER BY` *sname* to the query affect the plans produced?
6. How does adding `GROUP BY` *sname* to the query affect the plans produced?

Exercise 15.9 Consider the following scenario:

Emp(*eid:* integer, *sal:* integer, *age:* real, *did:* integer)
Dept(*did:* integer, *projid:* integer, *budget:* real, *status:* char(10))
Proj(*projid:* integer, *code:* integer, *report:* varchar)

Assume that each Emp record is 20 bytes long, each Dept record is 40 bytes long, and each Proj record is 2000 bytes long on average. There are 20,000 tuples in Emp, 5000 tuples in Dept (note that *did* is not a key), and 1000 tuples in Proj. Each department, identified by *did*, has 10 projects on average. The file system supports 4000 byte pages, and 12 buffer pages are available. All following questions are based on this information. You can assume uniform distribution of values. State any additional assumptions. The cost metric to use is *the number of page I/Os.* Ignore the cost of writing out the final result.

1. Consider the following two queries: "Find all employees with *age* = 30" and "Find all projects with *code* = 20." Assume that the number of qualifying tuples is the same in each case. If you are building indexes on the selected attributes to speed up these queries, for which query is a *clustered* index (in comparison to an *unclustered* index) more important?
2. Consider the following query: "Find all employees with *age* > 30." Assume that there is an unclustered index on *age*. Let the number of qualifying tuples be *N*. For what values of *N* is a sequential scan cheaper than using the index?
3. Consider the following query:

```
SELECT *
FROM   Emp E, Dept D
WHERE  E.did=D.did
```

   (a) Suppose that there is a clustered hash index on *did* on Emp. List all the plans that are considered and identify the plan with the lowest estimated cost.

   (b) Assume that both relations are sorted on the join column. List all the plans that are considered and show the plan with the lowest estimated cost.

   (c) Suppose that there is a clustered B+ tree index on *did* on Emp and Dept is sorted on *did*. List all the plans that are considered and identify the plan with the lowest estimated cost.

4. Consider the following query:

```
SELECT    D.did, COUNT(*)
FROM      Dept D, Proj P
WHERE     D.projid=P.projid
GROUP BY  D.did
```

   (a) Suppose that no indexes are available. Show the plan with the lowest estimated cost.

   (b) If there is a hash index on *P.projid* what is the plan with lowest estimated cost?

   (c) If there is a hash index on *D.projid* what is the plan with lowest estimated cost?

   (d) If there is a hash index on *D.projid* and *P.projid* what is the plan with lowest estimated cost?

   (e) Suppose that there is a clustered B+ tree index on *D.did* and a hash index on *P.projid*. Show the plan with the lowest estimated cost.

   (f) Suppose that there is a clustered B+ tree index on *D.did*, a hash index on *D.projid*, and a hash index on *P.projid*. Show the plan with the lowest estimated cost.

(g) Suppose that there is a clustered B+ tree index on ⟨*D.did, D.projid*⟩ and a hash index on *P.projid*. Show the plan with the lowest estimated cost.

(h) Suppose that there is a clustered B+ tree index on ⟨*D.projid, D.did*⟩ and a hash index on *P.projid*. Show the plan with the lowest estimated cost.

5. Consider the following query:

```
SELECT    D.did, COUNT(*)
FROM      Dept D, Proj P
WHERE     D.projid=P.projid AND D.budget>99000
GROUP BY  D.did
```

Assume that department budgets are uniformly distributed in the range 0 to 100,000.

(a) Show the plan with lowest estimated cost if no indexes are available.

(b) If there is a hash index on *P.projid* show the plan with lowest estimated cost.

(c) If there is a hash index on *D.budget* show the plan with lowest estimated cost.

(d) If there is a hash index on *D.projid* and *D.budget* show the plan with lowest estimated cost.

(e) Suppose that there is a clustered B+ tree index on ⟨*D.did,D.budget*⟩ and a hash index on *P.projid*. Show the plan with the lowest estimated cost.

(f) Suppose there is a clustered B+ tree index on *D.did*, a hash index on *D.budget*, and a hash index on *P.projid*. Show the plan with the lowest estimated cost.

(g) Suppose there is a clustered B+ tree index on ⟨*D.did, D.budget, D.projid*⟩ and a hash index on *P.projid*. Show the plan with the lowest estimated cost.

(h) Suppose there is a clustered B+ tree index on ⟨*D.did, D.projid, D.budget*⟩ and a hash index on *P.projid*. Show the plan with the lowest estimated cost.

6. Consider the following query:

```
SELECT E.eid, D.did, P.projid
FROM   Emp E, Dept D, Proj P
WHERE  E.sal=50,000 AND D.budget>20,000
       E.did=D.did AND D.projid=P.projid
```

Assume that employee salaries are uniformly distributed in the range 10,009 to 110,008 and that project budgets are uniformly distributed in the range 10,000 to 30,000. There is a clustered index on *sal* for Emp, a clustered index on *did* for Dept, and a clustered index on *projid* for Proj.

(a) List all the one-relation, two-relation, and three-relation subplans considered in optimizing this query.

(b) Show the plan with the lowest estimated cost for this query.

(c) If the index on Proj were unclustered, would the cost of the preceding plan change substantially? What if the index on Emp or on Dept were unclustered?

BIBLIOGRAPHIC NOTES

Query optimization is critical in a relational DBMS, and it has therefore been extensively studied. We concentrate in this chapter on the approach taken in System R, as described in [668], although our discussion incorporates subsequent refinements to the approach. [784] describes query optimization in Ingres. Good surveys can be found in [410] and [399]. [434] contains several articles on query processing and optimization.

From a theoretical standpoint, [155] shows that determining whether two *conjunctive queries* (queries involving only selections, projections, and cross-products) are equivalent is an NP-complete problem; if relations are *multisets*, rather than sets of tuples, it is not known whether the problem is decidable, although it is $\Pi_2{}^p$ hard. The equivalence problem is shown to be decidable for queries involving selections, projections, cross-products, and unions in [643]; surprisingly, this problem is undecidable if relations are multisets [404]. Equivalence of conjunctive queries in the presence of integrity constraints is studied in [30], and equivalence of conjunctive queries with inequality selections is studied in [440].

An important problem in query optimization is estimating the size of the result of a query expression. Approaches based on sampling are explored in [352, 353, 384, 481, 569]. The use of detailed statistics, in the form of histograms, to estimate size is studied in [405, 558, 598]. Unless care is exercised, errors in size estimation can quickly propagate and make cost estimates worthless for expressions with several operators. This problem is examined in [400]. [512] surveys several techniques for estimating result sizes and correlations between values in relations. There are a number of other papers in this area; for example, [26, 170, 594, 725], and our list is far from complete.

Semantic query optimization is based on transformations that preserve equivalence only when certain integrity constraints hold. The idea was introduced in [437] and developed further in [148, 682, 688].

In recent years, there has been increasing interest in complex queries for decision support applications. Optimization of nested SQL queries is discussed in [298, 426, 430, 557, 760]. The use of the Magic Sets technique for optimizing SQL queries is studied in [553, 554, 555, 670, 673]. Rule-based query optimizers are studied in [287, 326, 490, 539, 596]. Finding a good join order for queries with a large number of joins is studied in [401, 402, 453, 726]. Optimization of multiple queries for simultaneous execution is considered in [585, 633, 669]. Determining query plans at run-time is discussed in [327, 403]. Re-optimization of running queries based on statistics gathered during query execution is considered by Kabra and DeWitt [413]. Probabilistic optimization of queries is proposed in [183, 229].

PART V

TRANSACTION MANAGEMENT

16

OVERVIEW OF TRANSACTION MANAGEMENT

- What four properties of transactions does a DBMS guarantee?
- Why does a DBMS interleave transactions?
- What is the correctness criterion for interleaved execution?
- What kinds of anomalies can interleaving transactions cause?
- How does a DBMS use locks to ensure correct interleavings?
- What is the impact of locking on performance?
- What SQL commands allow programmers to select transaction characteristics and reduce locking overhead?
- How does a DBMS guarantee transaction atomicity and recovery from system crashes?
- **Key concepts:** ACID properties, atomicity, consistency, isolation, durability; schedules, serializability, recoverability, avoiding cascading aborts; anomalies, dirty reads, unrepeatable reads, lost updates; locking protocols, exclusive and shared locks, Strict Two-Phase Locking; locking performance, thrashing, hot spots; SQL transaction characteristics, savepoints, rollbacks, phantoms, access mode, isolation level; transaction manager, recovery manager, log, system crash, media failure; stealing frames, forcing pages; recovery phases, analysis, redo and undo.

I always say, keep a diary and someday it'll keep you.

—Mae West

In this chapter, we cover the concept of a *transaction*, which is the foundation for concurrent execution and recovery from system failure in a DBMS. A transaction is defined as *any one execution* of a user program in a DBMS and differs from an execution of a program outside the DBMS (e.g., a C program executing on Unix) in important ways. (Executing the same program several times generates several transactions.)

For performance reasons, a DBMS has to interleave the actions of several transactions. (We motivate interleaving of transactions in detail in Section 16.3.1.) However, to give users a simple way to understand the effect of running their programs, the interleaving is done carefully to ensure that the result of a concurrent execution of transactions is nonetheless equivalent (in its effect on the database) to some serial, or one-at-a-time, execution of the same set of transactions. How the DBMS handles concurrent executions is an important aspect of transaction management and the subject of *concurrency control*. A closely related issue is how the DBMS handles partial transactions, or transactions that are interrupted before they run to normal completion. The DBMS ensures that the changes made by such partial transactions are not seen by other transactions. How this is achieved is the subject of *crash recovery*. In this chapter, we provide a broad introduction to concurrency control and crash recovery in a DBMS. The details are developed further in the next two chapters.

In Section 16.1, we discuss four fundamental properties of database transactions and how the DBMS ensures these properties. In Section 16.2, we present an abstract way of describing an interleaved execution of several transactions, called a *schedule*. In Section 16.3, we discuss various problems that can arise due to interleaved execution. We introduce lock-based concurrency control, the most widely used approach, in Section 16.4. We discuss performance issues associated with lock-based concurrency control in Section 16.5. We consider locking and transaction properties in the context of SQL in Section 16.6. Finally, in Section 16.7, we present an overview of how a database system recovers from crashes and what steps are taken during normal execution to support crash recovery.

16.1 THE ACID PROPERTIES

We introduced the concept of database transactions in Section 1.7. To recapitulate briefly, a transaction is an execution of a user program, seen by the DBMS as a series of read and write operations.

A DBMS must ensure four important properties of transactions to maintain data in the face of concurrent access and system failures:

1. Users should be able to regard the execution of each transaction as **atomic**: Either all actions are carried out or none are. Users should not have to worry about the effect of incomplete transactions (say, when a system crash occurs).

2. Each transaction, run by itself with no concurrent execution of other transactions, must preserve the **consistency** of the database. The DBMS assumes that consistency holds for each transaction. Ensuring this property of a transaction is the responsibility of the user.

3. Users should be able to understand a transaction without considering the effect of other concurrently executing transactions, even if the DBMS interleaves the actions of several transactions for performance reasons. This property is sometimes referred to as **isolation**: Transactions are isolated, or protected, from the effects of concurrently scheduling other transactions.

4. Once the DBMS informs the user that a transaction has been successfully completed, its effects should persist even if the system crashes before all its changes are reflected on disk. This property is called **durability**.

The acronym ACID is sometimes used to refer to these four properties of transactions: atomicity, consistency, isolation and durability. We now consider how each of these properties is ensured in a DBMS.

16.1.1 Consistency and Isolation

Users are responsible for ensuring transaction consistency. That is, the user who submits a transaction must ensure that, when run to completion by itself against a 'consistent' database instance, the transaction will leave the database in a 'consistent' state. For example, the user may (naturally) have the consistency criterion that fund transfers between bank accounts should not change the total amount of money in the accounts. To transfer money from one account to another, a transaction must debit one account, temporarily leaving the database inconsistent in a global sense, even though the new account balance may satisfy any integrity constraints with respect to the range of acceptable account balances. The user's notion of a consistent database is preserved when the second account is credited with the transferred amount. If a faulty transfer program always credits the second account with one dollar less than the amount debited from the first account, the DBMS cannot be expected to detect inconsistencies due to such errors in the user program's logic.

The isolation property is ensured by guaranteeing that, even though actions of several transactions might be interleaved, the net effect is identical to executing all transactions one after the other in some serial order. (We discuss how the DBMS implements this guarantee in Section 16.4.) For example, if two transactions $T1$ and $T2$ are executed concurrently, the net effect is guaranteed to be equivalent to executing (all of) $T1$ followed by executing $T2$ or executing $T2$ followed by executing $T1$. (The DBMS provides no guarantees about which of these orders is effectively chosen.) If each transaction maps a consistent database instance to another consistent database instance, executing several transactions one after the other (on a consistent initial database instance) results in a consistent final database instance.

Database consistency is the property that every transaction sees a consistent database instance. Database consistency follows from transaction atomicity, isolation, and transaction consistency. Next, we discuss how atomicity and durability are guaranteed in a DBMS.

16.1.2 Atomicity and Durability

Transactions can be incomplete for three kinds of reasons. First, a transaction can be **aborted**, or terminated unsuccessfully, by the DBMS because some anomaly arises during execution. If a transaction is aborted by the DBMS for some internal reason, it is automatically restarted and executed anew. Second, the system may crash (e.g., because the power supply is interrupted) while one or more transactions are in progress. Third, a transaction may encounter an unexpected situation (for example, read an unexpected data value or be unable to access some disk) and decide to abort (i.e., terminate itself).

Of course, since users think of transactions as being atomic, a transaction that is interrupted in the middle may leave the database in an inconsistent state. Therefore, a DBMS must find a way to remove the effects of partial transactions from the database. That is, it must ensure transaction atomicity: Either all of a transaction's actions are carried out or none are. A DBMS ensures transaction atomicity by *undoing* the actions of incomplete transactions. This means that users can ignore incomplete transactions in thinking about how the database is modified by transactions over time. To be able to do this, the DBMS maintains a record, called the *log*, of all writes to the database. The log is also used to ensure durability: If the system crashes before the changes made by a completed transaction are written to disk, the log is used to remember and restore these changes when the system restarts.

The DBMS component that ensures atomicity and durability, called the *recovery manager*, is discussed further in Section 16.7.

16.2 TRANSACTIONS AND SCHEDULES

A transaction is seen by the DBMS as a series, or *list*, of **actions**. The actions that can be executed by a transaction include **reads** and **writes** of *database objects*. To keep our notation simple, we assume that an object O is always read into a program variable that is also named O. We can therefore denote the action of a transaction T reading an object O as $R_T(O)$; similarly, we can denote writing as $W_T(O)$. When the transaction T is clear from the context, we omit the subscript.

In addition to reading and writing, each transaction *must* specify as its final action either **commit** (i.e., complete successfully) or **abort** (i.e., terminate and undo all the actions carried out thus far). $Abort_T$ denotes the action of T aborting, and $Commit_T$ denotes T committing.

We make two important assumptions:

1. Transactions interact with each other *only* via database read and write operations; for example, they are not allowed to exchange messages.
2. A database is a *fixed* collection of *independent* objects. When objects are added to or deleted from a database or there are relationships between database objects that we want to exploit for performance, some additional issues arise.

If the first assumption is violated, the DBMS has no way to detect or prevent inconsistencies cause by such external interactions between transactions, and it is upto the writer of the application to ensure that the program is well-behaved. We relax the second assumption in Section 16.6.2.

A **schedule** is a list of actions (reading, writing, aborting, or committing) from a set of transactions, and the order in which two actions of a transaction T appear in a schedule must be the same as the order in which they appear in T. Intuitively, a schedule represents an actual or potential execution sequence. For example, the schedule in Figure 16.1 shows an execution order for actions of two transactions $T1$ and $T2$. We move forward in time as we go down from one row to the next. We emphasize that a schedule describes the actions of transactions *as seen by the DBMS*. In addition to these actions, a transaction may carry out other actions, such as reading or writing from operating system files, evaluating arithmetic expressions, and so on; however, we assume that these actions do not affect other transactions; that is, the effect of a transaction on another transaction can be understood solely in terms of the common database objects that they read and write.

$T1$	$T2$
$R(A)$	
$W(A)$	
	$R(B)$
	$W(B)$
$R(C)$	
$W(C)$	

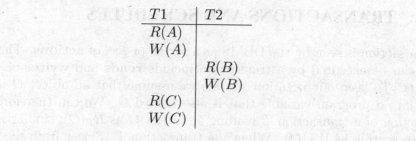

Figure 16.1 A Schedule Involving Two Transactions

Note that the schedule in Figure 16.1 does not contain an abort or commit action for either transaction. A schedule that contains either an abort or a commit for each transaction whose actions are listed in it is called a **complete schedule**. A complete schedule must contain all the actions of every transaction that appears in it. If the actions of different transactions are not interleaved—that is, transactions are executed from start to finish, one by one—we call the schedule a **serial schedule**.

16.3 CONCURRENT EXECUTION OF TRANSACTIONS

Now that we have introduced the concept of a schedule, we have a convenient way to describe interleaved executions of transactions. The DBMS interleaves the actions of different transactions to improve performance, but not all interleavings should be allowed. In this section, we consider what interleavings, or schedules, a DBMS should allow.

16.3.1 Motivation for Concurrent Execution

The schedule shown in Figure 16.1 represents an interleaved execution of the two transactions. Ensuring transaction isolation while permitting such concurrent execution is difficult but necessary for performance reasons. First, while one transaction is waiting for a page to be read in from disk, the CPU can process another transaction. This is because I/O activity can be done in parallel with CPU activity in a computer. Overlapping I/O and CPU activity reduces the amount of time disks and processors are idle and increases **system throughput** (the average number of transactions completed in a given time). Second, interleaved execution of a short transaction with a long transaction usually allows the short transaction to complete quickly. In serial execution, a short transaction could get stuck behind a long transaction, leading to unpredictable delays in **response time**, or average time taken to complete a transaction.

16.3.2 Serializability

A **serializable schedule** over a set S of committed transactions is a schedule whose effect on any consistent database instance is guaranteed to be identical to that of some complete serial schedule over S. That is, the database instance that results from executing the given schedule is identical to the database instance that results from executing the transactions in *some* serial order.[1]

As an example, the schedule shown in Figure 16.2 is serializable. Even though the actions of $T1$ and $T2$ are interleaved, the result of this schedule is equivalent to running $T1$ (in its entirety) and then running $T2$. Intuitively, $T1$'s read and write of B is not influenced by $T2$'s actions on A, and the net effect is the same if these actions are 'swapped' to obtain the serial schedule $T1; T2$.

$T1$	$T2$
$R(A)$	
$W(A)$	
	$R(A)$
	$W(A)$
$R(B)$	
$W(B)$	
	$R(B)$
	$W(B)$
	Commit
Commit	

Figure 16.2 A Serializable Schedule

Executing transactions serially in different orders may produce different results, but all are presumed to be acceptable; the DBMS makes no guarantees about which of them will be the outcome of an interleaved execution. To see this, note that the two example transactions from Figure 16.2 can be interleaved as shown in Figure 16.3. This schedule, also serializable, is equivalent to the serial schedule $T2; T1$. If $T1$ and $T2$ are submitted concurrently to a DBMS, either of these schedules (among others) could be chosen.

The preceding definition of a serializable schedule does not cover the case of schedules containing aborted transactions. We extend the definition of serializable schedules to cover aborted transactions in Section 16.3.4.

[1]If a transaction prints a value to the screen, this 'effect' is not directly captured in the database. For simplicity, we assume that such values are also written into the database.

$T1$	$T2$
	$R(A)$
	$W(A)$
$R(A)$	
	$R(B)$
	$W(B)$
$W(A)$	
$R(B)$	
$W(B)$	
	Commit
Commit	

Figure 16.3 Another Serializable Schedule

Finally, we note that a DBMS might sometimes execute transactions in a way that is not equivalent to any serial execution; that is, using a schedule that is not serializable. This can happen for two reasons. First, the DBMS might use a concurrency control method that ensures the executed schedule, though not itself serializable, is equivalent to some serializable schedule (e.g., see Section 17.6.2). Second, SQL gives application programmers the ability to instruct the DBMS to choose non-serializable schedules (see Section 16.6).

16.3.3 Anomalies Due to Interleaved Execution

We now illustrate three main ways in which a schedule involving two consistency preserving, committed transactions could run against a consistent database and leave it in an inconsistent state. Two actions on the same data object **conflict** if at least one of them is a write. The three anomalous situations can be described in terms of when the actions of two transactions $T1$ and $T2$ conflict with each other: In a **write-read (WR) conflict**, $T2$ reads a data object previously written by $T1$; we define **read-write (RW)** and **write-write (WW)** conflicts similarly.

Reading Uncommitted Data (WR Conflicts)

The first source of anomalies is that a transaction $T2$ could read a database object A that has been modified by another transaction $T1$, which has not yet committed. Such a read is called a **dirty read**. A simple example illustrates how such a schedule could lead to an inconsistent database state. Consider two transactions $T1$ and $T2$, each of which, run alone, preserves database consistency: $T1$ transfers \$100 from A to B, and $T2$ increments both A and B by 6% (e.g., annual interest is deposited into these two accounts). Suppose that the actions are interleaved so that (1) the account transfer program $T1$ deducts \$100 from account A, then (2) the interest deposit program $T2$ reads the current values of accounts A and B and adds 6% interest to each, and then (3) the account transfer program credits \$100 to account B. The corresponding schedule, which is the view the DBMS has of this series of events, is illustrated in Figure 16.4. The result of this schedule is different from any result that we would get by running one of the two transactions first and then the other. The problem can be traced to the fact that the value of A written by $T1$ is read by $T2$ before $T1$ has completed all its changes.

$T1$	$T2$
$R(A)$	
$W(A)$	
	$R(A)$
	$W(A)$
	$R(B)$
	$W(B)$
	Commit
$R(B)$	
$W(B)$	
Commit	

Figure 16.4 Reading Uncommitted Data

The general problem illustrated here is that $T1$ may write some value into A that makes the database inconsistent. As long as $T1$ overwrites this value with a 'correct' value of A before committing, no harm is done if $T1$ and $T2$ run in some serial order, because $T2$ would then not see the (temporary) inconsistency. On the other hand, interleaved execution can expose this inconsistency and lead to an inconsistent final database state.

Note that although a transaction must leave a database in a consistent state *after* it completes, it is not required to keep the database consistent while it is still in progress. Such a requirement would be too restrictive: To transfer money from one account to another, a transaction *must* debit one account, temporarily leaving the database inconsistent, and then credit the second account, restoring consistency.

Unrepeatable Reads (RW Conflicts)

The second way in which anomalous behavior could result is that a transaction $T2$ could change the value of an object A that has been read by a transaction $T1$, while $T1$ is still in progress.

If $T1$ tries to read the value of A again, it will get a different result, even though it has not modified A in the meantime. This situation could not arise in a serial execution of two transactions; it is called an **unrepeatable read**.

To see why this can cause problems, consider the following example. Suppose that A is the number of available copies for a book. A transaction that places an order first reads A, checks that it is greater than 0, and then decrements it. Transaction $T1$ reads A and sees the value 1. Transaction $T2$ also reads A and sees the value 1, decrements A to 0 and commits. Transaction $T1$ then tries to decrement A and gets an error (if there is an integrity constraint that prevents A from becoming negative).

This situation can never arise in a serial execution of $T1$ and $T2$; the second transaction would read A and see 0 and therefore not proceed with the order (and so would not attempt to decrement A).

Overwriting Uncommitted Data (WW Conflicts)

The third source of anomalous behavior is that a transaction $T2$ could overwrite the value of an object A, which has already been modified by a transaction $T1$, while $T1$ is still in progress. Even if $T2$ does not read the value of A written by $T1$, a potential problem exists as the following example illustrates.

Suppose that Harry and Larry are two employees, and their salaries must be kept equal. Transaction $T1$ sets their salaries to \$2000 and transaction $T2$ sets their salaries to \$1000. If we execute these in the serial order $T1$ followed by $T2$, both receive the salary \$1000; the serial order $T2$ followed by $T1$ gives each the salary \$2000. Either of these is acceptable from a consistency standpoint (although Harry and Larry may prefer a higher salary!). Note that neither transaction reads a salary value before writing it—such a write is called a **blind write**, for obvious reasons.

Now, consider the following interleaving of the actions of $T1$ and $T2$: $T2$ sets Harry's salary to \$1000, $T1$ sets Larry's salary to \$2000, $T2$ sets Larry's salary to \$1000 and commits, and finally $T1$ sets Harry's salary to \$2000 and commits. The result is not identical to the result of either of the two possible serial executions, and the interleaved schedule is therefore not serializable. It violates the desired consistency criterion that the two salaries must be equal.

The problem is that we have a **lost update**. The first transaction to commit, $T2$, overwrote Larry's salary as set by $T1$. In the serial order $T2$ followed by $T1$, Larry's salary should reflect $T1$'s update rather than $T2$'s, but $T1$'s update is 'lost'.

16.3.4 Schedules Involving Aborted Transactions

We now extend our definition of serializability to include aborted transactions.[2] Intuitively, all actions of aborted transactions are to be undone, and we can therefore imagine that they were never carried out to begin with. Using this intuition, we extend the definition of a serializable schedule as follows: A **serializable schedule** over a set S of transactions is a schedule whose effect on any consistent database instance is guaranteed to be identical to that of some complete serial schedule over the set of *committed* transactions in S.

This definition of serializability relies on the actions of aborted transactions being undone completely, which may be impossible in some situations. For example, suppose that (1) an account transfer program $T1$ deducts \$100 from account A, then (2) an interest deposit program $T2$ reads the current values of accounts A and B and adds 6% interest to each, then commits, and then (3) $T1$ is aborted. The corresponding schedule is shown in Figure 16.5.

$T1$	$T2$
$R(A)$	
$W(A)$	
	$R(A)$
	$W(A)$
	$R(B)$
	$W(B)$
	Commit
Abort	

Figure 16.5 An Unrecoverable Schedule

[2] We must also consider incomplete transactions for a rigorous discussion of system failures, because transactions that are active when the system fails are neither aborted nor committed. However, system recovery usually begins by aborting all active transactions, and for our informal discussion, considering schedules involving committed and aborted transactions is sufficient.

Now, $T2$ has read a value for A that should never have been there. (Recall that aborted transactions' effects are not supposed to be visible to other transactions.) If $T2$ had not yet committed, we could deal with the situation by *cascading* the abort of $T1$ and also aborting $T2$; this process recursively aborts any transaction that read data written by $T2$, and so on. But $T2$ has already committed, and so we cannot undo its actions. We say that such a schedule is *unrecoverable*. In a **recoverable schedule**, transactions commit only after (and if!) all transactions whose changes they read commit. If transactions read only the changes of committed transactions, not only is the schedule recoverable, but also aborting a transaction can be accomplished without cascading the abort to other transactions. Such a schedule is said to **avoid cascading aborts**.

There is another potential problem in undoing the actions of a transaction. Suppose that a transaction $T2$ overwrites the value of an object A that has been modified by a transaction $T1$, while $T1$ is still in progress, and $T1$ subsequently aborts. All of $T1$'s changes to database objects are undone by restoring the value of any object that it modified to the value of the object before $T1$'s changes. (We look at the details of how a transaction abort is handled in Chapter 18.) When $T1$ is aborted and its changes are undone in this manner, $T2$'s changes are lost as well, even if $T2$ decides to commit. So, for example, if A originally had the value 5, then was changed by $T1$ to 6, and by $T2$ to 7, if $T1$ now aborts, the value of A becomes 5 again. Even if $T2$ commits, its change to A is inadvertently lost. A concurrency control technique called Strict 2PL, introduced in Section 16.4, can prevent this problem (as discussed in Section 17.1).

16.4 LOCK-BASED CONCURRENCY CONTROL

A DBMS must be able to ensure that only serializable, recoverable schedules are allowed and that no actions of committed transactions are lost while undoing aborted transactions. A DBMS typically uses a *locking protocol* to achieve this. A **lock** is a small bookkeeping object associated with a database object. A **locking protocol** is a set of rules to be followed by each transaction (and enforced by the DBMS) to ensure that, even though actions of several transactions might be interleaved, the net effect is identical to executing all transactions in some serial order. Different locking protocols use different types of locks, such as shared locks or exclusive locks, as we see next, when we discuss the Strict 2PL protocol.

16.4.1 Strict Two-Phase Locking (Strict 2PL)

The most widely used locking protocol, called *Strict Two-Phase Locking*, or *Strict 2PL*, has two rules. The first rule is

1. If a transaction T wants to *read* (respectively, *modify*) an object, it first requests a **shared** (respectively, **exclusive**) lock on the object.

Of course, a transaction that has an exclusive lock can also read the object; an additional shared lock is not required. A transaction that requests a lock is suspended until the DBMS is able to grant it the requested lock. The DBMS keeps track of the locks it has granted and ensures that if a transaction holds an exclusive lock on an object, no other transaction holds a shared or exclusive lock on the same object. The second rule in Strict 2PL is

2. All locks held by a transaction are released when the transaction is completed.

Requests to acquire and release locks can be automatically inserted into transactions by the DBMS; users need not worry about these details. (We discuss how application programmers can select properties of transactions and control locking overhead in Section 16.6.3.)

In effect, the locking protocol allows only 'safe' interleavings of transactions. If two transactions access completely independent parts of the database, they concurrently obtain the locks they need and proceed merrily on their ways. On the other hand, if two transactions access the same object, and one wants to modify it, their actions are effectively ordered serially—all actions of one of these transactions (the one that gets the lock on the common object first) are completed before (this lock is released and) the other transaction can proceed.

We denote the action of a transaction T requesting a shared (respectively, exclusive) lock on object O as $S_T(O)$ (respectively, $X_T(O)$) and omit the subscript denoting the transaction when it is clear from the context. As an example, consider the schedule shown in Figure 16.4. This interleaving could result in a state that cannot result from any serial execution of the three transactions. For instance, $T1$ could change A from 10 to 20, then $T2$ (which reads the value 20 for A) could change B from 100 to 200, and then $T1$ would read the value 200 for B. If run serially, either $T1$ or $T2$ would execute first, and read the values 10 for A and 100 for B: Clearly, the interleaved execution is not equivalent to either serial execution.

If the Strict 2PL protocol is used, such interleaving is disallowed. Let us see why. Assuming that the transactions proceed at the same relative speed as before, $T1$ would obtain an exclusive lock on A first and then read and write A (Figure 16.6). Then, $T2$ would request a lock on A. However, this request

$T1$	$T2$
$X(A)$	
$R(A)$	
$W(A)$	

Figure 16.6 Schedule Illustrating Strict 2PL

cannot be granted until $T1$ releases its exclusive lock on A, and the DBMS therefore suspends $T2$. $T1$ now proceeds to obtain an exclusive lock on B, reads and writes B, then finally commits, at which time its locks are released. $T2$'s lock request is now granted, and it proceeds. In this example the locking protocol results in a serial execution of the two transactions, shown in Figure 16.7.

$T1$	$T2$
$X(A)$	
$R(A)$	
$W(A)$	
$X(B)$	
$R(B)$	
$W(B)$	
Commit	
	$X(A)$
	$R(A)$
	$W(A)$
	$X(B)$
	$R(B)$
	$W(B)$
	Commit

Figure 16.7 Schedule Illustrating Strict 2PL with Serial Execution

In general, however, the actions of different transactions could be interleaved. As an example, consider the interleaving of two transactions shown in Figure 16.8, which is permitted by the Strict 2PL protocol.

It can be shown that the Strict 2PL algorithm allows only serializable schedules. None of the anomalies discussed in Section 16.3.3 can arise if the DBMS implements Strict 2PL.

$T1$	$T2$
$S(A)$	
$R(A)$	
	$S(A)$
	$R(A)$
	$X(B)$
	$R(B)$
	$W(B)$
	Commit
$X(C)$	
$R(C)$	
$W(C)$	
Commit	

Figure 16.8 Schedule Following Strict 2PL with Interleaved Actions

16.4.2 Deadlocks

Consider the following example. Transaction $T1$ sets an exclusive lock on object A, $T2$ sets an exclusive lock on B, $T1$ requests an exclusive lock on B and is queued, and $T2$ requests an exclusive lock on A and is queued. Now, $T1$ is waiting for $T2$ to release its lock and $T2$ is waiting for $T1$ to release its lock. Such a cycle of transactions waiting for locks to be released is called a **deadlock**. Clearly, these two transactions will make no further progress. Worse, they hold locks that may be required by other transactions. The DBMS must either prevent or detect (and resolve) such deadlock situations; the common approach is to detect and resolve deadlocks.

A simple way to identify deadlocks is to use a timeout mechanism. If a transaction has been waiting too long for a lock, we can assume (pessimistically) that it is in a deadlock cycle and abort it. We discuss deadlocks in more detail in Section 17.2.

16.5 PERFORMANCE OF LOCKING

Lock-based schemes are designed to resolve conflicts between transactions and use two basic mechanisms: *blocking* and *aborting*. Both mechanisms involve a performance penalty: Blocked transactions may hold locks that force other transactions to wait, and aborting and restarting a transaction obviously wastes the work done thus far by that transaction. A deadlock represents an extreme instance of blocking in which a set of transactions is forever blocked unless one of the deadlocked transactions is aborted by the DBMS.

In practice, fewer than 1% of transactions are involved in a deadlock, and there are relatively few aborts. Therefore, the overhead of locking comes primarily from delays due to blocking.[3] Consider how blocking delays affect throughput. The first few transactions are unlikely to conflict, and throughput rises in proportion to the number of active transactions. As more and more transactions execute concurrently on the same number of database objects, the likelihood of their blocking each other goes up. Thus, delays due to blocking increase with the number of active transactions, and throughput increases more slowly than the number of active transactions. In fact, there comes a point when adding another active transaction actually reduces throughput; the new transaction is blocked and effectively competes with (and blocks) existing transactions. We say that the system **thrashes** at this point, which is illustrated in Figure 16.9.

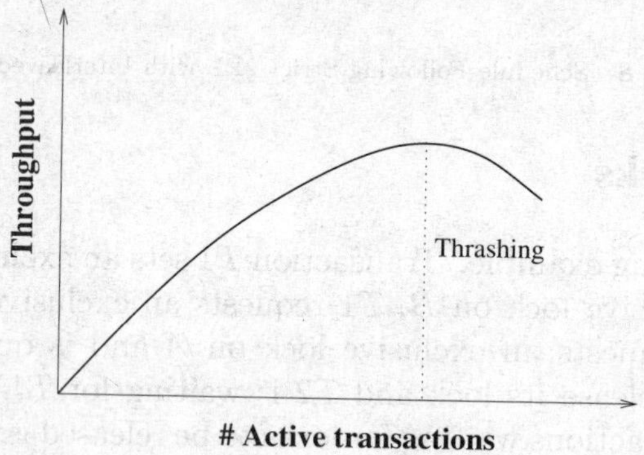

Figure 16.9 Lock Thrashing

If a database system begins to thrash, the database administrator should reduce the number of transactions allowed to run concurrently. Empirically, thrashing is seen to occur when 30% of active transactions are blocked, and a DBA should monitor the fraction of blocked transactions to see if the system is at risk of thrashing.

Throughput can be increased in three ways (other than buying a faster system):

- By locking the smallest sized objects possible (reducing the likelihood that two transactions need the same lock).
- By reducing the time that transaction hold locks (so that other transactions are blocked for a shorter time).

[3]Many common deadlocks can be avoided using a technique called *lock downgrades*, implemented in most commercial systems (Section 17.3).

- By reducing **hot spots**. A hot spot is a database object that is frequently accessed and modified, and causes a lot of blocking delays. Hot spots can significantly affect performance.

The granularity of locking is largely determined by the database system's implementation of locking, and application programmers and the DBA have little control over it. We discuss how to improve performance by minimizing the duration locks are held and using techniques to deal with hot spots in Section 20.10.

16.6 TRANSACTION SUPPORT IN SQL

We have thus far studied transactions and transaction management using an abstract model of a transaction as a sequence of read, write, and abort/commit actions. We now consider what support SQL provides for users to specify transaction-level behavior.

16.6.1 Creating and Terminating Transactions

A transaction is automatically started when a user executes a statement that accesses either the database or the catalogs, such as a `SELECT` query, an `UPDATE` command, or a `CREATE TABLE` statement.[4]

Once a transaction is started, other statements can be executed as part of this transaction until the transaction is terminated by either a `COMMIT` command or a `ROLLBACK` (the SQL keyword for abort) command.

In SQL:1999, two new features are provided to support applications that involve long-running transactions, or that must run several transactions one after the other. To understand these extensions, recall that all the actions of a given transaction are executed in order, regardless of how the actions of different transactions are interleaved. We can think of each transaction as a sequence of steps.

The first feature, called a **savepoint**, allows us to identify a point in a transaction and selectively roll back operations carried out after this point. This is especially useful if the transaction carries out what-if kinds of operations, and wishes to undo or keep the changes based on the results. This can be accomplished by defining savepoints.

[4]Some SQL statements—e.g., the `CONNECT` statement, which connects an application program to a database server—do not require the creation of a transaction.

SQL:1999 Nested Transactions: The concept of a transaction as an atomic sequence of actions has been extended in SQL:1999 through the introduction of the *savepoint* feature. This allows parts of a transaction to be selectively rolled back. The introduction of savepoints represents the first SQL support for the concept of **nested transactions**, which have been extensively studied in the research community. The idea is that a transaction can have several nested subtransactions, each of which can be selectively rolled back. Savepoints support a simple form of one-level nesting.

In a long-running transaction, we may want to define a series of savepoints. The savepoint command allows us to give each savepoint a name:

SAVEPOINT ⟨*savepoint name* ⟩

A subsequent rollback command can specify the savepoint to roll back to

ROLLBACK TO SAVEPOINT ⟨*savepoint name* ⟩

If we define three savepoints A, B, and C in that order, and then rollback to A, all operations since A are undone, including the creation of savepoints B and C. Indeed, the savepoint A is itself undone when we roll back to it, and we must re-establish it (through another savepoint command) if we wish to be able to roll back to it again. From a locking standpoint, locks obtained after savepoint A can be released when we roll back to A.

It is instructive to compare the use of savepoints with the alternative of executing a series of transactions (i.e., treat all operations in between two consecutive savepoints as a new transaction). The savepoint mechanism offers two advantages. First, we can roll back over several savepoints. In the alternative approach, we can roll back only the most recent transaction, which is equivalent to rolling back to the most recent savepoint. Second, the overhead of initiating several transactions is avoided.

Even with the use of savepoints, certain applications might require us to run several transactions one after the other. To minimize the overhead in such situations, SQL:1999 introduces another feature, called **chained transactions**. We can commit or roll back a transaction and immediately initiate another transaction. This is done by using the optional keywords `AND CHAIN` in the `COMMIT` and `ROLLBACK` statements.

16.6.2 What Should We Lock?

Until now, we have discussed transactions and concurrency control in terms of an abstract model in which a database contains a fixed collection of objects, and each transaction is a series of read and write operations on individual objects. An important question to consider in the context of SQL is what the DBMS should treat as an *object* when setting locks for a given SQL statement (that is part of a transaction).

Consider the following query:

```
SELECT S.rating, MIN (S.age)
FROM   Sailors S
WHERE  S.rating = 8
```

Suppose that this query runs as part of transaction $T1$ and an SQL statement that modifies the age of a given sailor, say Joe, with *rating=8* runs as part of transaction $T2$. What 'objects' should the DBMS lock when executing these transactions? Intuitively, we must detect a conflict between these transactions.

The DBMS could set a shared lock on the entire Sailors table for $T1$ and set an exclusive lock on Sailors for $T2$, which would ensure that the two transactions are executed in a serializable manner. However, this approach yields low concurrency, and we can do better by locking smaller objects, reflecting what each transaction actually accesses. Thus, the DBMS could set a shared lock on every row with *rating=8* for transaction $T1$ and set an exclusive lock on just the row for the modified tuple for transaction $T2$. Now, other read-only transactions that do not involve *rating=8* rows can proceed without waiting for $T1$ or $T2$.

As this example illustrates, the DBMS can lock objects at different **granularities**: We can lock entire tables or set row-level locks. The latter approach is taken in current systems because it offers much better performance. In practice, while row-level locking is generally better, the choice of locking granularity is complicated. For example, a transaction that examines several rows and modifies those that satisfy some condition might be best served by setting shared locks on the entire table and setting exclusive locks on those rows it wants to modify. We discuss this issue further in Section 17.5.3.

A second point to note is that SQL statements conceptually access a collection of rows described by a *selection predicate*. In the preceding example, transaction $T1$ accesses all rows with *rating=8*. We suggested that this could be dealt with by setting shared locks on all rows in Sailors that had *rating=8*. Unfortunately, this is a little too simplistic. To see why, consider an SQL statement that inserts a new sailor with *rating=8* and runs as transaction $T3$. (Observe that this example violates our assumption of a fixed number of objects in the database, but we must obviously deal with such situations in practice.)

Suppose that the DBMS sets shared locks on every existing Sailors row with *rating=8* for $T1$. This does not prevent transaction $T3$ from creating a brand new row with *rating=8* and setting an exclusive lock on this row. If this new row has a smaller *age* value than existing rows, $T1$ returns an answer that depends on when it executed relative to $T2$. However, our locking scheme imposes no relative order on these two transactions.

This phenomenon is called the **phantom** problem: A transaction retrieves a collection of objects (in SQL terms, a collection of tuples) twice and sees different results, even though it does not modify any of these tuples itself. To prevent phantoms, the DBMS must conceptually lock *all possible* rows with *rating=8* on behalf of $T1$. One way to do this is to lock the entire table, at the cost of low concurrency. It is possible to take advantage of indexes to do better, as we will see in Section 17.5.1, but in general preventing phantoms can have a significant impact on concurrency.

It may well be that the application invoking $T1$ can accept the potential inaccuracy due to phantoms. If so, the approach of setting shared locks on existing tuples for $T1$ is adequate, and offers better performance. SQL allows a programmer to make this choice—and other similar choices—explicitly, as we see next.

16.6.3 Transaction Characteristics in SQL

In order to give programmers control over the locking overhead incurred by their transactions, SQL allows them to specify three characteristics of a transaction: access mode, diagnostics size, and isolation level. The **diagnostics size** determines the number of error conditions that can be recorded; we will not discuss this feature further.

If the **access mode** is `READ ONLY`, the transaction is not allowed to modify the database. Thus, `INSERT`, `DELETE`, `UPDATE`, and `CREATE` commands cannot be executed. If we have to execute one of these commands, the access mode should be set to `READ WRITE`. For transactions with `READ ONLY` access mode, only shared locks need to be obtained, thereby increasing concurrency.

The **isolation level** controls the extent to which a given transaction is exposed to the actions of other transactions executing concurrently. By choosing one of four possible isolation level settings, a user can obtain greater concurrency at the cost of increasing the transaction's exposure to other transactions' uncommitted changes.

Isolation level choices are READ UNCOMMITTED, READ COMMITTED, REPEATABLE READ, and SERIALIZABLE. The effect of these levels is summarized in Figure 16.10. In this context, *dirty read* and *unrepeatable read* are defined as usual.

Level	Dirty Read	Unrepeatable Read	Phantom
READ UNCOMMITTED	Maybe	Maybe	Maybe
READ COMMITTED	No	Maybe	Maybe
REPEATABLE READ	No	No	Maybe
SERIALIZABLE	No	No	No

Figure 16.10 Transaction Isolation Levels in SQL-92

The highest degree of isolation from the effects of other transactions is achieved by setting the isolation level for a transaction T to SERIALIZABLE. This isolation level ensures that T reads only the changes made by committed transactions, that no value read or written by T is changed by any other transaction until T is complete, and that if T reads a set of values based on some search condition, this set is not changed by other transactions until T is complete (i.e., T avoids the phantom phenomenon).

In terms of a lock-based implementation, a SERIALIZABLE transaction obtains locks before reading or writing objects, including locks on sets of objects that it requires to be unchanged (see Section 17.5.1) and holds them until the end, according to Strict 2PL.

REPEATABLE READ ensures that T reads only the changes made by committed transactions and no value read or written by T is changed by any other transaction until T is complete. However, T could experience the phantom phenomenon; for example, while T examines all Sailors records with *rating=1*, another transaction might add a new such Sailors record, which is missed by T.

A REPEATABLE READ transaction sets the same locks as a SERIALIZABLE transaction, except that it does not do index locking; that is, it locks only individual objects, not sets of objects. We discuss index locking in detail in Section 17.5.1.

READ COMMITTED ensures that T reads only the changes made by committed transactions, and that no value written by T is changed by any other transaction until T is complete. However, a value read by T may well be modified by another transaction while T is still in progress, and T is exposed to the phantom problem.

A `READ COMMITTED` transaction obtains exclusive locks before writing objects and holds these locks until the end. It also obtains shared locks before reading objects, but these locks are released immediately; their only effect is to guarantee that the transaction that last modified the object is complete. (This guarantee relies on the fact that *every* SQL transaction obtains exclusive locks before writing objects and holds exclusive locks until the end.)

A `READ UNCOMMITTED` transaction T can read changes made to an object by an ongoing transaction; obviously, the object can be changed further while T is in progress, and T is also vulnerable to the phantom problem.

A `READ UNCOMMITTED` transaction does not obtain shared locks before reading objects. This mode represents the greatest exposure to uncommitted changes of other transactions; so much so that SQL prohibits such a transaction from making any changes itself—a `READ UNCOMMITTED` transaction is required to have an access mode of `READ ONLY`. Since such a transaction obtains no locks for reading objects and it is not allowed to write objects (and therefore never requests exclusive locks), it never makes any lock requests.

The `SERIALIZABLE` isolation level is generally the safest and is recommended for most transactions. Some transactions, however, can run with a lower isolation level, and the smaller number of locks requested can contribute to improved system performance. For example, a statistical query that finds the average sailor age can be run at the `READ COMMITTED` level or even the `READ UNCOMMITTED` level, because a few incorrect or missing values do not significantly affect the result if the number of sailors is large.

The isolation level and access mode can be set using the `SET TRANSACTION` command. For example, the following command declares the current transaction to be `SERIALIZABLE` and `READ ONLY`:

```
SET TRANSACTION ISOLATION LEVEL SERIALIZABLE READ ONLY
```

When a transaction is started, the default is `SERIALIZABLE` and `READ WRITE`.

16.7 INTRODUCTION TO CRASH RECOVERY

The **recovery manager** of a DBMS is responsible for ensuring transaction *atomicity* and *durability*. It ensures atomicity by undoing the actions of transactions that do not commit, and durability by making sure that all actions of committed transactions survive **system crashes**, (e.g., a core dump caused by a bus error) and **media failures** (e.g., a disk is corrupted).

When a DBMS is restarted after crashes, the recovery manager is given control and must bring the database to a consistent state. The recovery manager is also responsible for undoing the actions of an aborted transaction. To see what it takes to implement a recovery manager, it is necessary to understand what happens during normal execution.

The **transaction manager** of a DBMS controls the execution of transactions. Before reading and writing objects during normal execution, locks must be acquired (and released at some later time) according to a chosen locking protocol.[5] For simplicity of exposition, we make the following assumption:

> **Atomic Writes:** Writing a page to disk is an atomic action.

This implies that the system does not crash while a write is in progress and is unrealistic. In practice, disk writes do not have this property, and steps must be taken during restart after a crash (Section 18.6) to verify that the most recent write to a given page was completed successfully, and to deal with the consequences if not.

16.7.1 Stealing Frames and Forcing Pages

With respect to writing objects, two additional questions arise:

1. Can the changes made to an object O in the buffer pool by a transaction T be written to disk before T commits? Such writes are executed when another transaction wants to bring in a page and the buffer manager chooses to replace the frame containing O; of course, this page must have been unpinned by T. If such writes are allowed, we say that a **steal** approach is used. (Informally, the second transaction 'steals' a frame from T.)
2. When a transaction commits, must we ensure that all the changes it has made to objects in the buffer pool are immediately forced to disk? If so, we say that a **force** approach is used.

From the standpoint of implementing a recovery manager, it is simplest to use a buffer manager with a no-steal, force approach. If a no-steal approach is used, we do not have to undo the changes of an aborted transaction (because these changes have not been written to disk), and if a force approach is used, we do

[5] A concurrency control technique that does not involve locking could be used instead, but we assume that locking is used.

not have to redo the changes of a committed transaction if there is a subsequent crash (because all these changes are guaranteed to have been written to disk at commit time).

However, these policies have important drawbacks. The no-steal approach assumes that all pages modified by ongoing transactions can be accommodated in the buffer pool, and in the presence of large transactions (typically run in batch mode, e.g., payroll processing), this assumption is unrealistic. The force approach results in excessive page I/O costs. If a highly used page is updated in succession by 20 transactions, it would be written to disk 20 times. With a no-force approach, on the other hand, the in-memory copy of the page would be successively modified and written to disk just once, reflecting the effects of all 20 updates, when the page is eventually replaced in the buffer pool (in accordance with the buffer manager's page replacement policy).

For these reasons, most systems use a steal, no-force approach. Thus, if a frame is dirty and chosen for replacement, the page it contains is written to disk even if the modifying transaction is still active (*steal*); in addition, pages in the buffer pool that are modified by a transaction are not forced to disk when the transaction commits (*no-force*).

16.7.2 Recovery-Related Steps during Normal Execution

The recovery manager of a DBMS maintains some information during normal execution of transactions to enable it to perform its task in the event of a failure. In particular, a log of all modifications to the database is saved on **stable storage**, which is guaranteed[6] to survive crashes and media failures. Stable storage is implemented by maintaining multiple copies of information (perhaps in different locations) on nonvolatile storage devices such as disks or tapes.

As discussed earlier in Section 16.7, it is important to ensure that the log entries describing a change to the database are written to stable storage *before* the change is made; otherwise, the system might crash just after the change, leaving us without a record of the change. (Recall that this is the Write-Ahead Log, or WAL, property.)

The log enables the recovery manager to undo the actions of aborted and incomplete transactions and redo the actions of committed transactions. For example, a transaction that committed before the crash may have made updates

[6]Nothing in life is really guaranteed except death and taxes. However, we can reduce the chance of log failure to be vanishingly small by taking steps such as duplexing the log and storing the copies in different secure locations.

Tuning the Recovery Subsystem: DBMS performance can be greatly affected by the overhead imposed by the recovery subsystem. A DBA can take several steps to tune this subsystem, such as correctly sizing the log and how it is managed on disk, controlling the rate at which buffer pages are forced to disk, choosing a good frequency for checkpointing, and so forth.

to a copy (of a database object) in the buffer pool, and this change may not have been written to disk before the crash, because of a no-force approach. Such changes must be identified using the log and written to disk. Further, changes of transactions that did not commit prior to the crash might have been written to disk because of a steal approach. Such changes must be identified using the log and then undone.

The amount of work involved during recovery is proportional to the changes made by committed transactions that have not been written to disk at the time of the crash. To reduce the time to recover from a crash, the DBMS periodically forces buffer pages to disk during normal execution using a background process (while making sure that any log entries that describe changes these pages are written to disk first, i.e., following the WAL protocol). A process called *checkpointing*, which saves information about active transactions and dirty buffer pool pages, also helps reduce the time taken to recover from a crash. Checkpoints are discussed in Section 18.5.

16.7.3 Overview of ARIES

ARIES is a recovery algorithm that is designed to work with a steal, no-force approach. When the recovery manager is invoked after a crash, restart proceeds in three phases. In the **Analysis** phase, it identifies dirty pages in the buffer pool (i.e., changes that have not been written to disk) and active transactions at the time of the crash. In the **Redo** phase, it repeats all actions, starting from an appropriate point in the log, and restores the database state to what it was at the time of the crash. Finally, in the **Undo** phase, it undoes the actions of transactions that did not commit, so that the database reflects only the actions of committed transactions. The ARIES algorithm is discussed further in Chapter 18.

16.7.4 Atomicity: Implementing Rollback

It is important to recognize that the recovery subsystem is also responsible for executing the `ROLLBACK` command, which aborts a single transaction. Indeed, the logic (and code) involved in undoing a single transaction is identical to that used during the Undo phase in recovering from a system crash. All log records for a given transaction are organized in a linked list and can be efficiently accessed in reverse order to facilitate transaction rollback.

16.8 REVIEW QUESTIONS

Answers to the review questions can be found in the listed sections.

- What are the ACID properties? Define *atomicity*, *consistency*, *isolation*, and *durability* and illustrate them through examples. **(Section 16.1)**
- Define the terms *transaction*, *schedule*, *complete schedule*, and *serial schedule*. **(Section 16.2)**
- Why does a DBMS interleave concurrent transactions? **(Section 16.3)**
- When do two actions on the same data object *conflict*? Define the anomalies that can be caused by conflicting actions (*dirty reads, unrepeatable reads, lost updates*). **(Section 16.3)**
- What is a *serializable schedule*? What is a *recoverable schedule*? What is a schedule that *avoids cascading aborts*? What is a *strict schedule*? **(Section 16.3)**
- What is a *locking protocol*? Describe the *Strict Two-Phase Locking (Strict 2PL)* protocol. What can you say about the schedules allowed by this protocol? **(Section 16.4)**
- What overheads are associated with lock-based concurrency control? Discuss *blocking* and *aborting* overheads specifically and explain which is more important in practice. **(Section 16.5)**
- What is thrashing? What should a DBA do if the system thrashes? **(Section 16.5)**
- How can throughput be increased? **(Section 16.5)**
- How are transactions created and terminated in SQL? What are savepoints? What are chained transactions? Explain why savepoints and chained transactions are useful. **(Section 16.6)**
- What are the considerations in determining the locking granularity when executing SQL statements? What is the phantom problem? What impact does it have on performance? **(Section 16.6.2)**

- What transaction characteristics can a programmer control in SQL? Discuss the different *access modes* and *isolation levels* in particular. What issues should be considered in selecting an access mode and an isolation level for a transaction? **(Section 16.6.3)**
- Describe how different isolation levels are implemented in terms of the locks that are set. What can you say about the corresponding locking overheads? **(Section 16.6.3)**
- What functionality does the *recovery manager* of a DBMS provide? What does the *transaction manager* do? **(Section 16.7)**
- Describe the *steal* and *force* policies in the context of a buffer manager. What policies are used in practice and how does this affect recovery? **(Section 16.7.1)**
- What recovery-related steps are taken during normal execution? What can a DBA control to reduce the time to recover from a crash? **(Section 16.7.2)**
- How is the log used in transaction rollback and crash recovery? **(Sections 16.7.2, 16.7.3, and 16.7.4)**

EXERCISES

Exercise 16.1 Give brief answers to the following questions:

1. What is a transaction? In what ways is it different from an ordinary program (in a language such as C)?
2. Define these terms: *atomicity, consistency, isolation, durability, schedule, blind write, dirty read, unrepeatable read, serializable schedule, recoverable schedule, avoids-cascading-aborts schedule.*
3. Describe Strict 2PL.
4. What is the phantom problem? Can it occur in a database where the set of database objects is fixed and only the values of objects can be changed?

Exercise 16.2 Consider the following actions taken by transaction $T1$ on database objects X and Y:

R(X), W(X), R(Y), W(Y)

1. Give an example of another transaction $T2$ that, if run concurrently to transaction T without some form of concurrency control, could interfere with $T1$.
2. Explain how the use of Strict 2PL would prevent interference between the two transactions.
3. Strict 2PL is used in many database systems. Give two reasons for its popularity.

Exercise 16.3 Consider a database with objects X and Y and assume that there are two transactions $T1$ and $T2$. Transaction $T1$ reads objects X and Y and then writes object X. Transaction $T2$ reads objects X and Y and then writes objects X and Y.

1. Give an example schedule with actions of transactions $T1$ and $T2$ on objects X and Y that results in a write-read conflict.
2. Give an example schedule with actions of transactions $T1$ and $T2$ on objects X and Y that results in a read-write conflict.
3. Give an example schedule with actions of transactions $T1$ and $T2$ on objects X and Y that results in a write-write conflict.
4. For each of the three schedules, show that Strict 2PL disallows the schedule.

Exercise 16.4 We call a transaction that only reads database object a **read-only** transaction, otherwise the transaction is called a **read-write** transaction. Give brief answers to the following questions:

1. What is lock thrashing and when does it occur?
2. What happens to the database system throughput if the number of read-write transactions is increased?
3. What happens to the datbase system throughput if the number of read-only transactions is increased?
4. Describe three ways of tuning your system to increase transaction throughput.

Exercise 16.5 Suppose that a DBMS recognizes *increment*, which increments an integer-valued object by 1, and *decrement* as actions, in addition to reads and writes. A transaction that increments an object need not know the value of the object; increment and decrement are versions of blind writes. In addition to shared and exclusive locks, two special locks are supported: An object must be locked in I mode before incrementing it and locked in D mode before decrementing it. An I lock is compatible with another I or D lock on the same object, but not with S and X locks.

1. Illustrate how the use of I and D locks can increase concurrency. (Show a schedule allowed by Strict 2PL that only uses S and X locks. Explain how the use of I and D locks can allow more actions to be interleaved, while continuing to follow Strict 2PL.)
2. Informally explain how Strict 2PL guarantees serializability even in the presence of I and D locks. (Identify which pairs of actions conflict, in the sense that their relative order can affect the result, and show that the use of S, X, I, and D locks according to Strict 2PL orders all conflicting pairs of actions to be the same as the order in some serial schedule.)

Exercise 16.6 Answer the following questions: SQL supports four isolation-levels and two access-modes, for a total of eight combinations of isolation-level and access-mode. Each combination implicitly defines a class of transactions; the following questions refer to these eight classes:

1. Consider the four SQL isolation levels. Describe which of the phenomena can occur at each of these isolation levels: *dirty read, unrepeatable read, phantom problem.*
2. For each of the four isolation levels, give examples of transactions that could be run safely at that level.
3. Why does the access mode of a transaction matter?

Exercise 16.7 Consider the university enrollment database schema:

Student(*snum:* `integer`, *sname:* `string`, *major:* `string`, *level:* `string`, *age:* `integer`)
Class(*name:* `string`, *meets_at:* `time`, *room:* `string`, *fid:* `integer`)
Enrolled(*snum:* `integer`, *cname:* `string`)
Faculty(*fid:* `integer`, *fname:* `string`, *deptid:* `integer`)

The meaning of these relations is straightforward; for example, Enrolled has one record per student-class pair such that the student is enrolled in the class.

For each of the following transactions, state the SQL isolation level you would use and explain why you chose it.

1. Enroll a student identified by her *snum* into the class named 'Introduction to Database Systems'.
2. Change enrollment for a student identified by her *snum* from one class to another class.
3. Assign a new faculty member identified by his *fid* to the class with the least number of students.
4. For each class, show the number of students enrolled in the class.

Exercise 16.8 Consider the following schema:

Suppliers(*sid:* `integer`, *sname:* `string`, *address:* `string`)
Parts(*pid:* `integer`, *pname:* `string`, *color:* `string`)
Catalog(*sid:* `integer`, *pid:* `integer`, *cost:* `real`)

The Catalog relation lists the prices charged for parts by Suppliers.

For each of the following transactions, state the SQL isolation level that you would use and explain why you chose it.

1. A transaction that adds a new part to a supplier's catalog.
2. A transaction that increases the price that a supplier charges for a part.
3. A transaction that determines the total number of items for a given supplier.
4. A transaction that shows, for each part, the supplier that supplies the part at the lowest price.

Exercise 16.9 Consider a database with the following schema:

Suppliers(*sid:* `integer`, *sname:* `string`, *address:* `string`)
Parts(*pid:* `integer`, *pname:* `string`, *color:* `string`)
Catalog(*sid:* `integer`, *pid:* `integer`, *cost:* `real`)

The Catalog relation lists the prices charged for parts by Suppliers.

Consider three transactions $T1$, $T2$, and $T3$; $T1$ always has SQL isolation level `SERIALIZABLE`. We first run $T1$ concurrently with $T2$ and then we run $T1$ concurrently with $T2$ but we change the isolation level of $T2$ as specified below. Give a database instance and SQL statements for $T1$ and $T2$ such that result of running $T2$ with the first SQL isolation level is different from running $T2$ with the second SQL isolation level. Also specify the common schedule of $T1$ and $T2$ and explain why the results are different.

1. SERIALIZABLE versus REPEATABLE READ.
2. REPEATABLE READ versus READ COMMITTED.
3. READ COMMITTED versus READ UNCOMMITTED.

BIBLIOGRAPHIC NOTES

The transaction concept and some of its limitations are discussed in [332]. A formal transaction model that generalizes several earlier transaction models is proposed in [182].

Two-phase locking was introduced in [252], a fundamental paper that also discusses the concepts of transactions, phantoms, and predicate locks. Formal treatments of serializability appear in [92, 581].

Excellent in-depth presentations of transaction processing can be found in [90] and [770]. [338] is a classic, encyclopedic treatment of the subject.

17

CONCURRENCY CONTROL

- How does Strict 2PL ensure serializability and recoverability?
- How are locks implemented in a DBMS?
- What are lock conversions and why are they important?
- How does a DBMS resolve deadlocks?
- How do current systems deal with the phantom problem?
- Why are specialized locking techniques used on tree indexes?
- How does multiple-granularity locking work?
- What is Optimistic concurrency control?
- What is Timestamp-Based concurrency control?
- What is Multiversion concurrency control?
- **Key concepts:** Two-phase locking (2PL), serializability, recoverability, precedence graph, strict schedule, view equivalence, view serializable, lock manager, lock table, transaction table, latch, convoy, lock upgrade, deadlock, waits-for graph, conservative 2PL, index locking, predicate locking, multiple-granularity locking, lock escalation, SQL isolation level, phantom problem, optimistic concurrency control, Thomas Write Rule, recoverability

Pooh was sitting in his house one day, counting his pots of honey, when there came a knock on the door.
"Fourteen," said Pooh. "Come in. Fourteen. Or was it fifteen? Bother. That's muddled me."

"Hallo, Pooh," said Rabbit. "Hallo, Rabbit. Fourteen, wasn't it?"
"What was?" "My pots of honey what I was counting."
"Fourteen, that's right."
"Are you sure?"
"No," said Rabbit. "Does it matter?"

—A.A. Milne, *The House at Pooh Corner*

In this chapter, we look at concurrency control in more detail. We begin by looking at locking protocols and how they guarantee various important properties of schedules in Section 17.1. Section 17.2 is an introduction to how locking protocols are implemented in a DBMS. Section 17.3 discusses the issue of lock conversions, and Section 17.4 covers deadlock handling. Section 17.5 discusses three specialized locking protocols—for locking sets of objects identified by some predicate, for locking nodes in tree-structured indexes, and for locking collections of related objects. Section 17.6 examines some alternatives to the locking approach.

17.1 2PL, SERIALIZABILITY, AND RECOVERABILITY

In this section, we consider how locking protocols guarantee some important properties of schedules; namely, serializability and recoverability. Two schedules are said to be **conflict equivalent** if they involve the (same set of) actions of the same transactions and they order every pair of conflicting actions of two committed transactions in the same way.

As we saw in Section 16.3.3, two actions conflict if they operate on the same data object and at least one of them is a write. The outcome of a schedule depends only on the order of conflicting operations; we can interchange any pair of nonconflicting operations without altering the effect of the schedule on the database. If two schedules are conflict equivalent, it is easy to see that they have the same effect on a database. Indeed, because they order all pairs of conflicting operations in the same way, we can obtain one of them from the other by repeatedly swapping pairs of nonconflicting actions, that is, by swapping pairs of actions whose relative order does not alter the outcome.

A schedule is **conflict serializable** if it is conflict equivalent to some serial schedule. Every conflict serializable schedule is serializable, if we assume that the set of items in the database does not grow or shrink; that is, values can be modified but items are not added or deleted. We make this assumption for now and consider its consequences in Section 17.5.1. However, some serializable schedules are not conflict serializable, as illustrated in Figure 17.1. This schedule is equivalent to executing the transactions serially in the order $T1$, $T2$,

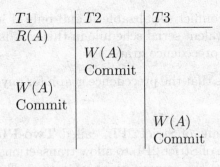

$T1$	$T2$	$T3$
$R(A)$		
	$W(A)$	
	Commit	
$W(A)$		
Commit		
		$W(A)$
		Commit

Figure 17.1 Serializable Schedule That Is Not Conflict Serializable

$T3$, but it is not conflict equivalent to this serial schedule because the writes of $T1$ and $T2$ are ordered differently.

It is useful to capture all potential conflicts between the transactions in a schedule in a **precedence graph**, also called a **serializability graph**. The precedence graph for a schedule S contains:

- A node for each committed transaction in S.
- An arc from Ti to Tj if an action of Ti precedes and conflicts with one of Tj's actions.

The precedence graphs for the schedules shown in Figures 16.7, 16.8, and 17.1 are shown in Figure 17.2 (parts a, b, and c, respectively).

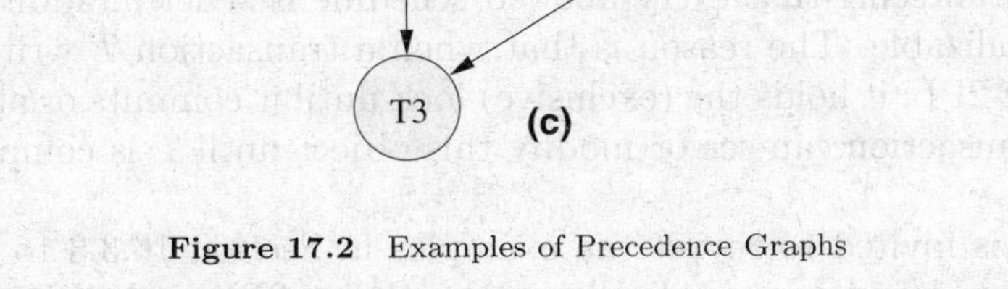

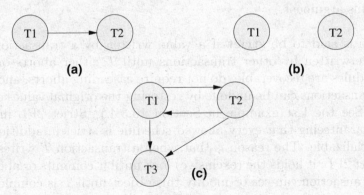

Figure 17.2 Examples of Precedence Graphs

The Strict 2PL protocol (introduced in Section 16.4) allows only conflict serializable schedules, as is seen from the following two results:

1. A schedule S is conflict serializable if and only if its precedence graph is acyclic. (An equivalent serial schedule in this case is given by any topological sort over the precedence graph.)

2. Strict 2PL ensures that the precedence graph for any schedule that it allows is acyclic.

A widely studied variant of Strict 2PL, called **Two-Phase Locking (2PL)**, relaxes the second rule of Strict 2PL to allow transactions to release locks before the end, that is, before the commit or abort action. For 2PL, the second rule is replaced by the following rule:

> **(2PL)** (2) A transaction cannot request additional locks once it releases *any* lock.

Thus, every transaction has a 'growing' phase in which it acquires locks, followed by a 'shrinking' phase in which it releases locks.

It can be shown that even nonstrict 2PL ensures acyclicity of the precedence graph and therefore allows only conflict serializable schedules. Intuitively, an equivalent serial order of transactions is given by the order in which transactions enter their shrinking phase: If $T2$ reads or writes an object written by $T1$, $T1$ must have released its lock on the object before $T2$ requested a lock on this object. Thus, $T1$ precedes $T2$. (A similar argument shows that $T1$ precedes $T2$ if $T2$ writes an object previously read by $T1$. A formal proof of the claim would have to show that there is no cycle of transactions that 'precede' each other by this argument.)

A schedule is said to be **strict** if a value written by a transaction T is not read or overwritten by other transactions until T either aborts or commits. Strict schedules are recoverable, do not require cascading aborts, and actions of aborted transactions can be undone by restoring the original values of modified objects. (See the last example in Section 16.3.4.) Strict 2PL improves on 2PL by guaranteeing that every allowed schedule is strict in addition to being conflict serializable. The reason is that when a transaction T writes an object under Strict 2PL, it holds the (exclusive) lock until it commits or aborts. Thus, no other transaction can see or modify this object until T is complete.

The reader is invited to revisit the examples in Section 16.3.3 to see how the corresponding schedules are disallowed by Strict 2PL and 2PL. Similarly, it would be instructive to work out how the schedules for the examples in Section 16.3.4 are disallowed by Strict 2PL but not by 2PL.

17.1.1 View Serializability

Conflict serializability is sufficient but not necessary for serializability. A more general sufficient condition is view serializability. Two schedules $S1$ and $S2$ over the same set of transactions—any transaction that appears in either $S1$ or $S2$ must also appear in the other—are **view equivalent** under these conditions:

1. If Ti reads the initial value of object A in $S1$, it must also read the initial value of A in $S2$.
2. If Ti reads a value of A written by Tj in $S1$, it must also read the value of A written by Tj in $S2$.
3. For each data object A, the transaction (if any) that performs the final write on A in $S1$ must also perform the final write on A in $S2$.

A schedule is **view serializable** if it is view equivalent to some serial schedule. Every conflict serializable schedule is view serializable, although the converse is not true. For example, the schedule shown in Figure 17.1 is view serializable, although it is not conflict serializable. Incidentally, note that this example contains blind writes. This is not a coincidence; it can be shown that any view serializable schedule that is not conflict serializable contains a blind write.

As we saw in Section 17.1, efficient locking protocols allow us to ensure that only conflict serializable schedules are allowed. Enforcing or testing view serializability turns out to be much more expensive, and the concept therefore has little practical use, although it increases our understanding of serializability.

17.2 INTRODUCTION TO LOCK MANAGEMENT

The part of the DBMS that keeps track of the locks issued to transactions is called the **lock manager**. The lock manager maintains a **lock table**, which is a hash table with the data object identifier as the key. The DBMS also maintains a descriptive entry for each transaction in a **transaction table**, and among other things, the entry contains a pointer to a list of locks held by the transaction. This list is checked before requesting a lock, to ensure that a transaction does not request the same lock twice.

A **lock table entry** for an object—which can be a page, a record, and so on, depending on the DBMS—contains the following information: the number of transactions currently holding a lock on the object (this can be more than one if the object is locked in shared mode), the nature of the lock (shared or exclusive), and a pointer to a queue of lock requests.

17.2.1 Implementing Lock and Unlock Requests

According to the Strict 2PL protocol, before a transaction T reads or writes a database object O, it must obtain a shared or exclusive lock on O and must hold on to the lock until it commits or aborts. When a transaction needs a lock on an object, it issues a lock request to the lock manager:

1. If a shared lock is requested, the queue of requests is empty, and the object is not currently locked in exclusive mode, the lock manager grants the lock and updates the lock table entry for the object (indicating that the object is locked in shared mode, and incrementing the number of transactions holding a lock by one).
2. If an exclusive lock is requested and no transaction currently holds a lock on the object (which also implies the queue of requests is empty), the lock manager grants the lock and updates the lock table entry.
3. Otherwise, the requested lock cannot be immediately granted, and the lock request is added to the queue of lock requests for this object. The transaction requesting the lock is suspended.

When a transaction aborts or commits, it releases all its locks. When a lock on an object is released, the lock manager updates the lock table entry for the object and examines the lock request at the head of the queue for this object. If this request can now be granted, the transaction that made the request is woken up and given the lock. Indeed, if several requests for a shared lock on the object are at the front of the queue, all of these requests can now be granted together.

Note that if $T1$ has a shared lock on O and $T2$ requests an exclusive lock, $T2$'s request is queued. Now, if $T3$ requests a shared lock, its request enters the queue behind that of $T2$, even though the requested lock is compatible with the lock held by $T1$. This rule ensures that $T2$ does not *starve*, that is, wait indefinitely while a stream of other transactions acquire shared locks and thereby prevent $T2$ from getting the exclusive lock for which it is waiting.

Atomicity of Locking and Unlocking

The implementation of *lock* and *unlock* commands must ensure that these are atomic operations. To ensure atomicity of these operations when several instances of the lock manager code can execute concurrently, access to the lock table has to be guarded by an operating system synchronization mechanism such as a semaphore.

To understand why, suppose that a transaction requests an exclusive lock. The lock manager checks and finds that no other transaction holds a lock on the object and therefore decides to grant the request. But, in the meantime, another transaction might have requested and *received* a conflicting lock. To prevent this, the entire sequence of actions in a lock request call (checking to see if the request can be granted, updating the lock table, etc.) must be implemented as an atomic operation.

Other Issues: Latches, Convoys

In addition to locks, which are held over a long duration, a DBMS also supports short-duration **latches**. Setting a latch before reading or writing a page ensures that the physical read or write operation is atomic; otherwise, two read/write operations might conflict if the objects being locked do not correspond to disk pages (the units of I/O). Latches are unset immediately after the physical read or write operation is completed.

We concentrated thus far on how the DBMS schedules transactions based on their requests for locks. This interleaving interacts with the operating system's scheduling of processes' access to the CPU and can lead to a situation called a convoy, where most of the CPU cycles are spent on process switching. The problem is that a transaction T holding a heavily used lock may be suspended by the operating system. Until T is resumed, every other transaction that needs this lock is queued. Such queues, called **convoys**, can quickly become very long; a convoy, once formed, tends to be stable. Convoys are one of the drawbacks of building a DBMS on top of a general-purpose operating system with preemptive scheduling.

17.3 LOCK CONVERSIONS

A transaction may need to acquire an exclusive lock on an object for which it already holds a shared lock. For example, a SQL update statement could result in shared locks being set on each row in a table. If a row satisfies the condition (in the `WHERE` clause) for being updated, an exclusive lock must be obtained for that row.

Such a **lock upgrade** request must be handled specially by granting the exclusive lock immediately if no other transaction holds a shared lock on the object and inserting the request at the front of the queue otherwise. The rationale for favoring the transaction thus is that it already holds a shared lock on the object and queuing it behind another transaction that wants an exclusive lock on the same object causes both a deadlock. Unfortunately, while favoring lock upgrades helps, it does not prevent deadlocks caused by two conflicting upgrade requests. For example, if two transactions that hold a shared lock on an object both request an upgrade to an exclusive lock, this leads to a deadlock.

A better approach is to avoid the need for lock upgrades altogether by obtaining exclusive locks initially, and **downgrading** to a shared lock once it is clear that this is sufficient. In our example of an SQL update statement, rows in a table are locked in exclusive mode first. If a row does *not* satisfy the condition for being updated, the lock on the row is downgraded to a shared lock. Does the downgrade approach violate the 2PL requirement? On the surface, it does, because downgrading reduces the locking privileges held by a transaction, and the transaction may go on to acquire other locks. However, this is a special case, because the transaction did nothing but read the object that it downgraded, even though it conservatively obtained an exclusive lock. We can safely expand our definition of 2PL from Section 17.1 to allow lock downgrades in the growing phase, provided that the transaction has not modified the object.

The downgrade approach reduces concurrency by obtaining write locks in some cases where they are not required. On the whole, however, it improves throughput by reducing deadlocks. This approach is therefore widely used in current commercial systems. Concurrency can be increased by introducing a new kind of lock, called an **update** lock, that is compatible with shared locks but not other update and exclusive locks. By setting an update lock initially, rather than exclusive locks, we prevent conflicts with other read operations. Once we are sure we need not update the object, we can downgrade to a shared lock. If we need to update the object, we must first upgrade to an exclusive lock. This upgrade does not lead to a deadlock because no other transaction can have an upgrade or exclusive lock on the object.

17.4 DEALING WITH DEADLOCKS

Deadlocks tend to be rare and typically involve very few transactions. In practice, therefore, database systems periodically check for deadlocks. When a transaction Ti is suspended because a lock that it requests cannot be granted, it must wait until all transactions Tj that currently hold conflicting locks release them. The lock manager maintains a structure called a **waits-for graph** to detect deadlock cycles. The nodes correspond to active transactions, and there is an arc from Ti to Tj if (and only if) Ti is waiting for Tj to release a lock. The lock manager adds edges to this graph when it queues lock requests and removes edges when it grants lock requests.

Consider the schedule shown in Figure 17.3. The last step, shown below the line, creates a cycle in the waits-for graph. Figure 17.4 shows the waits-for graph before and after this step.

$T1$	$T2$	$T3$	$T4$
$S(A)$			
$R(A)$			
	$X(B)$		
	$W(B)$		
$S(B)$			
		$S(C)$	
		$R(C)$	
	$X(C)$		
			$X(B)$
		$X(A)$	

Figure 17.3 Schedule Illustrating Deadlock

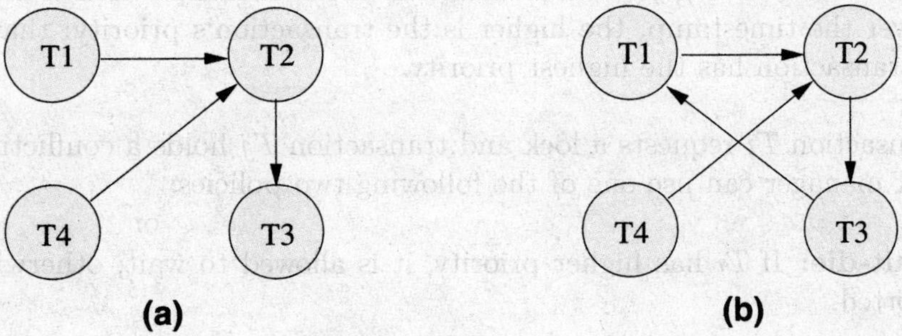

Figure 17.4 Waits-for Graph Before and After Deadlock

Observe that the waits-for graph describes all active transactions, some of which eventually abort. If there is an edge from Ti to Tj in the waits-for graph, and both Ti and Tj eventually commit, there is an edge in the opposite direction (from Tj to Ti) in the precedence graph (which involves only committed transactions).

The waits-for graph is periodically checked for cycles, which indicate deadlock. A deadlock is resolved by aborting a transaction that is on a cycle and releasing its locks; this action allows some of the waiting transactions to proceed. The choice of which transaction to abort can be made using several criteria: the one with the fewest locks, the one that has done the least work, the one that is farthest from completion, and so on. Further, a transaction might have been repeatedly restarted; if so, it should eventually be favored during deadlock detection and allowed to complete.

A simple alternative to maintaining a waits-for graph is to identify deadlocks through a timeout mechanism: If a transaction has been waiting too long for a lock, we assume (pessimistically) that it is in a deadlock cycle and abort it.

17.4.1 Deadlock Prevention

Empirical results indicate that deadlocks are relatively infrequent, and detection-based schemes work well in practice. However, if there is a high level of contention for locks and therefore an increased likelihood of deadlocks, prevention-based schemes could perform better. We can prevent deadlocks by giving each transaction a priority and ensuring that lower-priority transactions are not allowed to wait for higher-priority transactions (or vice versa). One way to assign priorities is to give each transaction a **timestamp** when it starts up. The lower the timestamp, the higher is the transaction's priority; that is, the oldest transaction has the highest priority.

If a transaction Ti requests a lock and transaction Tj holds a conflicting lock, the lock manager can use one of the following two policies:

- **Wait-die:** If Ti has higher priority, it is allowed to wait; otherwise, it is aborted.
- **Wound-wait:** If Ti has higher priority, abort Tj; otherwise, Ti waits.

In the wait-die scheme, lower-priority transactions can never wait for higher-priority transactions. In the wound-wait scheme, higher-priority transactions never wait for lower-priority transactions. In either case, no deadlock cycle develops.

A subtle point is that we must also ensure that no transaction is perennially aborted because it never has a sufficiently high priority. (Note that, in both schemes, the higher-priority transaction is never aborted.) When a transaction is aborted and restarted, it should be given the same timestamp it had originally. Reissuing timestamps in this way ensures that each transaction will eventually become the oldest transaction, and therefore the one with the highest priority, and will get all the locks it requires.

The wait-die scheme is nonpreemptive; only a transaction requesting a lock can be aborted. As a transaction grows older (and its priority increases), it tends to wait for more and more younger transactions. A younger transaction that conflicts with an older transaction may be repeatedly aborted (a disadvantage with respect to wound-wait), but on the other hand, a transaction that has all the locks it needs is never aborted for deadlock reasons (an advantage with respect to wound-wait, which is preemptive).

A variant of 2PL, called **Conservative 2PL**, can also prevent deadlocks. Under Conservative 2PL, a transaction obtains all the locks it will ever need when it begins, or blocks waiting for these locks to become available. This scheme ensures that there will be no deadlocks, and, perhaps more important, that a transaction that already holds some locks will not block waiting for other locks. If lock contention is heavy, Conservative 2PL can reduce the time that locks are held on average, because transactions that hold locks are never blocked. The trade-off is that a transaction acquires locks earlier, and if lock contention is low, locks are held longer under Conservative 2PL. From a practical perspective, it is hard to know exactly what locks are needed ahead of time, and this approach leads to setting more locks than necessary. It also has higher overhead for setting locks because a transaction has to release all locks and try to obtain them all over if it fails to obtain even one lock that it needs. This approach is therefore not used in practice.

17.5 SPECIALIZED LOCKING TECHNIQUES

Thus far we have treated a database as a *fixed* collection of *independent* data objects in our presentation of locking protocols. We now relax each of these restrictions and discuss the consequences.

If the collection of database objects is not fixed, but can grow and shrink through the insertion and deletion of objects, we must deal with a subtle complication known as the *phantom problem*, which was illustrated in Section 16.6.2. We discuss this problem in Section 17.5.1.

Although treating a database as an independent collection of objects is adequate for a discussion of serializability and recoverability, much better performance can sometimes be obtained using protocols that recognize and exploit the relationships between objects. We discuss two such cases, namely, locking in tree-structured indexes (Section 17.5.2) and locking a collection of objects with containment relationships between them (Section 17.5.3).

17.5.1 Dynamic Databases and the Phantom Problem

Consider the following example: Transaction $T1$ scans the Sailors relation to find the oldest sailor for each of the *rating* levels 1 and 2. First, $T1$ identifies and locks all pages (assuming that page-level locks are set) containing sailors with rating 1 and then finds the age of the oldest sailor, which is, say, 71. Next, transaction $T2$ inserts a new sailor with rating 1 and age 96. Observe that this new Sailors record can be inserted onto a page that does not contain other sailors with rating 1; thus, an exclusive lock on this page does not conflict with any of the locks held by $T1$. $T2$ also locks the page containing the oldest sailor with rating 2 and deletes this sailor (whose age is, say, 80). $T2$ then commits and releases its locks. Finally, transaction $T1$ identifies and locks pages containing (all remaining) sailors with rating 2 and finds the age of the oldest such sailor, which is, say, 63.

The result of the interleaved execution is that ages 71 and 63 are printed in response to the query. If $T1$ had run first, then $T2$, we would have gotten the ages 71 and 80; if $T2$ had run first, then $T1$, we would have gotten the ages 96 and 63. Thus, the result of the interleaved execution is not identical to any serial exection of $T1$ and $T2$, even though both transactions follow Strict 2PL and commit. The problem is that $T1$ assumes that the pages it has locked include *all* pages containing Sailors records with rating 1, and this assumption is violated when $T2$ inserts a new such sailor on a different page.

The flaw is not in the Strict 2PL protocol. Rather, it is in $T1$'s implicit assumption that it has locked the set of all Sailors records with *rating* value 1. $T1$'s semantics requires it to identify all such records, but locking pages that contain such records *at a given time* does not prevent new "phantom" records from being added on other pages. $T1$ has therefore *not* locked the set of desired Sailors records.

Strict 2PL guarantees conflict serializability; indeed, there are no cycles in the precedence graph for this example because conflicts are defined with respect to objects (in this example, pages) read/written by the transactions. However, because the set of objects that *should* have been locked by $T1$ was altered by the actions of $T2$, the outcome of the schedule differed from the outcome of any serial execution. This example brings out an important point about conflict serializability: If new items are added to the database, conflict serializability does not guarantee serializability.

A closer look at how a transaction identifies pages containing Sailors records with *rating* 1 suggests how the problem can be handled:

- If there is no index and all pages in the file must be scanned, $T1$ must somehow ensure that no new pages are added to the file, in addition to locking all existing pages.
- If there is an index on the *rating* field, $T1$ can obtain a lock on the index page—again, assuming that physical locking is done at the page level—that contains a data entry with *rating=1.* If there are no such data entries, that is, no records with this *rating* value, the page that *would* contain a data entry for *rating=1* is locked to prevent such a record from being inserted. Any transaction that tries to insert a record with *rating=1* into the Sailors relation must insert a data entry pointing to the new record into this index page and is blocked until $T1$ releases its locks. This technique is called **index locking**.

Both techniques effectively give $T1$ a lock on the set of Sailors records with *rating=1*: Each existing record with *rating=1* is protected from changes by other transactions, and additionally, new records with *rating=1* cannot be inserted.

An independent issue is how transaction $T1$ can efficiently identify and lock the index page containing *rating=1.* We discuss this issue for the case of tree-structured indexes in Section 17.5.2.

We note that index locking is a special case of a more general concept called **predicate locking**. In our example, the lock on the index page implicitly locked all Sailors records that satisfy the logical predicate *rating=1.* More generally, we can support implicit locking of all records that match an arbitrary predicate. General predicate locking is expensive to implement and therefore not commonly used.

17.5.2 Concurrency Control in B+ Trees

A straightforward approach to concurrency control for B+ trees and ISAM indexes is to ignore the index structure, treat each page as a data object, and use some version of 2PL. This simplistic locking strategy would lead to very high lock contention in the higher levels of the tree, because every tree search begins at the root and proceeds along some path to a leaf node. Fortunately, much more efficient locking protocols that exploit the hierarchical structure of a tree index are known to reduce the locking overhead while ensuring serializability and recoverability. We discuss some of these approaches briefly, concentrating on the search and insert operations.

Two observations provide the necessary insight:

1. The higher levels of the tree only direct searches. All the 'real' data is in the leaf levels (in the format of one of the three alternatives for data entries).

2. For inserts, a node must be locked (in exclusive mode, of course) only if a split can propagate up to it from the modified leaf.

Searches should obtain shared locks on nodes, starting at the root and proceeding along a path to the desired leaf. The first observation suggests that a lock on a node can be released as soon as a lock on a child node is obtained, because searches never go back up the tree.

A conservative locking strategy for inserts would be to obtain exclusive locks on all nodes as we go down from the root to the leaf node to be modified, because splits can propagate all the way from a leaf to the root. However, once we lock the child of a node, the lock on the node is required only in the event that a split propagates back to it. In particular, if the child of this node (on the path to the modified leaf) is not full when it is locked, any split that propagates up to the child can be resolved at the child, and does not propagate further to the current node. Therefore, when we lock a child node, we can release the lock on the parent if the child is not full. The locks held thus by an insert force any other transaction following the same path to wait at the earliest point (i.e., the node nearest the root) that might be affected by the insert. The technique of locking a child node and (if possible) releasing the lock on the parent is called **lock-coupling**, or **crabbing** (think of how a crab walks, and compare it to how we proceed down a tree, alternately releasing a lock on a parent and setting a lock on a child).

We illustrate B+ tree locking using the tree in Figure 17.5. To search for data entry 38*, a transaction Ti must obtain an S lock on node A, read the contents and determine that it needs to examine node B, obtain an S lock on node B and release the lock on A, then obtain an S lock on node C and release the lock on B, then obtain an S lock on node D and release the lock on C.

Ti always maintains a lock on one node in the path, to force new transactions that want to read or modify nodes on the same path to wait until the current transaction is done. If transaction Tj wants to delete 38*, for example, it must also traverse the path from the root to node D and is forced to wait until Ti

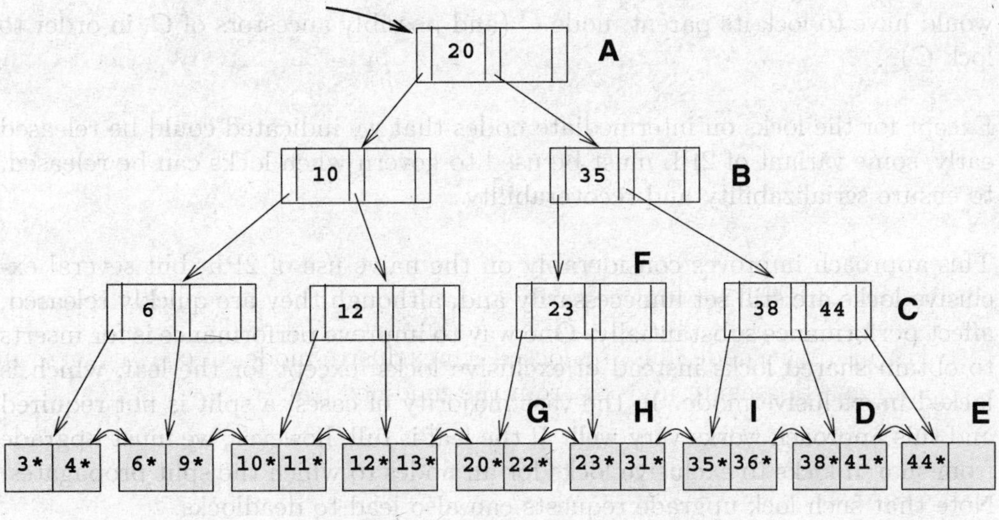

Figure 17.5 B+ Tree Locking Example

is done. Of course, if some transaction Tk holds a lock on, say, node C before Ti reaches this node, Ti is similarly forced to wait for Tk to complete.

To insert data entry 45*, a transaction must obtain an S lock on node A, obtain an S lock on node B and release the lock on A, then obtain an S lock on node C (observe that the lock on B is *not* released, because C is full), then obtain an X lock on node E and release the locks on C and then B. Because node E has space for the new entry, the insert is accomplished by modifying this node.

In contrast, consider the insertion of data entry 25*. Proceeding as for the insert of 45*, we obtain an X lock on node H. Unfortunately, this node is full and must be split. Splitting H requires that we also modify the parent, node F, but the transaction has only an S lock on F. Thus, it must request an upgrade of this lock to an X lock. If no other transaction holds an S lock on F, the upgrade is granted, and since F has space, the split does not propagate further and the insertion of 25* can proceed (by splitting H and locking G to modify the sibling pointer in I to point to the newly created node). However, if another transaction holds an S lock on node F, the first transaction is suspended until this transaction releases its S lock.

Observe that if another transaction holds an S lock on F and also wants to access node H, we have a deadlock because the first transaction has an X lock on H. The preceding example also illustrates an interesting point about sibling pointers: When we split leaf node H, the new node *must* be added to the *left* of H, since otherwise the node whose sibling pointer is to be changed would be node I, which has a different parent. To modify a sibling pointer on I, we would have to lock its parent, node C (and possibly ancestors of C, in order to lock C).

Except for the locks on intermediate nodes that we indicated could be released early, some variant of 2PL must be used to govern when locks can be released, to ensure serializability and recoverability.

This approach improves considerably on the naive use of 2PL, but several exclusive locks are still set unnecessarily and, although they are quickly released, affect performance substantially. One way to improve performance is for inserts to obtain shared locks instead of exclusive locks, except for the leaf, which is locked in exclusive mode. In the vast majority of cases, a split is not required and this approach works very well. If the leaf is full, however, we must upgrade from shared locks to exclusive locks for all nodes to which the split propagates. Note that such lock upgrade requests can also lead to deadlocks.

The tree locking ideas that we describe illustrate the potential for efficient locking protocols in this very important special case, but they are not the current state of the art. The interested reader should pursue the leads in the bibliography.

17.5.3 Multiple-Granularity Locking

Another specialized locking strategy, called **multiple-granularity locking**, allows us to efficiently set locks on objects that contain other objects.

For instance, a database contains several files, a file is a collection of pages, and a page is a collection of records. A transaction that expects to access most of the pages in a file should probably set a lock on the entire file, rather than locking individual pages (or records) when it needs them. Doing so reduces the locking overhead considerably. On the other hand, other transactions that require access to parts of the file—even parts not needed by this transaction—are blocked. If a transaction accesses relatively few pages of the file, it is better to lock only those pages. Similarly, if a transaction accesses several records on a page, it should lock the entire page, and if it accesses just a few records, it should lock just those records.

The question to be addressed is how a lock manager can efficiently ensure that a page, for example, is not locked by a transaction while another transaction holds a conflicting lock on the file containing the page (and therefore, implicitly, on the page).

The idea is to exploit the hierarchical nature of the 'contains' relationship. A database contains a set of files, each file contains a set of pages, and each page contains a set of records. This containment hierarchy can be thought of as a tree of objects, where each node contains all its children. (The approach can easily be extended to cover hierarchies that are not trees, but we do not discuss this extension.) A lock on a node locks that node and, implicitly, all its descendants. (Note that this interpretation of a lock is very different from B+ tree locking, where locking a node does *not* lock any descendants implicitly.)

In addition to shared (S) and exclusive (X) locks, multiple-granularity locking protocols also use two new kinds of locks, called **intention shared** (IS) and **intention exclusive** (IX) locks. IS locks conflict only with X locks. IX locks conflict with S and X locks. To lock a node in S (respectively, X) mode, a transaction must first lock all its ancestors in IS (respectively, IX) mode. Thus, if a transaction locks a node in S mode, no other transaction can have locked any ancestor in X mode; similarly, if a transaction locks a node in X mode, no other transaction can have locked any ancestor in S or X mode. This ensures that no other transaction holds a lock on an ancestor that conflicts with the requested S or X lock on the node.

A common situation is that a transaction needs to read an entire file and modify a few of the records in it; that is, it needs an S lock on the file and an IX lock so that it can subsequently lock some of the contained objects in X mode. It is useful to define a new kind of lock, called an SIX lock, that is logically equivalent to holding an S lock and an IX lock. A transaction can obtain a single SIX lock (which conflicts with any lock that conflicts with either S or IX) instead of an S lock and an IX lock.

A subtle point is that locks must be released in leaf-to-root order for this protocol to work correctly. To see this, consider what happens when a transaction Ti locks all nodes on a path from the root (corresponding to the entire database) to the node corresponding to some page p in IS mode, locks p in S mode, and then releases the lock on the root node. Another transaction Tj could now obtain an X lock on the root. This lock implicitly gives Tj an X lock on page p, which conflicts with the S lock currently held by Ti.

Multiple-granularity locking must be used with 2PL to ensure serializability. The 2PL protocol dictates when locks can be released. At that time, locks obtained using multiple-granularity locking can be released and must be released in leaf-to-root order.

Finally, there is the question of how to decide what granularity of locking is appropriate for a given transaction. One approach is to begin by obtaining fine granularity locks (e.g., at the record level) and, after the transaction requests

Lock Granularity: Some database systems allow programmers to override the default mechanism for choosing a lock granularity. For example, Microsoft SQL Server allows users to select page locking instead of table locking, using the keyword PAGLOCK. IBM's DB2 UDB allows for explicit table-level locking.

a certain number of locks at that granularity, to start obtaining locks at the next higher granularity (e.g., at the page level). This procedure is called **lock escalation**.

17.6 CONCURRENCY CONTROL WITHOUT LOCKING

Locking is the most widely used approach to concurrency control in a DBMS, but it is not the only one. We now consider some alternative approaches.

17.6.1 Optimistic Concurrency Control

Locking protocols take a pessimistic approach to conflicts between transactions and use either transaction abort or blocking to resolve conflicts. In a system with relatively light contention for data objects, the overhead of obtaining locks and following a locking protocol must nonetheless be paid.

In optimistic concurrency control, the basic premise is that most transactions do not conflict with other transactions, and the idea is to be as permissive as possible in allowing transactions to execute. Transactions proceed in three phases:

1. **Read:** The transaction executes, reading values from the database and writing to a private workspace.
2. **Validation:** If the transaction decides that it wants to commit, the DBMS checks whether the transaction could possibly have conflicted with any other concurrently executing transaction. If there is a possible conflict, the transaction is aborted; its private workspace is cleared and it is restarted.
3. **Write:** If validation determines that there are no possible conflicts, the changes to data objects made by the transaction in its private workspace are copied into the database.

If, indeed, there are few conflicts, and validation can be done efficiently, this approach should lead to better performance than locking. If there are many conflicts, the cost of repeatedly restarting transactions (thereby wasting the work they've done) hurts performance significantly.

Each transaction Ti is assigned a timestamp $TS(Ti)$ at the beginning of its validation phase, and the validation criterion checks whether the timestamp-ordering of transactions is an equivalent serial order. For every pair of transactions Ti and Tj such that $TS(Ti) < TS(Tj)$, one of the following **validation conditions** must hold:

1. Ti completes (all three phases) before Tj begins.
2. Ti completes before Tj starts its Write phase, and Ti does not write any database object read by Tj.
3. Ti completes its Read phase before Tj completes its Read phase, and Ti does not write any database object that is either read or written by Tj.

To validate Tj, we must check to see that one of these conditions holds with respect to each committed transaction Ti such that $TS(Ti) < TS(Tj)$. Each of these conditions ensures that Tj's modifications are not visible to Ti.

Further, the first condition allows Tj to see some of Ti's changes, but clearly, they execute completely in serial order with respect to each other. The second condition allows Tj to read objects while Ti is still modifying objects, but there is no conflict because Tj does not read any object modified by Ti. Although Tj might overwrite some objects written by Ti, all of Ti's writes precede all of Tj's writes. The third condition allows Ti and Tj to write objects at the same time and thus have even more overlap in time than the second condition, but the sets of objects written by the two transactions cannot overlap. Thus, no RW, WR, or WW conflicts are possible if any of these three conditions is met.

Checking these validation criteria requires us to maintain lists of objects read and written by each transaction. Further, while one transaction is being validated, no other transaction can be allowed to commit; otherwise, the validation of the first transaction might miss conflicts with respect to the newly committed transaction. The Write phase of a validated transaction must also be completed (so that its effects are visible outside its private workspace) before other transactions can be validated.

A synchronization mechanism such as a **critical section** can be used to ensure that at most one transaction is in its (combined) Validation/Write phases at any time. (When a process is executing a critical section in its code, the system suspends all other processes.) Obviously, it is important to keep these phases as short as possible in order to minimize the impact on concurrency. If copies of modified objects have to be copied from the private workspace, this can make the Write phase long. An alternative approach (which carries the penalty of poor physical locality of objects, such as B+ tree leaf pages, that must be clustered) is to use a level of indirection. In this scheme, every object is accessed via a logical pointer, and in the Write phase, we simply switch the logical pointer to point to the version of the object in the private workspace, instead of copying the object.

Clearly, it is not the case that optimistic concurrency control has no overheads; rather, the locking overheads of lock-based approaches are replaced with the overheads of recording read-lists and write-lists for transactions, checking for conflicts, and copying changes from the private workspace. Similarly, the implicit cost of blocking in a lock-based approach is replaced by the implicit cost of the work wasted by restarted transactions.

Improved Conflict Resolution[1]

Optimistic Concurrency Control using the three validation conditions described earlier is often overly conservative and unnecessarily aborts and restarts transactions. In particular, according to the validation conditions, Ti cannot write any object read by Tj. However, since the validation is aimed at ensuring that Ti logically executes before Tj, there is no harm if Ti writes all data items required by Tj before Tj reads them.

The problem arises because we have no way to tell when Ti wrote the object (relative to Tj's reading it) at the time we validate Tj, since all we have is the list of objects written by Ti and the list read by Tj. Such false conflicts can be alleviated by a finer-grain resolution of data conflicts, using mechanisms very similar to locking.

The basic idea is that each transaction in the Read phase tells the DBMS about items it is reading, and when a transaction Ti is committed (and its writes are accepted), the DBMS checks whether any of the items written by Ti are being read by any (yet to be validated) transaction Tj. If so, we know that Tj's validation must eventually fail. We can either allow Tj to discover this when it is validated (the **die** policy) or kill it and restart it immediately (the **kill** policy).

The details are as follows. Before reading a data item, a transaction T enters an **access entry** in a hash table. The access entry contains the *transaction id*, a *data object id*, and a *modified* flag (initially set to `false`), and entries are hashed on the data object id. A temporary exclusive lock is obtained on the

[1]We thank Alexander Thomasian for writing this section.

hash bucket containing the entry, and the lock is held while the read data item is copied from the database buffer into the private workspace of the transaction.

During validation of T the hash buckets of all data objects accessed by T are again locked (in exclusive mode) to check if T has encountered any data conflicts. T has encountered a conflict if the *modified* flag is set to `true` in one of its access entries. (This assumes that the 'die' policy is being used; if the 'kill' policy is used, T is restarted when the flag is set to `true`.)

If T is successfully validated, we lock the hash bucket of each object modified by T, retrieve all access entries for this object, set the *modified* flag to `true`, and release the lock on the bucket. If the 'kill' policy is used, the transactions that entered these access entries are restarted. We then complete T's Write phase.

It seems that the 'kill' policy is always better than the 'die' policy, because it reduces the overall response time and wasted processing. However, executing T to the end has the advantage that all of the data items required for its execution are prefetched into the database buffer, and restarted executions of T will not require disk I/O for reads. This assumes that the database buffer is large enough that prefetched pages are not replaced, and, more important, that **access invariance** prevails; that is, successive executions of T require the same data for execution. When T is restarted its execution time is much shorter than before because no disk I/O is required, and thus its chances of validation are higher. (Of course, if a transaction has already completed its Read phase once, subsequent conflicts should be handled using the 'kill' policy because all its data objects are already in the buffer pool.)

17.6.2 Timestamp-Based Concurrency Control

In lock-based concurrency control, conflicting actions of different transactions are ordered by the order in which locks are obtained, and the lock protocol extends this ordering on actions to transactions, thereby ensuring serializability. In optimistic concurrency control, a timestamp ordering is imposed on transactions and validation checks that all conflicting actions occurred in the same order.

Timestamps can also be used in another way: Each transaction can be assigned a timestamp at startup, and we can ensure, at execution time, that if action ai of transaction Ti conflicts with action aj of transaction Tj, ai occurs before aj if $TS(Ti) < TS(Tj)$. If an action violates this ordering, the transaction is aborted and restarted.

To implement this concurrency control scheme, every database object O is given a **read timestamp** $RTS(O)$ and a **write timestamp** $WTS(O)$. If transaction T wants to read object O, and $TS(T) < WTS(O)$, the order of this read with respect to the most recent write on O would violate the timestamp order between this transaction and the writer. Therefore, T is aborted and restarted *with a new, larger timestamp.* If $TS(T) > WTS(O)$, T reads O, and $RTS(O)$ is set to the larger of $RTS(O)$ and $TS(T)$. (Note that a physical change—the change to $RTS(O)$—is written to disk and recorded in the log for recovery purposes, even on reads. This write operation is a significant overhead.)

Observe that if T is restarted with the same timestamp, it is guaranteed to be aborted again, due to the same conflict. Contrast this behavior with the use of timestamps in 2PL for deadlock prevention, where transactions are restarted with the *same* timestamp as before to avoid repeated restarts. This shows that the two uses of timestamps are quite different and should not be confused.

Next, consider what happens when transaction T wants to write object O:

1. If $TS(T) < RTS(O)$, the write action conflicts with the most recent read action of O, and T is therefore aborted and restarted.
2. If $TS(T) < WTS(O)$, a naive approach would be to abort T because its write action conflicts with the most recent write of O and is out of timestamp order. However, we can safely ignore such writes and continue. Ignoring outdated writes is called the **Thomas Write Rule**.
3. Otherwise, T writes O and $WTS(O)$ is set to $TS(T)$.

The Thomas Write Rule

We now consider the justification for the Thomas Write Rule. If $TS(T) < WTS(O)$, the current write action has, in effect, been made obsolete by the most recent write of O, which *follows* the current write according to the timestamp ordering. We can think of T's write action as if it had occurred immediately *before* the most recent write of O and was never read by anyone.

If the Thomas Write Rule is not used, that is, T is aborted in case (2), the timestamp protocol, like 2PL, allows only conflict serializable schedules. If the Thomas Write Rule is used, some schedules are permitted that are not conflict serializable, as illustrated by the schedule in Figure 17.6.[2] Because $T2$'s write follows $T1$'s read and precedes $T1$'s write of the same object, this schedule is not conflict serializable.

[2] In the other direction, 2PL permits some schedules that are not allowed by the timestamp algorithm with the Thomas Write Rule; see Exercise 17.7.

$T1$	$T2$
$R(A)$	
	$W(A)$
	Commit
$W(A)$	
Commit	

Figure 17.6 A Serializable Schedule That Is Not Conflict Serializable

The Thomas Write Rule relies on the observation that $T2$'s write is never seen by any transaction and the schedule in Figure 17.6 is therefore equivalent to the serializable schedule obtained by deleting this write action, which is shown in Figure 17.7.

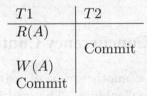

$T1$	$T2$
$R(A)$	
	Commit
$W(A)$	
Commit	

Figure 17.7 A Conflict Serializable Schedule

Recoverability

Unfortunately, the timestamp protocol just presented permits schedules that are not recoverable, as illustrated by the schedule in Figure 17.8. If $TS(T1) = 1$ and $TS(T2) = 2$, this schedule is permitted by the timestamp protocol (with or without the Thomas Write Rule). The timestamp protocol can be modified to disallow such schedules by **buffering** all write actions until the transaction commits. In the example, when $T1$ wants to write A, $WTS(A)$ is updated to reflect this action, but the change to A is not carried out immediately; instead, it is recorded in a private workspace, or buffer. When $T2$ wants to read A subsequently, its timestamp is compared with $WTS(A)$, and the read is seen to be permissible. However, $T2$ is blocked until $T1$ completes. If $T1$ commits, its change to A is copied from the buffer; otherwise, the changes in the buffer are discarded. $T2$ is then allowed to read A.

This blocking of $T2$ is similar to the effect of $T1$ obtaining an exclusive lock on A. Nonetheless, even with this modification, the timestamp protocol permits some schedules not permitted by 2PL; the two protocols are not quite the same. (See Exercise 17.7.)

$T1$	$T2$
$W(A)$	
	$R(A)$
	$W(B)$
	Commit

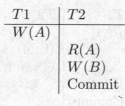

Figure 17.8 An Unrecoverable Schedule

Because recoverability is essential, such a modification must be used for the timestamp protocol to be practical. Given the added overhead this entails, on top of the (considerable) cost of maintaining read and write timestamps, timestamp concurrency control is unlikely to beat lock-based protocols in centralized systems. Indeed, it has been used mainly in the context of distributed database systems (Chapter 22).

17.6.3 Multiversion Concurrency Control

This protocol represents yet another way of using timestamps, assigned at startup time, to achieve serializability. The goal is to ensure that a transaction never has to wait to read a database object, and the idea is to maintain several versions of each database object, each with a write timestamp, and let transaction Ti read the most recent version whose timestamp precedes $TS(Ti)$.

If transaction Ti wants to write an object, we must ensure that the object has not already been read by some other transaction Tj such that $TS(Ti) < TS(Tj)$. If we allow Ti to write such an object, its change should be seen by Tj for serializability, but obviously Tj, which read the object at some time in the past, will not see Ti's change.

To check this condition, every object also has an associated read timestamp, and whenever a transaction reads the object, the read timestamp is set to the maximum of the current read timestamp and the reader's timestamp. If Ti wants to write an object O and $TS(Ti) < RTS(O)$, Ti is aborted and restarted with a new, larger timestamp. Otherwise, Ti creates a new version of O and sets the read and write timestamps of the new version to $TS(Ti)$.

The drawbacks of this scheme are similar to those of timestamp concurrency control, and in addition, there is the cost of maintaining versions. On the other hand, reads are never blocked, which can be important for workloads dominated by transactions that only read values from the database.

> **What Do Real Systems Do?** IBM DB2, Informix, Microsoft SQL Server, and Sybase ASE use Strict 2PL or variants (if a transaction requests a lower than `SERIALIZABLE` SQL isolation level; see Section 16.6). Microsoft SQL Server also supports modification timestamps so that a transaction can run without setting locks and validate itself (do-it-yourself Optimistic Concurrency Control!). Oracle 8 uses a multiversion concurrency control scheme in which readers never wait; in fact, readers never get locks and detect conflicts by checking if a block changed since they read it. All these systems support multiple-granularity locking, with support for table, page, and row level locks. All deal with deadlocks using waits-for graphs. Sybase ASIQ supports only table-level locks and aborts a transaction if a lock request fails—updates (and therefore conflicts) are rare in a data warehouse, and this simple scheme suffices.

17.7 REVIEW QUESTIONS

Answers to the review questions can be found in the listed sections.

- When are two schedules *conflict equivalent*? What is a *conflict serializable* schedule? What is a *strict* schedule? **(Section 17.1)**
- What is a *precedence graph* or *serializability graph*? How is it related to conflict serializability? How is it related to two-phase locking? **(Section 17.1)**
- What does the *lock manager* do? Describe the *lock table* and *transaction table* data structures and their role in lock management. **(Section 17.2)**
- Discuss the relative merits of *lock upgrades* and *lock downgrades.* **(Section 17.3)**
- Describe and compare deadlock detection and deadlock prevention schemes. Why are detection schemes more commonly used? **(Section 17.4)**
- If the collection of database objects is not fixed, but can grow and shrink through insertion and deletion of objects, we must deal with a subtle complication known as the *phantom problem.* Describe this problem and the index locking approach to solving the problem. **(Section 17.5.1)**
- In tree index structures, locking higher levels of the tree can become a performance bottleneck. Explain why. Describe specialized locking techniques that address the problem, and explain why they work correctly despite not being two-phase. **(Section 17.5.2)**
- *Multiple-granularity locking* enables us to set locks on objects that contain other objects, thus implicitly locking all contained objects. Why is this approach important and how does it work? **(Section 17.5.3)**

- In *optimistic concurrency control*, no locks are set and transactions read and modify data objects in a private workspace. How are conflicts between transactions detected and resolved in this approach? **(Section 17.6.1)**
- In *timestamp-based concurrency control*, transactions are assigned a timestamp at startup; how is it used to ensure serializability? How does the *Thomas Write Rule* improve concurrency? **(Section 17.6.2)**
- Explain why timestamp-based concurrency control allows schedules that are not recoverable. Describe how it can be modified through *buffering* to disallow such schedules. **(Section 17.6.2)**
- Describe *multiversion concurrency control*. What are its benefits and disadvantages in comparison to locking? **(Section 17.6.3)**

EXERCISES

Exercise 17.1 Answer the following questions:

1. Describe how a typical lock manager is implemented. Why must lock and unlock be atomic operations? What is the difference between a lock and a *latch*? What are *convoys* and how should a lock manager handle them?
2. Compare *lock downgrades* with upgrades. Explain why downgrades violate 2PL but are nonetheless acceptable. Discuss the use of *update* locks in conjunction with lock downgrades.
3. Contrast the timestamps assigned to restarted transactions when timestamps are used for deadlock prevention versus when timestamps are used for concurrency control.
4. State and justify the Thomas Write Rule.
5. Show that, if two schedules are conflict equivalent, then they are view equivalent.
6. Give an example of a serializable schedule that is not strict.
7. Give an example of a strict schedule that is not serialiable.
8. Motivate and describe the use of locks for improved conflict resolution in Optimistic Concurrency Control.

Exercise 17.2 Consider the following classes of schedules: *serializable, conflict-serializable, view-serializable, recoverable, avoids-cascading-aborts,* and *strict.* For each of the following schedules, state which of the preceding classes it belongs to. If you cannot decide whether a schedule belongs in a certain class based on the listed actions, explain briefly.

The actions are listed in the order they are scheduled and prefixed with the transaction name. If a commit or abort is not shown, the schedule is incomplete; assume that abort or commit must follow all the listed actions.

1. T1:R(X), T2:R(X), T1:W(X), T2:W(X)
2. T1:W(X), T2:R(Y), T1:R(Y), T2:R(X)

3. T1:R(X), T2:R(Y), T3:W(X), T2:R(X), T1:R(Y)
4. T1:R(X), T1:R(Y), T1:W(X), T2:R(Y), T3:W(Y), T1:W(X), T2:R(Y)
5. T1:R(X), T2:W(X), T1:W(X), T2:Abort, T1:Commit
6. T1:R(X), T2:W(X), T1:W(X), T2:Commit, T1:Commit
7. T1:W(X), T2:R(X), T1:W(X), T2:Abort, T1:Commit
8. T1:W(X), T2:R(X), T1:W(X), T2:Commit, T1:Commit
9. T1:W(X), T2:R(X), T1:W(X), T2:Commit, T1:Abort
10. T2: R(X), T3:W(X), T3:Commit, T1:W(Y), T1:Commit, T2:R(Y), T2:W(Z), T2:Commit
11. T1:R(X), T2:W(X), T2:Commit, T1:W(X), T1:Commit, T3:R(X), T3:Commit
12. T1:R(X), T2:W(X), T1:W(X), T3:R(X), T1:Commit, T2:Commit, T3:Commit

Exercise 17.3 Consider the following concurrency control protocols: 2PL, Strict 2PL, Conservative 2PL, Optimistic, Timestamp without the Thomas Write Rule, Timestamp with the Thomas Write Rule, and Multiversion. For each of the schedules in Exercise 17.2, state which of these protocols allows it, that is, allows the actions to occur in exactly the order shown.

For the timestamp-based protocols, assume that the timestamp for transaction Ti is i and that a version of the protocol that ensures recoverability is used. Further, if the Thomas Write Rule is used, show the equivalent serial schedule.

Exercise 17.4 Consider the following sequences of actions, listed in the order they are submitted to the DBMS:

- **Sequence S1:** T1:R(X), T2:W(X), T2:W(Y), T3:W(Y), T1:W(Y), T1:Commit, T2:Commit, T3:Commit
- **Sequence S2:** T1:R(X), T2:W(Y), T2:W(X), T3:W(Y), T1:W(Y), T1:Commit, T2:Commit, T3:Commit

For each sequence and for each of the following concurrency control mechanisms, describe how the concurrency control mechanism handles the sequence.

Assume that the timestamp of transaction Ti is i. For lock-based concurrency control mechanisms, add lock and unlock requests to the previous sequence of actions as per the locking protocol. The DBMS processes actions in the order shown. If a transaction is blocked, assume that all its actions are queued until it is resumed; the DBMS continues with the next action (according to the listed sequence) of an unblocked transaction.

1. Strict 2PL with timestamps used for deadlock prevention.
2. Strict 2PL with deadlock detection. (Show the waits-for graph in case of deadlock.)
3. Conservative (and Strict, i.e., with locks held until end-of-transaction) 2PL.
4. Optimistic concurrency control.
5. Timestamp concurrency control with buffering of reads and writes (to ensure recoverability) and the Thomas Write Rule.
6. Multiversion concurrency control.

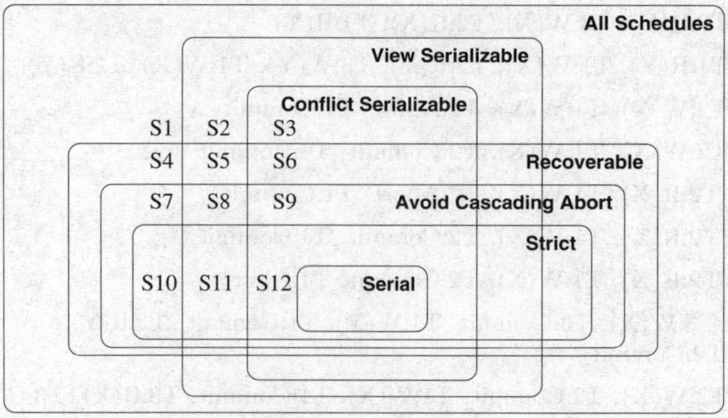

Figure 17.9 Venn Diagram for Classes of Schedules

Exercise 17.5 For each of the following locking protocols, assuming that every transaction follows that locking protocol, state which of these desirable properties are ensured: serializability, conflict-serializability, recoverability, avoidance of cascading aborts.

1. Always obtain an exclusive lock before writing; hold exclusive locks until end-of-transaction. No shared locks are ever obtained.
2. In addition to (1), obtain a shared lock before reading; shared locks can be released at any time.
3. As in (2), and in addition, locking is two-phase.
4. As in (2), and in addition, all locks held until end-of-transaction.

Exercise 17.6 The Venn diagram (from [76]) in Figure 17.9 shows the inclusions between several classes of schedules. Give one example schedule for each of the regions $S1$ through $S12$ in the diagram.

Exercise 17.7 Briefly answer the following questions:

1. Draw a Venn diagram that shows the inclusions between the classes of schedules permitted by the following concurrency control protocols: *2PL, Strict 2PL, Conservative 2PL, Optimistic, Timestamp without the Thomas Write Rule, Timestamp with the Thomas Write Rule,* and *Multiversion.*
2. Give one example schedule for each region in the diagram.
3. Extend the Venn diagram to include serializable and conflict-serializable schedules.

Exercise 17.8 Answer each of the following questions briefly. The questions are based on the following relational schema:

Emp(<u>*eid:* `integer`</u>, *ename:* `string`, *age:* `integer`, *salary:* `real`, *did:* `integer`)
Dept(<u>*did:* `integer`</u>, *dname:* `string`, *floor:* `integer`)

and on the following update command:

replace (salary = 1.1 * EMP.salary) where EMP.ename = 'Santa'

1. Give an example of a query that would conflict with this command (in a concurrency control sense) if both were run at the same time. Explain what could go wrong, and how locking tuples would solve the problem.
2. Give an example of a query or a command that would conflict with this command, such that the conflict could not be resolved by just locking individual tuples or pages but requires index locking.
3. Explain what index locking is and how it resolves the preceding conflict.

Exercise 17.9 SQL supports four isolation-levels and two access-modes, for a total of eight combinations of isolation-level and access-mode. Each combination implicitly defines a class of transactions; the following questions refer to these eight classes:

1. For each of the eight classes, describe a locking protocol that allows only transactions in this class. Does the locking protocol for a given class make any assumptions about the locking protocols used for other classes? Explain briefly.
2. Consider a schedule generated by the execution of several SQL transactions. Is it guaranteed to be conflict-serializable? to be serializable? to be recoverable?
3. Consider a schedule generated by the execution of several SQL transactions, each of which has `READ ONLY` access-mode. Is it guaranteed to be conflict-serializable? to be serializable? to be recoverable?
4. Consider a schedule generated by the execution of several SQL transactions, each of which has `SERIALIZABLE` isolation-level. Is it guaranteed to be conflict-serializable? to be serializable? to be recoverable?
5. Can you think of a timestamp-based concurrency control scheme that can support the eight classes of SQL transactions?

Exercise 17.10 Consider the tree shown in Figure 19.5. Describe the steps involved in executing each of the following operations according to the tree-index concurrency control algorithm discussed in Section 19.3.2, in terms of the order in which nodes are locked, unlocked, read, and written. Be specific about the kind of lock obtained and answer each part independently of the others, always starting with the tree shown in Figure 19.5.

1. Search for data entry 40*.
2. Search for all data entries $k*$ with $k \leq 40$.
3. Insert data entry 62*.
4. Insert data entry 40*.
5. Insert data entries 62* and 75*.

Exercise 17.11 Consider a database organized in terms of the following hierarachy of objects: The database itself is an object (D), and it contains two files ($F1$ and $F2$), each of which contains 1000 pages ($P1 \ldots P1000$ and $P1001 \ldots P2000$, respectively). Each page contains 100 records, and records are identified as $p : i$, where p is the page identifier and i is the slot of the record on that page.

Multiple-granularity locking is used, with S, X, IS, IX and SIX locks, and database-level, file-level, page-level and record-level locking. For each of the following operations, indicate the sequence of lock requests that must be generated by a transaction that wants to carry out (just) these operations:

1. Read record $P1200 : 5$.
2. Read records $P1200 : 98$ through $P1205 : 2$.
3. Read all (records on all) pages in file $F1$.
4. Read pages $P500$ through $P520$.
5. Read pages $P10$ through $P980$.
6. Read all pages in $F1$ and (based on the values read) modify 10 pages.
7. Delete record $P1200 : 98$. (This is a blind write.)
8. Delete the first record from each page. (Again, these are blind writes.)
9. Delete all records.

Exercise 17.12 Suppose that we have only two types of transactions, $T1$ and $T2$. Transactions preserve database consistency when run individually. We have defined several *integrity constraints* such that the DBMS never executes any SQL statement that brings the database into an inconsistent state. Assume that the DBMS does not perform *any* concurrency control. Give an example schedule of two transactions $T1$ and $T2$ that satisfies all these conditions, yet produces a database instance that is not the result of any serial execution of $T1$ and $T2$.

BIBLIOGRAPHIC NOTES

Concurrent access to B trees is considered in several papers, including [70, 456, 472, 505, 678]. Concurrency control techniques for Linear Hashing are presented in [240] and [543]. Multiple-granularity locking is introduced in [336] and studied further in [127, 449].

A concurrency control method that works with the ARIES recovery method is presented in [545]. Another paper that considers concurrency control issues in the context of recovery is [492]. Algorithms for building indexes without stopping the DBMS are presented in [548] and [9]. The performance of B tree concurrency control algorithms is studied in [704]. Performance of various concurrency control algorithms is discussed in [16, 729, 735]. A good survey of concurrency control methods and their performance is [734]. [455] is a comprehensive collection of papers on this topic.

Timestamp-based multiversion concurrency control is studied in [620]. Multiversion concurrency control algorithms are studied formally in [87]. Lock-based multiversion techniques are considered in [460]. Optimistic concurrency control is introduced in [457]. The use of access invariance to improve conflict resolution in high-contention environments is discussed in [281] and [280]. Transaction management issues for real-time database systems are discussed in [1, 15, 368, 382, 386, 448]. There is a large body of theoretical results on database concurrency control; [582, 89] offer thorough textbook presentations of this material.

18

CRASH RECOVERY

- What steps are taken in the ARIES method to recover from a DBMS crash?
- How is the log maintained during normal operation?
- How is the log used to recover from a crash?
- What information in addition to the log is used during recovery?
- What is a checkpoint and why is it used?
- What happens if repeated crashes occur during recovery?
- How is media failure handled?
- How does the recovery algorithm interact with concurrency control?
- **Key concepts:** steps in recovery, analysis, redo, undo; ARIES, repeating history; log, LSN, forcing pages, WAL; types of log records, update, commit, abort, end, compensation; transaction table, lastLSN; dirty page table, recLSN; checkpoint, fuzzy checkpointing, master log record; media recovery; interaction with concurrency control; shadow paging

Humpty Dumpty sat on a wall.
Humpty Dumpty had a great fall.
All the King's horses and all the King's men
Could not put Humpty together again.

—Old nursery rhyme

The **recovery manager** of a DBMS is responsible for ensuring two important properties of transactions: Atomicity and durability. It ensures *atomicity* by undoing the actions of transactions that do not commit and *durability* by making sure that all actions of committed transactions survive **system crashes** (e.g., a core dump caused by a bus error) and **media failures** (e.g., a disk is corrupted).

The recovery manager is one of the hardest components of a DBMS to design and implement. It must deal with a wide variety of database states because it is called on during system failures. In this chapter, we present the **ARIES** recovery algorithm, which is conceptually simple, works well with a wide range of concurrency control mechanisms, and is being used in an increasing number of database sytems.

We begin with an introduction to ARIES in Section 18.1. We discuss the log, which a central data structure in recovery, in Section 18.2, and other recovery-related data structures in Section 18.3. We complete our coverage of recovery-related activity during normal processing by presenting the Write-Ahead Logging protocol in Section 18.4, and checkpointing in Section 18.5.

We discuss recovery from a crash in Section 18.6. Aborting (or rolling back) a single transaction is a special case of Undo, discussed in Section 18.6.3. We discuss media failures in Section 18.7, and conclude in Section 18.8 with a discussion of the interaction of concurrency control and recovery and other approaches to recovery. In this chapter, we consider recovery only in a centralized DBMS; recovery in a distributed DBMS is discussed in Chapter 22.

18.1 INTRODUCTION TO ARIES

ARIES is a recovery algorithm designed to work with a steal, no-force approach. When the recovery manager is invoked after a crash, restart proceeds in three phases:

1. **Analysis:** Identifies dirty pages in the buffer pool (i.e., changes that have not been written to disk) and active transactions at the time of the crash.

2. **Redo:** Repeats all actions, starting from an appropriate point in the log, and restores the database state to what it was at the time of the crash.

3. **Undo:** Undoes the actions of transactions that did not commit, so that the database reflects only the actions of committed transactions.

Consider the simple execution history illustrated in Figure 18.1. When the system is restarted, the Analysis phase identifies $T1$ and $T3$ as transactions

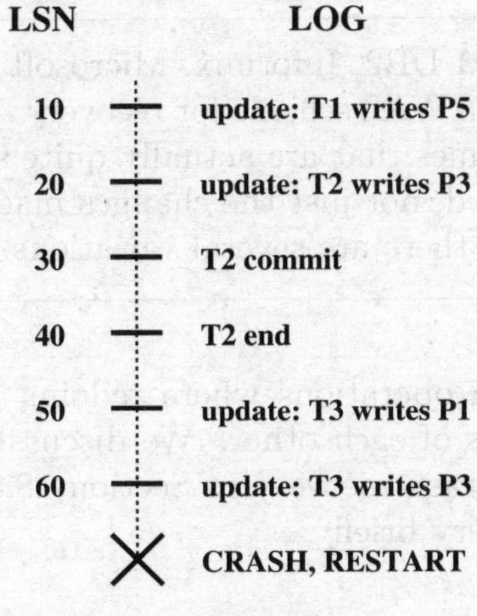

Figure 18.1 Execution History with a Crash

active at the time of the crash and therefore to be undone; $T2$ as a committed transaction, and all its actions therefore to be written to disk; and $P1$, $P3$, and $P5$ as potentially dirty pages. All the updates (including those of $T1$ and $T3$) are reapplied in the order shown during the Redo phase. Finally, the actions of $T1$ and $T3$ are undone in reverse order during the Undo phase; that is, $T3$'s write of $P3$ is undone, $T3$'s write of $P1$ is undone, and then $T1$'s write of $P5$ is undone.

Three main principles lie behind the ARIES recovery algorithm:

- **Write-Ahead Logging:** Any change to a database object is first recorded in the log; the record in the log must be written to stable storage before the change to the database object is written to disk.

- **Repeating History During Redo:** On restart following a crash, ARIES retraces all actions of the DBMS before the crash and brings the system back to the exact state that it was in at the time of the crash. Then, it undoes the actions of transactions still active at the time of the crash (effectively aborting them).

- **Logging Changes During Undo:** Changes made to the database while undoing a transaction are logged to ensure such an action is not repeated in the event of repeated (failures causing) restarts.

The second point distinguishes ARIES from other recovery algorithms and is the basis for much of its simplicity and flexibility. In particular, ARIES can support concurrency control protocols that involve locks of finer granularity than a page (e.g., record-level locks). The second and third points are also

Crash Recovery: IBM DB2, Informix, Microsoft SQL Server, Oracle 8, and Sybase ASE all use a WAL scheme for recovery. IBM DB2 uses ARIES, and the others use schemes that are actually quite similar to ARIES (e.g., all changes are re-applied, not just the changes made by transactions that are 'winners') although there are several variations.

important in dealing with operations where redoing and undoing the operation are not exact inverses of each other. We discuss the interaction between concurrency control and crash recovery in Section 18.8, where we also discuss other approaches to recovery briefly.

18.2 THE LOG

The log, sometimes called the **trail** or **journal**, is a history of actions executed by the DBMS. Physically, the log is a file of records stored in stable storage, which is assumed to survive crashes; this durability can be achieved by maintaining two or more copies of the log on different disks (perhaps in different locations), so that the chance of all copies of the log being simultaneously lost is negligibly small.

The most recent portion of the log, called the **log tail**, is kept in main memory and is periodically forced to stable storage. This way, log records and data records are written to disk at the same granularity (pages or sets of pages).

Every **log record** is given a unique *id* called the **log sequence number (LSN)**. As with any record id, we can fetch a log record with one disk access given the LSN. Further, LSNs should be assigned in monotonically increasing order; this property is required for the ARIES recovery algorithm. If the log is a sequential file, in principle growing indefinitely, the LSN can simply be the address of the first byte of the log record.[1]

For recovery purposes, every page in the database contains the LSN of the most recent log record that describes a change to this page. This LSN is called the **pageLSN**.

A log record is written for each of the following actions:

[1]In practice, various techniques are used to identify portions of the log that are 'too old' to be needed again to bound the amount of stable storage used for the log. Given such a bound, the log may be implemented as a 'circular' file, in which case the LSN may be the log record id plus a *wrap-count*.

- **Updating a Page**: After modifying the page, an *update* type record (described later in this section) is appended to the log tail. The pageLSN of the page is then set to the LSN of the update log record. (The page must be pinned in the buffer pool while these actions are carried out.)

- **Commit**: When a transaction decides to commit, it **force-writes** a *commit* type log record containing the transaction id. That is, the log record is appended to the log, and the log tail is written to stable storage, up to and including the commit record.[2] The transaction is considered to have committed at the instant that its commit log record is written to stable storage. (Some additional steps must be taken, e.g., removing the transaction's entry in the transaction table; these follow the writing of the commit log record.)

- **Abort**: When a transaction is aborted, an *abort* type log record containing the transaction id is appended to the log, and Undo is initiated for this transaction (Section 18.6.3).

- **End**: As noted above, when a transaction is aborted or committed, some additional actions must be taken beyond writing the abort or commit log record. After all these additional steps are completed, an *end* type log record containing the transaction id is appended to the log.

- **Undoing an update:** When a transaction is rolled back (because the transaction is aborted, or during recovery from a crash), its updates are undone. When the action described by an update log record is undone, a *compensation log record*, or CLR, is written.

Every log record has certain fields: **prevLSN**, **transID**, and **type**. The set of all log records for a given transaction is maintained as a linked list going back in time, using the **prevLSN** field; this list must be updated whenever a log record is added. The transID field is the id of the transaction generating the log record, and the type field obviously indicates the type of the log record.

Additional fields depend on the type of the log record. We already mentioned the additional contents of the various log record types, with the exception of the update and compensation log record types, which we describe next.

Update Log Records

The fields in an **update** log record are illustrated in Figure 18.2. The **pageID** field is the page id of the modified page; the length in bytes and the offset of the

[2]Note that this step requires the buffer manager to be able to selectively *force* pages to stable storage.

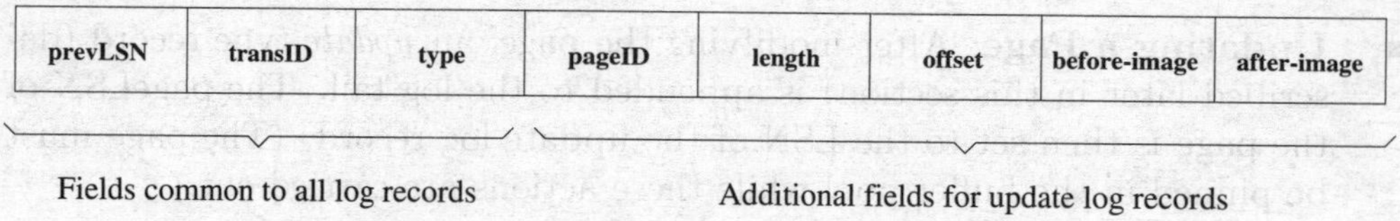

Figure 18.2 Contents of an Update Log Record

change are also included. The **before-image** is the value of the changed bytes before the change; the **after-image** is the value after the change. An update log record that contains both before- and after-images can be used to redo the change and undo it. In certain contexts, which we do not discuss further, we can recognize that the change will never be undone (or, perhaps, redone). A **redo-only update** log record contains just the after-image; similarly an **undo-only update** record contains just the before-image.

Compensation Log Records

A **compensation log record (CLR)** is written just before the change recorded in an update log record U is undone. (Such an undo can happen during normal system execution when a transaction is aborted or during recovery from a crash.) A compensation log record C describes the action taken to undo the actions recorded in the corresponding update log record and is appended to the log tail just like any other log record. The compensation log record C also contains a field called **undoNextLSN**, which is the LSN of the next log record that is to be undone for the transaction that wrote update record U; this field in C is set to the value of prevLSN in U.

As an example, consider the fourth update log record shown in Figure 18.3. If this update is undone, a CLR would be written, and the information in it would include the transID, pageID, length, offset, and before-image fields from the update record. Notice that the CLR records the (undo) action of changing the affected bytes back to the before-image value; thus, this value and the location of the affected bytes constitute the redo information for the action described by the CLR. The undoNextLSN field is set to the LSN of the first log record in Figure 18.3.

Unlike an update log record, a CLR describes an action that will never be *undone*, that is, we never undo an undo action. The reason is simple: An update log record describes a change made by a transaction during normal execution and the transaction may subsequently be aborted, whereas a CLR describes an action taken to rollback a transaction for which the decision to abort has already been made. Therefore, the transaction *must* be rolled back, and the undo action described by the CLR is definitely required. This observation is very useful because it bounds the amount of space needed for the log during restart from a crash: The number of CLRs that can be written during Undo is no more than the number of update log records for active transactions at the time of the crash.

A CLR may be written to stable storage (following WAL, of course) but the undo action it describes may not yet been written to disk when the system crashes again. In this case, the undo action described in the CLR is reapplied during the Redo phase, just like the action described in update log records.

For these reasons, a CLR contains the information needed to reapply, or redo, the change described but not to reverse it.

18.3 OTHER RECOVERY-RELATED STRUCTURES

In addition to the log, the following two tables contain important recovery-related information:

- **Transaction Table:** This table contains one entry for each active transaction. The entry contains (among other things) the transaction id, the status, and a field called **lastLSN**, which is the LSN of the most recent log record for this transaction. The **status** of a transaction can be that it is in progress, committed, or aborted. (In the latter two cases, the transaction will be removed from the table once certain 'clean up' steps are completed.)
- **Dirty page table:** This table contains one entry for each dirty page in the buffer pool, that is, each page with changes not yet reflected on disk. The entry contains a field **recLSN**, which is the LSN of the first log record that caused the page to become dirty. Note that this LSN identifies the earliest log record that might have to be redone for this page during restart from a crash.

During normal operation, these are maintained by the transaction manager and the buffer manager, respectively, and during restart after a crash, these tables are reconstructed in the Analysis phase of restart.

Consider the following simple example. Transaction $T1000$ changes the value of bytes 21 to 23 on page $P500$ from 'ABC' to 'DEF', transaction $T2000$ changes 'HIJ' to 'KLM' on page $P600$, transaction $T2000$ changes bytes 20 through 22 from 'GDE' to 'QRS' on page $P500$, then transaction $T1000$ changes 'TUV' to 'WXY' on page $P505$. The dirty page table, the transaction table,[3] and

[3]The status field is not shown in the figure for space reasons; all transactions are in progress.

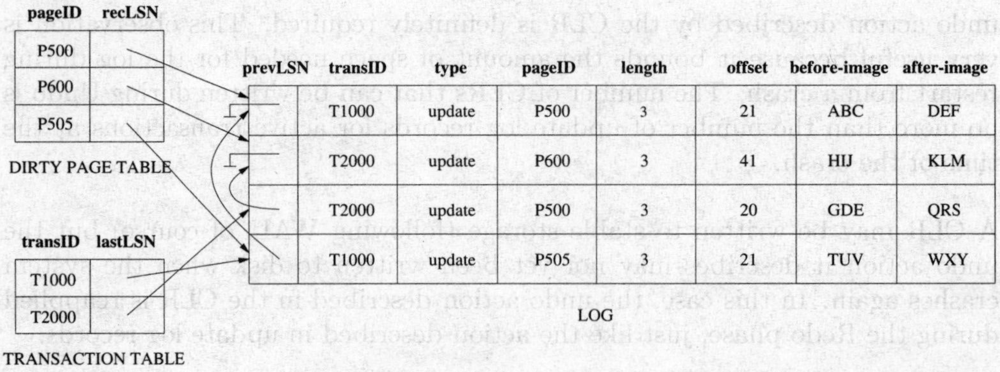
pageID recLSN
P500
P600
P505
DIRTY PAGE TABLE
transID lastLSN
T1000
T2000
TRANSACTION TABLE
prevLSN transID type pageID length offset before-image after-image
T1000 update P500 3 21 ABC DEF
T2000 update P600 3 41 HIJ KLM
T2000 update P500 3 20 GDE QRS
T1000 update P505 3 21 TUV WXY
LOG

Figure 18.3 Instance of Log and Transaction Table

the log at this instant are shown in Figure 18.3. Observe that the log is shown growing from top to bottom; older records are at the top. Although the records for each transaction are linked using the prevLSN field, the log as a whole also has a sequential order that is important—for example, $T2000$'s change to page $P500$ follows $T1000$'s change to page $P500$, and in the event of a crash, these changes must be redone in the same order.

18.4 THE WRITE-AHEAD LOG PROTOCOL

Before writing a page to disk, every update log record that describes a change to this page must be forced to stable storage. This is accomplished by forcing all log records up to and including the one with LSN equal to the pageLSN to stable storage before writing the page to disk.

The importance of the WAL protocol cannot be overemphasized—WAL is the fundamental rule that ensures that a record of every change to the database is available while attempting to recover from a crash. If a transaction made a change and committed, the no-force approach means that some of these changes may not have been written to disk at the time of a subsequent crash. Without a record of these changes, there would be no way to ensure that the changes of a committed transaction survive crashes. Note that the definition of a *committed transaction* is effectively 'a transaction all of whose log records, including a commit record, have been written to stable storage'.

When a transaction is committed, the log tail is forced to stable storage, even if a no-force approach is being used. It is worth contrasting this operation with the actions taken under a force approach: If a force approach is used, all the pages modified by the transaction, rather than a portion of the log that includes all its records, must be forced to disk when the transaction commits. The set of all changed pages is typically much larger than the log tail because the size of an update log record is close to (twice) the size of the changed bytes, which is likely to be much smaller than the page size. Further, the log is maintained as a sequential file, and all writes to the log are sequential writes. Consequently, the cost of forcing the log tail is much smaller than the cost of writing all changed pages to disk.

18.5 CHECKPOINTING

A **checkpoint** is like a snapshot of the DBMS state, and by taking checkpoints periodically, as we will see, the DBMS can reduce the amount of work to be done during restart in the event of a subsequent crash.

Checkpointing in ARIES has three steps. First, a **begin checkpoint** record is written to indicate when the checkpoint starts. Second, an **end checkpoint** record is constructed, including in it the current contents of the transaction table and the dirty page table, and appended to the log. The third step is carried out after the **end checkpoint** record is written to stable storage: A special **master** record containing the LSN of the *begin checkpoint* log record is written to a known place on stable storage. While the end checkpoint record is being constructed, the DBMS continues executing transactions and writing other log records; the only guarantee we have is that the transaction table and dirty page table are accurate *as of the time of the begin checkpoint record.*

This kind of checkpoint, called a **fuzzy checkpoint**, is inexpensive because it does not require quiescing the system or writing out pages in the buffer pool (unlike some other forms of checkpointing). On the other hand, the effectiveness of this checkpointing technique is limited by the earliest recLSN of pages in the dirty pages table, because during restart we must redo changes starting from the log record whose LSN is equal to this recLSN. Having a background process that periodically writes dirty pages to disk helps to limit this problem.

When the system comes back up after a crash, the restart process begins by locating the most recent checkpoint record. For uniformity, the system always begins normal execution by taking a checkpoint, in which the transaction table and dirty page table are both empty.

18.6 RECOVERING FROM A SYSTEM CRASH

When the system is restarted after a crash, the recovery manager proceeds in three phases, as shown in Figure 18.4.

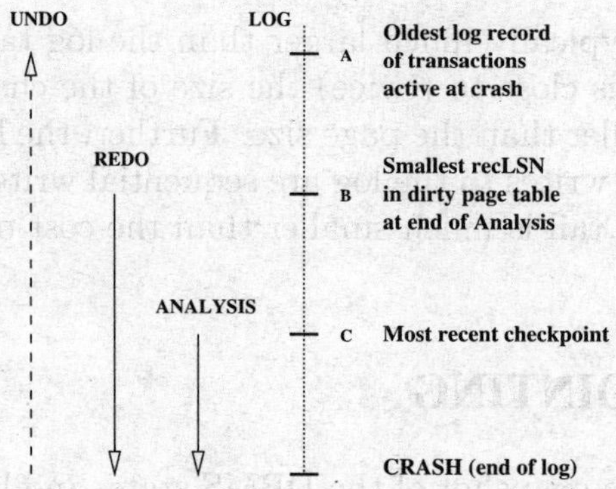

Figure 18.4 Three Phases of Restart in ARIES

The Analysis phase begins by examining the most recent begin checkpoint record, whose LSN is denoted C in Figure 18.4, and proceeds forward in the log until the last log record. The Redo phase follows Analysis and redoes all changes to any page that might have been dirty at the time of the crash; this set of pages and the starting point for Redo (the smallest recLSN of any dirty page) are determined during Analysis. The Undo phase follows Redo and undoes the changes of all transactions active at the time of the crash; again, this set of transactions is identified during the Analysis phase. Note that Redo reapplies changes in the order in which they were originally carried out; Undo reverses changes in the opposite order, reversing the most recent change first.

Observe that the relative order of the three points A, B, and C in the log may differ from that shown in Figure 18.4. The three phases of restart are described in more detail in the following sections.

18.6.1 Analysis Phase

The **Analysis** phase performs three tasks:

1. It determines the point in the log at which to start the Redo pass.
2. It determines (a conservative superset of the) pages in the buffer pool that were dirty at the time of the crash.
3. It identifies transactions that were active at the time of the crash and must be undone.

Analysis begins by examining the most recent begin checkpoint log record and initializing the dirty page table and transaction table to the copies of those structures in the next end checkpoint record. Thus, these tables are initialized to the set of dirty pages and active transactions at the time of the checkpoint.

(If additional log records are between the begin_checkpoint and end_checkpoint records, the tables must be adjusted to reflect the information in these records, but we omit the details of this step. See Exercise 18.9.) Analysis then scans the log in the forward direction until it reaches the end of the log:

- If an end log record for a transaction T is encountered, T is removed from the transaction table because it is no longer active.
- If a log record other than an end record for a transaction T is encountered, an entry for T is added to the transaction table if it is not already there. Further, the entry for T is modified:
  1. The lastLSN field is set to the LSN of this log record.
  2. If the log record is a commit record, the status is set to `C`, otherwise it is set to `U` (indicating that it is to be undone).
- If a redoable log record affecting page P is encountered, and P is not in the dirty page table, an entry is inserted into this table with page id P and recLSN equal to the LSN of this redoable log record. This LSN identifies the oldest change affecting page P that may not have been written to disk.

At the end of the Analysis phase, the transaction table contains an accurate list of all transactions that were active at the time of the crash—this is the set of transactions with status `U`. The dirty page table includes all pages that were dirty at the time of the crash but may also contain some pages that were written to disk. If an *end_write* log record were written at the completion of each write operation, the dirty page table constructed during Analysis could be made more accurate, but in ARIES, the additional cost of writing end_write log records is not considered to be worth the gain.

As an example, consider the execution illustrated in Figure 18.3. Let us extend this execution by assuming that $T2000$ commits, then $T1000$ modifies another page, say, $P700$, and appends an update record to the log tail, and then the system crashes (before this update log record is written to stable storage).

The dirty page table and the transaction table, held in memory, are lost in the crash. The most recent checkpoint was taken at the beginning of the execution, with an empty transaction table and dirty page table; it is not shown in Figure 18.3. After examining this log record, which we assume is just before the first log record shown in the figure, Analysis initializes the two tables to be empty. Scanning forward in the log, $T1000$ is added to the transaction table; in addition, $P500$ is added to the dirty page table with recLSN equal to the LSN of the first shown log record. Similarly, $T2000$ is added to the transaction table and $P600$ is added to the dirty page table. There is no change based on the third log record, and the fourth record results in the addition of $P505$ to the dirty page table. The commit record for $T2000$ (not in the figure) is now encountered, and $T2000$ is removed from the transaction table.

The Analysis phase is now complete, and it is recognized that the only active transaction at the time of the crash is $T1000$, with lastLSN equal to the LSN of the fourth record in Figure 18.3. The dirty page table reconstructed in the Analysis phase is identical to that shown in the figure. The update log record for the change to $P700$ is lost in the crash and not seen during the Analysis pass. Thanks to the WAL protocol, however, all is well—the corresponding change to page $P700$ cannot have been written to disk either!

Some of the updates may have been written to disk; for concreteness, let us assume that the change to $P600$ (and only this update) was written to disk before the crash. Therefore $P600$ is not dirty, yet it is included in the dirty page table. The pageLSN on page $P600$, however, reflects the write because it is now equal to the LSN of the second update log record shown in Figure 18.3.

18.6.2 Redo Phase

During the **Redo** phase, ARIES reapplies the updates of *all* transactions, committed or otherwise. Further, if a transaction was aborted before the crash and its updates were undone, as indicated by CLRs, the actions described in the CLRs are also reapplied. This **repeating history** paradigm distinguishes ARIES from other proposed WAL-based recovery algorithms and causes the database to be brought to the same state it was in at the time of the crash.

The Redo phase begins with the log record that has the smallest recLSN of all pages in the dirty page table constructed by the Analysis pass because this log record identifies the oldest update that may not have been written to disk prior to the crash. Starting from this log record, Redo scans forward until the end of the log. For each redoable log record (update or CLR) encountered, Redo checks whether the logged action must be redone. The action must be redone unless one of the following conditions holds:

- The affected page is not in the dirty page table.
- The affected page is in the dirty page table, but the recLSN for the entry is *greater than* the LSN of the log record being checked.
- The pageLSN (stored on the page, which must be retrieved to check this condition) is *greater than or equal* to the LSN of the log record being checked.

The first condition obviously means that all changes to this page have been written to disk. Because the recLSN is the first update to this page that may not have been written to disk, the second condition means that the update being checked was indeed propagated to disk. The third condition, which is checked last because it requires us to retrieve the page, also ensures that the update being checked was written to disk, because either this update or a later update to the page was written. (Recall our assumption that a write to a page is atomic; this assumption is important here!)

If the logged action must be redone:

1. The logged action is reapplied.

2. The pageLSN on the page is set to the LSN of the redone log record. No additional log record is written at this time.

Let us continue with the example discussed in Section 18.6.1. From the dirty page table, the smallest recLSN is seen to be the LSN of the first log record shown in Figure 18.3. Clearly, the changes recorded by earlier log records (there happen to be none in this example) have been written to disk. Now, Redo fetches the affected page, $P500$, and compares the LSN of this log record with the pageLSN on the page and, because we assumed that this page was not written to disk before the crash, finds that the pageLSN is less. The update is therefore reapplied; bytes 21 through 23 are changed to 'DEF', and the pageLSN is set to the LSN of this update log record.

Redo then examines the second log record. Again, the affected page, $P600$, is fetched and the pageLSN is compared to the LSN of the update log record. In this case, because we assumed that $P600$ was written to disk before the crash, they are equal, and the update does not have to be redone.

The remaining log records are processed similarly, bringing the system back to the exact state it was in at the time of the crash. Note that the first two conditions indicating that a redo is unnecessary never hold in this example. Intuitively, they come into play when the dirty page table contains a very old recLSN, going back to before the most recent checkpoint. In this case, as Redo scans forward from the log record with this LSN, it encounters log records for pages that were written to disk prior to the checkpoint and therefore not in the dirty page table in the checkpoint. Some of these pages may be dirtied again after the checkpoint; nonetheless, the updates to these pages prior to the checkpoint need not be redone. Although the third condition alone is sufficient to recognize that these updates need not be redone, it requires us to fetch the affected page. The first two conditions allow us to recognize this situation without fetching the page. (The reader is encouraged to construct examples that illustrate the use of each of these conditions; see Exercise 18.8.)

At the end of the Redo phase, end type records are written for all transactions with status `C`, which are removed from the transaction table.

18.6.3 Undo Phase

The Undo phase, unlike the other two phases, scans backward from the end of the log. The goal of this phase is to undo the actions of all transactions active at the time of the crash, that is, to effectively abort them. This set of transactions is identified in the transaction table constructed by the Analysis phase.

The Undo Algorithm

Undo begins with the transaction table constructed by the Analysis phase, which identifies all transactions active at the time of the crash, and includes the LSN of the most recent log record (the lastLSN field) for each such transaction. Such transactions are called **loser transactions**. All actions of losers must be undone, and further, these actions must be undone in the reverse of the order in which they appear in the log.

Consider the set of lastLSN values for all loser transactions. Let us call this set **ToUndo**. Undo repeatedly chooses the largest (i.e., most recent) LSN value in this set and processes it, until ToUndo is empty. To process a log record:

1. If it is a CLR and the undoNextLSN value is not *null*, the undoNextLSN value is added to the set ToUndo; if the undoNextLSN is *null*, an end record is written for the transaction because it is completely undone, and the CLR is discarded.

2. If it is an update record, a CLR is written and the corresponding action is undone, as described in Section 18.2, and the prevLSN value in the update log record is added to the set ToUndo.

When the set ToUndo is empty, the Undo phase is complete. Restart is now complete, and the system can proceed with normal operations.

Let us continue with the scenario discussed in Sections 18.6.1 and 18.6.2. The only active transaction at the time of the crash was determined to be $T1000$. From the transaction table, we get the LSN of its most recent log record, which is the fourth update log record in Figure 18.3. The update is undone, and a CLR is written with undoNextLSN equal to the LSN of the first log record in the figure. The next record to be undone for transaction $T1000$ is the first log record in the figure. After this is undone, a CLR and an end log record for $T1000$ are written, and the Undo phase is complete.

In this example, undoing the action recorded in the first log record causes the action of the third log record, which is due to a committed transaction, to be overwritten and thereby lost! This situation arises because $T2000$ overwrote a data item written by $T1000$ while $T1000$ was still active; if Strict 2PL were followed, $T2000$ would not have been allowed to overwrite this data item.

Aborting a Transaction

Aborting a transaction is just a special case of the Undo phase of Restart in which a single transaction, rather than a set of transactions, is undone. The example in Figure 18.5, discussed next, illustrates this point.

Crashes during Restart

It is important to understand how the Undo algorithm presented in Section 18.6.3 handles repeated system crashes. Because the details of precisely how the action described in an update log record is undone are straightforward, we discuss Undo in the presence of system crashes using an execution history, shown in Figure 18.5, that abstracts away unnecessary detail. This example illustrates how aborting a transaction is a special case of Undo and how the use of CLRs ensures that the Undo action for an update log record is not applied twice.

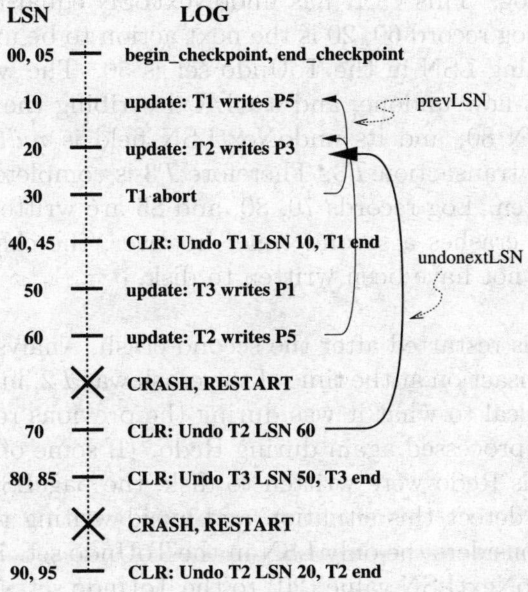

Figure 18.5 Example of Undo with Repeated Crashes

The log shows the order in which the DBMS executed various actions; note that the LSNs are in ascending order, and that each log record for a transaction has a prevLSN field that points to the previous log record for that transaction. We have not shown *null* prevLSNs, that is, some special value used in the prevLSN field of the first log record for a transaction to indicate that there is no previous log record. We also compacted the figure by occasionally displaying two log records (separated by a comma) on a single line.

Log record (with LSN) 30 indicates that $T1$ aborts. All actions of this transaction should be undone in reverse order, and the only action of $T1$, described by the update log record 10, is indeed undone as indicated by CLR 40.

After the first crash, Analysis identifies $P1$ (with recLSN 50), $P3$ (with recLSN 20), and $P5$ (with recLSN 10) as dirty pages. Log record 45 shows that $T1$ is a completed transaction; hence, the transaction table identifies $T2$ (with lastLSN 60) and $T3$ (with lastLSN 50) as active at the time of the crash. The Redo phase begins with log record 10, which is the minimum recLSN in the dirty page table, and reapplies all actions (for the update and CLR records), as per the Redo algorithm presented in Section 18.6.2.

The ToUndo set consists of LSNs 60, for $T2$, and 50, for $T3$. The Undo phase now begins by processing the log record with LSN 60 because 60 is the largest LSN in the ToUndo set. The update is undone, and a CLR (with LSN 70) is written to the log. This CLR has undoNextLSN equal to 20, which is the prevLSN value in log record 60; 20 is the next action to be undone for $T2$. Now the largest remaining LSN in the ToUndo set is 50. The write corresponding to log record 50 is now undone, and a CLR describing the change is written. This CLR has LSN 80, and its undoNextLSN field is *null* because 50 is the only log record for transaction $T3$. Therefore $T3$ is completely undone, and an end record is written. Log records 70, 80, and 85 are written to stable storage before the system crashes a second time; however, the changes described by these records may not have been written to disk.

When the system is restarted after the second crash, Analysis determines that the only active transaction at the time of the crash was $T2$; in addition, the dirty page table is identical to what it was during the previous restart. Log records 10 through 85 are processed again during Redo. (If some of the changes made during the previous Redo were written to disk, the pageLSNs on the affected pages are used to detect this situation and avoid writing these pages again.) The Undo phase considers the only LSN in the ToUndo set, 70, and processes it by adding the undoNextLSN value (20) to the ToUndo set. Next, log record 20 is processed by undoing $T2$'s write of page $P3$, and a CLR is written (LSN 90). Because 20 is the first of $T2$'s log records—and therefore, the last of its records to be undone—the undoNextLSN field in this CLR is *null*, an end record is written for $T2$, and the ToUndo set is now empty.

Recovery is now complete, and normal execution can resume with the writing of a checkpoint record.

This example illustrated repeated crashes during the Undo phase. For completeness, let us consider what happens if the system crashes while Restart is in the Analysis or Redo phase. If a crash occurs during the Analysis phase, all the work done in this phase is lost, and on restart the Analysis phase starts afresh with the same information as before. If a crash occurs during the Redo phase, the only effect that survives the crash is that some of the changes made during Redo may have been written to disk prior to the crash. Restart starts again with the Analysis phase and then the Redo phase, and some update log records that were redone the first time around will not be redone a second time because the pageLSN is now equal to the update record's LSN (although the pages have to be fetched again to detect this).

We can take checkpoints during Restart to minimize repeated work in the event of a crash, but we do not discuss this point.

18.7 MEDIA RECOVERY

Media recovery is based on periodically making a copy of the database. Because copying a large database object such as a file can take a long time, and the DBMS must be allowed to continue with its operations in the meantime, creating a copy is handled in a manner similar to taking a fuzzy checkpoint.

When a database object such as a file or a page is corrupted, the copy of that object is brought up-to-date by using the log to identify and reapply the changes of committed transactions and undo the changes of uncommitted transactions (as of the time of the media recovery operation).

The begin_checkpoint LSN of the most recent complete checkpoint is recorded along with the copy of the database object to minimize the work in reapplying changes of committed transactions. Let us compare the smallest recLSN of a dirty page in the corresponding end_checkpoint record with the LSN of the begin_checkpoint record and call the smaller of these two LSNs I. We observe that the actions recorded in all log records with LSNs less than I must be reflected in the copy. Thus, only log records with LSNs greater than I need be reapplied to the copy.

Finally, the updates of transactions that are incomplete at the time of media recovery or that were aborted after the fuzzy copy was completed need to be undone to ensure that the page reflects only the actions of committed transactions. The set of such transactions can be identified as in the Analysis pass, and we omit the details.

18.8 OTHER APPROACHES AND INTERACTION WITH CONCURRENCY CONTROL

Like ARIES, the most popular alternative recovery algorithms also maintain a log of database actions according to the WAL protocol. A major distinction between ARIES and these variants is that the Redo phase in ARIES *repeats history*, that is, redoes the actions of *all* transactions, not just the non-losers. Other algorithms redo only the non-losers, and the Redo phase follows the Undo phase, in which the actions of losers are rolled back.

Thanks to the repeating history paradigm and the use of CLRs, ARIES supports fine-granularity locks (record-level locks) and logging of logical operations rather than just byte-level modifications. For example, consider a transaction T that inserts a data entry $15*$ into a B+ tree index. Between the time this insert is done and the time that T is eventually aborted, other transactions may also insert and delete entries from the tree. If record-level locks are set rather than page-level locks, the entry $15*$ may be on a different physical page when T aborts from the one that T inserted it into. In this case, the undo operation for the insert of $15*$ must be recorded in logical terms because the physical (byte-level) actions involved in undoing this operation are not the inverse of the physical actions involved in inserting the entry.

Logging logical operations yields considerably higher concurrency, although the use of fine-granularity locks can lead to increased locking activity (because more locks must be set). Hence, there is a trade-off between different WAL-based recovery schemes. We chose to cover ARIES because it has several attractive properties, in particular, its simplicity and its ability to support fine-granularity locks and logging of logical operations.

One of the earliest recovery algorithms, used in the System R prototype at IBM, takes a very different approach. There is no logging and, of course, no WAL protocol. Instead, the database is treated as a collection of pages and accessed through a **page table**, which maps page ids to disk addresses. When a transaction makes changes to a data page, it actually makes a copy of the page, called the **shadow** of the page, and changes the shadow page. The transaction copies the appropriate part of the page table and changes the entry for the changed page to point to the shadow, so that it can see the changes; however, other transactions continue to see the original page table, and therefore the original page, until this transaction commits. Aborting a transaction is simple: Just discard its shadow versions of the page table and the data pages. Committing a transaction involves making its version of the page table public and discarding the original data pages that are superseded by shadow pages.

This scheme suffers from a number of problems. First, data becomes highly fragmented due to the replacement of pages by shadow versions, which may be located far from the original page. This phenomenon reduces data clustering and makes good garbage collection imperative. Second, the scheme does not yield a sufficiently high degree of concurrency. Third, there is a substantial storage overhead due to the use of shadow pages. Fourth, the process aborting a transaction can itself run into deadlocks, and this situation must be specially handled because the semantics of aborting an abort transaction gets murky.

For these reasons, even in System R, shadow paging was eventually superseded by WAL-based recovery techniques.

18.9 REVIEW QUESTIONS

Answers to the review questions can be found in the listed sections.

- What are the advantages of the ARIES recovery algorithm? **(Section 18.1)**
- Describe the three steps in crash recovery in ARIES? What is the goal of the Analysis phase? The redo phase? The undo phase? **(Section 18.1)**
- What is the LSN of a log record? **(Section 18.2)**
- What are the different types of log records and when are they written? **(Section 18.2)**
- What information is maintained in the transaction table and the dirty page table? **(Section 18.3)**
- What is Write-Ahead Logging? What is forced to disk at the time a transaction commits? **(Section 18.4)**
- What is a fuzzy checkpoint? Why is it useful? What is a master log record? **(Section 18.5)**
- In which direction does the Analysis phase of recovery scan the log? At which point in the log does it begin and end the scan? **(Section 18.6.1)**
- Describe what information is gathered in the Analysis phase and how. **(Section 18.6.1)**

- In which direction does the Redo phase of recovery process the log? At which point in the log does it begin and end? **(Section 18.6.2)**
- What is a redoable log record? Under what conditions is the logged action redone? What steps are carried out when a logged action is redone? **(Section 18.6.2)**
- In which direction does the Undo phase of recovery process the log? At which point in the log does it begin and end? **(Section 18.6.3)**
- What are loser transactions? How are they processed in the Undo phase and in what order? **(Section 18.6.3)**
- Explain what happens if there are crashes during the Undo phase of recovery. What is the role of CLRs? What if there are crashes during the Analysis and Redo phases? **(Section 18.6.3)**
- How does a DBMS recover from media failure without reading the complete log? **(Section 18.7)**
- Record-level logging increases concurrency. What are the potential problems, and how does ARIES address them? **(Section 18.8)**
- What is shadow paging? **(Section 18.8)**

EXERCISES

Exercise 18.1 Briefly answer the following questions:

1. How does the recovery manager ensure atomicity of transactions? How does it ensure durability?
2. What is the difference between stable storage and disk?
3. What is the difference between a system crash and a media failure?
4. Explain the WAL protocol.
5. Describe the steal and no-force policies.

Exercise 18.2 Briefly answer the following questions:

1. What are the properties required of LSNs?
2. What are the fields in an update log record? Explain the use of each field.
3. What are redoable log records?
4. What are the differences between update log records and CLRs?

Exercise 18.3 Briefly answer the following questions:

1. What are the roles of the Analysis, Redo, and Undo phases in ARIES?
2. Consider the execution shown in Figure 18.6.

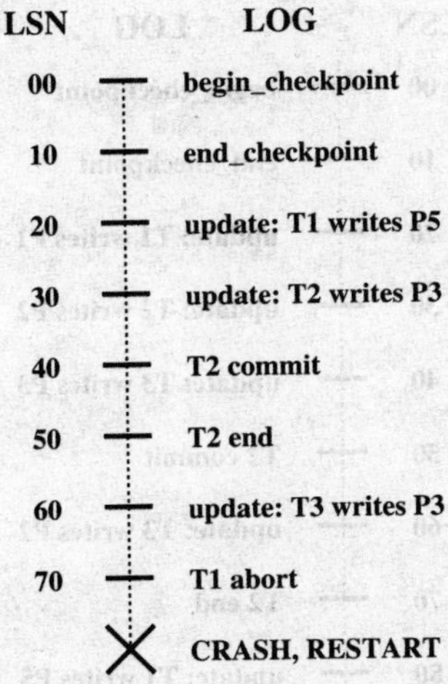

Figure 18.6 Execution with a Crash

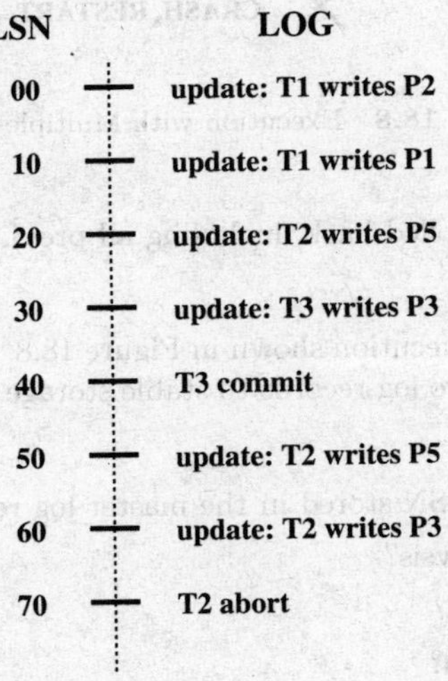

Figure 18.7 Aborting a Transaction

(a) What is done during Analysis? (Be precise about the points at which Analysis begins and ends and describe the contents of any tables constructed in this phase.)

(b) What is done during Redo? (Be precise about the points at which Redo begins and ends.)

(c) What is done during Undo? (Be precise about the points at which Undo begins and ends.)

Exercise 18.4 Consider the execution shown in Figure 18.7.

1. Extend the figure to show prevLSN and undonextLSN values.
2. Describe the actions taken to rollback transaction $T2$.

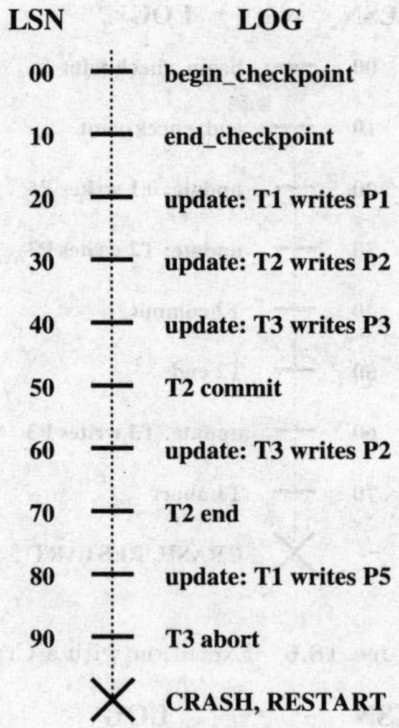

Figure 18.8 Execution with Multiple Crashes

3. Show the log after $T2$ is rolled back, including all prevLSN and undonextLSN values in log records.

Exercise 18.5 Consider the execution shown in Figure 18.8. In addition, the system crashes during recovery after writing two log records to stable storage and again after writing another two log records.

1. What is the value of the LSN stored in the master log record?
2. What is done during Analysis?
3. What is done during Redo?
4. What is done during Undo?
5. Show the log when recovery is complete, including all non-null prevLSN and undonextLSN values in log records.

Exercise 18.6 Briefly answer the following questions:

1. How is checkpointing done in ARIES?
2. Checkpointing can also be done as follows: Quiesce the system so that only checkpointing activity can be in progress, write out copies of all dirty pages, and include the dirty page table and transaction table in the checkpoint record. What are the pros and cons of this approach versus the checkpointing approach of ARIES?
3. What happens if a second begin checkpoint record is encountered during the Analysis phase?
4. Can a second end checkpoint record be encountered during the Analysis phase?
5. Why is the use of CLRs important for the use of undo actions that are not the physical inverse of the original update?

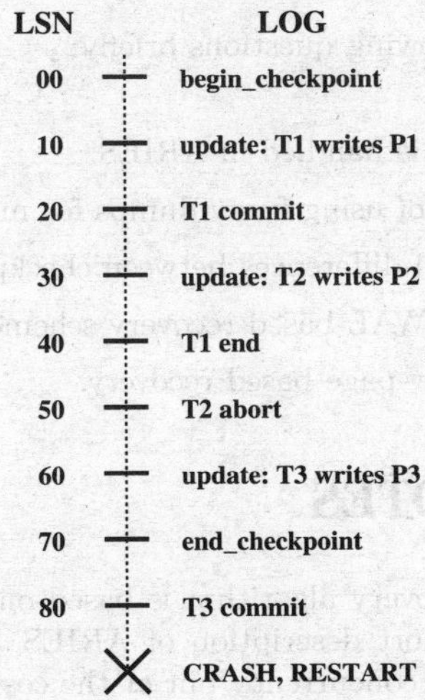

Figure 18.9 Log Records between Checkpoint Records

6. Give an example that illustrates how the paradigm of repeating history and the use of CLRs allow ARIES to support locks of finer granularity than a page.

Exercise 18.7 Briefly answer the following questions:

1. If the system fails repeatedly during recovery, what is the maximum number of log records that can be written (as a function of the number of update and other log records written before the crash) before restart completes successfully?
2. What is the oldest log record we need to retain?
3. If a bounded amount of stable storage is used for the log, how can we always ensure enough stable storage to hold all log records written during restart?

Exercise 18.8 Consider the three conditions under which a redo is unnecessary (Section 20.2.2).

1. Why is it cheaper to test the first two conditions?
2. Describe an execution that illustrates the use of the first condition.
3. Describe an execution that illustrates the use of the second condition.

Exercise 18.9 The description in Section 18.6.1 of the Analysis phase made the simplifying assumption that no log records appeared between the begin_checkpoint and end_checkpoint records for the most recent complete checkpoint. The following questions explore how such records should be handled.

1. Explain why log records could be written between the begin_checkpoint and end_checkpoint records.
2. Describe how the Analysis phase could be modified to handle such records.
3. Consider the execution shown in Figure 18.9. Show the contents of the end_checkpoint record.
4. Illustrate your modified Analysis phase on the execution shown in Figure 18.9.

Exercise 18.10 Answer the following questions briefly:

1. Explain how media recovery is handled in ARIES.
2. What are the pros and cons of using fuzzy dumps for media recovery?
3. What are the similarities and differences between checkpoints and fuzzy dumps?
4. Contrast ARIES with other WAL-based recovery schemes.
5. Contrast ARIES with shadow-page-based recovery.

BIBLIOGRAPHIC NOTES

Our discussion of the ARIES recovery algorithm is based on [544]. [282] is a survey article that contains a very readable, short description of ARIES. [541, 545] also discuss ARIES. Fine-granularity locking increases concurrency but at the cost of more locking activity; [542] suggests a technique based on LSNs for alleviating this problem. [458] presents a formal verification of ARIES.

[355] is an excellent survey that provides a broader treatment of recovery algorithms than our coverage, in which we chose to concentrate on one particular algorithm. [17] considers performance of concurrency control and recovery algorithms, taking into account their interactions. The impact of recovery on concurrency control is also discussed in [769]. [625] contains a performance analysis of various recovery techniques. [236] compares recovery techniques for main memory database systems, which are optimized for the case that most of the active data set fits in main memory.

[478] presents a description of a recovery algorithm based on write-ahead logging in which 'loser' transactions are first undone and then (only) transactions that committed before the crash are redone. Shadow paging is described in [493, 337]. A scheme that uses a combination of shadow paging and in-place updating is described in [624].

PART VI

DATABASE DESIGN AND TUNING

19

SCHEMA REFINEMENT AND NORMAL FORMS

- What problems are caused by redundantly storing information?
- What are functional dependencies?
- What are normal forms and what is their purpose?
- What are the benefits of BCNF and 3NF?
- What are the considerations in decomposing relations into appropriate normal forms?
- Where does normalization fit in the process of database design?
- Are more general dependencies useful in database design?
- **Key concepts:** redundancy, insert, delete, and update anomalies; functional dependency, Armstrong's Axioms; dependency closure, attribute closure; normal forms, BCNF, 3NF; decompositions, lossless-join, dependency-preservation; multivalued dependencies, join dependencies, inclusion dependencies, 4NF, 5NF

It is a melancholy truth that even great men have their poor relations.

—Charles Dickens

Conceptual database design gives us a set of relation schemas and integrity constraints (ICs) that can be regarded as a good starting point for the final database design. This initial design must be refined by taking the ICs into account more fully than is possible with just the ER model constructs and also by considering performance criteria and typical workloads. In this chapter, we discuss how ICs can be used to refine the conceptual schema produced by translating an ER model design into a collection of relations. Workload and performance considerations are discussed in Chapter 20.

We concentrate on an important class of constraints called *functional dependencies*. Other kinds of ICs, for example, *multivalued dependencies* and *join dependencies*, also provide useful information. They can sometimes reveal redundancies that cannot be detected using functional dependencies alone. We discuss these other constraints briefly.

This chapter is organized as follows. Section 19.1 is an overview of the schema refinement approach discussed in this chapter. We introduce functional dependencies in Section 19.2. In Section 19.3, we show how to reason with functional dependency information to infer additional dependencies from a given set of dependencies. We introduce normal forms for relations in Section 19.4; the normal form satisfied by a relation is a measure of the redundancy in the relation. A relation with redundancy can be refined by *decomposing it*, or replacing it with smaller relations that contain the same information but without redundancy. We discuss decompositions and desirable properties of decompositions in Section 19.5, and we show how relations can be decomposed into smaller relations in desirable normal forms in Section 19.6.

In Section 19.7, we present several examples that illustrate how relational schemas obtained by translating an ER model design can nonetheless suffer from redundancy, and we discuss how to refine such schemas to eliminate the problems. In Section 19.8, we describe other kinds of dependencies for database design. We conclude with a discussion of normalization for our case study, the Internet shop, in Section 19.9.

19.1 INTRODUCTION TO SCHEMA REFINEMENT

We now present an overview of the problems that schema refinement is intended to address and a refinement approach based on decompositions. Redundant storage of information is the root cause of these problems. Although decomposition can eliminate redundancy, it can lead to problems of its own and should be used with caution.

19.1.1 Problems Caused by Redundancy

Storing the same information **redundantly**, that is, in more than one place within a database, can lead to several problems:

- **Redundant Storage:** Some information is stored repeatedly.

- **Update Anomalies:** If one copy of such repeated data is updated, an inconsistency is created unless all copies are similarly updated.
- **Insertion Anomalies:** It may not be possible to store certain information unless some other, unrelated, information is stored as well.
- **Deletion Anomalies:** It may not be possible to delete certain information without losing some other, unrelated, information as well.

Consider a relation obtained by translating a variant of the Hourly_Emps entity set from Chapter 2:

Hourly_Emps(<u>*ssn*</u>, *name*, *lot*, *rating*, *hourly_wages*, *hours_worked*)

In this chapter, we omit attribute type information for brevity, since our focus is on the grouping of attributes into relations. We often abbreviate an attribute name to a single letter and refer to a relation schema by a string of letters, one per attribute. For example, we refer to the Hourly_Emps schema as *SNLRWH* (*W* denotes the *hourly_wages* attribute).

The key for Hourly_Emps is *ssn*. In addition, suppose that the *hourly_wages* attribute is determined by the *rating* attribute. That is, for a given *rating* value, there is only one permissible *hourly_wages* value. This IC is an example of a *functional dependency*. It leads to possible redundancy in the relation Hourly_Emps, as illustrated in Figure 19.1.

ssn	*name*	*lot*	*rating*	*hourly_wages*	*hours_worked*
123-22-3666	Attishoo	48	8	10	40
231-31-5368	Smiley	22	8	10	30
131-24-3650	Smethurst	35	5	7	30
434-26-3751	Guldu	35	5	7	32
612-67-4134	Madayan	35	8	10	40

Figure 19.1 An Instance of the Hourly_Emps Relation

If the same value appears in the *rating* column of two tuples, the IC tells us that the same value must appear in the *hourly_wages* column as well. This redundancy has the same negative consequences as before:

- *Redundant Storage:* The rating value 8 corresponds to the hourly wage 10, and this association is repeated three times.
- *Update Anomalies:* The *hourly_wages* in the first tuple could be updated without making a similar change in the second tuple.

- *Insertion Anomalies:* We cannot insert a tuple for an employee unless we know the hourly wage for the employee's rating value.
- *Deletion Anomalies:* If we delete all tuples with a given rating value (e.g., we delete the tuples for Smethurst and Guldu) we lose the association between that *rating* value and its *hourly_wage* value.

Ideally, we want schemas that do not permit redundancy, but at the very least we want to be able to identify schemas that do allow redundancy. Even if we choose to accept a schema with some of these drawbacks, perhaps owing to performance considerations, we want to make an informed decision.

Null Values

It is worth considering whether the use of *null* values can address some of these problems. As we will see in the context of our example, they cannot provide a complete solution, but they can provide some help. In this chapter, we do not discuss the use of *null* values beyond this one example.

Consider the example Hourly_Emps relation. Clearly, *null* values cannot help eliminate redundant storage or update anomalies. It appears that they can address insertion and deletion anomalies. For instance, to deal with the insertion anomaly example, we can insert an employee tuple with *null* values in the hourly wage field. However, *null* values cannot address all insertion anomalies. For example, we cannot record the hourly wage for a rating unless there is an employee with that rating, because we cannot store a null value in the *ssn* field, which is a primary key field. Similarly, to deal with the deletion anomaly example, we might consider storing a tuple with *null* values in all fields except *rating* and *hourly_wages* if the last tuple with a given *rating* would otherwise be deleted. However, this solution does not work because it requires the *ssn* value to be *null*, and primary key fields cannot be *null*. Thus, *null* values do not provide a general solution to the problems of redundancy, even though they can help in some cases.

19.1.2 Decompositions

Intuitively, redundancy arises when a relational schema forces an association between attributes that is not natural. Functional dependencies (and, for that matter, other ICs) can be used to identify such situations and suggest refinements to the schema. The essential idea is that many problems arising from redundancy can be addressed by replacing a relation with a collection of 'smaller' relations.

A **decomposition of a relation schema** R consists of replacing the relation schema by two (or more) relation schemas that each contain a subset of the attributes of R and together include all attributes in R. Intuitively, we want to store the information in any given instance of R by storing projections of the instance. This section examines the use of decompositions through several examples.

We can decompose Hourly_Emps into two relations:

Hourly_Emps2(*ssn*, *name*, *lot*, *rating*, *hours_worked*)
Wages(*rating*, *hourly_wages*)

The instances of these relations corresponding to the instance of Hourly_Emps relation in Figure 19.1 is shown in Figure 19.2.

ssn	*name*	*lot*	*rating*	*hours_worked*
123-22-3666	Attishoo	48	8	40
231-31-5368	Smiley	22	8	30
131-24-3650	Smethurst	35	5	30
434-26-3751	Guldu	35	5	32
612-67-4134	Madayan	35	8	40

rating	*hourly_wages*
8	10
5	7

Figure 19.2 Instances of Hourly_Emps2 and Wages

Note that we can easily record the hourly wage for any rating simply by adding a tuple to Wages, even if no employee with that rating appears in the current instance of Hourly_Emps. Changing the wage associated with a rating involves updating a single Wages tuple. This is more efficient than updating several tuples (as in the original design), and it eliminates the potential for inconsistency.

19.1.3 Problems Related to Decomposition

Unless we are careful, decomposing a relation schema can create more problems than it solves. Two important questions must be asked repeatedly:

1. Do we need to decompose a relation?

2. What problems (if any) does a given decomposition cause?

To help with the first question, several *normal forms* have been proposed for relations. If a relation schema is in one of these normal forms, we know that certain kinds of problems cannot arise. Considering the normal form of a given relation schema can help us to decide whether or not to decompose it further. If we decide that a relation schema must be decomposed further, we must choose a particular decomposition (i.e., a particular collection of smaller relations to replace the given relation).

With respect to the second question, two properties of decompositions are of particular interest. The *lossless-join* property enables us to recover any instance of the decomposed relation from corresponding instances of the smaller relations. The *dependency-preservation* property enables us to enforce any constraint on the original relation by simply enforcing some contraints on each of the smaller relations. That is, we need not perform joins of the smaller relations to check whether a constraint on the original relation is violated.

From a performance standpoint, queries over the original relation may require us to join the decomposed relations. If such queries are common, the performance penalty of decomposing the relation may not be acceptable. In this case, we may choose to live with some of the problems of redundancy and not decompose the relation. It is important to be aware of the potential problems caused by such residual redundancy in the design and to take steps to avoid them (e.g., by adding some checks to application code). In some situations, decomposition could actually *improve* performance. This happens, for example, if most queries and updates examine only one of the decomposed relations, which is smaller than the original relation. We do not discuss the impact of decompositions on query performance in this chapter; this issue is covered in Section 20.8.

Our goal in this chapter is to explain some powerful concepts and design guidelines based on the theory of functional dependencies. A good database designer should have a firm grasp of normal forms and what problems they (do or do not) alleviate, the technique of decomposition, and potential problems with decompositions. For example, a designer often asks questions such as these: Is a relation in a given normal form? Is a decomposition dependency-preserving? Our objective is to explain when to raise these questions and the significance of the answers.

19.2 FUNCTIONAL DEPENDENCIES

A **functional dependency** (FD) is a kind of IC that generalizes the concept of a *key*. Let R be a relation schema and let X and Y be nonempty sets of attributes in R. We say that an instance r of R satisfies the FD $X \rightarrow Y$[1] if the following holds for every pair of tuples t_1 and t_2 in r:

If $t1.X = t2.X$, then $t1.Y = t2.Y$.

We use the notation $t1.X$ to refer to the projection of tuple t_1 onto the attributes in X, in a natural extension of our TRC notation (see Chapter 4) $t.a$ for referring to attribute a of tuple t. An FD $X \rightarrow Y$ essentially says that if two tuples agree on the values in attributes X, they must also agree on the values in attributes Y.

Figure 19.3 illustrates the meaning of the FD $AB \rightarrow C$ by showing an instance that satisfies this dependency. The first two tuples show that an FD is not the same as a key constraint: Although the FD is not violated, AB is clearly not a key for the relation. The third and fourth tuples illustrate that if two tuples differ in either the A field or the B field, they can differ in the C field without violating the FD. On the other hand, if we add a tuple $\langle a1, b1, c2, d1\rangle$ to the instance shown in this figure, the resulting instance would violate the FD; to see this violation, compare the first tuple in the figure with the new tuple.

A	*B*	*C*	*D*
a1	b1	c1	d1
a1	b1	c1	d2
a1	b2	c2	d1
a2	b1	c3	d1

Figure 19.3 An Instance that Satisfies $AB \rightarrow C$

Recall that a *legal* instance of a relation must satisfy all specified ICs, including all specified FDs. As noted in Section 3.2, ICs must be identified and specified based on the semantics of the real-world enterprise being modeled. By looking at an instance of a relation, we might be able to tell that a certain FD does *not* hold. However, we can never deduce that an FD *does* hold by looking at one or more instances of the relation, because an FD, like other ICs, is a statement about *all* possible legal instances of the relation.

[1] $X \rightarrow Y$ is read as X *functionally determines* Y, or simply as X *determines* Y.

A primary key constraint is a special case of an FD. The attributes in the key play the role of X, and the set of all attributes in the relation plays the role of Y. Note, however, that the definition of an FD does not require that the set X be minimal; the additional minimality condition must be met for X to be a key. If $X \rightarrow Y$ holds, where Y is the set of all attributes, and there is some (strictly contained) subset V of X such that $V \rightarrow Y$ holds, then X is a *superkey*.

In the rest of this chapter, we see several examples of FDs that are not key constraints.

19.3 REASONING ABOUT FDS

Given a set of FDs over a relation schema R, typically several additional FDs hold over R whenever all of the given FDs hold. As an example, consider:

Workers(*ssn*, *name*, *lot*, *did*, *since*)

We know that $ssn \rightarrow did$ holds, since *ssn* is the key, and FD $did \rightarrow lot$ is given to hold. Therefore, in any legal instance of Workers, if two tuples have the same *ssn* value, they must have the same *did* value (from the first FD), and because they have the same *did* value, they must also have the same *lot* value (from the second FD). Therefore, the FD $ssn \rightarrow lot$ also holds on Workers.

We say that an FD f **is implied by** a given set F of FDs if f holds on every relation instance that satisfies all dependencies in F; that is, f holds whenever all FDs in F hold. Note that it is not sufficient for f to hold on some instance that satisfies all dependencies in F; rather, f must hold on *every* instance that satisfies all dependencies in F.

19.3.1 Closure of a Set of FDs

The set of all FDs implied by a given set F of FDs is called the **closure of F**, denoted as F^+. An important question is how we can **infer**, or compute, the closure of a given set F of FDs. The answer is simple and elegant. The following three rules, called **Armstrong's Axioms**, can be applied repeatedly to infer all FDs implied by a set F of FDs. We use X, Y, and Z to denote *sets* of attributes over a relation schema R:

- **Reflexivity:** If $X \supseteq Y$, then $X \rightarrow Y$.
- **Augmentation:** If $X \rightarrow Y$, then $XZ \rightarrow YZ$ for any Z.
- **Transitivity:** If $X \rightarrow Y$ and $Y \rightarrow Z$, then $X \rightarrow Z$.

Theorem 1 *Armstrong's Axioms are* **sound**, *in that they generate only FDs in F^+ when applied to a set* F *of FDs. They are also* **complete**, *in that repeated application of these rules will generate all FDs in the closure F^+.*

The soundness of Armstrong's Axioms is straightforward to prove. Completeness is harder to show; see Exercise 19.17.

It is convenient to use some additional rules while reasoning about F^+:

- **Union:** If $X \rightarrow Y$ and $X \rightarrow Z$, then $X \rightarrow YZ$.
- **Decomposition:** If $X \rightarrow YZ$, then $X \rightarrow Y$ and $X \rightarrow Z$.

These additional rules are not essential; their soundness can be proved using Armstrong's Axioms.

To illustrate the use of these inference rules for FDs, consider a relation schema ABC with FDs $A \rightarrow B$ and $B \rightarrow C$. In a **trivial FD**, the right side contains only attributes that also appear on the left side; such dependencies always hold due to reflexivity. Using reflexivity, we can generate all trivial dependencies, which are of the form:

$$X \rightarrow Y, \text{ where } Y \subseteq X,\ X \subseteq ABC, \text{ and } Y \subseteq ABC.$$

From transitivity we get $A \rightarrow C$. From augmentation we get the nontrivial dependencies:

$$AC \rightarrow BC,\ AB \rightarrow AC,\ AB \rightarrow CB.$$

As another example, we use a more elaborate version of Contracts:

Contracts(<u>*contractid*</u>, *supplierid*, *projectid*, *deptid*, *partid*, *qty*, *value*)

We denote the schema for Contracts as $CSJDPQV$. The meaning of a tuple is that the contract with *contractid* C is an agreement that supplier S (*supplierid*) will supply Q items of part P (*partid*) to project J (*projectid*) associated with department D (*deptid*); the value V of this contract is equal to *value*.

The following ICs are known to hold:

1. The contract id C is a key: $C \rightarrow CSJDPQV$.
2. A project purchases a given part using a single contract: $JP \rightarrow C$.

3. A department purchases at most one part from a supplier: $SD \rightarrow P$.

Several additional FDs hold in the closure of the set of given FDs:

From $JP \rightarrow C$, $C \rightarrow CSJDPQV$, and transitivity, we infer $JP \rightarrow CSJDPQV$.

From $SD \rightarrow P$ and augmentation, we infer $SDJ \rightarrow JP$.

From $SDJ \rightarrow JP$, $JP \rightarrow CSJDPQV$, and transitivity, we infer $SDJ \rightarrow CSJDPQV$. (Incidentally, while it may appear tempting to do so, we *cannot* conclude $SD \rightarrow CSDPQV$, canceling J on both sides. FD inference is not like arithmetic multiplication!)

We can infer several additional FDs that are in the closure by using augmentation or decomposition. For example, from $C \rightarrow CSJDPQV$, using decomposition, we can infer:

$C \rightarrow C$, $C \rightarrow S$, $C \rightarrow J$, $C \rightarrow D$, and so forth

Finally, we have a number of trivial FDs from the reflexivity rule.

19.3.2 Attribute Closure

If we just want to check whether a given dependency, say, $X \rightarrow Y$, is in the closure of a set F of FDs, we can do so efficiently without computing F^+. We first compute the **attribute closure** X^+ with respect to F, which is the set of attributes A such that $X \rightarrow A$ can be inferred using the Armstrong Axioms. The algorithm for computing the attribute closure of a set X of attributes is shown in Figure 19.4.

```
closure = X;
repeat until there is no change: {
        if there is an FD U → V in F such that U ⊆ closure,
            then set closure = closure ∪ V
        }
```

Figure 19.4 Computing the Attribute Closure of Attribute Set X

Theorem 2 *The algorithm shown in Figure 19.4 computes the attribute closure X^+ of the attribute set X with respect to the set of FDs F.*

The proof of this theorem is considered in Exercise 19.15. This algorithm can be modified to find keys by starting with set X containing a single attribute and stopping as soon as *closure* contains all attributes in the relation schema. By varying the starting attribute and the order in which the algorithm considers FDs, we can obtain all candidate keys.

19.4 NORMAL FORMS

Given a relation schema, we need to decide whether it is a good design or we need to decompose it into smaller relations. Such a decision must be guided by an understanding of what problems, if any, arise from the current schema. To provide such guidance, several **normal forms** have been proposed. If a relation schema is in one of these normal forms, we know that certain kinds of problems cannot arise.

The normal forms based on FDs are *first normal form (1NF)*, *second normal form (2NF)*, *third normal form (3NF)*, and *Boyce-Codd normal form (BCNF)*. These forms have increasingly restrictive requirements: Every relation in BCNF is also in 3NF, every relation in 3NF is also in 2NF, and every relation in 2NF is in 1NF. A relation is in **first normal form** if every field contains only atomic values, that is, no lists or sets. This requirement is implicit in our definition of the relational model. Although some of the newer database systems are relaxing this requirement, in this chapter we assume that it always holds. 2NF is mainly of historical interest. 3NF and BCNF are important from a database design standpoint.

While studying normal forms, it is important to appreciate the role played by FDs. Consider a relation schema R with attributes ABC. In the absence of any ICs, any set of ternary tuples is a legal instance and there is no potential for redundancy. On the other hand, suppose that we have the FD $A \rightarrow B$. Now if several tuples have the same A value, they must also have the same B value. This potential redundancy can be predicted using the FD information. If more detailed ICs are specified, we may be able to detect more subtle redundancies as well.

We primarily discuss redundancy revealed by FD information. In Section 19.8, we discuss more sophisticated ICs called *multivalued dependencies* and *join dependencies* and normal forms based on them.

19.4.1 Boyce-Codd Normal Form

Let R be a relation schema, F be the set of FDs given to hold over R, X be a subset of the attributes of R, and A be an attribute of R. R is in **Boyce-Codd**

normal form if, for every FD $X \rightarrow A$ in F, one of the following statements is true:

- $A \in X$; that is, it is a trivial FD, or
- X is a superkey.

Intuitively, in a BCNF relation, the only nontrivial dependencies are those in which a key determines some attribute(s). Therefore, each tuple can be thought of as an entity or relationship, identified by a key and described by the remaining attributes. Kent (in [425]) puts this colorfully, if a little loosely: "Each attribute must describe [an entity or relationship identified by] the key, the whole key, and nothing but the key." If we use ovals to denote attributes or sets of attributes and draw arcs to indicate FDs, a relation in BCNF has the structure illustrated in Figure 19.5, considering just one key for simplicity. (If there are several candidate keys, each candidate key can play the role of KEY in the figure, with the other attributes being the ones not in the chosen candidate key.)

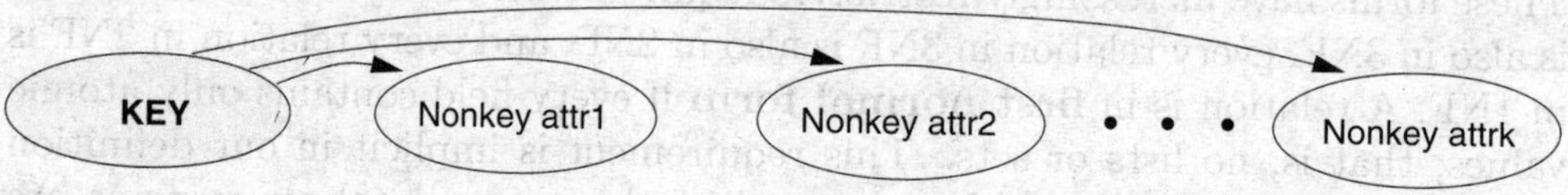

Figure 19.5 FDs in a BCNF Relation

BCNF ensures that no redundancy can be detected using FD information alone. It is thus the most desirable normal form (from the point of view of redundancy) if we take into account only FD information. This point is illustrated in Figure 19.6.

X	Y	A
x	y_1	a
x	y_2	?

Figure 19.6 Instance Illustrating BCNF

This figure shows (two tuples in) an instance of a relation with three attributes X, Y, and A. There are two tuples with the same value in the X column. Now suppose that we know that this instance satisfies an FD $X \rightarrow A$. We can see that one of the tuples has the value a in the A column. What can we infer about the value in the A column in the second tuple? Using the FD, we can conclude that the second tuple also has the value a in this column. (Note that this is really the only kind of inference we can make about values in the fields of tuples by using FDs.)

But is this situation not an example of redundancy? We appear to have stored the value a twice. Can such a situation arise in a BCNF relation? The answer is No! If this relation is in BCNF, because A is distinct from X, it follows that X must be a key. (Otherwise, the FD $X \rightarrow A$ would violate BCNF.) If X is a key, then $y_1 = y_2$, which means that the two tuples are identical. Since a relation is defined to be a *set* of tuples, we cannot have two copies of the same tuple and the situation shown in Figure 19.6 cannot arise.

Therefore, if a relation is in BCNF, every field of every tuple records a piece of information that cannot be inferred (using only FDs) from the values in all other fields in (all tuples of) the relation instance.

19.4.2 Third Normal Form

Let R be a relation schema, F be the set of FDs given to hold over R, X be a subset of the attributes of R, and A be an attribute of R. R is in **third normal form** if, for every FD $X \rightarrow A$ in F, one of the following statements is true:

- $A \in X$; that is, it is a trivial FD, or
- X is a superkey, or
- A is part of some key for R.

The definition of 3NF is similar to that of BCNF, with the only difference being the third condition. Every BCNF relation is also in 3NF. To understand the third condition, recall that a key for a relation is a *minimal* set of attributes that uniquely determines all other attributes. A must be part of a key (any key, if there are several). It is not enough for A to be part of a superkey, because the latter condition is satisfied by every attribute! Finding all keys of a relation schema is known to be an NP-complete problem, and so is the problem of determining whether a relation schema is in 3NF.

Suppose that a dependency $X \rightarrow A$ causes a violation of 3NF. There are two cases:

- X *is a proper subset of some key* K. Such a dependency is sometimes called a **partial dependency**. In this case, we store *(X, A)* pairs redundantly. As an example, consider the Reserves relation with attributes *SBDC* from Section 19.7.4. The only key is *SBD*, and we have the FD $S \rightarrow C$. We store the credit card number for a sailor as many times as there are reservations for that sailor.
- X *is not a proper subset of any key.* Such a dependency is sometimes called a **transitive dependency**, because it means we have a chain of

dependencies $K \to X \to A$. The problem is that we cannot associate an X value with a K value unless we also associate an A value with an X value. As an example, consider the Hourly Emps relation with attributes *SNLRWH* from Section 19.7.1. The only key is S, but there is an FD $R \to W$, which gives rise to the chain $S \to R \to W$. The consequence is that we cannot record the fact that employee S has rating R without knowing the hourly wage for that rating. This condition leads to insertion, deletion, and update anomalies.

Partial dependencies are illustrated in Figure 19.7, and transitive dependencies are illustrated in Figure 19.8. Note that in Figure 19.8, the set X of attributes may or may not have some attributes in common with KEY; the diagram should be interpreted as indicating only that X is not a subset of KEY.

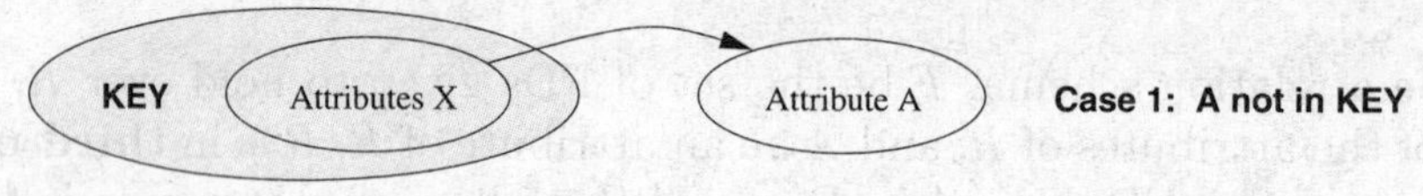

Figure 19.7 Partial Dependencies

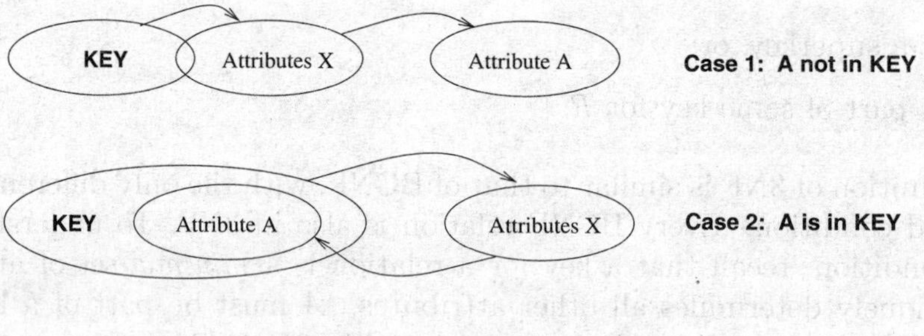

Figure 19.8 Transitive Dependencies

The motivation for 3NF is rather technical. By making an exception for certain dependencies involving key attributes, we can ensure that every relation schema can be decomposed into a collection of 3NF relations using only decompositions that have certain desirable properties (Section 19.5). Such a guarantee does not exist for BCNF relations; the 3NF definition weakens the BCNF requirements just enough to make this guarantee possible. We may therefore compromise by settling for a 3NF design. As we see in Chapter 20, we may sometimes accept this compromise (or even settle for a non-3NF schema) for other reasons as well.

Unlike BCNF, however, some redundancy is possible with 3NF. The problems associated with partial and transitive dependencies persist if there is a nontrivial dependency $X \to A$ and X is not a superkey, even if the relation is in 3NF because A is part of a key. To understand this point, let us revisit the Reserves relation with attributes *SBDC* and the FD $S \rightarrow C$, which states that a sailor uses a unique credit card to pay for reservations. *S* is not a key, and *C* is not part of a key. (In fact, the only key is *SBD*.) Hence, this relation is not in 3NF; *(S, C)* pairs are stored redundantly. However, if we also know that credit cards uniquely identify the owner, we have the FD $C \rightarrow S$, which means that *CBD* is also a key for Reserves. Therefore, the dependency $S \rightarrow C$ does not violate 3NF, and Reserves is in 3NF. Nonetheless, in all tuples containing the same *S* value, the same *(S, C)* pair is redundantly recorded.

For completeness, we remark that the definition of **second normal form** is essentially that partial dependencies are not allowed. Thus, if a relation is in 3NF (which precludes both partial and transitive dependencies), it is also in 2NF.

19.5 PROPERTIES OF DECOMPOSITIONS

Decomposition is a tool that allows us to eliminate redundancy. As noted in Section 19.1.3, however, it is important to check that a decomposition does not introduce new problems. In particular, we should check whether a decomposition allows us to recover the original relation, and whether it allows us to check integrity constraints efficiently. We discuss these properties next.

19.5.1 Lossless-Join Decomposition

Let *R* be a relation schema and let *F* be a set of FDs over *R*. A decomposition of *R* into two schemas with attribute sets *X* and *Y* is said to be a **lossless-join decomposition with respect to *F*** if, for every instance *r* of *R* that satisfies the dependencies in *F*, $\pi_X(r) \bowtie \pi_Y(r) = r$. In other words, we can recover the original relation from the decomposed relations.

This definition can easily be extended to cover a decomposition of *R* into more than two relations. It is easy to see that $r \subseteq \pi_X(r) \bowtie \pi_Y(r)$ always holds. In general, though, the other direction does not hold. If we take projections of a relation and recombine them using natural join, we typically obtain some tuples that were not in the original relation. This situation is illustrated in Figure 19.9.

By replacing the instance *r* shown in Figure 19.9 with the instances $\pi_{SP}(r)$ and $\pi_{PD}(r)$, we lose some information. In particular, suppose that the tuples in *r* denote relationships. We can no longer tell that the relationships (s_1, p_1, d_3) and (s_3, p_1, d_1) do not hold. The decomposition of schema *SPD* into *SP* and *PD* is therefore lossy if the instance *r* shown in the figure is legal, that is, if this

S	P	D
s1	p1	d1
s2	p2	d2
s3	p1	d3

Instance r

S	P
s1	p1
s2	p2
s3	p1

$\pi_{SP}(r)$

P	D
p1	d1
p2	d2
p1	d3

$\pi_{PD}(r)$

S	P	D
s1	p1	d1
s2	p2	d2
s3	p1	d3
s1	p1	d3
s3	p1	d1

$\pi_{SP}(r) \bowtie \pi_{PD}(r)$

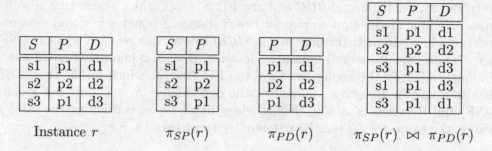

Figure 19.9 Instances Illustrating Lossy Decompositions

instance could arise in the enterprise being modeled. (Observe the similarities between this example and the Contracts relationship set in Section 2.5.3.)

All decompositions used to eliminate redundancy **must** *be lossless.* The following simple test is very useful:

Theorem 3 *Let* R *be a relation and* F *be a set of FDs that hold over* R. *The decomposition of* R *into relations with attribute sets* R_1 *and* R_2 *is lossless if and only if* F^+ *contains either the FD* $R_1 \cap R_2 \rightarrow R_1$ *or the FD* $R_1 \cap R_2 \rightarrow R_2$.

In other words, the attributes common to R_1 and R_2 must contain a key for either R_1 or R_2.[2] If a relation is decomposed into more than two relations, an efficient (time polynomial in the size of the dependency set) algorithm is available to test whether or not the decomposition is lossless, but we will not discuss it.

Consider the Hourly_Emps relation again. It has attributes *SNLRWH*, and the FD $R \rightarrow W$ causes a violation of 3NF. We dealt with this violation by decomposing the relation into *SNLRH* and *RW*. Since R is common to both decomposed relations and $R \rightarrow W$ holds, this decomposition is lossless-join.

This example illustrates a general observation that follows from Theorem 3:

> If an FD $X \rightarrow Y$ holds over a relation R and $X \cap Y$ is empty, the decomposition of R into $R - Y$ and XY is lossless.

X appears in both $R - Y$ (since $X \cap Y$ is empty) and XY, and it is a key for XY.

---

[2]See Exercise 19.19 for a proof of Theorem 3. Exercise 19.11 illustrates that the 'only if' claim depends on the assumption that only functional dependencies can be specified as integrity constraints.

Another important observation, which we state without proof, has to do with repeated decompositions. Suppose that a relation *R* is decomposed into *R1* and *R2* through a lossless-join decomposition, and that *R1* is decomposed into *R11* and *R12* through another lossless-join decomposition. Then, the decomposition of *R* into *R11*, *R12*, and *R2* is lossless-join; by joining *R11* and *R12*, we can recover *R1*, and by then joining *R1* and *R2*, we can recover *R*.

19.5.2 Dependency-Preserving Decomposition

Consider the Contracts relation with attributes *CSJDPQV* from Section 19.3.1. The given FDs are $C \rightarrow CSJDPQV$, $JP \rightarrow C$, and $SD \rightarrow P$. Because *SD* is not a key the dependency $SD \rightarrow P$ causes a violation of BCNF.

We can decompose Contracts into two relations with schemas *CSJDQV* and *SDP* to address this violation; the decomposition is lossless-join. There is one subtle problem, however. We can enforce the integrity constraint $JP \rightarrow C$ easily when a tuple is inserted into Contracts by ensuring that no existing tuple has the same *JP* values (as the inserted tuple) but different *C* values. Once we decompose Contracts into *CSJDQV* and *SDP*, enforcing this constraint requires an expensive join of the two relations whenever a tuple is inserted into *CSJDQV*. We say that this decomposition is not dependency-preserving.

Intuitively, a *dependency-preserving decomposition* allows us to enforce all FDs by examining a single relation instance on each insertion or modification of a tuple. (Note that deletions cannot cause violation of FDs.) To define dependency-preserving decompositions precisely, we have to introduce the concept of a projection of FDs.

Let *R* be a relation schema that is decomposed into two schemas with attribute sets *X* and *Y*, and let *F* be a set of FDs over *R*. The **projection of *F* on *X*** is the set of FDs in the closure F^+ (not just *F*!) that involve only attributes in *X*. We denote the projection of *F* on attributes *X* as F_X. Note that a dependency $U \rightarrow V$ in F^+ is in F_X only if *all* the attributes in *U* and *V* are in *X*.

The decomposition of relation schema *R* with FDs *F* into schemas with attribute sets *X* and *Y* is **dependency-preserving** if $(F_X \cup F_Y)^+ = F^+$. That is, if we take the dependencies in F_X and F_Y and compute the closure of their union, we get back all dependencies in the closure of *F*. Therefore, we need to enforce only the dependencies in F_X and F_Y; all FDs in F^+ are then sure to be satisfied. To enforce F_X, we need to examine only relation *X* (on inserts to that relation). To enforce F_Y, we need to examine only relation *Y*.

To appreciate the need to consider the closure F^+ while computing the projection of F, suppose that a relation R with attributes ABC is decomposed into relations with attributes AB and BC. The set F of FDs over R includes $A \rightarrow B$, $B \rightarrow C$, and $C \rightarrow A$. Of these, $A \rightarrow B$ is in F_{AB} and $B \rightarrow C$ is in F_{BC}. But is this decomposition dependency-preserving? What about $C \rightarrow A$? This dependency is not implied by the dependencies listed (thus far) for F_{AB} and F_{BC}.

The closure of F contains all dependencies in F plus $A \rightarrow C$, $B \rightarrow A$, and $C \rightarrow B$. Consequently, F_{AB} also contains $B \rightarrow A$, and F_{BC} contains $C \rightarrow B$. Therefore, $F_{AB} \cup F_{BC}$ contains $A \rightarrow B$, $B \rightarrow C$, $B \rightarrow A$, and $C \rightarrow B$. The closure of the dependencies in F_{AB} and F_{BC} now includes $C \rightarrow A$ (which follows from $C \rightarrow B$, $B \rightarrow A$, and transitivity). Thus, the decomposition preserves the dependency $C \rightarrow A$.

A direct application of the definition gives us a straightforward algorithm for testing whether a decomposition is dependency-preserving. (This algorithm is exponential in the size of the dependency set. A polynomial algorithm is available; see Exercise 19.9.)

We began this section with an example of a lossless-join decomposition that was not dependency-preserving. Other decompositions are dependency-preserving, but not lossless. A simple example consists of a relation ABC with FD $A \rightarrow B$ that is decomposed into AB and BC.

19.6 NORMALIZATION

Having covered the concepts needed to understand the role of normal forms and decompositions in database design, we now consider algorithms for converting relations to BCNF or 3NF. If a relation schema is not in BCNF, it is possible to obtain a lossless-join decomposition into a collection of BCNF relation schemas. Unfortunately, there may be no dependency-preserving decomposition into a collection of BCNF relation schemas. However, there is always a dependency-preserving, lossless-join decomposition into a collection of 3NF relation schemas.

19.6.1 Decomposition into BCNF

We now present an algorithm for decomposing a relation schema R with a set of FDs F into a collection of BCNF relation schemas:

1. Suppose that R is not in BCNF. Let $X \subset R$, A be a single attribute in R, and $X \rightarrow A$ be an FD that causes a violation of BCNF. Decompose R into $R - A$ and XA.

2. If either $R - A$ or XA is not in BCNF, decompose them further by a recursive application of this algorithm.

$R - A$ denotes the set of attributes other than A in R, and XA denotes the union of attributes in X and A. Since $X \rightarrow A$ violates BCNF, it is not a trivial dependency; further, A is a single attribute. Therefore, A is not in X; that is, $X \cap A$ is empty. Therefore, each decomposition carried out in Step 1 is lossless-join.

The set of dependencies associated with $R - A$ and XA is the projection of F onto their attributes. If one of the new relations is not in BCNF, we decompose it further in Step 2. Since a decomposition results in relations with strictly fewer attributes, this process terminates, leaving us with a collection of relation schemas that are all in BCNF. Further, joining instances of the (two or more) relations obtained through this algorithm yields precisely the corresponding instance of the original relation (i.e., the decomposition into a collection of relations each of which in BCNF is a lossless-join decomposition).

Consider the Contracts relation with attributes $CSJDPQV$ and key C. We are given FDs $JP \rightarrow C$ and $SD \rightarrow P$. By using the dependency $SD \rightarrow P$ to guide the decomposition, we get the two schemas SDP and $CSJDQV$. SDP is in BCNF. Suppose that we also have the constraint that each project deals with a single supplier: $J \rightarrow S$. This means that the schema $CSJDQV$ is not in BCNF. So we decompose it further into JS and $CJDQV$. $C \rightarrow JDQV$ holds over $CJDQV$; the only other FDs that hold are those obtained from this FD by augmentation, and therefore all FDs contain a key in the left side. Thus, each of the schemas SDP, JS, and $CJDQV$ is in BCNF, and this collection of schemas also represents a lossless-join decomposition of $CSJDQV$.

The steps in this decomposition process can be visualized as a tree, as shown in Figure 19.10. The root is the original relation $CSJDPQV$, and the leaves are the BCNF relations that result from the decomposition algorithm: SDP, JS, and $CSDQV$. Intuitively, each internal node is replaced by its children through a single decomposition step guided by the FD shown just below the node.

Redundancy in BCNF Revisited

The decomposition of $CSJDQV$ into SDP, JS, and $CJDQV$ is not dependency-preserving. Intuitively, dependency $JP \rightarrow C$ cannot be enforced without a join. One way to deal with this situation is to add a relation with attributes CJP. In

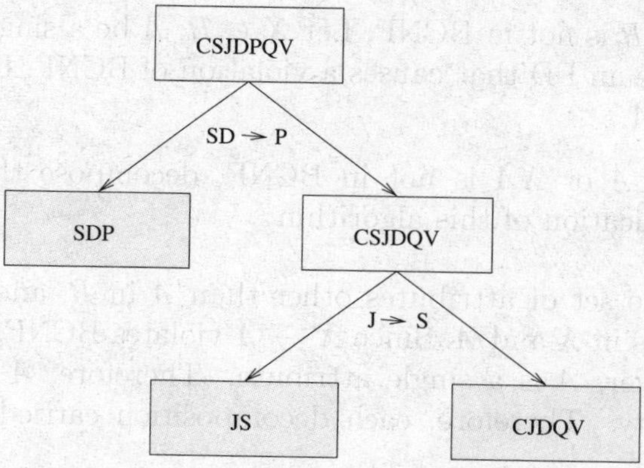

Figure 19.10 Decomposition of *CSJDQV* into *SDP*, *JS*, and *CJDQV*

effect, this solution amounts to storing some information redundantly to make the dependency enforcement cheaper.

This is a subtle point: Each of the schemas *CJP*, *SDP*, *JS*, and *CJDQV* is in BCNF, yet some redundancy can be predicted by FD information. In particular, if we join the relation instances for *SDP* and *CJDQV* and project the result onto the attributes *CJP*, we must get exactly the instance stored in the relation with schema *CJP*. We saw in Section 19.4.1 that there is no such redundancy within a single BCNF relation. This example shows that redundancy can still occur across relations, even though there is no redundancy within a relation.

Alternatives in Decomposing to BCNF

Suppose several dependencies violate BCNF. Depending on which of these dependencies we choose to guide the next decomposition step, we may arrive at quite different collections of BCNF relations. Consider Contracts. We just decomposed it into *SDP*, *JS*, and *CJDQV*. Suppose we choose to decompose the original relation *CSJDPQV* into *JS* and *CJDPQV*, based on the FD $J \rightarrow S$. The only dependencies that hold over *CJDPQV* are $JP \rightarrow C$ and the key dependency $C \rightarrow CJDPQV$. Since *JP* is a key, *CJDPQV* is in BCNF. Thus, the schemas *JS* and *CJDPQV* represent a lossless-join decomposition of Contracts into BCNF relations.

The lesson to be learned here is that the theory of dependencies can tell us when there is redundancy and give us clues about possible decompositions to address the problem, but it cannot discriminate among decomposition alternatives. A designer has to consider the alternatives and choose one based on the semantics of the application.

BCNF and Dependency-Preservation

Sometimes, there simply is no decomposition into BCNF that is dependency-preserving. As an example, consider the relation schema *SBD*, in which a tuple denotes that sailor S has reserved boat B on date D. If we have the FDs $SB \rightarrow D$ (a sailor can reserve a given boat for at most one day) and $D \rightarrow B$ (on any given day at most one boat can be reserved), *SBD* is not in BCNF because D is not a key. If we try to decompose it, however, we cannot preserve the dependency $SB \rightarrow D$.

19.6.2 Decomposition into 3NF

Clearly, the approach we outlined for lossless-join decomposition into BCNF also gives us a lossless-join decomposition into 3NF. (Typically, we can stop a little earlier if we are satisfied with a collection of 3NF relations.) But this approach does not ensure dependency-preservation.

A simple modification, however, yields a decomposition into 3NF relations that is lossless-join and dependency-preserving. Before we describe this modification, we need to introduce the concept of a minimal cover for a set of FDs.

Minimal Cover for a Set of FDs

A **minimal cover** for a set F of FDs is a set G of FDs such that:

1. Every dependency in G is of the form $X \rightarrow A$, where A is a single attribute.
2. The closure F^+ is equal to the closure G^+.
3. If we obtain a set H of dependencies from G by deleting one or more dependencies or by deleting attributes from a dependency in G, then $F^+ \neq H^+$.

Intuitively, a minimal cover for a set F of FDs is an equivalent set of dependencies that is *minimal* in two respects: (1) Every dependency is as small as possible; that is, each attribute on the left side is necessary and the right side is a single attribute. (2) Every dependency in it is required for the closure to be equal to F^+.

As an example, let F be the set of dependencies:

$$A \rightarrow B,\ ABCD \rightarrow E,\ EF \rightarrow G,\ EF \rightarrow H, \text{ and } ACDF \rightarrow EG.$$

First, let us rewrite $ACDF \rightarrow EG$ so that every right side is a single attribute:

$ACDF \to E$ and $ACDF \to G$.

Next consider $ACDF \to G$. This dependency is implied by the following FDs:

$A \to B$, $ABCD \to E$, and $EF \to G$.

Therefore, we can delete it. Similarly, we can delete $ACDF \to E$. Next consider $ABCD \to E$. Since $A \to B$ holds, we can replace it with $ACD \to E$. (At this point, the reader should verify that each remaining FD is minimal and required.) Thus, a minimal cover for F is the set:

$A \to B$, $ACD \to E$, $EF \to G$, and $EF \to H$.

The preceding example illustrates a general algorithm for obtaining a minimal cover of a set F of FDs:

1. **Put the FDs in a Standard Form:** Obtain a collection G of equivalent FDs with a single attribute on the right side (using the decomposition axiom).

2. **Minimize the Left Side of Each FD:** For each FD in G, check each attribute in the left side to see if it can be deleted while preserving equivalence to F^+.

3. **Delete Redundant FDs:** Check each remaining FD in G to see if it can be deleted while preserving equivalence to F^+.

Note that the order in which we consider FDs while applying these steps could produce different minimal covers; there could be several minimal covers for a given set of FDs.

More important, it is necessary to minimize the left sides of FDs *before* checking for redundant FDs. If these two steps are reversed, the final set of FDs could still contain some redundant FDs (i.e., not be a minimal cover), as the following example illustrates. Let F be the set of dependencies, each of which is already in the standard form:

$ABCD \to E$, $E \to D$, $A \to B$, and $AC \to D$.

Observe that none of these FDs is redundant; if we checked for redundant FDs first, we would get the same set of FDs F. The left side of $ABCD \to E$ can be replaced by AC while preserving equivalence to F^+, and we would stop here if we checked for redundant FDs in F before minimizing the left sides. However, the set of FDs we have is not a minimal cover:

$AC \to E$, $E \to D$, $A \to B$, and $AC \to D$.

From transitivity, the first two FDs imply the last FD, which can therefore be deleted while preserving equivalence to F^+. The important point to note is that $AC \to D$ becomes redundant only after we replace $ABCD \to E$ with $AC \to E$. If we minimize left sides of FDs first and then check for redundant FDs, we are left with the first three FDs in the preceding list, which is indeed a minimal cover for F.

Dependency-Preserving Decomposition into 3NF

Returning to the problem of obtaining a lossless-join, dependency-preserving decomposition into 3NF relations, let R be a relation with a set F of FDs that is a minimal cover, and let $R_1, R_2, \ldots, R_n$ be a lossless-join decomposition of R. For $1 \leq i \leq n$, suppose that each R_i is in 3NF and let F_i denote the projection of F onto the attributes of R_i. Do the following:

- Identify the set N of dependencies in F that is not **preserved**, that is, not included in the closure of the union of F_is.
- For each FD $X \to A$ in N, create a relation schema XA and add it to the decomposition of R.

Obviously, every dependency in F is preserved if we replace R by the R_is plus the schemas of the form XA added in this step. The R_is are given to be in 3NF. We can show that each of the schemas XA is in 3NF as follows: Since $X \to A$ is in the minimal cover F, $Y \to A$ does not hold for any Y that is a strict subset of X. Therefore, X is a key for XA. Further, if any other dependencies hold over XA, the right side can involve only attributes in X because A is a single attribute (because $X \to A$ is an FD in a minimal cover). Since X is a key for XA, none of these additional dependencies causes a violation of 3NF (although they might cause a violation of BCNF).

As an optimization, if the set N contains several FDs with the same left side, say, $X \to A_1$, $X \to A_2$, $\ldots$, $X \to A_n$, we can replace them with a single equivalent FD $X \to A_1 \ldots A_n$. Therefore, we produce one relation schema $XA_1 \ldots A_n$, instead of several schemas $XA_1, \ldots, XA_n$, which is generally preferable.

Consider the Contracts relation with attributes *CSJDPQV* and FDs $JP \to C$, $SD \to P$, and $J \to S$. If we decompose *CSJDPQV* into *SDP* and *CSJDQV*, then *SDP* is in BCNF, but *CSJDQV* is not even in 3NF. So we decompose it further into *JS* and *CJDQV*. The relation schemas *SDP*, *JS*, and *CJDQV* are in 3NF (in fact, in BCNF), and the decomposition is lossless-join. However, the dependency $JP \rightarrow C$ is not preserved. This problem can be addressed by adding a relation schema CJP to the decomposition.

3NF Synthesis

We assumed that the design process starts with an ER diagram, and that our use of FDs is primarily to guide decisions about decomposition. The algorithm for obtaining a lossless-join, dependency-preserving decomposition was presented in the previous section from this perspective—a lossless-join decomposition into 3NF is straightforward, and the algorithm addresses dependency-preservation by adding extra relation schemas.

An alternative approach, called **synthesis**, is to take all the attributes over the original relation R and a minimal cover F for the FDs that hold over it and add a relation schema XA to the decomposition of R for each FD $X \rightarrow A$ in F.

The resulting collection of relation schemas is in 3NF and preserves all FDs. If it is not a lossless-join decomposition of R, we can make it so by adding a relation schema that contains just those attributes that appear in some key. This algorithm gives us a lossless-join, dependency-preserving decomposition into 3NF and has polynomial complexity—polynomial algorithms are available for computing minimal covers, and a key can be found in polynomial time (even though finding all keys is known to be NP-complete). The existence of a polynomial algorithm for obtaining a lossless-join, dependency-preserving decomposition into 3NF is surprising when we consider that testing whether a given schema is in 3NF is NP-complete.

As an example, consider a relation ABC with FDs $F = \{A \rightarrow B,\ C \rightarrow B\}$. The first step yields the relation schemas AB and BC. This is not a lossless-join decomposition of ABC; $AB \cap BC$ is B, and neither $B \rightarrow A$ nor $B \rightarrow C$ is in F^+. If we add a schema AC, we have the lossless-join property as well. Although the collection of relations AB, BC, and AC is a dependency-preserving, lossless-join decomposition of ABC, we obtained it through a process of *synthesis*, rather than through a process of repeated decomposition. We note that the decomposition produced by the synthesis approach heavily dependends on the minimal cover used.

As another example of the synthesis approach, consider the Contracts relation with attributes $CSJDPQV$ and the following FDs:

$$C \rightarrow CSJDPQV,\ JP \rightarrow C,\ SD \rightarrow P, \text{ and } J \rightarrow S.$$

This set of FDs is not a minimal cover, and so we must find one. We first replace $C \rightarrow CSJDPQV$ with the FDs:

$$C \to S,\ C \to J,\ C \to D,\ C \to P,\ C \to Q, \text{ and } C \to V.$$

The FD $C \to P$ is implied by $C \to S$, $C \to D$, and $SD \to P$; so we can delete it. The FD $C \to S$ is implied by $C \to J$ and $J \to S$; so we can delete it. This leaves us with a minimal cover:

$$C \to J,\ C \to D,\ C \to Q,\ C \to V,\ JP \to C,\ SD \to P, \text{ and } J \to S.$$

Using the algorithm for ensuring dependency-preservation, we obtain the relational schema *CJ*, *CD*, *CQ*, *CV*, *CJP*, *SDP*, and *JS*. We can improve this schema by combining relations for which *C* is the key into *CDJPQV*. In addition, we have *SDP* and *JS* in our decomposition. Since one of these relations (*CDJPQV*) is a superkey, we are done.

Comparing this decomposition with that obtained earlier in this section, we find they are quite close, with the only difference being that one of them has *CDJPQV* instead of *CJP* and *CJDQV*. In general, however, there could be significant differences.

19.7 SCHEMA REFINEMENT IN DATABASE DESIGN

We have seen how normalization can eliminate redundancy and discussed several approaches to normalizing a relation. We now consider how these ideas are applied in practice.

Database designers typically use a conceptual design methodology, such as ER design, to arrive at an initial database design. Given this, the approach of repeated decompositions to rectify instances of redundancy is likely to be the most natural use of FDs and normalization techniques.

In this section, we motivate the need for a schema refinement step following ER design. It is natural to ask whether we even need to decompose relations produced by translating an ER diagram. Should a good ER design not lead to a collection of relations free of redundancy problems? Unfortunately, ER design is a complex, subjective process, and certain constraints are not expressible in terms of ER diagrams. The examples in this section are intended to illustrate why decomposition of relations produced through ER design might be necessary.

19.7.1 Constraints on an Entity Set

Consider the Hourly Emps relation again. The constraint that attribute *ssn* is a key can be expressed as an FD:

$$\{ssn\} \rightarrow \{ssn,\ name,\ lot,\ rating,\ hourly\ wages,\ hours\ worked\}$$

For brevity, we write this FD as $S \rightarrow SNLRWH$, using a single letter to denote each attribute and omitting the set braces, but the reader should remember that both sides of an FD contain sets of attributes. In addition, the constraint that the *hourly wages* attribute is determined by the *rating* attribute is an FD: $R \rightarrow W$.

As we saw in Section 19.1.1, this FD led to redundant storage of rating–wage associations. *It cannot be expressed in terms of the ER model. Only FDs that determine all attributes of a relation (i.e., key constraints) can be expressed in the ER model.* Therefore, we could not detect it when we considered Hourly Emps as an entity set during ER modeling.

We could argue that the problem with the original design was an artifact of a poor ER design, which could have been avoided by introducing an entity set called Wage Table (with attributes *rating* and *hourly wages*) and a relationship set Has Wages associating Hourly Emps and Wage Table. The point, however, is that we could easily arrive at the original design given the subjective nature of ER modeling. Having formal techniques to identify the problem with this design and guide us to a better design is very useful. The value of such techniques cannot be underestimated when designing large schemas—schemas with more than a hundred tables are not uncommon.

19.7.2 Constraints on a Relationship Set

The previous example illustrated how FDs can help to refine the subjective decisions made during ER design, but one could argue that the best possible ER diagram would have led to the same final set of relations. Our next example shows how FD information can lead to a set of relations unlikely to be arrived at solely through ER design.

We revisit an example from Chapter 2. Suppose that we have entity sets Parts, Suppliers, and Departments, as well as a relationship set Contracts that involves all of them. We refer to the schema for Contracts as *CQPSD*. A contract with contract id *C* specifies that a supplier *S* will supply some quantity *Q* of a part *P* to a department *D*. (We have added the contract id field *C* to the version of the Contracts relation discussed in Chapter 2.)

We might have a policy that a department purchases at most one part from any given supplier. Therefore, if there are several contracts between the same supplier and department, we know that the same part must be involved in all of them. This constraint is an FD, $DS \rightarrow P$.

Again we have redundancy and its associated problems. We can address this situation by decomposing Contracts into two relations with attributes *CQSD* and *SDP*. Intuitively, the relation *SDP* records the part supplied to a department by a supplier, and the relation *CQSD* records additional information about a contract. It is unlikely that we would arrive at such a design solely through ER modeling, since it is hard to formulate an entity or relationship that corresponds naturally to *CQSD*.

19.7.3 Identifying Attributes of Entities

This example illustrates how a careful examination of FDs can lead to a better understanding of the entities and relationships underlying the relational tables; in particular, it shows that attributes can easily be associated with the 'wrong' entity set during ER design. The ER diagram in Figure 19.11 shows a relationship set called Works In that is similar to the Works In relationship set of Chapter 2 but with an additional key constraint indicating that an employee can work in at most one department. (Observe the arrow connecting Employees to Works In.)

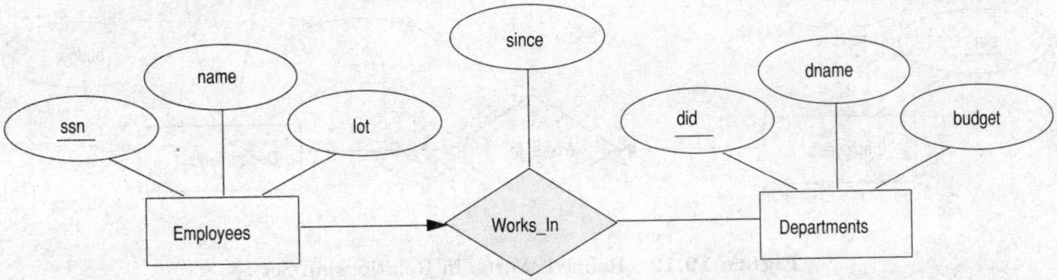

Figure 19.11 The Works In Relationship Set

Using the key constraint, we can translate this ER diagram into two relations:

Workers(*ssn*, *name*, *lot*, *did*, *since*)
Departments(*did*, *dname*, *budget*)

The entity set Employees and the relationship set Works In are mapped to a single relation, Workers. This translation is based on the second approach discussed in Section 2.4.1.

Now suppose employees are assigned parking lots based on their department, and that all employees in a given department are assigned to the same lot. This constraint is not expressible with respect to the ER diagram of Figure 19.11. It is another example of an FD: *did* → *lot*. The redundancy in this design can be eliminated by decomposing the Workers relation into two relations:

Workers2(*ssn*, *name*, *did*, *since*)
Dept Lots(*did*, *lot*)

The new design has much to recommend it. We can change the lots associated with a department by updating a single tuple in the second relation (i.e., no update anomalies). We can associate a lot with a department even if it currently has no employees, without using *null* values (i.e., no deletion anomalies). We can add an employee to a department by inserting a tuple to the first relation even if there is no lot associated with the employee's department (i.e., no insertion anomalies).

Examining the two relations Departments and Dept Lots, which have the same key, we realize that a Departments tuple and a Dept Lots tuple with the same key value describe the same entity. This observation is reflected in the ER diagram shown in Figure 19.12.

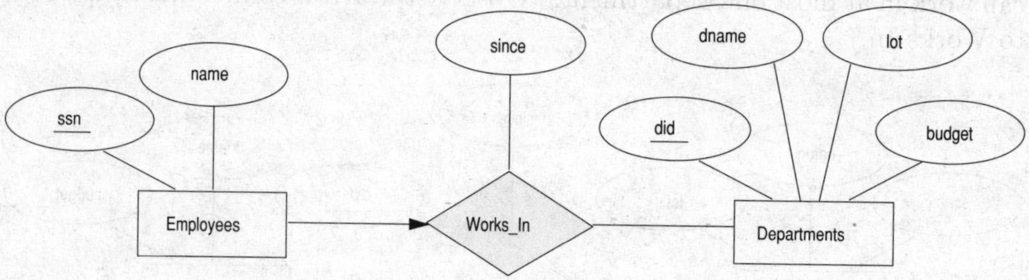

Figure 19.12 Refined Works In Relationship Set

Translating this diagram into the relational model would yield:

Workers2(*ssn*, *name*, *did*, *since*)
Departments(*did*, *dname*, *budget*, *lot*)

It seems intuitive to associate lots with employees; on the other hand, the ICs reveal that in this example lots are really associated with departments. The subjective process of ER modeling could miss this point. The rigorous process of normalization would not.

19.7.4 Identifying Entity Sets

Consider a variant of the Reserves schema used in earlier chapters. Let Reserves contain attributes S, B, and D as before, indicating that sailor S has a reservation for boat B on day D. In addition, let there be an attribute C denoting the credit card to which the reservation is charged. We use this example to illustrate how FD information can be used to refine an ER design. In particular, we discuss how FD information can help decide whether a concept should be modeled as an entity or as an attribute.

Suppose every sailor uses a unique credit card for reservations. This constraint is expressed by the FD $S \rightarrow C$. This constraint indicates that, in relation Reserves, we store the credit card number for a sailor as often as we have reservations for that sailor, and we have redundancy and potential update anomalies. A solution is to decompose Reserves into two relations with attributes SBD and SC. Intuitively, one holds information about reservations, and the other holds information about credit cards.

It is instructive to think about an ER design that would lead to these relations. One approach is to introduce an entity set called Credit_Cards, with the sole attribute *cardno*, and a relationship set Has_Card associating Sailors and Credit_Cards. By noting that each credit card belongs to a single sailor, we can map Has_Card and Credit_Cards to a single relation with attributes SC. We would probably not model credit card numbers as entities if our main interest in card numbers is to indicate how a reservation is to be paid for; it suffices to use an attribute to model card numbers in this situation.

A second approach is to make *cardno* an attribute of Sailors. But this approach is not very natural—a sailor may have several cards, and we are not interested in all of them. Our interest is in the one card that is used to pay for reservations, which is best modeled as an attribute of the relationship Reserves.

A helpful way to think about the design problem in this example is that we first make *cardno* an attribute of Reserves and then refine the resulting tables by taking into account the FD information. (Whether we refine the design by adding *cardno* to the table obtained from Sailors or by creating a new table with attributes SC is a separate issue.)

19.8 OTHER KINDS OF DEPENDENCIES

FDs are probably the most common and important kind of constraint from the point of view of database design. However, there are several other kinds of dependencies. In particular, there is a well-developed theory for database design using *multivalued dependencies* and *join dependencies.* By taking such dependencies into account, we can identify potential redundancy problems that cannot be detected using FDs alone.

This section illustrates the kinds of redundancy that can be detected using multivalued dependencies. Our main observation, however, is that simple guidelines (which can be checked using only FD reasoning) can tell us whether we even need to worry about complex constraints such as multivalued and join dependencies. We also comment on the role of *inclusion dependencies* in database design.

19.8.1 Multivalued Dependencies

Suppose that we have a relation with attributes *course*, *teacher*, and *book*, which we denote as *CTB*. The meaning of a tuple is that teacher *T* can teach course *C*, and book *B* is a recommended text for the course. There are no FDs; the key is *CTB*. However, the recommended texts for a course are independent of the instructor. The instance shown in Figure 19.13 illustrates this situation.

course	*teacher*	*book*
Physics101	Green	Mechanics
Physics101	Green	Optics
Physics101	Brown	Mechanics
Physics101	Brown	Optics
Math301	Green	Mechanics
Math301	Green	Vectors
Math301	Green	Geometry

Figure 19.13 BCNF Relation with Redundancy That Is Revealed by MVDs

Note three points here:

- The relation schema *CTB* is in BCNF; therefore we would not consider decomposing it further if we looked only at the FDs that hold over *CTB*.
- There is redundancy. The fact that Green can teach Physics101 is recorded once per recommended text for the course. Similarly, the fact that Optics is a text for Physics101 is recorded once per potential teacher.
- The redundancy can be eliminated by decomposing *CTB* into *CT* and *CB*.

The redundancy in this example is due to the constraint that the texts for a course are independent of the instructors, which cannot be expressed in terms of FDs. This constraint is an example of a *multivalued dependency*, or MVD. Ideally, we should model this situation using two binary relationship sets, Instructors with attributes *CT* and Text with attributes *CB*. Because these are two essentially independent relationships, modeling them with a single ternary relationship set with attributes *CTB* is inappropriate. (See Section 2.5.3 for a further discussion of ternary versus binary relationships.) Given the subjectivity of ER design, however, we might create a ternary relationship. A careful analysis of the MVD information would then reveal the problem.

Let R be a relation schema and let X and Y be subsets of the attributes of R. Intuitively, the **multivalued dependency** $X \to\to Y$ is said to hold over R if, in every legal instance r of R, each X value is associated with a set of Y values and this set is independent of the values in the other attributes.

Formally, if the MVD $X \to\to Y$ holds over R and $Z = R - XY$, the following must be true for every legal instance r of R:

> If $t_1 \in r$, $t_2 \in r$ and $t_1.X = t_2.X$, then there must be some $t_3 \in r$ such that $t_1.XY = t_3.XY$ and $t_2.Z = t_3.Z$.

Figure 19.14 illustrates this definition. If we are given the first two tuples and told that the MVD $X \to\to Y$ holds over this relation, we can infer that the relation instance must also contain the third tuple. Indeed, by interchanging the roles of the first two tuples—treating the first tuple as t_2 and the second tuple as t_1—we can deduce that the tuple t_4 must also be in the relation instance.

X	Y	Z	
a	b_1	c_1	— tuple t_1
a	b_2	c_2	— tuple t_2
a	b_1	c_2	— tuple t_3
a	b_2	c_1	— tuple t_4

Figure 19.14 Illustration of MVD Definition

This table suggests another way to think about MVDs: If $X \to\to Y$ holds over R, then $\pi_{YZ}(\sigma_{X=x}(R)) = \pi_Y(\sigma_{X=x}(R)) \times \pi_Z(\sigma_{X=x}(R))$ in every legal instance of R, for any value x that appears in the X column of R. In other words, consider groups of tuples in R with the same X-value. In each such group consider the projection onto the attributes YZ. This projection must be equal to the cross-product of the projections onto Y and Z. That is, for a given X-value, the Y-values and Z-values are independent. (From this definition it is easy to see that $X \to\to Y$ must hold whenever $X \to Y$ holds. If the FD $X \to$

Y holds, there is exactly one Y-value for a given X-value, and the conditions in the MVD definition hold trivially. The converse does not hold, as Figure 19.14 illustrates.)

Returning to our CTB example, the constraint that course texts are independent of instructors can be expressed as $C \rightarrow\rightarrow T$. In terms of the definition of MVDs, this constraint can be read as follows:

> If (there is a tuple showing that) C is taught by teacher T,
> and (there is a tuple showing that) C has book B as text,
> then (there is a tuple showing that) C is taught by T and has text B.

Given a set of FDs and MVDs, in general, we can infer that several additional FDs and MVDs hold. A sound and complete set of inference rules consists of the three Armstrong Axioms plus five additional rules. Three of the additional rules involve only MVDs:

- **MVD Complementation:** If $X \rightarrow\rightarrow Y$, then $X \rightarrow\rightarrow R - XY$.
- **MVD Augmentation:** If $X \rightarrow\rightarrow Y$ and $W \supseteq Z$, then $WX \rightarrow\rightarrow YZ$.
- **MVD Transitivity:** If $X \rightarrow\rightarrow Y$ and $Y \rightarrow\rightarrow Z$, then $X \rightarrow\rightarrow (Z - Y)$.

As an example of the use of these rules, since we have $C \rightarrow\rightarrow T$ over CTB, MVD complementation allows us to infer that $C \rightarrow\rightarrow CTB - CT$ as well, that is, $C \rightarrow\rightarrow B$. The remaining two rules relate FDs and MVDs:

- **Replication:** If $X \rightarrow Y$, then $X \rightarrow\rightarrow Y$.
- **Coalescence:** If $X \rightarrow\rightarrow Y$ and there is a W such that $W \cap Y$ is empty, $W \rightarrow Z$, and $Y \supseteq Z$, then $X \rightarrow Z$.

Observe that replication states that every FD is also an MVD.

19.8.2 Fourth Normal Form

Fourth normal form is a direct generalization of BCNF. Let R be a relation schema, X and Y be nonempty subsets of the attributes of R, and F be a set of dependencies that includes both FDs and MVDs. R is said to be in **fourth normal form (4NF)**, if, for every MVD $X \rightarrow\rightarrow Y$ that holds over R, one of the following statements is true:

- $Y \subseteq X$ or $XY = R$, or
- X is a superkey.

In reading this definition, it is important to understand that the definition of a *key* has not changed—the key must uniquely determine all attributes through FDs alone. $X \rightarrow\rightarrow Y$ is a **trivial MVD** if $Y \subseteq X \subseteq R$ or $XY = R$; such MVDs always hold.

The relation *CTB* is not in 4NF because $C \rightarrow\rightarrow T$ is a nontrivial MVD and C is not a key. We can eliminate the resulting redundancy by decomposing *CTB* into *CT* and *CB*; each of these relations is then in 4NF.

To use MVD information fully, we must understand the theory of MVDs. However, the following result due to Date and Fagin identifies conditions—detected using only FD information!—under which we can safely ignore MVD information. That is, using MVD information in addition to the FD information will not reveal any redundancy. Therefore, if these conditions hold, we do not even need to identify all MVDs.

> If a relation schema is in BCNF, and at least one of its keys consists of a single attribute, it is also in 4NF.

An important assumption is implicit in any application of the preceding result: *The set of FDs identified thus far is indeed the set of all FDs that hold over the relation.* This assumption is important because the result relies on the relation being in BCNF, which in turn depends on the set of FDs that hold over the relation.

We illustrate this point using an example. Consider a relation schema *ABCD* and suppose that the FD $A \rightarrow BCD$ and the MVD $B \rightarrow\rightarrow C$ are given. Considering only these dependencies, this relation schema appears to be a counterexample to the result. The relation has a simple key, appears to be in BCNF, and yet is not in 4NF because $B \rightarrow\rightarrow C$ causes a violation of the 4NF conditions. Let us take a closer look.

B	C	A	D	
b	c_1	a_1	d_1	— tuple t_1
b	c_2	a_2	d_2	— tuple t_2
b	c_1	a_2	d_2	— tuple t_3

Figure 19.15 Three Tuples from a Legal Instance of *ABCD*

Figure 19.15 shows three tuples from an instance of *ABCD* that satisfies the given MVD $B \rightarrow\rightarrow C$. From the definition of an MVD, given tuples t_1 and t_2, it follows that tuple t_3 must also be included in the instance. Consider tuples t_2 and t_3. From the given FD $A \rightarrow BCD$ and the fact that these tuples have the same A-value, we can deduce that $c_1 = c_2$. Therefore, we see that the FD $B \rightarrow C$ must hold over $ABCD$ whenever the FD $A \rightarrow BCD$ and the MVD $B \rightarrow\rightarrow C$ hold. If $B \rightarrow C$ holds, the relation $ABCD$ is not in BCNF (unless additional FDs make B a key)!

Thus, the apparent counterexample is really not a counterexample—rather, it illustrates the importance of correctly identifying all FDs that hold over a relation. In this example, $A \rightarrow BCD$ is not the only FD; the FD $B \rightarrow C$ also holds but was not identified initially. Given a set of FDs and MVDs, the inference rules can be used to infer additional FDs (and MVDs); to apply the Date-Fagin result without first using the MVD inference rules, we must be certain that we have identified all the FDs.

In summary, the Date-Fagin result offers a convenient way to check that a relation is in 4NF (without reasoning about MVDs) if we are confident that we have identified all FDs. At this point, the reader is invited to go over the examples we have discussed in this chapter and see if there is a relation that is not in 4NF.

19.8.3 Join Dependencies

A join dependency is a further generalization of MVDs. A **join dependency** (JD) $\bowtie \{R_1, \ldots, R_n\}$ is said to hold over a relation R if $R_1, \ldots, R_n$ is a lossless-join decomposition of R.

An MVD $X \rightarrow\rightarrow Y$ over a relation R can be expressed as the join dependency $\bowtie$ {XY, X(R−Y)}. As an example, in the *CTB* relation, the MVD $C \rightarrow\rightarrow T$ can be expressed as the join dependency $\bowtie$ {CT, CB}.

Unlike FDs and MVDs, there is no set of sound and complete inference rules for JDs.

19.8.4 Fifth Normal Form

A relation schema R is said to be in **fifth normal form (5NF)** if, for every JD $\bowtie \{R_1, \ldots, R_n\}$ that holds over R, one of the following statements is true:

- $R_i = R$ for some i, or
- The JD is implied by the set of those FDs over R in which the left side is a key for R.

The second condition deserves some explanation, since we have not presented inference rules for FDs and JDs taken together. Intuitively, we must be able to show that the decomposition of R into $\{R_1, \ldots, R_n\}$ is lossless-join whenever the **key dependencies** (FDs in which the left side is a key for R) hold. JD $\bowtie \{R_1, \ldots, R_n\}$ is a **trivial JD** if $R_i = R$ for some i; such a JD always holds.

The following result, also due to Date and Fagin, identifies conditions—again, detected using only FD information—under which we can safely ignore JD information:

> If a relation schema is in 3NF and each of its keys consists of a single attribute, it is also in 5NF.

The conditions identified in this result are sufficient for a relation to be in 5NF but not necessary. The result can be very useful in practice because it allows us to conclude that a relation is in 5NF *without ever identifying the MVDs and JDs that may hold over the relation.*

19.8.5 Inclusion Dependencies

MVDs and JDs can be used to guide database design, as we have seen, although they are less common than FDs and harder to recognize and reason about. In contrast, inclusion dependencies are very intuitive and quite common. However, they typically have little influence on database design (beyond the ER design stage).

Informally, an inclusion dependency is a statement of the form that some columns of a relation are contained in other columns (usually of a second relation). A foreign key constraint is an example of an inclusion dependency; the referring column(s) in one relation must be contained in the primary key column(s) of the referenced relation. As another example, if R and S are two relations obtained by translating two entity sets that every R entity is also an S entity, we would have an inclusion dependency; projecting R on its key attributes yields a relation contained in the relation obtained by projecting S on its key attributes.

The main point to bear in mind is that we should not split groups of attributes that participate in an inclusion dependency. For example, if we have an inclusion dependency $AB \subseteq CD$, while decomposing the relation schema containing AB, we should ensure that at least one of the schemas obtained in the decomposition contains both A and B. Otherwise, we cannot check the inclusion dependency $AB \subseteq CD$ without reconstructing the relation containing AB.

Most inclusion dependencies in practice are *key-based*, that is, involve only keys. Foreign key constraints are a good example of key-based inclusion dependencies. An ER diagram that involves ISA hierarchies (see Section 2.4.4) also leads to key-based inclusion dependencies. If all inclusion dependencies are key-based, we rarely have to worry about splitting attribute groups that participate in inclusion dependencies, since decompositions usually do not split the primary key. Note, however, that going from 3NF to BCNF always involves splitting some key (ideally not the primary key!), since the dependency guiding the split is of the form $X \rightarrow A$ where A is part of a key.

19.9 CASE STUDY: THE INTERNET SHOP

Recall from Section 3.8 that DBDudes settled on the following schema:

> Books(*isbn:* CHAR(10), *title:* CHAR(8), *author:* CHAR(80),
> *qty_in_stock:* INTEGER, *price:* REAL, *year_published:* INTEGER)
> Customers(*cid:* INTEGER, *cname:* CHAR(80), *address:* CHAR(200))
> Orders(*ordernum:* INTEGER, *isbn:* CHAR(10), *cid:* INTEGER,
> *cardnum:* CHAR(16), *qty:* INTEGER, *order_date:* DATE, *ship_date:* DATE)

DBDudes analyzes the set of relations for possible redundancy. The Books relation has only one key, (*isbn*), and no other functional dependencies hold over the table. Thus, Books is in BCNF. The Customers relation also has only one key, (*cid*), and no other functional depedencies hold over the table. Thus, Customers is also in BCNF.

DBDudes has already identified the pair $\langle$*ordernum*, *isbn*$\rangle$ as the key for the Orders table. In addition, since each order is placed by one customer on one specific date with one specific credit card number, the following three functional dependencies hold:

> *ordernum* → *cid*, *ordernum* → *order_date*, and *ordernum* → *cardnum*

The experts at DBDudes conclude that Orders is not even in 3NF. (Can you see why?) They decide to decompose Orders into the following two relations:

> Orders(*ordernum*, *cid*, *order_date*, *cardnum*, and
> Orderlists(*ordernum*, *isbn*, *qty*, *ship_date*)

The resulting two relations, Orders and Orderlists, are both in BCNF, and the decomposition is lossless-join since *ordernum* is a key for (the new) Orders. The reader is invited to check that this decomposition is also dependency-preserving. For completeness, we give the SQL DDL for the Orders and Orderlists relations below:

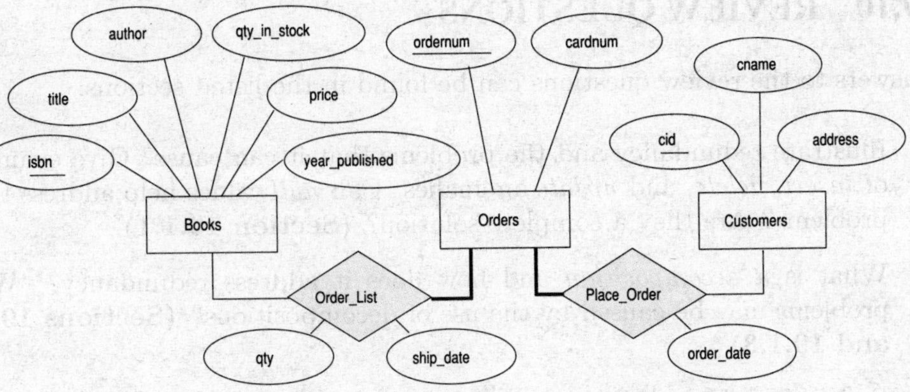

Figure 19.16 ER Diagram Reflecting the Final Design

```
CREATE TABLE Orders ( ordernum    INTEGER,
                      cid         INTEGER,
                      order date  DATE,
                      cardnum     CHAR(16),
                      PRIMARY KEY (ordernum),
                      FOREIGN KEY (cid) REFERENCES Customers )
```

```
CREATE TABLE Orderlists ( ordernum   INTEGER,
                          isbn       CHAR(10),
                          qty        INTEGER,
                          ship date  DATE,
                          PRIMARY KEY (ordernum, isbn),
                          FOREIGN KEY (isbn) REFERENCES Books)
```

Figure 19.16 shows an updated ER diagram that reflects the new design. Note that DBDudes could have arrived immediately at this diagram if they had made Orders an entity set instead of a relationship set right at the beginning. But at that time they did not understand the requirements completely, and it seemed natural to model Orders as a relationship set. This iterative refinement process is typical of real-life database design processes. As DBDudes has learned over time, it is rare to achieve an initial design that is not changed as a project progresses.

The DBDudes team celebrates the successful completion of logical database design and schema refinement by opening a bottle of champagne and charging it to B&N. After recovering from the celebration, they move on to the physical design phase.

19.10 REVIEW QUESTIONS

Answers to the review questions can be found in the listed sections.

- Illustrate redundancy and the problems that it can cause. Give examples of *insert, delete,* and *update* anomalies. Can *null* values help address these problems? Are they a complete solution? **(Section 19.1.1)**
- What is a *decomposition* and how does it address redundancy? What problems may be caused by the use of decompositions? **(Sections 19.1.2 and 19.1.3)**
- Define *functional dependencies.* How are *primary keys* related to FDs? **(Section 19.2)**
- When is an FD f *implied by* a set F of FDs? Define *Armstrong's Axioms*, and explain the statement that "they are a sound and complete set of rules for FD inference." **(Section 19.3)**
- What is the *dependency closure* F^+ of a set F of FDs? What is the *attribute closure* X^+ of a set of attributes X with respect to a set of FDs F? **(Section 19.3)**
- Define 1NF, 2NF, 3NF, and BCNF. What is the motivation for putting a relation in BCNF? What is the motivation for 3NF? **(Section 19.4)**
- When is the decomposition of a relation schema R into two relation schemas X and Y said to be a *lossless-join* decomposition? Why is this property so important? Give a necessary and sufficient condition to test whether a decomposition is lossless-join. **(Section 19.5.1)**
- When is a decomposition said to be *dependency-preserving*? Why is this property useful? **(Section 19.5.2)**
- Describe how we can obtain a lossless-join decomposition of a relation into BCNF. Give an example to show that there may not be a dependency-preserving decomposition into BCNF. Illustrate how a given relation could be decomposed in different ways to arrive at several alternative decompositions, and discuss the implications for database design. **(Section 19.6.1)**
- Give an example that illustrates how a collection of relations in BCNF could have redundancy even though each relation, by itself, is free from redundancy. **(Section 19.6.1)**
- What is a *minimal cover* for a set of FDs? Describe an algorithm for computing the minimal cover of a set of FDs, and illustrate it with an example. **(Section 19.6.2)**

- Describe how the algorithm for lossless-join decomposition into BCNF can be adapted to obtain a lossless-join, dependency-preserving decomposition into 3NF. Describe the alternative *synthesis* approach to obtaining such a decomposition into 3NF. Illustrate both approaches using an example. **(Section 19.6.2)**

- Discuss how schema refinement through dependency analysis and normalization can improve schemas obtained through ER design. **(Section 19.7)**

- Define *multivalued dependencies*, *join dependencies*, and *inclusion dependencies.* Discuss the use of such dependencies for database design. Define 4NF and 5NF, and explain how they prevent certain kinds of redundancy that BCNF does not eliminate. Describe tests for 4NF and 5NF that use only FDs. What key assumption is involved in these tests? **(Section 19.8)**

EXERCISES

Exercise 19.1 Briefly answer the following questions:

1. Define the term *functional dependency.*
2. Why are some functional dependencies called *trivial*?
3. Give a set of FDs for the relation schema $R(A,B,C,D)$ with primary key AB under which R is in 1NF but not in 2NF.
4. Give a set of FDs for the relation schema $R(A,B,C,D)$ with primary key AB under which R is in 2NF but not in 3NF.
5. Consider the relation schema $R(A,B,C)$, which has the FD $B \rightarrow C$. If A is a candidate key for R, is it possible for R to be in BCNF? If so, under what conditions? If not, explain why not.
6. Suppose we have a relation schema $R(A,B,C)$ representing a relationship between two entity sets with keys A and B, respectively, and suppose that R has (among others) the FDs $A \rightarrow B$ and $B \rightarrow A$. Explain what such a pair of dependencies means (i.e., what they imply about the relationship that the relation models).

Exercise 19.2 Consider a relation R with five attributes $ABCDE$. You are given the following dependencies: $A \rightarrow B$, $BC \rightarrow E$, and $ED \rightarrow A$.

1. List all keys for R.
2. Is R in 3NF?
3. Is R in BCNF?

Exercise 19.3 Consider the relation shown in Figure 19.17.

1. List all the functional dependencies that this relation instance satisfies.
2. Assume that the value of attribute Z of the last record in the relation is changed from z_3 to z_2. Now list all the functional dependencies that this relation instance satisfies.

Exercise 19.4 Assume that you are given a relation with attributes $ABCD$.

X	Y	Z
x_1	y_1	z_1
x_1	y_1	z_2
x_2	y_1	z_1
x_2	y_1	z_3

Figure 19.17 Relation for Exercise 19.3.

1. Assume that no record has NULL values. Write an SQL query that checks whether the functional dependency $A \rightarrow B$ holds.
2. Assume again that no record has NULL values. Write an SQL assertion that enforces the functional dependency $A \rightarrow B$.
3. Let us now assume that records could have NULL values. Repeat the previous two questions under this assumption.

Exercise 19.5 Consider the following collection of relations and dependencies. Assume that each relation is obtained through decomposition from a relation with attributes *ABCDEFGHI* and that all the known dependencies over relation *ABCDEFGHI* are listed for each question. (The questions are independent of each other, obviously, since the given dependencies over *ABCDEFGHI* are different.) For each (sub)relation: (a) State the strongest normal form that the relation is in. (b) If it is not in BCNF, decompose it into a collection of BCNF relations.

1. *R1(A,C,B,D,E)*, $A \rightarrow B$, $C \rightarrow D$
2. *R2(A,B,F)*, $AC \rightarrow E$, $B \rightarrow F$
3. *R3(A,D)*, $D \rightarrow G$, $G \rightarrow H$
4. *R4(D,C,H,G)*, $A \rightarrow I$, $I \rightarrow A$
5. *R5(A,I,C,E)*

Exercise 19.6 Suppose that we have the following three tuples in a legal instance of a relation schema *S* with three attributes *ABC* (listed in order): (1,2,3), (4,2,3), and (5,3,3).

1. Which of the following dependencies can you infer does *not* hold over schema *S*?

   (a) $A \rightarrow B$, (b) $BC \rightarrow A$, (c) $B \rightarrow C$

2. Can you identify any dependencies that hold over *S*?

Exercise 19.7 Suppose you are given a relation *R* with four attributes *ABCD*. For each of the following sets of FDs, assuming those are the only dependencies that hold for *R*, do the following: (a) Identify the candidate key(s) for *R*. (b) Identify the best normal form that *R* satisfies (1NF, 2NF, 3NF, or BCNF). (c) If *R* is not in BCNF, decompose it into a set of BCNF relations that preserve the dependencies.

1. $C \rightarrow D$, $C \rightarrow A$, $B \rightarrow C$
2. $B \rightarrow C$, $D \rightarrow A$
3. $ABC \rightarrow D$, $D \rightarrow A$
4. $A \rightarrow B$, $BC \rightarrow D$, $A \rightarrow C$
5. $AB \rightarrow C$, $AB \rightarrow D$, $C \rightarrow A$, $D \rightarrow B$

Exercise 19.8 Consider the attribute set $R = ABCDEGH$ and the FD set $F = \{AB \rightarrow C, AC \rightarrow B, AD \rightarrow E, B \rightarrow D, BC \rightarrow A, E \rightarrow G\}$.

1. For each of the following attribute sets, do the following: (i) Compute the set of dependencies that hold over the set and write down a minimal cover. (ii) Name the strongest normal form that is not violated by the relation containing these attributes. (iii) Decompose it into a collection of BCNF relations if it is not in BCNF.

   (a) ABC, (b) $ABCD$, (c) $ABCEG$, (d) $DCEGH$, (e) $ACEH$

2. Which of the following decompositions of $R = ABCDEG$, with the same set of dependencies F, is (a) dependency-preserving? (b) lossless-join?

   (a) $\{AB, BC, ABDE, EG\}$

   (b) $\{ABC, ACDE, ADG\}$

Exercise 19.9 Let R be decomposed into $R_1, R_2, \ldots, R_n$. Let F be a set of FDs on R.

1. Define what it means for F to *be preserved* in the set of decomposed relations.
2. Describe a polynomial-time algorithm to test dependency-preservation.
3. Projecting the FDs stated over a set of attributes X onto a subset of attributes Y requires that we consider the closure of the FDs. Give an example where considering the closure is important in testing dependency-preservation, that is, considering just the given FDs gives incorrect results.

Exercise 19.10 Suppose you are given a relation $R(A,B,C,D)$. For each of the following sets of FDs, assuming they are the only dependencies that hold for R, do the following: (a) Identify the candidate key(s) for R. (b) State whether or not the proposed decomposition of R into smaller relations is a good decomposition and briefly explain why or why not.

1. $B \rightarrow C$, $D \rightarrow A$; decompose into BC and AD.
2. $AB \rightarrow C$, $C \rightarrow A$, $C \rightarrow D$; decompose into ACD and BC.
3. $A \rightarrow BC$, $C \rightarrow AD$; decompose into ABC and AD.
4. $A \rightarrow B$, $B \rightarrow C$, $C \rightarrow D$; decompose into AB and ACD.
5. $A \rightarrow B$, $B \rightarrow C$, $C \rightarrow D$; decompose into AB, AD and CD.

Exercise 19.11 Consider a relation R that has three attributes ABC. It is decomposed into relations R_1 with attributes AB and R_2 with attributes BC.

1. State the definition of a lossless-join decomposition with respect to this example. Answer this question concisely by writing a relational algebra equation involving R, R_1, and R_2.
2. Suppose that $B \rightarrow\rightarrow C$. Is the decomposition of R into R_1 and R_2 lossless-join? Reconcile your answer with the observation that neither of the FDs $R_1 \cap R_2 \rightarrow R_1$ nor $R_1 \cap R_2 \rightarrow R_2$ hold, in light of the simple test offering a necessary and sufficient condition for lossless-join decomposition into two relations in Section 15.6.1.
3. If you are given the following instances of R_1 and R_2, what can you say about the instance of R from which these were obtained? Answer this question by listing tuples that are definitely in R and tuples that are possibly in R.

   Instance of $R_1 = \{(5,1), (6,1)\}$
   Instance of $R_2 = \{(1,8), (1,9)\}$

   Can you say that attribute B definitely *is* or *is not* a key for R?

Exercise 19.12 Suppose that we have the following four tuples in a relation S with three attributes ABC: (1,2,3), (4,2,3), (5,3,3), (5,3,4). Which of the following functional ($\rightarrow$) and multivalued ($\rightarrow\rightarrow$) dependencies can you infer does *not* hold over relation S?

1. $A \rightarrow B$
2. $A \rightarrow\rightarrow B$
3. $BC \rightarrow A$
4. $BC \rightarrow\rightarrow A$
5. $B \rightarrow C$
6. $B \rightarrow\rightarrow C$

Exercise 19.13 Consider a relation R with five attributes $ABCDE$.

1. For each of the following instances of R, state whether it violates (a) the FD $BC \rightarrow D$ and (b) the MVD $BC \rightarrow\rightarrow D$:
   (a) { } (i.e., empty relation)
   (b) {(a,2,3,4,5), (2,a,3,5,5)}
   (c) {(a,2,3,4,5), (2,a,3,5,5), (a,2,3,4,6)}
   (d) {(a,2,3,4,5), (2,a,3,4,5), (a,2,3,6,5)}
   (e) {(a,2,3,4,5), (2,a,3,7,5), (a,2,3,4,6)}
   (f) {(a,2,3,4,5), (2,a,3,4,5), (a,2,3,6,5), (a,2,3,6,6)}
   (g) {(a,2,3,4,5), (a,2,3,6,5), (a,2,3,6,6), (a,2,3,4,6)}
2. If each instance for R listed above is legal, what can you say about the FD $A \rightarrow B$?

Exercise 19.14 JDs are motivated by the fact that sometimes a relation that cannot be decomposed into two smaller relations in a lossless-join manner can be so decomposed into three or more relations. An example is a relation with attributes *supplier*, *part*, and *project*, denoted SPJ, with no FDs or MVDs. The JD $\bowtie \{SP,\ PJ,\ JS\}$ holds.

From the JD, the set of relation schemes SP, PJ, and JS is a lossless-join decomposition of SPJ. Construct an instance of SPJ to illustrate that no two of these schemes suffice.

Exercise 19.15 Answer the following questions

1. Prove that the algorithm shown in Figure 19.4 correctly computes the attribute closure of the input attribute set X.
2. Describe a linear-time (in the size of the set of FDs, where the size of each FD is the number of attributes involved) algorithm for finding the attribute closure of a set of attributes with respect to a set of FDs. Prove that your algorithm correctly computes the attribute closure of the input attribute set.

Exercise 19.16 Let us say that an FD $X \rightarrow Y$ is *simple* if Y is a single attribute.

1. Replace the FD $AB \rightarrow CD$ by the smallest equivalent collection of simple FDs.
2. Prove that every FD $X \rightarrow Y$ in a set of FDs F can be replaced by a set of simple FDs such that F^+ is equal to the closure of the new set of FDs.

Exercise 19.17 Prove that Armstrong's Axioms are sound and complete for FD inference. That is, show that repeated application of these axioms on a set F of FDs produces exactly the dependencies in F^+.

Exercise 19.18 Consider a relation R with attributes $ABCDE$. Let the following FDs be given: $A \rightarrow BC$, $BC \rightarrow E$, and $E \rightarrow DA$. Similarly, let S be a relation with attributes $ABCDE$ and let the following FDs be given: $A \rightarrow BC$, $B \rightarrow E$, and $E \rightarrow DA$. (Only the second dependency differs from those that hold over R.) You do not know whether or which other (join) dependencies hold.

1. Is R in BCNF?
2. Is R in 4NF?
3. Is R in 5NF?
4. Is S in BCNF?
5. Is S in 4NF?
6. Is S in 5NF?

Exercise 19.19 Let R be a relation schema with a set F of FDs. Prove that the decomposition of R into R_1 and R_2 is lossless-join if and only if F^+ contains $R_1 \cap R_2 \rightarrow R_1$ or $R_1 \cap R_2 \rightarrow R_2$.

Exercise 19.20 Consider a scheme R with FDs F that is decomposed into schemes with attributes X and Y. Show that this is dependency-preserving if $F \subseteq (F_X \cup F_Y)^+$.

Exercise 19.21 Prove that the optimization of the algorithm for lossless-join, dependency-preserving decomposition into 3NF relations (Section 19.6.2) is correct.

Exercise 19.22 Prove that the 3NF synthesis algorithm produces a lossless-join decomposition of the relation containing all the original attributes.

Exercise 19.23 Prove that an MVD $X \rightarrow\rightarrow Y$ over a relation R can be expressed as the join dependency $\bowtie \{XY,\ X(R-Y)\}$.

Exercise 19.24 Prove that, if R has only one key, it is in BCNF if and only if it is in 3NF.

Exercise 19.25 Prove that, if R is in 3NF and every key is simple, then R is in BCNF.

Exercise 19.26 Prove these statements:

1. If a relation scheme is in BCNF and at least one of its keys consists of a single attribute, it is also in 4NF.
2. If a relation scheme is in 3NF and each key has a single attribute, it is also in 5NF.

Exercise 19.27 Give an algorithm for testing whether a relation scheme is in BCNF. The algorithm should be polynomial in the size of the set of given FDs. (The *size* is the sum over all FDs of the number of attributes that appear in the FD.) Is there a polynomial algorithm for testing whether a relation scheme is in 3NF?

Exercise 19.28 Give an algorithm for testing whether a relation scheme is in BCNF. The algorithm should be polynomial in the size of the set of given FDs. (The 'size' is the sum over all FDs of the number of attributes that appear in the FD.) Is there a polynomial algorithm for testing whether a relation scheme is in 3NF?

Exercise 19.29 Prove that the algorithm for decomposing a relation schema with a set of FDs into a collection of BCNS relation schemas as described in Section 19.6.1 is correct (i.e., it produces a collection of BCNF relations, and is lossless-join) and terminates.

BIBLIOGRAPHIC NOTES

Textbook presentations of dependency theory and its use in database design include [3, 45, 501, 509, 747]. Good survey articles on the topic include [755, 415].

FDs were introduced in [187], along with the concept of 3NF, and axioms for inferring FDs were presented in [38]. BCNF was introduced in [188]. The concept of a legal relation instance and dependency satisfaction are studied formally in [328]. FDs were generalized to semantic data models in [768].

Finding a key is shown to be NP-complete in [497]. Lossless-join decompositions were studied in [28, 502, 627]. Dependency-preserving decompositions were studied in [74]. [81] introduced minimal covers. Decomposition into 3NF is studied by [81, 98] and decomposition into BCNF is addressed in [742]. [412] shows that testing whether a relation is in 3NF is NP-complete. [253] introduced 4NF and discussed decomposition into 4NF. Fagin introduced other normal forms in [254] (project-join normal form) and [255] (domain-key normal form). In contrast to the extensive study of vertical decompositions, there has been relatively little formal investigation of horizontal decompositions. [209] investigates horizontal decompositions.

MVDs were discovered independently by Delobel [211], Fagin [253], and Zaniolo [789]. Axioms for FDs and MVDs were presented in [73]. [593] shows that there is no axiomatization for JDs, although [662] provides an axiomatization for a more general class of dependencies. The sufficient conditions for 4NF and 5NF in terms of FDs that were discussed in Section 19.8 are from [205]. An approach to database design that uses dependency information to construct sample relation instances is described in [508, 509].

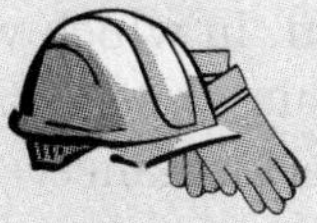

20

PHYSICAL DATABASE DESIGN AND TUNING

- What is physical database design?
- What is a query workload?
- How do we choose indexes? What tools are available?
- What is co-clustering and how is it used?
- What are the choices in tuning a database?
- How do we tune queries and view?
- What is the impact of concurrency on performance?
- How can we reduce lock contention and hotspots?
- What are popular database benchmarks and how are they used?
- **Key concepts:** Physical database design, database tuning, workload, co-clustering, index tuning, tuning wizard, index configuration, hot spot, lock contention, database benchmark, transactions per second

> Advice to a client who complained about rain leaking through the roof onto the dining table: "Move the table."
>
> —Architect Frank Lloyd Wright

The performance of a DBMS on commonly asked queries and typical update operations is the ultimate measure of a database design. A DBA can improve performance by identifying performance bottlenecks and adjusting some DBMS parameters (e.g., the size of the buffer pool or the frequency of checkpointing) or adding hardware to eliminate such bottlenecks. The first step in achieving good performance, however, is to make good database design choices, which is the focus of this chapter.

After we design the *conceptual* and *external* schemas, that is, create a collection of relations and views along with a set of integrity constraints, we must address performance goals through **physical database design**, in which we design the *physical* schema. As user requirements evolve, it is usually necessary to **tune**, or adjust, all aspects of a database design for good performance.

This chapter is organized as follows. We give an overview of physical database design and tuning in Section 20.1. The most important physical design decisions concern the choice of indexes. We present guidelines for deciding which indexes to create in Section 20.2. These guidelines are illustrated through several examples and developed further in Sections 20.3. In Section 20.4, we look closely at the important issue of clustering; we discuss how to choose clustered indexes and whether to store tuples from different relations near each other (an option supported by some DBMSs). In Section 20.5, we emphasize how well-chosen indexes can enable some queries to be answered without ever looking at the actual data records. Section 20.6 discusses tools that can help the DBA to automatically select indexes.

In Section 20.7, we survey the main issues of database tuning. In addition to tuning indexes, we may have to tune the conceptual schema as well as frequently used query and view definitions. We discuss how to refine the conceptual schema in Section 20.8 and how to refine queries and view definitions in Section 20.9. We briefly discuss the performance impact of concurrent access in Section 20.10. We illustrate tuning on our Internet shop example in Section 20.11. We conclude the chapter with a short discussion of DBMS benchmarks in Section 20.12; benchmarks help evaluate the performance of alternative DBMS products.

20.1 INTRODUCTION TO PHYSICAL DATABASE DESIGN

Like all other aspects of database design, physical design must be guided by the nature of the data and its intended use. In particular, it is important to understand the typical **workload** that the database must support; the workload consists of a mix of queries and updates. Users also have certain requirements about how fast certain queries or updates must run or how many transactions must be processed per second. The workload description and users' performance requirements are the basis on which a number of decisions have to be made during physical database design.

Identifying Performance Bottlenecks: All commercial systems provide a suite of tools for monitoring a wide range of system parameters. These tools, used properly, can help identify performance bottlenecks and suggest aspects of the database design and application code that need to be tuned for performance. For example, we can ask the DBMS to monitor the execution of the database for a certain period of time and report on the number of clustered scans, open cursors, lock requests, checkpoints, buffer scans, average wait time for locks, and many such statistics that give detailed insight into a *snapshot* of the live system. In Oracle, a report containing this information can be generated by running a script called `UTLBSTAT.SQL` to initiate monitoring and a script `UTLBSTAT.SQL` to terminate monitoring. The system catalog contains details about the sizes of tables, the distribution of values in index keys, and the like. The plan generated by the DBMS for a given query can be viewed in a graphical display that shows the estimated cost for each plan operator. While the details are specific to each vendor, all major DBMS products on the market today provide a suite of such tools.

To create a good physical database design and tune the system for performance in response to evolving user requirements, a designer must understand the workings of a DBMS, especially the indexing and query processing techniques supported by the DBMS. If the database is expected to be accessed concurrently by many users, or is a *distributed database*, the task becomes more complicated and other features of a DBMS come into play. We discuss the impact of concurrency on database design in Section 20.10 and distributed databases in Chapter 22.

20.1.1 Database Workloads

The key to good physical design is arriving at an accurate description of the expected workload. A **workload description** includes the following:

1. A list of queries (with their frequency, as a ratio of all queries / updates).
2. A list of updates and their frequencies.
3. Performance goals for each type of query and update.

For each query in the workload, we must identify

- Which relations are accessed.
- Which attributes are retained (in the `SELECT` clause).

- Which attributes have selection or join conditions expressed on them (in the `WHERE` clause) and how selective these conditions are likely to be.

Similarly, for each update in the workload, we must identify

- Which attributes have selection or join conditions expressed on them (in the `WHERE` clause) and how selective these conditions are likely to be.
- The type of update (`INSERT`, `DELETE`, or `UPDATE`) and the updated relation.
- For `UPDATE` commands, the fields that are modified by the update.

Remember that queries and updates typically have parameters, for example, a debit or credit operation involves a particular account number. The values of these parameters determine selectivity of selection and join conditions.

Updates have a query component that is used to find the target tuples. This component can benefit from a good physical design and the presence of indexes. On the other hand, updates typically require additional work to maintain indexes on the attributes that they modify. Thus, while queries can only benefit from the presence of an index, an index may either speed up or slow down a given update. Designers should keep this trade-off in mind when creating indexes.

20.1.2 Physical Design and Tuning Decisions

Important decisions made during physical database design and database tuning include the following:

1. **Choice of indexes to create:**
   - Which relations to index and which field or combination of fields to choose as index search keys.
   - For each index, should it be clustered or unclustered?
2. *Tuning the conceptual schema:*
   - *Alternative normalized schemas:* We usually have more than one way to decompose a schema into a desired normal form (BCNF or 3NF). A choice can be made on the basis of performance criteria.
   - *Denormalization:* We might want to reconsider schema decompositions carried out for normalization during the conceptual schema design process to improve the performance of queries that involve attributes from several previously decomposed relations.

- *Vertical partitioning:* Under certain circumstances we might want to further decompose relations to improve the performance of queries that involve only a few attributes.
- *Views:* We might want to add some views to mask the changes in the conceptual schema from users.

3. *Query and transaction tuning:* Frequently executed queries and transactions might be rewritten to run faster.

In parallel or distributed databases, which we discuss in Chapter 22, there are additional choices to consider, such as whether to partition a relation across different sites or whether to store copies of a relation at multiple sites.

20.1.3 Need for Database Tuning

Accurate, detailed workload information may be hard to come by while doing the initial design of the system. Consequently, tuning a database after it has been designed and deployed is important—we must refine the initial design in the light of actual usage patterns to obtain the best possible performance.

The distinction between database design and database tuning is somewhat arbitrary. We could consider the design process to be over once an initial conceptual schema is designed and a set of indexing and clustering decisions is made. Any subsequent changes to the conceptual schema or the indexes, say, would then be regarded as tuning. Alternatively, we could consider some refinement of the conceptual schema (and physical design decisions affected by this refinement) to be part of the physical design process.

Where we draw the line between design and tuning is not very important, and we simply discuss the issues of index selection and database tuning without regard to when the tuning is carried out.

20.2 GUIDELINES FOR INDEX SELECTION

In considering which indexes to create, we begin with the list of queries (including queries that appear as part of update operations). Obviously, only relations accessed by some query need to be considered as candidates for indexing, and the choice of attributes to index is guided by the conditions that appear in the `WHERE` clauses of the queries in the workload. The presence of suitable indexes can significantly improve the evaluation plan for a query, as we saw in Chapters 8 and 12.

One approach to index selection is to consider the most important queries in turn, and, for each, determine which plan the optimizer would choose given the indexes currently on our list of (to be created) indexes. Then we consider whether we can arrive at a substantially better plan by adding more indexes; if so, these additional indexes are candidates for inclusion in our list of indexes. In general, range retrievals benefit from a B+ tree index, and exact-match retrievals benefit from a hash index. Clustering benefits range queries, and it benefits exact-match queries if several data entries contain the same key value.

Before adding an index to the list, however, we must consider the impact of having this index on the updates in our workload. As we noted earlier, although an index can speed up the query component of an update, all indexes on an updated attribute—on *any* attribute, in the case of inserts and deletes—must be updated whenever the value of the attribute is changed. Therefore, we must sometimes consider the trade-off of slowing some update operations in the workload in order to speed up some queries.

Clearly, choosing a good set of indexes for a given workload requires an understanding of the available indexing techniques, and of the workings of the query optimizer. The following guidelines for index selection summarize our discussion:

Whether to Index (Guideline 1): The obvious points are often the most important. Do not build an index unless some query—including the query components of updates—benefits from it. Whenever possible, choose indexes that speed up more than one query.

Choice of Search Key (Guideline 2): Attributes mentioned in a `WHERE` clause are candidates for indexing.

- An exact-match selection condition suggests that we consider an index on the selected attributes, ideally, a hash index.
- A range selection condition suggests that we consider a B+ tree (or ISAM) index on the selected attributes. A B+ tree index is usually preferable to an ISAM index. An ISAM index may be worth considering if the relation is infrequently updated, but we assume that a B+ tree index is always chosen over an ISAM index, for simplicity.

Multi-Attribute Search Keys (Guideline 3): Indexes with multiple-attribute search keys should be considered in the following two situations:

- A `WHERE` clause includes conditions on more than one attribute of a relation.

- They enable index-only evaluation strategies (i.e., accessing the relation can be avoided) for important queries. (This situation could lead to attributes being in the search key even if they do not appear in `WHERE` clauses.)

When creating indexes on search keys with multiple attributes, if range queries are expected, be careful to order the attributes in the search key to match the queries.

Whether to Cluster (Guideline 4): At most one index on a given relation can be clustered, and clustering affects performance greatly; so the choice of clustered index is important.

- As a rule of thumb, range queries are likely to benefit the most from clustering. If several range queries are posed on a relation, involving different sets of attributes, consider the selectivity of the queries and their relative frequency in the workload when deciding which index should be clustered.

- If an index enables an index-only evaluation strategy for the query it is intended to speed up, the index need not be clustered. (Clustering matters only when the index is used to retrieve tuples from the underlying relation.)

Hash versus Tree Index (Guideline 5): A B+ tree index is usually preferable because it supports range queries as well as equality queries. A hash index is better in the following situations:

- The index is intended to support index nested loops join; the indexed relation is the inner relation, and the search key includes the join columns. In this case, the slight improvement of a hash index over a B+ tree for equality selections is magnified, because an equality selection is generated for each tuple in the outer relation.

- There is a very important equality query, and no range queries, involving the search key attributes.

Balancing the Cost of Index Maintenance (Guideline 6): After drawing up a 'wishlist' of indexes to create, consider the impact of each index on the updates in the workload.

- If maintaining an index slows down frequent update operations, consider dropping the index.

- Keep in mind, however, that adding an index may well speed up a given update operation. For example, an index on employee IDs could speed up the operation of increasing the salary of a given employee (specified by ID).

20.3 BASIC EXAMPLES OF INDEX SELECTION

The following examples illustrate how to choose indexes during database design, continuing the discussion from Chapter 8, where we focused on index selection for single-table queries. The schemas used in the examples are not described in detail; in general, they contain the attributes named in the queries. Additional information is presented when necessary.

Let us begin with a simple query:

```
SELECT E.ename, D.mgr
FROM   Employees E, Departments D
WHERE  D.dname='Toy' AND E.dno=D.dno
```

The relations mentioned in the query are Employees and Departments, and both conditions in the WHERE clause involve equalities. Our guidelines suggest that we should build hash indexes on the attributes involved. It seems clear that we should build a hash index on the *dname* attribute of Departments. But consider the equality *E.dno=D.dno*. Should we build an index (hash, of course) on the *dno* attribute of Departments or Employees (or both)? Intuitively, we want to retrieve Departments tuples using the index on *dname* because few tuples are likely to satisfy the equality selection *D.dname='Toy'*.[1] For each qualifying Departments tuple, we then find matching Employees tuples by using an index on the *dno* attribute of Employees. So, we should build an index on the *dno* field of Employees. (Note that nothing is gained by building an additional index on the *dno* field of Departments because Departments tuples are retrieved using the *dname* index.)

Our choice of indexes was guided by the query evaluation plan we wanted to utilize. This consideration of a potential evaluation plan is common while making physical design decisions. Understanding query optimization is very useful for physical design. We show the desired plan for this query in Figure 20.1.

As a variant of this query, suppose that the WHERE clause is modified to be WHERE *D.dname='Toy'* AND *E.dno=D.dno* AND *E.age=25*. Let us consider alternative evaluation plans. One good plan is to retrieve Departments tuples that satisfy the selection on *dname* and retrieve matching Employees tuples by using an index on the *dno* field; the selection on *age* is then applied on-the-fly. However, unlike the previous variant of this query, we do not really need to have an index on the *dno* field of Employees if we have an index on *age*. In this

[1] This is only a heuristic. If *dname* is not the key, and we have no statistics to verify this claim, it is possible that several tuples satisfy this condition.

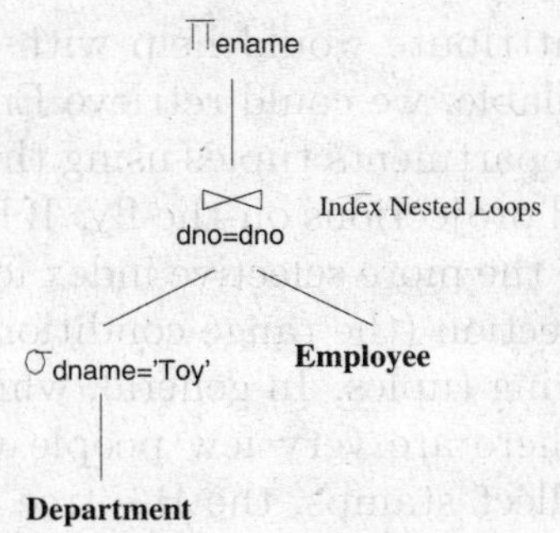

Figure 20.1 A Desirable Query Evaluation Plan

case we can retrieve Departments tuples that satisfy the selection on *dname* (by using the index on *dname*, as before), retrieve Employees tuples that satisfy the selection on *age* by using the index on *age*, and join these sets of tuples. Since the sets of tuples we join are small, they fit in memory and the join method is unimportant. This plan is likely to be somewhat poorer than using an index on *dno*, but it is a reasonable alternative. Therefore, if we have an index on *age* already (prompted by some other query in the workload), this variant of the sample query does not justify creating an index on the *dno* field of Employees.

Our next query involves a range selection:

```
SELECT E.ename, D.dname
FROM   Employees E, Departments D
WHERE  E.sal BETWEEN 10000 AND 20000
       AND E.hobby='Stamps' AND E.dno=D.dno
```

This query illustrates the use of the BETWEEN operator for expressing range selections. It is equivalent to the condition:

$10000 \leq$ E.sal AND E.sal ≤ 20000

The use of BETWEEN to express range conditions is recommended; it makes it easier for both the user and the optimizer to recognize both parts of the range selection.

Returning to the example query, both (nonjoin) selections are on the Employees relation. Therefore, it is clear that a plan in which Employees is the outer relation and Departments is the inner relation is the best, as in the previous query, and we should build a hash index on the *dno* attribute of Departments. But which index should we build on Employees? A B+ tree index on the *sal* attribute would help with the range selection, especially if it is clustered. A hash index on the *hobby* attribute would help with the equality selection. If one of these indexes is available, we could retrieve Employees tuples using this index, retrieve matching Departments tuples using the index on *dno*, and apply all remaining selections and projections on-the-fly. If both indexes are available, the optimizer would choose the more selective index for the given query; that is, it would consider which selection (the range condition on *salary* or the equality on *hobby*) has fewer qualifying tuples. In general, which index is more selective depends on the data. If there are very few people with salaries in the given range and many people collect stamps, the B+ tree index is best. Otherwise, the hash index on *hobby* is best.

If the query constants are known (as in our example), the selectivities can be estimated if statistics on the data are available. Otherwise, as a rule of thumb, an equality selection is likely to be more selective, and a reasonable decision would be to create a hash index on *hobby*. Sometimes, the query constants are not known—we might obtain a query by expanding a query on a view at run-time, or we might have a query in Dynamic SQL, which allows constants to be specified as *wild-card variables* (e.g., *%X*) and instantiated at run-time (see Sections 6.1.3 and 6.2). In this case, if the query is very important, we might choose to create a B+ tree index on *sal* and a hash index on *hobby* and leave the choice to be made by the optimizer at run-time.

20.4 CLUSTERING AND INDEXING

Clustered indexes can be especially important while accessing the inner relation in an index nested loops join. To understand the relationship between clustered indexes and joins, let us revisit our first example:

```
SELECT E.ename, D.mgr
FROM   Employees E, Departments D
WHERE  D.dname='Toy' AND E.dno=D.dno
```

We concluded that a good evaluation plan is to use an index on *dname* to retrieve Departments tuples satisfying the condition on *dname* and to find matching Employees tuples using an index on *dno*. Should these indexes be clustered? Given our assumption that the number of tuples satisfying *D.dname='Toy'* is likely to be small, we should build an unclustered index on *dname*. On the other hand, Employees is the inner relation in an index nested loops join and *dno* is not a candidate key. This situation is a strong argument that the index on the *dno* field of Employees should be clustered. In fact, because the join consists of repeatedly posing equality selections on the *dno* field of the inner relation, this type of query is a stronger justification for making the index on *dno* clustered than a simple selection query such as the previous selection on *hobby*. (Of course, factors such as selectivities and frequency of queries have to be taken into account as well.)

The following example, very similar to the previous one, illustrates how clustered indexes can be used for sort-merge joins:

```
SELECT E.ename, D.mgr
FROM   Employees E, Departments D
WHERE  E.hobby='Stamps' AND E.dno=D.dno
```

This query differs from the previous query in that the condition *E.hobby='Stamps'* replaces *D.dname='Toy'*. Based on the assumption that there are few employees in the Toy department, we chose indexes that would facilitate an indexed nested loops join with Departments as the outer relation. Now, let us suppose that many employees collect stamps. In this case, a block nested loops or sort-merge join might be more efficient. A sort-merge join can take advantage of a clustered B+ tree index on the *dno* attribute in Departments to retrieve tuples and thereby avoid sorting Departments. Note that an unclustered index is not useful—since all tuples are retrieved, performing one I/O per tuple is likely to be prohibitively expensive. If there is no index on the *dno* field of Employees, we could retrieve Employees tuples (possibly using an index on *hobby*, especially if the index is clustered), apply the selection *E.hobby='Stamps'* on-the-fly, and sort the qualifying tuples on *dno*.

As our discussion has indicated, when we retrieve tuples using an index, the impact of clustering depends on the number of retrieved tuples, that is, the number of tuples that satisfy the selection conditions that match the index. An unclustered index is just as good as a clustered index for a selection that retrieves a single tuple (e.g., an equality selection on a candidate key). As the number of retrieved tuples increases, the unclustered index quickly becomes more expensive than even a sequential scan of the entire relation. Although the sequential scan retrieves all tuples, each page is retrieved exactly once, whereas a page may be retrieved as often as the number of tuples it contains if an unclustered index is used. If blocked I/O is performed (as is common), the relative advantage of sequential scan versus an unclustered index increases further. (Blocked I/O also speeds up access using a clustered index, of course.)

We illustrate the relationship between the number of retrieved tuples, viewed as a percentage of the total number of tuples in the relation, and the cost of various access methods in Figure 20.2. We assume that the query is a selection on a single relation, for simplicity. (Note that this figure reflects the cost of writing out the result; otherwise, the line for sequential scan would be flat.)

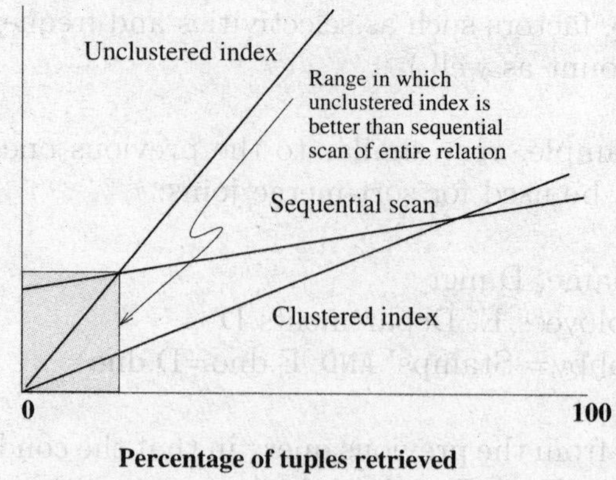

Figure 20.2 The Impact of Clustering

20.4.1 Co-clustering Two Relations

In our description of a typical database system architecture in Chapter 9, we explained how a relation is stored as a file of records. Although a file usually contains only the records of some one relation, some systems allow records from more than one relation to be stored in a single file. The database user can request that the records from two relations be interleaved physically in this manner. This data layout is sometimes referred to as **co-clustering** the two relations. We now discuss when co-clustering can be beneficial.

As an example, consider two relations with the following schemas:

Parts(*pid:* `integer`, *pname:* `string`, *cost:* `integer`, *supplierid:* `integer`)
Assembly(*partid:* `integer`, *componentid:* `integer`, *quantity:* `integer`)

In this schema the *componentid* field of Assembly is intended to be the *pid* of some part that is used as a component in assembling the part with *pid* equal to *partid*. Therefore, the Assembly table represents a 1:N relationship between parts and their subparts; a part can have many subparts, but each part is the subpart of at most one part. In the Parts table, *pid* is the key. For composite parts (those assembled from other parts, as indicated by the contents of Assembly), the *cost* field is taken to be the cost of assembling the part from its subparts.

Suppose that a frequent query is to find the (immediate) subparts of all parts supplied by a given supplier:

```
SELECT P.pid, A.componentid
FROM   Parts P, Assembly A
```

```
WHERE  P.pid = A.partid AND P.supplierid = 'Acme'
```

A good evaluation plan is to apply the selection condition on Parts and then retrieve matching Assembly tuples through an index on the *partid* field. Ideally, the index on *partid* should be clustered. This plan is reasonably good. However, if such selections are common and we want to optimize them further, we can *co-cluster* the two tables. In this approach, we store records of the two tables together, with each Parts record P followed by all the Assembly records A such that *P.pid* = *A.partid*. This approach improves on storing the two relations separately and having a clustered index on *partid* because it does not need an index lookup to find the Assembly records that match a given Parts record. Thus, for each selection query, we save a few (typically two or three) index page I/Os.

If we are interested in finding the immediate subparts of *all* parts (i.e., the preceding query with no selection on *supplierid*), creating a clustered index on *partid* and doing an index nested loops join with Assembly as the inner relation offers good performance. An even better strategy is to create a clustered index on the *partid* field of Assembly and the *pid* field of Parts, then do a sort-merge join, using the indexes to retrieve tuples in sorted order. This strategy is comparable to doing the join using a co-clustered organization, which involves just one scan of the set of tuples (of Parts and Assembly, which are stored together in interleaved fashion).

The real benefit of co-clustering is illustrated by the following query:

```
SELECT P.pid, A.componentid
FROM   Parts P, Assembly A
WHERE  P.pid = A.partid AND P.cost=10
```

Suppose that many parts have *cost* = 10. This query essentially amounts to a collection of queries in which we are given a Parts record and want to find matching Assembly records. If we have an index on the *cost* field of Parts, we can retrieve qualifying Parts tuples. For each such tuple, we have to use the index on Assembly to locate records with the given *pid*. The index access for Assembly is avoided if we have a co-clustered organization. (Of course, we still require an index on the *cost* attribute of Parts tuples.)

Such an optimization is especially important if we want to traverse several levels of the part-subpart hierarchy. For example, a common query is to find the total cost of a part, which requires us to repeatedly carry out joins of Parts and Assembly. Incidentally, if we do not know the number of levels in the hierarchy in advance, the number of joins varies and the query cannot be expressed in SQL. The query can be answered by embedding an SQL statement for the join inside an iterative host language program. How to express the query is orthogonal to our main point here, which is that co-clustering is especially beneficial when the join in question is carried out very frequently (either because it arises repeatedly in an important query such as finding total cost, or because the join query itself is asked frequently).

To summarize co-clustering:

- It can speed up joins, in particular key–foreign key joins corresponding to 1:N relationships.
- A sequential scan of either relation becomes slower. (In our example, since several Assembly tuples are stored in between consecutive Parts tuples, a scan of all Parts tuples becomes slower than if Parts tuples were stored separately. Similarly, a sequential scan of all Assembly tuples is also slower.)
- All inserts, deletes, and updates that alter record lengths become slower, thanks to the overheads involved in maintaining the clustering. (We do not discuss the implementation issues involved in co-clustering.)

20.5 INDEXES THAT ENABLE INDEX-ONLY PLANS

This section considers a number of queries for which we can find efficient plans that avoid retrieving tuples from one of the referenced relations; instead, these plans scan an associated index (which is likely to be much smaller). An index that is used (only) for index-only scans does *not* have to be clustered because tuples from the indexed relation are not retrieved.

This query retrieves the managers of departments with at least one employee:

```
SELECT D.mgr
FROM   Departments D, Employees E
WHERE  D.dno=E.dno
```

Observe that no attributes of Employees are retained. If we have an index on the *dno* field of Employees, the optimization of doing an index nested loops join using an index-only scan for the inner relation is applicable. Given this variant of the query, the correct decision is to build an unclustered index on the *dno* field of Employees, rather than a clustered index.

The next query takes this idea a step further:

```
SELECT D.mgr, E.eid
FROM   Departments D, Employees E
WHERE  D.dno=E.dno
```

If we have an index on the *dno* field of Employees, we can use it to retrieve Employees tuples during the join (with Departments as the outer relation), but unless the index is clustered, this approach is not be efficient. On the other hand, suppose that we have a B+ tree index on $\langle dno, eid \rangle$. Now all the information we need about an Employees tuple is contained in the data entry for this tuple in the index. We can use the index to find the first data entry with a given *dno*; all data entries with the same *dno* are stored together in the index. (Note that a hash index on the composite key $\langle dno, eid \rangle$ cannot be used to locate an entry with just a given *dno*!) We can therefore evaluate this query using an index nested loops join with Departments as the outer relation and an index-only scan of the inner relation.

20.6 TOOLS TO ASSIST IN INDEX SELECTION

The number of possible indexes to consider building is potentially very large: For each relation, we can potentially consider all possible subsets of attributes as an index key; we have to decide on the ordering of the attributes in the index; and we also have to decide which indexes should be clustered and which unclustered. Many large applications—for example enterprise resource planning systems—create tens of thousands of different relations, and manual tuning of such a large schema is a daunting endeavor.

The difficulty and importance of the index selection task motivated the development of tools that help database administrators select appropriate indexes for a given workload. The first generation of such **index tuning wizards**, or **index advisors**, were separate tools outside the database engine; they suggested indexes to build, given a workload of SQL queries. The main drawback of these systems was that they had to replicate the database query optimizer's cost model in the tuning tool to make sure that the optimizer would choose the same query evaluation plans as the design tool. Since query optimizers change from release to release of a commercial database system, considerable effort was needed to keep the tuning tool and the database optimizer synchronized. The most recent generation of tuning tools are integrated with the database engine and use the database query optimizer to estimate the cost of a workload given a set of indexes, avoiding duplication of the query optimizer's cost model into an external tool.

20.6.1 Automatic Index Selection

We call a set of indexes for a given database schema an **index configuration**. We assume that a query workload is a set of queries over a database schema where each query has a frequency of occurrence assigned to it. Given a database schema and a workload, the **cost of an index configuration** is the expected cost of running the queries in the workload given the index configuration — taking the different frequencies of queries in the workload into account. Given a database schema and a query workload, we can now define the problem of **automatic index selection** as finding an index configuration with minimal cost. As in query optimization, in practice our goal is to find a *good* index configuration rather than the true optimal configuration.

Why is automatic index selection a hard problem? Let us calculate the number of different indexes with c attributes, assuming that the table has n attributes. For the first attribute in the index, there are n choices, for the second attribute $n-1$, and thus for a c attribute index, there are overall $n \cdot (n-1) \cdots (n-c+1) = \frac{n!}{(n-c)!}$ different indexes possible. The total number of different indexes with up to c attributes is

$$\sum_{i=1}^{c} \frac{n!}{(n-i)!}.$$

For a table with 10 attributes, there are 10 different one-attribute indexes, 90 different two-attribute indexes, and 30240 different five-attribute indexes. For a complex workload involving hundreds of tables, the number of possible index configurations is clearly very large.

The efficiency of automatic index selection tools can be separated into two components: (1) the number of candidate index configurations considered, and (2) the number of optimizer calls necessary to evaluate the cost for a configuration. Note that reducing the search space of candidate indexes is analogous to restricting the search space of the query optimizer to left-deep plans. In many cases, the optimal plan is not left-deep, but among all left-deep plans there is usually a plan whose cost is close to the optimal plan.

We can easily reduce the time taken for automatic index selection by reducing the number of candidate index configurations, but the smaller the space of index configurations considered, the farther away the final index configuration is from the optimal index configuration. Therefore, different index tuning wizards prune the search space differently, for example, by considering only one- or two-attribute indexes.

20.6.2 How Do Index Tuning Wizards Work?

All index tuning wizards search a set of candidate indexes for an index configuration with lowest cost. Tools differ in the space of candidate index configurations they consider and how they search this space. We describe one representative algorithm; existing tools implement variants of this algorithm, but their implementations have the same basic structure.

The DB2 Index Advisor. The DB2 Index Advisor is a tool for automatic index recommendation given a workload. The workload is stored in the database system in a table called ADVISE_WORKLOAD. It is populated either (1) by SQL statements from the DB2 dynamic SQL statement cache, a cache for recently executed SQL statements, (2) with SQL statements from packages —groups of statically compiled SQL statements, or (3) with SQL statements from an online monitor called the Query Patroller. The DB2 Advisor allows the user to specify the maximum amount of disk space for new indexes and a maximum time for the computation of the recommended index configuration.

The DB2 Index Advisor consists of a program that intelligently searches a subset of index configurations. Given a candidate configuration, it calles the query optimizer for each query in the ADVISE_WORKLOAD table first in the RECOMMEND_INDEXES mode, where the optimizer recommends a set of indexes and stores them in the ADVISE_INDEXES table. In the EVALUATE_INDEXES mode, the optimizer evaluates the benefit of the index configuration for each query in the ADVISE-WORKLOAD table. The output of the index tuning step is are SQL DDL statements whose execution creates the recommended indexes.

The Microsoft SQL Server 2000 Index Tuning Wizard. Microsoft pioneered the implementation of a tuning wizard integrated with the database query optimizer. The Microsoft Tuning Wizard has three tuning modes that permit the user to trade off running time of the analysis and number of candidate index configurations examined: *fast*, *medium*, and *thorough*, with *fast* having the lowest running time and *thorough* examining the largest number of configurations. To further reduce the running time, the tool has a sampling mode in which the tuning wizard randomly samples queries from the input workload to speed up analysis. Other parameters include the maximum space allowed for the recommended indexes, the maximum number of attributes per index considered, and the tables on which indexes can be generated. The Microsoft Index Tuning Wizard also permits *table scaling*, where the user can specify an anticipated number of records for the tables involved in the workload. This allows users to plan for future growth of the tables.

Before we describe the index tuning algorithm, let us consider the problem of estimating the cost of a configuration. Note that it is not feasible to actually create the set of indexes in a candidate configuration and then optimize the query workload given the physical index configuration. Creation of even a single candidate configuration with several indexes might take hours for large databases and put considerable load on the database system itself. Since we want to examine a large number of possible candidate configurations, this approach is not feasible.

Therefore index tuning algorithms usually *simulate* the effect of indexes in a candidate configuration (unless such indexes already exist). Such **what-if** indexes look to the query optimizer like any other index and are taken into account when calculating the cost of the workload for a given configuration, but the creation of what-if indexes does not incur the overhead of actual index creation. Commercial database systems that support index tuning wizards using the database query optimizer have been extended with a module that permits the creation and deletion of what-if indexes with the necessary statistics about the indexes (that are used when estimating the cost of a query plan).

We now describe a representative index tuning algorithm. The algorithm proceeds in two steps, *candidate index selection* and *configuration enumeration*. In the first step, we select a set of candidate indexes to consider during the second step as building blocks for index configurations. Let us discuss these two steps in more detail.

Candidate Index Selection

We saw in the previous section that it is impossible to consider every possible index, due to the huge number of candidate indexes available for larger database schemas. One heuristic to prune the large space of possible indexes is to first tune each query in the workload independently and then select the union of the indexes selected in this first step as input to the second step.

For a query, let us introduce the notion of an indexable attribute, which is an attribute whose appearance in an index could change the cost of the query. An **indexable attribute** is an attribute on which the `WHERE`-part of the query has a condition (e.g., an equality predicate) or the attribute appears in a `GROUP BY` or `ORDER BY` clause of the SQL query. An **admissible index** for a query is an index that contains only indexable attributes in the query.

How do we select candidate indexes for an individual query? One approach is a basic enumeration of all indexes with up to k attributes. We start with all indexable attributes as single attribute candidate indexes, then add all combinations of two indexable attributes as candidate indexes, and repeat this procedure until a user-defined size threshold k. This procedure is obviously very expensive as we add overall $n + n \cdot (n-1) + \cdots + n \cdot (n-1) \cdots (n-k+1)$ candidate indexes, but it guarantees that the best index with up to k attributes is among the candidate indexes. The references at the end of this chapter contain pointers to faster (but less exhaustive) heuristical search algorithms.

Enumerating Index Configurations

In the second phase, we use the candidate indexes to enumerate index configurations. As in the first phase, we can exhaustively enumerate all index configurations up to size k, this time combining candidate indexes. As in the previous phase, more sophisticated search strategies are possible that cut down the number of configurations considered while still generating a final configuration of high quality (i.e., low execution cost for the final workload).

20.7 OVERVIEW OF DATABASE TUNING

After the initial phase of database design, actual use of the database provides a valuable source of detailed information that can be used to refine the initial design. Many of the original assumptions about the expected workload can be replaced by observed usage patterns; in general, some of the initial workload specification is validated, and some of it turns out to be wrong. Initial guesses about the size of data can be replaced with actual statistics from the system catalogs (although this information keeps changing as the system evolves). Careful monitoring of queries can reveal unexpected problems; for example, the optimizer may not be using some indexes as intended to produce good plans.

Continued database tuning is important to get the best possible performance. In this section, we introduce three kinds of tuning: *tuning indexes, tuning the conceptual schema,* and *tuning queries.* Our discussion of index selection also applies to index tuning decisions. Conceptual schema and query tuning are discussed further in Sections 20.8 and 20.9.

20.7.1 Tuning Indexes

The initial choice of indexes may be refined for one of several reasons. The simplest reason is that the observed workload reveals that some queries and updates considered important in the initial workload specification are not very frequent. The observed workload may also identify some new queries and updates that *are* important. The initial choice of indexes has to be reviewed in light of this new information. Some of the original indexes may be dropped and new ones added. The reasoning involved is similar to that used in the initial design.

It may also be discovered that the optimizer in a given system is not finding some of the plans that it was expected to. For example, consider the following query, which we discussed earlier:

```
SELECT D.mgr
FROM   Employees E, Departments D
WHERE  D.dname='Toy' AND E.dno=D.dno
```

A good plan here would be to use an index on *dname* to retrieve Departments tuples with *dname='Toy'* and to use an index on the *dno* field of Employees as the inner relation, using an index-only scan. Anticipating that the optimizer would find such a plan, we might have created an unclustered index on the *dno* field of Employees.

Now suppose queries of this form take an unexpectedly long time to execute. We can ask to see the plan produced by the optimizer. (Most commercial systems provide a simple command to do this.) If the plan indicates that an index-only scan is not being used, but that Employees tuples are being retrieved, we have to rethink our initial choice of index, given this revelation about our system's (unfortunate) limitations. An alternative to consider here would be to drop the unclustered index on the *dno* field of Employees and replace it with a clustered index.

Some other common limitations of optimizers are that they do not handle selections involving string expressions, arithmetic, or *null* values effectively. We discuss these points further when we consider query tuning in Section 20.9.

In addition to re-examining our choice of indexes, it pays to periodically reorganize some indexes. For example, a static index, such as an ISAM index, may have developed long overflow chains. Dropping the index and rebuilding it—if feasible, given the interrupted access to the indexed relation—can substantially improve access times through this index. Even for a dynamic structure such as a B+ tree, if the implementation does not merge pages on deletes, space occupancy can decrease considerably in some situations. This in turn makes the size of the index (in pages) larger than necessary, and could increase the height and therefore the access time. Rebuilding the index should be considered. Extensive updates to a clustered index might also lead to overflow pages being allocated, thereby decreasing the degree of clustering. Again, rebuilding the index may be worthwhile.

Finally, note that the query optimizer relies on statistics maintained in the system catalogs. These statistics are updated only when a special utility program is run; be sure to run the utility frequently enough to keep the statistics reasonably current.

20.7.2 Tuning the Conceptual Schema

In the course of database design, we may realize that our current choice of relation schemas does not enable us meet our performance objectives for the given workload with any (feasible) set of physical design choices. If so, we may have to redesign our conceptual schema (and re-examine physical design decisions affected by the changes we make).

We may realize that a redesign is necessary during the initial design process or later, after the system has been in use for a while. Once a database has been designed and populated with tuples, changing the conceptual schema requires a significant effort in terms of mapping the contents of the relations affected. Nonetheless, it may be necessary to revise the conceptual schema in light of experience with the system. (Such changes to the schema of an operational system are sometimes referred to as **schema evolution**.) We now consider the issues involved in conceptual schema (re)design from the point of view of performance.

The main point to understand is that *our choice of conceptual schema should be guided by a consideration of the queries and updates in our workload,* in addition to the issues of redundancy that motivate normalization (which we discussed in Chapter 19). Several options must be considered while tuning the conceptual schema:

- We may decide to settle for a 3NF design instead of a BCNF design.
- If there are two ways to decompose a given schema into 3NF or BCNF, our choice should be guided by the workload.
- Sometimes we might decide to further decompose a relation that is *already* in BCNF.
- In other situations, we might *denormalize.* That is, we might choose to replace a collection of relations obtained by a decomposition from a larger relation with the original (larger) relation, even though it suffers from some redundancy problems. Alternatively, we might choose to add some fields to certain relations to speed up some important queries, even if this leads to a redundant storage of some information (and, consequently, a schema that is in neither 3NF nor BCNF).

- This discussion of normalization has concentrated on the technique of *decomposition*, which amounts to vertical partitioning of a relation. Another technique to consider is *horizontal partitioning* of a relation, which would lead to having two relations with identical schemas. Note that we are not talking about physically partitioning the tuples of a single relation; rather, we want to create two distinct relations (possibly with different constraints and indexes on each).

Incidentally, when we redesign the conceptual schema, especially if we are tuning an existing database schema, it is worth considering whether we should create views to mask these changes from users for whom the original schema is more natural. We discuss the choices involved in tuning the conceptual schema in Section 20.8.

20.7.3 Tuning Queries and Views

If we notice that a query is running much slower than we expected, we have to examine the query carefully to find the problem. Some rewriting of the query, perhaps in conjunction with some index tuning, can often fix the problem. Similar tuning may be called for if queries on some view run slower than expected. We do not discuss view tuning separately; just think of queries on views as queries in their own right (after all, queries on views are expanded to account for the view definition before being optimized) and consider how to tune them.

When tuning a query, the first thing to verify is that the system uses the plan you expect it to use. Perhaps the system is not finding the best plan for a variety of reasons. Some common situations not handled efficiently by many optimizers follow:

- A selection condition involving *null* values.
- Selection conditions involving arithmetic or string expressions or conditions using the `OR` connective. For example, if we have a condition $E.age = 2*D.age$ in the `WHERE` clause, the optimizer may correctly utilize an available index on $E.age$ but fail to utilize an available index on $D.age$. Replacing the condition by $E.age/2 = D.age$ would reverse the situation.
- Inability to recognize a sophisticated plan such as an index-only scan for an aggregation query involving a `GROUP BY` clause. Of course, virtually no optimizer looks for plans outside the plan space described in Chapters 12 and 15, such as nonleft-deep join trees. So a good understanding of what an optimizer typically does is important. In addition, the more aware you are of a given system's strengths and limitations, the better off you are.

If the optimizer is not smart enough to find the best plan (using access methods and evaluation strategies supported by the DBMS), some systems allow users to guide the choice of a plan by providing hints to the optimizer; for example, users might be able to force the use of a particular index or choose the join order and join method. A user who wishes to guide optimization in this manner should have a thorough understanding of both optimization and the capabilities of the given DBMS. We discuss query tuning further in Section 20.9.

20.8 CHOICES IN TUNING THE CONCEPTUAL SCHEMA

We now illustrate the choices involved in tuning the conceptual schema through several examples using the following schemas:

Contracts(*cid:* `integer`, *supplierid:* `integer`, *projectid:* `integer`,
deptid: `integer`, *partid:* `integer`, *qty:* `integer`, *value:* `real`)
Departments(*did:* `integer`, *budget:* `real`, *annualreport:* `varchar`)
Parts(*pid:* `integer`, *cost:* `integer`)
Projects(*jid:* `integer`, *mgr:* `char(20)`)
Suppliers(*sid:* `integer`, *address:* `char(50)`)

For brevity, we often use the common convention of denoting attributes by a single character and denoting relation schemas by a sequence of characters. Consider the schema for the relation Contracts, which we denote as CSJDPQV, with each letter denoting an attribute. The meaning of a tuple in this relation is that the contract with *cid* C is an agreement that supplier S (with *sid* equal to *supplierid*) will supply Q items of part P (with *pid* equal to *partid*) to project J (with *jid* equal to *projectid*) associated with department D (with *deptid* equal to *did*), and that the value V of this contract is equal to *value*.[2]

There are two known integrity constraints with respect to Contracts. A project purchases a given part using a single contract; thus, there cannnot be two distinct contracts in which the same project buys the same part. This constraint is represented using the FD $JP \rightarrow C$. Also, a department purchases at most one part from any given supplier. This constraint is represented using the FD $SD \rightarrow P$. In addition, of course, the contract ID C is a key. The meaning of the other relations should be obvious, and we do not describe them further because we focus on the Contracts relation.

[2]If this schema seems complicated, note that real-life situations often call for considerably more complex schemas!

20.8.1 Settling for a Weaker Normal Form

Consider the Contracts relation. Should we decompose it into smaller relations? Let us see what normal form it is in. The candidate keys for this relation are C and JP. (C is given to be a key, and JP functionally determines C.) The only nonkey dependency is $SD \rightarrow P$, and P is a *prime* attribute because it is part of candidate key JP. Thus, the relation is not in BCNF—because there is a nonkey dependency—but it is in 3NF.

By using the dependency $SD \rightarrow P$ to guide the decomposition, we get the two schemas SDP and CSJDQV. This decomposition is lossless, but it is not dependency-preserving. However, by adding the relation scheme CJP, we obtain a lossless-join, dependency-preserving decomposition into BCNF. Using the guideline that such a decomposition into BCNF is good, we might decide to replace Contracts by three relations with schemas CJP, SDP, and CSJDQV.

However, suppose that the following query is very frequently asked: Find the number of copies Q of part P ordered in contract C. This query requires a join of the decomposed relations CJP and CSJDQV (or SDP and CSJDQV), whereas it can be answered directly using the relation Contracts. The added cost for this query could persuade us to settle for a 3NF design and not decompose Contracts further.

20.8.2 Denormalization

The reasons motivating us to settle for a weaker normal form may lead us to take an even more extreme step: deliberately introduce some redundancy. As an example, consider the Contracts relation, which is in 3NF. Now, suppose that a frequent query is to check that the value of a contract is less than the budget of the contracting department. We might decide to add a budget field B to Contracts. Since *did* is a key for Departments, we now have the dependency $D \rightarrow B$ in Contracts, which means Contracts is not in 3NF any more. Nonetheless, we might choose to stay with this design if the motivating query is sufficiently important. Such a decision is clearly subjective and comes at the cost of significant redundancy.

20.8.3 Choice of Decomposition

Consider the Contracts relation again. Several choices are possible for dealing with the redundancy in this relation:

- We can leave Contracts as it is and accept the redundancy associated with its being in 3NF rather than BCNF.

- We might decide that we want to avoid the anomalies resulting from this redundancy by decomposing Contracts into BCNF using one of the following methods:
  - We have a lossless-join decomposition into PartInfo with attributes SDP and ContractInfo with attributes CSJDQV. As noted previously, this decomposition is not dependency-preserving, and to make it so would require us to add a third relation CJP, whose sole purpose is to allow us to check the dependency $JP \rightarrow C$.
  - We could choose to replace Contracts by just PartInfo and ContractInfo even though this decomposition is not dependency-preserving.

Replacing Contracts by just PartInfo and ContractInfo does not prevent us from enforcing the constraint $JP \rightarrow C$; it only makes this more expensive. We could create an assertion in SQL-92 to check this constraint:

```
CREATE ASSERTION checkDep
CHECK      ( NOT EXISTS
           ( SELECT   *
           FROM       PartInfo PI, ContractInfo CI
           WHERE      PI.supplierid=CI.supplierid
                      AND PI.deptid=CI.deptid
           GROUP BY   CI.projectid, PI.partid
           HAVING     COUNT (cid) > 1 ) )
```

This assertion is expensive to evaluate because it involves a join followed by a sort (to do the grouping). In comparison, the system can check that JP is a primary key for table CJP by maintaining an index on JP. This difference in integrity-checking cost is the motivation for dependency-preservation. On the other hand, if updates are infrequent, this increased cost may be acceptable; therefore, we might choose not to maintain the table CJP (and quite likely, an index on it).

As another example illustrating decomposition choices, consider the Contracts relation again, and suppose that we also have the integrity constraint that a department uses a given supplier for at most one of its projects: $SPQ \rightarrow V$. Proceeding as before, we have a lossless-join decomposition of Contracts into SDP and CSJDQV. Alternatively, we could begin by using the dependency $SPQ \rightarrow V$ to guide our decomposition, and replace Contracts with SPQV and CSJDPQ. We can then decompose CSJDPQ, guided by $SD \rightarrow P$, to obtain SDP and CSJDQ.

We now have two alternative lossless-join decompositions of Contracts into BCNF, neither of which is dependency-preserving. The first alternative is to replace Contracts with the relations SDP and CSJDQV. The second alternative is to replace it with SPQV, SDP, and CSJDQ. The addition of CJP makes the second decomposition (but not the first) dependency-preserving. Again, the cost of maintaining the three relations CJP, SPQV, and CSJDQ (versus just CSJDQV) may lead us to choose the first alternative. In this case, enforcing the given FDs becomes more expensive. We might consider not enforcing them, but we then risk a violation of the integrity of our data.

20.8.4 Vertical Partitioning of BCNF Relations

Suppose that we have decided to decompose Contracts into SDP and CSJDQV. These schemas are in BCNF, and there is no reason to decompose them further from a normalization standpoint. However, suppose that the following queries are very frequent:

- Find the contracts held by supplier S.
- Find the contracts placed by department D.

These queries might lead us to decompose CSJDQV into CS, CD, and CJQV. The decomposition is lossless, of course, and the two important queries can be answered by examining much smaller relations. Another reason to consider such a decomposition is concurrency control *hot spots.* If these queries are common, and the most common updates involve changing the quantity of products (and the value) involved in contracts, the decomposition improves performance by reducing lock contention. Exclusive locks are now set mostly on the CJQV table, and reads on CS and CD do not conflict with these locks.

Whenever we decompose a relation, we have to consider which queries the decomposition might adversely affect, especially if the only motivation for the decomposition is improved performance. For example, if another important query is to find the total value of contracts held by a supplier, it would involve a join of the decomposed relations CS and CJQV. In this situation, we might decide against the decomposition.

20.8.5 Horizontal Decomposition

Thus far, we have essentially considered how to replace a relation with a collection of vertical decompositions. Sometimes, it is worth considering whether to replace a relation with two relations that have the same attributes as the original relation, each containing a subset of the tuples in the original. Intuitively, this technique is useful when different subsets of tuples are queried in very distinct ways.

For example, different rules may govern large contracts, which are defined as contracts with values greater than 10,000. (Perhaps, such contracts have to be awarded through a bidding process.) This constraint could lead to a number of queries in which Contracts tuples are selected using a condition of the form $value > 10,000$. One way to approach this situation is to build a clustered B+ tree index on the *value* field of Contracts. Alternatively, we could replace Contracts with two relations called LargeContracts and SmallContracts, with the obvious meaning. If this query is the only motivation for the index, horizontal decomposition offers all the benefits of the index without the overhead of index maintenance. This alternative is especially attractive if other important queries on Contracts also require clustered indexes (on fields other than *value*).

If we replace Contracts by two relations LargeContracts and SmallContracts, we could mask this change by defining a view called Contracts:

```
CREATE VIEW Contracts(cid, supplierid, projectid, deptid, partid, qty, value)
     AS ((SELECT *
         FROM   LargeContracts)
         UNION
         (SELECT  *
         FROM   SmallContracts))
```

However, any query that deals solely with LargeContracts should be expressed directly on LargeContracts and not on the view. Expressing the query on the view Contracts with the selection condition $value > 10,000$ is equivalent to expressing the query on LargeContracts but less efficient. This point is quite general: Although we can mask changes to the conceptual schema by adding view definitions, users concerned about performance have to be aware of the change.

As another example, if Contracts had an additional field *year* and queries typically dealt with the contracts in some one year, we might choose to partition Contracts by year. Of course, queries that involved contracts from more than one year might require us to pose queries against each of the decomposed relations.

20.9 CHOICES IN TUNING QUERIES AND VIEWS

The first step in tuning a query is to understand the plan used by the DBMS to evaluate the query. Systems usually provide some facility for identifying the plan used to evaluate a query. Once we understand the plan selected by the system, we can consider how to improve performance. We can consider a different choice of indexes or perhaps co-clustering two relations for join queries, guided by our understanding of the old plan and a better plan that we want the DBMS to use. The details are similar to the initial design process.

One point worth making is that before creating new indexes we should consider whether rewriting the query achieves acceptable results with existing indexes. For example, consider the following query with an OR connective:

```
SELECT E.dno
FROM   Employees E
WHERE  E.hobby='Stamps' OR E.age=10
```

If we have indexes on both *hobby* and *age*, we can use these indexes to retrieve the necessary tuples, but an optimizer might fail to recognize this opportunity. The optimizer might view the conditions in the WHERE clause as a whole as not matching either index, do a sequential scan of Employees, and apply the selections on-the-fly. Suppose we rewrite the query as the union of two queries, one with the clause WHERE *E.hobby='Stamps'* and the other with the clause WHERE *E.age=10*. Now each query is answered efficiently with the aid of the indexes on *hobby* and *age*.

We should also consider rewriting the query to avoid some expensive operations. For example, including DISTINCT in the SELECT clause leads to duplicate elimination, which can be costly. Thus, we should omit DISTINCT whenever possible. For example, for a query on a single relation, we can omit DISTINCT whenever either of the following conditions holds:

- We do not care about the presence of duplicates.
- The attributes mentioned in the SELECT clause include a candidate key for the relation.

Sometimes a query with GROUP BY and HAVING can be replaced by a query without these clauses, thereby eliminating a sort operation. For example, consider:

```
SELECT   MIN (E.age)
FROM     Employees E
GROUP BY E.dno
HAVING   E.dno=102
```

This query is equivalent to

```
SELECT   MIN (E.age)
FROM     Employees E
WHERE    E.dno=102
```

Complex queries are often written in steps, using a temporary relation. We can usually rewrite such queries without the temporary relation to make them run faster. Consider the following query for computing the average salary of departments managed by Robinson:

```
SELECT    *
INTO      Temp
FROM      Employees E, Departments D
WHERE     E.dno=D.dno AND D.mgrname='Robinson'

SELECT    T.dno, AVG (T.sal)
FROM      Temp T
GROUP BY  T.dno
```

This query can be rewritten as

```
SELECT    E.dno, AVG (E.sal)
FROM      Employees E, Departments D
WHERE     E.dno=D.dno AND D.mgrname='Robinson'
GROUP BY  E.dno
```

The rewritten query does not materialize the intermediate relation Temp and is therefore likely to be faster. In fact, the optimizer may even find a very efficient index-only plan that never retrieves Employees tuples if there is a composite B+ tree index on $\langle dno, sal \rangle$. This example illustrates a general observation: *By rewriting queries to avoid unnecessary temporaries, we not only avoid creating the temporary relations, we also open up more optimization possibilities for the optimizer to explore.*

In some situations, however, if the optimizer is unable to find a good plan for a complex query (typically a nested query with correlation), it may be worthwhile to rewrite the query using temporary relations to guide the optimizer toward a good plan.

In fact, nested queries are a common source of inefficiency because many optimizers deal poorly with them, as discussed in Section 15.5. Whenever possible, it is better to rewrite a nested query without nesting and a correlated query without correlation. As already noted, a good reformulation of the query may require us to introduce new, temporary relations, and techniques to do so systematically (ideally, to be done by the optimizer) have been widely studied. Often though, it is possible to rewrite nested queries without nesting or the use of temporary relations, as illustrated in Section 15.5.

20.10 IMPACT OF CONCURRENCY

In a system with many concurrent users, several additional points must be considered. Transactions obtain *locks* on the pages they access, and other transactions may be blocked waiting for locks on objects they wish to access.

We observed in Section 16.5 that blocking delays must be minimized for good performance and identified two specific ways to reduce blocking:

- Reducing the time that transactions hold locks.
- Reducing hot spots.

We now discuss techniques for achieving these goals.

20.10.1 Reducing Lock Durations

Delay Lock Requests: Tune transactions by writing to local program variables and deferring changes to the database until the end of the transaction. This delays the acquisition of the corresponding locks and reduces the time the locks are held.

Make Transactions Faster: The sooner a transaction completes, the sooner its locks are released. We have already discussed several ways to speed up queries and updates (e.g., tuning indexes, rewriting queries). In addition, a careful partitioning of the tuples in a relation and its associated indexes across a collection of disks can significantly improve concurrent access. For example, if we have the relation on one disk and an index on another, accesses to the index can proceed without interfering with accesses to the relation, at least at the level of disk reads.

Replace Long Transactions by Short Ones: Sometimes, just too much work is done within a transaction, and it takes a long time and holds locks a long time. Consider rewriting the transaction as two or more smaller transactions; holdable cursors (see Section 6.1.2) can be helpful in doing this. The advantage is that each new transaction completes quicker and releases locks sooner. The disadvantage is that the original list of operations is no longer executed atomically, and the application code must deal with situations in which one or more of the new transactions fail.

Build a Warehouse: Complex queries can hold shared locks for a long time. Often, however, these queries involve statistical analysis of business trends and it is acceptable to run them on a copy of the data that is a little out of date. This led to the popularity of *data warehouses*, which are databases that complement the operational database by maintaining a copy of data used in complex queries (Chapter 25). Running these queries against the warehouse relieves the burden of long-running queries from the operational database.

Consider a Lower Isolation Level: In many situations, such as queries generating aggregate information or statistical summaries, we can use a lower SQL isolation level such as `REPEATABLE READ` or `READ COMMITTED` (Section 16.6). Lower isolation levels incur lower locking overheads, and the application programmer must make good design trade-offs.

20.10.2 Reducing Hot Spots

Delay Operations on Hot Spots: We already discussed the value of delaying lock requests. Obviously, this is especially important for requests involving frequently used objects.

Optimize Access Patterns: The *pattern* of updates to a relation can also be significant. For example, if tuples are inserted into the Employees relation in *eid* order and we have a B+ tree index on *eid*, each insert goes to the last leaf page of the B+ tree. This leads to hot spots along the path from the root to the rightmost leaf page. Such considerations may lead us to choose a hash index over a B+ tree index or to index on a different field. Note that this pattern of access leads to poor performance for ISAM indexes as well, since the last leaf page becomes a hot spot. This is not a problem for hash indexes because the hashing process randomizes the bucket into which a record is inserted.

Partition Operations on Hot Spots: Consider a data entry transaction that appends new records to a file (e.g., inserts into a table stored as a heap file). Instead of appending records one-per-transaction and obtaining a lock on the last page for each record, we can replace the transaction by several other transactions, each of which writes records to a local file and periodically appends a batch of records to the main file. While we do more work overall, this reduces the lock contention on the last page of the original file.

As a further illustration of partitioning, suppose we track the number of records inserted in a counter. Instead of updating this counter once per record, the preceding approach results in updating several counters and periodically updating the main counter. This idea can be adapted to many uses of counters, with varying degrees of effort. For example, consider a counter that tracks the number of reservations, with the rule that a new reservation is allowed only if the counter is below a maximum value. We can replace this by three counters, each with one-third the original maximum threshold, and three transactions that use these counters rather than the original. We obtain greater concurrency, but have to deal with the case where one of the counters is at the maximum value but some other counter can still be incremented. Thus, the price of greater concurrency is increased complexity in the logic of the application code.

Choice of Index: If a relation is updated frequently, B+ tree indexes can become a concurrency control bottleneck, because all accesses through the index must go through the root. Thus, the root and index pages just below it can become hot spots. If the DBMS uses specialized locking protocols for tree indexes, and in particular, sets fine-granularity locks, this problem is greatly alleviated. Many current systems use such techniques.

Nonetheless, this consideration may lead us to choose an ISAM index in some situations. Because the index levels of an ISAM index are static, we need not obtain locks on these pages; only the leaf pages need to be locked. An ISAM index may be preferable to a B+ tree index, for example, if frequent updates occur but we expect the relative distribution of records and the number (and size) of records with a given range of search key values to stay approximately the same. In this case the ISAM index offers a lower locking overhead (and reduced contention for locks), and the distribution of records is such that few overflow pages are created.

Hashed indexes do not create such a concurrency bottleneck, unless the data distribution is very skewed and many data items are concentrated in a few buckets. In this case, the directory entries for these buckets can become a hot spot.

20.11 CASE STUDY: THE INTERNET SHOP

Revisiting our running case study, DBDudes considers the expected workload for the B&N bookstore. The owner of the bookstore expects most of his customers to search for books by ISBN number before placing an order. Placing an order involves inserting one record into the Orders table and inserting one or more records into the Orderlists relation. If a sufficient number of books is available, a shipment is prepared and a value for the *ship_date* in the Orderlists relation is set. In addition, the available quantities of books in stock changes all the time, since orders are placed that decrease the quantity available and new books arrive from suppliers and increase the quantity available.

The DBDudes team begins by considering searches for books by ISBN. Since *isbn* is a key, an equality query on *isbn* returns at most one record. Therefore, to speed up queries from customers who look for books with a given ISBN, DBDudes decides to build an unclustered hash index on *isbn*.

Next, it considers updates to book quantities. To update the *qty in stock* value for a book, we must first search for the book by ISBN; the index on *isbn* speeds this up. Since the *qty in stock* value for a book is updated quite frequently, DBDudes also considers partitioning the Books relation vertically into the following two relations:

BooksQty(*isbn*, *qty*)
BookRest(*isbn*, *title*, *author*, *price*, *year published*)

Unfortunately, this vertical partitioning slows down another very popular query: Equality search on ISBN to retrieve all information about a book now requires a join between BooksQty and BooksRest. So DBDudes decides not to vertically partition Books.

DBDudes thinks it is likely that customers will also want to search for books by title and by author, and decides to add unclustered hash indexes on *title* and *author*—these indexes are inexpensive to maintain because the set of books is rarely changed even though the quantity in stock for a book changes often.

Next, DBDudes considers the Customers relation. A customer is first identified by the unique customer identifaction number. So the most common queries on Customers are equality queries involving the customer identification number, and DBDudes decides to build a clustered hash index on *cid* to achieve maximum speed for this query.

Moving on to the Orders relation, DBDudes sees that it is involved in two queries: insertion of new orders and retrieval of existing orders. Both queries involve the *ordernum* attribute as search key and so DBDudes decides to build an index on it. What type of index should this be—a B+ tree or a hash index? Since order numbers are assigned sequentially and correspond to the order date, sorting by *ordernum* effectively sorts by order date as well. So DBDudes decides to build a clustered B+ tree index on *ordernum*. Although the operational requirements mentioned until now favor neither a B+ tree nor a hash index, B&N will probably want to monitor daily activities and the clustered B+ tree is a better choice for such range queries. Of course, this means that retrieving all orders for a given customer could be expensive for customers with many orders, since clustering by *ordernum* precludes clustering by other attributes, such as *cid*.

The Orderlists relation involves mostly insertions, with an occasional update of a shipment date or a query to list all components of a given order. If Orderlists is kept sorted on *ordernum*, all insertions are appends at the end of the relation and thus very efficient. A clustered B+ tree index on *ordernum* maintains this sort order and also speeds up retrieval of all items for a given order. To update a shipment date, we need to search for a tuple by *ordernum* and *isbn*. The index on *ordernum* helps here as well. Although an index on ⟨*ordernum, isbn*⟩ would be better for this purpose, insertions would not be as efficient as with an index on just *ordernum*; DBDudes therefore decides to index Orderlists on just *ordernum*.

20.11.1 Tuning the Database

Several months after the launch of the B&N site, DBDudes is called in and told that customer enquiries about pending orders are being processed very slowly. B&N has become very successful, and the Orders and Orderlists tables have grown huge.

Thinking further about the design, DBDudes realizes that there are two types of orders: *completed orders*, for which all books have already shipped, and *partially completed orders*, for which some books are yet to be shipped. Most customer requests to look up an order involve partially completed orders, which are a small fraction of all orders. DBDudes therefore decides to horizontally partition both the Orders table and the Orderlists table by *ordernum*. This results in four new relations: NewOrders, OldOrders, NewOrderlists, and OldOrderlists.

An order and its components are always in exactly one pair of relations—and we can determine which pair, old or new, by a simple check on *ordernum*—and queries involving that order can always be evaluated using only the relevant relations. Some queries are now slower, such as those asking for all of a customer's orders, since they require us to search two sets of relations. However, these queries are infrequent and their performance is acceptable.

20.12 DBMS BENCHMARKING

Thus far, we considered how to improve the design of a database to obtain better performance. As the database grows, however, the underlying DBMS may no longer be able to provide adequate performance, even with the best possible design, and we have to consider upgrading our system, typically by buying faster hardware and additional memory. We may also consider migrating our database to a new DBMS.

When evaluating DBMS products, performance is an important consideration. A DBMS is a complex piece of software, and different vendors may target their systems toward different market segments by putting more effort into optimizing certain parts of the system or choosing different system designs. For example, some systems are designed to run complex queries efficiently, while others are designed to run many simple transactions per second. Within each category of systems, there are many competing products. To assist users in choosing a DBMS that is well suited to their needs, several **performance benchmarks** have been developed. These include benchmarks for measuring the performance of a certain class of applications (e.g., the TPC benchmarks) and benchmarks for measuring how well a DBMS performs various operations (e.g., the Wisconsin benchmark).

Benchmarks should be portable, easy to understand, and scale naturally to larger problem instances. They should measure *peak performance* (e.g., *transactions per second*, or *tps*) as well as *price/performance ratios* (e.g., \$/*tps*) for typical workloads in a given application domain. The Transaction Processing Council (TPC) was created to define benchmarks for transaction processing and database systems. Other well-known benchmarks have been proposed by academic researchers and industry organizations. Benchmarks that are proprietary to a given vendor are not very useful for comparing different systems (although they may be useful in determining how well a given system would handle a particular workload).

20.12.1 Well-Known DBMS Benchmarks

Online Transaction Processing Benchmarks: The TPC-A and TPC-B benchmarks constitute the standard definitions of the *tps* and \$/*tps* measures. TPC-A measures the performance and price of a computer network in addition to the DBMS, whereas the TPC-B benchmark considers the DBMS by itself. These benchmarks involve a simple transaction that updates three data records, from three different tables, and appends a record to a fourth table. A number of details (e.g., transaction arrival distribution, interconnect method, system properties) are rigorously specified, ensuring that results for different systems can be meaningfully compared. The TPC-C benchmark is a more complex suite of transactional tasks than TPC-A and TPC-B. It models a warehouse that tracks items supplied to customers and involves five types of transactions. Each TPC-C transaction is much more expensive than a TPC-A or TPC-B transaction, and TPC-C exercises a much wider range of system capabilities, such as use of secondary indexes and transaction aborts. It has more or less completely replaced TPC-A and TPC-B as the standard transaction processing benchmark.

Query Benchmarks: The Wisconsin benchmark is widely used for measuring the performance of simple relational queries. The Set Query benchmark measures the performance of a suite of more complex queries, and the AS^3AP benchmark measures the performance of a mixed workload of transactions, relational queries, and utility functions. The TPC-D benchmark is a suite of complex SQL queries intended to be representative of the decision-support application domain. The OLAP Council also developed a benchmark for complex decision-support queries, including some queries that cannot be expressed easily in SQL; this is intended to measure systems for *online analytic processing (OLAP)*, which we discuss in Chapter 25, rather than traditional SQL systems. The Sequoia 2000 benchmark is designed to compare DBMS support for geographic information systems.

Object-Database Benchmarks: The 001 and 007 benchmarks measure the performance of object-oriented database systems. The Bucky benchmark measures the performance of object-relational database systems. (We discuss object-database systems in Chapter 23.)

20.12.2 Using a Benchmark

Benchmarks should be used with a good understanding of what they are designed to measure and the application environment in which a DBMS is to be used. When you use benchmarks to guide your choice of a DBMS, keep the following guidelines in mind:

- **How Meaningful is a Given Benchmark?** Benchmarks that try to distill performance into a single number can be overly simplistic. A DBMS is a complex piece of software used in a variety of applications. A good benchmark should have a suite of tasks that are carefully chosen to cover a particular application domain and test DBMS features important for that domain.

- **How Well Does a Benchmark Reflect Your Workload?** Consider your expected workload and compare it with the benchmark. Give more weight to the performance of those benchmark tasks (i.e., queries and updates) that are similar to important tasks in your workload. Also consider how benchmark numbers are measured. For example, elapsed time for individual queries might be misleading if considered in a multiuser setting: A system may have higher elapsed times because of slower I/O. On a multiuser workload, given sufficient disks for parallel I/O, such a system might outperform a system with a lower elapsed time.

- **Create Your Own Benchmark:** Vendors often tweak their systems in ad hoc ways to obtain good numbers on important benchmarks. To counter this, create your own benchmark by modifying standard benchmarks slightly or by replacing the tasks in a standard benchmark with similar tasks from your workload.

20.13 REVIEW QUESTIONS

Answers to the review questions can be found in the listed sections.

- What are the components of a workload description? **(Section 20.1.1)**
- What decisions need to be made during physical design? **(Section 20.1.2)**
- Describe six high-level guidelines for index selection. **(Section 20.2)**
- When should we create clustered indexes? **(Section 20.4)**
- What is co-clustering, and when should we use it? **(Section 20.4.1)**
- What is an index-only plan, and how do we create indexes for index-only plans? **(Section 20.5)**
- Why is automatic index tuning a hard problem? Give an example. **(Section 20.6.1)**
- Give an example of one algorithm for automatic index tuning. **(Section 20.6.2)**
- Why is database tuning important? **(Section 20.7)**
- How do we tune indexes, the conceptual schema, and queries and views? **(Sections 20.7.1 to 20.7.3)**
- What are our choices in tuning the conceptual schema? What are the following techniques and when should we apply them: settling for a weaker normal form, denormalization, and horizontal and vertiacal decompositions. **(Section 20.8)**
- What choices do we have in tuning queries and views? **(Section 20.9)**
- What is the impact of locking on database performance? How can we reduce lock contention and hot spots? **(Section 20.10)**
- Why do we have standardized database benchmarks, and what common metrics are used to evaluate database systems? Can you describe a few popular database benchmarks? **(Section 20.12)**

EXERCISES

Exercise 20.1 Consider the following BCNF schema for a portion of a simple corporate database (type information is not relevant to this question and is omitted):

Emp (*eid*, *ename, addr, sal, age, yrs, deptid*)
Dept (*did*, *dname, floor, budget*)

Suppose you know that the following queries are the six most common queries in the workload for this corporation and that all six are roughly equivalent in frequency and importance:

- List the id, name, and address of employees in a user-specified age range.
- List the id, name, and address of employees who work in the department with a user-specified department name.
- List the id and address of employees with a user-specified employee name.
- List the overall average salary for employees.
- List the average salary for employees of each age; that is, for each age in the database, list the age and the corresponding average salary.
- List all the department information, ordered by department floor numbers.

1. Given this information, and assuming that these queries are more important than any updates, design a physical schema for the corporate database that will give good performance for the expected workload. In particular, decide which attributes will be indexed and whether each index will be a clustered index or an unclustered index. Assume that B+ tree indexes are the only index type supported by the DBMS and that both single- and multiple-attribute keys are permitted. Specify your physical design by identifying the attributes you recommend indexing on via clustered or unclustered B+ trees.
2. Redesign the physical schema assuming that the set of important queries is changed to be the following:
   - List the id and address of employees with a user-specified employee name.
   - List the overall maximum salary for employees.
   - List the average salary for employees by department; that is, for each *deptid* value, list the *deptid* value and the average salary of employees in that department.
   - List the sum of the budgets of all departments by floor; that is, for each floor, list the floor and the sum.
   - Assume that this workload is to be tuned with an automatic index tuning wizard. Outline the main steps in the execution of the index tuning algorithm and the set of candidate configurations that would be considered.

Exercise 20.2 Consider the following BCNF relational schema for a portion of a university database (type information is not relevant to this question and is omitted):

Prof(*ssno*, *pname, office, age, sex, specialty, dept_did*)
Dept(*did*, *dname, budget, num_majors, chair_ssno*)

Suppose you know that the following queries are the five most common queries in the workload for this university and that all five are roughly equivalent in frequency and importance:

- List the names, ages, and offices of professors of a user-specified sex (male or female) who have a user-specified research specialty (e.g., *recursive query processing*). Assume that the university has a diverse set of faculty members, making it very uncommon for more than a few professors to have the same research specialty.
- List all the department information for departments with professors in a user-specified age range.
- List the department id, department name, and chairperson name for departments with a user-specified number of majors.

- List the lowest budget for a department in the university.
- List all the information about professors who are department chairpersons.

These queries occur much more frequently than updates, so you should build whatever indexes you need to speed up these queries. However, you should not build any unnecessary indexes, as updates will occur (and would be slowed down by unnecessary indexes). Given this information, design a physical schema for the university database that will give good performance for the expected workload. In particular, decide which attributes should be indexed and whether each index should be a clustered index or an unclustered index. Assume that both B+ trees and hashed indexes are supported by the DBMS and that both single- and multiple-attribute index search keys are permitted.

1. Specify your physical design by identifying the attributes you recommend indexing on, indicating whether each index should be clustered or unclustered and whether it should be a B+ tree or a hashed index.
2. Assume that this workload is to be tuned with an automatic index tuning wizard. Outline the main steps in the algorithm and the set of candidate configurations considered.
3. Redesign the physical schema, assuming that the set of important queries is changed to be the following:
   - List the number of different specialties covered by professors in each department, by department.
   - Find the department with the fewest majors.
   - Find the youngest professor who is a department chairperson.

Exercise 20.3 Consider the following BCNF relational schema for a portion of a company database (type information is not relevant to this question and is omitted):

Project(*pno, proj_name, proj_base_dept, proj_mgr, topic, budget*)
Manager(*mid, mgr_name, mgr_dept, salary, age, sex*)

Note that each project is based in some department, each manager is employed in some department, and the manager of a project need not be employed in the same department (in which the project is based). Suppose you know that the following queries are the five most common queries in the workload for this university and all five are roughly equivalent in frequency and importance:

- List the names, ages, and salaries of managers of a user-specified sex (male or female) working in a given department. You can assume that, while there are many departments, each department contains very few project managers.
- List the names of all projects with managers whose ages are in a user-specified range (e.g., younger than 30).
- List the names of all departments such that a manager in this department manages a project based in this department.
- List the name of the project with the lowest budget.
- List the names of all managers in the same department as a given project.

These queries occur much more frequently than updates, so you should build whatever indexes you need to speed up these queries. However, you should not build any unnecessary indexes, as updates will occur (and would be slowed down by unnecessary indexes). Given this information, design a physical schema for the company database that will give good performance for the expected workload. In particular, decide which attributes should be indexed and whether each index should be a clustered index or an unclustered index. Assume that both B+ trees and hashed indexes are supported by the DBMS, and that both single- and multiple-attribute index keys are permitted.

1. Specify your physical design by identifying the attributes you recommend indexing on, indicating whether each index should be clustered or unclustered and whether it should be a B+ tree or a hashed index.
2. Assume that this workload is to be tuned with an automatic index tuning wizard. Outline the main steps in the algorithm and the set of candidate configurations considered.
3. Redesign the physical schema assuming the set of important queries is changed to be the following:
   - Find the total of the budgets for projects managed by each manager; that is, list *proj_mgr* and the total of the budgets of projects managed by that manager, for all values of *proj_mgr*.
   - Find the total of the budgets for projects managed by each manager but only for managers who are in a user-specified age range.
   - Find the number of male managers.
   - Find the average age of managers.

Exercise 20.4 The Globetrotters Club is organized into chapters. The president of a chapter can never serve as the president of any other chapter, and each chapter gives its president some salary. Chapters keep moving to new locations, and a new president is elected when (and only when) a chapter moves. This data is stored in a relation *G(C,S,L,P)*, where the attributes are chapters (C), salaries (S), locations (L), and presidents (P). Queries of the following form are frequently asked, and you *must* be able to answer them without computing a join: "Who was the president of chapter X when it was in location Y?"

1. List the FDs that are given to hold over G.
2. What are the candidate keys for relation G?
3. What normal form is the schema G in?
4. Design a good database schema for the club. (Remember that your design *must* satisfy the stated query requirement!)
5. What normal form is your good schema in? Give an example of a query that is likely to run slower on this schema than on the relation G.
6. Is there a lossless-join, dependency-preserving decomposition of G into BCNF?
7. Is there ever a good reason to accept something less than 3NF when designing a schema for a relational database? Use this example, if necessary adding further constraints, to illustrate your answer.

Exercise 20.5 Consider the following BCNF relation, which lists the ids, types (e.g., nuts or bolts), and costs of various parts, along with the number available or in stock:

Parts (<u>*pid*</u>, *pname, cost, num_avail*)

You are told that the following two queries are extremely important:

- Find the total number available by part type, for all types. (That is, the sum of the *num_avail* value of all nuts, the sum of the *num_avail* value of all bolts, and so forth)
- List the *pids* of parts with the highest cost.

1. Describe the physical design that you would choose for this relation. That is, what kind of a file structure would you choose for the set of Parts records, and what indexes would you create?
2. Suppose your customers subsequently complain that performance is still not satisfactory (given the indexes and file organization you chose for the Parts relation in response to the previous question). Since you cannot afford to buy new hardware or software, you have to consider a schema redesign. Explain how you would try to obtain better performance by describing the schema for the relation(s) that you would use and your choice of file organizations and indexes on these relations.
3. How would your answers to the two questions change, if at all, if your system did not support indexes with multiple-attribute search keys?

Exercise 20.6 Consider the following BCNF relations, which describe employees and the departments they work in:

Emp (<u>*eid*</u>, *sal, did*)
Dept (<u>*did*</u>, *location, budget*)

You are told that the following queries are extremely important:

- Find the location where a user-specified employee works.
- Check whether the budget of a department is greater than the salary of each employee in that department.

1. Describe the physical design you would choose for this relation. That is, what kind of a file structure would you choose for these relations, and what indexes would you create?
2. Suppose that your customers subsequently complain that performance is still not satisfactory (given the indexes and file organization that you chose for the relations in response to the previous question). Since you cannot afford to buy new hardware or software, you have to consider a schema redesign. Explain how you would try to obtain better performance by describing the schema for the relation(s) that you would use and your choice of file organizations and indexes on these relations.
3. Suppose that your database system has very inefficient implementations of index structures. What kind of a design would you try in this case?

Exercise 20.7 Consider the following BCNF relations, which describe departments in a company and employees:

Dept(<u>*did*</u>, *dname, location, managerid*)
Emp(<u>*eid*</u>, *sal*)

You are told that the following queries are extremely important:

- List the names and ids of managers for each department in a user-specified location, in alphabetical order by department name.
- Find the average salary of employees who manage departments in a user-specified location. You can assume that no one manages more than one department.

1. Describe the file structures and indexes that you would choose.
2. You subsequently realize that updates to these relations are frequent. Because indexes incur a high overhead, can you think of a way to improve performance on these queries without using indexes?

Exercise 20.8 For each of the following queries, identify one possible reason why an optimizer might not find a good plan. Rewrite the query so that a good plan is likely to be found. Any available indexes or known constraints are listed before each query; assume that the relation schemas are consistent with the attributes referred to in the query.

1. An index is available on the *age* attribute:

```
SELECT E.dno
FROM   Employee E
WHERE  E.age=20 OR E.age=10
```

2. A B+ tree index is available on the *age* attribute:

```
SELECT E.dno
FROM   Employee E
WHERE  E.age<20 AND E.age>10
```

3. An index is available on the *age* attribute:

```
SELECT E.dno
FROM   Employee E
WHERE  2*E.age<20
```

4. No index is available:

```
SELECT DISTINCT *
FROM   Employee E
```

5. No index is available:

```
SELECT    AVG (E.sal)
FROM      Employee E
GROUP BY  E.dno
HAVING    E.dno=22
```

6. The *sid* in Reserves is a foreign key that refers to Sailors:

```
SELECT  S.sid
FROM    Sailors S, Reserves R
WHERE   S.sid=R.sid
```

Exercise 20.9 Consider two ways to compute the names of employees who earn more than \$100,000 and whose age is equal to their manager's age. First, a nested query:

```
SELECT  E1.ename
FROM    Emp E1
WHERE   E1.sal > 100 AND E1.age = ( SELECT E2.age
                                     FROM   Emp E2, Dept D2
                                     WHERE  E1.dname = D2.dname
                                            AND D2.mgr = E2.ename )
```

Second, a query that uses a view definition:

```
SELECT   E1.ename
FROM     Emp E1, MgrAge A
WHERE    E1.dname = A.dname AND E1.sal > 100 AND E1.age = A.age

CREATE VIEW MgrAge (dname, age)
       AS SELECT D.dname, E.age
          FROM   Emp E, Dept D
          WHERE  D.mgr = E.ename
```

1. Describe a situation in which the first query is likely to outperform the second query.
2. Describe a situation in which the second query is likely to outperform the first query.
3. Can you construct an equivalent query that is likely to beat both these queries when every employee who earns more than $100,000 is either 35 or 40 years old? Explain briefly.

BIBLIOGRAPHIC NOTES

[658] is an early discussion of physical database design. [659] discusses the performance implications of normalization and observes that denormalization may improve performance for certain queries. The ideas underlying a physical design tool from IBM are described in [272]. The Microsoft AutoAdmin tool that performs automatic index selection according to a query workload is described in several papers [163, 164]. The DB2 Advisor is described in [750]. Other approaches to physical database design are described in [146, 639]. [679] considers *transaction tuning*, which we discussed only briefly. The issue is how an application should be structured into a collection of transactions to maximize performance.

The following books on database design cover physical design issues in detail; they are recommended for further reading. [274] is largely independent of specific products, although many examples are based on DB2 and Teradata systems. [779] deals primarily with DB2. Shasha and Bonnet give an in-depth, readable introduction to database tuning [104].

[334] contains several papers on benchmarking database systems and has accompanying software. It includes articles on the AS^3AP, Set Query, TPC-A, TPC-B, Wisconsin, and 001 benchmarks written by the original developers. The Bucky benchmark is described in [132], the 007 benchmark is described in [131], and the TPC-D benchmark is described in [739]. The Sequoia 2000 benchmark is described in [720].

21

SECURITY AND AUTHORIZATION

- What are the main security considerations in designing a database application?
- What mechanisms does a DBMS provide to control a user's access to data?
- What is discretionary access control and how is it supported in SQL?
- What are the weaknesses of discretionary access control? How are these addressed in mandatory access control?
- What are covert channels and how do they compromise mandatory access control?
- What must the DBA do to ensure security?
- What is the added security threat when a database is accessed remotely?
- What is the role of encryption in ensuring secure access? How is it used for certifying servers and creating digital signatures?

- **Key concepts:** security, integrity, availability; discretionary access control, privileges, `GRANT`, `REVOKE`; mandatory access control, objects, subjects, security classes, multilevel tables, polyinstantiation; covert channels, DoD security levels; statistical databases, inferring secure information; authentication for remote access, securing servers, digital signatures; encyption, public-key encryption.

I know that's a secret, for it's whispered everywhere.

—William Congreve

The data stored in a DBMS is often vital to the business interests of the organization and is regarded as a corporate asset. In addition to protecting the intrinsic value of the data, corporations must consider ways to ensure privacy and control access to data that must not be revealed to certain groups of users for various reasons.

In this chapter, we discuss the concepts underlying access control and security in a DBMS. After introducing database security issues in Section 21.1, we consider two distinct approaches, called *discretionary* and *mandatory*, to specifying and managing access controls. An **access control** mechanism is a way to control the data accessible by a given user. After introducing access controls in Section 21.2, we cover discretionary access control, which is supported in SQL, in Section 21.3. We briefly cover mandatory access control, which is not supported in SQL, in Section 21.4.

In Section 21.6, we discuss some additional aspects of database security, such as security in a statistical database and the role of the database administrator. We then consider some of the unique challenges in supporting secure access to a DBMS over the Internet, which is a central problem in e-commerce and other Internet database applications, in Section 21.5. We conclude this chapter with a discussion of security aspects of the Barns and Nobble case study in Section 21.7.

21.1 INTRODUCTION TO DATABASE SECURITY

There are three main objectives when designing a secure database application:

1. **Secrecy:** Information should not be disclosed to unauthorized users. For example, a student should not be allowed to examine other students' grades.
2. **Integrity:** Only authorized users should be allowed to modify data. For example, students may be allowed to see their grades, yet not allowed (obviously) to modify them.
3. **Availability:** Authorized users should not be denied access. For example, an instructor who wishes to change a grade should be allowed to do so.

To achieve these objectives, a clear and consistent **security policy** should be developed to describe what security measures must be enforced. In particular, we must determine what part of the data is to be protected and which users get access to which portions of the data. Next, the **security mechanisms** of the underlying DBMS and operating system, as well as external mechanisms, such as securing access to buildings, must be utilized to enforce the policy. We emphasize that security measures must be taken at several levels.

Security leaks in the OS or network connections can circumvent database security mechanisms. For example, such leaks could allow an intruder to log on as the database administrator, with all the attendant DBMS access rights. Human factors are another source of security leaks. For example, a user may choose a password that is easy to guess, or a user who is authorized to see sensitive data may misuse it. Such errors account for a large percentage of security breaches. We do not discuss these aspects of security despite their importance because they are not specific to database management systems; our main focus is on database access control mechanisms to support a security policy.

We observe that views are a valuable tool in enforcing security policies. The view mechanism can be used to create a 'window' on a collection of data that is appropriate for some group of users. Views allow us to limit access to sensitive data by providing access to a restricted version (defined through a view) of that data, rather than to the data itself.

We use the following schemas in our examples:

> Sailors(*sid:* `integer`, *sname:* `string`, *rating:* `integer`, *age:* `real`)
> Boats(*bid:* `integer`, *bname:* `string`, *color:* `string`)
> Reserves(*sid:* `integer`, *bid:* `integer`, *day:* `dates`)

Increasingly, as database systems become the backbone of e-commerce applications requests originate over the Internet. This makes it important to be able to **authenticate** a user to the database system. After all, enforcing a security policy that allows user Sam to read a table and Elmer to write the table is not of much use if Sam can masquerade as Elmer. Conversely, we must be able to assure users that they are communicating with a legitimate system (e.g., the real Amazon.com server, and not a spurious application intended to steal sensitive information such as a credit card number). While the details of authentication are outside the scope of our coverage, we discuss the role of authentication and the basic ideas involved in Section 21.5, after covering database access control mechanisms.

21.2 ACCESS CONTROL

A database for an enterprise contains a great deal of information and usually has several groups of users. Most users need to access only a small part of the database to carry out their tasks. Allowing users unrestricted access to all the data can be undesirable, and a DBMS should provide mechanisms to control access to data.

A DBMS offers two main approaches to access control. **Discretionary access control** is based on the concept of access rights, or **privileges**, and mechanisms for giving users such privileges. A privilege allows a user to access some data object in a certain manner (e.g., to read or modify). A user who creates a database object such as a table or a view automatically gets all applicable privileges on that object. The DBMS subsequently keeps track of how these privileges are granted to other users, and possibly revoked, and ensures that at all times only users with the necessary privileges can access an object. SQL supports discretionary access control through the `GRANT` and `REVOKE` commands. The `GRANT` command gives privileges to users, and the `REVOKE` command takes away privileges. We discuss discretionary access control in Section 21.3.

Discretionary access control mechanisms, while generally effective, have certain weaknesses. In particular, a devious unauthorized user can trick an authorized user into disclosing sensitive data. **Mandatory access control** is based on systemwide policies that cannot be changed by individual users. In this approach each database object is assigned a *security class*, each user is assigned *clearance* for a security class, and rules are imposed on reading and writing of database objects by users. The DBMS determines whether a given user can read or write a given object based on certain rules that involve the security level of the object and the clearance of the user. These rules seek to ensure that sensitive data can never be 'passed on' to a user without the necessary clearance. The SQL standard does not include any support for mandatory access control. We discuss mandatory access control in Section 21.4.

21.3 DISCRETIONARY ACCESS CONTROL

SQL supports discretionary access control through the `GRANT` and `REVOKE` commands. The `GRANT` command gives users privileges to base tables and views. The syntax of this command is as follows:

`GRANT` **privileges** `ON` **object** `TO` **users** [`WITH GRANT OPTION`]

For our purposes **object** is either a base table or a view. SQL recognizes certain other kinds of objects, but we do not discuss them. Several privileges can be specified, including these:

- `SELECT`: The right to access (read) all columns of the table specified as the **object**, *including columns added later* through `ALTER TABLE` commands.

- `INSERT`(*column-name*): The right to insert rows with (non-*null* or non-default) values in the named column of the table named as **object**. If this right is to be granted with respect to all columns, including columns that might be added later, we can simply use `INSERT`. The privileges `UPDATE`(*column-name*) and `UPDATE` are similar.
- `DELETE`: The right to delete rows from the table named as **object**.
- `REFERENCES`(*column-name*): The right to define foreign keys (in other tables) that refer to the specified column of the table **object**. `REFERENCES` without a column name specified denotes this right with respect to all columns, including any that are added later.

If a user has a privilege with the **grant option**, he or she can pass it to another user (with or without the grant option) by using the `GRANT` command. A user who creates a base table automatically has all applicable privileges on it, along with the right to grant these privileges to other users. A user who creates a view has precisely those privileges on the view that he or she has on *every* one of the views or base tables used to define the view. The user creating the view must have the `SELECT` privilege on each underlying table, of course, and so is always granted the `SELECT` privilege on the view. The creator of the view has the `SELECT` privilege with the grant option only if he or she has the `SELECT` privilege with the grant option on every underlying table. In addition, if the view is updatable and the user holds `INSERT`, `DELETE`, or `UPDATE` privileges (with or without the grant option) on the (single) underlying table, the user automatically gets the same privileges on the view.

Only the owner of a schema can execute the data definition statements `CREATE`, `ALTER`, and `DROP` on that schema. The right to execute these statements cannot be granted or revoked.

In conjunction with the `GRANT` and `REVOKE` commands, views are an important component of the security mechanisms provided by a relational DBMS. By defining views on the base tables, we can present needed information to a user while *hiding* other information that the user should not be given access to. For example, consider the following view definition:

```
CREATE VIEW ActiveSailors (name, age, day)
        AS SELECT S.sname, S.age, R.day
           FROM   Sailors S, Reserves R
           WHERE  S.sid = R.sid AND S.rating > 6
```

A user who can access ActiveSailors but not Sailors or Reserves knows the names of sailors who have reservations but cannot find out the *bid*s of boats reserved by a given sailor.

Role-Based Authorization in SQL: Privileges are assigned to users (authorization IDs, to be precise) in SQL-92. In the real world, privileges are often associated with a user's job or *role* within the organization. Many DBMSs have long supported the concept of a **role** and allowed privileges to be assigned to roles. Roles can then be granted to users and other roles. (Of courses, privileges can also be granted directly to users.) The SQL:1999 standard includes support for roles. Roles can be created and destroyed using the `CREATE ROLE` and `DROP ROLE` commands. Users can be granted roles (optionally, with the ability to pass the role on to others). The standard `GRANT` and `REVOKE` commands can assign privileges to (and revoke from) roles or authorization IDs.
What is the benefit of including a feature that many systems already support? This ensures that, over time, all vendors who comply with the standard support this feature. Thus, users can use the feature without worrying about portability of their application across DBMSs.

Privileges are assigned in SQL to **authorization IDs**, which can denote a single user or a group of users; a user must specify an authorization ID and, in many systems, a corresponding *password* before the DBMS accepts any commands from him or her. So, technically, *Joe*, *Michael*, and so on are authorization IDs rather than user names in the following examples.

Suppose that user Joe has created the tables Boats, Reserves, and Sailors. Some examples of the `GRANT` command that Joe can now execute follow:

```
GRANT INSERT, DELETE ON Reserves TO Yuppy WITH GRANT OPTION
GRANT SELECT ON Reserves TO Michael
GRANT SELECT ON Sailors TO Michael WITH GRANT OPTION
GRANT UPDATE (rating) ON Sailors TO Leah
GRANT REFERENCES (bid) ON Boats TO Bill
```

Yuppy can insert or delete Reserves rows and authorize someone else to do the same. Michael can execute `SELECT` queries on Sailors and Reserves, and he can pass this privilege to others for Sailors but not for Reserves. With the `SELECT` privilege, Michael can create a view that accesses the Sailors and Reserves tables (for example, the ActiveSailors view), but he cannot grant `SELECT` on ActiveSailors to others.

On the other hand, suppose that Michael creates the following view:

```
CREATE VIEW YoungSailors (sid, age, rating)
       AS SELECT S.sid, S.age, S.rating
```

```
FROM    Sailors S
WHERE   S.age < 18
```

The only underlying table is Sailors, for which Michael has SELECT with the grant option. He therefore has SELECT with the grant option on YoungSailors and can pass on the SELECT privilege on YoungSailors to Eric and Guppy:

```
GRANT SELECT ON YoungSailors TO Eric, Guppy
```

Eric and Guppy can now execute SELECT queries on the view YoungSailors—note, however, that Eric and Guppy do *not* have the right to execute SELECT queries directly on the underlying Sailors table.

Michael can also define constraints based on the information in the Sailors and Reserves tables. For example, Michael can define the following table, which has an associated table constraint:

```
CREATE TABLE Sneaky (maxrating   INTEGER,
                     CHECK ( maxrating >=
                           ( SELECT MAX (S.rating )
                             FROM   Sailors S )))
```

By repeatedly inserting rows with gradually increasing *maxrating* values into the Sneaky table until an insertion finally succeeds, Michael can find out the highest *rating* value in the Sailors table. This example illustrates why SQL requires the creator of a table constraint that refers to Sailors to possess the SELECT privilege on Sailors.

Returning to the privileges granted by Joe, Leah can update only the *rating* column of Sailors rows. She can execute the following command, which sets all ratings to 8:

```
UPDATE Sailors S
SET    S.rating = 8
```

However, she cannot execute the same command if the SET clause is changed to be SET *S.age = 25*, because she is not allowed to update the *age* field. A more subtle point is illustrated by the following command, which decrements the rating of all sailors:

```
UPDATE Sailors S
SET    S.rating = S.rating-1
```

Leah cannot execute this command because it requires the SELECT privilege on the *S.rating* column and Leah does not have this privilege.

Bill can refer to the *bid* column of Boats as a foreign key in another table. For example, Bill can create the Reserves table through the following command:

```
CREATE TABLE Reserves ( sid   INTEGER,
                        bid   INTEGER,
                        day   DATE,
                        PRIMARY KEY (bid, day),
                        FOREIGN KEY (sid) REFERENCES Sailors ),
                        FOREIGN KEY (bid) REFERENCES Boats )
```

If Bill did not have the REFERENCES privilege on the *bid* column of Boats, he would not be able to execute this CREATE statement because the FOREIGN KEY clause requires this privilege. (A similar point holds with respect to the foreign key reference to Sailors.)

Specifying just the INSERT privilege (similarly, REFERENCES and other privileges) in a GRANT command is not the same as specifying SELECT(*column-name*) for each column currently in the table. Consider the following command over the Sailors table, which has columns *sid*, *sname*, *rating*, and *age*:

GRANT INSERT ON Sailors TO Michael

Suppose that this command is executed and then a column is added to the Sailors table (by executing an ALTER TABLE command). Note that Michael has the INSERT privilege with respect to the newly added column. If we had executed the following GRANT command, instead of the previous one, Michael would not have the INSERT privilege on the new column:

GRANT INSERT ON Sailors(*sid*), Sailors(*sname*), Sailors(*rating*),
Sailors(*age*), TO Michael

There is a complementary command to GRANT that allows the withdrawal of privileges. The syntax of the REVOKE command is as follows:

REVOKE [GRANT OPTION FOR] **privileges**
ON **object** FROM **users** { RESTRICT | CASCADE }

The command can be used to revoke either a privilege or just the grant option on a privilege (by using the optional GRANT OPTION FOR clause). One of the two alternatives, RESTRICT or CASCADE, must be specified; we see what this choice means shortly.

The intuition behind the GRANT command is clear: The creator of a base table or a view is given all the appropriate privileges with respect to it and is allowed to pass these privileges—including the right to pass along a privilege—to other users. The REVOKE command is, as expected, intended to achieve the reverse: A user who has granted a privilege to another user may change his or her mind and want to withdraw the granted privilege. The intuition behind exactly what effect a REVOKE command has is complicated by the fact that a user may be granted the same privilege multiple times, possibly by different users.

When a user executes a REVOKE command with the CASCADE keyword, the effect is to withdraw the named privileges or grant option from all users who currently hold these privileges *solely* through a GRANT command that was previously executed by the same user who is now executing the REVOKE command. If these users received the privileges with the grant option and passed it along, those recipients in turn lose their privileges as a consequence of the REVOKE command, unless they received these privileges through an additional GRANT command.

We illustrate the REVOKE command through several examples. First, consider what happens after the following sequence of commands, where Joe is the creator of Sailors.

```
GRANT SELECT ON Sailors TO Art WITH GRANT OPTION    (executed by Joe)
GRANT SELECT ON Sailors TO Bob WITH GRANT OPTION    (executed by Art)
REVOKE SELECT ON Sailors FROM Art CASCADE           (executed by Joe)
```

Art loses the SELECT privilege on Sailors, of course. Then Bob, who received this privilege from Art, and only Art, also loses this privilege. Bob's privilege is said to be **abandoned** when the privilege from which it was derived (Art's SELECT privilege with grant option, in this example) is revoked. When the CASCADE keyword is specified, all abandoned privileges are also revoked (possibly causing privileges held by other users to become abandoned and thereby revoked recursively). If the RESTRICT keyword is specified in the REVOKE command, the command is rejected if revoking the privileges *just* from the users specified in the command would result in other privileges becoming abandoned.

Consider the following sequence, as another example:

```
GRANT SELECT ON Sailors TO Art WITH GRANT OPTION    (executed by Joe)
GRANT SELECT ON Sailors TO Bob WITH GRANT OPTION    (executed by Joe)
GRANT SELECT ON Sailors TO Bob WITH GRANT OPTION    (executed by Art)
REVOKE SELECT ON Sailors FROM Art CASCADE           (executed by Joe)
```

As before, Art loses the SELECT privilege on Sailors. But what about Bob? Bob received this privilege from Art, but he also received it independently (coincidentally, directly from Joe). So Bob retains this privilege. Consider a third example:

```
GRANT SELECT ON Sailors TO Art WITH GRANT OPTION    (executed by Joe)
GRANT SELECT ON Sailors TO Art WITH GRANT OPTION    (executed by Joe)
REVOKE SELECT ON Sailors FROM Art CASCADE           (executed by Joe)
```

Since Joe granted the privilege to Art twice and only revoked it once, does Art get to keep the privilege? As per the SQL standard, no. Even if Joe absentmindedly granted the same privilege to Art several times, he can revoke it with a single `REVOKE` command.

It is possible to revoke just the grant option on a privilege:

```
GRANT SELECT ON Sailors TO Art WITH GRANT OPTION    (executed by Joe)
REVOKE GRANT OPTION FOR SELECT ON Sailors
      FROM Art CASCADE                              (executed by Joe)
```

This command would leave Art with the `SELECT` privilege on Sailors, but Art no longer has the grant option on this privilege and therefore cannot pass it on to other users.

These examples bring out the intuition behind the `REVOKE` command, and they highlight the complex interaction between `GRANT` and `REVOKE` commands. When a `GRANT` is executed, a **privilege descriptor** is added to a table of such descriptors maintained by the DBMS. The privilege descriptor specifies the following: the *grantor* of the privilege, the *grantee* who receives the privilege, the *granted privilege* (including the name of the object involved), and whether the grant option is included. When a user creates a table or view and 'automatically' gets certain privileges, a privilege descriptor with *system* as the grantor is entered into this table.

The effect of a series of `GRANT` commands can be described in terms of an **authorization graph** in which the nodes are users—technically, they are authorization IDs—and the arcs indicate how privileges are passed. There is an arc from (the node for) user 1 to user 2 if user 1 executed a `GRANT` command giving a privilege to user 2; the arc is labeled with the descriptor for the `GRANT` command. A `GRANT` command has no effect if the same privileges have already been granted to the same grantee by the same grantor. The following sequence of commands illustrates the semantics of `GRANT` and `REVOKE` commands when there is a *cycle* in the authorization graph:

```
GRANT SELECT ON Sailors TO Art WITH GRANT OPTION    (executed by Joe)
GRANT SELECT ON Sailors TO Bob WITH GRANT OPTION    (executed by Art)
```

```
GRANT SELECT ON Sailors TO Art WITH GRANT OPTION   (executed by Bob)
GRANT SELECT ON Sailors TO Cal WITH GRANT OPTION   (executed by Joe)
GRANT SELECT ON Sailors TO Bob WITH GRANT OPTION   (executed by Cal)
REVOKE SELECT ON Sailors FROM Art CASCADE          (executed by Joe)
```

The authorization graph for this example is shown in Figure 21.1. Note that we indicate how Joe, the creator of Sailors, acquired the SELECT privilege from the DBMS by introducing a *System* node and drawing an arc from this node to Joe's node.

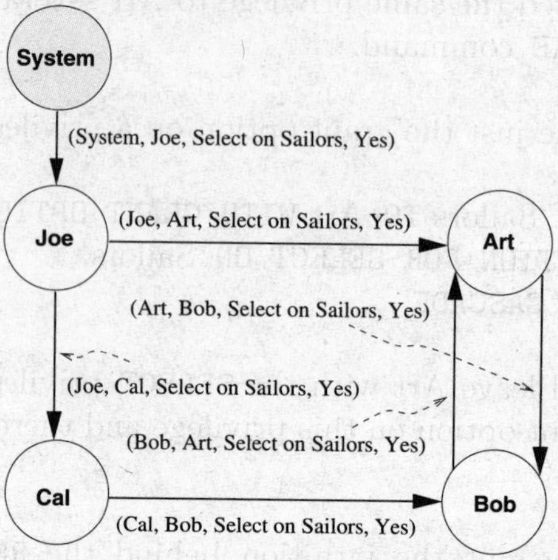

Figure 21.1 Example Authorization Graph

As the graph clearly indicates, Bob's grant to Art and Art's grant to Bob (of the same privilege) creates a cycle. Bob is subsequently given the same privilege by Cal, who received it independently from Joe. At this point Joe decides to revoke the privilege he granted Art.

Let us trace the effect of this revocation. The arc from Joe to Art is removed because it corresponds to the granting action that is revoked. All remaining nodes have the following property: *If node N has an outgoing arc labeled with a privilege, there is a path from the System node to node N in which each arc label contains the same privilege plus the grant option.* That is, any remaining granting action is justified by a privilege received (directly or indirectly) from the System. The execution of Joe's REVOKE command therefore stops at this point, with everyone continuing to hold the SELECT privilege on Sailors.

This result may seem unintuitive because Art continues to have the privilege only because he received it from Bob, and at the time that Bob granted the privilege to Art, he had received it only from Art. Although Bob acquired the privilege through Cal subsequently, should we not undo the effect of his grant to Art when executing Joe's REVOKE command? The effect of the grant from Bob to Art is *not* undone in SQL. In effect, if a user acquires a privilege multiple times from different grantors, SQL treats each of these grants to the user as having occurred *before* that user passed on the privilege to other users. This implementation of REVOKE is convenient in many real-world situations. For example, if a manager is fired after passing on some privileges to subordinates (who may in turn have passed the privileges to others), we can ensure that only the manager's privileges are removed by first redoing all of the manager's granting actions and then revoking his or her privileges. That is, we need not recursively redo the subordinates' granting actions.

To return to the saga of Joe and his friends, let us suppose that Joe decides to revoke Cal's SELECT privilege as well. Clearly, the arc from Joe to Cal corresponding to the grant of this privilege is removed. The arc from Cal to Bob is removed as well, since there is no longer a path from System to Cal that gives Cal the right to pass the SELECT privilege on Sailors to Bob. The authorization graph at this intermediate point is shown in Figure 21.2.

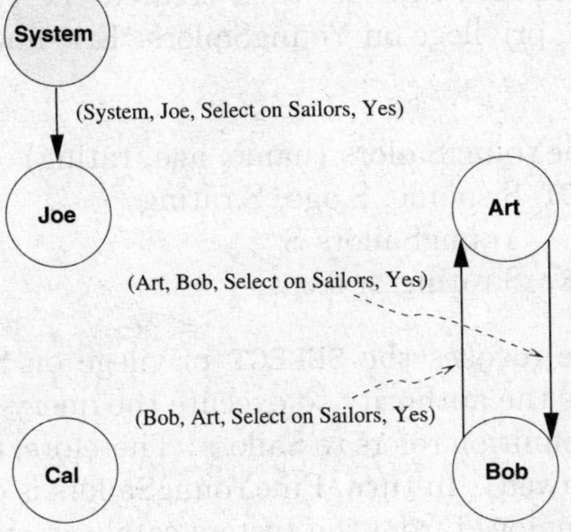

Figure 21.2 Example Authorization Graph during Revocation

The graph now contains two nodes (Art and Bob) for which there are outgoing arcs with labels containing the SELECT privilege on Sailors; therefore, these users have granted this privilege. However, although each node contains an incoming arc carrying the same privilege, *there is no such path from System to either of these nodes*; so these users' right to grant the privilege has been abandoned. We therefore remove the outgoing arcs as well. In general, these nodes might have other arcs incident on them, but in this example, they now have no incident arcs. Joe is left as the only user with the SELECT privilege on Sailors; Art and Bob have lost their privileges.

21.3.1 Grant and Revoke on Views and Integrity Constraints

The privileges held by the creator of a view (with respect to the view) change over time as he or she gains or loses privileges on the underlying tables. If the creator loses a privilege held with the grant option, users who were given that privilege on the view lose it as well. There are some subtle aspects to the GRANT and REVOKE commands when they involve views or integrity constraints. We consider some examples that highlight the following important points:

1. A view may be dropped because a SELECT privilege is revoked from the user who created the view.

2. If the creator of a view gains additional privileges on the underlying tables, he or she automatically gains additional privileges on the view.

3. The distinction between the REFERENCES and SELECT privileges is important.

Suppose that Joe created Sailors and gave Michael the SELECT privilege on it with the grant option, and Michael then created the view YoungSailors and gave Eric the SELECT privilege on YoungSailors. Eric now defines a view called FineYoungSailors:

```
CREATE VIEW FineYoungSailors (name, age, rating)
       AS SELECT S.sname, S.age, S.rating
          FROM   YoungSailors S
          WHERE  S.rating > 6
```

What happens if Joe revokes the SELECT privilege on Sailors from Michael? Michael no longer has the authority to execute the query used to define YoungSailors because the definition refers to Sailors. Therefore, the view YoungSailors is dropped (i.e., destroyed). In turn, FineYoungSailors is dropped as well. Both view definitions are removed from the system catalogs; even if a remorseful Joe decides to give back the SELECT privilege on Sailors to Michael, the views are gone and must be created afresh if they are required.

On a more happy note, suppose that everything proceeds as just described until Eric defines FineYoungSailors; then, instead of revoking the SELECT privilege on Sailors from Michael, Joe decides to also give Michael the INSERT privilege on Sailors. Michael's privileges on the view YoungSailors are upgraded to what he would have if he were to create the view *now*. He therefore acquires the INSERT privilege on YoungSailors as well. (Note that this view is updatable.) What about Eric? His privileges are unchanged.

Whether or not Michael has the INSERT privilege on YoungSailors with the grant option depends on whether or not Joe gives him the INSERT privilege on

Sailors with the grant option. To understand this situation, consider Eric again. If Michael has the `INSERT` privilege on YoungSailors with the grant option, he can pass this privilege to Eric. Eric could then insert rows into the Sailors table because inserts on YoungSailors are effected by modifying the underlying base table, Sailors. Clearly, we do not want Michael to be able to authorize Eric to make such changes unless Michael has the `INSERT` privilege on Sailors with the grant option.

The `REFERENCES` privilege is very different from the `SELECT` privilege, as the following example illustrates. Suppose that Joe is the creator of Boats. He can authorize another user, say, Fred, to create Reserves with a foreign key that refers to the *bid* column of Boats by giving Fred the `REFERENCES` privilege with respect to this column. On the other hand, if Fred has the `SELECT` privilege on the *bid* column of Boats but not the `REFERENCES` privilege, Fred *cannot* create Reserves with a foreign key that refers to Boats. If Fred creates Reserves with a foreign key column that refers to *bid* in Boats and later loses the `REFERENCES` privilege on the *bid* column of boats, the foreign key constraint in Reserves is dropped; however, the Reserves table is *not* dropped.

To understand why the SQL standard chose to introduce the `REFERENCES` privilege rather than to simply allow the `SELECT` privilege to be used in this situation, consider what happens if the definition of Reserves specified the `NO ACTION` option with the foreign key—Joe, the owner of Boats, may be prevented from deleting a row from Boats because a row in Reserves refers to this Boats row. Giving Fred, the creator of Reserves, the right to constrain updates on Boats in this manner goes beyond simply allowing him to read the values in Boats, which is all that the `SELECT` privilege authorizes.

21.4 MANDATORY ACCESS CONTROL

Discretionary access control mechanisms, while generally effective, have certain weaknesses. In particular they are susceptible to *Trojan horse* schemes whereby a devious unauthorized user can trick an authorized user into disclosing sensitive data. For example, suppose that student Tricky Dick wants to break into the grade tables of instructor Trustin Justin. Dick does the following:

- He creates a new table called MineAllMine and gives `INSERT` privileges on this table to Justin (who is blissfully unaware of all this attention, of course).
- He modifies the code of some DBMS application that Justin uses often to do a couple of additional things: first, read the Grades table, and next, write the result into MineAllMine.

Then he sits back and waits for the grades to be copied into MineAllMine and later undoes the modifications to the application to ensure that Justin does not somehow find out later that he has been cheated. Thus, despite the DBMS enforcing all discretionary access controls—only Justin's authorized code was allowed to access Grades—sensitive data is disclosed to an intruder. The fact that Dick could surreptitiously modify Justin's code is outside the scope of the DBMS's access control mechanism.

Mandatory access control mechanisms are aimed at addressing such loopholes in discretionary access control. The popular model for mandatory access control, called the Bell-LaPadula model, is described in terms of **objects** (e.g., tables, views, rows, columns), **subjects** (e.g., users, programs), **security classes**, and **clearances**. Each database object is assigned a *security class*, and each subject is assigned *clearance* for a security class; we denote the class of an object or subject A as *class(A)*. The security classes in a system are organized according to a partial order, with a **most secure class** and a **least secure class**. For simplicity, we assume that there are four classes: *top secret (TS), secret (S), confidential (C), and unclassified (U)*. In this system, $TS > S > C > U$, where $A > B$ means that class A data is more sensitive than class B data.

The Bell-LaPadula model imposes two restrictions on all reads and writes of database objects:

1. **Simple Security Property:** Subject S is allowed to read object O only if $class(S) \geq class(O)$. For example, a user with TS clearance can read a table with C clearance, but a user with C clearance is not allowed to read a table with TS classification.

2. ***-Property:** Subject S is allowed to write object O only if $class(S) \leq class(O)$. For example, a user with S clearance can write only objects with S or TS classification.

If discretionary access controls are also specified, these rules represent additional restrictions. Therefore, to read or write a database object, a user must have the necessary privileges (obtained via `GRANT` commands) *and* the security classes of the user and the object must satisfy the preceding restrictions. Let us consider how such a mandatory control mechanism might have foiled Tricky Dick. The Grades table could be classified as S, Justin could be given clearance for S, and Tricky Dick could be given a lower clearance (C). Dick can create objects of only C or lower classification; so the table MineAllMine can have at most the classification C. When the application program running on behalf of Justin (and therefore with clearance S) tries to copy Grades into MineAllMine, it is not allowed to do so because $class(MineAllMine) < class(application)$, and the *-Property is violated.

21.4.1 Multilevel Relations and Polyinstantiation

To apply mandatory access control policies in a relational DBMS, a security class must be assigned to each database object. The objects can be at the granularity of tables, rows, or even individual column values. Let us assume that each row is assigned a security class. This situation leads to the concept of a **multilevel table**, which is a table with the surprising property that users with different security clearances see a different collection of rows when they access the same table.

Consider the instance of the Boats table shown in Figure 21.3. Users with *S* and *TS* clearance get both rows in the answer when they ask to see all rows in Boats. A user with *C* clearance gets only the second row, and a user with *U* clearance gets no rows.

bid	*bname*	*color*	**Security Class**
101	Salsa	Red	*S*
102	Pinto	Brown	*C*

Figure 21.3 An Instance *B1* of Boats

The Boats table is defined to have *bid* as the primary key. Suppose that a user with clearance *C* wishes to enter the row ⟨*101, Picante, Scarlet, C*⟩. We have a dilemma:

- If the insertion is permitted, two distinct rows in the table have key 101.
- If the insertion is not permitted because the primary key constraint is violated, the user trying to insert the new row, who has clearance *C*, can infer that there is a boat with *bid=101* whose security class is higher than *C*. This situation compromises the principle that users should not be able to infer any information about objects that have a higher security classification.

This dilemma is resolved by effectively treating the security classification as part of the key. Thus, the insertion is allowed to continue, and the table instance is modified as shown in Figure 21.4.

bid	*bname*	*color*	**Security Class**
101	Salsa	Red	*S*
101	Picante	Scarlet	*C*
102	Pinto	Brown	*C*

Figure 21.4 Instance *B1* after Insertion

Users with clearance *C* or *U* see just the rows for Picante and Pinto, but users with clearance *S* or *TS* see all three rows. The two rows with *bid=101* can be interpreted in one of two ways: only the row with the higher classification (Salsa, with classification *S*) actually exists, or both exist and their presence is revealed to users according to their clearance level. The choice of interpretation is up to application developers and users.

The presence of data objects that appear to have different values to users with different clearances (for example, the boat with *bid* 101) is called **polyinstantiation**. If we consider security classifications associated with individual columns, the intuition underlying polyinstantiation can be generalized in a straightforward manner, but some additional details must be addressed. We remark that the main drawback of mandatory access control schemes is their rigidity; policies are set by system administrators, and the classification mechanisms are not flexible enough. A satisfactory combination of discretionary and mandatory access controls is yet to be achieved.

21.4.2 Covert Channels, DoD Security Levels

Even if a DBMS enforces the mandatory access control scheme just discussed, information can flow from a higher classification level to a lower classification level through indirect means, called **covert channels**. For example, if a transaction accesses data at more than one site in a distributed DBMS, the actions at the two sites must be coordinated. The process at one site may have a lower clearance (say, *C*) than the process at another site (say, *S*), and both processes have to agree to commit before the transaction can be committed. This requirement can be exploited to pass information with an *S* classification to the process with a *C* clearance: The transaction is repeatedly invoked, and the process with the *C* clearance always agrees to commit, whereas the process with the *S* clearance agrees to commit if it wants to transmit a 1 bit and does not agree if it wants to transmit a 0 bit.

In this (admittedly tortuous) manner, information with an *S* clearance can be sent to a process with a *C* clearance as a stream of bits. This covert channel is an indirect violation of the intent behind the *-Property. Additional examples of covert channels can be found readily in statistical databases, which we discuss in Section 21.6.2.

DBMS vendors recently started implementing mandatory access control mechanisms (although they are not part of the SQL standard) because the United States Department of Defense (DoD) requires such support for its systems. The DoD requirements can be described in terms of **security levels** *A*, *B*, *C*, and *D*, of which *A* is the most secure and *D* is the least secure.

> **Current Systems:** Commercial RDBMSs are available that support discretionary controls at the *C2* level and mandatory controls at the *B1* level. IBM DB2, Informix, Microsoft SQL Server, Oracle 8, and Sybase ASE all support SQL's features for discretionary access control. In general, they do not support mandatory access control; Oracle offers a version of their product with support for mandatory access control.

Level *C* requires support for discretionary access control. It is divided into sublevels *C1* and *C2*; *C2* also requires some degree of accountability through procedures such as login verification and audit trails. Level *B* requires support for mandatory access control. It is subdivided into levels *B1*, *B2*, and *B3*. Level *B2* additionally requires the identification and elimination of covert channels. Level *B3* additionally requires maintenance of audit trails and the designation of a **security administrator** (usually, but not necessarily, the DBA). Level *A*, the most secure level, requires a mathematical proof that the security mechanism enforces the security policy!

21.5 SECURITY FOR INTERNET APPLICATIONS

When a DBMS is accessed from a secure location, we can rely upon a simple password mechanism for authenticating users. However, suppose our friend Sam wants to place an order for a book over the Internet. This presents some unique challenges: Sam is not even a known user (unless he is a repeat customer). From Amazon's point of view, we have an individual asking for a book and offering to pay with a credit card registered to Sam, but is this individual really Sam? From Sam's point of view, he sees a form asking for credit card information, but is this indeed a legitimate part of Amazon's site, and not a rogue application designed to trick him into revealing his credit card number?

This example illustrates the need for a more sophisticated approach to authentication than a simple password mechanism. Encryption techniques provide the foundation for modern authentication.

21.5.1 Encryption

The basic idea behind encryption is to apply an **encryption algorithm** to the data, using a user-specified or DBA-specified **encryption key**. The output of the algorithm is the encrypted version of the data. There is also a **decryption algorithm**, which takes the encrypted data and a **decryption key** as input and then returns the original data. Without the correct decryption key, the decryption algorithm produces gibberish. The encryption and decryption

DES and AES: The DES standard, adopted in 1977, has a 56-bit encryption key. Over time, computers have become so fast that, in 1999, a special-purpose chip and a network of PCs were used to crack DES in under a day. The system was testing 245 billion keys per second when the correct key was found! It is estimated that a special-purpose hardware device can be built for under a million dollars that can crack DES in under four hours. Despite growing concerns about its vulnerability, DES is still widely used. In 2000, a successor to DES, called the **Advanced Encryption Standard (AES)**, was adopted as the new (symmetric) encryption standard. AES has three possible key sizes: 128, 192, and 256 bits. With a 128 bit key size, there are over $3 \cdot 10^{38}$ possible AES keys, which is on the order of 10^{24} more than the number of 56-bit DES keys. Assume that we could build a computer fast enough to crack DES in 1 second. This computer would compute for about 149 trillion years to crack a 128-bit AES key. (Experts think the universe is less than 20 billion years old.)

algorithms themselves are assumed to be publicly known, but one or both keys are secret (depending upon the encryption scheme).

In **symmetric encryption**, the encryption key is also used as the decryption key. The ANSI **Data Encryption Standard** (DES), which has been in use since 1977, is a well-known example of symmetric encryption. It uses an encryption algorithm that consists of character substitutions and permutations. The main weakness of symmetric encryption is that all authorized users must be told the key, increasing the likelihood of its becoming known to an intruder (e.g., by simple human error).

Another approach to encryption, called **public-key encryption**, has become increasingly popular in recent years. The encryption scheme proposed by Rivest, Shamir, and Adleman, called RSA, is a well-known example of public-key encryption. Each authorized user has a **public encryption key**, known to everyone, and a private **decryption key**, known only to him or her. Since the private decryption keys are known only to their owners, the weakness of DES is avoided.

A central issue for public-key encryption is how encryption and decryption keys are chosen. Technically, public-key encryption algorithms rely on the existence of **one-way functions**, whose inverses are computationally very hard to determine. The RSA algorithm, for example, is based on the observation that, although checking whether a given number is prime is easy, determining the prime factors of a nonprime number is extremely hard. (Determining the

> **Why RSA Works:** The essential point of the scheme is that it is easy to compute d given e, p, and q, but *very* hard to compute d given just e and L. In turn, this difficulty depends on the fact that it is hard to determine the prime factors of L, which happen to be p and q. *A caveat:* Factoring is widely believed to be hard, but there is no proof that this is so. Nor is there a proof that factoring is the only way to crack RSA; that is, to compute d from e and L.

prime factors of a number with over 100 digits can take years of CPU time on the fastest available computers today.)

We now sketch the idea behind the RSA algorithm, assuming that the data to be encrypted is an integer I. To choose an encryption key and a decryption key for a given user, we first choose a very large integer L, larger than the largest integer we will ever need to encode.[1] We then select a number e as the encryption key and compute the decryption key d based on e and L; how this is done is central to the approach, as we see shortly. Both L and e are made public and used by the encryption algorithm. However, d is kept secret and is necessary for decryption.

- The encryption function is $S = I^e \texttt{ mod } L$.
- The decryption function is $I = S^d \texttt{ mod } L$.

We choose L to be the product of two large (e.g., 1024-bit), distinct prime numbers, $p * q$. The encryption key e is a randomly chosen number between 1 and L that is relatively prime to $(p-1)*(q-1)$. The decryption key d is computed such that $d*e = 1 \texttt{ mod } ((p-1)*(q-1))$. Given these choices, results in number theory can be used to prove that the decryption function recovers the original message from its encrypted version.

A very important property of the encryption and decryption algorithms is that the roles of the encryption and decryption keys can be reversed:

$$\textit{decrypt}(\text{d}, (\textit{encrypt}(\text{e}, \text{I}))) = \text{I} = \textit{decrypt}(\text{e}, (\textit{encrypt}(\text{d}, \text{I})))$$

Since many protocols rely on this property, we henceforth simply refer to public and private keys (since both keys can be used for encryption as well as decryption).

---

[1] A message that is to be encrypted is decomposed into blocks such that each block can be treated as an integer less than L.

While we introduced encryption in the context of authentication, we note that it is a fundamental tool for enforcing security. A DBMS can use *encryption* to protect information in situations where the normal security mechanisms of the DBMS are not adequate. For example, an intruder may steal tapes containing some data or tap a communication line. By storing and transmitting data in an encrypted form, the DBMS ensures that such stolen data is not intelligible to the intruder.

21.5.2 Certifying Servers: The SSL Protocol

Suppose we associate a public key and a decryption key with Amazon. Anyone, say, user Sam, can send Amazon an order by encrypting the order using Amazon's public key. Only Amazon can decrypt this secret order because the decryption algorithm requires Amazon's private key, known only to Amazon.

This hinges on Sam's ability to reliably find out Amazon's public key. A number of companies serve as **certification authorities**, e.g., Verisign. Amazon generates a public encryption key e_A (and a private decryption key) and sends the public key to Verisign. Verisign then issues a **certificate** to Amazon that contains the following information:

$$\langle \textit{Verisign, Amazon, https://www.amazon.com}, e_A \rangle$$

The certificate is encrypted using Verisign's own *private* key, which is known to (i.e., stored in) Internet Explorer, Netscape Navigator, and other browsers.

When Sam comes to the Amazon site and wants to place an order, his browser, running the SSL protocol,[2] asks the server for the Verisign certificate. The browser then validates the certificate by decrypting it (using Verisign's public key) and checking that the result is a certificate with the name Verisign, and that the URL it contains is that of the server it is talking to. (Note that an attempt to forge a certificate will fail because certificates are encrypted using Verisign's private key, which is known only to Verisign.) Next, the browser generates a random **session key**, encrypt it using Amazon's public key (which it obtained from the validated certificate and therefore trusts), and sends it to the Amazon server.

From this point on, the Amazon server and the browser can use the session key (which both know and are confident that only they know) and a *symmetric* encryption protocol like AES or DES to exchange securely encrypted messages: Messages are encrypted by the sender and decrypted by the receiver using the same session key. The encrypted messages travel over the Internet and may be

[2]A browser uses the SSL protocol if the target URL begins with *https*.

intercepted, but they cannot be decrypted without the session key. It is useful to consider why we need a session key; after all, the browser could simply have encrypted Sam's original request using Amazon's public key and sent it securely to the Amazon server. The reason is that, without the session key, the Amazon server has no way to securely send information back to the browser. A further advantage of session keys is that symmetric encryption is computationally much faster than public key encryption. The session key is discarded at the end of the session.

Thus, Sam can be assured that only Amazon can see the information he types into the form shown to him by the Amazon server and the information sent back to him in responses from the server. However, at this point, Amazon has no assurance that the user running the browser is actually Sam, and not someone who has stolen Sam's credit card. Typically, merchants accept this situation, which also arises when a customer places an order over the phone.

If we want to be sure of the user's identity, this can be accomplished by additionally requiring the user to login. In our example, Sam must first establish an account with Amazon and select a password. (Sam's identity is originally established by calling him back on the phone to verify the account information or by sending email to an email address; in the latter case, all we establish is that the owner of the account is the individual with the given email address.) Whenever he visits the site and Amazon needs to verify his identity, Amazon redirects him to a login form *after* using SSL to establish a session key. The password typed in is transmitted securely by encrypting it with the session key.

One remaining drawback in this approach is that Amazon now knows Sam's credit card number, and he must trust Amazon not to misuse it. The **Secure Electronic Transaction** protocol addresses this limitation. Every customer must now obtain a certificate, with his or her own private and public keys, and every transaction involves the Amazon server, the customer's browser, and the server of a trusted third party, such as Visa for credit card transactions. The basic idea is that the browser encodes non-credit card information using Amazon's public key and the credit card information using Visa's public key and sends these to the Amazon server, which forwards the credit card information (which it cannot decrypt) to the Visa server. If the Visa server approves the information, the transaction goes through.

21.5.3 Digital Signatures

Suppose that Elmer, who works for Amazon, and Betsy, who works for McGraw-Hill, need to communicate with each other about inventory. Public key encryption can be used to create **digital signatures** for messages. That is, messages can be encoded in such a way that, if Elmer gets a message supposedly from Betsy, he can verify that it is from Betsy (in addition to being able to decrypt the message) and, further, *prove* that it is from Betsy at McGraw-Hill, even if the message is sent from a Hotmail account when Betsy is traveling. Similarly, Betsy can authenticate the originator of messages from Elmer.

If Elmer encrypts messages for Betsy using her public key, and vice-versa, they can exchange information securely but cannot authenticate the sender. Someone who wishes to impersonate Betsy could use her public key to send a message to Elmer, pretending to be Betsy.

A clever use of the encryption scheme, however, allows Elmer to verify whether the message was indeed sent by Betsy. Betsy encrypts the message using her *private* key and then encrypts the result using Elmer's public key. When Elmer receives such a message, he first decrypts it using his private key and then decrypts the result using Betsy's public key. This step yields the original unencrypted message. Furthermore, Elmer can be certain that the message was composed and encrypted by Betsy because a forger could not have known her private key, and without it the final result would have been nonsensical, rather than a legible message. Further, because even Elmer does not know Betsy's private key, Betsy cannot claim that Elmer forged the message.

If authenticating the sender is the objective and hiding the message is not important, we can reduce the cost of encryption by using a **message signature**. A signature is obtained by applying a one-way function (e.g., a hashing scheme) to the message and is considerably smaller. We encode the signature as in the basic digital signature approach, and send the encoded signature together with the full, unencoded message. The recipient can verify the sender of the signature as just described, and validate the message itself by applying the one-way function and comparing the result with the signature.

21.6 ADDITIONAL ISSUES RELATED TO SECURITY

Security is a broad topic, and our coverage is necessarily limited. This section briefly touches on some additional important issues.

21.6.1 Role of the Database Administrator

The database administrator (DBA) plays an important role in enforcing the security-related aspects of a database design. In conjunction with the owners of the data, the DBA also contributes to developing a security policy. The DBA has a special account, which we call the **system account**, and is responsible for the overall security of the system. In particular, the DBA deals with the following:

1. **Creating New Accounts:** Each new user or group of users must be assigned an authorization ID and a password. Note that application programs that access the database have the same authorization ID as the user executing the program.
2. **Mandatory Control Issues:** If the DBMS supports mandatory control—some customized systems for applications with very high security requirements (for example, military data) provide such support—the DBA must assign security classes to each database object and assign security clearances to each authorization ID in accordance with the chosen security policy.

The DBA is also responsible for maintaining the **audit trail**, which is essentially the log of updates with the authorization ID (of the user executing the transaction) added to each log entry. This log is just a minor extension of the log mechanism used to recover from crashes. Additionally, the DBA may choose to maintain a log of *all* actions, including reads, performed by a user. Analyzing such histories of how the DBMS was accessed can help prevent security violations by identifying suspicious patterns before an intruder finally succeeds in breaking in, or it can help track down an intruder after a violation has been detected.

21.6.2 Security in Statistical Databases

A **statistical database** contains specific information on individuals or events but is intended to permit only statistical queries. For example, if we maintained a statistical database of information about sailors, we would allow statistical queries about average ratings, maximum age, and so on, but not queries about individual sailors. Security in such databases poses new problems because it is possible to **infer** protected information (such as a sailor's rating) from answers to permitted statistical queries. Such inference opportunities represent covert channels that can compromise the security policy of the database.

Suppose that sailor Sneaky Pete wants to know the rating of Admiral Horntooter, the esteemed chairman of the sailing club, and happens to know that Horntooter is the oldest sailor in the club. Pete repeatedly asks queries of the form "How many sailors are there whose age is greater than X?" for various values of X, until the answer is 1. Obviously, this sailor is Horntooter, the oldest sailor. Note that each of these queries is a valid statistical query and is permitted. Let the value of X at this point be, say, 65. Pete now asks the query, "What is the maximum rating of all sailors whose age is greater than

65?" Again, this query is permitted because it is a statistical query. However, the answer to this query reveals Horntooter's rating to Pete, and the security policy of the database is violated.

One approach to preventing such violations is to require that each query must involve at least some minimum number, say, N, of rows. With a reasonable choice of N, Pete would not be able to isolate the information about Horntooter, because the query about the maximum rating would fail. This restriction, however, is easy to overcome. By repeatedly asking queries of the form, "How many sailors are there whose age is greater than X?" until the system rejects one such query, Pete identifies a set of N sailors, including Horntooter. Let the value of X at this point be 55. Now, Pete can ask two queries:

- "What is the sum of the ratings of all sailors whose age is greater than 55?" Since N sailors have age greater than 55, this query is permitted.
- "What is the sum of the ratings of all sailors, other than Horntooter, whose age is greater than 55, and sailor Pete?" Since the set of sailors whose ratings are added up now includes Pete instead of Horntooter, but is otherwise the same, the number of sailors involved is still N, and this query is also permitted.

From the answers to these two queries, say, A_1 and A_2, Pete, who knows his rating, can easily calculate Horntooter's rating as $A_1 - A_2 + \textit{Pete's rating}$.

Pete succeeded because he was able to ask two queries that involved many of the same sailors. The number of rows examined in common by two queries is called their **intersection**. If a limit were to be placed on the amount of intersection permitted between any two queries issued by the same user, Pete could be foiled. Actually, a truly fiendish (and patient) user can generally find out information about specific individuals even if the system places a minimum number of rows bound (N) and a maximum intersection bound (M) on queries, but the number of queries required to do this grows in proportion to N/M. We can try to additionally limit the total number of queries that a user is allowed to ask, but two users could still conspire to breach security. By maintaining a log of all activity (including read-only accesses), such query patterns can be detected, ideally before a security violation occurs. This discussion should make it clear, however, that security in statistical databases is difficult to enforce.

21.7 DESIGN CASE STUDY: THE INTERNET STORE

We return to our case study and our friends at DBDudes to consider security issues. There are three groups of users: customers, employees, and the owner of the book shop. (Of course, there is also the database administrator, who has universal access to all data and is responsible for regular operation of the database system.)

The owner of the store has full privileges on all tables. Customers can query the Books table and place orders online, but they should not have access to other customers' records nor to other customers' orders. DBDudes restricts access in two ways. First, it designs a simple Web page with several forms similar to the page shown in Figure 7.1 in Chapter 7. This allows customers to submit a small collection of valid requests without giving them the ability to directly access the underlying DBMS through an SQL interface. Second, DBDudes uses the security features of the DBMS to limit access to sensitive data.

The webpage allows customers to query the Books relation by ISBN number, name of the author, and title of a book. The webpage also has two buttons. The first button retrieves a list of all of the customer's orders that are not completely fulfilled yet. The second button displays a list of all completed orders for that customer. Note that customers cannot specify actual SQL queries through the Web but only fill in some parameters in a form to instantiate an automatically generated SQL query. All queries generated through form input have a `WHERE` clause that includes the *cid* attribute value of the current customer, and evaluation of the queries generated by the two buttons requires knowledge of the customer identification number. Since all users have to log on to the website before browsing the catalog, the business logic (discussed in Section 7.7) must maintain state information about a customer (i.e., the customer identification number) during the customer's visit to the website.

The second step is to configure the database to limit access according to each user group's need to know. DBDudes creates a special `customer` account that has the following privileges:

```
SELECT ON Books, NewOrders, OldOrders, NewOrderlists, OldOrderlists
INSERT ON NewOrders, OldOrders, NewOrderlists, OldOrderlists
```

Employees should be able to add new books to the catalog, update the quantity of a book in stock, revise customer orders if necessary, and update all customer information *except the credit card information.* In fact, employees should not even be able to see a customer's credit card number. Therefore, DBDudes creates the following view:

```
CREATE VIEW CustomerInfo (cid,cname,address)
       AS SELECT C.cid, C.cname, C.address
          FROM   Customers C
```

DBDudes gives the `employee` account the following privileges:

```
SELECT ON CustomerInfo, Books,
          NewOrders, OldOrders, NewOrderlists, OldOrderlists
INSERT ON CustomerInfo, Books,
          NewOrders, OldOrders, NewOrderlists, OldOrderlists
UPDATE ON CustomerInfo, Books,
          NewOrders, OldOrders, NewOrderlists, OldOrderlists
DELETE ON Books, NewOrders, OldOrders, NewOrderlists, OldOrderlists
```

Observe that employees can modify CustomerInfo and even insert tuples into it. This is possible because they have the necessary privileges, and further, the view is updatable and insertable-into. While it seems reasonable that employees can update a customer's address, it does seem odd that they can insert a tuple into CustomerInfo even though they cannot see related information about the customer (i.e., credit card number) in the Customers table. The reason for this is that the store wants to be able to take orders from first-time customers over the phone without asking for credit card information over the phone. Employees can insert into CustomerInfo, effectively creating a new Customers record without credit card information, and customers can subsequently provide the credit card number through a Web interface. (Obviously, the order is not shipped until they do this.)

In addition, there are security issues when the user first logs on to the website using the customer identification number. Sending the number unencrypted over the Internet is a security hazard, and a secure protocol such as SSL should be used.

Companies such as CyberCash and DigiCash offer electronic commerce payment solutions, even including *electronic cash.* Discussion of how to incorporate such techniques into the website are outside the scope of this book.

21.8 REVIEW QUESTIONS

Answers to the review questions can be found in the listed sections.

- What are the main objectives in designing a secure database application? Explain the terms *secrecy*, *integrity*, *availability*, and *authentication*. **(Section 21.1)**

- Explain the terms *security policy* and *security mechanism* and how they are related. **(Section 21.1)**

- What is the main idea behind *discretionary access control*? What is the idea behind *mandatory access control*? What are the relative merits of these two approaches? **(Section 21.2)**

- Describe the privileges recognized in SQL? In particular, describe SELECT, INSERT, UPDATE, DELETE, and REFERENCES. For each privilege, indicate who acquires it automatically on a given table. **(Section 21.3)**
- How are the owners of privileges identified? In particular, discuss *authorization IDs* and *roles*. **(Section 21.3)**
- What is an *authorization graph*? Explain SQL's GRANT and REVOKE commands in terms of their effect on this graph. In particular, discuss what happens when users pass on privileges that they receive from someone else. **(Section 21.3)**
- Discuss the difference between having a privilege on a table and on a view defined over the table. In particular, how can a user have a privilege (say, SELECT) over a view without also having it on all underlying tables? Who must have appropriate privileges on all underlying tables of the view? **(Section 21.3.1)**
- What are *objects*, *subjects*, *security classes*, and *clearances* in mandatory access control? Discuss the Bell-LaPadula restrictions in terms of these concepts. Specifically, define the *simple security property* and the **-property*. **(Section 21.4)**
- What is a *Trojan horse* attack and how can it compromise discretionary access control? Explain how mandatory access control protects against Trojan horse attacks. **(Section 21.4)**
- What do the terms *multilevel table* and *polyinstantiation* mean? Explain their relationship, and how they arise in the context of mandatory access control. **(Section 21.4.1)**
- What are *covert channels* and how can they arise when both discretionary and mandatory access controls are in place? **(Section 21.4.2)**
- Discuss the DoD security levels for database systems. **(Section 21.4.2)**
- Explain why a simple password mechanism is insufficient for authentication of users who access a database remotely, say, over the Internet. **(Section 21.5)**
- What is the difference between *symmetric* and *public-key encryption*? Give examples of well-known encryption algorithms of both kinds. What is the main weakness of symmetric encryption and how is this addressed in public-key encryption? **(Section 21.5.1)**
- Discuss the choice of encryption and decryption keys in public-key encryption and how they are used to encrypt and decrypt data. Explain the role of *one-way functions*. What assurance do we have that the RSA scheme cannot be compromised? **(Section 21.5.1)**

- What are *certification authorities* and why are they needed? Explain how *certificates* are issued to sites and validated by a browser using the *SSL protocol*; discuss the role of the *session key*. **(Section 21.5.2)**
- If a user connects to a site using the SSL protocol, explain why there is still a need to login the user. Explain the use of SSL to protect passwords and other sensitive information being exchanged. What is the *secure electronic transaction protocol*? What is the added value over SSL? **(Section 21.5.2)**
- A *digital signature* facilitates secure exchange of messages. Explain what it is and how it goes beyond simply encrypting messages. Discuss the use of *message signatures* to reduce the cost of encryption. **(Section 21.5.3)**
- What is the role of the database administrator with respect to security? **(Section 21.6.1)**
- Discuss the additional security loopholes introduced in *statistical databases*. **(Section 21.6.2)**

EXERCISES

Exercise 21.1 Briefly answer the following questions:

1. Explain the intuition behind the two rules in the Bell-LaPadula model for mandatory access control.
2. Give an example of how covert channels can be used to defeat the Bell-LaPadula model.
3. Give an example of polyinstantiation.
4. Describe a scenario in which mandatory access controls prevent a breach of security that cannot be prevented through discretionary controls.
5. Describe a scenario in which discretionary access controls are required to enforce a security policy that cannot be enforced using only mandatory controls.
6. If a DBMS already supports discretionary and mandatory access controls, is there a need for encryption?
7. Explain the need for each of the following limits in a statistical database system:
   (a) A maximum on the number of queries a user can pose.
   (b) A minimum on the number of tuples involved in answering a query.
   (c) A maximum on the intersection of two queries (i.e., on the number of tuples that both queries examine).
8. Explain the use of an audit trail, with special reference to a statistical database system.
9. What is the role of the DBA with respect to security?
10. Describe AES and its relationship to DES.
11. What is public-key encryption? How does it differ from the encryption approach taken in the Data Encryption Standard (DES), and in what ways is it better than DES?

12. Explain how a company offering services on the Internet could use encryption-based techniques to make its order-entry process secure. Discuss the role of DES, AES, SSL, SET, and digital signatures. Search the Web to find out more about related techniques such as *electronic cash.*

Exercise 21.2 You are the DBA for the VeryFine Toy Company and create a relation called Employees with fields *ename*, *dept*, and *salary.* For authorization reasons, you also define views EmployeeNames (with *ename* as the only attribute) and DeptInfo with fields *dept* and *avgsalary.* The latter lists the average salary for each department.

1. Show the view definition statements for EmployeeNames and DeptInfo.
2. What privileges should be granted to a user who needs to know only average department salaries for the Toy and CS departments?
3. You want to authorize your secretary to fire people (you will probably tell him whom to fire, but you want to be able to delegate this task), to check on who is an employee, and to check on average department salaries. What privileges should you grant?
4. Continuing with the preceding scenario, you do not want your secretary to be able to look at the salaries of individuals. Does your answer to the previous question ensure this? Be specific: Can your secretary possibly find out salaries of *some* individuals (depending on the actual set of tuples), or can your secretary always find out the salary of any individual he wants to?
5. You want to give your secretary the authority to allow other people to read the EmployeeNames view. Show the appropriate command.
6. Your secretary defines two new views using the EmployeeNames view. The first is called AtoRNames and simply selects names that begin with a letter in the range A to R. The second is called HowManyNames and counts the number of names. You are so pleased with this achievement that you decide to give your secretary the right to insert tuples into the EmployeeNames view. Show the appropriate command and describe what privileges your secretary has after this command is executed.
7. Your secretary allows Todd to read the EmployeeNames relation and later quits. You then revoke the secretary's privileges. What happens to Todd's privileges?
8. Give an example of a view update on the preceding schema that cannot be implemented through updates to Employees.
9. You decide to go on an extended vacation, and to make sure that emergencies can be handled, you want to authorize your boss Joe to read and modify the Employees relation and the EmployeeNames relation (and Joe must be able to delegate authority, of course, since he is too far up the management hierarchy to actually do any work). Show the appropriate SQL statements. Can Joe read the DeptInfo view?
10. After returning from your (wonderful) vacation, you see a note from Joe, indicating that he authorized his secretary Mike to read the Employees relation. You want to revoke Mike's `SELECT` privilege on Employees, but you do not want to revoke the rights you gave to Joe, even temporarily. Can you do this in SQL?
11. Later you realize that Joe has been quite busy. He has defined a view called AllNames using the view EmployeeNames, defined another relation called StaffNames that he has access to (but you cannot access), and given his secretary Mike the right to read from the AllNames view. Mike has passed this right on to his friend Susan. You decide that, even at the cost of annoying Joe by revoking some of his privileges, you simply have to take away Mike and Susan's rights to see your data. What `REVOKE` statement would you execute? What rights does Joe have on Employees after this statement is executed? What views are dropped as a consequence?

Exercise 21.3 You are a painter and have an Internet store where you sell your paintings directly to the public. You would like customers to pay for their purchases with credit cards, and wish to ensure that these electronic transactions are secure.

Assume that Mary wants to purchase your recent painting of the Cornell Uris Library. Answer the following questions.

1. How can you ensure that the user who is purchasing the painting is really Mary?
2. Explain how SSL ensures that the communication of the credit card number is secure. What is the role of a certification authority in this case?
3. Assume that you would like Mary to be able to verify that all your email messages are really sent from you. How can you authenticate your messages without encrypting the actual text?
4. Assume that your customers can also negotiate the price of certain paintings and assume that Mary wants to negotiate the price of your painting of the Madison Terrace. You would like the text of this communication to be private between you and Mary. Explain the advantages and disadvantages of different methods of encrypting your communication with Mary.

Exercise 21.4 Consider Exercises 6.6 to 6.9 from Chapter 6. For each exercise, identify what data should be accessible to different groups of users, and write the SQL statements to enforce these access control policies.

Exercise 21.5 Consider Exercises 7.7 to 7.10 from Chapter 7. For each exercise, discuss where encryption, SSL, and digital signatures are appropriate.

PROJECT-BASED EXERCISES

Exercise 21.6 Is there any support for views or authorization in Minibase?

BIBLIOGRAPHIC NOTES

The authorization mechanism of System R, which greatly influenced the `GRANT` and `REVOKE` paradigm in SQL, is described in [341]. A good general treatment of security and cryptography is presented in [213], and an overview of database security can be found in [140] and [467]. Security in statistical databases is investigated in several papers, including [212] and [178]. Multilevel security is discussed in several papers, including [409, 499, 694, 710].

A classic reference on crytography is the book by Schneier [661]. Diffie and Hellman proposed the first public key cryptographic technique [227]. The widely-used RSA encryption scheme was introduced by Rivest, Shamir, and Adleman [629]. AES is based on Daemen and Rijmen's Rijndael algorithm [200]. There are many introductory books on SSL, such as [623] and [733]. More information on ditigal signatures can be found in the book by Ford and Baum [276].

PART VII

ADDITIONAL TOPICS

22

PARALLEL AND DISTRIBUTED DATABASES

- What is the motivation for parallel and distributed DBMSs?
- What are the alternative architectures for parallel database systems?
- How are pipelining and data partitioning used to gain parallelism?
- How are dataflow concepts used to parallelize existing sequential code?
- What are alternative architectures for distributed DBMSs?
- How is data distributed across sites?
- How can we evaluate and optimize queries over distributed data?
- What are the merits of synchronous vs. asynchronous replication?
- How are transactions managed in a distributed environment?

➥ **Key concepts:** parallel DBMS architectures; performance, speed-up and scale-up; pipelined versus data-partitioned parallelism, blocking; partitioning strategies; dataflow operators; distributed DBMS architectures; heterogeneous systems; gateway protocols; data distribution, distributed catalogs; semijoins, data shipping; synchronous versus asynchronous replication; distributed transactions, lock management, deadlock detection, two-phase commit, Presumed Abort

No man is an island, entire of itself; every man is a piece of the continent, a part of the main.

—John Donne

In this chapter we look at the issues of parallelism and data distribution in a DBMS. We begin by introducing parallel and distributed database systems in Section 22.1. In Section 22.2, we discuss alternative hardware configurations for a parallel DBMS. In Section 22.3, we introduce the concept of data partitioning and consider its influence on parallel query evaluation. In Section 22.4, we show how data partitioning can be used to parallelize several relational operations. In Section 22.5, we conclude our treatment of parallel query processing with a discussion of parallel query optimization.

The rest of the chapter is devoted to distributed databases. We present an overview of distributed databases in Section 22.6. We discuss some alternative architectures for a distributed DBMS in Section 22.7 and describe options for distributing data in Section 22.8. We describe distributed catalog management in Section 22.9, then in Section 22.10, we discuss query optimization and evaluation for distributed databases. In Section 22.11, we discuss updating distributed data, and finally, in Sections 22.12 to 22.14 we describe distributed transaction management.

22.1 INTRODUCTION

We have thus far considered centralized database management systems in which all the data is maintained at a single site and assumed that the processing of individual transactions is essentially sequential. One of the most important trends in databases is the increased use of parallel evaluation techniques and data distribution.

A **parallel database system** seeks to improve performance through parallelization of various operations, such as loading data, building indexes, and evaluating queries. Although data may be stored in a distributed fashion in such a system, the distribution is governed solely by performance considerations.

In a **distributed database system**, data is physically stored across several sites, and each site is typically managed by a DBMS capable of running independent of the other sites. The location of data items and the degree of autonomy of individual sites have a significant impact on all aspects of the system, including query optimization and processing, concurrency control, and recovery. In contrast to parallel databases, the distribution of data is governed by factors such as local ownership and increased availability, in addition to performance issues.

While parallelism is motivated by performance considerations, several distinct issues motivate data distribution:

- **Increased Availability:** If a site containing a relation goes down, the relation continues to be available if a copy is maintained at another site.
- **Distributed Access to Data:** An organization may have branches in several cities. Although analysts may need to access data corresponding to different sites, we usually find locality in the access patterns (e.g., a bank manager is likely to look up the accounts of customers at the local branch), and this locality can be exploited by distributing the data accordingly.
- **Analysis of Distributed Data:** Organizations want to examine all the data available to them, even when it is stored across multiple sites and on multiple database systems. Support for such integrated access involves many issues; even enabling access to widely distributed data can be a challenge.

22.2 ARCHITECTURES FOR PARALLEL DATABASES

The basic idea behind parallel databases is to carry out evaluation steps in parallel whenever possible, and there are many such opportunities in a relational DBMS; databases represent one of the most successful instances of parallel computing.

Figure 22.1 Physical Architectures for Parallel Database Systems

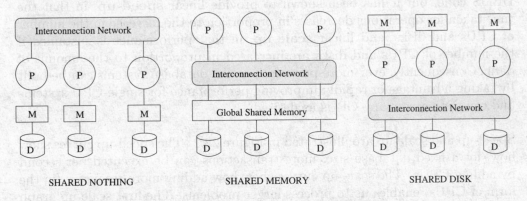

Three main architectures have been proposed for building parallel DBMSs. In a **shared-memory** system, multiple CPUs are attached to an interconnection network and can access a common region of main memory. In a **shared-disk** system, each CPU has a private memory and direct access to all disks through an interconnection network. In a **shared-nothing** system, each CPU has local main memory and disk space, but no two CPUs can access the same storage area; all communication between CPUs is through a network connection. The three architectures are illustrated in Figure 22.1.

The shared-memory architecture is closer to a conventional machine, and many commercial database systems have been ported to shared memory platforms with relative ease. Communication overhead is low, because main memory can be used for this purpose, and operating system services can be leveraged to utilize the additional CPUs. Although this approach is attractive for achieving moderate parallelism—a few tens of CPUs can be exploited in this fashion—memory contention becomes a bottleneck as the number of CPUs increases. The shared-disk architecture faces a similar problem because large amounts of data are shipped through the interconnection network.

The basic problem with the shared-memory and shared-disk architectures is **interference**: As more CPUs are added, existing CPUs are slowed down because of the increased contention for memory accesses and network bandwidth. It has been noted that even an average 1 percent slowdown per additional CPU means that the maximum speed-up is a factor of 37, and adding additional CPUs actually slows down the system; a system with 1000 CPUs is only 4 percent as effective as a *single-CPU* system! This observation has motivated the development of the shared-nothing architecture, which is now widely considered to be the best architecture for large parallel database systems.

The shared-nothing architecture requires more extensive reorganization of the DBMS code, but it has been shown to provide linear **speed-up**, in that the time taken for operations decreases in proportion to the increase in the number of CPUs and disks, and linear **scale-up**, in that performance is sustained if the number of CPUs and disks are increased in proportion to the amount of data. Consequently, ever-more-powerful parallel database systems can be built by taking advantage of rapidly improving performance for single-CPU systems and connecting as many CPUs as desired.

Speed-up and scale-up are illustrated in Figure 22.2. The speed-up curves show how, for a fixed database size, more transactions can be executed per second by adding CPUs. The scale-up curves show how adding more resources (in the form of CPUs) enables us to process larger problems. The first scale-up graph measures the number of transactions executed per second as the database size is increased and the number of CPUs is correspondingly increased. An alternative way to measure scale-up is to consider the time taken per transaction as more CPUs are added to process an increasing number of transactions per second; the goal here is to sustain the response time per transaction.

22.3 PARALLEL QUERY EVALUATION

In this section, we discuss parallel evaluation of a relational query in a DBMS with a shared-nothing architecture. While it is possible to consider parallel

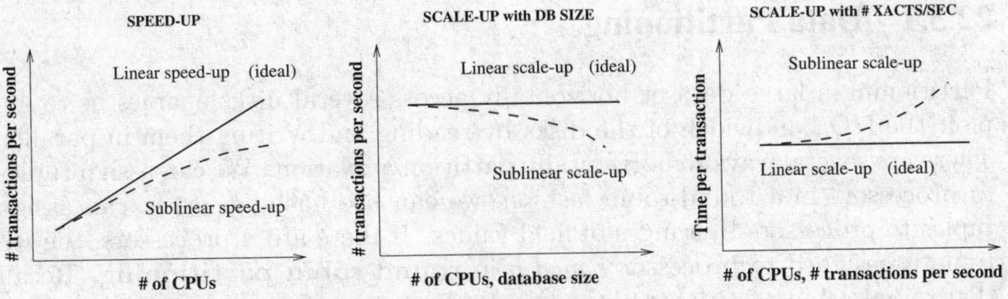

Figure 22.2 Speed-up and Scale-up

execution of multiple queries, it is hard to identify in advance which queries will run concurrently. So the emphasis has been on parallel execution of a single query.

A relational query execution plan is a graph of relational algebra operators, and the operators in a graph can be executed in parallel. If one operator consumes the output of a second operator, we have **pipelined parallelism** (the output of the second operator is worked on by the first operator as soon as it is generated); if not, the two operators can proceed essentially independently. An operator is said to **block** if it produces no output until it has consumed all its inputs. Pipelined parallelism is limited by the presence of operators (e.g., sorting or aggregation) that block.

In addition to evaluating different operators in parallel, we can evaluate each individual operator in a query plan in a parallel fashion. The key to evaluating an operator in parallel is to *partition* the input data; we can then work on each partition in parallel and combine the results. This approach is called **data-partitioned parallel evaluation**. By exercising some care, existing code for sequentially evaluating relational operators can be ported easily for data-partitioned parallel evaluation.

An important observation, which explains why shared-nothing parallel database systems have been very successful, is that database query evaluation is very amenable to data-partitioned parallel evaluation. The goal is to minimize data shipping by partitioning the data and structuring the algorithms to do most of the processing at individual processors. (We use *processor* to refer to a CPU together with its local disk.)

We now consider data partitioning and parallelization of existing operator evaluation code in more detail.

22.3.1 Data Partitioning

Partitioning a large dataset horizontally across several disks enables us to exploit the I/O bandwidth of the disks by reading and writing them in parallel. There are several ways to horizontally partition a relation. We can assign tuples to processors in a round-robin fashion, we can use hashing, or we can assign tuples to processors by ranges of field values. If there are n processors, the ith tuple is assigned to processor $i \bmod n$ in **round-robin partitioning**. Recall that round-robin partitioning is used in RAID storage systems (see Section 9.2). In **hash partitioning**, a hash function is applied to (selected fields of) a tuple to determine its processor. In **range partitioning**, tuples are sorted (conceptually), and n ranges are chosen for the sort key values so that each range contains roughly the same number of tuples; tuples in range i are assigned to processor i.

Round-robin partitioning is suitable for efficiently evaluating queries that access the entire relation. If only a subset of the tuples (e.g., those that satisfy the selection condition $age = 20$) is required, hash partitioning and range partitioning are better than round-robin partitioning because they enable us to access only those disks that contain matching tuples. (Of course, this statement assumes that the tuples are partitioned on the attributes in the selection condition; if $age = 20$ is specified, the tuples must be partitioned on *age*.) If range selections such as $15 < age < 25$ are specified, range partitioning is superior to hash partitioning because qualifying tuples are likely to be clustered together on a few processors. On the other hand, range partitioning can lead to **data skew**; that is, partitions with widely varying numbers of tuples across partitions or disks. Skew causes processors dealing with large partitions to become performance bottlenecks. Hash partitioning has the additional virtue that it keeps data evenly distributed even if the data grows and shrinks over time.

To reduce skew in range partitioning, the main question is how to choose the ranges by which tuples are distributed. One effective approach is to take samples from each processor, collect and sort all samples, and divide the sorted set of samples into equally sized subsets. If tuples are to be partitioned on *age*, the *age* ranges of the sampled subsets of tuples can be used as the basis for redistributing the entire relation.

22.3.2 Parallelizing Sequential Operator Evaluation Code

An elegant software architecture for parallel DBMSs enables us to readily parallelize existing code for sequentially evaluating a relational operator. The basic idea is to use parallel data streams. Streams (from different disks or the output of other operators) are **merged** as needed to provide the inputs for a relational operator, and the output of an operator is **split** as needed to parallelize subsequent processing.

A parallel evaluation plan consists of a dataflow network of relational, merge, and split operators. The merge and split operators should be able to buffer some data and should be able to halt the operators producing their input data. They can then regulate the speed of the execution according to the execution speed of the operator that consumes their output.

As we will see, obtaining good parallel versions of algorithms for sequential operator evaluation requires careful consideration; there is no magic formula for taking sequential code and producing a parallel version. Good use of split and merge in a dataflow software architecture, however, can greatly reduce the effort of implementing parallel query evaluation algorithms, as we illustrate in Section 22.4.3.

22.4 PARALLELIZING INDIVIDUAL OPERATIONS

This section shows how various operations can be implemented in parallel in a shared-nothing architecture. We assume that each relation is horizontally partitioned across several disks, although this partitioning may or may not be appropriate for a given query. The evaluation of a query must take the initial partitioning criteria into account and repartition if necessary.

22.4.1 Bulk Loading and Scanning

We begin with two simple operations: *scanning* a relation and *loading* a relation. Pages can be read in parallel while scanning a relation, and the retrieved tuples can then be merged, if the relation is partitioned across several disks. More generally, the idea also applies when retrieving all tuples that meet a selection condition. If hashing or range partitioning is used, selection queries can be answered by going to just those processors that contain relevant tuples.

A similar observation holds for bulk loading. Further, if a relation has associated indexes, any sorting of data entries required for building the indexes during bulk loading can also be done in parallel (see later).

22.4.2 Sorting

A simple idea is to let each CPU sort the part of the relation that is on its local disk and then merge these sorted sets of tuples. The degree of parallelism is likely to be limited by the merging phase.

A better idea is to first redistribute all tuples in the relation using range partitioning. For example, if we want to sort à collection of employee tuples by salary, salary values range from 10 to 210, and we have 20 processors, we could send all tuples with salary values in the range 10 to 20 to the first processor, all in the range 21 to 30 to the second processor, and so on. (Prior to the redistribution, while tuples are distributed across the processors, we cannot assume that they are distributed according to salary ranges.)

Each processor then sorts the tuples assigned to it, using some sequential sorting algorithm. For example, a processor can collect tuples until its memory is full, then sort these tuples and write out a run, until all incoming tuples have been written to such sorted runs on the local disk. These runs can then be merged to create the sorted version of the set of tuples assigned to this processor. The entire sorted relation can be retrieved by visiting the processors in an order corresponding to the ranges assigned to them and simply scanning the tuples.

The basic challenge in parallel sorting is to do the range partitioning so that each processor receives roughly the same number of tuples; otherwise, a processor that receives a disproportionately large number of tuples to sort becomes a bottleneck and limits the scalability of the parallel sort. One good approach to range partitioning is to obtain a sample of the entire relation by taking samples at each processor that initially contains part of the relation. The (relatively small) sample is sorted and used to identify ranges with equal numbers of tuples. This set of range values, called a **splitting vector**, is then distributed to all processors and used to range partition the entire relation.

A particularly important application of parallel sorting is sorting the data entries in tree-structured indexes. Sorting data entries can significantly speed up the process of bulk-loading an index.

22.4.3 Joins

In this section, we consider how the join operation can be parallelized. We present the basic idea behind the parallelization and illustrate the use of the merge and split operators described in Section 22.3.2. We focus on parallel hash join, which is widely used, and briefly outline how sort-merge join can be similarly parallelized. Other join algorithms can be parallelized as well, although not as effectively as these two algorithms.

Suppose that we want to join two relations, say, A and B, on the *age* attribute. We assume that they are initially distributed across several disks in some way that is not useful for the join operation; that is, the initial partitioning is not based on the join attribute. The basic idea for joining A and B in parallel is to decompose the join into a collection of k smaller joins. We can decompose the join by partitioning both A and B into a collection of k logical buckets or partitions. By using the same partitioning function for both A and B, we ensure that the union of the k smaller joins computes the join of A and B; this idea is similar to intuition behind the partitioning phase of a sequential hash join, described in Section 14.4.3. Because A and B are initially distributed across several processors, the partitioning step itself can be done in parallel at these processors. At each processor, all local tuples are retrieved and hashed into one of k partitions, with the same hash function used at all sites, of course.

Alternatively, we can partition A and B by dividing the range of the join attribute *age* into k disjoint subranges and placing A and B tuples into partitions according to the subrange to which their *age* values belong. For example, suppose that we have 10 processors, the join attribute is *age*, with values from 0 to 100. Assuming uniform distribution, A and B tuples with $0 \leq age < 10$ go to processor 1, $10 \leq age < 20$ go to processor 2, and so on. This approach is likely to be more susceptible than hash partitioning to data skew (i.e., the number of tuples to be joined can vary widely across partitions), unless the subranges are carefully determined; we do not discuss how good subrange boundaries can be identified.

Having decided on a partitioning strategy, we can assign each partition to a processor and carry out a local join, using any join algorithm we want, at each processor. In this case, the number of partitions k is chosen to be equal to the number of processors n available for carrying out the join, and during partitioning, each processor sends tuples in the ith partition to processor i. After partitioning, each processor joins the A and B tuples assigned to it. Each join process executes sequential join code and receives input A and B tuples from several processors; a merge operator merges all incoming A tuples, and another merge operator merges all incoming B tuples. Depending on how we want to distribute the result of the join of A and B, the output of the join process may be split into several data streams. The network of operators for parallel join is shown in Figure 22.3. To simplify the figure, we assume that the processors doing the join are distinct from the processors that initially contain tuples of A and B and show only four processors.

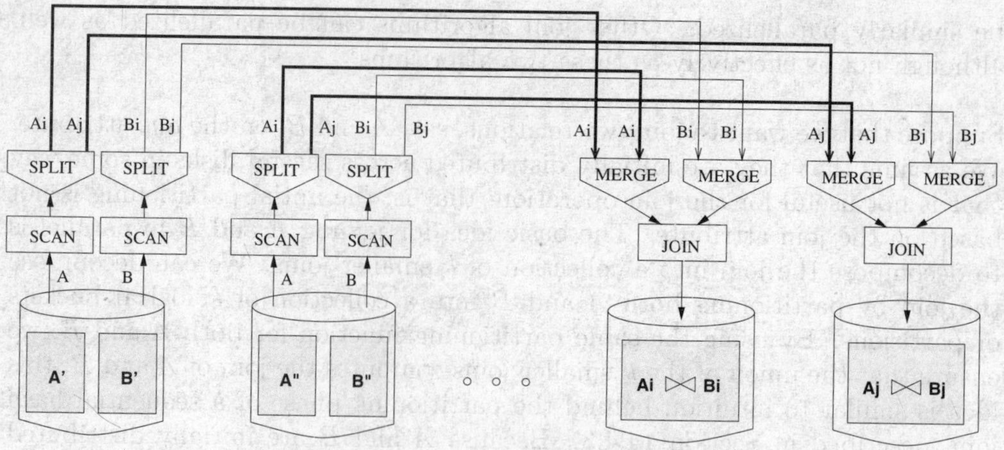

Figure 22.3 Dataflow Network of Operators for Parallel Join

If range partitioning is used, this algorithm leads to a parallel version of a sort-merge join, with the advantage that the output is available in sorted order. If hash partitioning is used, we obtain a parallel version of a hash join.

Improved Parallel Hash Join

A hash-based refinement of the approach offers improved performance. The main observation is that, if A and B are very large and the number of partitions k is chosen to be equal to the number of processors n, the size of each partition may still be large, leading to a high cost for each local join at the n processors.

An alternative is to execute the smaller joins $A_i \bowtie B_i$, for $i = 1 \ldots k$, one after the other, but with each join executed in parallel using all processors. This approach allows us to utilize the total available main memory at all n processors in each join $A_i \bowtie B_i$ and is described in more detail as follows:

1. At each site, apply a hash function $h1$ to partition the A and B tuples at this site into partitions $i = 1 \ldots k$. Let A be the smaller relation. The number of partitions k is chosen such that each partition of A fits into the *aggregate* or combined memory of all n processors.

2. For $i = 1 \ldots k$, process the join of the ith partitions of A and B. To compute $A_i \bowtie B_i$, do the following at every site:
   (a) Apply a second hash function $h2$ to all A_i tuples to determine where they should be joined and send tuple t to site $h2(t)$.
   (b) As A_i tuples arrive to be joined, add them to an in-memory hash table.

(c) After all A_i tuples have been distributed, apply $h2$ to B_i tuples to determine where they should be joined and send tuple t to site $h2(t)$.

(d) As B_i tuples arrive to be joined, probe the in-memory table of A_i tuples and output result tuples.

The use of the second hash function $h2$ ensures that tuples are (more or less) uniformly distributed across all n processors participating in the join. This approach greatly reduces the cost for each of the smaller joins and therefore reduces the overall join cost. Observe that all available processors are fully utilized, even though the smaller joins are carried out one after the other.

The reader is invited to adapt the network of operators shown in Figure 22.3 to reflect the improved parallel join algorithm.

22.5 PARALLEL QUERY OPTIMIZATION

In addition to parallelizing individual operations, we can obviously execute different operations in a query in parallel and execute multiple queries in parallel. Optimizing a single query for parallel execution has received more attention; systems typically optimize queries without regard to other queries that might be executing at the same time.

Two kinds of interoperation parallelism can be exploited within a query:

- The result of one operator can be pipelined into another. For example, consider a left-deep plan in which all the joins use index nested loops. The result of the first (i.e., the bottommost) join is the outer relation tuples for the next join node. As tuples are produced by the first join, they can be used to probe the inner relation in the second join. The result of the second join can similarly be pipelined into the next join, and so on.
- Multiple independent operations can be executed concurrently. For example, consider a (bushy) plan in which relations A and B are joined, relations C and D are joined, and the results of these two joins are finally joined. Clearly, the join of A and B can be executed concurrently with the join of C and D.

An optimizer that seeks to parallelize query evaluation has to consider several issues, and we only outline the main points. The cost of executing individual operations in parallel (e.g., parallel sorting) obviously differs from executing them sequentially, and the optimizer should estimate operation costs accordingly.

Next, the plan that returns answers quickest may not be the plan with the least cost. For example, the cost of $A \bowtie B$ plus the cost of $C \bowtie D$ plus the cost of joining their results may be more than the cost of the cheapest left-deep plan. However, the time taken is the time for the more expensive of $A \bowtie B$ and $C \bowtie D$ plus the time to join their results. This time may be less than the time taken by the cheapest left-deep plan. This observation suggests that a parallelizing optimizer should not restrict itself to left-deep trees and should also consider *bushy* trees, which significantly enlarge the space of plans to be considered.

Finally, a number of parameters, such as available buffer space and the number of free processors, are known only at run-time. This comment holds in a multiuser environment even if only sequential plans are considered; a multiuser environment is a simple instance of interquery parallelism.

22.6 INTRODUCTION TO DISTRIBUTED DATABASES

As we observed earlier, data in a distributed database system is stored across several sites, and each site is typically managed by a DBMS that can run independent of the other sites. The classical view of a distributed database system is that the system should make the impact of data distribution **transparent**. In particular, the following properties are considered desirable:

- **Distributed Data Independence:** Users should be able to ask queries without specifying where the referenced relations, or copies or fragments of the relations, are located. This principle is a natural extension of physical and logical data independence; we discuss it in Section 22.8. Further, queries that span multiple sites should be optimized systematically in a cost-based manner, taking into account communication costs and differences in local computation costs. We discuss distributed query optimization in Section 22.10.

- **Distributed Transaction Atomicity:** Users should be able to write transactions that access and update data at several sites just as they would write transactions over purely local data. In particular, the effects of a transaction across sites should continue to be atomic; that is, all changes persist if the transaction commits and none persist if it aborts. We discuss this distributed transaction processing in Sections 22.11, 22.13, and 22.14.

Although most people would agree that these properties are in general desirable, in certain situations, such as when sites are connected by a slow long-distance network, these properties are not efficiently achievable. Indeed, it has been argued that, when sites are globally distributed, these properties are not even desirable. The argument essentially is that the administrative overhead of supporting a system with distributed data independence and transaction atomicity—in effect, coordinating all activities across all sites to support the view of the whole as a unified collection of data—is prohibitive, over and above DBMS performance considerations.

Keep these remarks about distributed databases in mind as we cover the topic in more detail in the rest of this chapter. There is no real consensus on what the design objectives of distributed databases should be, and the field is evolving in response to users' needs.

22.6.1 Types of Distributed Databases

If data is distributed but all servers run the same DBMS software, we have a **homogeneous distributed database system**. If different sites run under the control of different DBMSs, essentially autonomously, and are connected somehow to enable access to data from multiple sites, we have a **heterogeneous distributed database system**, also referred to as a **multidatabase system**.

The key to building heterogeneous systems is to have well-accepted standards for **gateway protocols**. A gateway protocol is an API that exposes DBMS functionality to external applications. Examples include ODBC and JDBC (see Section 6.2). By accessing database servers through gateway protocols, their differences (in capability, data format, etc.) are masked, and the differences between the different servers in a distributed system are bridged to a large degree.

Gateways are not a panacea, however. They add a layer of processing that can be expensive, and they do not completely mask the differences among servers. For example, a server may not be capable of providing the services required for distributed transaction management (see Sections 22.13 and 22.14), and even if it is capable, standardizing gateway protocols all the way down to this level of interaction poses challenges that have not yet been resolved satisfactorily.

Distributed data management, in the final analysis, comes at a significant cost in terms of performance, software complexity, and administration difficulty. This observation is especially true of heterogeneous systems.

22.7 DISTRIBUTED DBMS ARCHITECTURES

Three alternative approaches are used to separate functionality across different DBMS-related processes; these alternative distributed DBMS architectures are called *Client-Server*, *Collaborating Server*, and *Middleware*.

22.7.1 Client-Server Systems

A **Client-Server** system has one or more client processes and one or more server processes, and a client process can send a query to any one server process. Clients are responsible for user-interface issues, and servers manage data and execute transactions. Thus, a client process could run on a personal computer and send queries to a server running on a mainframe.

This architecture has become very popular for several reasons. First, it is relatively simple to implement due to its clean separation of functionality and because the server is centralized. Second, expensive server machines are not underutilized by dealing with mundane user-interactions, which are now relegated to inexpensive client machines. Third, users can run a graphical user interface that they are familiar with, rather than the (possibly unfamiliar and unfriendly) user interface on the server.

While writing Client-Server applications, it is important to remember the boundary between the client and the server and keep the communication between them as set-oriented as possible. In particular, opening a cursor and fetching tuples one at a time generates many messages and should be avoided. (Even if we fetch several tuples and cache them at the client, messages must be exchanged when the cursor is advanced to ensure that the current row is locked.) Techniques to exploit client-side caching to reduce communication overhead have been studied extensively, although we do not discuss them further.

22.7.2 Collaborating Server Systems

The Client-Server architecture does not allow a single query to span multiple servers because the client process would have to be capable of breaking such a query into appropriate subqueries to be executed at different sites and then piecing together the answers to the subqueries. The client process would therefore be quite complex, and its capabilities would begin to overlap with the server; distinguishing between clients and servers becomes harder. Eliminating this distinction leads us to an alternative to the Client-Server architecture: a **Collaborating Server** system. We can have a collection of database servers, each capable of running transactions against local data, which cooperatively execute transactions spanning multiple servers.

When a server receives a query that requires access to data at other servers, it generates appropriate subqueries to be executed by other servers and puts the results together to compute answers to the original query. Ideally, the decomposition of the query should be done using cost-based optimization, taking into account the cost of network communication as well as local processing costs.

22.7.3 Middleware Systems

The Middleware architecture is designed to allow a single query to span multiple servers, without requiring all database servers to be capable of managing such multi-site execution strategies. It is especially attractive when trying to integrate several legacy systems, whose basic capabilities cannot be extended.

The idea is that we need just one database server capable of managing queries and transactions spanning multiple servers; the remaining servers need to handle only local queries and transactions. We can think of this special server as a layer of software that coordinates the execution of queries and transactions across one or more independent database servers; such software is often called **middleware**. The middleware layer is capable of executing joins and other relational operations on data obtained from the other servers but, typically, does not itself maintain any data.

22.8 STORING DATA IN A DISTRIBUTED DBMS

In a distributed DBMS, relations are stored across several sites. Accessing a relation stored at a remote site incurs message-passing costs and, to reduce this overhead, a single relation may be *partitioned* or *fragmented* across several sites, with fragments stored at the sites where they are most often accessed or *replicated* at each site where the relation is in high demand.

22.8.1 Fragmentation

Fragmentation consists of breaking a relation into smaller relations or fragments and storing the fragments (instead of the relation itself), possibly at different sites. In **horizontal fragmentation**, each fragment consists of a subset of *rows* of the original relation. In **vertical fragmentation**, each fragment consists of a subset of *columns* of the original relation. Horizontal and vertical fragments are illustrated in Figure 22.4.

Typically, the tuples that belong to a given horizontal fragment are identified by a selection query; for example, employee tuples might be organized into fragments by city, with all employees in a given city assigned to the same fragment. The horizontal fragment shown in Figure 22.4 corresponds to Chicago. By storing fragments in the database site at the corresponding city, we achieve locality of reference—Chicago data is most likely to be updated and queried

TID	eid	name	city	age	sal
t1	53666	Jones	Madras	18	35
t2	53688	Smith	Chicago	18	32
t3	53650	Smith	Chicago	19	48
t4	53831	Madayan	Bombay	11	20
t5	53832	Guldu	Bombay	12	20

Vertical Fragment **Horizontal Fragment**

Figure 22.4 Horizontal and Vertical Fragmentation

from Chicago, and storing this data in Chicago makes it local (and reduces communication costs) for most queries. Similarly, the tuples in a given vertical fragment are identified by a projection query. The vertical fragment in the figure results from projection on the first two columns of the employees relation.

When a relation is fragmented, we must be able to recover the original relation from the fragments:

- **Horizontal Fragmentation:** The union of the horizontal fragments must be equal to the original relation. Fragments are usually also required to be disjoint.

- **Vertical Fragmentation:** The collection of vertical fragments should be a lossless-join decomposition, as per the definition in Chapter 19.

To ensure that a vertical fragmentation is lossless-join, systems often assign a unique tuple id to each tuple in the original relation, as shown in Figure 22.4, and attach this id to the projection of the tuple in each fragment. If we think of the original relation as containing an additional tuple-id field that is a key, this field is added to each vertical fragment. Such a decomposition is guaranteed to be lossless-join.

In general, a relation can be (horizontally or vertically) fragmented, and each resulting fragment can be further fragmented. For simplicity of exposition, in the rest of this chapter, we assume that fragments are not recursively partitioned in this manner.

22.8.2 Replication

Replication means that we store several copies of a relation or relation fragment. An entire relation can be replicated at one or more sites. Similarly, one or more fragments of a relation can be replicated at other sites. For example, if a relation R is fragmented into $R1$, $R2$, and $R3$, there might be just one copy of $R1$, whereas $R2$ is replicated at two other sites and $R3$ is replicated at all sites.

The motivation for replication is twofold:

- **Increased Availability of Data:** If a site that contains a replica goes down, we can find the same data at other sites. Similarly, if local copies of remote relations are available, we are less vulnerable to failure of communication links.
- **Faster Query Evaluation:** Queries can execute faster by using a local copy of a relation instead of going to a remote site.

The two kinds of replication, called *synchronous* and *asynchronous* replication, differ primarily in how replicas are kept current when the relation is modified (see Section 22.11).

22.9 DISTRIBUTED CATALOG MANAGEMENT

Keeping track of data distributed across several sites can get complicated. We must keep track of how relations are fragmented and replicated—that is, how relation fragments are distributed across several sites and where copies of fragments are stored—in addition to the usual schema, authorization, and statistical information.

22.9.1 Naming Objects

If a relation is fragmented and replicated, we must be able to uniquely identify each replica of each fragment. Generating such unique names requires some care. If we use a global name-server to assign globally unique names, local autonomy is compromised; we want (users at) each site to be able to assign names to local objects without reference to names systemwide.

The usual solution to the naming problem is to use names consisting of several fields. For example, we could have:

- A *local name* field, which is the name assigned locally at the site where the relation is created. Two objects at different sites could have the same local name, but two objects at a given site cannot have the same local name.
- A *birth site* field, which identifies the site where the relation was created, and where information is maintained about all fragments and replicas of the relation.

These two fields identify a relation uniquely; we call the combination a **global relation name**. To identify a replica (of a relation or a relation fragment), we take the global relation name and add a *replica-id* field; we call the combination a **global replica name**.

22.9.2 Catalog Structure

A centralized system catalog can be used but is vulnerable to failure of the site containing the catalog. An alternative is to maintain a copy of a global system catalog, which describes all the data at every site. Although this approach is not vulnerable to a single-site failure, it compromises site autonomy, just like the first solution, because every change to a local catalog must now be broadcast to all sites.

A better approach, which preserves local autonomy and is not vulnerable to a single-site failure, was developed in the R* distributed database project, which was a successor to the System R project at IBM. Each site maintains a local catalog that describes all copies of data stored at that site. In addition, the catalog at the birth site for a relation is responsible for keeping track of where replicas of the relation (in general, of fragments of the relation) are stored. In particular, a precise description of each replica's contents—a list of columns for a vertical fragment or a selection condition for a horizontal fragment—is stored in the birth site catalog. Whenever a new replica is created or a replica is moved across sites, the information in the birth site catalog for the relation must be updated.

To locate a relation, the catalog at its birth site must be looked up. This catalog information can be cached at other sites for quicker access, but the cached information may become out of date if, for example, a fragment is moved. We would discover that the locally cached information is out of date when we use it to access the relation, and at that point, we must update the cache by looking up the catalog at the birth site of the relation. (The birth site of a relation is recorded in each local cache that describes the relation, and the birth site never changes, even if the relation is moved.)

22.9.3 Distributed Data Independence

Distributed data independence means that users should be able to write queries without regard to how a relation is fragmented or replicated; it is the responsibility of the DBMS to compute the relation as needed (by locating suitable copies of fragments, joining the vertical fragments, and taking the union of horizontal fragments).

In particular, this property implies that users should not have to specify the full name for the data objects accessed while evaluating a query. Let us see how users can be enabled to access relations without considering how the relations are distributed. The *local name* of a relation in the system catalog (Section 22.9.1) is really a combination of a *user name* and a user-defined *relation name*. Users can give whatever names they wish to their relations, without regard to the relations created by other users. When a user writes a program or SQL statement that refers to a relation, he or she simply uses the relation name. The DBMS adds the user name to the relation name to get a local name, then adds the user's site-id as the (default) birth site to obtain a global relation name. By looking up the global relation name—in the local catalog if it is cached there or in the catalog at the birth site—the DBMS can locate replicas of the relation.

A user may want to create objects at several sites or refer to relations created by other users. To do this, a user can create a **synonym** for a global relation name, using an SQL-style command (although such a command is not currently part of the SQL:1999 standard) and subsequently refer to the relation using the synonym. For each user known at a site, the DBMS maintains a table of synonyms as part of the system catalog at that site and uses this table to find the global relation name. Note that a user's program runs unchanged even if replicas of the relation are moved, because the global relation name is never changed until the relation itself is destroyed.

Users may want to run queries against specific replicas, especially if asynchronous replication is used. To support this, the synonym mechanism can be adapted to also allow users to create synonyms for global replica names.

22.10 DISTRIBUTED QUERY PROCESSING

We first discuss the issues involved in evaluating relational algebra operations in a distributed database through examples and then outline distributed query optimization. Consider the following two relations:

Sailors(<u>*sid:* `integer`</u>, *sname:* `string`, *rating:* `integer`, *age:* `real`)
Reserves(<u>*sid:* `integer`, *bid:* `integer`, *day:* `date`</u>, *rname:* `string`)

As in Chapter 14, assume that each tuple of Reserves is 40 bytes long, that a page can hold 100 Reserves tuples, and that we have 1000 pages of such tuples. Similarly, assume that each tuple of Sailors is 50 bytes long, that a page can hold 80 Sailors tuples, and that we have 500 pages of such tuples.

To estimate the cost of an evaluation strategy, in addition to counting the number of page I/Os, we must count the number of pages sent from one site to another because communication costs are a significant component of overall cost in a distributed database. We must also change our cost model to count the cost of shipping the result tuples to the site where the query is posed from the site where the result is assembled! In this chapter, we denote the time taken to read one page from disk (or to write one page to disk) as t_d and the time taken to ship one page (from any site to another site) as t_s.

22.10.1 Nonjoin Queries in a Distributed DBMS

Even simple operations such as scanning a relation, selection, and projection are affected by fragmentation and replication. Consider the following query:

```
SELECT S.age
FROM   Sailors S
WHERE  S.rating > 3 AND S.rating < 7
```

Suppose that the Sailors relation is horizontally fragmented, with all tuples having a rating less than 5 at Shanghai and all tuples having a rating greater than 5 at Tokyo.

The DBMS must answer this query by evaluating it at both sites and taking the union of the answers. If the `SELECT` clause contained `AVG` *(S.age)*, combining the answers could not be done by simply taking the union—the DBMS must compute the sum and count of *age* values at the two sites and use this information to compute the average age of all sailors.

If the `WHERE` clause contained just the condition *S.rating* > 6, on the other hand, the DBMS should recognize that this query could be answered by just executing it at Tokyo.

As another example, suppose that the Sailors relation were vertically fragmented, with the *sid* and *rating* fields at Shanghai and the *sname* and *age* fields at Tokyo. No field is stored at both sites. This vertical fragmentation would therefore be a lossy decomposition, except that a field containing the id of the corresponding Sailors tuple is included by the DBMS in both fragments! Now, the DBMS has to reconstruct the Sailors relation by joining the two fragments on the common tuple-id field and execute the query over this reconstructed relation.

Finally, suppose that the entire Sailors relation were stored at both Shanghai and Tokyo. We could answer any of the previous queries by executing it at either Shanghai or Tokyo. Where should the query be executed? This depends on the cost of shipping the answer to the query site (which may be Shanghai, Tokyo, or some other site) as well as the cost of executing the query at Shanghai and at Tokyo—the local processing costs may differ depending on what indexes are available on Sailors at the two sites, for example.

22.10.2 Joins in a Distributed DBMS

Joins of relations at different sites can be very expensive, and we now consider the evaluation options that must be considered in a distributed environment. Suppose that the Sailors relation were stored at London, and the Reserves relation were stored at Paris. We consider the cost of various strategies for computing *Sailors* $\bowtie$ *Reserves.*

Fetch As Needed

We could do a page-oriented nested loops join in London with Sailors as the outer, and for each Sailors page, fetch all Reserves pages from Paris. If we cache the fetched Reserves pages in London until the join is complete, pages are fetched only once, but assume that Reserves pages are not cached, just to see how bad things can get. (The situation can get much worse if we use a tuple-oriented nested loops join!)

The cost is $500t_d$ to scan Sailors plus, for each Sailors page, the cost of scanning and shipping all of Reserves, which is $1000(t_d + t_s)$. The total cost is therefore $500t_d + 500{,}000(t_d + t_s)$.

In addition, if the query was not submitted at the London site, we must add the cost of shipping the result to the query site; this cost depends on the size of the result. Because *sid* is a key for Sailors, the number of tuples in the result is 100,000 (the number of tuples in Reserves) and each tuple is 40 + 50 = 90 bytes long; thus 4000/90 = 44 result tuples fit on a page, and the result size is 100,000/44=2273 pages. The cost of shipping the answer to another site, if necessary, is 2273 t_s. In the rest of this section, we assume that the query is posed at the site where the result is computed; if not, the cost of shipping the result to the query site must be added to the cost.

In this example, observe that, if the query site is not London or Paris, the cost of shipping the result is greater than the cost of shipping both Sailors and Reserves to the query site! Therefore, it would be cheaper to ship both relations to the query site and compute the join there.

Alternatively, we could do an index nested loops join in London, fetching all matching Reserves tuples for each Sailors tuple. Suppose we have an unclustered hash index on the *sid* column of Reserves. Because there are 100,000 Reserves tuples and 40,000 Sailors tuples, each sailor has on average 2.5 reservations. The cost of finding the 2.5 Reservations tuples that match a given Sailors tuple is $(1.2 + 2.5)t_d$, assuming 1.2 I/Os to locate the appropriate bucket in the index. The total cost is the cost of scanning Sailors plus the cost of finding and fetching matching Reserves tuples for each Sailors tuple, $500t_d + 40,000(3.7t_d + 2.5t_s)$.

Both algorithms fetch required Reserves tuples from a remote site as needed. Clearly, this is not a good idea; the cost of shipping tuples dominates the total cost even for a fast network.

Ship to One Site

We can ship Sailors from London to Paris and carry out the join there, ship Reserves to London and carry out the join there, or ship both to the site where the query was posed and compute the join there. Note again that the query could have been posed in London, Paris, or perhaps a third site, say, Timbuktu!

The cost of scanning and shipping Sailors, saving it at Paris, then doing the join at Paris is $500(2t_d + t_s) + 4500t_d$, assuming that the version of the sort-merge join described in Section 14.10 is used and we have an adequate number of buffer pages. In the rest of this section we assume that sort-merge join is the join method used when both relations are at the same site.

The cost of shipping Reserves and doing the join at London is $1000(2t_d + t_s) + 4500t_d$.

Semijoins and Bloomjoins

Consider the strategy of shipping Reserves to London and computing the join at London. Some tuples in (the current instance of) Reserves do not join with any tuple in (the current instance of) Sailors. If we could somehow identify

Reserves tuples that are guaranteed not to join with any Sailors tuples, we could avoid shipping them.

Two techniques, *Semijoin* and *Bloomjoin*, have been proposed for reducing the number of Reserves tuples to be shipped. The first technique is called **Semijoin**. The idea is to proceed in three steps:

1. At London, compute the projection of Sailors onto the join columns (in this case just the *sid* field) and ship this projection to Paris.
2. At Paris, compute the natural join of the projection received from the first site with the Reserves relation. The result of this join is called the **reduction** of Reserves with respect to Sailors. Clearly, only those Reserves tuples in the reduction will join with tuples in the Sailors relation. Therefore, ship the reduction of Reserves to London, rather than the entire Reserves relation.
3. At London, compute the join of the reduction of Reserves with Sailors.

Let us compute the cost of using this technique for our example join query. Suppose we have a straightforward implementation of projection based on first scanning Sailors and creating a temporary relation with tuples that have only an *sid* field, then sorting the temporary and scanning the sorted temporary to eliminate duplicates. If we assume that the size of the *sid* field is 10 bytes, the cost of projection is $500t_d$ for scanning Sailors, plus $100t_d$ for creating the temporary, plus $400t_d$ for sorting it (in two passes), plus $100t_d$ for the final scan, plus $100t_d$ for writing the result into another temporary relation; a total of $1200t_d$. (Because *sid* is a key, no duplicates need be eliminated; if the optimizer is good enough to recognize this, the cost of projection is just $(500 + 100)t_d$.)

The cost of computing the projection and shipping it to Paris is therefore $1200t_d + 100t_s$. The cost of computing the reduction of Reserves is $3 \cdot (100 + 1000) = 3300t_d$, assuming that sort-merge join is used. (The cost does not reflect that the projection of Sailors is already sorted; the cost would decrease slightly if the refined sort-merge join exploited this.)

What is the size of the reduction? If every sailor holds at least one reservation, the reduction includes every tuple of Reserves! The effort invested in shipping the projection and reducing Reserves is a total waste. Indeed, because of this observation, we note that Semijoin is especially useful in conjunction with a selection on one of the relations. For example, if we want to compute the join of Sailors tuples with a *rating* greater than 8 with the Reserves relation, the size of the projection on *sid* for tuples that satisfy the selection would be just 20 percent of the original projection, that is, 20 pages.

Let us now continue the example join, with the assumption that we have the additional selection on *rating*. (The cost of computing the projection of Sailors goes down a bit, the cost of shipping it goes down to $20t_s$, and the cost of the reduction of Reserves also goes down a little, but we ignore these reductions for simplicity.) We assume that only 20 percent of the Reserves tuples are included in the reduction, thanks to the selection. Hence, the reduction contains 200 pages, and the cost of shipping it is $200t_s$.

Finally, at London, the reduction of Reserves is joined with Sailors, at a cost of $3 \cdot (200 + 500) = 21100t_d$. Observe that there are over 6500 page I/Os versus about 200 pages shipped, using this join technique. In contrast, to ship Reserves to London and do the join there costs $1000t_s$ plus $4500t_d$. With a high-speed network, the cost of Semijoin may be more than the cost of shipping Reserves in its entirety, even though the shipping cost itself is much less ($200t_s$ versus $1000t_s$).

The second technique, called **Bloomjoin**, is quite similar. The main difference is that a bit-vector is shipped in the first step, instead of the projection of Sailors. A bit-vector of (some chosen) size k is computed by hashing each tuple of Sailors into the range 0 to $k-1$ and setting bit i to 1 if some tuple hashes to i, and 0 otherwise. In the second step, the reduction of Reserves is computed by hashing each tuple of Reserves (using the *sid* field) into the range 0 to $k-1$, using the same hash function used to construct the bit-vector and discarding tuples whose hash value i corresponds to a 0 bit. Because no Sailors tuples hash to such an i, no Sailors tuple can join with any Reserves tuple that is not in the reduction.

The costs of shipping a bit-vector and reducing Reserves using the vector are less than the corresponding costs in Semijoin. On the other hand, the size of the reduction of Reserves is likely to be larger than in Semijoin; so, the costs of shipping the reduction and joining it with Sailors are likely to be higher.

Let us estimate the cost of this approach. The cost of computing the bit-vector is essentially the cost of scanning Sailors, which is $500t_d$. The cost of sending the bit-vector depends on the size we choose for the bit-vector, which is certainly smaller than the size of the projection; we take this cost to be $20t_s$, for concreteness. The cost of reducing Reserves is just the cost of scanning Reserves, $1000t_d$. The size of the reduction of Reserves is likely to be about the same as or a little larger than the size of the reduction in the Semijoin approach; instead of 200, we will take this size to be 220 pages. (We assume that the selection on Sailors is included, to permit a direct comparison with the cost of Semijoin.) The cost of shipping the reduction is therefore $220t_s$. The cost of the final join at London is $3 \cdot (500 + 220) = 2160t_d$.

Thus, in comparison to Semijoin, the shipping cost of this approach is about the same, although it could be higher if the bit-vector were not as selective as the projection of Sailors in terms of reducing Reserves. Typically, though, the reduction of Reserves is no more than 10 to 20 percent larger than the size of the reduction in Semijoin. In exchange for this slightly higher shipping cost, Bloomjoin achieves a significantly lower processing cost: less than $3700t_d$ versus more than $6500t_d$ for Semijoin. Indeed, Bloomjoin has a lower I/O cost and a lower shipping cost than the strategy of shipping all of Reserves to London! These numbers indicate why Bloomjoin is an attractive distributed join method; but the sensitivity of the method to the effectiveness of bit-vector hashing (in reducing Reserves) should be kept in mind.

22.10.3 Cost-Based Query Optimization

We have seen how data distribution can affect the implementation of individual operations, such as selection, projection, aggregation, and join. In general, of course, a query involves several operations, and optimizing queries in a distributed database poses the following additional challenges:

- Communication costs must be considered. If we have several copies of a relation, we must also decide which copy to use.
- If individual sites are run under the control of different DBMSs, the autonomy of each site must be respected while doing global query planning.

Query optimization proceeds essentially as in a centralized DBMS, as described in Chapter 12, with information about relations at remote sites obtained from the system catalogs. Of course, there are more alternative methods to consider for each operation (e.g., consider the new options for distributed joins), and the cost metric must account for communication costs as well, but the overall planning process is essentially unchanged if we take the cost metric to be the total cost of all operations. (If we consider response time, the fact that certain subqueries can be carried out in parallel at different sites would require us to change the optimizer as per the discussion in Section 22.5.)

In the overall plan, local manipulation of relations at the site where they are stored (to compute an intermediate relation to be shipped elsewhere) is encapsulated into a *suggested* local plan. The overall plan includes several such local plans, which we can think of as subqueries executing at different sites. While generating the global plan, the suggested local plans provide realistic cost estimates for the computation of the intermediate relations; the suggested local plans are constructed by the optimizer mainly to provide these local cost estimates. A site is free to ignore the local plan suggested to it if it is able to find a cheaper plan by using more current information in the local catalogs. Thus, site autonomy is respected in the optimization and evaluation of distributed queries.

22.11 UPDATING DISTRIBUTED DATA

The classical view of a distributed DBMS is that it should behave just like a centralized DBMS from the point of view of a user; issues arising from distribution of data should be transparent to the user, although, of course, they must be addressed at the implementation level.

With respect to queries, this view of a distributed DBMS means that users should be able to ask queries without worrying about how and where relations are stored; we have already seen the implications of this requirement on query evaluation.

With respect to updates, this view means that transactions should continue to be atomic actions, regardless of data fragmentation and replication. In particular, all copies of a modified relation must be updated before the modifying transaction commits. We refer to replication with this semantics as **synchronous replication**; before an update transaction commits, it synchronizes all copies of modified data.

An alternative approach to replication, called **asynchronous replication**, has come to be widely used in commercial distributed DBMSs. Copies of a modified relation are updated only periodically in this approach, and a transaction that reads different copies of the same relation may see different values. Thus, asynchronous replication compromises distributed data independence, but it can be implemented more efficiently than synchronous replication.

22.11.1 Synchronous Replication

There are two basic techniques for ensuring that transactions see the same value regardless of which copy of an object they access. In the first technique, called **voting**, a transaction must write a majority of copies to modify an object and read at least enough copies to make sure that one of the copies is current. For example, if there are 10 copies and 7 copies are written by update transactions, then at least 4 copies must be read. Each copy has a version number, and the copy with the highest version number is current. This technique is not attractive in most situations because reading an object requires reading multiple copies; in most applications, objects are read much more frequently than they are updated, and efficient performance on reads is very important.

In the second technique, called **read-any write-all**, to read an object, a transaction can read any one copy, but to write an object, it must write all copies. Reads are fast, especially if we have a local copy, but writes are slower, relative to the first technique. This technique is attractive when reads are much more frequent than writes, and it is usually adopted for implementing synchronous replication.

22.11.2 Asynchronous Replication

Synchronous replication comes at a significant cost. Before an update transaction can commit, it must obtain exclusive locks on all copies—assuming that the read-any write-all technique is used—of modified data. The transaction may have to send lock requests to remote sites and wait for the locks to be granted, and during this potentially long period, it continues to hold all its other locks. If sites or communication links fail, the transaction cannot commit until all the sites at which it has modified data recover and are reachable. Finally, even if locks are obtained readily and there are no failures, committing a transaction requires several additional messages to be sent as part of a *commit protocol* (Section 22.14.1).

For these reasons, synchronous replication is undesirable or even unachievable in many situations. Asynchronous replication is gaining in popularity, even though it allows different copies of the same object to have different values for short periods of time. This situation violates the principle of distributed data independence; users must be aware of which copy they are accessing, recognize that copies are brought up-to-date only periodically, and live with this reduced level of data consistency. Nonetheless, this seems to be a practical compromise that is acceptable in many situations.

Primary Site versus Peer-to-Peer Replication

Asynchronous replication comes in two flavors. In **primary site** asynchronous replication, one copy of a relation is designated the **primary** or **master** copy. Replicas of the entire relation or fragments of the relation can be created at other sites; these are **secondary** copies, and unlike the primary copy, they cannot be updated. A common mechanism for setting up primary and secondary copies is that users first **register** or **publish** the relation at the primary site and subsequently **subscribe** to a fragment of a registered relation from another (secondary) site.

In **peer-to-peer** asynchronous replication, more than one copy (although perhaps not all) can be designated as updatable, that is, a master copy. In addition to propagating changes, a **conflict resolution** strategy must be used to deal with conflicting changes made at different sites. For example, Joe's age may be changed to 35 at one site and to 38 at another. Which value is 'correct'? Many more subtle kinds of conflicts can arise in peer-to-peer replication, and in general peer-to-peer replication leads to ad hoc conflict resolution. Some special situations in which peer-to-peer replication does not lead to conflicts arise quite often, and in such situations peer-to-peer replication is best utilized. For example:

- Each master is allowed to update only a fragment (typically a horizontal fragment) of the relation, and any two fragments updatable by different masters are disjoint. For example, it may be that salaries of German employees are updated only in Frankfurt, and salaries of Indian employees are updated only in Madras, even though the entire relation is stored at both Frankfurt and Madras.
- Updating rights are held by only one master at a time. For example, one site is designated a *backup* to another site. Changes at the master site are propagated to other sites and updates are not allowed at other sites (including the backup). But, if the master site fails, the backup site takes over and updates are now permitted at (only) the backup site.

We will not discuss peer-to-peer replication further.

Implementing Primary Site Asynchronous Replication

The main issue in implementing primary site replication is determining how changes to the primary copy are propagated to the secondary copies. Changes are usually propagated in two steps, called *Capture* and *Apply.* Changes made by committed transactions to the primary copy are somehow identified during the Capture step and subsequently propagated to secondary copies during the Apply step.

In contrast to synchronous replication, a transaction that modifies a replicated relation directly locks and changes only the primary copy. It is typically committed long before the Apply step is carried out. Systems vary considerably in their implementation of these steps. We present an overview of some of the alternatives.

Capture

The **Capture** step is implemented using one of two approaches. In **log-based** Capture, the log maintained for recovery purposes is used to generate a record of updates. Basically, when the log tail is written to stable storage, all log records that affect replicated relations are also written to a separate **change data table (CDT)**. Since the transaction that generated the update log record may still be active when the record is written to the CDT, it may subsequently abort. Update log records written by transactions that subsequently abort must be removed from the CDT to obtain a stream of updates due (only) to committed transactions. This stream can be obtained as part of the Capture step or subsequently in the Apply step if commit log records are added to the CDT; for concreteness, we assume that the committed update stream is obtained as part of the Capture step and that the CDT sent to the Apply step contains only update log records of committed transactions.

In **procedural** Capture, a procedure automatically invoked by the DBMS or an application program initiates the Capture process, which consists typically of taking a **snapshot** of the primary copy. A snapshot is just a copy of the relation as it existed at some instant in time. (A procedure that is automatically invoked by the DBMS, such as the one that initiates Capture, is called a *trigger*. We covered triggers in Chapter 5.)

Log-based Capture has a smaller overhead than procedural Capture and, because it is driven by changes to the data, results in a smaller delay between the time the primary copy is changed and the time that the change is propagated to the secondary copies. (Of course, this delay also depends on how the Apply step is implemented.) In particular, only changes are propagated, and related changes (e.g., updates to two tables with a referential integrity constraint between them) are propagated together. The disadvantage is that implementing log-based Capture requires a detailed understanding of the structure of the log, which is quite system specific. Therefore, a vendor cannot easily implement a log-based Capture mechanism that will capture changes made to data in another vendor's DBMS.

Apply

The **Apply** step takes the changes collected by the Capture step, which are in the CDT table or a snapshot, and propagates them to the secondary copies. This can be done by having the primary site continuously send the CDT or periodically requesting (the latest portion of) the CDT or a snapshot from the primary site. Typically, each secondary site runs a copy of the Apply process and 'pulls' the changes in the CDT from the primary site using periodic requests. The interval between such requests can be controlled by a timer or a user's application program. Once the changes are available at the secondary site, they can be applied directly to the replica.

In some systems, the replica need not be just a fragment of the original relation—it can be a view defined using SQL, and the replication mechanism is sufficiently sophisticated to maintain such a view at a remote site incrementally (by reevaluating only the part of the view affected by changes recorded in the CDT).

Log-based Capture in conjunction with continuous Apply minimizes the delay in propagating changes. It is the best combination in situations where the primary and secondary copies are both used as part of an operational DBMS and replicas must be as closely synchronized with the primary copy as possible. Log-based Capture with continuous Apply is essentially a less expensive substitute for synchronous replication. Procedural Capture and application-driven Apply offer the most flexibility in processing source data and changes before altering the replica; this flexibility is often useful in data warehousing applications where the ability to 'clean' and filter the retrieved data is more important than the currency of the replica.

Data Warehousing: An Example of Replication

Complex decision support queries that look at data from multiple sites are becoming very important. The paradigm of executing queries that span multiple sites is simply inadequate for performance reasons. One way to provide such complex query support over data from multiple sources is to create a copy of all the data at some one location and use the copy rather than going to the individual sources. Such a copied collection of data is called a **data warehouse**. Specialized systems for building, maintaining, and querying data warehouses have become important tools in the marketplace.

Data warehouses can be seen as one instance of asynchronous replication, in which copies are updated relatively infrequently. When we talk of replication, we typically mean copies maintained under the control of a single DBMS, whereas with data warehousing, the original data may be on different software platforms (including database systems and OS file systems) and even belong to different organizations. This distinction, however, is likely to become blurred as vendors adopt more 'open' strategies to replication. For example, some products already support the maintenance of replicas of relations stored in one vendor's DBMS in another vendor's DBMS.

We note that data warehousing involves more than just replication. We discuss other aspects of data warehousing in Chapter 25.

22.12 DISTRIBUTED TRANSACTIONS

In a distributed DBMS, a given transaction is submitted at some one site, but it can access data at other sites as well. In this chapter we refer to the activity of a transaction at a given site as a **subtransaction**. When a transaction is submitted at some site, the transaction manager at that site breaks it up into a collection of one or more subtransactions that execute at different sites, submits them to transaction managers at the other sites, and coordinates their activity.

We now consider aspects of concurrency control and recovery that require additional attention because of data distribution. As we saw in Chapter 16, there are many concurrency control protocols; in this chapter, for concreteness, we assume that Strict 2PL with deadlock detection is used. We discuss the following issues in subsequent sections:

- **Distributed Concurrency Control:** How can locks for objects stored across several sites be managed? How can deadlocks be detected in a distributed database?
- **Distributed Recovery:** Transaction atomicity must be ensured—when a transaction commits, all its actions, across all the sites at which it executes, must persist. Similarly, when a transaction aborts, none of its actions must be allowed to persist.

22.13 DISTRIBUTED CONCURRENCY CONTROL

In Section 22.11.1, we described two techniques for implementing synchronous replication, and in Section 22.11.2, we discussed various techniques for implementing asynchronous replication. The choice of technique determines *which* objects are to be locked. *When* locks are obtained and released is determined by the concurrency control protocol. We now consider how lock and unlock requests are implemented in a distributed environment.

Lock management can be distributed across sites in many ways:

- **Centralized:** A single site is in charge of handling lock and unlock requests for all objects.
- **Primary Copy:** One copy of each object is designated the primary copy. All requests to lock or unlock a copy of this object are handled by the lock manager at the site where the primary copy is stored, regardless of where the copy itself is stored.

- **Fully Distributed:** Requests to lock or unlock a copy of an object stored at a site are handled by the lock manager at the site where the copy is stored.

The centralized scheme is vulnerable to failure of the single site that controls locking. The primary copy scheme avoids this problem, but in general, reading an object requires communication with two sites: the site where the primary copy resides and the site where the copy to be read resides. This problem is avoided in the fully distributed scheme, because locking is done at the site where the copy to be read resides. However, while writing, locks must be set at all sites where copies are modified in the fully distributed scheme, whereas locks need be set only at one site in the other two schemes.

Clearly, the fully distributed locking scheme is the most attractive scheme if reads are much more frequent than writes, as is usually the case.

22.13.1 Distributed Deadlock

One issue that requires special attention when using either primary copy or fully distributed locking is deadlock detection. (Of course, a deadlock prevention scheme can be used instead, but we focus on deadlock detection, which is widely used.) As in a centralized DBMS, deadlocks must be detected and resolved (by aborting some deadlocked transaction).

Each site maintains a local waits-for graph, and a cycle in a local graph indicates a deadlock. However, there can be a deadlock even if no local graph contains a cycle. For example, suppose that two sites, A and B, both contain copies of objects $O1$ and $O2$, and that the read-any write-all technique is used. $T1$, which wants to read $O1$ and write $O2$, obtains an S lock on $O1$ and an X lock on $O2$ at Site A, then requests an X lock on $O2$ at Site B. $T2$, which wants to read $O2$ and write $O1$, meanwhile, obtains an S lock on $O2$ and an X lock on $O1$ at Site B, then requests an X lock on $O1$ at Site A. As Figure 22.5 illustrates, $T2$ is waiting for $T1$ at Site A and $T1$ is waiting for $T2$ at Site B; thus, we have a deadlock, which neither site can detect based solely on its local waits-for graph.

To detect such deadlocks, a **distributed deadlock detection** algorithm must be used. We describe three such algorithms.

The first algorithm, which is centralized, consists of periodically sending all local waits-for graphs to one site that is responsible for global deadlock detection. At this site, the global waits-for graph is generated by combining all the local graphs; the set of nodes is the union of nodes in the local graphs, and there is

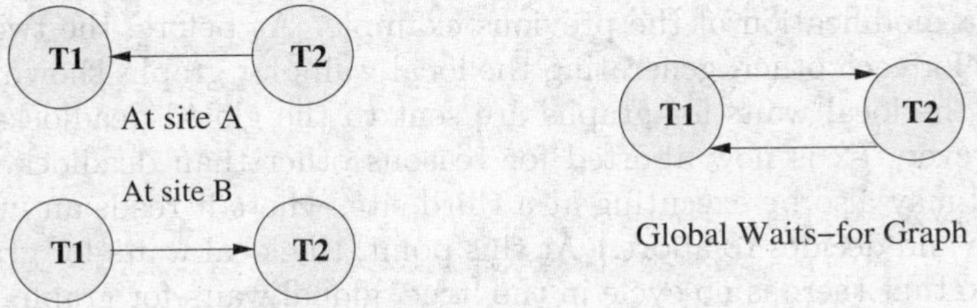

Figure 22.5 Distributed Deadlock

an edge from one node to another if there is such an edge in any of the local graphs.

The second algorithm, which is hierarchical, groups sites into a hierarchy. For instance, sites might be grouped by state, then by country, and finally into a single group that contains all sites. Every node in this hierarchy constructs a waits-for graph that reveals deadlocks involving only sites contained in (the subtree rooted at) this node. All sites periodically (e.g., every 10 seconds) send their local waits-for graph to the site responsible for constructing the waits-for graph for their state. The sites constructing waits-for graphs at the state level periodically (e.g., every minute) send the state waits-for graph to the site constructing the waits-for graph for their country. The sites constructing waits-for graphs at the country level periodically (e.g., every 10 minutes) send the country waits-for graph to the site constructing the global waits-for graph. This scheme is based on the observation that more deadlocks are likely across closely related sites than across unrelated sites, and it puts more effort into detecting deadlocks across related sites. All deadlocks are eventually detected, but a deadlock involving two different countries may take a while to detect.

The third algorithm is simple: If a transaction waits longer than some chosen time-out interval, it is aborted. Although this algorithm may cause many unnecessary restarts, the overhead of deadlock detection is (obviously!) low, and in a heterogeneous distributed database, if the participating sites cannot cooperate to the extent of sharing their waits-for graphs, it may be the only option.

A subtle point to note with respect to distributed deadlock detection is that delays in propagating local information might cause the deadlock detection algorithm to identify 'deadlocks' that do not really exist. Such situations, called **phantom deadlocks**, lead to unnecessary aborts. For concreteness, we discuss the centralized algorithm, although the hierarchical algorithm suffers from the same problem.

Consider a modification of the previous example. As before, the two transactions wait for each other, generating the local waits-for graphs shown in Figure 22.5, and the local waits-for graphs are sent to the global deadlock-detection site. However, $T2$ is now aborted for reasons other than deadlock. (For example, $T2$ may also be executing at a third site, where it reads an unexpected data value and decides to abort.) At this point, the local waits-for graphs have changed so that there is no cycle in the 'true' global waits-for graph. However, the constructed global waits-for graph will contain a cycle, and $T1$ may well be picked as the victim!

22.14 DISTRIBUTED RECOVERY

Recovery in a distributed DBMS is more complicated than in a centralized DBMS for the following reasons:

- New kinds of failure can arise: failure of communication links and failure of a remote site at which a subtransaction is executing.
- Either all subtransactions of a given transaction must commit or none must commit, and this property must be guaranteed despite any combination of site and link failures. This guarantee is achieved using a **commit protocol**.

As in a centralized DBMS, certain actions are carried out as part of normal execution to provide the necessary information to recover from failures. A log is maintained at each site, and in addition to the kinds of information maintained in a centralized DBMS, actions taken as part of the commit protocol are also logged. The most widely used commit protocol is called *Two-Phase Commit (2PC)*. A variant called *2PC with Presumed Abort*, which we discuss next, has been adopted as an industry standard.

In this section, we first describe the steps taken during normal execution, concentrating on the commit protocol, and then discuss recovery from failures.

22.14.1 Normal Execution and Commit Protocols

During normal execution, each site maintains a log, and the actions of a subtransaction are logged at the site where it executes. The regular logging activity described in Chapter 18 is carried out and, in addition, a commit protocol is followed to ensure that all subtransactions of a given transaction either commit or abort uniformly. The transaction manager at the site where the transaction originated is called the **coordinator** for the transaction; transaction managers at sites where its subtransactions execute are called **subordinates** (with respect to the coordination of this transaction).

We now describe the **Two-Phase Commit (2PC)** protocol, in terms of the messages exchanged and the log records written. When the user decides to commit a transaction, the commit command is sent to the coordinator for the transaction. This initiates the 2PC protocol:

1. The coordinator sends a *prepare* message to each subordinate.

2. When a subordinate receives a *prepare* message, it decides whether to abort or commit its subtransaction. It force-writes an abort or **prepare** log record, and *then* sends a *no* or *yes* message to the coordinator. Note that a prepare log record is not used in a centralized DBMS; it is unique to the distributed commit protocol.

3. If the coordinator receives *yes* messages from all subordinates, it force-writes a commit log record and then sends a *commit* message to all subordinates. If it receives even one *no* message or receives no response from some subordinate for a specified time-out interval, it force-writes an abort log record, and then sends an *abort* message to all subordinates.[1]

4. When a subordinate receives an *abort* message, it force-writes an abort log record, sends an *ack* message to the coordinator, and aborts the subtransaction. When a subordinate receives a *commit* message, it force-writes a commit log record, sends an *ack* message to the coordinator, and commits the subtransaction.

5. After the coordinator has received *ack* messages from all subordinates, it writes an end log record for the transaction.

The name *Two-Phase Commit* reflects the fact that two rounds of messages are exchanged: first a voting phase, then a termination phase, both initiated by the coordinator. The basic principle is that any of the transaction managers involved (including the coordinator) can unilaterally abort a transaction, whereas there must be unanimity to commit a transaction. When a message is sent in 2PC, it signals a decision by the sender. To ensure that this decision survives a crash at the sender's site, the log record describing the decision is always forced to stable storage *before* the message is sent.

A transaction is officially committed at the time the coordinator's commit log record reaches stable storage. Subsequent failures cannot affect the outcome of the transaction; it is irrevocably committed. Log records written to record the commit protocol actions contain the type of the record, the transaction id, and the identity of the coordinator. A coordinator's commit or abort log record also contains the identities of the subordinates.

[1] As an optimization, the coordinator need not send *abort* messages to subordinates who voted *no*.

22.14.2 Restart after a Failure

When a site comes back up after a crash, we invoke a recovery process that reads the log and processes all transactions executing the commit protocol at the time of the crash. The transaction manager at this site could have been the coordinator for some of these transactions and a subordinate for others. We do the following in the recovery process:

- If we have a commit or abort log record for transaction T, its status is clear; we redo or undo T, respectively. If this site is the coordinator, which can be determined from the commit or abort log record, we must periodically resend—because there may be other link or site failures in the system—a *commit* or *abort* message to each subordinate until we receive an *ack*. After we have received *ack*s from all subordinates, we write an end log record for T.

- If we have a prepare log record for T but no commit or abort log record, this site is a subordinate, and the coordinator can be determined from the prepare record. We must repeatedly contact the coordinator site to determine the status of T. Once the coordinator responds with either commit or abort, we write a corresponding log record, redo or undo the transaction, and then write an end log record for T.

- If we have no prepare, commit, or abort log record for transaction T, T certainly could not have voted to commit before the crash; so we can unilaterally abort and undo T and write an end log record. In this case, we have no way to determine whether the current site is the coordinator or a subordinate for T. However, if this site is the coordinator, it might have sent a *prepare* message prior to the crash, and if so, other sites may have voted *yes*. If such a subordinate site contacts the recovery process at the current site, we now know that the current site is the coordinator for T, and given that there is no commit or abort log record, the response to the subordinate should be to abort T.

Observe that, if the coordinator site for a transaction T fails, subordinates who voted *yes* cannot decide whether to commit or abort T until the coordinator site recovers; we say that T is **blocked**. In principle, the active subordinate sites could communicate among themselves, and if at least one of them contains an abort or commit log record for T, its status becomes globally known. To communicate among themselves, all subordinates must be told the identity of the other subordinates at the time they are sent the *prepare* message. However, 2PC is still vulnerable to coordinator failure during recovery because even if all subordinates voted *yes*, the coordinator (who also has a vote!) may have decided to abort T, and this decision cannot be determined until the coordinator site recovers.

We covered how a site recovers from a crash, but what should a site that is involved in the commit protocol do if a site that it is communicating with fails? If the current site is the coordinator, it should simply abort the transaction. If the current site is a subordinate, and it has not yet responded to the coordinator's *prepare* message, it can (and should) abort the transaction. If it is a subordinate and has voted *yes*, then it cannot unilaterally abort the transaction, and it cannot commit either; it is blocked. It must periodically contact the coordinator until it receives a reply.

Failures of communication links are seen by active sites as failure of other sites that they are communicating with, and therefore the solutions just outlined apply to this case as well.

22.14.3 Two-Phase Commit Revisited

Now that we examined how a site recovers from a failure, and saw the interaction between the 2PC protocol and the recovery process, it is instructive to consider how 2PC can be refined further. In doing so, we arrive at a more efficient version of 2PC, but equally important perhaps, we understand the role of the various steps of 2PC more clearly. Consider three basic observations:

1. The *ack* messages in 2PC are used to determine when a coordinator (or the recovery process at a coordinator site following a crash) can 'forget' about a transaction T. Until the coordinator knows that all subordinates are aware of the commit or abort decision for T, it must keep information about T in the transaction table.

2. If the coordinator site fails after sending out *prepare* messages but before writing a commit or abort log record, when it comes back up, it has no information about the transaction's commit status prior to the crash. However, it is still free to abort the transaction unilaterally (because it has not written a commit record, it can still cast a *no* vote itself). If another site inquires about the status of the transaction, the recovery process, as we have seen, responds with an *abort* message. Therefore, in the absence of information, a transaction is *presumed to have aborted.*

3. If a subtransaction does no updates, it has no changes to either redo or undo; in other words, its commit or abort status is irrelevant.

The first two observations suggest several refinements:

- When a coordinator aborts a transaction T, it can undo T and remove it from the transaction table immediately. After all, removing T from the table results in a 'no information' state with respect to T, and the default response (to an enquiry about T) in this state, which is *abort*, is the correct response for an aborted transaction.

- By the same token, if a subordinate receives an *abort* message, it need not send an *ack* message. The coordinator is not waiting to hear from subordinates after sending an *abort* message! If, for some reason, a subordinate that receives a *prepare* message (and voted *yes*) does not receive an *abort* or *commit* message for a specified time-out interval, it contacts the coordinator again. If the coordinator decided to abort, there may no longer be an entry in the transaction table for this transaction, but the subordinate receives the default *abort* message, which is the correct response.
- Because the coordinator is not waiting to hear from subordinates after deciding to abort a transaction, the names of subordinates need not be recorded in the abort log record for the coordinator.
- All abort log records (for the coordinator as well as subordinates) can simply be appended to the log tail, instead of doing a force-write. After all, if they are not written to stable storage before a crash, the default decision is to abort the transaction.

The third basic observation suggests some additional refinements:

- If a subtransaction does no updates (which can be easily detected by keeping a count of update log records), the subordinate can respond to a *prepare* message from the coordinator with a *reader* message, instead of *yes* or *no*. The subordinate writes no log records in this case.
- When a coordinator receives a *reader* message, it treats the message as a *yes* vote, but with the optimization that it does not send any more messages to the subordinate, because the subordinate's commit or abort status is irrelevant.
- If all subtransactions, including the subtransaction at the coordinator site, send a *reader* message, we do not need the second phase of the commit protocol. Indeed, we can simply remove the transaction from the transaction table, without writing any log records at any site for this transaction.

The Two-Phase Commit protocol with the refinements discussed in this section is called **Two-Phase Commit with Presumed Abort**.

22.14.4 Three-Phase Commit

A commit protocol called **Three-Phase Commit (3PC)** can avoid blocking even if the coordinator site fails during recovery. The basic idea is that, when the coordinator sends out *prepare* messages and receives *yes* votes from all subordinates, it sends all sites a *precommit* message, rather than a *commit* message. When a sufficient number—more than the maximum number of failures that must be handled—of *acks* have been received, the coordinator force-writes a *commit* log record and sends a *commit* message to all subordinates. In 3PC, the coordinator effectively postpones the decision to commit until it is sure that enough sites know about the decision to commit; if the coordinator subsequently fails, these sites can communicate with each other and detect that the transaction must be committed—conversely, aborted, if none of them has received a *precommit* message—without waiting for the coordinator to recover.

The 3PC protocol imposes a significant additional cost during normal execution and requires that communication link failures do not lead to a network partition (wherein some sites cannot reach some other sites through any path) to ensure freedom from blocking. For these reasons, it is not used in practice.

22.15 REVIEW QUESTIONS

Answers to the review questions can be found in the listed sections.

- Discuss the different motivations behind parallel and distributed databases. **(Section 22.1)**
- Describe the three main architectures for parallel DBMSs. Explain why the *shared-memory* and *shared-disk* approaches suffer from *interference*. What can you say about the *speed-up* and *scale-up* of the *shared-nothing* architecture? **(Section 22.2)**
- Describe and differentiate *pipelined parallelism* and *data-partitioned parallelism*. **(Section 22.3)**
- Discuss the following techniques for partitioning data: *round-robin*, *hash*, and *range*. **(Section 22.3.1)**
- Explain how existing code can be parallelized by introducing *split* and *merge* operators. **(Section 22.3.2)**
- Discuss how each of the following operators can be parallized using data partitioning: *scanning, sorting, join*. Compare the use of sorting versus hashing for partitioning. **(Section 22.4)**
- What do we need to consider in optimizing queries for parallel execution? Discuss interoperation parallelism, left-deep trees versus bushy trees, and cost estimation. **(Section 22.5)**

- Define the terms *distributed data independence* and *distributed transaction atomicity*. Are these concepts supported in current commercial systems? Why not? What is the difference between *homogeneous* and *heterogeneous* distributed databases? **(Section 22.6)**
- Describe the three main architectures for distributed DBMSs. **(Section 22.7)**
- A relation can be distributed by *fragmenting* it or *replicating* it across several sites. Explain these concepts and how they differ. Also, distinguish between *horizontal* and *vertical* fragmentation. **(Section 22.8)**
- If a relation is fragmented and replicated, each partition needs a globally unique name called the *relation name*. Explain how such global names are created and the motivation behind the described approach to naming. **(Section 22.9.1)**
- Explain how metadata about such distributed data is maintained in a *distributed catalog*. **(Section 22.9.2)**
- Describe a naming scheme that supports distributed data independence. **(Section 22.9.3)**
- When processing queries in a distributed DBMS, the location of partitions of the relation needs to be taken into account. Discuss the alternatives when joining two two relations that reside on different sites. In particular, explain and describe the motivation behind the *Semijoin* and *Bloomjoin* techniques. **(Section 22.10.2)**
- What issues must be considered in optimizing queries over distributed data, in addition to where the data is located? **(Section 22.10.3)**
- What is the difference between *synchronous asynchronous* replication? Why has asynchronous replication gained in popularity? **(Section 22.11)**
- Describe the *voting* and *read-any write-all* approaches to synchronous replication. **(Section 22.11.1)**
- Summarize the *peer-to-peer* and *primary site* approaches to asynchronous replication. **(Section 22.11.2)**
- In primary site replication, changes to the primary copy must be propagated to secondary copies. What is done in the *Capture* and *Apply* steps? Describe *log-based* and *procedural* approaches to Capture and compare them. What are the variations in scheduling the Apply step? Illustrate the use of asynchronous replication in a data warehouse. **(Section 22.11.2)**
- What is a *subtransaction*? **(Section 22.12)**

- What are the choices for managing locks in a distributed DBMS? **(Section 22.13)**
- Discuss deadlock detection in a distributed database. Contrast the *centralized*, *hierarchical*, and *time-out* approaches. **(Section 22.13.1)**
- Why is recovery in a distributed DBMS more complicated than in a centralized system? **(Section 22.14)**
- What is a *commit protocol* and why is it required in a distributed database? Describe and compare *Two-Phase* and *Three-Phase Commit*. What is *blocking*, and how does the Three-Phase protocol prevent it? Why is it nonetheless not used in practice? **(Section 22.14)**

EXERCISES

Exercise 22.1 Give brief answers to the following questions:

1. What are the similarities and differences between parallel and distributed database management systems?
2. Would you expect to see a parallel database built using a wide-area network? Would you expect to see a distributed database built using a wide-area network? Explain.
3. Define the terms *scale-up* and *speed-up*.
4. Why is a shared-nothing architecture attractive for parallel database systems?
5. The idea of building specialized hardware to run parallel database applications received considerable attention but has fallen out of favor. Comment on this trend.
6. What are the advantages of a distributed DBMS over a centralized DBMS?
7. Briefly describe and compare the Client-Server and Collaborating Servers architectures.
8. In the Collaborating Servers architecture, when a transaction is submitted to the DBMS, briefly describe how its activities at various sites are coordinated. In particular, describe the role of transaction managers at the different sites, the concept of *subtransactions*, and the concept of *distributed transaction atomicity*.

Exercise 22.2 Give brief answers to the following questions:

1. Define the terms *fragmentation* and *replication*, in terms of where data is stored.
2. What is the difference between *synchronous* and *asynchronous* replication?
3. Define the term *distributed data independence*. What does this mean with respect to querying and updating data in the presence of data fragmentation and replication?
4. Consider the *voting* and *read-any write-all* techniques for implementing synchronous replication. What are their respective pros and cons?
5. Give an overview of how asynchronous replication can be implemented. In particular, explain the terms *Capture* and *Apply*.
6. What is the difference between log-based and procedural implementations of capture?
7. Why is giving database objects unique names more complicated in a distributed DBMS?

8. Describe a catalog organization that permits any replica (of an entire relation or a fragment) to be given a unique name and provides the naming infrastructure required for ensuring distributed data independence.
9. If information from remote catalogs is cached at other sites, what happens if the cached information becomes outdated? How can this condition be detected and resolved?

Exercise 22.3 Consider a parallel DBMS in which each relation is stored by horizontally partitioning its tuples across all disks:

Employees(*eid:* `integer`, *did:* `integer`, *sal:* `real`)
Departments(*did:* `integer`, *mgrid:* `integer`, *budget:* `integer`)

The *mgrid* field of Departments is the *eid* of the manager. Each relation contains 20-byte tuples, and the *sal* and *budget* fields both contain uniformly distributed values in the range 0 to 1 million. The Employees relation contains 100,000 pages, the Departments relation contains 5,000 pages, and each processor has 100 buffer pages of 4,000 bytes each. The cost of one page I/O is t_d, and the cost of shipping one page is t_s; tuples are shipped in units of one page by waiting for a page to be filled before sending a message from processor i to processor j. There are no indexes, and all joins that are local to a processor are carried out using a sort-merge join. Assume that the relations are initially partitioned using a round-robin algorithm and that there are 10 processors.

For each of the following queries, describe the evaluation plan briefly and give its cost in terms of t_d and t_s. You should compute the total cost across all sites as well as the 'elapsed time' cost (i.e., if several operations are carried out concurrently, the time taken is the maximum over these operations).

1. Find the highest paid employee.
2. Find the highest paid employee in the department with *did* 55.
3. Find the highest paid employee over all departments with *budget* less than 100,000.
4. Find the highest paid employee over all departments with *budget* less than 300,000.
5. Find the average salary over all departments with *budget* less than 300,000.
6. Find the salaries of all managers.
7. Find the salaries of all managers who manage a department with a budget less than 300,000 and earn more than 100,000.
8. Print the *eids* of all employees, ordered by increasing salaries. Each processor is connected to a separate printer, and the answer can appear as several sorted lists, each printed by a different processor, as long as we can obtain a fully sorted list by concatenating the printed lists (in some order).

Exercise 22.4 Consider the same scenario as in Exercise 22.3, except that the relations are originally partitioned using range partitioning on the *sal* and *budget* fields.

Exercise 22.5 Repeat Exercises 22.3 and 22.4 with (i) 1 processor, and (ii) 100 processors.

Exercise 22.6 Consider the Employees and Departments relations described in Exercise 22.3. They are now stored in a distributed DBMS with all of Employees stored at Naples and all of Departments stored at Berlin. There are no indexes on these relations. The cost of various operations is as described in Exercise 22.3. Consider the query:

```
SELECT *
FROM   Employees E, Departments D
WHERE  E.eid = D.mgrid
```

The query is posed at Delhi, and you are told that only 1 percent of employees are managers. Find the cost of answering this query using each of the following plans:

1. Ship Departments to Naples, compute the query at Naples, then ship the result to Delhi.
2. Ship Employees to Berlin, compute the query at Berlin, then ship the result to Delhi.
3. Compute the query at Delhi by shipping both relations to Delhi.
4. Compute the query at Naples using Bloomjoin; then ship the result to Delhi.
5. Compute the query at Berlin using Bloomjoin; then ship the result to Delhi.
6. Compute the query at Naples using Semijoin; then ship the result to Delhi.
7. Compute the query at Berlin using Semijoin; then ship the result to Delhi.

Exercise 22.7 Consider your answers in Exercise 22.6. Which plan minimizes shipping costs? Is it necessarily the cheapest plan? Which do you expect to be the cheapest?

Exercise 22.8 Consider the Employees and Departments relations described in Exercise 22.3. They are now stored in a distributed DBMS with 10 sites. The Departments tuples are horizontally partitioned across the 10 sites by *did*, with the same number of tuples assigned to each site and no particular order to how tuples are assigned to sites. The Employees tuples are similarly partitioned, by *sal* ranges, with $sal \leq 100{,}000$ assigned to the first site, $100{,}000 < sal \leq 200{,}000$ assigned to the second site, and so on. In addition, the partition $sal \leq 100{,}000$ is frequently accessed and infrequently updated, and it is therefore replicated at every site. No other Employees partition is replicated.

1. Describe the best plan (unless a plan is specified) and give its cost:
   (a) Compute the natural join of Employees and Departments by shipping all fragments of the smaller relation to every site containing tuples of the larger relation.
   (b) Find the highest paid employee.
   (c) Find the highest paid employee with salary less than 100,000.
   (d) Find the highest paid employee with salary between 400,000 and 500,000.
   (e) Find the highest paid employee with salary between 450,000 and 550,000.
   (f) Find the highest paid manager for those departments stored at the query site.
   (g) Find the highest paid manager.
2. Assuming the same data distribution, describe the sites visited and the locks obtained for the following update transactions, assuming that *synchronous* replication is used for the replication of Employees tuples with $sal \leq 100{,}000$:
   (a) Give employees with salary less than 100,000 a 10 percent raise, with a maximum salary of 100,000 (i.e., the raise cannot increase the salary to more than 100,000).
   (b) Give all employees a 10 percent raise. The conditions of the original partitioning of Employees must still be satisfied after the update.
3. Assuming the same data distribution, describe the sites visited and the locks obtained for the following update transactions, assuming that *asynchronous* replication is used for the replication of Employees tuples with $sal \leq 100{,}000$.

(a) For all employees with salary less than 100,000 give them a 10 percent raise, with a maximum salary of 100,000.

(b) Give all employees a 10 percent raise. After the update is completed, the conditions of the original partitioning of Employees must still be satisfied.

Exercise 22.9 Consider the Employees and Departments tables from Exercise 22.3. You are a DBA and you need to decide how to distribute these two tables across two sites, Manila and Nairobi. Your DBMS supports only unclustered B+ tree indexes. You have a choice between synchronous and asynchronous replication. For each of the following scenarios, describe how you would distribute them and what indexes you would build at each site. If you feel that you have insufficient information to make a decision, explain briefly.

1. Half the departments are located in Manila and the other half are in Nairobi. Department information, including that for employees in the department, is changed only at the site where the department is located, but such changes are quite frequent. (Although the location of a department is not included in the Departments schema, this information can be obtained from another table.)
2. Half the departments are located in Manila and the other half are in Nairobi. Department information, including that for employees in the department, is changed only at the site where the department is located, but such changes are infrequent. Finding the average salary for each department is a frequently asked query.
3. Half the departments are located in Manila and the other half are in Nairobi. Employees tuples are frequently changed (only) at the site where the corresponding department is located, but the Departments relation is almost never changed. Finding a given employee's manager is a frequently asked query.
4. Half the employees work in Manila and the other half work in Nairobi. Employees tuples are frequently changed (only) at the site where they work.

Exercise 22.10 Suppose that the Employees relation is stored in Madison and the tuples with $sal \leq 100{,}000$ are replicated at New York. Consider the following three options for lock management: all locks managed at a *single site*, say, Milwaukee; *primary copy* with Madison being the primary for Employees; and *fully distributed*. For each of the lock management options, explain what locks are set (and at which site) for the following queries. Also state from which site the page is read.

1. A query at Austin wants to read a page of Employees tuples with $sal \leq 50{,}000$.
2. A query at Madison wants to read a page of Employees tuples with $sal \leq 50{,}000$.
3. A query at New York wants to read a page of Employees tuples with $sal \leq 50{,}000$.

Exercise 22.11 Briefly answer the following questions:

1. Compare the relative merits of centralized and hierarchical deadlock detection in a distributed DBMS.
2. What is a *phantom deadlock*? Give an example.
3. Give an example of a distributed DBMS with three sites such that no two local waits-for graphs reveal a deadlock, yet there is a global deadlock.
4. Consider the following modification to a local waits-for graph: Add a new node T_{ext}, and for every transaction T_i that is waiting for a lock at another site, add the edge $T_i \rightarrow T_{ext}$. Also add an edge $T_{ext} \rightarrow T_i$ if a transaction executing at another site is waiting for T_i to release a lock at this site.

(a) If there is a cycle in the modified local waits-for graph that does not involve T_{ext}, what can you conclude? If every cycle involves T_{ext}, what can you conclude?

(b) Suppose that every site is assigned a unique integer *site-id*. Whenever the local waits-for graph suggests that there might be a global deadlock, send the local waits-for graph to the site with the next higher site-id. At that site, combine the received graph with the local waits-for graph. If this combined graph does not indicate a deadlock, ship it on to the next site, and so on, until either a deadlock is detected or we are back at the site that originated this round of deadlock detection. Is this scheme guaranteed to find a global deadlock if one exists?

Exercise 22.12 Timestamp-based concurrency control schemes can be used in a distributed DBMS, but we must be able to generate globally unique, monotonically increasing timestamps without a bias in favor of any one site. One approach is to assign timestamps at a single site. Another is to use the local clock time and to append the site-id. A third scheme is to use a counter at each site. Compare these three approaches.

Exercise 22.13 Consider the multiple-granularity locking protocol described in Chapter 18. In a distributed DBMS, the site containing the root object in the hierarchy can become a bottleneck. You hire a database consultant who tells you to modify your protocol to allow only intention locks on the root and implicitly grant all possible intention locks to every transaction.

1. Explain why this modification works correctly, in that transactions continue to be able to set locks on desired parts of the hierarchy.
2. Explain how it reduces the demand on the root.
3. Why is this idea not included as part of the standard multiple-granularity locking protocol for a centralized DBMS?

Exercise 22.14 Briefly answer the following questions:

1. Explain the need for a commit protocol in a distributed DBMS.
2. Describe 2PC. Be sure to explain the need for force-writes.
3. Why are *ack* messages required in 2PC?
4. What are the differences between 2PC and 2PC with Presumed Abort?
5. Give an example execution sequence such that 2PC and 2PC with Presumed Abort generate an identical sequence of actions.
6. Give an example execution sequence such that 2PC and 2PC with Presumed Abort generate different sequences of actions.
7. What is the intuition behind 3PC? What are its pros and cons relative to 2PC?
8. Suppose that a site gets no response from another site for a long time. Can the first site tell whether the connecting link has failed or the other site has failed? How is such a failure handled?
9. Suppose that the coordinator includes a list of all subordinates in the *prepare* message. If the coordinator fails after sending out either an *abort* or *commit* message, can you suggest a way for active sites to terminate this transaction without waiting for the coordinator to recover? Assume that some but not all of the *abort* or *commit* messages from the coordinator are lost.

10. Suppose that 2PC with Presumed Abort is used as the commit protocol. Explain how the system recovers from failure and deals with a particular transaction T in each of the following cases:
    (a) A subordinate site for T fails before receiving a *prepare* message.
    (b) A subordinate site for T fails after receiving a *prepare* message but before making a decision.
    (c) A subordinate site for T fails after receiving a *prepare* message and force-writing an abort log record but before responding to the *prepare* message.
    (d) A subordinate site for T fails after receiving a *prepare* message and force-writing a prepare log record but before responding to the *prepare* message.
    (e) A subordinate site for T fails after receiving a *prepare* message, force-writing an abort log record, and sending a *no* vote.
    (f) The coordinator site for T fails before sending a *prepare* message.
    (g) The coordinator site for T fails after sending a *prepare* message but before collecting all votes.
    (h) The coordinator site for T fails after writing an *abort* log record but before sending any further messages to its subordinates.
    (i) The coordinator site for T fails after writing a *commit* log record but before sending any further messages to its subordinates.
    (j) The coordinator site for T fails after writing an *end* log record. Is it possible for the recovery process to receive an inquiry about the status of T from a subordinate?

Exercise 22.15 Consider a heterogeneous distributed DBMS.

1. Define the terms *multidatabase system* and *gateway.*
2. Describe how queries that span multiple sites are executed in a multidatabase system. Explain the role of the gateway with respect to catalog interfaces, query optimization, and query execution.
3. Describe how transactions that update data at multiple sites are executed in a multidatabase system. Explain the role of the gateway with respect to lock management, distributed deadlock detection, Two-Phase Commit, and recovery.
4. Schemas at different sites in a multidatabase system are probably designed independently. This situation can lead to *semantic heterogeneity*; that is, units of measure may differ across sites (e.g., inches versus centimeters), relations containing essentially the same kind of information (e.g., employee salaries and ages) may have slightly different schemas, and so on. What impact does this heterogeneity have on the end user? In particular, comment on the concept of distributed data independence in such a system.

BIBLIOGRAPHIC NOTES

Work on parallel algorithms for sorting and various relational operations is discussed in the bibliographies for Chapters 13 and 14. Our discussion of parallel joins follows [220], and our discussion of parallel sorting follows [223]. DeWitt and Gray make the case that for future high performance database systems, parallelism will be the key [221]. Scheduling in parallel database systems is discussed in [522]. [496] contains a good collection of papers on query processing in parallel database systems.

Textbook discussions of distributed databases include [78, 144, 580]. Good survey articles include [85], which focuses on concurrency control; [637], which is about distributed databases in general; and [785], which concentrates on distributed query processing. Two major projects in the area were SDD-1 [636] and R* [777]. Fragmentation in distributed databases is considered in [157, 207]. Replication is considered in [11, 14, 137, 239, 238, 388, 385, 335, 552, 600]. For good overviews of current trends in asynchronous replication, see [234, 709, 772]. Papers on view maintenance mentioned in the bibliographic notes of Chapter 21 are also relevant in this context. Olston considers techniques for trading of performance versus precision in a replicated environment [571, 572, 573].

Query processing in the SDD-1 distributed database is described in [88]. One of the notable aspects of SDD-1 query processing was the extensive use of Semijoins. Theoretical studies of Semijoins are presented in [83, 86, 414]. Query processing in R* is described in [667]. The R* query optimizer is validated in [500]; much of our discussion of distributed query processing is drawn from the results reported in this paper. Query processing in Distributed Ingres is described in [247]. Optimization of queries for parallel execution is discussed in [297, 323, 383]. Franklin, Jonsson, and Kossman discuss the trade-offs between *query shipping*, the more traditional approach in relational databases, and *data shipping*, which consists of shipping data to the client for processing and is widely used in object-oriented systems [284]. A good recent survey of distributed query processing techniques can be found in [450].

Concurrency control in the SDD-1 distributed database is described in [91]. Transaction management in R* is described in [547]. Concurrency control in Distributed Ingres is described in [714]. [740] provides an introduction to distributed transaction management and various notions of distributed data independence. Optimizations for read-only transactions are discussed in [306]. Multiversion concurrency control algorithms based on timestamps were proposed in [620]. Timestamp-based concurrency control is discussed in [84, 356]. Concurrency control algorithms based on voting are discussed in [303, 318, 408, 452, 732]. The rotating primary copy scheme is described in [538]. Optimistic concurrency control in distributed databases is discussed in [660], and adaptive concurrency control is discussed in [488].

Two-Phase Commit was introduced in [466, 331]. 2PC with Presumed Abort is described in [546], along with an alternative called *2PC with Presumed Commit*. A variation of Presumed Commit is proposed in [465]. Three-Phase Commit is described in [692]. The deadlock detection algorithms in R* are described in [567]. Many papers discuss deadlocks, for example, [156, 243, 526, 632]. [441] is a survey of several algorithms in this area. Distributed clock synchronization is discussed by [464]. [333] argues that distributed data independence is not always a good idea, due to processing and administrative overheads. The ARIES algorithm is applicable for distributed recovery, but the details of how messages should be handled are not discussed in [544]. The approach taken to recovery in SDD-1 is described in [43]. [114] also addresses distributed recovery. [444] is a survey article that discusses concurrency control and recovery in distributed systems. [95] contains several articles on these topics.

Multidatabase systems are discussed in [10, 113, 230, 231, 242, 476, 485, 519, 520, 599, 641, 765, 797]; see [112, 486, 684] for surveys.

23

OBJECT-DATABASE SYSTEMS

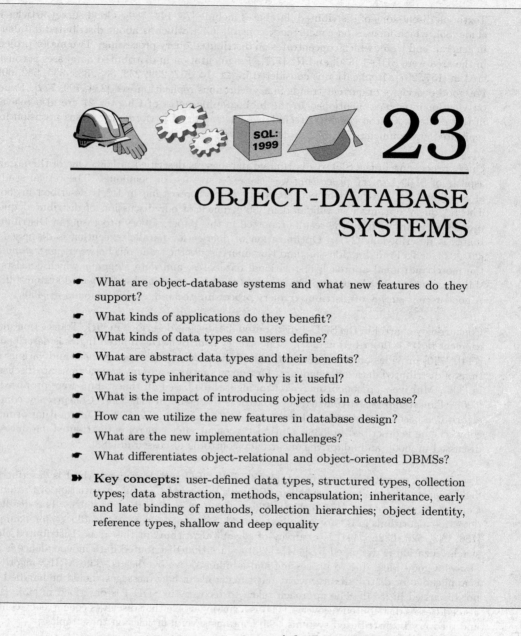

- What are object-database systems and what new features do they support?
- What kinds of applications do they benefit?
- What kinds of data types can users define?
- What are abstract data types and their benefits?
- What is type inheritance and why is it useful?
- What is the impact of introducing object ids in a database?
- How can we utilize the new features in database design?
- What are the new implementation challenges?
- What differentiates object-relational and object-oriented DBMSs?

➽ **Key concepts:** user-defined data types, structured types, collection types; data abstraction, methods, encapsulation; inheritance, early and late binding of methods, collection hierarchies; object identity, reference types, shallow and deep equality

with Joseph M. Hellerstein
University of California–Berkeley

You know my methods, Watson. Apply them.

—Arthur Conan Doyle, *The Memoirs of Sherlock Holmes*

Relational database systems support a small, fixed collection of data types (e.g., integers, dates, strings), which has proven adequate for traditional application domains such as administrative data processing. In many application domains, however, much more complex kinds of data must be handled. Typically this complex data has been stored in OS file systems or specialized data structures, rather than in a DBMS. Examples of domains with complex data include computer-aided design and modeling (CAD/CAM), multimedia repositories, and document management.

As the amount of data grows, the many features offered by a DBMS—for example, reduced application development time, concurrency control and recovery, indexing support, and query capabilities—become increasingly attractive and, ultimately, necessary. To support such applications, a DBMS must support complex data types. Object-oriented concepts strongly influenced efforts to enhance database support for complex data and led to the development of object-database systems, which we discuss in this chapter.

Object-database systems have developed along two distinct paths:

- **Object-Oriented Database Systems:** Object-oriented database systems are proposed as an alternative to relational systems and are aimed at application domains where complex objects play a central role. The approach is heavily influenced by object-oriented programming languages and can be understood as an attempt to add DBMS functionality to a programming language environment. The Object Database Management Group (ODMG) has developed a standard **Object Data Model (ODM)** and **Object Query Language (OQL)**, which are the equivalent of the SQL standard for relational database systems.

- **Object-Relational Database Systems:** Object-relational database systems can be thought of as an attempt to extend relational database systems with the functionality necessary to support a broader class of applications and, in many ways, provide a bridge between the relational and object-oriented paradigms. The SQL:1999 standard extends SQL to incorporate support for the object-relational model of data.

We use acronyms for relational, object-oriented, and object-relational database management systems **(RDBMS, OODBMS, ORDBMS)**. In this chapter, we focus on ORDBMSs and emphasize how they can be viewed as a development of RDBMSs, rather than as an entirely different paradigm, as exemplified by the evolution of SQL:1999.

We concentrate on developing the fundamental concepts rather than presenting SQL:1999; some of the features we discuss are not included in SQL:1999.

Nonetheless, we have chosen to emphasize concepts relevant to SQL:1999 and its likely future extensions. We also try to be consistent with SQL:1999 for notation, although we occasionally diverge slightly for clarity. It is important to recognize that the main concepts discussed are common to both ORDBMSs and OODBMSs; we discuss how they are supported in the ODL/OQL standard proposed for OODBMSs in Section 23.9.

RDBMS vendors, including IBM, Informix, and Oracle, are adding ORDBMS functionality (to varying degrees) in their products, and it is important to recognize how the existing body of knowledge about the design and implementation of relational databases can be leveraged to deal with the ORDBMS extensions. It is also important to understand the challenges and opportunities these extensions present to database users, designers, and implementors.

In this chapter, Sections 23.1 through 23.6 introduce object-oriented concepts. The concepts discussed in these sections are common to both OODBMSs and ORDBMSs. We begin by presenting an example in Section 23.1 that illustrates why extensions to the relational model are needed to cope with some new application domains. This is used as a running example throughout the chapter. We discuss the use of type constructors to support user-defined structured data types in Section 23.2. We consider what operations are supported on these new types of data in Section 23.3. Next, we discuss data encapsulation and abstract data types in Section 23.4. We cover inheritance and related issues, such as method binding and collection hierarchies, in Section 23.5. We then consider objects and object identity in Section 23.6.

We consider how to take advantage of the new object-oriented concepts to do ORDBMS database design in Section 23.7. In Section 23.8, we discuss some of the new implementation challenges posed by object-relational systems. We discuss ODL and OQL, the standards for OODBMSs, in Section 23.9, and then present a brief comparison of ORDBMSs and OODBMSs in Section 23.10.

23.1 MOTIVATING EXAMPLE

As a specific example of the need for object-relational systems, we focus on a new business data processing problem that is both harder and (in our view) more entertaining than the dollars and cents bookkeeping of previous decades. Today, companies in industries such as entertainment are in the business of selling *bits*; their basic corporate assets are not tangible products, but rather software artifacts such as video and audio.

We consider the fictional Dinky Entertainment Company, a large Hollywood conglomerate whose main assets are a collection of cartoon characters, especially the cuddly and internationally beloved Herbert the Worm. Dinky has several Herbert the Worm films, many of which are shown in theaters around the world at any given time. Dinky also makes a good deal of money licensing Herbert's image, voice, and video footage for various purposes: action figures, video games, product endorsements, and so on. Dinky's database is used to manage the sales and leasing records for the various Herbert-related products, as well as the video and audio data that make up Herbert's many films.

23.1.1 New Data Types

The basic problem confronting Dinky's database designers is that they need support for considerably richer data types than is available in a relational DBMS:

- **User-defined data types:** Dinky's assets include Herbert's image, voice, and video footage, and these must be stored in the database. To handle these new types, we need to be able to represent richer structure. (See Section 23.2.) Further, we need special functions to manipulate these objects. For example, we may want to write functions that produce a compressed version of an image or a lower-resolution image. By hiding the details of the data structure through the functions that capture the behavior, we achieve *data abstraction*, leading to cleaner code design. (See Section 23.4.)

- **Inheritance:** As the number of data types grows, it is important to take advantage of the commonality between different types. For example, both compressed images and lower-resolution images are, at some level, just images. It is therefore desirable to *inherit* some features of image objects while defining (and later manipulating) compressed image objects and lower-resolution image objects. (See Section 23.5.)

- **Object Identity:** Given that some of the new data types contain very large instances (e.g., videos), it is important not to store copies of objects; instead, we must store *references*, or *pointers*, to such objects. In turn, this underscores the need for giving objects a unique *object identity*, which can be used to refer or 'point' to them from elsewhere in the data. (See Section 23.6.)

How might we address these issues in an RDBMS? We could store images, videos, and so on as BLOBs in current relational systems. A **binary large object (BLOB)** is just a long stream of bytes, and the DBMS's support consists of storing and retrieving BLOBs in such a manner that a user does not have to worry about the size of the BLOB; a BLOB can span several pages, unlike a traditional attribute. All further processing of the BLOB has to be done by the user's application program, in the host language in which the

The SQL/MM Standard: SQL/MM is an emerging standard that builds upon SQL:1999's new data types to define extensions of SQL:1999 that facilitate handling of complex multimedia data types. SQL/MM is a multipart standard. Part 1, SQL/MM Framework, identifies the SQL:1999 concepts that are the foundation for SQL/MM extensions. Each of the remaining parts addresses a specific type of complex data: **Full Text, Spatial, Still Image,** and **Data Mining**. SQL/MM anticipates that these new complex types can be used in columns of tables as field values.

Large Objects: SQL:1999 includes a new data type called `LARGE OBJECT` or `LOB`, with two variants called `BLOB` (binary large object) and `CLOB` (character large object). This standardizes the large object support found in many current relational DBMSs. LOBs cannot be included in primary keys, `GROUP BY`, or `ORDER BY` clauses. They can be compared using equality, inequality, and substring operations. A LOB has a **locator** that is essentially a unique id and allows LOBs to be manipulated without extensive copying.
LOBs are typically stored separately from the data records in whose fields they appear. IBM DB2, Informix, Microsoft SQL Server, Oracle 8, and Sybase ASE all support LOBs.

SQL code is embedded. This solution is not efficient because we are forced to retrieve all BLOBs in a collection even if most of them could be filtered out of the answer by applying user-defined functions (within the DBMS). It is not satisfactory from a data consistency standpoint either, because the semantics of the data now depends heavily on the host language application code and cannot be enforced by the DBMS.

As for structured types and inheritance, there is simply no support in the relational model. We are forced to map data with such complex structure into a collection of flat tables. (We saw examples of such mappings when we discussed the translation from ER diagrams with inheritance to relations in Chapter 2.)

This application clearly requires features not available in the relational model. As an illustration of these features, Figure 23.1 presents SQL:1999 DDL statements for a portion of Dinky's ORDBMS schema used in subsequent examples. Although the DDL is very similar to that of a traditional relational system, some important distinctions highlight the new data modeling capabilities of an ORDBMS. A quick glance at the DDL statements is sufficient for now; we study them in detail in the next section, after presenting some of the basic concepts that our sample application suggests are needed in a next-generation DBMS.

1. `CREATE TABLE` Frames
    (*frameno* `integer`, *image* `jpeg image`, *category* `integer`);
2. `CREATE TABLE` Categories
    (*cid* `integer`, *name* `text`, *lease price* `float`, *comments* `text`);
3. `CREATE TYPE theater t AS`
    `ROW(`*tno* `integer`, *name* `text`, *address* `text`, *phone* `text`)
    `REF IS SYSTEM GENERATED;`
4. `CREATE TABLE` Theaters `OF theater t REF is` tid `SYSTEM GENERATED;`
5. `CREATE TABLE` Nowshowing
    (*film* `integer`, *theater* `REF`(theater t) `SCOPE` Theaters, *start* `date`, *end* `date`);
6. `CREATE TABLE` Films
    (*filmno* `integer`, *title* `text`, *stars* `VARCHAR(25) ARRAY [10]`),
    director `text`, *budget* `float`);
7. `CREATE TABLE` Countries
    (*name* `text`, *boundary* `polygon`, *population* `integer`, *language* `text`);

Figure 23.1 SQL:1999 DDL Statements for Dinky Schema

23.1.2 Manipulating the New Data

Thus far, we described the new kinds of data that must be stored in the Dinky database. We have not yet said anything about how to *use* these new types in queries, so let us study two queries that Dinky's database needs to support. The syntax of the queries is not critical; it is sufficient to understand what they express. We return to the specifics of the queries' syntax later.

Our first challenge comes from the Clog breakfast cereal company. Clog produces a cereal called Delirios and it wants to lease an image of Herbert the Worm in front of a sunrise to incorporate in the Delirios box design. A query to present a collection of possible images and their lease prices can be expressed in SQL-like syntax as in Figure 23.2. Dinky has a number of methods written in an imperative language like Java and registered with the database system. These methods can be used in queries in the same way as built-in methods, such as $=, +, -, <, >$, are used in a relational language like SQL. The *thumbnail* method in the `Select` clause produces a small version of its full-size input image. The *is sunrise* method is a boolean function that analyzes an image and returns *true* if the image contains a sunrise; the *is herbert* method returns *true* if the image contains a picture of Herbert. The query produces the frame code number, image thumbnail, and price for all frames that contain Herbert and a sunrise.

```
SELECT F.frameno, thumbnail(F.image), C.lease_price
FROM   Frames F, Categories C
WHERE  F.category = C.cid AND is_sunrise(F.image) AND is_herbert(F.image)
```

Figure 23.2 Extended SQL to Find Pictures of Herbert at Sunrise

The second challenge comes from Dinky's executives. They know that Delirios is exceedingly popular in the tiny country of Andorra, so they want to make sure that a number of Herbert films are playing at theaters near Andorra when the cereal hits the shelves. To check on the current state of affairs, the executives want to find the names of all theaters showing Herbert films within 100 kilometers of Andorra. Figure 23.3 shows this query in an SQL-like syntax.

```
SELECT N.theater->name, N.theater->address, F.title
FROM   Nowshowing N, Films F, Countries C
WHERE  N.film = F.filmno AND
       overlaps(C.boundary, radius(N.theater->address, 100)) AND
       C.name = 'Andorra' AND 'Herbert the Worm' = F.stars[1]
```

Figure 23.3 Extended SQL to Find Herbert Films Playing near Andorra

The *theater* attribute of the Nowshowing table is a reference to an object in another table, which has attributes *name*, *address*, and *location*. This object referencing allows for the notation *N.theater->name* and *N.theater->address*, each of which refers to attributes of the `theater_t` object referenced in the Nowshowing row *N*. The *stars* attribute of the *films* table is a set of names of each film's stars. The *radius* method returns a circle centered at its first argument with radius equal to its second argument. The `overlaps` method tests for spatial overlap. Nowshowing and Films are joined by the equijoin clause, while Nowshowing and Countries are joined by the spatial overlap clause. The selections to 'Andorra' and films containing 'Herbert the Worm' complete the query.

These two object-relational queries are similar to SQL-92 queries but have some unusual features:

- **User-Defined Methods:** User-defined abstract types are manipulated via their methods, for example, *is_herbert* (Section 23.2).
- **Operators for Structured Types:** Along with the structured types available in the data model, ORDBMSs provide the natural methods for those types. For example, the `ARRAY` type supports the standard array

operation of accessing an array element by specifying the index; *F.stars*[1] returns the first element of the array in the *stars* column of film *F* (Section 23.3).

- **Operators for Reference Types:** Reference types are *dereferenced* via an arrow (->) notation (Section 23.6.2).

To summarize the points highlighted by our motivating example, traditional relational systems offer limited flexibility in the data types available. Data is stored in tables and the type of each field value is limited to a simple atomic type (e.g., integer or string), with a small, fixed set of such types to choose from. This limited type system can be extended in three main ways: user-defined abstract data types, structured types, and reference types. Collectively, we refer to these new types as **complex types**. In the rest of this chapter, we consider how a DBMS can be extended to provide support for defining new complex types and manipulating objects of these new types.

23.2 STRUCTURED DATA TYPES

SQL:1999 allows users to define new data types, in addition to the built-in types (e.g., integers). In Section 5.7.2, we discussed the definition of new *distinct* types. Distinct types stay within the standard relational model, since values of these types must be atomic.

SQL:1999 also introduced two **type constructors** that allow us to define new types with internal structure. Types defined using type constructors are called **structured types**. This takes us beyond the relational model, since field values need no longer be atomic:

- `ROW`(n_1 t_1, ..., n_n t_n): A type representing a row, or tuple, of n fields with fields $n_1, ..., n_n$ of types $t_1, ..., t_n$ respectively.

- `base ARRAY [`i`]`): A type representing an array of (up to) i `base`-type items.

The `theater_t` type in Figure 23.1 illustrates the new `ROW` data type. In SQL:1999, the `ROW` type has a special role because every table is a collection of rows—every table is a set of rows or a multiset of rows. Values of other types can appear only as field values.

The *stars* field of table Films illustrates the new `ARRAY` type. It is an array of upto 10 elements, each of which is of type `VARCHAR(25)`. Note that 10 is the maximum number of elements in the array; at any time, the array (unlike, say,

SQL:1999 Structured Data Types: Several commercial systems, including IBM DB2, Informix UDS, and Oracle 9i support the `ROW` and `ARRAY` constructors. The `listof`, `bagof`, and `setof` type constructors are not included in SQL:1999. Nonetheless, commercial systems support some of these constructors to varying degrees. Oracle supports nested relations and arrays, but does not support fully composing these constructors. Informix supports the `setof`, **bagof**, and **listof** constructors and allows them to be composed. Support in this area varies widely across vendors.

in C) can contain fewer elements. Since SQL:1999 does not support multidimensional arrays, *vector* might have been a more accurate name for the array constructor.

The power of type constructors comes from the fact that they can be composed. The following row type contains a field that is an array of at most 10 strings:

`ROW`(*filmno:* `integer`, *stars:* `VARCHAR(25) ARRAY` [10])

The row type in SQL:1999 is quite general; its fields can be of any SQL:1999 data type. Unfortunately, the array type is restricted; elements of an array cannot be arrays themselves. Therefore, the following definition is illegal:

(`integer ARRAY` [5]) `ARRAY` [10]

23.2.1 Collection Types

SQL:1999 supports only the `ROW` and `ARRAY` type constructors. Other common type constructors include

- `listof(base)`: A type representing a sequence of `base`-type items.
- `setof(base)`: A type representing a *set* of `base`-type items. Sets cannot contain duplicate elements.
- `bagof(base)`: A type representing a *bag* or *multiset* of `base`-type items.

Types using `listof`, `ARRAY`, `bagof`, or `setof` as the outermost type constructor are sometimes referred to as **collection types** or **bulk data types**.

The lack of support for these collection types is recognized as a weakness of SQL:1999's support for complex objects and it is quite possible that some of these collection types will be added in future revisions of the SQL standard.[1]

23.3 OPERATIONS ON STRUCTURED DATA

The DBMS provides built-in methods for the types defined using type constructors. These methods are analogous to built-in operations such as addition and multiplication for atomic types such as integers. In this section we present the methods for various type constructors and illustrate how SQL queries can create and manipulate values with structured types.

23.3.1 Operations on Rows

Given an item i whose type is `ROW`$(n_1\ t_1, ..., n_n\ t_n)$, the field extraction method allows us to access an individual field n_k using the traditional dot notation $i.n_k$. If row constructors are nested in a type definition, dots may be nested to access the fields of the nested row; for example $i.n_k.m_l$. If we have a collection of rows, the dot notation gives us a collection as a result. For example, if i is a list of rows, $i.n_k$ gives us a list of items of type t_n; if i is a set of rows, $i.n_k$ gives us a set of items of type t_n.

This nested-dot notation is often called a **path expression**, because it describes a path through the nested structure.

23.3.2 Operations on Arrays

Array types support an 'array index' method to allow users to access array items at a particular offset. A postfix 'square bracket' syntax is usually used. Since the number of elements can vary, there is an operator (`CARDINALITY`) that returns the number of elements in the array. The variable number of elements also motivates an operator to concatenate two arrays. The following example illustrates these operations on SQL:1999 arrays.

```
SELECT F.filmno, (F.stars || ['Brando', 'Pacino'])
FROM   Films F
WHERE  CARDINALITY(F.stars) < 3 AND F.stars[1]='Redford'
```

[1]According to Jim Melton, the editor of the SQL:1999 standard, these collection types were considered for inclusion but omitted because some problems with their specifications were discovered too late for correction in the SQL:1999 time-frame.

For each film with Redford as the first star[2] and fewer than three stars, the result of the query contains the film's array of stars concatenated with the array containing the two elements 'Brando' and 'Pacino'. Observe how a value of type array (containing Brando and Pacino) is constructed through the use of square brackets in the `SELECT` clause.

23.3.3 Operations on Other Collection Types

Although only arrays are supported in SQL:1999, future versions of SQL are expected to support other collection types, and we consider what operations are appropriate over these types of data. provide such operations. Our discussion is illustrative and not meant to be comprehensive. For example, one could additionally allow aggregate operators *count*, *sum*, *avg*, *max*, and *min* to be applied to any object of a collection type with an appropriate base type (e.g., `INTEGER`). One could also support operators for type conversions. For example, one could provide operators to convert a multiset object to a set object by eliminating duplicates.

Sets and Multisets

Set objects can be compared using the traditional set methods $\subset, \subseteq, =, \supseteq, \supset$. An item of type `setof(foo)` can be compared with an item of type `foo` using the $\in$ method, as illustrated in Figure 23.3, which contains the comparison *'Herbert the Worm'* $\in$ *F.stars*. Two set objects (having elements of the same type) can be combined to form a new object using the $\cup$, $\cap$, and $-$ operators.

Each of the methods for sets can be defined for multisets, taking the number of copies of elements into account. The $\cup$ operation simply adds up the number of copies of an element, the $\cap$ operation counts the lesser number of times a given element appears in the two input multisets, and $-$ subtracts the number of times a given element appears in the second multiset from the number of times it appears in the first multiset. For example, using multiset semantics $\cup$ ({1,2,2,2}, {2,2,3}) = {1,2,2,2,2,2,3}; $\cap$ ({1,2,2,2}, {2,2,3}) = {2,2}; and $-$ ({1,2,2,2}, {2,2,3}) = {1,2}.

Lists

Traditional list operations include *head*, which returns the first element; *tail*, which returns the list obtained by removing the first element; *prepend*, which

[2]Note that the first element in an SQL array has index value 1 (not 0, as in some languages).

takes an element and inserts it as the first element in a list; and *append*, which appends one list to another.

23.3.4 Queries Over Nested Collections

We now present some examples to illustrate how relations that contain nested collections can be queried, using SQL syntax. In particular, extensions of the relational model with nested sets and multisets have been widely studied and we focus on these collection types.

We consider a variant of the Films relation from Figure 23.1 in this section, with the *stars* field defined as a `setof (VARCHAR[25])`, rather than an array. Each tuple describes a film, uniquely identified by *filmno*, and contains a set (of stars in the film) as a field value.

Our first example illustrates how we can apply an aggregate operator to such a nested set. It identifies films with more than two stars by counting the number of stars; the `CARDINALITY` operator is applied once per Films tuple. [3]

```
SELECT F.filmno
FROM   Films F
WHERE  CARDINALITY(F.stars) > 2
```

Our second query illustrates an operation called **unnesting**. Consider the instance of Films shown in Figure 23.4; we have omitted the *director* and *budget* fields (included in the Films schema in Figure 23.1) for simplicity. A flat version of the same information is shown in Figure 23.5; for each film and star in the film, we have a tuple in Films_flat.

filmno	*title*	*stars*
98	Casablanca	{Bogart, Bergman}
54	Earth Worms Are Juicy	{Herbert, Wanda}

Figure 23.4 A Nested Relation, Films

The following query generates the instance of Films_flat from Films:

```
SELECT F.filmno, F.title, S AS star
FROM   Films F, F.stars AS S
```

[3]SQL:1999 does not support set or multiset values, as we noted earlier. If it did, it would be natural to allow the `CARDINALITY` operator to be applied to a set-value to count the number of elements; we have used the operator in this spirit.

filmno	*title*	*star*
98	Casablanca	Bogart
98	Casablanca	Bergman
54	Earth Worms Are Juicy	Herbert
54	Earth Worms Are Juicy	Wanda

Figure 23.5 A Flat Version, Films_flat

The variable F is successively bound to tuples in Films, and for each value of F, the variable S is successively bound to the set in the *stars* field of F. Conversely, we may want to generate the instance of Films from Films_flat. We can generate the Films instance using a generalized form of SQL's `GROUP BY` construct, as the following query illustrates:

```
SELECT    F.filmno, F.title, set_gen(F.star)
FROM      Films_flat F
GROUP BY  F.filmno, F.title
```

This example introduces a new operator *set_gen*, to be used with `GROUP BY`, that requires some explanation. The `GROUP BY` clause partitions the Films_flat table by sorting on the *filmno* attribute; all tuples in a given partition have the same *filmno* (and therefore the same *title*). Consider the set of values in the *star* column of a given partition. In an SQL-92 query, this set must be summarized by applying an aggregate operator such as `COUNT`. Now that we allow relations to contain sets as field values, however, we can return the set of *star* values as a field value in a single answer tuple; the answer tuple also contains the *filmno* of the corresponding partition. The *set_gen* operator collects the set of *star* values in a partition and creates a set-valued object. This operation is called **nesting**. We can imagine similar generator functions for creating multisets, lists, and so on. However, such generators are not included in SQL:1999.

23.4 ENCAPSULATION AND ADTS

Consider the Frames table of Figure 23.1. It has a column *image* of type `jpeg_image`, which stores a compressed image representing a single frame of a film. The `jpeg_image` type is not one of the DBMS's built-in types and was defined by a user for the Dinky application to store image data compressed using the JPEG standard. As another example, the Countries table defined in Line 7 of Figure 23.1 has a column *boundary* of type `polygon`, which contains representations of the shapes of countries' outlines on a world map.

Allowing users to define arbitrary new data types is a key feature of ORDBMSs. The DBMS allows users to store and retrieve objects of type `jpeg_image`, just like an object of any other type, such as `integer`. New atomic data types usually need to have type-specific operations defined by the user who creates them. For example, one might define operations on an image data type such as `compress`, `rotate`, `shrink`, and `crop`. The combination of an atomic data type and its associated methods is called an **abstract data type**, or **ADT**. Traditional SQL comes with built-in ADTs, such as integers (with the associated arithmetic methods) or strings (with the equality, comparison, and `LIKE` methods). Object-relational systems include these ADTs and also allow users to define their own ADTs.

The label *abstract* is applied to these data types because the database system does not need to know how an ADT's data is stored nor how the ADT's methods work. It merely needs to know what methods are available and the input and output types for the methods. Hiding ADT internals is called **encapsulation**.[4] Note that even in a relational system, atomic types such as integers have associated methods that encapsulate them. In the case of integers, the standard methods for the ADT are the usual arithmetic operators and comparators. To evaluate the addition operator on integers, the database system need not understand the laws of addition—it merely needs to know how to invoke the addition operator's code and what type of data to expect in return.

In an object-relational system, the simplification due to encapsulation is critical because it hides any substantive distinctions between data types and allows an ORDBMS to be implemented without anticipating the types and methods that users might want to add. For example, adding integers and overlaying images can be treated uniformly by the system, with the only significant distinctions being that different code is invoked for the two operations and differently typed objects are expected to be returned from that code.

23.4.1 Defining Methods

To register a new method for a user-defined data type, users must write the code for the method and then inform the database system about the method. The code to be written depends on the languages supported by the DBMS and, possibly, the operating system in question. For example, the ORDBMS may handle Java code in the Linux operating system. In this case, the method code must be written in Java and compiled into a Java bytecode file stored in a Linux file system. Then an SQL-style method registration command is given to the ORDBMS so that it recognizes the new method:

[4]Some ORDBMSs actually refer to ADTs as **opaque types** because they are encapsulated and hence one cannot see their details.

Packaged ORDBMS Extensions: Developing a set of user-defined types and methods for a particular application—say, image management—can involve a significant amount of work and domain-specific expertise. As a result, most ORDBMS vendors partner with third parties to sell prepackaged sets of ADTs for particular domains. Informix calls these extensions *DataBlades*, Oracle calls them *Data Cartridges*, IBM calls them *DB2 Extenders*, and so on. These packages include the ADT method code, DDL scripts to automate loading the ADTs into the system, and in some cases specialized access methods for the data type. Packaged ADT extensions are analogous to the class libraries available for object-oriented programming languages: They provide a set of objects that together address a common task.
SQL:1999 has an extension called SQL/MM that consists of several independent parts, each of which specifies a type library for a particular kind of data. The SQL/MM parts for Full-Text, Spatial, Still Image, and Data Mining are available, or nearing publication.

```
CREATE FUNCTION is_sunrise(jpeg_image) RETURNS boolean
        AS EXTERNAL NAME '/a/b/c/dinky.class' LANGUAGE 'java';
```

This statement defines the salient aspects of the method: the type of the associated ADT, the return type, and the location of the code. Once the method is registered, the DBMS uses a Java virtual machine to execute the code[5]. Figure 23.6 presents a number of method registration commands for our Dinky database.

```
1. CREATE FUNCTION thumbnail(jpeg_image) RETURNS jpeg_image
        AS EXTERNAL NAME '/a/b/c/dinky.class' LANGUAGE 'java';
2. CREATE FUNCTION is_sunrise(jpeg_image) RETURNS boolean
        AS EXTERNAL NAME '/a/b/c/dinky.class' LANGUAGE 'java';
3. CREATE FUNCTION is_herbert(jpeg_image) RETURNS boolean
        AS EXTERNAL NAME '/a/b/c/dinky.class' LANGUAGE 'java';
4. CREATE FUNCTION radius(polygon, float) RETURNS polygon
        AS EXTERNAL NAME '/a/b/c/dinky.class' LANGUAGE 'java';
5. CREATE FUNCTION overlaps(polygon, polygon) RETURNS boolean
        AS EXTERNAL NAME '/a/b/c/dinky.class' LANGUAGE 'java';
```

Figure 23.6 Method Registration Commands for the Dinky Database

[5]In the case of non-portable compiled code—written, for example, in a language like C++—the DBMS uses the operating system's dynamic linking facility to link the method code into the database system so that it can be invoked.

Type definition statements for the user-defined atomic data types in the Dinky schema are given in Figure 23.7.

1. `CREATE ABSTRACT DATA TYPE jpeg_image`
   (*internallength* = `VARIABLE`, *input* = jpeg_in, *output* = jpeg_out);
2. `CREATE ABSTRACT DATA TYPE polygon`
   (*internallength* = `VARIABLE`, *input* = poly_in, *output* = poly_out);

Figure 23.7 Atomic Type Declaration Commands for Dinky Database

23.5 INHERITANCE

We considered the concept of inheritance in the context of the ER model in Chapter 2 and discussed how ER diagrams with inheritance were translated into tables. In object-database systems, unlike relational systems, inheritance is supported directly and allows type definitions to be reused and refined very easily. It can be very helpful when modeling similar but slightly different classes of objects. In object-database systems, inheritance can be used in two ways: for reusing and refining types and for creating hierarchies of collections of similar but not identical objects.

23.5.1 Defining Types with Inheritance

In the Dinky database, we model movie theaters with the type `theater_t`. Dinky also wants their database to represent a new marketing technique in the theater business: the *theater-cafe*, which serves pizza and other meals while screening movies. Theater-cafes require additional information to be represented in the database. In particular, a theater-cafe is just like a theater, but has an additional attribute representing the theater's menu. Inheritance allows us to capture this 'specialization' explicitly in the database design with the following DDL statement:

```
CREATE TYPE theatercafe_t UNDER theater_t (menu text);
```

This statement creates a new type, `theatercafe_t`, which has the same attributes and methods as `theater_t`, plus one additional attribute *menu* of type `text`. Methods defined on `theater_t` apply to objects of type `theatercafe_t`, but not vice versa. We say that `theatercafe_t` **inherits** the attributes and methods of `theater_t`.

Note that the inheritance mechanism is not merely a macro to shorten `CREATE` statements. It creates an explicit relationship in the database between the **subtype** (`theatercafe_t`) and the **supertype** (`theater_t`): *An object of the* *subtype is also considered to be an object of the supertype.* This treatment means that any operations that apply to the supertype (methods as well as query operators, such as projection or join) also apply to the subtype. This is generally expressed in the following principle:

> **The Substitution Principle**: Given a supertype A and a subtype B, it is always possible to substitute an object of type B into a legal expression written for objects of type A, without producing type errors.

This principle enables easy code reuse because queries and methods written for the supertype can be applied to the subtype without modification.

Note that inheritance can also be used for atomic types, in addition to row types. Given a supertype `image_t` with methods *title(), number_of_colors(),* and *display()*, we can define a subtype `thumbnail_image_t` for small images that inherits the methods of `image_t`.

23.5.2 Binding Methods

In defining a subtype, it is sometimes useful to replace a method for the supertype with a new version that operates differently on the subtype. Consider the `image_t` type and the subtype `jpeg_image_t` from the Dinky database. Unfortunately, the *display()* method for standard images does not work for JPEG images, which are specially compressed. Therefore, in creating type `jpeg_image_t`, we write a special *display()* method for JPEG images and register it with the database system using the `CREATE FUNCTION` command:

```
CREATE FUNCTION display(jpeg_image) RETURNS jpeg_image
        AS EXTERNAL NAME '/a/b/c/jpeg.class' LANGUAGE 'java';
```

Registering a new method with the same name as an old method is called **overloading** the method name.

Because of overloading, the system must understand which method is intended in a particular expression. For example, when the system needs to invoke the *display()* method on an object of type `jpeg_image_t`, it uses the specialized *display* method. When it needs to invoke *display* on an object of type `image_t` that is not otherwise subtyped, it invokes the standard *display* method. The process of deciding which method to invoke is called **binding** the method to the object. In certain situations, this binding can be done when an expression is parsed (**early binding**), but in other cases the most specific type of an object cannot be known until run-time, so the method cannot be bound until then (**late binding**). Late binding facilties add flexibility but can make it harder for the user to reason about the methods that get invoked for a given query expression.

23.5.3 Collection Hierarchies

Type inheritance was invented for object-oriented programming languages, and our discussion of inheritance up to this point differs little from the discussion one might find in a book on an object-oriented language such as C++ or Java.

However, because database systems provide query languages over tabular data sets, the mechanisms from programming languages are enhanced in object databases to deal with tables and queries as well. In particular, in object-relational systems, we can define a table containing objects of a particular type, such as the Theaters table in the Dinky schema. Given a new subtype, such as `theatercafe t`, we would like to create another table Theater cafes to store the information about theater cafes. But, when writing a query over the Theaters table, it is sometimes desirable to ask the same query over the Theater cafes table; after all, if we project out the additional columns, an instance of the Theater cafes table can be regarded as an instance of the Theaters table.

Rather than requiring the user to specify a separate query for each such table, we can inform the system that a new table of the subtype is to be treated as part of a table of the supertype, with respect to queries over the latter table. In our example, we can say

`CREATE TABLE` Theater Cafes `OF TYPE theatercafe t UNDER` Theaters;

This statement tells the system that queries over the Theaters table should actually be run over all tuples in both the Theaters and Theater Cafes tables. In such cases, if the subtype definition involves method overloading, late-binding is used to ensure that the appropriate methods are called for each tuple.

In general, the `UNDER` clause can be used to generate an arbitrary tree of tables, called a **collection hierarchy**. Queries over a particular table T in the hierarchy are run over all tuples in T and its descendants. Sometimes, a user may want the query to run only on T and not on the descendants; additional syntax, for example, the keyword `ONLY`, can be used in the query's `FROM` clause to achieve this effect.

23.6 OBJECTS, OIDS, AND REFERENCE TYPES

In object-database systems, data objects can be given an **object identifier (oid)**, which is some value that is unique in the database across time. The

OIDs: IBM DB2, Informix UDS, and Oracle 9i support REF types.

DBMS is responsible for generating oids and ensuring that an oid identifies an object uniquely over its entire lifetime. In some systems, all tuples stored in any table are objects and automatically assigned unique oids; in other systems, a user can specify the tables for which the tuples are to be assigned oids. Often, there are also facilities for generating oids for larger structures (e.g., tables) as well as smaller structures (e.g., instances of data values such as a copy of the integer 5 or a JPEG image).

An object's oid can be used to refer to it from elsewhere in the data. An oid has a type similar to the type of a pointer in a programming language.

In SQL:1999 every tuple in a table can be given an oid by defining the table in terms of a structured type and declaring that a REF type is associated with it, as in the definition of the Theaters table in Line 4 of Figure 23.1. Contrast this with the definition of the Countries table in Line 7; Countries tuples do not have associated oids. (SQL:1999 also assigns 'oids' to large objects: This is the locator for the object.)

REF types have values that are unique identifiers or oids. SQL:1999 requires that a given REF type must be associated with a specific table. For example, Line 5 of Figure 23.1 defines a column *theater* of type REF(theater_t). The SCOPE clause specifies that items in this column are references to rows in the Theaters table, which is defined in Line 4.

23.6.1 Notions of Equality

The distinction between reference types and reference-free structured types raises another issue: the definition of equality. Two objects having the same type are defined to be **deep equal** if and only if

1. The objects are of atomic type and have the same value.

2. The objects are of reference type and the *deep equals* operator is true for the two referenced objects.

3. The objects are of structured type and the *deep equals* operator is true for all the corresponding subparts of the two objects.

Two objects that have the same reference type are defined to be **shallow equal** if both refer to the same object (i.e., both references use the same oid). The definition of shallow equality can be extended to objects of arbitrary type by taking the definition of deep equality and replacing *deep equals* by *shallow equals* in parts (2) and (3).

As an example, consider the complex objects `ROW(`538, *t89*, 6-3-97, 8-7-97`)` and `ROW(`538, *t33*, 6-3-97, 8-7-97`)`, whose type is the type of rows in the table Nowshowing (Line 5 of Figure 23.1). These two objects are not shallow equal because they differ in the second attribute value. Nonetheless, they might be deep equal, if, for instance, the oids *t89* and *t33* refer to objects of type `theater t` that have the same value; for example, `tuple(`54, 'Majestic', '115 King', '2556698'`)`.

While two deep equal objects may not be shallow equal, as the example illustrates, two shallow equal objects are always deep equal, of course. The default choice of deep versus shallow equality for reference types is different across systems, although typically we are given syntax to specify either semantics.

23.6.2 Dereferencing Reference Types

An item of reference type `REF(basetype)` is not the same as the `basetype` item to which it points. To access the referenced `basetype` item, a built-in `deref()` method is provided along with the `REF` type constructor. For example, given a tuple from the Nowshowing table, one can access the *name* field of the referenced `theater t` object with the syntax Nowshowing.`deref`*(theater).name*. Since references to tuple types are common, SQL:1999 uses a Java-style arrow operator, which combines a postfix version of the dereference operator with a tuple-type dot operator. The name of the referenced theater can be accessed with the equivalent syntax Nowshowing.*theater–>name*, as in Figure 23.3.

At this point we have covered all the basic type extensions used in the Dinky schema in Figure 23.1. The reader is invited to revisit the schema and examine the structure and content of each table and how the new features are used in the various sample queries.

23.6.3 URLs and OIDs in SQL:1999

It is instructive to note the differences between Internet URLs and the oids in object systems. First, oids uniquely identify a single object over all time (at least, until the object is deleted, when the oid is undefined), whereas the Web resource pointed at by an URL can change over time. Second, oids are simply identifiers and carry no physical information about the objects they identify—this makes it possible to change the storage location of an object without modifying pointers to the object. In contrast, URLs include network addresses and often file-system names as well, meaning that if the resource identified by the URL has to move to another file or network address, then all links to that resource are either incorrect or require a 'forwarding' mechanism. Third, oids are automatically generated by the DBMS for each object, whereas URLs are user-generated. Since users generate URLs, they often embed semantic information into the URL via machine, directory, or file names; this can become confusing if the object's properties change over time.

For URLs, deletions can be troublesome: This leads to the notorious '404 Page Not Found' error. For oids, SQL:1999 allows us to say `REFERENCES ARE CHECKED` as part of the `SCOPE` clause and choose one of several actions when a referenced object is deleted. This is a direct extension of referential integrity that covers oids.

23.7 DATABASE DESIGN FOR AN ORDBMS

The rich variety of data types in an ORDBMS offers a database designer many opportunities for a more natural or more efficient design. In this section we illustrate the differences between RDBMS and ORDBMS database design through several examples.

23.7.1 Collection Types and ADTs

Our first example involves several space probes, each of which continuously records a video. A single video stream is associated with each probe, and while this stream was collected over a certain time period, we assume that it is now a complete object associated with the probe. During the time period over which the video was collected, the probe's location was periodically recorded (such information can easily be piggy-backed onto the header portion of a video stream conforming to the MPEG standard). The information associated with a probe has three parts: (1) a *probe ID* that identifies a probe uniquely, (2) a *video stream*, and (3) a *location sequence* of ⟨*time, location*⟩ pairs. What kind of a database schema should we use to store this information?

An RDBMS Database Design

In an RDBMS, we must store each video stream as a BLOB and each location sequence as tuples in a table. A possible RDBMS database design follows:

Probes(*pid:* `integer`, *time:* `timestamp`, *lat:* `real`, *long:* `real`,
camera: `string`, *video:* `BLOB`)

There is a single table called Probes and it has several rows for each probe. Each of these rows has the same *pid*, *camera*, and *video* values, but different *time*, *lat*, and *long* values. (We have used latitude and longitude to denote location.) The key for this table can be represented as a functional dependency: $PTLN \rightarrow CV$, where N stands for longitude. There is another dependency: $P \rightarrow CV$. This relation is therefore not in BCNF; indeed, it is not even in 3NF. We can decompose Probes to obtain a BCNF schema:

Probes_Loc(*pid:* `integer`, *time:* `timestamp`, *lat:* `real`, *long:* `real`)
Probes_Video(*pid:* `integer`, *camera:* `string`, *video:* `BLOB`)

This design is about the best we can achieve in an RDBMS. However, it suffers from several drawbacks.

First, representing videos as BLOBs means that we have to write application code in an external language to manipulate a video object in the database. Consider this query: "For probe 10, display the video recorded between 1:10 P.M. and 1:15 P.M. on May 10 1996." We must retrieve the entire video object associated with probe 10, recorded over several hours, to display a segment recorded over five minutes.

Next, the fact that each probe has an associated sequence of location readings is obscured, and the sequence information associated with a probe is dispersed across several tuples. A third drawback is that we are forced to separate the video information from the sequence information for a probe. These limitations are exposed by queries that require us to consider all the information associated with each probe; for example, "For each probe, print the earliest time at which it recorded, and the camera type." This query now involves a join of Probes_Loc and Probes_Video on the *pid* field.

An ORDBMS Database Design

An ORDBMS supports a much better solution. First, we can store the video as an ADT object and write methods that capture any special manipulation we wish to perform. Second, because we are allowed to store structured types such as lists, we can store the location sequence for a probe in a single tuple, along with the video information. This layout eliminates the need for joins in queries that involve both the sequence and video information. An ORDBMS design for our example consists of a single relation called Probes_AllInfo:

Probes_AllInfo(*pid:* `integer`, *locseq:* `location_seq`, *camera:* `string`,
video: `mpeg_stream`)

This definition involves two new types, `location_seq` and `mpeg_stream`. The `mpeg_stream` type is defined as an ADT, with a method *display()* that takes a start time and an end time and displays the portion of the video recorded during that interval. This method can be implemented efficiently by looking at the total recording duration and the total length of the video and interpolating to extract the segment recorded during the interval specified in the query.

Our first query in extended SQL using this *display* method follows. We now retrieve only the required segment of the video rather than the entire video.

```
SELECT  display(P.video, 1:10 P.M. May 10 1996, 1:15 P.M. May 10 1996)
FROM    Probes_AllInfo P
WHERE   P.pid = 10
```

Now consider the `location_seq` type. We could define it as a `list` type, containing a list of `ROW` type objects:

```
CREATE TYPE location_seq listof
        (row (time: timestamp, lat: real, long: real))
```

Consider the *locseq* field in a row for a given probe. This field contains a list of rows, each of which has three fields. If the ORDBMS implements collection types in their full generality, we should be able to extract the *time* column from this list to obtain a list of `timestamp` values and apply the `MIN` aggregate operator to this list to find the earliest time at which the given probe recorded. Such support for collection types would enable us to express our second query thus:

```
SELECT  P.pid, MIN(P.locseq.time)
FROM    Probes_AllInfo P
```

Current ORDBMSs are not as general and clean as this example query suggests. For instance, the system may not recognize that projecting the *time* column from a list of rows gives us a list of timestamp values; or the system may allow us to apply an aggregate operator only to a table and not to a nested list value.

Continuing with our example, we may want to do specialized operations on our location sequences that go beyond the standard aggregate operators. For instance, we may want to define a method that takes a time interval and computes the distance traveled by the probe during this interval. The code for this method must understand details of a probe's trajectory and geospatial coordinate systems. For these reasons, we might choose to define `location_seq` as an ADT.

Clearly, an (ideal) ORDBMS gives us many useful design options that are not available in an RDBMS.

23.7.2 Object Identity

We now discuss some of the consequences of using reference types or oids. The use of oids is especially significant when the size of the object is large, either because it is a structured data type or because it is a big object such as an image.

Although reference types and structured types seem similar, they are actually quite different. For example, consider a structured type `my_theater tuple(`*tno* `integer`, *name* `text`, *address* `text`, *phone* `text)` and the reference type `theater ref(theater_t)` of Figure 23.1. There are important differences in the way that database updates affect these two types:

- **Deletion:** Objects with references can be affected by the deletion of objects that they reference, while reference-free structured objects are not affected by deletion of other objects. For example, if the Theaters table were dropped from the database, an object of type `theater` might change value to *null*, because the `theater_t` object it refers to has been deleted, while a similar object of type `my_theater` would not change value.

- **Update:** Objects of reference types change value if the referenced object is updated. Objects of reference-free structured types change value only if updated directly.

- **Sharing versus Copying:** An identified object can be referenced by multiple reference-type items, so that each update to the object is reflected in many places. To get a similar effect in reference-free types requires updating all 'copies' of an object.

There are also important storage distinctions between reference types and non-reference types, which might affect performance:

- **Storage Overhead:** Storing copies of a large value in multiple structured type objects may use much more space than storing the value once and referring to it elsewhere through reference type objects. This additional storage requirement can affect both disk usage and buffer management (if many copies are accessed at once).

- **Clustering:** The subparts of a structured object are typically stored together on disk. Objects with references may point to other objects that are far away on the disk, and the disk arm may require significant movement

> **OIDs and Referential Integrity:** In SQL:1999, all the oids that appear in a column of a relation are required to reference the same target relation. This 'scoping' makes it possible to check oid references for 'referential integrity' just like foreign key references are checked. While current ORDBMS products supporting oids do not support such checks, it is likely that they will in future releases. This will make it much safer to use oids.

to assemble the object and its references together. Structured objects can thus be more efficient than reference types if they are typically accessed in their entirety.

Many of these issues also arise in traditional programming languages such as C or Pascal, which distinguish between the notions of referring to objects *by value* and *by reference*. In database design, the choice between using a structured type or a reference type typically includes consideration of the storage costs, clustering issues, and the effect of updates.

Object Identity versus Foreign Keys

Using an oid to refer to an object is similar to using a foreign key to refer to a tuple in another relation but not quite the same: An oid can point to an object of `theater_t` that is stored *anywhere* in the database, even in a field, whereas a foreign key reference is constrained to point to an object in a particular referenced relation. This restriction makes it possible for the DBMS to provide much greater support for referential integrity than for arbitrary oid pointers. In general, if an object is deleted while there are still oid-pointers to it, the best the DBMS can do is to recognize the situation by maintaining a reference count. (Even this limited support becomes impossible if oids can be copied freely.) Therefore, the responsibility for avoiding dangling references rests largely with the user if oids are used to refer to objects. This burdensome responsibility suggests that we should use oids with great caution and use foreign keys instead whenever possible.

23.7.3 Extending the ER Model

The ER model, as described in Chapter 2, is not adequate for ORDBMS design. We have to use an extended ER model that supports structured attributes (i.e., sets, lists, arrays as attribute values), distinguishes whether entities have object ids, and allows us to model entities whose attributes include methods. We illustrate these comments using an extended ER diagram to describe the space probe data in Figure 23.8; our notational conventions are ad hoc and only for illustrative purposes.

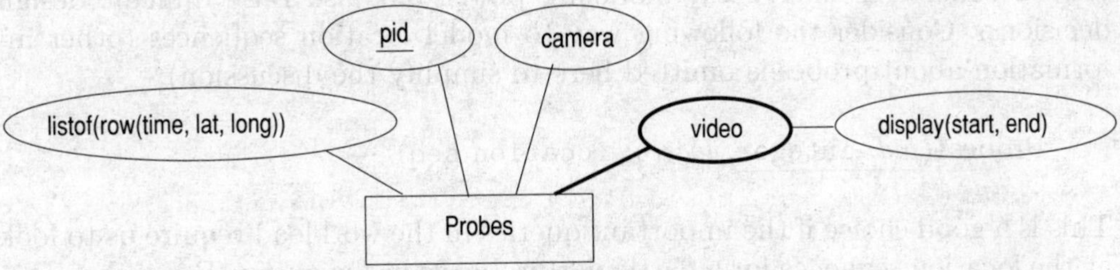

Figure 23.8 The Space Probe Entity Set

The definition of Probes in Figure 23.8 has two new aspects. First, it has a structured-type attribute `listof(row(`*time, lat, long*`))`; each value assigned to this attribute in a Probes entity is a list of tuples with three fields. Second, Probes has an attribute called *video* that is an abstract data type object, which is indicated by a dark oval for this attribute with a dark line connecting it to Probes. Further, this attribute has an 'attribute' of its own, which is a method of the ADT.

Alternatively, we could model each video as an entity by using an entity set called Videos. The association between Probes entities and Videos entities could then be captured by defining a relationship set that links them. Since each video is collected by precisely one probe and every video is collected by some probe, this relationship can be maintained by simply storing a reference to a probe object with each Videos entity; this technique is essentially the second translation approach from ER diagrams to tables discussed in Section 2.4.1.

If we also make Videos a weak entity set in this alternative design, we can add a referential integrity constraint that causes a Videos entity to be deleted when the corresponding Probes entity is deleted. More generally, this alternative design illustrates a strong similarity between storing references to objects and foreign keys; the foreign key mechanism achieves the same effect as storing oids, but in a controlled manner. If oids are used, the user must ensure that there are no dangling references when an object is deleted, with very little support from the DBMS.

Finally, we note that a significant extension to the ER model is required to support the design of nested collections. For example, if a location sequence is modeled as an entity, and we want to define an attribute of Probes that contains a set of such entities, there is no way to do this without extending the ER model. We do not discuss this point further at the level of ER diagrams, but consider an example next that illustrates when to use a nested collection.

23.7.4 Using Nested Collections

Nested collections offer great modeling power but also raise difficult design decisions. Consider the following way to model location sequences (other information about probes is omitted here to simplify the discussion):

Probes1(*pid:* `integer`, *locseq:* `location_seq`)

This is a good choice if the important queries in the workload require us to look at the location sequence for a particular probe, as in the query "For each probe, print the earliest time at which it recorded and the camera type." On the other hand, consider a query that requires us to look at all location sequences: "Find the earliest time at which a recording exists for *lat=5, long=90.*" This query can be answered more efficiently if the following schema is used:

Probes2(*pid:* `integer`, *time:* `timestamp`, *lat:* `real`, *long:* `real`)

The choice of schema must therefore be guided by the expected workload (as always). As another example, consider the following schema:

Can_Teach1(*cid:* `integer`, *teachers:* `setof`(*ssn:* `string`), *sal:* `integer`)

If tuples in this table are to be interpreted as "Course *cid* can be taught by any of the teachers in the *teachers* field, at a cost *sal.*" then we have the option of using the following schema instead:

Can_Teach2(*cid:* `integer`, *teacher_ssn:* `string`, *sal:* `integer`)

A choice between these two alternatives can be made based on how we expect to query this table. On the other hand, suppose that tuples in Can_Teach1 are to be interpreted as "Course *cid* can be taught by the team *teachers,* at a combined cost of *sal.*" Can_Teach2 is no longer a viable alternative. If we wanted to flatten Can_Teach1, we would have to use a separate table to encode teams:

Can_Teach2(*cid:* `integer`, *team_id:* `oid`, *sal:* `integer`)
Teams(*tid:* `oid`, *ssn:* `string`)

As these examples illustrate, nested collections are appropriate in certain situations, but this feature can easily be misused; nested collections should therefore be used with care.

23.8 ORDBMS IMPLEMENTATION CHALLENGES

The enhanced functionality of ORDBMSs raises several implementation challenges. Some of these are well understood and solutions have been implemented in products; others are subjects of current research. In this section we examine a few of the key challenges that arise in implementing an efficient, fully functional ORDBMS. Many more issues are involved than those discussed here; the interested reader is encouraged to revisit the previous chapters in this book and consider whether the implementation techniques described there apply naturally to ORDBMSs or not.

23.8.1 Storage and Access Methods

Since object-relational databases store new types of data, ORDBMS implementors need to revisit some of the storage and indexing issues discussed in earlier chapters. In particular, the system must efficiently store ADT objects and structured objects and provide efficient indexed access to both.

Storing Large ADT and Structured Type Objects

Large ADT objects and structured objects complicate the layout of data on disk. This problem is well understood and has been solved in essentially all ORDBMSs and OODBMSs. We present some of the main issues here.

User-defined ADTs can be quite large. In particular, they can be bigger than a single disk page. Large ADTs, like BLOBs, require special storage, typically in a different location on disk from the tuples that contain them. Disk-based pointers are maintained from the tuples to the objects they contain.

Structured objects can also be large, but unlike ADT objects, they often vary in size during the lifetime of a database. For example, consider the *stars* attribute of the *films* table in Figure 23.1. As the years pass, some of the 'bit actors' in an old movie may become famous.[6] When a bit actor becomes famous, Dinky might want to advertise his or her presence in the earlier films. This involves an insertion into the *stars* attribute of an individual tuple in *films*. Because these bulk attributes can grow arbitrarily, flexible disk layout mechanisms are required.

[6] A famous example is Marilyn Monroe, who had a bit part in the Bette Davis classic *All About Eve*.

An additional complication arises with array types. Traditionally, array elements are stored sequentially on disk in a row-by-row fashion; for example

$$A_{11}, \ldots, A_{1n}, A_{21}, \ldots, A_{2n}, \ldots, A_{m1}, \ldots, A_{mn}$$

However, queries may often request subarrays that are not stored contiguously on disk (e.g., $A_{11}, A_{21}, \ldots, A_{m1}$). Such requests can result in a very high I/O cost for retrieving the subarray. To reduce the number of I/Os required, arrays are often broken into contiguous *chunks*, which are then stored in some order on disk. Although each chunk is some contiguous region of the array, chunks need not be row-by-row or column-by-column. For example, a chunk of size 4 might be $A_{11}, A_{12}, A_{21}, A_{22}$, which is a square region if we think of the array as being arranged row-by-row in two dimensions.

Indexing New Types

One important reason for users to place their data in a database is to allow for efficient access via indexes. Unfortunately, the standard RDBMS index structures support only equality conditions (B+ trees and hash indexes) and range conditions (B+ trees). An important issue for ORDBMSs is to provide efficient indexes for ADT methods and operators on structured objects.

Many specialized index structures have been proposed by researchers for particular applications such as cartography, genome research, multimedia repositories, Web search, and so on. An ORDBMS company cannot possibly implement every index that has been invented. Instead, the set of index structures in an ORDBMS should be user-extensible. Extensibility would allow an expert in cartography, for example, to not only register an ADT for points on a map (i.e., latitude–longitude pairs) but also implement an index structure that supports natural map queries (e.g., the R-tree, which matches conditions such as "Find me all theaters within 100 miles of Andorra"). (See Chapter 28 for more on R-trees and other spatial indexes.)

One way to make the set of index structures extensible is to publish an *access method interface* that lets users implement an index structure *outside* the DBMS. The index and data can be stored in a file system and the DBMS simply issues the *open*, *next*, and *close* iterator requests to the user's external index code. Such functionality makes it possible for a user to connect a DBMS to a Web search engine, for example. A main drawback of this approach is that data in an external index is not protected by the DBMS's support for concurrency and recovery. An alternative is for the ORDBMS to provide a generic 'template' index structure that is sufficiently general to encompass most index structures that users might invent. Because such a structure is implemented within the DBMS, it can support high concurrency and recovery. The *Gener-*

alized Search Tree (GiST) is such a structure. It is a template index structure based on B+ trees, which allows most of the tree index structures invented so far to be implemented with only a few lines of user-defined ADT code.

23.8.2 Query Processing

ADTs and structured types call for new functionality in processing queries in ORDBMSs. They also change a number of assumptions that affect the efficiency of queries. In this section we look at two functionality issues (user-defined aggregates and security) and two efficiency issues (method caching and pointer swizzling).

User-Defined Aggregation Functions

Since users are allowed to define new methods for their ADTs, it is not unreasonable to expect them to want to define new aggregation functions for their ADTs as well. For example, the usual SQL aggregates—`COUNT`, `SUM`, `MIN`, `MAX`, `AVG`—are not particularly appropriate for the `image` type in the Dinky schema.

Most ORDBMSs allow users to register new aggregation functions with the system. To register an aggregation function, a user must implement three methods, which we call *initialize*, *iterate*, and *terminate*. The *initialize* method initializes the internal state for the aggregation. The *iterate* method updates that state for every tuple seen, while the *terminate* method computes the aggregation result based on the final state and then cleans up. As an example, consider an aggregation function to compute the second-highest value in a field. The *initialize* call would allocate storage for the top two values, the *iterate* call would compare the current tuple's value with the top two and update the top two as necessary, and the *terminate* call would delete the storage for the top two values, returning a copy of the second-highest value.

Method Security

ADTs give users the power to add code to the DBMS; this power can be abused. A buggy or malicious ADT method can bring down the database server or even corrupt the database. The DBMS must have mechanisms to prevent buggy or malicious user code from causing problems. It may make sense to override these mechanisms for efficiency in production environments with vendor-supplied methods. However, it is important for the mechanisms to exist, if only to support debugging of ADT methods; otherwise method writers would have to write bug-free code before registering their methods with the DBMS—not a very forgiving programming environment.

One mechanism to prevent problems is to have the user methods be *interpreted* rather than *compiled*. The DBMS can check that the method is well behaved either by restricting the power of the interpreted language or by ensuring that each step taken by a method is safe before executing it. Typical interpreted languages for this purpose include Java and the procedural portions of SQL:1999.

An alternative mechanism is to allow user methods to be compiled from a general-purpose programming language, such as C++, but to run those methods in a different address space than the DBMS. In this case, the DBMS sends explicit interprocess communications (IPCs) to the user method, which sends IPCs back in return. This approach prevents bugs in the user methods (e.g., stray pointers) from corrupting the state of the DBMS or database and prevents malicious methods from reading or modifying the DBMS state or database as well. Note that the user writing the method need not know that the DBMS is running the method in a separate process: The user code can be linked with a 'wrapper' that turns method invocations and return values into IPCs.

Method Caching

User-defined ADT methods can be very expensive to execute and can account for the bulk of the time spent in processing a query. During query processing, it may make sense to cache the results of methods, in case they are invoked multiple times with the same argument. Within the scope of a single query, one can avoid calling a method twice on duplicate values in a column by either sorting the table on that column or using a hash-based scheme much like that used for aggregation (see Section 14.6). An alternative is to maintain a *cache* of method inputs and matching outputs as a table in the database. Then, to find the value of a method on particular inputs, we essentially join the input tuples with the cache table. These two approaches can also be combined.

Pointer Swizzling

In some applications, objects are retrieved into memory and accessed frequently through their oids; dereferencing must be implemented very efficiently. Some systems maintain a table of oids of objects that are (currently) in memory. When an object O is brought into memory, they check each oid contained in O and replace oids of in-memory objects by in-memory pointers to those objects. This technique, called **pointer swizzling**, makes references to in-memory objects very fast. The downside is that when an object is paged out,

> **Optimizer Extensibility:** As an example, consider the Oracle 9i optimizer, which is extensible and supports user-defined 'domain' indexes and methods. The support includes user-defined statistics and cost functions that the optimizer uses in tandem with system statistics. Suppose that there is a domain index for text on the *resume* column and a regular Oracle B-tree index on *hiringdate*. A query with a selection on both these fields can be evaluated by converting the rids from the two indexes into bitmaps, performing a bitmap `AND`, and converting the resulting bitmap to rids before accessing the table. Of course, the optimizer also considers using the two indexes individually, as well as a full table scan.

in-memory references to it must somehow be invalidated and replaced with its oid.

23.8.3 Query Optimization

New indexes and query processing techniques widen the choices available to a query optimizer. To handle the new query processing functionality, an optimizer must know about the new functionality and use it appropriately. In this section, we discuss two issues in exposing information to the optimizer (new indexes and ADT method estimation) and an issue in query planning that was ignored in relational systems (expensive selection optimization).

Registering Indexes with the Optimizer

As new index structures are added to a system—either via external interfaces or built-in template structures like GiSTs—the optimizer must be informed of their existence and their costs of access. In particular, for a given index structure, the optimizer must know (1) what `WHERE`-clause conditions are matched by that index, and (2) what the cost of fetching a tuple is for that index. Given this information, the optimizer can use any index structure in constructing a query plan. Different ORDBMSs vary in the syntax for registering new index structures. Most systems require users to state a number representing the cost of access, but an alternative is for the DBMS to measure the structure as it is used and maintain running statistics on cost.

Reduction Factor and Cost Estimation for ADT Methods

In Section 15.2.1, we discussed how to estimate the reduction factor of various selection and join conditions including =, <, and so on. For user-defined conditions such as *is herbert()*, the optimizer also needs to be able to estimate reduction factors. Estimating reduction factors for user-defined conditions is a difficult problem and actively studied. The currently popular approach is to leave it up to the user—a user who registers a method can also register an auxiliary function to estimate the method's reduction factor. If such a function is not registered, the optimizer uses an arbitrary value such as $\frac{1}{10}$.

ADT methods can be quite expensive and it is important for the optimizer to know just how much these methods cost to execute. Again, estimating method costs is open research. In current systems, users who register a method can specify the method's cost as a number, typically in units of the cost of an I/O in the system. Such estimation is hard for users to do accurately. An attractive alternative is for the ORDBMS to run the method on objects of various sizes and attempt to estimate the method's cost automatically, but this approach has not been investigated in detail and is not implemented in commercial ORDBMSs.

Expensive Selection Optimization

In relational systems, selection is expected to be a zero-time operation. For example, it requires no I/Os and few CPU cycles to test if $emp.salary < 10$. However, conditions such as *is herbert(Frames.image)* can be quite expensive because they may fetch large objects off the disk and process them in memory in complicated ways.

ORDBMS optimizers must consider carefully how to order selection conditions. For example, consider a selection query that tests tuples in the Frames table with two conditions: $Frames.frameno < 100 \wedge is\ herbert(Frame.image)$. It is probably preferable to check the *frameno* condition before testing *is herbert*. The first condition is quick and may often return false, saving the trouble of checking the second condition. In general, the best ordering among selections is a function of their costs and reduction factors. It can be shown that selections should be ordered by increasing *rank*, where rank = (reduction factor − 1)/cost. If a selection with very high rank appears in a multitable query, it may even make sense to postpone the selection until after performing joins. Note that this approach is the opposite of the heuristic for pushing selections presented in Section 15.3. The details of optimally placing expensive selections among joins are somewhat complicated, adding to the complexity of optimization in ORDBMSs.

23.9 OODBMS

In the introduction of this chapter, we defined an OODBMS as a programming language with support for persistent objects. While this definition reflects the origins of OODBMSs accurately, and to a certain extent the implementation focus of OODBMSs, the fact that OODBMSs support *collection types* (see Section 23.2.1) makes it possible to provide a query language over collections. Indeed, a standard has been developed by the Object Database Management Group and is called **Object Query Language**.

OQL is similar to SQL, with a `SELECT–FROM–WHERE`–style syntax (even `GROUP BY`, `HAVING`, and `ORDER BY` are supported) and many of the proposed SQL:1999 extensions. Notably, OQL supports structured types, including sets, bags, arrays, and lists. The OQL treatment of collections is more uniform than SQL:1999 in that it does not give special treatment to collections of rows; for example, OQL allows the aggregate operation `COUNT` to be applied to a list to compute the length of the list. OQL also supports reference types, path expressions, ADTs and inheritance, type extents, and SQL-style nested queries. There is also a standard Data Definition Language for OODBMSs (**Object Data Language**, or **ODL**) that is similar to the DDL subset of SQL but supports the additional features found in OODBMSs, such as ADT definitions.

23.9.1 The ODMG Data Model and ODL

The ODMG data model is the basis for an OODBMS, just like the relational data model is the basis for an RDBMS. A database contains a collection of **objects**, which are similar to entities in the ER model. Every object has a unique oid, and a database contains collections of objects with similar properties; such a collection is called a **class**.

The properties of a class are specified using ODL and are of three kinds: attributes, relationships, and methods. **Attributes** have an atomic type or a structured type. ODL supports the `set`, `bag`, `list`, `array`, and `struct` type constructors; these are just `setof`, `bagof`, `listof`, `ARRAY`, and `ROW` in the terminology of Section 23.2.1.

Relationships have a type that is either a reference to an object or a collection of such references. A relationship captures how an object is related to one or more objects of the same class or of a different class. A relationship in the ODMG model is really just a binary relationship in the sense of the ER model. A relationship has a corresponding **inverse relationship**; intuitively, it is the relationship 'in the other direction.' For example, if a movie is being

> **Class = Interface + Implementation:** Properly speaking, a class consists of an interface together with an implementation of the interface. An ODL interface definition is implemented in an OODBMS by translating it into declarations of the object-oriented language (e.g., C++, Smalltalk or Java) supported by the OODBMS. If we consider C++, for instance, there is a library of classes that implement the ODL constructs. There is also an **Object Manipulation Language (OML)** specific to the programming language (in our example, C++), which specifies how database objects are manipulated in the programming language. The goal is to seamlessly integrate the programming language and the database features.

shown at several theaters and each theater shows several movies, we have two relationships that are inverses of each other: *shownAt* is associated with the class of movies and is the set of theaters at which the given movie is being shown, and *nowShowing* is associated with the class of theaters and is the set of movies being shown at that theater.

Methods are functions that can be applied to objects of the class. There is no analog to methods in the ER or relational models.

The keyword `interface` is used to define a class. For each interface, we can declare an **extent**, which is the name for the current set of objects of that class. The extent is analogous to the instance of a relation and the interface is analogous to the schema. If the user does not anticipate the need to work with the set of objects of a given class—it is sufficient to manipulate individual objects—the extent declaration can be omitted.

The following ODL definitions of the Movie and Theater classes illustrate these concepts. (While these classes bear some resemblance to the Dinky database schema, the reader should not look for an exact parallel, since we have modified the example to highlight ODL features.)

```
interface Movie
    (extent Movies key movieName)
    { attribute date start;
    attribute date end;
    attribute string moviename;
    relationship Set⟨Theater⟩ shownAt inverse Theater::nowShowing;
    }
```

The collection of database objects whose class is Movie is called Movies. No two objects in Movies have the same *movieName* value, as the key declaration indicates. Each movie is shown at a set of theaters and is shown during the specified period. (It would be more realistic to associate a different period with each theater, since a movie is typically played at different theaters over different periods. While we can define a class that captures this detail, we have chosen a simpler definition for our discussion.) A theater is an object of class Theater, defined as:

```
interface Theater
    (extent Theaters key theaterName)
    { attribute string theaterName;
    attribute string address;
    attribute integer ticketPrice;
    relationship Set⟨Movie⟩ nowShowing inverse Movie::shownAt;
    float numshowing() raises(errorCountingMovies);
    }
```

Each theater shows several movies and charges the same ticket price for every movie. Observe that the *shownAt* relationship of Movie and the *nowShowing* relationship of Theater are declared to be inverses of each other. Theater also has a method *numshowing()* that can be applied to a theater object to find the number of movies being shown at that theater.

ODL also allows us to specify inheritance hierarchies, as the following class definition illustrates:

```
interface SpecialShow extends Movie
    (extent SpecialShows)
    { attribute integer maximumAttendees;
    attribute string benefitCharity;
    }
```

An object of class SpecialShow is an object of class Movie, with some additional properties, as discussed in Section 23.5.

23.9.2 OQL

The ODMG query language OQL was deliberately designed to have syntax similar to SQL to make it easy for users familiar with SQL to learn OQL. Let us begin with a query that finds pairs of movies and theaters such that the movie is shown at the theater and the theater is showing more than one movie:

```
SELECT mname: M.movieName, tname: T.theaterName
```

```
FROM     Movies M, M.shownAt T
WHERE    T.numshowing() > 1
```

The SELECT clause indicates how we can give names to fields in the result: The two result fields are called *mname* and *tname*. The part of this query that differs from SQL is the FROM clause. The variable M is bound in turn to each movie in the extent Movies. For a given movie M, we bind the variable T in turn to each theater in the collection *M.shownAt*. Thus, the use of the path expression *M.shownAt* allows us to easily express a nested query. The following query illustrates the grouping construct in OQL:

```
SELECT   T.ticketPrice,
         avgNum: AVG(SELECT P.T.numshowing() FROM partition P)
FROM     Theaters T
GROUP BY T.ticketPrice
```

For each ticket price, we create a group of theaters with that ticket price. This group of theaters is the partition for that ticket price, referred to using the OQL keyword partition. In the SELECT clause, for each ticket price, we compute the average number of movies shown at theaters in the partition for that ticketPrice. OQL supports an interesting variation of the grouping operation that is missing in SQL:

```
SELECT   low, high,
         avgNum: AVG(SELECT P.T.numshowing() FROM partition P)
FROM     Theaters T
GROUP BY low: T.ticketPrice < 5, high: T.ticketPrice >= 5
```

The GROUP BY clause now creates just two partitions called *low* and *high*. Each theater object T is placed in one of these partitions based on its ticket price. In the SELECT clause, *low* and *high* are boolean variables, exactly one of which is true in any given output tuple; partition is instantiated to the corresponding partition of theater objects. In our example, we get two result tuples. One of them has *low* equal to true and *avgNum* equal to the average number of movies shown at theaters with a low ticket price. The second tuple has *high* equal to true and *avgNum* equal to the average number of movies shown at theaters with a high ticket price.

The next query illustrates OQL support for queries that return collections other than set and multiset:

```
(SELECT  T.theaterName
FROM     Theaters T
ORDER BY T.ticketPrice DESC) [0:4]
```

The `ORDER BY` clause makes the result a list of theater names ordered by ticket price. The elements of a list can be referred to by position, starting with position 0. Therefore, the expression [0:4] extracts a list containing the names of the five theaters with the highest ticket prices.

OQL also supports `DISTINCT`, `HAVING`, explicit nesting of subqueries, view definitions, and other SQL features.

23.10 COMPARING RDBMS, OODBMS, AND ORDBMS

Now that we have covered the main object-oriented DBMS extensions, it is time to consider the two main variants of object-databases, OODBMSs and ORDBMSs, and compare them with RDBMSs. Although we presented the concepts underlying object-databases, we still need to define the terms OODBMS and ORDBMS.

An **ORDBMS** is a relational DBMS with the extensions discussed in this chapter. (Not all ORDBMS systems support all the extensions in the general form that we have discussed them, but our concern in this section is the paradigm itself rather than specific systems.) An **OODBMS** is a programming language with a type system that supports the features discussed in this chapter and allows any data object to be **persistent**; that is, to survive across different program executions. Many current systems conform to neither definition entirely but are much closer to one or the other and can be classified accordingly.

23.10.1 RDBMS versus ORDBMS

Comparing an RDBMS with an ORDBMS is straightforward. An RDBMS does not support the extensions discussed in this chapter. The resulting simplicity of the data model makes it easier to optimize queries for efficient execution, for example. A relational system is also easier to use because there are fewer features to master. On the other hand, it is less versatile than an ORDBMS.

23.10.2 OODBMS versus ORDBMS: Similarities

OODBMSs and ORDBMSs both support user-defined ADTs, structured types, object identity and reference types, and inheritance. Both support a query language for manipulating collection types. ORDBMSs support an extended form of SQL, and OODBMSs support ODL/OQL. The similarities are by no means accidental: ORDBMSs consciously try to add OODBMS features to an RDBMS, and OODBMSs in turn have developed query languages based on relational query languages. Both OODBMSs and ORDBMSs provide DBMS functionality such as concurrency control and recovery.

23.10.3 OODBMS versus ORDBMS: Differences

The fundamental difference is really a philosophy that is carried all the way through: OODBMSs try to add DBMS functionality to a programming language, whereas ORDBMSs try to add richer data types to a relational DBMS. Although the two kinds of object-databases are converging in terms of functionality, this difference in their underlying philosophy (and for most systems, their implementation approach) has important consequences in terms of the issues emphasized in the design of these DBMSs and the efficiency with which various features are supported, as the following comparison indicates:

- OODBMSs aim to achieve seamless integration with a programming language such as C++, Java, or Smalltalk. Such integration is not an important goal for an ORDBMS. SQL:1999, like SQL-92, allows us to embed SQL commands in a host language, but the interface is very evident to the SQL programer. (SQL:1999 also provides extended programming language constructs of its own, as we saw in Chapter 6.)

- An OODBMS is aimed at applications where an object-centric viewpoint is appropriate; that is, typical user sessions consist of retrieving a few objects and working on them for long periods, with related objects (e.g., objects referenced by the original objects) fetched occasionally. Objects may be extremely large and may have to be fetched in pieces; therefore, attention must be paid to buffering parts of objects. It is expected that most applications can cache the objects they require in memory, once the objects are retrieved from disk. Therefore, considerable attention is paid to making references to in-memory objects efficient. Transactions are likely to be of very long duration and holding locks until the end of a transaction may lead to poor performance; therefore, alternatives to Two-Phase Locking must be used.

  An ORDBMS is optimized for applications in which large data collections are the focus, even though objects may have rich structure and be fairly large. It is expected that applications will retrieve data from disk extensively and optimizing disk access is still the main concern for efficient execution. Transactions are assumed to be relatively short and traditional RDBMS techniques are typically used for concurrency control and recovery.

- The query facilities of OQL are not supported efficiently in most OODBMSs, whereas the query facilities are the centerpiece of an ORDBMS. To some extent, this situation is the result of different concentrations of effort in the development of these systems. To a significant extent, it is also a consequence of the systems' being optimized for very different kinds of applications.

23.11 REVIEW QUESTIONS

Answers to the review questions can be found in the listed sections.

- Consider the extended Dinky example from Section 23.1. Explain how it motivates the need for each of the following object-database features: *user-defined structured types*, *abstract data types (ADTs)*, *inheritance*, and *object identity*. **(Section 23.1)**
- What are *structured data types*? What are *collection types*, in particular? Discuss the extent to which these concepts are supported in SQL:1999. What important type constructors are missing? What are the limitations on the ROW and ARRAY constructors? **(Section 23.2)**
- What kinds of operations should be provided for each of the structured data types? To what extent is such support included in SQL:1999? **(Section 23.3)**
- What is an *abstract data type*? How are methods of an abstract data type defined in an external programming language? **(Section 23.4)**
- Explain *inheritance* and how new types (called *subtypes*) extend existing types (called *supertypes*). What are *method overloading* and *late binding*? What is a *collection hierarchy*? Contrast this with inheritance in programming languages. **(Section 23.5)**
- How is an *object identifier (oid)* different from a record id in a relational DBMS? How is it different from a URL? What is a *reference type*? Define *deep* and *shallow* equality and illustrate them through an example. **(Section 23.6)**
- The multitude of data types in an ORDBMS allows us to design a more natural and efficient database schema but introduces some new design choices. Discuss ORDBMS database design issues and illustrate your discussion using an example application. **(Section 23.7)**
- Implementing an ORDBMS brings new challenges. The system must store large ADTs and structured types that might be very large. Efficient and extensible index mechanisms must be provided. Examples of new functionality include *user-defined aggregation functions* (we can define new aggregation functions for our ADTs) and *method security* (the system has to prevent user-defined methods from compromising the security of the DBMS). Examples of new techniques to increase performance include

method caching and *pointer swizzling.* The optimizer must know about the new functionality and use it appropriately. Illustrate each of these challenges through an example. **(Section 23.8)**

- Compare OODBMSs with ORDBMSs. In particular, compare OQL and SQL:1999 and discuss the underlying data model. **(Sections 23.9 and 23.10)**

EXERCISES

Exercise 23.1 Briefly answer the following questions:

1. What are the new kinds of data types supported in object-database systems? Give an example of each and discuss how the example situation would be handled if only an RDBMS were available.
2. What must a user do to define a new ADT?
3. Allowing users to define methods can lead to efficiency gains. Give an example.
4. What is late binding of methods? Give an example of inheritance that illustrates the need for dynamic binding.
5. What are collection hierarchies? Give an example that illustrates how collection hierarchies facilitate querying.
6. Discuss how a DBMS exploits encapsulation in implementing support for ADTs.
7. Give an example illustrating the nesting and unnesting operations.
8. Describe two objects that are deep equal but not shallow equal or explain why this is not possible.
9. Describe two objects that are shallow equal but not deep equal or explain why this is not possible.
10. Compare RDBMSs with ORDBMSs. Describe an application scenario for which you would choose an RDBMS and explain why. Similarly, describe an application scenario for which you would choose an ORDBMS and explain why.

Exercise 23.2 Consider the Dinky schema shown in Figure 23.1 and all related methods defined in the chapter. Write the following queries in SQL:1999:

1. How many films were shown at theater $tno = 5$ between January 1 and February 1 of 2002?
2. What is the lowest budget for a film with at least two stars?
3. Consider theaters at which a film directed by Steven Spielberg started showing on January 1, 2002. For each such theater, print the names of all countries within a 100-mile radius. (You can use the *overlap* and *radius* methods illustrated in Figure 23.2.)

Exercise 23.3 In a company database, you need to store information about employees, departments, and children of employees. For each employee, identified by *ssn*, you must record *years* (the number of years that the employee has worked for the company), *phone*, and *photo* information. There are two subclasses of employees: contract and regular. Salary is computed by invoking a method that takes *years* as a parameter; this method has a different implementation for each subclass. Further, for each regular employee, you must record the name and age of every child. The most common queries involving children are similar to "Find the average age of Bob's children" and "Print the names of all of Bob's children."

A photo is a large image object and can be stored in one of several image formats (e.g., gif, jpeg). You want to define a *display* method for image objects; display must be defined differently for each image format. For each department, identified by *dno*, you must record *dname*, *budget*, and *workers* information. *Workers* is the set of employees who work in a given department. Typical queries involving workers include, "Find the average salary of all workers (across all departments)."

1. Using extended SQL, design an ORDBMS schema for the company database. Show all type definitions, including method definitions.
2. If you have to store this information in an RDBMS, what is the best possible design?
3. Compare the ORDBMS and RDBMS designs.
4. If you are told that a common request is to display the images of all employees in a given department, how would you use this information for physical database design?
5. If you are told that an employee's image must be displayed whenever any information about the employee is retrieved, would this affect your schema design?
6. If you are told that a common query is to find all employees who look similar to a given image and given code that lets you create an index over all images to support retrieval of similar images, what would you do to utilize this code in an ORDBMS?

Exercise 23.4 ORDBMSs need to support efficient access over collection hierarchies. Consider the collection hierarchy of Theaters and Theater_cafes presented in the Dinky example. In your role as a DBMS implementor (not a DBA), you must evaluate three storage alternatives for these tuples:

- All tuples for all kinds of theaters are stored together on disk in an arbitrary order.
- All tuples for all kinds of theaters are stored together on disk, with the tuples that are from Theater_cafes stored directly after the last of the non-cafe tuples.
- Tuples from Theater_cafes are stored separately from the rest of the (non-cafe) theater tuples.

1. For each storage option, describe a mechanism for distinguishing plain theater tuples from Theater_cafe tuples.
2. For each storage option, describe how to handle the insertion of a new non-cafe tuple.
3. Which storage option is most efficient for queries over all theaters? Over just Theater_cafes? In terms of the number of I/Os, how much more efficient is the best technique for each type of query compared to the other two techniques?

Exercise 23.5 Different ORDBMSs use different techniques for building indexes to evaluate queries over collection hierarchies. For our Dinky example, to index theaters by name there are two common options:

- Build one B+ tree index over Theaters.*name* and another B+ tree index over Theater_cafes.*name*.
- Build one B+ tree index over the union of Theaters.*name* and Theater_cafes.*name*.

1. Describe how to efficiently evaluate the following query using each indexing option (this query is over all kinds of theater tuples):

   `SELECT * FROM Theaters T WHERE T.name = 'Majestic'`

   Give an estimate of the number of I/Os required in the two different scenarios, assuming there are 1 million standard theaters and 1000 theater-cafes. Which option is more efficient?
2. Perform the same analysis over the following query:

   `SELECT * FROM Theater_cafes T WHERE T.name = 'Majestic'`
3. For clustered indexes, does the choice of indexing technique interact with the choice of storage options? For unclustered indexes?

Exercise 23.6 Consider the following query:

```
SELECT thumbnail(I.image)
FROM   Images I
```

Given that the *I.image* column may contain duplicate values, describe how to use hashing to avoid computing the *thumbnail* function more than once per distinct value in processing this query.

Exercise 23.7 You are given a two-dimensional, $n \times n$ array of objects. Assume that you can fit 100 objects on a disk page. Describe a way to lay out (chunk) the array onto pages so that retrievals of square $m \times m$ subregions of the array are efficient. (Different queries request subregions of different sizes, i.e., different m values, and your arrangement of the array onto pages should provide good performance, on average, for all such queries.)

Exercise 23.8 An ORDBMS optimizer is given a single-table query with n expensive selection conditions, $\sigma_n(...(\sigma_1(T)))$. For each condition σ_i, the optimizer can estimate the cost c_i of evaluating the condition on a tuple and the reduction factor of the condition r_i. Assume that there are t tuples in T.

1. How many tuples appear in the output of this query?
2. Assuming that the query is evaluated as shown (without reordering selections), what is the total cost of the query? Be sure to include the cost of scanning the table and applying the selections.
3. In Section 23.8.2, it was asserted that the optimizer should reorder selections so that they are applied to the table in order of increasing rank, where $\text{rank}_i = (r_i - 1)/c_i$. Prove that this assertion is optimal. That is, show that no other ordering could result in a query of lower cost. (Hint: It may be easiest to consider the special case where $n = 2$ first and generalize from there.)

Exercise 23.9 ORDBMSs support references as a data type. It is often claimed that using references instead of key–foreign key relationships will give much higher performance for joins. This question asks you to explore this issue.

- Consider the following SQL:1999 DDL which only uses straight relational constructs:

  ```
  CREATE TABLE R(rkey integer, rdata text);
  CREATE TABLE S(skey integer, rfkey integer);
  ```

Assume that we have the following straightforward join query:

```
SELECT S.skey, R.rdata
FROM   S, R
WHERE  S.rfkey = R.rkey
```

- Now consider the following SQL:1999 ORDBMS schema:

```
CREATE TYPE r_t AS ROW(rkey integer, rdata text);
CREATE TABLE R OF r_t REF is SYSTEM GENERATED;
CREATE TABLE S (skey integer, r REF(r_t) SCOPE R);
```

Assume we have the following query:

```
SELECT S.skey, S.r.rkey
FROM   S
```

What algorithm would you suggest to evaluate the pointer join in the ORDBMS schema? How do you think it will perform versus a relational join on the previous schema?

Exercise 23.10 Many object-relational systems support set-valued attributes using some variant of the setof constructor. For example, assuming we have a type person_t, we could have created the table Films in the Dinky Schema in Figure 23.1 as follows:

```
CREATE TABLE Films(filmno integer, title text, stars setof Person);
```

1. Describe two ways of implementing set-valued attributes. One way requires variable-length records, even if the set elements are all fixed-length.
2. Discuss the impact of the two strategies on optimizing queries with set-valued attributes.
3. Suppose you would like to create an index on the column stars in order to look up films by the name of the star that has starred in the film. For both implementation strategies, discuss alternative index structures that could help speed up this query.
4. What types of statistics should the query optimizer maintain for set-valued attributes? How do we obtain these statistics?

BIBLIOGRAPHIC NOTES

A number of the object-oriented features described here are based in part on fairly old ideas in the programming languages community. [42] provides a good overview of these ideas in a database context. Stonebraker's book [719] describes the vision of ORDBMSs embodied by his company's early product, Illustra (now a product of Informix). Current commercial DBMSs with object-relational support include Informix Universal Server, IBM DB/2 CS V2, and UniSQL. An new version of Oracle is scheduled to include ORDBMS features as well.

Many of the ideas in current object-relational systems came out of a few prototypes built in the 1980s, especially POSTGRES [723], Starburst [351], and O2 [218].

The idea of an object-oriented database was first articulated in [197], which described the GemStone prototype system. Other prototypes include DASDBS [657], EXODUS [130], IRIS [273], ObjectStore [463], ODE, [18] ORION [432], SHORE [129], and THOR [482]. O2 is actually an early example of a system that was beginning to merge the themes of ORDBMSs and OODBMSs—it could fit in this list as well. [41] lists a collection of features that are generally considered to belong in an OODBMS. Current commercially available OODBMSs include GemStone, Itasca, O2, Objectivity, ObjectStore, Ontos, Poet, and Versant. [431] compares OODBMSs and RDBMSs.

Database support for ADTs was first explored in the INGRES and POSTGRES projects at U.C. Berkeley. The basic ideas are described in [716], including mechanisms for query processing and optimization with ADTs as well as extensible indexing. Support for ADTs was also investigated in the Darmstadt database system, [480]. Using the POSTGRES index extensibility correctly required intimate knowledge of DBMS-internal transaction mechanisms. Generalized search trees were proposed to solve this problem; they are described in [376], with concurrency and ARIES-based recovery details presented in [447]. [672] proposes that users must be allowed to define operators over ADT objects and properties of these operators that can be utilized for query optimization, rather than just a collection of methods.

Array chunking is described in [653]. Techniques for method caching and optimizing queries with expensive methods are presented in [373, 165]. Client-side data caching in a client-server OODBMS is studied in [283]. Clustering of objects on disk is studied in [741]. Work on nested relations was an early precursor of recent research on complex objects in OODBMSs and ORDBMSs. One of the first nested relation proposals is [504]. MVDs play an important role in reasoning about reduncancy in nested relations; see, for example, [579]. Storage structures for nested relations were studied in [215].

Formal models and query languages for object-oriented databases have been widely studied; papers include [4, 56, 75, 125, 391, 392, 428, 578, 724]. [427] proposes SQL extensions for querying object-oriented databases. An early and elegant extension of SQL with path expressions and inheritance was developed in GEM [791]. There has been much interest in combining deductive and object-oriented features. Papers in this area include [44, 288, 495, 556, 706, 793]. See [3] for a thorough textbook discussion of formal aspects of object-orientation and query languages.

[433, 435, 721, 796] include papers on DBMSs that would now be termed object-relational and/or object-oriented. [794] contains a detailed overview of schema and database evolution in object-oriented database systems. A thorough presentation of SQL:1999 can be found in [525], and advanced features, including the object extensions, are covered in [523]. A short survey of new SQL:1999 features can be found in [237]. The incorporation of several SQL:1999 features into IBM DB2 is described in [128]. OQL is described in [141]. It is based to a large extent on the O2 query language, which is described, together with other aspects of O2, in the collection of papers [55].

24

DEDUCTIVE DATABASES

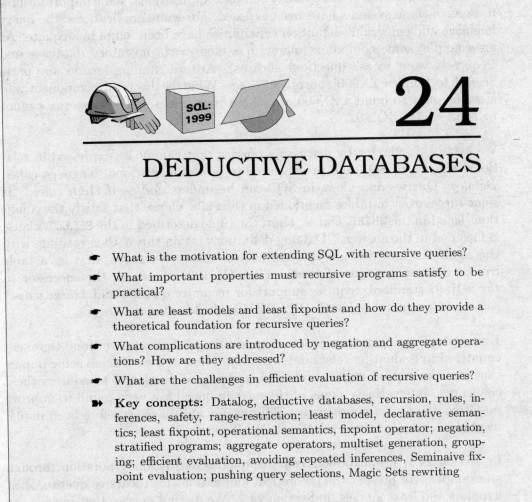

- What is the motivation for extending SQL with recursive queries?
- What important properties must recursive programs satisfy to be practical?
- What are least models and least fixpoints and how do they provide a theoretical foundation for recursive queries?
- What complications are introduced by negation and aggregate operations? How are they addressed?
- What are the challenges in efficient evaluation of recursive queries?
- **Key concepts:** Datalog, deductive databases, recursion, rules, inferences, safety, range-restriction; least model, declarative semantics; least fixpoint, operational semantics, fixpoint operator; negation, stratified programs; aggregate operators, multiset generation, grouping; efficient evaluation, avoiding repeated inferences, Seminaive fixpoint evaluation; pushing query selections, Magic Sets rewriting

For 'Is' and 'Is-Not' though with Rule and Line,
And 'Up-and-Down' by Logic I define,
Of all that one should care to fathom, I
Was never deep in anything but—Wine.

—*Rubaiyat of Omar Khayyam*, Translated by Edward Fitzgerald

Relational database management systems have been enormously successful for administrative data processing. In recent years, however, as people have tried to use database systems in increasingly complex applications, some important limitations of these systems have been exposed. For some applications, the query language and constraint definition capabilities have been found inadequate. As an example, some companies maintain a huge parts inventory database and frequently want to ask questions such as, "Are we running low on any parts needed to build a ZX600 sports car?" or "What is the total component and assembly cost to build a ZX600 at today's part prices?" These queries cannot be expressed in SQL-92.

We begin this chapter by discussing queries that cannot be expressed in relational algebra or SQL and present a more powerful relational language called *Datalog*. Queries and views in SQL can be understood as **if–then** rules: "**If** some tuples exist in tables mentioned in the `FROM` clause that satisfy the conditions listed in the `WHERE` clause, **then** the tuple described in the `SELECT` clause is included in the answer." Datalog definitions retain this if–then reading, with the significant new feature that definitions can be *recursive*, that is, a table can be defined in terms of itself. The SQL:1999 standard, the successor to the SQL-92 standard, requires support for recursive queries, and a large subset some systems, notably IBM's DB2 DBMS, already support them.

Evaluating Datalog queries poses some additional challenges, beyond those encountered in evaluating relational algebra queries, and we discuss some important implementation and optimization techniques developed to address these challenges. Interestingly, some of these techniques have been found to improve performance of even nonrecursive SQL queries and have therefore been implemented in several current relational DBMS products.

In Section 24.1, we introduce recursive queries and Datalog notation through an example. We present the theoretical foundations for recursive queries, least fixpoints and least models, in Section 24.2. We discuss queries that involve the use of negation or set-difference in Section 24.3. Finally, we consider techniques for evaluating recursive queries efficiently in Section 24.5.

24.1 INTRODUCTION TO RECURSIVE QUERIES

We begin with a simple example that illustrates the limits of SQL-92 queries and the power of recursive definitions. Let Assembly be a relation with three fields *part*, *subpart*, and *qty*. An example instance of Assembly is shown in Figure 24.1. Each tuple in Assembly indicates how many copies of a particular subpart are contained in a given part. The first tuple indicates, for example, that a trike contains three wheels. The Assembly relation can be visualized as a tree, as shown in Figure 24.2. A tuple is shown as an edge going from the part to the subpart, with the *qty* value as the edge label.

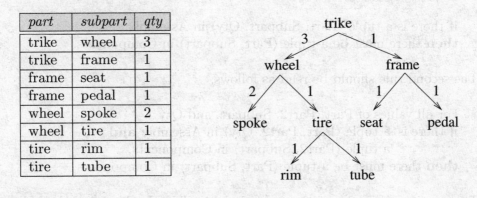

part	*subpart*	*qty*
trike	wheel	3
trike	frame	1
frame	seat	1
frame	pedal	1
wheel	spoke	2
wheel	tire	1
tire	rim	1
tire	tube	1

Figure 24.1 An Instance of Assembly

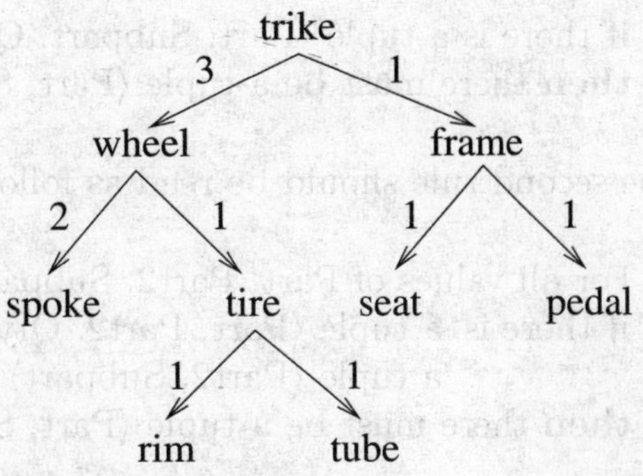

Figure 24.2 Assembly Instance Seen as a Tree

A natural question to ask is, "What are the components of a trike?" Rather surprisingly, this query is impossible to write in SQL-92. Of course, if we look at a given instance of the Assembly relation, we can write a 'query' that takes the union of the parts that are used in a trike. But such a query is not interesting—we want a query that identifies all components of a trike for *any* instance of Assembly, and such a query cannot be written in relational algebra or in SQL-92. Intuitively, the problem is that we are forced to join the Assembly relation with itself to recognize that *trike* contains *spoke* and *tire*, that is, to go one level down the Assembly tree. For each additional level, we need an additional join; two joins are needed to recognize that *trike* contains *rim*, which is a subpart of *tire*. Thus, the number of joins needed to identify all subparts of *trike* depends on the height of the Assembly tree, that is, on the given instance of the Assembly relation. No relational algebra query works for all instances; given any query, we can construct an instance whose height is greater than the number of joins in the query.

24.1.1 Datalog

We now define a relation called Components that identifies the components of every part. Consider the following **program**, or collection of **rules**:

```
Components(Part, Subpart) :-  Assembly(Part, Subpart, Qty).
Components(Part, Subpart) :-  Assembly(Part, Part2, Qty),
                              Components(Part2, Subpart).
```

These are rules in **Datalog**, a relational query language inspired by Prolog, the well-known logic programming language; indeed, the notation follows Prolog. The first rule should be read as follows:

For all values of Part, Subpart, and Qty,

if there is a tuple ⟨Part, Subpart, Qty⟩ in Assembly,
then there must be a tuple ⟨Part, Subpart⟩ in Components.

The second rule should be read as follows:

For all values of Part, Part2, Subpart, and Qty,
if there is a tuple ⟨Part, Part2, Qty⟩ in Assembly **and**
a tuple ⟨Part2, Subpart⟩ in Components,
then there must be a tuple ⟨Part, Subpart⟩ in Components.

The part to the right of the :- symbol is called the **body** of the rule, and the part to the left is called the **head** of the rule. The symbol :- denotes logical implication; if the tuples mentioned in the body exist in the database, it is implied that the tuple mentioned in the head of the rule must also be in the database. (Note that the body could be empty; in this case, the tuple mentioned in the head of the rule must be included in the database.) Therefore, if we are given a set of Assembly and Components tuples, each rule can be used to **infer**, or **deduce**, some new tuples that belong in Components. This is why database systems that support Datalog rules are often called **deductive database systems**.

By assigning constants to the variables that appear in a rule, we can infer a specific Components tuple. For example, by setting Part=*trike*, Subpart=*wheel*, and Qty=*3*, we can infer that ⟨*trike*, *wheel*⟩ is in Components. Each rule is really a *template* for making **inferences**: An inference is the use of a rule to generate a new tuple (for the relation in the head of the rule) by substituting constants for variables in such a way that every tuple in the rule body (after the substitution) is in the corresponding relation instance.

By considering each tuple in Assembly in turn, the first rule allows us to infer that the set of tuples obtained by taking the projection of Assembly onto its first two fields is in Components.

The second rule then allows us to combine previously discovered Components tuples with Assembly tuples to infer new Components tuples. We can apply the second rule by considering the cross-product of Assembly and (the current instance of) Components and assigning values to the variables in the rule for each row of the cross-product, one row at a time. Observe how the repeated use of the variable Part2 prevents certain rows of the cross-product from contributing any new tuples; in effect, it specifies an equality join condition on Assembly and Components. The tuples obtained by one application of this rule are shown in Figure 24.3. (In addition, Components contains the tuples obtained by applying the first rule; these are not shown.)

part	*subpart*
trike	spoke
trike	tire
trike	seat
trike	pedal
wheel	rim
wheel	tube

Figure 24.3 Components Tuples Obtained by Applying the Second Rule Once

part	*subpart*
trike	spoke
trike	tire
trike	seat
trike	pedal
wheel	rim
wheel	tube
trike	rim
trike	tube

Figure 24.4 Components Tuples Obtained by Applying the Second Rule Twice

The tuples obtained by a second application of this rule are shown in Figure 24.4. Note that each tuple shown in Figure 24.3 is reinferred. Only the last two tuples are new.

Applying the second rule a third time does not generate additional tuples. The set of Components tuples shown in Figure 24.4 includes all the tuples that can be inferred using the two Datalog rules defining Components and the given instance of Assembly. The components of a trike can now be obtained by selecting all Components tuples with the value *trike* in the first field.

Each application of a Datalog rule can be understood in terms of relational algebra. The first rule in our example program simply applies projection to the Assembly relation and adds the resulting tuples to the Components relation, which is initially empty. The second rule joins Assembly with Components and then does a projection. The result of each rule application is combined with the existing set of Components tuples using union.

The only Datalog operation that goes beyond relational algebra is the *repeated* application of the rules defining Components until no new tuples are generated. This repeated application of a set of rules is called the *fixpoint* operation, and we develop this idea further in the next section.

We conclude this section by rewriting the Datalog definition of Components using SQL:1999 syntax:

```
WITH RECURSIVE Components(Part, Subpart) AS
    (SELECT A1.Part, A1.Subpart FROM Assembly A1)
    UNION
    (SELECT A2.Part, C1.Subpart
    FROM    Assembly A2, Components C1
```

```
        WHERE  A2.Subpart = C1.Part)

SELECT * FROM Components C2
```

The WITH clause introduces a relation that is part of a query definition; this relation is similar to a view, but the scope of a relation introduced using WITH is local to the query definition. The RECURSIVE keyword signals that the table (in our example, Components) is recursively defined. The structure of the definition closely parallels the Datalog rules. Incidentally, if we wanted to find the components of a particular part, for example, *trike*, we can simply replace the last line with the following:

```
SELECT * FROM Components C2
WHERE  C2.Part = 'trike'
```

24.2 THEORETICAL FOUNDATIONS

We classify the relations in a Datalog program as either output relations or input relations. **Output relations** are defined by rules (e.g., Components), and **input relations** have a set of tuples explicitly listed (e.g., Assembly). Given instances of the input relations, we must compute instances for the output relations. The meaning of a Datalog program is usually defined in two different ways, both of which essentially describe the relation instances for the output relations. Technically, a **query** is a selection over one of the output relations (e.g., all Components tuples C with $C.part = trike$). However, the meaning of a query is clear once we understand how relation instances are associated with the output relations in a Datalog program.

The first approach to defining the semantics of a Datalog program, called the *least model semantics*, gives users a way to understand the program without thinking about how the program is to be executed. That is, the semantics is *declarative*, like the semantics of relational calculus, and not *operational* like relational algebra semantics. This is important because recursive rules make it difficult to understand a program in terms of an evaluation strategy.

The second approach, called the *least fixpoint semantics*, gives a conceptual evaluation strategy to compute the desired relation instances. This serves as the basis for recursive query evaluation in a DBMS. More efficient evaluation strategies are used in an actual implementation, but their correctness is shown by demonstrating their equivalence to the least fixpoint approach. The fixpoint semantics is thus operational and plays a role analogous to that of relational algebra semantics for nonrecursive queries.

24.2.1 Least Model Semantics

We want users to be able to understand a Datalog program by understanding each rule independent of other rules, with the meaning: *If the body is true, the head is also true.* This intuitive reading of a rule suggests that, given certain relation instances for the relation names that appear in the body of a rule, the relation instance for the relation mentioned in the head of the rule must contain a certain set of tuples. If a relation name R appears in the heads of several rules, the relation instance for R must satisfy the intuitive reading of all these rules. However, we do not want tuples to be included in the instance for R unless they are necessary to satisfy one of the rules defining R. That is, we want to compute only tuples for R that are supported by some rule for R.

To make these ideas precise, we need to introduce the concepts of models and least models. A **model** is a collection of relation instances, one instance for each relation in the program, that satisfies the following condition. For every rule in the program, whenever we replace each variable in the rule by a corresponding constant, the following holds:

> *If* every tuple in the body (obtained by our replacement of variables with constants) is in the corresponding relation instance,
>
> *Then* the tuple generated for the head (by the assignment of constants to variables that appear in the head) is also in the corresponding relation instance.

Observe that the instances for the input relations are given, and the definition of a model essentially restricts the instances for the output relations.

Consider the rule

```
Components(Part, Subpart) :-  Assembly(Part, Part2, Qty),
                              Components(Part2, Subpart).
```

Suppose we replace the variable Part by the constant *wheel*, Part2 by *tire*, Qty by 1, and Subpart by *rim*:

```
Components(wheel, rim) :- Assembly(wheel, tire, 1),
                          Components(tire, rim).
```

Let A be an instance of Assembly and C be an instance of Components. If A contains the tuple $\langle$*wheel*, *tire*, 1$\rangle$ and C contains the tuple $\langle$*tire*, *rim*$\rangle$, then C must also contain the tuple $\langle$*wheel*, *rim*$\rangle$ for the pair of instances A and C to be a model. Of course, the instances A and C must satisfy the inclusion requirement just illustrated for *every* assignment of constants to the variables in the rule: If the tuples in the rule body are in A and C, the tuple in the head must be in C.

As an example, the instances of Assembly shown in Figure 24.1 and Components shown in Figure 24.4 together form a model for the Components program.

Given the instance of Assembly shown in Figure 24.1, there is no justification for including the tuple $\langle spoke,\ pedal\rangle$ to the Components instance. Indeed, if we add this tuple to the components instance in Figure 24.4, we no longer have a model for our program, as the following instance of the recursive rule demonstrates, since $\langle wheel,\ pedal\rangle$ is not in the Components instance:

```
Components(wheel, pedal) :-  Assembly(wheel, spoke, 2),
                             Components(spoke, pedal).
```

However, by also adding the tuple $\langle wheel,\ pedal\rangle$ to the Components instance, we obtain another model of the Components program. Intuitively, this is unsatisfactory since there is no justification for adding the tuple $\langle spoke,\ pedal\rangle$ in the first place, given the tuples in the Assembly instance and the rules in the program.

We address this problem by using the concept of a least model. A **least model** of a program is a model M such that for every other model M2 of the same program, for each relation R in the program, the instance for R in M is contained in the instance of R in M2. The model formed by the instances of Assembly and Components shown in Figures 24.1 and 24.4 is the least model for the Components program with the given Assembly instance.

24.2.2 The Fixpoint Operator

A **fixpoint** of a function f is a value v such that the function applied to the value returns the same value, that is, $f(v) = v$. Consider a function applied to a set of values that also returns a set of values. For example, we can define *double* to be a function that multiplies every element of the input set by two and *double+* to be *double* ∪ *identity*. Thus, *double*({1,2,5}) = {2,4,10}, and *double+*({1,2,5}) = {1,2,4,5,10}. The set of all even integers—which happens to be an infinite set—is a fixpoint of the function *double+*. Another fixpoint of the function *double+* is the set of all integers. The first fixpoint (the set of all even integers) is *smaller* than the second fixpoint (the set of all integers) because it is contained in the latter.

The **least fixpoint** of a function is the fixpoint that is smaller than every other fixpoint of that function. In general, it is not guaranteed that a function has a least fixpoint. For example, there may be two fixpoints, neither of which is smaller than the other. (Does *double* have a least fixpoint? What is it?)

Now let us turn to functions over sets of tuples, in particular, functions defined using relational algebra expressions. The Components relation can be defined by an equation of the form

$$Components \;=\; \pi_{1,5}(Assembly \bowtie_{2=1} Components) \;\cup\; \pi_{1,2}(Assembly)$$

This equation has the form

$$Components \;=\; f(Components, Assembly)$$

where the function f is defined using a relational algebra expression. For a given instance of the input relation Assembly, this can be simplified to

$$Components \;=\; f(Components)$$

The least fixpoint of f is an instance of Components that satisfies this equation. Clearly the projection of the first two fields of the tuples in the given instance of the input relation Assembly must be included in the (instance that is the) least fixpoint of Components. In addition, any tuple obtained by joining Components with Assembly and projecting the appropriate fields must also be in Components.

A little thought shows that the instance of Components that is the least fixpoint of f can be computed using repeated applications of the Datalog rules shown in the previous section. Indeed, applying the two Datalog rules is identical to evaluating the relational expression used in defining Components. If an application generates Components tuples that are not in the current instance of the Components relation, the current instance cannot be the fixpoint. Therefore, we add the new tuples to Components and evaluate the relational expression (equivalently, the two Datalog rules) again. This process is repeated until every tuple generated is already in the current instance of Components. When applying the rules to the current set of tuples does not produce any new tuples, we have reached a fixpoint. If Components is initialized to the empty set of tuples, intuitively we infer only tuples that are necessary by the definition of a fixpoint, and the fixpoint computed is the least fixpoint.

24.2.3 Safe Datalog Programs

Consider the following program:

```
Complex_Parts(Part) :- Assembly(Part, Subpart, Qty), Qty > 2.
```

According to this rule, a complex part is defined to be any part that has more than two copies of any one subpart. For each part mentioned in the Assembly relation, we can easily check whether it is a complex part. In contrast, consider the following program:

```
Price_Parts(Part,Price) :-
            Assembly(Part, Subpart, Qty), Qty > 2.
```

This variation seeks to associate a price with each complex part. However, the variable *Price* does not appear in the body of the rule. This means that an infinite number of tuples must be included in any model of this program. To see this, suppose we replace the variable Part by the constant *trike*, SubPart by *wheel*, and Qty by 3. This gives us a version of the rule with the only remaining variable being *Price*:

```
Price_Parts(trike,Price) :- Assembly(trike, wheel, 3), 3 > 2.
```

Now, any assignment of a constant to *Price* gives us a tuple to be included in the output relation Price_Parts. For example, replacing *Price* by 100 gives us the tuple Price_Parts(trike,100). If the least model of a program is not finite, for even one instance of its input relations, then we say the program is **unsafe**.

Database systems disallow unsafe programs by requiring that every variable in the head of a rule also appear in the body. Such programs are said to be **range-restricted**, and every range-restricted Datalog program has a finite least model if the input relation instances are finite. In the rest of this chapter, we assume that programs are range-restricted.

24.2.4 Least Model = Least Fixpoint

Does a Datalog program always have a least model? Or is it possible that there are two models, neither of which is contained in the other? Similarly, does every Datalog program have a least fixpoint? What is the relationship between the least model and the least fixpoint of a Datalog program?

As we noted earlier, not every function has a least fixpoint. Fortunately, every function defined in terms of relational algebra expressions that do not contain set-difference is guaranteed to have a least fixpoint, and the least fixpoint can be computed by repeatedly evaluating the function. This tells us that every Datalog program has a least fixpoint and that it can be computed by repeatedly applying the rules of the program on the given instances of the input relations.

Further, every Datalog program is guaranteed to have a least model and the least model is equal to the least fixpoint of the program. These results (whose proofs we do not discuss) provide the basis for Datalog query processing. Users can understand a program in terms of 'If the body is true, the head is also true,' thanks to the least model semantics. The DBMS can compute the answer by repeatedly applying the program rules, thanks to the least fixpoint semantics and the fact that the least model and the least fixpoint are identical.

24.3 RECURSIVE QUERIES WITH NEGATION

Unfortunately, once set-difference is allowed in the body of a rule, there may be no least model or least fixpoint for a program. Consider the following rules:

```
Big(Part) :-    Assembly(Part, Subpart, Qty), Qty > 2,
                NOT Small(Part).
Small(Part) :-  Assembly(Part, Subpart, Qty), NOT Big(Part).
```

These two rules can be thought of as an attempt to divide parts (those that are mentioned in the first column of the Assembly table) into two classes, Big and Small. The first rule defines Big to be the set of parts that use at least three copies of some subpart and are not classified as small parts. The second rule defines Small as the set of parts not classified as big parts.

If we apply these rules to the instance of Assembly shown in Figure 24.1, *trike* is the only part that uses at least three copies of some subpart. Should the tuple $\langle trike \rangle$ be in Big or Small? If we apply the first rule and then the second rule, this tuple is in Big. To apply the first rule, we consider the tuples in Assembly, choose those with Qty > 2 (which is just $\langle trike \rangle$), discard those in the current instance of Small (both Big and Small are initially empty), and add the tuples that are left to Big. Therefore, an application of the first rule adds $\langle trike \rangle$ to Big. Proceeding similarly, we can see that if the second rule is applied before the first, $\langle trike \rangle$ is added to Small instead of Big.

This program has two fixpoints, neither of which is smaller than the other, as shown in Figure 24.5. The first fixpoint has a Big tuple that does not appear in the second fixpoint; therefore, it is not smaller than the second fixpoint. The second fixpoint has a Small tuple that does not appear in the first fixpoint; therefore, it is not smaller than the first fixpoint. The order in which we apply the rules determines which fixpoint is computed; this situation is very unsatisfactory. We want users to be able to understand their queries without thinking about exactly how the evaluation proceeds.

The root of the problem is the use of `NOT`. When we apply the first rule, some inferences are disallowed because of the presence of tuples in Small. Parts

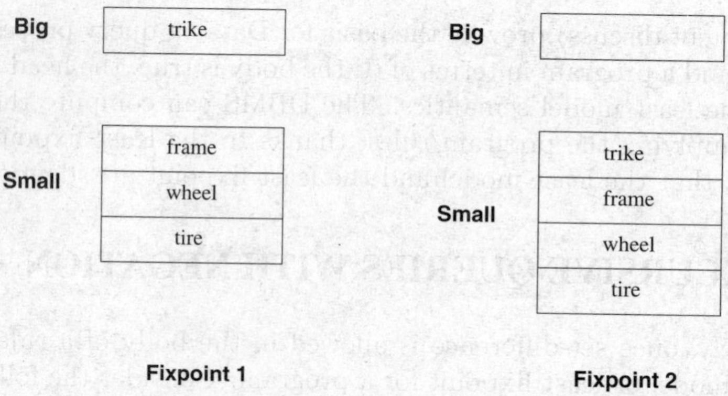

Figure 24.5 Two Fixpoints for the Big/Small Program

that satisfy the other conditions in the body of the rule are candidates for addition to Big; we remove the parts in Small from this set of candidates. Thus, some inferences that are possible if Small is empty (as it is before the second rule is applied) are disallowed if Small contains tuples (generated by applying the second rule before the first rule). Here is the difficulty: If NOT is used, the addition of tuples to a relation can *disallow* the inference of other tuples. Without NOT, this situation can never arise; the addition of tuples to a relation can *never* disallow the inference of other tuples.

Range-Restriction and Negation

If rules are allowed to contain NOT in the body, the definition of range-restriction must be extended ensure that all range-restricted programs are safe. If a relation appears in the body of a rule preceded by NOT, we call this a **negated occurrence**. Relation occurrences in the body that are not negated are called **positive occurrences**. A program is **range-restricted** if every variable in the head of the rule appears in some positive relation occurrence in the body.

24.3.1 Stratification

A widely used solution to the problem caused by negation, or the use of NOT, is to impose certain syntactic restrictions on programs. These restrictions can be easily checked and programs that satisfy them have a natural meaning.

We say that a table T **depends on** a table S if some rule with T in the head contains S, or (recursively) contains a predicate that depends on S, in the body. A recursively defined predicate always depends on itself. For example, Big depends on Small (and on itself). Indeed, the tables Big and Small are

mutually recursive, that is, the definition of Big depends on Small and vice versa. We say that a table T **depends negatively on** a table S if some rule with T in the head contains `NOT` S, or (recursively) contains a predicate that depends negatively on S, in the body.

Suppose we classify the tables in a program into **strata** or **layers** as follows. The tables that do not depend on any other tables are in stratum 0. In our Big/Small example, Assembly is the only table in stratum 0. Next, we identify tables in stratum 1; these are tables that depend only on tables in stratum 0 or stratum 1 and depend negatively only on tables in stratum 0. Higher strata are similarly defined: The tables in stratum i are those that do not belong to lower strata, depend only on tables in stratum i or lower strata, and depend negatively only on tables in lower strata. A **stratified program** is one whose tables can be classified into strata according to the above algorithm.

The Big/Small program is not stratified. Since Big and Small depend on each other, they must be in the same stratum. However, they depend negatively on each other, violating the requirement that a table can depend negatively only on tables in lower strata. Consider the following variant of the Big/Small program, in which the first rule has been modified:

```
Big2(Part) :- Assembly(Part, Subpart, Qty), Qty > 2.
Small2(Part) :- Assembly(Part, Subpart, Qty), NOT Big2(Part).
```

This program is stratified. Small2 depends on Big2 but Big2 does not depend on Small2. Assembly is in stratum 0, Big is in stratum 1, and Small2 is in stratum 2.

A stratified program is evaluated stratum-by-stratum, starting with stratum 0. To evaluate a stratum, we compute the fixpoint of all rules defining tables in this stratum. When evaluating a stratum, any occurrence of `NOT` involves a table from a lower stratum, which has therefore been completely evaluated by now. The tuples in the negated table still disallow some inferences, but the effect is completely deterministic, given the stratum-by-stratum evaluation. In the example, Big2 is computed before Small2 because it is in a lower stratum than Small2; $\langle trike \rangle$ is added to Big2. Next, when we compute Small2, we recognize that $\langle trike \rangle$ is not in Small2 because it is already in Big2.

Incidentally, note that the stratified Big/Small program is not even recursive. If we replace Assembly by Components, we obtain a recursive, stratified program: Assembly is in stratum 0, Components is in stratum 1, Big2 is also in stratum 1, and Small2 is in stratum 2.

Intuition behind Stratification

Consider the stratified version of the Big/Small program. The rule defining Big2 forces us to add ⟨*trike*⟩ to Big2 and it is natural to assume that ⟨*trike*⟩ is the only tuple in Big2, because we have no supporting evidence for any other tuple being in Big2. The minimal fixpoint computed by stratified fixpoint evaluation is consistent with this intuition. However, there is another minimal fixpoint: We can place every part in Big2 and make Small2 be empty. While this assignment of tuples to relations seems unintuitive, it is nonetheless a minimal fixpoint.

The requirement that programs be stratified gives us a natural order for evaluating rules. When the rules are evaluated in this order, the result is a unique fixpoint that is one of the minimal fixpoints of the program. The fixpoint computed by the stratified fixpoint evaluation usually corresponds well to our intuitive reading of a stratified program, even if the program has more than one minimal fixpoint.

For nonstratified Datalog programs, it is harder to identify a natural model from among the alternative minimal models, especially when we consider that the meaning of a program must be clear even to users who lack expertise in mathematical logic. Although considerable research has been done on identifying natural models for nonstratified programs, practical implementations of Datalog have concentrated on stratified programs.

Relational Algebra and Stratified Datalog

Every relational algebra query can be written as a range-restricted, stratified Datalog program. (Of course, not all Datalog programs can be expressed in relational algebra; for example, the Components program.) We sketch the translation from algebra to stratified Datalog by writing a Datalog program for each of the basic algebra operations, in terms of two example tables R and S, each with two fields:

Selection:	Result(Y) :- R(X,Y), X=*c*.
Projection:	Result(Y) :- R(X,Y).
Cross-product:	Result(X,Y,U,V) :- R(X,Y), S(U,V).
Set-difference:	Result(X,Y) :- R(X,Y), `NOT` S(U,V).
Union:	Result(X,Y) :- R(X,Y).
	Result(X,Y) :- S(X,Y).

We conclude our discussion of stratification by noting that SQL:1999 requires programs to be stratified. The stratified Big/Small program is shown below in SQL:1999 notation, with a final additional selection on Big2:

SQL:1999 and Datalog Queries: A Datalog rule is **linear recursive** if the body contains at most one occurrence of any table that depends on the table in the head of the rule. A **linear recursive program** contains only linear recursive rules. All linear recursive Datalog programs can be expressed using the recursive features of SQL:1999. However, these features are not in Core SQL.

```
WITH
Big2(Part) AS
        (SELECT   A1.Part FROM Assembly A1 WHERE Qty > 2)
Small2(Part) AS
        ((SELECT  A2.Part FROM Assembly A2)
        EXCEPT
        (SELECT   B1.Part from Big2 B1))

SELECT * FROM Big2 B2
```

24.4 FROM DATALOG TO SQL

To support recursive queries in SQL, we must take into account the features of SQL that are not found in Datalog. Two central SQL features missing in Datalog are (1) SQL treats tables as *multisets* of tuples, rather than sets, and (2) SQL permits grouping and aggregate operations.

The multiset semantics of SQL queries can be preserved if we do not check for duplicates after applying rules. Every relation instance, including instances of the recursively defined tables, is a multiset. The number of occurrences of a tuple in a relation is equal to the number of distinct inferences that generate this tuple.

The second point can be addressed by extending Datalog with grouping and aggregation operations. This must be done with multiset semantics in mind, as we now illustrate. Consider the following program:

```
NumParts(Part, SUM(⟨Qty⟩)) :- Assembly(Part, Subpart, Qty).
```

This program is equivalent to the SQL query

```
SELECT    A.Part, SUM (A.Qty)
FROM      Assembly A
GROUP BY  A.Part
```

The angular brackets $\langle \ldots \rangle$ notation was introduced in the LDL deductive system, one of the pioneering deductive database prototypes developed at MCC in the late 1980s. We use it to denote *multiset generation*, or the creation of multiset-values. In principle, the rule defining NumParts is evaluated by first creating the temporary relation shown in Figure 24.6. We create the temporary relation by sorting on the *part* attribute (which appears on the left side of the rule, along with the $\langle \ldots \rangle$ term) and collecting the multiset of *qty* values for each *part* value. We then apply the SUM aggregate to each multiset-value in the second column to obtain the answer, which is shown in Figure 24.7.

part	$\langle qty \rangle$
trike	{3,1}
frame	{1,1}
wheel	{2,1}
tire	{1,1}

Figure 24.6 Temporary Relation

part	SUM($\langle qty \rangle$)
trike	4
frame	2
wheel	3
tire	2

Figure 24.7 The Tuples in NumParts

The temporary relation shown in Figure 24.6 need not be materialized to compute NumParts; for example, SUM can be applied on-the-fly or Assembly can simply be sorted and aggregated as described in Section 14.6.

The use of grouping and aggregation, like negation, causes complications when applied to a partially computed relation. The difficulty is overcome by adopting the same solution used for negation, stratification. Consider the following program:[1]

```
TotParts(Part, Subpart, SUM(⟨Qty⟩)) :- BOM(Part, Subpart, Qty).
BOM(Part, Subpart, Qty) :- Assembly(Part, Subpart, Qty).
BOM(Part, Subpart, Qty) :- Assembly(Part, Part2, Qty2),
            BOM(Part2, Subpart, Qty3), Qty=Qty2*Qty3.
```

The idea is to count the number of copies of Subpart for each Part. By aggregating over BOM rather than Assembly, we count subparts at any level in the hierarchy instead of just immediate subparts. This program is a version of a well-known problem called *Bill-of-Materials* and variants of it are probably the most widely used recursive queries in practice.

The important point to note in this example is that we must wait until the relation BOM has been completely evaluated before we apply the TotParts rule. Otherwise, we obtain incomplete counts. This situation is analogous to the problem we faced with negation; we have to evaluate the negated relation

[1]The reader should write this in SQL:1999 syntax, as a simple exercise.

SQL:1999 Cycle Detection: Safe Datalog queries that do not use arithmetic operations have finite answers and the fixpoint evaluation is guaranteed to halt. Unfortunately, recursive SQL queries may have infinite answer sets and query evaluation may not halt. There are two independent reasons for this: (1) the use of arithmetic operations to generate data values that are not stored in input tables of a query, and (2) multiset semantics for rule applications; intuitively, problems arise from *cycles* in the data. (To see this, consider the Components program on the Assembly instance shown in Figure 24.1 plus the tuple ⟨*tube, wheel, 1*⟩.) SQL:1999 provides special constructs to check for such cycles.

completely before applying a rule that involves the use of `NOT`. If a program is stratified with respect to uses of ⟨...⟩ as well as `NOT`, stratified fixpoint evaluation gives us meaningful results.

There are two further aspects to this example. First, we must understand the cardinality of each tuple in BOM, based on the multiset semantics for rule application. Second, we must understand the cardinality of the multiset of *Qty* values for each ⟨*Part, Subpart*⟩ group in TotParts.

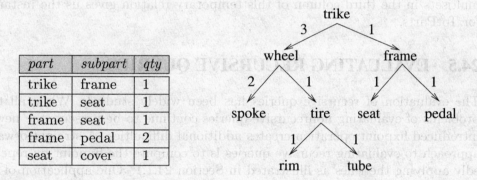

part	*subpart*	*qty*
trike	frame	1
trike	seat	1
frame	seat	1
frame	pedal	2
seat	cover	1

Figure 24.8 Another Instance of Assembly

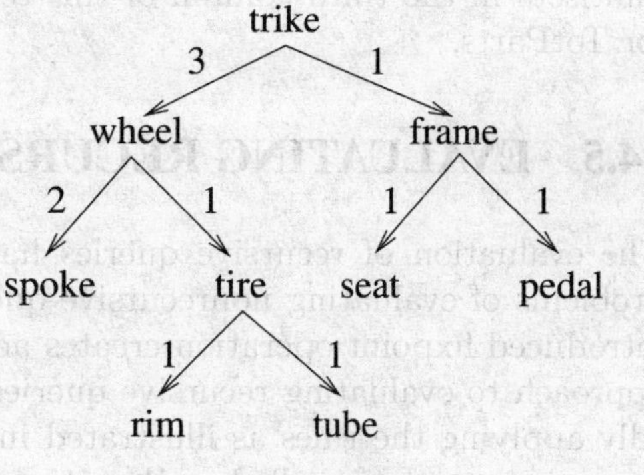

Figure 24.9 Assembly Instance Seen as a Graph

We illustrate these two points using the instance of Assembly shown in Figures 24.8 and 24.9. Applying the first BOM rule, we add (one copy of) every tuple in Assembly to BOM. Applying the second BOM rule, we add the following four tuples to BOM: ⟨*trike, seat, 1*⟩, ⟨*trike, pedal, 2*⟩, ⟨*trike, cover, 1*⟩, and ⟨*frame, cover, 1*⟩. Observe that the tuple ⟨*trike, seat, 1*⟩ was already in BOM because it was generated by applying the first rule; therefore, multiset semantics for rule application gives us two copies of this tuple. Applying the second BOM rule on the new tuples, we generate the tuple ⟨*trike, cover, 1*⟩ (using the tuple ⟨*frame, cover, 1*⟩ for BOM in the body of the rule); this is our second copy of the tuple. Applying the second rule again on this tuple does not generate any tuples, and the computation of the BOM relation is now complete. The BOM instance at this stage is shown in Figure 24.10.

part	*subpart*	*qty*
trike	frame	1
trike	seat	1
frame	seat	1
frame	pedal	2
seat	cover	1
trike	seat	1
trike	pedal	2
trike	cover	1
frame	cover	1
trike	cover	1

Figure 24.10 Instance of BOM Table

part	*subpart*	*qty*
trike	frame	{1}
trike	seat	{1,1}
trike	cover	{1,1}
trike	pedal	{2}
frame	seat	{1}
frame	pedal	{2}
seat	cover	{1}
frame	cover	{1}

Figure 24.11 Temporary Relation

Multiset grouping on this instance yields the temporary relation instance shown in Figure 24.11. (This step is only conceptual; the aggregation can be done on the fly without materializing this temporary relation.) Applying `SUM` to the multisets in the third column of this temporary relation gives us the instance for TotParts.

24.5 EVALUATING RECURSIVE QUERIES

The evaluation of recursive queries has been widely studied. While all the problems of evaluating nonrecursive queries continue to be present, the newly introduced fixpoint operation creates additional difficulties. A straightforward approach to evaluating recursive queries is to compute the fixpoint by repeatedly applying the rules as illustrated in Section 24.1.1. One application of all the program rules is called an **iteration**; we perform as many iterations as necessary to reach the least fixpoint. This approach has two main disadvantages:

- **Repeated Inferences:** As Figures 24.3 and 24.4 illustrate, inferences are repeated across iterations. That is, the same tuple is inferred repeatedly in *the same way*, using the same rule and the same tuples for tables in the body of the rule.
- **Unnecessary Inferences:** Suppose we want to find the components of only a *wheel*. Computing the entire Components table is wasteful and does not take advantage of information in the query.

In this section, we discuss how each of these difficulties can be overcome. We consider only Datalog programs without negation.

24.5.1 Fixpoint Evaluation without Repeated Inferences

Computing the fixpoint by repeatedly applying all rules is called **Naive fixpoint evaluation**. Naive evaluation is guaranteed to compute the least fixpoint, but every application of a rule repeats all inferences made by earlier applications of this rule. We illustrate this point using the following rule:

```
Components(Part, Subpart) :-  Assembly(Part, Part2, Qty),
                              Components(Part2, Subpart).
```

When this rule is applied for the first time, after applying the first rule defining Components, the Components table contains the projection of Assembly on the first two fields. Using these Components tuples in the body of the rule, we generate the tuples shown in Figure 24.3. For example, the tuple ⟨*wheel*, *rim*⟩ is generated through the following inference:

```
Components(wheel, rim) :- Assembly(wheel, tire, 1),
                          Components(tire, rim).
```

When this rule is applied a second time, the Components table contains the tuples shown in Figure 24.3 in addition to the tuples that it contained before the first application. Using the Components tuples shown in Figure 24.3 leads to new inferences; for example,

```
Components(trike, rim) :- Assembly(trike, wheel, 3),
                          Components(wheel, rim).
```

However, every inference carried out in the first application of this rule is also repeated in the second application of the rule, since all the Assembly and Components tuples used in the first rule application are considered again. For example, the inference of ⟨*wheel*, *rim*⟩ shown above is repeated in the second application of this rule.

The solution to this repetition of inferences consists of remembering which inferences were carried out in earlier rule applications and not carrying them out again. We can 'remember' previously executed inferences efficiently by simply keeping track of which Components tuples were generated for the first time in the most recent application of the recursive rule. Suppose we keep track by introducing a new relation called *delta Components* and storing just the newly generated Components tuples in it. Now, we can use only the tuples in *delta_Components* in the next application of the recursive rule; any inference using other Components tuples should have been carried out in earlier rule applications.

This refinement of fixpoint evaluation is called **Seminaive fixpoint evaluation**. Let us trace Seminaive fixpoint evaluation on our example program. The first application of the recursive rule produces the Components tuples shown in Figure 24.3, just like Naive fixpoint evaluation, and these tuples are placed in *delta_Components*. In the second application, however, only *delta_Components* tuples are considered, which means that only the following inferences are carried out in the second application of the recursive rule:

```
Components(trike, rim) :- Assembly(trike, wheel, 3),
                          delta_Components(wheel, rim).
Components(trike, tube) :-Assembly(trike, wheel, 3),
                          delta_Components(wheel, tube).
```

Next, the bookkeeping relation *delta_Components* is updated to contain just these two Components tuples. In the third application of the recursive rule, only these two *delta_Components* tuples are considered and therefore no additional inferences can be made. The fixpoint of Components has been reached.

To implement Seminaive fixpoint evaluation for general Datalog programs, we apply all the recursive rules in a program together in an **iteration**. Iterative application of all recursive rules is repeated until no new tuples are generated in some iteration. To summarize how Seminaive fixpoint evaluation is carried out, there are two important differences with respect to Naive fixpoint evaluation:

- We maintain a *delta* version of every recursive predicate to keep track of the tuples generated for this predicate in the most recent iteration; for example, *delta_Components* for Components. The *delta* versions are updated at the end of each iteration.
- The original program rules are rewritten to ensure that every inference uses at least one *delta* tuple; that is, one tuple that was not known before the previous iteration. This property guarantees that the inference could not have been carried out in earlier iterations.

We do not discuss details of Seminaive fixpoint evaluation (such as the algorithm for rewriting program rules to ensure the use of a *delta* tuple in each inference).

24.5.2 Pushing Selections to Avoid Irrelevant Inferences

Consider a nonrecursive view definition. If we want only those tuples in the view that satisfy an additional selection condition, the selection can be added to the plan as a final operation, and the relational algebra transformations for commuting selections with other relational operators allow us to 'push' the selection ahead of more expensive operations such as cross-products and joins. In effect, we restrict the computation by utilizing selections in the query specification. The problem is more complicated for recursively defined queries.

We use the following program as an example in this section:

```
SameLevel(S1, S2) :-  Assembly(P1, S1, Q1),
                      Assembly(P1, S2, Q2).
SameLevel(S1, S2) :-  Assembly(P1, S1, Q1),
                      SameLevel(P1, P2), Assembly(P2, S2, Q2).
```

Consider the tree representation of Assembly tuples illustrated in Figure 24.2. There is a tuple $\langle S1, S2\rangle$ in SameLevel if there is a path from $S1$ to $S2$ that goes up a certain number of edges in the tree and then comes down the same number of edges.

Suppose we want to find all SameLevel tuples with the first field equal to *spoke*. Since SameLevel tuples can be used to compute other SameLevel tuples, we cannot just compute those tuples with *spoke* in the first field. For example, the tuple $\langle wheel, frame\rangle$ in SameLevel allows us to infer a SameLevel tuple with *spoke* in the first field:

```
SameLevel(spoke, seat) :-  Assembly(wheel, spoke, 2),
                           SameLevel(wheel, frame),
                           Assembly(frame, seat, 1).
```

Intuitively, we have to compute all SameLevel tuples whose first field contains a value on the path from *spoke* to the root in Figure 24.2. Each such tuple has the potential to contribute to answers for the given query. On the other hand, computing the entire SameLevel table is wasteful; for example, the SameLevel tuple $\langle tire, seat\rangle$ cannot be used to infer any answer to the given query (or, indeed, to infer any tuple that can in turn be used to infer an answer tuple). We define a new table, which we call Magic_SameLevel, such that each tuple in this table identifies a value m for which we have to compute all SameLevel tuples with m in the first column to answer the given query:

```
Magic_SameLevel(P1) :- Magic_SameLevel(S1), Assembly(P1, S1, Q1).
Magic_SameLevel(spoke) :- .
```

Consider the tuples in Magic_SameLevel. Obviously we have ⟨*spoke*⟩. Using this Magic_SameLevel tuple and the Assembly tuple ⟨*wheel*, *spoke*, 2⟩, we can infer that the tuple ⟨*wheel*⟩ is in Magic_SameLevel. Using this tuple and the Assembly tuple ⟨*trike*, *wheel*, 3⟩, we can infer that the tuple ⟨*trike*⟩ is in Magic_SameLevel. Thus, Magic_SameLevel contains each node that is on the path from *spoke* to the root in Figure 24.2. The Magic_SameLevel table can be used as a filter to restrict the computation:

```
SameLevel(S1, S2) :- Magic_SameLevel(S1),
          Assembly(P1, S1, Q1), Assembly(P2, S2, Q2).
SameLevel(S1, S2) :- Magic_SameLevel(S1), Assembly(P1, S1, Q1),
          SameLevel(P1, P2), Assembly(P2, S2, Q2).
```

These rules together with the rules defining Magic_SameLevel give us a program for computing all SameLevel tuples with *spoke* in the first column. Notice that the new program depends on the query constant *spoke* only in the second rule defining Magic_SameLevel. Therefore, the program for computing all SameLevel tuples with *seat* in the first column, for instance, is identical except that the second Magic_SameLevel rule is

```
Magic_SameLevel(seat) :- .
```

The number of inferences made using the Magic program can be far fewer than the number of inferences made using the original program, depending on just how much the selection in the query restricts the computation.

24.5.3 The Magic Sets Algorithm

We illustrated the intuition behind the **Magic Sets** algorithm on the SameLevel program, which contains just one output relation and one recursive rule.

The intuition behind the rewriting is that the rows in the Magic tables correspond to the subqueries whose answers are relevant to the original query. By evaluating the rewritten program instead of the original program, we can restrict computation by intuitively pushing the selection condition in the query into the recursion.

The algorithm, however, can be applied to any Datalog program. The input to the algorithm consists of the program and a **query pattern**, which is a relation we want to query plus the fields for which a query will provide constants. The output of the algorithm is a rewritten program.

The Magic Sets program rewriting algorithm can be summarized as follows:

1. **Generate the Adorned Program:** In this step, the program is rewritten to make the pattern of queries and subqueries explicit.
2. **Add Magic Filters:** Modify each rule in the Adorned Program by adding a Magic condition to the body that acts as a filter on the set of tuples generated by this rule.
3. **Define the Magic Tables:** We create new rules to define the Magic tables. Intuitively, from each occurrence of a table R in the body of an Adorned Program rule, we obtain a rule defining the table Magic_R.

When a query is posed, we add the corresponding Magic tuple to the rewritten program and evaluate the least fixpoint of the program (using Seminaive evaluation).

We remark that the Magic Sets algorithm has turned out to be quite effective for computing correlated nested SQL queries, even if there is no recursion, and is used for this purpose in many commercial DBMSs, even systems that do not currently support recursive queries.

We now describe the three steps in the Magic Sets algorithm using the SameLevel program as a running example.

Adorned Program

We consider the query pattern $SameLevel^{bf}$. Thus, given a value c, we want to compute all rows in *SameLevel* in which c appears in the first column. We generate the Adorned Program P^{ad} from the given program P by repeatedly generating adorned versions of rules in P for every **reachable query pattern**, with the given query pattern as the only reachable pattern to begin with; additional reachable patterns are identified during the course of generating the Adorned Program as described next.

Consider a rule in P whose head contains the same table as some reachable pattern. The adorned version of the rule depends on the order in which we consider the predicates in the body of the rule. To simplify our discussion, we assume that this is always left-to-right. First, we replace the head of the rule with the matching query pattern. After this step, the recursive SameLevel rule looks like this:

```
SameLevel^bf(S1, S2) :- Assembly(P1, S1, Q1),
        SameLevel(P1, P2), Assembly(P2, S2, Q2).
```

Next, we proceed left-to-right in the body of the rule until we encounter the first recursive predicate. All columns that contain a constant or a variable that appears to the left are marked *b* (for *bound*) and the rest are marked *f* (for *free*) in the query pattern for this occurrence of the predicate. We add this pattern to the set of reachable patterns and modify the rule accordingly:

$SameLevel^{bf}$`(S1, S2) :- Assembly(P1, S1, Q1),`
    $SameLevel^{bf}$`(P1, P2), Assembly(P2, S2, Q2).`

If there are additional occurrences of recursive predicates in the body of the recursive rule, we continue (adding the query patterns to the reachable set and modifying the rule). (Of course, in linear recursive programs, there is at most one occurrence of a recursive predicate in a rule body.)

We repeat this until we have generated the adorned version of every rule in P for every reachable query pattern that contains the same table as the head of the rule. The result is the Adorned Program P^{ad}, which, in our example, is

$SameLevel^{bf}$`(S1, S2) :- Assembly(P1, S1, Q1),`
    `Assembly(P1, S2, Q2).`
$SameLevel^{bf}$`(S1, S2) :- Assembly(P1, S1, Q1),`
    $SameLevel^{bf}$`(P1, P2), Assembly(P2, S2, Q2).`

In our example, there is only one reachable query pattern. In general, there can be several.[2]

Adding Magic Filters

Every rule in the Adorned Program is modified by adding a 'magic filter' predicate to obtain the rewritten program:

$SameLevel^{bf}$`(S1, S2) :-` $Magic\_SameLevel^{bf}$`(S1),`
    `Assembly(P1, S1, Q1), Assembly(P2, S2, Q2).`
$SameLevel^{bf}$`(S1, S2) :-` $Magic\_SameLevel^{bf}$`(S1),`
    `Assembly(P1, S1, Q1),` $SameLevel^{bf}$`(P1, P2),`
    `Assembly(P2, S2, Q2).`

The filter predicate is a copy of the head of the rule, with 'Magic' as a prefix for the table name and the variables in columns corresponding to *free* deleted, as illustrated in these two rules.

[2] As an example, consider a variant of the SameLevel program in which the variables $P1$ and $P2$ are interchanged in the body of the recursive rule (Exercise 24.5)

Defining Magic Filter Tables

Consider the Adorned Program after every rule has been modified as described. From each occurrence O of a recursive predicate in the body of a rule in this modified program, we generate a rule that defines a Magic predicate. The algorithm for generating this rule is as follows: (1) Delete everything to the right of occurrence O in the body of the modified rule. (2) Add the prefix 'Magic' and delete the free columns of O. (3) Move O, with these changes, into the head of the rule.

From the recursive rule in our example, after steps (1) and (2) we get:

$SameLevel^{bf}$(S1, S2) :- $Magic\_SameLevel^{bf}$(S1),
    Assembly(P1, S1, Q1), $Magic\_SameLevel^{bf}$(P1).

After step (3), we get:

$Magic\_SameLevel^{bf}$(P1) :- $Magic\_SameLevel^{bf}$(S1),
    Assembly(P1, S1, Q1).

The query itself generates a row in the corresponding Magic table, for example, $Magic\_SameLevel^{bf}$(seat).

24.6 REVIEW QUESTIONS

Answers to the review questions can be found in the listed sections.

- Describe *Datalog* programs. Use an example Datalog program to explain why it is not possible to write recursive rules in SQL-92. **(Section 24.1)**
- Define the terms *model* and *least model*. What can you say about least models for Datalog programs? Why is this approach to defining the meaning of a Datalog program called *declarative*? **(Section 24.2.1)**
- Define the terms *fixpoint* and *least fixpoint*. What can you say about least fixpoints for Datalog programs? Why is this approach to defining the meaning of a Datalog program said to be *operational*? **(Section 24.2.2)**
- What is a *safe* program? Why is this property important? What is *range-restriction* and how does it ensure safety? **(Section 24.2.3)**
- What is the connection between least models and least fixpoints for Datalog programs? **(Section 24.2.4)**

- Explain why programs with negation may not have a least model or least fixpoint. Extend the definition of *range-restriction* to programs with negation. **(Section 24.3)**
- What is a *stratified* program? How does stratification address the problem of identifying a desired fixpoint? Show how every relational algebra query can be written as a stratified Datalog program. **(Section 24.3.1)**
- Two important aspects of SQL, *multiset tables* and *aggregation with grouping*, are missing in Datalog. How can we extend Datalog to support these features? Discuss the interaction of these two new features and the need for stratification of aggregation. **(Section 24.4)**
- Define the terms *inference* and *iteration*. What are the two main challenges in efficient evaluation of recursive Datalog programs? **(Section 24.5)**
- Describe *Seminaive fixpoint evaluation* and explain how it avoids repeated inferences. **(Section 24.5.1)**
- Describe the *Magic Sets* program transformation and explain how it avoids unnecessary inferences. **(Sections 24.5.2 and 24.5.3)**

EXERCISES

Exercise 24.1 Consider the Flights relation:

Flights(*<u>flno</u>:* `integer`, *from:* `string`, *to:* `string`, *distance:* `integer`,
departs: `time`, *arrives:* `time`)

Write the following queries in Datalog and SQL:1999 syntax:

1. Find the *flno* of all flights that depart from Madison.
2. Find the *flno* of all flights that leave Chicago after Flight 101 arrives in Chicago and no later than 1 hour after.
3. Find the *flno* of all flights that do not depart from Madison.
4. Find all cities reachable from Madison through a series of one or more connecting flights.
5. Find all cities reachable from Madison through a chain of one or more connecting flights, with no more than 1 hour spent on any connection. (That is, every connecting flight must depart within an hour of the arrival of the previous flight in the chain.)
6. Find the shortest time to fly from Madison to Madras, using a chain of one or more connecting flights.
7. Find the *flno* of all flights that do not depart from Madison or a city that is reachable from Madison through a chain of flights.

Exercise 24.2 Consider the definition of Components in Section 24.1.1. Suppose that the second rule is replaced by

```
Components(Part, Subpart) :-Components(Part, Part2),
                            Components(Part2, Subpart).
```

1. If the modified program is evaluated on the Assembly relation in Figure 24.1, how many iterations does Naive fixpoint evaluation take and what Components facts are generated in each iteration?
2. Extend the given instance of Assembly so that Naive fixpoint iteration takes two more iterations.
3. Write this program in SQL:1999 syntax, using the `WITH` clause.
4. Write a program in Datalog syntax to find the part with the most distinct subparts; if several parts have the same maximum number of subparts, your query should return all these parts.
5. How would your answer to the previous part be changed if you also wanted to list the number of subparts for the part with the most distinct subparts?
6. Rewrite your answers to the previous two parts in SQL:1999 syntax.
7. Suppose that you want to find the part with the most subparts, taking into account the quantity of each subpart used in a part, how would you modify the Components program? (*Hint:* To write such a query you reason about the number of inferences of a fact. For this, you have to rely on SQL's maintaining as many copies of each fact as the number of inferences of that fact and take into account the properties of Seminaive evaluation.)

Exercise 24.3 Consider the definition of Components in Exercise 24.2. Suppose that the recursive rule is rewritten as follows for Seminaive fixpoint evaluation:

```
Components(Part, Subpart) :-  delta Components(Part, Part2, Qty),
                              delta Components(Part2, Subpart).
```

1. At the end of an iteration, what steps must be taken to update *delta* Components to contain just the new tuples generated in this iteration? Can you suggest an index on Components that might help to make this faster?
2. Even if the *delta* relation is correctly updated, fixpoint evaluation using the preceding rule does not always produce all answers. Show an instance of Assembly that illustrates the problem.
3. Can you suggest a way to rewrite the recursive rule in terms of *delta* Components so that Seminaive fixpoint evaluation always produces all answers and no inferences are repeated across iterations?
4. Show how your version of the rewritten program performs on the example instance of Assembly that you used to illustrate the problem with the given rewriting of the recursive rule.

Exercise 24.4 Consider the definition of SameLevel in Section 24.5.2 and the Assembly instance shown in Figure 24.1.

1. Rewrite the recursive rule for Seminaive fixpoint evaluation and show how Seminaive evaluation proceeds.
2. Consider the rules defining the relation Magic, with *spoke* as the query constant. For Seminaive evaluation of the 'Magic' version of the SameLevel program, all tuples in Magic are computed first. Show how Seminaive evaluation of the Magic relation proceeds.

3. After the Magic relation is computed, it can be treated as a fixed database relation, just like Assembly, in the Seminaive fixpoint evaluation of the rules defining SameLevel in the 'Magic' version of the program. Rewrite the recursive rule for Seminaive evaluation and show how Seminaive evaluation of these rules proceeds.

Exercise 24.5 Consider the definition of SameLevel in Section 24.5.2 and a query in which the first argument is bound. Suppose that the recursive rule is rewritten as follows, leading to multiple binding patterns in the adorned program:

```
SameLevel(S1, S2) :- Assembly(P1, S1, Q1),
          Assembly(P1, S2, Q2).
SameLevel(S1, S2) :- Assembly(P1, S1, Q1),
          SameLevel(P2, P1), Assembly(P2, S2, Q2).
```

1. Show the adorned program.
2. Show the Magic program.
3. Show the Magic program after applying Seminaive rewriting.
4. Construct an example instance of Assembly such that the evaluating the optimized program generates less than 1% of the facts generated by evaluating the original program (and finally selecting the query result).

Exercise 24.6 Again, consider the definition of SameLevel in Section 24.5.2 and a query in which the first argument is bound. Suppose that the recursive rule is rewritten as follows:

```
SameLevel(S1, S2) :- Assembly(P1, S1, Q1),
          Assembly(P1, S2, Q2).
SameLevel(S1, S2) :- Assembly(P1, S1, Q1),
          SameLevel(P1, R1), SameLevel(R1, P2), Assembly(P2, S2, Q2).
```

1. Show the adorned program.
2. Show the Magic program.
3. Show the Magic program after applying Seminaive rewriting.
4. Construct an example instance of Assembly such that the evaluating the optimized program generates less than 1% of the facts generated by evaluating the original program (and finally selecting the query result).

BIBLIOGRAPHIC NOTES

The use of logic as a query language is discussed in several papers [296, 537], which arose out of influential workshops. Good textbook discussions of deductive databases can be found in [747, 3, 143, 794, 503]. [614] is a recent survey article that provides an overview and covers the major prototypes in the area, including LDL [177], Glue-Nail! [214, 549] EKS-V1 [758], Aditi [615], Coral [612], LOLA [804], and XSB [644].

The fixpoint semantics of logic programs (and deductive databases as a special case) is presented in [751], which also shows equivalence of the fixpoint semantics to a *least-model* semantics. The use of stratification to give a natural semantics to programs with negation was developed independently in [37, 154, 559, 752].

Efficient evaluation of deductive database queries has been widely studied, and [58] is a survey and comparison of several early techniques; [611] is a more recent survey. Seminaive fixpoint evaluation was independently proposed several times; a good treatment appears in [54]. The Magic Sets technique is proposed in [57] and generalized to cover all deductive database queries without negation in [77]. The Alexander method [631] was independently developed and is equivalent to a variant of Magic Sets called *Supplementary Magic Sets* in [77]. [553] shows how Magic Sets offers significant performance benefits even for nonrecursive SQL queries. [673] describes a version of Magic Sets designed for SQL queries with correlation, and its implementation in the Starburst system (which led to its implementation in IBM's DB2 DBMS). [670] discusses how Magic Sets can be incorporated into a System R style cost-based optimization framework. The Magic Sets technique is extended to programs with stratified negation in [53, 76]. [121] compares Magic Sets with top-down evaluation strategies derived from Prolog.

[642] develops a program rewriting technique related to Magic Sets called *Magic Counting.* Other related methods that are not based on program rewriting but rather on run-time control strategies for evaluation include [226, 429, 756, 757]. The ideas in [226] have been developed further to design an *abstract machine* for logic program evaluation using tabling in [609, 727]; this is the basis for the XSB system [644].

25

DATA WAREHOUSING AND DECISION SUPPORT

- Why are traditional DBMSs inadequate for decision support?
- What is the multidimensional data model and what kinds of analysis does it facilitate?
- What SQL:1999 features support multidimensional queries?
- How does SQL:1999 support analysis of sequences and trends?
- How are DBMSs being optimized to deliver early answers for interactive analysis?
- What kinds of index and file organizations do OLAP systems require?
- What is data warehousing and why is it important for decision support?
- Why have materialized views become important?
- How can we efficiently maintain materialized views?

- **Key concepts:** OLAP, multimensional model, dimensions, measures; roll-up, drill-down, pivoting, cross-tabulation, `CUBE`; `WINDOW` queries, frames, order; top N queries, online aggregation; bitmap indexes, join indexes; data warehouses, extract, refresh, purge; materialized views, incremental maintenance, maintaining warehouse views

Nothing is more difficult, and therefore more precious, than to be able to decide.

—Napoleon Bonaparte

Database management systems are widely used by organizations for maintaining data that documents their everyday operations. In applications that update such *operational data*, transactions typically make small changes (for example, adding a reservation or depositing a check) and a large number of transactions must be reliably and efficiently processed. Such **online transaction processing (OLTP)** applications have driven the growth of the DBMS industry in the past three decades and will doubtless continue to be important. DBMSs have traditionally been optimized extensively to perform well in such applications.

Recently, however, organizations have increasingly emphasized applications in which current and historical data is comprehensively analyzed and explored, identifying useful trends and creating summaries of the data, in order to support high-level decision making. Such applications are referred to as **decision support**. Mainstream relational DBMS vendors have recognized the importance of this market segment and are adding features to their products to support it. In particular, SQL has been extended with new constructs and novel indexing and query optimization techniques are being added to support complex queries.

The use of views has gained rapidly in popularity because of their utility in applications involving complex data analysis. While queries on views can be answered by evaluating the view definition when the query is submitted, precomputing the view definition can make queries run much faster. Carrying the motivation for precomputed views one step further, organizations can consolidate information from several databases into a *data warehouse* by copying tables from many sources into one location or materializing a view defined over tables from several sources. Data warehousing has become widespread, and many specialized products are now available to create and manage warehouses of data from multiple databases.

We begin this chapter with an overview of decision support in Section 25.1. We introduce the multimensional model of data in Section 25.2 and consider database design issues in 25.2.1. We discuss the rich class of queries that it naturally supports in Section 25.3. We discuss how new SQL:1999 constructs allow us to express multidimensional queries in 25.3.1. In Section 25.4, we discuss SQL:1999 extensions that support queries over relations as ordered collections. We consider how to optimize for fast generation of initial answers in Section 25.5. The many query language extensions required in the OLAP environment prompted the development of new implementation techniques; we discuss these in Section 25.6. In Section 25.7, we examine the issues involved in creating and maintaining a data warehouse. From a technical standpoint, a key issue is how to maintain warehouse information (replicated tables or views) when the underlying source information changes. After covering the important role played by views in OLAP and warehousing in Section 25.8, we consider maintenance of materialized views in Sections 25.9 and 25.10.

25.1 INTRODUCTION TO DECISION SUPPORT

Organizational decision making requires a comprehensive view of all aspects of an enterprise, so many organizations created consolidated **data warehouses** that contain data drawn from several databases maintained by different business units together with historical and summary information.

The trend toward data warehousing is complemented by an increased emphasis on powerful analysis tools. Many characteristics of decision support queries make traditional SQL systems inadequate:

- The `WHERE` clause often contains many `AND` and `OR` conditions. As we saw in Section 14.2.3, `OR` conditions, in particular, are poorly handled in many relational DBMSs.
- Applications require extensive use of statistical functions, such as standard deviation, that are not supported in SQL-92. Therefore, SQL queries must frequently be embedded in a host language program.
- Many queries involve conditions over time or require aggregating over time periods. SQL-92 provides poor support for such time-series analysis.
- Users often need to pose several related queries. Since there is no convenient way to express these commonly occurring families of queries, users have to write them as a collection of independent queries, which can be tedious. Further, the DBMS has no way to recognize and exploit optimization opportunities arising from executing many related queries together.

Three broad classes of analysis tools are available. First, some systems support a class of stylized queries that typically involve group-by and aggregation operators and provide excellent support for complex boolean conditions, statistical functions, and features for time-series analysis. Applications dominated by such queries are called **online analytic processing (OLAP)**. These systems support a querying style in which the data is best thought of as a multidimensional array and are influenced by end-user tools, such as spreadsheets, in addition to database query languages.

Second, some DBMSs support traditional SQL-style queries but are designed to also support OLAP queries efficiently. Such systems can be regarded as relational DBMSs optimized for decision support applications. Many vendors of relational DBMSs are currently enhancing their products in this direction and, over time, the distinction between specialized OLAP systems and relational DBMSs enhanced to support OLAP queries is likely to diminish.

The third class of analysis tools is motivated by the desire to find interesting or unexpected trends and patterns in large data sets rather than the complex

SQL:1999 and OLAP: In this chapter, we discuss a number of features introduced in SQL:1999 to support OLAP. In order not to delay publication of the SQL:1999 standard, these features were actually added to the standard through an *amendment* called SQL/OLAP.

query characteristics just listed. In **exploratory data analysis**, although an analyst can recognize an 'interesting pattern' when shown such a pattern, it is very difficult to formulate a query that captures the essence of an interesting pattern. For example, an analyst looking at credit-card usage histories may want to detect unusual activity indicating misuse of a lost or stolen card. A catalog merchant may want to look at customer records to identify promising customers for a new promotion; this identification would depend on income level, buying patterns, demonstrated interest areas, and so on. The amount of data in many applications is too large to permit manual analysis or even traditional statistical analysis, and the goal of **data mining** is to support exploratory analysis over very large data sets. We discuss data mining further in Chapter 26.

Clearly, evaluating OLAP or data mining queries over globally distributed data is likely to be excruciatingly slow. Further, for such complex analysis, often statistical in nature, it is not essential that the most current version of the data be used. The natural solution is to create a centralized repository of all the data; that is, a data warehouse. Thus, the availability of a warehouse facilitates the application of OLAP and data mining tools and, conversely, the desire to apply such analysis tools is a strong motivation for building a data warehouse.

25.2 OLAP: MULTIDIMENSIONAL DATA MODEL

OLAP applications are dominated by ad hoc, complex queries. In SQL terms, these are queries that involve group-by and aggregation operators. The natural way to think about typical OLAP queries, however, is in terms of a multidimensional data model. In this section, we present the multidimensional data model and compare it with a relational representation of data. In subsequent sections, we describe OLAP queries in terms of the multidimensional data model and consider some new implementation techniques designed to support such queries.

In the multidimensional data model, the focus is on a collection of numeric **measures**. Each measure depends on a set of **dimensions**. We use a running example based on sales data. The measure attribute in our example is *sales*. The dimensions are Product, Location, and Time. Given a product, a location, and a time, we have at most one associated sales value. If we identify a product by a unique identifier *pid* and, similarly, identify location by *locid* and time by *timeid*, we can think of sales information as being arranged in a three-dimensional array Sales. This array is shown in Figure 25.1; for clarity, we show only the values for a single *locid* value, *locid*= 1, which can be thought of as a slice orthogonal to the *locid* axis.

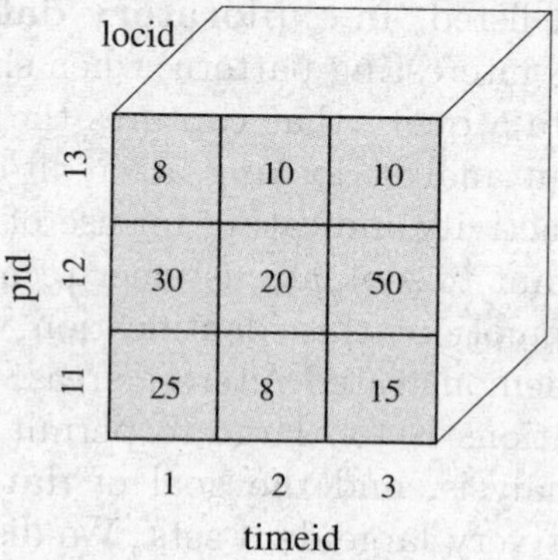

Figure 25.1 Sales: A Multidimensional Dataset

This view of data as a multidimensional array is readily generalized to more than three dimensions. In OLAP applications, the bulk of the data can be represented in such a multidimensional array. Indeed, some OLAP systems actually store data in a multidimensional array (of course, implemented without the usual programming language assumption that the entire array fits in memory). OLAP systems that use arrays to store multidimensional datasets are called **multidimensional OLAP (MOLAP)** systems.

The data in a multidimensional array can also be represented as a relation, as illustrated in Figure 25.2, which shows the same data as in Figure 25.1, with additional rows corresponding to the 'slice' *locid*= 2. This relation, which relates the dimensions to the measure of interest, is called the **fact table**.

Now let us turn to dimensions. Each dimension can have a set of associated attributes. For example, the Location dimension is identified by the *locid* attribute, which we used to identify a location in the Sales table. We assume that it also has attributes *country, state*, and *city*. We further assume that the Product dimension has attributes *pname, category*, and *price* in addition to the identifier *pid*. The *category* of a product indicates its general nature; for example, a product *pant* could have category value *apparel*. We assume that the Time dimension has attributes *date, week, month, quarter, year,* and *holiday_flag* in addition to the identifier *timeid*.

locid	*city*	*state*	*country*
1	Madison	WI	USA
2	Fresno	CA	USA
5	Chennai	TN	India

Locations

pid	*pname*	*category*	*price*
11	Lee Jeans	Apparel	25
12	Zord	Toys	18
13	Biro Pen	Stationery	2

Products

pid	*timeid*	*locid*	*sales*
11	1	1	25
11	2	1	8
11	3	1	15
12	1	1	30
12	2	1	20
12	3	1	50
13	1	1	8
13	2	1	10
13	3	1	10
11	1	2	35
11	2	2	22
11	3	2	10
12	1	2	26
12	2	2	45
12	3	2	20
13	1	2	20
13	2	2	40
13	3	2	5

Sales

Figure 25.2 Locations, Products, and Sales Represented as Relations

For each dimension, the set of associated values can be structured as a hierarchy. For example, cities belong to states, and states belong to countries. Dates belong to weeks and months, both weeks and months are contained in quarters, and quarters are contained in years. (Note that a week could span two months; therefore, weeks are not contained in months.) Some of the attributes of a dimension describe the position of a dimension value with respect to this underlying hierarchy of dimension values. The hierarchies for the Product, Location, and Time hierarchies in our example are shown at the attribute level in Figure 25.3.

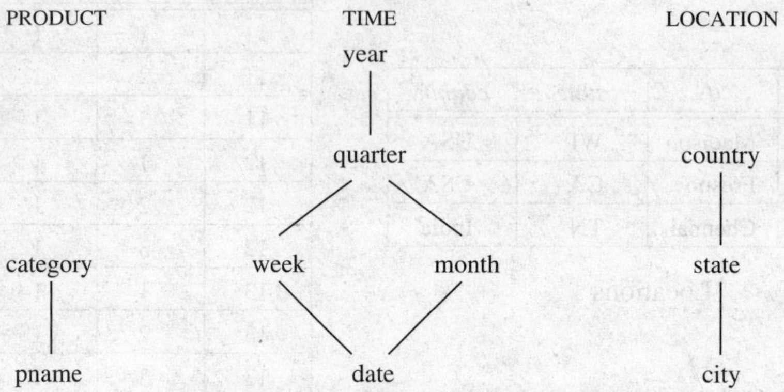

Figure 25.3 Dimension Hierarchies

Information about dimensions can also be represented as a collection of relations:

Locations(<u>*locid:* `integer`</u>, *city:* `string`, *state:* `string`, *country:* `string`)
Products(<u>*pid:* `integer`</u>, *pname:* `string`, *category:* `string`, *price:* `real`)
Times(<u>*timeid:* `integer`</u>, *date:* `string`, *week:* `integer`, *month:* `integer`,
quarter: `integer`, *year:* `integer`, *holiday_flag:* `boolean`)

These relations are much smaller than the fact table in a typical OLAP application; they are called the **dimension tables**. OLAP systems that store all information, including fact tables, as relations are called **relational OLAP (ROLAP)** systems.

The Times table illustrates the attention paid to the Time dimension in typical OLAP applications. SQL's date and timestamp data types are not adequate; to support summarizations that reflect business operations, information such as fiscal quarters, holiday status, and so on is maintained for each time value.

25.2.1 Multidimensional Database Design

Figure 25.4 shows the tables in our running sales example. It suggests a star, centered at the fact table Sales; such a combination of a fact table and dimension tables is called a **star schema**. This schema pattern is very common in databases designed for OLAP. The bulk of the data is typically in the fact table, which has no redundancy; it is usually in BCNF. In fact, to minimize the size of the fact table, dimension identifiers (such as *pid* and *timeid*) are system-generated identifiers.

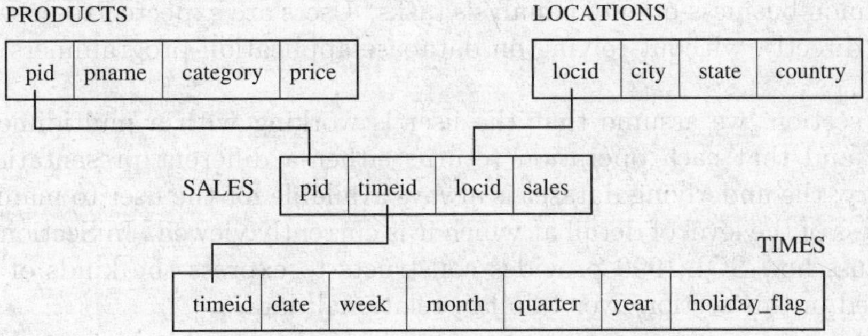

Figure 25.4 An Example of a Star Schema

Information about dimension values is maintained in the dimension tables. Dimension tables are usually not normalized. The rationale is that the dimension tables in a database used for OLAP are static and update, insertion, and deletion anomalies are not important. Further, because the size of the database is dominated by the fact table, the space saved by normalizing dimension tables is negligible. Therefore, minimizing the computation time for combining facts in the fact table with dimension information is the main design criterion, which suggests that we avoid breaking a dimension table into smaller tables (which might lead to additional joins).

Small response times for interactive querying are important in OLAP, and most systems support the materialization of summary tables (typically generated through queries using grouping). Ad hoc queries posed by users are answered using the original tables along with precomputed summaries. A very important design issue is which summary tables should be materialized to achieve the best use of available memory and answer commonly asked ad hoc queries with interactive response times. In current OLAP systems, deciding which summary tables to materialize may well be the most important design decision.

Finally, new storage structures and indexing techniques have been developed to support OLAP and they present the database designer with additional physical design choices. We cover some of these implementation techniques in Section 25.6.

25.3 MULTIDIMENSIONAL AGGREGATION QUERIES

Now that we have seen the multidimensional model of data, let us consider how such data can be queried and manipulated. The operations supported by this model are strongly influenced by end user tools such as spreadsheets. The goal is to give end users who are not SQL experts an intuitive and powerful interface for common business-oriented analysis tasks. Users are expected to pose ad hoc queries directly, without relying on database application programmers.

In this section, we assume that the user is working with a multidimensional dataset and that each operation returns either a different presentation or a summary; the underlying dataset is always available for the user to manipulate, regardless of the level of detail at which it is currently viewed. In Section 25.3.1, we discuss how SQL:1999 provides constructs to express the kinds of queries presented in this section over tabular, relational data.

A very common operation is aggregating a measure over one or more dimensions. The following queries are typical:

- Find the total sales.
- Find total sales for each city.
- Find total sales for each state.

These queries can be expressed as SQL queries over the fact and dimension tables. When we aggregate a measure on one or more dimensions, the aggregated measure depends on fewer dimensions than the original measure. For example, when we compute the total sales by city, the aggregated measure is *total sales* and it depends only on the Location dimension, whereas the original *sales* measure depended on the Location, Time, and Product dimensions.

Another use of aggregation is to summarize at different levels of a dimension hierarchy. If we are given total sales per city, we can aggregate on the Location dimension to obtain sales per state. This operation is called **roll-up** in the OLAP literature. The inverse of roll-up is **drill-down**: Given total sales by state, we can ask for a more detailed presentation by drilling down on Location. We can ask for sales by city or just sales by city for a selected state (with sales presented on a per-state basis for the remaining states, as before). We can also drill down on a dimension other than Location. For example, we can ask for total sales for each product for each state, drilling down on the Product dimension.

Another common operation is **pivoting**. Consider a tabular presentation of the Sales table. If we pivot it on the Location and Time dimensions, we obtain a table of total sales for each location for each time value. This information can be presented as a two-dimensional chart in which the axes are labeled with location and time values; the entries in the chart correspond to the total sales for that location and time. Therefore, values that appear in columns of the original presentation become labels of axes in the result presentation. The result of pivoting, called a **cross-tabulation**, is illustrated in Figure 25.5. Observe that in spreadsheet style, in addition to the total sales by year and state (taken together), we also have additional summaries of sales by year and sales by state.

	WI	CA	Total
1995	63	81	144
1996	38	107	145
1997	75	35	110
Total	176	223	399

Figure 25.5 Cross-Tabulation of Sales by Year and State

Pivoting can also be used to change the dimensions of the cross-tabulation; from a presentation of sales by year and state, we can obtain a presentation of sales by product and year.

Clearly, the OLAP framework makes it convenient to pose a broad class of queries. It also gives catchy names to some familiar operations: **Slicing** a dataset amounts to an equality selection on one or more dimensions, possibly also with some dimensions projected out. **Dicing** a dataset amounts to a range selection. These terms come from visualizing the effect of these operations on a cube or cross-tabulated representation of the data.

A Note on Statistical Databases

Many OLAP concepts are present in earlier work on **statistical databases (SDBs)**, which are database systems designed to support statistical applications, although this connection has not been sufficiently recognized because of differences in application domains and terminology. The multidimensional data model, with the notions of a measure associated with dimensions and classification hierarchies for dimension values, is also used in SDBs. OLAP operations such as roll-up and drill-down have counterparts in SDBs. Indeed, some implementation techniques developed for OLAP are also applied to SDBs.

Nonetheless, some differences arise from the different domains OLAP and SDBs were developed to support. For example, SDBs are used in socioeconomic applications, where classification hierarchies and privacy issues are very important. This is reflected in the greater complexity of classification hierarchies in SDBs, along with issues such as potential breaches of privacy. (The privacy issue concerns whether a user with access to summarized data can reconstruct the original, unsummarized data.) In contrast, OLAP has been aimed at business applications with large volumes of data and efficient handling of very large datasets has received more attention than in the SDB literature.

25.3.1 ROLLUP and CUBE in SQL:1999

In this section, we discuss how many of the query capabilities of the multidimensional model are supported in SQL:1999. Typically, a single OLAP operation leads to several closely related SQL queries with aggregation and grouping. For example, consider the cross-tabulation shown in Figure 25.5, which was obtained by pivoting the Sales table. To obtain the same information, we would issue the following queries:

```
SELECT   T.year, L.state, SUM (S.sales)
FROM     Sales S, Times T, Locations L
WHERE    S.timeid=T.timeid AND S.locid=L.locid
GROUP BY T.year, L.state
```

This query generates the entries in the body of the chart (outlined by the dark lines). The summary column on the right is generated by the query:

```
SELECT   T.year, SUM (S.sales)
FROM     Sales S, Times T
WHERE    S.timeid=T.timeid
GROUP BY T.year
```

The summary row at the bottom is generated by the query:

```
SELECT   L.state, SUM (S.sales)
FROM     Sales S, Locations L
WHERE    S.locid=L.locid
GROUP BY L.state
```

The cumulative sum in the bottom-right corner of the chart is produced by the query:

```
SELECT   SUM (S.sales)
FROM     Sales S, Locations L
WHERE    S.locid=L.locid
```

The example cross-tabulation can be thought of as roll-up on the entire dataset (i.e., treating everything as one big group), on the Location dimension, on the Time dimension, and on the Location and Time dimensions together. Each roll-up corresponds to a single SQL query with grouping. In general, given a measure with k associated dimensions, we can roll up on any subset of these k dimensions; so we have a total of 2^k such SQL queries.

Through high-level operations such as pivoting, users can generate many of these 2^k SQL queries. Recognizing the commonalities between these queries enables more efficient, coordinated computation of the set of queries.

SQL:1999 extends the `GROUP BY` construct to provide better support for roll-up and cross-tabulation queries. The `GROUP BY` clause with the `CUBE` keyword is equivalent to a collection of `GROUP BY` statements, with one `GROUP BY` statement for each subset of the k dimensions.

Consider the following query:

```
SELECT   T.year, L.state, SUM (S.sales)
FROM     Sales S, Times T, Locations L
WHERE    S.timeid=T.timeid AND S.locid=L.locid
GROUP BY CUBE (T.year, L.state)
```

The result of this query, shown in Figure 25.6, is just a tabular representation of the cross-tabulation in Figure 25.5.

SQL:1999 also provides variants of `GROUP BY` that enable computation of subsets of the cross-tabulation computed using `GROUP BY CUBE`. For example, we can replace the grouping clause in the previous query with

```
GROUP BY ROLLUP (T.year, L.state)
```

In contrast to `GROUP BY CUBE`, we aggregate by all pairs of year and state values and by each year, and compute an overall sum for the entire dataset (the last row in Figure 25.6), but we do not aggregate for each state value. The result is identical to that shown in Figure 25.6, except that the rows with *null* in the *T.year* column and non-*null* values in the *L.state* column are not computed.

```
CUBE pid, locid, timeid BY SUM Sales
```

T.year	*L.state*	*SUM(S.sales)*
1995	WI	63
1995	CA	81
1995	*null*	144
1996	WI	38
1996	CA	107
1996	*null*	145
1997	WI	75
1997	CA	35
1997	*null*	110
null	WI	176
null	CA	223
null	*null*	399

Figure 25.6 The Result of GROUP BY CUBE on Sales

This query rolls up the table Sales on all eight subsets of the set {pid, locid, timeid} (including the empty subset). It is equivalent to eight queries of the form

```
SELECT    SUM (S.sales)
FROM      Sales S
GROUP BY  grouping-list
```

The queries differ only in the *grouping-list*, which is some subset of the set {pid, locid, timeid}. We can think of these eight queries as being arranged in a lattice, as shown in Figure 25.7. The result tuples at a node can be aggregated further to compute the result for any child of the node. This relationship between the queries arising in a CUBE can be exploited for efficient evaluation.

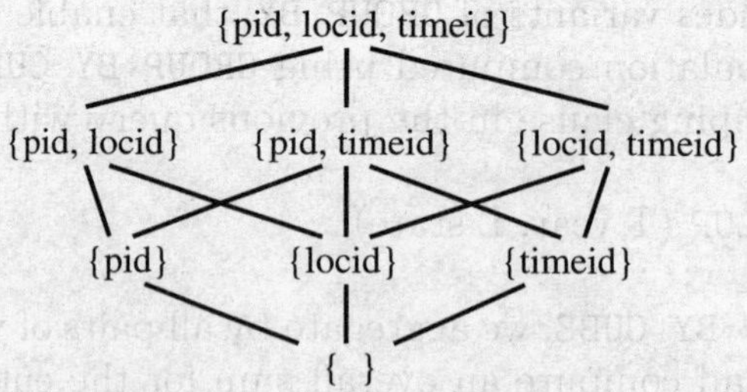

Figure 25.7 The Lattice of GROUP BY Queries in a CUBE Query

25.4 WINDOW QUERIES IN SQL:1999

The time dimension is very important in decision support and queries involving trend analysis have traditionally been difficult to express in SQL. To address this, SQL:1999 introduced a fundamental extension called a **query window**. Examples of queries that can be written using this extension, but are either difficult or impossible to write in SQL without it, include

1. Find total sales by month.
2. Find total sales by month for each city.
3. Find the percentage change in the total monthly sales for each product.
4. Find the top five products ranked by total sales.
5. Find the trailing n day moving average of sales. (For each day, we must compute the average daily sales over the preceding n days.)
6. Find the top five products ranked by cumulative sales, for every month over the past year.
7. Rank all products by total sales over the past year, and, for each product, print the difference in total sales relative to the product ranked behind it.

The first two queries can be expressed as SQL queries using `GROUP BY` over the fact and dimension tables. The next two queries can be expressed too, but are quite complicated in SQL-92. The fifth query cannot be expressed in SQL-92 if n is to be a parameter of the query. The last query cannot be expressed in SQL-92.

In this section, we discuss the features of SQL:1999 that allow us to express all these queries and, obviously, a rich class of similar queries.

The main extension is the `WINDOW` clause, which intuitively identifies an ordered 'window' of rows 'around' each tuple in a table. This allows us to apply a rich collection of aggregate functions to the window of a row and extend the row with the results. For example, we can associate the average sales over the past 3 days with every Sales tuple (each of which records 1 day's sales). This gives us a 3-day moving average of sales.

While there is some similarity to the `GROUP BY` and `CUBE` clauses, there are important differences as well. For example, like the `WINDOW` operator, `GROUP BY` allows us to create partitions of rows and apply aggregate functions such as `SUM` to the rows in a partition. However, unlike `WINDOW`, there is a single output row per partition, rather than one output row for each row, and each partition is an unordered collection of rows.

We now illustrate the window concept through an example:

```
SELECT L.state, T.month, AVG (S.sales) OVER W AS movavg
FROM   Sales S, Times T, Locations L
WHERE  S.timeid=T.timeid AND S.locid=L.locid
WINDOW W AS (PARTITION BY L.state
       ORDER BY T.month
       RANGE BETWEEN INTERVAL '1' MONTH PRECEDING
       AND INTERVAL '1' MONTH FOLLOWING)
```

The FROM and WHERE clauses are processed as usual to (conceptually) generate an intermediate table, which we refer to as Temp. Windows are created over the Temp relation.

There are three steps in defining a window. First, we define *partitions* of the table, using the PARTITION BY clause. In the example, partitions are based on the *L.state* column. Partitions are similar to groups created with GROUP BY, but there is a very important difference in how they are processed. To understand the difference, observe that the SELECT clause contains a column, *T.month*, which is not used to define the partitions; different rows in a given partition could have different values in this column. Such a column cannot appear in the SELECT clause in conjunction with grouping, but it is allowed for partitions. The reason is that there is one answer row for *each* row in a partition of Temp, rather than just one answer row per partition. The window around a given row is used to compute the aggregate functions in the corresponding answer row.

The second step in defining a window is to specify the *ordering* of rows within a partition. We do this using the ORDER BY clause; in the example, the rows within each partition are ordered by *T.month*.

The third step in window definition is to *frame* windows; that is, to establish the boundaries of the window associated with each row in terms of the ordering of rows within partitions. In the example, the window for a row includes the row itself plus all rows whose month value is within a month before or after; therefore, a row whose *month* value is June 2002 has a window containing all rows with *month* equal to May, June, or July 2002.

The answer row corresponding to a given row is constructed by first identifying its window. Then, for each answer column defined using a window aggregate function, we compute the aggregate using the rows in the window.

In our example, each row of Temp is essentially a row of Sales, tagged with extra details (about the location and time dimensions). There is one partition for each state and every row of Temp belongs to exactly one partition. Consider a row for a store in Wisconsin. The row states the sales for a given product, in that store, at a certain time. The window for this row includes all rows that describe sales in Wisconsin within the previous or next month and *movavg* is the average of sales (over all products) in Wisconsin within this period.

We note that the ordering of rows within a partition for the purposes of window definition does not extend to the table of answer rows. The ordering of answer rows is nondeterministic, unless, of course, we fetch them through a cursor and use `ORDER BY` to order the cursor's output.

25.4.1 Framing a Window

There are two distinct ways to frame a window in SQL:1999. The example query illustrated the `RANGE` construct, which defines a window based on the values in some column (*month* in our example). The ordering column has to be a numeric type, a datetime type, or an interval type since these are the only types for which addition and subtraction are defined.

The second approach is based on using the ordering directly and specifying how many rows before and after the given row are in its window. Thus, we could say

```
SELECT L.state, T.month, AVG (S.sales) OVER W AS movavg
FROM   Sales S, Times T, Locations L
WHERE  S.timeid=T.timeid AND S.locid=L.locid
WINDOW W AS (PARTITION BY L.state
             ORDER BY T.month
             ROWS BETWEEN 1 PRECEDING AND 1 FOLLOWING)
```

If there is exactly one row in Temp for each month, this is equivalent to the previous query. However, if a given month has no rows or multiple rows, the two queries produce different results. In this case, the result of the second query is hard to understand because the windows for different rows do not align in a natural way.

The second approach is appropriate if, in terms of our example, there is exactly one row per month. Generalizing from this, it is also appropriate if there is exactly one row for every value in the sequence of ordering column values. Unlike the first approach, where the ordering has to be specified over a single (numeric, datetime, or interval type) column, the ordering can be based on a composite key.

We can also define windows that include all rows that are before a given row (`UNBOUNDED PRECEDING`) or all rows after a given row (`UNBOUNDED FOLLOWING`) within the row's partition.

25.4.2 New Aggregate Functions

While the standard aggregate functions that apply to multisets of values (e.g., `SUM, AVG`) can be used in conjunction with windowing, there is a need for a new class of functions that operate on a *list* of values.

The `RANK` function returns the position of a row within its partition. If a partition has 15 rows, the first row (according to the ordering of rows in the window definition over this partition) has rank 1 and the last row has rank 15. The rank of intermediate rows depends on whether there are multiple (or no) rows for a given value of the ordering column.

Consider our running example. If the first row in the Wisconsin partition has the month January 2002, and the second and third rows both have the month February 2002, then their ranks are 1, 2, and 2, respectively. If the next row has month March 2002 its rank is 4.

In contrast, the `DENSE RANK` function generates ranks without gaps. In our example, the four rows are given ranks 1, 2, 2, and 3. The only change is in the fourth row, whose rank is now 3 rather than 4.

The `PERCENT RANK` function gives a measure of the relative position of a row within a partition. It is defined as (`RANK`-1) divided by the number of rows in the partition. `CUME DIST` is similar but based on actual position within the ordered partition rather than rank.

25.5 FINDING ANSWERS QUICKLY

A recent trend, fueled in part by the popularity of the Internet, is an emphasis on queries for which a user wants only the first few, or the 'best' few, answers quickly. When users pose queries to a search engine such as AltaVista, they rarely look beyond the first or second page of results. If they do not find what they are looking for, they refine their query and resubmit it. The same phenomenon occurs in decision support applications and some DBMS products (e.g., DB2) already support extended SQL constructs to specify such queries. A related trend is that, for complex queries, users would like to see an approximate answer quickly and then have it be continually refined, rather than wait until the exact answer is available. We now discuss these two trends briefly.

25.5.1 Top N Queries

An analyst often wants to identify the top-selling handful of products, for example. We can sort by sales for each product and return answers in this order. If we have a million products and the analyst is interested only in the top 10, this straightforward evaluation strategy is clearly wasteful. It is desirable for users to be able to explicitly indicate how many answers they want, making it possible for the DBMS to optimize execution. The following example query asks for the top 10 products ordered by sales in a given location and time:

```
SELECT     P.pid, P.pname, S.sales
FROM       Sales S, Products P
WHERE      S.pid=P.pid AND S.locid=1 AND S.timeid=3
ORDER BY   S.sales DESC
OPTIMIZE FOR 10 ROWS
```

The `OPTIMIZE FOR` N `ROWS` construct is not in SQL-92 (or even SQL:1999), but it is supported in IBM's DB2 product, and other products (e.g., Oracle 9i) have similar constructs. In the absence of a cue such as `OPTIMIZE FOR 10 ROWS`, the DBMS computes sales for all products and returns them in descending order by sales. The application can close the result cursor (i.e., terminate the query execution) after consuming 10 rows, but considerable effort has already been expended in computing sales for all products and sorting them.

Now let us consider how a DBMS can use the `OPTIMIZE FOR` cue to execute the query efficiently. The key is to somehow compute sales only for products that are likely to be in the top 10 by sales. Suppose that we know the distribution of sales values because we maintain a histogram on the *sales* column of the Sales relation. We can then choose a value of *sales*, say, c, such that only 10 products have a larger sales value. For those Sales tuples that meet this condition, we can apply the location and time conditions as well and sort the result. Evaluating the following query is equivalent to this approach:

```
SELECT     P.pid, P.pname, S.sales
FROM       Sales S, Products P
WHERE      S.pid=P.pid AND S.locid=1 AND S.timeid=3 AND S.sales > c
ORDER BY   S.sales DESC
```

This approach is, of course, much faster than the alternative of computing all product sales and sorting them, but there are some important problems to resolve:

1. *How do we choose the sales cutoff value c?* Histograms and other system statistics can be used for this purpose, but this can be a tricky issue. For

one thing, the statistics maintained by a DBMS are only approximate. For another, even if we choose the cutoff to reflect the top 10 sales values accurately, other conditions in the query may eliminate some of the selected tuples, leaving us with fewer than 10 tuples in the result.

2. *What if we have more than 10 tuples in the result?* Since the choice of the cutoff c is approximate, we could get more than the desired number of tuples in the result. This is easily handled by returning just the top 10 to the user. We still save considerably with respect to the approach of computing sales for all products, thanks to the conservative pruning of irrelevant sales information, using the cutoff c.

3. *What if we have fewer than 10 tuples in the result?* Even if we choose the sales cutoff c conservatively, we could still compute fewer than 10 result tuples. In this case, we can re-execute the query with a smaller cutoff value c_2 or simply re-execute the original query with no cutoff.

The effectiveness of the approach depends on how well we can estimate the cutoff and, in particular, on minimizing the number of times we obtain fewer than the desired number of result tuples.

25.5.2 Online Aggregation

Consider the following query, which asks for the average sales amount by state:

```
SELECT    L.state, AVG (S.sales)
FROM      Sales S, Locations L
WHERE     S.locid=L.locid
GROUP BY  L.state
```

This can be an expensive query if Sales and Locations are large relations. We cannot achieve fast response times with the traditional approach of computing the anwer in its entirety when the query is presented. One alternative, as we have seen, is to use precomputation. Another alternative is to compute the answer to the query when the query is presented but return an approximate answer to the user as soon as possible. As the computation progresses, the answer quality is continually refined. This approach is called **online aggregation**. It is very attractive for queries involving aggregation, because efficient techniques for computing and refining approximate answers are available.

Online aggregation is illustrated in Figure 25.8: For each state—the grouping criterion for our example query—the current value for average sales is displayed, together with a confidence interval. The entry for Alaska tells us that the

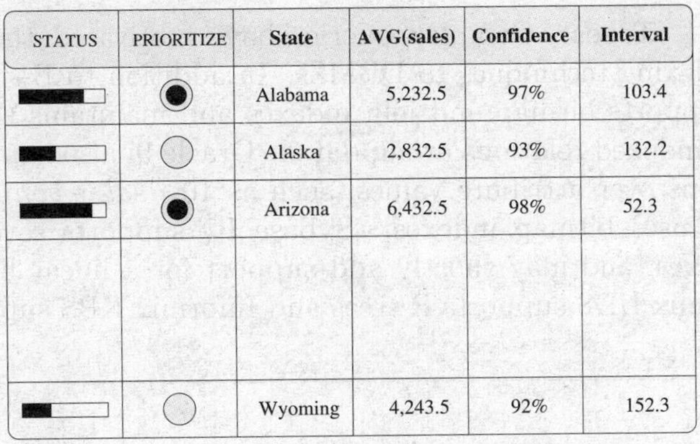
STATUS
PRIORITIZE
State
AVG(sales)
Confidence
Interval
Alabama
5,232.5
97%
103.4
Alaska
2,832.5
93%
132.2
Arizona
6,432.5
98%
52.3
Wyoming
4,243.5
92%
152.3

Figure 25.8 Online Aggregation

current estimate of average per-store sales in Alaska is $2,832.50, and that this is within the range $2,700.30 to $2,964.70 with 93% probability. The status bar in the first column indicates how close we are to arriving at an exact value for the average sales and the second column indicates whether calculating the average sales for this state is a priority. Estimating average sales for Alaska is not a priority, but estimating it for Arizona is a priority. As the figure indicates, the DBMS devotes more system resources to estimating the average sales for high-priority states; the estimate for Arizona is much tighter than that for Alaska and holds with a higher probability. Users can set the priority for a state by clicking on the Prioritize button at any time during the execution. This degree of interactivity, together with the continuous feedback provided by the visual display, makes online aggregation an attractive technique.

To implement online aggregation, a DBMS must incorporate statistical techniques to provide confidence intervals for approximate answers and use **non-blocking algorithms** for the relational operators. An algorithm is said to block if it does not produce output tuples until it has consumed all its input tuples. For example, the sort-merge join algorithm blocks because sorting requires all input tuples before determining the first output tuple. Nested loops join and hash join are therefore preferable to sort-merge join for online aggregation. Similarly, hash-based aggregation is better than sort-based aggregation.

25.6 IMPLEMENTATION TECHNIQUES FOR OLAP

In this section we survey some implementation techniques motivated by the OLAP environment. The goal is to provide a feel for how OLAP systems differ from more traditional SQL systems; our discussion is far from comprehensive.

Beyond B+ Trees: Complex queries have motivated the addition of powerful indexing techniques to DBMSs. In addition to B+ tree indexes, Oracle 9i supports bitmap and join indexes and maintains these dynamically as the indexed relations are updated. Oracle 9i also supports indexes on expressions over attribute values, such as $10 * sal + bonus$. Microsoft SQL Server uses bitmap indexes. Sybase IQ supports several kinds of bitmap indexes, and may shortly add support for a linear hashing based index. Informix UDS supports R trees and Informix XPS supports bitmap indexes.

The mostly-read environment of OLAP systems makes the CPU overhead of maintaining indexes negligible and the requirement of interactive response times for queries over very large datasets makes the availability of suitable indexes very important. This combination of factors has led to the development of new indexing techniques. We discuss several of these techniques. We then consider file organizations and other OLAP implementation issues briefly.

We note that the emphasis on query processing and decision support applications in OLAP systems is being complemented by a greater emphasis on evaluating complex SQL queries in traditional SQL systems. Traditional SQL systems are evolving to support OLAP-style queries more efficiently, supporting constructs (e.g., `CUBE` and window functions) and incorporating implementation techniques previously found only in specialized OLAP systems.

25.6.1 Bitmap Indexes

Consider a table that describes customers:

Customers(*custid:* `integer`, *name:* `string`, *gender:* `boolean`, *rating:* `integer`)

The *rating* value is an integer in the range 1 to 5, and only two values are recorded for *gender*. Columns with few possible values are called **sparse**. We can exploit sparsity to construct a new kind of index that greatly speeds up queries on these columns.

The idea is to record values for sparse columns as a sequence of bits, one for each possible value. For example, a *gender* value is either 10 or 01; a 1 in the first position denotes male, and 1 in the second position denotes female. Similarly, 10000 denotes the *rating* value 1, and 00001 denotes the *rating* value 5.

If we consider the *gender* values for all rows in the Customers table, we can treat this as a collection of two **bit vectors**, one of which has the associated value M(ale) and the other the associated value F(emale). Each bit vector has one bit per row in the Customers table, indicating whether the value in that row is the value associated with the bit vector. The collection of bit vectors for a column is called a **bitmap index** for that column.

An example instance of the Customers table, together with the bitmap indexes for *gender* and *rating*, is shown in Figure 25.9.

M	*F*
1	0
1	0
0	1
1	0

custid	*name*	*gender*	*rating*
112	Joe	M	3
115	Ram	M	5
119	Sue	F	5
112	Woo	M	4

1	*2*	*3*	*4*	*5*
0	0	1	0	0
0	0	0	0	1
0	0	0	0	1
0	0	0	1	0

Figure 25.9 Bitmap Indexes on the Customers Relation

Bitmap indexes offer two important advantages over conventional hash and tree indexes. First, they allow the use of efficient bit operations to answer queries. For example, consider the query, "How many male customers have a rating of 5?" We can take the first bit vector for *gender* and do a bitwise `AND` with the fifth bit vector for *rating* to obtain a bit vector that has 1 for every male customer with rating 5. We can then count the number of 1s in this bit vector to answer the query. Second, bitmap indexes can be much more compact than a traditional B+ tree index and are very amenable to the use of compression techniques.

Bit vectors correspond closely to the rid-lists used to represent data entries in Alternative (3) for a traditional B+ tree index (see Section 8.2). In fact, we can think of a bit vector for a given *age* value, say, as an alternative representation of the rid-list for that value.

This suggests a way to combine bit vectors (and their advantages of bitwise processing) with B+ tree indexes: We can use Alternative (3) for data entries, using a bit vector representation of rid-lists. A caveat is that, if an rid-list is very small, the bit vector representation may be much larger than a list of rid values, even if the bit vector is compressed. Further, the use of compression leads to decompression costs, offsetting some of the computational advantages of the bit vector representation.

A more flexible approach is to use a standard list representation of the rid-list for some key values (intuitively, those that contain few elements) and a bit vector representation for other key values (those that contain many elements, and therefore lend themselves to a compact bit vector representation).

This hybrid approach, which can easily be adapted to work with hash indexes as well as B+ tree indexes, has both advantages and disadvantages relative to a standard list of rids approach:

1. It can be applied even to columns that are not sparse; that is, in which are many possible values can appear. The index levels (or the hashing scheme) allow us to quickly find the 'list' of rids, in a standard list or bit vector representation, for a given key value.
2. Overall, the index is more compact because we can use a bit vector representation for long rid lists. We also have the benefits of fast bit vector processing.
3. On the other hand, the bit vector representation of an rid list relies on a mapping from a position in the vector to an rid. (This is true of any bit vector representation, not just the hybrid approach.) If the set of rows is static, and we do not worry about inserts and deletes of rows, it is straightforward to ensure this by assigning contiguous rids for rows in a table. If inserts and deletes must be supported, additional steps are required. For example, we can continue to assign rids contiguously on a per-table basis and simply keep track of which rids correspond to deleted rows. Bit vectors can now be longer than the current number of rows, and periodic reorganization is required to compact the 'holes' in the assignment of rids.

25.6.2 Join Indexes

Computing joins with small response times is extremely hard for very large relations. One approach to this problem is to create an index designed to speed up specific join queries. Suppose that the Customers table is to be joined with a table called Purchases (recording purchases made by customers) on the *custid* field. We can create a collection of $\langle c, p \rangle$ pairs, where p is the rid of a Purchases record that joins with a Customers record with *custid* c.

This idea can be generalized to support joins over more than two relations. We discuss the special case of a star schema, in which the fact table is likely to be joined with several dimension tables. Consider a join query that joins fact table F with dimension tables D1 and D2 and includes selection conditions on column C_1 of table D1 and column C_2 of table D2. We store a tuple $\langle r_1, r_2, r \rangle$ in the join index if r_1 is the rid of a tuple in table D1 with value c_1 in column C_1, r_2 is the rid of a tuple in table D2 with value c_2 in column C_2, and r is the rid of a tuple in the fact table F, and these three tuples join with each other.

> **Complex Queries:** The IBM DB2 optimizer recognizes star join queries and performs rid-based semijoins (using Bloom filters) to filter the fact table. Then fact table rows are rejoined to the dimension tables. Complex (multitable) dimension queries (called *snowflake queries*) are supported. DB2 also supports `CUBE` using smart algorithms that minimize sorts. Microsoft SQL Server optimizes star join queries extensively. It considers taking the cross-product of small dimension tables before joining with the fact table, the use of join indexes, and rid-based semijoins. Oracle 9i also allows users to create dimensions to declare hierarchies and functional dependencies. It supports the `CUBE` operator and optimizes star join queries by eliminating joins when no column of a dimension table is part of the query result. DBMS products have also been developed specifically for decision support applications, such as Sybase IQ.

The drawback of a join index is that the number of indexes can grow rapidly if several columns in each dimension table are involved in selections and joins with the fact table. An alternative kind of join index avoids this problem. Consider our example involving fact table F and dimension tables D1 and D2. Let C_1 be a column of D1 on which a selection is expressed in some query that joins D1 with F. Conceptually, we now join F with D1 to extend the fields of F with the fields of D1, and index F on the 'virtual field' C_1: If a tuple of D1 with value c_1 in column C_1 joins with a tuple of F with rid r, we add a tuple $\langle c_1, r \rangle$ to the join index. We create one such join index for each column of either D1 or D2 that involves a selection in some join with F; C_1 is an example of such a column.

The price paid with respect to the previous version of join indexes is that join indexes created in this way have to be combined (rid intersection) to deal with the join queries of interest to us. This can be done efficiently if we make the new indexes *bitmap* indexes; the result is called a **bitmapped join index**. The idea works especially well if columns such as C_1 are sparse, and therefore well suited to bitmap indexing.

25.6.3 File Organizations

Since many OLAP queries involve just a few columns of a large relation, vertical partitioning becomes attractive. However, storing a relation column-wise can degrade performance for queries that involve several columns. An alternative in a mostly-read environment is to store the relation row-wise, but also store each column separately.

A more radical file organization is to regard the fact table as a large multidimensional array and store it and index it as such. This approach is taken in MOLAP systems. Since the array is much larger than available main memory, it is broken up into contiguous chunks, as discussed in Section 23.8. In addition, traditional B+ tree indexes are created to enable quick retrieval of chunks that contain tuples with values in a given range for one or more dimensions.

25.7 DATA WAREHOUSING

Data warehouses contain consolidated data from many sources, augmented with summary information and covering a long time period. Warehouses are much larger than other kinds of databases; sizes ranging from several gigabytes to terabytes are common. Typical workloads involve ad hoc, fairly complex queries and fast response times are important. These characteristics differentiate warehouse applications from OLTP applications, and different DBMS design and implementation techniques must be used to achieve satisfactory results. A distributed DBMS with good scalability and high availability (achieved by storing tables redundantly at more than one site) is required for very large warehouses.

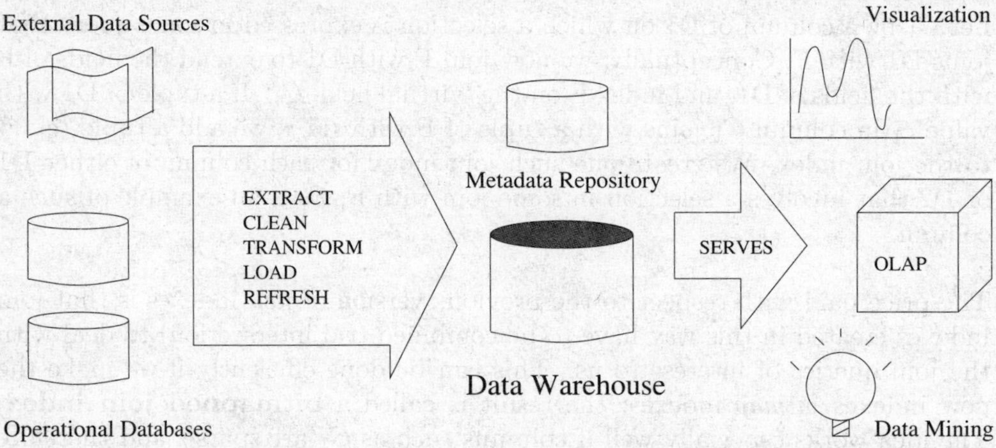

Figure 25.10 A Typical Data Warehousing Architecture

A typical data warehousing architecture is illustrated in Figure 25.10. An organization's daily operations access and modify **operational databases**. Data from these operational databases and other external sources (e.g., customer profiles supplied by external consultants) are **extracted** by using interfaces such as JDBC (see Section 6.2).

25.7.1 Creating and Maintaining a Warehouse

Many challenges must be met in creating and maintaining a large data warehouse. A good database schema must be designed to hold an integrated collection of data copied from diverse sources. For example, a company warehouse might include the inventory and personnel departments' databases, together with sales databases maintained by offices in different countries. Since the source databases are often created and maintained by different groups, there are a number of semantic mismatches across these databases, such as different currency units, different names for the same attribute, and differences in how tables are normalized or structured; these differences must be reconciled when data is brought into the warehouse. After the warehouse schema is designed, the warehouse must be populated, and over time, it must be kept consistent with the source databases.

Data is **extracted** from operational databases and external sources, **cleaned** to minimize errors and fill in missing information when possible, and **transformed** to reconcile semantic mismatches. Transforming data is typically accomplished by defining a relational view over the tables in the data sources (the operational databases and other external sources). **Loading** data consists of materializing such views and storing them in the warehouse. Unlike a standard view in a relational DBMS, therefore, the view is stored in a database (the warehouse) that is different from the database(s) containing the tables it is defined over.

The cleaned and transformed data is finally **loaded** into the warehouse. Additional preprocessing such as sorting and generation of summary information is carried out at this stage. Data is partitioned and indexes are built for efficiency. Due to the large volume of data, loading is a slow process. Loading a terabyte of data sequentially can take weeks, and loading even a gigabyte can take hours. Parallelism is therefore important for loading warehouses.

After data is loaded into a warehouse, additional measures must be taken to ensure that the data in the warehouse is periodically **refreshed** to reflect updates to the data sources and periodically **purge** old data (perhaps onto archival media). Observe the connection between the problem of refreshing warehouse tables and asynchronously maintaining replicas of tables in a distributed DBMS. Maintaining replicas of source relations is an essential part of warehousing, and this application domain is an important factor in the popularity of asynchronous replication (Section 22.11.2), even though asynchronous replication violates the principle of distributed data independence. The problem of refreshing warehouse tables (which are materialized views over tables in the source databases) has also renewed interest in incremental maintenance of materialized views. (We discuss materialized views in Section 25.8.)

An important task in maintaining a warehouse is keeping track of the data currently stored in it; this bookkeeping is done by storing information about the warehouse data in the system catalogs. The system catalogs associated with a warehouse are very large and often stored and managed in a separate database called a **metadata repository**. The size and complexity of the catalogs is in part due to the size and complexity of the warehouse itself and in part because a lot of administrative information must be maintained. For example, we must keep track of the source of each warehouse table and when it was last refreshed, in addition to describing its fields.

The value of a warehouse is ultimately in the analysis it enables. The data in a warehouse is typically accessed and analyzed using a variety of tools, including OLAP query engines, data mining algorithms, information visualization tools, statistical packages, and report generators.

25.8 VIEWS AND DECISION SUPPORT

Views are widely used in decision support applications. Different groups of analysts within an organization are typically concerned with different aspects of the business, and it is convenient to define views that give each group insight into the business details that concern it. Once a view is defined, we can write queries or new view definitions that use it, as we saw in Section 3.6; in this respect a view is just like a base table. Evaluating queries posed against views is very important for decision support applications. In this section, we consider how such queries can be evaluated efficiently after placing views within the context of decision support applications.

25.8.1 Views, OLAP, and Warehousing

Views are closely related to OLAP and data warehousing.

OLAP queries are typically aggregate queries. Analysts want fast answers to these queries over very large datasets, and it is natural to consider precomputing views (see Sections 25.9 and 25.10). In particular, the `CUBE` operator—discussed in Section 25.3—gives rise to several aggregate queries that are closely related. The relationships that exist between the many aggregate queries that arise from a single `CUBE` operation can be exploited to develop very effective precomputation strategies. The idea is to choose a subset of the aggregate queries for materialization in such a way that typical `CUBE` queries can be quickly answered by using the materialized views and doing some additional computation. The choice of views to materialize is influenced by how many queries they can potentially speed up and by the amount of space required to store the materialized view (since we have to work with a given amount of storage space).

A data warehouse is just a collection of asynchronously replicated tables and periodically synchronized views. A warehouse is characterized by its size, the number of tables involved, and the fact that most of the underlying tables are from external, independently maintained databases. Nonetheless, the fundamental problem in warehouse maintenance is asynchronous maintenance of replicated tables and materialized views (see Section 25.10).

25.8.2 Queries over Views

Consider the following view, RegionalSales, which computes sales of products by category and state:

```
CREATE VIEW RegionalSales (category, sales, state)
        AS SELECT P.category, S.sales, L.state
           FROM   Products P, Sales S, Locations L
           WHERE  P.pid = S.pid AND S.locid = L.locid
```

The following query computes the total sales for each category by state:

```
SELECT    R.category, R.state, SUM (R.sales)
FROM      RegionalSales R
GROUP BY  R.category, R.state
```

While the SQL standard does not specify how to evaluate queries on views, it is useful to think in terms of a process called **query modification**. The idea is to replace the occurrence of RegionalSales in the query by the view definition. The result on this query is

```
SELECT    R.category, R.state, SUM (R.sales)
FROM      ( SELECT P.category, S.sales, L.state
            FROM   Products P, Sales S, Locations L
            WHERE  P.pid = S.pid AND S.locid = L.locid ) AS R
GROUP BY  R.category, R.state
```

25.9 VIEW MATERIALIZATION

We can answer a query on a view by using the query modification technique just described. Often, however, queries against complex view definitions must be answered very fast because users engaged in decision support activities require interactive response times. Even with sophisticated optimization and evaluation techniques, there is a limit to how fast we can answer such queries. Also, if the underlying tables are in a remote database, the query modification approach may not even be feasible because of issues like connectivity and availability.

An alternative to query modification is to precompute the view definition and store the result. When a query is posed on the view, the (unmodified) query is executed directly on the precomputed result. This approach, called **view materialization**, is likely to be much faster than the query modification approach because the complex view need not be evaluated when the query is computed. Materialized views can be used during query processing in the same way as regular relations; for example, we can create indexes on materialized views to further speed up query processing. The drawback, of course, is that we must maintain the consistency of the precomputed (or *materialized*) view whenever the underlying tables are updated.

25.9.1 Issues in View Materialization

Three questions must be considered with regard to view materialization:

1. What views should we materialize and what indexes should we build on the materialized views?
2. Given a query on a view and a set of materialized views, can we exploit the materialized views to answer the query?
3. How should we synchronize materialized views with changes to the underlying tables? The choice of synchronization technique depends on several factors, such as whether the underlying tables are in a remote database. We discuss this issue in Section 25.10.

The answers to the first two questions are related. The choice of views to materialize and index is governed by the expected workload, and the discussion of indexing in Chapter 20 is relevant to this question as well. The choice of views to materialize is more complex than just choosing indexes on a set of database tables, however, because the range of alternative views to materialize is wider. The goal is to materialize a small, carefully chosen set of views that can be utilized to quickly answer most of the important queries. Conversely, once we have chosen a set of views to materialize, we have to consider how they can be used to answer a given query.

Consider the RegionalSales view. It involves a join of Sales, Products, and Locations and is likely to be expensive to compute. On the other hand, if it is materialized and stored with a clustered B+ tree index on the search key ⟨category, state, sales⟩, we can answer the example query by an index-only scan.

Given the materialized view and this index, we can also answer queries of the following form efficiently:

```
SELECT    R.state, SUM (R.sales)
FROM      RegionalSales R
WHERE     R.category = 'Laptop'
GROUP BY  R.state
```

To answer such a query, we can use the index on the materialized view to locate the first index leaf entry with *category* = 'Laptop' and then scan the leaf level until we come to the first entry with *category* not equal to Laptop.

The given index is less effective on the following query, for which we are forced to scan the entire leaf level:

```
SELECT    R.state, SUM (R.sales)
FROM      RegionalSales R
WHERE     R.state = 'Wisconsin'
GROUP BY  R.category
```

This example indicates how the choice of views to materialize and the indexes to create are affected by the expected workload. This point is illustrated further by our next example.

Consider the following two queries:

```
SELECT    P.category, SUM (S.sales)
FROM      Products P, Sales S
WHERE     P.pid = S.pid
GROUP BY  P.category

SELECT    L.state, SUM (S.sales)
FROM      Locations L, Sales S
WHERE     L.locid = S.locid
GROUP BY  L.state
```

These two queries require us to join the Sales table (which is likely to be very large) with another table and aggregate the result. How can we use materialization to speed up these queries? The straightforward approach is to precompute each of the joins involved (Products with Sales and Locations with Sales) or to precompute each query in its entirety. An alternative approach is to define the following view:

```
CREATE  VIEW TotalSales (pid, locid, total)
        AS SELECT  S.pid, S.locid, SUM (S.sales)
           FROM    Sales S
           GROUP BY S.pid, S.locid
```

The view TotalSales can be materialized and used instead of Sales in our two example queries:

```
SELECT    P.category, SUM (T.total)
FROM      Products P, TotalSales T
WHERE     P.pid = T.pid
GROUP BY  P.category
```

```
SELECT    L.state, SUM (T.total)
FROM      Locations L, TotalSales T
WHERE     L.locid = T.locid
GROUP BY  L.state
```

25.10 MAINTAINING MATERIALIZED VIEWS

A materialized view is said to be **refreshed** when we make it consistent with changes to its underlying tables. The process of refreshing a view to keep it consistent with changes to the underlying table is often referred to as **view maintenance**. Two questions to consider are

1. *How* do we refresh a view when an underlying table is modified? Two issues of particular interest are how to maintain views *incrementally*, that is, without recomputing from scratch when there is a change to an underlying table; and how to maintain views in a distributed environment such as a data warehouse.

2. *When* should we refresh a view in response to a change to an underlying table?

25.10.1 Incremental View Maintenance

A straightforward approach to refreshing a view is to simply recompute the view when an underlying table is modified. This may, in fact, be a reasonable strategy in some cases. For example, if the underlying tables are in a remote database, the view can be periodically recomputed and sent to the data warehouse where the view is materialized. This has the advantage that the underlying tables need not be replicated at the warehouse.

Whenever possible, however, algorithms for refreshing a view should be **incremental**, in that the cost is proportional to the extent of the change rather than the cost of recomputing the view from scratch.

To understand the intuition behind incremental view maintenance algorithms, observe that a given row in the materialized view can appear several times, depending on how often it was derived. (Recall that duplicates are not eliminated from the result of an SQL query unless the `DISTINCT` clause is used. In this section, we discuss multiset semantics, even when relational algebra notation is used.) The main idea behind incremental maintenance algorithms is to efficiently compute changes to the rows of the view, either new rows or changes to the count associated with a row; if the count of a row becomes 0, the row is deleted from the view.

We present an incremental maintenance algorithm for views defined using projection, binary join, and aggregation; we cover these operations because they illustrate the main ideas. The approach can be extended to other operations such as selection, union, intersection, and (multiset) difference, as well as expressions containing several operators. The key idea is still to maintain the number of derivations for each view row, but the details of how to efficiently compute the changes in view rows and associated counts differ.

Projection Views

Consider a view V defined in terms of a projection on a table R; that is, $V = \pi(R)$. Every row v in V has an associated count, corresponding to the number of times it can be derived, which is the number of rows in R that yield v when the projection is applied. Suppose we modify R by inserting a collection of rows R_i and deleting a collection of existing rows R_d.[1] We compute $\pi(R_i)$ and add it to V. If the multiset $\pi(R_i)$ contains a row r with count c and r does not appear in V, we add it to V with count c. If r is in V, we add c to its count. We also compute $\pi(R_d)$ and subtract it from V. Observe that if r appears in $\pi(R_d)$ with count c, it must also appear in V with a higher count;[2] we subtract c from r's count in V.

---

[1]These collections can be multisets of rows. We can treat a row modification as an insert followed by a delete, for simplicity.

[2]As a simple exercise, consider why this must be so.

As an example, consider the view $\pi_{sales}(Sales)$ and the instance of Sales shown in Figure 25.2. Each row in the view has a single column; the (row with) value 25 appears with count 1, and the value 10 appears with count 3. If we delete one of the rows in Sales with *sales* 10, the count of the (row with) value 10 in the view becomes 2. If we insert a new row into Sales with *sales* 99, the view now has a row with value 99.

An important point is that we have to maintain the counts associated with rows even if the view definition uses the `DISTINCT` clause, meaning that duplicates are eliminated from the view. Consider the same view with set semantics—the `DISTINCT` clause is used in the SQL view definition—and suppose that we delete one of the rows in Sales with *sales* 10. Does the view now contain a row with value 10? To determine that the answer is yes, we need to maintain the row counts, even though each row (with a nonzero count) is displayed only once in the materialized view.

Join Views

Next, consider a view V defined as a join of two tables, $R \bowtie S$. Suppose we modify R by inserting a collection of rows R_i and deleting a collection of rows R_d. We compute $R_i \bowtie S$ and add the result to V. We also compute $R_d \bowtie S$ and subtract the result from V. Observe that if r appears in $R_d \bowtie S$ with count c, it must also appear in V with a higher count.[3]

Views with Aggregation

Consider a view V defined over R using `GROUP BY` on column G and an aggregate operation on column A. Each row v in the view summarizes a group of tuples in R and is of the form $\langle g, \mathit{summary}\rangle$, where g is the value of the grouping column G and the summary information depends on the aggregate operation. To maintain such a view incrementally, in general, we have to keep a more detailed summary than just the information included in the view. If the aggregate operation is `COUNT`, we need to maintain only a count c for each row v in the view. If a row r is inserted into R, and there is no row v in V with $v.G = r.G$, we add a new row $\langle r.G, 1\rangle$. If there is a row v with $v.G = r.G$, we increment its count. If a row r is deleted from R, we decrement the count for the row v with $v.G = r.G$; v can be deleted if its count becomes 0, because then the last row in this group has been deleted from R.

If the aggregate operation is `SUM`, we have to maintain a sum s and also a count c. If a row r is inserted into R and there is no row v in V with $v.G = r.G$,

[3]As another simple exercise, consider why this must be so.

we add a new row $\langle r.G, a, 1\rangle$. If there is a row $\langle r.G, s, c\rangle$, we replace it by $\langle r.G, s+a, c+1\rangle$. If a row r is deleted from R, we replace the row $\langle r.G, s, c\rangle$ with $\langle r.G, s-a, c-1\rangle$; v can be deleted if its count becomes 0. Observe that without the count, we do not know when to delete v, since the sum for a group could be 0 even if the group contains some rows.

If the aggregate operation is `AVG`, we have to maintain a sum s, a count c, and the average for each row in the view. The sum and count are maintained incrementally as already described, and the average is computed as s/c.

The aggregate operations `MIN` and `MAX` are potentially expensive to maintain. Consider `MIN`. For each group in R, we maintain $\langle g, m, c\rangle$, where m is the minimum value for column A in the group g, and c is the count of the number of rows r in R with $r.G = g$ and $r.A = m$. If a row r is inserted into R and $r.G = g$, if $r.A$ is greater than the minimum m for group g, we can ignore r. If $r.A$ is equal to the minimum m for r's group, we replace the summary row for the group with $\langle g, m, c+1\rangle$. If $r.A$ is less than the minimum m for r's group, we replace the summary for the group with $\langle g, r.A, 1\rangle$. If a row r is deleted from R and $r.A$ is equal to the minimum m for r's group, then we must decrement the count for the group. If the count is greater than 0, we simply replace the summary for the group with $\langle g, m, c-1\rangle$. However, if the count becomes 0, this means the last row with the recorded minimum A value has been deleted from R and we have to retrieve the smallest A value among the remaining rows in R with group value $r.G$—and this might require retrieval of all rows in R with group value $r.G$.

25.10.2 Maintaining Warehouse Views

The views materialized in a data warehouse can be based on source tables in remote databases. The asynchronous replication techniques discussed in Section 22.11.2 allow us to communicate changes at the source to the warehouse, but refreshing views incrementally in a distributed setting presents some unique challenges. To illustrate this, we consider a simple view that identifies suppliers of Toys.

```
CREATE VIEW ToySuppliers (sid)
    AS SELECT S.sid
       FROM   Suppliers S, Products P
       WHERE  S.pid = P.pid AND P.category = 'Toys'
```

Suppliers is a new table introduced for this example; let us assume that it has just two fields, *sid* and *pid*, indicating that supplier *sid* supplies part *pid*. The location of the tables Products and Suppliers and the view ToySuppliers influences how we maintain the view. Suppose that all three are maintained at a single site. We can maintain the view incrementally using the techniques discussed in Section 25.10.1. If a replica of the view is created at another site, we can monitor changes to the materialized view and apply them at the second site using the asynchronous replication techniques from Section 22.11.2.

But, what if Products and Suppliers are at one site and the view is materialized (only) at a second site? To motivate this scenario, we observe that, if the first site is used for operational data and the second site supports complex analysis, the two sites may well be administered by different groups. The option of materializing ToySuppliers (a view of interest to the second group) at the first site (run by a different group) is not attractive and may not even be possible; the administrators of the first site may not want to deal with someone else's views, and the administrators of the second site may not want to coordinate with someone else whenever they modify view definitions. As another motivation for materializing views at a different location from source tables, observe that Products and Suppliers may be at two different sites. Even if we materialize ToySuppliers at one of these sites, one of the two source tables is remote.

Now that we have presented motivation for maintaining ToySuppliers at a location (say, Warehouse) different from the one (say, Source) that contains Products and Suppliers, let us consider the difficulties posed by data distribution. Suppose that a new Products record (with *category* = 'Toys') is inserted. We could try to maintain the view incrementally as follows:

1. The Warehouse site sends this update to the Source site.
2. To refresh the view, we need to check the Suppliers table to find suppliers of the item, and so the Warehouse site asks the Source site for this information.
3. The Source site returns the set of suppliers for the sold item, and the Warehouse site incrementally refreshes the view.

This works when there are no additional changes at the Source site in between steps (1) and (3). If there are changes, however, the materialized view can become incorrect—reflecting a state that can never arise except for anomalies introduced by the preceding, naive, incremental refresh algorithm. To see this, suppose that Products is empty and Suppliers contains just the row $\langle s1, 5\rangle$ initially, and consider the following sequence of events:

1. Product *pid* = 5 is inserted with *category* = 'Toys'; Source notifies Warehouse.
2. Warehouse asks Source for suppliers of product *pid* = 5. *(The only such supplier at this instant is s1.)*

3. The row $\langle s2, 5\rangle$ is inserted into Suppliers; Source notifies Warehouse.

4. To decide whether $s2$ should be added to the view, we need to know the category of product $pid = 5$, and Warehouse asks Source. *(Warehouse has not received an answer to its previous question.)*

5. Source now processes the first query from Warehouse, finds two suppliers for part 5, and returns this information to Warehouse.

6. Warehouse gets the answer to its first question: suppliers $s1$ and $s2$, and adds these to the view, each with count 1.

7. Source processes the second query from Warehouse and responds with the information that part 5 is a toy.

8. Warehouse gets the answer to its second question and accordingly increments the count for supplier $s2$ in the view.

9. Product $pid = 5$ is now deleted; Source notifies Warehouse.

10. Since the deleted part is a toy, Warehouse decrements the counts of matching view tuples; $s1$ has count 0 and is removed, but $s2$ has count 1 and is retained.

Clearly, $s2$ should not remain in the view after part 5 is deleted. This example illustrates the added subtleties of incremental view maintenance in a distributed environment, and this is a topic of ongoing research.

25.10.3 When Should We Synchronize Views?

A **view maintenance policy** is a decision about when a view is refreshed, independent of whether the refresh is incremental or not. A view can be refreshed within the same transaction that updates the underlying tables. This is called **immediate view maintenance**. The update transaction is slowed by the refresh step, and the impact of refresh increases with the number of materialized views that depend on the updated table.

Alternatively, we can defer refreshing the view. Updates are captured in a log and applied subsequently to the materialized views. There are several **deferred view maintenance policies**:

1. **Lazy:** The materialized view V is refreshed at the time a query is evaluated using V, if V is not already consistent with its underlying base tables. This approach slows down queries rather than updates, in contrast to immediate view maintenance.

Views for Decision Support: DBMS vendors are enhancing their main relational products to support decision support queries. IBM DB2 supports materialized views with transaction-consistent or user-invoked maintenance. Microsoft SQL Server supports **partition views**, which are unions of (many) horizontal partitions of a table. These are aimed at a warehousing environment where each partition could be, for example, a monthly update. Queries on partition views are optimized so that only relevant partitions are accessed. Oracle 9i supports materialized views with transaction-consistent, user-invoked, or time-scheduled maintenance.

2. **Periodic:** The materialized view is refreshed periodically, say, once a day. The discussion of the Capture and Apply steps in asynchronous replication (see Section 22.11.2) should be reviewed at this point, since it is very relevant to periodic view maintenance. In fact, many vendors are extending their asynchronous replication features to support materialized views. Materialized views that are refreshed periodically are also called **snapshots**.
3. **Forced:** The materialized view is refreshed after a certain number of changes have been made to the underlying tables.

In periodic and forced view maintenance, queries may see an instance of the materialized view that is not consistent with the current state of the underlying tables. That is, the queries would see a different set of rows if the view definition was recomputed. This is the price paid for fast updates and queries, and the trade-off is similar to the trade-off made in using asynchronous replication.

25.11 REVIEW QUESTIONS

Answers to the review questions can be found in the listed sections.

- What are *decision support* applications? Discuss the relationship of *complex SQL queries*, *OLAP*, *data mining*, and *data warehousing*. **(Section 25.1)**
- Describe the multidimensional data model. Explain the distinction between *measures* and *dimensions* and between *fact tables* and *dimension tables*. What is a *star schema*? **(Sections 25.2 and 25.2.1)**
- Common OLAP operations have received special names: *roll-up, drill-down, pivoting, slicing,* and *dicing*. Describe each of these operations and illustrate them using examples. **(Section 25.3)**
- Describe the SQL:1999 `ROLLUP` and `CUBE` features and their relationship to the OLAP operations. **(Section 25.3.1)**

- Describe the SQL:1999 `WINDOW` feature, in particular, framing and ordering of windows. How does it support queries over ordered data? Give examples of queries that are hard to express without this feature. **(Section 25.4)**

- New query paradigms include *top N queries* and *online aggregation*. Explain the motivation behind these concepts and illustrate them through examples. **(Section 25.5)**

- Index structures that are especially suitable for OLAP systems include *bitmap indexes* and *join indexes*. Describe these structures. How are bitmap indexes related to B+ trees? **(Section 25.6)**

- Information about daily operations of an organization is stored in *operational databases*. Why is a *data warehouse* used to store data from operational databases? What issues arise in data warehousing? Discuss *data extraction*, *cleaning*, *transformation*, and *loading*. Discuss the challenges in efficiently *refreshing* and *purging* data. **(Section 25.7)**

- Why are views important in decision support environments? How are views related to data warehousing and OLAP? Explain the *query modification* technique for answering queries over views and discuss why this is not adequate in decision support environments. **(Section 25.8)**

- What are the main issues to consider in maintaining materialized views? Discuss how to select views to materialize and how to use materialized views to answer a query. **(Section 25.9)**

- How can views be maintained *incrementally*? Discuss all the relational algebra operators and aggregation. **(Section 25.10.1)**

- Use an example to illustrate the added complications for incremental view maintenance introduced by data distribution. **(Section 25.10.2)**

- Discuss the choice of an appropriate *maintenance policy* for when to refresh a view. **(Section 25.10.3)**

EXERCISES

Exercise 25.1 Briefly answer the following questions:

1. How do warehousing, OLAP, and data mining complement each other?
2. What is the relationship between data warehousing and data replication? Which form of replication (synchronous or asynchronous) is better suited for data warehousing? Why?
3. What is the role of the metadata repository in a data warehouse? How does it differ from a catalog in a relational DBMS?
4. What considerations are involved in designing a data warehouse?

5. Once a warehouse is designed and loaded, how is it kept current with respect to changes to the source databases?
6. One of the advantages of a warehouse is that we can use it to track how the contents of a relation change over time; in contrast, we have only the current snapshot of a relation in a regular DBMS. Discuss how you would maintain the history of a relation *R*, taking into account that 'old' information must somehow be purged to make space for new information.
7. Describe dimensions and measures in the multidimensional data model.
8. What is a fact table, and why is it so important from a performance standpoint?
9. What is the fundamental difference between MOLAP and ROLAP systems?
10. What is a star schema? Is it typically in BCNF? Why or why not?
11. How is data mining different from OLAP?

Exercise 25.2 Consider the instance of the Sales relation shown in Figure 25.2.

1. Show the result of pivoting the relation on *pid* and *timeid.*
2. Write a collection of SQL queries to obtain the same result as in the previous part.
3. Show the result of pivoting the relation on *pid* and *locid.*

Exercise 25.3 Consider the cross-tabulation of the Sales relation shown in Figure 25.5.

1. Show the result of roll-up on *locid* (i.e., state).
2. Write a collection of SQL queries to obtain the same result as in the previous part.
3. Show the result of roll-up on *locid* followed by drill-down on *pid.*
4. Write a collection of SQL queries to obtain the same result as in the previous part, starting with the cross-tabulation shown in Figure 25.5.

Exercise 25.4 Briefly answer the following questions:

1. What is the differences between the `WINDOW` clause and the `GROUP BY` clause?
2. Give an example query that cannot be expressed in SQL without the `WINDOW` clause but that can be expressed with the `WINDOW` clause.
3. What is the *frame* of a window in SQL:1999?
4. Consider the following simple `GROUP BY` query.

```
SELECT    T.year, SUM (S.sales)
FROM      Sales S, Times T
WHERE     S.timeid=T.timeid
GROUP BY  T.year
```

Can you write this query in SQL:1999 without using a `GROUP BY` clause? (Hint: Use the SQL:1999 `WINDOW` clause.)

Exercise 25.5 Consider the Locations, Products, and Sales relations shown in Figure 25.2. Write the following queries in SQL:1999 using the `WINDOW` clause whenever you need it.

1. Find the percentage change in the total monthly sales for each location.
2. Find the percentage change in the total quarterly sales for each product.

3. Find the average daily sales over the preceding 30 days for each product.
4. For each week, find the maximum moving average of sales over the preceding four weeks.
5. Find the top three locations ranked by total sales.
6. Find the top three locations ranked by cumulative sales, for every month over the past year.
7. Rank all locations by total sales over the past year, and for each location print the difference in total sales relative to the location behind it.

Exercise 25.6 Consider the Customers relation and the bitmap indexes shown in Figure 25.9.

1. For the same data, if the underlying set of rating values is assumed to range from 1 to 10, show how the bitmap indexes would change.
2. How would you use the bitmap indexes to answer the following queries? If the bitmap indexes are not useful, explain why.
   (a) How many customers with a rating less than 3 are male?
   (b) What percentage of customers are male?
   (c) How many customers are there?
   (d) How many customers are named Woo?
   (e) Find the rating value with the greatest number of customers and also find the number of customers with that rating value; if several rating values have the maximum number of customers, list the requested information for all of them. (Assume that very few rating values have the same number of customers.)

Exercise 25.7 In addition to the Customers table of Figure 25.9 with bitmap indexes on *gender* and *rating*, assume that you have a table called Prospects, with fields *rating* and *prospectid*. This table is used to identify potential customers.

1. Suppose that you also have a bitmap index on the *rating* field of Prospects. Discuss whether or not the bitmap indexes would help in computing the join of Customers and Prospects on *rating*.
2. Suppose you have *no* bitmap index on the *rating* field of Prospects. Discuss whether or not the bitmap indexes on Customers would help in computing the join of Customers and Prospects on *rating*.
3. Describe the use of a join index to support the join of these two relations with the join condition *custid=prospectid*.

Exercise 25.8 Consider the instances of the Locations, Products, and Sales relations shown in Figure 25.2.

1. Consider the basic join indexes described in Section 25.6.2. Suppose you want to optimize for the following two kinds of queries: Query 1 finds sales in a given city, and Query 2 finds sales in a given state. Show the indexes you would create on the example instances shown in Figure 25.2.
2. Consider the bitmapped join indexes described in Section 25.6.2. Suppose you want to optimize for the following two kinds of queries: Query 1 finds sales in a given city, and Query 2 finds sales in a given state. Show the indexes that you would create on the example instances shown in Figure 25.2.

3. Consider the basic join indexes described in Section 25.6.2. Suppose you want to optimize for these two kinds of queries: Query 1 finds sales in a given city for a given product name, and Query 2 finds sales in a given state for a given product category. Show the indexes that you would create on the example instances shown in Figure 25.2.
4. Consider the bitmapped join indexes described in Section 25.6.2. Suppose you want to optimize for these two kinds of queries: Query 1 finds sales in a given city for a given product name, and Query 2 finds sales in a given state for a given product category. Show the indexes that you would create on the example instances shown in Figure 25.2.

Exercise 25.9 Consider the view NumReservations defined as:

```
CREATE VIEW NumReservations (sid, sname, numres)
       AS SELECT S.sid, S.sname, COUNT (*)
          FROM     Sailors S, Reserves R
          WHERE    S.sid = R.sid
          GROUP BY S.sid, S.sname
```

1. How is the following query, which is intended to find the highest number of reservations made by some one sailor, rewritten using query modification?

```
SELECT   MAX (N.numres)
FROM     NumReservations N
```

2. Consider the alternatives of computing on demand and view materialization for the preceding query. Discuss the pros and cons of materialization.
3. Discuss the pros and cons of materialization for the following query:

```
SELECT   N.sname, MAX (N.numres)
FROM     NumReservations N
GROUP BY N.sname
```

Exercise 25.10 Consider the Locations, Products, and Sales relations in Figure 25.2.

1. To decide whether to materialize a view, what factors do we need to consider?
2. Assume that we have defined the following materialized view:

```
SELECT   L.state, S.sales
FROM     Locations L, Sales S
WHERE    S.locid=L.locid
```

   (a) Describe what auxiliary information the algorithm for incremental view maintenance from Section 25.10.1 maintains and how this data helps in maintaining the view incrementally.

   (b) Discuss the pros and cons of materializing this view.

3. Consider the materialized view in the previous question. Assume that the relations Locations and Sales are stored at one site, but the view is materialized on a second site. Why would we ever want to maintain the view at a second site? Give a concrete example where the view could become inconsistent.
4. Assume that we have defined the following materialized view:

```
SELECT   T.year, L.state, SUM (S.sales)
FROM     Sales S, Times T, Locations L
WHERE    S.timeid=T.timeid AND S.locid=L.locid
GROUP BY T.year, L.state
```

(a) Describe what auxiliary information the algorithm for incremental view maintenance from Section 25.10.1 maintains, and how this data helps in maintaining the view incrementally.

(b) Discuss the pros and cons of materializing this view.

BIBLIOGRAPHIC NOTES

A good survey of data warehousing and OLAP is presented in [161], which is the source of Figure 25.10. [686] provides an overview of OLAP and statistical database research, showing the strong parallels between concepts and research in these two areas. The book by Kimball [436], one of the pioneers in warehousing, and the collection of papers in [62] offer a good practical introduction to the area. The term OLAP was popularized by Codd's paper [191]. For a recent discussion of the performance of algorithms utilizing bitmap and other nontraditional index structures, see [575].

Stonebraker discusses how queries on views can be converted to queries on the underlying tables through query modification [713]. Hanson compares the performance of query modification versus immediate and deferred view maintenance [365]. Srivastava and Rotem present an analytical model of materialized view maintenance algorithms [707]. A number of papers discuss how materialized views can be incrementally maintained as the underlying relations are changed. Research into this area has become very active recently, in part because of the interest in *data warehouses*, which can be thought of as collections of views over relations from various sources. An excellent overview of the state of the art can be found in [348], which contains a number of influential papers together with additional material that provides context and background. The following partial list should provide pointers for further reading: [100, 192, 193, 349, 369, 570, 601, 635, 664, 705, 800].

Gray et al. introduced the `CUBE` operator [335], and optimization of `CUBE` queries and efficient maintenance of the result of a `CUBE` query have been addressed in several papers, including [12, 94, 216, 367, 380, 451, 634, 638, 687, 799]. Related algorithms for processing queries with aggregates and grouping are presented in [160, 166]. Rao, Badia, and Van Gucht address the implementation of queries involving generalized quantifiers such as *a majority of* [618]. Srivastava, Tan, and Lum describe an access method to support processing of aggregate queries [708]. Shanmugasundaram et al. discuss how to maintain compressed cubes for approximate answering of aggregate queries in [675].

SQL:1999's support for OLAP, including `CUBE` and `WINDOW` constructs, is described in [523]. The windowing extensions are very similar to SQL extension for querying sequence data, called SRQL, proposed in [610]. Sequence queries have received a lot of attention recently. Extending relational systems, which deal with sets of records, to deal with sequences of records is investigated in [473, 665, 671].

There has been recent interest in one-pass query evaluation algorithms and database management for data streams. A recent survey of data management for data streams and algorithms for data stream processing can be found in [49]. Examples include quantile and order-statistics computation [340, 506], estimating frequency moments and join sizes [34, 35], estimating correlated aggregates [310], multidimensional regression analysis [173], and computing one-dimensional (i.e., single-attribute) histograms and Haar wavelet decompositions [319, 345].

Other work includes techniques for incrementally maintaining equi-depth histograms [313] and Haar wavelets [515], maintaining samples and simple statistics over sliding windows [201], as well as general, high-level architectures for stream database systems [50]. Zdonik et al. describe the architecture of a database system for monitoring data streams [795]. A language infrastructure for developing data stream applications is described by Cortes et al. [199].

Carey and Kossmann discuss how to evaluate queries for which only the first few answers are desired [135, 136]. Donjerkovic and Ramakrishnan consider how a probabilistic approach to query optimization can be applied to this problem [229]. [120] compares several strategies for evaluating Top N queries. Hellerstein et al. discuss how to return approximate answers to aggregate queries and to refine them 'online.' [47, 374]. This work has been extended to online computation of joins [354], online reordering [617] and to adaptive query processing [48].

There has been recent interest in approximate query answering, where a small synopsis data structure is used to give fast approximate query answers with provable performance guarantees [7, 8, 61, 159, 167, 314, 759].

26

DATA MINING

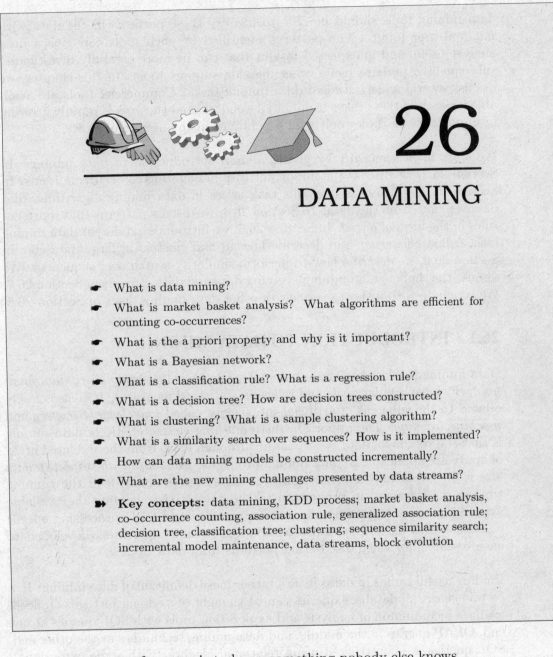

- What is data mining?
- What is market basket analysis? What algorithms are efficient for counting co-occurrences?
- What is the a priori property and why is it important?
- What is a Bayesian network?
- What is a classification rule? What is a regression rule?
- What is a decision tree? How are decision trees constructed?
- What is clustering? What is a sample clustering algorithm?
- What is a similarity search over sequences? How is it implemented?
- How can data mining models be constructed incrementally?
- What are the new mining challenges presented by data streams?
- **Key concepts:** data mining, KDD process; market basket analysis, co-occurrence counting, association rule, generalized association rule; decision tree, classification tree; clustering; sequence similarity search; incremental model maintenance, data streams, block evolution

The secret of success is to know something nobody else knows.

—Aristotle Onassis

Data mining consists of finding interesting trends or patterns in large datasets to guide decisions about future activities. There is a general expectation that data mining tools should be able to identify these patterns in the data with minimal user input. The patterns identified by such tools can give a data analyst useful and unexpected insight that can be more carefully investigated subsequently, perhaps using other decision support tools. In this chapter, we discuss several widely studied data mining tasks. Commercial tools are available for each of these tasks from major vendors, and the area is rapidly growing in importance as these tools gain acceptance in the user community.

We start in Section 26.1 by giving a short introduction to data mining. In Section 26.2, we discuss the important task of counting co-occurring items. In Section 26.3, we discuss how this task arises in data mining algorithms that discover rules from the data. In Section 26.4, we discuss patterns that represent rules in the form of a tree. In Section 26.5, we introduce a different data mining task, called *clustering*, and describe how to find clusters in large datasets. In Section 26.6, we describe how to perform similarity search over sequences. We discuss the challenges in mining evolving data and data streams in Section 26.7. We conclude with a short overview of other data mining tasks in Section 26.8.

26.1 INTRODUCTION TO DATA MINING

Data mining is related to the subarea of statistics called *exploratory data analysis*, which has similar goals and relies on statistical measures. It is also closely related to the subareas of artificial intelligence called *knowledge discovery* and *machine learning*. The important distinguishing characteristic of data mining is that the volume of data is very large; although ideas from these related areas of study are applicable to data mining problems, *scalability with respect to data size* is an important new criterion. An algorithm is **scalable** if the running time grows (linearly) in proportion to the dataset size, holding the available system resources (e.g., amount of main memory and CPU processing speed) constant. Old algorithms must be adapted or new algorithms developed to ensure scalability when discovering patterns from data.

Finding useful trends in datasets is a rather loose definition of data mining: In a certain sense, all database queries can be thought of as doing just this. Indeed, we have a continuum of analysis and exploration tools with SQL queries at one end, OLAP queries in the middle, and data mining techniques at the other end. SQL queries are constructed using relational algebra (with some extensions), OLAP provides higher-level querying idioms based on the multidimensional data model, and data mining provides the most abstract analysis operations. We can think of different data mining tasks as complex 'queries' specified at a high level, with a few parameters that are user-definable, and for which specialized algorithms are implemented.

SQL/MM: Data Mining SQL/MM: The SQL/MM: Data Mining extension of the SQL:1999 standard supports four kinds of data mining models: *frequent itemsets and association rules*, *clusters of records*, *regression trees*, and *classification trees*. Several new data types are introduced. These data types play several roles. Some represent a particular class of model (e.g., `DM_RegressionModel`, `DM_ClusteringModel`); some specify the input parameters for a mining algorithm (e.g., `DM_RegTask`, `DM_ClusTask`); some describe the input data (e.g., `DM_LogicalDataSpec`, `DM_MiningData`); and some represent the result of executing a mining algorithm (e.g., `DM_RegResult`, `DM_ClusResult`). Taken together, these classes and their methods provide a standard interface to data mining algorithms that can be invoked from any SQL:1999 database system. The data mining models can be exported in a standard XML format called **Predictive Model Markup Language (PMML)**; models represented using PMML can be imported as well.

In the real world, data mining is much more than simply applying one of these algorithms. Data is often noisy or incomplete, and unless this is understood and corrected for, it is likely that many interesting patterns will be missed and the reliability of detected patterns will be low. Further, the analyst must decide what kinds of mining algorithms are called for, apply them to a well-chosen subset of data samples and variables (i.e., tuples and attributes), digest the results, apply other decision support and mining tools, and iterate the process.

26.1.1 The Knowledge Discovery Process

The **knowledge discovery and data mining (KDD) process** can roughly be separated into four steps.

1. **Data Selection:** The target subset of data and the attributes of interest are identified by examining the entire raw dataset.

2. **Data Cleaning:** Noise and outliers are removed, field values are transformed to common units and some new fields are created by combining existing fields to facilitate analysis. The data is typically put into a relational format, and several tables might be combined in a *denormalization* step.

3. **Data Mining:** We apply data mining algorithms to extract interesting patterns.

4. **Evaluation:** The patterns are presented to end-users in an understandable form, for example, through visualization.

The results of any step in the KDD process might lead us back to an earlier step to redo the process with the new knowledge gained. In this chapter, however, we limit ourselves to looking at algorithms for some specific data mining tasks. We do not discuss other aspects of the KDD process.

26.2 COUNTING CO-OCCURRENCES

We begin by considering the problem of counting co-occurring items, which is motivated by problems such as market basket analysis. A **market basket** is a collection of items purchased by a customer in a single **customer transaction**. A customer transaction consists of a single visit to a store, a single order through a mail-order catalog, or an order at a store on the Web. (In this chapter, we often abbreviate *customer transaction* to *transaction* when there is no confusion with the usual meaning of *transaction* in a DBMS context, which is an execution of a user program.) A common goal for retailers is to identify items that are purchased together. This information can be used to improve the layout of goods in a store or the layout of catalog pages.

transid	*custid*	*date*	*item*	*qty*
111	201	5/1/99	pen	2
111	201	5/1/99	ink	1
111	201	5/1/99	milk	3
111	201	5/1/99	juice	6
112	105	6/3/99	pen	1
112	105	6/3/99	ink	1
112	105	6/3/99	milk	1
113	106	5/10/99	pen	1
113	106	5/10/99	milk	1
114	201	6/1/99	pen	2
114	201	6/1/99	ink	2
114	201	6/1/99	juice	4
114	201	6/1/99	water	1

Figure 26.1 The Purchases Relation

26.2.1 Frequent Itemsets

We use the Purchases relation shown in Figure 26.1 to illustrate frequent itemsets. The records are shown sorted into groups by transaction. All tuples in a group have the same *transid*, and together they describe a customer transaction, which involves purchases of one or more items. A transaction occurs on a given date, and the name of each purchased item is recorded, along with the purchased quantity. Observe that there is redundancy in Purchases: It can be decomposed by storing *transid–custid–date* triples in a separate table and dropping *custid* and *date* from Purchases; this may be how the data is actually stored. However, it is convenient to consider the Purchases relation, as shown in Figure 26.1, to compute frequent itemsets. Creating such 'denormalized' tables for ease of data mining is commonly done in the data cleaning step of the KDD process.

By examining the set of transaction groups in Purchases, we can make observations of the form: "In 75% of the transactions a pen and ink are purchased together." This statement describes the transactions in the database. Extrapolation to future transactions should be done with caution, as discussed in Section 26.3.6. Let us begin by introducing the terminology of market basket analysis. An **itemset** is a set of items. The **support** of an itemset is the fraction of transactions in the database that contain all the items in the itemset. In our example, the itemset {pen, ink} has 75% support in Purchases. We can therefore conclude that pens and ink are frequently purchased together. If we consider the itemset {milk, juice}, its support is only 25%; milk and juice are not purchased together frequently.

Usually the number of sets of items frequently purchased together is relatively small, especially as the size of the itemsets increases. We are interested in all itemsets whose support is higher than a user-specified minimum support called *minsup*; we call such itemsets **frequent itemsets**. For example, if the minimum support is set to 70%, then the frequent itemsets in our example are {pen}, {ink}, {milk}, {pen, ink}, and {pen, milk}. Note that we are also interested in itemsets that contain only a single item since they identify frequently purchased items.

We show an algorithm for identifying frequent itemsets in Figure 26.2. This algorithm relies on a simple yet fundamental property of frequent itemsets:

> **The a Priori Property:** Every subset of a frequent itemset is also a frequent itemset.

The algorithm proceeds iteratively, first identifying frequent itemsets with just one item. In each subsequent iteration, frequent itemsets identified in the previous iteration are extended with another item to generate larger candidate itemsets. By considering only itemsets obtained by enlarging frequent itemsets, we greatly reduce the number of candidate frequent itemsets; this optimization is crucial for efficient execution. The a priori property guarantees that this optimization is correct; that is, we do not miss any frequent itemsets. A single scan of all transactions (the Purchases relation in our example) suffices to

```
foreach item,                                          // Level 1
    check if it is a frequent itemset  // appears in > minsup transactions
k = 1
repeat          // Iterative, level-wise identification of frequent itemsets
    foreach new frequent itemset I_k with k items           // Level k + 1
        generate all itemsets I_{k+1} with k + 1 items, I_k ⊂ I_{k+1}
    Scan all transactions once and check if
    the generated k + 1-itemsets are frequent
    k = k + 1
until no new frequent itemsets are identified
```

Figure 26.2 An Algorithm for Finding Frequent Itemsets

determine which candidate itemsets generated in an iteration are frequent. The algorithm terminates when no new frequent itemsets are identified in an iteration.

We illustrate the algorithm on the Purchases relation in Figure 26.1, with *minsup* set to 70%. In the first iteration (Level 1), we scan the Purchases relation and determine that each of these one-item sets is a frequent itemset: {*pen*} (appears in all four transactions), {*ink*} (appears in three out of four transactions), and {*milk*} (appears in three out of four transactions).

In the second iteration (Level 2), we extend each frequent itemset with an additional item and generate the following candidate itemsets: {*pen, ink*}, {*pen, milk*}, {*pen, juice*}, {*ink, milk*}, {*ink, juice*}, and {*milk, juice*}. By scanning the Purchases relation again, we determine that the following are frequent itemsets: {*pen, ink*} (appears in three out of four transactions), and {*pen, milk*} (appears in three out of four transactions).

In the third iteration (Level 3), we extend these itemsets with an additional item and generate the following candidate itemsets: {*pen, ink, milk*}, {*pen, ink, juice*}, and {*pen, milk, juice*}. (Observe that {*ink, milk, juice*} is not generated.) A third scan of the Purchases relation allows us to determine that none of these is a frequent itemset.

The simple algorithm presented here for finding frequent itemsets illustrates the principal feature of more sophisticated algorithms, namely, the iterative generation and testing of candidate itemsets. We consider one important refinement of this simple algorithm. Generating candidate itemsets by adding an item to a known frequent itemset is an attempt to limit the number of candidate itemsets using the a priori property. The a priori property implies that a candidate itemset can be frequent only if all its subsets are frequent. Thus, we can reduce the number of candidate itemsets further—*a priori*, or before scanning the Purchases database—by checking whether all subsets of a newly generated candidate itemset are frequent. Only if all subsets of a candidate itemset are frequent do we compute its support in the subsequent database scan. Compared to the simple algorithm, this refined algorithm generates fewer candidate itemsets at each level and thus reduces the amount of computation performed during the database scan of Purchases.

Consider the refined algorithm on the Purchases table in Figure 26.1 with *minsup*= 70%. In the first iteration (Level 1), we determine the frequent itemsets of size one: {*pen*}, {*ink*}, and {*milk*}. In the second iteration (Level 2), only the following candidate itemsets remain when scanning the Purchases table: {*pen, ink*}, {*pen, milk*}, and {*ink, milk*}. Since {*juice*} is not frequent, the itemsets {*pen, juice*}, {*ink, juice*}, and {*milk, juice*} cannot be frequent as well and we can eliminate those itemsets a priori, that is, without considering them during the subsequent scan of the Purchases relation. In the third iteration (Level 3), no further candidate itemsets are generated. The itemset {*pen, ink, milk*} cannot be frequent since its subset {*ink, milk*} is not frequent. Thus, the improved version of the algorithm does not need a third scan of Purchases.

26.2.2 Iceberg Queries

We introduce iceberg queries through an example. Consider again the Purchases relation shown in Figure 26.1. Assume that we want to find pairs of customers and items such that the customer has purchased the item more than five times. We can express this query in SQL as follows:

```
SELECT    P.custid, P.item, SUM (P.qty)
FROM      Purchases P
GROUP BY  P.custid, P.item
HAVING    SUM (P.qty) > 5
```

Think about how this query would be evaluated by a relational DBMS. Conceptually, for each (*custid, item*) pair, we need to check whether the sum of the *qty* field is greater than 5. One approach is to make a scan over the Purchases relation and maintain running sums for each (*custid, item*) pair. This is a feasible execution strategy as long as the number of pairs is small enough to fit into main memory. If the number of pairs is larger than main memory, more expensive query evaluation plans, which involve either sorting or hashing, have to be used.

The query has an important property not exploited by the preceding execution strategy: Even though the Purchases relation is potentially very large and the number of (*custid*, *item*) groups can be huge, the output of the query is likely to be relatively small because of the condition in the `HAVING` clause. Only groups where the customer has purchased the item more than five times appear in the output. For example, there are nine groups in the query over the Purchases relation shown in Figure 26.1, although the output contains only three records. The number of groups is very large, but the answer to the query—the tip of the iceberg—is usually very small. Therefore, we call such a query an **iceberg query**. In general, given a relational schema R with attributes *A1, A2, ..., Ak,* and *B* and an aggregation function **aggr**, an iceberg query has the following structure:

```
SELECT    R.A1, R.A2, ..., R.Ak, aggr(R.B)
FROM      Relation R
GROUP BY  R.A1, ..., R.Ak
HAVING    aggr(R.B) >= constant
```

Traditional query plans for this query that use sorting or hashing first compute the value of the aggregation function for all groups and then eliminate groups that do not satisfy the condition in the `HAVING` clause.

Comparing the query with the problem of finding frequent itemsets discussed in the previous section, there is a striking similarity. Consider again the Purchases relation shown in Figure 26.1 and the iceberg query from the beginning of this section. We are interested in (*custid*, *item*) pairs that have `SUM` (P.qty) > 5. Using a variation of the a priori property, we can argue that we only have to consider values of the *custid* field where the customer has purchased at least five items. We can generate such items through the following query:

```
SELECT    P.custid
FROM      Purchases P
GROUP BY  P.custid
HAVING    SUM (P.qty) > 5
```

Similarly, we can restrict the candidate values for the *item* field through the following query:

```
SELECT    P.item
FROM      Purchases P
GROUP BY  P.item
HAVING    SUM (P.qty) > 5
```

If we restrict the computation of the original iceberg query to (*custid*, *item*) groups where the field values are in the output of the previous two queries, we eliminate a large number of (*custid*, *item*) pairs a priori. So, a possible evaluation strategy is to first compute candidate values for the *custid* and *item* fields, and use combinations of only these values in the evaluation of the original iceberg query. We first generate candidate field values for individual fields and use only those values that survive the a priori pruning step as expressed in the two previous queries. Thus, the iceberg query is amenable to the same bottom-up evaluation strategy used to find frequent itemsets. In particular, we can use the a priori property as follows: We keep a counter for a group only if each individual component of the group satisfies the condition expressed in the `HAVING` clause. The performance improvements of this alternative evaluation strategy over traditional query plans can be very significant in practice.

Even though the bottom-up query processing strategy eliminates many groups a priori, the number of (*custid*, *item*) pairs can still be very large in practice; even larger than main memory. Efficient strategies that use sampling and more sophisticated hashing techniques have been developed; the bibliographic notes at the end of the chapter provide pointers to the relevant literature.

26.3 MINING FOR RULES

Many algorithms have been proposed for discovering various forms of rules that succinctly describe the data. We now look at some widely discussed forms of rules and algorithms for discovering them.

26.3.1 Association Rules

We use the Purchases relation shown in Figure 26.1 to illustrate association rules. By examining the set of transactions in Purchases, we can identify rules of the form:

$$\{pen\} \Rightarrow \{ink\}$$

This rule should be read as follows: "If a pen is purchased in a transaction, it is likely that ink is also be purchased in that transaction." It is a statement that describes the transactions in the database; extrapolation to future transactions should be done with caution, as discussed in Section 26.3.6. More generally, an **association rule** has the form *LHS* $\Rightarrow$ *RHS*, where both *LHS* and *RHS* are sets of items. The interpretation of such a rule is that if every item in *LHS* is purchased in a transaction, then it is likely that the items in *RHS* are purchased as well.

There are two important measures for an association rule:

- **Support:** The support for a set of items is the percentage of transactions that contain all these items. The support for a rule *LHS* $\Rightarrow$ *RHS* is the support for the set of items *LHS* $\cup$ *RHS*. For example, consider the rule {*pen*} $\Rightarrow$ {*ink*}. The support of this rule is the support of the itemset {*pen*, *ink*}, which is 75%.

- **Confidence:** Consider transactions that contain all items in *LHS*. The confidence for a rule *LHS* $\Rightarrow$ *RHS* is the percentage of such transactions that also contain all items in *RHS*. More precisely, let *sup*(*LHS*) be the percentage of transactions that contain *LHS* and let *sup*(*LHS* $\cup$ *RHS*) be the percentage of transactions that contain both *LHS* and *RHS*. Then the confidence of the rule *LHS* $\Rightarrow$ *RHS* is *sup*(*LHS* $\cup$ *RHS*) / *sup*(*LHS*). The confidence of a rule is an indication of the strength of the rule. As an example, consider again the rule {*pen*} $\Rightarrow$ {*ink*}. The confidence of this rule is 75%; 75% of the transactions that contain the itemset {*pen*} also contain the itemset {*ink*}.

26.3.2 An Algorithm for Finding Association Rules

A user can ask for all association rules that have a specified minimum support *(minsup)* and minimum confidence *(minconf)*, and various algorithms have been developed for finding such rules efficiently. These algorithms proceed in two steps. In the first step, all frequent itemsets with the user-specified minimum support are computed. In the second step, rules are generated using the frequent itemsets as input. We discussed an algorithm for finding frequent itemsets in Section 26.2; we concentrate here on the rule generation part.

Once frequent itemsets are identified, the generation of all possible candidate rules with the user-specified minimum support is straightforward. Consider a frequent itemset X with support s_X identified in the first step of the algorithm. To generate a rule from X, we divide X into two itemsets, *LHS* and *RHS*. The confidence of the rule *LHS* $\Rightarrow$ *RHS* is s_X/s_{LHS}, the ratio of the support of X and the support of *LHS*. From the a priori property, we know that the support of *LHS* is larger than *minsup*, and thus we have computed the support of *LHS* during the first step of the algorithm. We can compute the confidence values for the candidate rule by calculating the ratio support(X)/support(*LHS*) and then check how the ratio compares to *minconf*.

In general, the expensive step of the algorithm is the computation of the frequent itemsets, and many different algorithms have been developed to perform this step efficiently. Rule generation—given that all frequent itemsets have been identified—is straightforward.

In the rest of this section, we discuss some generalizations of the problem.

26.3.3 Association Rules and ISA Hierarchies

In many cases, an **ISA hierarchy** or **category hierarchy** is imposed on the set of items. In the presence of a hierarchy, a transaction contains, for each of its items, implicitly all the item's ancestors in the hierarchy. For example, consider the category hierarchy shown in Figure 26.3. Given this hierarchy, the Purchases relation is conceptually enlarged by the eight records shown in Figure 26.4. That is, the Purchases relation has all tuples shown in Figure 26.1 in addition to the tuples shown in Figure 26.4.

The hierarchy allows us to detect relationships between items at different levels of the hierarchy. As an example, the support of the itemset {*ink*, *juice*} is 50%, but if we replace *juice* with the more general category *beverage*, the support of the resulting itemset {*ink*, *beverage*} increases to 75%. In general, the support of an itemset can increase only if an item is replaced by one of its ancestors in the ISA hierarchy.

Assuming that we actually physically add the eight records shown in Figure 26.4 to the Purchases relation, we can use any algorithm for computing frequent itemsets on the augmented database. Assuming that the hierarchy fits into main memory, we can also perform the addition on-the-fly while we scan the database, as an optimization.

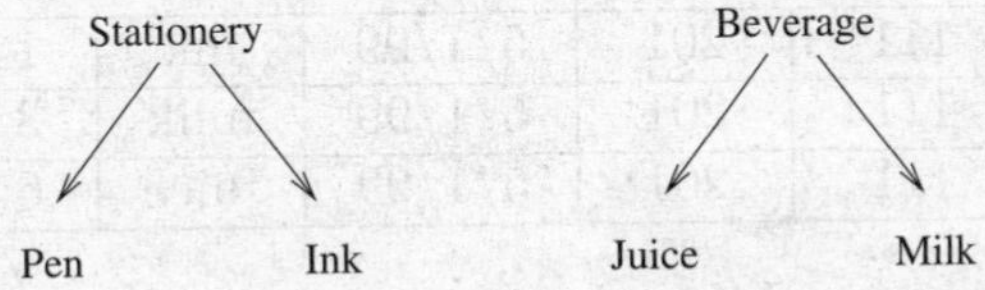

Figure 26.3 An ISA Category Taxonomy

transid	*custid*	*date*	*item*	*qty*
111	201	5/1/99	stationery	3
111	201	5/1/99	beverage	9
112	105	6/3/99	stationery	2
112	105	6/3/99	beverage	1
113	106	5/10/99	stationery	1
113	106	5/10/99	beverage	1
114	201	6/1/99	stationery	4
114	201	6/1/99	beverage	5

Figure 26.4 Conceptual Additions to the Purchases Relation with ISA Hierarchy

26.3.4 Generalized Association Rules

Although association rules have been most widely studied in the context of market basket analysis, or analysis of customer transactions, the concept is more general. Consider the Purchases relation as shown in Figure 26.5, grouped by *custid*. By examining the set of customer groups, we can identify association rules such as {pen} ⇒ {milk}. This rule should now be read as follows: "If a pen is purchased by a customer, it is likely that milk is also be purchased by that customer." In the Purchases relation shown in Figure 26.5, this rule has both support and confidence of 100%.

transid	*custid*	*date*	*item*	*qty*
112	105	6/3/99	pen	1
112	105	6/3/99	ink	1
112	105	6/3/99	milk	1
113	106	5/10/99	pen	1
113	106	5/10/99	milk	1
114	201	5/15/99	pen	2
114	201	5/15/99	ink	2
114	201	5/15/99	juice	4
114	201	6/1/99	water	1
111	201	5/1/99	pen	2
111	201	5/1/99	ink	1
111	201	5/1/99	milk	3
111	201	5/1/99	juice	6

Figure 26.5 The Purchases Relation Sorted on Customer ID

Similarly, we can group tuples by date and identify association rules that describe purchase behavior on the same day. As an example consider again the Purchases relation. In this case, the rule {pen} ⇒ {milk} is now interpreted as follows: "On a day when a pen is purchased, it is likely that milk is also be purchased."

If we use the *date* field as grouping attribute, we can consider a more general problem called **calendric market basket analysis**. In calendric market basket analysis, the user specifies a collection of **calendars**. A calendar is any group of dates, such as *every Sunday in the year 1999*, or *every first of the month.* A rule holds if it holds on every day in the calendar. Given a calendar, we can compute association rules over the set of tuples whose *date* field falls within the calendar.

By specifying interesting calendars, we can identify rules that might not have enough support and confidence with respect to the entire database but have enough support and confidence on the subset of tuples that fall within the calendar. On the other hand, even though a rule might have enough support and confidence with respect to the complete database, it might gain its support only from tuples that fall within a calendar. In this case, the support of the rule over the tuples within the calendar is significantly higher than its support with respect to the entire database.

As an example, consider the Purchases relation with the calendar *every first of the month.* Within this calendar, the association rule *pen* ⇒ *juice* has support and confidence of 100%, whereas over the entire Purchases relation, this rule only has 50% support. On the other hand, within the calendar, the rule *pen* ⇒ *milk* has support of confidence of 50%, whereas over the entire Purchases relation it has support and confidence of 75%.

More general specifications of the conditions that must be true within a group for a rule to hold (for that group) have also been proposed. We might want to say that all items in the *LHS* have to be purchased in a quantity of less than two items, and all items in the *RHS* must be purchased in a quantity of more than three.

Using different choices for the grouping attribute and sophisticated conditions as in the preceding examples, we can identify rules more complex than the basic association rules discussed earlier. These more complex rules, nonetheless, retain the essential structure of an association rule as a condition over a group of tuples, with support and confidence measures defined as usual.

26.3.5 Sequential Patterns

Consider the Purchases relation shown in Figure 26.1. Each group of tuples, having the same *custid* value, can be thought of as a *sequence* of transactions ordered by *date*. This allows us to identify frequently arising buying patterns over time.

We begin by introducing the concept of a sequence of itemsets. Each transaction is represented by a set of tuples, and by looking at the values in the *item* column, we get a set of items purchased in that transaction. Therefore, the sequence of transactions associated with a customer corresponds naturally to a sequence of itemsets purchased by the customer. For example, the sequence of purchases for customer 201 is ⟨{*pen, ink, milk, juice*}, {*pen, ink, juice*}⟩.

A **subsequence** of a sequence of itemsets is obtained by deleting one or more itemsets, and is also a sequence of itemsets. We say that a sequence $\langle a_1, \ldots, a_m \rangle$ is **contained** in another sequence S if S has a subsequence $\langle b_1, \ldots, b_m \rangle$ such that $a_i \subseteq b_i$, for $1 \leq i \leq m$. Thus, the sequence $\langle\{pen\}, \{ink, milk\}, \{pen, juice\}\rangle$ is contained in $\langle\{pen, ink\}, \{shirt\}, \{juice, ink, milk\}, \{juice, pen, milk\}\rangle$. Note that the order of items within each itemset does not matter. However, the order of itemsets does matter: the sequence $\langle\{pen\}, \{ink, milk\}, \{pen, juice\}\rangle$ is not contained in $\langle\{pen, ink\}, \{shirt\}, \{juice, pen, milk\}, \{juice, milk, ink\}\rangle$.

The **support** for a sequence S of itemsets is the percentage of customer sequences of which S is a subsequence. The problem of identifying sequential patterns is to find all sequences that have a user-specified minimum support. A sequence $\langle a_1, a_2, a_3, \ldots, a_m \rangle$ with minimum support tells us that customers often purchase the items in set a_1 in a transaction, then in some subsequent transaction buy the items in set a_2, then the items in set a_3 in a later transaction, and so on.

Like association rules, sequential patterns are statements about groups of tuples in the current database. Computationally, algorithms for finding frequently occurring sequential patterns resemble algorithms for finding frequent itemsets. Longer and longer sequences with the required minimum support are identified iteratively in a manner very similar to the iterative identification of frequent itemsets.

26.3.6 The Use of Association Rules for Prediction

Association rules are widely used for prediction, but it is important to recognize that such predictive use is not justified without additional analysis or domain knowledge. Association rules describe existing data accurately but can be misleading when used naively for prediction. For example, consider the rule

$$\{pen\} \Rightarrow \{ink\}$$

The confidence associated with this rule is the conditional probability of an ink purchase given a pen purchase *over the given database*; that is, it is a *descriptive* measure. We might use this rule to guide future sales promotions. For example, we might offer a discount on pens to increase the sales of pens and, therefore, also increase sales of ink.

However, such a promotion assumes that pen purchases are good indicators of ink purchases in *future* customer transactions (in addition to transactions in the current database). This assumption is justified if there is a *causal link* between pen purchases and ink purchases; that is, if buying pens causes the buyer to also buy ink. However, we can infer association rules with high support and confidence in some situations where there is no causal link between *LHS* and *RHS*. For example, suppose that pens are always purchased together with pencils, perhaps because of customers' tendency to order writing instruments together. We would then infer the rule

$$\{pencil\} \Rightarrow \{ink\}$$

with the same support and confidence as the rule

$$\{pen\} \Rightarrow \{ink\}$$

However, there is no causal link between pencils and ink. If we promote pencils, a customer who purchases several pencils due to the promotion has no reason to buy more ink. Therefore, a sales promotion that discounted pencils in order to increase the sales of ink would fail.

In practice, one would expect that, by examining a large database of past transactions (collected over a long time and a variety of circumstances) and restricting attention to rules that occur often (i.e., that have high support), we minimize inferring misleading rules. However, we should bear in mind that misleading, noncausal rules might still be generated. Therefore, we should treat the generated rules as possibly, rather than conclusively, identifying causal relationships. Although association rules do not indicate causal relationships between the *LHS* and *RHS*, we emphasize that they provide a useful starting point for identifying such relationships, using either further analysis or a domain expert's judgment; this is the reason for their popularity.

26.3.7 Bayesian Networks

Finding causal relationships is a challenging task, as we saw in Section 26.3.6. In general, if certain events are highly correlated, there are many possible explanations. For example, suppose that pens, pencils, and ink are purchased together frequently. It might be that the purchase of one of these items (e.g., ink) depends causally on the purchase of another item (e.g., pen). Or it might be that the purchase of one of these items (e.g., pen) is strongly correlated with the purchase of another (e.g., pencil) because of some underlying phenomenon (e.g., users' tendency to think about writing instruments together) that causally influences both purchases. How can we identify the true causal relationships that hold between these events in the real world?

One approach is to consider each possible combination of causal relationships among the variables or events of interest to us and evaluate the likelihood of each combination on the basis of the data available to us. If we think of each combination of causal relationships as a *model* of the real world underlying the collected data, we can assign a score to each model by considering how consistent it is (in terms of probabilities, with some simplifying assumptions) with the observed data. Bayesian networks are graphs that can be used to describe a class of such models, with one node per variable or event, and arcs between nodes to indicate causality. For example, a good model for our running example of pens, pencils, and ink is shown in Figure 26.6. In general, the number of possible models is exponential in the number of variables, and considering all models is expensive, so some subset of all possible models is evaluated.

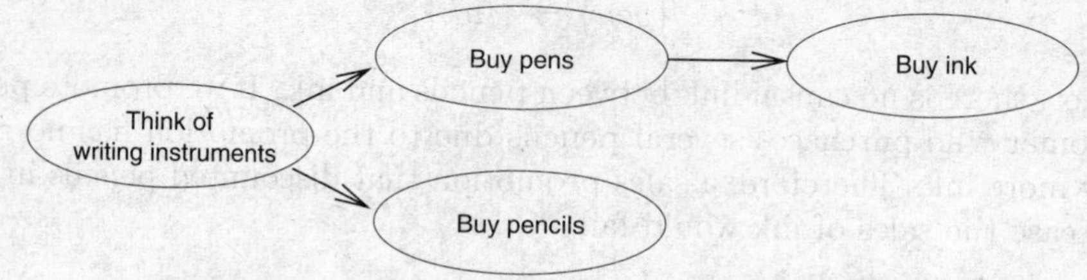

Figure 26.6 Bayesian Network Showing Causality

26.3.8 Classification and Regression Rules

Consider the following view that contains information from a mailing campaign performed by an insurance company:

InsuranceInfo(*age:* `integer`, *cartype:* `string`, *highrisk:* `boolean`)

The InsuranceInfo view has information about current customers. Each record contains a customer's age and type of car as well as a flag indicating whether the person is considered a high-risk customer. If the flag is true, the customer is considered high-risk. We would like to use this information to identify rules that predict the insurance risk of new insurance applicants whose age and car type are known. For example, one such rule could be: "If *age* is between 16 and 25 and *cartype* is either Sports or Truck, then the risk is high."

Note that the rules we want to find have a specific structure. We are not interested in rules that predict the age or type of car of a person; we are interested only in rules that predict the insurance risk. Thus, there is one designated attribute whose value we wish to predict, and we call this attribute the **dependent** attribute. The other attributes are called **predictor** attributes. In our example, the dependent attribute in the InsuranceInfo view is the *highrisk* attribute and the predictor attributes are *age* and *cartype*. The general form of the types of rules we want to discover is

$$P_1(X_1) \land P_2(X_2) \ldots \land P_k(X_k) \Rightarrow Y = c$$

The predictor attributes $X_1, \ldots, X_k$ are used to predict the value of the dependent attribute Y. Both sides of a rule can be interpreted as conditions on fields of a tuple. The $P_i(X_i)$ are predicates that involve attribute X_i. The form of the predicate depends on the type of the predictor attribute. We distinguish two types of attributes: numerical and categorical. For **numerical** attributes, we can perform numerical computations, such as computing the average of two values; whereas for **categorical** attributes, the only allowed operation is testing whether two values are equal. In the InsuranceInfo view, *age* is a numerical attribute whereas *cartype* and *highrisk* are categorical attributes. Returning to the form of the predicates, if X_i is a numerical attribute, its predicate P_i is of the form $li \leq X_i \leq hi$; if X_i is a categorical attribute, P_i is of the form $X_i \in \{v_1, \ldots, v_j\}$.

If the dependent attribute is categorical, we call such rules **classification rules.** If the dependent attribute is numerical, we call such rules **regression rules.**

For example, consider again our example rule: "If *age* is between 16 and 25 and *cartype* is either Sports or Truck, then *highrisk* is true." Since *highrisk* is a categorical attribute, this rule is a classification rule. We can express this rule formally as follows:

$$(16 \leq age \leq 25) \wedge (cartype \in \{\text{Sports, Truck}\}) \Rightarrow highrisk = \texttt{true}$$

We can define support and confidence for classification and regression rules, as for association rules:

- **Support:** The support for a condition C is the percentage of tuples that satisfy C. The support for a rule $C1 \Rightarrow C2$ is the support for the condition $C1 \wedge C2$.

- **Confidence:** Consider those tuples that satisfy condition $C1$. The confidence for a rule $C1 \Rightarrow C2$ is the percentage of such tuples that also satisfy condition $C2$.

As a further generalization, consider the right-hand side of a classification or regression rule: $Y = c$. Each rule predicts a value of Y for a given tuple based on the values of predictor attributes $X1, \ldots, Xk$. We can consider rules of the form

$$P_1(X_1) \wedge \ldots \wedge P_k(X_k) \Rightarrow Y = f(X_1, \ldots, X_k)$$

where f is some function. We do not discuss such rules further.

Classification and regression rules differ from association rules by considering continuous and categorical fields, rather than only one field that is set-valued. Identifying such rules efficiently presents a new set of challenges; we do not discuss the general case of discovering such rules. We discuss a special type of such rules in Section 26.4.

Classification and regression rules have many applications. Examples include classification of results of scientific experiments, where the type of object to be recognized depends on the measurements taken; direct mail prospecting, where the response of a given customer to a promotion is a function of his or her income level and age; and car insurance risk assessment, where a customer could be classified as risky depending on age, profession, and car type. Example applications of regression rules include financial forecasting, where the price of coffee futures could be some function of the rainfall in Colombia a month ago, and medical prognosis, where the likelihood of a tumor being cancerous is a function of measured attributes of the tumor.

26.4 TREE-STRUCTURED RULES

In this section, we discuss the problem of discovering classification and regression rules from a relation, but we consider only rules that have a very special structure. The type of rules we discuss can be represented by a tree, and typically the tree itself is the output of the data mining activity. Trees that represent classification rules are called **classification trees** or **decision trees** and trees that represent regression rules are called **regression trees**

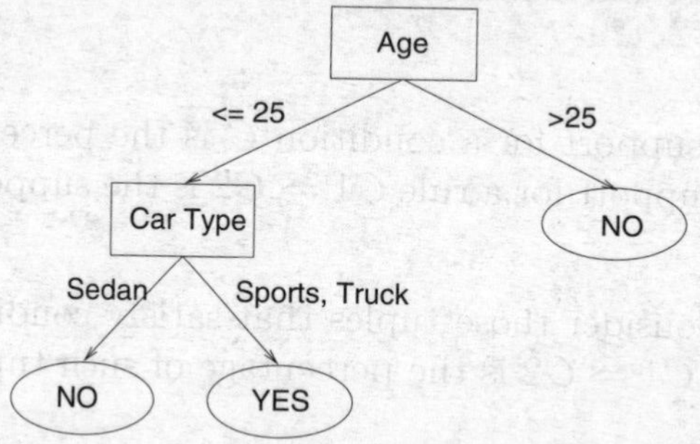

Figure 26.7 Insurance Risk Example Decision Tree

As an example, consider the decision tree shown in Figure 26.7. Each path from the root node to a leaf node represents one classification rule. For example, the path from the root to the leftmost leaf node represents the classification rule: "If a person is 25 years or younger and drives a sedan, then he or she is likely to have a low insurance risk." The path from the root to the right-most leaf node represents the classification rule: "If a person is older than 25 years, then he or she is likely to have a low insurance risk."

Tree-structured rules are very popular since they are easy to interpret. Ease of understanding is very important because the result of any data mining activity needs to be comprehensible by nonspecialists. In addition, studies have shown that, despite limitations in structure, tree-structured rules are very accurate. There exist efficient algorithms to construct tree-structured rules from large databases. We discuss a sample algorithm for decision tree construction in the remainder of this section.

26.4.1 Decision Trees

A decision tree is a graphical representation of a collection of classification rules. Given a data record, the tree directs the record from the root to a leaf. Each internal node of the tree is labeled with a predictor attribute. This attribute is often called a **splitting attribute**, because the data is 'split' based on conditions over this attribute. The outgoing edges of an internal node are labeled with predicates that involve the splitting attribute of the node; every data record entering the node must satisfy the predicate labeling exactly one outgoing edge. The combined information about the splitting attribute and the predicates on the outgoing edges is called the **splitting criterion** of the node. A node with no outgoing edges is called a **leaf node**. Each leaf node of the tree is labeled with a value of the dependent attribute. We consider only binary trees where internal nodes have two outgoing edges, although trees of higher degree are possible.

Consider the decision tree shown in Figure 26.7. The splitting attribute of the root node is *age*, the splitting attribute of the left child of the root node is *cartype*. The predicate on the left outgoing edge of the root node is $age \leq 25$, the predicate on the right outgoing edge is $age > 25$.

We can now associate a classification rule with each leaf node in the tree as follows. Consider the path from the root of the tree to the leaf node. Each edge on that path is labeled with a predicate. The conjunction of all these predicates makes up the left-hand side of the rule. The value of the dependent attribute at the leaf node makes up the right-hand side of the rule. Thus, the decision tree represents a collection of classification rules, one for each leaf node.

A decision tree is usually constructed in two phases. In phase one, the **growth phase**, an overly large tree is constructed. This tree represents the records in the input database very accurately; for example, the tree might contain leaf nodes for individual records from the input database. In phase two, the **pruning phase**, the final size of the tree is determined. The rules represented by the tree constructed in phase one are usually overspecialized. By reducing the size of the tree, we generate a smaller number of more general rules that are better than a very large number of very specialized rules. Algorithms for tree pruning are beyond our scope of discussion here.

Classification tree algorithms build the tree greedily top-down in the following way. At the root node, the database is examined and the locally 'best' splitting criterion is computed. The database is then partitioned, according to the root node's splitting criterion, into two parts, one partition for the left child and one partition for the right child. The algorithm then recurses on each child. This schema is depicted in Figure 26.8.

Input: node n, partition D, split selection method $\mathcal{S}$
Output: decision tree for D rooted at node n

Top-Down Decision Tree Induction Schema:
BuildTree(Node n, data partition D, split selection method $\mathcal{S}$)
(1) Apply $\mathcal{S}$ to D to find the splitting criterion
(2) **if** (a good splitting criterion is found)
(3) Create two children nodes n_1 and n_2 of n
(4) Partition D into D_1 and D_2
(5) BuildTree(n_1, D_1, $\mathcal{S}$)
(6) BuildTree(n_2, D_2, $\mathcal{S}$)
(7) **endif**

Figure 26.8 Decision Tree Induction Schema

The splitting criterion at a node is found through application of a **split selection method**. A split selection method is an algorithm that takes as input (part of) a relation and outputs the locally 'best' splitting criterion. In our example, the split selection method examines the attributes *cartype* and *age*, selects one of them as splitting attribute, and then selects the splitting predicates. Many different, very sophisticated split selection methods have been developed; the references provide pointers to the relevant literature.

26.4.2 An Algorithm to Build Decision Trees

If the input database fits into main memory, we can directly follow the classification tree induction schema shown in Figure 26.8. How can we construct decision trees when the input relation is larger than main memory? In this case, step (1) in Figure 26.8 fails, since the input database does not fit in memory. But we can make one important observation about split selection methods that helps us to reduce the main memory requirements.

Consider a node of the decision tree. The split selection method has to make two decisions after examining the partition at that node: It has to select the splitting attribute, and it has to select the splitting predicates for the outgo-

age	*cartype*	*highrisk*
23	Sedan	false
30	Sports	false
36	Sedan	false
25	Truck	true
30	Sedan	false
23	Truck	true
30	Truck	false
25	Sports	true
18	Sedan	false

Figure 26.9 The InsuranceInfo Relation

ing edges. After selecting the splitting criterion at a node, the algorithm is recursively applied to each of the children of the node. Does a split selection method actually need the complete database partition as input? Fortunately, the answer is no.

Split selection methods that compute splitting criteria that involve a single predictor attribute at each node evaluate each predictor attribute individually. Since each attribute is examined separately, we can provide the split selection method with aggregated information about the database instead of loading the complete database into main memory. Chosen correctly, this aggregated information enables us to compute the same splitting criterion as we would obtain by examining the complete database.

Since the split selection method examines all predictor attributes, we need aggregated information about each predictor attribute. We call this aggregated information the **AVC set** of the predictor attribute. The AVC set of a predictor attribute X at node n is the projection of n's database partition onto X and the dependent attribute where counts of the individual values in the domain of the dependent attribute are aggregated. (AVC stands for **A**ttribute-**V**alue, **C**lass label, because the values of the dependent attribute are often called **class labels**.) For example, consider the InsuranceInfo relation as shown in Figure 26.9. The AVC set of the root node of the tree for predictor attribute *age* is the result of the following database query:

```
SELECT    R.age, R.highrisk, COUNT (*)
FROM      InsuranceInfo R
GROUP BY  R.age, R.highrisk
```

The AVC set for the left child of the root node for predictor attribute *cartype* is the result of the following query:

```
SELECT   R.cartype, R.highrisk, COUNT (*)
FROM     InsuranceInfo R
WHERE    R.age <= 25
GROUP BY R.cartype, R.highrisk
```

The two AVC sets of the root node of the tree are shown in Figure 26.10.

Car type	highrisk	
	true	false
Sedan	0	4
Sports	1	1
Truck	2	1

Age	highrisk	
	true	false
18	0	1
23	1	1
25	2	0
30	0	3
36	0	1

Figure 26.10 AVC Group of the Root Node for the InsuranceInfo Relation

We define the **AVC group** of a node n to be the set of the AVC sets of all predictor attributes at node n. Our example of the InsuranceInfo relation has two predictor attributes; therefore, the AVC group of any node consists of two AVC sets.

How large are AVC sets? Note that the size of the AVC set of a predictor attribute X at node n depends only on the number of distinct attribute values of X and the size of the domain of the dependent attribute. For example, consider the AVC sets shown in Figure 26.10. The AVC set for the predictor attribute *cartype* has three entries, and the AVC set for predictor attribute *age* has five entries, although the InsuranceInfo relation as shown in Figure 26.9 has nine records. For large databases, the size of the AVC sets is independent of the number of tuples in the database, except if there are attributes with very large domains, for example, a real-valued field recorded at a very high precision with many digits after the decimal point.

If we make the simplifying assumption that all the AVC sets of the root node together fit into main memory, then we can construct decision trees from very large databases as follows: We make a scan over the database and construct the AVC group of the root node in memory. Then we run the split selection method of our choice with the AVC group as input. After the split selection method computes the splitting attribute and the splitting predicates on the outgoing nodes, we partition the database and recurse. Note that this algorithm is very similar to the original algorithm shown in Figure 26.8; the only modification necessary is shown in Figure 26.11. In addition, this algorithm is still independent of the actual split selection method involved.

Input: node n, partition D, split selection method $\mathcal{S}$
Output: decision tree for D rooted at node n

Top-Down Decision Tree Induction Schema:
BuildTree(Node n, data partition D, split selection method $\mathcal{S}$)
(1a) Make a scan over D and construct the AVC group of n in-memory
(1b) Apply $\mathcal{S}$ to the AVC group to find the splitting criterion

Figure 26.11 Classification Tree Induction Refinement with AVC Groups

26.5 CLUSTERING

In this section we discuss the **clustering problem**. The goal is to partition a set of records into groups such that records within a group are similar to each other and records that belong to two different groups are dissimilar. Each such group is called a **cluster** and each record belongs to exactly one cluster.[1] Similarity between records is measured computationally by a **distance function**. A distance function takes two input records and returns a value that is a measure of their similarity. Different applications have different notions of similarity, and no one measure works for all domains.

As an example, consider the schema of the CustomerInfo view:

CustomerInfo(*age:* `int`, *salary:* `real`)

We can plot the records in the view on a two-dimensional plane as shown in Figure 26.12. The two coordinates of a record are the values of the record's *salary* and *age* fields. We can visually identify three clusters: Young customers who have low salaries, young customers with high salaries, and older customers with high salaries.

Usually, the output of a clustering algorithm consists of a **summarized representation** of each cluster. The type of summarized representation depends strongly on the type and shape of clusters the algorithm computes. For example, assume that we have spherical clusters as in the example shown in Figure 26.12. We can summarize each cluster by its *center* (often also called the *mean*) and its *radius*, which are defined as follows. Given a collection of records $r_1, \ldots, r_n$, their **center** C and **radius** R are defined as follows:

$$C = \frac{1}{n}\sum_{i=1}^{n} r_i, \text{ and } R = \sqrt{\frac{\sum_{i=1}^{n}(r_i - C)}{n}}$$

[1]There are clustering algorithms that allow overlapping clusters, where a record could belong to several clusters.

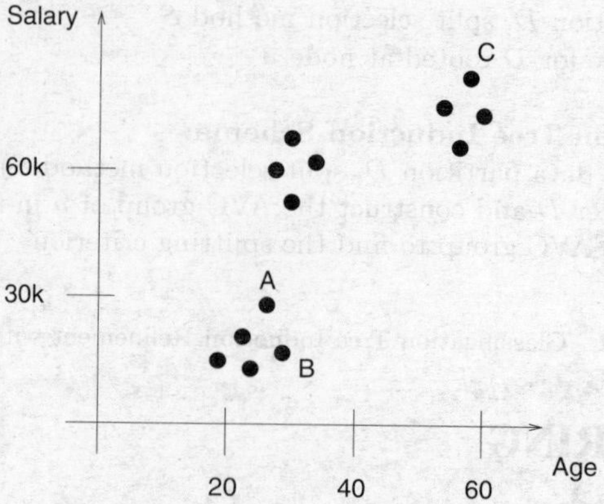

Figure 26.12 Records in CustomerInfo

There are two types of clustering algorithms. A **partitional** clustering algorithm partitions the data into k groups such that some criterion that evaluates the clustering quality is optimized. The number of clusters k is a parameter whose value is specified by the user. A **hierarchical** clustering algorithm generates a sequence of partitions of the records. Starting with a partition in which each cluster consists of one single record, the algorithm merges two partitions in each step until only one single partition remains in the end.

26.5.1 A Clustering Algorithm

Clustering is a very old problem, and numerous algorithms have been developed to cluster a collection of records. Traditionally, the number of records in the input database was assumed to be relatively small and the complete database was assumed to fit into main memory. In this section, we describe a clustering algorithm called BIRCH that handles very large databases. The design of BIRCH reflects the following two assumptions:

- The number of records is potentially very large, and therefore we want to make only one scan over the database.
- Only a limited amount of main memory is available.

A user can set two parameters to control the BIRCH algorithm. The first is a threshold on the amount of main memory available. This main memory threshold translates into a maximum number of cluster summaries k that can be maintained in memory. The second parameter ϵ is an initial threshold for the radius of any cluster. The value of ϵ is an upper bound on the radius of any cluster and controls the number of clusters that the algorithm discovers. If ϵ is small, we discover many small clusters; if ϵ is large, we discover very few clusters, each of which is relatively large. We say that a cluster is **compact** if its radius is smaller than ϵ.

BIRCH always maintains k or fewer cluster summaries (C_i, R_i) in main memory, where C_i is the center of cluster i and R_i is the radius of cluster i. The algorithm always maintains compact clusters; that is, the radius of each cluster is less than ϵ. If this invariant cannot be maintained with the given amount of main memory, ϵ is increased as described next.

The algorithm reads records from the database sequentially and processes them as follows:

1. Compute the distance between record r and each of the existing cluster centers. Let i be the cluster index such that the distance between r and C_i is the smallest.

2. Compute the value of the new radius R'_i of the ith cluster under the assumption that r is inserted into it. If $R'_i \leq \epsilon$, then the ith cluster remains compact, and we assign r to the ith cluster by updating its center and setting its radius to R'_i. If $R'_i > \epsilon$, then the ith cluster would no longer be compact if we insert r into it. Therefore, we start a new cluster containing only the record r.

The second step presents a problem if we already have the maximum number of cluster summaries, k. If we now read a record that requires us to create a new cluster, we lack the main memory required to hold its summary. In this case, we increase the radius threshold ϵ—using some heuristic to determine the increase—in order to *merge* existing clusters: An increase of ϵ has two consequences. First, existing clusters can accommodate more records, since their maximum radius has increased. Second, it might be possible to merge existing clusters such that the resulting cluster is still compact. Thus, an increase in ϵ usually reduces the number of existing clusters.

The complete BIRCH algorithm uses a balanced in-memory tree, which is similar to a B+ tree in structure, to quickly identify the closest cluster center for a new record. A description of this data structure is beyond the scope of our discussion.

26.6 SIMILARITY SEARCH OVER SEQUENCES

A lot of information stored in databases consists of sequences. In this section, we introduce the problem of similarity search over a collection of sequences. Our query model is very simple: We assume that the user specifies a **query sequence** and wants to retrieve all data sequences that are similar to the

Commercial Data Mining Systems: There are a number of data mining products on the market today, such as SAS Enterprise Miner, SPSS Clementine, CART from Salford Systems, Megaputer PolyAnalyst, ANGOSS KnowledgeStudio. We highlight two that have strong database ties.

IBM's Intelligent Miner offers a wide range of algorithms, including association rules, regression, classification, and clustering. The emphasis of Intelligent Miner is on scalability—the product contains versions of all algorithms for parallel computers and is tightly integrated with IBM's DB2 database system. DB2's object-relational capabilities can be used to define the data mining classes of SQL/MM. Of course, other data mining vendors can use these capabilities to add their own data mining models and algorithms to DB2.

Microsoft's SQL Server 2000 has a component called the Analysis Server that makes it possible to create, apply, and manage data mining models within the DBMS. (SQL Server's OLAP capabilities are also packaged in the Analysis Server component.) The basic approach taken is to represent a mining model as a table; clustering and decision tree models are currently supported. The table conceptually has one row for each possible combination of input (predictor) attribute values. The model is created using a statement analogous to SQL's `CREATE TABLE` that describes the input on which the model is to be trained and the algorithm to use in constructing the model. An interesting feature is that the input table can be defined, using a specialized view mechanism, to be a *nested table.* For example, we can define an input table with one row per customer, where one of the fields is a nested table that describes the customer's purchases. The SQL/MM extensions for data mining do not provide this capability because SQL:1999 does not currently support nested tables (Section 23.2.1). Several properties of attributes, such as whether they are discrete or continuous, can also be specified.

A model is trained by inserting rows into it, using the `INSERT` command. It is applied to a new dataset to make predictions using a new kind of join called `PREDICTION JOIN`; in principle, each input tuple is matched with the corresponding tuple in the mining model to determine the value of the predicted attribute. Thus, end users can create, train, and apply decision trees and clustering using extended SQL. There are also commands to browse models. Unfortunately, users cannot add new models or new algorithms for models, a capability that is supported in the SQL/MM proposal.

query sequence. Similarity search is different from 'normal' queries in that we are interested not only in sequences that match the query sequence exactly but also those that differ only slightly from the query sequence.

We begin by describing sequences and similarity between sequences. A **data sequence** X is a series of numbers $X = \langle x_1, \ldots, x_k \rangle$. Sometimes X is also called a **time series**. We call k the **length** of the sequence. A **subsequence** $Z = \langle z_1, \ldots, z_j \rangle$ is obtained from another sequence $X = \langle x_1, \ldots, x_k \rangle$ by deleting numbers from the front and back of the sequence X. Formally, Z is a subsequence of X if $z_1 = x_i, z_2 = x_{i+1}, \ldots, z_j = z_{i+j-1}$ for some $i \in \{1, \ldots, k-j+1\}$. Given two sequences $X = \langle x_1, \ldots, x_k \rangle$ and $Y = \langle y_1, \ldots, y_k \rangle$, we can define the **Euclidean norm** as the distance between the two sequences as follows:

$$\|X - Y\| = \sum_{i=1}^{k} (x_i - y_i)^2$$

Given a user-specified query sequence and a threshold parameter ϵ, our goal is to retrieve all data sequences that are within ϵ-distance of the query sequence.

Similarity queries over sequences can be classified into two types.

- **Complete Sequence Matching:** The query sequence and the sequences in the database have the same length. Given a user-specified threshold parameter ϵ, our goal is to retrieve all sequences in the database that are within ϵ-distance to the query sequence.
- **Subsequence Matching:** The query sequence is shorter than the sequences in the database. In this case, we want to find all subsequences of sequences in the database such that the subsequence is within distance ϵ of the query sequence. We do not discuss subsequence matching.

26.6.1 An Algorithm to Find Similar Sequences

Given a collection of data sequences, a query sequence, and a distance threshold ϵ, how can we efficiently find all sequences within ϵ-distance of the query sequence?

One possibility is to scan the database, retrieve each data sequence, and compute its distance to the query sequence. While this algorithm has the merit of being simple, it always retrieves every data sequence.

Because we consider the complete sequence matching problem, all data sequences and the query sequence have the same length. We can think of this similarity search as a high-dimensional indexing problem. Each data sequence and the query sequence can be represented as a point in a k-dimensional space. Therefore, if we insert all data sequences into a multidimensional index, we can retrieve data sequences that exactly match the query sequence by querying the index. But since we want to retrieve not only data sequences that match the query exactly but also all sequences within ϵ-distance of the query sequence, we do not use a point query as defined by the query sequence. Instead, we query the index with a hyper-rectangle that has side-length 2ϵ and the query sequence as center, and we retrieve all sequences that fall within this hyper-rectangle. We then discard sequences that are actually further than ϵ away from the query sequence.

Using the index allows us to greatly reduce the number of sequences we consider and decreases the time to evaluate the similarity query significantly. The bibliographic notes at the end of the chapter provide pointers to further improvements.

26.7 INCREMENTAL MINING AND DATA STREAMS

Real-life data is not static, but is constantly evolving through additions or deletions of records. In some applications, such as network monitoring, data arrives in such high-speed streams that it is infeasible to store the data for offline analysis. We describe both evolving and streaming data in terms of a framework called **block evolution**. In block evolution, the input dataset to the data mining process is not static but periodically updated with a new block of tuples, for example, every day at midnight or in a continuous stream. A **block** is a set of tuples added simultaneously to the database. For large blocks, this model captures common practice in many of today's data warehouse installations, where updates from operational databases are batched together and performed in a block update. For small blocks of data—at the extreme, each block consists of a single record—this model captures streaming data.

In the block evolution model, the database consists of a (conceptually infinite) sequence of data blocks $D_1, D_2, \ldots$ that arrive at times $1, 2, \ldots$, where each block D_i consists of a set of records.[2] We call i the *block identifier* of block B_i. Therefore, at any time t, the database consists of a finite sequence of blocks of data $\langle D_1, \ldots, D_t \rangle$ that arrived at times $\{1, 2, \ldots, t\}$. The database at time t, which we denote by $D[1, t]$, is the union of the database at time $t - 1$ and the block that arrives at time t, D_t.

For evolving data, two classes of problems are of particular interest: model maintenance and change detection. The goal of **model maintenance** is to

[2] In general, a block specifies records to change or delete, in addition to records to insert. We only consider inserts.

maintain a data mining model under insertion and deletions of blocks of data. To incrementally compute the data mining model at time t, which we denote by $M(D[1,t])$, we must consider only $M(D[1,t-1])$ and D_t; we cannot consider the data that arrived prior to time t. Further, a data analyst might specify time-dependent subsets of $D[1,t]$, such as a window of interest (e.g., all the data seen thus far or last week's data). More general selections are also possible, for example, all weekend data over the past year. Given such selections, we must incrementally compute the model on the appropriate subset of $D[1,t]$ by considering only D_t and the model on the appropriate subset of $D[1,t-1]$. 'Almost' incremental algorithms that occasionally examine older data might be acceptable in warehouse applications, where incrementality is motivated by efficiency considerations and older data is available to us if necessary. This option is not available for high-speed data streams, where older data may not be available at all.

The goal of **change detection** is to quantify the difference, in terms of their data characteristics, between two sets of data and determine whether the change is meaningful (i.e., statistically significant). In particular, we must quantify the difference between the models of the data as it existed at some time t_1 and the evolved version at a subsequent time t_2; that is, we must quantify the difference between $M(D[1,t_1])$ and $M(D[1,t_2])$. We can also measure changes with respect to selected subsets of data. Several natural variants of the problem exist; for example, the difference between $M(D[1,t-1])$ and $M(D_t)$ indicates whether the latest block differs substantially from previously existing data. In the rest of this chapter, we focus on model maintenance and do not discuss change detection.

Incremental model maintenance has received much attention. Since the quality of the data mining model is of utmost importance, incremental model maintenance algorithms have concentrated on computing exactly the same model as computed by running the basic model construction algorithm on the union of old and new data. One widely used scalability technique is localization of changes due to new blocks. For example, for density-based clustering algorithms, the insertion of a new record affects only clusters in the neighborhood of the record, and thus efficient algorithms can *localize* the change to a few clusters and avoid recomputing all clusters. As another example, in decision tree construction, we might be able to show that the split criterion at a node of the tree changes only within acceptably small confidence intervals when records are inserted, if we assume that the underlying distribution of training records is static.

One-pass model construction over data streams has received particular attention, since data arrives and must be processed continuously in several emerging application domains. For example, network installations of large Telecom

and Internet service providers have detailed usage information (e.g., call-detail-records, router packet-flow and trace data) from different parts of the underlying network that needs to be continuously analyzed to detect interesting trends. Other examples include webserver logs, streams of transactional data from large retail chains, and financial stock tickers.

When working with high-speed data streams, algorithms must be designed to construct data mining models while looking at the relevant data items *only once and in a fixed order* (determined by the stream-arrival pattern), with a limited amount of main memory. Data-stream computation has given rise to several recent (theoretical and practical) studies of online or one-pass algorithms with bounded memory. Algorithms have been developed for one-pass computation of quantiles and order-statistics, estimation of frequency moments and join sizes, clustering and decision tree construction, estimating correlated aggregates, and computing one-dimensional (i.e., single-attribute) histograms and Haar wavelet decompositions. Next, we discuss one such algorithm, for incremental maintenance of frequent itemsets.

26.7.1 Incremental Maintenance of Frequent Itemsets

Consider the Purchases Relation shown in Figure 26.1 and assume that the minimum support threshold is 60%. It can be easily seen that the set of frequent itemsets of size 1 consists of {*pen* }, {*ink*}, and {*milk*} with supports of 100%, 75%, and 75%, respectively. The set of frequent itemsets of size 2 consists of {*pen, ink*} and {*pen, milk*}, both with supports of 75%. The Purchases relation is our first block of data. Our goal is to develop an algorithm that maintains the set of frequent itemsets under insertion of new blocks of data.

As a first example, let us consider the addition of the block of data shown in Figure 26.13 to our original database (Figure 26.1). Under this addition, the set of frequent itemsets does not change, although their support values do: {*pen*}, {*ink*}, and {*milk*} now have support values of 100%, 60%, and 60%, respectively, and {*pen, ink*} and {*pen, milk*} now have 60% support. Note that we could detect this case of 'no change' simply by maintaining the number of market baskets in which each itemset occured. In this example, we update the (absolute) support of itemset {*pen*} by 1.

transid	*custid*	*date*	*item*	*qty*
115	201	7/1/99	pen	2

Figure 26.13 The Purchases Relation Block 2

transid	*custid*	*date*	*item*	*qty*
115	201	7/1/99	water	1
115	201	7/1/99	milk	1

Figure 26.14 The Purchases Relation Block 2a

In general, the set of frequent itemsets may change. As an example, consider the addition of the block shown in Figure 26.14 to the original database shown in Figure 26.1. We see a transaction containing the item water, but we do not know the support of the itemset {*water*}, since water was not above the minimum support in our original database. A simple solution in this case is to make an additional scan over the original database and compute the support of the itemset {*water*}. But can we do better? Another immediate solution is to keep counters for *all* possible itemsets, but the number of all possible itemsets is exponential in the number of items—and most of these counters would be 0 anyway. Can we design an intelligent strategy that tells us *which* counters to maintain?

We introduce the notion of the **negative border** of a set of itemsets to help decide which counters to keep. The negative border of a set of frequent itemsets consists of all itemsets X such that X itself is not frequent, but all subsets of X are frequent. For example, in the case of the database shown in Figure 26.1, the following itemsets make up the negative border: {*juice*}, {*water*}, and {*ink, milk*}. Now we can design a more efficient algorithm for maintaining frequent itemsets by keeping counters for all currently frequent itemsets *and* all itemsets currently in the negative border. Only if an itemset in the negative border becomes frequent do we need to read the original dataset again, to find the support for new candidate itemsets that might be frequent.

We illustrate this point through the following two examples. If we add Block 2a shown in Figure 26.14 to the original database shown in Figure 26.1, we increase the support of the frequent itemset {*milk*} by one, and we increase the support of the itemset {*water*}, which is in the negative border, by one as well. But since no itemset in the negative border became frequent, we do not have to re-scan the original database.

In contrast, consider the addition of Block 2b shown in Figure 26.15 to the original database shown in Figure 26.1. In this case, the itemset {*juice*}, which was originally in the negative border, becomes frequent with a support of 60%. This means that now the following itemsets of size two enter the negative border: {*juice, pen*}, {*juice, ink*}, and {*juice, milk*}. (We know that {*juice, water*} cannot be frequent since the itemset {*water*} is not frequent.)

transid	*custid*	*date*	*item*	*qty*
115	201	7/1/99	juice	2
115	201	7/1/99	water	2

Figure 26.15 The Purchases Relation Block 2b

26.8 ADDITIONAL DATA MINING TASKS

We focused on the problem of discovering patterns from a database, but there are several other equally important data mining tasks. We now discuss some of these briefly. The bibliographic references at the end of the chapter provide many pointers for further study.

- **Dataset and Feature Selection:** It is often important to select the 'right' dataset to mine. Dataset selection is the process of finding which datasets to mine. Feature selection is the process of deciding which attributes to include in the mining process.

- **Sampling:** One way to explore a large dataset is to obtain one or more *samples* and analyze them. The advantage of sampling is that we can carry out detailed analysis on a sample that would be infeasible on the entire dataset, for very large datasets. The disadvantage of sampling is that obtaining a representative sample for a given task is difficult; we might miss important trends or patterns because they are not reflected in the sample. Current database systems also provide poor support for efficiently obtaining samples. Improving database support for obtaining samples with various desirable statistical properties is relatively straightforward and likely to be available in future DBMSs. Applying sampling for data mining is an area for further research.

- **Visualization:** Visualization techniques can significantly assist in understanding complex datasets and detecting interesting patterns, and the importance of visualization in data mining is widely recognized.

26.9 REVIEW QUESTIONS

Answers to the review questions can be found in the listed sections.

- What is the role of data mining in the KDD process? **(Section 26.1)**
- What is the a priori property? Describe an algorithm for finding frequent itemsets. **(Section 26.2.1)**

- How are iceberg queries related to frequent itemsets? **(Section 26.2.2)**
- Give the definition of an *association rule*. What is the difference between support and confidence of a rule? **(Setion 26.3.1)**
- Can you explain extensions of association rules to ISA hierarchies? What other extensions of association rules are you familiar with? **(Sections 26.3.3 and 26.3.4)**
- What is a sequential pattern? How can we compute sequential patterns? **(Section 26.3.5)**
- Can we use association rules for prediction? **(Section 26.3.6)**
- What is the difference between Bayesian Networks and association rules? **(Section 26.3.7)**
- Can you give examples of classification and regression rules? How is support and confidence for such rules defined? **(Section 26.3.8)**
- What are the components of a decision tree? How are decision trees constructed? **(Sections 26.4.1 and 26.4.2)**
- What is a cluster? What information do we usually output for a cluster? **(Section 26.5)**
- How can we define the distance between two sequences? Describe an algorithm to find all sequences similar to a query sequence. **(Section 26.6)**
- Describe the block evolution model and define the problems of incremental model maintenance and change detection. What is the added challenge in mining data streams? **(Section 26.7)**
- Describe an incremental algorithm for computing frequent itemsets. **(Section 26.7.1)**
- Give examples of other tasks related to data mining. **(Section 26.8)**

EXERCISES

Exercise 26.1 Briefly answer the following questions:

1. Define *support* and *confidence* for an association rule.
2. Explain why association rules cannot be used directly for prediction, without further analysis or domain knowledge.
3. What are the differences between *association rules*, *classification rules*, and *regression rules*?
4. What is the difference between *classification* and *clustering*?

transid	*custid*	*date*	*item*	*qty*
111	201	5/1/2002	ink	1
111	201	5/1/2002	milk	2
111	201	5/1/2002	juice	1
112	105	6/3/2002	pen	1
112	105	6/3/2002	ink	1
112	105	6/3/2002	water	1
113	106	5/10/2002	pen	1
113	106	5/10/2002	water	2
113	106	5/10/2002	milk	1
114	201	6/1/2002	pen	2
114	201	6/1/2002	ink	2
114	201	6/1/2002	juice	4
114	201	6/1/2002	water	1
114	201	6/1/2002	milk	1

Figure 26.16 The Purchases2 Relation

5. What is the role of information visualization in data mining?
6. Give examples of queries over a database of stock price quotes, stored as sequences, one per stock, that cannot be expressed in SQL.

Exercise 26.2 Consider the Purchases table shown in Figure 26.1.

1. Simulate the algorithm for finding frequent itemsets on the table in Figure 26.1 with *minsup*=90 percent, and then find association rules with *minconf*=90 percent.
2. Can you modify the table so that the same frequent itemsets are obtained with *minsup*=90 percent as with *minsup*=70 percent on the table shown in Figure 26.1?
3. Simulate the algorithm for finding frequent itemsets on the table in Figure 26.1 with *minsup*=10 percent and then find association rules with *minconf*=90 percent.
4. Can you modify the table so that the same frequent itemsets are obtained with *minsup*=10 percent as with *minsup*=70 percent on the table shown in Figure 26.1?

Exercise 26.3 Assume we are given a dataset D of market baskets and have computed the set of frequent itemsets $\mathcal{X}$ in D for a given support threshold *minsup*. Assume that we would like to add another dataset D' to D, and maintain the set of frequent itemsets with support threshold *minsup* in $D \cup D'$. Consider the following algorithm for incremental maintenance of a set of frequent itemsets:

1. We run the *a priori* algorithm on D' and find all frequent itemsets in D' and their support. The result is a set of itemsets $\mathcal{X}'$. We also compute the support of all itemsets $X \in \mathcal{X}$ in D'.
2. We then make a scan over D to compute the support of all itemsets in $\mathcal{X}'$.

Answer the following questions about the algorithm:

- The last step of the algorithm is missing; that is, what should the algorithm output?
- Is this algorithm more efficient than the algorithm described in Section 26.7.1?

Exercise 26.4 Consider the Purchases2 table shown in Figure 26.16.

- List all itemsets in the negative border of the dataset.
- List all frequent itemsets for a support threshold of 50%.
- Give an example of a database in which the addition of this database does not change the negative border.
- Give an example of a database in which the addition of this database would change the negative border.

Exercise 26.5 Consider the Purchases table shown in Figure 26.1. Find all (generalized) association rules that indicate the likelihood of items being purchased on the same date by the same customer, with *minsup* set to 10% and *minconf* set to 70%.

Exercise 26.6 Let us develop a new algorithm for the computation of all large itemsets. Assume that we are given a relation D similar to the Purchases table shown in Figure 26.1. We partition the table horizontally into k parts $D_1, \ldots, D_k$.

1. Show that, if itemset X is frequent in D, then it is frequent in at least one of the k parts.
2. Use this observation to develop an algorithm that computes all frequent itemsets in two scans over D. (Hint: In the first scan, compute the locally frequent itemsets for each part D_i, $i \in \{1, \ldots, k\}$.)
3. Illustrate your algorithm using the Purchases table shown in Figure 26.1. The first partition consists of the two transactions with *transid* 111 and 112, the second partition consists of the two transactions with *transid* 113 and 114. Assume that the minimum support is 70 percent.

Exercise 26.7 Consider the Purchases table shown in Figure 26.1. Find all sequential patterns with *minsup* set to 60%. (The text only sketches the algorithm for discovering sequential patterns, so use brute force or read one of the references for a complete algorithm.)

Exercise 26.8 Consider the SubscriberInfo Relation shown in Figure 26.17. It contains information about the marketing campaign of the *DB Aficionado* magazine. The first two columns show the age and salary of a potential customer and the *subscription* column shows whether the person subscribes to the magazine. We want to use this data to construct a decision tree that helps predict whether a person will subscribe to the magazine.

1. Construct the AVC-group of the root node of the tree.
2. Assume that the spliting predicate at the root node is $age \leq 50$. Construct the AVC-groups of the two children nodes of the root node.

Exercise 26.9 Assume you are given the following set of six records: $\langle 7, 55\rangle$, $\langle 21, 202\rangle$, $\langle 25, 220\rangle$, $\langle 12, 73\rangle$, $\langle 8, 61\rangle$, and $\langle 22, 249\rangle$.

1. Assuming that all six records belong to a single cluster, compute its center and radius.
2. Assume that the first three records belong to one cluster and the second three records belong to a different cluster. Compute the center and radius of the two clusters.
3. Which of the two clusterings is 'better' in your opinion and why?

Exercise 26.10 Assume you are given the three sequences $\langle 1, 3, 4\rangle$, $\langle 2, 3, 2\rangle$, $\langle 3, 3, 7\rangle$. Compute the Euclidian norm between all pairs of sequences.

age	*salary*	*subscription*
37	45k	No
39	70k	Yes
56	50k	Yes
52	43k	Yes
35	90k	Yes
32	54k	No
40	58k	No
55	85k	Yes
43	68k	Yes

Figure 26.17 The SubscriberInfo Relation

BIBLIOGRAPHIC NOTES

Discovering useful knowledge from a large database is more than just applying a collection of data mining algorithms, and the point of view that it is an iterative process guided by an analyst is stressed in [265] and [666]. Work on exploratory data analysis in statistics, for example [745], and on machine learning and knowledge discovery in artificial intelligence was a precursor to the current focus on data mining; the added emphasis on large volumes of data is the important new element. Good recent surveys of data mining algorithms include [267, 397, 507]. [266] contains additional surveys and articles on many aspects of data mining and knowledge discovery, including a tutorial on Bayesian networks [371]. The book by Piatetsky-Shapiro and Frawley [595] contains an interesting collection of data mining papers. The annual SIGKDD conference, run by the ACM special interest group in knowledge discovery in databases, is a good resource for readers interested in current research in data mining [25, 162, 268, 372, 613, 691], as is the *Journal of Knowledge Discovery and Data Mining.* [363, 370, 511, 781] are good, in-depth textbooks on data mining.

The problem of mining association rules was introduced by Agrawal, Imielinski, and Swami [20]. Many efficient algorithms have been proposed for the computation of large itemsets, including [21, 117, 364, 683, 738, 786].

Iceberg queries have been introduced by Fang et al. [264]. There is also a large body of research on generalized forms of association rules; for example, [700, 701, 703]. The problem of finding maximal frequent itemsets has also received significant attention [13, 67, 126, 346, 347, 479, 787]. Algorithms for mining association rules with constraints are considered in [68, 462, 563, 590, 591, 703].

Parallel algorithms are described in [23] and [655]. Recent papers on parallel data mining can be found in [788], and work on distributed data mining can be found in [417].

[291] presents an algorithm for discovering association rules over a continuous numeric attribute; association rules over numeric attributes are also discussed in [783]. The general form of association rules, in which attributes other than the transaction id are grouped is developed in [529]. Association rules over items in a hierarchy are discussed in [361, 700]. Further

extensions and generalization of association rules are proposed in [67, 115, 563]. Integration of mining for frequent itemsets into database systems has been addressed in [654, 743]. The problem of mining sequential patterns is discussed in [24], and further algorithms for mining sequential patterns can be found in [510, 702].

General introductions to classification and regression rules can be found in [362, 532]. The classic reference for decision and regression tree construction is the CART book by Breiman, Friedman, Olshen, and Stone [111]. A machine learning perspective of decision tree construction is given by Quinlan [603]. Recently, several scalable algorithms for decision tree construction have been developed [309, 311, 521, 619, 674].

The clustering problem has been studied for decades in several disciplines. Sample textbooks include [232, 407, 418]. Scalable clustering algorithms include CLARANS [562], DBSCAN [249, 250], BIRCH [798], and CURE [344]. Bradley, Fayyad, and Reina address the problem of scaling the K-Means clustering algorithm to large databases [108, 109]. The problem of finding clusters in subsets of the fields is addressed in [19]. Ganti et al. examine the problem of clustering data in arbitrary metric spaces [302]. Algorithms for clustering caterogical data include STIRR [315] and CACTUS [301]. [651] is a clustering algorithm for spatial data.

Finding similar sequences from a large database of sequences is discussed in [22, 262, 446, 606, 680].

Work on incremental maintenance of association rules is considered in [174, 175, 736]. Ester et al. describe how to maintain clusters incrementally [248], and Hidber describes how to maintain large itemsets incrementally [378]. There has also been recent work on mining data streams, such as the construction of decision trees over data streams [228, 309, 393] and clustering data streams [343, 568]. A general framework for mining evolving data is presented in [299]. A framework for measuring change in data characteristics is proposed in [300].

27

INFORMATION RETRIEVAL AND XML DATA

- How are DBMSs evolving in response to the growing amounts of text data?
- What is the vector space model and how does it support text search?
- How are text collections indexed?
- Compared to IR systems, what is new in Web search?
- How is XML data different from plain text and relational tables?
- What are the main features of XQuery?
- What are the implementation challenges posed by XML data?
- **Key concepts:** information retrieval, boolean and ranked queries; relevance, precision, recall; vector space model, TF/IDF term weighting, document similarity; inverted index, signature file; Web crawler, hubs and authorities, Pigeon Rank of a webpage; semistructured data model, XML; XQuery, path expressions, FLWR queries; XML storage and indexing

with Raghav Kaushik
University of Wisconsin–Madison

A *memex* is a device in which an individual stores all his books, records, and communications, and which is mechanized so that it may be consulted with exceeding speed and flexibility.

—Vannevar Bush, *As We May Think, 1945*

The field of **information retrieval (IR)** has studied the problem of searching collections of text documents since the 1950s and developed largely independently of database systems. The proliferation of text documents on the Web made document search an everyday operation for most people and led to renewed research on the topic.

The database field's desire to expand the kinds of data that can be managed in a DBMS is well-established and reflected in developments like object-relational extensions (Chapter 23). Documents on the Web represent one of the most rapidly growing sources of data, and the challenge of managing such documents in a DBMS has naturally become a focal point for database research.

The Web, therefore, brought the two fields of database management systems and information retrieval closer together than ever before, and, as we will see, XML sits squarely in the middle ground between them. We introduce IR systems as well as a data model and query language for XML data and discuss the relationship with (object-)relational database systems.

In this chapter, we present an overview of information retrieval, Web search, and the emerging XML data model and query language standards. We begin in Section 27.1 with a discussion of how these text-oriented trends fit within the context of current object-relational database systems. We introduce information retrieval concepts in Section 27.2 and discuss specialized indexing techniques for text in Section 27.3. We discuss Web search engines in Section 27.4. In Section 27.5, we briefly outline current trends in extending database systems to support text data and identify some of the important issues involved. In Section 27.6, we present the XML data model, building on the XML concepts introduced in Chapter 7. We describe the XQuery language in Section 27.7. In Section 27.8, we consider efficient evaluation of XQuery queries.

27.1 COLLIDING WORLDS: DATABASES, IR, AND XML

The Web is the most widely used document collection today, and search on the Web differs from traditional IR-style document retrieval in important ways. First, there is great emphasis on scalability to very large document collections. IR systems typically dealt with tens of thousands of documents, whereas the Web contains billions of pages.

Second, the Web has significantly changed how document collections are created and used. Traditionally, IR systems were aimed at professionals like librarians and legal researchers, who were trained in using sophisticated retrieval engines. Documents were carefully prepared, and documents in a given collection were typically on related topics. On the Web, documents are created by an infinite

variety of individuals for equally many purposes, and reflect this diversity in size and content. Searches are carried out by ordinary people with no training in using retrieval software.

The emergence of XML has added a third interesting dimension to text search: Every document can now be marked up to reflect additional information of interest, such as authorship, source, and even details about the intrinsic content. This has changed the nature of a "document" from free text to textual objects with associated fields containing **metadata** (data about data) or descriptive information. Links to other documents are a particularly important kind of metadata, and they can have great value in searching document collections on the Web.

The Web also changed the notion of what constitutes a document. Documents on the Web may be multimedia objects such as images or video clips, with text appearing only in descriptive tags. We must be able to manage such heterogeneous data collections and support searches over them.

Database management systems traditionally dealt with simple tabular data. In recent years, object-relational database systems (ORDBMSs) were designed to support complex data types. Images, videos, and textual objects have been explicitly mentioned as examples of the data types ORDBMSs are intended to support. Nonetheless, current database systems have a long way to go before they can support such complex data types satisfactorily. In the context of text and XML data, challenges include efficient support for searches over textual content and support for searches that exploit the loose structure of XML data.

27.1.1 DBMS versus IR Systems

Database and IR systems have the common objective of supporting searches over collections of data. However, many important differences have influenced their development.

- **Searches versus Queries:** IR systems are designed to support a specialized class of queries that we also call **searches**. Searches are specified in terms of a few **search terms**, and the underlying data is usually a collection of unstructured text documents. In addition, an important feature of IR searches is that search results may be **ranked**, or ordered, in terms of how 'well' the search results match the search terms. In contrast, database systems support a very general class of queries, and the underlying data is rigidly structured. Unlike IR systems, database systems have traditionally returned unranked sets of results. (Even the recent SQL/OLAP extensions that support early results and searches over ordered data (see Chapter 25)

do not order results in terms of how well they match the query. Relational queries are *precise* in that a row is either in the answer or it is not ; there is no notion of 'how well a row matches' the query.) In other words, a relational query only assigns two ranks to a row, indicating whether the row is in the answer or not.

- **Updates and Transactions:** IR systems are optimized for a read-mostly workload and do not support the notion of a transaction. In traditional IR systems, new documents are added to the document collection from time to time, and index structures that speed up searches are periodically rebuilt or updated. Therefore, documents that are highly relevant for a search might exist in the IR system, but not be retrievable yet because of outdated index structures. In contrast, database systems are designed to handle a wide range of workloads, including update-intensive transaction processing workloads.

These differences in design objectives have led, not surprisingly, to very different research emphases and system designs. Research in IR studied ranking functions extensively. For example, among other topics, research in IR investigated how to incorporate feedback from a user's behavior to modify a ranking function and how to apply linguistic processing techniques to improve searches. Database research concentrated on query processing, concurrency control and recovery, and other topics, as covered in this book.

The differences between a DBMS and an IR system from a design and implementation standpoint should become clear as we introduce IR systems in the next few sections.

27.2 INTRODUCTION TO INFORMATION RETRIEVAL

There are two common types of searches, or queries, over text collections: boolean queries and ranked queries. In a **boolean query**, the user specifies an expression constructed using terms and boolean operators (`And`, `Or`, `Not`). For example,

database `And` (*Microsoft* `Or` *IBM*)

This query asks for all documents that contain the term *database* and in addition, either *Microsoft* or *IBM.*

In a **ranked query** the user specifies one or more terms, and the result of the query is a list of documents ranked by their relevance to the query. Intuitively, documents at the top of the result list are expected to 'match' the search

docid	Document
1	agent James Bond good agent
2	agent mobile computer
3	James Madison movie
4	James Bond movie

Figure 27.1 A Text Database with Four Records

condition more closely, or be 'more relevant', than documents lower in the result list. While a document that contains *Microsoft* satisfies the search '*Microsoft, IBM*,' a document that also contains *IBM* is considered to be a better match. Similarly, a document that contains several occurrences of *Microsoft* might be a better match than a document that contains a single occurence. Ranking the documents that satisfy the boolean search condition is an important aspect of an IR search engine, and we discuss how this is done in Sections 27.2.3 and 27.4.2.

An important extension of ranked queries is to ask for documents that are most relevant to a given natural language sentence. Since a sentence has linguistic structure (e.g., subject-verb-object relationships), it provides more information than just the list of words that it contains. We do not discuss **natural language search**.

27.2.1 Vector Space Model

We now describe a widely-used framework for representing documents and searching over document collections. Consider the set of all terms that appear in a given collection of documents. We can represent each document as a vector with one entry per term. In the simplest form of document vectors, if term j appears k times in document i, the **document vector** for document i contains value k in position j. The document vector for i contains the value 0 in positions corresponding to terms that do not appear in i.

Consider the example collection of four documents shown in Figure 27.1. The document vector representation is illustrated in Figure 27.2; each row represents a document. This representation of documents as term vectors is called the **vector space model**.

docid	agent	Bond	computer	good	James	Madison	mobile	movie
1	2	1	0	1	1	0	0	0
2	1	0	1	0	0	0	1	0
3	0	0	0	0	1	1	0	1
4	0	1	0	0	1	0	0	1

Figure 27.2 Document Vectors for the Example Collection

27.2.2 TF/IDF Weighting of Terms

We described the value for a term in a document vector as simply the **term frequency (TF)**, or number of occurrences of that term in the given document. This reflects the intuition that a term which appears often is more important in characterizing the document than a term that appears only once (or a term that does not appear at all).

However, some terms appear very frequently in the document collection, and others are relatively rare. The frequency of terms is empirically observed to follow a Zipfian distribution, as illustrated in Figure 27.3. In this figure, each position on the X-axis corresponds to a term and the Y-axis corresponds to the number of occurrences of the term. Terms are arranged on the X-axis in decreasing order by the number of times they occur (in the document collection as a whole).

As might be expected, it turns out that extremely common terms are not very useful in searches. Examples of such common terms include *a, an, the* etc. Terms that occur extremely often are called **stop words**, and documents are pre-processed to eliminate stop words.

Even after eliminating stop words, we have the phenomenon that some words appear much more often than others in the document collection. Consider the words *Linux* and *kernel* in the context of a collection of documents about the Linux operating system. While neither is common enough to be a stop word, *Linux* is likely to appear much more often. Given a search that contains both these keywords, we are likely to get better results if we give more importance to documents that contain *kernel* than documents that contain *Linux*.

We can capture this intuition by refining the document vector representation as follows. The value associated with term j in the document vector for document i, denoted as w_{ij}, is obtained by multiplying the term frequency t_{ij} (the number of times term j appears in document i) by the **inverse document frequency (IDF)** of term j in the document collection. IDF of a term j is defined as

$log(N/n_j)$, where N is the total number of documents, and n_j is the number of documents that term j appears in. This effectively increases the weight given to rare terms. As an example, in a collection of 10,000 documents, a term that appears in half the documents has an IDF of 0.3, and a term that occurs in just one document has an IDF of 4.

Length Normalization

Consider a document D. Suppose that we modify it by adding a large number of new terms. Should a the weight of a term t that appears in D be the same in the document vectors for D and the modified document? Although the TF/IDF weight for t is indeed the same in the two document vector, our intuition suggests that the weight should be less in the modified document. Longer documents tend to have more terms, and more occurrences of any given term. Thus, if two documents contain the same number of occurrences of a given term, the importance of the term in characterizing the document also depends on the length of the document.

Several approaches to **length normalization** have been proposed. Intuitively, all of them reduce the importance given to how often a term occurs as the frequency grows. In traditional IR systems, a popular way to refine the similarity metric is **cosine length normalization**:

$$w_{ij}^{*} = \frac{w_{ij}}{\sqrt{\sum_{k=1}^{t} w_{ik}^{2}}}$$

In this formula, t is the number of terms in the document collection, w_{ij} is the TF/IDF weight without length normalization, and w_{ij}^{*} is the length adjusted TF/IDF weight.

Terms that occur frequently in a document are particularly problematic on the Web because webpages are often deliberately modified by adding many copies of certain words—for example, sale, free, sex —to increase the likelihood of their being returned in response to queries. For this reason, Web search engines typically normalize for length by imposing a maximum value (usually 2 or 3) for term frequencies.

27.2.3 Ranking Document Similarity

We now consider how the vector space representation allows us to rank documents in the result of a ranked query. A key observation is that a ranked query can itself be thought of as a document, since it is just a collection of terms. This allows us to use **document similarity** as the basis for ranking query

results—the document that is most similar to the query is ranked highest, and the one that is least similar is ranked lowest.

If a total of t terms appear in the collection of documents (t is 8 in the example shown in Figure 27.2), we can visualize document vectors in a t-dimensional space in which each axis is labeled with a term. This is illustrated in Figure 27.4, for a two-dimensional space. The figure shows document vectors for two documents, D_1 and D_2, as well as a query Q.

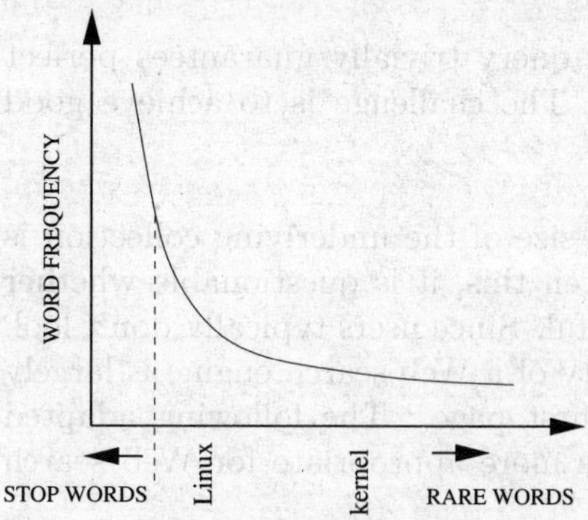

Figure 27.3 Zipfian Distribution of Term Frequencies

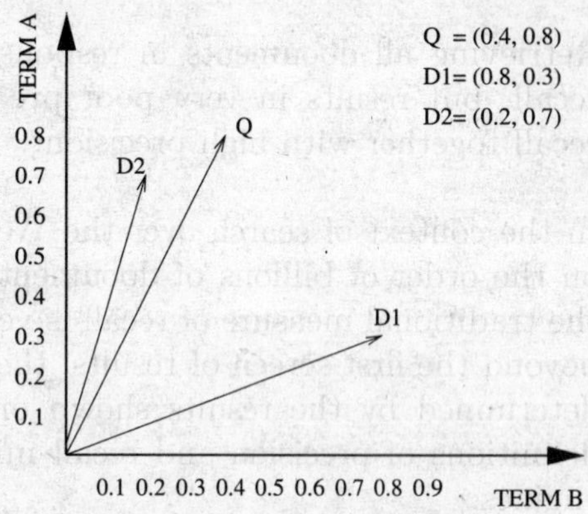

Figure 27.4 Document Similarity

The traditional measure of closeness between two vectors, their *dot product*, is used as a measure of document similarity. The similarity of query Q to a document D_i is measured by their dot product:

$$sim(Q, D_i) = \sum_{j=1}^{t} q_j^*.w_{ij}^*$$

In the example shown in Figure 27.4, $sim(Q, D_1) = (0.4 * 0.8) + (0.8 * 0.3) = 0.56$, and $sim(Q, D_2) = (0.4 * 0.2) + (0.8 * 0.7) = 0.64$. Accordingly, D_2 is ranked higher than D_1 in the search result.

In the context of the Web, document similarity is one of several measures that can be used to rank results, but should not be used exclusively. First, it is questionable whether users want documents that are similar to the query (which typically consists of one or two words) or documens that contain useful information related to the query terms. Intuitively, we want to give importance to the *quality* of a Web page while ranking it, in addition to reflecting the similarity of the page to a given query. Links between pages provide valuable

additional information that can be used to obtain high-quality results. We discuss this issue in Section 27.4.2.

27.2.4 Measuring Success: Precision and Recall

Two criteria are commonly used to evaluate information retrieval systems. **Precision** is the percentage of retrieved documents that are relevant to the query. **Recall** is the percentage of relevant documents in the database that are retrieved in response to a query.

Retrieving all documents in response to a query trivially guarantees perfect recall, but results in very poor precision. The challenge is to achieve good recall together with high precision.

In the context of search over the Web, the size of the underlying collection is on the order of billions of documents. Given this, it is questionable whether the traditional measure of recall is very useful. Since users typically don't look beyond the first screen of results, the quality of a Web search engine is largely determined by the results shown on the first page. The following adapted definitions of precision and recall might be more appropriate for Web search engines:

- **Web Search Precision:** The percentage of results on the first page that are relevant to the query.
- **Web Search Recall:** The fraction N/M, expressed as a percentage, where M is the number of results displayed on the front page, and of the M most relevant documents, N is the number displayed on the front page.

27.3 INDEXING FOR TEXT SEARCH

In this section, we introduce two indexing techniques that support the evaluation of boolean and ranked queries. The *inverted index* structure discussed in Section 27.3.1 is widely used due to its simplicity and good performance. Its main disadvantage is that it imposes a significant space overhead: The size can be up to 300 percent the size of the original file. The *signature file* index discussed in Section 27.3.2 has a small space overhead and offers a quick filter that eliminates most nonqualifying documents. However, does not scale as well to larger database sizes because the index has to be sequentially scanned.

Before a document is indexed, it is typically pre-processed to eliminate stop words. Since the size of the indexes is very sensitive to the number of terms in the document collection, eliminating stop words can greatly reduce index

size. IR systems also do certain other kinds of pre-processing. For instance, they apply **stemming** to reduce related terms to a canonical form. This step also reduces the number of terms to be indexed, but equally importantly, it allows us to retrieve documents that may not contain the exact query term but contain some variant. As an example, the terms *run, running,* and *runner* all stem to *run.* The term *run* is indexed, and every occurrence of a variant of this term is treated as an occurrence of *run.* A query that specifies *runner* finds documents that contain any word that stems to *run.*

27.3.1 Inverted Indexes

An **inverted index** is a data structure that enables fast retrieval of all documents that contain a query term. For each term, the index maintains a list (called the **inverted list**) of entries describing occurrences of the term, with one entry per document that contains the term.

Consider the inverted index for our running example shown in Figure 27.5. The term 'James' has an inverted list with one entry each for documents 1, 3, and 4; the term 'agent' has entries for documents 1 and 2.

The entry for document d in the inverted list for term t contains details about the occurrences of term t in document d. In Figure 27.5, this information consists of a list of locations within the document that contain term t. Thus, the entry for document 1 in the inverted list for term 'agent' lists the locations 1 and 5, since 'agent' is the first and fifth word of document 1. In general, we can store additional information about each occurrence (e.g., in an HTML document, is the occurrence in the TITLE tag?) in the inverted list. We can also store the length of the document if this is used for length normalization (see below).

The collection of inverted lists is called the **postings file**. Inverted lists can be very large for large document collections. In fact, Web search engines typically store each inverted list on a separate page, and most lists span multiple pages (and if so, are maintained as a linked list of pages). In order to quickly find the inverted list for a query term, all possible query terms are organized in a second index structure such as a B+ tree or a hash index.

The second index, called the **lexicon**, is much smaller than the postings file since it only contains one entry per term, and further, only contains entries for the set of terms that are retained after eliminating stop words, and applying stemming rules. An entry consists of the term, some summary information about its inverted list, and the address (on disk) of the inverted list. In Figure 27.5, the summary information consists of the number of entries in the inverted

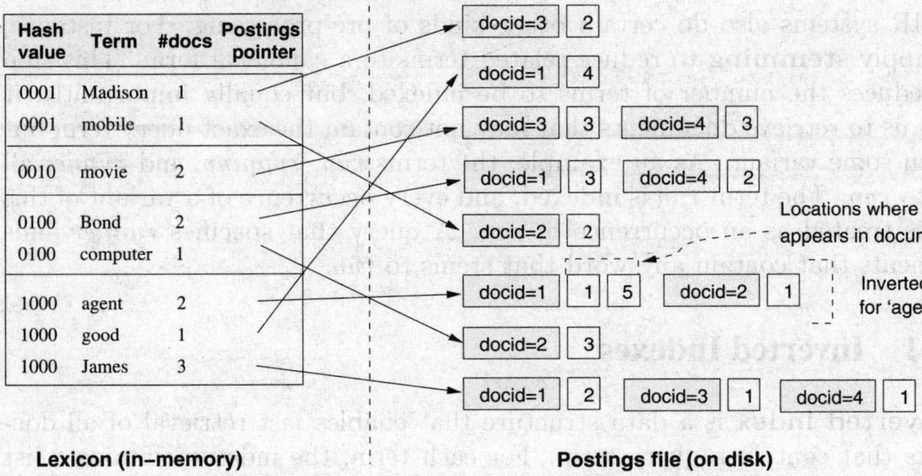

Figure 27.5 Inverted Index for Example Collection

list (i.e., the number of documents that the term appears in). In general, it could contain additional information such as the IDF for the term, but it is important to keep the entry's size as small as possible.

The lexicon is maintained in-memory, and enables fast retrieval of the inverted list for a query term. The lexicon in Figure 27.5 uses a hash index, and is sketched by showing the hash value for the term; entries for terms are grouped into hash buckets by their hash value.

Using an Inverted Index

A query containing a single term is evaluated by first searching the lexicon to find the address of the inverted list for the term. Then the inverted list is retrieved, the docids in it are mapped to physical document addresses, and the corresponding documents are retrieved. If the results are to be ranked, the relevance of each document in the inverted list to the query term is computed, and documents are then retrieved in order of their relevance rank. Observe that the information needed to compute the relevance measure described in Section 27.2—the frequency of the query term in the document, the IDF of the term in the document collection, and the length of the document if it is used for length normalization—are all available in either the lexicon or the inverted list.

When inverted lists are very long, as in Web search engines, it is useful to consider whether we should precompute the relevance of each document in the inverted list for a term (with respect to that term) and sort the list by relevance rather than document id. This would speed up querying because we can just

look at a prefix of the inverted list, since users rarely look at more than the first few results. However, maintaining lists in sorted order by relevance can be expensive. (Sorting by document id is convenient because new documents are assigned increasing ids, and we can therefore simply append entries for new documents at the end of the inverted list. Further, if the similarity function is changed, we do not have to rebuild the index.)

A query with a conjunction of several terms is evaluated by retrieving the inverted lists of the query terms one at a time and intersecting them. In order to minimize memory usage, the inverted lists should be retrieved in order of increasing length. A query with a disjunction of several terms is evaluated by merging all relevant inverted lists.

Consider the example inverted index shown in Figure 27.5. To evaluate the query 'James', we probe the lexicon to find the address of the inverted list for 'James', fetch it from disk and then retrieve document 1. To evaluate the query 'James' `AND` 'Bond', we first retrieve the inverted list for the term 'Bond' and intersect it with the inverted list for the term 'James.' (The inverted list of the term 'Bond' has length two, whereas the inverted list of the term 'James' has length three.) The result of the intersection of the list $\langle 1, 4\rangle$ with the list $\langle 1, 3, 4\rangle$ is the list $\langle 1, 4\rangle$ and documents 1 and 4 are therefore retrieved. To evaluate the query 'James' `OR` 'Bond,' we retrieve the two inverted lists in any order and merge the results.

For ranked queries with multiple terms, we must fetch the inverted lists for all terms, compute the relevance of every document that appears in one of these lists with respect to the given collection of query terms, and then sort the document ids by their relevance before fetching the documents in relevance rank order. Again, if the inverted lists are sorted by the relevance measure, we can support ranked queries by typically processing only small prefixes of the the inverted lists. (Observe that the relevance of a document with respect to the query is easily computed from its relevance with respect to each query term.)

27.3.2 Signature Files

A **signature file** is another index structure for text database systems that supports efficient evaluation of boolean queries. A signature file contains an index record for each document in the database. This index record is called the **signature** of the document. Each signature has a fixed size of b bits; b is called the **signature width**. The bits that are set depend on the words that appear in the document. We map words to bits by applying a hash function to each word in the document and we set the bits that appear in the result of

docid	Document	Signature
1	agent James Bond good agent	1100
2	agent mobile computer	1101
3	James Madison movie	1011
4	James Bond movie	1110

Figure 27.6 Signature File for Example Collection

the hash function. Note that unless we have a bit for each possible word in the vocabulary, the same bit could be set twice by different words because the hash function maps both words to the same bit. We say that a signature S_1 matches another signature S_2 if all the bits that are set in signature S_2 are also set in signature S_1. If signature S_1 matches signature S_2, then signature S_1 has at least as many bits set as signature S_2.

For a query consisting of a conjunction of terms, we first generate the query signature by applying the hash function to each word in the query. We then scan the signature file and retrieve all documents whose signatures match the query signature, because every such document is a potential result to the query. Since the signature does not uniquely identify the words that a document contains, we have to retrieve each potential match and check whether the document actually contains the query terms. A document whose signature matches the query signature but that does not contain all terms in the query is called a **false positive**. A false positive is an expensive mistake since the document has to be retrieved from disk, parsed, stemmed, and checked to determine whether it contains the query terms.

For a query consisting of a disjunction of terms, we generate a list of query signatures, one for each term in the query. The query is evaluated by scanning the signature file to find documents whose signatures match any signature in the list of query signatures.

As an example, consider the signature file of width 4 for our running example shown in Figure 27.6. The bits set by the hashed values of all query terms are shown in the figure. To evaluate the query 'James,' we first compute the hash value of the term; this is 1000. Then we scan the signature file and find matching index records. As we can see from Figure 27.6, the signatures of all records have the first bit set. We retrieve all documents and check for false positives; the only false positive for this query is document with rid 2. (Unfortunately, the hashed value of the term 'agent' also happened to set the very first bit in the signature.) Consider the query 'James' `And` 'Bond.' The query signature is 1100 and three document signatures match the query signature. Again, we retrieve one false positive. As another example of a conjunctive query, con-

sider the query 'movie' And 'Madison.' The query signature is 0011, and only one document signature matches the query signature. No false positives are retrieved.

Note that for each query we have to scan the complete signature file, and there are as many records in the signature file as there are documents in the database. To reduce the amount of data that has to be retrieved for each query, we can vertically partition a signature file into a set of **bit slices**, and we call such an index a **bit-sliced signature file**. The length of each bit slice is still equal to the number of documents in the database, but for a query with q bits set in the query signature we need only to retrieve q bit slices. The reader is invited to construct a bit-sliced signature file and to evaluate the example queries in this paragraph using the bit slices.

27.4 WEB SEARCH ENGINES

Web search engines must contend with extremely large numbers of documents, and have to be highly scalable. Documents are also linked to each other, and this link information turns out to be very valuable in finding pages relevant to a given search. These factors have caused search engines to differ from traditional IR systems in important ways. Nonetheless, they rely on some form of inverted indexes as the basic indexing mechanism. In this section, we discuss Web search engines, using Google as a typical example.

27.4.1 Search Engine Architecture

Web search engines **crawl** the web to collect documents to index. The crawling algorithm is simple, but crawler software can be complex because of the details of connecting to millions of sites, minimizing network latencies, parallelizing the crawling, dealing with timeouts and other connection failures, ensuring that crawled sites are not unduly stressed by the crawler, and other practical concerns.

The search algorithm used by a crawler is a graph traversal. Starting at a collection of pages with many links (e.g., Yahoo directory pages), all links on crawled pages are followed to identify new pages. This step is iterated, keeping track of which pages have been visited in order to avoid re-visiting them.

The collection of pages retrieved through crawling can be enormous, on the order of billions of pages. Indexing them is a very expensive task. Fortunately, the task is highly parallelizable: Each document is independently analyzed to create inverted lists for the terms that appear in the document. These per-document lists are then sorted by term and merged to create complete per-

term inverted lists that span all documents. Term statistics such as IDF can be computed during the merge phase.

Supporting searches over such vast indexes is another mammoth undertaking. Fortunately, again, the task is readily parallelized using a cluster of inexpensive machines: We can deal with the amount of data by partitioning the index across several machines. Each machine contains the inverted index for those terms that are mapped to that machine (e.g., by hashing the term). Queries may have to be sent to multiple machines if the terms they contain are handled by different machines, but given that Web queries rarely contain more than two terms, this is not a serious problem in practice.

We must also deal with a huge volume of queries; Google supports over 150 million searches each day, and the number is growing. This is accomplished by replicating the data across several machines. We already described how the data is partitioned across machines. For each partition, we now assign several machines, each of which contains an exact copy of the data for that partition. Queries on this partition can be handled by any machine in the partition. Queries can be distributed across machines on the basis of load, by hashing on IP addresses, etc. Replication also addresses the problem of high-availability, since the failure of a machine only increases the load on the remaining machines in the partition, and if partitions contain several machines the impact is small. Failures can be made transparent to users by routing queries to other machines through the load balancer.

27.4.2 Using Link Information

webpages are created by a variety of users for a variety of purposes, and their content does not always lend itself to effective retrieval. The most relevant pages for a search may not contain the search terms at all and are therefore not returned by a boolean keyword search! For example, consider the query term 'Web browser.' A boolean text query using the terms does not return the relevant pages of Netscape Corporation or Microsoft, because these pages do not contain the term 'Web browser' at all. Similarly, the home page of Yahoo does not contain the term 'search engine.' The problem is that relevant sites do not necessarily describe their contents in a way that is useful for boolean text queries.

Until now, we only considered information within a single webpage to estimate its relevance to a query. But webpages are connected through hyperlinks, and it is quite likely that there is a webpage containing the term 'search engine' that has a link to Yahoo's home page. Can we use the information hidden in such links?

Building on research in the sociology literature, an interesting analogy between links and bibliographic citations suggests a way to exploit link information: Just as influential authors and pubications are cited often, good webpages are likely to be often linked to. It is useful to distinguish between two types of pages, *authorities* and *hubs.* An **authority** is a page that is very relevant to a certain topic and that is recognized by other pages as authoritative on the subject. These other pages, called hubs, usually have a significant number of hyperlinks to authorities, although they themselves are not very well known and do not necessarily carry a lot of content relevant to the given query. **Hub** pages could be compilations of resources about a topic on a site for professionals, lists of recommended sites for the hobbies of an individual user, or even a part of the bookmarks of an individual user that are relevant to one of the user's interests; their main property is that they have many outgoing links to relevant pages. Good hub pages are often not well known and there may be few links pointing to a good hub. In contrast, good authorities are 'endorsed' by many good hubs and thus have many links from good hub pages.

This symbiotic relationship between hubs and authorities is the basis for the HITS algorithm, a link-based search algorithm that discovers high-quality pages that are relevant to a user's query terms. The HITS algorithm models Web as a directed graph. Each webpage represents a node in the graph, and a hyperlink from page A to page B is represented as an edge between the two corresponding nodes.

Assume that we are given a user query with several terms. The algorithm proceeds in two steps. In the first step, the *sampling step*, we collect a set of pages called the **base set**. The base set most likely includes very relevant pages to the user's query, but the base set can still be quite large. In the second step, the *iteration step*, we find good authorities and good hubs among the pages in the base set.

The sampling step retrieves a set of webpages that contain the query terms, using some traditional technique. For example, we can evaluate the query as a boolean keyword search and retrieve all webpages that contain the query terms. We call the resulting set of pages the **root set**. The root set might not contain all relevant pages because some authoritative pages might not include the user query words. But we expect that at least some of the pages in the root set contain hyperlinks to the most relevant authoritative pages or that some authoritative pages link to pages in the root set. This motivates our notion of a **link page**. We call a page a link page if it has a hyperlink to some page in the root set or if a page in the root set has a hyperlink to it. In order not to miss potentially relevant pages, we augment the root set by all link pages and we call the resulting set of pages the **base set**. Thus, the base set includes all

root pages and all link pages; we refer to a webpage in the base set as a **base page**.

Our goal in the second step of the algorithm is to find out which base pages are good hubs and good authorities and to return the best authorities and hubs as the answers to the query. To quantify the quality of a base page as a hub and as an authority, we associate with each base page in the base set a **hub weight** and an **authority weight**. The hub weight of the page indicates the quality of the page as a hub, and the authority weight of the page indicates the quality of the page as an authority. We compute the weights of each page according to the intuition that a page is a good authority if many good hubs have hyperlinks to it, and that a page is a good hub if it has many outgoing hyperlinks to good authorities. Since we do not have any a priori knowledge about which pages are good hubs and authorities, we initialize all weights to one. We then update the authority and hub weights of base pages iteratively as described below.

Consider a base page p with hub weight h_p and with authority weight a_p. In one iteration, we update a_p to be the sum of the hub weights of all pages that have a hyperlink to p. Formally:

$$a_p = \sum_{\text{All base pages } q \text{ that have a link to } p} h_q$$

Analogously, we update h_p to be the sum of the weights of all pages that p points to:

$$h_p = \sum_{\text{All base pages } q \text{ such that } p \text{ has a link to } q} a_q$$

Comparing the algorithm with the other approaches to querying text that we discussed in this chapter, we note that the iteration step of the HITS algorithm—the distribution of the weights—does not take into account the words on the base pages. In the iteration step, we are only concerned about the relationship between the base pages as represented by hyperlinks.

The HITS algorithm usually produces very good results. For example, the five highest ranked results from Google (which uses a variant of the HITS algorithm) for the query 'Raghu Ramakrishnan' are the following webpages:

```
www.cs.wisc.edu/~raghu/raghu.html
www.cs.wisc.edu/~dbbook/dbbook.html
www.informatik.uni-trier.de/
    ~ley/db/indices/a-tree/r/Ramakrishnan:Raghu.html
www.informatik.uni-trier.de/
```

Computing hub and authority weights: We can use matrix notation to write the updates for all hub and authority weights in one step. Assume that we number all pages in the base set $\{1, 2, ..., n\}$. The adjacency matrix B of the base set is an $n \times n$ matrix whose entries are either 0 or 1. The matrix entry (i, j) is set to 1 if page i has a hyperlink to page j; it is set to 0 otherwise. We can also write the hub weights h and authority weights a in vector notation: $h = \langle h_1, \ldots, h_n \rangle$ and $a = \langle a_1, \ldots, a_n \rangle$. We can now rewrite our update rules as follows:

$$h = B \cdot a, \quad \text{and} \quad a = B^T \cdot h \ .$$

Unfolding this equation once, corresponding to the first iteration, we obtain:

$$h = BB^T h = (BB^T)h, \quad \text{and} \quad a = B^T Ba = (B^T B)a \ .$$

After the second iteration, we arrive at:

$$h = (BB^T)^2 h, \quad \text{and} \quad a = (B^T B)^2 a \ .$$

Results from linear algebra tell us that the sequence of iterations for the hub (resp. authority) weights converges to the principal eigenvectors of BB^T (resp. $B^T B$) if we normalize the weights before each iteration so that the sum of the squares of all weights is always $2 \cdot n$. Furthermore, results from linear algebra tell us that this convergence is independent of the choice of initial weights, as long as the initial weights are positive. Thus, our rather arbitrary choice of initial weights—we initialized all hub and authority weights to 1—does not change the outcome of the algorithm.

Google's Pigeon Rank: Google computes the *pigeon rank (PR)* for a webpage A using the following formula, which is very similar to the Hub-Authority ranking functions:

$$PR(A) = (1 - d) + d(PR(T_1)/C(T_1) + ... + PR(T_n)/C(T_n))$$

$T_1 \ldots T_n$ are the pages that link (or 'point') to A, $C(T_i)$ is the number of links going out of page T_i, and d is a heuristically chosen constant (Google uses 0.85). Pigeon ranks form a probability distribution over all webpages; the sum of ranks over all pages is 1. If we consider a model of user behavior in which a user randomly chooses a page and then repeatedly clicks on links until he gets bored and randomly chooses a new page, the probability that the user visits a page is its Pigeon rank. The pages in the result of a search are ranked using a combination of an IR-style relevance metric and Pigeon rank.

SQL/MM: Full Text 'Full text' is described as data that can be searched, unlike simple character strings, and a new data type called `FullText` is introduced to support it. The methods associated with this type support searching for individual words, phrases, words that 'sound like' a query term, etc. Three methods are of particular interest. `CONTAINS` checks if a FullText object contains a specified search term (word or phrase). `RANK` returns the relevance rank of a FullText object with respect to a specified search term. (How the rank is defined is left to the implementation.) `IS ABOUT` determines whether the FullText object is sufficiently related to the specified search term. (The behavior of `IS ABOUT` is also left to the implementation.)
Relational DBMSs from IBM, Microsoft, and Oracle all support text fields, although they do not currently conform to the SQL/MM standard.

```
~ley/db/indices/a-tree/s/Seshadri:Praveen.html
www.acm.org/awards/fellows_citations_n-z/ramakrishnan.html
```

The first result is Ramakrishnan's home page; the second is the home page for this book; the third is the page listing his publications in the popular DBLP bibliography; and the fourth (initially puzzling) result is the list of publications for a former student of his.

27.5 MANAGING TEXT IN A DBMS

In preceding sections, we saw how large text collections are indexed and queried in IR systems and Web search engines. We now consider the additional challenges raised by integrating text data into database systems.

The basic approach being pursued by the SQL standards community is to treat text documents as a new data type, `FullText`, that can appear as the value of a field in a table. If we define a table with a single column of type FullText, each row in the table corresponds to a document in a document collection. Methods of FullText can be used in the `WHERE` clause of SQL queries to retrieve rows containing text objects that match an IR-style search criterion. The relevance rank of a FullText object can be explicitly retrieved using the `RANK` method, and this can be used to sort results by relevance.

Several points must be kept in mind as we consider this approach:

- This is an extremely general approach, and the performance of a SQL system that supports such an extension is likely to be inferior to a specialized IR system.

- The model of data does not adequately reflect documents with additional metadata. If we store documents in a table with a FullText column and use additional columns to store metadata—for example, author, title, summary, rating, popularity—relevance measures that combine metadata with IR similarity measures must be expressed using new user-defined methods, because the `RANK` method only has access to the FullText object, and not the metadata. The emergence of XML documents, which have non-uniform, partial metadata, further complicates matters.
- The handling of updates is unclear. As we have seen, IR indexes are complex, and expensive to maintain. Requiring a system to update the indexes before the updating transaction commits can impose a severe performance penalty.

27.5.1 Loosely Coupled Inverted Index

The implementation approach used in current relational DBMSs that support text fields is to have a separate text-search engine that is loosely coupled to the DBMS. The engine periodically updates the indexes, but provides no transactional guarantees. Thus, a transaction could insert (a row containing) a text object and commit, and a subsequent transaction that issues a matching search might not retrieve the (row containing the) object.

27.6 A DATA MODEL FOR XML

As we saw in Section 7.4.1, XML provides a way to mark up a document with meaningful tags that impart some partial structure to the document. *Semistructured data models*, which we introduce in this section, capture much of the structure in XML documents, while abstracting away many details.[1] Semistructured data models have the potential to serve as a formal foundation for XML and enable us to rigorously define the semantics of queries over XML, which we discuss in Section 27.7.

27.6.1 Motivation for Loose Structure

Consider a set of documents on the Web that contain hyperlinks to other documents. These documents, although not completely unstructured, cannot be modeled naturally in the relational data model because the pattern of hyperlinks is not regular across documents. In fact, every HTML document has

[1]An important aspect of XML that is *not* captured is the ordering of elements. A more complete data model called XData has been proposed by the W3C committee that is developing XML standards, but we do not discuss it here.

XML Data Models: A number of data models for XML are being considered by standards committees such as ISO and W3C. W3C's **Infoset** is a tree-structured model, and each node can be retrieved through an **accessor function**. A version called **Post-Validation Infoset (PSVI)** serves as the data model for XML Schema. The XQuery language has yet another data model associated with it. The plethora of models is due to parallel development in some cases, and due to different objectives in others. Nonetheless, all these models have loosely-structured trees as their central feature.

some minimal structure, such as the text in the `TITLE` tag versus the text in the document body, or text that is highlighted versus text that is not. As another example, a bibliography file also has a certain degree of structure due to fields such as *author* and *title*, but is otherwise unstructured text. Even data that is 'unstructured', such as free text or an image or a video clip, typically has some associated information such as timestamp or author information that contributes partial structure.

We refer to data with such partial structure as **semistructured data**. There are many reasons why data might be semistructured. First, the structure of data might be implicit, hidden, unknown, or the user might choose to ignore it. Second, when integrating data from several heterogeneous sources, data exchange and transformation are important problems. We need a highly flexible data model to integrate data from all types of data sources including flat files and legacy systems; a structured data model such as the relational model is often too rigid. Third, we cannot query a structured database without knowing the schema, but sometimes we want to query the data without full knowledge of the schema. For example, we cannot express the query "Where in the database can we find the string *Malgudi?*" in a relational database system without knowing the schema, and knowing which fields contain such text values.

27.6.2 A Graph Model

All data models proposed for semistructured data represent the data as some kind of labeled graph. Nodes in the graph correspond to compound objects or atomic values. Each edge indicates an object-subobject or object-value relationship. Leaf nodes, i.e, nodes with no outgoing edges have a value associated with them. There is no separate schema and no auxiliary description; the data in the graph is self describing. For example, consider the graph shown in Figure 27.7, which represents part of the XML data from Figure 7.2. The root node of the graph represents the outermost element, `BOOKLIST`. The node has three children that are labeled with the element name `BOOK`, since the list of books

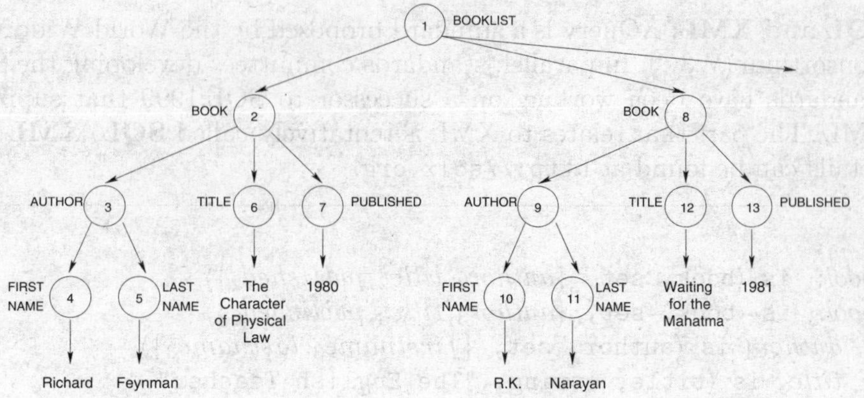

Figure 27.7 The Semistructured Data Model

consists of three individual books. The numbers within the nodes indicate the object identifier associated with the corresponding object.

We now describe one of the proposed data models for semistructured data, called the **object exchange model (OEM)**. Each object is described by a quadruple consisting of a *label*, a *type*, the *value* of the object, and an *object identifier* which is a unique identifier for the object. Since each object has a label that can be thought of as a column name in the relational model, and each object has a type that can be thought of as the column type in the relational model, the object exchange model is self-describing. Labels in OEM should be as informative as possible, since they serve two purposes—they can be used to identify an object as well as to convey the meaning of an object. For example, we can represent the last name of an author as follows:

⟨lastName, string, "Feynman"⟩

More complex objects are decomposed hierarchically into smaller objects. For example, an author name can contain a first name and a last name. This object is described as follows:

⟨authorName, set, $\{firstname_1, lastname_1\}$⟩
  $firstname_1$ is ⟨firstName, string, "Richard"⟩
  $lastname_1$ is ⟨lastName, string, "Feynman"⟩

As another example, an object representing a set of books is described as follows:

⟨bookList, set, $\{book_1, book_2, book_3\}$⟩
  $book_1$ is ⟨book, set, $\{author_1, title_1, published_1\}$⟩

SQL and XML: XQuery is a standard proposed by the World-Wide Web Consortium (W3C). In parallel, standards committees developing the SQL standards have been working on a successor to SQL:1999 that supports XML. The part that relates to XML is tentatively called **SQL/XML** and details can be found at `http://sqlx.org`.

$book_2$ `is` ⟨`book, set,` $\{author_2, title_2, published_2\}$⟩
$book_3$ `is` ⟨`book, set,` $\{author_3, title_3, published_3\}$⟩
  $author_3$ `is` ⟨`author, set,` $\{firstname_3, lastname_3\}$⟩
  $title_3$ `is` ⟨`title, string, "The English Teacher"`⟩
  $published_3$ `is` ⟨`published, integer, 1980`⟩

27.7 XQUERY: QUERYING XML DATA

Given that XML documents are encoded in a way that reflects (a considerable amount of) structure, we have the opportunity to use a high-level language that exploits this structure to conveniently retrieve data from within such documents. Such a language would also allow us to easily translate XML data between different DTDs, as we must when integrating data from multiple sources. At the time of writing of this book, **XQuery** is the W3C standard query language for XML data. In this section, we give a brief overview of XQuery.

27.7.1 Path Expressions

Consider the XML document shown in Figure 7.2. The following example query returns the last names of all authors, assuming that our XML document resides at the location `www.ourbookstore.com/books.xml`.

```
FOR
  $l IN doc(www.ourbookstore.com/books.xml)//AUTHOR/LASTNAME
RETURN <RESULT> $l </RESULT>
```

This example illustrates some of the basic constructs of XQuery. The `FOR` clause in XQuery is roughly analogous to the `FROM` clause in SQL. The `RETURN` clause is similar to the `SELECT` clause. We return to the general form of queries shortly, after introducing an important concept called a **path expression**.

The expression

```
doc(www.ourbookstore.com/books.xml)//AUTHOR/LASTNAME
```

XPath and Other XML Query Languages: Path expressions in XQuery are derived from XPath, an earlier XML query facility. Path expressions in XPath can be qualified with selection conditions, and can utilize several built-in functions (e.g., counting the number of nodes matched by the expression). Many of XQuery's features are borrowed from earlier languages, including XML-QL and Quilt.

in the `FOR` clause is an example of a path expression. It specifies a **path** involving three entities: the document itself, the `AUTHOR` elements and the `LASTNAME` elements.

The path relationship is expressed through separators / and //. The separator // specifies that the `AUTHOR` element can be nested anywhere within the document whereas the separator / constrains the `LASTNAME` element to be nested immediately under (in terms of the graph structure of the document) the `AUTHOR` element. Evaluating a path expression returns a *set* of elements that match the expression. The variable l in the example query is bound in turn to each `LASTNAME` element returned by evaluating the path expression. (To distinguish variable names from normal text, variable names in XQuery are prefixed with a dollar sign $.)

The `RETURN` clause constructs the query result—which is also an XML document—by bracketing each value to which the variable l is bound with the tag `RESULT`. If the example query is applied to the sample data shown in Figure 7.2, the result would be the following XML document:

```
<RESULT><LASTNAME>Feynman </LASTNAME></RESULT>
<RESULT><LASTNAME>Narayan </LASTNAME></RESULT>
```

We use the document in Figure 7.2 as our input in the rest of this chapter.

27.7.2 FLWR Expressions

The basic form of an XQuery consists of a **FLWR expression**, where the letters denote the `FOR`, `LET`, `WHERE` and `RETURN` clauses. The `FOR` and `LET` clauses bind variables to values through path expressions. These values are qualified by the `WHERE` clause, and the result XML fragment is constructed by the `RETURN` clause.

The difference between a `FOR` and `LET` clause is that while `FOR` binds a variable to each element specified by the path expression, `LET` binds a variable to the whole *collection* of elements. Thus, if we change our example query to:

```
LET
  $l IN doc(www.ourbookstore.com/books.xml)//AUTHOR/LASTNAME
RETURN <RESULT> $l </RESULT>
```

then the result of the query becomes:

```
<RESULT>
  <LASTNAME>Feynman</LASTNAME>
  <LASTNAME>Narayan</LASTNAME>
</RESULT>
```

Selection conditions are expressed using the WHERE clause. Also, the output of a query is not limited to a single element. These points are illustrated by the following query, which finds the first and last names of all authors who wrote a book that was published in 1980:

```
FOR $b IN doc(www.ourbookstore.com/books.xml)/BOOKLIST/BOOK
WHERE $b/PUBLISHED='1980'
RETURN
  <RESULT> $b/AUTHOR/FIRSTNAME, $b/AUTHOR/LASTNAME </RESULT>
```

The result of the above query is the following XML document:

```
<RESULT>
  <FIRSTNAME>Richard </FIRSTNAME><LASTNAME>Feynman </LASTNAME>
</RESULT>
<RESULT>
  <FIRSTNAME>R.K. </FIRSTNAME><LASTNAME>Narayan </LASTNAME>
</RESULT>
```

For the specific DTD in this example, where a BOOK element has only one AUTHOR, the above query can be written by using a different path expression in the FOR clause, as follows.

```
FOR $a IN
  doc(www.ourbookstore.com/books.xml)
    /BOOKLIST/BOOK[PUBLISHED='1980']/AUTHOR
RETURN <RESULT> $a/FIRSTNAME, $a/LASTNAME </RESULT>
```

The path expression in this query is an instance of a **branching path expression**. The variable l is now bound to every AUTHOR element that matches the path doc/BOOKLIST/BOOK/AUTHOR where the intermediate BOOK element is constrained to have a PUBLISHED element nested immediately within it with the value 1980.

27.7.3 Ordering of Elements

XML data consists of *ordered* documents and so the query language must return data in some order. The semantics of XQuery is that a path expression returns results sorted in document order. Thus, variables in the `FOR` clause are bound in document order. If however, we desire a different order, we can explicitly order the output as shown in the following query, which returns `TITLE` elements sorted lexicographically.

```
FOR
  $b IN doc(www.ourbookstore.com/books.xml)/BOOKLIST/BOOK
RETURN <BOOKTITLES> $b/TITLE </BOOKTITLES>
SORT BY TITLE
```

27.7.4 Grouping and Generation of Collection Values

Our next example illustrates grouping in XQuery, which allows us to generate a new collection value for each group. (Contrast this with grouping in SQL, which only allows us to generate an aggregate value (e.g., `SUM`) per group.) Suppose that for each year we want to find the last names of authors who wrote a book published in that year. We group by year of publication and generate a list of last names for each year:

```
FOR $p IN DISTINCT
  doc(www.ourbookstore.com/books.xml)/BOOKLIST/BOOK/PUBLISHED
  RETURN
  <RESULT>
    $p,
    FOR $a IN DISTINCT /BOOKLIST/BOOK[PUBLISHED=$p]/AUTHOR
      RETURN $a
  </RESULT>
```

The keyword *DISTINCT* eliminates duplicates from the collection returned by a path expression. Using the XML document in Figure 7.2 as input, the above query produces the following result:

```
<RESULT> <PUBLISHED>1980</PUBLISHED>
  <LASTNAME>Feynman</LASTNAME>
  <LASTNAME>Narayan</LASTNAME>
</RESULT>
<RESULT> <PUBLISHED>1981</PUBLISHED>
  <LASTNAME>Narayan</LASTNAME>
</RESULT>
```

27.8 EFFICIENT EVALUATION OF XML QUERIES

XQuery operates on XML data and produces XML data as output. In order to be able to evaluate queries efficiently, we need to address the following issues.

- **Storage**: We can use an existing storage system like a relational or object oriented system or design a new storage format for XML documents. There are several ways to use a relational system to store XML. One of them is to store the XML data as Character Large Objects (CLOBs). (CLOBS were discussed in Chapter 23.) In this case, however, we cannot exploit the query processing infrastructure provided by the relational system and would instead have to process XQuery outside the database system. In order to circumvent this problem, we need to identify a schema according to which the XML data can be stored. These points are discussed in Section 27.8.1.
- **Indexing**: Path expressions add a lot of richness to XQuery and yield many new access patterns over the data. If we use a relational system for storing XML data, then we are constrained to use only relational indexes like the B-Tree. However, if we use a native storage engine, then we have the option of building novel index structures for path expressions, some of which are discussed in Section 27.8.2.
- **Query Optimization**: Optimization of queries in XQuery is an open problem. The work so far in this area can be divided into three parts. The first is developing an algebra for XQuery, analogous to relational algebra. The second research direction is providing statistics for path expression queries. Finally, some work has addressed simplification of queries by exploiting constraints on the data. Since query optimization for XQuery is still at a preliminary stage, we do not cover it in this chapter.

Another issue to be considered while designing a new storage system for XML data is the verbosity of repeated tags. As we see in Section 27.8.1, using a relational storage system addresses this problem since tag names are not stored repeatedly. If on the other hand, we want to build a native storage system, then the manner in which the XML data is compressed becomes significant. Several compression algorithms are known that achieve compression ratios close to relational storage, but we do not discuss them here.

27.8.1 Storing XML in RDBMS

One natural candidate for storing XML data is a relational database system. The main issues involved in storing XML data in a relational system are:

Commercial database systems and XML: Many relational and object-relational database system vendors are currently looking into support for XML in their database engines. Several vendors of object-oriented database management systems already offer database engines that can store XML data whose contents can be accessed through graphical user interfaces or server-side Java extensions.

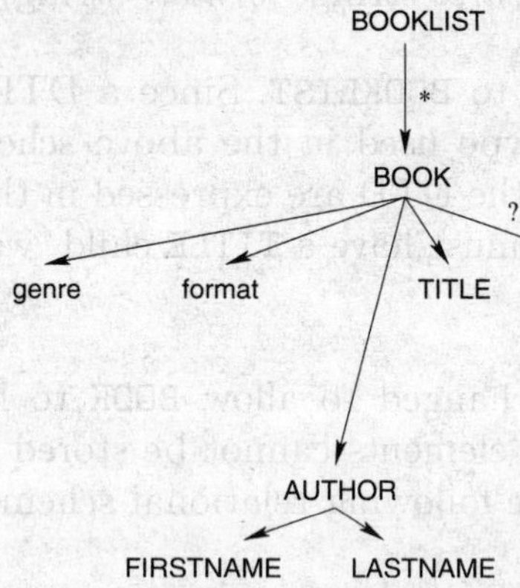

Figure 27.8 Bookstore XML DTD Element Relationships

- *Choice of relational schema*: In order to use an RDBMS, we need a schema. What relational schema should we use even assuming that the XML data comes with an associated schema?

- *Queries*: Queries on XML data are in XQuery whereas a relational system can only handle SQL. Queries in XQuery therefore need to be *translated* into SQL.

- *Reconstruction*: The output of XQuery is XML. Thus, the result of a SQL query needs to be converted back into XML.

Mapping XML Data to Relations

We illustrate the mapping process through our bookstore example. The nesting relationships among the different elements in the DTD is shown in Figure 27.8. The edges indicate the nature of the nesting.

One way to derive a relational schema is as follows. We begin at the `BOOKLIST` element and create a relation to store it. Traversing down from `BOOKLIST`, we get `BOOK` following a * edge. This edge indicates that we store the `BOOK` elements in a separate relation. Traversing further down, we see that all elements and

attributes nested within BOOK occur at most once. Hence, we can store them in the same relation as BOOK. The resulting relational schema *Relschema1* is shown below.

BOOKLIST(<u>*id*</u>: integer)
BOOK(*booklistid*: integer, *author_firstname*: string,
author_lastname: string, *title*: string,
published: string, *genre*: string, *format*: string)

BOOK.*booklistid* connects BOOK to BOOKLIST. Since a DTD has only one base type, `string`, the only base type used in the above schema is `string`. The constraints expressed through the DTD are expressed in the relational schema. For instance, since every BOOK must have a TITLE child, we must constrain the *title* column to be non-*null*.

Alternatively, if the DTD is changed to allow BOOK to have more than one AUTHOR child, then the AUTHOR elements cannot be stored in the same relation as BOOK. This change yields the following relational schema *Relschema2*.

BOOKLIST(<u>*id*</u>: integer)
BOOK(<u>*id*</u>: integer, *booklistid*: integer,
title: string, *published*: string, *genre*: string, *format*: string)
AUTHOR(*bookid*: integer, *firstname*: string, *lastname*: string)

The column AUTHOR.*bookid* connects AUTHOR to BOOK.

Query Processing

Consider the following example query again:

```
FOR
  $b IN doc(www.ourbookstore.com/books.xml)/BOOKLIST/BOOK
WHERE $b/PUBLISHED='1980'
RETURN
  <RESULT> $b/AUTHOR/FIRSTNAME, $b/AUTHOR/LASTNAME </RESULT>
```

If the mapping between the XML data and relational tables is known, then we can construct a SQL query that returns all columns that are needed to reconstruct the result XML document for this query. Conditions enforced by the path expressions and the WHERE clause are translated into equivalent conditions in the SQL query. We obtain the following equivalent SQL query if we use *Relschema1* as our relational schema.

```
SELECT BOOK.author_firstname, BOOK.author_lastname
```

```
FROM   BOOK, BOOKLIST
WHERE  BOOKLIST.id = BOOK.booklistid
          AND BOOK.published='1980'
```

The results thus returned by the relational query processor are then tagged, outside the relational system, as specified by the RETURN clause. This is the result of the *reconstruction* phase.

In order to understand this better, consider what happens if we allow a BOOK to have multiple AUTHOR children. Assume that we use *Relschema2* as our relational schema. Processing the FOR and WHERE clauses tells us that it is necessary to join relations BOOKLIST and BOOK with a selection on the BOOK relation corresponding to the year condition in the above query. Since the RETURN clause needs information about AUTHOR elements, we need to further join the BOOK relation with the AUTHOR relation and project the *firstname* and *lastname* columns in the latter. Finally, since each binding of the variable $b in the above query produces one RESULT element, and since each BOOK is now allowed to have more than one AUTHOR, we need to project the *id* column of the BOOK relation. Based on these observations, we obtain the following equivalent SQL query:

```
SELECT   BOOK.id, AUTHOR.firstname, AUTHOR.lastname
FROM     BOOK, BOOKLIST, AUTHOR
WHERE    BOOKLIST.id = BOOK.booklistid AND
            BOOK.id = AUTHOR.bookid AND BOOK.published='1980'
GROUP BY BOOK.id
```

The result is grouped by BOOK.id. The tagger outside the database system now receives results clustered by the BOOK element and can tag the resulting tuples on the fly.

Publishing Relational Data as XML

Since XML has emerged as the standard data exchange format for business applications, it is necessary to publish existing business data as XML. Most operational business data is stored in relational systems. Consequently, mechanisms have been proposed to publish such data as XML documents. These involve a language for specifying how to tag and structure relational data and an implementation to carry out the conversion. This mapping is in some sense the reverse of the XML-to-relational mapping used to store XML data. The conversion process mimics the reconstruction phase when we execute XQuery using a relational system. The published XML data can be thought of as an XML view of relational data. This view can be queried using XQuery. One

method of executing XQuery on such views is to translate them into SQL and then construct the XML result.

27.8.2 Indexing XML Repositories

Path expressions are at the heart of all proposed XML query languages, in particular XQuery. A natural question that arises is how to index XML data to support path expression evaluation. The aim of this section is to give a flavor of the indexing techniques proposed for this problem. We consider the OEM model of semistructured data, where the data is self-describing and there is no separate schema.

Using a B+ Tree to Index Values

Consider the following XQuery example, which we discussed earlier on the bookstore XML data in Figure 7.2. The OEM representation of this data is shown in Figure 27.7.

```
FOR
  $b IN doc(www.ourbookstore.com/books.xml)/BOOKLIST/BOOK
WHERE $b/PUBLISHED='1980'
RETURN
  <RESULT> $b/AUTHOR/FIRSTNAME, $b/AUTHOR/LASTNAME </RESULT>
```

This query specifies joins among the objects with labels BOOKLIST, BOOK, AUTHOR, FIRSTNAME, LASTNAME and PUBLISHED with a selection condition on PUBLISHED objects.

Let us suppose that we are evaluating this query in the absence of any indexes for path expressions. However, we do have a value index such as a B-Tree that enables us to find the ids of all objects with label PUBLISHED and value 1980. There are several ways of executing this query under these assumptions.

For instance, we could begin at the document root and traverse down the data graph through the BOOKLIST object to the BOOK objects. By further traversing the data graph downwards, for each BOOK object we can check whether it satisfies the value predicate (PUBLISHED='1980'). Finally, for those BOOK objects that satisfy the predicate, we can find the relevant FIRSTNAME and LASTNAME objects. This approach corresponds to a top-down evaluation of the query.

Alternatively, we could begin by using the value index to find all PUBLISHED objects that satisfy PUBLISHED='1980'. If the data graph can be traversed in the reverse direction—that is, given an object, we can find its parent—then we

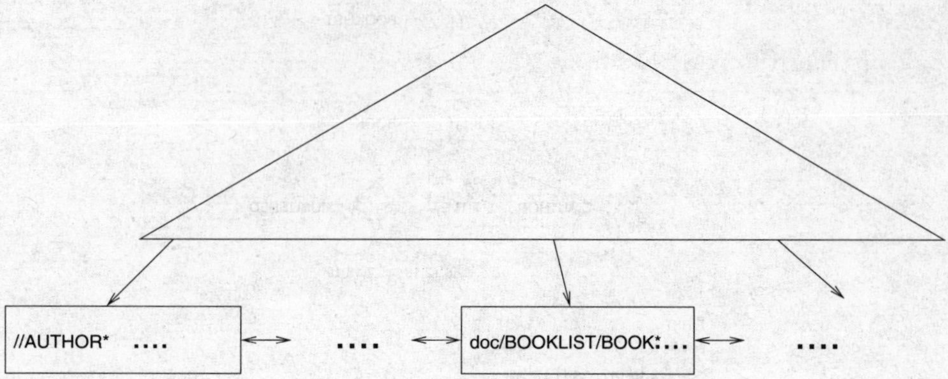

Figure 27.9 Path Expressions in a B-Tree

can find all parents of the `PUBLISHED` objects retaining only those that have label `BOOK`. We can continue in this manner until we find the `FIRSTNAME` and `LASTNAME` objects of interest. Observe that we need to perform all joins in the query on the fly.

Indexing on Structure vs. Value

Now let us ask ourselves whether traditional indexing solutions like the B-Tree can be used to index path expressions. We can use the B-Tree to map a path expression to the ids of all objects returned by it. The idea is to treat all path expressions as strings and order them lexicographically. Every leaf entry in the B-Tree contains a string representing a path expression and a list of ids corresponding to its result. Figure 27.9 shows how such a B-Tree would look. Let us contrast this with the traditional problem of indexing a well-ordered domain like integers for point queries. In the latter case, the number of distinct point queries that can be posed is just the number of data values and so is linear in the data size.

The scenario with path indexing is fundamentally different—the variety of ways in which we can combine tags to form (simple) path expressions coupled with the power of placing // separators leads to a much larger number of possible path expressions. For instance, an `AUTHOR` element in the example in Figure 27.7 is returned as part of the queries `BOOKLIST/BOOK/AUTHOR`, `//AUTHOR`, `//BOOK//AUTHOR`, `BOOKLIST//AUTHOR` and so on. The number of distinct queries can in fact be exponential in the data size (measured in terms of the number of XML elements) in the worst case. This is what motivates the search for alternative strategies to index path expressions.

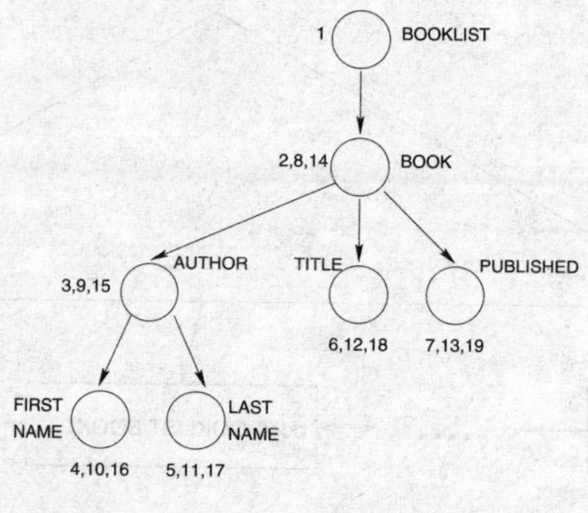

Figure 27.10 Example Path Index

The approach taken is to represent the mapping between a path expression and its result by means of a structural summary which takes the form of another labeled, directed graph. The idea is to preserve all the paths in the data graph in the summary graph, while having far fewer nodes and edges. An **extent** is associated with each node in the summary. The extent of an index node is a subset of the data nodes. The summary graph along with the extents constitutes a path index. A path expression is evaluated using the index by evaluating it against the summary graph and then taking the union of the extents of all matching nodes. This yields the index result of the path expression query. The index **covers** a path expression if the index result is the correct result; obviously, we can use an index to evaluate a path expression only if the index covers it.

Consider the structural summary shown in Figure 27.10. This is a path index for the data in Figure 27.7. The numbers shown beside the nodes correspond to the respective extents. Let us now examine how this index can change the top-down evaluation of the example query used earlier to illustrate B+ tree value indexes.

The top-down evaluation as outlined above begins at the document root and traverses down to the `BOOK` objects. This can be achieved more efficiently by the path index. Instead of traversing the data graph, we can traverse the path index down to the `BOOK` object in the index and look up its extent, which gives us the ids of all `BOOK` objects that match the path expression in the `FOR` clause. The rest of the evaluation then proceeds as before. Thus, the path index saves us from performing joins by essentially precomputing them. We note here that the path index shown in Figure 27.10 is isomorphic to the DTD schema graph shown in Figure 27.8. This drives home the point that the path index without the extents is a structural summary of the data.

The above path index is the **Strong Dataguide**. If we treat path expressions as strings, then the dataguide is the **trie** representing them. The trie is a well-known data structure used to search regular expressions over text. This shows the deeper unity between the research on indexing text and the XML path indexing work. Several other path indexes have been also proposed for semi-structured data, and this is an active area of research.

27.9 REVIEW QUESTIONS

Answers to the review questions can be found in the listed sections.

- What is information retrieval? **(Section 27.1)**
- What are some of the differences between DBMS and IR systems? Describe the differences between a ranked query and a boolean query. **(Section 27.2)**
- What is the vector space model, and what are its advantages? **(Section 27.2.1)**
- What is TF/IDF term weighting, and why do we weigh by both? We do we eliminate stop words? What is length normalization, and why is it done? **(Section 27.2.2)**
- How can we measure document similarity? **(Sections 27.2.3)**
- What are *precision* and *recall*, and how do they relate to each other? **(Section 27.2.4)**
- Describe the following two index structures for text: Inverted index and signature file. What is a bit-sliced signature file? **(Section 27.3)**
- How are web search engines architected? How does the "hubs and authorities" algorithm work? Can you illustrate it on a small set of pages? **(Section 27.4)**
- What support is there for managing text in a DBMS? **(Section 27.5)**
- Descibe the OEM data model for semistructured data. **(Section 27.6)**
- What are the elements of XQuery? What is a path expression? What is an FLWR expression? How can we order the output of query? How do we group query outputs? **(Section 27.7)**
- Describe how XML data can be stored in a relational DBMS. How do we map XML data to relations? Can we use the query processing infrastructure of the relational DBMS? How do we publish relational data as XML? **(Section 27.8.1)**

- How do we index collections of XML documents? What is the difference between indexing on structure versus indexing on value? What is a path index? **(Section 27.8.2)**

EXERCISES

Exercise 27.1 Carry out the following tasks.

1. Given an ASCII file, compute the frequency of each word and create a plot similar to Figure 27.3. (Feel free to use public domain plotting software.) Run the program on the collection of files currently in your directory and see whether the distribution of frequencies is Zipfian. How can you use such plots to create lists of stop words?
2. The Porter stemmer is widely used, and code implementing it is freely available. Download a copy, and run it on your collection of documents.
3. One criticism of the vector space model and its use in similarity checking is that it treats terms as occurring independently of each other. In practice, many words tend to occur together (e.g., ambulance and emergency). Write a program that scans an ASCII file and lists all pairs of words that occur within 5 words of each other. For each pair of words, you now have a frequency, and should be able to create a plot like Figure 27.3 with pairs of words on the X-axis. Run this program on some sample document collections. What do the results suggest about co-occurrences of words?

Exercise 27.2 Assume you are given a document database that contains six documents. After stemming, the documents contain the following terms:

Document	Terms
1	car manufacturer Honda auto
2	auto computer navigation
3	Honda navigation
4	manufacturer computer IBM
5	IBM personal computer
6	car Beetle VW

Answer the following questions.

1. Show the result of creating an inverted file on the documents.
2. Show the result of creating a signature file with a width of 5 bits. Construct your own hashing function that maps terms to bit positions.
3. Evaluate the following boolean queries using the inverted file and the signature file that you created: 'car', 'IBM' `AND` 'computer', 'IBM' `AND` 'car', 'IBM' `OR` 'auto', and 'IBM' `AND` 'computer' `AND` 'manufacturer'.
4. Assume that the query load against the document database consists of exactly the queries that were stated in the previous question. Also assume that each of these queries is evaluated exactly once.
   (a) Design a signature file with a width of 3 bits and design a hashing function that minimizes the overall number of false positives retrieved when evaluating the

(b) Design a signature file with a width of 6 bits and a hashing function that minimizes the overall number of false positives.

(c) Assume you want to construct a signature file. What is the smallest signature width that allows you to evaluate all queries without retrieving any false positives?

5. Consider the following ranked queries: 'car, 'IBM computer', 'IBM car', 'IBM auto', and 'IBM computer manufacturer'.

(a) Calculate the IDF for every term in the database.

(b) For each document, show its document vector.

(c) For each query, calculate the relevance of each document in the database, with and without the length normalization step.

(d) Describe how you would use the inverted index to identify the top two documents that match each query.

(e) How would having the inverted lists sorted by relevance instead of document id affect your answer to the previous question?

(f) Replace each document with a variation that contains 10 copies of the same document. For each query, recompute the relevance of each document, with and without the length normalization step.

Exercise 27.3 Assume you are given the following stemmed document database:

Document	Terms
1	car car manufacturer car car Honda auto
2	auto computer navigation
3	Honda navigation auto
4	manufacturer computer IBM graphics
5	IBM personal IBM computer IBM IBM IBM IBM
6	car Beetle VW Honda

Using this database, repeat the previous exercise.

Exercise 27.4 You are in charge of the Genghis ('We execute fast') search engine. You are designing your server cluster to handle 500 million hits a day and 10 billion pages of indexed data. Each machine costs $1000, and can store 10 million pages and respond to 200 queries per second (against these pages).

1. If you were given a budget of $500,000 dollars for purchasing machines, and were required to index all 10 billion pages, could you do it?
2. What is the minimum budget to index all pages? If you assume that each query can be answered by looking at data in just one (10 million page) partition, and that queries are uniformly distributed across partitions, what peak load (in number of queries per second) can such a cluster handle?
3. How would your answer to the previous question change if each query, on average, accessed two partitions?
4. What is the minimum budget required to handle the desired load of 500 million hits per day if all queries are on a *single partition*? Assume that queries are uniformly distributed with respect to time of day.

5. How would your answer to the previous question change if the number of queries per day went up to 5 billion hits per day? How would it change if the number of pages went up to 100 billion?
6. Assume that each query accesses just one partition, that queries are uniformly distributed across partitions, but that at any given time, the peak load on a partition is upto 10 times the average load. What is the minimum budget for purchasing machines in this scenario?
7. Take the cost for machines from the previous question and multiply it by 10 to reflect the costs of maintenance, administration, network bandwidth, etc. This amount is your annual cost of operation. Assume that you charge advertisers 2 cents per page. What fraction of your inventory (i.e., the total number of pages that you serve over the course of a year) do you have to sell in order to make a profit?

Exercise 27.5 Assume that the base set of the HITS algorithm consists of the set of Web pages displayed in the following table. An entry should be interpreted as follows: Web page 1 has hyperlinks to pages 5 and 6.

Webpage	*Pages that this page has links to*
1	5, 6, 7
2	5, 7
3	6, 8
4	
5	1, 2
6	1, 3
7	1, 2
8	4

1. Run five iterations of the HITS algorithm and find the highest ranked authority and the highest ranked hub.
2. Compute Google's Pigeon Rank for each page.

Exercise 27.6 Consider the following description of items shown in the Eggface computer mail-order catalog.

"Eggface sells hardware and software. We sell the new Palm Pilot V for $400; its part number is 345. We also sell the IBM ThinkPad 570 for only $1999; its part number is 3784. We sell both business and entertainment software. Microsoft Office 2000 has just arrived and you can purchase the Standard Edition for only $140, part number 974; the Professional Edition is $200, part 975. The new desktop publishing software from Adobe called InDesign is here for only $200, part 664. We carry the newest games from Blizzard software. You can start playing Diablo II for only $30, part number 12, and you can purchase Starcraft for only $10, part number 812. Our goal is complete customer satisfaction—if we don't have what you want in stock, we'll give you $10 off your next purchase!"

1. Design an HTML document that depicts the items offered by Eggface.
2. Create a well-formed XML document that describes the contents of the Eggface catalog.
3. Create a DTD for your XML document and make sure that the document you created in the last question is valid with respect to this DTD.

4. Write an XQuery query that lists all software items in the catalog, sorted by price.
5. Write an XQuery query that, for each vendor, lists all software items from that vendor (i.e., one row in the result per vendor).
6. Write an XQuery query that lists the prices of all hardware items in the catalog.
7. Depict the catalog data in the semistructured data model as shown in Figure 27.7.
8. Build a dataguide for this data. Discuss how it can be used (or not) for each of the above queries.
9. Design a relational schema to publish this data.

Exercise 27.7 A university database contains information about professors and the courses they teach. The university has decided to publish this information on the Web and you are in charge of the execution. You are given the following information about the contents of the database:

In the fall semester 1999, the course 'Introduction to Database Management Systems' was taught by Professor Ioannidis. The course took place Mondays and Wednesdays from 9–10 a.m. in room 101. The discussion section was held on Fridays from 9–10 a.m. Also in the fall semester 1999, the course 'Advanced Database Management Systems' was taught by Professor Carey. Thirty five students took that course which was held in room 110 Tuesdays and Thursdays from 1–2 p.m. In the spring semester 1999, the course 'Introduction to Database Management Systems' was taught by U.N. Owen on Tuesdays and Thursdays from 3–4 p.m. in room 110. Sixty three students were enrolled; the discussion section was on Thursdays from 4–5 p.m. The other course taught in the spring semester was 'Advanced Database Management Systems' by Professor Ioannidis, Monday, Wednesday, and Friday from 8–9 a.m.

1. Create a well-formed XML document that contains the university database.
2. Create a DTD for your XML document. Make sure that the XML document is valid with respect to this DTD.
3. Write an XQuery query that lists the names of all professors in the order they are listed on the Web.
4. Write an XQuery query that lists all courses taught in 1999. The result should be grouped by professor, with one row per professor, sorted by last name. For a given professor, courses should be ordered by name and should not contain duplicates (i.e., even if a professor teaches the same course twice in 1999, it should appear only once in the result).
5. Build a dataguide for this data. Discuss how it can be used (or not) for each of the above queries.
6. Design a relational schema to publish this data.
7. Describe the information in a different XML document—a document that has a different structure. Create a corresponding DTD and make sure that the document is valid. Reformulate the queries you wrote for preceding parts of this exercise to work with the new DTD.

Exercise 27.8 Consider the database of the FamilyWear clothes manufacturer. FamilyWear produces three types of clothes: women's clothes, men's clothes, and children's clothes. Men can choose between polo shirts and T-shirts. Each polo shirt has a list of available colors, sizes, and a uniform price. Each T-shirt has a price, a list of available colors, and a list of

available sizes. Women have the same choice of polo shirts and T-shirts as men. In addition women can choose between three types of jeans: slim fit, easy fit, and relaxed fit jeans. Each pair of jeans has a list of possible waist sizes and possible lengths. The price of a pair of jeans only depends on its type. Children can choose between T-shirts and baseball caps. Each T-shirt has a price, a list of available colors, and a list of available patterns. T-shirts for children all have the same size. Baseball caps come in three different sizes: small, medium, and large. Each item has an optional sales price that is offered on special occasions. Write all queries in XQuery.

1. Design an XML DTD for FamilyWear so that FamilyWear can publish its catalog on the Web.
2. Write a query to find the most expensive item sold by FamilyWear.
3. Write a query to find the average price for each clothes type.
4. Write a query to list all items that cost more than the average for their type; the result must contain one row per type in the order that types are listed on the Web. For each type, the items must be listed in increasing order by price.
5. Write a query to find all items whose sale price is more than twice the normal price of some other item.
6. Write a query to find all items whose sale price is more than twice the normal price of some other item within the same clothes type.
7. Build a dataguide for this data. Discuss how it can be used (or not) for each of the above queries.
8. Design a relational schema to publish this data.

Exercise 27.9 With every element e in an XML document, suppose we associate a triplet of numbers <begin, end, level>, where begin denotes the start position of e in the document in terms of the byte offset in the file, end denotes the end position of the element, and level indicates the nesting level of e, with the root element starting at nesting level 0.

1. Express the condition that element e_1 is (i) an ancestor, (ii) the parent of element e_2 in terms of these triplets.
2. Suppose every element has an internal system-generated id and, for every tag name l, we store a list of ids of all elements in the document having tag l, that is, an inverted list of ids per tag. Along with the element id, we also store the triplet associated with it, and sort the list by the *begin* positions of elements. Now, suppose we wish to evaluate a path expression a//b. The output of the join must be $<id_a, id_b>$ pairs such that id_a and id_b are ids of elements e_a with tag name a and e_b with tag name b respectively, and e_a is an ancestor of e_b. It must be sorted by the composite key $<$ *begin* position of e_a, *begin* position of e_b $>$.

   Design an algorithm that merges the lists for a and b and performs this join. The number of position comparisons must be linear in the input and output sizes. *Hint:* The approach is similar to a sort-merge of two sorted lists of integers.
3. Suppose that we have k sorted lists of integers where k is a constant. Assume there are no duplicates; that is, each value occurs in exactly one list and exactly once. Design an algorithm to merge these lists where the number of comparisons is linear in the input size.
4. Next, suppose we wish to perform the join $a_1//a_2//...//a_k$ (again, k is a constant). The output of the join must be a list of k-tuples $<id_1, id_2, \ldots, id_k>$ such that id_i is the id

of an element e_i with tag name a_i and e_i is an ancestor of e_{i+1} for all $1 \leq i \leq k-1$. The list must be sorted by the composite key $<$ *begin* position of $e_1, \ldots$ *begin* position of $e_k >$. Extend the algorithms you designed in parts (2) and (3) to compute this join. The number of position comparisons must be linear in the combined input and output size.

Exercise 27.10 This exercise examines why path indexing for XML data is different from conventional indexing problems such as indexing a linearly ordered domain for point and range queries. The following model has been proposed for the problem of indexing in general: The input to the problem consists of (i) a domain of elements $\mathcal{D}$, (ii) a data instance I which is a finite subset of $\mathcal{D}$, and (iii) a finite set of queries $\mathcal{Q}$; each query is a non-empty subset of I. This triplet $< \mathcal{D}, I, \mathcal{Q} >$ represents the indexed workload. An indexing scheme $\mathcal{S}$ for this workload essentially groups the data elements into fixed size blocks of size B. Formally, $\mathcal{S}$ is a collection of blocks $\{S_1, S_2, \ldots, S_k\}$, where each block is a subset of I containing exactly B elements. These blocks must together exhaust I; that is, $I = S_1 \cup S_2 \ldots \cup S_k$.

1. Suppose $\mathcal{D}$ is the set of positive integers and I consists of integers from 1 to n. $\mathcal{Q}$ consists of all point queries; that is, of singletons $\{1\}, \{2\}, \ldots, \{n\}$. Suppose we want to index this workload using a B+ tree in which each leaf level block can hold exactly l integers. What is the block size of this indexing scheme? What is the number of blocks used?
2. The *storage redundancy* of an indexing scheme $\mathcal{S}$ is the maximum number of blocks that contain an element of I. What is the storage redundancy of the B+ tree used in part (1) above?
3. Define the *access cost* of a query Q in $\mathcal{Q}$ under scheme $\mathcal{S}$ to be the minimum number of blocks of $\mathcal{S}$ that cover it. The access overhead of Q is its access cost divided by its ideal access cost, which is $\lceil |Q|/B \rceil$. What is the access cost of any query under the B+ tree scheme of part (1)? What about the access overhead?
4. The access overhead of the indexing scheme itself is the maximum access overhead among all queries in $\mathcal{Q}$. Show that this value can never be higher than B. What is the access overhead of the B+ tree scheme?
5. We now define a workload for path indexing. The domain $\mathcal{D} = \{i : i \text{ is a positive integer}\}$. This is intuitively the set of all object identifiers. An instance can be any finite subset of $\mathcal{D}$. In order to define $\mathcal{Q}$, we impose a tree structure on the set of object identifiers in I. Thus, if there are n identifiers in I, we define a tree T with n nodes and associate every node with exactly one identifier from I. The tree is rooted and node-labeled where the node labels come from an infinite set of labels Σ. The root of T has a distinguished label called root. Now, $\mathcal{Q}$ contains a subset S of the object identifiers in I if S is the result of some path expression on T. The class of path expressions we consider involves only simple path expressions; that is, expressions of the form $PE = \mathsf{root} s_1 l_1 s_2 l_2 \ldots l_n$ where each s_i is a separator which can either be / or // and each l_i is a label from Σ. This expression returns the set of all object identifiers corresponding to nodes in T that have a path matching PE coming in to them.
   Show that for any r, there is a path indexing workload such that any indexing scheme with redundancy at most r will have access overhead $B - 1$.

Exercise 27.11 This exercise introduces the notion of *graph simulation* in the context of query minimization. Consider the following kind of constraints on the data: (1) Required parent constraints, where we can specify that the parent of an element of tag b always has tag a, and (2) Required ancestor constraints, where we can specify that that an element of tag b always has an ancestor of tag a.

1. We represent a path expression query $PE = \mathsf{root}s_1l_1s_2l_2\ldots l_n$, where each s_i is a separator and each l_i is a label, as a directed graph with one node for root and one for each l_i. Edges go from root to l_1 and from l_i to l_{i+1}. An edge is a parent edge or an ancestor edge according to whether the respective separator is / or //. We represent a parent edge from u to v in the text as $u \rightarrow v$ and an ancestor edge as $u \Rightarrow v$.

   Represent the path expression root//a/b/c as a graph, as a simple exercise.
2. The constraints are also represented as a directed graph in the following manner. Create a node for each tag name. A parent (ancestor) edge is present from tag name a to tag name b if there is a constraint asserting that every b element must have an a parent (ancestor). Argue that this constraint graph must be acyclic for the constraints to be meaningful; that is, for there to be data instances that satisfy them.
3. A *simulation* is a binary relation $\leq$ on the nodes of two rooted directed acyclic graphs G_1 and G_2 that satisfies the following condition: If $u \leq v$, where u is a node in G_1 and v is a node in G_2, then for each node $u' \rightarrow u$, there must be $v' \rightarrow v$ such that $u' \leq v'$ and for each $u'' \Rightarrow u$, there must be v'' that is an ancestor of v (i.e., has some path to v) such that $u'' \leq v''$. Show that there is a unique largest simulation relation $\leq^m$. If $u \leq^m v$ then u is said to be *simulated by* v.
4. Show that the path expression root//b//c can be rewritten as //c if and only if the c node in the query graph can be simulated by the c node in the constraint graph.
5. The path expression $//l_js_{j+1}l_{j+1}\ldots l_n$ $(j > 1)$ is a *suffix* of $\mathsf{root}s_1l_1s_2l_2\ldots l_n$. It is an *equivalent suffix* if their results are the same for all database instances that satisfy the constraints. Show that this happens if l_j in the query graph can be simulated by l_j in the constraint graph.

BIBLIOGRAPHIC NOTES

Introductory reading material on information retrieval includes the standard textbooks by Salton and McGill [646] and by van Rijsbergen [753]. Collections of articles for the more advanced reader have been edited by Jones and Willett [411] and by Frakes and Baeza-Yates [279]. Querying text repositories has been studied extensively in information retrieval; see [626] for a recent survey. Faloutsos overviews indexing methods for text databases [257]. Inverted files are discussed in [540] and signature files are discussed in [259]. Zobel, Moffat, and Ramamohanarao give a comparison of inverted files and signature files [802]. A survey of incremental updates to inverted indexes is presented in [179]. Other aspects of information retrieval and indexing in the context of databases are addressed in [604], [290], [656], and [803],, among others. [330] studies the problem of discovering text resources on the Web. The book by Witten, Moffat, and Bell has a lot of material on compression techniques for document databases [780].

The number of citation counts as a measure of scientific impact has first been studied by Garfield [307]; see also [763]. Usage of hypertextual information to improve the quality of search engines has been proposed by Spertus [699] and by Weiss et al. [771]. The HITS algorithm was developed by Jon Kleinberg [438]. Concurrently, Brin and Page developed the Pagerank (now called PigeonRank) algorithm, which also takes hyperlinks between pages into account [116]. A thorough analysis and comparison of several recently proposed algorithms for determining authoritative pages is presented in [106]. The discovery of structure in the World Wide Web is currently a very active area of research; see for example the work by Gibson et al. [316].

There is a lot of research on semistructured data in the database community. The Tsimmis data integration system uses a semistructured data model to cope with possible heterogeneity of data sources [584, 583]. Work on describing the structure of semistructured databases can be found in [561]. Wang and Liu consider schema discovery for semistructured documents [766]. Mapping between relational and XML representations is discussed in [271, 676, 103] and [134].

Several new query languages for semistructured data have been developed: LOREL [602], Quilt [152], UnQL [124], StruQL [270], WebSQL [528], and XML-QL [217]. The current W3C standard, XQuery, is described in [153]. The latest version of several standards mentioned in this chapter, including XML, XSchema, XPath, and XQuery, can be found at the website of the World Wide Web Consortium (`www.w3.org`). Kweelt [645] is an open source system that supports Quilt, and is a convenient platform for systems experimentation that can be obtained online at `http://kweelt.sourceforge.net`.

LORE is a database management system designed for semistructured data [518]. Query optimization for semistructured data is addressed in [5] and [321], which proposed the Strong Dataguide. The 1-Index was proposed in [536] to address the size-explosion issue for dataguides. Another XML indexing scheme is proposed in [196]. Recent work [419] aims to extend the framework of structure indexes to cover specific subsets of path expressions. Selectivity estimation for XML path expressions is discussed in [6]. The theory of indexability proposed by Hellerstein et al. in [375] enables a formal analysis of the path indexing problem, which turns out to be harder than traditional indexing.

There has been a lot of work on using semistructured data models for Web data and several Web query systems have been developed: WebSQL [528], W3QS [445], WebLog [461], WebOQL [39], STRUDEL [269], ARANEUS [46], and FLORID [379]. [275] is a good overview of database research in the context of the Web.

28

SPATIAL DATA MANAGEMENT

- What is spatial data, and how can we classify it?
- What applications drive the need for spatial data management?
- What are spatial indexes and how are they different in structure from non-spatial data?
- How can we use space-filling curves for indexing spatial data?
- What are directory-based approaches to indexing spatial data?
- What are R trees and how to they work?
- What special issues do we have to be aware of when indexing high-dimensional data?
- **Key concepts:** Spatial data, spatial extent, location, boundary, point data, region data, raster data, feature vector, vector data, spatial query, nearest neighbor query, spatial join, content-based image retrieval, spatial index, space-filling curve, Z-ordering, grid file, R tree, R+ tree, R* tree, generalized search tree, contrast.

Nothing puzzles me more than time and space; and yet nothing puzzles me less, as I never think about them.

—Charles Lamb

Many applications involve large collections of spatial objects; and querying, indexing, and maintaining such collections requires some specialized techniques. In this chapter, we motivate spatial data management and provide an introduction to the required techniques.

SQL/MM: Spatial The SQL/MM standard supports points, lines, and 2-dimensional (planar or surface) data. Future extensions are expected to support 3-dimensional (volumetric) and 4-dimensional (spatio-temporal) data as well. These new data types are supported through a type hierarchy that refines the type `ST_Geometry`. Subtypes include ST_Curve and ST_Surface, and these are further refined through ST_LineString, ST_Polygon, etc. The methods defined for the type ST_Geometry support (point set) intersection of objects, union, difference, equality, containment, computation of the convex hull, and other similar spatial operations. The SQL/MM: Spatial standard has been designed with an eye to compatibility with related standards such as those proposed by the Open GIS (Geographic Information Systems) Consortium.

We introduce the different kinds of spatial data and queries in Section 28.1 and discuss several important applications in Section 28.2. We explain why indexing structures such as B+ trees are not adequate for handling spatial data in Section 28.3. We discuss three approaches to indexing spatial data in Sections 28.4 through 28.6: In Section 28.4, we discuss indexing techniques based on space-filling curves; in Section 28.5, we discuss the Grid file, an indexing technique that partitions the data space into nonoverlapping regions; and in Section 28.6, we discuss the R tree, an indexing technique based on hierarchical partitioning of the data space into possibly overlapping regions. Finally, in Section 28.7 we discuss some issues that arise in indexing datasets with a large number of dimensions.

28.1 TYPES OF SPATIAL DATA AND QUERIES

We use the term **spatial data** in a broad sense, covering multidimensional points, lines, rectangles, polygons, cubes, and other geometric objects. A spatial data object occupies a certain region of space, called its **spatial extent**, which is characterized by its **location** and **boundary**.

From the point of view of a DBMS, we can classify spatial data as being either *point data* or *region data.*

Point Data: A **point** has a spatial extent characterized completely by its location; intuitively, it occupies no space and has no associated area or volume. Point data consists of a collection of *points* in a multidimensional space. Point data stored in a database can be based on direct measurements or generated by transforming data obtained through measurements for ease of storage and querying. **Raster data** is an example of directly measured point data and

includes bitmaps or pixel maps such as satellite imagery. Each pixel stores a measured value (e.g., temperature or color) for a corresponding location in space. Another example of such measured point data is medical imagery such as three-dimensional magnetic resonance imaging (MRI) brain scans. *Feature vectors* extracted from images, text, or signals, such as time series are examples of point data obtained by transforming a data object. As we will see, it is often easier to use such a representation of the data, instead of the actual image or signal, to answer queries.

Region Data: A **region** has a spatial extent with a location and a boundary. The location can be thought of as the position of a fixed 'anchor point' for the region, such as its centroid. In two dimensions, the boundary can be visualized as a line (for finite regions, a closed loop), and in three dimensions, it is a surface. Region data consists of a collection of *regions*. Region data stored in a database is typically a simple geometric approximation to an actual data object. **Vector data** is the term used to describe such geometric approximations, constructed using points, line segments, polygons, spheres, cubes, and the like. Many examples of region data arise in geographic applications. For instance, roads and rivers can be represented as a collection of line segments, and countries, states, and lakes can be represented as polygons. Other examples arise in computer-aided design applications. For instance, an airplane wing might be modeled as a *wire frame* using a collection of polygons (that intuitively tile the wire frame surface approximating the wing), and a tubular object may be modeled as the difference between two concentric cylinders.

Queries that arise over spatial data are of three main types: *spatial range queries*, *nearest neighbor queries*, and *spatial join queries*.

Spatial Range Queries: In addition to multidimensional queries, such as, "Find all employees with salaries between $50,000 and $60,000 and ages between 40 and 50," we can ask queries such as "Find all cities within 50 miles of Madison" or "Find all rivers in Wisconsin." A spatial range query has an associated region (with a location and boundary). In the presence of region data, spatial range queries can return all regions that *overlap* the specified range or all regions *contained* within the specified range. Both variants of spatial range queries are useful, and algorithms for evaluating one variant are easily adapted to solve the other. Range queries occur in a wide variety of applications, including relational queries, GIS queries, and CAD/CAM queries.

Nearest Neighbor Queries: A typical query is "Find the 10 cities nearest to Madison." We usually want the answers ordered by distance to Madison, that is, by proximity. Such queries are especially important in the context of multimedia databases, where an object (e.g., images) is represented by a point,

and 'similar' objects are found by retrieving objects whose representative points are closest to the point representing the query object.

Spatial Join Queries: Typical examples include "Find pairs of cities within 200 miles of each other" and "Find all cities near a lake." These queries can be quite expensive to evaluate. If we consider a relation in which each tuple is a point representing a city or a lake, the preceding queries can be answered by a join of this relation with itself, where the join condition specifies the distance between two matching tuples. Of course, if cities and lakes are represented in more detail and have a spatial extent, both the meaning of such queries (are we looking for cities whose centroids are within 200 miles of each other or cities whose boundaries come within 200 miles of each other?), and the query evaluation strategies become more complex. Still, the essential character of a spatial join query is retained.

These kinds of queries are very common and arise in most applications of spatial data. Some applications also require specialized operations such as interpolation of measurements at a set of locations to obtain values for the measured attribute over an entire region.

28.2 APPLICATIONS INVOLVING SPATIAL DATA

Many applications involve spatial data. Even a traditional relation with k fields can be thought of as a collection of k-dimensional points, and as we see in Section 28.3, certain relational queries can be executed faster by using indexing techniques designed for spatial data. In this section, however, we concentrate on applications in which spatial data plays a central role and in which efficient handling of spatial data is essential for good performance.

Geographic Information Systems (GIS) deal extensively with spatial data, including points, lines, and two- or three-dimensional regions. For example, a map contains locations of small objects (points), rivers and highways (lines), and cities and lakes (regions). A GIS system must efficiently manage two-dimensional and three-dimensional datasets. All the classes of spatial queries we described arise naturally, and both point data and region data must be handled. Commercial GIS systems such as ArcInfo are in wide use today, and object database systems aim to support GIS applications as well.

Computer-aided design and manufacturing (CAD/CAM) systems and *medical imaging* systems store spatial objects, such as surfaces of design objects (e.g., the fuselage of an aircraft). As with GIS systems, both point and region data must be stored. Range queries and spatial join queries are probably the most common queries, and **spatial integrity constraints**, such as "There must be

a minimum clearance of one foot between the wheel and the fuselage," can be very useful. (CAD/CAM was a major reason behind the development of object databases.)

Multimedia databases, which contain multimedia objects such as images, text, and various kinds of time-series data (e.g., audio), also require spatial data management. In particular, finding objects similar to a given object is a common query in a multimedia system, and a popular approach to answering similarity queries involves first mapping multimedia data to a collection of points, called **feature vectors**. A similarity query is then converted to the problem of finding the nearest neighbors of the point that represents the query object.

In medical image databases, we store digitized two-dimensional and three-dimensional images such as X-rays or MRI images. Fingerprints (together with information identifying the fingerprinted individual) can be stored in an image database, and we can search for fingerprints that match a given fingerprint. Photographs from driver's licenses can be stored in a database, and we can search for faces that match a given face. Such image database applications rely on **content-based image retrieval** (e.g., find images similar to a given image). Going beyond images, we can store a database of video clips and search for clips in which a scene changes, or in which there is a particular kind of object. We can store a database of *signals* or *time-series* and look for similar time-series. We can store a collection of text documents and search for similar documents (i.e., dealing with similar topics).

Feature vectors representing multimedia objects are typically points in a high-dimensional space. For example, we can obtain feature vectors from a text object by using a list of keywords (or concepts) and noting which keywords are present; we thus get a vector of 1s (the corresponding keyword is present) and 0s (the corresponding keyword is missing in the text object) whose length is equal to the number of keywords in our list. Lists of several hundred words are commonly used. We can obtain feature vectors from an image by looking at its color distribution (the levels of red, green, and blue for each pixel) or by using the first several coefficients of a mathematical function (e.g., the Hough transform) that closely approximates the shapes in the image. In general, given an arbitrary signal, we can represent it using a mathematical function having a standard series of terms and approximate it by storing the coefficients of the most significant terms.

When mapping multimedia data to a collection of points, it is important to ensure that a there is a measure of distance between two points that captures the notion of similarity between the corresponding multimedia objects. Thus, two images that map to two nearby points must be more similar than two images that map to two points far from each other. Once objects are mapped

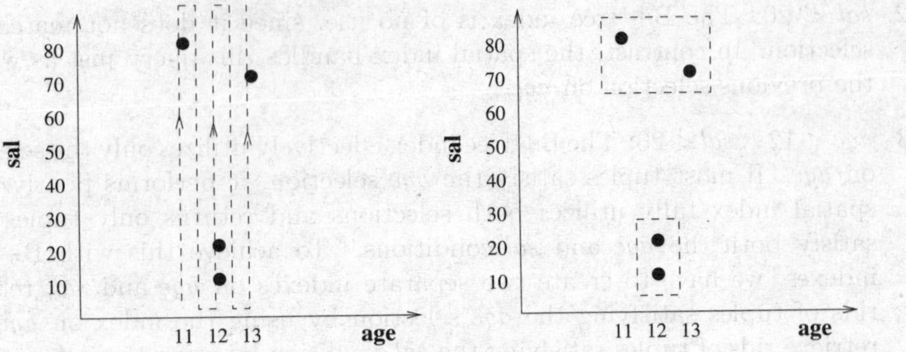

Figure 28.1 Clustering of Data Entries in B+ Tree vs. Spatial Indexes

into a suitable coordinate space, finding similar images, similar documents, or similar time-series can be modeled as finding points that are close to each other: We map the query object to a point and look for its nearest neighbors. The most common kind of spatial data in multimedia applications is point data, and the most common query is nearest neighbor. In contrast to GIS and CAD/CAM, the data is of high dimensionality (usually 10 or more dimensions).

28.3 INTRODUCTION TO SPATIAL INDEXES

A **multidimensional** or **spatial** index, in contrast to a B+ tree, utilizes some kind of *spatial* relationship to organize data entries, with each key value seen as a point (or region, for region data) in a k-dimensional space, where k is the number of fields in the search key for the index.

In a B+ tree index, the two-dimensional space of $\langle$*age, sal*$\rangle$ values is linearized—that is, points in the two-dimensional domain are totally ordered—by sorting on *age* first and then on *sal*. In Figure 28.1, the dotted line indicates the linear order in which points are stored in a B+ tree. In contrast, a spatial index stores data entries based on their proximity in the underlying two-dimensional space. In Figure 28.1, the boxes indicate how points are stored in a spatial index.

Let us compare a B+ tree index on key $\langle$*age, sal*$\rangle$ with a spatial index on the space of *age* and *sal* values, using several example queries:

1. *age* < 12: The B+ tree index performs very well. As we will see, a spatial index handles such a query quite well, although it cannot match a B+ tree index in this case.

2. *sal* < 20: The B+ tree index is of no use, since it does not match this selection. In contrast, the spatial index handles this query just as well as the previous selection on *age*.

3. *age* < 12 ∧ *sal* < 20: The B+ tree index effectively utilizes only the selection on *age*. If most tuples satisfy the *age* selection, it performs poorly. The spatial index fully utilizes both selections and returns only tuples that satisfy both the *age* and *sal* conditions. To achieve this with B+ tree indexes, we have to create two separate indexes on *age* and *sal*, retrieve rids of tuples satisfying the *age* selection by using the index on *age* and retrieve rids of tuples satisfying the *sal* condition by using the index on *sal*, intersect these rids, then retrieve the tuples with these rids.

Spatial indexes are ideal for queries such as "Find the 10 nearest neighbors of a given point" and, "Find all points within a certain distance of a given point." The drawback with respect to a B+ tree index is that if (almost) all data entries are to be retrieved in *age* order, a spatial index is likely to be slower than a B+ tree index in which *age* is the first field in the search key.

28.3.1 Overview of Proposed Index Structures

Many spatial index structures have been proposed. Some are designed primarily to index collections of points although they can be adapted to handle regions, and some handle region data naturally. Examples of index structures for point data include *Grid files*, *hB trees*, *KD trees*, *Point Quad trees*, and *SR trees*. Examples of index structures that handle regions as well as point data include *Region Quad trees*, *R trees*, and *SKD trees*. These lists are far from complete; there are many variants of these index structures and many entirely distinct index structures.

There is as yet no consensus on the 'best' spatial index structure. However, R trees have been widely implemented and found their way into commercial DBMSs. This is due to their relative simplicity, their ability to handle both point and region data, and their performance, which is at least comparable to more complex structures.

We discuss three approaches that are distinct and, taken together, illustrate of many of the proposed indexing alternatives. First, we discuss index structures that rely on *space-filling curves* to organize points. We begin by discussing *Z-ordering* for point data, and then for region data, which is essentially the idea behind Region Quad trees. Region Quad trees illustrate an indexing approach based on recursive subdivision of the multidimensional space, independent of the actual dataset. There are several variants of Region Quad trees.

Second, we discuss Grid files, which illustrate how an Extendible Hashing style directory can be used to index spatial data. Many index structures such as *Bang files*, *Buddy trees*, and *Multilevel Grid files* have been proposed refining the basic idea. Finally, we discuss R trees, which also recursively subdivide the multidimensional space. In contrast to Region Quad trees, the decomposition of space utilized in an R tree depends on the indexed dataset. We can think of R trees as an adaptation of the B+ tree idea to spatial data. Many variants of R trees have been proposed, including *Cell trees*, *Hilbert R trees*, *Packed R trees*, *R* trees*, *R+ trees*, *TV trees*, and *X trees*.

28.4 INDEXING BASED ON SPACE-FILLING CURVES

Space-filling curves are based on the assumption that any attribute value can be represented with some fixed number of bits, say k bits. The maximum number of values along each dimension is therefore 2^k. We consider a two-dimensional dataset for simplicity, although the approach can handle any number of dimensions.

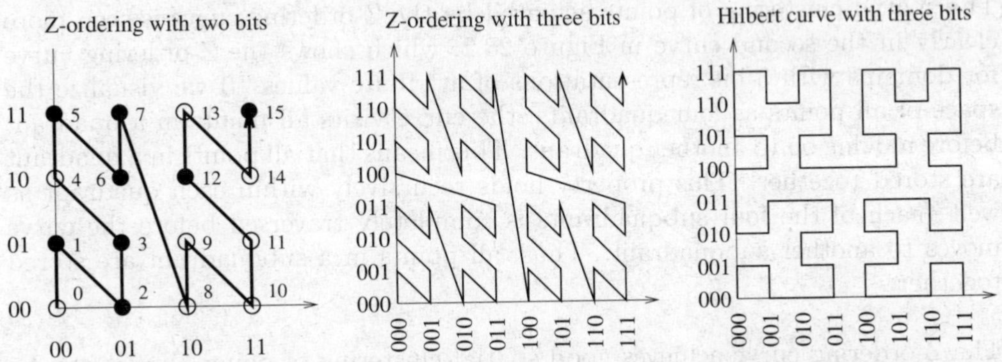

Figure 28.2 Space Filling Curves

A space-filling curve imposes a linear ordering on the domain, as illustrated in Figure 28.2. The first curve shows the **Z-ordering** curve for domains with 2-bit representations of attribute values. A given dataset contains a subset of the points in the domain, and these are shown as filled circles in the figure. Domain points not in the given dataset are shown as unfilled circles. Consider the point with $X = 01$ and $Y = 11$ in the first curve. The point has **Z-value** 0111, obtained by interleaving the bits of the X and Y values; we take the first X bit (0), then the first Y bit (1), then the second X bit (1), and finally the second Y bit (1). In decimal representation, the Z-value 0111 is equal to 7, and the point $X = 01$ and $Y = 11$ has the Z-value 7 shown next to it in Figure

28.2. This is the eighth domain point 'visited' by the space-filling curve, which starts at point $X = 00$ and $Y = 00$ (Z-value 0).

The points in a dataset are stored in Z-value order and indexed by a traditional indexing structure such as a B+ tree. That is, the Z-value of a point is stored together with the point and is the search key for the B+ tree. (Actually, we need not need store the X and Y values for a point if we store the Z-value, since we can compute them from the Z-value by extracting the interleaved bits.) To insert a point, we compute its Z-value and insert it into the B+ tree. Deletion and search are similarly based on computing the Z-value and using the standard B+ tree algorithms.

The advantage of this approach over using a B+ tree index on some combination of the X and Y fields is that points are clustered together by spatial proximity in the X–Y space. Spatial queries over the X–Y space now translate into linear range queries over the ordering of Z-values and are efficiently answered using the B+ tree on Z-values.

The spatial clustering of points achieved by the Z-ordering curve is seen more clearly in the second curve in Figure 28.2, which shows the Z-ordering curve for domains with 3-bit representations of attribute values. If we visualize the space of all points as four quadrants, the curve visits all points in a quadrant before moving on to another quadrant. This means that all points in a quadrant are stored together. This property holds recursively within each quadrant as well—each of the four subquadrants is completely traversed before the curve moves to another subquadrant. Thus, all points in a subquadrant are stored together.

The Z-ordering curve achieves good spatial clustering of points, but it can be improved on. Intuitively, the curve occasionally makes long diagonal 'jumps,' and the points connected by the jumps, while far apart in the X–Y space of points, are nonetheless close in Z-ordering. The Hilbert curve, shown as the third curve in Figure 28.2, addresses this problem.

28.4.1 Region Quad Trees and Z-Ordering: Region Data

Z-ordering gives us a way to group points according to spatial proximity. What if we have region data? The key is to understand how Z-ordering recursively decomposes the data space into quadrants and subquadrants, as illustrated in Figure 28.3.

The Region Quad tree structure corresponds directly to the recursive decomposition of the data space. Each node in the tree corresponds to a square-shaped

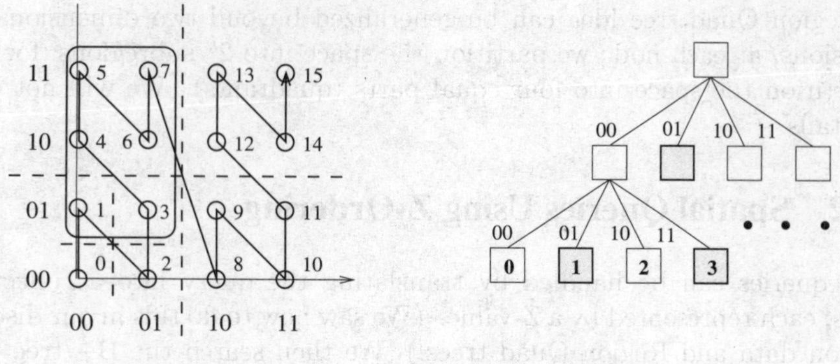

Figure 28.3 Z-Ordering and Region Quad Trees

region of the data space. As special cases, the root corresponds to the entire data space, and some leaf nodes correspond to exactly one point. Each internal node has four children, corresponding to the four quadrants into which the space corresponding to the node is partitioned: 00 identifies the bottom left quadrant, 01 identifies the top left quadrant, 10 identifies the bottom right quadrant, and 11 identifies the top right quadrant.

In Figure 28.3, consider the children of the root. All points in the quadrant corresponding to the 00 child have Z-values that begin with 00, all points in the quadrant corresponding to the 01 child have Z-values that begin with 01, and so on. In fact, the Z-value of a point can be obtained by traversing the path from the root to the leaf node for the point and concatenating all the edge labels.

Consider the region represented by the rounded rectangle in Figure 28.3. Suppose that the rectangle object is stored in the DBMS and given the unique identifier (oid) R. R includes all points in the 01 quadrant of the root as well as the points with Z-values 1 and 3, which are in the 00 quadrant of the root. In the figure, the nodes for points 1 and 3 and the 01 quadrant of the root are shown with dark boundaries. Together, the dark nodes represent the rectangle R. The three records ⟨0001, R⟩, ⟨0011, R⟩, and ⟨01, R⟩ can be used to store this information. The first field of each record is a Z-value; the records are clustered and indexed on this column using a B+ tree. Thus, a B+ tree is used to implement a Region Quad tree, just as it was used to implement Z-ordering.

Note that a region object can usually be stored using fewer records if it is sufficient to represent it at a coarser level of detail. For example, rectangle R can be represented using two records ⟨00, R⟩ and ⟨01, R⟩. This approximates R by using the bottom-left and top-left quadrants of the root.

The Region Quad tree idea can be generalized beyond two dimensions. In k dimensions, at each node we partition the space into 2^k subregions; for $k = 2$, we partition the space into four equal parts (quadrants). We will not discuss the details.

28.4.2 Spatial Queries Using Z-Ordering

Range queries can be handled by translating the query into a collection of regions, each represented by a Z-value. (We saw how to do this in our discussion of region data and Region Quad trees.) We then search the B+ tree to find matching data items.

Nearest neighbor queries can also be handled, although they are a little trickier because distance in the Z-value space does not always correspond well to distance in the original X–Y coordinate space (recall the diagonal jumps in the Z-order curve). The basic idea is to first compute the Z-value of the query and find the data point with the closest Z-value by using the B+ tree. Then, to make sure we are not overlooking any points that are closer in the X–Y space, we compute the actual distance r between the query point and the retrieved data point and issue a range query centered at the query point and with radius r. We check all retrieved points and return the one closest to the query point.

Spatial joins can be handled by extending the approach to range queries.

28.5 GRID FILES

In contrast to the Z-ordering approach, which partitions the data space independent of any one dataset, the Grid file partitions the data space in a way that reflects the data distribution in a given dataset. The method is designed to guarantee that any *point query* (a query that retrieves the information associated with the query point) can be answered in; at most, two disk accesses.

Grid files rely upon a **grid directory** to identify the data page containing a desired point. The grid directory is similar to the directory used in Extendible Hashing (see Chapter 11). When searching for a point, we first find the corresponding entry in the grid directory. The grid directory entry, like the directory entry in Extendible Hashing, identifies the page on which the desired point is stored, if the point is in the database. To understand the Grid file structure, we need to understand how to find the grid directory entry for a given point.

We describe the Grid file structure for two-dimensional data. The method can be generalized to any number of dimensions, but we restrict ourselves to the two-dimensional case for simplicity. The Grid file partitions space into

rectangular regions using lines parallel to the axes. Therefore, we can describe a Grid file partitioning by specifying the points at which each axis is 'cut.' If the X axis is cut into i segments and the Y axis is cut into j segments, we have a total of $i \times j$ partitions. The grid directory is an i by j array with one entry per partition. This description is maintained in an array called a **linear scale**; there is one linear scale per axis.

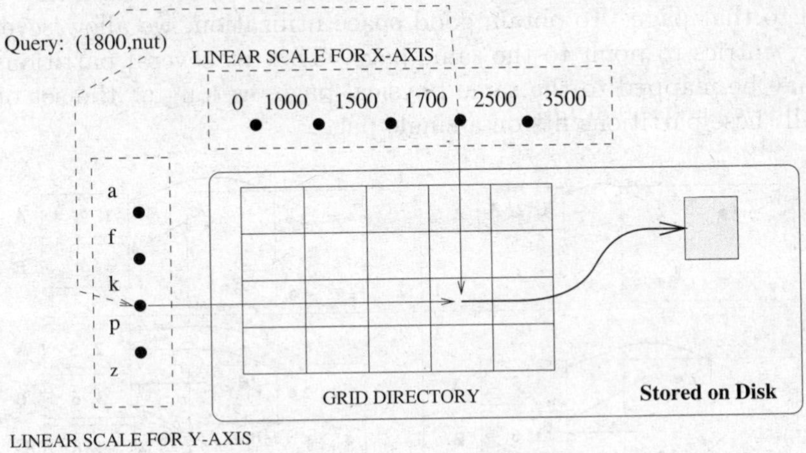

Figure 28.4 Searching for a Point in a Grid File

Figure 28.4 illustrates how we search for a point using a Grid file index. First, we use the linear scales to find the X segment to which the X value of the given point belongs and the Y segment to which the Y value belongs. This identifies the entry of the grid directory for the given point. We assume that all linear scales are stored in main memory, and therefore this step does not require any I/O. Next, we fetch the grid directory entry. Since the grid directory may be too large to fit in main memory, it is stored on disk. However, we can identify the disk page containing a given entry and fetch it in one I/O because the grid directory entries are arranged sequentially in either rowwise or columnwise order. The grid directory entry gives us the ID of the data page containing the desired point, and this page can now be retrieved in one I/O. Thus, we can retrieve a point in two I/Os—one I/O for the directory entry and one for the data page.

Range queries and nearest neighbor queries are easily answered using the Grid file. For range queries, we use the linear scales to identify the set of grid directory entries to fetch. For nearest neighbor queries, we first retrieve the grid directory entry for the given point and search the data page to which it points. If this data page is empty, we use the linear scales to retrieve the data entries for grid partitions that are adjacent to the partition that contains the

query point. We retrieve all the data points within these partitions and check them for nearness to the given point.

The Grid file relies upon the property that a grid directory entry points to a page that contains the desired data point (if the point is in the database). This means that we are forced to split the grid directory—and therefore a linear scale along the splitting dimension—if a data page is full and a new point is inserted to that page. To obtain good space utilization, we allow several grid directory entries to point to the same page. That is, several partitions of the space may be mapped to the same physical page, as long as the set of points across all these partitions fits on a single page.

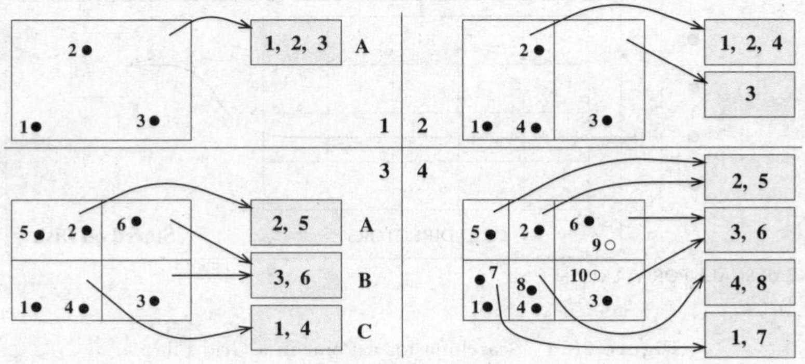

Figure 28.5 Inserting Points into a Grid File

Insertion of points into a Grid file is illustrated in Figure 28.5, which has four parts, each illustrating a snapshot of a Grid file. Each snapshot shows just the grid directory and the data pages; the linear scales are omitted for simplicity. Initially (the top-left part of the figure), there are only three points, all of which fit into a single page (A). The grid directory contains a single entry, which covers the entire data space and points to page A.

In this example, we assume that the capacity of a data page is three points. Therefore, when a new point is inserted, we need an additional data page. We are also forced to split the grid directory to accommodate an entry for the new page. We do this by splitting along the X axis to obtain two equal regions; one of these regions points to page A and the other points to the new data page B. The data points are redistributed across pages A and B to reflect the partitioning of the grid directory. The result is shown in the top-right part of Figure 28.5.

The next part (bottom left) of Figure 28.5 illustrates the Grid file after two more insertions. The insertion of point 5 forces us to split the grid directory again, because point 5 is in the region that points to page A, and page A is

already full. Since we split along the X axis in the previous split, we now split along the Y axis, and redistribute the points in page A across page A and a new data page, C. (Choosing the axis to split in a round-robin fashion is one of several possible splitting policies.) Observe that splitting the region that points to page A also causes a split of the region that points to page B, leading to two regions pointing to page B. Inserting point 6 next is straightforward because it is in a region that points to page B, and page B has space for the new point.

Next, consider the bottom right part of the figure. It shows the example file after the insertion of two additional points, 7 and 8. The insertion of point 7 fills page C, and the subsequent insertion of point 8 causes another split. This time, we split along the X axis and redistribute the points in page C across C and the new data page, D. Observe how the grid directory is partitioned the most in those parts of the data space that contain the most points—the partitioning is sensitive to data distribution, like the partitioning in Extendible Hashing, and handles skewed distributions well.

Finally, consider the potential insertion of points 9 and 10, which are shown as light circles to indicate that the result of these insertions is not reflected in the data pages. Inserting point 9 fills page B, and subsequently inserting point 10 requires a new data page. However, the grid directory does not have to be split further—points 6 and 9 can be in page B, points 3 and 10 can go to a new page E, and the second grid directory entry that points to page B can be reset to point to page E.

Deletion of points from a Grid file is complicated. When a data page falls below some occupancy threshold, such as, less than half-full, it must be merged with some other data page to maintain good space utilization. We do not go into the details beyond noting that, to simplify deletion, a *convexity requirement* is placed on the set of grid directory entries that point to a single data page: *The region defined by this set of grid directory entries must be convex.*

28.5.1 Adapting Grid Files to Handle Regions

There are two basic approaches to handling region data in a Grid file, neither of which is satisfactory. First, we can represent a region by a point in a higher-dimensional space. For example, a box in two dimensions can be represented as a four-dimensional point by storing two diagonal corner points of the box. This approach does not support nearest neighbor and spatial join queries, since distances in the original space are not reflected in the distances between points in the higher-dimensional space. Further, this approach increases the dimensionality of the stored data, which leads to various problems (see Section 28.7).

The second approach is to store a record representing the region object in each grid partition that overlaps the region object. This is unsatisfactory because it leads to a lot of additional records and makes insertion and deletion expensive.

In summary, the Grid file is not a good structure for storing region data.

28.6 R TREES: POINT AND REGION DATA

The R tree is an adaptation of the B+ tree to handle spatial data, and it is a height-balanced data structure, like the B+ tree. The search key for an R tree is a collection of intervals, with one interval per dimension. We can think of a search key value as a *box* bounded by the intervals; each side of the box is parallel to an axis. We refer to search key values in an R tree as **bounding boxes**.

A data entry consists of a pair ⟨*n-dimensional box, rid*⟩, where *rid* identifies an object and the box is the smallest box that contains the object. As a special case, the box is a point if the data object is a point instead of a region. Data entries are stored in leaf nodes. Non-leaf nodes contain index entries of the form ⟨*n-dimensional box, pointer to a child node*⟩. The box at non-leaf node N is the smallest box that contains all boxes associated with the child nodes; intuitively, it bounds the region containing all data objects stored in the subtree rooted at node N.

Figure 28.6 shows two views of an example R tree. In the first view, we see the tree structure. In the second view, we see how the data objects and bounding boxes are distributed in space.

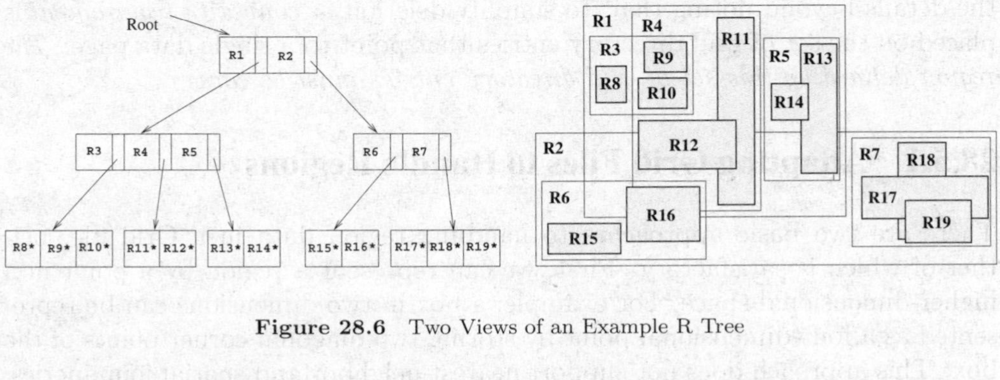

Figure 28.6 Two Views of an Example R Tree

There are 19 regions in the example tree. Regions R8 through R19 represent data objects and are shown in the tree as data entries at the leaf level. The entry R8*, for example, consists of the bounding box for region R8 and the rid of the underlying data object. Regions R1 through R7 represent bounding

boxes for internal nodes in the tree. Region R1, for example, is the bounding box for the space containing the left subtree, which includes data objects R8, R9, R10, R11, R12, R13, and R14.

The bounding boxes for two children of a given node can overlap; for example, the boxes for the children of the root node, R1 and R2, overlap. This means that more than one leaf node could accommodate a given data object while satisfying all bounding box constraints. However, every data object is stored in exactly one leaf node, even if its bounding box falls within the regions corresponding to two or more higher-level nodes. For example, consider the data object represented by R9. It is contained within both R3 and R4 and could be placed in either the first or the second leaf node (going from left to right in the tree). We have chosen to insert it into the left-most leaf node; it is not inserted anywhere else in the tree. (We discuss the criteria used to make such choices in Section 28.6.2.)

28.6.1 Queries

To search for a point, we compute its bounding box B, which is just the point, and start at the root of the tree. We test the bounding box for each child of the root to see if it overlaps the query box B, and if so, we search the subtree rooted at the child. If more than one child of the root has a bounding box that overlaps B, we must search all the corresponding subtrees. This is an important difference with respect to B+ trees: *The search for even a single point can lead us down several paths in the tree.* When we get to the leaf level, we check to see if the node contains the desired point. It is possible that we do not visit *any* leaf node—this happens when the query point is in a region not covered by any of the boxes associated with leaf nodes. If the search does not visit any leaf pages, we know that the query point is not in the indexed dataset.

Searches for region objects and range queries are handled similarly by computing a bounding box for the desired region and proceeding as in the search for an object. For a range query, when we get to the leaf level we must retrieve all region objects that belong there and test whether they overlap (or are contained in, depending on the query) the given range. The reason for this test is that, even if the bounding box for an object overlaps the query region, the object itself may not!

As an example, suppose we want to find all objects that overlap our query region, and the query region happens to be the box representing object R8. We start at the root and find that the query box overlaps R1 but not R2. Therefore, we search the left subtree but not the right subtree. We then find

that the query box overlaps R3 but not R4 or R5. So we search the left-most leaf and find object R8. As another example, suppose that the query region coincides with R9 rather than R8. Again, the query box overlaps R1 but not R2 and so we search (only) the left subtree. Now we find that the query box overlaps both R3 and R4 but not R5. We therefore search the children pointed to by the entries for R3 and R4.

As a refinement to the basic search strategy, we can approximate the query region by a convex region defined by a collection of linear constraints, rather than a bounding box, and test this convex region for overlap with the bounding boxes of internal nodes as we search down the tree. The benefit is that a convex region is a tighter approximation than a box, and therefore we can sometimes detect that there is no overlap although the intersection of bounding boxes is nonempty. The cost is that the overlap test is more expensive, but this is a pure CPU cost and negligible in comparison to the potential I/O savings.

Note that using convex regions to approximate the regions associated with nodes in the R tree would also reduce the likelihood of false overlaps—the bounding regions overlap, but the data object does not overlap the query region—but the cost of storing convex region descriptions is much higher than the cost of storing bounding box descriptions.

To search for the nearest neighbors of a given point, we proceed as in a search for the point itself. We retrieve all points in the leaves that we examine as part of this search and return the point closest to the query point. If we do not visit any leaves, then we replace the query point by a small box centered at the query point and repeat the search. If we still do not visit any leaves, we increase the size of the box and search again, continuing in this fashion until we visit a leaf node. We then consider all points retrieved from leaf nodes in this iteration of the search and return the point closest to the query point.

28.6.2 Insert and Delete Operations

To insert a data object with rid r, we compute the bounding box B for the object and insert the pair $\langle B, r\rangle$ into the tree. We start at the root node and traverse a single path from the root to a leaf (in contrast to searching, where we could traverse several such paths). At each level, we choose the child node whose bounding box needs the least enlargement (in terms of the increase in its area) to cover the box B. If several children have bounding boxes that cover B (or that require the same enlargement in order to cover B), from these children, we choose the one with the smallest bounding box.

At the leaf level, we insert the object, and if necessary we enlarge the bounding box of the leaf to cover box B. If we have to enlarge the bounding box for the leaf, this must be propagated to ancestors of the leaf—after the insertion is completed, the bounding box for every node must cover the bounding box for all descendants. If the leaf node lacks space for the new object, we must split the node and redistribute entries between the old leaf and the new node. We must then adjust the bounding box for the old leaf and insert the bounding box for the new leaf into the parent of the leaf. Again, these changes could propagate up the tree.

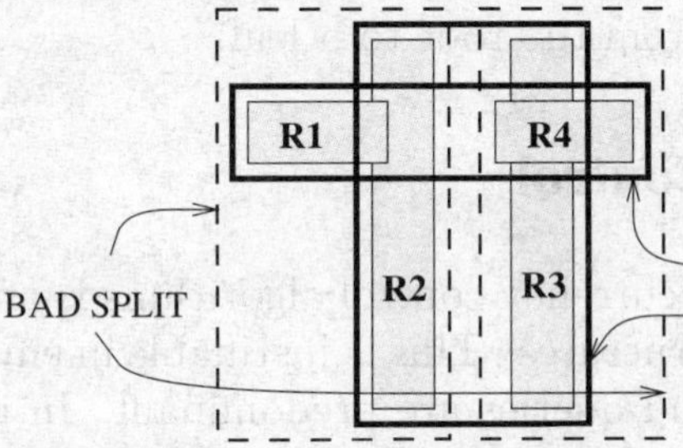

Figure 28.7 Alternative Redistributions in a Node Split

It is important to minimize the overlap between bounding boxes in the R tree because overlap causes us to search down multiple paths. The amount of overlap is greatly influenced by how entries are distributed when a node is split. Figure 28.7 illustrates two alternative redistributions during a node split. There are four regions, R1, R2, R3, and R4, to be distributed across two pages. The first split (shown in broken lines) puts R1 and R2 on one page and R3 and R4 on the other. The second split (shown in solid lines) puts R1 and R4 on one page and R2 and R3 on the other. Clearly, the total area of the bounding boxes for the new pages is much less with the second split.

Minimizing overlap using a good insertion algorithm is very important for good search performance. A variant of the R tree, called the **R* tree**, introduces the concept of **forced reinserts** to reduce overlap: When a node overflows, rather than split it immediately, we remove some number of entries (about 30 percent of the node's contents works well) and reinsert them into the tree. This may result in all entries fitting inside some existing page and eliminate the need for a split. The R* tree insertion algorithms also try to minimize *box perimeters* rather than *box areas.*

To delete a data object from an R tree, we have to proceed as in the search algorithm and potentially examine several leaves. If the object is in the tree, we remove it. In principle, we can try to shrink the bounding box for the

leaf containing the object and the bounding boxes for all ancestor nodes. In practice, deletion is often implemented by simply removing the object.

Another variant, called the **R+ tree**, avoids overlap by inserting an object into multiple leaves if necessary. Consider the insertion of an object with bounding box B at a node N. If box B overlaps the boxes associated with more than one child of N, the object is inserted into the subtree associated with each such child. For the purposes of insertion into child C with bounding box B_C, the object's bounding box is considered to be the overlap of B and B_C.[1] The advantage of the more complex insertion strategy is that searches can now proceed along a single path from the root to a leaf.

28.6.3 Concurrency Control

The cost of implementing concurrency control algorithms is often overlooked in discussions of spatial index structures. This is justifiable in environments where the data is rarely updated and queries are predominant. In general, however, this cost can greatly influence the choice of index structure.

We presented a simple concurrency control algorithm for B+ trees in Section 17.5.2: Searches proceed from root to a leaf obtaining shared locks on nodes; a node is unlocked as soon as a child is locked. Inserts proceed from root to a leaf obtaining exclusive locks; a node is unlocked after a child is locked if the child is not full. This algorithm can be adapted to R trees by modifying the insert algorithm to release a lock on a node only if the locked child has space *and* its region contains the region for the inserted entry (thus ensuring that the region modifications do not propagate to the node being unlocked).

We presented an index locking technique for B+ trees in Section 17.5.1, which locks a range of values and prevents new entries in this range from being inserted into the tree. This technique is used to avoid the phantom problem. Now let us consider how to adapt the index locking approach to R trees. The basic idea is to lock the index page that contains or would contain entries with key values in the locked range. In R trees, overlap between regions associated with the children of a node could force us to lock several (non-leaf) nodes on different paths from the root to some leaf. Additional complications arise from having to deal with changes—in particular, enlargements due to insertions—in the regions of locked nodes. Without going into further detail, it should be clear that index locking to avoid phantom insertions in R trees is both harder and less efficient than in B+ trees. Further, ideas such as forced reinsertion in R* trees and

[1]Insertion into an R+ tree involves additional details. For example, if box B is not contained in the collection of boxes associated with the children of N whose boxes B overlaps, one of the children must have its box enlarged so that B is contained in the collection of boxes associated with the children.

multiple insertions of an object in R+ trees make index locking prohibitively expensive.

28.6.4 Generalized Search Trees

The B+ tree and R tree index structures are similar in many respects: Both are height-balanced, in which searches start at the root of the tree and proceed toward the leaves; each node covers a portion of the underlying data space, and the children of a node cover a subregion of the region associated with the node. There are important differences of course—for example, the space is linearized in the B+ tree representation but not in the R tree—but the common features lead to striking similarities in the algorithms for insertion, deletion, search, and even concurrency control.

The **generalized search tree (GiST)** abstracts the essential features of tree index structures and provides 'template' algorithms for insertion, deletion, and searching. The idea is that an ORDBMS can support these template algorithms and thereby make it easy for an advanced database user to implement specific index structures, such as R trees or variants, without making changes to any system code. The effort involved in writing the extension methods is much less than that involved in implementing a new indexing method from scratch, and the performance of the GiST template algorithms is comparable to specialized code. (For concurrency control, more efficient approaches are applicable if we exploit the properties that distinguish B+ trees from R trees. However, B+ trees are implemented directly in most commercial DBMSs, and the GiST approach is intended to support more complex tree indexes.)

The template algorithms call on a set of extension methods specific to a particular index structure, and these must be supplied by the implementor. For example, the search template searches all children of a node whose region is consistent with the query. In a B+ tree the region associated with a node is a range of key values, and in an R tree, the region is spatial. The check to see whether a region is consistent with the query region is specific to the index structure and is an example of an extension method. As another example of an extension method, consider how to choose the child of an R tree node to insert a new entry into. This choice can be made based on which candidate child's region needs expanded the least; an extension method is required to calculate the required expansions for candidate children and choose the child into which to insert the entry.

28.7 ISSUES IN HIGH-DIMENSIONAL INDEXING

The spatial indexing techniques just discussed work quite well for two- and three-dimensional datasets, which are encountered in many applications of spatial data. In some applications, such as content-based image retrieval or text indexing, however, the number of dimensions can be large (tens of dimensions are not uncommon). Indexing such high-dimensional data presents unique challenges, and new techniques are required. For example, sequential scan becomes superior to R trees even when searching for a single point for datasets with more than about a dozen dimensions.

High-dimensional datasets are typically collections of points, not regions, and nearest neighbor queries are the most common kind of queries. Searching for the nearest neighbor of a query point is meaningful when the distance from the query point to its nearest neighbor is less than the distance to other points. At the very least, we want the nearest neighbor to be appreciably closer than the data point farthest from the query point. High-dimensional data poses a potential problem: For a wide range of data distributions, as dimensionality d increases, the distance (from any given query point) to the nearest neighbor grows closer and closer to the distance to the farthest data point! Searching for nearest neighbors is not meaningful in such situations.

In many applications, high-dimensional data may not suffer from these problems and may be amenable to indexing. However, it is advisable to check high-dimensional datasets to make sure that nearest neighbor queries are meaningful. Let us call the ratio of the distance (from a query point) to the nearest neighbor to the distance to the farthest point the **contrast** in the dataset. We can measure the contrast of a dataset by generating a number of sample queries, measuring distances to the nearest and farthest points for each of these sample queries and computing the ratios of these distances, and taking the average of the measured ratios. In applications that call for the nearest neighbor, we should first ensure that datasets have good contrast by empirical tests of the data.

28.8 REVIEW QUESTIONS

Answers to the review questions can be found in the listed sections.

- What are the characteristics of spatial data? What is a spatial extent? What are the differences between spatial range queries, nearest neighbor queries, and spatial join queries? **(Section 28.1)**

- Name several applications that deal with spatial data and specify their requirements on a database system. What is a feature vector and how is it used? **(Section 28.2)**
- What is a multi-dimensional index? What is a spatial index? What are the differences between a spatial index and a B+ tree? **(Section 28.3)**
- What is a space-filling curve, and how can it be used to design a spatial index? Describe a spatial index structure based on space-filling curves. **(Section 28.4)**
- What data structures are maintained for the Grid file index? How do insertion and deletion in a Grid file work? For what types of queries and data are Grid files especially suitable and why? **(Section 28.5)**
- What is an R tree? What is the structure of data entries in R trees? How can we minimize the overlap between bounding boxes when splitting nodes? How does concurrency control in a R tree work? Describe a generic template for tree-structured indexes. **(Section 28.6)**
- Why is indexing high-dimensional data very difficult? What is the impact of the dimensionality on nearest neighbor queries? What is the *contrast* of a dataset? **(Section 28.7)**

EXERCISES

Exercise 28.1 Answer the following questions briefly:

1. How is point spatial data different from nonspatial data?
2. How is point data different from region data?
3. Describe three common kinds of spatial queries.
4. Why are nearest neighbor queries important in multimedia applications?
5. How is a B+ tree index different from a spatial index? When would you use a B+ tree index over a spatial index for point data? When would you use a spatial index over a B+ tree index for point data?
6. What is the relationship between Z-ordering and Region Quad trees?
7. Compare Z-ordering and Hilbert curves as techniques to cluster spatial data.

Exercise 28.2 Consider Figure 28.3, which illustrates Z-ordering and Region Quad trees. Answer the following questions.

1. Consider the region composed of the points with these Z-values: 4, 5, 6, and 7. Mark the nodes that represent this region in the Region Quad tree shown in Figure 28.3. (Expand the tree if necessary.)
2. Repeat the preceding exercise for the region composed of the points with Z-values 1 and 3.

3. Repeat it for the region composed of the points with Z-values 1 and 2.
4. Repeat it for the region composed of the points with Z-values 0 and 1.
5. Repeat it for the region composed of the points with Z-values 3 and 12.
6. Repeat it for the region composed of the points with Z-values 12 and 15.
7. Repeat it for the region composed of the points with Z-values 1, 3, 9, and 11.
8. Repeat it for the region composed of the points with Z-values 3, 6, 9, and 12.
9. Repeat it for the region composed of the points with Z-values 9, 11, 12, and 14.
10. Repeat it for the region composed of the points with Z-values 8, 9, 10, and 11.

Exercise 28.3 This exercise also refers to Figure 28.3.

1. Consider the region represented by the 01 child of the root in the Region Quad tree shown in Figure 28.3. What are the Z-values of points in this region?
2. Repeat the preceding exercise for the region represented by the 10 child of the root and the 01 child of the 00 child of the root.
3. List the Z-values of four adjacent data points distributed across the four children of the root in the Region Quad tree.
4. Consider the alternative approaches of indexing a two-dimensional point dataset using a B+ tree index: (i) on the composite search key $\langle X, Y \rangle$, (ii) on the Z-ordering computed over the X and Y values. Assuming that X and Y values can be represented using two bits each, show an example dataset and query illustrating each of these cases:

   (a) The alternative of indexing on the composite query is faster.

   (b) The alternative of indexing on the Z-value is faster.

Exercise 28.4 Consider the Grid file instance with three points 1, 2, and 3 shown in the first part of Figure 28.5.

1. Show the Grid file after inserting each of these points, in the order they are listed: 6, 9, 10, 7, 8, 4, and 5.
2. Assume that deletions are handled by simply removing the deleted points, with no attempt to merge empty or underfull pages. Can you suggest a simple concurrency control scheme for Grid files?
3. Discuss the use of Grid files to handle region data.

Exercise 28.5 Answer each of the following questions independently with respect to the R tree shown in Figure 28.6. (That is, don't consider the insertions corresponding to other questions when answering a given question.)

1. Show the bounding box of a new object that can be inserted into R4 but not into R3.
2. Show the bounding box of a new object that is contained in both R1 and R6 but is inserted into R6.
3. Show the bounding box of a new object that is contained in both R1 and R6 and is inserted into R1. In which leaf node is this object placed?
4. Show the bounding box of a new object that could be inserted into either R4 or R5 but is placed in R5 based on the principle of least expansion of the bounding box area.

5. Given an example of an object such that searching for the object takes us to both the R1 and R2 subtrees.
6. Give an example query that takes us to nodes R3 and R5. (Explain if there is no such query.)
7. Give an example query that takes us to nodes R3 and R4 but not to R5. (Explain if there is no such query.)
8. Give an example query that takes us to nodes R3 and R5 but not to R4. (Explain if there is no such query.)

BIBLIOGRAPHIC NOTES

Several multidimensional indexing techniques have been proposed. These include Bang files [286], Grid files [565], hB trees [491], KDB trees [630], Pyramid trees [80] Quad trees[649], R trees [350], R* trees [72], R+ trees, the TV tree, and the VA file [767]. [322] discusses how to search R trees for regions defined by linear constraints. Several variations of these, and several other distinct techniques, have also been proposed; Samet's text [650] deals with many of them. A good recent survey is [294].

The use of Hilbert curves for linearizing multidimensional data is proposed in [263]. [118] is an early paper discussing spatial joins. Hellerstein, Naughton, and Pfeffer propose a generalized tree index that can be specialized to obtain many of the specific tree indexes mentioned earlier [376]. Concurrency control and recovery issues for this generalized index are discussed in [447]. Hellerstein, Koutsoupias, and Papadimitriou discuss the complexity of indexing schemes [377], in particular range queries, and Beyer et al. discuss the problems arising with high dimensionality [93]. Faloutsos provides a good overview of how to search multimedia databases by content [258]. A recent trend is towards spatiotemporal applications, such as tracking moving objects [782].

29

FURTHER READING

- ☛ What is next?
- ➽ **Key concepts:** TP monitors, real-time transactions; data integration; mobile data; main memory databases; multimedia databases; GIS; temporal databases; Bioinformatics; information visualization

> This is not the end. It is not even the beginning of the end. But it is, perhaps, the end of the beginning.
>
> —Winston Churchill

In this book, we concentrated on relational database systems and discussed several fundamental issues in detail. However, our coverage of the database area, and indeed even the relational database area, is far from exhaustive. In this chapter, we look briefly at several topics we did not cover, with the goal of giving the reader some perspective and indicating directions for further study.

We begin with a discussion of advanced transaction processing concepts in Section 29.1. We discuss integrated access to data from multiple databases in Section 29.2 and touch on mobile applications that connect to databases in Section 29.3. We consider the impact of increasingly larger main memory sizes in Section 29.4. We discuss multimedia databases in Section 29.5, geographic information systems in Section 29.6, temporal data in Section 29.7, and sequence data in Section 29.8. We conclude with a look at information visualization in Section 29.9.

The applications covered in this chapter push the limits of currently available database technology and drive the development of new techniques. As even our brief coverage indicates, much work lies ahead for the database field!

29.1 ADVANCED TRANSACTION PROCESSING

The concept of a transaction has wide applicability for a variety of distributed computing tasks, such as airline reservations, inventory management, and electronic commerce.

29.1.1 Transaction Processing Monitors

Complex applications are often built on top of several **resource managers**, such as database management systems, operating systems, user interfaces, and messaging software. A **transaction processing (TP) monitor** glues together the services of several resource managers and provides application programmers a uniform interface for developing transactions with the ACID properties. In addition to providing a uniform interface to the services of different resource managers, a TP monitor also routes transactions to the appropriate resource managers. Finally, a TP monitor ensures that an application behaves as a transaction by implementing concurrency control, logging, and recovery functions and by exploiting the transaction processing capabilities of the underlying resource managers.

TP monitors are used in environments where applications require advanced features, such as access to multiple resource managers, sophisticated request routing (also called **workflow management**); assigning priorities to transactions and doing priority-based load-balancing across servers, and so on. A DBMS provides many of the functions supported by a TP monitor in addition to processing queries and database updates efficiently. A DBMS is appropriate for environments where the wealth of transaction management capabilities provided by a TP monitor is not necessary and, in particular, where very high scalability (with respect to transaction processing activity) and interoperability are not essential.

The transaction processing capabilities of database systems are improving continually. For example, many vendors offer distributed DBMS products today in which a transaction can execute across several resource managers, each of which is a DBMS. Currently, all the DBMSs must be from the same vendor; however, as transaction-oriented services from different vendors become more standardized, distributed, heterogeneous DBMSs should become available. Eventually, perhaps, the functions of current TP monitors will also be available in many

DBMSs; for now, TP monitors provide essential infrastructure for high-end transaction processing environments.

29.1.2 New Transaction Models

Consider an application such as computer-aided design, in which users retrieve large design objects from a database and interactively analyze and modify them. Each transaction takes a long time—minutes or even hours, whereas the TPC benchmark transactions take under a millisecond—and holding locks this long affects performance. Further, if a crash occurs, undoing an active transaction completely is unsatisfactory, since considerable user effort may be lost. Ideally, we want to restore most of the actions of an active transaction and resume execution. Finally, if several users are concurrently developing a design, they may want to see changes being made by others without waiting until the end of the transaction that changes the data.

To address the needs of long-duration activities, several refinements of the transaction concept have been proposed. The basic idea is to treat each transaction as a collection of related **subtransactions**. Subtransactions can acquire locks, and the changes made by a subtransaction become visible to other transactions after the subtransaction ends (and before the main transaction of which it is a part commits). In **multilevel transactions**, locks held by a subtransaction are released when the subtransaction ends. In **nested transactions**, locks held by a subtransaction are assigned to the parent (sub)transaction when the subtransaction ends. These refinements to the transaction concept have a significant effect on concurrency control and recovery algorithms.

29.1.3 Real-Time DBMSs

Some transactions must be executed within a user-specified **deadline**. A **hard deadline** means the value of the transaction is zero after the deadline. For example, in a DBMS designed to record bets on horse races, a transaction placing a bet is worthless once the race begins. Such a transaction should not be executed; the bet should not be placed. A **soft deadline** means the value of the transaction decreases after the deadline, eventually going to zero. For example, in a DBMS designed to monitor some activity (e.g., a complex reactor), a transaction that looks up the current reading of a sensor must be executed within a short time, say, one second. The longer it takes to execute the transaction, the less useful the reading becomes. In a real-time DBMS, the goal is to maximize the value of executed transactions, and the DBMS must prioritize transactions, taking their deadlines into account.

29.2 DATA INTEGRATION

As databases proliferate, users want to access data from more than one source. For example, if several travel agents market their travel packages through the Web, customers would like to compare packages from different agents. A more traditional example is that large organizations typically have several databases, created (and maintained) by different divisions, such as Sales, Production, and Purchasing. While these databases contain much common information, determining the exact relationship between tables in different databases can be a complicated problem. For example, prices in one database might be in dollars per dozen items, while prices in another database might be in dollars per item. The development of XML DTDs (see Section 7.4.3) offers the promise that such *semantic mismatches* can be avoided if all parties conform to a single standard DTD. However, there are many legacy databases and most domains still do not have agreed-upon DTDs; the problem of semantic mismatches will be encountered frequently for the foreseeable future.

Semantic mismatches can be resolved and hidden from users by defining relational views over the tables from the two databases. Defining a collection of views to give a group of users a uniform presentation of relevant data from multiple databases is called **semantic integration**. Creating views that mask semantic mismatches in a natural manner is a difficult task and has been widely studied. In practice, the task is made harder because the schemas of existing databases are often poorly documented; hence, it is difficult to even understand the meaning of rows in existing tables, let alone define unifying views across several tables from different databases.

If the underlying databases are managed using different DBMSs, as is often the case, some kind of 'middleware' must be used to evaluate queries over the integrating views, retrieving data at query execution time by using protocols such as Open Database Connectivity (ODBC) to give each underlying database a uniform interface, as discussed in Chapter 6. Alternatively, the integrating views can be materialized and stored in a data warehouse, as discussed in Chapter 25. Queries can then be executed over the warehoused data without accessing the source DBMSs at run-time.

29.3 MOBILE DATABASES

The availability of portable computers and wireless communications has created a new breed of nomadic database users. At one level, these users are simply accessing a database through a network, which is similar to distributed DBMSs. At another level, the network as well as data and user characteristics now have several novel properties, which affect basic assumptions in many components

of a DBMS, including the query engine, transaction manager, and recovery manager:

- Users are connected through a wireless link whose bandwidth is 10 times less than Ethernet and 100 times less than ATM networks. Communication costs are therefore significantly higher in proportion to I/O and CPU costs.
- Users' locations constantly change, and mobile computers have a limited battery life. Therefore, the true communication costs reflect connection time and battery usage in addition to bytes transferred and change constantly depending on location. Data is frequently replicated to minimize the cost of accessing it from different locations.
- As a user moves around, data could be accessed from multiple database servers within a single transaction. The likelihood of losing connections is also much greater than in a traditional network. Centralized transaction management may therefore be impractical, especially if some data is resident at the mobile computers. We may in fact have to give up on ACID transactions and develop alternative notions of consistency for user programs.

29.4 MAIN MEMORY DATABASES

The price of main memory is now low enough that we can buy enough main memory to hold the entire database for many applications; with 64-bit addressing, modern CPUs also have very large address spaces. Some commercial systems now have several *gigabytes* of main memory. This shift prompts a reexamination of some basic DBMS design decisions, since disk accesses no longer dominate processing time for a memory-resident database:

- Main memory does not survive system crashes, and so we still have to implement logging and recovery to ensure transaction atomicity and durability. Log records must be written to stable storage at commit time, and this process could become a bottleneck. To minimize this problem, rather than commit each transaction as it completes, we can collect completed transactions and commit them in batches; this is called **group commit**. Recovery algorithms can also be optimized, since pages rarely have to be written out to make room for other pages.
- The implementation of in-memory operations has to be optimized carefully, since disk accesses are no longer the limiting factor for performance.
- A new criterion must be considered while optimizing queries, the amount of space required to execute a plan. It is important to minimize the space

overhead because exceeding available physical memory would lead to swapping pages to disk (through the operating system's virtual memory mechanisms), greatly slowing down execution.

- Page-oriented data structures become less important (since pages are no longer the unit of data retrieval), and clustering is not important (since the cost of accessing any region of main memory is uniform).

29.5 MULTIMEDIA DATABASES

In an object-relational DBMS, users can define ADTs with appropriate methods, which is an improvement over an RDBMS. Nonetheless, supporting just ADTs falls short of what is required to deal with very large collections of **multimedia objects**, including audio, images, free text, text marked up in HTML or variants, sequence data, and videos. Illustrative applications include NASA's EOS project, which aims to create a repository of satellite imagery; the Human Genome project, which is creating databases of genetic information such as GenBank; and NSF/DARPA's Digital Libraries project, which aims to put entire libraries into database systems and make them accessible through computer networks. Industrial applications, such as collaborative development of engineering designs, also require multimedia database management and are being addressed by several vendors.

We outline some applications and challenges in this area:

- **Content-Based Retrieval:** Users must be able to specify selection conditions based on the contents of multimedia objects. For example, users may search for images using queries such as "Find all images that are similar to this image" and "Find all images that contain at least three airplanes." As images are inserted into the database, the DBMS must analyze them and automatically *extract features* that help answer such content-based queries. This information can then be used to search for images that satisfy a given query, as discussed in Chapter 28. As another example, users would like to search for documents of interest using information retrieval techniques and keyword searches. Vendors are moving toward incorporating such techniques into DBMS products. It is still not clear how these domain-specific retrieval and search techniques can be combined effectively with traditional DBMS queries. Research into abstract data types and ORDBMS query processing has provided a starting point, but more work is needed.

- **Managing Repositories of Large Objects:** Traditionally, DBMSs have concentrated on tables that contain a large number of tuples, each of which is relatively small. Once multimedia objects such as images, sound clips, and videos are stored in a database, individual objects of very large size

have to be handled efficiently. For example, compression techniques must be carefully integrated into the DBMS environment. As another example, distributed DBMSs must develop techniques to efficiently retrieve such objects. Retrieval of multimedia objects in a distributed system has been addressed in limited contexts, such as client-server systems, but in general remains a difficult problem.

- **Video-On-Demand:** Many companies want to provide video-on-demand services that enable users to dial into a server and request a particular video. The video must then be delivered to the user's computer in real time, reliably and inexpensively. Ideally, users must be able to perform familiar VCR functions such as fast-forward and reverse. From a database perspective, the server has to contend with specialized real-time constraints; video delivery rates must be synchronized at the server and at the client, taking into account the characteristics of the communication network.

29.6 GEOGRAPHIC INFORMATION SYSTEMS

Geographic Information Systems (GIS) contain spatial information about cities, states, countries, streets, highways, lakes, rivers, and other geographical features and support applications to combine such spatial information with non-spatial data. As discussed in Chapter 28, spatial data is stored in either raster or vector formats. In addition, there is often a temporal dimension, as when we measure rainfall at several locations over time. An important issue with spatial datasets is how to integrate data from multiple sources, since each source may record data using a different coordinate system to identify locations.

Now let us consider how spatial data in a GIS is analyzed. Spatial information is most naturally thought of as being overlaid on maps. Typical queries include "What cities lie on I-94 between Madison and Chicago?" and "What is the shortest route from Madison to St. Louis?" These kinds of queries can be addressed using the techniques discussed in Chapter 28. An emerging application is in-vehicle navigation aids. With Global Positioning System (GPS) technology, a car's location can be pinpointed, and by accessing a database of local maps, a driver can receive directions from his or her current location to a desired destination; this application also involves mobile database access!

In addition, many applications involve interpolating measurements at certain locations across an entire region to obtain a *model* and combining overlapping models. For example, if we have measured rainfall at certain locations, we can use the **Triangulated Irregular Network (TIN)** approach to triangulate the region, with the locations at which we have measurements being the vertices of the triangles. Then, we use some form of interpolation to estimate

the rainfall at points within triangles. Interpolation, triangulation, map overlays, visualization of spatial data, and many other domain-specific operations are supported in GIS products such as ESRI Systems' ARC-Info. Therefore, while spatial query processing techniques as discussed in Chapter 28 are an important part of a GIS product, considerable additional functionality must be incorporated as well. How best to extend ORDBMS systems with this additional functionality is an important problem yet to be resolved. Agreeing on standards for data representation formats and coordinate systems is another major challenge facing the field.

29.7 TEMPORAL DATABASES

Consider the following query: "Find the longest interval in which the same person managed two different departments." Many issues are associated with representing temporal data and supporting such queries. We need to be able to distinguish the times during which something is true in the real world (**valid time**) from the times it is true in the database (**transaction time**). The period during which a given person managed a department can be indicated by two fields *from* and *to*, and queries must reason about time intervals. Further, temporal queries require the DBMS to be aware of the anomalies associated with calendars (such as leap years).

29.8 BIOLOGICAL DATABASES

BioInformatics is an emerging field at the intersection of Biology and Computer Science. From a database standpoint, the rapidly growing data in this area has (at least) two interesting characteristics. First, a lot of *loosely structured data* is widely exchanged, leading to interest in integration of such data. This has motivated some of the research in the area of XML repositories.

The second interesting feature is *sequence data.* DNA sequences are being generated at a rapid pace by the biological community. The field of biological information management and analysis has become very popular in recent years, called **bioinformatics**. Biological data, such as DNA sequence data, characterized by complex structure and numerous relationships among data elements, many overlapping and incomplete or erroneous data fragments (because experimentally collected data from several groups, often working on related problems, is stored in the databases), a need to frequently change the database *schema* itself as new kinds of relationships in the data are discovered, and the need to maintain several versions of data for archival and reference.

29.9 INFORMATION VISUALIZATION

As computers become faster and main memory cheaper, it becomes increasingly feasible to create visual presentations of data, rather than just text-based reports. Data visualization makes it easier for users to understand the information in large complex datasets. The challenge here is to make it easy for users to develop visual presentations of their data and interactively query such presentations. Although a number of data visualization tools are available, efficient visualization of large datasets presents many challenges.

The need for visualization is especially important in the context of decision support; when confronted with large quantities of high-dimensional data and various kinds of data summaries produced by using analysis tools such as SQL, OLAP, and data mining algorithms, the information can be overwhelming. Visualizing the data, together with the generated summaries, can be a powerful way to sift through this information and spot interesting trends or patterns. The human eye, after all, is very good at finding patterns. A good framework for data mining must combine analytic tools to process data and bring out latent anomalies or trends with a visualization environment in which a user can notice these patterns and interactively drill down to the original data for further analysis.

29.10 SUMMARY

The database area continues to grow vigorously, in terms of both technology and applications. The fundamental reason for this growth is that the amount of information stored and processed using computers is growing rapidly. Regardless of the nature of the data and the intended applications, users need database management systems and their services (concurrent access, crash recovery, easy and efficient querying, etc.) as the volume of data increases. As the range of applications is broadened, however, some shortcomings of current DBMSs become serious limitations. These problems are being actively studied in the database research community.

The coverage in this book provides an introduction, but is not intended to cover all aspects of database systems. Ample material is available for further study, as this chapter illustrates, and we hope that the reader is motivated to pursue the leads in the bibliography. Bon voyage!

BIBLIOGRAPHIC NOTES

[338] contains a comprehensive treatment of all aspects of transaction processing. See [241] for several papers that describe new transaction models for nontraditional applications such as CAD/CAM. [1, 577, 696, 711, 761] are some of the many papers on real-time databases.

Determining which entities are the same across different databases is a difficult problem; it is an example of a semantic mismatch. Resolving such mismatches has been addressed in many papers, including [424, 476, 641, 663]. [389] is an overview of theoretical work in this area. Also see the bibliographic notes for Chapter 22 for references to related work on multidatabases, and see the notes for Chapter 2 for references to work on view integration.

[304] is an early paper on main memory databases. [102, 406] describe the Dali main memory storage manager. [421] surveys visualization idioms designed for large databases, and [342] discusses visualization for data mining.

Visualization systems for databases include DataSpace [592], DEVise [489], IVEE [27], the Mineset suite from SGI, Tioga [31], and VisDB [420]. In addition, a number of general tools are available for data visualization.

Querying text repositories has been studied extensively in information retrieval; see [626] for a recent survey. This topic has generated considerable interest in the database community recently because of the widespread use of the Web, which contains many text sources. In particular, HTML documents have some structure if we interpret links as edges in a graph. Such documents are examples of semistructured data; see [2] for a good overview. Recent papers on queries over the Web include [2, 445, 527, 564].

See [576] for a survey of multimedia issues in database management. There has been much recent interest in database issues in a mobile computing environment; for example, [387, 398]. See [395] for a collection of articles on this subject. [728] contains several articles that cover all aspects of temporal databases. The use of constraints in databases has been actively investigated in recent years; [416] is a good overview. Geographic Information Systems have also been studied extensively; [586] describes the Paradise system, which is notable for its scalability.

The book [794] contains detailed discussions of temporal databases (including the TSQL2 language, which is influencing the SQL standard), spatial and multimedia databases, and uncertainty in databases.

30

THE MINIBASE SOFTWARE

Practice is the best of all instructors.

—Publius Syrus, 42 B.C.

Minibase is a small relational DBMS, together with a suite of visualization tools, that has been developed for use with this book. While the book makes no direct reference to the software and can be used independently, Minibase offers instructors an opportunity to design a variety of hands-on assignments, with or without programming. To see an online description of the software, visit this URL:

`http://www.cs.wisc.edu/~dbbook/minibase.html`

The software is available freely through ftp. By registering themselves as users at the URL for the book, instructors can receive prompt notification of any major bug reports and fixes. Sample project assignments, which elaborate on some of the briefly sketched ideas in the *project-based exercises* at the end of chapters, can be seen at

`http://www.cs.wisc.edu/~dbbook/minihwk.html`

Instructors should consider making small modifications to each assignment to discourage undesirable 'code reuse' by students; assignment handouts formatted using Latex are available by ftp. Instructors can also obtain solutions to these assignments by contacting the authors (`raghu@cs.wisc.edu`, `johannes@cs.cornell.edu`).

30.1 WHAT IS AVAILABLE

Minibase is intended to supplement the use of a commercial DBMS such as Oracle or Sybase in course projects, not to replace them. While a commercial DBMS is ideal for SQL assignments, it does not help students understand how the DBMS works. Minibase is intended to address the latter issue; the subset of SQL that it supports is intentionally kept small, and students should also be asked to use a commercial DBMS for writing SQL queries and programs.

Minibase is provided on an as-is basis with no warranties or restrictions for educational or personal use. It includes the following:

- Code for a small single-user relational DBMS, including a parser and query optimizer for a subset of SQL, and components designed to be (re)written by students as project assignments: *heap files, buffer manager, B+ trees, sorting*, and *joins*.

30.2 OVERVIEW OF MINIBASE ASSIGNMENTS

Several assignments involving the use of Minibase are described here. Each of these has been tested in a course already, but the details of how Minibase is set up might vary at your school, so you may have to modify the assignments accordingly. If you plan to use these assignments, you are advised to download and try them at your site well in advance of handing them to students. We have done our best to test and document these assignments and the Minibase software, but bugs undoubtedly persist. Please report bugs at this URL:

`http://www.cs.wisc.edu/~dbbook/minibase.comments.html`

We hope users will contribute bug fixes, additional project assignments, and extensions to Minibase. These will be made publicly available through the Minibase site, together with pointers to the authors.

In several assignments, students are asked to rewrite a component of Minibase. The book provides the necessary background for all these assignments, and the assignment handout provides additional system-level details. The online HTML documentation provides an overview of the software, in particular the component interfaces, and can be downloaded and installed at each school that uses Minibase. The projects that follow should be assigned after covering the relevant material from the indicated chapter:

- **Buffer Manager (Chapter 9):** Students are given code for the layer that manages space on disk and supports the concept of pages with page ids. They are asked to implement a buffer manager that brings requested pages into memory if they are not already there. One variation of this assignment could use different replacement policies. Students are asked to assume a single-user environment, with no concurrency control or recovery management.

- **HF Page (Chapter 9):** Students must write code that manages records on a page using a slot-directory page format to keep track of the records. Possible variants include fixed-length versus variable-length records and other ways to keep track of records on a page.

- **Heap Files (Chapter 9):** Using the HF page and buffer manager code, students are asked to implement a layer that supports the abstraction of files of unordered pages, that is, heap files.
- **B+ Trees (Chapter 10):** This is one of the more complex assignments. Students have to implement a page class that maintains records in sorted order within a page and implement the B+ tree index structure to impose a sort order across several leaf-level pages. Indexes store ⟨*key, record-pointer*⟩ pairs in leaf pages, and data records are stored separately (in heap files). Similar assignments can easily be created for Linear Hashing or Extendible Hashing index structures.
- **External sorting (Chapter 13):** Building on the buffer manager and heap file layers, students are asked to implement external merge-sort. The emphasis is on minimizing I/O rather than on the in-memory sort used to create sorted runs.
- **Sort-Merge Join (Chapter 14):** Building upon the code for external sorting, students are asked to implement the sort-merge join algorithm. This assignment can be easily modified to create assignments that involve other join algorithms.
- **Index Nested-Loop Join (Chapter 14):** This assignment is similar to the sort-merge join assignment, but relies on B+ tree (or other indexing) code, instead of sorting code.

30.3 ACKNOWLEDGMENTS

The Minibase software was inpired by Minirel, a small relational DBMS developed by David DeWitt for instructional use. Minibase was developed by a large number of dedicated students over a long time, and the design was guided by Mike Carey and R. Ramakrishnan. See the online documentation for more on Minibase's history.

REFERENCES

[1] R. Abbott and H. Garcia-Molina. Scheduling real-time transactions: A performance evaluation. *ACM Transactions on Database Systems*, 17(3), 1992.

[2] S. Abiteboul. Querying semi-structured data. In *Intl. Conf. on Database Theory*, 1997.

[3] S. Abiteboul, R. Hull, and V. Vianu. *Foundations of Databases*. Addison-Wesley, 1995.

[4] S. Abiteboul and P. Kanellakis. Object identity as a query language primitive. In *Proc. ACM SIGMOD Conf. on the Management of Data*, 1989.

[5] S. Abiteboul and V. Vianu. Regular path queries with constraints. In *Proc. ACM Symp. on Principles of Database Systems*, 1997.

[6] A. Aboulnaga, A. R. Alameldeen, and J. F. Naughton. Estimating the selectivity of XML path expressions for Internet scale applications. In *Proceedings of VLDB*, 2001.

[7] S. Acharya, P. B. Gibbons, V. Poosala, and S. Ramaswamy. The Aqua approximate query answering system. In *Proc. ACM SIGMOD Conf. on the Management of Data*, pages 574–576. ACM Press, 1999.

[8] S. Acharya, P. B. Gibbons, V. Poosala, and S. Ramaswamy. Join synopses for approximate query answering. In *Proc. ACM SIGMOD Conf. on the Management of Data*, pages 275–286. ACM Press, 1999.

[9] K. Achyutuni, E. Omiecinski, and S. Navathe. Two techniques for on-line index modification in shared nothing parallel databases. In *Proc. ACM SIGMOD Conf. on the Management of Data*, 1996.

[10] S. Adali, K. Candan, Y. Papakonstantinou, and V. Subrahmanian. Query caching and optimization in distributed mediator systems. In *Proc. ACM SIGMOD Conf. on the Management of Data*, 1996.

[11] M. E. Adiba. Derived relations: A unified mechanism for views, snapshots and distributed data. In *Proc. Intl. Conf. on Very Large Databases*, 1981.

[12] S. Agarwal, R. Agrawal, P. Deshpande, A. Gupta, J. Naughton, R. Ramakrishnan, and S. Sarawagi. On the computation of multidimensional aggregates. In *Proc. Intl. Conf. on Very Large Databases*, 1996.

[13] R. C. Agarwal, C. C. Aggarwal, and V. V. V. Prasad. A tree projection algorithm for generation of frequent item sets. *Journal of Parallel and Distributed Computing*, 61(3):350–371, 2001.

[14] D. Agrawal and A. El Abbadi. The generalized tree quorum protocol: An efficient approach for managing replicated data. *ACM Transactions on Database Systems*, 17(4), 1992.

[15] D. Agrawal, A. El Abbadi, and R. Jeffers. Using delayed commitment in locking protocols for real-time databases. In *Proc. ACM SIGMOD Conf. on the Management of Data*, 1992.

[16] R. Agrawal, M. Carey, and M. Livny. Concurrency control performance-modeling: Alternatives and implications. In *Proc. ACM SIGMOD Conf. on the Management of Data*, 1985.

[17] R. Agrawal and D. DeWitt. Integrated concurrency control and recovery mechanisms: Design and performance evaluation. *ACM Transactions on Database Systems*, 10(4):529–564, 1985.

[18] R. Agrawal and N. Gehani. ODE (Object Database and Environment): The language and the data model. In *Proc. ACM SIGMOD Conf. on the Management of Data*, 1989.

[19] R. Agrawal, J. E. Gehrke, D. Gunopulos, and P. Raghavan. Automatic subspace clustering of high dimensional data for data mining. In *Proc. ACM SIGMOD Conf. on Management of Data*, 1998.

[20] R. Agrawal, T. Imielinski, and A. Swami. Database mining: A performance perspective. *IEEE Transactions on Knowledge and Data Engineering*, 5(6):914–925, December 1993.

[21] R. Agrawal, H. Mannila, R. Srikant, H. Toivonen, and A. I. Verkamo. Fast discovery of association rules. In U. M. Fayyad, G. Piatetsky-Shapiro, P. Smyth, and R. Uthurusamy, editors, *Advances in Knowledge Discovery and Data Mining*, chapter 12, pages 307–328. AAAI/MIT Press, 1996.

[22] R. Agrawal, G. Psaila, E. Wimmers, and M. Zaot. Querying shapes of histories. In *Proc. Intl. Conf. on Very Large Databases*, 1995.

[23] R. Agrawal and J. Shafer. Parallel mining of association rules. *IEEE Transactions on Knowledge and Data Engineering*, 8(6):962–969, 1996.

[24] R. Agrawal and R. Srikant. Mining sequential patterns. In *Proc. IEEE Intl. Conf. on Data Engineering*, 1995.

[25] R. Agrawal, P. Stolorz, and G. Piatetsky-Shapiro, editors. *Proc. Intl. Conf. on Knowledge Discovery and Data Mining.* AAAI Press, 1998.

[26] R. Ahad, K. BapaRao, and D. McLeod. On estimating the cardinality of the projection of a database relation. *ACM Transactions on Database Systems*, 14(1):28–40, 1989.

[27] C. Ahlberg and E. Wistrand. IVEE: An information visualization exploration environment. In *Intl. Symp. on Information Visualization*, 1995.

[28] A. Aho, C. Beeri, and J. Ullman. The theory of joins in relational databases. *ACM Transactions on Database Systems*, 4(3):297–314, 1979.

[29] A. Aho, J. Hopcroft, and J. Ullman. *The Design and Analysis of Computer Algorithms.* Addison-Wesley, 1983.

[30] A. Aho, Y. Sagiv, and J. Ullman. Equivalences among relational expressions. *SIAM Journal of Computing*, 8(2):218–246, 1979.

[31] A. Aiken, J. Chen, M. Stonebraker, and A. Woodruff. Tioga-2: A direct manipulation database visualization environment. In *Proc. IEEE Intl. Conf. on Data Engineering*, 1996.

[32] A. Aiken, J. Widom, and J. Hellerstein. Static analysis techniques for predicting the behavior of active database rules. *ACM Transactions on Database Systems*, 20(1):3–41, 1995.

[33] A. Ailamaki, D. DeWitt, M. Hill, and M. Skounakis. Weaving relations for cache performance. In *Proc. Intl. Conf. on Very Large Data Bases*, 2001.

[34] N. Alon, P. B. Gibbons, Y. Matias, and M. Szegedy. Tracking join and self-join sizes in limited storage. In *Proc. ACM Symposium on Principles of Database Systems*, Philadeplphia, Pennsylvania, 1999.

[35] N. Alon, Y. Matias, and M. Szegedy. The space complexity of approximating the frequency moments. In *Proc. of the ACM Symp. on Theory of Computing*, pages 20–29, 1996.

[36] E. Anwar, L. Maugis, and U. Chakravarthy. A new perspective on rule support for object-oriented databases. In *Proc. ACM SIGMOD Conf. on the Management of Data*, 1993.

[37] K. Apt, H. Blair, and A. Walker. Towards a theory of declarative knowledge. In J. Minker, editor, *Foundations of Deductive Databases and Logic Programming.* Morgan Kaufmann, 1988.

[38] W. Armstrong. Dependency structures of database relationships. In *Proc. IFIP Congress*, 1974.

[39] G. Arocena and A. O. Mendelzon. WebOQL: restructuring documents, databases and webs. In *Proc. Intl. Conf. on Data Engineering*, 1988.

[40] M. Astrahan, M. Blasgen, D. Chamberlin, K. Eswaran, J. Gray, P. Griffiths, W. King, R. Lorie, P. McJones, J. Mehl, G. Putzolu, I. Traiger, B. Wade, and V. Watson. System R: a relational approach to database management. *ACM Transactions on Database Systems*, 1(2):97–137, 1976.

[41] M. Atkinson, P. Bailey, K. Chisholm, P. Cockshott, and R. Morrison. An approach to persistent programming. In *Readings in Object-Oriented Databases.* eds. S.B. Zdonik and D. Maier, Morgan Kaufmann, 1990.

[42] M. Atkinson and P. Buneman. Types and persistence in database programming languages. *ACM Computing Surveys*, 19(2):105–190, 1987.

[43] R. Attar, P. Bernstein, and N. Goodman. Site initialization, recovery, and back-up in a distributed database system. *IEEE Transactions on Software Engineering*, 10(6):645–650, 1983.

[44] P. Atzeni, L. Cabibbo, and G. Mecca. Isalog: A declarative language for complex objects with hierarchies. In *Proc. IEEE Intl. Conf. on Data Engineering*, 1993.

[45] P. Atzeni and V. De Antonellis. *Relational Database Theory.* Benjamin-Cummings, 1993.

[46] P. Atzeni, G. Mecca, and P. Merialdo. To weave the web. In *Proc. Intl. Conf. Very Large Data Bases*, 1997.

[47] R. Avnur, J. Hellerstein, B. Lo, C. Olston, B. Raman, V. Raman, T. Roth, and K. Wylie. Control: Continuous output and navigation technology with refinement online In *Proc. ACM SIGMOD Conf. on the Management of Data*, 1998.

[48] R. Avnur and J. M. Hellerstein. Eddies: Continuously adaptive query processing. In *Proc. ACM SIGMOD Conf. on the Management of Data*, pages 261–272. ACM, 2000.

[49] B. Babcock, S. Babu, M. Datar, R. Motwani, and J. Widom. Models and issues in data stream systems. In *Proc. ACM Symp. on on Principles of Database Systems*, 2002.

[50] S. Babu and J. Widom. Continous queries over data streams. *ACM SIGMOD Record*, 30(3):109–120, 2001.

[51] D. Badal and G. Popek. Cost and performance analysis of semantic integrity validation methods. In *Proc. ACM SIGMOD Conf. on the Management of Data*, 1979.

[52] A. Badia, D. Van Gucht, and M. Gyssens. Querying with generalized quantifiers. In *Applications of Logic Databases.* ed. R. Ramakrishnan, Kluwer Academic, 1995.

[53] I. Balbin, G. Port, K. Ramamohanarao, and K. Meenakshi. Efficient bottom-up computation of queries on stratified databases. *Journal of Logic Programming*, 11(3):295–344, 1991.

[54] I. Balbin and K. Ramamohanarao. A generalization of the differential approach to recursive query evaluation. *Journal of Logic Programming*, 4(3):259–262, 1987.

[55] F. Bancilhon, C. Delobel, and P. Kanellakis. *Building an Object-Oriented Database System.* Morgan Kaufmann, 1991.

[56] F. Bancilhon and S. Khoshafian. A calculus for complex objects. *Journal of Computer and System Sciences*, 38(2):326–340, 1989.

[57] F. Bancilhon, D. Maier, Y. Sagiv, and J. Ullman. Magic sets and other strange ways to implement logic programs. In *ACM Symp. on Principles of Database Systems*, 1986.

[58] F. Bancilhon and R. Ramakrishnan. An amateur's introduction to recursive query processing strategies. In *Proc. ACM SIGMOD Conf. on the Management of Data*, 1986.

[59] F. Bancilhon and N. Spyratos. Update semantics of relational views. *ACM Transactions on Database Systems*, 6(4):557–575, 1981.

[60] E. Baralis, S. Ceri, and S. Paraboschi. Modularization techniques for active rules design. *ACM Transactions on Database Systems*, 21(1):1–29, 1996.

[61] D. Barbará, W. DuMouchel, C. Faloutsos, P. J. Haas, J. M. Hellerstein, Y. E. Ioannidis, H. V. Jagadish, T. Johnson, R. T. Ng, V. Poosala, K. A. Ross, and K. C. Sevcik. The New Jersey data reduction report. *Data Engineering Bulletin*, 20(4):3–45, 1997.

[62] R. Barquin and H. Edelstein. *Planning and Designing the Data Warehouse.* Prentice-Hall, 1997.

[63] C. Batini, S. Ceri, and S. Navathe. *Database Design: An Entity Relationship Approach.* Benjamin/Cummings Publishers, 1992.

[64] C. Batini, M. Lenzerini, and S. Navathe. A comparative analysis of methodologies for database schema integration. *ACM Computing Surveys*, 18(4):323–364, 1986.

[65] D. Batory, J. Barnett, J. Garza, K. Smith, K. Tsukuda, B. Twichell, and T. Wise. GENESIS: An extensible database management system. In S. Zdonik and D. Maier, editors, *Readings in Object-Oriented Databases.* Morgan Kaufmann, 1990.

[66] B. Baugsto and J. Greipsland. Parallel sorting methods for large data volumes on a hypercube database computer. In *Proc. Intl. Workshop on Database Machines*, 1989.

[67] R. J. Bayardo. Efficiently mining long patterns from databases. In *Proc. ACM SIGMOD Intl. Conf. on Management of Data*, pages 85–93. ACM Press, 1998.

[68] R. J. Bayardo, R. Agrawal, and D. Gunopulos. Constraint-based rule mining in large, dense databases. *Data Mining and Knowledge Discovery*, 4(2/3):217–240, 2000.

[69] R. Bayer and E. McCreight. Organization and maintenance of large ordered indexes. *Acta Informatica*, 1(3):173–189, 1972.

[70] R. Bayer and M. Schkolnick. Concurrency of operations on B-trees. *Acta Informatica*, 9(1):1–21, 1977.

[71] M. Beck, D. Bitton, and W. Wilkinson. Sorting large files on a backend multiprocessor. *IEEE Transactions on Computers*, 37(7):769–778, 1988.

[72] N. Beckmann, H.-P. Kriegel, R. Schneider, and B. Seeger. The R∗ tree: An efficient and robust access method for points and rectangles. In *Proc. ACM SIGMOD Conf. on the Management of Data*, 1990.

[73] C. Beeri, R. Fagin, and J. Howard. A complete axiomatization of functional and multivalued dependencies in database relations. In *Proc. ACM SIGMOD Conf. on the Management of Data*, 1977.

[74] C. Beeri and P. Honeyman. Preserving functional dependencies. *SIAM Journal of Computing*, 10(3):647–656, 1982.

[75] C. Beeri and T. Milo. A model for active object-oriented database. In *Proc. Intl. Conf. on Very Large Databases*, 1991.

[76] C. Beeri, S. Naqvi, R. Ramakrishnan, O. Shmueli, and S. Tsur. Sets and negation in a logic database language (LDL1). In *ACM Symp. on Principles of Database Systems*, 1987.

[77] C. Beeri and R. Ramakrishnan. On the power of magic. In *ACM Symp. on Principles of Database Systems*, 1987.

[78] D. Bell and J. Grimson. *Distributed Database Systems.* Addison-Wesley, 1992.

[79] J. Bentley and J. Friedman. Data structures for range searching. *ACM Computing Surveys*, 13(3):397–409, 1979.

[80] S. Berchtold, C. Bohm, and H.-P. Kriegel. The pyramid-tree: breaking the curse of dimensionality. In *ACM SIGMOD Conf. on the Management of Data*, 1998.

[81] P. Bernstein. Synthesizing third normal form relations from functional dependencies. *ACM Transactions on Database Systems*, 1(4):277–298, 1976.

[82] P. Bernstein, B. Blaustein, and E. Clarke. Fast maintenance of semantic integrity assertions using redundant aggregate data. In *Proc. Intl. Conf. on Very Large Databases*, 1980.

[83] P. Bernstein and D. Chiu. Using semi-joins to solve relational queries. *Journal of the ACM*, 28(1):25–40, 1981.

[84] P. Bernstein and N. Goodman. Timestamp-based algorithms for concurrency control in distributed database systems. In *Proc. Intl. Conf. on Very Large Databases*, 1980.

[85] P. Bernstein and N. Goodman. Concurrency control in distributed database systems. *ACM Computing Surveys*, 13(2):185–222, 1981.

[86] P. Bernstein and N. Goodman. Power of natural semijoins. *SIAM Journal of Computing*, 10(4):751–771, 1981.

[87] P. Bernstein and N. Goodman. Multiversion concurrency control—Theory and algorithms. *ACM Transactions on Database Systems*, 8(4):465–483, 1983.

[88] P. Bernstein, N. Goodman, E. Wong, C. Reeve, and J. Rothnie. Query processing in a system for distributed databases (SDD-1). *ACM Transactions on Database Systems*, 6(4):602–625, 1981.

[89] P. Bernstein, V. Hadzilacos, and N. Goodman. *Concurrency Control and Recovery in Database Systems.* Addison-Wesley, 1987.

[90] P. Bernstein and E. Newcomer. *Principles of Transaction Processing.* Morgan Kaufmann, 1997.

[91] P. Bernstein, D. Shipman, and J. Rothnie. Concurrency control in a system for distributed databases (SDD-1). *ACM Transactions on Database Systems*, 5(1):18–51, 1980.

[92] P. Bernstein, D. Shipman, and W. Wong. Formal aspects of serializability in database concurrency control. *IEEE Transactions on Software Engineering*, 5(3):203–216, 1979.

[93] K. Beyer, J. Goldstein, R. Ramakrishnan, and U. Shaft. When is nearest neighbor meaningful? In *IEEE International Conference on Database Theory*, 1999.

[94] K. Beyer and R. Ramakrishnan. Bottom-up computation of sparse and iceberg cubes In *Proc. ACM SIGMOD Conf. on the Management of Data*, 1999.

[95] B. Bhargava, editor. *Concurrency Control and Reliability in Distributed Systems.* Van Nostrand Reinhold, 1987.

[96] A. Biliris. The performance of three database storage structures for managing large objects. In *Proc. ACM SIGMOD Conf. on the Management of Data*, 1992.

[97] J. Biskup and B. Convent. A formal view integration method. In *Proc. ACM SIGMOD Conf. on the Management of Data*, 1986.

[98] J. Biskup, U. Dayal, and P. Bernstein. Synthesizing independent database schemas. In *Proc. ACM SIGMOD Conf. on the Management of Data*, 1979.

[99] D. Bitton and D. DeWitt. Duplicate record elimination in large data files. *ACM Transactions on Database Systems*, 8(2):255–265, 1983.

[100] J. Blakeley, P.-A. Larson, and F. Tompa. Efficiently updating materialized views. In *Proc. ACM SIGMOD Conf. on the Management of Data*, 1986.

[101] M. Blasgen and K. Eswaran. On the evaluation of queries in a database system. Technical report, IBM FJ (RJ1745), San Jose, 1975.

[102] P. Bohannon, D. Leinbaugh, R. Rastogi, S. Seshadri, A. Silberschatz, and S. Sudarshan. Logical and physical versioning in main memory databases. In *Proc. Intl. Conf. on Very Large Databases*, 1997.

[103] P. Bohannon, J. Freire, P. Roy, and J. Simeon. From XML schema to relations: A cost-based approach to XML storage. In *Proceedings of ICDE*, 2002.

[104] P. Bonnet and D. E. Shasha. *Database Tuning: Principles, Experiments, and Troubleshooting Techniques.* Morgan Kaufmann Publishers, 2002.

[105] G. Booch, I. Jacobson, and J. Rumbaugh. *The Unified Modeling Language User Guide.* Addison-Wesley, 1998.

[106] A. Borodin, G. Roberts, J. Rosenthal, and P. Tsaparas. Finding authorities and hubs from link structures on Roberts G.O. the world wide web. In *World Wide Web Conference*, pages 415–429, 2001.

[107] R. Boyce and D. Chamberlin. SEQUEL: A structured English query language. In *Proc. ACM SIGMOD Conf. on the Management of Data*, 1974.

[108] P. S. Bradley and U. M. Fayyad. Refining initial points for K-Means clustering. In *Proc. Intl. Conf. on Machine Learning*, pages 91–99. Morgan Kaufmann, San Francisco, CA, 1998.

[109] P. S. Bradley, U. M. Fayyad, and C. Reina. Scaling clustering algorithms to large databases. In *Proc. Intl. Conf. on Knowledge Discovery and Data Mining*, 1998.

[110] K. Bratbergsengen. Hashing methods and relational algebra operations. In *Proc. Intl. Conf. on Very Large Databases*, 1984.

[111] L. Breiman, J. H. Friedman, R. A. Olshen, and C. J. Stone. *Classification and Regression Trees.* Wadsworth, Belmont. CA, 1984.

[112] Y. Breitbart, H. Garcia-Molina, and A. Silberschatz. Overview of multidatabase transaction management. In *Proc. Intl. Conf. on Very Large Databases*, 1992.

[113] Y. Breitbart, A. Silberschatz, and G. Thompson. Reliable transaction management in a multidatabase system. In *Proc. ACM SIGMOD Conf. on the Management of Data*, 1990.

[114] Y. Breitbart, A. Silberschatz, and G. Thompson. An approach to recovery management in a multidatabase system. In *Proc. Intl. Conf. on Very Large Databases*, 1992.

[115] S. Brin, R. Motwani, and C. Silverstein. Beyond market baskets: Generalizing association rules to correlations. In *Proc. ACM SIGMOD Conf. on the Management of Data*, 1997.

[116] S. Brin and L. Page. The anatomy of a large-scale hypertextual web search engine. In *Proceedings of 7th World Wide Web Conference*, 1998.

[117] S. Brin, R. Motwani, J. D. Ullman, and S. Tsur. Dynamic itemset counting and implication rules for market basket data. In *Proc. ACM SIGMOD Intl. Conf. on Management of Data*, pages 255–264. ACM Press, 1997.

[118] T. Brinkhoff, H.-P. Kriegel, and R. Schneider. Comparison of approximations of complex objects used for approximation-based query processing in spatial database systems. In *Proc. IEEE Intl. Conf. on Data Engineering*, 1993.

[119] K. Brown, M. Carey, and M. Livny. Goal-oriented buffer management revisited. In *Proc. ACM SIGMOD Conf. on the Management of Data*, 1996.

[120] N. Bruno, S. Chaudhuri, and L. Gravano. Top-k selection queries over relational databases: Mapping strategies and performance evaluation. *ACM Transactions on Database Systems*, To appear, 2002.

[121] F. Bry. Towards an efficient evaluation of general queries: Quantifier and disjunction processing revisited. In *Proc. ACM SIGMOD Conf. on the Management of Data*, 1989.

[122] F. Bry and R. Manthey. Checking consistency of database constraints: A logical basis. In *Proc. Intl. Conf. on Very Large Databases*, 1986.

[123] P. Buneman and E. Clemons. Efficiently monitoring relational databases. *ACM Transactions on Database Systems*, 4(3), 1979.

[124] P. Buneman, S. Davidson, G. Hillebrand, and D. Suciu. A query language and optimization techniques for unstructured data. In *Proc. ACM SIGMOD Conf. on Management of Data*, 1996.

[125] P. Buneman, S. Naqvi, V. Tannen, and L. Wong. Principles of programming with complex objects and collection types. *Theoretical Computer Science*, 149(1):3–48, 1995.

[126] D. Burdick, M. Calimlim, and J. E. Gehrke. Mafia: A maximal frequent itemset algorithm for transactional databases. In *Proc. Intl. Conf. on Data Engineering (ICDE)*. IEEE Computer Society, 2001.

[127] M. Carey. Granularity hierarchies in concurrency control. In *ACM Symp. on Principles of Database Systems*, 1983.

[128] M. Carey, D. Chamberlin, S. Narayanan, B. Vance, D. Doole, S. Rielau, R. Swagerman, and N. Mattos. O-O, what's happening to DB2? In *Proc. ACM SIGMOD Conf. on the Management of Data*, 1999.

[129] M. Carey, D. DeWitt, M. Franklin, N. Hall, M. McAuliffe, J. Naughton, D. Schuh, M. Solomon, C. Tan, O. Tsatalos, S. White, and M. Zwilling. Shoring up persistent applications. In *Proc. ACM SIGMOD Conf. on the Management of Data*, 1994.

[130] M. Carey, D. DeWitt, G. Graefe, D. Haight, J. Richardson, D. Schuh, E. Shekita, and S. Vandenberg. The EXODUS Extensible DBMS project: An overview. In S. Zdonik and D. Maier, editors, *Readings in Object-Oriented Databases*. Morgan Kaufmann, 1990.

[131] M. Carey, D. DeWitt, and J. Naughton. The 007 benchmark. In *Proc. ACM SIGMOD Conf. on the Management of Data*, 1993.

[132] M. Carey, D. DeWitt, J. Naughton, M. Asgarian, J. Gehrke, and D. Shah. The BUCKY object-relational benchmark. In *Proc. ACM SIGMOD Conf. on the Management of Data*, 1997.

[133] M. Carey, D. DeWitt, J. Richardson, and E. Shekita. Object and file management in the Exodus extensible database system. In *Proc. Intl. Conf. on Very Large Databases*, 1986.

[134] M. Carey, D. Florescu, Z. Ives, Y. Lu, J. Shanmugasundaram, E. Shekita, and S. Subramanian. XPERANTO: publishing object-relational data as XML. In *Proceedings of the Third International Workshop on the Web and Databases*, May 2000.

[135] M. Carey and D. Kossman. On saying "Enough Already!" in SQL In *Proc. ACM SIGMOD Conf. on the Management of Data*, 1997.

[136] M. Carey and D. Kossman. Reducing the braking distance of an SQL query engine In *Proc. Intl. Conf. on Very Large Databases*, 1998.

[137] M. Carey and M. Livny. Conflict detection tradeoffs for replicated data. *ACM Transactions on Database Systems*, 16(4), 1991.

[138] M. Casanova, L. Tucherman, and A. Furtado. Enforcing inclusion dependencies and referential integrity. In *Proc. Intl. Conf. on Very Large Databases*, 1988.

[139] M. Casanova and M. Vidal. Towards a sound view integration methodology. In *ACM Symp. on Principles of Database Systems*, 1983.

[140] S. Castano, M. Fugini, G. Martella, and P. Samarati. *Database Security.* Addison-Wesley, 1995.

[141] R. Cattell. *The Object Database Standard: ODMG-93 (Release 1.1).* Morgan Kaufmann, 1994.

[142] S. Ceri, P. Fraternali, S. Paraboschi, and L. Tanca. Active rule management in Chimera. In J. Widom and S. Ceri, editors, *Active Database Systems.* Morgan Kaufmann, 1996.

[143] S. Ceri, G. Gottlob, and L. Tanca. *Logic Programming and Databases.* Springer Verlag, 1990.

[144] S. Ceri and G. Pelagatti. *Distributed Database Design: Principles and Systems.* McGraw-Hill, 1984.

[145] S. Ceri and J. Widom. Deriving production rules for constraint maintenance. In *Proc. Intl. Conf. on Very Large Databases*, 1990.

[146] F. Cesarini, M. Missikoff, and G. Soda. An expert system approach for database application tuning. *Data and Knowledge Engineering*, 8:35–55, 1992.

[147] U. Chakravarthy. Architectures and monitoring techniques for active databases: An evaluation. *Data and Knowledge Engineering*, 16(1):1–26, 1995.

[148] U. Chakravarthy, J. Grant, and J. Minker. Logic-based approach to semantic query optimization. *ACM Transactions on Database Systems*, 15(2):162–207, 1990.

[149] D. Chamberlin. *Using the New DB2.* Morgan Kaufmann, 1996.

[150] D. Chamberlin, M. Astrahan, M. Blasgen, J. Gray, W. King, B. Lindsay, R. Lorie, J. Mehl, T. Price, P. Selinger, M. Schkolnick, D. Slutz, I. Traiger, B. Wade, and R. Yost. A history and evaluation of System R. *Communications of the ACM*, 24(10):632–646, 1981.

[151] D. Chamberlin, M. Astrahan, K. Eswaran, P. Griffiths, R. Lorie, J. Mehl, P. Reisner, and B. Wade. Sequel 2: a unified approach to data definition, manipulation, and control. *IBM Journal of Research and Development*, 20(6):560–575, 1976.

[152] D. Chamberlin, D. Florescu, and J. Robie. Quilt: an XML query language for heterogeneous data sources. In *Proceedings of WebDB,* Dallas, TX, May 2000.

[153] D. Chamberlin, D. Florescu, J. Robie, J. Simeon, and M. Stefanescu. XQuery: A query language for XML. World Wide Web Consortium, `http://www.w3.org/TR/xquery`, Feb 2000.

[154] A. Chandra and D. Harel. Structure and complexity of relational queries. *J. Computer and System Sciences*, 25:99–128, 1982.

[155] A. Chandra and P. Merlin. Optimal implementation of conjunctive queries in relational databases. In *Proc. ACM SIGACT Symp. on Theory of Computing*, 1977.

[156] M. Chandy, L. Haas, and J. Misra. Distributed deadlock detection. *ACM Transactions on Computer Systems*, 1(3):144–156, 1983.

[157] C. Chang and D. Leu. Multi-key sorting as a file organization scheme when queries are not equally likely. In *Proc. Intl. Symp. on Database Systems for Advanced Applications*, 1989.

[158] D. Chang and D. Harkey. *Client/ server data access with Java and XML.* John Wiley and Sons, 1998.

[159] M. Charikar, S. Chaudhuri, R. Motwani, and V. R. Narasayya. Towards estimation error guarantees for distinct values. In *Proc. ACM Symposium on Principles of Database Systems*, pages 268–279. ACM, 2000.

[160] D. Chatziantoniou and K. Ross. Groupwise processing of relational queries. In *Proc. Intl. Conf. on Very Large Databases*, 1997.

[161] S. Chaudhuri and U. Dayal. An overview of data warehousing and OLAP technology. *SIGMOD Record*, 26(1):65–74, 1997.

[162] S. Chaudhuri and D. Madigan, editors. *Proc. ACM SIGKDD Intl. Conference on Knowledge Discovery and Data Mining.* ACM Press, 1999.

[163] S. Chaudhuri and V. Narasayya. An efficient cost-driven index selection tool for Microsoft SQL Server. In *Proc. Intl. Conf. on Very Large Databases*, 1997.

[164] S. Chaudhuri and V. R. Narasayya. Autoadmin 'what-if' index analysis utility. In *Proc. ACM SIGMOD Intl. Conf. on Management of Data*, 1998.

[165] S. Chaudhuri and K. Shim. Optimization of queries with user-defined predicates. In *Proc. Intl. Conf. on Very Large Databases*, 1996.

[166] S. Chaudhuri and K. Shim. Optimization queries with aggregate views. In *Intl. Conf. on Extending Database Technology*, 1996.

[167] S. Chaudhuri, G. Das, and V. R. Narasayya. A robust, optimization-based approach for approximate answering of aggregate queries. In *Proc. ACM SIGMOD Conf. on the Management of Data*, 2001.

[168] J. Cheiney, P. Faudemay, R. Michel, and J. Thevenin. A reliable parallel backend using multiattribute clustering and select-join operator. In *Proc. Intl. Conf. on Very Large Databases*, 1986.

[169] C. Chen and N. Roussopoulos. Adaptive database buffer management using query feedback. In *Proc. Intl. Conf. on Very Large Databases*, 1993.

[170] C. Chen and N. Roussopoulos. Adaptive selectivity estimation using query feedback. In *Proc. ACM SIGMOD Conf. on the Management of Data*, 1994.

[171] P. M. Chen, E. K. Lee, G. A. Gibson, R. H. Katz, and D. A. Patterson. RAID: High-performance, reliable secondary storage. *ACM Computing Surveys*, 26(2):145–185, June 1994.

[172] P. P. Chen. The entity-relationship model—toward a unified view of data. *ACM Transactions on Database Systems*, 1(1):9–36, 1976.

[173] Y. Chen, G. Dong, J. Han, B. W. Wah, and J. Wang. Multi-dimensional regression analysis of time-series data streams. In *Proc. Intl. Conf. on Very Large Data Bases*, 2002.

[174] D. W. Cheung, J. Han, V. T. Ng, and C. Y. Wong. Maintenance of discovered association rules in large databases: An incremental updating technique. In *Proc. Int. Conf. Data Engineering*, 1996.

[175] D. W. Cheung, V. T. Ng, and B. W. Tam Maintenance of discovered knowledge: A case in multi-level association rules. In *Proc. Intl. Conf. on Knowledge Discovery and Data Mining.* AAAI Press, 1996.

[176] D. Childs. Feasibility of a set theoretical data structure—A general structure based on a reconstructed definition of relation. *Proc. Tri-annual IFIP Conference*, 1968.

[177] D. Chimenti, R. Gamboa, R. Krishnamurthy, S. Naqvi, S. Tsur, and C. Zaniolo. The ldl system prototype. *IEEE Transactions on Knowledge and Data Engineering*, 2(1):76–90, 1990.

[178] F. Chin and G. Ozsoyoglu. Statistical database design. *ACM Transactions on Database Systems*, 6(1):113–139, 1981.

[179] T.-C. Chiueh and L. Huang. Efficient real-time index updates in text retrieval systems.

[180] J. Chomicki. Real-time integrity constraints. In *ACM Symp. on Principles of Database Systems*, 1992.

[181] H.-T. Chou and D. DeWitt. An evaluation of buffer management strategies for relational database systems. In *Proc. Intl. Conf. on Very Large Databases*, 1985.

[182] P. Chrysanthis and K. Ramamritham. Acta: A framework for specifying and reasoning about transaction structure and behavior. In *Proc. ACM SIGMOD Conf. on the Management of Data*, 1990.

[183] F. Chu, J. Halpern, and P. Seshadri. Least expected cost query optimization: An exercise in utility *ACM Symp. on Principles of Database Systems*, 1999.

[184] F. Civelek, A. Dogac, and S. Spaccapietra. An expert system approach to view definition and integration. In *Proc. Entity-Relationship Conference*, 1988.

[185] R. Cochrane, H. Pirahesh, and N. Mattos. Integrating triggers and declarative constraints in SQL database systems. In *Proc. Intl. Conf. on Very Large Databases*, 1996.

[186] CODASYL. *Report of the CODASYL Data Base Task Group.* ACM, 1971.

[187] E. Codd. A relational model of data for large shared data banks. *Communications of the ACM*, 13(6):377–387, 1970.

[188] E. Codd. Further normalization of the data base relational model. In R. Rustin, editor, *Data Base Systems.* Prentice Hall, 1972.

[189] E. Codd. Relational completeness of data base sub-languages. In R. Rustin, editor, *Data Base Systems.* Prentice Hall, 1972.

[190] E. Codd. Extending the database relational model to capture more meaning. *ACM Transactions on Database Systems*, 4(4):397–434, 1979.

[191] E. Codd. Twelve rules for on-line analytic processing. *Computerworld*, April 13 1995.

[192] L. Colby, T. Griffin, L. Libkin, I. Mumick, and H. Trickey. Algorithms for deferred view maintenance. In *Proc. ACM SIGMOD Conf. on the Management of Data*, 1996.

[193] L. Colby, A. Kawaguchi, D. Lieuwen, I. Mumick, and K. Ross. Supporting multiple view maintenance policies: Concepts, algorithms, and performance analysis. In *Proc. ACM SIGMOD Conf. on the Management of Data*, 1997.

[194] D. Comer. The ubiquitous B-tree. *ACM C. Surveys*, 11(2):121–137, 1979.

[195] D. Connolly, editor. *XML Principles, Tools and Techniques.* O'Reilly & Associates, Sebastopol, USA, 1997.

[196] B. Cooper, N. Sample, M. J. Franklin, G. R. Hjaltason, and M. Shadmon. A fast index for semistructured data. In *Proceedings of VLDB*, 2001.

[197] D. Copeland and D. Maier. Making SMALLTALK a database system. In *Proc. ACM SIGMOD Conf. on the Management of Data*, 1984.

[198] G. Cornell and K. Abdali. *CGI Programming With Java.* PrenticeHall, 1998.

[199] C. Cortes, K. Fisher, D. Pregibon, and A. Rogers. Hancock: a language for extracting signatures from data streams. In *Proc. ACM SIGKDD Intl. Conference on Knowledge Discovery and Data Mining*, pages 9–17. AAAI Press, 2000.

[200] J. Daemen and V. Rijmen. *The Design of Rijndael: AES –The Advanced Encryption Standard (Information Security and Cryptography).* Springer Verlag, 2002.

[201] M. Datar, A. Gionis, P. Indyk, and R. Motwani. Maintaining stream statistics over sliding windows. In *Proc. of the Annual ACM-SIAM Symp. on Discrete Algorithms*, 2002.

[202] C. Date. A critique of the SQL database language. *ACM SIGMOD Record*, 14(3):8–54, 1984.

[203] C. Date. *Relational Database: Selected Writings.* Addison-Wesley, 1986.

[204] C. Date. *An Introduction to Database Systems.* Addison-Wesley, 7 edition, 1999.

[205] C. Date and R. Fagin. Simple conditions for guaranteeing higher normal forms in relational databases. *ACM Transactions on Database Systems*, 17(3), 1992.

[206] C. Date and D. McGoveran. *A Guide to Sybase and SQL Server.* Addison-Wesley, 1993.

[207] U. Dayal and P. Bernstein. On the updatability of relational views. In *Proc. Intl. Conf. on Very Large Databases*, 1978.

[208] U. Dayal and P. Bernstein. On the correct translation of update operations on relational views. *ACM Transactions on Database Systems*, 7(3), 1982.

[209] P. DeBra and J. Paredaens. Horizontal decompositions for handling exceptions to FDs. In H. Gallaire, J. Minker, and J.-M. Nicolas, editors, *Advances in Database Theory*,. Plenum Press, 1981.

[210] J. Deep and P. Holfelder. *Developing CGI applications with Perl.* Wiley, 1996.

[211] C. Delobel. Normalization and hierarchial dependencies in the relational data model. *ACM Transactions on Database Systems*, 3(3):201–222, 1978.

[212] D. Denning. Secure statistical databases with random sample queries. *ACM Transactions on Database Systems*, 5(3):291–315, 1980.

[213] D. E. Denning. *Cryptography and Data Security.* Addison-Wesley, 1982.

[214] M. Derr, S. Morishita, and G. Phipps. The glue-nail deductive database system: Design, implementation, and evaluation. *VLDB Journal*, 3(2):123–160, 1994.

[215] A. Deshpande. An implementation for nested relational databases. Technical report, PhD thesis, Indiana University, 1989.

[216] P. Deshpande, K. Ramasamy, A. Shukla, and J. F. Naughton. Caching multidimensional queries using chunks. In *Proc. ACM SIGMOD Intl. Conf. on Management of Data*, 1998.

[217] A. Deutsch, M. Fernandez, D. Florescu, A. Levy, and D. Suciu. XML-QL: A query language for XML. World Wide Web Consortium, `http://www.w3.org/TR/NOTE-xml-ql`, Aug 1998.

[218] O. e. a. Deux. The story of O2. *IEEE Transactions on Knowledge and Data Engineering*, 2(1), 1990.

[219] D. DeWitt, H.-T. Chou, R. Katz, and A. Klug. Design and implementation of the Wisconsin Storage System. *Software Practice and Experience*, 15(10):943–962, 1985.

[220] D. DeWitt, R. Gerber, G. Graefe, M. Heytens, K. Kumar, and M. Muralikrishna. Gamma—A high performance dataflow database machine. In *Proc. Intl. Conf. on Very Large Databases*, 1986.

[221] D. DeWitt and J. Gray. Parallel database systems: The future of high-performance database systems. *Communications of the ACM*, 35(6):85–98, 1992.

[222] D. DeWitt, R. Katz, F. Olken, L. Shapiro, M. Stonebraker, and D. Wood. Implementation techniques for main memory databases. In *Proc. ACM SIGMOD Conf. on the Management of Data*, 1984.

[223] D. DeWitt, J. Naughton, and D. Schneider. Parallel sorting on a shared-nothing architecture using probabilistic splitting. In *Proc. Conf. on Parallel and Distributed Information Systems*, 1991.

[224] D. DeWitt, J. Naughton, D. Schneider, and S. Seshadri. Practical skew handling in parallel joins. In *Proc. Intl. Conf. on Very Large Databases*, 1992.

[225] O. Diaz, N. Paton, and P. Gray. Rule management in object-oriented databases: A uniform approach. In *Proc. Intl. Conf. on Very Large Databases*, 1991.

[226] S. Dietrich. Extension tables: Memo relations in logic programming. In *Proc. Intl. Symp. on Logic Programming*, 1987.

[227] W. Diffie and M. E. Hellman. New directions in cryptography. *IEEE Transactions on Information Theory*, 22(6):644–654, 1976.

[228] P. Domingos and G. Hulten. Mining high-speed data streams. In *Proc. ACM SIGKDD Intl. Conference on Knowledge Discovery and Data Mining.* AAAI Press, 2000.

[229] D. Donjerkovic and R. Ramakrishnan. Probabilistic optimization of top N queries In *Proc. Intl. Conf. on Very Large Databases*, 1999.

[230] W. Du and A. Elmagarmid. Quasi-serializability: A correctness criterion for global concurrency control in interbase. In *Proc. Intl. Conf. on Very Large Databases*, 1989.

[231] W. Du, R. Krishnamurthy, and M.-C. Shan. Query optimization in a heterogeneous DBMS. In *Proc. Intl. Conf. on Very Large Databases*, 1992.

[232] R. C. Dubes and A. Jain. *Clustering Methodologies in Exploratory Data Analysis, Advances in Computers.* Academic Press, New York, 1980.

[233] N. Duppel. Parallel SQL on TANDEM 's NonStop SQL. *IEEE COMPCON*, 1989.

[234] H. Edelstein. The challenge of replication, Parts 1 and 2. *DBMS: Database and Client-Server Solutions*, 1995.

[235] W. Effelsberg and T. Haerder. Principles of database buffer management. *ACM Transactions on Database Systems*, 9(4):560–595, 1984.

[236] M. H. Eich. A classification and comparison of main memory database recovery techniques. In *Proc. IEEE Intl. Conf. on Data Engineering*, 1987.

[237] A. Eisenberg and J. Melton. SQL:1999 , formerly known as SQL 3 *ACM SIGMOD Record*, 28(1):131–138, 1999.

[238] A. El Abbadi. Adaptive protocols for managing replicated distributed databases. In *IEEE Symp. on Parallel and Distributed Processing*, 1991.

[239] A. El Abbadi, D. Skeen, and F. Cristian. An efficient, fault-tolerant protocol for replicated data management. In *ACM Symp. on Principles of Database Systems*, 1985.

[240] C. Ellis. Concurrency in Linear Hashing. *ACM Transactions on Database Systems*, 12(2):195–217, 1987.

[241] A. Elmagarmid. *Database Transaction Models for Advanced Applications.* Morgan Kaufmann, 1992.

[242] A. Elmagarmid, J. Jing, W. Kim, O. Bukhres, and A. Zhang. Global commitability in multidatabase systems. *IEEE Transactions on Knowledge and Data Engineering*, 8(5):816–824, 1996.

[243] A. Elmagarmid, A. Sheth, and M. Liu. Deadlock detection algorithms in distributed database systems. In *Proc. IEEE Intl. Conf. on Data Engineering*, 1986.

[244] R. Elmasri and S. Navathe. Object integration in database design. In *Proc. IEEE Intl. Conf. on Data Engineering*, 1984.

[245] R. Elmasri and S. Navathe. *Fundamentals of Database Systems.* Benjamin-Cummings, 3 edition, 2000.

[246] R. Epstein. Techniques for processing of aggregates in relational database systems. Technical report, UC-Berkeley, Electronics Research Laboratory, M798, 1979.

[247] R. Epstein, M. Stonebraker, and E. Wong. Distributed query processing in a relational data base system. In *Proc. ACM SIGMOD Conf. on the Management of Data*, 1978.

[248] M. Ester, H.-P. Kriegel, J. Sander, M. Wimmer, and X. Xu. Incremental clustering for mining in a data warehousing environment. In *Proc. Intl. Conf. On Very Large Data Bases*, 1998.

[249] M. Ester, H.-P. Kriegel, J. Sander, and X. Xu. A density-based algorithm for discovering clusters in large spatial databases with noise. In *Proc. Intl. Conf. on Knowledge Discovery in Databases and Data Mining*, 1995.

[250] M. Ester, H.-P. Kriegel, and X. Xu. A database interface for clustering in large spatial databases. In *Proc. Intl. Conf. on Knowledge Discovery in Databases and Data Mining*, 1995.

[251] K. Eswaran and D. Chamberlin. Functional specification of a subsystem for data base integrity. In *Proc. Intl. Conf. on Very Large Databases*, 1975.

[252] K. Eswaran, J. Gray, R. Lorie, and I. Traiger. The notions of consistency and predicate locks in a data base system. *Communications of the ACM*, 19(11):624–633, 1976.

[253] R. Fagin. Multivalued dependencies and a new normal form for relational databases. *ACM Transactions on Database Systems*, 2(3):262–278, 1977.

[254] R. Fagin. Normal forms and relational database operators. In *Proc. ACM SIGMOD Conf. on the Management of Data*, 1979.

[255] R. Fagin. A normal form for relational databases that is based on domains and keys. *ACM Transactions on Database Systems*, 6(3):387–415, 1981.

[256] R. Fagin, J. Nievergelt, N. Pippenger, and H. Strong. Extendible Hashing—a fast access method for dynamic files. *ACM Transactions on Database Systems*, 4(3), 1979.

[257] C. Faloutsos. Access methods for text. *ACM Computing Surveys*, 17(1):49–74, 1985.

[258] C. Faloutsos. *Searching Multimedia Databases by Content* Kluwer Academic, 1996.

[259] C. Faloutsos and S. Christodoulakis. Signature files: An access method for documents and its analytical performance evaluation. *ACM Transactions on Office Information Systems*, 2(4):267–288, 1984.

[260] C. Faloutsos and H. Jagadish. On B-Tree indices for skewed distributions. In *Proc. Intl. Conf. on Very Large Databases*, 1992.

[261] C. Faloutsos, R. Ng, and T. Sellis. Predictive load control for flexible buffer allocation. In *Proc. Intl. Conf. on Very Large Databases*, 1991.

[262] C. Faloutsos, M. Ranganathan, and Y. Manolopoulos. Fast subsequence matching in time-series databases. In *Proc. ACM SIGMOD Conf. on the Management of Data*, 1994.

[263] C. Faloutsos and S. Roseman. Fractals for secondary key retrieval. In *ACM Symp. on Principles of Database Systems*, 1989.

[264] M. Fang, N. Shivakumar, H. Garcia-Molina, R. Motwani, and J. D. Ullman. Computing iceberg queries efficiently. In *Proc. Intl. Conf. On Very Large Data Bases*, 1998.

[265] U. Fayyad, G. Piatetsky-Shapiro, and P. Smyth. The KDD process for extracting useful knowledge from volumes of data. *Communications of the ACM*, 39(11):27–34, 1996.

[266] U. Fayyad, G. Piatetsky-Shapiro, P. Smyth, and R. Uthurusamy, editors. *Advances in Knowledge Discovery and Data Mining.* MIT Press, 1996.

[267] U. Fayyad and E. Simoudis. Data mining and knowledge discovery: Tutorial notes. In *Intl. Joint Conf. on Artificial Intelligence*, 1997.

[268] U. M. Fayyad and R. Uthurusamy, editors. *Proc. Intl. Conf. on Knowledge Discovery and Data Mining.* AAAI Press, 1995.

[269] M. Fernandez, D. Florescu, J. Kang, A. Y. Levy, and D. Suciu. STRUDEL: A Web site management system. In *Proc. ACM SIGMOD Conf. on Management of Data*, 1997.

[270] M. Fernandez, D. Florescu, A. Y. Levy, and D. Suciu. A query language for a Web -site management system. *SIGMOD Record (ACM Special Interest Group on Management of Data)*, 26(3):4–11, 1997.

[271] M. Fernandez, D. Suciu, and W. Tan. SilkRoute: trading between relations and XML. In *Proceedings of the WWW9*, 2000.

[272] S. Finkelstein, M. Schkolnick, and P. Tiberio. Physical database design for relational databases. *IBM Research Review RJ5034*, 1986.

[273] D. Fishman, D. Beech, H. Cate, E. Chow, T. Connors, J. Davis, N. Derrett, C. Hoch, W. Kent, P. Lyngbaek, B. Mahbod, M.-A. Neimat, T. Ryan, and M.-C. Shan. Iris: an object-oriented database management system *ACM Transactions on Office Information Systems*, 5(1):48–69, 1987.

[274] C. Fleming and B. von Halle. *Handbook of Relational Database Design.* Addison-Wesley, 1989.

[275] D. Florescu, A. Y. Levy, and A. O. Mendelzon. Database techniques for the World-Wide Web: A survey. *SIGMOD Record (ACM Special Interest Group on Management of Data)*, 27(3):59–74, 1998.

[276] W. Ford and M. S. Baum. *Secure Electronic Commerce: Building the Infrastructure for Digital Signatures and Encryption (2nd Edition).* Prentice Hall, 2000.

[277] F. Fotouhi and S. Pramanik. Optimal secondary storage access sequence for performing relational join. *IEEE Transactions on Knowledge and Data Engineering*, 1(3):318–328, 1989.

[278] M. Fowler and K. Scott. *UML Distilled: Applying the Standard Object Modeling Language.* Addison-Wesley, 1999.

[279] W. B. Frakes and R. Baeza-Yates, editors. *Information Retrieval: Data Structures and Algorithms.* PrenticeHall, 1992.

[280] P. Franaszek, J. Robinson, and A. Thomasian. Concurrency control for high contention environments. *ACM Transactions on Database Systems*, 17(2), 1992.

[281] P. Franazsek, J. Robinson, and A. Thomasian. Access invariance and its use in high contention environments. In *Proc. IEEE International Conference on Data Engineering*, 1990.

[282] M. Franklin. Concurrency control and recovery. In *Handbook of Computer Science, A.B. Tucker (ed.), CRC Press*, 1996.

[283] M. Franklin, M. Carey, and M. Livny. Local disk caching for client-server database systems. In *Proc. Intl. Conf. on Very Large Databases*, 1993.

[284] M. Franklin, B. Jonsson, and D. Kossman. Performance tradeoffs for client-server query processing. In *Proc. ACM SIGMOD Conf. on the Management of Data*, 1996.

[285] P. Fraternali and L. Tanca. A structured approach for the definition of the semantics of active databases. *ACM Transactions on Database Systems*, 20(4):414–471, 1995.

[286] M. W. Freeston. The BANG file: A new kind of Grid File. In *Proc. ACM SIGMOD Conf. on the Management of Data*, 1987.

[287] J. Freytag. A rule-based view of query optimization. In *Proc. ACM SIGMOD Conf. on the Management of Data*, 1987.

[288] O. Friesen, A. Lefebvre, and L. Vieille. VALIDITY: Applications of a DOOD system. In *Intl. Conf. on Extending Database Technology*, 1996.

[289] J. Fry and E. Sibley. Evolution of data-base management systems. *ACM Computing Surveys*, 8(1):7–42, 1976.

[290] N. Fuhr. A decision-theoretic approach to database selection in networked ir. *ACM Transactions on Database Systems*, 17(3), 1999.

[291] T. Fukuda, Y. Morimoto, S. Morishita, and T. Tokuyama. Mining optimized association rules for numeric attributes. In *ACM Symp. on Principles of Database Systems*, 1996.

[292] A. Furtado and M. Casanova. Updating relational views. In *Query Processing in Database Systems*. eds. W. Kim, D.S. Reiner and D.S. Batory, Springer-Verlag, 1985.

[293] S. Fushimi, M. Kitsuregawa, and H. Tanaka. An overview of the systems software of a parallel relational database machine: Grace. In *Proc. Intl. Conf. on Very Large Databases*, 1986.

[294] V. Gaede and O. Guenther. Multidimensional access methods. *Computing Surveys*, 30(2):170–231, 1998.

[295] H. Gallaire, J. Minker, and J.-M. Nicolas (eds.). *Advances in Database Theory, Vols. 1 and 2.* Plenum Press, 1984.

[296] H. Gallaire and J. Minker (eds.). *Logic and Data Bases.* Plenum Press, 1978.

[297] S. Ganguly, W. Hasan, and R. Krishnamurthy. Query optimization for parallel execution. In *Proc. ACM SIGMOD Conf. on the Management of Data*, 1992.

[298] R. Ganski and H. Wong. Optimization of nested SQL queries revisited. In *Proc. ACM SIGMOD Conf. on the Management of Data*, 1987.

[299] V. Ganti, J. Gehrke, and R. Ramakrishnan. Demon: mining and monitoring evolving data. *IEEE Transactions on Knowledge and Data Engineering*, 13(1), 2001.

[300] V. Ganti, J. Gehrke, R. Ramakrishnan, and W.-Y. Loh. Focus: a framework for measuring changes in data characteristics. In *Proc. ACM Symposium on Principles of Database Systems*, 1999.

[301] V. Ganti, J. E. Gehrke, and R. Ramakrishnan. Cactus–clustering categorical data using summaries. In *Proc. ACM Intl. Conf. on Knowledge Discovery in Databases*, 1999.

[302] V. Ganti, R. Ramakrishnan, J. E. Gehrke, A. Powell, and J. French. Clustering large datasets in arbitrary metric spaces. In *Proc. IEEE Intl. Conf. Data Engineering*, 1999.

[303] H. Garcia-Molina and D. Barbara. How to assign votes in a distributed system. *Journal of the ACM*, 32(4), 1985.

[304] H. Garcia-Molina, R. Lipton, and J. Valdes. A massive memory system machine. *IEEE Transactions on Computers*, C33(4):391–399, 1984.

[305] H. Garcia-Molina, J. Ullman, and J. Widom. *Database Systems: The Complete Book* Prentice Hall, 2001.

[306] H. Garcia-Molina and G. Wiederhold. Read-only transactions in a distributed database. *ACM Transactions on Database Systems*, 7(2):209–234, 1982.

[307] E. Garfield. Citation analysis as a tool in journal evaluation. *Science*, 178(4060):471–479, 1972.

[308] A. Garg and C. Gotlieb. Order preserving key transformations. *ACM Transactions on Database Systems*, 11(2):213–234, 1986.

[309] J. E. Gehrke, V. Ganti, R. Ramakrishnan, and W.-Y. Loh. Boat: Optimistic decision tree construction. In *Proc. ACM SIGMOD Conf. on Managment of Data*, 1999.

[310] J. E. Gehrke, F. Korn, and D. Srivastava. On computing correlated aggregates over continual data streams. In *Proc. ACM SIGMOD Conf. on the Management of Data*, 2001.

[311] J. E. Gehrke, R. Ramakrishnan, and V. Ganti. Rainforest: A framework for fast decision tree construction of large datasets. In *Proc. Intl. Conf. on Very Large Databases*, 1998.

[312] S. P. Ghosh. *Data Base Organization for Data Management (2nd ed.)*. Academic Press, 1986.

[313] P. B. Gibbons, Y. Matias, and V. Poosala. Fast incremental maintenance of approximate histograms. In *Proc. of the Conf. on Very Large Databases*, 1997.

[314] P. B. Gibbons and Y. Matias. New sampling-based summary statistics for improving approximate query answers. In *Proc. ACM SIGMOD Conf. on the Management of Data*, pages 331–342. ACM Press, 1998.

[315] D. Gibson, J. M. Kleinberg, and P. Raghavan. Clustering categorical data: An approach based on dynamical systems. In *Proc. Intl. Conf. Very Large Data Bases*, 1998.

[316] D. Gibson, J. M. Kleinberg, and P. Raghavan. Inferring web communities from link topology. In *Proc. ACM Conf. on Hypertext*, 1998.

[317] G. A. Gibson. *Redundant Disk Arrays: Reliable, Parallel Secondary Storage*. An ACM Distinguished Dissertation 1991. MIT Press, 1992.

[318] D. Gifford. Weighted voting for replicated data. In *ACM Symp. on Operating Systems Principles*, 1979.

[319] A. C. Gilbert, Y. Kotidis, S. Muthukrishnan, and M. J. Strauss. Surfing wavelets on streams: One-pass summaries for approximate aggregate queries. In *Proc. of the Conf. on Very Large Databases*, 2001.

[320] C. F. Goldfarb and P. Prescod. *The XML Handbook*. PrenticeHall, 1998.

[321] R. Goldman and J. Widom. DataGuides: enabling query formulation and optimization in semistructured databases. In *Proc. Intl. Conf. on Very Large Data Bases*, pages 436–445, 1997.

[322] J. Goldstein, R. Ramakrishnan, U. Shaft, and J.-B. Yu. Processing queries by linear constraints. In *Proc. ACM Symposium on Principles of Database Systems*, 1997.

[323] G. Graefe. Encapsulation of parallelism in the Volcano query processing system. In *Proc. ACM SIGMOD Conf. on the Management of Data*, 1990.

[324] G. Graefe. Query evaluation techniques for large databases. *ACM Computing Surveys*, 25(2), 1993.

[325] G. Graefe, R. Bunker, and S. Cooper. Hash joins and hash teams in microsoft SQL Server: In *Proc. Intl. Conf. on Very Large Databases*, 1998.

[326] G. Graefe and D. DeWitt. The Exodus optimizer generator. In *Proc. ACM SIGMOD Conf. on the Management of Data*, 1987.

[327] G. Graefe and K. Ward. Dynamic query optimization plans. In *Proc. ACM SIGMOD Conf. on the Management of Data*, 1989.

[328] M. Graham, A. Mendelzon, and M. Vardi. Notions of dependency satisfaction. *Journal of the ACM*, 33(1):105–129, 1986.

[329] G. Grahne. *The Problem of Incomplete Information in Relational Databases.* Springer-Verlag, 1991.

[330] L. Gravano, H. Garcia-Molina, and A. Tomasic. Gloss: text-source discovery over the internet. *ACM Transactions on Database Systems*, 24(2), 1999.

[331] J. Gray. Notes on data base operating systems. In *Operating Systems: An Advanced Course.* eds. Bayer, Graham, and Seegmuller, Springer-Verlag, 1978.

[332] J. Gray. The transaction concept: Virtues and limitations. In *Proc. Intl. Conf. on Very Large Databases*, 1981.

[333] J. Gray. Transparency in its place—the case against transparent access to geographically distributed data. *Tandem Computers, TR-89-1*, 1989.

[334] J. Gray. *The Benchmark Handbook: for Database and Transaction Processing Systems.* Morgan Kaufmann, 1991.

[335] J. Gray, A. Bosworth, A. Layman, and H. Pirahesh. Data cube: A relational aggregation operator generalizing group-by, cross-tab and sub-totals. In *Proc. IEEE Intl. Conf. on Data Engineering*, 1996.

[336] J. Gray, R. Lorie, G. Putzolu, and I. Traiger. Granularity of locks and degrees of consistency in a shared data base. In *Proc. of IFIP Working Conf. on Modelling of Data Base Management Systems*, 1977.

[337] J. Gray, P. McJones, M. Blasgen, B. Lindsay, R. Lorie, G. Putzolu, T. Price, and I. Traiger. The recovery manager of the System R database manager. *ACM Computing Surveys*, 13(2):223–242, 1981.

[338] J. Gray and A. Reuter. *Transaction Processing: Concepts and Techniques.* Morgan Kaufmann, 1992.

[339] P. Gray. *Logic, Algebra, and Databases.* John Wiley, 1984.

[340] M. Greenwald and S. Khanna. Space-efficient online computation of quantile summaries. In *Proc. ACM SIGMOD Conf. on Management of Data*, 2001.

[341] P. Griffiths and B. Wade. An authorization mechanism for a relational database system. *ACM Transactions on Database Systems*, 1(3):242–255, 1976.

[342] G. Grinstein. Visualization and data mining. In *Intl. Conf. on Knowledge Discovery in Databases*, 1996.

[343] S. Guha, N. Mishra, R. Motwani, and L. O'Callaghan. Clustering data streams. In *Proc. of the Annual Symp. on Foundations of Computer Science*, 2000.

[344] S. Guha, R. Rastogi, and K. Shim. Cure: an efficient clustering algorithm for large databases. In *Proc. ACM SIGMOD Conf. on Management of Data*, 1998.

[345] S. Guha, N. Koudas, and K. Shim. Data streams and histograms. In *Proc. of the ACM Symp. on Theory of Computing*, 2001.

[346] D. Gunopulos, H. Mannila, R. Khardon, and H. Toivonen. Data mining, hypergraph transversals, and machine learning. In *Proc. ACM Symposium on Principles of Database Systems*, pages 209–216, 1997.

[347] D. Gunopulos, H. Mannila, and S. Saluja. Discovering all most specific sentences by randomized algorithms. In *Proc. of the Intl. Conf. on Database Theory*, volume 1186 of *Lecture Notes in Computer Science*, pages 215–229. Springer, 1997.

[348] A. Gupta and I. Mumick. *Materialized Views: Techniques, Implementations, and Applications* MIT Press, 1999.

[349] A. Gupta, I. Mumick, and V. Subrahmanian. Maintaining views incrementally. In *Proc. ACM SIGMOD Conf. on the Management of Data*, 1993.

[350] A. Guttman. R-trees: a dynamic index structure for spatial searching. In *Proc. ACM SIGMOD Conf. on the Management of Data*, 1984.

[351] L. Haas, W. Chang, G. Lohman, J. McPherson, P. Wilms, G. Lapis, B. Lindsay, H. Pirahesh, M. Carey, and E. Shekita. Starburst mid-flight: As the dust clears. *IEEE Transactions on Knowledge and Data Engineering*, 2(1), 1990.

[352] P. Haas, J. Naughton, S. Seshadri, and L. Stokes. Sampling-based estimation of the number of distinct values of an attribute. In *Proc. Intl. Conf. on Very Large Databases*, 1995.

[353] P. Haas and A. Swami. Sampling-based selectivity estimation for joins using augmented frequent value statistics. In *Proc. IEEE Intl. Conf. on Data Engineering*, 1995.

[354] P. J. Haas and J. M. Hellerstein. Ripple joins for online aggregation. In *Proc. ACM SIGMOD Conf. on the Management of Data*, pages 287–298. ACM Press, 1999.

[355] T. Haerder and A. Reuter. Principles of transaction oriented database recovery—a taxonomy. *ACM Computing Surveys*, 15(4), 1982.

[356] U. Halici and A. Dogac. Concurrency control in distributed databases through time intervals and short-term locks. *IEEE Transactions on Software Engineering*, 15(8):994–1003, 1989.

[357] M. Hall. *Core Web Programming: HTML , Java , CGI , & Javascript.* Prentice-Hall, 1997.

[358] P. Hall. Optimization of a simple expression in a relational data base system. *IBM Journal of Research and Development*, 20(3):244–257, 1976.

[359] G. Hamilton, R. G. Cattell, and M. Fisher. *JDBC Database Access With Java: A Tutorial and Annotated Reference.* Java Series. Addison-Wesley, 1997.

[360] M. Hammer and D. McLeod. Semantic integrity in a relational data base system. In *Proc. Intl. Conf. on Very Large Databases*, 1975.

[361] J. Han and Y. Fu. Discovery of multiple-level association rules from large databases. In *Proc. Intl. Conf. on Very Large Databases*, 1995.

[362] D. Hand. *Construction and Assessment of Classification Rules.* John Wiley & Sons, Chichester, England, 1997.

[363] J. Han and M. Kamber. *Data Mining: Concepts and Techniques.* Morgan Kaufmann Publishers, 2000.

[364] J. Han, J. Pei, and Y. Yin. Mining frequent patterns without candidate generation. In *Proc. ACM SIGMOD Intl. Conf. on Management of Data*, pages 1–12, 2000.

[365] E. Hanson. A performance analysis of view materialization strategies. In *Proc. ACM SIGMOD Conf. on the Management of Data*, 1987.

[366] E. Hanson. Rule condition testing and action execution in Ariel. In *Proc. ACM SIGMOD Conf. on the Management of Data*, 1992.

[367] V. Harinarayan, A. Rajaraman, and J. Ullman. Implementing data cubes efficiently. In *Proc. ACM SIGMOD Conf. on the Management of Data*, 1996.

[368] J. Haritsa, M. Carey, and M. Livny. On being optimistic about real-time constraints. In *ACM Symp. on Principles of Database Systems*, 1990.

[369] J. Harrison and S. Dietrich. Maintenance of materialized views in deductive databases: An update propagation approach. In *Proc. Workshop on Deductive Databases*, 1992.

[370] T. Hastie, R. Tibshirani, and J. H. Friedman. *The Elements of Statistical Learning: Data Mining, Inference, and Prediction.* Springer Verlag, 2001.

[371] D. Heckerman. Bayesian networks for knowledge discovery. In *Advances in Knowledge Discovery and Data Mining.* eds. U.M. Fayyad, G. Piatetsky-Shapiro, P. Smyth, and R. Uthurusamy, MIT Press, 1996.

[372] D. Heckerman, H. Mannila, D. Pregibon, and R. Uthurusamy, editors. *Proc. Intl. Conf. on Knowledge Discovery and Data Mining.* AAAI Press, 1997.

[373] J. Hellerstein. Optimization and execution techniques for queries with expensive methods. *Ph.D. thesis, University of Wisconsin-Madison*, 1995.

[374] J. Hellerstein, P. Haas, and H. Wang. Online aggregation In *Proc. ACM SIGMOD Conf. on the Management of Data*, 1997.

[375] J. Hellerstein, E. Koutsoupias, and C. Papadimitriou. On the analysis of indexing schemes. In *Proceedings of the ACM Symposium on Principles of Database Systems*, pages 249–256. ACM Press, 1997.

[376] J. Hellerstein, J. Naughton, and A. Pfeffer. Generalized search trees for database systems. In *Proc. Intl. Conf. on Very Large Databases*, 1995.

[377] J. M. Hellerstein, E. Koutsoupias, and C. H. Papadimitriou. On the analysis of indexing schemes. In *Proc. ACM Symposium on Principles of Database Systems*, pages 249–256, 1997.

[378] C. Hidber Online association rule mining. In *Proc. ACM SIGMOD Conf. on the Management of Data*, pages 145–156, 1999.

[379] R. Himmeroeder, G. Lausen, B. Ludaescher, and C. Schlepphorst. On a declarative semantics for Web queries. *Lecture Notes in Computer Science*, 1341:386–398, 1997.

[380] C.-T. Ho, R. Agrawal, N. Megiddo, and R. Srikant. Range queries in OLAP data cubes. In *Proc. ACM SIGMOD Conf. on the Management of Data*, 1997.

[381] S. Holzner. *XML Complete.* Mc Graw-Hill, 1998.

[382] D. Hong, T. Johnson, and U. Chakravarthy. Real-time transaction scheduling: A cost conscious approach. In *Proc. ACM SIGMOD Conf. on the Management of Data*, 1993.

[383] W. Hong and M. Stonebraker. Optimization of parallel query execution plans in XPRS. In *Proc. Intl. Conf. on Parallel and Distributed Information Systems*, 1991.

[384] W.-C. Hou and G. Ozsoyoglu. Statistical estimators for aggregate relational algebra queries. *ACM Transactions on Database Systems*, 16(4), 1991.

[385] H. Hsiao and D. DeWitt. A performance study of three high availability data replication strategies. In *Proc. Intl. Conf. on Parallel and Distributed Information Systems*, 1991.

[386] J. Huang, J. Stankovic, K. Ramamritham, and D. Towsley. Experimental evaluation of real-time optimistic concurrency control schemes. In *Proc. Intl. Conf. on Very Large Databases*, 1991.

[387] Y. Huang, A. Sistla, and O. Wolfson. Data replication for mobile computers. In *Proc. ACM SIGMOD Conf. on the Management of Data*, 1994.

[388] Y. Huang and O. Wolfson. A competitive dynamic data replication algorithm. In *Proc. IEEE CS IEEE Intl. Conf. on Data Engineering*, 1993.

[389] R. Hull. Managing semantic heterogeneity in databases: A theoretical perspective. In *ACM Symp. on Principles of Database Systems*, 1997.

[390] R. Hull and R. King. Semantic database modeling: Survey, applications, and research issues. *ACM Computing Surveys*, 19(19):201–260, 1987.

[391] R. Hull and J. Su. Algebraic and calculus query languages for recursively typed complex objects. *Journal of Computer and System Sciences*, 47(1):121–156, 1993.

[392] R. Hull and M. Yoshikawa. ILOG: Declarative creation and manipulation of object-identifiers. In *Proc. Intl. Conf. on Very Large Databases*, 1990.

[393] G. Hulten, L. Spencer, and P. Domingos. Mining time-changing data streams. In *Proc. ACM SIGKDD Intl. Conference on Knowledge Discovery and Data Mining*, pages 97–106. AAAI Press, 2001.

[394] J. Hunter. *Java Servlet Programming.* O'Reilly Associates, Inc., 1998.

[395] T. Imielinski and H. Korth (eds.). *Mobile Computing.* Kluwer Academic, 1996.

[396] T. Imielinski and W. Lipski. Incomplete information in relational databases. *Journal of the ACM*, 31(4):761–791, 1984.

[397] T. Imielinski and H. Mannila. A database perspective on knowledge discovery. *Communications of the ACM*, 38(11):58–64, 1996.

[398] T. Imielinski, S. Viswanathan, and B. Badrinath. Energy efficient indexing on air. In *Proc. ACM SIGMOD Conf. on the Management of Data*, 1994.

[399] Y. Ioannidis. Query optimization. In *Handbook of Computer Science.* ed. A.B. Tucker, CRC Press, 1996.

[400] Y. Ioannidis and S. Christodoulakis. Optimal histograms for limiting worst-case error propagation in the size of join results. *ACM Transactions on Database Systems*, 1993.

[401] Y. Ioannidis and Y. Kang. Randomized algorithms for optimizing large join queries. In *Proc. ACM SIGMOD Conf. on the Management of Data*, 1990.

[402] Y. Ioannidis and Y. Kang. Left-deep vs. bushy trees: An analysis of strategy spaces and its implications for query optimization. In *Proc. ACM SIGMOD Conf. on the Management of Data*, 1991.

[403] Y. Ioannidis, R. Ng, K. Shim, and T. Sellis. Parametric query processing. In *Proc. Intl. Conf. on Very Large Databases*, 1992.

[404] Y. Ioannidis and R. Ramakrishnan. Containment of conjunctive queries: Beyond relations as sets. *ACM Transactions on Database Systems*, 20(3):288–324, 1995.

[405] Y. E. Ioannidis. Universality of serial histograms. In *Proc. Intl. Conf. on Very Large Databases*, 1993.

[406] H. Jagadish, D. Lieuwen, R. Rastogi, A. Silberschatz, and S. Sudarshan. Dali: A high performance main-memory storage manager. In *Proc. Intl. Conf. on Very Large Databases*, 1994.

[407] A. K. Jain and R. C. Dubes. *Algorithms for Clustering Data.* PrenticeHall, 1988.

[408] S. Jajodia and D. Mutchler. Dynamic voting algorithms for maintaining the consistency of a replicated database. *ACM Transactions on Database Systems*, 15(2):230–280, 1990.

[409] S. Jajodia and R. Sandhu. Polyinstantiation integrity in multilevel relations. In *Proc. IEEE Symp. on Security and Privacy*, 1990.

[410] M. Jarke and J. Koch. Query optimization in database systems. *ACM Computing Surveys*, 16(2):111–152, 1984.

[411] K. S. Jones and P. Willett, editors. *Readings in Information Retrieval.* Multimedia Information and Systems. Morgan Kaufmann Publishers, 1997.

[412] J. Jou and P. Fischer. The complexity of recognizing 3NF schemes. *Information Processing Letters*, 14(4):187–190, 1983.

[413] N. Kabra and D. J. DeWitt. Efficient mid-query re-optimization of sub-optimal query execution plans. In *Proc. ACM SIGMOD Intl. Conf. on Management of Data*, 1998.

[414] Y. Kambayashi, M. Yoshikawa, and S. Yajima. Query processing for distributed databases using generalized semi-joins. In *Proc. ACM SIGMOD Conf. on the Management of Data*, 1982.

[415] P. Kanellakis. Elements of relational database theory. In *Handbook of Theoretical Computer Science.* ed. J. Van Leeuwen, Elsevier, 1991.

[416] P. Kanellakis. Constraint programming and database languages: A tutorial. In *ACM Symp. on Principles of Database Systems*, 1995.

[417] H. Kargupta and P. Chan, editors. *Advances in Distributed and Parallel Knowledge Discovery.* MIT Press, 2000.

[418] L. Kaufman and P. Rousseeuw. *Finding Groups in Data: An Introduction to Cluster Analysis.* John Wiley and Sons, 1990.

[419] R. Kaushik, P. Bohannon, J. F. Naughton, and H. F. Korth. Covering indexes for branching path expression queries. In *Proceedings of SIGMOD*, 2002.

[420] D. Keim and H.-P. Kriegel. VisDB: a system for visualizing large databases. In *Proc. ACM SIGMOD Conf. on the Management of Data*, 1995.

[421] D. Keim and H.-P. Kriegel. Visualization techniques for mining large databases: A comparison. *IEEE Transactions on Knowledge and Data Engineering*, 8(6):923–938, 1996.

[422] A. Keller. Algorithms for translating view updates to database updates for views involving selections, projections, and joins. *ACM Symp. on Principles of Database Systems*, 1985.

[423] W. Kent. *Data and Reality, Basic Assumptions in Data Processing Reconsidered.* North-Holland, 1978.

[424] W. Kent, R. Ahmed, J. Albert, M. Ketabchi, and M.-C. Shan. Object identification in multi-database systems. In *IFIP Intl. Conf. on Data Semantics*, 1992.

[425] L. Kerschberg, A. Klug, and D. Tsichritzis. A taxonomy of data models. In *Systems for Large Data Bases.* eds. P.C. Lockemann and E.J. Neuhold, North-Holland, 1977.

[426] W. Kiessling. On semantic reefs and efficient processing of correlation queries with aggregates. In *Proc. Intl. Conf. on Very Large Databases*, 1985.

[427] M. Kifer, W. Kim, and Y. Sagiv. Querying object-oriented databases. In *Proc. ACM SIGMOD Conf. on the Management of Data*, 1992.

[428] M. Kifer, G. Lausen, and J. Wu. Logical foundations of object-oriented and frame-based languages. *Journal of the ACM*, 42(4):741–843, 1995.

[429] M. Kifer and E. Lozinskii. Sygraf: Implementing logic programs in a database style. *IEEE Transactions on Software Engineering*, 14(7):922–935, 1988.

[430] W. Kim. On optimizing an SQL -like nested query. *ACM Transactions on Database Systems*, 7(3), 1982.

[431] W. Kim. Object-oriented database systems: Promise, reality, and future. In *Proc. Intl. Conf. on Very Large Databases*, 1993.

[432] W. Kim, J. Garza, N. Ballou, and D. Woelk. Architecture of the ORION next-generation database system. *IEEE Transactions on Knowledge and Data Engineering*, 2(1):109–124, 1990.

[433] W. Kim and F. Lochovsky (eds.). *Object-Oriented Concepts, Databases, and Applications.* Addison-Wesley, 1989.

[434] W. Kim, D. Reiner, and D. Batory (eds.). *Query Processing in Database Systems.* Springer Verlag, 1984.

[435] W. Kim (ed.). *Modern Database Systems.* ACM Press and Addison-Wesley, 1995.

[436] R. Kimball. *The Data Warehouse Toolkit.* John Wiley and Sons, 1996.

[437] J. King. Quist: A system for semantic query optimization in relational databases. In *Proc. Intl. Conf. on Very Large Databases*, 1981.

[438] J. M. Kleinberg. Authoritative sources in a hyperlinked environment. In *Proc. ACM -SIAM Symp. on Discrete Algorithms*, 1998.

[439] A. Klug. Equivalence of relational algebra and relational calculus query languages having aggregate functions. *Journal of the ACM*, 29(3):699–717, 1982.

[440] A. Klug. On conjunctive queries containing inequalities. *Journal of the ACM*, 35(1):146–160, 1988.

[441] E. Knapp. Deadlock detection in distributed databases. *ACM Computing Surveys*, 19(4):303–328, 1987.

[442] D. Knuth. *The Art of Computer Programming, Vol.3—Sorting and Searching.* Addison-Wesley, 1973.

[443] G. Koch and K. Loney. *Oracle: The Complete Reference.* Oracle Press, Osborne-McGraw-Hill, 1995.

[444] W. Kohler. A survey of techniques for synchronization and recovery in decentralized computer systems. *ACM Computing Surveys*, 13(2):149–184, 1981.

[445] D. Konopnicki and O. Shmueli. W3QS: A system for WWW querying. In *Proc. IEEE Intl. Conf. on Data Engineering*, 1997.

[446] F. Korn, H. Jagadish, and C. Faloutsos. Efficiently supporting ad hoc queries in large datasets of time sequences. In *Proc. ACM SIGMOD Conf. on Management of Data*, 1997.

[447] M. Kornacker, C. Mohan, and J. Hellerstein. Concurrency and recovery in generalized search trees. In *Proc. ACM SIGMOD Conf. on the Management of Data*, 1997.

[448] H. Korth, N. Soparkar, and A. Silberschatz. Triggered real-time databases with consistency constraints. In *Proc. Intl. Conf. on Very Large Databases*, 1990.

[449] H. F. Korth. Deadlock freedom using edge locks. *ACM Transactions on Database Systems*, 7(4):632–652, 1982.

[450] D. Kossmann. The state of the art in distributed query processing. *ACM Computing Surveys*, 32(4):422–469, 2000.

[451] Y. Kotidis and N. Roussopoulos. An alternative storage organization for ROLAP aggregate views based on cubetrees. In *Proc. ACM SIGMOD Intl. Conf. on Management of Data*, 1998.

[452] N. Krishnakumar and A. Bernstein. High throughput escrow algorithms for replicated databases. In *Proc. Intl. Conf. on Very Large Databases*, 1992.

[453] R. Krishnamurthy, H. Boral, and C. Zaniolo. Optimization of nonrecursive queries. In *Proc. Intl. Conf. on Very Large Databases*, 1986.

[454] J. Kuhns. Logical aspects of question answering by computer. Technical report, Rand Corporation, RM-5428-Pr., 1967.

[455] V. Kumar. *Performance of Concurrency Control Mechanisms in Centralized Database Systems*. PrenticeHall, 1996.

[456] H. Kung and P. Lehman. Concurrent manipulation of binary search trees. *ACM Transactions on Database Systems*, 5(3):354–382, 1980.

[457] H. Kung and J. Robinson. On optimistic methods for concurrency control. *Proc. Intl. Conf. on Very Large Databases*, 1979.

[458] D. Kuo. Model and verification of a data manager based on ARIES. In *Intl. Conf. on Database Theory*, 1992.

[459] M. LaCroix and A. Pirotte. Domain oriented relational languages. In *Proc. Intl. Conf. on Very Large Databases*, 1977.

[460] M.-Y. Lai and W. Wilkinson. Distributed transaction management in Jasmin. In *Proc. Intl. Conf. on Very Large Databases*, 1984.

[461] L. Lakshmanan, F. Sadri, and I. N. Subramanian. A declarative query language for querying and restructuring the web. In *Proc. Intl. Conf. on Research Issues in Data Engineering*, 1996.

[462] L. V. S. Lakshmanan, Raymond T. Ng, J. Han, and A. Pang. Optimization of constrained frequent set queries with 2-variable constraints. In *Proc. ACM SIGMOD Intl. Conf. on Management of Data*, pages 157–168. ACM Press, 1999.

[463] C. Lam, G. Landis, J. Orenstein, and D. Weinreb. The Objectstore database system. *Communications of the ACM*, 34(10), 1991.

[464] L. Lamport. Time, clocks and the ordering of events in a distributed system. *Communications of the ACM*, 21(7):558–565, 1978.

[465] B. Lampson and D. Lomet. A new presumed commit optimization for two phase commit. In *Proc. Intl. Conf. on Very Large Databases*, 1993.

[466] B. Lampson and H. Sturgis. Crash recovery in a distributed data storage system. Technical report, Xerox PARC, 1976.

[467] C. Landwehr. Formal models of computer security. *ACM Computing Surveys*, 13(3):247–278, 1981.

[468] R. Langerak. View updates in relational databases with an independent scheme. *ACM Transactions on Database Systems*, 15(1):40–66, 1990.

[469] P.-A. Larson. Linear hashing with overflow-handling by linear probing. *ACM Transactions on Database Systems*, 10(1):75–89, 1985.

[470] P.-A. Larson. Linear hashing with separators—A dynamic hashing scheme achieving one-access retrieval. *ACM Transactions on Database Systems*, 13(3):366–388, 1988.

[471] P.-A. Larson and G. Graefe. Memory Management During Run Generation in External Sorting. In *Proc. ACM SIGMOD Conf. on Management of Data*, 1998.

[472] P. Lehman and S. Yao. Efficient locking for concurrent operations on b trees. *ACM Transactions on Database Systems*, 6(4):650–670, 1981.

[473] T. Leung and R. Muntz. Temporal query processing and optimization in multiprocessor database machines. In *Proc. Intl. Conf. on Very Large Databases*, 1992.

[474] M. Leventhal, D. Lewis, and M. Fuchs. *Designing XML Internet applications.* The Charles F. Goldfarb series on open information management. PrenticeHall, 1998.

[475] P. Lewis, A. Bernstein, and M. Kifer. *Databases and Transaction Processing.* Addison Wesley, 2001.

[476] E.-P. Lim and J. Srivastava. Query optimization and processing in federated database systems. In *Proc. Intl. Conf. on Intelligent Knowledge Management*, 1993.

[477] B. Lindsay, J. McPherson, and H. Pirahesh. A data management extension architecture. In *Proc. ACM SIGMOD Conf. on the Management of Data*, 1987.

[478] B. Lindsay, P. Selinger, C. Galtieri, J. Gray, R. Lorie, G. Putzolu, I. Traiger, and B. Wade. Notes on distributed databases. Technical report, RJ2571, San Jose, CA, 1979.

[479] D.-I. Lin and Z. M. Kedem. Pincer search: A new algorithm for discovering the maximum frequent set. *Lecture Notes in Computer Science*, 1377:105–??, 1998.

[480] V. Linnemann, K. Kuspert, P. Dadam, P. Pistor, R. Erbe, A. Kemper, N. Sudkamp, G. Walch, and M. Wallrath. Design and implementation of an extensible database management system supporting user defined data types and functions. In *Proc. Intl. Conf. on Very Large Databases*, 1988.

[481] R. Lipton, J. Naughton, and D. Schneider. Practical selectivity estimation through adaptive sampling. In *Proc. ACM SIGMOD Conf. on the Management of Data*, 1990.

[482] B. Liskov, A. Adya, M. Castro, M. Day, S. Ghemawat, R. Gruber, U. Maheshwari, A. Myers, and L. Shrira. Safe and efficient sharing of persistent objects in Thor. In *Proc. ACM SIGMOD Conf. on the Management of Data*, 1996.

[483] W. Litwin. Linear Hashing: A new tool for file and table addressing. In *Proc. Intl. Conf. on Very Large Databases*, 1980.

[484] W. Litwin. Trie Hashing. In *Proc. ACM SIGMOD Conf. on the Management of Data*, 1981.

[485] W. Litwin and A. Abdellatif. Multidatabase interoperability. *IEEE Computer*, 12(19):10–18, 1986.

[486] W. Litwin, L. Mark, and N. Roussopoulos. Interoperability of multiple autonomous databases. *ACM Computing Surveys*, 22(3), 1990.

[487] W. Litwin, M.-A. Neimat, and D. Schneider. LH *—A scalable, distributed data structure. *ACM Transactions on Database Systems*, 21(4):480–525, 1996.

[488] M. Liu, A. Sheth, and A. Singhal. An adaptive concurrency control strategy for distributed database system. In *Proc. IEEE Intl. Conf. on Data Engineering*, 1984.

[489] M. Livny, R. Ramakrishnan, K. Beyer, G. Chen, D. Donjerkovic, S. Lawande, J. Myllymaki, and K. Wenger. DEVise: Integrated querying and visual exploration of large datasets. In *Proc. ACM SIGMOD Conf. on the Management of Data*, 1997.

[490] G. Lohman. Grammar-like functional rules for representing query optimization alternatives. In *Proc. ACM SIGMOD Conf. on the Management of Data*, 1988.

[491] D. Lomet and B. Salzberg. The hB-T ree: A multiattribute indexing method with good guaranteed performance. *ACM Transactions on Database Systems*, 15(4), 1990.

[492] D. Lomet and B. Salzberg. Access method concurrency with recovery. In *Proc. ACM SIGMOD Conf. on the Management of Data*, 1992.

[493] R. Lorie. Physical integrity in a large segmented database. *ACM Transactions on Database Systems*, 2(1):91–104, 1977.

[494] R. Lorie and H. Young. A low communication sort algorithm for a parallel database machine. In *Proc. Intl. Conf. on Very Large Databases*, 1989.

[495] Y. Lou and Z. Ozsoyoglu. LLO: An object-oriented deductive language with methods and method inheritance. In *Proc. ACM SIGMOD Conf. on the Management of Data*, 1991.

[496] H. Lu, B.-C. Ooi, and K.-L. Tan (eds.). *Query Processing in Parallel Relational Database Systems.* IEEE Computer Society Press, 1994.

[497] C. Lucchesi and S. Osborn. Candidate keys for relations. *J. Computer and System Sciences*, 17(2):270–279, 1978.

[498] V. Lum. Multi-attribute retrieval with combined indexes. *Communications of the ACM*, 1(11):660–665, 1970.

[499] T. Lunt, D. Denning, R. Schell, M. Heckman, and W. Shockley. The seaview security model. *IEEE Transactions on Software Engineering*, 16(6):593–607, 1990.

[500] L. Mackert and G. Lohman. R* optimizer validation and performance evaluation for local queries. Technical report, IBM RJ-4989, San Jose, CA, 1986.

[501] D. Maier. *The Theory of Relational Databases.* Computer Science Press, 1983.

[502] D. Maier, A. Mendelzon, and Y. Sagiv. Testing implication of data dependencies. *ACM Transactions on Database Systems*, 4(4), 1979.

[503] D. Maier and D. Warren. *Computing with Logic: Logic Programming with Prolog.* Benjamin/Cummings Publishers, 1988.

[504] A. Makinouchi. A consideration on normal form of not-necessarily-normalized relation in the relational data model. In *Proc. Intl. Conf. on Very Large Databases*, 1977.

[505] U. Manber and R. Ladner. Concurrency control in a dynamic search structure. *ACM Transactions on Database Systems*, 9(3):439–455, 1984.

[506] G. Manku, S. Rajagopalan, and B. Lindsay. Random sampling techniques for space efficient online computation of order statistics of large datasets. In *Proc. ACM SIGMOD Conf. on Management of Data*, 1999.

[507] H. Mannila. Methods and problems in data mining. In *Intl. Conf. on Database Theory*, 1997.

[508] H. Mannila and K.-J. Raiha. Design by Example: An application of Armstrong relations. *Journal of Computer and System Sciences*, 33(2):126–141, 1986.

[509] H. Mannila and K.-J. Raiha. *The Design of Relational Databases.* Addison-Wesley, 1992.

[510] H. Mannila, H. Toivonen, and A. I. Verkamo. Discovering frequent episodes in sequences. In *Proc. Intl. Conf. on Knowledge Discovery in Databases and Data Mining*, 1995.

[511] H. Mannila, P. Smyth, and D. J. Hand. *Principles of Data Mining.* MIT Press, 2001.

[512] M. Mannino, P. Chu, and T. Sager. Statistical profile estimation in database systems. *ACM Computing Surveys*, 20(3):191–221, 1988.

[513] V. Markowitz. Representing processes in the extended entity-relationship model. In *Proc. IEEE Intl. Conf. on Data Engineering*, 1990.

[514] V. Markowitz. Safe referential integrity structures in relational databases. In *Proc. Intl. Conf. on Very Large Databases*, 1991.

[515] Y. Matias, J. S. Vitter, and M. Wang. Dynamic maintenance of wavelet-based histograms. In *Proc. of the Conf. on Very Large Databases*, 2000.

[516] D. McCarthy and U. Dayal. The architecture of an active data base management system. In *Proc. ACM SIGMOD Conf. on the Management of Data*, 1989.

[517] W. McCune and L. Henschen. Maintaining state constraints in relational databases: A proof theoretic basis. *Journal of the ACM*, 36(1):46–68, 1989.

[518] J. McHugh, S. Abiteboul, R. Goldman, D. Quass, and J. Widom. Lore: A database management system for semistructured data. *ACM SIGMOD Record*, 26(3):54–66, 1997.

[519] S. Mehrotra, R. Rastogi, Y. Breitbart, H. Korth, and A. Silberschatz. Ensuring transaction atomicity in multidatabase systems. In *ACM Symp. on Principles of Database Systems*, 1992.

[520] S. Mehrotra, R. Rastogi, H. Korth, and A. Silberschatz. The concurrency control problem in multidatabases: Characteristics and solutions. In *Proc. ACM SIGMOD Conf. on the Management of Data*, 1992.

[521] M. Mehta, R. Agrawal, and J. Rissanen. SLIQ: A fast scalable classifier for data mining. In *Proc. Intl. Conf. on Extending Database Technology*, 1996.

[522] M. Mehta, V. Soloviev, and D. DeWitt. Batch scheduling in parallel database systems. In *Proc. IEEE Intl. Conf. on Data Engineering*, 1993.

[523] J. Melton. *Advanced SQL:1999, Understanding Understanding Object-Relational and Other Advanced Features.* Morgan Kaufmann, 2002.

[524] J. Melton and A. Simon. *Understanding the New SQL: A Complete Guide.* Morgan Kaufmann, 1993.

[525] J. Melton and A. Simon. *SQL:1999, Understanding Relational Language Components.* Morgan Kaufmann, 2002.

[526] D. Menasce and R. Muntz. Locking and deadlock detection in distributed data bases. *IEEE Transactions on Software Engineering*, 5(3):195–222, 1979.

[527] A. Mendelzon and T. Milo. Formal models of web queries. In *ACM Symp. on Principles of Database Systems*, 1997.

[528] A. O. Mendelzon, G. A. Mihaila, and T. Milo. Querying the World Wide Web. *Journal on Digital Libraries*, 1:54–67, 1997.

[529] R. Meo, G. Psaila, and S. Ceri. A new SQL -like operator for mining association rules. In *Proc. Intl. Conf. on Very Large Databases*, 1996.

[530] T. Merrett. The extended relational algebra, a basis for query languages. In *Databases.* ed. Shneiderman, Academic Press, 1978.

[531] T. Merrett. *Relational Information Systems.* Reston Publishing Company, 1983.

[532] D. Michie, D. Spiegelhalter, and C. Taylor, editors. *Machine Learning, Neural and Statistical Classification.* Ellis Horwood, London, 1994.

[533] Microsoft. *Microsoft ODBC 3.0 Software Development Kit and Programmer's Reference.* Microsoft Press, 1997.

[534] K. Mikkilineni and S. Su. An evaluation of relational join algorithms in a pipelined query processing environment. *IEEE Transactions on Software Engineering*, 14(6):838–848, 1988.

[535] R. Miller, Y. Ioannidis, and R. Ramakrishnan. The use of information capacity in schema integration and translation. In *Proc. Intl. Conf. on Very Large Databases*, 1993.

[536] T. Milo and D. Suciu. Index structures for path expressions. In *ICDT: 7th International Conference on Database Theory*, 1999.

[537] J. Minker (ed.). *Foundations of Deductive Databases and Logic Programming.* Morgan Kaufmann, 1988.

[538] T. Minoura and G. Wiederhold. Resilient extended true-copy token scheme for a distributed database. *IEEE Transactions in Software Engineering*, 8(3):173–189, 1982.

[539] G. Mitchell, U. Dayal, and S. Zdonik. Control of an extensible query optimizer: A planning-based approach. In *Proc. Intl. Conf. on Very Large Databases*, 1993.

[540] A. Moffat and J. Zobel. Self-indexing inverted files for fast text retrieval. *ACM Transactions on Information Systems*, 14(4):349–379, 1996.

[541] C. Mohan. ARIES/NT: A recovery method based on write-ahead logging for nested. In *Proc. Intl. Conf. on Very Large Databases*, 1989.

[542] C. Mohan. Commit LSN: A novel and simple method for reducing locking and latching in transaction processing systems. In *Proc. Intl. Conf. on Very Large Databases*, 1990.

[543] C. Mohan. ARIES/LHS: A concurrency control and recovery method using write-ahead logging for linear hashing with separators. In *Proc. IEEE Intl. Conf. on Data Engineering*, 1993.

[544] C. Mohan, D. Haderle, B. Lindsay, H. Pirahesh, and P. Schwarz. ARIES: a transaction recovery method supporting fine-granularity locking and partial rollbacks using write-ahead logging. *ACM Transactions on Database Systems*, 17(1):94–162, 1992.

[545] C. Mohan and F. Levine. ARIES/IM An efficient and high concurrency index management method using write-ahead logging. In *Proc. ACM SIGMOD Conf. on the Management of Data*, 1992.

[546] C. Mohan and B. Lindsay. Efficient commit protocols for the tree of processes model of distributed transactions. In *ACM SIGACT-SIGOPS Symp. on Principles of Distributed Computing*, 1983.

[547] C. Mohan, B. Lindsay, and R. Obermarck. Transaction management in the R* distributed database management system. *ACM Transactions on Database Systems*, 11(4):378–396, 1986.

[548] C. Mohan and I. Narang. Algorithms for creating indexes for very large tables without quiescing updates. In *Proc. ACM SIGMOD Conf. on the Management of Data*, 1992.

[549] K. Morris, J. Naughton, Y. Saraiya, J. Ullman, and A. Van Gelder. YAWN ! (Yet Another Window on NAIL!). *Database Engineering*, 6:211–226, 1987.

[550] A. Motro. Superviews: Virtual integration of multiple databases. *IEEE Transactions on Software Engineering*, 13(7):785–798, 1987.

[551] A. Motro and P. Buneman. Constructing superviews. In *Proc. ACM SIGMOD Conf. on the Management of Data*, 1981.

[552] R. Mukkamala. Measuring the effect of data distribution and replication models on performance evaluation of distributed database systems. In *Proc. IEEE Intl. Conf. on Data Engineering*, 1989.

[553] I. Mumick, S. Finkelstein, H. Pirahesh, and R. Ramakrishnan. Magic is relevant. In *Proc. ACM SIGMOD Conf. on the Management of Data*, 1990.

[554] I. Mumick, S. Finkelstein, H. Pirahesh, and R. Ramakrishnan. Magic conditions. *ACM Transactions on Database Systems*, 21(1):107–155, 1996.

[555] I. Mumick, H. Pirahesh, and R. Ramakrishnan. Duplicates and aggregates in deductive databases. In *Proc. Intl. Conf. on Very Large Databases*, 1990.

[556] I. Mumick and K. Ross. Noodle: A language for declarative querying in an object-oriented database. In *Intl. Conf. on Deductive and Object-Oriented Databases*, 1993.

[557] M. Muralikrishna. Improved unnesting algorithms for join aggregate SQL queries. In *Proc. Intl. Conf. on Very Large Databases*, 1992.

[558] M. Muralikrishna and D. DeWitt. Equi-depth histograms for estimating selectivity factors for multi-dimensional queries. In *Proc. ACM SIGMOD Conf. on the Management of Data*, 1988.

[559] S. Naqvi. Negation as failure for first-order queries. In *ACM Symp. on Principles of Database Systems*, 1986.

[560] M. Negri, G. Pelagatti, and L. Sbattella. Formal semantics of SQL queries. *ACM Transactions on Database Systems*, 16(3), 1991.

[561] S. Nestorov, J. Ullman, J. Weiner, and S. Chawathe. Representative objects: Concise representations of semistructured, hierarchical data. In *Proc. Intl. Conf. on Data Engineering*. IEEE Computer Society, 1997.

[562] R. T. Ng and J. Han. Efficient and effective clustering methods for spatial data mining. In *Proc. Intl. Conf. on Very Large Databases*, Santiago, Chile, September 1994.

[563] R. T. Ng, L. V. S. Lakshmanan, J. Han, and A. Pang. Exploratory mining and pruning optimizations of constrained association rules. In *Proc. ACM SIGMOD Intl. Conf. on Management of Data*, pages 13–24. ACM Press, 1998.

[564] T. Nguyen and V. Srinivasan. Accessing relational databases from the World Wide Web. In *Proc. ACM SIGMOD Conf. on the Management of Data*, 1996.

[565] J. Nievergelt, H. Hinterberger, and K. Sevcik. The Grid File: An adaptable symmetric multikey file structure. *ACM Transactions on Database Systems*, 9(1):38–71, 1984.

[566] C. Nyberg, T. Barclay, Z. Cvetanovic, J. Gray, and D. Lomet. Alphasort: a cache-sensitive parallel external sort. *VLDB Journal*, 4(4):603–627, 1995.

[567] R. Obermarck. Global deadlock detection algorithm. *ACM Transactions on Database Systems*, 7(2):187–208, 1981.

[568] L. O'Callaghan, N. Mishra, A. Meyerson, S. Guha, and R. Motwani. Streaming-data algorithms for high-quality clustering. In *Proc. of the Intl. Conference on Data Engineering*. IEEE, 2002.

[569] F. Olken and D. Rotem. Simple random sampling from relational databases. In *Proc. Intl. Conf. on Very Large Databases*, 1986.

[570] F. Olken and D. Rotem. Maintenance of materialized views of sampling queries. In *Proc. IEEE Intl. Conf. on Data Engineering*, 1992.

[571] C. Olston, B. T. Loo, and J. Widom. Adaptive precision setting for cached approximate values. In *Proc. ACM SIGMOD Conf. on the Management of Data*, 2001.

[572] C. Olston and J. Widom. Offering a precision-performance tradeoff for aggregation queries over replicated data. In *Proc. of the Conf. on Very Large Databases*, pages 144–155, 2000.

[573] C. Olston and J. Widom. Best-effort cache synchronization with source cooperation. In *Proc. ACM SIGMOD Conf. on the Management of Data*, 2002.

[574] P. O'Neil and E. O'Neil. *Database Principles, Programming, and Performance.* Addison Wesley, 2 edition, 2000.

[575] P. O'Neil and D. Quass. Improved query performance with variant indexes. In *Proc. ACM SIGMOD Conf. on the Management of Data*, 1997.

[576] B. Ozden, R. Rastogi, and A. Silberschatz. Multimedia support for databases. In *ACM Symp. on Principles of Database Systems*, 1997.

[577] G. Ozsoyoglu, K. Du, S. Guruswamy, and W.-C. Hou. Processing real-time, non-aggregate queries with time-constraints in case-db. In *Proc. IEEE Intl. Conf. on Data Engineering*, 1992.

[578] G. Ozsoyoglu, Z. Ozsoyoglu, and V. Matos. Extending relational algebra and relational calculus with set-valued attributes and aggregate functions. *ACM Transactions on Database Systems*, 12(4):566–592, 1987.

[579] Z. Ozsoyoglu and L.-Y. Yuan. A new normal form for nested relations. *ACM Transactions on Database Systems*, 12(1):111–136, 1987.

[580] M. Ozsu and P. Valduriez. *Principles of Distributed Database Systems.* PrenticeHall, 1991.

[581] C. Papadimitriou. The serializability of concurrent database updates. *Journal of the ACM*, 26(4):631–653, 1979.

[582] C. Papadimitriou. *The Theory of Database Concurrency Control.* Computer Science Press, 1986.

[583] Y. Papakonstantinou, S. Abiteboul, and H. Garcia-Molina. Object fusion in mediator systems. In *Proc. Intl. Conf. on Very Large Data Bases*, 1996.

[584] Y. Papakonstantinou, H. Garcia-Molina, and J. Widom. Object exchange across heterogeneous information sources. In *Proc. Intl. Conf. on Data Engineering*, 1995.

[585] J. Park and A. Segev. Using common subexpressions to optimize multiple queries. In *Proc. IEEE Intl. Conf. on Data Engineering*, 1988.

[586] J. Patel, J.-B. Yu, K. Tufte, B. Nag, J. Burger, N. Hall, K. Ramasamy, R. Lueder, C. Ellman, J. Kupsch, S. Guo, D. DeWitt, and J. Naughton. Building a scaleable geo-spatial DBMS: Technology, implementation, and evaluation. In *Proc. ACM SIGMOD Conf. on the Management of Data*, 1997.

[587] D. Patterson, G. Gibson, and R. Katz. RAID: redundant arrays of inexpensive disks. In *Proc. ACM SIGMOD Conf. on the Management of Data*, 1988.

[588] H.-B. Paul, H.-J. Schek, M. Scholl, G. Weikum, and U. Deppisch. Architecture and implementation of the Darmstadt database kernel system. In *Proc. ACM SIGMOD Conf. on the Management of Data*, 1987.

[589] J. Peckham and F. Maryanski. Semantic data models. *ACM Computing Surveys*, 20(3):153–189, 1988.

[590] J. Pei and J. Han. Can we push more constraints into frequent pattern mining? In *ACM SIGKDD Conference*, pages 350–354, 2000.

[591] J. Pei, J. Han, and L. V. S. Lakshmanan. Mining frequent item sets with convertible constraints. In *Proc. Intl. Conf. on Data Engineering (ICDE)*, pages 433–442. IEEE Computer Society, 2001.

[592] E. Petajan, Y. Jean, D. Lieuwen, and V. Anupam. DataSpace: An automated visualization system for large databases. In *Proc. of SPIE, Visual Data Exploration and Analysis*, 1997.

[593] S. Petrov. Finite axiomatization of languages for representation of system properties. *Information Sciences*, 47:339–372, 1989.

[594] G. Piatetsky-Shapiro and C. Cornell. Accurate estimation of the number of tuples satisfying a condition. In *Proc. ACM SIGMOD Conf. on the Management of Data*, 1984.

[595] G. Piatetsky-Shapiro and W. J. Frawley, editors. *Knowledge Discovery in Databases.* AAAI/MIT Press, Menlo Park, CA, 1991.

[596] H. Pirahesh and J. Hellerstein. Extensible/rule-based query rewrite optimization in starburst. In *Proc. ACM SIGMOD Conf. on the Management of Data*, 1992.

[597] N. Pitts-Moultis and C. Kirk. *XML black book: Indispensable problem solver.* Coriolis Group, 1998.

[598] V. Poosala, Y. Ioannidis, P. Haas, and E. Shekita. Improved histograms for selectivity estimation of range predicates. In *Proc. ACM SIGMOD Conf. on the Management of Data*, 1996.

[599] C. Pu. Superdatabases for composition of heterogeneous databases. In *Proc. IEEE Intl. Conf. on Data Engineering*, 1988.

[600] C. Pu and A. Leff. Replica control in distributed systems: An asynchronous approach. In *Proc. ACM SIGMOD Conf. on the Management of Data*, 1991.

[601] X.-L. Qian and G. Wiederhold. Incremental recomputation of active relational expressions. *IEEE Transactions on Knowledge and Data Engineering*, 3(3):337–341, 1990.

[602] D. Quass, A. Rajaraman, Y. Sagiv, and J. Ullman. Querying semistructured heterogeneous information. In *Proc. Intl. Conf. on Deductive and Object-Oriented Databases*, 1995.

[603] J. R. Quinlan. *C4.5: Programs for Machine Learning.* Morgan Kaufman, 1993.

[604] H. G. M. R. Alonso, D. Barbara. Data caching issues in an information retrieval system. *ACM Transactions on Database Systems*, 15(3), 1990.

[605] The RAIDBook: A source book for RAID technology. The RAID Advisory Board, `http://www.raid-advisory.com`, North Grafton, MA, Dec. 1998. Sixth Edition.

[606] D. Rafiei and A. Mendelzon. Similarity-based queries for time series data. In *Proc. ACM SIGMOD Conf. on the Management of Data*, 1997.

[607] M. Ramakrishna. An exact probability model for finite hash tables. In *Proc. IEEE Intl. Conf. on Data Engineering*, 1988.

[608] M. Ramakrishna and P.-A. Larson. File organization using composite perfect hashing. *ACM Transactions on Database Systems*, 14(2):231–263, 1989.

[609] I. Ramakrishnan, P. Rao, K. Sagonas, T. Swift, and D. Warren. Efficient tabling mechanisms for logic programs. In *Intl. Conf. on Logic Programming*, 1995.

[610] R. Ramakrishnan, D. Donjerkovic, A. Ranganathan, K. Beyer, and M. Krishnaprasad. SRQL: Sorted relational query language In *Proc. IEEE Intl. Conf. on Scientific and Statistical DBMS*, 1998.

[611] R. Ramakrishnan, D. Srivastava, and S. Sudarshan. Efficient bottom-up evaluation of logic programs. In *The State of the Art in Computer Systems and Software Engineering.* ed. J. Vandewalle, Kluwer Academic, 1992.

[612] R. Ramakrishnan, D. Srivastava, S. Sudarshan, and P. Seshadri. The CORAL: deductive system. *VLDB Journal*, 3(2):161–210, 1994.

[613] R. Ramakrishnan, S. Stolfo, R. J. Bayardo., and I. Parsa, editors. *Proc. ACM SIGKDD Intl. Conference on Knowledge Discovery and Data Mining.* AAAI Press, 2000.

[614] R. Ramakrishnan and J. Ullman. A survey of deductive database systems. *Journal of Logic Programming*, 23(2):125–149, 1995.

[615] K. Ramamohanarao. Design overview of the Aditi deductive database system. In *Proc. IEEE Intl. Conf. on Data Engineering*, 1991.

[616] K. Ramamohanarao, J. Shepherd, and R. Sacks-Davis. Partial-match retrieval for dynamic files using linear hashing with partial expansions. In *Intl. Conf. on Foundations of Data Organization and Algorithms*, 1989.

[617] V. Raman, B. Raman, and J. M. Hellerstein. Online dynamic reordering for interactive data processing. In *Proc. of the Conf. on Very Large Databases*, pages 709–720. Morgan Kaufmann, 1999.

[618] S. Rao, A. Badia, and D. Van Gucht. Providing better support for a class of decision support queries. In *Proc. ACM SIGMOD Conf. on the Management of Data*, 1996.

[619] R. Rastogi and K. Shim. Public: A decision tree classifier that integrates building and pruning. In *Proc. Intl. Conf. on Very Large Databases*, 1998.

[620] D. Reed. Implementing atomic actions on decentralized data. *ACM Transactions on Database Systems*, 1(1):3–23, 1983.

[621] G. Reese. *Database Programming With JDBC and Java.* O'Reilly & Associates, 1997.

[622] R. Reiter. A sound and sometimes complete query evaluation algorithm for relational databases with null values. *Journal of the ACM*, 33(2):349–370, 1986.

[623] E. Rescorla. *SSL and TLS: Designing and Building Secure Systems.* Addison Wesley Professional, 2000.

[624] A. Reuter. A fast transaction-oriented logging scheme for undo recovery. *IEEE Transactions on Software Engineering*, 6(4):348–356, 1980.

[625] A. Reuter. Performance analysis of recovery techniques. *ACM Transactions on Database Systems*, 9(4):526–559, 1984.

[626] E. Riloff and L. Hollaar. Text databases and information retrieval. In *Handbook of Computer Science.* ed. A.B. Tucker, CRC Press, 1996.

[627] J. Rissanen. Independent components of relations. *ACM Transactions on Database Systems*, 2(4):317–325, 1977.

[628] R. Rivest. Partial match retrieval algorithms. *SIAM Journal on Computing*, 5(1):19–50, 1976.

[629] R. L. Rivest, A. Shamir, and L. M. Adleman. A method for obtaining digital signatures and public-key cryptosystems. *Communications of the ACM*, 21(2):120–126, 1978.

[630] J. T. Robinson. The KDB tree: A search structure for large multidimensional dynamic indexes. In *Proc. ACM SIGMOD Int. Conf. on Management of Data*, 1981.

[631] J. Rohmer, F. Lescoeur, and J. Kerisit. The Alexander method, a technique for the processing of recursive queries. *New Generation Computing*, 4(3):273–285, 1986.

[632] D. Rosenkrantz, R. Stearns, and P. Lewis. System level concurrency control for distributed database systems. *ACM Transactions on Database Systems*, 3(2), 1978.

[633] A. Rosenthal and U. Chakravarthy. Anatomy of a modular multiple query optimizer. In *Proc. Intl. Conf. on Very Large Databases*, 1988.

[634] K. Ross and D. Srivastava. Fast computation of sparse datacubes. In *Proc. Intl. Conf. on Very Large Databases*, 1997.

[635] K. Ross, D. Srivastava, and S. Sudarshan. Materialized view maintenance and integrity constraint checking: Trading space for time. In *Proc. ACM SIGMOD Conf. on the Management of Data*, 1996.

[636] J. Rothnie, P. Bernstein, S. Fox, N. Goodman, M. Hammer, T. Landers, C. Reeve, D. Shipman, and E. Wong. Introduction to a system for distributed databases (SDD -1). *ACM Transactions on Database Systems*, 5(1), 1980.

[637] J. Rothnie and N. Goodman. An overview of the preliminary design of SDD -1: A system for distributed data bases. In *Proc. Berkeley Workshop on Distributed Data Management and Computer Networks*, 1977.

[638] N. Roussopoulos, Y. Kotidis, and M. Roussopoulos. Cubetree: Organization of and bulk updates on the data cube. In *Proc. ACM SIGMOD Conf. on the Management of Data*, 1997.

[639] S. Rozen and D. Shasha. Using feature set compromise to automate physical database design. In *Proc. Intl. Conf. on Very Large Databases*, 1991.

[640] J. Rumbaugh, I. Jacobson, and G. Booch. *The Unified Modeling Language Reference Manual (Addison-Wesley Object Technology Series)*. Addison-Wesley, 1998.

[641] M. Rusinkiewicz, A. Sheth, and G. Karabatis. Specifying interdatabase dependencies in a multidatabase environment. *IEEE Computer*, 24(12), 1991.

[642] D. Sacca and C. Zaniolo. Magic counting methods. In *Proc. ACM SIGMOD Conf. on the Management of Data*, 1987.

[643] Y. Sagiv and M. Yannakakis. Equivalence among expressions with the union and difference operators. *Journal of the ACM*, 27(4):633–655, 1980.

[644] K. Sagonas, T. Swift, and D. Warren. XSB as an efficient deductive database engine. In *Proc. ACM SIGMOD Conf. on the Management of Data*, 1994.

[645] A. Sahuguet, L. Dupont, and T. Nguyen. Kweelt: Querying XML in the new millenium. `http://kweelt.sourceforge.net`, Sept 2000.

[646] G. Salton and M. J. McGill. *Introduction to Modern Information Retrieval*. McGraw-Hill, 1983.

[647] B. Salzberg, A. Tsukerman, J. Gray, M. Stewart, S. Uren, and B. Vaughan. Fastsort: A distributed single-input single-output external sort. In *Proc. ACM SIGMOD Conf. on the Management of Data*, 1990.

[648] B. J. Salzberg. *File Structures*. PrenticeHall, 1988.

[649] H. Samet. The Quad T ree and related hierarchical data structures. *ACM Computing Surveys*, 16(2), 1984.

[650] H. Samet. *The Design and Analysis of Spatial Data Structures*. Addison-Wesley, 1990.

[651] J. Sander, M. Ester, H.-P. Kriegel, and X. Xu. Density-based clustering in spatial databases. *J. of Data Mining and Knowledge Discovery*, 2(2), 1998.

[652] R. E. Sanders. *ODBC 3.5 Developer's Guide*. McGraw-Hill Series on Data Warehousing and Data Management. McGraw-Hill, 1998.

[653] S. Sarawagi and M. Stonebraker. Efficient organization of large multidimensional arrays. In *Proc. IEEE Intl. Conf. on Data Engineering*, 1994.

[654] S. Sarawagi, S. Thomas, and R. Agrawal. Integrating mining with relational database systems: Alternatives and implications. In *Proc. ACM SIGMOD Intl. Conf. on Management of Data*, 1998.

[655] A. Savasere, E. Omiecinski, and S. Navathe. An efficient algorithm for mining association rules in large databases. In *Proc. Intl. Conf. on Very Large Databases*, 1995.

[656] P. Schauble. Spider: A multiuser information retrieval system for semistructured and dynamic data. In *Proc. ACM SIGIR Conference on Research and Development in Information Retrieval*, pages 318 – 327, 1993.

[657] H.-J. Schek, H.-B. Paul, M. Scholl, and G. Weikum. The DASDBS project: Objects, experiences, and future projects. *IEEE Transactions on Knowledge and Data Engineering*, 2(1), 1990.

[658] M. Schkolnick. Physical database design techniques. In *NYU Symp. on Database Design*, 1978.

[659] M. Schkolnick and P. Sorenson. The effects of denormalization on database performance. Technical report, IBM RJ3082, San Jose, CA, 1981.

[660] G. Schlageter. Optimistic methods for concurrency control in distributed database systems. In *Proc. Intl. Conf. on Very Large Databases*, 1981.

[661] B. Schneier. *Applied Cryptography: Protocols, Algorithms, and Source Code in C.* John Wiley & Sons, 1995.

[662] E. Sciore. A complete axiomatization of full join dependencies. *Journal of the ACM*, 29(2):373–393, 1982.

[663] E. Sciore, M. Siegel, and A. Rosenthal. Using semantic values to facilitate interoperability among heterogeneous information systems. *ACM Transactions on Database Systems*, 19(2):254–290, 1994.

[664] A. Segev and J. Park. Maintaining materialized views in distributed databases. In *Proc. IEEE Intl. Conf. on Data Engineering*, 1989.

[665] A. Segev and A. Shoshani. Logical modeling of temporal data. *Proc. ACM SIGMOD Conf. on the Management of Data*, 1987.

[666] P. Selfridge, D. Srivastava, and L. Wilson. IDEA: Interactive data exploration and analysis. In *Proc. ACM SIGMOD Conf. on the Management of Data*, 1996.

[667] P. Selinger and M. Adiba. Access path selections in distributed data base management systems. In *Proc. Intl. Conf. on Databases, British Computer Society*, 1980.

[668] P. Selinger, M. Astrahan, D. Chamberlin, R. Lorie, and T. Price. Access path selection in a relational database management system. In *Proc. ACM SIGMOD Conf. on the Management of Data*, 1979.

[669] T. K. Sellis. Multiple query optimization. *ACM Transactions on Database Systems*, 13(1):23–52, 1988.

[670] P. Seshadri, J. Hellerstein, H. Pirahesh, T. Leung, R. Ramakrishnan, D. Srivastava, P. Stuckey, and S. Sudarshan. Cost-based optimization for Magic: Algebra and implementation. In *Proc. ACM SIGMOD Conf. on the Management of Data*, 1996.

[671] P. Seshadri, M. Livny, and R. Ramakrishnan. The design and implementation of a sequence database system. In *Proc. Intl. Conf. on Very Large Databases*, 1996.

[672] P. Seshadri, M. Livny, and R. Ramakrishnan. The case for enhanced abstract data types. In *Proc. Intl. Conf. on Very Large Databases*, 1997.

[673] P. Seshadri, H. Pirahesh, and T. Leung. Complex query decorrelation. In *Proc. IEEE Intl. Conf. on Data Engineering*, 1996.

[674] J. Shafer and R. Agrawal. SPRINT: a scalable parallel classifier for data mining. In *Proc. Intl. Conf. on Very Large Databases*, 1996.

[675] J. Shanmugasundaram, U. Fayyad, and P. Bradley. Compressed data cubes for olap aggregate query approximation on continuous dimensions. In *Proc. Intl. Conf. on Knowledge Discovery and Data Mining (KDD)*, 1999.

[676] J. Shanmugasundaram, J. Kiernan, E. J. Shekita, C. Fan, and J. Funderburk. Querying XML views of relational data. In *Proc. Intl. Conf. on Very Large Data Bases*, 2001.

[677] L. Shapiro. Join processing in database systems with large main memories. *ACM Transactions on Database Systems*, 11(3):239–264, 1986.

[678] D. Shasha and N. Goodman. Concurrent search structure algorithms. *ACM Transactions on Database Systems*, 13:53–90, 1988.

[679] D. Shasha, E. Simon, and P. Valduriez. Simple rational guidance for chopping up transactions. In *Proc. ACM SIGMOD Conf. on the Management of Data*, 1992.

[680] H. Shatkay and S. Zdonik. Approximate queries and representations for large data sequences. In *Proc. IEEE Intl. Conf. on Data Engineering*, 1996.

[681] T. Sheard and D. Stemple. Automatic verification of database transaction safety. *ACM Transactions on Database Systems*, 1989.

[682] S. Shenoy and Z. Ozsoyoglu. Design and implementation of a semantic query optimizer. *IEEE Transactions on Knowledge and Data Engineering*, 1(3):344–361, 1989.

[683] P. Shenoy, J. Haritsa, S. Sudarshan, G. Bhalotia, M. Bawa, and D. Shah. Turbo-charging vertical mining of large databases. In *Proc. ACM SIGMOD Intl. Conf. on Management of Data*, pages 22–33, May 2000.

[684] A. Sheth and J. Larson. Federated database systems for managing distributed, heterogeneous, and autonomous databases. *Computing Surveys*, 22(3):183–236, 1990.

[685] A. Sheth, J. Larson, A. Cornelio, and S. Navathe. A tool for integrating conceptual schemas and user views. In *Proc. IEEE Intl. Conf. on Data Engineering*, 1988.

[686] A. Shoshani. OLAP and statistical databases: Similarities and differences. In *ACM Symp. on Principles of Database Systems*, 1997.

[687] A. Shukla, P. Deshpande, J. Naughton, and K. Ramasamy. Storage estimation for multidimensional aggregates in the presence of hierarchies. In *Proc. Intl. Conf. on Very Large Databases*, 1996.

[688] M. Siegel, E. Sciore, and S. Salveter. A method for automatic rule derivation to support semantic query optimization. *ACM Transactions on Database Systems*, 17(4), 1992.

[689] A. Silberschatz, H. Korth, and S. Sudarshan. *Database System Concepts (4th ed.)*. McGraw-Hill, 4 edition, 2001.

[690] E. Simon, J. Kiernan, and C. de Maindreville. Implementing high-level active rules on top of relational databases. In *Proc. Intl. Conf. on Very Large Databases*, 1992.

[691] E. Simoudis, J. Wei, and U. M. Fayyad, editors. *Proc. Intl. Conf. on Knowledge Discovery and Data Mining.* AAAI Press, 1996.

[692] D. Skeen. Nonblocking commit protocols. In *Proc. ACM SIGMOD Conf. on the Management of Data*, 1981.

[693] J. Smith and D. Smith. Database abstractions: Aggregation and generalization. *ACM Transactions on Database Systems*, 1(1):105–133, 1977.

[694] K. Smith and M. Winslett. Entity modeling in the MLS relational model. In *Proc. Intl. Conf. on Very Large Databases*, 1992.

[695] P. Smith and M. Barnes. *Files and Databases: An Introduction.* Addison-Wesley, 1987.

[696] N. Soparkar, H. Korth, and A. Silberschatz. Databases with deadline and contingency constraints. *IEEE Transactions on Knowledge and Data Engineering*, 7(4):552–565, 1995.

[697] S. Spaccapietra, C. Parent, and Y. Dupont. Model independent assertions for integration of heterogeneous schemas. In *Proc. Intl. Conf. on Very Large Databases*, 1992.

[698] S. Spaccapietra (ed.). *Entity-Relationship Approach: Ten Years of Experience in Information Modeling, Proc. Entity-Relationship Conf.* North-Holland, 1987.

[699] E. Spertus. ParaSite: mining structural information on the web. In *Intl. World Wide Web Conference*, 1997.

[700] R. Srikant and R. Agrawal. Mining generalized association rules. In *Proc. Intl. Conf. on Very Large Databases*, 1995.

[701] R. Srikant and R. Agrawal. Mining Quantitative Association Rules in Large Relational Tables. In *Proc. ACM SIGMOD Conf. on Management of Data*, 1996.

[702] R. Srikant and R. Agrawal. Mining Sequential Patterns: Generalizations and Performance Improvements. In *Proc. Intl. Conf. on Extending Database Technology*, 1996.

[703] R. Srikant, Q. Vu, and R. Agrawal. Mining Association Rules with Item Constraints. In *Proc. Intl. Conf. on Knowledge Discovery in Databases and Data Mining*, 1997.

[704] V. Srinivasan and M. Carey. Performance of B-Tree concurrency control algorithms. In *Proc. ACM SIGMOD Conf. on the Management of Data*, 1991.

[705] D. Srivastava, S. Dar, H. Jagadish, and A. Levy. Answering queries with aggregation using views. In *Proc. Intl. Conf. on Very Large Databases*, 1996.

[706] D. Srivastava, R. Ramakrishnan, P. Seshadri, and S. Sudarshan. Coral++: Adding object-orientation to a logic database language. In *Proc. Intl. Conf. on Very Large Databases*, 1993.

[707] J. Srivastava and D. Rotem. Analytical modeling of materialized view maintenance. In *ACM Symp. on Principles of Database Systems*, 1988.

[708] J. Srivastava, J. Tan, and V. Lum. Tbsam: An access method for efficient processing of statistical queries. *IEEE Transactions on Knowledge and Data Engineering*, 1(4):414–423, 1989.

[709] D. Stacey. Replication: DB2 , Oracle or Sybase? *Database Programming and Design*, pages 42–50, December 1994.

[710] P. Stachour and B. Thuraisingham. Design of LDV: A multilevel secure relational database management system. *IEEE Transactions on Knowledge and Data Engineering*, 2(2), 1990.

[711] J. Stankovic and W. Zhao. On real-time transactions. In *Proc. ACM SIGMOD Conf. on the Management of Data Record*, 1988.

[712] T. Steel. Interim report of the ANSI-SPARC study group. In *Proc. ACM SIGMOD Conf. on the Management of Data*, 1975.

[713] M. Stonebraker. Implementation of integrity constraints and views by query modification. In *Proc. ACM SIGMOD Conf. on the Management of Data*, 1975.

[714] M. Stonebraker. Concurrency control and consistency of multiple copies of data in Distributed Ingres. *IEEE Transactions on Software Engineering*, 5(3), 1979.

[715] M. Stonebraker. Operating system support for database management. *Communications of the ACM*, 14(7):412–418, 1981.

[716] M. Stonebraker. Inclusion of new types in relational database systems. In *Proc. IEEE Intl. Conf. on Data Engineering*, 1986.

[717] M. Stonebraker. *The INGRES Papers: Anatomy of a Relational Database System.* Addison-Wesley, 1986.

[718] M. Stonebraker. The design of the Postgres storage system. In *Proc. Intl. Conf. on Very Large Databases*, 1987.

[719] M. Stonebraker. *Object-relational DBMSs—The Next Great Wave.* Morgan Kaufmann, 1996.

[720] M. Stonebraker, J. Frew, K. Gardels, and J. Meredith. The Sequoia 2000 storage benchmark. In *Proc. ACM SIGMOD Conf. on the Management of Data*, 1993.

[721] M. Stonebraker and J. Hellerstein (eds). *Readings in Database Systems.* Morgan Kaufmann, 2 edition, 1994.

[722] M. Stonebraker, A. Jhingran, J. Goh, and S. Potamianos. On rules, procedures, caching and views in data base systems. In *UCBERL M9036*, 1990.

[723] M. Stonebraker and G. Kemnitz. The Postgres next-generation database management system. *Communications of the ACM*, 34(10):78–92, 1991.

[724] B. Subramanian, T. Leung, S. Vandenberg, and S. Zdonik. The AQUA approach to querying lists and trees in object-oriented databases. In *Proc. IEEE Intl. Conf. on Data Engineering*, 1995.

[725] W. Sun, Y. Ling, N. Rishe, and Y. Deng. An instant and accurate size estimation method for joins and selections in a retrieval-intensive environment. In *Proc. ACM SIGMOD Conf. on the Management of Data*, 1993.

[726] A. Swami and A. Gupta. Optimization of large join queries: Combining heuristics and combinatorial techniques. In *Proc. ACM SIGMOD Conf. on the Management of Data*, 1989.

[727] T. Swift and D. Warren. An abstract machine for SLG resolution: Definite programs. In *Intl. Logic Programming Symposium*, 1994.

[728] A. Tansel, J. Clifford, S. Gadia, S. Jajodia, A. Segev, and R. Snodgrass. *Temporal Databases: Theory, Design and Implementation.* Benjamin-Cummings, 1993.

[729] Y. Tay, N. Goodman, and R. Suri. Locking performance in centralized databases. *ACM Transactions on Database Systems*, 10(4):415–462, 1985.

[730] T. Teorey. *Database Modeling and Design: The E-R Approach.* Morgan Kaufmann, 1990.

[731] T. Teorey, D.-Q. Yang, and J. Fry. A logical database design methodology for relational databases using the extended entity-relationship model. *ACM Computing Surveys*, 18(2):197–222, 1986.

[732] R. Thomas. A majority consensus approach to concurrency control for multiple copy databases. *ACM Transactions on Database Systems*, 4(2):180–209, 1979.

[733] S. A. Thomas. *SSL & TLS Essentials: Securing the Web.* John Wiley & Sons, 2000.

[734] A. Thomasian. Concurrency control: Methods, performance, and analysis. *ACM Computing Surveys*, 30(1):70–119, 1998.

[735] A. Thomasian. Two-phase locking performance and its thrashing behavior *ACM Computing Surveys*, 30(1):70–119, 1998.

[736] S. Thomas, S. Bodagala, K. Alsabti, and S. Ranka. An efficient algorithm for the incremental updation of association rules in large databases. In *Proc. Intl. Conf. on Knowledge Discovery and Data Mining.* AAAI Press, 1997.

[737] S. Todd. The Peterlee relational test vehicle. *IBM Systems Journal*, 15(4):285–307, 1976.

[738] H. Toivonen. Sampling large databases for association rules. In *Proc. Intl. Conf. on Very Large Databases*, 1996.

[739] TP Performance Council. TPC Benchmark D: Standard specification, rev. 1.2. Technical report, `http://www.tpc.org/dspec.html`, 1996.

[740] I. Traiger, J. Gray, C. Galtieri, and B. Lindsay. Transactions and consistency in distributed database systems. *ACM Transactions on Database Systems*, 25(9), 1982.

[741] M. Tsangaris and J. Naughton. On the performance of object clustering techniques. In *Proc. ACM SIGMOD Conf. on the Management of Data*, 1992.

[742] D.-M. Tsou and P. Fischer. Decomposition of a relation scheme into Boyce-C odd normal form. *SIGACT News*, 14(3):23–29, 1982.

[743] D. Tsur, J. D. Ullman, S. Abiteboul, C. Clifton, R. Motwani, S. Nestorov, and A. Rosenthal. Query flocks: A generalization of association-rule mining. In *Proc. ACM SIGMOD Conf. on Management of Data*, pages 1–12, 1998.

[744] A. Tucker (ed.). *Computer Science and Engineering Handbook.* CRC Press, 1996.

[745] J. W. Tukey. *Exploratory Data Analysis.* Addison-Wesley, 1977.

[746] J. Ullman. The U.R. strikes back. In *ACM Symp. on Principles of Database Systems*, 1982.

[747] J. Ullman. *Principles of Database and Knowledgebase Systems, Vols. 1 and 2.* Computer Science Press, 1989.

[748] J. Ullman. Information integration using logical views. In *Intl. Conf. on Database Theory*, 1997.

[749] S. Urban and L. Delcambre. An analysis of the structural, dynamic, and temporal aspects of semantic data models. In *Proc. IEEE Intl. Conf. on Data Engineering*, 1986.

[750] G. Valentin, M. Zuliani, D. C. Zilio, G. M. Lohman, and A. Skelley. Db2 advisor: An optimizer smart enough to recommend its own indexes. In *Proc. Intl. Conf. on Data Engineering (ICDE)*, pages 101–110. IEEE Computer Society, 2000.

[751] M. Van Emden and R. Kowalski. The semantics of predicate logic as a programming language. *Journal of the ACM*, 23(4):733–742, 1976.

[752] A. Van Gelder. Negation as failure using tight derivations for general logic programs. In J. Minker, editor, *Foundations of Deductive Databases and Logic Programming.* Morgan Kaufmann, 1988.

[753] C. J. van Rijsbergen. *Information Retrieval.* Butterworths, London, United Kingdom, 1990.

[754] M. Vardi. Incomplete information and default reasoning. In *ACM Symp. on Principles of Database Systems*, 1986.

[755] M. Vardi. Fundamentals of dependency theory. In *Trends in Theoretical Computer Science.* ed. E. Borger, Computer Science Press, 1987.

[756] L. Vieille. Recursive axioms in deductive databases: The query-subquery approach. In *Intl. Conf. on Expert Database Systems*, 1986.

[757] L. Vieille. From QSQ towards QoSaQ: global optimization of recursive queries. In *Intl. Conf. on Expert Database Systems*, 1988.

[758] L. Vieille, P. Bayer, V. Kuchenhoff, and A. Lefebvre. EKS-V1 , a short overview. In *AAAI-90 Workshop on Knowledge Base Management Systems*, 1990.

[759] J. S. Vitter and M. Wang. Approximate computation of multidimensional aggregates of sparse data using wavelets. In *Proc. ACM SIGMOD Conf. on the Management of Data*, pages 193–204. ACM Press, 1999.

[760] G. von Bultzingsloewen. Translating and optimizing SQL queries having aggregates. In *Proc. Intl. Conf. on Very Large Databases*, 1987.

[761] G. von Bultzingsloewen, K. Dittrich, C. Iochpe, R.-P. Liedtke, P. Lockemann, and M. Schryro. Kardamom—A dataflow database machine for real-time applications. In *Proc. ACM SIGMOD Conf. on the Management of Data*, 1988.

[762] G. Vossen. *Data Models, Database Languages and Database Management Systems.* Addison-Wesley, 1991.

[763] N. Wade. Citation analysis: A new tool for science administrators. *Science*, 188(4183):429–432, 1975.

[764] R. Wagner. Indexing design considerations. *IBM Systems Journal*, 12(4):351–367, 1973.

[765] X. Wang, S. Jajodia, and V. Subrahmanian. Temporal modules: An approach toward federated temporal databases. In *Proc. ACM SIGMOD Conf. on the Management of Data*, 1993.

[766] K. Wang and H. Liu. Schema discovery for semistructured data. In *Third International Conference on Knowledge Discovery and Data Mining (KDD -97)*, pages 271–274, 1997.

[767] R. Weber, H. Schek, and S. Blott. A quantitative analysis and performance study for similarity-search methods in high-dimensional spaces. In *Proc. Intl. Conf. on Very Large Data Bases*, 1998.

[768] G. Weddell. Reasoning about functional dependencies generalized for semantic data models. *ACM Transactions on Database Systems*, 17(1), 1992.

[769] W. Weihl. The impact of recovery on concurrency control. In *ACM Symp. on Principles of Database Systems*, 1989.

[770] G. Weikum and G. Vossen. *Transactional Information Systems.* Morgan Kaufmann, 2001.

[771] R. Weiss, B. V. lez, M. A. Sheldon, C. Manprempre, P. Szilagyi, A. Duda, and D. K. Gifford. HyPursuit: A hierarchical network search engine that exploits content-link hypertext clustering. In *Proc. ACM Conf. on Hypertext*, 1996.

[772] C. White. Let the replication battle begin. In *Database Programming and Design*, pages 21–24, May 1994.

[773] S. White, M. Fisher, R. Cattell, G. Hamilton, and M. Hapner. *JDBC API Tutorial and Reference: Universal Data Access for the Java 2 Platform.* Addison-Wesley, 2 edition, 1999.

[774] J. Widom and S. Ceri. *Active Database Systems.* Morgan Kaufmann, 1996.

[775] G. Wiederhold. *Database Design (2nd ed.).* McGraw-Hill, 1983.

[776] G. Wiederhold, S. Kaplan, and D. Sagalowicz. Physical database design research at Stanford. *IEEE Database Engineering*, 1:117–119, 1983.

[777] R. Williams, D. Daniels, L. Haas, G. Lapis, B. Lindsay, P. Ng, R. Obermarck, P. Selinger, A. Walker, P. Wilms, and R. Yost. R*: An overview of the architecture. Technical report, IBM RJ3325, San Jose, CA, 1981.

[778] M. S. Winslett. A model-based approach to updating databases with incomplete information. *ACM Transactions on Database Systems*, 13(2):167–196, 1988.

[779] G. Wiorkowski and D. Kull. *DB2: Design and Development Guide (3rd ed.)*. Addison-Wesley, 1992.

[780] I. H. Witten, A. Moffat, and T. C. Bell. *Managing Gigabytes: Compressing and Indexing Documents and Images.* Van Nostrand Reinhold, 1994.

[781] I. H. Witten and E. Frank. *Data Mining: Practical Machine Learning Tools and Techniques with Java Implementations.* Morgan Kaufmann Publishers, 1999.

[782] O. Wolfson, A. Sistla, , B. Xu, J. Zhou, and S. Chamberlain. Domino: Databases for moving objects tracking. In *Proc. ACM SIGMOD Int. Conf. on Management of Data*, 1999.

[783] Y. Yang and R. Miller. Association rules over interval data. In *Proc. ACM SIGMOD Conf. on the Management of Data*, 1997.

[784] K. Youssefi and E. Wong. Query processing in a relational database management system. In *Proc. Intl. Conf. on Very Large Databases*, 1979.

[785] C. Yu and C. Chang. Distributed query processing. *ACM Computing Surveys*, 16(4):399–433, 1984.

[786] O. R. Zaiane, M. El-Hajj, and P. Lu. Fast Parallel Association Rule Mining Without Candidacy Generation. In *Proc. IEEE Intl. Conf. on Data Mining (ICDM)*, 2001.

[787] M. J. Zaki. Scalable algorithms for association mining. In *IEEE Transactions on Knowledge and Data Engineering*, volume 12, pages 372–390, May/June 2000.

[788] M. J. Zaki and C.-T. Ho, editors. *Large-Scale Parallel Data Mining.* Springer Verlag, 2000.

[789] C. Zaniolo. Analysis and design of relational schemata. Technical report, Ph.D. Thesis, UCLA, TR UCLA-ENG-7669, 1976.

[790] C. Zaniolo. Database relations with null values. *Journal of Computer and System Sciences*, 28(1):142–166, 1984.

[791] C. Zaniolo. The database language GEM. In *Readings in Object-Oriented Databases.* eds. S.B. Zdonik and D. Maier, Morgan Kaufmann, 1990.

[792] C. Zaniolo. Active database rules with transaction-conscious stable-model semantics. In *Intl. Conf. on Deductive and Object-Oriented Databases*, 1996.

[793] C. Zaniolo, N. Arni, and K. Ong. Negation and aggregates in recursive rules: the LDL++ approach. In *Intl. Conf. on Deductive and Object-Oriented Databases*, 1993.

[794] C. Zaniolo, S. Ceri, C. Faloutsos, R. Snodgrass, V. Subrahmanian, and R. Zicari. *Advanced Database Systems.* Morgan Kaufmann, 1997.

[795] S. Zdonik, U. Cetintemel, M. Cherniack, C. Convey, S. Lee, G. Seidman, M. Stonebraker, N. Tatbul, and D. Carney Monitoring streams—A new class of data management applications. In *Proc. Intl. Conf. on Very Large Data Bases*, 2002.

[796] S. Zdonik and D. Maier (eds.). *Readings in Object-Oriented Databases.* Morgan Kaufmann, 1990.

[797] A. Zhang, M. Nodine, B. Bhargava, and O. Bukhres. Ensuring relaxed atomicity for flexible transactions in multidatabase systems. In *Proc. ACM SIGMOD Conf. on the Management of Data*, 1994.

[798] T. Zhang, R. Ramakrishnan, and M. Livny. BIRCH: an efficient data clustering method for very large databases. In *Proc. ACM SIGMOD Conf. on Management of Data*, 1996.

[799] Y. Zhao, P. Deshpande, J. F. Naughton, and A. Shukla. Simultaneous optimization and evaluation of multiple dimensional queries. In *Proc. ACM SIGMOD Intl. Conf. on Management of Data*, 1998.

[800] Y. Zhuge, H. Garcia-Molina, J. Hammer, and J. Widom. View maintenance in a warehousing environment. In *Proc. ACM SIGMOD Conf. on the Management of Data*, 1995.

[801] M. M. Zloof. Query-by-example: a database language. *IBM Systems Journal*, 16(4):324–343, 1977.

[802] J. Zobel, A. Moffat, and K. Ramamohanarao. Inverted files versus signature files for text indexing. *ACM Transactions on Database Systems*, 23, 1998.

[803] J. Zobel, A. Moffat, and R. Sacks-Davis. An efficient indexing technique for full text databases. In *Proc. Intl. Conf. on Very Large Databases, Morgan Kaufman pubs. (San Francisco, CA) 18, Vancouver*, 1992.

[804] U. Zukowski and B. Freitag. The deductive database system LOLA. In *Proc. Intl. Conf. on Logic Programming and Non-Monotonic Reasoning*, 1997.

AUTHOR INDEX

SUBJECT INDEX

Online Learning Center Available

at **www.mhhe.com/ramakrishnan** and at **www.cs.wisc.edu/~dbbook**

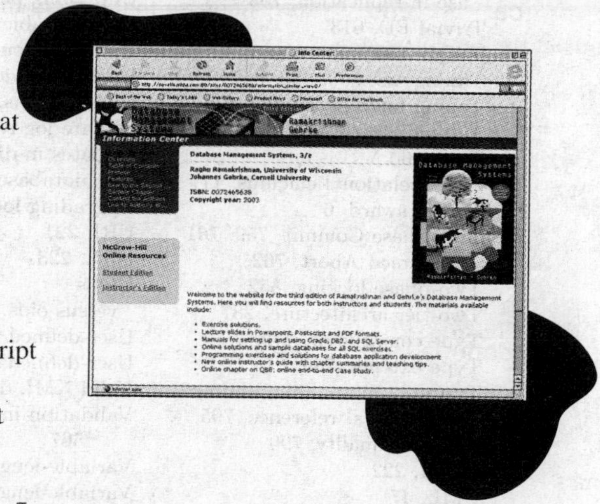

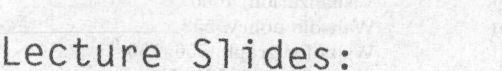

Lecture Slides:

- ***For Students:*** Slides in Postscript and PDF format
- ***For Instructors:*** Slides in PowerPoint format for easy modification

Solutions to Chapter Exercises:

- ***For Students:*** Odd-numbered solutions in Postscript and PDF format
- ***For Instructors:*** Complete solutions in Postscript and PDF format

Online Instructor's Manual:

- ***For Instructors:*** Provides a short overview of the goals of each chapter and identifies choices for material to emphasize or omit. It discusses the online resources available for that chapter and offers suggestions for hands-on exercises and projects. It includes sample exams from courses that the authors have taught using the book.

Code for SQL and Internet Database Applications:

- ***For Students:*** Complete source code for one database-backed website (online bookstore).
  Scripts to set up sample databases for all SQL exercises.
- ***For Instructors:*** Complete solutions for all SQL exercises, available for Oracle, DB2, SQL Server, Access, and MySQL. Complete design documents, complete source code, skeleton design documents, and skeleton source code for website assignments are available for instructors.

Hands-on Internet Course Projects

- Online Record Store
- Online Pharmacy
- Student Enrollment System
- Airline Reservation System

Installation and Getting-Started Manuals:

- ***For Instructors and Students:*** Directions for getting students up and running on Apache Tomcat, as well as the most popular databases, including Oracle, DB2, SQL Server, Access, and MySQL.

Minibase Software:

- ***For Instructors and Students:*** Minibase is a small relational Database Management System intended for use in systems-oriented courses. Minibase comes with sample assignments and solutions.

It's your choice!

New Modular Organization!

Applications emphasis: A course that covers the principles of database systems and emphasizes how they are used in developing data-intensive applications.

Systems emphasis: A course that has a strong systems emphasis and assumes that students have good programming skills in C and C++.

Hybrid course: Modular organization allows you to teach the course with the emphasis you want.

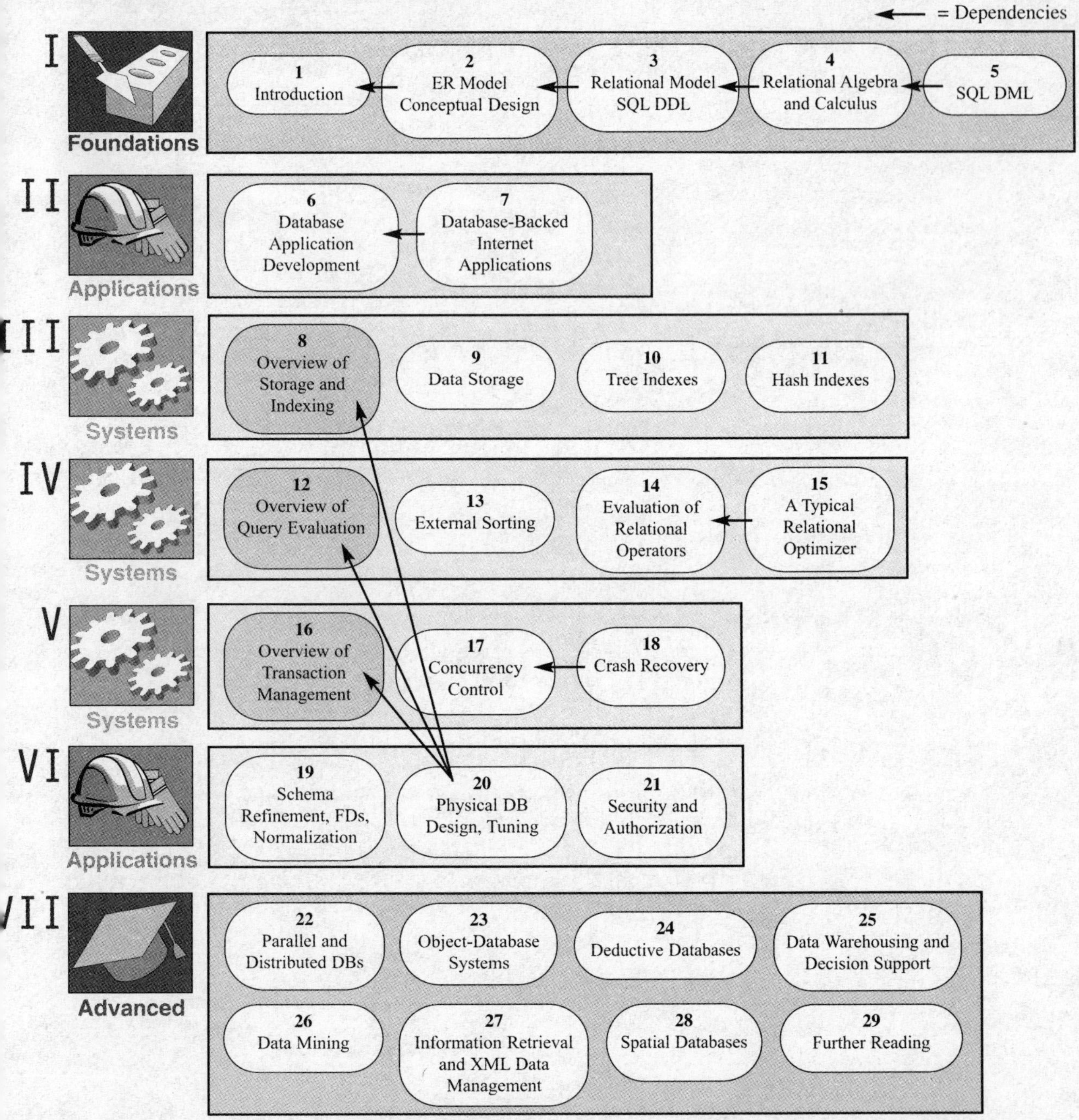